C-Ch Volume 3

The World Book Encyclopedia

World Book, Inc.
a Scott Fetzer company
Chicago

The World Book Encyclopedia

World Book, Inc.
233 North Michigan Avenue
Chicago, IL 60601
U.S.A.

www.worldbook.com

About the cover design

The encyclopedia is available in both traditional and SPINESCAPE bindings. The SPINESCAPE design for the 2007 edition—*Undersea World of Wonders*—shows the beauty and rich wildlife of Australia's Great Barrier Reef, the largest group of coral reefs in the world. The image highlights a major goal of *World Book,* to describe and explain the wonders of the natural world to its readers.

Library of Congress Cataloging-in-Publication Data

The World Book encyclopedia.
p. cm.
2007 ed.
Summary: "A 22-volume, highly illustrated, A-Z general encyclopedia for all ages, featuring the sections *How to Use WORLD BOOK, Other Research Aids, Key to Pronunciation,* and *A Student Guide to Better Writing, Speaking, and Research Skills,* and a comprehensive index"-- Provided by publisher.
Includes bibliographical references and index.
ISBN-13: 978-0-7166-0107-4
ISBN-10: 0-7166-0107-9
1. Encyclopedias and dictionaries. I. World Book, Inc.
AE5.W55 2007
031--dc22

2006013005

Printed in the United States of America

07 5 4 3 2 1

Cc

C is the third letter of our alphabet. It was also the third letter in the alphabet used by the Semites, who once lived in Syria and Palestine. *C* comes from the same letter as our *G* or *g*. The Semites named it *gimel,* their word for a throwing stick. The sign is possibly adapted from an Egyptian *hieroglyphic* (picture symbol) for a boomerang. The Romans gave the letter its capital C form, and used it to indicate two sounds, that of *g* and that of *k*. The Romans finally made two different letters by adding a vertical stroke to the C to make G. See **Alphabet**.

Uses. *C* or *c* is about the 13th most frequently used letter in books, newspapers, and other printed material in English. As a grade, *C* means average on a school report card. In Roman numerals, *C* means *100;* in chemistry, the element *carbon.* Used with other letters, *C* may represent a number of words, such as *CBC,* for *Canadian Broadcasting Corporation; C.O.D.,* for *cash on delivery;* and *L.C.,* for *Library of Congress.* It is also used for *cent;* for *capacity* in electricity; for *Celsius* in temperature; and in Latin, for *circa,* meaning *about.*

Pronunciation. In English, *C* is pronounced two ways, like *s* as in *city* and *face,* and like *k* as in *camp.* For the *s* sound, a person places the tongue against the edges of the lower front teeth and forces breath through open lips. For the *k* sound, a person places the tongue back, with its sides touching the velum, or soft palate. The velum is closed, and the vocal cords do not vibrate. *C* is silent in such words as *indict* and *fascinate.* See **Pronunciation**.

Marianne Cooley

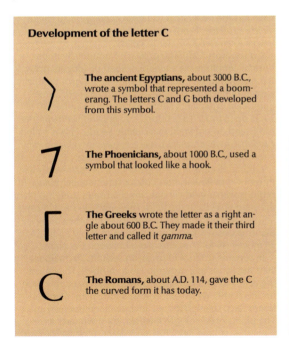

Development of the letter C

The ancient Egyptians, about 3000 B.C., wrote a symbol that represented a boomerang. The letters C and G both developed from this symbol.

The Phoenicians, about 1000 B.C., used a symbol that looked like a hook.

The Greeks wrote the letter as a right angle about 600 B.C. They made it their third letter and called it *gamma.*

The Romans, about A.D. 114, gave the C the curved form it has today.

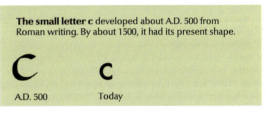

The small letter c developed about A.D. 500 from Roman writing. By about 1500, it had its present shape.

A.D. 500

Today

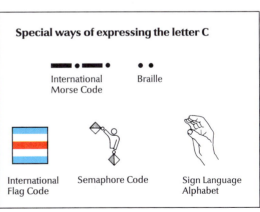

Special ways of expressing the letter C

International Morse Code

Braille

International Flag Code

Semaphore Code

Sign Language Alphabet

Common forms of the letter C

Handwritten letters vary from person to person. *Manuscript* (printed) letters have simple curves, *left,* and straight lines. Cursive letters, *right,* have flowing lines.

Roman letters have small finishing strokes called *serifs* that extend from the main strokes. The type face shown above is Baskerville. The italic form appears at the right.

Sans-serif letters are also called *gothic letters.* They have no serifs. The type face shown above is called Futura. The italic form of Futura appears at the right.

Computer letters have special shapes. Computers can "read" these letters either optically or by means of the magnetic ink with which the letters may be printed.

C-reactive protein is a substance found in the blood of human beings and other animals. The protein, often called CRP, plays an important role in *inflammation,* the redness, swelling, and heat with which the body responds to injury or infection. Inflammation, together with the disease-fighting process known as the *immune response,* is how the body recognizes and removes infectious agents or damaged tissues, and begins healing.

Medical researchers are interested in CRP because high levels are associated with increased risk of heart attacks and strokes. Scientists believe that cholesterol deposits called *plaques* within the arteries will more likely rupture when CRP levels are high. When plaques rupture, blood clots form inside the arteries. A clot can block arteries of the heart, causing heart attack, or arteries to the brain, causing stroke. High levels of CRP are also a risk factor for *type 2 diabetes,* a disease in which blood sugar levels are abnormal. Many patients with diabetes also have heart disease. CRP levels are high in many patients with arthritis and other disorders that result from inappropriate or uncontrolled inflammation.

Physicians recommend regular exercise, not smoking, and a healthy diet to prevent heart disease, stroke, and diabetes. All these activities also reduce CRP levels. Certain drugs, such as statins, that lower heart attack risk also lower CRP levels. CRP can be measured by a blood test. A CRP level less than 1.0 milligram per liter of blood is considered desirable. A level greater than 3 milligrams per liter is considered high. Paul M. Ridker

See also **Diabetes; Heart** (Coronary artery disease); **Inflammation; Stroke** (Causes).

Caaba. See **Kaaba**.

Cabal, *kuh BAL* or *kuh BAHL,* is a close-knit group of people who work privately or secretly to carry out their own plans. The word has become a term of reproach, and implies plotting, scheming, and conspiring to overthrow legitimate authority.

The term *cabal* is frequently associated with five members of the Privy Council under King Charles II of England. However, the group actually carried out many popular foreign policy projects and did not fit what has become the common meaning of the term.

The *Conway cabal* is a name given to a group of American army officers and congressmen who wished to remove George Washington from his post as commander in chief in 1777 and 1778, during the Revolutionary War. The name is taken from that of Major General Thomas Conway, who regarded Washington's military skills with contempt and questioned his ability to lead. But many historians question whether an organized plot against Washington ever existed. Stephen Goode

Cabbage is a common vegetable native to England and northwestern France, but grown throughout Europe, Asia, and America. Other leafy vegetables closely related to the cabbage include cauliflower, Brussels sprouts, broccoli, and turnips.

Kinds of cabbage. There are three kinds of cabbage, *white, red,* and *savoy.* The leaves of the plant grow close together to form a hard, round head. The leaves of the white and red cabbage are usually quite smooth, but have rather prominent veins. Those of the savoy appear wrinkled or blistered. White cabbage, which has pale green leaves, is the most popular type in the United States. People eat it raw in salads, cooked as a hot vegetable, or pickled as sauerkraut. Red cabbage, with its reddish-purple leaves, is not so popular as the white, but it can be eaten raw or cooked. The savoy type perhaps has the best flavor. *Chinese cabbage,* also called *celery cabbage,* is not a true cabbage. Its long, thin leaves form stalks similar to celery.

WORLD BOOK illustration by Kate Lloyd-Jones, Linden Artists Ltd.

Cabbage is a vegetable with leaves that grow close together to form a hard, round head. It is a nutritious food.

Cultivation. Cabbage grown commercially under normal conditions is a biennial. Seed producers grow the plants one year and leave them in the ground during winter. In the spring the plants produce seed. Sometimes cabbage plants subjected to cool weather (50 to 55 °F, or 10 to 13 °C) produce flowers and seeds prematurely and do not yield marketable heads. This is called *bolting.* However, plant breeders have developed varieties that are resistant to cold temperatures.

Cabbage seeds are small and look almost exactly like those of cauliflower, broccoli, or other similar plants. In regions with a mild climate, most farmers prefer to plant the seed directly in the field. They sow the seed in rows about 3 feet (91 centimeters) apart. When the young plants grow, workers thin the rows to allow about 18 to 24 inches (46 to 61 centimeters) between the plants.

In regions with short growing seasons, farmers may start the seeds in a greenhouse or hotbed. They plant the seeds in small, shallow boxes called *flats.* Shortly after the seedlings sprout, workers transplant them to larger flats, spacing them 2 inches (5 centimeters) apart. The plants grow for 4 to 6 weeks, then workers transplant them to the field. But each plant must reestablish itself every time it is transplanted, so growth is retarded. Therefore, most farmers, particularly in mild climates, seed cabbage in the field. Field seeding is much less expensive than transplanting. Also, seedlings establish a better root system than do transplanted cabbage plants. But transplanting is a more reliable method of growing. Home gardeners often prefer to buy the small plants.

Insects and diseases. Cabbage plants are attacked by aphids, cabbage loopers, maggots, cabbageworms, and other insects. Some insects eat the leaves, destroying the head's shape. Insecticides can control insects.

Diseases that affect cabbage include blackleg, club root, mildew, mosaic, black rot, and yellows. Club root and yellows are soilborne. Scientists have developed cabbage varieties resistant to yellows. Hugh C. Price

Scientific classification. Cabbage is in the mustard family, Brassicaceae or Cruciferae. It is *Brassica oleracea,* variety *capitata.* Chinese cabbage is *B. pekinensis.*

Related articles in *World Book* include:

Broccoli	Chinese cabbage	Mustard
Brussels sprouts	Kale	Turnip
Cauliflower	Kohlrabi	

Cabbage palm is a type of palm tree that grows in Cuba, the Bahamas, and the Southeastern United States. It may grow from 20 to 90 feet (6 to 27 meters) tall and has ribbed, fan-shaped leaves that are 5 to 8 feet (1.5 to 2.4 meters) in length. The tree bears a round black fruit that measures ½ inch (13 millimeters) in diameter.

Cabbage palms have edible leaf buds. The buds are formed of new leaves that are developing in the center of the leaf cluster and have not yet opened. The buds may be roasted, boiled, or eaten raw. But they are not often harvested, because harvesting the buds can damage and even kill the tree. Another species of palm tree that is sometimes called cabbage palm produces buds that are harvested and sold as "hearts of palm." Hearts of palm are eaten in salads or served as a vegetable.

Michael G. Barbour

Scientific classification. The cabbage palm belongs to the palm family, Arecaceae. Its scientific name is *Sabal palmetto.* The palm that produces hearts of palm is *Euterpe oleracea.*

See also **Palm; Palmetto.**

Cabell, *CAB uhl,* **James Branch** (1879-1958), was an American author. His unusual fiction is a sophisticated combination of romance, legend, fantasy, satire, mythology, symbolism, and irony. Cabell's books, though often filled with whimsy and humor, are the work of an essentially serious philosophic writer.

Cabell's major achievement was an 18-volume series he called "Biography of the Life of Manuel." The series deals imaginatively with Dom Manuel, a medieval nobleman in the mythical French province of Poictesme, and his descendants over a period of several centuries. The most famous work in the series is the novel *Jurgen* (1919). Attempts were made to ban the book on a charge of obscenity. Other well-known volumes in the "Biography" include *The Rivet in Grandfather's Neck* (1915), *The Cream of the Jest* (1917), *Figures of Earth* (1921), *The High Place* (1923), *The Silver Stallion* (1926), and *Something About Eve* (1927).

Cabell was born on April 14, 1879, in Richmond, Virginia. His writings reflect his knowledge of languages and literature and interest in history and genealogy. He died on May 5, 1958. Bert Hitchcock

Cabeza de Vaca, *kah VAY thah thay VAH kah,* **Álvar Núñez,** *AHL vahr NOO nyayth* (1490?-1557?), was a Spanish explorer in the Americas. He was the first European to describe the American buffalo, or *bison.* In 1527, Cabeza joined an expedition to Florida. After landing, he became separated from the ships. Cabeza and a few companions, including the black explorer Estevanico, sailed on a barge from northern Florida to an island off the Texas coast. They lived with Indians for several years before reaching northwestern Mexico on foot. The explorers' reports that great wealth lay north of Mexico attracted other Spanish explorers to the area, including Francisco Vásquez de Coronado and Hernando de Soto.

In 1540, Cabeza was appointed governor of Paraguay. He was a failure as governor, and the colonists later deposed him. Helen Delpar

Cabinda, *kuh BEEN duh,* is a district of Angola and a major oil-producing area. It is separated from the rest of Angola by the western end of Congo (Kinshasa) and the Congo River (see **Angola** [map]). Cabinda covers 2,807 square miles (7,270 square kilometers) and has a population of about 114,000. Its capital and largest city, also called Cabinda, is an important seaport. Cabinda produces most of Angola's chief export, oil. Cabinda also produces coffee, palm oil, timber, and various minerals.

Black Africans inhabited the Cabinda area more than 2,000 years ago. During the 1500's, Portuguese settlers claimed possession of Cabinda and other parts of Angola. In the 1960's, the discovery of oil off Cabinda's coast and on the mainland gave the area new economic importance. Angola—including Cabinda—was controlled by Portugal until 1975, when it gained independence. Members of a nationalist movement in Cabinda tried to gain independence from Angola. Angolan forces defeated most of these rebels. But some fighting has continued between rebel groups and Angolan forces.

Ian S. Spears

Cabinet is a group of advisers who help the head of a government establish policies and make decisions. It nearly always consists of the officials who supervise the executive or administrative work of a government. These officials usually have the title of *minister,* or *secretary,* of a department or office. The term *cabinet* is also used to describe a system of government in which officials who direct the executive work of the government are directly responsible to the legislature.

Cabinet of the United States

Development of the Cabinet. The Constitution of the United States makes no mention of a Cabinet. In describing the powers of the president, it states that "he may require the opinion, in writing, of the principal officer in each of the executive departments, upon any subject relating to the duties of their respective offices." In 1789, Congress established three departments—State, War, and Treasury—and the office of the attorney general. President George Washington frequently consulted with the department heads and the attorney general. The first recorded meeting of this group, held in 1791, included the three secretaries and the vice president. Later, the attorney general and the secretary of the Navy also attended the meetings.

By the early 1800's, the Cabinet was commonly regarded as consisting of the heads of the existing executive offices. But not until 1907 did a federal statute first use the term *cabinet.* Some presidents discontinued Cabinet meetings. Andrew Jackson, for example, had a group of advisers known as the "Kitchen Cabinet."

Membership in the Cabinet is determined by the president. Today, most people call the heads of the 15 executive departments "the Cabinet." These heads are the secretaries of agriculture; commerce; defense; education; energy; health and human services; homeland security; housing and urban development; the interior;

labor; state; transportation; the treasury; veterans affairs; and the attorney general.

Various presidents have asked other officials in the executive branch of government to take part in Cabinet meetings regularly. In 1961, for example, President John F. Kennedy began to have the U.S. ambassador to the United Nations attend Cabinet meetings.

The president calls Cabinet meetings. The meetings usually take place weekly in the Cabinet Room of the White House.

As department heads, Cabinet members are legal officers of the federal government. The president appoints them with the advice and consent of the Senate, and may dismiss them at any time. They are responsible for administering their departments and carrying out government policies.

By custom, Cabinet members resign when a new president takes office. This procedure enables the new chief executive to select his or her own Cabinet.

Policymaking role of the Cabinet has varied with different presidents. That role has diminished since the 1960's because presidents have relied increasingly on smaller advisory groups in making important foreign and domestic policy decisions. For example, economic policy is largely shaped by four people. Of this group, only the secretary of the treasury belongs to the Cabinet. The others are the chairman of the Council of Economic Advisers, the director of the Office of Management and Budget, and the head of the Federal Reserve Board. In matters of foreign policy and defense, the National Security Council plays a more important role than the Cabinet. Many of these smaller, influential groups, including the White House Office, are agencies in the Executive Office of the President.

See the separate articles on each executive department, such as **State, Department of**. For the order in which Cabinet members succeed to the presidency, see **Presidential succession**. For the flags of the Cabinet members, see **Flag** (pictures: Flags of the United States government).

For lists of Cabinet members, see the tables with the biographies of U.S. presidents. For example, see **Nixon, Richard M.** (table: Vice presidents and Cabinet).

The cabinet system of government

The cabinet system of government is often called the *parliamentary system of government.* The officers who direct the executive work of the government are directly responsible to the *parliament* (legislature). In some countries with cabinet systems, the cabinet officials are members of the parliament.

The official head of the government, such as a king, queen, or president, selects the *prime minister* (sometimes called the *chancellor* or *premier)* from the parliament. The prime minister has executive authority in the government (see **Prime minister**). Advisers to the prime minister help form the ministry (see **Ministry**). If one party has a majority in the parliament, that party's leader usually becomes prime minister. The prime minister selects members of his or her party to head the government departments. If no party has a majority, the monarch or president picks a person who can gain the support of a *coalition,* or combination of parties (see **Coalition**). In such a cabinet, the prime minister divides the cabinet posts among the supporting parties so that the cabinet will have the support of a majority in the parliament.

A cabinet resigns if it no longer has the support of the parliament. For example, the parliament may refuse to approve a program that the prime minister considers basic. Or it may vote "no confidence" in the cabinet. In each of these cases, the cabinet resigns. The prime minister or his or her successor forms a new cabinet that has the support of the parliament. In the United Kingdom, a prime minister who believes that the people support his or her program can dissolve Parliament instead of resigning. The British people are then asked to elect a new one. Even with the support of Parliament, a British Cabinet cannot stay in power indefinitely. A prime minister must call a general election after five years in office. Canada and most Commonwealth and European nations have the cabinet system of government. Charles E. Jacob

See also the *Government* section of articles on countries that have the cabinet system of government, such as **United Kingdom** (Government).

Additional resources

Blondel, Jean, and Müller-Rommel, Ferdinand, eds. *Cabinets in Eastern Europe.* Palgrave, 2001. *Cabinets in Western Europe.* 2nd ed. St. Martin's, 1997.

Grossman, Mark. *Encyclopedia of the United States Cabinet.* 3 vols. ABC-CLIO, 2000.

White, Graham. *Cabinets and First Ministers.* UBC Pr., 2005. Focuses on Canada.

Cabinetmaker. See **Carpentry**.

Cable, for electric and communications use, is an insulated wire or bundle of wires that carry electric current, or a bundle of glass fibers that carry pulses of light. Billions of miles of cable carry communications signals and electric power throughout the world. Millions of feet of specialized cables are used in computers as well as in a wide variety of other electrical and electronic devices. The terms *cable* and *wire* are sometimes used interchangeably.

Communications systems that transmit radio signals through the air have begun to take the place of some cables. But in many cases, cables still provide the most practical means of transmitting communications signals.

Cable construction

Most cables consist of *conductors* (metal wires capable of carrying electric current) covered with insulation and other protective materials. The most common conductor materials are copper and aluminum. Copper has low *resistance* (opposition to the passage of electric charges) and does not corrode easily. Aluminum has properties that are less ideal, but it is lighter and less expensive than copper. Conductors of small diameter, such as those of cables used in computers, carry low-voltage, low-amperage electric currents. Large-diameter conductors, such as those used in electric power transmission, carry currents with high voltage and high amperage.

Insulation prevents electric current from escaping the conductor, protects the conductor from damage, and helps prevent *interference.* Interference occurs when a conductor picks up electric signals from other nearby conductors or from the air. The most common insula-

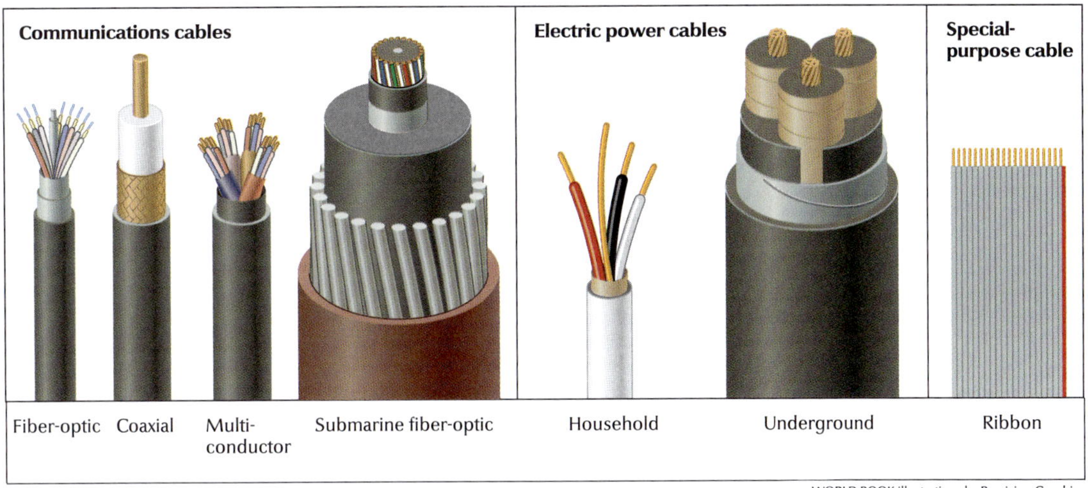

WORLD BOOK illustrations by Precision Graphics

Various types of cables play an important role in everyday life. Communications cables carry telephone and television signals. Electric power cables distribute electric power from utility companies to customers. Special-purpose cables are used in computers and other electronic devices.

tion materials are plastics. However, some electric power cables are insulated using paper saturated with oil. The insulation thickness of some computer cables is less than 1/100 inch (0.2 millimeter). Cable used for long-distance electric power transmission often has insulation more than 1 inch (25 millimeters) thick.

Simple cables are made of a single pair of insulated wires twisted together. *Multiconductor cables* have three or more insulated conductors. Some multiconductor cables used in communications, such as telephone lines, can contain hundreds, or even thousands, of insulated conductors bound together. Multiconductor cables are usually enclosed in a heavy sheath made of several layers of aluminum or plastic. Some thick cables also contain steel wire to provide strength. Low-energy multiconductor cables, such as *ribbon cables* (flat cables used to make connections in computers) require no special protection because they are installed in an enclosed, protected environment.

Types and functions of cables

Two widely used types of cables are (1) coaxial cables and (2) fiber-optic cables.

Coaxial cables are made up of two conductors. The outer conductor is a rigid or flexible metal tube, and the inner conductor is a wire running through the tube's center. Insulation holds the wire in place and separates the two conductors. The cables are called *coaxial* because the tube and the wire have the same *axis* (center). A typical coaxial cable has about the same diameter as a pencil. Several such cables may be bundled together.

Many telephone conversations travel over coaxial cables. When used for phone conversations, coaxial cables normally work in pairs that carry signals in opposite directions. Coaxial cables are also used in some parts of cable television systems. A single cable can carry as many as several hundred television signals or thousands of telephone conversations at once. Individual signals do not interfere with each other because they are carried by electric currents *oscillating* (moving back and forth) at different *frequencies* (numbers of cycles per second).

Most cables used to transmit or distribute electric power are also coaxial cables. The inner conductor carries the electric current. The outer conductor is connected to a neutral ground point in the system to maintain a uniform electric field on the cable surface and to prevent electric shocks.

Coaxial electric power cables are made with great care. The insulation of these cables must hold in high levels of electric power. Contamination, such as small metal particles within the insulation, can result in electrical stresses that will cause the cable to eventually fail.

Fiber-optic cables carry signals in the form of light. Such cables consist of a bundle of threadlike transparent glass or plastic *optical fibers.* Signals coded as pulses of light are sent into one end of an optical fiber by a laser, and the light travels through the core. *Cladding,* a thin covering usually made of glass, surrounds the core of each fiber and helps prevent the light from escaping. A photosensitive device at the other end of the fiber receives the coded signals, which another device then converts to the original signals.

The largest fiber-optic cables can carry hundreds of thousands of telephone conversations or hundreds of television channels. Many communications companies have begun installing fiber-optic cables in place of coaxial cables. No electrical interference occurs in fiber-optic cables, and there is less *signal loss* (gradual weakening of signals as they travel along a cable) than there is in coaxial cables. Fiber-optic cables measure only 1/25 to 1/2 inch (1 to 13 millimeters) in diameter and thus take up much less space than coaxial cables.

Cable installation

Cables can be laid underground or along the ocean floor, or they can be mounted on poles. Underground cables can be laid directly in the earth, or they can be

© Corbis

Laying an underwater cable requires a ship outfitted with special equipment. Underwater cables are commonly used to carry communications signals between continents.

pulled through *conduits.* Conduits are pipes or tubes that are laid in the ground and covered before the cable is installed. Burying cable protects it from harsh weather and keeps the land surface uncluttered. As a result, few new cables are strung aboveground. Underwater communications cables serve as a link between continents. Special amplifiers installed at various points along a cable system strengthen signals to prevent signal loss.

During installation, it is often necessary to *splice* (connect) two cables together. Fiber-optic and high-energy electric power cables are spliced in specially constructed temporary rooms with filtered, extra clean air.

Chief parts of coaxial and fiber-optic cables

A coaxial cable has an inner and an outer conductor that share the same axis. A fiber-optic cable has a number of transparent fibers of glass and a central wire that strengthens the cable.

WORLD BOOK illustrations by Precision Graphics

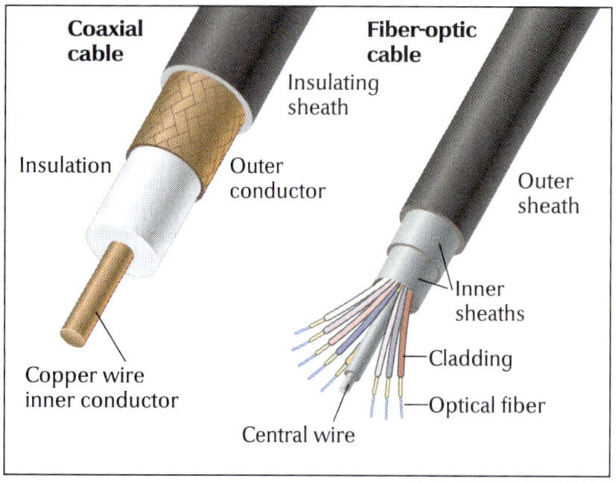

History

Telegraph cables. In 1844, the American painter and inventor Samuel F. B. Morse completed the first long-distance telegraph cable in the United States. Morse's cable extended from Baltimore to Washington, D.C. It was strung on wooden poles and insulated with glass plates.

During the late 1840's, numerous attempts were made to lay telegraph cables along the bottom of various bodies of water. Many of these attempts failed because the insulation on the cables could not shield the conductors from the water. In 1851, two English brothers, Jacob and John Brett, succeeded in laying a telegraph cable across the English Channel. In making their cable, they used a tough insulation consisting of a fiber called *hemp* and a rubberlike substance called *gutta-percha.* They also used iron to strengthen their cable.

The Atlantic Telegraph Company, organized by the American businessman Cyrus W. Field, laid the first telegraph cables across the bottom of the Atlantic Ocean. From 1857 to 1866, the company made four attempts to lay a transatlantic cable, but the cables either broke while being laid or failed after a short time. Success finally came in 1866, when the British steamship *Great Eastern* laid a cable from Valentia, Ireland, to Heart's Content, Newfoundland, Canada. Much of the success of the transatlantic cable was due to the work of the British physicist William Thomson (later Lord Kelvin), who supervised the project. By 1900, 15 transatlantic telegraph cables were in operation.

Electric power cables. In mid-1880, Thomas Edison planned the installation of his first incandescent-lighting system in New York. Because the cables would encompass all the individual wires leading to houses, they would be too large to suspend from poles. Edison determined that they would have to be buried. He initially thought wood would serve as a good insulator for his cables, and so he performed tests using wires laid in

Forte Power Systems, Inc.

Burying cable protects it from weather damage and helps keep the landscape uncluttered. A power cable like the one shown here may be laid in a concrete channel for additional protection.

wood moldings in shallow trenches. However, Edison soon found that wood lost its insulating properties when it became wet. He tried various other insulating materials, eventually settling on asphalt mixed with linseed oil and small amounts of paraffin and beeswax. This compound was heated, and then strips of muslin were dipped into it and wrapped around the conductors. This method worked, and by the end of November 1880, Edison's new system was lighting 400 street lamps.

Telephone cables. The Scottish-born inventor Alexander Graham Bell patented the telephone in 1876. Thousands of telephones quickly came into use, and many cities became cluttered with telephone lines consisting of single insulated wires. In the late 1880's, engineers found that, by twisting wires together, they could produce a stronger cable and limit the clutter. The first underground telephone cable was installed in 1902 between New York City and Newark, New Jersey.

In 1931, two American engineers, Lloyd Espenschied and Herman A. Affel, patented the coaxial cable. Coaxial cables were first used commercially in 1941.

The laying of the first transatlantic telephone cable was finished in 1956. The cable extended from Clarenville, on the island of Newfoundland, to Oban, Scotland. The first long-distance fiber-optic cable was completed in 1983. It carries telephone conversations between New York City and Washington, D.C. The first fiber-optic cables to span the Atlantic and Pacific oceans joined the United States with France and the United Kingdom in 1988 and the United States with Japan in 1989.

Recent developments. Cable manufacturers have begun developing "intelligent" electric power cables. Optical fibers in such cables can provide information on the performance and soundness of the cables. Such properties will help cable operators avoid damage during cable installation and operation.

Advances in technology have led to the development of highly efficient *superconducting cables* that are able to carry vast amounts of electric power. Superconductors are conductors that have almost no resistance to the flow of electric current. Superconducting cables are made from special ceramic fibers that become superconducting when cooled with liquid nitrogen. Electric utilities have begun to test this type of cable for use in large cities that lack space for new power lines.

Richard A. Hartlein

Related articles in *World Book* include:

Coaxial cable
Communication
Fiber optics
Field, Cyrus West
Insulator, Electric
Kelvin, Lord
Maury, Matthew F.
Telecommunications
Telegraph
Telephone

Cable, George Washington (1844-1925), was an American writer known for his books about *Creoles,* who were Louisiana natives descended from French and Spanish settlers. Cable's reputation rests primarily on his portrayal of Creole customs and speech and his examination of Southern racial attitudes.

Cable was part of a movement in American literature called *local color writing.* This movement tried to capture the feeling of a particular region through descriptions of local speech and manners. Like other local color writers, Cable wrote for many magazines. His first book, *Old Creole Days* (1879), was a collection of magazine stories. The novel *The Grandissimes* (1880) combines the themes of slavery and prejudice toward people of mixed racial ancestry. His novelette *Madame Delphine* (1881) also deals with people of mixed racial ancestry. Cable supported civil rights reform in the South in such nonfiction books as *The Silent South* (1885) and *The Negro Question* (1890). Cable was born on Oct. 12, 1844, in New Orleans. He died on Jan. 31, 1925. Ronald T. Curran

Cable car is a passenger vehicle that is pulled by a constantly moving wire cable. Some cable cars, such as ski lifts, run on cables suspended between towers. However, most cable cars ride on rails. In such systems, the cable runs in a channel beneath the street. An engine in a central station propels the cable at about 9 miles (14 kilometers) per hour. A cable car moves when its operator pushes a lever that causes the car's heavy metal *grip* to latch onto the moving cable.

Andrew S. Hallidie, an American manufacturer, invented the cable car, and in 1873 he helped install the first cable-car line, in San Francisco. Cable cars soon became popular throughout the world. During the 1890's, however, electric streetcars began to replace them (see **Streetcar**). Darwin H. Stapleton

See also **San Francisco** (Transportation and communication; Continued prosperity; picture).

Cable television. See **Television** (Cable television systems).

Cabot, John, was an Italian navigator who sailed the Atlantic Ocean from Europe to North America in 1497. His was the first recorded voyage across the North Atlantic since the Vikings explored Canada about A.D. 1000. Cabot wanted to reach East Asia by sailing west, but he did not realize that America lay in his path. He explored the island of Newfoundland, and possibly the coasts of southeastern Labrador and Cape Breton Island, in what is today eastern Canada.

The date and place of Cabot's birth are unknown. Some records suggest he was born in Italy as Zuan Chabotto. Cabot grew up in Venice, Italy, a city famous for the skill of its sailors.

In 1492, the Italian navigator Christopher Columbus sailed from Spain to the West Indies. People assumed he had reached Asia. Cabot believed there was a shorter route than the one Columbus had taken. About 1495, he went to Bristol, England, seeking merchants to invest in a voyage to East Asia. Although this effort was unsuccessful, he managed to find investors for another voyage. In 1496, King Henry VII of England gave Cabot permission to explore lands "unknown to all Christians" for England.

Cabot set sail from Bristol in May 1497 on a small ship, the *Mathew.* He took a crew of about 20 men. On June 24, 1497, Cabot sighted land somewhere in Atlantic Canada. His son Sebastian later claimed that this was Cape Breton, in present-day Nova Scotia, but his claim is questionable.

Cabot and his crew landed only once. Armed with crossbows, they remained close to the shore. They planted the flags of England and Venice and raised a cross for the Roman Catholic Church. They also found animal traps, fishnets, and a weaving tool. Cabot and his crew were probably in Newfoundland, where the Beothuk people lived. Cabot believed he had reached Asia. He recorded the latitude of what is now the tip of Newfoundland's Great Northern Peninsula.

After Cabot returned to England in August 1497, King Henry gave him a handsome reward. The king also decided to invest in a second, larger expedition in 1498. Meanwhile, the *Mathew's* crew told of huge schools of fish off the mysterious coasts they had explored.

Cabot's second voyage ended in disaster, and he and his ships were lost. Although he did not discover a new route to Asia, Cabot reopened European contact with North America and discovered rich fishing areas. From 1500 to 1800, thousands of Europeans crossed the Atlantic to fish along the Newfoundland coast.

Peter E. Pope

See also **Cabot, Sebastian; Exploration** (Exploring the New World).

Cabot, Sebastian (? -1557) was an influential Italian mapmaker and navigator. He explored the coast of Labrador, in what is now northeastern Canada.

Cabot was born in Venice, Italy. The year of his birth is unknown, but it was probably sometime before 1486. His father was the famous Italian explorer John Cabot (see **Cabot, John**). His family moved to Bristol, England, about 1495. Cabot claimed he was on his father's first expedition to North America, in 1497, but no other evidence supports his claim.

In 1508, Cabot led an English expedition up the coast of Labrador in search of a Northwest Passage—that is, a route around or through North America to Asia. The expedition encountered a great deal of ice, suggesting there was no easy passage through the Arctic Ocean. Later, Cabot's mapmaking skills earned him a position as *pilot major* for Spain. As pilot major, he was in charge of recording Spain's effort to explore the world. In 1526, he led another expedition bound for Asia. On this voyage, he explored the Río de la Plata in present-day Argentina.

In 1544, Cabot prepared one of the first printed maps of the world. In 1553, he became governor of the Muscovy Company, an association of London merchants. During his final years, he is said to have taught English sea captains how to navigate using the stars and the sun.

Peter E. Pope

Cabral, *kuh BRAHL,* **Pedro Álvares,** *PAY throo AHL vuh reesh* (1467?-1528?), was a Portuguese navigator who sailed to Brazil in 1500 and claimed it for Portugal. His voyage helped Portugal develop a large overseas empire in the 1500's.

Cabral was born near Covilhã, Portugal. He was educated at the royal court and became a member of the King's Council. In 1499, King Manuel I appointed him commander of a fleet to carry on the work of Portuguese explorer Vasco da Gama (see **Da Gama, Vasco**). Cabral probably had never sailed a ship before.

Cabral and his fleet of 13 ships sailed from Belem, near Lisbon, on March 9, 1500. He headed for India and planned to follow the route taken by Da Gama. The fleet sailed southwest and passed the Canary and Cape Verde islands. The sailors hoped for winds that would carry them around the Cape of Good Hope at the bottom of the African continent. However, for some reason, probably the weather, the fleet sailed off course.

On April 22, the crew sighted what is now southeastern Brazil. Cabral claimed the area for Portugal. The land lay within Portuguese territory as determined by the Treaty of Tordesillas in 1494 (see **Line of Demarcation**). Cabral had lost one ship, and another returned to Portugal with news of the landing. The remaining ships stayed in Brazil for eight days and then continued the voyage to India.

On May 24, a storm scattered the fleet. Four of the vessels were lost, but one reached Madagascar. The other six ships met at Mozambique and followed the African coast northward. The fleet crossed the Indian Ocean and arrived in Kozhikode (also called Calicut), India, on September 13. There, many crew members were killed in a battle with a band of Arab merchants. Cabral's fleet then sailed to the Indian towns of Cochin and Cannanore, where the ships were loaded with spices.

Cabral's fleet returned to Lisbon on June 23, 1501. Manuel I considered Cabral for command of another expedition to India but chose Da Gama instead. Cabral then retired from royal service. John Parker

See also **Exploration** (map: The great age of discovery).

Cabrillo, *kah BREE yoh,* **Juan Rodríguez,** *hwahn roh THREE gayth* (? -1543), led the first European expedition to explore the coast of what is now California. His explorations aided the Spanish in settling California.

Cabrillo was born in Portugal. Scholars know little about his early life. He came to Cuba about 1520 and joined the Spanish army there. Cabrillo participated in the Spanish conquest of what is now Mexico in 1521 and of present-day Guatemala in 1523 and 1524.

In 1541, Antonio de Mendoza, the Spanish ruler of Mexico, ordered Cabrillo to explore the Pacific coast north of Mexico. Cabrillo commanded two ships, the *San Salvador* and the *Victoria.* The expedition set out from Navidad, Mexico, near Manzanillo, in June 1542. Three months later, the explorers reached San Diego Bay. They then continued to sail northward along the coast and met Indians from several villages. Some of the Indians gave Cabrillo fish and other supplies.

In November 1542, a storm blew Cabrillo's ships past the Golden Gate, the entrance to San Francisco Bay. Soon afterward, the expedition turned south. The explorers anchored at San Miguel Island, about 50 miles (80 kilometers) west of Santa Barbara. Cabrillo died on San Miguel Island on Jan. 3, 1543. John Parker

See also **California** (Spanish and English exploration).

Cabrillo National Monument, *kuh BRIHL oh* or *kah BREE yoh,* in California, honors the Portuguese-born explorer Juan Rodríguez Cabrillo, who served Spain. Cabrillo sailed into San Diego Bay on Sept. 28, 1542, and claimed for Spain the west coast of what became the United States. The monument was established in 1913. For area, see **National Park System** (table: National monuments). Critically reviewed by the National Park Service

Cabrini, Saint Frances Xavier, *kuh BREE nee, saynt FRAN sihs ZAY vih ur* (1850-1917), was the first United States citizen to be made a saint by the Roman Catholic Church. She was *canonized* (declared a saint) in 1946. In 1950, Pope Pius XII named her patron saint of emigrants.

She was born Maria Francesca Cabrini on July 15, 1850, in the Lombardy region of Italy. She was the 13th and youngest child of a farmer. During the early part of her life, she wanted to be a missionary in China. She was trained to be a schoolteacher. When Cabrini was 30, she established the Missionary Sisters of the Sacred Heart, an order originally formed for the instruction of poor children.

Cabrini League

Saint Frances Cabrini

In 1889, the nun came to the United States, where she immediately displayed the courage, hope, vision, and endurance of a pioneer. Cabrini lived in New York City and Chicago, and traveled in Latin America. She and her followers opened many charitable institutions, including orphanages, schools, and free clinics. Cabrini founded Columbus Hospital in New York City in 1892 and Columbus Hospital in Chicago in 1905. In 1909, she became a United States citizen.

Four miracles were credited to her from the time she died on Dec. 22, 1917, until she was canonized. Her feast day is November 13. She is buried at Mother Cabrini High School in New York City. Anne E. Carr

Cacao, *kuh KAY oh,* is an evergreen tree whose seeds, or beans, are used to make chocolate and cocoa. Cultivated cacao trees grow about 25 feet (7.6 meters) high. In the wild, cacao trees can reach a height of 40 feet (12 meters). Their fruit is a melonlike pod that may be 12 inches (30 centimeters) long. The cacao seeds, imbedded in the pod, are about the size of lima beans. They range from light brown to purple. Cacao trees are cultivated in Central and South America, the East and West Indies, and West Africa. The beans supply not only chocolate and cocoa, but also cocoa butter, used in candies and medicines. The people of Mexico and Central America once used cacao beans as money.

David S. Seigler

WORLD BOOK illustration by Chris Skilton

The cacao tree bears pods on short stems close to the trunk. The pods contain the beans used to make chocolate and cocoa.

Scientific classification. The cacao tree belongs to the sterculia family, Sterculiaceae. It is *Theobroma cacao.*

Cachalot. See Sperm whale.

Cactus is any of a family of North and South American plants that usually have clusters of spines. There are hundreds of *species* (kinds) of cactuses. Most species grow in hot, dry regions in Mexico and the southwestern United States. But cactuses also inhabit such areas as rain forests in Central America and cold, high regions in the Andes Mountains of South America.

Richard Parker, NAS

The saguaro, or giant cactus, may reach a height of 60 feet (18 meters) and a diameter of 2 feet (0.6 meter). In spring, flowers bloom on the tips of its branches and stem.

Cactuses vary widely in size and shape. For example, the giant saguaro looks like a bare tree with a thick trunk and long, upturned branches. It can grow as tall as 60 feet (18 meters). Some tiny South American cactuses measure less than 1 inch (2.5 centimeters) high. Certain cactuses look like pincushions or starfish, while others have flat, papery spines that resemble blades of grass.

Scientists believe cactuses may have grown on Earth for millions of years. The first cactuses had leaves, branches, and woody stems like those of a tree. These features are still found in some primitive cactuses. Most cactus species, however, changed in appearance over the years. The branches became shorter, and the leaves developed into spines. The woody stem became softer and more able to absorb and store water.

Parts of the cactus. The structure of a cactus helps the plant survive in dry climates. Most cactuses have

Allan D. Cruickshank, NAS

The barrel cactus has tough, curved spines that Native Americans once used as fishhooks. Its juicy pulp has saved the life of many thirsty travelers in the desert.

David Muench

The organ-pipe cactus has stems that resemble the pipes of an organ. It may grow 25 feet (7.6 meters) high. Some people enclose their property with rows of these cactuses.

Norman Myers, Bruce Coleman Inc.

The old man cactus has a coat of white hair that shields it from the sun. This thornless cactus is a popular house plant.

E. S. Ross

The prickly pear has thorny, leaflike stems. This cactus grows in dry or rocky ground in many parts of North America. The plant bears pear-shaped fruit that is good to eat.

thick, fleshy stems with waxy skin. The stem holds water, and the skin keeps the water from evaporating. In addition, the surfaces of many cactuses can expand and contract like an accordion, which accommodates the changes of water content in the stem.

Cactuses have extremely long roots. The roots grow close to the surface and collect as much water as possible for storage. The roots of a large saguaro may grow 50 feet (15 meters) in length. Some cactuses store their water in thick, fleshy roots that look like carrots.

The spines of a cactus protect the juicy plant from being eaten by animals. They also provide some shade for the plant. The spines may be long or short and soft or sharp. They may have straight or hooked tips. Spines grow in clusters out of small lumps or mounds, called *areoles,* on the stem. Areoles occur in regular patterns on the stem. In some species, such as the saguaro and the barrel cactus, the areoles merge to form ribs that run along the length of the stem. The ribs give the plant shade and help the stem store water.

All cactuses produce flowers. Like the spines, flowers grow out of the areoles. The flowers may be white or a bright color, such as yellow, orange, or red. In dry weather cactuses, the flowers remain open for only a day or two. Some open only at night. They then wither and fall off. This short blooming period keeps water from evaporating from the big, soft petals. Cactuses that live in rain forests, where water is more abundant, have flowers that stay open for several days.

Life cycle of the cactus. All cactuses reproduce sexually. They bear flowers with male and female parts. The male part produces a yellow powder, called *pollen.* For a cactus to reproduce, its pollen must fertilize an egg cell in the female part of the plant. Insects, birds, or bats are attracted to the flowers' bright colors or scent. As they feed, these creatures carry pollen from one part of the plant to the other. This process is called *pollination.*

After pollen has fertilized an egg cell, a fruit develops. The cactus fruit is a fleshy berry that contains black or brown seeds. Cactus seeds are scattered by wind, rain, and animals. One cactus plant may produce a million seeds during its lifetime. But only one or two seeds will live long enough to produce a new cactus plant.

Some cactuses reproduce both sexually and *asexually* (without seeds and flowers). For example, prickly pear and cholla (pronounced *CHOY uh)* cactuses have stems with weak connecting joints. If part of a stem is knocked off and sticks in the ground, it can grow new roots and become a new plant. It will then make its own stems and flowers. Most cactuses grow slowly. Young plants may take a year to reach a height of 1 inch (2.5 centimeters). Older plants may grow from 3 to 4 inches (7.5 to 10 centimeters) a year. Cactuses live from 50 to 200 years.

Kinds of cactuses. Common cactuses in Mexico and the southwestern United States include the organ pipe, old man, cholla, barrel, prickly pear, and saguaro cactuses. The organ pipe cactus has tall stems that grow in groups. They look like a set of organ pipes. The old man cactus has spines that resemble long white hair. The stems of the jumping cholla fall off so easily that they seem to jump on people passing by. Another type of cholla, called the teddy bear cholla, has brown and tan spines. From far away, the plant's shape and color make it look like a teddy bear.

The common barrel cactus has a barrel shape and long, tough spines. The Engelmann's prickly pear features large, circular or oval stems and pear-shaped fruit. The saguaro may have as many as a dozen armlike branches.

South American cactuses include the snow cactuses, which live high in the Andes Mountains. These small plants clump together in mounds. Snow cactuses have many long, white hairs, which make the mounds look like snow drifts.

The importance of cactuses. Insects, birds, and other small animals feed on the stems and flowers of cactus plants. Many of these animals hide from enemies in cactuses, where they are protected by the plants' spines. Numerous birds also build their nests in cactus stems. Certain woodpeckers live inside larger cactus species.

Cactuses also provide food for people. After the spines are scraped off, prickly pear stems can be fried and eaten. Some people eat cactus fruits or grind the seeds into a kind of meal for cakes. Manufacturers use some cactuses to make a red food dye. Certain cactuses can be used for lumber.

People in all parts of the world grow cactus plants for sale. Sometimes people sell cactuses that they dig out of natural areas. This *cactus rustling* has become illegal in most countries. Certain species of cactus are in danger of becoming extinct. National parks and preserves have been established to protect them. James D. Mauseth

Scientific classification. Cactuses make up the cactus family, Cactaceae. Chollas, prickly pears, and snow cactuses belong to the subfamily Opuntioideae. Saguaro, organ pipe, old man, and barrel cactuses belong to the subfamily Cactoideae.

Related articles in *World Book* include:

Arizona (Plant and animal life; pictures)
Flower (pictures: Flowers of the desert)
Mescaline
Plant (Water storage; pictures)
Prickly pear
Saguaro

Caddisfly is any of a large group of mothlike insects that live in and around water. Adult caddisflies have two pairs of wings that extend over their abdomens like a tent when at rest. Fine, hairlike structures cover the wings. Most adults have brownish or grayish coloring and grow up to about 1 ¼ inches (3 centimeters) long.

Adult caddisflies are weak flyers that become most active at night. They have poorly developed mouthparts. Instead of eating solid food, they sip water, plant juices, or *honeydew* (a liquid produced by certain insects).

Caddisfly *larvae* (young) resemble caterpillars. They live mainly in lakes, rivers, and other bodies of fresh water, absorbing oxygen through threadlike gills on their abdomens. A few species live on land. Unlike the adults, the larvae consume solid food. Most species eat plants or scavenge for meat. These species build portable protective cases in which to live. To make the cases, they glue together sticks, stones, leaves, or sand grains with a silklike substance produced in their bodies. Some caddisflies spin silklike webs or tunnels in the water that both provide shelter and trap prey.

Caddisfly larvae serve as food for fish and other water animals. People often use the larvae as fishing bait. Most caddisflies are sensitive to polluted water, and biologists use them to assess water quality. John R. Meyer

Scientific classification. Caddisflies belong to the order Trichoptera.

Caddo Indians, *KAD oh,* formed a group of allied tribes that once lived in Louisiana, Arkansas, and Texas. Caddo is an abbreviation of the native name *Kadohadacho,* meaning *real chiefs.*

The Caddo lived in large houses of post framework covered with grass. Each house held several families. The Caddo cultivated fields of corn, beans, and pumpkins, and collected wild grapes and berries. They also hunted deer, bear, wild fowl, and buffalo. The men cut and traded the wood of the Osage orange, the favorite bowwood among tribes of the Western plains. The women made excellent pottery. Caddo chiefs were highly respected and were carried from place to place on litters or on the shoulders of their subjects.

Early Spanish explorers learned to respect the Caddo warriors, who bravely hurled fire-hardened lances at the invading soldiers. But explorers who came from Mexico in the middle 1600's knew these Indians as *Texas* or *Tejas,* meaning *friends.* When French explorers met the Caddo in the 1680's, they found the Indians riding swift Spanish horses. During the 1700's, warfare between the Spanish and French in Caddo territory killed many of the Caddo, and most of the remainder moved to Texas.

In 1855, the United States government assigned the Caddo a reservation on the Brazos River in Texas. The Caddo were moved in 1859 to southwestern Oklahoma, where many of their descendants still live. C. B. Clark

See also **Texas** (Indian days).

Cadence, *KAY duhns,* is rhythm of sound or motion. In music, it is the closing air or tune of a song, or of a phrase or movement within the composition. In present-day music, a *perfect cadence* is the progression of the dominant chord to the tonic.

See also **Music** (Harmony; illustration: Cadences).

Cadet, *kuh DEHT,* is a student in officer's training at the United States Military and Air Force academies. Students in the United States Navy and Air Force flying schools are also called cadets, as are students enrolled in Reserve Officers Training Corps (ROTC) programs. English and Canadian military academies also use the term. Some private military schools call their students cadets. *Cadet* is a French word meaning *younger son.* See also **Reserve Officers Training Corps; United States Air Force Academy; United States Military Academy.** Allan R. Millett

Cadillac, *KAD uh LAK,* **Antoine de Lamothe,** *ahn TWAN duh la MAWT* (1658-1730), was a French colonizer, administrator, and fur trader. He founded Detroit and served as governor of the French colony of Louisiana.

Cadillac was born Antoine Laumet on March 5, 1658, at Les Laumets, France. He falsely claimed to belong to the nobility, and he awarded himself a coat of arms and the title "de Lamothe Cadillac." In 1683, Cadillac arrived in Nova Scotia, where he served on a *privateer* (private warship) and traded for furs. From 1694 to 1697, he commanded Fort Michilimackinac (in what is now Michigan), the most important French outpost in the West.

In 1701, Cadillac founded Fort Pontchartrain at the site of present-day Detroit. He served as commandant there until 1710, when he was dismissed for incompetence and corruption. Cadillac was governor of Louisiana from 1711 until 1716, when he was recalled to France. He died on Oct. 15, 1730. D. Peter MacLeod

Cádiz, *kuh DIHZ* or *KAY dihz* (pop. 133,363), is a major port city in southern Spain. It lies on the Atlantic Ocean, 60 miles (97 kilometers) northwest of Gibraltar (see

Spain [political map]). Cádiz has long been Spain's chief naval station, and ships of many nations use its harbor. The city is the capital of Cádiz province.

The Phoenicians founded Cádiz in 1130 B.C., and many experts believe it to be the oldest city in Europe. The settlement prospered and became one of the great outposts of Phoenician power. About 550 B.C., Cádiz found itself threatened by local Iberian tribes, and called on Carthage for help. Carthage sent forces to Cádiz, but the Carthaginians captured the city. The Romans seized Cádiz from the Carthaginians in 205 B.C. Hundreds of years later, the city became a Moorish stronghold.

In 1262, King Alfonso X of Castile and León drove the Moors out of Cádiz. Christopher Columbus sailed from Cádiz in 1493 on his second voyage to America. During the next 300 years, when Spain had a worldwide empire, the riches of the American colonies poured into the city, and Cádiz became wealthy. Stanley G. Payne

Cadmium, *KAD mee uhm,* is a soft, silvery-white metallic element used for plating and in *alloys* (mixtures of metals). Friedrich Stromeyer of Germany discovered it in 1817. For every billion atoms of Earth's crust, only about 30 are cadmium. Cadmium is similar to the element zinc. It occurs with zinc minerals and is obtained as a by-product of zinc refining. Japan is the leading producer of cadmium.

Cadmium is poisonous. People have become seriously ill or have died soon after breathing cadmium dust or fumes of cadmium oxide. Also, small amounts of cadmium entering the body over long periods may damage the kidneys and deform bones. Some people fear that hazardous amounts of cadmium have reached the environment from widespread industrial use of the metal.

Industry uses cadmium in alloys for high-speed bearings, and as a protective coating for other metals. Cadmium is often used instead of zinc for *galvanizing* iron and steel—that is, for coating them to prevent rust. Cadmium provides poorer long-term protection than zinc. But it keeps a brighter color for longer periods. Cadmium rods are used in nuclear reactors to control nuclear reactions. Nickel-cadmium and silver-cadmium batteries, which can be recharged, are used in watches, calculators, and many other small devices.

Its *atomic number* (number of protons in its nucleus) is 48. Its *relative atomic mass* is 112.411. An element's relative atomic mass equals its *mass* (amount of matter) divided by $\frac{1}{12}$ of the mass of carbon 12, the most abundant form of carbon. The density of cadmium is 8.65 grams per cubic centimeter at 20 °C. Cadmium melts at 320.9 °C and boils at 765 °C. Raymond E. Davis

See also **Battery** (Rechargeable alkaline batteries).

Cadmus, *KAD muhs,* in Greek mythology, was the son of Agenor, the king of Tyre, a city in Phoenicia. He set out to find his sister Europa, whom Zeus had stolen. But an oracle told him his search was useless, and directed him instead to follow a cow. Cadmus was to build a city where the cow lay down. A dragon was guarding the spot. Cadmus killed the dragon and sowed its teeth in the ground. At once, armed men sprang up and fought with each other until only five were left. These five helped Cadmus build the city of Thebes in Boeotia (see **Thebes**). Cadmus is also said to have brought the alphabet from Phoenicia to Greece. William F. Hansen

See also **Europa.**

Caduceus. See **Mercury** (mythology).

Caecilian. See **Amphibian.**

Caedmon, *KAD muhn,* was an English poet who lived in England in the late 600's. An uneducated herdsman, Caedmon entered the monastery of Whitby late in life. Saint Bede reported in his *Ecclesiastical History* that Caedmon dreamed he was commanded to sing the praises of God (see **Bede, Saint**). To the monks' surprise, Caedmon sang what is now known as Caedmon's *Hymn.* This song, the only authentic poem Caedmon left, praised God in the heroic tradition of Anglo-Saxon poetry (see **English literature** [Old English literature]). The monks believed that they had witnessed a miracle.

The *Hymn* influenced much later Anglo-Saxon poetry. Scholars once credited paraphrases of the books of Genesis, Exodus, and part of Daniel to Caedmon, but they now believe these paraphrases confirm his influence, not his authorship. William Harmon

Caesar, *SEE zuhr,* was a title which came from the family name of Julius Caesar, who ruled Rome as a monarch without a crown from 49 to 44 B.C. Octavian, Caesar's great-nephew and adopted son, took Caesar's name and also the title of Augustus. The next four Roman emperors all had some claim, by family or adoption, to the name of Caesar, which became so closely associated with the idea of the emperor that it was a kind of title. In choosing the person to follow him as supreme ruler, the emperor would give his heir the title *Caesar.* In the days of the Byzantine Empire, anyone chosen as ruler of a country under the empire might be called Caesar. In the Russian language, the title became *czar.* In German, Caesar became *kaiser.* See also **Kaiser.** Arthur M. Eckstein

Caesar, *SEE zuhr,* **Julius** (100?-44 B.C.), was one of ancient Rome's greatest generals and statesmen. He became a brilliant military leader and helped make Rome the center of an empire that stretched across Europe. Caesar also won fame as an orator, politician, and writer. Caesar's victories in civil war helped him become dictator of the Roman people. But his power frightened many of his political opponents, and a group of them assassinated him.

Early life. Gaius Julius Caesar was born in Rome of an aristocratic family. At the age of 17, he married Cornelia, the daughter of Lucius Cornelius Cinna. Cinna had been an associate of Gaius Marius, a great popular leader. Lucius Sulla, the aristocratic dictator of Rome, ordered Caesar to divorce Cornelia. But Caesar refused to do so. He then went to Greece to study philosophy and oratory. Sulla later pardoned Caesar, and he returned to Rome. Caesar and Cornelia had a daughter, Julia. Cornelia died about 68 B.C.

Caesar became increasingly interested in public affairs, and tried to gain the people's favor. In 65 B.C., he was elected to the office of *aedile* and organized public games. He won favor because he spent much money to provide recreation for the people, although he went heavily into debt to do so. In 62 B.C., Caesar became *praetor,* the office next in rank to consul (see **Praetor**).

Alliance with Pompey. Catiline, a dissatisfied Roman politician, plotted a revolt. In breaking up this plot, leading aristocrats sought to disgrace the entire group of popular leaders, including Caesar (see **Catiline**). But they failed to hurt his political prospects.

In 60 B.C., Caesar allied himself with Marcus Licinius

Crassus and Gnaeus Pompey in the *First Triumvirate,* an alliance that held considerable power in Rome. Crassus was a man of enormous wealth and political ambition. Pompey had returned from Asia Minor in 62 B.C. as a great military leader and the idol of the people. The three gained a major victory when, through violence and bribery, Caesar was elected a consul in 59 B.C. He used force to push through the triumvirate's program, and won the hatred of the conservatives. He was awarded the post of proconsul of three provinces north of Italy. In 59 B.C., Caesar married Calpurnia, daughter of Lucius Piso of Rome. Also that year, Pompey married Caesar's daughter, Julia.

Campaigns in Gaul. By training, Caesar was a politician rather than a soldier. But he knew he needed military victories to gain greater fame. In 58 B.C., Caesar began a campaign to conquer Gaul (now mainly France). It soon became clear that he was a military genius. During his nine years in Gaul, Caesar lost only two battles in which he personally took part. He conquered all territory east to the Rhine River, drove the Germans out of Gaul, and crossed the Rhine to show them the might of Rome. He also invaded Britain twice, in 55 and 54 B.C.

Civil war. Although great public thanksgiving celebrations were held in Rome for his victories, not everyone rejoiced over Caesar's conquests. Pompey became alarmed at Caesar's success. Pompey's growing suspicions of Caesar threw him into an alliance with the conservatives. In 49 B.C., the conservatives ordered Caesar to give up his army.

Caesar had no intention of surrendering his army and leaving himself defenseless. He led 5,000 soldiers across the Rubicon, a stream that separated his provinces from Italy. After this hostile act, there was no turning back. Caesar had provoked, or had been provoked into, a civil war. As Caesar dashed south, he met little opposition. Pompey's troops surrendered, forcing Pompey to flee to the Balkans. The conservatives who had ordered Caesar to give up his army fled with Pompey.

Within 60 days, Caesar became master of Italy. But it took him nearly five years to complete the conquest of Pompey and his followers. In 49 B.C., Caesar had himself appointed dictator and consul. He met Pompey's army in Greece where, at Pharsalus in 48 B.C., he defeated Pompey's forces. Pompey escaped to Egypt. Caesar followed Pompey to Egypt and found that his enemy had been murdered. There, Caesar met Cleopatra.

Last victories. Before returning to Rome, Caesar won the war he fought to make Cleopatra ruler of Egypt. He later brought her to Rome. Caesar won his next victory in 47 B.C., over Pharnaces II, King of Pontus. *Veni, vidi, vici* ("I came, I saw, I conquered") was Caesar's brief but meaningful dispatch to the Roman Senate, reporting this victory at Zela in what is now northwestern Turkey.

Pompey's forces reorganized after the death of their leader. But, in 46 B.C., at Thapsus in northern Africa, Caesar defeated them decisively. Cato the Younger, one of Pompey's supporters, killed himself when he heard of the defeat. In 45 B.C. at Munda, in Spain, Caesar defeated the two sons of Pompey. This was his last battle.

Caesar had now become undisputed master of the Roman world. He pardoned the followers of Pompey. The people honored Caesar for his leadership and triumphs by granting him the powers of dictator for 10 years. Later, he was made dictator for life. At a public festival, Mark Antony tested popular feeling by offering Caesar the crown of a king. Because the Romans hated kings, Caesar refused the crown.

Assassination. Even though Caesar refused the crown, many Romans suspected that he intended to make himself king someday. Marcus Junius Brutus and Gaius Cassius, both of whom Caesar had pardoned after the battle of Pharsalus, led a group of aristocrats in a plot to kill the dictator. On March 15 (the Ides of March), 44 B.C., they stabbed Caesar to death as he entered a Senate meeting. He received more than 20 wounds from men who had accepted his favors and who he had believed were his friends. In Shakespeare's play *Julius Caesar,* Mark Antony says at the funeral of Caesar:

> You all did see that on the Lupercal
> I thrice presented him a kingly crown,
> Which he did thrice refuse: was this ambition?
> Yet Brutus says he was ambitious;
> And, sure, he is an honorable man.
> I speak not to disprove what Brutus spoke,
> But here I am to speak what I do know.

His reforms. Caesar used wisely the power he had won, and made many important reforms. He tried to control dishonest practices in the Roman and provincial governments. He improved the calendar, clearing up confusion that had existed for hundreds of years in computing time. He established a plan for reorganizing city government in Italy. He tried to reconcile his opponents

Julius Caesar was one of the great military leaders of all time. This statue shows Caesar in the uniform of a Roman general.

Marble statue carved between 99 B.C. and 1 B.C. by an unknown Roman sculptor; Museo Capitolino, Rome (Oscar Savio)

by appointing them to public office. Caesar granted Roman citizenship to many people who lived in the provinces.

Caesar gave poor people in Rome an outlet to improve their way of living by establishing colonies, notably at Carthage and Corinth. He continued to distribute free grain but reduced the number of people eligible for it. He is said to have planned many other reforms, such as the founding of public libraries and the construction of a canal across the Isthmus of Corinth.

Caesar had proved he was capable of governing Rome and its vast possessions. Yet many of Caesar's actions offended Roman pride. Caesar treated the Senate as a mere advisory council, and the senators resented this disrespect. He also offended many Romans by assuming the office of dictator. In addition, some Romans objected to measures that gave full citizenship to peoples they regarded as their subjects.

Other talents. As an orator, Caesar ranked second only to Cicero, the great Roman statesman and philosopher. Caesar is also famous as a writer. His *Commentaries on the Gallic War* describes his conquests in Gaul. The clear, direct style of this work makes it a model of historical writing. Erich S. Gruen

Related articles in *World Book* include:

Antony, Mark	Cleopatra
Augustus	Crassus, Marcus Licinius
Brutus, Marcus Junius	Pompey the Great
Cassius Longinus, Gaius	Sulla, Lucius Cornelius

Additional resources

Meier, Christian. *Caesar.* Basic Bks., 1995.
Thorne, James. *Julius Caesar.* Rosen Central, 2003. Younger readers.

Cafeteria. See **Restaurant.**

Caffeine, *KAF een, KAF ee ihn,* or *ka FEEN,* is an odorless, slightly bitter solid. It is a stimulant, and is found in small amounts in coffee, tea, and colas. Caffeine dissolves in water and alcohol, and has crystals that look like needles. When taken in small amounts, caffeine stimulates the nervous system. In this way, caffeine increases alertness and energy. When taken in large amounts, however, it causes nervousness and loss of sleep. The use of caffeine also may cause headaches and digestive disturbances. Caffeine has been linked to the development of birth defects in laboratory animals. Pregnant women are advised to avoid excessive caffeine consumption.

Caffeine was produced from plants in the pure form in 1820. It can now be made in the laboratory. Caffeine is used as a stimulant of the heart and nervous system in certain disorders and is found in a number of nonprescription analgesic preparations. It is also a remedy for poisoning by alcohol, opium, and other drugs that *depress* (slow down) the nervous system. Its chemical formula is $C_8H_{10}N_4O_2$. Barbara M. Bayer

See also **Alkaloid; Coffee; Maté; Tea.**

Cage, John (1912-1992), was perhaps the most radical and controversial modern American composer. He was best known for his experiments with *aleatoric* (random or chance) music. Cage's *Imaginary Landscape No. 4* (1951) was written for 12 radios with two performers at each, one manipulating the knob that changes stations and the other the volume control. The composition's notation is precise, but the sound cannot be predicted and varies with each performance according to what is on the air.

Cage was born on Sept. 5, 1912, in Los Angeles. In 1938, he first composed music for *prepared piano.* This music calls for various objects—bolts, screws, or rubber strips—to be inserted between some of the piano strings. When the performer hits the keys for these strings, the sounds resemble a percussion instrument, as in *Sonatas and Interludes for Prepared Piano* (1948).

Cage believed that any sound or noise surrounding us is music and thus the distinctions between life and art should be broken down. In *4′33″* (1952) for piano, the performer sits silently at the instrument for 4 minutes and 33 seconds, inviting the audience to listen to any sounds and noises in the hall and those from outside. Cage's books include *Silence* (1961). He died on Aug. 12, 1992. Stephen Jaffe

See also **Aleatory music.**

Cagliari, Paolo. See **Veronese, Paolo.**

Cagney, James (1899-1986), an American motion-picture actor, became famous for his roles as a cocky tough guy. Cagney also was an accomplished dancer. He won an Academy Award as best actor for his performance in *Yankee Doodle Dandy* (1942). This motion picture portrayed the life of the Broadway showman George M. Cohan.

Cagney appeared in more than 60 motion pictures, of which the first was *Sinner's Holiday* (1930). His performance as a gangster in *The Public Enemy* (1931) established him as a star. Cagney made several other gangster films, including *G-Men* (1935), *Angels with Dirty Faces* (1938), *The Roaring Twenties* (1939), and *White Heat* (1949). Cagney's other films included *Footlight Parade* (1933), *Mister Roberts* (1955), *Love Me or Leave Me* (1955), *Man of a Thousand Faces* (1957), and *One, Two, Three* (1961).

James Francis Cagney, Jr., was born on July 17, 1899, in New York City. During the 1920's, he performed in vaudeville and on Broadway in New York City. He died on March 30, 1986. Roger Ebert

Bettmann

James Cagney won the 1942 Academy Award as best actor for his performance in the musical *Yankee Doodle Dandy.* Cagney was also known for his roles in action and gangster movies.

Cain was the eldest son of Adam and Eve in the Old Testament, or Hebrew Bible. According to the story in Genesis, Cain became angry when the Lord liked his brother Abel's sacrifice of sheep better than Cain's sacrifice of "the fruit of the ground." He killed Abel. After the Lord asked Cain where Abel was, Cain said, "I know not: am I my brother's keeper?" (Genesis 4:9). To punish Cain, the Lord sent him away to be a wanderer. Cain feared that he would be killed, so the Lord placed a mark on him and commanded that no one harm him. Parallels to the story of Cain and Abel are found in a much earlier Sumerian story in which a farmer (Enkimdu) and a shepherd (Dumuzi) compete for the love of the fertility goddess Inanna. Carole R. Fontaine

Cain, James M. (1892-1977), was an American author known for his tough, realistic crime fiction. Cain gained immediate fame with his first novel, *The Postman Always Rings Twice* (1934). The story deals with a drifter who stops at a roadside diner, falls in love with the owner's wife, and conspires with her to kill her husband. The novel is recognized as a classic of "hard-boiled" fiction.

Cain's best novels and stories are set in California. They are known for their terse prose, unsentimental depiction of sexual relationships between men and women, and frank exploration of the human potential for violence. Cain also gained praise for his ability in his novels to describe in detail the specialized workings of various businesses. *Double Indemnity* (1936) has an insurance background, and *Mildred Pierce* (1941) concerns restaurants. His other novels include *Serenade* (1937) and *The Butterfly* (1947).

James Mallahan Cain was born on July 1, 1892, in Annapolis, Maryland. He worked as a journalist for newspapers in Baltimore and New York City from 1917 to 1931. He moved to California in 1931 to become a screenwriter. Cain returned to Maryland in 1948 and continued to write books into his 80's. Most of his later work is considered inferior to the novels of his California period. He died on Oct. 27, 1977. Jon L. Breen

Cairn terrier is a breed of dog that originated in the highlands and island regions of Scotland. It received its name because of its ability to dig under *cairns* (heaps of stones) to hunt rats and other animals. The terrier's broad, short head looks more like that of a cat than that of a dog. Its ears are wide apart, and the dog holds them erect. The cairn has a hard wiry topcoat and an undercoat of soft fur. Its coat may be any color but white. It weighs from 13 to 14 pounds (6 to 6.4 kilograms). See also **Dog** (picture: Terriers).

Critically reviewed by the Cairn Terrier Club of America

Cairo, *KY roh* (pop. 6,800,992), is the capital of Egypt. It has more people than any other city in Africa and the Middle East. Cairo covers about 83 square miles (215 square kilometers) on the east bank of the Nile River in northeastern Egypt. Most Egyptians call the city *Masr,* which is also the name for Egypt itself. The metropolitan area includes densely populated suburbs that surround the historic city center. Some suburbs, including Giza, are on the Nile's west bank. About 15 million people live in greater Cairo. A political and cultural center of the Arab world, Cairo is home to the headquarters of the Arab League.

Cairo lies in the Nile Valley at the southern edge of the Nile Delta. The Nile River divides into two channels just north of the city. Huge deserts lie east and west of the city. Some famous reminders of ancient Egypt, including pyramids and the Great Sphinx, stand on the Giza plateau west of Cairo (see **Pyramids; Sphinx**).

The city. In general, the oldest and most historic sections of Cairo are in the eastern part of the city. Newer, more modern areas are on the Nile's west bank, in Giza. Other modern suburbs lie north, east, and south of the city and on the island of Gezira in the river. Many government offices, foreign embassies, clubs, restaurants, and hotels are on or near the banks of the Nile.

Most buildings in the modern sections of Cairo were built in the 1900's. Their design is in the style of present-day American and European architecture. The newer areas of Cairo have public squares and wide boulevards, which make these areas somewhat less crowded than the older sections. However, even these newer areas have become congested, with most people living in large blocks of apartments.

Cairo's older areas are famous for their narrow, winding streets and historic buildings. Lively markets known as *suqs* fill almost all the available space in some streets.

© Simon Harris, eStock Photo

Cairo is the capital of Egypt and has more people than any other city in Africa and the Middle East. The city lies on the east bank of the Nile River, one of the most important waterways in Africa. Many of Cairo's modern skyscrapers stand on or near the river.

© Superstock

Many mosques in Cairo are outstanding examples of Islamic architecture. The Mosque of Sultan Hassan, *left,* was built in the 1300's. It is considered one of the finest mosques built by the Mamelukes, who ruled Egypt from 1250 to 1517. The Mosque of ar-Rifai, *right,* was built in the 1800's.

In many of the buildings of the old sections, open-front shops occupy the ground floor. Small apartments take up the upper floors. The old sections are also known for their beautiful *mosques* (Islamic houses of worship). *Minarets* (tall, slender towers) are important features of the mosques. Public criers called *muezzins* announce prayer time by loudspeakers on the minarets five times a day. Several minarets can be seen from almost any place in Cairo's old sections.

Many of Cairo's mosques are outstanding examples of Islamic architecture. Some of the most famous mosques and their construction dates are Ahmed Ibn Tulun (A.D. 870's), al-Azhar (about 970), Sultan Hassan (mid-1300's), Qayt Bey (about 1475), and Muhammad Ali (early 1800's). The Mosque of al-Azhar is part of a university, and the Muhammad Ali Mosque is part of a walled fortress called the Citadel.

Cairo has hot summers and mild winters. During the summer, many families leave the city and go to seaside resorts to escape the heat. Cairo's mild winters attract many tourists from colder places. Cairo receives only about 1 inch (2.5 centimeters) of rain a year. The sun shines almost every day. For more details on Cairo's climate, see **Egypt** (Climate).

People. The people of Cairo are called *Cairenes.* Many are poor, unskilled workers employed in factories or small shops. They live in crowded apartments in older areas of the city. Some dress in long, flowing robes, the traditional Arab garment. But most wear Western-style clothes made in Egypt. Most middle-class and wealthy Cairenes live in newer areas. These people include doctors, factory managers, engineers, government officials, lawyers, and teachers. They dress in Western-style clothing.

Nearly all Cairenes are Arabs who speak Arabic. Many educated Cairenes can speak English, French, or both. Most Cairenes are Muslims who practice the *Sunni* (orthodox) form of Islam. A minority of Cairenes are Christians, most of whom belong to the Coptic church.

Until the mid-1900's, influential European and Jewish communities flourished in Cairo. An Egyptian nationalist government came to power in 1952, and many foreign-owned businesses were seized. Many foreigners lost the legal and financial privileges they had enjoyed. As a result, their communities dwindled away.

Education and cultural life. Most of Egypt's schools of higher learning are in or near Cairo. Al-Azhar University, in Cairo, is a major center for the study of Islam. This university was founded about 970 and ranks among the world's oldest. Other universities in the area include Cairo University, the largest university in the country, in Giza; Ain Shams University, in Cairo; and the American University in Cairo, a small English-language institution.

Cairo's museums house priceless treasures from many periods in history. The city's Egyptian Museum contains the mummy of Ramses II and the gold mask and other belongings of King Tutankhamun (see **Tutankhamun** [picture]). The Museum of Islamic Art contains copies of the Qur'ān (the holy book of Islam), manuscripts, metalware, and other objects that date from the 600's to the 1800's.

Economy. Cairo is an important manufacturing center. A factory at Hulwan, south of the city, makes iron and steel. Other industries in and near Cairo process

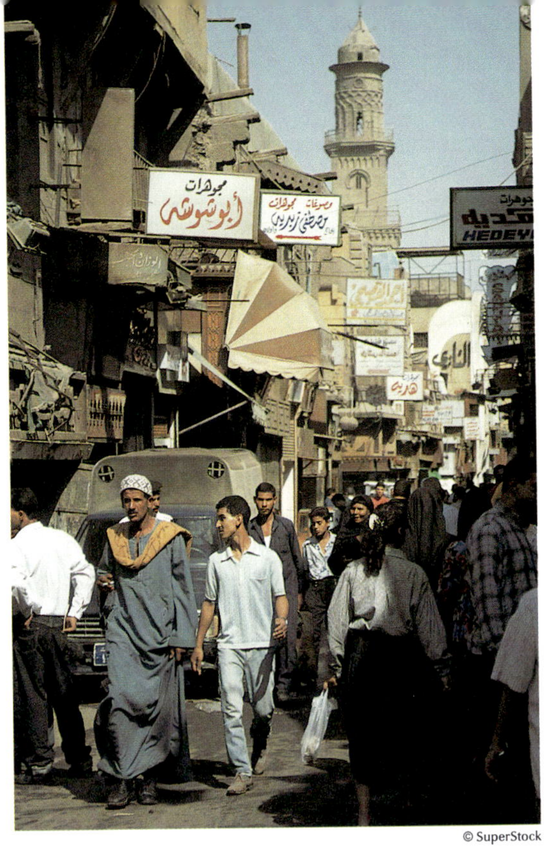

© SuperStock

Clothing styles in Cairo vary. Most people wear European- or American-style clothes made in Egypt. But some people dress in long, flowing robes, the traditional Arab garment.

food and tobacco and manufacture chemicals, paper, textiles, and other products. Many small companies and shops make such items as jewelry and statues that are sold as souvenirs. In the mid-1900's, the government took over virtually all important industries. Some of these have been returned to private ownership, but the government still owns some of the largest plants.

Tourism is a key part of Cairo's economy. Each year, millions of visitors come to see the mosques, museums, pyramids, Great Sphinx, and other attractions.

History. The ancient city of Memphis stood near the site of present-day Cairo. According to tradition, it was founded about 3100 B.C. as ancient Egypt's first capital. Between A.D. 639 and 642, Arab Muslims from the east conquered Egypt. At the time, Egypt was a province of the Byzantine Empire. Its people were descendants of the ancient Egyptians, and most were Christians. In 640, the Arabs set up a large military camp near what is now southern Cairo. They later built houses, mosques, and palaces. The camp became the Arab capital, al-Fustat.

The Fatimid dynasty took over Egypt in 969. The Fatimids belonged to the minority Shiah branch of Islam. General Jawhar established a new capital at Cairo for al-Muizz, the Fatimid *caliph* (ruler). Jawhar built up the area north of the first Arab settlement, and Cairo soon became one of the Islamic world's most important cities. The Fatimids founded al-Azhar University, which attracted students of Islam from many countries. The Fatimids called their city *Al Qahirah,* perhaps because the planet Mars (*al-Qahir* in Arabic) was rising in the sky when they began building. The name *Cairo* comes from *Al Qahirah.*

WORLD BOOK maps

Cairo

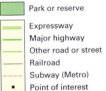

Location of Cairo

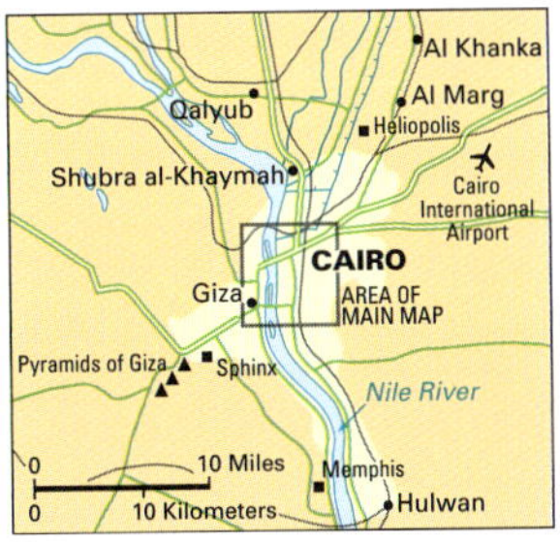

Cairo metro area

© Digital Vision/Getty Images

The famous Pyramids of Giza stand on the Giza plateau west of Cairo. There are 10 pyramids at Giza, including 3 of the largest and best preserved of all Egyptian pyramids. These 3 large pyramids are shown here. The pyramids were built for kings about 2600 to 2500 B.C.

Saladin, the founder of Egypt's Ayyubid dynasty (family of rulers), expanded the city's boundaries and built the Citadel in the late 1100's. He restored the dominance of Sunni Islam in Egypt. The Mamelukes, who had been the Ayyubids' bodyguards, ruled Egypt from 1250 to 1517. They built many of Cairo's finest mosques and further extended the city's boundaries. The Ottomans gained control of Egypt in 1517.

Many treasures of ancient Egypt were discovered in the early 1800's. Thousands of people visited Cairo to see these wonders. Many Europeans settled in Cairo during the 1800's, when European nations became more involved in Egypt's affairs. During this period, Egypt's rulers worked to make Cairo more like a European city.

© SIME, eStock Photo

The Egyptian Museum in Cairo houses many historical items, such as the sphinx statue shown here. Many of the museum's holdings date back to ancient Egyptian times.

The United Kingdom gained effective control of Egypt in 1882. Egypt became an independent monarchy in 1922. The government has done much to modernize Cairo, especially since a *republican* (elected) form of government was established in 1953. But great poverty continues to exist in many parts of the city.

The rapid population growth of Cairo and the surrounding area has contributed to the poverty problem. The city's population increased from about 375,000 in 1882 to more than 3 ½ million in the 1960's to nearly 7 million in the 1990's. This population growth has resulted from three causes—(1) a high birth rate, (2) thousands of Egyptian families moving from rural areas to Cairo, and (3) refugees coming from Ismailia, Port Said, and Suez. These cities were heavily damaged in fighting between Egyptian and Israeli forces along the Suez Canal in the late 1960's and early 1970's.

Since the 1970's, important improvements have been made in many of Cairo's city services. The city now has an excellent underground rail network, many new bridges and overpasses, a fine international airport, reliable telephone and Internet access, and a revamped sewage system. But the ever-growing number of people and vehicles burdens local facilities, damages the environment, creates health hazards, and makes daily life difficult for many Cairenes. Michael J. Reimer

See also **Giza.**

Caisson, *KAY son,* in building, is a watertight chamber used in the construction of building foundations, tunnels, bridges, and other structures. Caissons provide a place where crews can safely work underground or underwater. In addition, caissons may be filled with concrete and become part of the finished structure.

Most caissons have the shape of a cylinder or a box. The walls may be made of steel, concrete, or timber. All caissons are open at the bottom, where digging takes place. But they may be open or closed on top. The two main types of caissons are *open* and *pneumatic.*

An open caisson has an open top and bottom. The bottom edges, called *cutting edges,* are constructed so they can cut into the ground. The caisson sinks deeper

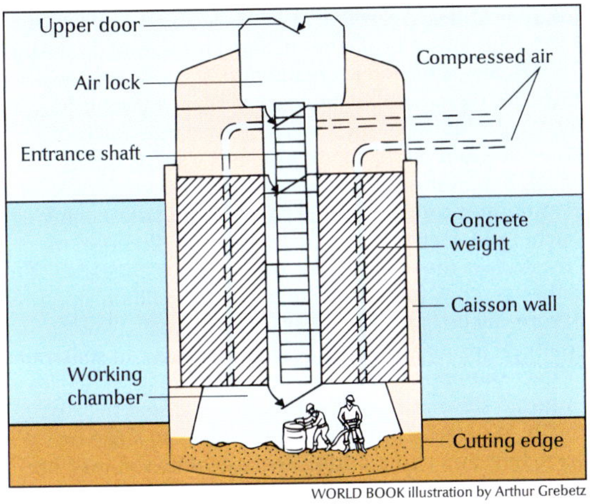

WORLD BOOK illustration by Arthur Grebetz

A pneumatic caisson uses compressed air to keep water out of an excavation site. Workers pass through an air lock to enter the pressurized working chamber. As earth is removed, the caisson sinks under the weight of concrete in its upper section.

into the ground as earth is removed beneath it.

A pneumatic caisson is closed at the top. It uses compressed air to keep water out of the working chamber and to provide oxygen for the workers. This type of caisson consists of two sections. The lower section, where the workers are, has cutting edges like those of open caissons. Concrete is poured into the upper section. Its weight helps drive the caisson deeper into the ground. Workers and materials move in and out of the lower section through a shaft. Pneumatic caissons are usually used to support bridge piers located in deep water.

Before workers enter a pneumatic caisson, they must enter an airtight chamber called an *air lock.* The air pressure in the air lock is gradually raised until it is the same as the pressure in the working chamber. When workers prepare to leave the caisson, they again pass through the air lock and the pressure is gradually lowered. If workers go through a change of pressure too fast, they may develop *bends,* a painful and sometimes fatal condition also known as *caisson disease.* William E. Saul

See also **Air lock; Bends.**

Caisson disease. See **Bends.**

Cajuns, *KAY juhn,* are a group of people in southern Louisiana and Texas who are descendants of French settlers called Acadians. The Acadians came from the Acadia region of Canada, which included New Brunswick and Nova Scotia (see **Acadia**). The word *Cajuns* comes from *Acadians.*

During the 1750's, British troops drove the Acadians from Canada. At that time, the British and French were fighting the French and Indian War, a struggle for control of eastern North America. Many Acadians eventually settled in southern Louisiana, where swamps and slow-moving streams called *bayous* cover much of the land. The American poet Henry Wadsworth Longfellow described their journey in his poem *Evangeline.* The Cajuns lived in relative isolation in the bayou area. They continued to regard themselves as a separate people and maintained a unique culture that had many Acadian French characteristics.

Today, most Cajuns speak both English and a French dialect that includes many words no longer used by other French-speaking peoples. The majority of the people are Roman Catholics. Many Cajun families live by fishing and trapping. Others raise cattle or such crops as rice, sugar, and sweet potatoes. Cajun cooking is spicy and includes much seafood. Favorite foods include a thick soup called *gumbo* and a rice dish called *jambalaya.* Traditional Cajun music is played by a band consisting of a fiddle, accordion, and triangle.

Since the mid-1900's, better communication and transportation have put the Cajuns into closer contact with other people. Many young Cajuns do not speak French or follow Cajun customs. Some Cajuns worry about losing their cultural heritage and have led a movement to preserve it. For example, Louisiana schools once discouraged Cajun children from speaking French. Today, most pupils study the language in elementary school.

James H. Dormon

Calabash, *KAL uh bash,* is a gourd that grows on a long tropical vine. The gourd ranges from 3 to 30 inches (8 to 76 centimeters) long. It is often called *bottle gourd* or *dipper gourd,* depending on the shape. See **Gourd.**

The gourdlike fruit of the calabash tree, an evergreen tree of tropical America, is also called *calabash.* The round fruit may be 12 inches (30 centimeters) across. Its hard, tough outer shell can be used as a cooking pot. The pulp and seeds may be eaten. W. E. Splittstoesser

© Heather Angel

The calabash fruit has a hard, tough shell. It grows on the calabash tree, an evergreen found in tropical America.

Scientific classification. The calabash vine belongs to the gourd family, Cucurbitaceae. Its scientific name is *Lagenaria siceraria.* The calabash tree belongs to the bignonia family, Bignoniaceae. It is *Crescentia cujete.*

Caladium, *kuh LAY dee uhm,* is a group of foliage plants that grow in tropical America. They have huge, arrow-shaped leaves beautifully marked in various colors and patterns. Thousands of varieties are grown commercially in Florida. They are shipped to florists early in

E. R. Degginger

The caladium has beautifully colored leaves.

spring for potting. Caladiums grow well in shady, protected sites such as window boxes. David A. Francko

Scientific classification. Caladiums belong to the arum family, Araceae.

Calais, *KAL ay* (pop. 78,170), a seaport in northern France, is closer to England than any other city in mainland Europe. It lies on the English Channel coast at the Strait of Dover, 26 miles (42 kilometers) southeast of Dover, England (see **France** [political map]). Calais is a leading shipping center for trade between mainland Europe and the United Kingdom. It is also a major port for travel between the mainland and the United Kingdom.

Calais's industries include distilling, food processing, and the manufacture of chemicals, electric appliances, paper, plastics, textiles—especially lace—and tiles. Calais is France's largest lace-manufacturing center.

Calais's founding date is unknown. Originally a fishing village, it became a major port during the Middle Ages. Modern port facilities were installed in the 1800's. Calais suffered heavy damage during World Wars I (1914-1918) and II (1939-1945) but was rebuilt. Mark Kesselman

Calamity Jane (1852-1903) was the nickname of Martha Canary (or Cannary), a notorious American frontierswoman. There are many stories about how she got her nickname. According to one, she used to warn men that to offend her was to court calamity.

Canary was born on May 1, 1852, near Princeton, Missouri. In 1865, her family moved to Virginia City, Montana. They separated, and Martha was raised there and in other mining camps in Wyoming and Utah. She became a skilled horsewoman and an expert with a rifle and revolver. She usually dressed in men's clothes.

Many wild stories exist about Canary, most of which she made up herself. She may have become associated with the 7th Cavalry of the United States Army near Rawlins, Wyoming. Some writers believe that because of her knowledge of the frontier, she was a scout for Lieutenant Colonel George A. Custer. She may have spent some time at Fort Bridger and Fort Russell in Wyoming.

In 1875, Canary went to the Black Hills area of South Dakota. She lived in Deadwood at the time of a gold rush in the area, and she was praised as a heroine for helping treat victims of a smallpox outbreak in 1878.

Calamity Jane appeared in Wild West shows until about 1902. Alcoholism broke her health, and she died on Aug. 1, 1903. She is buried in Deadwood. William W. Savage, Jr.

Calcite is a mineral that occurs in small amounts in most types of rocks and makes up the largest part of limestone and marble. Pure calcite is transparent or white, but a variety of impurities can give it colors. Nickel impurities produce green calcite; manganese, pink calcite; and iron, brown calcite. Calcite in the form of limestone is the chief source of lime. Limestone also serves as a raw material in cement and building stone.

Pure calcite is a form of calcium carbonate, whose chemical formula is $CaCO_3$. Calcite crystals can split into perfect *rhombohedrons,* six-sided objects in which the opposite sides are parallel. The crystal structure causes calcite to polarize light. Calcite is fairly soft; it can be scratched by a copper coin. Because of its softness, calcite serves as a scratchless scouring ingredient in some cleaning powders. Calcite fizzes in a weak acid solution.

Many *invertebrates* (animals without backbones) have skeletons of calcite. Some beaches in Florida along the Gulf of Mexico consist primarily of calcite shells and coral from marine invertebrates. David L. Bish

See also **Calcium carbonate; Chalk; Lime; Limestone; Marble; Mineral** (picture: Common minerals with nonmetallic luster); **Polarized light.**

Calcium, *KAL see uhm,* is a soft, silvery-white metallic element found most widely in such rocks as limestone and marble. It is one of the most abundant metals and makes up about 3 ½ percent of Earth's crust. It reacts readily with both oxygen and water. In nature, it occurs

Culver

Calamity Jane was an expert with a horse and rifle.

only in compounds—chiefly as calcium carbonate, calcium fluoride, and calcium sulfate.

Calcium has an *atomic number* (number of protons in its nucleus) of 20. Its *relative atomic mass* is 40.078. An element's relative atomic mass equals its *mass* (amount of matter) divided by $\frac{1}{12}$ of the mass of carbon 12, the most abundant form of carbon. Calcium's chemical symbol is Ca. It is one of the *alkaline earth metals* (see **Element, Chemical** [Periodic table of the elements]). Calcium melts at 839 °C and boils at 1484 °C. It has a density of 1.55 grams per cubic centimeter at 20 °C (see **Density**).

Calcium and its compounds have many industrial uses. Pure calcium metal, used in certain alloys, is obtained from molten calcium chloride through a process called *electrolysis.* Various industrial processes, such as leather tanning and petroleum refining, involve calcium oxide. This compound is made by heating calcium carbonate in *kilns* (furnaces). Calcium fluoride and calcium sulfate are used in making cement and plaster for construction work. Other calcium compounds are used in a variety of products ranging from fertilizer to paint.

Calcium is essential to all living things. It is the most abundant metal in the body. Calcium is vital for the growth and protection of the bones and teeth and helps the blood to clot and muscles to contract. A daily diet that includes green vegetables, milk, and milk products supplies enough calcium for the body's normal needs.

British chemist Sir Humphry Davy first isolated pure calcium in 1808. But ancient Egyptians, Greeks, and Romans used calcium compounds to make *mortar,* a material that holds bricks or stones together. Iain C. Paul

See also **Calcite; Calcium carbide; Calcium carbonate; Lime; Limestone; Nutrition** (Minerals).

Calcium carbide, *KAL see uhm KAHR byd,* is a hard, brittle, crystalline compound made of calcium and carbon. Its chemical formula is CaC_2. Calcium carbide is used in industry to make acetylene, a gas used in welding or cutting metal. It also is the source of calcium cyanamide, which is used in the making of fertilizer. Calcium carbide is produced by heating lime and coke in an electric furnace at a temperature of 2800 °C. This method was discovered in 1892 by T. L. Willson, an American chemist. See also **Acetylene.** Harriet V. Taylor

Calcium carbonate, *KAL see uhm KAHR buh nayt,* is a white, crystalline mineral. It is widely distributed in nature and is the main ingredient in limestone, marble, and coral. In caves, ground waters deposit calcium carbonate over time to form stalactites and stalagmites. Calcium carbonate is an ingredient of some toothpastes and toothpowders. It is also used in some medicines to reduce acidity in the stomach. Calcium carbonate dissolves only slightly in pure water but forms calcium bicarbonate if carbon dioxide is present. The chemical formula of calcium carbonate is $CaCO_3$. Robert J. Ouellette

See also **Calcite; Chalk; Salt, Chemical.**

Calcium channel blocker is a drug used to treat certain disorders of the heart and blood vessels. Calcium channel blockers, also called *calcium antagonists,* include *diltiazem,* sold under such trade names as Cardizem and Dilacor; and *nifedipine,* often sold under the trade names Procardia and Adalat. These drugs stop calcium from entering muscle cells in the heart and blood vessels. Blocking the entry of calcium interferes with muscle cell contraction. As a result, blood vessels expand and carry more blood and oxygen to tissues.

These drugs are used to prevent severe chest pains called *angina pectoris* that are caused by lack of oxygen in the heart. These pains occur when arteries in the heart become narrowed due to fatty deposits, abnormal contractions, or a combination of these conditions. Narrowed vessels cannot supply the heart with enough oxygen during exercise, stress, or other periods of hard work. Calcium channel blockers expand the heart's arteries and restore its supply of oxygen.

Calcium channel blockers also reduce blood pressure by expanding blood vessels throughout the body. This drop in pressure lessens the heart's workload and reduces the heart's need for oxygen.

Calcium channel blocker

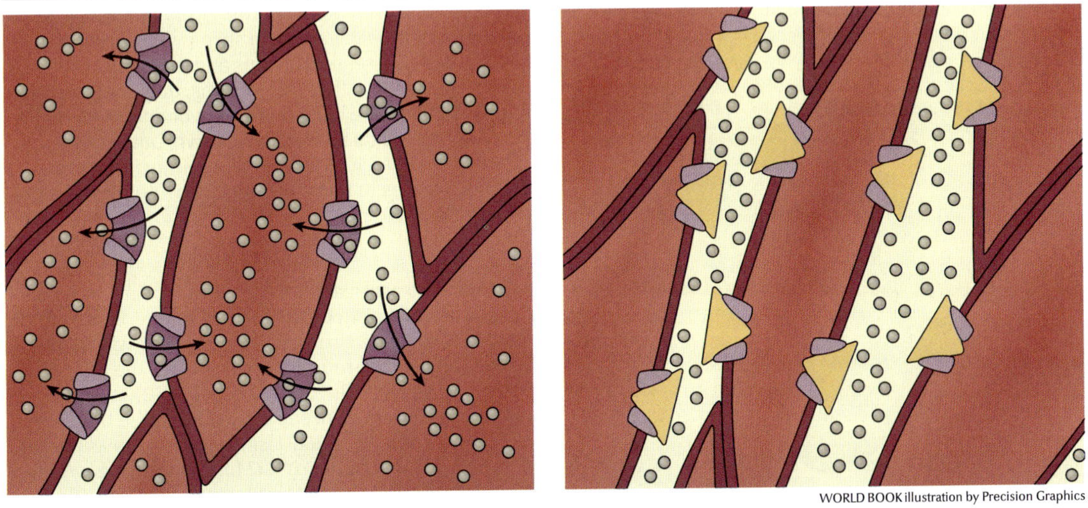

WORLD BOOK illustration by Precision Graphics

Calcium molecules, *shown as dots,* flow through channels (purple) into muscle cells lining blood vessels. The muscles then contract, narrowing the vessels and reducing blood flow.

Calcium channel blockers (yellow triangles) stop the flow of calcium into the muscle cells. The muscles relax and the blood vessel expands, allowing blood to flow more easily.

Some calcium channel blockers, called *short-acting* forms, act quickly. Other types, called *long-acting* or *extended-release* forms, act more slowly. Studies show that the different forms vary in their safety and effectiveness in treating certain disorders. For example, several studies suggest that treating high blood pressure with short-acting nifedipine raises the risk of heart attack or death. The increased risk may occur because this drug lowers blood pressure too rapidly. Michael H. Crawford

See also **Angina pectoris.**

Calculator is a device that adds, subtracts, multiplies, divides, and performs many other mathematical operations quickly and accurately. Many people use a small, inexpensive calculator to help balance checkbooks, figure percentages, or quickly total columns of numbers. Manufacturers also produce many types of specialized calculators that perform complex functions necessary for such fields as accounting, engineering, and statistics.

People developed the first calculating devices more than 2,500 years ago. Ancient merchants kept count by grouping small objects on a *counting board* or by sliding beads along the grooves or rods of an *abacus.* In the 1620's, the English mathematician William Oughtred invented an early *slide rule.* Oughtred's device used sliding scales of numbers known as *logarithms* to quickly estimate the results of complicated multiplication calculations (see **Logarithms**). In the early 1640's, the French mathematician Blaise Pascal invented a calculating machine that performed addition and subtraction.

Most calculators today are *electronic calculators.* These devices use miniature circuits to perform calculations automatically. Manufacturers began producing electronic calculators commercially during the mid-1960's. Many early electronic calculators were bulky and stood on a desktop. By the 1970's, many desktop calculators had some features in common with computers, such as storing data on hard disks or magnetic tape. *Printing calculators* provided output on paper tape that showed the numbers involved in operations, enabling operators to verify entries and to keep a permanent record of the results.

Handheld calculators became popular during the 1970's because of their convenience. Until the invention of these devices, most engineers, scientists, and other professionals had relied on slide rules to perform computations. Some handheld calculators provide printed output, but most are *display calculators,* which show entries and results in a small window.

© Alex Tossi, Alamy

A handheld calculator solves and displays the answer to many kinds of mathematical problems. Most such calculators can perform a wide range of both simple and complicated functions.

Since the 1970's, calculators have become cheaper, smaller, and more powerful. Many modern calculators handle logarithms, cube roots, and other complex mathematical functions. Most have a *memory,* which can store numbers and instructions for solving problems at a later time.

Many high school and college students use *graphing calculators* to solve equations whose solutions can be plotted on graphs. *Programmable calculators* can handle complicated, multistep tasks similar to those performed by computers. Users can store sets of instructions called *programs* in these calculators to automatically direct the calculators through the proper steps to solve certain kinds of problems. Amy Sue Bix

See also **Abacus; Electronics** (picture: Parts of an electronic device).

Calculus, *KAL kyuh luhs,* is the branch of mathematics that deals with changing quantities. Students usually learn it in college after they have mastered algebra, geometry, and trigonometry.

Calculus is the language in which engineers, physicists, and other scientists develop theories and solve practical problems. For example, the laws of aerodynamics are expressed in terms of calculus. An airplane designer can use these laws to calculate the changing forces that affect an airplane during flight. Calculus has also stimulated many new directions in mathematics since its development in the 1600's.

Calculus was invented to answer questions that could not be solved using algebra or geometry. One branch of calculus, called *differential calculus,* began with questions about the speed of moving objects. For example, How fast does a stone fall two seconds after it has been dropped from a cliff? How fast is Earth moving around the sun on July 4? The other branch of calculus, *integral calculus,* was invented to answer a very different kind of question: What is the area of a shape with curved sides?

Although differential calculus and integral calculus began by solving different problems, their methods are closely related. The central problem of differential calculus is to find the rate at which a known, but varying, quantity changes. Integral calculus has just the reverse problem. It tries to find a quantity knowing the rate at which it is changing.

Differential calculus

Imagine an astronaut hovering in a landing craft near the surface of a planet with no atmosphere. Due to gravitational pull, a ball dropped from the craft will fall toward the planet. Through measurements, the astronaut finds that the ball falls 7 feet in 1 second, 28 feet in 2 seconds, and 700 feet in 10 seconds. Clearly, the ball is not falling at a constant speed. Using algebra, the astronaut determines the formula $d = 7t^2$ for the distance (d) in feet that the ball falls from the landing craft in t seconds.

But assume that the astronaut wants to know the rate at which the ball's distance from the landing craft is changing and so be able to determine the ball's speed at any instant. Differential calculus can provide the astronaut with the formula $s = 14t$ for the ball's speed *(s)* in feet per second t seconds after it is dropped. Thus, the ball has a speed of 14 feet per second after 1 second, 28 feet per second after 2 seconds, and 140 feet per second after 10 seconds. From the formula $s = 14t$, differential calculus shows that the ball has a constant acceleration of 14 feet per second per second, written 14 ft/sec/sec or 14 ft^2. That is, in each second the speed of the ball increases 14 feet per second (14 ft/sec).

Functions. Calculus deals with functions. A formula is often used to define a function. More precisely, a function *(f)* is a correspondence that associates with each number *t* some number *f(t)*, read "*f* of *t*." For example, the formula $d = 7t^2$ associates with each number *t* some number *d*. If we use *f* to label this function, then $f(t) = 7t^2$. Thus, $f(1) = 7 \times 1^2 = 7$, $f(2) = 7 \times 2^2 = 28$, $f(10) = 7 \times 10^2 = 700$.

Rate of change of a function is the concern of differential calculus. If *f(a)* and *f(b)* are two values of the function *f*, then $f(b) - f(a)$ equals the *change* in *f* brought about by the change from *a* to *b* in the number at which *f* is evaluated. The *average rate of change* of *f* between *a* and *b* is $\frac{f(b)-f(a)}{b-a}$

The function $f(t) = 7t^2$ describes the motion of the ball falling from the landing craft. The change in *f* from $t = 2$ to $t = 10$ equals $f(10) - f(2) = 700 - 28 = 672$. The average rate of change of *f* between 2 and 10 is

$$\frac{f(10) - f(2)}{10 - 2} = \frac{672}{8} = 84$$

Thus, the ball falls 672 feet in 8 seconds, and the average speed of the ball during the 8-second period is 84 ft/sec. In a problem such as this where *t* is time and *f(t)* is distance, we use the term *speed* for the rate of change of *f*.

Limits. Suppose a jet airplane makes a flight in which its average speed is 1,100 kilometers an hour. Also suppose that you wanted to know the speed of the airplane at any instant during its flight. You could not find this out by merely knowing the average speed of the jet. You would need other calculations.

Similarly, knowing the average speed of the ball dropped from the landing craft tells us little about its speed at any single instant. We need the idea of a *limit* to find this speed. Limits allow us to calculate the *instantaneous rate of change* of a function, such as the ball's speed at a particular instant.

Consider the formula $d = 7t^2$ for the distance the ball falls toward the planet in the situation already described. The average speed, *s(t)*, of the ball between 2 seconds and *t* seconds after it is dropped is given by the following:

$$s(t) = \frac{f(t) - f(2)}{t-2} = \frac{7t^2 - 7 \times 2^2}{t-2} = 7(t+2) \text{ft./sec.}$$

The following table of values gives the average speed of the ball over a time interval from 2 to *t* as the values of *t* get closer and closer to 2.

t	10	8	4	3	2.5	2.1	2.01	2.001
s(t)	84	70	42	35	31.5	28.7	28.07	28.007

What is the average speed of the ball, *s(t)*, close to when *t* is close to 2? From the table, we can clearly see that the answer is 28. In calculus, we would say that the limit of *s(t)* as *t* approaches 2 is 28 ft/sec. That is, the closer that *t* comes to 2, the closer the average speed comes to 28 ft/sec. The instantaneous speed of the ball 2 seconds after it is released is 28 ft/sec. In calculus, the fact that the instantaneous speed of the ball at $t = 2$ is 28 ft/sec is written $\lim_{t \to 2} s(t) = 28$ ft/sec.

In general, the instantaneous rate of change of a function *f* at the number *a* is defined as follows:

$$\lim_{x \to a} \frac{f(x)-f(a)}{x-a}$$

Derivatives. The instantaneous rate of change of a function is so important that mathematicians have given it the special name *derivative*. One of the most common symbols for the derivative of the function *f* at *a* is *f'(a)*, which is read "f prime of a." Other notations for the derivative are $D_x f$ and *df/dx*. If we let $y = f(x)$, then the notation *dy/dx* is used. The derivative is defined as follows:

$$f'(a) = \lim_{x \to a} \frac{f(x)-f(a)}{x-a}$$

All calculus books contain rules for finding derivatives of common functions. One of the most useful rules tells how to find the derivative of a power function, such as $f(x) = cx^n$, where *c* is a constant. In this kind of function, $f'(x) = cnx^{n-1}$. This is the rule the astronaut should follow to find the speed of the falling ball. From $f(t) = 7t^2$, it follows that $f'(t) = 7 \times 2t^1 = 14t$. Therefore, $s = 14t$ is the formula for the speed of the ball at any time, *t* seconds, after it starts to fall.

Many functions can be shown as curved lines on a graph. At any point on a curve, we can draw a line *tangent* to the curve—that is, a straight line that touches the curve only at that point. The derivative provides the formula for the tangent line. The fact that the derivative is the slope of the tangent makes it a powerful tool for graphing functions.

Suppose we have a graph that shows the distance of the falling ball from the landing craft. The vertical axis of the graph indicates the distance *(d)* and the horizontal axis indicates the time *(t)*. The curve of the graph shows us how the ball's distance from the landing craft changes over time. The steepness, or slope, of the tangent line to the curve at any particular point is the ball's speed at that instant.

Integral calculus

In physics, work is measured by the formula $W = Fd$, where *W* is the work done in foot-pounds, *F* is a constant force, and *d* is the distance through which the force acts. For example, if a constant force of 50 pounds is needed to push a box 20 feet across a room, then the work done is 20 × 50, or 1,000 foot-pounds. But if the force varies as the box is pushed, then the formula $W = Fd$ does not apply. For example, you could not use the formula if the box was pushed with an ever-increasing force. But you could find the work done by using integral calculus. Integral calculus also solves many geometrical problems. For example, it is used to find the area of a region with a curved boundary. In fact, finding such areas is basic to integral calculus because it helps solve many problems, including the one of finding the work done by a variable force.

Finding areas. The curve *BC* shown below is part of a parabola, a shape commonly found in the reflectors of automobile headlights and in the mirrors used in telescopes. Suppose we want to find the area of the region

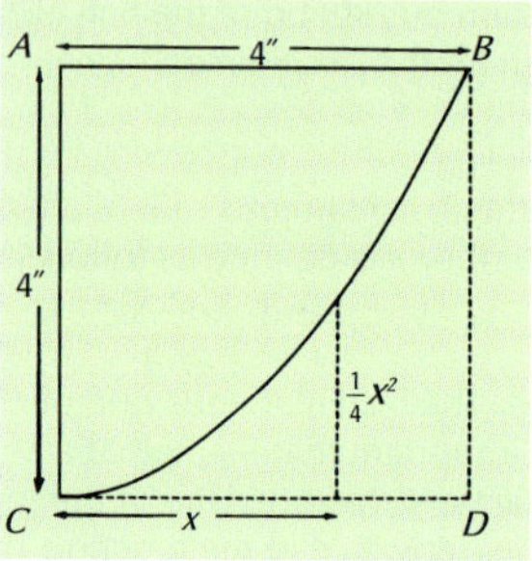

BCD, which has sides *BD* and *CD* that are 4 inches long.

We can find the approximate area of *BCD* by drawing it on graph paper. In the graph below on the left, suppose the lines are 1 inch apart and each square therefore has an area of 1 square inch. In the graph below on the right, the lines are $\frac{1}{2}$ inch apart and each square has

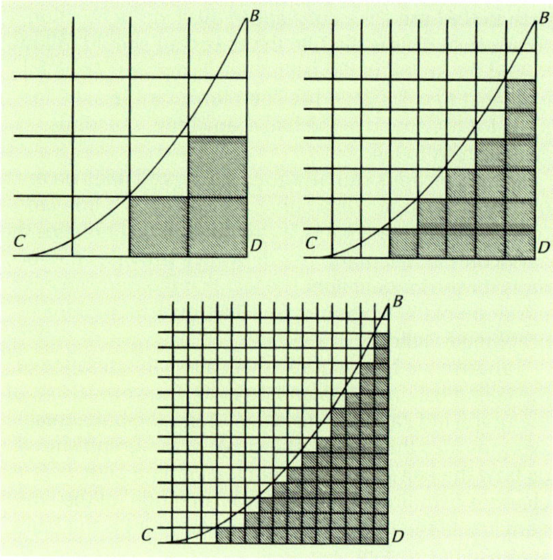

an area of $\frac{1}{4}$ square inch. In the bottom graph, the lines are $\frac{1}{4}$ inch apart, and each square has an area of $\frac{1}{16}$ square inch.

In the left-hand graph, *BCD* contains three squares with some area left over. Thus, *BCD* has an area of at least 3 square inches. In the right-hand graph, *BCD* contains 16 squares with some space left over. Since each square has an area of $\frac{1}{4}$ square inch, *BCD* has an area of at least 4 square inches. In the bottom graph, each of the 74 small squares has an area of $\frac{1}{16}$ square inch. Thus, *BCD* has an area of at least 4 $\frac{5}{8}$ square inches. If we kept plotting *BCD* on graph paper with smaller and smaller squares, we could get a closer approximation of its actual area. But we cannot get the exact area this way. Integral calculus does give us the exact area.

A different way of approximating the area of *BCD* is shown at the top of the next column. Divide the line seg-

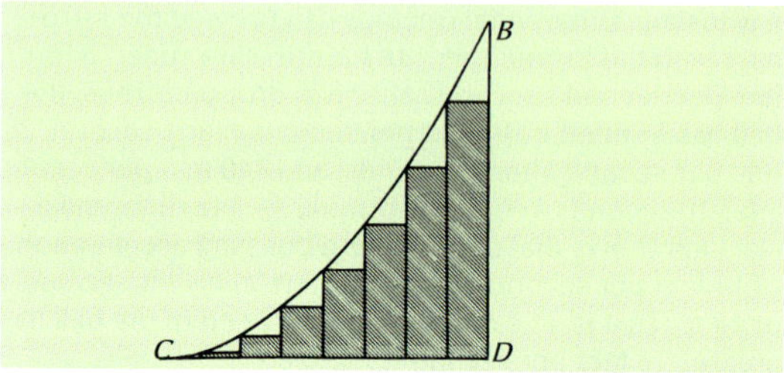

ment *CD* into eight parts, each $\frac{1}{2}$ inch long. In the original parabola, any point on the parabola *BC* is $\frac{1}{4}x^2$ inches above the line *CD* at any point x inches from *C*. Using this fact, we find that the eight rectangles drawn in *BCD* have heights of 0, $\frac{1}{16}$, $\frac{1}{4}$, $\frac{9}{16}$, 1, $\frac{25}{16}$, $\frac{9}{4}$, and $\frac{49}{16}$ inches. The sum of their areas is given by the following:

$$S_n = 0 \times \frac{1}{2} + \frac{1}{16} \times \frac{1}{2} + \frac{1}{4} \times \frac{1}{2} + \frac{9}{16} \times \frac{1}{2} + 1 \times \frac{1}{2} + \frac{25}{16} \times \frac{1}{2} + \frac{9}{4} \times \frac{1}{2} + \frac{49}{16} \times \frac{1}{2} = \frac{35}{8} = 4\,\frac{3}{8} \text{ square inches}$$

Thus, the area of *BCD* must be more than $4\frac{3}{8}$ square inches using this method.

If we divide the segment *CD* into *n* equal parts, where *n* is a positive whole number, each part has a length of $\frac{4}{n}$ inches. If we draw *n* rectangles in *BCD* just as we did above for $n = 8$, the sum, S_n, of the areas of the *n* rectangles is given by the following:

$$S_n = 0 \times \frac{4}{n} + \frac{1}{4}\left(\frac{4}{n}\right)^2 \times \frac{4}{n} + \frac{1}{4}\left(\frac{12}{n}\right)^2 \times \frac{4}{n} +$$

$$\ldots \frac{1}{4}\left(\frac{4(n-1)}{n}\right)^2 \times \frac{4}{n}$$

In this equation, the three dots indicate that some of the terms may have been left out. For example, if $n = 100$, 95 more terms should be included.

You can show by algebra that $Sn = \frac{16}{3} - \frac{8}{n} + \frac{8}{3n^2}$

As *n* gets larger and larger, the last two terms of this equation get closer and closer to 0. Thus, mathematicians say the limit of S_n as *n* approaches infinity (∞) is $\frac{16}{3}$. They write this:

$$\lim_{n^2 \to \infty} Sn = \frac{16}{3}$$

Since S_n is getting closer and closer to the area of *BCD* as *n* gets larger and larger, then the limit of S_n as *n* approaches infinity is the exact area of *BCD.* That is, the area of *BCD* is $\frac{16}{3}$, or $5\frac{1}{3}$ square inches.

The definite integral. A method similar to that used in the last example can be used to find the area of a more general region such as *ABDC* shown below.

The area of *ABDC* may be approximated by drawing rectangles in it as we did for the parabola. The height of

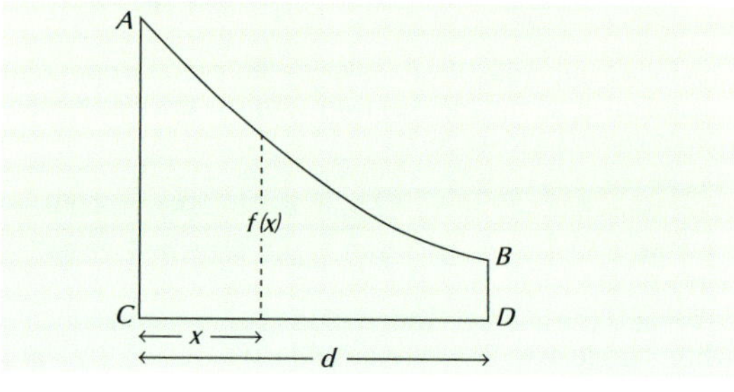

each rectangle is defined by the function $f(x)$, which is the height of the curve x units from C. Therefore, if we draw four rectangles with equal bases, the sum of their areas is given by the following equation:

$$S_4 = f(x_1)\Delta x + f(x_2)\Delta x + f(x_3)\Delta x + f(x_4)\Delta x$$

In this equation, Δx (spoken "delta x") equals $\frac{d}{4}$, the length of each base.

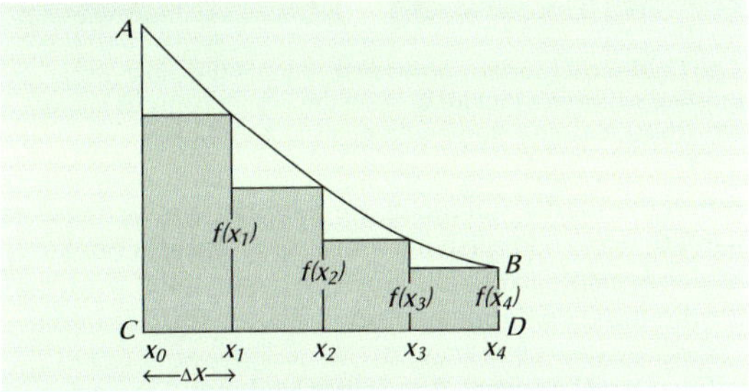

If we divide line segment CD into n equal parts by the points $x_0, x_1, \ldots, x_n$, and if we draw n rectangles in region $ABDC$, the sum, S_n, of the areas of the n rectangles is given by the following equation:

$$S_n = f(x_1)\Delta x + f(x_2)\Delta x + \ldots + f(x_n)\Delta x$$

Again, $\Delta x = \frac{d}{n}$, or the length of each base.

You can see that S_n is an approximation of the area of $ABDC$. As we divide line segment CD into more and more parts, making n larger and larger and Δx smaller and smaller, S_n becomes closer and closer to the actual area of $ABDC$. The actual area a is the limit of S_n as n approaches infinity: $a = \lim_{n \to \infty} S_n$

In words, a is the number that S_n is approaching as we divide segment CD into more and more parts, thereby making n larger and larger and Δx smaller and smaller.

The limit of S_n as n approaches infinity is called the definite integral of the function f from 0 to d. It is written with a stretched-out S as follows:

$$\int_0^d f(x)dx$$

In this equation, dx indicates that a change in the value of x is the basis for change in the value of $f(x)$.

For a function f, defined between the numbers a and b where a is less than b, we can divide the segment between a and b into n equal parts and find the sum S_n as shown. The limit of S_n as n approaches infinity is called the definite integral of f from a to b and is written:

$$\int_a^b f(x)dx$$

The fundamental theorem of calculus. The area of a region with a curved boundary, such as the area under the graph of a function f between the numbers a and b, can be found by a method that does not use the limits of sums of the areas of rectangles. First, suppose there is a function g that gives the area of the region between the numbers a and x. If we can find g, we can calculate the area between a and b. Mathematicians have discovered that the derivative of the function for the area, g', always equals the function that defines the curve, f. This relationship is known as the *fundamental theorem of calculus.* It states that

$$\int_a^b f(x)dx = g(b) - g(a)$$

where g is any function whose derivative is the function f. For example, $f(x) = \frac{1}{4}x^2$ is the height function of the parabola we have been studying. The function g, defined by $g(x) = \frac{1}{12}x^3$, has f as its derivative. This is because $g'(x) = \frac{1}{12}3x^2 = \frac{1}{4}x^2 = f(x)$. By the fundamental theorem of calculus:

$$\int \frac{1}{4}x^2dx = g(4) - g(0) = \frac{1}{12}4^3 - \frac{1}{12}0^3 = \frac{63}{12} = \frac{16}{3}$$

This is the area of region BCD under the parabola.

The fundamental theorem of calculus unites differential and integral calculus into one system that can solve a broad range of problems. The problem of finding an area becomes the problem of finding a function with a given derivative. The ability to find a function once the derivative is known enabled scientists to determine the speed of objects from the gravitational forces acting upon them. In the example of the falling ball, the speed increases by 14 feet each second, $s = 14t$. The fundamental theorem shows that the total distance the ball falls is given by the function whose derivative is $s = 14t$. That function is $d = 7t^2$.

History

In solving problems of area, the Greek mathematician Archimedes used methods that foreshadowed those used today in integral calculus. In the 1600's, differential calculus was developed to find tangents to curves and solve problems connected with the motions of planets and other objects. Then, the English scientist Sir Isaac Newton and the German philosopher Gottfried W. Leibniz independently discovered the fundamental theorem of calculus. For this discovery, Newton and Leibniz are called the founders of calculus. Thomas J. Brieske

See also **Leibniz, Gottfried Wilhelm; Mathematics** (History); **Newton, Sir Isaac.**

Calcutta. See **Kolkata.**

Caldecott, Randolph (1846-1886), was a British illustrator of children's books. He became known for lively scenes of the English countryside and humorous portrayals of those who lived there. He is considered the originator of children's picture books.

Caldecott was born on March 22, 1846, in Chester. He began drawing animals at an early age. Caldecott first won fame for illustrating Washington Irving's *Old Christmas* (1875).

From 1878 to 1886, he produced two picture books a year at Christmas with Edmund Evans, an English engraver and printer. They included *An Elegy on the Death of a Mad Dog* (1879), *Three Jovial Huntsmen* (1880), *Sing a Song for Sixpence* (1880), *The Queen of Hearts* (1881), *The Milkmaid* (1882), *Hey Diddle Diddle: and Baby Bunting* (1882), and *A Frog He Would A-Wooing Go* (1883). In them, he made bold use of reds and greens. The Caldecott Medal, an annual award for the best picture book of the year, is named for him. Jill P. May

See also **Caldecott Medal; Literature for children** (The rise of illustration; picture: Great illustrators).

Caldecott Medal is an annual award for the most distinguished picture book for children published during the previous year. It was the first award recognizing the work of the illustrator of a book. The selection is made by a committee consisting of 15 members of the Association for Library Service to Children (ALSC) of the American Library Association. The winner is announced in January. The ALSC presents the award to the illustrator at the association's annual conference.

The award is limited to artists who are U.S. citizens or residents, and whose work was published within the past year. The book must be the artist's original creation. If two artists worked on it, the award is given to both. The artist does not have to write the story. The pictures, rather than the text, should be the heart of the book.

The face of the Caldecott Medal has a reproduction of Randolph Caldecott's original illustration of John Gilpin's ride from the famous narrative poem "The Diverting History of John Gilpin" by William Cowper. The other side has an illustration of "four and twenty blackbirds baked in a pie." The engraving reads "For the most distinguished American picture book for children."

Frederic G. Melcher, coeditor of *Publishers' Weekly* magazine and founder of Children's Book Week, established the medal. Caldecott, for whom the award was named, was an English illustrator of children's books. Melcher also established the Newbery Medal, awarded for the most distinguished book written for children.

Critically reviewed by the Association for Library Service to Children

See also **Caldecott, Randolph; Melcher, Frederic G.; Newbery Medal.**

American Library Association

The Caldecott Medal, *shown here,* honors the most distinguished children's picture book of the year. It pictures characters from children's storybooks on its face and back.

Calder, Alexander (1898-1976), was one of the first American sculptors of international significance, and one of the best-known American artists of the 1900's. Calder became famous for his witty and elegant sculptures called *mobiles.* The works received this name because they actually move when they are pushed by air

Winners of the Caldecott Medal

Year	Illustrator	Winning book
1938	Dorothy P. Lathrop	*Animals of the Bible*
1939	Thomas Handforth	*Mei Li*
1940	Ingri and Edgar Parin d'Aulaire	*Abraham Lincoln*
1941	Robert Lawson	*They Were Strong and Good*
1942	Robert McCloskey	*Make Way for Ducklings*
1943	Virginia Lee Burton	*The Little House*
1944	Louis Slobodkin	*Many Moons*
1945	Elizabeth Orton Jones	*Prayer for a Child*
1946	Maud and Miska Petersham	*The Rooster Crows*
1947	Leonard Weisgard	*The Little Island*
1948	Roger Duvoisin	*White Snow, Bright Snow*
1949	Berta and Elmer Hader	*The Big Snow*
1950	Leo Politi	*Song of the Swallows*
1951	Katherine Milhous	*The Egg Tree*
1952	Nicolas Mordvinoff	*Finders Keepers*
1953	Lynd K. Ward	*The Biggest Bear*
1954	Ludwig Bemelmans	*Madeline's Rescue*
1955	Marcia Brown	*Cinderella; or The Little Glass Slipper*
1956	Feodor Rojankovsky	*Frog Went A-Courtin'*
1957	Marc Simont	*A Tree Is Nice*
1958	Robert McCloskey	*Time of Wonder*
1959	Barbara Cooney	*Chanticleer and the Fox*
1960	Marie Hall Ets	*Nine Days to Christmas*
1961	Nicolas Sidjakov	*Baboushka and the Three Kings*
1962	Marcia Brown	*Once a Mouse*
1963	Ezra Jack Keats	*The Snowy Day*
1964	Maurice Sendak	*Where the Wild Things Are*
1965	Beni Montresor	*May I Bring a Friend?*
1966	Nonny Hogrogian	*Always Room for One More*
1967	Evaline Ness	*Sam, Bangs, & Moonshine*
1968	Ed Emberley	*Drummer Hoff*
1969	Uri Shulevitz	*The Fool of the World and the Flying Ship*
1970	William Steig	*Sylvester and the Magic Pebble*
1971	Gail E. Haley	*A Story, a Story*
1972	Nonny Hogrogian	*One Fine Day*
1973	Blair Lent	*The Funny Little Woman*
1974	Margot Zemach	*Duffy and the Devil: A Cornish Tale*

Year	Illustrator	Winning book
1975	Gerald McDermott	*Arrow to the Sun: A Pueblo Indian Tale*
1976	Leo and Diane Dillon	*Why Mosquitoes Buzz in People's Ears: A West African Tale*
1977	Leo and Diane Dillon	*Ashanti to Zulu: African Traditions*
1978	Peter Spier	*Noah's Ark*
1979	Paul Goble	*The Girl Who Loved Wild Horses*
1980	Barbara Cooney	*Ox-Cart Man*
1981	Arnold Lobel	*Fables*
1982	Chris Van Allsburg	*Jumanji*
1983	Marcia Brown	*Shadow*
1984	Alice and Martin Provensen	*The Glorious Flight: Across the Channel with Louis Blériot*
1985	Trina Schart Hyman	*Saint George and the Dragon*
1986	Chris Van Allsburg	*The Polar Express*
1987	Richard Egielski	*Hey, Al*
1988	John Schoenherr	*Owl Moon*
1989	Stephen Gammell	*Song and Dance Man*
1990	Ed Young	*Lon Po Po: A Red-Riding Hood Story from China*
1991	David Macaulay	*Black and White*
1992	David Wiesner	*Tuesday*
1993	Emily Arnold McCully	*Mirette on the High Wire*
1994	Allen Say	*Grandfather's Journey*
1995	David Diaz	*Smoky Night*
1996	Peggy Rathmann	*Officer Buckle and Gloria*
1997	David Wisniewski	*Golem*
1998	Paul O. Zelinsky	*Rapunzel*
1999	Mary Azarian	*Snowflake Bentley*
2000	Simms Taback	*Joseph Had a Little Overcoat*
2001	David Small	*So You Want to Be President?*
2002	David Wiesner	*The Three Pigs*
2003	Eric Rohmann	*My Friend Rabbit*
2004	Mordicai Gerstein	*The Man Who Walked Between the Towers*
2005	Kevin Henkes	*Kitten's First Full Moon*
2006	Chris Raschka	*The Hello, Goodbye Window*

Calder in his studio in Roxbury, Connecticut; John Lewis Stage from *Holiday Magazine* © 1959

Alexander Calder became famous for his delicate and playful metal sculpture. He created both *mobiles* (moving sculpture) and *stabiles* (stationary sculpture).

currents. Earlier sculptors had given movement to sculpture by using motors or clockworks. Calder's mobiles are delicately suspended abstract constructions of sheet metal parts and wires.

Calder was born in Philadelphia on July 22, 1898. His father and grandfather were sculptors, and his mother was a painter. He received an engineering degree from the Stevens Institute of Technology in 1919. He then studied painting at the Art Students League in New York City and moved to Paris in 1926. Calder divided his time between Paris and New York until 1933, when he established his first American studio in Roxbury, Connecticut.

The early work of Calder in Paris included wooden toys, miniature circuses, and wire sculptures. In the early 1930's, he began constructing mobiles, a term invented by the French artist Marcel Duchamp. Calder also started to build *stabiles,* a name first used by his friend and fellow artist, the German-born French sculptor Jean Arp. Stabiles resemble mobiles except they do not move. Calder later created works that combine the elements of both mobiles and stabiles. See **Mobile**.

Major displays of Calder's works included those in New York City at the Museum of Modern Art in 1964 and 1965, and at the Whitney Museum of Art in 1976. Among his many important public sculptures are those at UNESCO Headquarters in Paris, Kennedy International Airport and Lincoln Center for the Performing Arts in New York City, and the Festival of Two Worlds in Spoleto, Italy. Calder's sculpture *Red Petals* appears in the **Sculpture** article. He also created many lithographs. Calder died on Nov. 11, 1976. George Gurney

Calderón de la Barca, *KAHL duh ROHN day lah BAHR kuh,* **Pedro,** *PAY droh* (1600-1681), was a Spanish playwright and the last great writer of Spain's Golden Age. Calderón wrote about 200 plays, including more than 70 *autos sacramentales* (religious plays on the theme of the Eucharist). Calderón dealt with traditional Roman Catholic moral and religious attitudes. He filled his plays with symbolism and elaborate figures of speech. *Life Is a Dream* (1635), his best-known play, explores the mysteries of human destiny and the conflict between free will and predestination. He also wrote tragedies based on the Spanish honor code, including *The Surgeon of His Honor,* and "cloak-and-sword" plays of intrigue.

Calderón was born in Madrid on Jan. 17, 1600. He received a university education in law, logic, and theology. Calderón became a priest at the age of 50. He died on May 25, 1681. Harry Sieber

See also **Drama** (The Golden Age of Spanish drama); **Spanish literature** (The 1600's).

Calderone, Mary Steichen (1904-1998), an American physician, won fame for her efforts to promote sex education in schools. She helped establish the Sex Information and Education Council of the United States (SIECUS) in 1964 and was its executive director until 1982. SIECUS provides information about sex education to counselors, physicians, religious groups, and schools. It also publishes books and study guides.

Calderone was born in New York City on July 1, 1904. She earned an M.D. at the University of Rochester. She and her husband, also a physician, both worked in the field of public health. Calderone formerly served as physician to the public schools in Great Neck, New York. From 1953 to 1964, she was medical director of the Planned Parenthood Federation of America. Calderone became convinced that a thorough understanding of sex would help people handle their sexual problems responsibly and achieve greater health and happiness. She died on Oct. 24, 1998. Daniel J. Kevles

Caldwell, Erskine, *UR skihn* (1903-1987), was an American author best known for the sensationalism of his novels about rural Southern life. His most famous works portray the impact of changing cultural and economic conditions on poverty-stricken white tenant farmers. Caldwell told about men and women reduced to the basic hungers of life and starved of the satisfaction of these hungers. His emphasis on sex and violence, even when combined with humor, was condemned by some people as crude, vulgar, sensationalistic, and immoral.

Caldwell wrote more than 50 books. He first became famous with *Tobacco Road* (1932), which features his best-known character, Jeeter Lester. *Tobacco Road* was adapted into a play that ran from 1933 to 1941 on Broadway. Caldwell's next novel, *God's Little Acre* (1933), increased his fame. His other novels include *Journeyman* (1935), *Georgia Boy* (1943), and *Tragic Ground* (1944). His *Complete Stories* appeared in 1953. His nonfiction includes two volumes of autobiography, *Call It Experience* (1951) and *With All My Might* (1987). He wrote the text for Margaret Bourke-White's book of photographs of the Great Depression, *You Have Seen Their Faces* (1937). Caldwell was born on Dec. 17, 1903, in White Oak, Georgia. He died on April 11, 1987. Noel Polk

Caldwell, Sarah (1924-2006), was an American opera director and conductor. She founded the Opera Company of Boston in 1957 and served as its artistic director and frequently as its conductor until the company suspended operations in 1991.

Caldwell emphasized the dramatic elements in her productions, and many of her stagings included spectacular visual effects. She was also known for producing rarely performed operas or alternative versions of familiar works.

Peter Benjamin

Sarah Caldwell

Caldwell was born on March 6, 1924, in Maryville, Missouri. She taught at the Berkshire Music Center from 1948 to 1952 and headed the Opera Workshop at Boston University from 1952 to 1960. Starting in the 1970's, Caldwell was in great demand as a guest conductor. In 1976, she became the first woman to conduct at the Metropolitan Opera House in New York City.

From the late 1970's to the early 2000's, Caldwell often worked outside the United States. In the early 1990's, she was named principal guest conductor of the Sverdlovsk Philharmonic Orchestra in Yekaterinburg, Russia, where she served until 2001. Caldwell died on March 23, 2006. Ellen Pfeifer

Caledonia, *KAL ih DOH nee uh,* is the ancient Roman name for northeast Scotland. Much later, it became a poetic name for all Scotland. The Roman general Agricola invaded Caledonia three times between A.D. 80 and 84. The first Caledonians were a single Highland tribe. Later, all the tribes of northeast Scotland became known together as Caledonians. The Romans called the Caledonians *Picts.* Eventually, this name replaced *Caledonians.* See also **Scotland** (The Roman invasion). James E. Fraser

Calendar is a system of measuring and recording the passage of time. A major scientific advance occurred when people realized that nature furnishes a regular sequence of seasons. The seasons governed their lives, determined their needs, and controlled the supply of their natural foods. They needed a calendar so they could prepare for the hardships of winter.

Before the invention of the clock, people watched the sun, the moon, and the stars to tell time. The daily rising of the sun provided a short unit of time, the solar day. The cycle of seasons roughly indicated a longer unit of time, the solar year. But early people did not know that Earth's revolution around the sun caused the different seasons. The changing position and shape of the moon was easier for them to observe. As a result, the early calendars used the interval between the successive full moons, the lunar month, as an intermediate unit of time.

We now know that the lunar month lasts about 29 ½ days. Twelve such months amount to about 354 days. This interval is almost 11 days shorter than the true solar year, which has 365 days, 5 hours, 48 minutes, and 46 seconds. But a year of 13 lunar months would amount to about 383 ½ days and would be more than 18 days longer than the solar year. The solar year, therefore, does not equal any whole number of lunar months.

The discrepancy between whole lunar months and

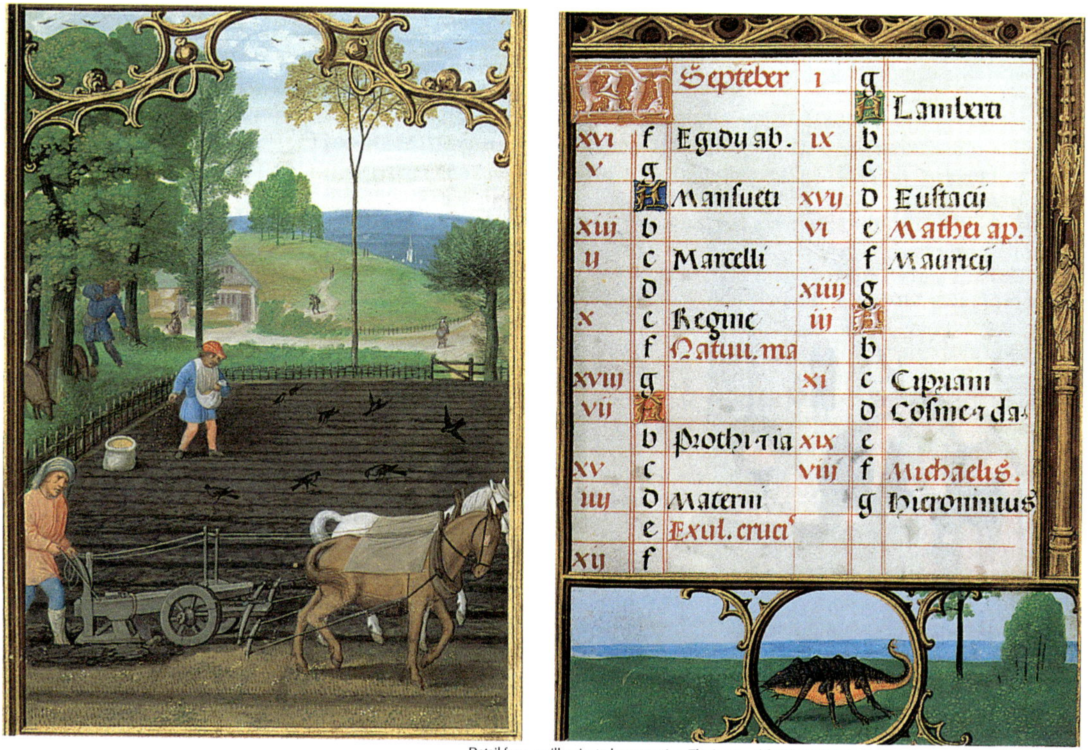

Detail from an illuminated manuscript, *The Hours of the Virgin* (1515); Pierpont Morgan Library, New York City

A Flemish calendar from the 1500's shows the month of September illustrated with a farming scene.

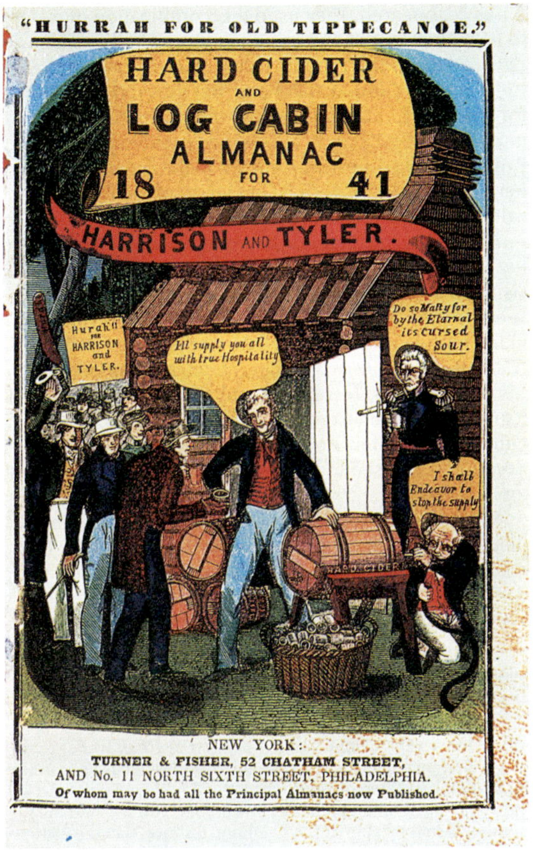

Granger Collection

An American calendar of 1841 shows a cartoon supporting the presidential candidacy of William Henry Harrison.

days in a solar year explains the confusion over calendar keeping during thousands of years. A calendar based on 12 lunar months becomes out of step with the seasons. Some people who used lunar calendars kept them roughly in step with the seasons by making some years 12 months long and other years 13 months long.

Some calendars today

Most people in the Western world use the *Gregorian calendar,* worked out in the 1580's by Pope Gregory XIII. It has 12 months, 11 with 30 or 31 days. The other month, February, normally has 28 days. Every fourth year, called a leap year, it has 29 days. However, century years that cannot be divided evenly by 400 lose the extra day, though they are leap years. For example, February had 28 days in 1900 but 29 days in 2000.

The Gregorian calendar is based on the year of Jesus Christ's birth, according to a dating system started in 532 by the monk Dionysius Exiguus. In this system, the year of Christ's birth was A.D. 1., and the year before that was 1 B.C. The abbreviation *A.D.* stands for *anno Domini* (in the year of our Lord), and *B.C.* means *before Christ.* But modern scholars believe Christ was born no later than 1 B.C. He was born during the lifetime of Herod the Great, who died in either 4 B.C. or 1 B.C. An alternative system uses Gregorian numbering, but does not refer to Christ. In that system, *C.E.* (common era) replaces A.D., and *B.C.E.* (before the common era) replaces B.C. See **B.C.; A.D.**

The Christian church calendar is regulated partly by the sun and partly by the moon. *Immovable feasts* include Christmas and such feasts as the Nativity of the Blessed Virgin. They are based on the solar year. Such days as Ash Wednesday, Palm Sunday, and Easter are called *movable feasts,* because their dates vary from year to year, according to the phases of the moon.

The Hebrew calendar begins with an estimated moment of the world's creation. Hebrew tradition has placed this moment at 3,760 years and 3 months before the birth of Jesus Christ. To find a year in the Hebrew calendar, we must add 3,760 to the date in the Gregorian calendar. For example, 2000 in the Gregorian calendar is 5760 in the Hebrew calendar. But this system will not work to the exact month, because the Hebrew year begins in September or October in the Gregorian calendar. By November 2000, for instance, the Hebrew year had become 5761.

The Hebrew year is based on the moon and normally consists of 12 months. The months are *Tishri, Heshvan, Kislev, Tebet, Shebat, Adar, Nisan, Iyar, Sivan, Tammuz, Ab,* and *Elul.* They are alternately 30 and 29 days long. Seven times during every 19-year period, an *embolismic* or extra 29-day month, called *Veadar,* is inserted between Adar and Nisan. At the same time, Adar is given 30 days instead of 29. These additions keep the Hebrew calendar and holidays in agreement with the seasons of the solar year.

The Islamic calendar begins with Muhammad's flight from Mecca to Medina. This flight, called *the Hijra,* took place in A.D. 622 by the Gregorian calendar. The Islamic year is based on the moon, and has 12 months, alternately 30 and 29 days long. These months are *Muharram, Safar, Rabi I, Rabi II, Jumada I, Jumada II, Rajab, Shaban, Ramadan, Shawwal, Zulkadah,* and *Dhul-Hijja.*

The Islamic year is much shorter than the solar year, with only 354 days. As a result, the Islamic New Year moves backward through the seasons. It moves completely backward in a course of 32 $\frac{1}{2}$ years. The Islamic calendar divides time into cycles 30 years long. During each cycle, 19 years have the regular 354 days, and 11 years have an extra day each. This method of counting time makes the Islamic year nearly as accurate in measuring the lunar year as the Gregorian year is in measuring the solar year.

The Chinese calendar begins at 2637 B.C., the year in which the legendary Emperor Huangdi is said to have invented it. This calendar counts years in cycles of 60. For example, the year 2000 in the Gregorian calendar is the 17th year in the 78th cycle. The years within each cycle of the Chinese calendar are broken down into repeating 12-year cycles. In these cycles, each year is named after 10 Chinese constellations and 12 animals. The animals are the rat, ox, tiger, hare, dragon, snake, horse, sheep, monkey, rooster, dog, and pig. The year 2000 is the *year of the dragon.*

The Chinese year is based on the moon and generally consists of 12 months. Each month begins at new moon and has 29 or 30 days. A month is repeated seven times during each 19-year period, so that the calendar stays approximately in line with the seasons. The year starts at the second new moon after the beginning of winter in the Northern Hemisphere. Thus, the Chinese New Year occurs no earlier than January 21 and no later than February 20.

History

Early calendars usually represented some sort of compromise between the lunar and solar years. Some years lasted 12 months, and others lasted 13 months.

The Babylonians, who lived in what is now Iraq, added an extra month to their years at irregular intervals. Their calendar, composed of alternate 29-day and 30-day months, kept roughly in step with the lunar year. To balance the calendar with the solar year, the early Babylonians calculated that they needed to add an extra month three times every eight years. But this system still did not accurately make up for the accumulated differences between the solar year and the lunar year. Whenever the king felt that the calendar had slipped too far out of step with the seasons, he ordered another extra month. However, the Babylonian calendar was quite confused until the 300's B.C., when the Babylonians began to use a more reliable system.

The Egyptians were probably the first group to adopt a mainly solar calendar. They noted that the Dog Star, Sirius, reappeared in the eastern sky just before sunrise after several months of invisibility. They also observed that the annual flood of the Nile River came soon after Sirius reappeared. They used this combination of events to fix their calendar and came to recognize a year of 365 days, made up of 12 months each 30 days long, and an extra five days added at the end. But they did not allow for the extra fourth of a day, and their calendar drifted into error. According to the famed Egyptologist J. H. Breasted, the earliest date known in the Egyptian calendar corresponds to 4236 B.C. in terms of the Gregorian calendar.

The Romans apparently borrowed parts of their earliest known calendar from the Greeks. The calendar consisted of 10 months in a year of 304 days. The Romans seem to have ignored the remaining 61 days, which fell in the middle of winter. The 10 months were named *Martius, Aprilis, Maius, Junius, Quintilis, Sextilis, September, October, November,* and *December.* The last six names were taken from the words for five, six, seven, eight, nine, and ten. Romulus, the legendary first ruler of Rome, is supposed to have introduced this calendar in the 700's B.C.

According to tradition, the Roman ruler Numa Pompilius added January and February to the calendar. This made the Roman year 355 days long. To make the calendar correspond approximately to the solar year, Numa also ordered the addition every other year of a month called Mercedinus. Mercedinus was inserted after February 23 or 24, and the last days of February were

A perpetual calendar will show the day of the week for any year desired. This calendar begins with A.D. 1753, the year after Britain adopted the calendar used widely in the Western world. This perpetual calendar is easy to use. The letters in the *Table of Years (on the opposite page)* refer to the first column of the *Table of Months (next to it).* The figures in the Table of Months refer to one of the seven columns in the *Table of Days (below).* For example, to find on what day of the week Christmas fell in 1900, look for **1900** in the Table of Years. The letter **a** follows. Look for **a** in the Table of Months, and, under December, you will find the number **6**. In the Table of Days, column **6** shows that the 25th day, Christmas, fell on Tuesday in 1900.

1		2		3		4		5		6		7	
Monday	1	Tuesday	1	Wednesday	1	Thursday	1	Friday	1	Saturday	1	**Sunday**	1
Tuesday	2	Wednesday	2	Thursday	2	Friday	2	Saturday	2	**Sunday**	2	Monday	2
Wednesday	3	Thursday	3	Friday	3	Saturday	3	**Sunday**	3	Monday	3	Tuesday	3
Thursday	4	Friday	4	Saturday	4	**Sunday**	4	Monday	4	Tuesday	4	Wednesday	4
Friday	5	Saturday	5	**Sunday**	5	Monday	5	Tuesday	5	Wednesday	5	Thursday	5
Saturday	6	**Sunday**	6	Monday	6	Tuesday	6	Wednesday	6	Thursday	6	Friday	6
Sunday	7	Monday	7	Tuesday	7	Wednesday	7	Thursday	7	Friday	7	Saturday	7
Monday	8	Tuesday	8	Wednesday	8	Thursday	8	Friday	8	Saturday	8	**Sunday**	8
Tuesday	9	Wednesday	9	Thursday	9	Friday	9	Saturday	9	**Sunday**	9	Monday	9
Wednesday	10	Thursday	10	Friday	10	Saturday	10	**Sunday**	10	Monday	10	Tuesday	10
Thursday	11	Friday	11	Saturday	11	**Sunday**	11	Monday	11	Tuesday	11	Wednesday	11
Friday	12	Saturday	12	**Sunday**	12	Monday	12	Tuesday	12	Wednesday	12	Thursday	12
Saturday	13	**Sunday**	13	Monday	13	Tuesday	13	Wednesday	13	Thursday	13	Friday	13
Sunday	14	Monday	14	Tuesday	14	Wednesday	14	Thursday	14	Friday	14	Saturday	14
Monday	15	Tuesday	15	Wednesday	15	Thursday	15	Friday	15	Saturday	15	**Sunday**	15
Tuesday	16	Wednesday	16	Thursday	16	Friday	16	Saturday	16	**Sunday**	16	Monday	16
Wednesday	17	Thursday	17	Friday	17	Saturday	17	**Sunday**	17	Monday	17	Tuesday	17
Thursday	18	Friday	18	Saturday	18	**Sunday**	18	Monday	18	Tuesday	18	Wednesday	18
Friday	19	Saturday	19	**Sunday**	19	Monday	19	Tuesday	19	Wednesday	19	Thursday	19
Saturday	20	**Sunday**	20	Monday	20	Tuesday	20	Wednesday	20	Thursday	20	Friday	20
Sunday	21	Monday	21	Tuesday	21	Wednesday	21	Thursday	21	Friday	21	Saturday	21
Monday	22	Tuesday	22	Wednesday	22	Thursday	22	Friday	22	Saturday	22	**Sunday**	22
Tuesday	23	Wednesday	23	Thursday	23	Friday	23	Saturday	23	**Sunday**	23	Monday	23
Wednesday	24	Thursday	24	Friday	24	Saturday	24	**Sunday**	24	Monday	24	Tuesday	24
Thursday	25	Friday	25	Saturday	25	**Sunday**	25	Monday	25	Tuesday	25	Wednesday	25
Friday	26	Saturday	26	**Sunday**	26	Monday	26	Tuesday	26	Wednesday	26	Thursday	26
Saturday	27	**Sunday**	27	Monday	27	Tuesday	27	Wednesday	27	Thursday	27	Friday	27
Sunday	28	Monday	28	Tuesday	28	Wednesday	28	Thursday	28	Friday	28	Saturday	28
Monday	29	Tuesday	29	Wednesday	29	Thursday	29	Friday	29	Saturday	29	**Sunday**	29
Tuesday	30	Wednesday	30	Thursday	30	Friday	30	Saturday	30	**Sunday**	30	Monday	30
Wednesday	31	Thursday	31	Friday	31	Saturday	31	**Sunday**	31	Monday	31	Tuesday	31

moved to the end of Mercedinus. In years when it was inserted, Mercedinus added 22 or 23 days to the year.

The Julian calendar. By the time of Julius Caesar, the accumulated error caused by the incorrect length of the Roman year—and by the occasional failure to add extra days at the proper times—had made the calendar about three months ahead of the seasons. Winter occurred in September, and autumn came in the month now called July.

In 46 B.C., Caesar asked the astronomer Sosigenes to review the calendar and suggest ways for improving it. Acting on Sosigenes's suggestions, Caesar ordered the Romans to disregard the moon in calculating their calendars. He divided the year into 12 months of 31 and 30 days, except for February, which had only 29 days. Every fourth year, it would have 30 days. To realign the calendar with the seasons, Caesar ruled that the year we know as 46 B.C. should have 445 days. The Romans called it *the year of confusion.*

The Romans renamed Quintilis to honor Julius Caesar, giving us *July.* Sextilis was renamed *August* by the Roman Senate to honor the Emperor Augustus. The Senate also moved a day from February to August to make August as long as July.

The Julian calendar was widely used for more than 1,500 years. A Julian year lasted 365 $\frac{1}{4}$ days. But it was actually about 11 minutes and 14 seconds longer than the solar year. This difference led to a gradual change in the dates on which the seasons began. By A.D. 1580, the spring equinox fell 10 days earlier on the Julian calendar than its appointed date.

The Gregorian calendar was designed to correct the errors of the Julian calendar. In 1582, on the advice of astronomers, Pope Gregory XIII corrected the difference between sun and calendar by ordering 10 days dropped from October, the month with the fewest Roman Catholic holy days. The day that would have been Oct. 5, 1582, became October 15. This procedure restored the next equinox to its proper date. To correct the Julian calendar's error regularly, the pope decreed that February would have an extra day in century years that could be divided evenly by 400, such as 1600 and 2000, but not in others, such as 1700, 1800, and 1900.

The Gregorian calendar is so accurate that the difference between the calendar and solar years is now only about 26 seconds. This difference will increase by 0.53 second every hundred years, because the solar year is gradually becoming shorter.

Years 1753 to 2030

	1786g	1821a	1856k	1891d	1926e	1961g	1996h
	1787a	1822b	1857d	1892n	1927f	1962a	1997c
1753a	1788k	1823c	1858e	1893g	1928q	1963b	1998d
1754b	1789d	1824m	1859f	1894a	1929b	1964l	1999e
1755c	1790e	1825f	1860q	1895b	1930c	1965e	2000p
1756m	1791f	1826g	1861b	1896l	1931d	1966f	2001a
1757f	1792q	1827a	1862c	1897e	1932n	1967g	2002b
1758g	1793b	1828k	1863d	1898f	1933g	1968h	2003c
1759a	1794c	1829d	1864n	1899g	1934a	1969c	2004m
1760k	1795d	1830e	1865g	1900a	1935b	1970d	2005f
1761d	1796n	1831f	1866a	1901b	1936l	1971e	2006g
1762e	1797g	1832q	1867b	1902c	1937e	1972p	2007a
1763f	1798a	1833b	1868l	1903d	1938f	1973a	2008k
1764q	1799b	1834c	1869e	1904n	1939g	1974b	2009d
1765b	1800c	1835d	1870f	1905g	1940h	1975c	2010e
1766c	1801d	1836n	1871g	1906a	1941c	1976m	2011f
1767d	1802e	1837g	1872h	1907b	1942d	1977f	2012q
1768n	1803f	1838a	1873c	1908l	1943e	1978g	2013b
1769g	1804q	1839b	1874d	1909e	1944p	1979a	2014c
1770a	1805b	1840l	1875e	1910f	1945a	1980k	2015d
1771b	1806c	1841e	1876p	1911g	1946b	1981d	2016n
1772l	1807d	1842f	1877a	1912h	1947c	1982e	2017g
1773e	1808n	1843g	1878b	1913c	1948m	1983f	2018a
1774f	1809g	1844h	1879c	1914d	1949f	1984q	2019b
1775g	1810a	1845c	1880m	1915e	1950g	1985b	2020l
1776h	1811b	1846d	1881f	1916p	1951a	1986c	2021e
1777c	1812l	1847e	1882g	1917a	1952k	1987d	2022f
1778d	1813e	1848p	1883a	1918b	1953d	1988n	2023g
1779e	1814f	1849a	1884k	1919c	1954e	1989g	2024h
1780p	1815g	1850b	1885d	1920m	1955f	1990a	2025c
1781a	1816h	1851c	1886e	1921f	1956q	1991b	2026d
1782b	1817c	1852m	1887f	1922g	1957b	1992l	2027e
1783c	1818d	1853f	1888q	1923a	1958c	1993e	2028p
1784m	1819e	1854g	1889b	1924k	1959d	1994f	2029a
1785f	1820p	1855a	1890c	1925d	1960n	1995g	2030b

	Jan.	Feb.	March	April	May	June	July	Aug.	Sept.	Oct.	Nov.	Dec.
a	1	4	4	7	2	5	7	3	6	1	4	6
b	2	5	5	1	3	6	1	4	7	2	5	7
c	3	6	6	2	4	7	2	5	1	3	6	1
d	4	7	7	3	5	1	3	6	2	4	7	2
e	5	1	1	4	6	2	4	7	3	5	1	3
f	6	2	2	5	7	3	5	1	4	6	2	4
g	7	3	3	6	1	4	6	2	5	7	3	5
h	1	4	5	1	3	6	1	4	7	2	5	7
k	2	5	6	2	4	7	2	5	1	3	6	1
l	3	6	7	3	5	1	3	6	2	4	7	2
m	4	7	1	4	6	2	4	7	3	5	1	3
n	5	1	2	5	7	3	5	1	4	6	2	4
p	6	2	3	6	1	4	6	2	5	7	3	5
q	7	3	4	7	2	5	7	3	6	1	4	6

The Roman Catholic nations of Europe adopted the Gregorian calendar almost immediately after Gregory XIII devised it. Various German states kept the Julian calendar until 1700. Britain (now the United Kingdom) and the American Colonies changed to the Gregorian calendar in 1752. Russia and Turkey did not adopt the Gregorian calendar until the early 1900's.

Calendar reform would simplify the present calendar. Two proposed calendars have received considerable support. In each, months and years would begin on the same day of the week every year. All months would contain the same or nearly the same number of days. The Fixed Calendar, also called the Thirteen-Month Calendar, would provide 13 months exactly four weeks long. The extra month, Sol, would come before July. A year day placed at the end of the year would belong to no week or month. Every four years, a leap-year day would be added just before July 1. The World Calendar would have 12 months of 30 or 31 days, a year day at the end of each year, and a leap-year day before July 1 every four years. Irene Cockroft

Related articles in *World Book* include:

April Fools' Day	Julian calendar	Moon
Century	Leap year	Olympiad
Day	Maya (Communication and learning)	Season
Equinox		Time
Gregorian calendar		Week
	Month	Year

Additional resources

Bourgoing, Jacqueline de. *The Calendar.* Abrams, 2001.
Duncan, David E. *Calendar: Humanity's Epic Struggle to Determine a True and Accurate Year.* 1998. Reprint. Avon, 1999.
Kummer, Patricia K. *The Calendar.* Watts, 2005. Younger readers.
Richards, E. G. *Mapping Time: The Calendar and Its History.* 1998. Reprint. Oxford, 1999.

Calendering. See **Paper** (Sheet formation; picture: How paper is made); **Plastics** (Making plastic products; diagram); **Rubber** (Shaping); **Textile** (Finishing the fabric).

Calendula, *kuh LEHN juh luh,* is a group of herbs of the composite family. Most kinds of calendula grow in the temperate zone from the Canary Islands to Asia Minor. Calendulas grow from 1 to 2 feet (30 to 60 centimeters) high. The leaves lie one above the other on the stem. The flower heads have yellow or orange rays.

WORLD BOOK illustration by Carol A. Brozman

Calendulas are common garden flowers in temperate regions around the world. The flowers have yellow or orange petals.

Some calendulas, such as the pot marigold, are favorite annual garden flowers in many parts of the world. Gardeners usually grow them from seeds. The calendula is the flower-of-the-month for October. In the 1500's and 1600's, the calendula blossom was used in cooking to flavor soups and stews. David J. Keil

Scientific classification. Calendulas belong to the composite family, Asteraceae or Compositae. A common calendula is *Calendula officinalis.*

Calf, in anatomy. See **Leg** (The leg).

Calf. See **Cattle; Elephant** (Reproduction); **Whale** (Reproduction).

Calgary, *KAL guh ree,* is the oil center of Canada and the largest city in the province of Alberta. According to the 2001 census, Calgary also has the largest metropolitan area population in Alberta. Edmonton ranks second in both city and metropolitan area population. The oil in-

City of Calgary

Calgary, the center of Canada's oil industry, lies at the junction of the Bow and Elbow rivers in southwestern Alberta.

City boundary
Expressway
Other road
Railroad
Point of interest
Park

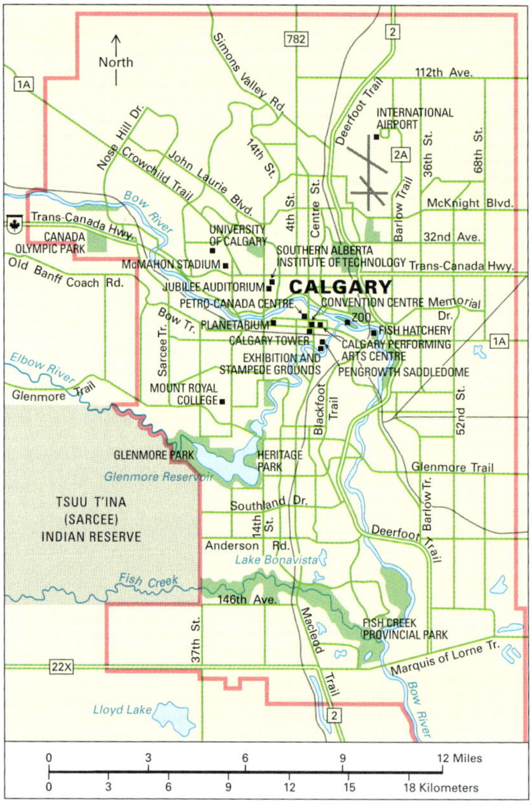

WORLD BOOK maps

dustry has made Calgary one of Canada's fastest-growing cities.

Calgary lies in the eastern foothills of the Canadian Rocky Mountains and is often called the *Foothills City.* Its location has made it a major transportation and distribution center of western Canada. Calgary grew up as a cattle town and is still a major cattle center in Alberta. The city has won fame for the yearly Calgary Exhibition and Stampede, which features chuck wagon races, livestock shows, rodeo events, and carnival rides and games.

The city seal of Calgary shows the city's symbols—the Rockies, a buffalo, a horse, and a steer.

The North-West Mounted Police (NWMP)—now the Royal Canadian Mounted Police—set up a fort on the site of Calgary in 1875. NWMP Colonel James F. Macleod named the fort after his ancestors' home, Calgary, in Scotland. The Gaelic word *calgary* was thought to mean *bay farm.*

The city. Calgary lies at the junction of the Bow and Elbow rivers, which run through the heart of the city. In Calgary, streets run north and south, and avenues run east and west. Many streets and avenues in the city have numbers instead of names. The intersection of Centre Street and the Bow River is the starting point of the numbering system. Centre Street divides the east and west numbers, and the Bow divides the north and south numbers. The intersection also divides Calgary into quarters—northeast (N.E.), northwest (N.W.), southeast

Facts in brief

Population: *City*—878,866. *Metropolitan area*—951,395.
Area: *City*—271 mi^2 (702 km^2). *Metropolitan area*—1,963 mi^2 (5,083 km^2).
Altitude: 3,441 ft (1,049 m) above sea level.
Climate: *Average temperature*—January, 16 °F (−9 °C); July, 63 °F (17 °C). *Average annual precipitation* (rainfall, melted snow, and other forms of moisture)—$17\frac{1}{2}$ in (44.5 cm). For the monthly weather in Calgary, see **Alberta** (Climate).
Government: Mayor-council. *Terms*—3 years for the mayor and 14 aldermen.
Founded: 1875. Incorporated as a town in 1884. Incorporated as a city in 1893.

(S.E.), and southwest (S.W.)—that help locate most addresses.

The Bow River curves around the city and forms the northern border of downtown Calgary. City Hall stands at the corner of 7th Avenue S.E. and Macleod Trail (also called 2nd Street S.E.). Many historic buildings line Stephen Avenue (8th Avenue S.E. and S.W.). The Calgary Tower, a city landmark, rises 626 feet (191 meters) at the intersection of 9th Avenue S.E. and Centre Street. Atop this building are an observation deck, a revolving restaurant, and a flame that is lit on special occasions.

The Petro-Canada Centre, completed in 1984, consists of two office buildings, 35 and 55 stories tall. The 55-story tower is the highest structure in Calgary, standing 689 feet (210 meters) tall. Many of Calgary's downtown office buildings are connected by a system of enclosed elevated walkways. The walkway system provides comfort for people moving about in the area.

The people. About half the people in Calgary have some British ancestry. After World War II ended in 1945, many Europeans moved to Canada. These immigrants included Dutch, French, Germans, and Scandinavians,

© Mach 2 Stock Exchange

Calgary is Alberta's largest city and the center of Canada's oil industry. Calgary Tower, *background, with red top,* a city landmark, rises 626 feet (191 meters) over the downtown area. The Pengrowth Saddledome, *foreground,* opened in 1983 and was originally called the Olympic Saddledome. It was constructed for the 1988 Winter Olympic Games and is home to the Calgary Flames of the National Hockey League.

many of whom settled in Calgary. People of Chinese descent make up Calgary's largest nonwhite ethnic group. Many South Asians, Filipinos, blacks, and other minorities also live in the city. About 900 Indians live on the Tsuu T'ina (Sarcee) reserve southwest of Calgary.

Economy. Calgary is an international oil center. Hundreds of oil and natural gas companies have their headquarters in Calgary. The city's many refineries process petroleum from the Turner Valley oil fields and other wells in southern Alberta. Calgary also is a center for the processing and distribution of other energy resources, such as coal.

A large number of Canada's engineering, geological, geophysical, and surveying consultant firms are based in Calgary. Most Canadian banks have western headquarters in the city, making it a major financial center.

Calgary is a leading cattle center. Large ranches in southern Alberta send their cattle to slaughterhouses and processing plants in the Calgary area. Calgary lies in a wheat-growing region, and grain elevators and flour mills operate in and near the city.

The city's location makes it a center for transportation and shipping. About 20 airlines serve Calgary International Airport. The city is served by two transcontinental railways. One of them, Canadian Pacific Railway (CPR), has its headquarters in Calgary. Several branch railways and transcontinental truck lines also serve the city. The Trans-Canada Highway runs through Calgary.

Calgary also has become a center for manufacturing and technology. Many plants in the city produce products for the agricultural, oil, and natural gas industries. Other leading products include building materials, chemicals, clothing, electrical and electronic products, furniture, fabricated metal products, paper, plastics, and wood products. Technology companies engage in such activities as telecommunications equipment production, software development, and biotechnology research.

Education. Calgary has more than 200 public schools and more than 80 Roman Catholic schools. Public funds support both systems. The University of Calgary is the city's major institution of higher learning. Mount Royal College, the Southern Alberta Institute of Technology, Bow Valley College, and the Alberta College of Art and Design also serve the city.

The Calgary Public Library, which opened in 1912, was the first public library in Alberta. It has 16 branches.

Cultural life of the city is highlighted by the Calgary Exhibition and Stampede in July. Contestants from throughout North America take part in this 10-day festival, which attracts about 1 million people annually. See **Alberta** (picture: Chuck wagon race).

The *Calgary Herald* and *The Calgary Sun,* both daily newspapers, serve the city. The city also has three local television stations and several radio stations.

The Calgary Performing Arts Centre contains five stages. The Calgary Philharmonic Orchestra, Alberta Theatre Projects, and Theatre Calgary perform in the Calgary Centre. The Southern Alberta Jubilee Auditorium hosts concerts. The Glenbow-Alberta Institute, a cultural organization, houses an art gallery, a historical library, and a museum. The institute owns the largest collection of Indian artifacts in Canada.

The Calgary Zoo, one of the largest zoos in Canada, opened in 1918. The zoo's $7\frac{1}{2}$-acre (3-hectare) Prehistoric Park features life-sized models of the prehistoric animals that once roamed the area. In the city's Chinatown district, the Chinese Cultural Centre hosts numerous exhibits and celebrations. This center was designed to resemble the Temple of Heaven in Beijing, China.

In addition, Calgary has a planetarium and more than 100 public parks. The Calgary Stampeders of the Canadian Football League and the Calgary Flames of the National Hockey League make their home in the city.

Government. Calgary has a mayor-council form of government. Voters elect the mayor to a three-year term. The city is divided into 14 *wards* (voting areas), each of which elects one alderman to the city council. The aldermen also serve three-year terms. The city council appoints a chief executive officer who oversees the city's five executive departments. Calgary gets much of its income from business licenses, property taxes, and provincial and federal grants.

History. The Blackfoot, Sarcee, and Assiniboine Indians lived in the Calgary region before white people came. White traders and trappers first came to the area in the 1700's. By the late 1800's, illegal whiskey trading was common, and disputes often broke out between traders and Indians. Because of the unrest, the North-West Mounted Police established Fort Calgary in 1875.

The Canadian Pacific Railway reached Calgary in 1883 while building a railroad across Canada. The Canadian government offered free land to attract settlers to Calgary, and many people moved there from the United States. Calgary was incorporated as a town in 1884. Its population jumped to almost 3,900 by 1891, and Calgary received a city charter in 1893.

Many large ranches developed in southern Alberta after cattle herds were moved north in search of ungrazed land. Calgary became the center of Canada's meat-packing industry. The city's first annual agricultural exhibition was held in 1886. In 1912, four ranchers, known as the Big Four, organized a rodeo. They called this event the Calgary Stampede, and it also became an annual affair. In 1923, the exhibition and the rodeo merged, forming the Calgary Exhibition and Stampede.

Oil was discovered at nearby Turner Valley in 1914. This discovery led to even more important oil strikes, including one at Leduc, near Edmonton, in 1947. These oil strikes attracted thousands of people from the United States and from other parts of Canada.

In 1967, Calgary announced plans for major urban renewal in the downtown area. From the early 1970's to the early 1980's, millions of dollars' worth of construction projects were completed. A medical school at the University of Calgary opened in 1970. The Calgary Convention Centre opened in 1974. Bow Valley Square, a four-tower office complex, was completed in 1982. The Calgary Performing Arts Centre opened in 1985.

The Olympic Saddledome, an indoor arena, opened in 1983. It was renamed the Pengrowth Saddledome in 2000. It was built as the new home of the Calgary Flames and as one of the facilities for the 1988 Winter Olympic Games. Calgary was the first Canadian city to host the Winter Olympics. The city's 400-meter (1,300-foot) indoor speed skating oval, the first of its kind, was used during the 1988 Olympics. Canada Olympic Park, also used for the Olympics, includes two ski jumps, a luge track, a bobsled run, and a museum. Donna J. Bloomfield

Calgary, University of, is a coeducational university in Calgary, Canada. It is primarily supported by the province of Alberta. The university's *faculties* (divisions) include communication and culture, continuing education, education, engineering, environmental design, fine arts, graduate studies, humanities, kinesiology, law, management, medicine, nursing, science, social sciences, and social work. The university grants bachelor's, master's, and doctor's degrees.

The university operates an Environmental Sciences Centre in Kananaskis and an astrophysical observatory near Priddis. Several research institutes on or near the campus are affiliated with the university.

The University of Alberta set up a branch in Calgary in 1945. This branch became the University of Calgary in 1966. Critically reviewed by the University of Calgary

Calhoun, John Caldwell (1782-1850), of South Carolina, was a major American political figure before the American Civil War. Calhoun played an important part in national affairs for 40 years. He was vice president of the United States from 1825 to 1832, and he ran for president several times but never won. He also served as a member of the U.S. House of Representatives and of the Senate, and as secretary of war and secretary of state.

Calhoun is best known for his doctrine of states' rights, in which he claimed that each U.S. state had a right to *nullify* (reject) national laws. He wished to use the doctrine to protect slavery and other Southern interests without requiring the Southern States to *secede* (withdraw) from the Union. Later, however, the doctrine helped bring on the Civil War (1861-1865).

Detail of an oil portrait (about 1845) by G. P. A. Healy; Virginia Museum of Fine Arts, Richmond

John C. Calhoun

Early career. Calhoun entered national politics as a member of the House of Representatives from 1811 to 1817. He was an ardent nationalist and, together with other young congressmen, was called a *War Hawk* for advocating the War of 1812 (see **War of 1812** [The War Hawks]). He actively supported the government's postwar program, which included a protective tariff, a national bank, and an enlarged army and navy. He improved the army's organization while secretary of war from 1817 to 1825.

Calhoun was the vice presidential running mate of both Andrew Jackson and John Quincy Adams in 1824. He won by a landslide, but the vote for president was indecisive. The House of Representatives picked Adams. In 1828, Jackson again opposed Adams for president, and Calhoun served as Jackson's vice presidential running mate. Jackson and Calhoun won the election. But after Jackson became president, the two men quarreled, especially over Calhoun's support of nullification (see **Jackson, Andrew** [Split with Calhoun]).

Southern leader. Calhoun felt that South Carolina, and the South in general, were being exploited by the *protective tariff,* a high tax on imported goods. The tax allowed Northern manufacturers to compete with more efficient European producers, but it forced Southerners to pay higher prices for manufactured goods.

Calhoun argued that because state conventions had originally ratified the Constitution of the United States, such conventions could also nullify any national law by declaring it unconstitutional. He hoped to use nullification to defeat protective tariffs and to preserve slavery and other Southern interests.

After Congress adopted another protective tariff in 1832, South Carolina acted on Calhoun's theory of states' rights and nullified the new tariff. This action caused a constitutional crisis. Calhoun resigned as vice president in December 1832 and entered the Senate as the elected spokesman of South Carolina. He had no wish to destroy the Union and worked hard for Henry Clay's compromise of 1833. This compromise took the attention away from the tariff issue but did not resolve the states' rights problem Calhoun had raised (see **Nullification**).

Calhoun served in the Senate until 1843. In 1844, he became secretary of state under President John Tyler. He served until March 1845 and then returned to the Senate, serving there until his death on March 31, 1850. In his later years, Calhoun supported slavery and its extension and encouraged the annexation of Texas.

Calhoun was born on March 18, 1782, near Abbeville District, South Carolina. He was an honor graduate at Yale College in 1804. He practiced law in Abbeville District until his election to the South Carolina Legislature in 1808. A statue of Calhoun represents South Carolina in the U.S. Capitol. William W. Freehling

See also **Compromise of 1850.**

Additional resources

Bartlett, Irving H. *John C. Calhoun.* Norton, 1993.
Brown, Warren. *John C. Calhoun.* Chelsea Hse., 1993. Younger readers.

Calico is a cotton fabric of plain weave. It is related to chintz and percale. It is usually printed on rotary presses. The name *calico* comes from Calicut (now Kozhikode), India, where calico was first developed. Calico was originally a fine cloth, but today it is a coarse fabric. Christine W. Cole

Califano, Joseph Anthony, Jr. (1931-   ), served as United States secretary of health, education, and welfare (HEW) from 1977 to 1979 under President Jimmy Carter. One of Califano's chief concerns as secretary of HEW was to streamline the huge department.

Califano was born on May 15, 1931, in New York City. He graduated from Holy Cross College and from Harvard Law School. He served in the U.S. Navy from 1955 to 1958 and then practiced law. From 1961 to 1965, Califano held a series of posts in the Department of Defense. He became a special assistant to President Lyndon B. Johnson in 1965. Califano helped develop the Model Cities project and other programs of what Johnson called the Great Society. He practiced law from 1969 to 1977 and returned to law practice again after he left his Cabinet post. In 1992, Califano founded the National Center on Addiction and Substance Abuse at Columbia University and became its chairman and president.

Califano has written several books. They include *The Student Revolution: A Global Confrontation* (1969); *A Presidential Nation* (1975), a discussion of the U.S. presidency; and *The Triumph and Tragedy of Lyndon Johnson* (2000), a study of Johnson's presidency. Lee Thornton

© John Elk III

Yosemite National Park lies in the Sierra Nevada in east-central California. Several national parks preserve the natural beauty of the state's scenic mountains, valleys, lakes, and forests.

California *The Golden State*

California has more people than any other state of the United States. Many visitors and new residents are attracted by California's outdoor way of life. The warm, dry climate of southern California permits outdoor recreation almost all the year around.

California ranks first among the states in manufacturing. More goods are made there than in any other state. California is the nation's leader in the manufacture of electronic equipment. Its products also include aircraft and such food products as baked goods and wines. California is a leading mining state as well. For example, its fields of oil and natural gas yield thousands of barrels of fuel a day.

California also ranks first among the states in agriculture. A vast farming region, the Central Valley, extends about 450 miles (720 kilometers) through the center of the state. The valley is the leading region in the United States for growing fruits, nuts, and vegetables.

California is a center of the motion-picture and television industries. Its entertainment products are distributed throughout the world.

The contributors of this article are William A. Bowen, Professor of Geography at California State University, Northridge, and Clark Davis, Assistant Professor of History at California State University, Fullerton.

California has 4 of the nation's 20 largest cities—Los Angeles, San Diego, San Jose, and San Francisco. The state capital is Sacramento, another large city.

The international airports at Los Angeles and San Francisco are among the busiest in the world. The ports along California's Pacific Coast make the state a leading area for international trade with Latin America and Asia.

Hundreds of computer and electronics companies have their headquarters in California. Research laboratories, computer companies, and engineering firms cluster around universities in and near the largest cities. They take advantage of the "brain power" of scientists and engineers from the universities.

California covers a larger area than any other state except Alaska and Texas. The high Sierra Nevada rises near the eastern border. Rocky cliffs and sandy beaches line the shore of the Pacific Ocean in the west. Thick forests of Douglas-firs and redwoods cover the Coast Ranges and the Klamath Mountains in the northwest. Barren deserts stretch across the southeast.

The Spaniards were the first Europeans to colonize California. Franciscan friars from Spain established the first of a chain of missions there in 1769. California is known as the *Golden State.* Its gold fields attracted thousands of miners, known as the "Forty-Niners," during the gold rush of 1849. The nickname also suggests the brilliant sunshine the state enjoys.

© Craig Aurness, West Light

Beverly Hills, a fashionable city near the Hollywood district of Los Angeles, has many beautiful homes with swimming pools.

Interesting facts about California

WORLD BOOK illustrations by Kevin Chadwick

The highest temperature ever recorded in the United States, 134 °F (57 °C), was measured in Death Valley on July 10, 1913. In addition, the lowest elevation in the Western Hemisphere is located near Badwater in Death Valley. It lies 282 feet (86 meters) below sea level.

Death Valley

The world's tallest living tree rises 368 feet (112 meters) in the Tall Trees Grove in Redwood National Park.

The first cable car street railway system was installed in San Francisco in 1873.

The General Sherman Tree, in Sequoia National Park, is one of the world's largest living things. It has a circumference of 103 feet (31.4 meters) at the base and rises 275 feet (83.8 meters). The tree is estimated to be about 2,500 years old.

The first synchronized sound cartoon was Walt Disney's *Steamboat Willie,* produced in Hollywood in 1928. It featured Mickey Mouse.

First cable car system

© John Elk III

The Golden Gate Bridge spans a channel at the entrance of San Francisco Bay. One of the world's longest suspension bridges, it has a total length of 8,981 feet (2,737 meters).

California in brief

Symbols of California

The state flag, adopted in 1911, shows a grizzly bear and a single red star. On the state seal, adopted in 1849, appears Minerva, the Roman goddess of wisdom. Next to Minerva are a grizzly bear and clusters of grapes, symbolizing wildlife and agriculture. A miner labors along the Sacramento River, below the Sierra Nevada. The word Eureka (Greek for *I have found it*) probably refers to the miner's discovery of gold.

State flag

State seal

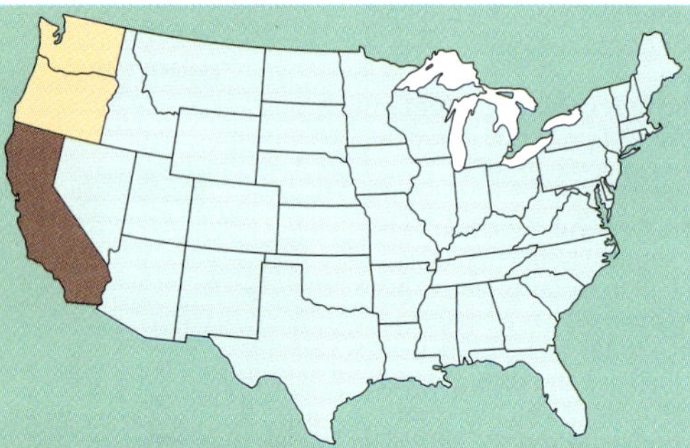

California (brown) ranks third in size among all the states and is the largest of the Pacific Coast States (yellow).

General information

Statehood: Sept. 9, 1850, the 31st state.
State abbreviations: Calif. (traditional); CA (postal).
State motto: *Eureka* (I Have Found It).
State song: "I Love You, California." Words by F. B. Silverwood; music by A. F. Frankenstein

The State Capitol is in Sacramento, California's capital since 1854. Monterey, San Jose, Vallejo, Benicia, and San Francisco were temporary capitals between 1850 and 1854.

Land and climate

Area: 158,648 mi² (410,896 km²), including 2,674 mi² (6,925 km²) of inland water but excluding 222 mi² (574 km²) of Pacific coastal water.
Elevation: *Highest*—Mount Whitney, 14,494 ft (4,418 m) above sea level. *Lowest*—282 ft (86 m) below sea level in Death Valley.
Coastline: 840 mi (1,352 km).
Record high temperature: 134 °F (57 °C) at Greenland Ranch in Death Valley on July 10, 1913.
Record low temperature: −45 °F (−43 °C) at Boca, near Truckee, on Jan. 20, 1937.
Average July temperature: 75 °F (24 °C).
Average January temperature: 44 °F (7 °C).
Average yearly precipitation: 22 in (56 cm).

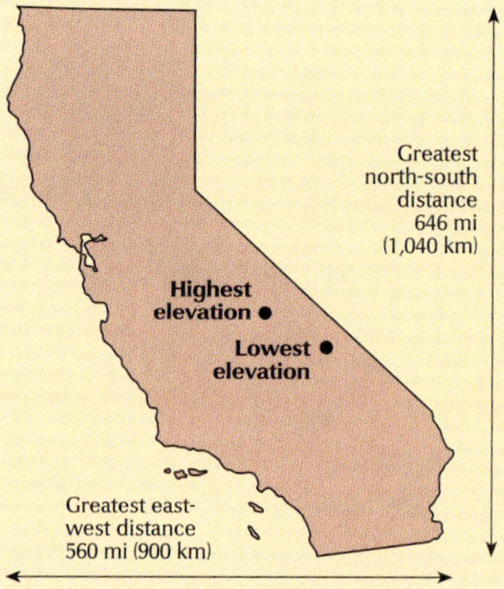

Important dates

1542 Juan Rodríguez Cabrillo, a Portuguese sailor employed by Spain, explored San Diego Bay.

1769 Junípero Serra established the first Franciscan mission in California in what is now San Diego.

1822 California became a part of Mexico.

1846 U.S. forces conquered California during the Mexican War.

1848 James W. Marshall discovered gold at Sutter's Mill.

State bird
California quail

State flower
Golden poppy

State tree
California redwood

People

Population: 33,871,648
Rank among the states: 1st
Density: 214 per mi² (82 per km²), U.S. average 78 per mi² (30 per km²)
Distribution: 94 percent urban, 6 percent rural

Largest cities in California

Los Angeles	3,694,820
San Diego	1,223,400
San Jose	894,943
San Francisco	776,733
Long Beach	461,522
Fresno	427,652

Source: 2000 census.

Population trend

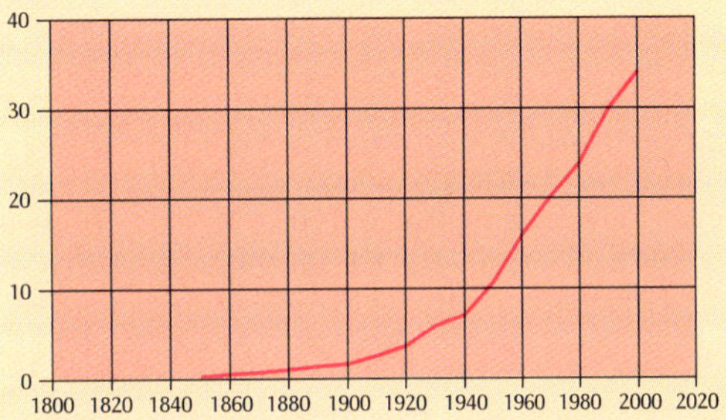

Year	Population
2000	33,871,648
1990	29,760,021
1980	23,667,826
1970	19,971,069
1960	15,717,204
1950	10,586,223
1940	6,907,387
1930	5,677,251
1920	3,426,861
1910	2,377,549
1900	1,485,053
1890	1,213,398
1880	864,694
1870	560,247
1860	379,994
1850	92,597

Source: U.S. Census Bureau.

Economy

Chief products

Agriculture: milk, grapes, greenhouse and nursery products, lettuce, beef cattle, hay, strawberries, tomatoes.
Manufacturing: computer and electronic products, food products, chemicals, transportation equipment, fabricated metal products.
Mining: petroleum, natural gas, sand and gravel, boron.

Gross state product

Value of goods and services produced in 2002: $1,367,785,000,000. *Services* include community, business, and personal services; finance; government; trade; and transportation and communication. *Industry* includes construction, manufacturing, mining, and utilities. *Agriculture* includes agriculture, fishing, and forestry.

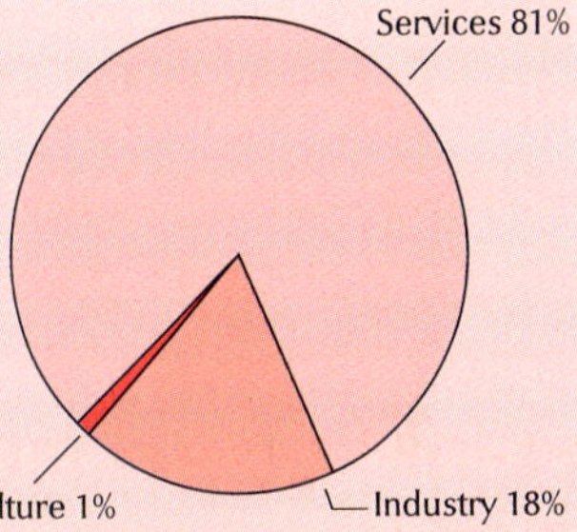

Source: U.S. Bureau of Economic Analysis.

Government

State government

Governor: 4-year term
State senators: 40; 4-year terms
Members of the Assembly: 80; 2-year terms
Counties: 58

Federal government

United States senators: 2
United States representatives: 53
Electoral votes: 55

Sources of information

For information about tourism, write to: California Tourism, 980 9th Street, Suite 480, Sacramento, CA 95814. The Web site at www.visitcalifornia.com also provides information.
For information on the economy, write to: Department of Finance, 915 L Street, Sacramento, CA 95814.
The state's official Web site at www.ca.gov also provides a gateway to much information on California's economy, government, and history.

1850 California became the 31st state on September 9.
1915 International expositions at San Diego and San Francisco marked the opening of the Panama Canal.
1963 California became the state with the largest population.
1994 A destructive earthquake struck Los Angeles. Another quake had hit San Francisco-Oakland-San Jose in 1989.
2003 Voters recalled Governor Gray Davis.

People

Population. The 2000 United States census reported that California had 33,871,648 people. The population had increased 14 percent over the 1990 figure, 29,760,021. According to the 2000 census, California ranks first in population among the 50 states.

In 1960, California ranked second to New York in population. Unofficial figures indicated that California passed New York early in 1963. By 2000, California had about 15 million more people than New York and 13 million more than Texas, which passed New York in population during the 1990's.

About 98 percent of the people of California live in metropolitan statistical areas (see **Metropolitan area**). More than 35 percent of California's population lives in the largest metropolitan area—Los Angeles-Long Beach-Santa Ana. For the populations of the state's metropolitan areas, see the *Index* to the political map of California.

Los Angeles is the largest city, both in area and in population. It covers 465 square miles (1,204 square kilometers). The United States Census Bureau reported that Los Angeles had a population of 3,694,820 in 2000.

California has 10 other cities of more than 250,000. Only two—Fresno and Sacramento—are inland. The others lie on or near the Pacific Coast. Oakland, San Francisco, and San Jose are in the San Francisco Bay area. Anaheim, Long Beach, Riverside, and Santa Ana are part of the Los Angeles population cluster. San Diego is on the coast near the Mexican border.

About 74 of every 100 Californians were born in the United States. Mexicans make up the largest group of Californians born in another country. More people of Mexican ancestry live in the Los Angeles area than in any other urban area in the world outside Mexico. Many Californians of Chinese and Japanese ancestry live in their own communities in Los Angeles and San Francisco. Chinatown in San Francisco has one of the largest Chinese communities outside Asia. California also is home to many people born in the Philippines, Vietnam, El Salvador, North and South Korea, Guatemala, India, Iran, Canada, and the United Kingdom. California also has about 333,000 American Indians—more than any other state.

Schools. In the late 1700's and early 1800's, Franciscan friars taught farming, weaving, and other crafts to the Indians of California. A few small schools were established in the region. But most children of the early settlers received instruction from private teachers.

The first tax-supported school in California opened in San Francisco in 1850. It was financed by the city. In 1849, the California Constitution provided for a system of public schools. The California Legislature passed a tax law in 1852 to support public schools. But the schools did not become free to all children until 1867. At that time, the school system did not include high schools. The state's first public high school opened in 1856 in San Francisco. In 1910, California established in Fresno the first tax-supported junior college in the United States.

An 11-member state Board of Education sets policies for California's elementary and secondary school system. The members of the board are appointed by the governor, subject to the approval of the state Senate. Members serve four-year terms, except for one student representative, who serves one year. The California Department of Education provides assistance to the state's local school districts and county offices of education, and it divides state and federal funds among them. An elected superintendent of public instruction heads the department.

With some exceptions, California law requires children from age 6 to 18 to attend school. Students between the ages of 16 and 18 may leave school if they graduate from high school or if they pass a special examination and have parental permission. For the number of students of students and teachers in California, see **Education** (table).

California State University is the largest state-supported system of four-year and graduate-level education in the United States. It has more than 20 campuses and about 400,000 students. Another state-supported university, the University of California, has 10 campuses and more than 208,000 students. California also has an outstanding system of community colleges. A master plan, which was approved by the State Legislature in 1960, provides for the orderly expansion of the system of state colleges and universities.

Libraries. California's outstanding public library system was founded in 1909. Today, public libraries exist throughout the state. In addition, all types of libraries in California have formal and informal cooperative arrangements between them for sharing resources. The University of California at Berkeley has the largest university library in the state. It includes the Bancroft Library collections of rare materials on the American West. The Hoover Institution on War, Revolution, and

Population density

California has more people than any other state. About 98 percent of its people live in one of the state's 26 metropolitan areas. Over a third live in or near Los Angeles, the state's largest city.

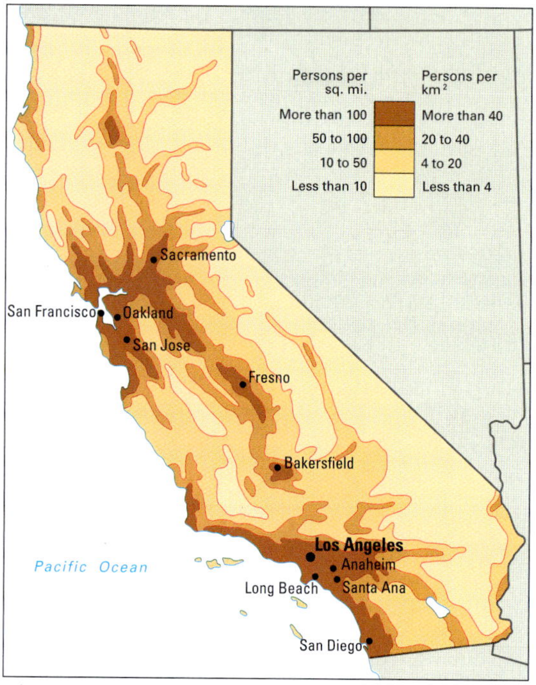

WORLD BOOK map; based on U.S. Census Bureau data.

Universities and colleges

This table lists the universities and colleges in California that grant bachelor's or advanced degrees and are accredited by the Western Association of Schools and Colleges.

Name	Mailing address
Alliant International University	*
American Conservatory Theater	San Francisco
American Film Institute Conservatory	Los Angeles
American InterContinental University	Los Angeles
Antioch University Southern California	Culver City
Argosy University	†
Art Center College of Design	Pasadena
Azusa Pacific University	Azusa
Bethany University	Scotts Valley
Biola University	La Mirada
California, University of	‡
California Baptist University	Riverside
California College of the Arts	San Francisco
California Institute of Integral Studies	San Francisco
California Institute of Technology	Pasadena
California Institute of the Arts	Valencia
California Lutheran University	Thousand Oaks
California Maritime Academy	Vallejo
California Polytechnic State University	San Luis Obispo
California State Polytechnic University	Pomona
California State University	§
Chapman University	Orange
Charles R. Drew University of Medicine and Science	Los Angeles
Church Divinity School of the Pacific	Berkeley
City of Hope	Duarte
Claremont Graduate University	Claremont
Claremont McKenna College	Claremont
Claremont School of Theology	Claremont
Cleveland Chiropractic College	Los Angeles
Cogswell Polytechnical College	Sunnyvale
Concordia University	Irvine
DeVry University	#
Dominican School of Philosophy and Theology	Berkeley
Dominican University of California	San Rafael
Fashion Institute of Design and Merchandising	Los Angeles
Fielding Graduate Institute	Santa Barbara
Franciscan School of Theology	Berkeley
Fresno Pacific University	Fresno
Fuller Theological Seminary	Pasadena
Golden Gate Baptist Theological Seminary	Mill Valley
Golden Gate University	San Francisco
Graduate Theological Union	Berkeley
Harvey Mudd College	Claremont
Hebrew Union College—Jewish Institute of Religion	Los Angeles
Holy Names University	Oakland
Hope International University	Fullerton
Humboldt State University	Arcata
Humphreys College	Stockton
Jesuit School of Theology at Berkeley	Berkeley
John F. Kennedy University	Pleasant Hill
Judaism, University of	Los Angeles
Keck Graduate Institute	Claremont
Keller Graduate School of Management at DeVry University	**
La Sierra University	Riverside
La Verne, University of	La Verne
Laguna College of Art and Design	Laguna Beach
Life Pacific College	San Dimas
Loma Linda University	Loma Linda
Loyola Marymount University	Los Angeles
Master's College and Seminary	Santa Clarita
Menlo College	Atherton
Mennonite Brethren Biblical Seminary	Fresno
Mills College	Oakland
Monterey Institute of International Studies	Monterey
Mount St. Mary's College	Los Angeles
National Hispanic University	San Jose
National University	La Jolla
Naval Postgraduate School	Monterey
New College School of Law	San Francisco
Notre Dame de Namur University	Belmont
Occidental College	Los Angeles
Otis College of Art and Design	Westchester
Pacific, University of the	Stockton
Pacific Graduate School of Psychology	Palo Alto
Pacific Oaks College	Pasadena
Pacific School of Religion	Berkeley
Pacific Union College	Angwin
Pacifica Graduate Institute	Carpinteria
Pardee RAND Graduate School of Policy Studies	Santa Monica
Patten University	Oakland
Pepperdine University	Malibu
Phillips Graduate Institute	Encino
Pitzer College	Claremont
Point Loma Nazarene University	San Diego
Pomona College	Claremont
Redlands, University of	Redlands
St. John's Seminary	Camarillo
St. Mary's College of California	Moraga
St. Patrick's Seminary & University	Menlo Park
Samuel Merritt College	Oakland
San Diego, University of	San Diego
San Diego Christian College	El Cajon
San Diego State University	San Diego
San Francisco, University of	San Francisco
San Francisco Art Institute	San Francisco
San Francisco Conservatory of Music	San Francisco
San Francisco State University	San Francisco
San Francisco Theological Seminary	San Anselmo
San Joaquin College of Law	Clovis
San Jose State University	San Jose
Santa Clara University	Santa Clara
Saybrook Graduate School and Research Center	San Francisco
Scripps College	Claremont
Scripps Research Institute	La Jolla
Simpson University	Redding
Soka University of America	Aliso Viejo
Sonoma State University	Rohnert Park
Southern California, University of	Los Angeles
Southern California College of Optometry	Fullerton
Southern California Institute of Architecture	Los Angeles
Southern California University of Health Sciences	Whittier
Stanford University	Stanford
Thomas Aquinas College	Santa Paula
Thomas Jefferson School of Law	San Diego
Touro University-California	Vallejo
Touro University International	Cypress
Transpersonal Psychology, Institute of	Palo Alto
Vanguard University of Southern California	Costa Mesa
West Los Angeles, University of	Inglewood
Western State University College of Law	Fullerton
Western University of Health Sciences	Pomona
Westminster Theological Seminary in California	Escondido
Westmont College	Santa Barbara
Whittier College	Whittier
William Jessup University	Rocklin
Woodbury University	Burbank
Wright Institute	Berkeley

*Campuses at Alhambra, Fresno, Irvine, San Diego, and San Francisco.
†Campuses at Point Richmond and Santa Ana.
‡For campuses, see **California, University of.**
§For campuses, see **California State University.**
#Campuses at Fremont, Irvine, Long Beach, Pomona, and West Hills.
**Campuses at San Diego and San Francisco.

Peace at Stanford University has books and documents on world affairs since 1900.

Museums. The de Young Museum in San Francisco has art objects from many lands. Exhibits include famous paintings by European artists and items made by early American Indians. The Legion of Honor in San Francisco displays antique furniture, paintings, porcelain, sculpture, and tapestries. The Hollywood Entertainment Museum in Los Angeles displays objects and exhibits on Hollywood's motion-picture and television industries.

The Huntington Gallery in San Marino exhibits British paintings and French furniture and tapestries of the 1700's and early 1800's. The California State Railroad Museum in Sacramento is one of the largest of its kind in the world. The Southwest Museum in Los Angeles displays items of American Indians who lived in the Southwest. The J. Paul Getty Museum in Los Angeles houses an outstanding collection of fine art and antiques. The Page Museum in Los Angeles owns perhaps the best collection of Pleistocene Ice Age fossils in the world. The fossils owned by the museum came from the La Brea tar pits in Los Angeles (see **La Brea tar pits**).

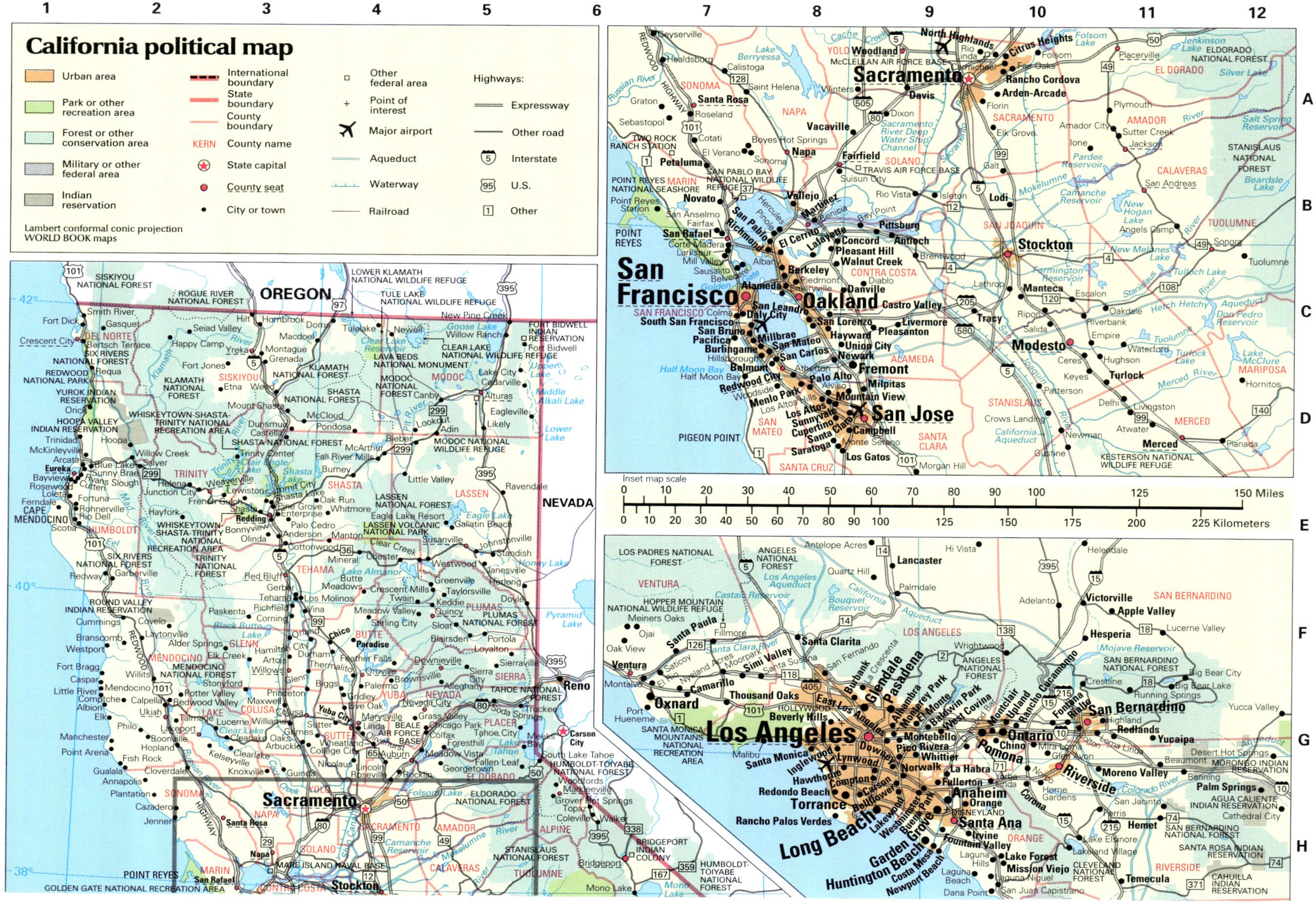
California political map
Urban area
Park or other recreation area
Forest or other conservation area
Military or other federal area
Indian reservation
International boundary
State boundary
County boundary
KERN County name
State capital
County seat
City or town
Other federal area
Point of interest
Major airport
Aqueduct
Waterway
Railroad
Highways:
Expressway
Other road
Interstate
U.S.
Other
Lambert conformal conic projection
WORLD BOOK maps
Inset map scale
150 Miles
225 Kilometers
OREGON
NEVADA
Sacramento
San Francisco
Oakland
San Jose
Stockton
Modesto
Los Angeles
Long Beach
San Bernardino
Riverside
Santa Ana
Anaheim
Reno
Carson City

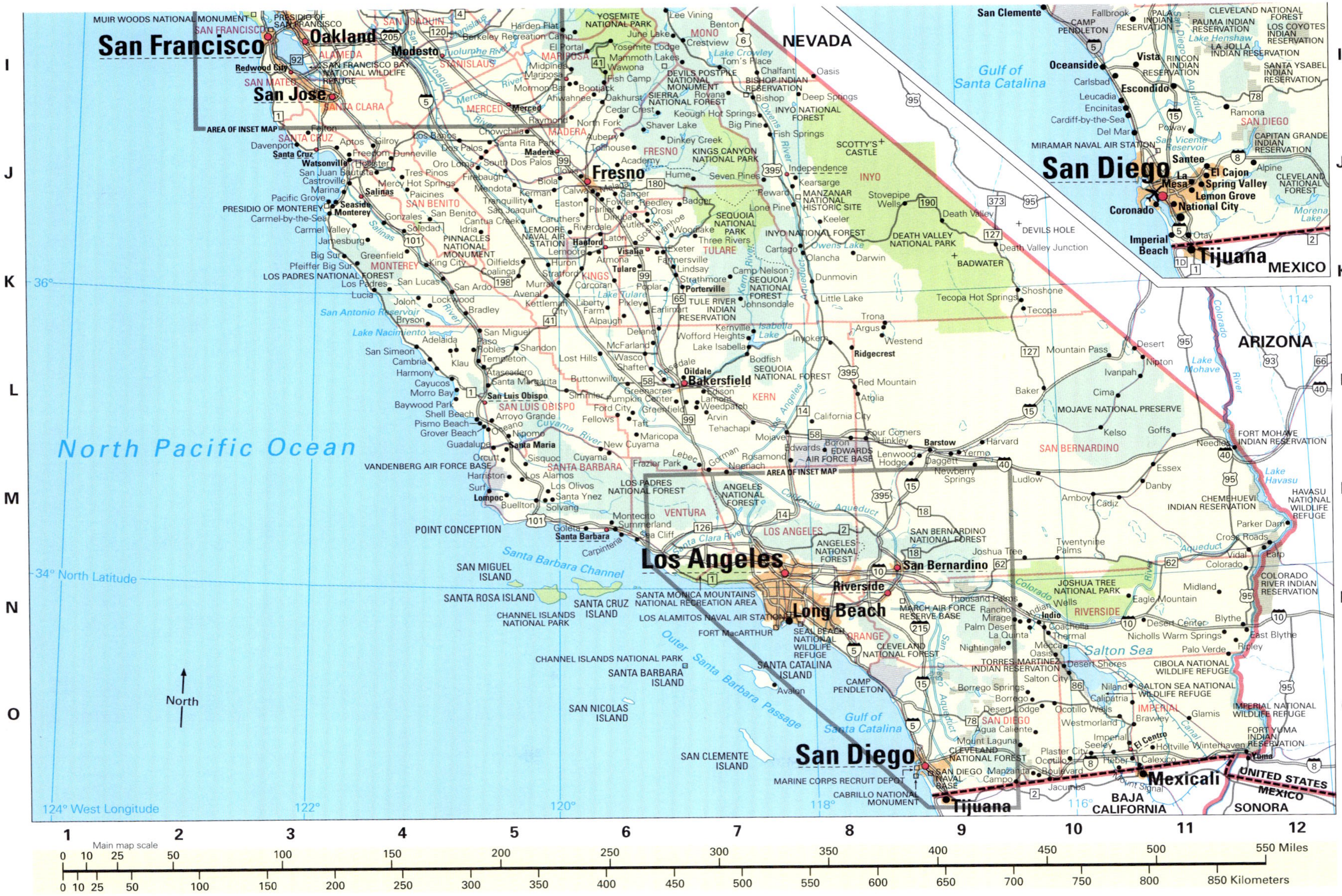
North Pacific Ocean
San Francisco
Oakland
San Jose
Modesto
Fresno
Bakersfield
Los Angeles
Long Beach
Riverside
San Bernardino
San Diego
Tijuana
Mexicali
NEVADA
ARIZONA
MEXICO
BAJA CALIFORNIA
SONORA
UNITED STATES
Salton Sea
Gulf of Santa Catalina
Santa Barbara Channel
Outer Santa Barbara Passage
SAN MIGUEL ISLAND
SANTA ROSA ISLAND
SANTA CRUZ ISLAND
SANTA BARBARA ISLAND
SAN NICOLAS ISLAND
SANTA CATALINA ISLAND
SAN CLEMENTE ISLAND
CHANNEL ISLANDS NATIONAL PARK
POINT CONCEPTION
VANDENBERG AIR FORCE BASE
DEATH VALLEY NATIONAL PARK
MOJAVE NATIONAL PRESERVE
JOSHUA TREE NATIONAL PARK
SEQUOIA NATIONAL PARK
KINGS CANYON NATIONAL PARK
YOSEMITE NATIONAL PARK
AREA OF INSET MAP
North
34° North Latitude
36°
124° West Longitude
122°
120°
118°
116°
114°
I
J
K
L
M
N
O
1
2
3
4
5
6
7
8
9
10
11
12
Main map scale
550 Miles
850 Kilometers

California map index

Metropolitan areas

Bakersfield 661,645
Chico 203,171
El Centro 142,361
Fresno 799,407
Hanford-Corcoran 129,461
Los Angeles-Long Beach-Santa Ana 12,365,627
Madera 123,109
Merced 210,554
Modesto 446,997
Napa 124,279
Oxnard-Thousand Oaks-Ventura 753,197
Redding 163,256
Riverside-San Bernardino-Ontario 3,254,821
Sacramento-Arden-Arcade-Roseville 1,796,857
Salinas 401,762
San Diego-Carlsbad-San Marcos 2,813,833
San Francisco-Oakland-Fremont 4,123,740
San Jose-Sunnyvale-Santa Clara 1,735,819
San Luis Obispo-Paso Robles 246,681
Santa Barbara-Santa Maria-Goleta 399,347
Santa Cruz-Watsonville 255,602
Santa Rosa-Petaluma 458,614
Stockton 563,598
Vallejo-Fairfield 394,542
Visalia-Porterville 368,021
Yuba City 139,149

Metropolitan divisions

Los Angeles-Long Beach-Glendale 9,519,338
Oakland-Fremont-Hayward 2,392,557
San Francisco-San Mateo-Redwood City 1,731,183
Santa Ana-Anaheim-Irvine 2,846,289

Counties

Alameda 1,443,741 I 3
Alpine 1,208 H 6
Amador 35,100 H 5
Butte 203,701 F 4
Calaveras 40,554 H 5
Colusa 18,804 G 3
Contra Costa 948,816 H 3
Del Norte 27,507 C 2
El Dorado 156,299 G 5
Fresno 799,407 J 6
Glenn 26,453 F 3
Humboldt 126,518 E 2
Imperial 142,361 O 11
Inyo 17,945 J 8
Kern 661,645 L 7
Kings 129,461 K 6
Lake 58,309 F 2
Lassen 33,828 E 5
Los Angeles 9,519,338 M 7
Madera 123,109 J 5
Marin 247,289 H 2
Mariposa 17,130 I 6
Mendocino 86,265 F 2
Merced 210,554 I 5
Modoc 9,449 D 5
Mono 12,853 I 7
Monterey 401,762 K 4
Napa 124,279 H 3
Nevada 92,033 G 5
Orange 2,846,289 N 8
Placer 248,399 G 5
Plumas 20,824 F 5
Riverside 1,545,387 N 10
Sacramento 1,223,499 H 4
San Benito 53,234 J 4
San Bernardino 1,709,434 M 10
San Diego 2,813,833 O 9
San Francisco 776,733 I 3
San Joaquin 563,598 I 4
San Luis Obispo 246,681 L 5
San Mateo 707,161 I 3
Santa Barbara 399,347 M 5
Santa Clara 1,682,585 I 3
Santa Cruz 255,602 J 3
Shasta 163,256 E 4
Sierra 3,555 F 5
Siskiyou 44,301 D 3
Solano 394,542 H 3
Sonoma 458,614 H 2
Stanislaus 446,997 I 5
Sutter 78,930 G 4
Tehama 56,039 E 3
Trinity 13,022 E 2
Tulare 368,021 K 7
Tuolumne 54,501 H 5
Ventura 753,197 M 7
Yolo 168,660 H 4
Yuba 60,219 G 4

Cities and towns and other populated places

Adelanto 18,130 F 10
Agoura Hills* 20,537 G 7
Agua Caliente, see Fetters Hot Springs [-Agua Caliente]
Agua Caliente Indian Reservation 21,358 H 12
Alameda 72,259 C 8
Alamo*† 15,626 C 8
Albany 16,444 C 8
Alhambra 85,804 G 9
Aliso Viejo*† 40,166 H 10
Alondra Park*† 8,622 H 8
Alpine† 13,143 J 12
Alta Sierra*† 6,522 G 4
Altadena*† 42,610 G 9
Alturas° 2,892 D 5
American Canyon*† 9,774 B 8
Anaheim 328,014 H 9
Anderson 9,022 F 3
Angels Camp 3,004 B 11
Angwin*† 3,148 A 7
Antioch 90,532 B 9
Apple Valley 54,239 F 11
Aptos† 9,396 J 4
Aptos Hills-Larkin Valley*† 2,361 J 8
Arbuckle† 2,332 G 3
Arcade, see Arden-Arcade
Arcadia* 53,054 G 9
Arcata 16,651 D 1
Arden-Arcade† 96,025 A 10
Armona† 3,239 K 6
Arnold*† 4,218 B 12
Aromas*† 2,797 J 4
Arroyo Grande 15,851 L 5
Artesia* 16,380 G 9
Arvin 12,956 L 7
Ashland*† 20,793 C 8
Atascadero 26,411 L 5
Atherton 7,194 D 8
Atwater 23,113 D 11
Auberry† 2,053 J 6
Auburn° 12,462 G 4
August*† 7,808 B 10
Avalon 3,127 O 7
Avenal 14,674 K 5
Avocado Heights*† 15,148 G 9
Azusa* 44,712 G 9
Bakersfield° 247,057 L 7
Baldwin Park 75,837 G 9
Banning 23,562 G 11
Barstow 21,119 M 9
Bay Point† 21,534 B 8
Bayview† 2,359 E 1
Bayview [-Montalvin]*† 5,004 B 8
Baywood [-Los Osos]*† 14,351 L 5
Beale AFB† 5,115 G 4
Beaumont 11,384 G 11
Bell* 36,664 G 9
Bell Gardens* 44,054 G 9
Bellflower 72,878 G 9
Belmont 25,123 D 8
Belvedere 2,125 C 7
Ben Lomond*† 2,364 J 3
Benicia 26,865 B 8
Berkeley 102,743 C 8
Bermuda Dunes*† 6,229 N 10
Bethel Island*† 2,312 B 9
Beverly Hills 33,784 G 8
Big Bear City 5,779 F 11
Big Bear Lake 5,438 F 11
Big Oak Flat, see Groveland-Big Oak Flat
Biggs 1,793 G 4
Bishop 3,575 I 7
Bishop Ind. Res. 1,441 I 7
Blackhawk-Camino Tassajara*† 10,048 C 8
Bloomington*† 19,318 G 10
Blue Lake 1,135 D 1
Blythe 12,155 N 11
Bodfish† 1,823 I 7
Bonadelle Ranchos-Madera Ranchos*† 7,300 J 6
Bonita*† 12,401 K 11
Bonsall*† 3,401 I 11
Bootjack† 1,588 I 6
Boron† 2,025 M 8
Borrego Springs† 2,535 O 10
Bostonia*† 15,169 J 11
Boulder Creek*† 4,081 J 3
Boyes Hot Springs† 6,665 A 7
Brawley 22,052 O 11
Brea* 35,410 G 9
Brentwood 23,302 B 9
Bridgeport° H 6
Broadmoor*† 4,026 C 7
Buellton† 3,828 M 5
Buena Park 78,282 H 9
Burbank 100,316 G 8
Burbank*† 5,239 D 8
Burlingame 28,158 C 7
Burney† 3,217 E 4
Buttonwillow† 1,266 L 6
Calexico 27,109 O 11
California City 8,385 L 8
Calipatria 7,289 O 10
Calistoga 5,190 A 7
Camarillo 57,077 G 7
Cambria† 6,232 L 4
Cambrian Park*† 3,258 H 9
Cameron Park*† 14,549 A 10
Camp Pendleton North*† 8,197 I 11
Camp Pendleton South*† 8,854 I 11
Campbell 38,138 D 8
Canyon Lake* 9,952 H 10
Capitola* 10,033 J 3
Carlsbad 78,247 I 10
Carmel-by-the-Sea 4,081 J 3
Carmel Valley† 4,700 J 4
Carmichael† 49,742 A 10
Carpinteria 14,194 M 6
Carson 89,730 G 8
Caruthers† 2,103 J 6
Casa Conejo† 3,180 G 7
Casa de Oro-Mount Helix*† 18,874 J 11
Castro Valley† 57,292 C 8
Castroville† 6,724 J 4
Cathedral City 42,647 H 12
Cayucos† 2,943 L 4
Cedar Ridge, see Phoenix Lake-Cedar Ridge
Ceres 34,609 C 10
Cerritos* 51,488 G 9
Channel Islands Beach*† 3,142 G 6
Charter Oak*† 9,027 G 9
Cherry Valley*† 5,891 G 11
Cherryland*† 13,837 C 8
Chester† 2,316 E 4
Chico 59,954 F 4
Chino 67,168 G 10
Chino Hills† 66,787 G 9
Chowchilla 11,127 J 5
Chula Vista 173,556 J 11
Citrus*† 10,581 G 9
Citrus Heights 85,071 A 10
Claremont* 33,998 G 10
Clayton* 10,762 J 8
Clearlake 13,142 G 3
Clearlake Oaks† 2,402 G 3
Cloverdale 6,831 G 2
Clovis 68,468 J 6
Coachella 22,724 N 10
Coalinga 11,668 K 5
Colfax 1,496 G 5
Colma 1,191 C 7
Colorado River Indian Res.‡ 1,735 N 12
Colton 47,662 G 10
Colusa° 5,402 G 3
Commerce* 12,568 G 9
Compton 93,493 G 9
Concord 121,780 B 8
Corcoran 14,458 K 6
Corning 6,741 F 3
Corona 124,966 G 10
Coronado 24,100 J 11
Corralitos*† 2,431 J 4
Corte Madera 9,100 B 7
Costa Mesa 108,724 H 9
Cotati 6,471 A 7
Coto de Caza*† 13,057 H 10
Cotton Center, see Poplar [-Cotton Center]
Cottonwood† 2,960 E 3
Country Club† 9,462 I 4
Covelo† 1,175 F 2
Covina* 46,837 G 9
Crescent City° 4,006 C 1
Crescent North*† 4,028 C 1
Crestline† 10,218 F 10
Crockett*† 3,194 B 8
Cudahy* 24,208 G 9
Culver City* 38,816 G 8
Cupertino 50,546 D 8
Cutler† 4,491 J 6
Cutten† 2,933 E 1
Cypress* 46,229 H 9
Daly City 103,621 C 7
Dana Point 35,110 H 10
Danville 41,715 C 8
Davis 60,308 A 9
Day Valley*† 3,587 J 4
Deer Park*† 1,433 A 7
Del Aire*† 9,012 G 8
Delano 38,824 K 6
Delhi† 8,022 D 11
Del Mar 4,389 J 11
Del Monte Forest*† 4,531 J 3
Denair*† 3,446 C 10
Desert Hot Springs 16,582 G 12
Desert View Highlands*† 2,337 F 9
Devonshire, see Glenshire-Devonshire
Diamond Bar 56,287 G 9
Diamond Springs*† 4,888 A 11
Dinuba 16,844 J 6
Discovery Bay*† 8,981 C 9
Dixon 16,103 A 9
Dixon Lane-Meadow Creek*† 2,702 I 7
Dos Palos 4,581 J 5
Downey 107,323 G 9
Downieville° F 5
Duarte* 21,486 G 9
Dublin* 29,973 C 8
Dunsmuir 1,923 D 3
Durham† 5,220 F 4
Earlimart† 6,583 K 6
East Blythe† 3 N 12
East Compton*† 9,286 G 9
East Foothills*† 8,133 D 9
East Hemet*† 14,823 H 11
East La Mirada*† 9,538 G 9
East Los Angeles† 124,283 G 9
East Palo Alto* 29,506 D 8
East Pasadena*† 6,045 G 9
East Porterville*† 6,730 K 7
East Quincy*† 2,398 F 5
East Richmond Heights*† 3,357 B 8
East San Gabriel† 14,512 G 9
Easton† 1,966 J 6
Edwards AFB† 5,909 M 8
El Cajon 94,869 J 11
El Centro° 37,835 O 11
El Cerrito 23,171 B 8
El Cerrito*† 4,590 H 10
El Dorado Hills*† 18,016 G 10
El Granada*† 5,724 A 10
Elk Grove† 59,984 C 7
El Monte 115,965 G 9
El Rio† 6,193 F 7
El Segundo* 16,033 G 8
El Sobrante*† 12,260 B 8
El Verano† 3,954 B 7
Emerald Lake Hills*† 3,899 D 8
Emeryville 6,882 C 8
Encinitas 58,014 J 10
Escalon 5,963 C 10
Escondido 133,559 I 11
Eureka° 26,128 E 1
Exeter 9,168 K 6
Fair Oaks† 28,008 A 10
Fairfax 7,319 B 7
Fairfield° 96,178 B 8
Fairview*† 9,470 C 8
Fallbrook† 29,100 I 11
Farmersville 8,737 K 6
Felton† 1,051 J 3
Ferndale 1,382 E 1
Fetters Hot Springs-Agua Caliente*† 2,505 A 7
Fillmore 13,643 F 7
Firebaugh 5,743 J 5
Florence [-Graham]*† 60,197 G 9
Florin*† 27,653 A 10
Folsom 51,884 A 10
Fontana 128,929 G 10
Foothill Farms*† 17,426 A 10
Ford City† 3,512 L 6
Forest Knolls, see Lagunitas [-Forest Knolls]
Forestville*† 2,370 A 6
Fort Bragg 7,026 F 2
Fort Yuma Indian Res.§ 2,340 O 12
Fortuna 10,497 E 1
Foster City* 28,803 C 8
Fountain Valley 54,978 H 9
Fowler 3,979 J 6
Frazier Park† 2,348 M 7
Freedom† 6,000 J 4
Fremont 203,413 D 8
French Camp*† 4,109 C 10
Fresno° 427,652 J 6
Fullerton 126,003 G 9
Galt 19,472 B 10
Garden Acres*† 9,747 B 10
Garden Grove 165,196 H 9
Gardena* 57,746 G 8
Gerber [-Las Flores]† 1,389 F 3
Gilroy 41,464 J 4
Glen Avon† 14,853 G 10
Glendale 194,973 G 8
Glendora* 49,415 G 9
Golden Hills*† 7,434 C 7
Gonzales 7,525 J 4
Graham, see Florence [-Graham]
Granite Hills*† 3,246 J 11
Grass Valley 10,922 G 4
Graton† 1,815 A 7
Greenacres L 6
Greenfield 12,583 K 4
Greenville† 1,160 F 5
Gridley 5,382 G 4
Groveland-Big Oak Flat*† 3,388 C 11
Grover Beach 13,067 L 5
Guadalupe 5,659 M 5
Guerneville*† 2,441 A 7
Gustine 4,698 D 10
Hacienda Heights*† 53,122 G 9
Half Moon Bay 11,842 D 7
Hamilton City† 1,903 F 3
Hanford° 41,686 K 6
Harbison Canyon*† 3,645 J 12
Hawaiian Gardens* 14,779 H 9
Hawthorne 84,112 G 8
Hayfork† 2,315 E 2
Hayward 140,030 C 8
Healdsburg 10,722 A 6
Heber† 2,988 O 10
Hemet 58,812 H 11
Hercules 19,488 B 8
Hermosa Beach* 18,566 G 8
Hesperia 62,582 F 10
Hidden Meadows*† 3,463 I 11
Highgrove*† 3,445 G 11
Highland 44,605 G 11
Highlands-Baywood Park*† 4,210 D 7
Hillmar-Irwin*† 4,807 D 10
Hillsborough 10,825 C 7
Hollister° 34,413 J 4
Holtville 5,612 O 11
Home Gardens† 9,461 G 10
Homeland*† 3,710 H 11
Homestead Valley, see Tamalpias-Homestead Valley
Hoopa Valley Indian Res. 2,633 D 2
Hughson 3,980 D 10
Humboldt*† 3,246 E 1
Huntington Beach 189,594 H 9
Huntington Park* 61,348 G 8
Huron 6,306 K 5
Idyllwild-Pine Cove*† 3,504 G 12
Imperial 7,560 O 10
Imperial Beach 26,992 K 11
Independence†° 574 J 8
Indian Wells 3,816 N 10
Indio 49,116 N 10
Inglewood 112,580 G 8
Interlaken*† 7,328 J 4
Ione 7,129 A 10
Irvine* 143,072 H 9
Irwin, see Hillmar-Irwin
Isla Vista*† 18,344 M 6
Ivanhoe† 4,474 K 6
Jackson° 3,989 A 11
Jamestown*† 3,017 B 12
Jamul*† 5,920 J 12
Joshua Tree† 4,207 N 10
Kelseyville† 2,928 J 12
Kensington*† 4,936 B 8
Kentfield*† 6,351 B 7
Kerman 8,551 J 5
Kernville† 1,736 K 7
Kettleman City*† 1,499 K 5
Keyes† 4,575 D 10
King City 11,094 K 4
Kings Beach*† 4,037 G 6
Kingsburg* 9,199 J 6
La Canada Flintridge* 20,318 G 9
La Crescenta-Montrose*† 18,532 G 9
Ladera Heights*† 6,568 G 8
Lafayette 23,908 B 8
Laguna*† 34,309 A 10
Laguna Beach 23,727 H 10
Laguna Hills*† 31,178 H 10
Laguna Niguel 61,891 H 10
Lagunitas [-Forest Knolls]*† 1,835 B 7
La Habra 58,974 G 9
Lake Arrowhead*† 8,934 G 11
Lake Elsinore 28,928 H 10
Lake Forest 58,707 H 10
Lake Isabella† 3,315 L 7
Lake Los Angeles*† 11,523 F 9
Lake of the Pines*† 3,956 G 4

Lake San Marcos*† ......4,138 ..I 11
Lakeland Village† ....5,626 ..H 10
Lakeport○ ....4,820 ..G 2
Lakeside*† ......19,560 ..J 11
Lakewood ......79,345 ..H 9
La Mesa ....54,749 ..J 11
La Mirada* ......46,783 ..G 9
Lamont† ....13,296 ..L 6
Lancaster ......118,718 ..E 9
La Palma* ....15,408 ..G 9
La Puente* ......41,063 ..G 9
La Quinta ....23,694 ..N 10
La Riviera*† .....10,273 ..A 10
Larkfield -Wikiup*† ......7,479 ..A 7
Larkin Valley, see Aptos Hills-Larkin Valley
Larkspur ....12,014 ..B 7
Las Flores see Gerber [-Las Flores]
Las Lomas*†.......3,078 ..J 4
Lathrop ....10,445 ..C 10
Laton† ....1,236 ..K 6
La Verne*.......31,638 ..G 10
Lawndale* ......31,711 ..G 8
Laytonville†......1,301 ..F 2
Lemon Grove...24,918 ..J 11
Lemoore........19,712 ..K 6
Lennox*†........22,950 ..G 8
Lenwood† ....3,222 ..M 9
Lewiston†........1,305 ..E 7
Lexington Hills*† ....2,454 ..D 8
Lincoln..........11,205 ..G 4
Lincoln Village*† ......4,216 ..B 10
Linda† ....13,474 ..G 4
Lindsay ....10,297 ..K 7
Live Oak ....6,229 ..G 4
Live Oak*† ......16,628 ..J 3
Livermore ......73,345 ..C 9
Livingston ......10,473 ..D 11
Lockeford*†......3,179 ..B 10
Lodi.............56,999 ..B 10
Loma Linda .....18,681 ..G 11
Loma Rica*†......2,075 ..G 4
Lomita* ....20,046 ..H 8
Lompoc.........41,103 ..M 5
Lone Pine†.......1,655 ..J 7
Long Beach....461,522 ..N 8
Los Alamitos*...11,536 ..H 9
Los Altos........27,693 ..D 8
Los Altos Hills....7,902 ..D 8
Los Angeles○.....3,694,820 ..N 7
Los Banos.......25,869 ..J 5
Los Gatos ....28,592 ..D 8
Los Molinos† .....1,952 ..F 3
Los Nietos, see West Whittier-Los Nietos
Los Osos, see Baywood-Los Osos
Lost Hills†........1,938 ..L 6
Loyola*†..........3,478 ..D 8
Lucas Valley-Marinwood*†......6,357 ..B 7
Lucerne†.........2,870 ..G 3
Lynwood........69,845 ..G 9
Madera○........43,207 ..J 5
Madera Acres*†........7,741 ..J 5
Madera Ranchos, see Bonadelle Ranchos-Madera Ranchos]
Magalia*†.......10,569 ..F 4
Mammoth Lakes..........7,093 ..I 7
Manhattan Beach* ....33,852 ..G 8
Manteca........49,258 ..C 10
March AFB†.......370 ..N 9
Maricopa ....1,111 ..L 6
Marina..........25,101 ..K 4
Marina Del Ray*†..........8,176 ..G 8
Marinwood, see Lucas Valley-Marinwood
Mariposa†○......1,373 ..I 6
Markleeville†○.....197 ..H 6
Martinez○.......35,866 ..B 8
Marysville○.....12,268 ..G 4
Mayflower Village*† ......5,081 ..G 9
Maywood*......28,083 ..G 9
McCloud† ....1,343 ..D 3
McFarland ....9,618 ..L 6
McKinleyville†..13,599 ..D 1
Meadow Creek, see Dixon Lane-Meadow Creek
Meadow Vista† ..3,096 ..G 5
Mecca† ....5,402 ..N 10
Meiners Oaks† ..3,750 ..F 6
Mendota.........7,890 ..J 5
Menlo Park .....30,785 ..D 8
Mentone*†.......7,803 ..G 11
Merced○........63,893 ..I 5
Mill Valley ......13,600 ..C 7
Millbrae ....20,718 ..C 7
Milpitas.........62,698 ..D 8
Mira Loma†.....17,617 ..G 10
Mira Monte*†....7,177 ..J 7
Mission Hills*†...3,142 ..G 9
Mission Viejo*..93,102 ..H 10
Modesto○ .....188,856 ..I 10
Mojave† ....3,836 ..L 7
Mono Vista*† ....3,072 ..B 12
Monrovia* ......36,929 ..G 9
Montague.........1,456 ..C 3
Montalvin, see Bayview [-Montalvin]
Montara*† ....2,950 ..G 7
Montclair.......33,049 ..G 10
Monte Sereno ...3,483 ..D 8
Montebello .....62,150 ..G 9
Monterey.......29,674 ..J 3
Monterey Park..60,051 ..G 9
Montrose, see La Crescenta [-Montrose]
Moorpark ......31,415 ..F 7
Morada*† ....3,726 ..B 10
Moraga* ....16,290 ..C 8
Moreno Valley* ......142,381 ..G 11
Morgan Hill.....33,556 ..D 9
Morongo Valley Indian Reservation*†.......954 ..G 12
Morro Bay......10,350 ..L 5
Moss Beach*†....1,953 ..C 7
Mount Helix, see Casa Oro [-Mount Helix]
Mount Shasta....3,621 ..D 3
Mountain View ....70,708 ..D 8
Mountain View Acres*†........2,521 ..F 10
Murrieta* ....44,282 ..H 11
Murrieta Hot Springs*†......2,948 ..H 11
Muscoy*† ....8,919 ..G 10
Myrtletown*† ....4,459 ..E 1
Napa○...........72,585 ..H 3
National City....54,260 ..J 11
Needles...........4,830 ..M 11
Nevada City○.....3,001 ..G 5
Newark ....42,471 ..C 8
Newman ....7,093 ..D 10
Newport Beach........70,032 ..H 9
Nice*†............2,509 ..G 3
Niland† ....1,143 ..O 10
Nipomo†........12,626 ..L 5
Norco...........24,157 ..G 10
North Auburn*† ....11,847 ..G 4
North El Monte*† ....3,703 ..G 9
North Fair Oaks*† ....15,440 ..D 8
North Highlands†........44,187 ..A 10
Norwalk ....103,298 ..G 9
Novato..........47,630 ..B 7
Nuevo*†..........4,135 ..H 11
Oak Park*†.......2,320 ..G 7
Oak View† ....4,199 ..F 6
Oakdale.........15,503 ..C 11
Oakhurst†........2,868 ..I 6
Oakland○......399,484 ..I 3
Oakley* ....25,619 ..B 9
Oceano† ....7,260 ..L 5
Oceanside.....161,029 ..I 10
Oildale†.........27,885 ..L 7
Ojai ....7,862 ..F 6
Olivehurst† .....11,061 ..G 4
Ontario ....158,007 ..G 10
Opal Cliffs*†......6,458 ..J 3
Orange ....128,821 ..H 9
Orangevale*†...26,705 ..A 10
Orinda* ....17,599 ..B 8
Orland ....6,281 ..F 3
Orosi† ....7,318 ..J 6
Oroville○ ....13,004 ..F 4
Oroville East*†...8,680 ..F 4
Oxnard ....170,358 ..G 7
Pacheco*† ....3,562 ..B 8
Pacific Grove ...15,522 ..J 3
Pacifica ....38,390 ..C 7
Pajaro*†..........3,384 ..J 4
Pala Ind. Res......1,573 ..I 11
Palermo† ....5,720 ..G 4
Palm Desert ....41,155 ..N 9
Palm Springs ...42,807 ..G 12
Palmdale ......116,670 ..F 9
Palo Alto........58,598 ..D 8
Palos Verdes Estates*.......13,340 ..H 8
Paradise ....26,408 ..F 4
Paramount* .....55,266 ..G 9
Parksdale*† ....2,688 ..J 5
Parkway-South Sacramento*†......36,468 ..A 9
Parkwood*†.......2,119 ..J 5
Parlier ....11,145 ..J 6
Pasadena......133,936 ..G 9
Paso Robles ....24,297 ..L 5
Patterson ......11,606 ..D 10
Pedley*† ....11,207 ..G 10
Perris...........36,189 ..H 11
Petaluma........54,548 ..B 7
Phoenix Lake-Cedar Ridge*†........5,123 ..B 12
Pico Rivera .....63,428 ..G 9
Piedmont ....10,952 ..C 8
Pine Cove, see Idyllwild [-Pine Cove]
Pine Hills*†.......3,108 ..E 1
Pinole...........19,039 ..B 8
Pismo Beach.....8,551 ..L 5
Pittsburg........56,769 ..B 9
Pixley† ....2,586 ..K 6
Placentia*.......46,488 ..G 9
Placerville○......9,610 ..A 11
Planada† ....4,369 ..D 12
Pleasant Hill ....32,837 ..B 8
Pleasanton......63,654 ..C 9
Pollock Pines*† ..4,728 ..A 11
Pomona ....149,473 ..G 8
Poplar [-Cotton Center]† ....1,496 ..K 6
Port Hueneme..21,845 ..G 7
Porterville ......39,615 ..K 7
Portola...........2,227 ..F 5
Portola Hills*†....6,391 ..G 9
Portola Valley*...4,462 ..D 8
Poway ....48,044 ..J 11
Prunedale*† ....16,432 ..J 3
Quail Valley*†....1,639 ..G 10
Quartz Hill†......9,890 ..E 9
Quincy†○ ....1,879 ..F 5
Rainbow*† ....2,026 ..I 11
Ramona† ....15,691 ..J 11
Rancho Cordova† ....55,060 ..A 10
Rancho Cucamonga......127,743 ..G 10
Rancho Mirage.......13,249 ..N 9
Rancho Murieta*† .....4,193 ..A 10
Rancho Palos Verdes*......41,145 ..H 8
Rancho San Diego*† ......20,155 ..J 11
Rancho Santa Margarita* ...47,214 ..H 10
Red Bluff○ ......13,147 ..F 3
Redding○ ....80,865 ..E 3
Redlands........63,591 ..G 11
Redondo Beach........63,261 ..H 8
Redway†.........1,188 ..F 2
Redwood City○ ....75,402 ..I 3
Reedley.........20,756 ..J 6
Rialto ....91,873 ..G 10
Richgrove*†.......2,723 ..K 6
Richmond.......99,216 ..B 8
Ridgecrest ......24,927 ..L 8
Rincon Indian Res.*†..........1,495 ..I 11
Rio Del Mar*†....9,198 ..J 4
Rio Dell ....3,174 ..E 1
Rio Linda† ....10,466 ..A 9
Rio Vista ....4,571 ..B 9
Ripon ....10,146 ..C 10
Riverbank.......15,826 ..C 10
Riverdale† ....2,416 ..K 5
Riverside○......255,166 ..N 8
Rocklin ....36,330 ..G 4
Rodeo*†..........8,717 ..B 8
Rohnert Park*..42,236 ..A 7
Rolling Hills Estates*........7,676 ..H 8
Romoland*†......2,764 ..H 11
Rosamond†.....14,349 ..M 7
Rosedale†........8,445 ..L 6
Roseland*†.......6,369 ..A 7
Rosemead* .....53,505 ..G 9
Rosemont*†.....22,904 ..A 10
Roseville........79,921 ..G 4
Ross*.............2,329 ..B 7
Rossmoor*†.....10,298 ..G 9
Round Valley Indian Res........82 ..F 2
Rowland Heights*†....48,553 ..G 9
Rubidoux*† .....29,180 ..G 10
Running Springs† ......5,125 ..G 11
Sacramento○..407,018 ..H 4
St. Helena........5,950 ..A 7
Salida†..........12,560 ..C 10
Salinas○ ....151,060 ..J 3
San Andreas†○ ..2,615 ..B 11
San Anselmo ...12,378 ..B 7
San Antonio Heights*†......3,122 ..G 10
San Bernardino○ ....185,401 ..N 9
San Buenaventura, see Ventura (San Buenaventura)
San Bruno ......40,165 ..C 7
San Carlos ......27,718 ..C 8
San Clemente...49,936 ..I 10
San Diego○ ..1,223,400 ..O 9
San Diego Country Estates*† ...9,262 ..J 12
San Dimas* .....34,980 ..G 9
San Fernando...23,564 ..F 8
San Francisco○.......776,733 ..I 3
San Gabriel* ....39,804 ..G 9
San Jacinto.......23,779 ..H 11
San Joaquin......3,270 ..J 5
San Jose○......894,943 ..I 3
San Juan Bautista ....1,549 ..J 4
San Juan Capistrano ....33,826 ..H 10
San Leandro....79,452 ..C 8
San Lorenzo† ...21,898 ..C 8
San Luis Obispo○......44,174 ..L 5
San Marcos* ....54,977 ..I 11
San Marino* ....12,945 ..G 9
San Mateo......92,482 ..C 8
San Miguel† .....1,427 ..K 5
San Pablo.......30,215 ..B 8
San Rafael○ .....56,063 ..H 3
San Ramon*.....44,722 ..C 8
San Simeon ....L 4
Sanger...........18,931 ..J 6
Santa Ana○ ....337,977 ..H 9
Santa Barbara○.....92,325 ..M 6
Santa Clara .....102,361 ..D 8
Santa Clarita....151,088 ..F 8
Santa Cruz○.....54,593 ..J 3
Santa Fe Springs*......17,438 ..G 9
Santa Maria.....77,423 ..M 5
Santa Monica...84,084 ..G 8
Santa Paula .....28,598 ..F 7
Santa Rosa○ ...147,595 ..H 3
Santa Venetia*†......4,298 ..B 7
Santa Ynez†......4,584 ..M 5
Santee* ....52,975 ..J 11
Saratoga ....29,843 ..D 8
Sausalito.........7,330 ..C 7
Scotts Valley* ...11,385 ..J 3
Seal Beach*......24,157 ..H 9
Searles Valley*†..1,885 ..L 8
Seaside ....31,696 ..J 3
Sebastopol.......7,774 ..A 7
Sedco Hills*†.....3,078 ..H 10
Seeley† ....1,624 ..O 10
Selma*..........19,444 ..J 6
Shafter.........12,736 ..L 6
Shasta Lake......9,008 ..E 3
Shingle Springs*†......2,643 ..A 10
Sierra Madre* ..10,578 ..G 9
Simi Valley ....111,351 ..F 7
Solana Beach* ..12,979 ..J 11
Soledad.........11,263 ..K 4
Solvang..........5,332 ..M 5
Sonoma...........9,128 ..B 7
Sonora○ ....4,423 ..B 12
Soquel*† ....5,081 ..J 3
Soulsbyville*†....1,729 ..H 12
South El Monte*.......21,144 ..G 9
South Gate* .....96,375 ..G 9
South Lake Tahoe........23,609 ..G 6
South Oroville*† .7,695 ..F 4
South Pasadena*.........24,292 ..G 9
South Sacramento, see Parkway-South Sacramento
South San Francisco ....60,552 ..C 7
South San Gabriel*† ......7,595 ..G 9
South San Jose Hills*†...20,218 ..G 9
South Taft*†......1,898 ..L 6
South Whittier*†....55,193 ..G 9
South Yuba City*†.........12,651 ..G 4
Spring Valley*† .26,663 ..J 11
Squaw Valley*† ..2,691 ..J 7
Stanford*† ......13,315 ..D 8
Stanton* ....37,403 ..H 9
Stockton○ .....243,771 ..H 4
Strathmore† .....2,584 ..K 7
Strawberry*†.....5,302 ..C 7
Suisun City......26,118 ..B 8
Sun City*†.......17,773 ..H 10
Sunnyslope*†.....4,437 ..G 10
Sunnyvale .....131,760 ..D 8
Susanville○ .....13,541 ..E 5
Sutter† ....2,885 ..G 4
Sutter Creek .....2,303 ..A 11
Taft..............6,400 ..L 6
Taft Heights*† .....1,865 ..L 6
Tamalpias-Homestead Valley*† ......10,691 ..C 7
Tara Hills*† ......5,332 ..B 8
Tehachapi ......10,957 ..L 7
Temecula*.......57,716 ..H 11
Temple City*....33,377 ..G 9
Templeton†.......4,687 ..L 5
Terra Bella*†.....3,466 ..K 7
Thermalito†......6,045 ..F 4
Thousand Oaks ....117,005 ..G 7
Thousand Palms† ....5,120 ..N 10
Tiburon* ....8,666 ..C 7
Tierra Buena*†...4,587 ..K 6
Torrance ......137,946 ..H 8
Torres-Martinez Indian Res.....4,146 ..O 10
Tracy ....56,929 ..C 9
Truckee ....13,864 ..G 5
Tulare ....43,994 ..K 6
Tulelake ....1,020 ..C 4
Tuolumne† ......1,865 ..B 12
Turlock.........55,810 ..D 11
Tustin* ....67,504 ..H 9
Tustin Foothills*†....24,044 ..H 9
Twain Harte*†....2,586 ..B 12
Twentynine Palms ....14,764 ..N 9
Twentynine Palms Base*†.........8,413 ..N 9
Twin Lakes*†.....5,533 ..J 3
Ukiah○ ....15,497 ..G 2
Union City ......66,869 ..C 8
Upland..........68,393 ..G 10
Vacaville........88,625 ..A 8
Valinda*† ....21,776 ..G 9
Valle Vista*† ....10,488 ..H 11
Vallejo.........116,760 ..B 8
Vandenburg AFB† ....6,151 ..M 5
Vandenberg Village*† ......5,802 ..M 5
Ventura (San Buenaventura)○....100,916 ..F 6
Victorville ......64,029 ..F 10
View Park -Windsor Hills*† ....10,958 ..G 8
Villa Park*........5,999 ..H 9
Vincent*† ....15,097 ..G 9
Vine Hill*† ....3,260 ..B 8
Visalia○ ....91,565 ..K 6
Vista ....89,857 ..I 11
Walnut*.........30,004 ..G 9
Walnut Creek...64,296 ..C 8
Walnut Park*† ..16,180 ..G 9
Wasco ....21,263 ..L 6
Waterford........6,924 ..C 11
Watsonville.....44,265 ..J 4
Weaverville†○ ...3,554 ..E 3
Weed ....2,978 ..D 3
Weedpatch† ......2,726 ..L 7
West Athens*† ...9,101 ..G 8
West Bishop*† ...2,807 ..I 7
West Carson*† .....21,138 ..H 8
West Compton*† ....5,435 ..G 9
West Covina...105,080 ..G 9
West Hollywood*........35,716 ..G 8
West Menlo Park*† ....3,629 ..D 8
West Puente Valley*† ......22,589 ..G 9
West Sacramento* ....31,615 ..A 9
West Whittier [-Los Nietos]*† .....25,129 ..G 9
Westlake Village*........8,368 ..G 7
Westminster....88,207 ..H 9
Westmont*† ....31,623 ..G 8
Westmorland ....2,131 ..O 10
Westwood†.......1,998 ..E 5
Wheatland ....2,275 ..G 4
Whittier.........83,680 ..G 9
Wikiup, see Larkfield-Wikiup
Wildomar*†.....14,064 ..H 10
Williams ....3,670 ..G 3
Willits............5,073 ..F 2
Willowbrook*† ......34,138 ..G 9
Willow Creek† ...1,743 ..D 2
Willows○..........6,220 ..F 3
Wilton*† ....4,551 ..A 9
Windsor* ....22,744 ..A 7
Windsor Hills, see View Park-Windsor Hills
Winters ....6,125 ..A 8
Winton*†.........8,832 ..D 11
Wofford Heights*†......2,276 ..L 7
Woodcrest*†......8,342 ..G 10
Woodlake........6,651 ..K 7
Woodland○.......49,151 ..A 9
Woodside.........5,352 ..D 8
Woodville*†.......1,678 ..K 6
Wrightwood*† ...3,837 ..F 10
Yorba Linda.....58,918 ..G 10
Yosemite Lakes*†........4,160 ..J 6
Yreka○ ....7,290 ..C 3
Yuba City○ ......36,758 ..G 4
Yucaipa.........41,207 ..G 11
Yucca Valley†...16,865 ..G 12
Yurok Ind. Res....1,103 ..D 2

*Does not appear on map; key shows general location.
†Census designated place—unincorporated, but recognized as a significant settled community by the U.S. Census Bureau.
‡Reservation on California-Arizona border; total population 2,376.
§ Reservation on California-Arizona border; total population 9,201.
○County seat.
Source: 2000 census. Metropolitan area and metropolitan division figures are based on 2003 Office of Management and Budget reorganization of 2000 census data. Places without population figures are unincorporated areas.

Visitor's guide

Many people visit California to see such natural wonders as redwood groves and volcanic cones. California also has famous golf courses, resorts, beaches, ski areas, and many other recreational facilities.

California's largest cities, Los Angeles, San Diego, and San Francisco, play host to millions of visitors every year. For information on things to see and do in these cities, see **Los Angeles; San Diego; San Francisco.**

California's most famous annual event is the Tournament of Roses, held in Pasadena on New Year's Day or January 2. Colorful floats, decorated with thousands of flowers, compete for prizes in the Tournament of Roses Parade. A beauty contest and the Rose Bowl football game are also part of the festivities.

Phil and Loretta Hermann, Hillstrom Stock Photo

Fantasy Castle at Disneyland in Anaheim

© John Elk III

Hearst Castle near San Luis Obispo

Places to visit

Following are brief descriptions of some of California's many interesting places to visit:

Disneyland, in Anaheim, is an amusement park designed by the famous American motion-picture producer Walt Disney. Its attractions include a fairyland castle, a boat trip through "jungle" waters, and "Mickey's ToonTown."

Hearst Castle, near San Luis Obispo, is the former estate of newspaper owner William Randolph Hearst. It includes a castle with ancient works of art, a Roman temple, a private theater, and huge swimming pools. Its official name is Hearst San Simeon State Historical Monument.

Knott's Berry Farm, in Buena Park, is California's oldest amusement park. It has rides, a ghost town, and an Indian village.

Missions were built in California by Franciscan friars beginning in 1769. For information about these missions, see *The California missions* heading in the *History* section of this article.

Monterey Bay National Marine Sanctuary is a vast area set aside to preserve marine life in its natural habitat. It extends from Marin County south to Cambria.

Monterey Peninsula includes the communities of Carmel, Monterey, Pacific Grove, and Pebble Beach. Carmel is an art colony. Monterey has Monterey Bay Aquarium and buildings from Spanish colonial days.

Redwood Highway (U.S. 101), from San Francisco to Oregon, passes through magnificent groves of redwood trees. These trees are the tallest living trees in the world.

San Diego Zoo has a large collection of birds, mammals, and reptiles. Its monkey and ape exhibits rank among the finest in North America.

Six Flags Marine World, in Vallejo, is the first combination wildlife park, oceanarium, and theme park in the United States. It includes rides, shows, and animal attractions.

Parklands in California include eight national parks. The state's national parks are Channel Islands, Death Valley, Joshua Tree, Kings Canyon, Lassen Volcanic, Redwood, Sequoia, and Yosemite. Thousands of miles of trails wind through the parks. In addition, the state of California has several national monuments, including California Coastal, Lava Beds, Muir Woods, and Pinnacles. For more information on these and other California parklands, see the map and tables in the *World Book* article on **National Park System.**

National forests. California has 18 national forests. Congress has set aside several areas in these national forests to be preserved in their natural condition.

State parks, forests, and monuments offer numerous historic and scenic attractions. For information, write to Department of Parks and Recreation, P.O. Box 942896, Sacramento, CA 94296.

Annual events

January-June
Chinese New Year Celebration in San Francisco and Los Angeles (January, February, or March); Whiskey Flat Days in Kernville (February); Aleutian Goose Festival in Crescent City (April); Northern California Cherry Blossom Festival in San Francisco (April); Godwit Days Spring Migration Bird Festival in Arcata (April); Monterey Wine Festival (April); Red Bluff Round-Up in Red Bluff (April); Stockton Asparagus Festival (April); Calaveras County Fair & Jumping Frog Jubilee in Angels Camp (May); Kinetic Sculpture Race from Arcata to Ferndale (May); Oakdale Chocolate Festival (May); Sacramento Jazz Jubilee (May); Salinas Valley Fair in King City (May); Strawberry Festival in Galt (May).

July-December
California WorldFest in Grass Valley (July); Garlic Festival in Gilroy (July); Mozart Festival in San Luis Obispo (July); Shakespeare Santa Cruz (July-August); Rolex Monterey Historical Automobile Races in Monterey (August); Old Spanish Days Fiesta in Santa Barbara (August); State Fair in Sacramento (August-September); Lodi Grape Festival and Harvest Fair (September); Monterey Jazz Festival (September); Stater Bros. Route 66 Rendezvous® in San Bernadino (September); Oktoberfest in Hayward (September); Clam Festival in Pismo Beach (October); Lone Pine Film Festival (October); Christmas Boat Parade in Newport Beach (December).

David Frazier

San Diego Zoo

© Steve Morris, Hillstrom Stock Photo

Old Spanish Days Fiesta in Santa Barbara

Berg & Associates

Tournament of Roses Parade in Pasadena

Gerald French, Photofile

A California redwood forest

Land and climate

California is larger than any other state except Alaska and Texas. San Bernardino County, California's largest county, covers more than 20,000 square miles (51,800 square kilometers). It is one of the largest counties in area in the United States.

Land regions. California has eight main land regions: (1) the Klamath Mountains, (2) the Coast Ranges, (3) the Central Valley, (4) the Sierra Nevada, (5) the Cascade Mountains, (6) the Basin and Range Region, (7) the Transverse Ranges, and (8) the Peninsular Ranges.

The Klamath Mountains include several small, forest-covered ranges in the northwestern corner of California. These ranges are higher and more rugged than the coastal mountains to the south. Many peaks are from 6,000 to 8,000 feet (1,800 to 2,400 meters) high. Deep canyons break up the ranges.

The Coast Ranges extend southward along the Pacific Coast from the Klamath Mountains to Santa Barbara County. Individual sections of this mountain chain have names of their own. These include the Diablo, Santa Cruz, and Santa Lucia ranges. Livestock ranches, orchards, vineyards, and truck gardens dot the beautiful valleys that separate the ranges. These valleys include the Napa Valley north of San Francisco, and the Santa Clara and Salinas valleys to the south. California's famous redwood trees grow in the coastal areas of the Coast Ranges.

An important feature of the region is the San Andreas Fault. A *fault* is a break in the earth's rocky outer shell, along which movements of the rock have taken place. The San Andreas Fault enters northern California from the Pacific Ocean near Point Arena and extends southeastward into southern California. Movements of the earth's crust along this fault cause earthquakes.

The Central Valley, sometimes called the *Great Valley,* lies between the Coast Ranges and the Sierra Nevada. It has two major river systems—the Sacramento in the north and the San Joaquin in the south. The valley extends about 450 miles (720 kilometers) from northwest to southeast. Much of it is level and looks like a broad, open plain. This fertile valley forms the largest and most important farming area west of the Rocky Mountains. It has three-fifths of California's farmland and produces a great variety of crops.

The Sierra Nevada, located east of the Central Valley, forms a massive rock wall more than 400 miles (640 kilometers) long and about 40 to 70 miles (64 to 110 kilometers) wide. Several peaks of the Sierra Nevada rise more than 14,000 feet (4,270 meters). These peaks include Mount Whitney (14,494 feet, or 4,418 meters), the highest point in the United States south of Alaska. Rushing mountain rivers have cut deep canyons in the western part of the Sierra. Yosemite Valley is the most outstanding of these canyons. Yosemite originally was cut by streams. Later, glaciers moved down the valley and eroded it further.

The Cascade Mountains extend northward from the Sierra Nevada. Unlike other California ranges, the Cascades were formed by volcanoes. Lassen Peak (10,457

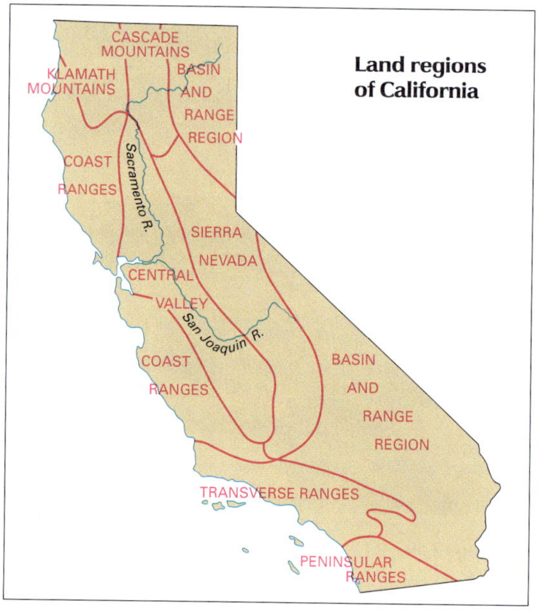

WORLD BOOK map

Map index

Agua Tibia Mts.	H	6
Amargosa Range	F	6
American R.	C	3
Black Butte	C	2
Black Butte Lake	C	2
Bodega Head	D	1
Boulder Peak	A	2
Breckinridge Mtn.	F	4
Bristol Lake	G	7
Buena Vista Lake	G	4
Camanche Res.	D	3
Cape San Martin	F	2
Cascade Mts.	A	2
Chanchelulla Peak	B	2
Channel Islands Natl. Park	H	3
Chocolate Mts.	H	7
Clair Engle Lake	B	2
Clear Lake	C	2
Clear Lake Res.	A	3
Coachella Canal	I	7
Coast Ranges	C	2
Colorado Desert	H	6
Colorado R.	H	7
Colorado R. Aqueduct	H	6
Cuyama R.	G	3
Death Valley (lowest point in U.S.)	F	6
Death Valley Natl. Park	F	6
Devils Postpile Natl. Mon.	E	4
Diablo Range	E	3
Donner Pass	C	3
Eagle Lake	B	3
Eagle Peak	B	3
Echo Summit	D	4
Eel R.	C	1
Estero Bay	F	2
Farallon Is.	D	1
Feather R.	C	2
Folsom Lake	D	3
Fredonyer Peak	B	3
Goose Lake	A	3
Greenhorn Mts.	F	4
Gulf of Santa Catalina	H	5
Hetch Hetchy Aqueduct	E	2
Honey Lake	C	3
Hot Springs Peak	B	4
Imperial Valley	I	7
Iron Gate Res.	A	2
Isabella Lake	F	4
Joshua Tree Natl. Park	H	6
Kern R.	F	4
Kings Canyon Natl. Park	E	5
Kings R.	F	4
Klamath Mts.	A	2
Klamath R.	A	1
Laguna Mts.	I	6
Lake Almanor	B	3
Lake Berryessa	D	2
Lake Havasu	G	7
Lake Mendocino	C	1
Lake Oroville	C	3
Lake Success	F	4
Lake Tahoe	D	4
Lake Tulare	F	4
Lassen Peak	B	2
Lassen Volcanic Natl. Park	B	3
Lava Beds Natl. Mon.	A	3
Los Angeles Aqueduct	G	5
Mammoth Pool Res.	E	3
Merced R.	E	3
Mojave Desert	G	5
Mojave R.	G	6
Mokelumne R.	D	3
Mono Lake	D	4
Monterey Bay	E	2
Mt. Bidwell	A	4
Mt. Conness	D	4
Mt. Patterson	D	4
Mt. Pinos	G	4
Mt. Ritter	E	4
Mt. Shasta	A	2
Mt. Whitney (highest point in Calif.)	F	5
Nacimiento Res.	F	3
Napa R.	D	2
North Palisade (Mtn.)	E	5
Outer Santa Barbara Channel	H	4
Owens Lake	F	5
Panamint Range	F	5
Picacho Peak	I	7
Pigeon Pt.	E	2
Pinnacles Natl. Mon.	E	3
Pit R.	B	3
Pt. Arguello	G	3
Pt. Arena	C	1
Pt. Buchon	G	3
Pt. Conception	G	3
Pt. Loma	I	5
Pt. Piedras Blancas	F	2
Pt. Pinos	E	2
Pt. Reyes	D	I
Pt. Reyes Natl. Seashore	D	I
Pt. St. George	A	1
Pt. Sal	G	3
Pt. San Luis	G	3
Pt. Sur	F	2
Punta Gorda	B	1
Redwood Natl Park	A	1
Rogers Lake	G	5
Russian R.	C	2
Sacramento R.	C	2
Sacramento Valley	C	2
Salinas R.	F	2
Salmon Mts.	B	2
Salton Sea	H	6
San Benito Mountain	F	3
San Bernardino Mts.	H	6
San Clemente Island	I	4
San Diego Aqueduct	H	5
San Francisco Bay	E	2
San Gabriel Mts.	G	5
San Gorgonio Mountain	H	6
San Jacinto Mts.	H	6
San Joaquin R.	E	3
San Joaquin Valley	E	3
San Luis Res.	E	3
San Miguel Island	H	3
San Nicolas Island	H	3
San Pedro Channel	H	4
San Rafael Mts.	G	3
Santa Barbara Channel	G	3
Santa Barbara Island	H	4
Santa Catalina Island	H	4
Santa Clara R.	G	4
Santa Cruz Island	H	3
Santa Cruz Mts.	E	2
Santa Lucia Range	F	2
Santa Monica Mts.	G	4
Santa Rosa Island	H	3
Santa Ynez Mts.	G	3
Searles Lake	F	5
Sequoia Natl. Park	F	4
Shasta Lake	B	2
Sierra Nevada (mts.)	C	3
Siskiyou Mts.	A	1
Soda Lake	G	6
S. Yolla Bolly Mtn.	A	1
Stanislaus R.	D	3
Telescope Peak	F	5
Temblor Range	G	4
Trinidad Head	B	1
Trinity Mts.	B	2
Trinity R.	B	1
Tulloch Res.	D	3
Tuolumne R.	E	3
Vallecito Mts.	I	6
Warner Mts.	A	4
Whiskeytown Res.	B	2
Wishon Res.	E	4
Yosemite Natl. Park	E	4
Yuba R.	C	3

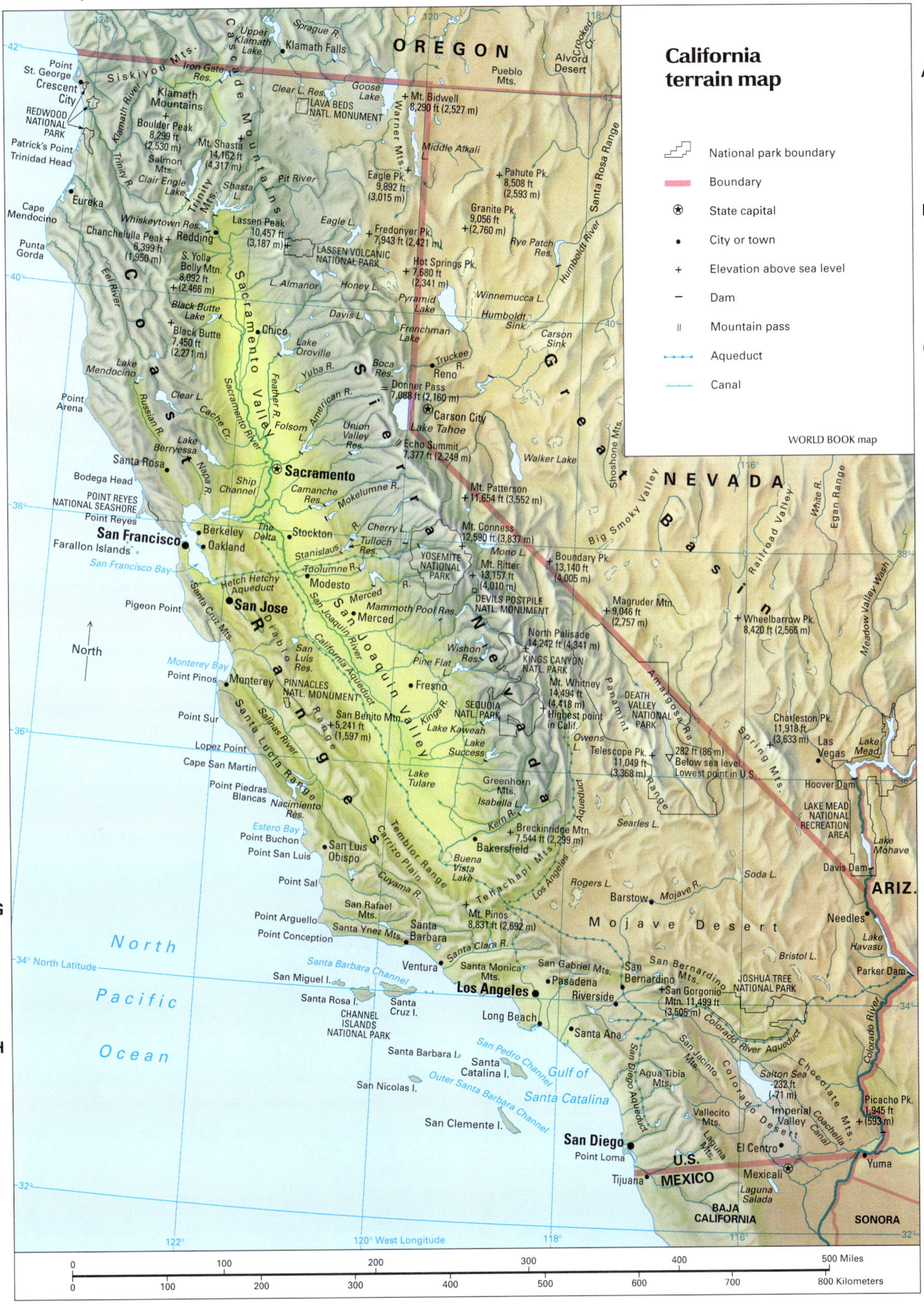

California terrain map
National park boundary
Boundary
State capital
City or town
Elevation above sea level
Dam
Mountain pass
Aqueduct
Canal
WORLD BOOK map
1
2
3
4
5
6
7
A
B
C
D
E
F
G
H
I
OREGON
NEVADA
ARIZ.
U.S.
MEXICO
BAJA CALIFORNIA
SONORA
North Pacific Ocean
North
Point St. George
Crescent City
REDWOOD NATIONAL PARK
Patrick's Point
Trinidad Head
Eureka
Cape Mendocino
Punta Gorda
Siskiyou Mts.
Klamath River
Klamath Mountains
Boulder Peak 8,299 ft (2,530 m)
Salmon Mts.
Trinity R.
Clair Engle Lake
Trinity Mts.
Mt. Shasta 14,162 ft (4,317 m)
Shasta L.
Iron Gate Res.
Upper Klamath Lake
Klamath Falls
Sprague R.
Cascade Mountains
Clear L. Res.
LAVA BEDS NATL. MONUMENT
Goose Lake
Mt. Bidwell 8,290 ft (2,527 m)
Warner Mts.
Middle Alkali L.
Pit River
Eagle Pk. 9,892 ft (3,015 m)
Whiskeytown Res.
Redding
Chanchelulla Peak 6,399 ft (1,950 m)
Lassen Peak 10,457 ft (3,187 m)
LASSEN VOLCANIC NATIONAL PARK
Eagle L.
Fredonyer Pk. 7,943 ft (2,421 m)
Hot Springs Pk. 7,680 ft (2,341 m)
S. Yolla Bolly Mtn. 8,092 ft (2,466 m)
Eel River
L. Almanor
Honey L.
Pyramid Lake
Black Butte Lake
Black Butte 7,450 ft (2,271 m)
Coast Ranges
Sacramento Valley
Chico
Lake Oroville
Davis L.
Frenchman Lake
Lake Mendocino
Feather R.
Yuba R.
Boca Res.
Truckee R.
Reno
Donner Pass 7,088 ft (2,160 m)
Carson City
Lake Tahoe
Point Arena
Russian R.
Clear L.
Cache Cr.
Sacramento River
American R.
Folsom L.
Union Valley Res.
Echo Summit 7,377 ft (2,248 m)
Lake Berryessa
Santa Rosa
Napa R.
Sierra Nevada
Bodega Head
POINT REYES NATIONAL SEASHORE
Point Reyes
Ship Channel
Sacramento
Camanche Res.
Mokelumne R.
San Francisco
Farallon Islands
Berkeley
Oakland
San Francisco Bay
The Delta
Stockton
Cherry L.
Tulloch Res.
Stanislaus R.
Tuolumne R.
Hetch Hetchy Aqueduct
Modesto
YOSEMITE NATIONAL PARK
Mt. Conness 12,590 ft (3,837 m)
Mono L.
Mt. Ritter 13,157 ft (4,010 m)
DEVILS POSTPILE NATL. MONUMENT
Mt. Patterson 11,654 ft (3,552 m)
Walker Lake
Pigeon Point
San Jose
Santa Cruz Mts.
Diablo Range
Merced R.
Merced
Mammoth Pool Res.
San Joaquin River
San Joaquin Valley
California Aqueduct
Monterey Bay
Point Pinos
Monterey
San Luis Res.
PINNACLES NATL. MONUMENT
Fresno
Pine Flat L.
Wishon Res.
North Palisade 14,242 ft (4,341 m)
KINGS CANYON NATL. PARK
Mt. Whitney 14,494 ft (4,418 m) Highest point in Calif.
SEQUOIA NATL. PARK
Kings R.
Lake Kaweah
Lake Success
Point Sur
Santa Lucia Range
Salinas River
San Benito Mtn. 5,241 ft (1,597 m)
Lopez Point
Cape San Martin
Point Piedras Blancas
Nacimiento Res.
Lake Tulare
Greenhorn Mts.
Isabella L.
Kern R.
Owens L.
Panamint Range
DEATH VALLEY NATIONAL PARK
Telescope Pk. 11,049 ft (3,368 m)
Amargosa Ra.
282 ft (86 m) Below sea level. Lowest point in U.S.
Spring Mts.
Charleston Pk. 11,918 ft (3,633 m)
Las Vegas
Lake Mead
Hoover Dam
LAKE MEAD NATIONAL RECREATION AREA
Lake Mohave
Davis Dam
Estero Bay
Point Buchon
Point San Luis
San Luis Obispo
Carrizo Plain
Temblor Range
Breckinridge Mtn. 7,544 ft (2,299 m)
Bakersfield
Buena Vista Lake
Tehachapi Mts.
Los Angeles Aqueduct
Searles L.
Point Sal
Cuyama R.
San Rafael Mts.
Mt. Pinos 8,831 ft (2,692 m)
Point Arguello
Point Conception
Santa Ynez Mts.
Santa Barbara
Santa Clara R.
Rogers L.
Barstow
Mojave R.
Soda L.
Mojave Desert
Needles
Bristol L.
Lake Havasu
Parker Dam
Santa Barbara Channel
Ventura
Santa Monica Mts.
San Gabriel Mts.
Pasadena
Los Angeles
San Bernardino
San Bernardino Mts.
San Gorgonio Mtn. 11,499 ft (3,505 m)
Riverside
JOSHUA TREE NATIONAL PARK
Colorado River Aqueduct
Colorado River
San Miguel I.
Santa Rosa I.
Santa Cruz I.
CHANNEL ISLANDS NATIONAL PARK
Long Beach
Santa Ana
San Jacinto Mts.
Chocolate Mts.
Salton Sea -232 ft (-71 m)
Picacho Pk. 1,945 ft (593 m)
Santa Barbara I.
San Pedro Channel
Santa Catalina I.
Gulf of Santa Catalina
Outer Santa Barbara Channel
San Nicolas I.
San Clemente I.
Agua Tibia Mts.
San Diego Aqueduct
Colorado Desert
Vallecito Mts.
Imperial Valley
Coachella Canal
Laguna Mts.
San Diego
Point Loma
El Centro
Tijuana
Mexicali
Yuma
Laguna Salada
Alvord Desert
Pueblo Mts.
Crooked Cr.
Pahute Pk. 8,508 ft (2,593 m)
Santa Rosa Range
Granite Pk. 9,056 ft (2,760 m)
Rye Patch Res.
Humboldt River
Winnemucca L.
Humboldt Sink
Carson Sink
Great Basin
Shoshone Mts.
Big Smoky Valley
Railroad Valley
White R.
Egan Range
Boundary Pk. 13,140 ft (4,005 m)
Magruder Mtn. 9,046 ft (2,757 m)
Wheelbarrow Pk. 8,420 ft (2,566 m)
Meadow Valley Wash
42°
40°
38°
36°
34° North Latitude
32°
124°
122°
120°
120° West Longitude
118°
116°
0
100
200
300
400
500 Miles
600
700
800 Kilometers

The Sierra Nevada in eastern California has jagged granite peaks and clear mountain streams. Several peaks in the Sierra Nevada rise more than 14,000 feet (4,270 meters).

© John Elk III

feet, or 3,187 meters) is an active volcano in the southern Cascades. Another famous peak, Mount Shasta (14,162 feet, or 4,317 meters), was once an active volcano.

The Basin and Range Region is part of a larger region that extends into Nevada, Oregon, and several other states. It is an area of mountains and valleys created by movement along fault lines. Much of the northern section of the Basin and Range Region is a lava plateau called the Modoc Plateau. Thousands of years ago, lava flowed out of great cracks in the earth's surface and flooded the area.

In southern California, much of the Basin and Range Region is a wasteland. South of the Garlock Fault lies the Mojave Desert. The Mojave covers a large area between the southern Sierra and the Colorado River. The Colorado Desert lies to the south. Irrigation has made several valleys in the region suitable for raising crops. These valleys include the fertile Imperial and Coachella valleys near the Mexican border.

Death Valley is in the Basin and Range Region near the California-Nevada border. Part of Death Valley lies 282 feet (86 meters) below sea level and is the lowest point in North America.

The Transverse Ranges are a group of small mountain ranges between Santa Barbara and San Diego counties. They are called the Transverse Ranges because they extend generally in an east-west direction, along fault lines. Other ranges in California run generally north and south. The Transverse Ranges include the Santa Ynez, Santa Monica, San Gabriel, and San Bernardino mountains. Some geographers consider the San Jacinto and Santa Ana Mountains to be a part of this group. Most of the city of Los Angeles and its suburbs lie on a broad lowland between the San Gabriel Mountains and the Pacific Ocean. The hilly slopes of the Santa Monica Mountains extend into parts of the city.

The Peninsular Ranges, also called the *San Diego Ranges,* cover most of San Diego County at the southwestern tip of the state. They include the Agua Tibia, Laguna, and Vallecito mountains. This mountain system extends southward into the Mexican peninsula known as Baja (Lower) California.

Coastline. California's general coastline measures 840 miles (1,352 kilometers). California's *tidal shoreline* (including small bays and inlets) is 3,427 miles (5,515 kilometers) long. Along much of the coast, the Coast Ranges rise from the shore in steep cliffs and terraces. Southern California has many wide, sandy beaches. The California coast has two great natural harbors—San Francisco and San Diego bays. There are smaller natural harbors at Humboldt and Monterey bays.

Two groups of islands are located near the California coast. The small, rocky Farallon Islands rise from the ocean about 30 miles (48 kilometers) west of San Francisco. The eight Channel Islands lie scattered off the coast of southern California. Catalina Island, the best known of the Channel Islands, attracts many vacationers.

Rivers, waterfalls, and lakes. California's two longest rivers are the Sacramento and the San Joaquin. The Sacramento rises near Mount Shasta and flows south through the Central Valley. The San Joaquin rises in the

David Muench, Alpha Photo Assoc.

The Mojave Desert covers a large area in southeastern California and forms part of the state's Basin and Range Region. Much of the southern part of this region is barren wasteland.

The Coast Ranges rise from the Pacific Ocean. This mountain chain creates ruggedly beautiful coastline from the Klamath Mountains to Santa Barbara County. A scenic bridge spans Bixby Creek where it empties into the ocean near Big Sur, *shown here.*

© Baron Wolman

Sierra Nevada and flows northwest through the Central Valley. The two rivers meet northeast of San Francisco and flow west into San Francisco Bay. The place where the two rivers meet is the Delta, a maze of channels and islands. Smaller rivers, such as the Feather and the Mokelumne, begin in the eastern mountains and flow west into the Sacramento or the San Joaquin.

The Colorado River forms the border between southern California and Arizona. It is an important source of water for southern California cities. Water from the Colorado is also used to irrigate desert farmlands. Many rivers in southern California dry up or run underground during the dry season. Water may suddenly pour into the dry riverbeds during the rainy season and cause serious floods. In desert areas, most rivers have no outlets to other streams or to the sea. They flow above ground for a certain distance, then dry up or sink into the sand.

Yosemite National Park has several of the highest waterfalls in North America. Ribbon Falls (1,612 feet, or 491 meters) is the highest on the continent. Yosemite's other high waterfalls include Bridalveil, Illilouette, Nevada, Silver Strand, Vernal, and Upper and Lower Yosemite.

California has about 8,000 lakes. Lake Tahoe, the deepest, averages 1,500 feet (427 meters) in depth. It lies in the Sierra on the California-Nevada border and reflects the surrounding mountain peaks. Most of the desert lakes east of the Sierra contain dissolved minerals that give the water a disagreeable taste. Potash, salt, and other minerals are taken from Owens Lake, Searles Lake, and other dry or partly dry lakes in this region. The Salton Sea is a large, shallow lake in southern California. It was formed between 1905 and 1907 by floodwaters from the Colorado River.

Plant and animal life. California's widely varied climate and terrain combine to produce a wide variety of plant and animal life. Some of the world's most unusual living things are found in the state. The coast redwood tree is the tallest living thing in the world, and the bristlecone pine tree of the White Mountains is the oldest. The rare California condor is the largest bird in North America.

Forests cover about 40 percent of California. Softwood trees make up most of the forests. These trees include cedars, firs, hemlocks, giant sequoias, pines, and redwoods. The most common hardwood trees are oaks.

Desert plants cover much of the southeastern section of the state. These plants include burroweeds, creosote bushes, indigo bushes, Joshua trees, and several kinds of cactuses. Desert wild flowers include desert evening primrose and sand verbena. Patches of *chaparral* (thick and often thorny shrubs and small trees) cover the foothills. In the foothills and valleys of northern California, a spectacular array of wildflowers blooms after the winter rainy season. These flowers include beard-tongue, California poppy, evening primroses, fiddlenecks, and lupine. Fireweed and Washington lily bloom in the mountains.

Desert wildlife in California includes coyotes, lizards, and rattlesnakes. Beavers, bears, deer, foxes, minks, muskrats, rabbits, wildcats, wolverines, and a few mountain sheep roam the mountain and forest areas. Small herds of pronghorns and elk are found chiefly in the northern part of the state. California game birds include ducks, geese, grouse, mourning doves, quail, and turkey. Game fishes in the state's streams include black bass, salmon, striped bass, and trout. Abalones, clams, crabs, shrimps, lobsters, oysters, scallops, and other shellfishes are found along the California coast.

Average monthly weather

	Los Angeles						San Francisco				
	Temperatures °F		°C		Days of rain or snow		Temperatures °F		°C		Days of rain or snow
	High	Low	High	Low			High	Low	High	Low	
Jan.	65	45	18	7	7	Jan.	56	40	13	4	12
Feb.	66	47	19	8	5	Feb.	59	43	15	6	10
Mar.	69	49	21	9	6	Mar.	61	44	16	7	9
Apr.	71	52	22	11	4	Apr.	63	45	17	7	6
May	74	55	23	13	2	May	65	48	18	9	3
June	77	58	25	14	1	June	69	50	21	10	2
July	83	62	28	17	0	July	69	52	21	11	0
Aug.	84	62	29	17	1	Aug.	70	52	21	11	0
Sept.	82	60	28	16	1	Sept.	72	52	22	11	1
Oct.	77	56	25	13	2	Oct.	69	49	21	9	4
Nov.	73	51	23	11	4	Nov.	64	45	18	7	6
Dec.	67	48	19	9	6	Dec.	57	42	14	6	11

Average January temperatures

California's winters vary widely from mild temperatures in the south and on the coast to below freezing inland.

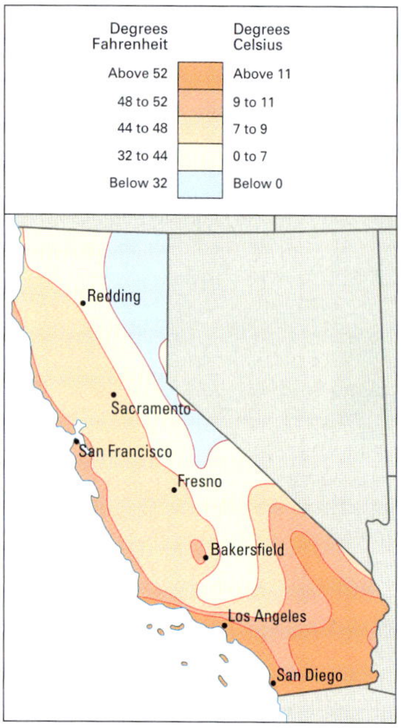

Average July temperatures

Summers in California can be very hot in the desert areas and mild along the coast and in the mountains.

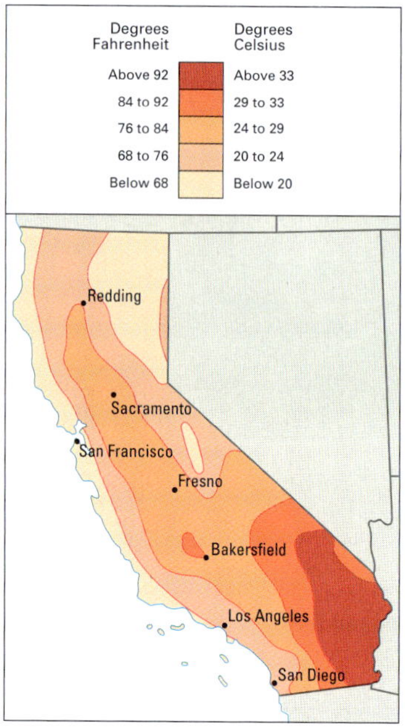

Average yearly precipitation

Precipitation is greatest along the northern coast. Parts of the southeastern desert basins receive almost no moisture.

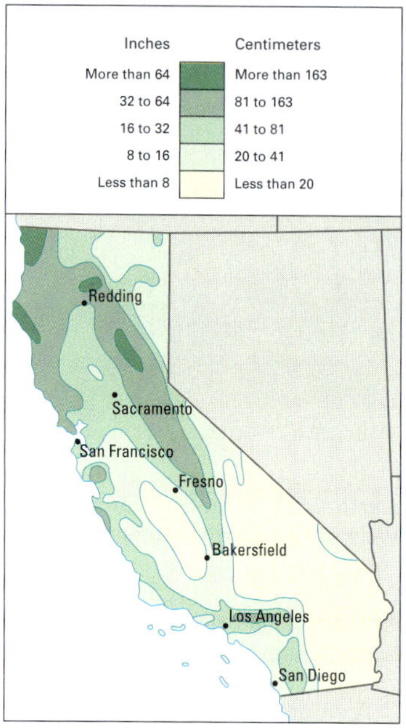

WORLD BOOK maps

Climate. California has a great variety of climates. The southern coast has a mild climate. The climate along the coast of northern and central California is also mild, but this region is generally cooler than the southern coast. The climate of southeastern California is hot and dry.

January temperatures in California average 44 °F (7 °C). Boca, near Truckee, recorded the state's lowest temperature, −45 °F (−43 °C), on Jan. 20, 1937. July temperatures average 75 °F (24 °C). The highest temperature ever recorded in the United States, 134 °F (57 °C), occurred at Greenland Ranch in Death Valley on July 10, 1913.

Most parts of California have only two well-marked seasons—a rainy season and a dry season. The rainy season lasts from October to April in the north, and from November to March or April in the south. Yearly precipitation is greatest along the northern coast, where it averages over 80 inches (200 centimeters). At San Francisco, the yearly average is about 22 inches (56 centimeters); at Los Angeles, 15 inches (38 centimeters); and at San Diego, 10 inches (25 centimeters). Some desert basins in the southeast receive almost no rain. From Oct. 3, 1912, to Nov. 8, 1914, Bagdad, in Death Valley, had no measurable precipitation. This 760-day rainless period set the United States record.

Snowfall is rare along the central and southern coast of California. But at Tamarack, in the Sierra Nevada, the yearly snowfall averages about 450 inches (1,140 centimeters).

Economy

The value of California's total economic production is higher than that of any other state. If California were a separate country, it would rank among the 10 leading countries in total value of goods and services produced. California's economy benefits from the state's abundant resources and strategic location. Important resources include a mild climate, plentiful minerals and timber, and fertile soils. California's location on the West Coast makes it a leading area for international trade with Asia and Latin America. California has long been a center of the motion-picture and television industries. Its films and entertainment products are distributed throughout the world.

Service industries provide the largest portion of California's *gross state product*—the total value of goods and services produced in a state annually. But goods-producing industries are also important for the state.

California ranks first among the states in both agriculture and manufacturing. The Central Valley region is one of the world's great farming areas. Most of the state's manufactured goods are products of modern science and engineering. These include airplanes, computers, electronic components, missiles, and scientific instruments. Private companies maintain several hundred laboratories for conducting research and testing new products. Most laboratories are near large universities. They are thus able to draw upon the ideas and skills of university biologists, chemists, engineers, and physicists.

Natural resources. California is unusually rich in minerals and timber. The state's soil and climate make it possible for farmers to grow a wide variety of crops.

Soils. Many parts of California, especially in the Central Valley, have *alluvial* (water deposited) soils. These soils make the best farmland. The Imperial Valley in southern California has rich alluvial soils that produce outstanding crops when irrigated. *Residual* (upland) soils cover the mountain slopes. These soils support forests in areas that have enough rain. In many other places, they provide grazing land.

Minerals. California has important fields of petroleum and natural gas in the southern part of the Central Valley, near the southern coast, and in coastal waters off Long Beach and Santa Barbara. Valuable deposits of boron exist in southeastern California. Commercially important quantities of sand and gravel occur in most California counties. Gemstones, including agate, benitoite, diamond, quartz, and tourmaline, are found in various counties. Other nonmetallic mined products found in the state include clays, diatomite, feldspar, gypsum, pumice, salt, soda ash, stone, and talc.

California's tungsten deposits are among the nation's largest. They occur mainly in Inyo County. Gold deposits are found in several parts of the state, from the western slopes of the northern Sierra Nevada to Imperial County, in the southeast.

Forests cover about 40 percent of California. The state has two main timber regions, each named for an important tree in the region. The *redwood region* is a narrow belt that extends south along the coast from Oregon to San Luis Obispo County. The *pine region* covers the Cascades and the Sierra Nevada. It extends along the inland parts of the Klamath Mountains and the Coast Ranges as far south as Lake County. The Douglas-fir, which is one of California's most valuable timber trees, grows in the redwood region and the pine region. Other important timber trees that grow in the state include incense-cedar, red fir, white fir, Jeffrey pine, ponderosa pine, sugar pine, and redwood.

California's most famous trees are its two types of sequoias, the redwood and the giant sequoia. The redwood is the state tree. Redwoods are the world's tallest living things. They grow near the coast in northern and central California. Giant sequoias, often called *big trees,* have larger trunks than redwoods but are not as tall. They grow on the western slopes of the Sierra Nevada. Bristlecone pines in the White Mountains of eastern California are the world's oldest living things. Some are more than 4,000 years old. See **Bristlecone pine** (with picture).

California's forests are important for timber production and for recreation. But they are especially important for preserving the state's precious water supply. Water does not run off or evaporate so quickly in forest areas as it does in treeless regions. The logging industry and the government work to protect California's forests from fire, harmful insects, and tree diseases. Landowners also grow trees on tree farms so there will be a constant supply of timber to replace the trees that are cut.

Water is one of California's most important natural resources. The mountain areas, especially in the north, have plenty of water from rain and melted snow. But most farms, industries, and homes are in the dry southern valleys. One of the state's greatest problems is to transport water from rainy areas to dry places where it is needed. Many *aqueducts* (channels and large pipelines) and canals have been built for that purpose. The Owens Valley Aqueduct brings water from the east side of the Sierra Nevada to Los Angeles. Water from the Colorado River has long been supplied to farms and cities in southern California by canals and aqueducts. The Central Valley Project brings water from the Sacramento Valley to the San Joaquin Valley. The water is used to irrigate the state's farms. The Hetch Hetchy Aqueduct brings water from the Tuolumne River to San Francisco.

The state's largest water-transfer program is the California State Water Project. It includes dams and reservoirs to store water, and aqueducts to carry it from rivers in northern California to coastal cities and to southern California. Oroville Dam on the Feather River is the most important part of the project. Water from the Feather, Sacramento, and other northern rivers is sent southward in the long California Aqueduct. Some of the water is pumped over mountain ranges into the Los Angeles and San Diego areas.

Service industries account for the largest part of California's gross state product. Service industries are most important in the state's largest cities. California's service industries receive much income from the tourist industry.

Community, business, and personal services form California's leading service industry in terms of the gross state product. This industry employs more people than any other activity in the state. It consists of a variety of establishments, such as entertainment companies, hotels, private health care, law firms and engineering companies, computer programming services, and repair shops. Tenet Healthcare, one of the largest hospital chains in the United States, is based in the Los Angeles area. Burbank is home to the Walt Disney Company, a major entertainment firm. Bechtel and Fluor, two of the world's leading engineering companies, have headquarters in California.

Production and workers by economic activities

Economic activities	Percent of GSP* produced	Employed workers: Number of people	Employed workers: Percent of total
Community, business, & personal services	24	6,673,700	34
Finance, insurance, & real estate	22	1,729,400	9
Trade, restaurants, & hotels	16	4,012,900	20
Government	11	2,677,900	14
Manufacturing	11	1,734,600	9
Transportation & communication	8	1,126,700	6
Construction	4	1,056,800	5
Utilities	2	56,800	†
Agriculture	1	563,400	3
Mining	1	33,500	†
Total	100	19,665,700	100

*GSP = gross state product, the total value of goods and services produced in a year.
†Less than one-half of 1 percent.
Figures are for 2002; employment figures include full- and part-time workers.
Source: *World Book* estimates based on data from U.S. Bureau of Economic Analysis.

© Chuck O'Rear, West Light

An electronics plant near Milpitas manufactures microchips for computers. Milpitas is located in the Silicon Valley area, the nation's leading computer-manufacturing region.

Boeing Company

At an aircraft factory in Long Beach, workers install the nose section of a Boeing jet airplane. Aircraft and other transportation equipment are among California's chief manufactured products.

Finance, insurance, and real estate form the second-ranking service industry in California. This industry is one of the fastest-growing economic activities in California. Real estate is the most important part of this industry. Property prices in the San Francisco and Los Angeles areas are among the highest in the nation. These two areas are also major United States financial centers. Several of the nation's largest banking companies are based in San Francisco and Los Angeles. San Diego and San Jose are also major U.S. financial centers.

Trade, restaurants, and hotels ranks third among California's service industries. This industry group employs about a fifth of the state's workers. Wholesale trade consists of buying goods from producers and selling these goods to other businesses.

The wholesale trade of food products, medical supplies, motor vehicles, and petroleum products is important in California. Dole Food Company, based near Los Angeles, is a leading wholesale distributor of fruit. AmerisourceBergen, with offices in nearby Orange, is a major distributor of medical supplies.

Retail trade involves selling goods directly to consumers. Leading types of retail businesses include automobile dealerships, department stores, food stores, and service stations. Safeway, a major food store chain, is based in California.

Restaurants and hotels benefit from California having more tourists each year than any other state.

Government ranks fourth among California service industries in terms of the gross state product. Government services include public schools and hospitals, and military establishments. California has one of the world's largest public school systems, and its schools employ many people. Public universities in California operate many fine medical facilities and research laboratories. Edwards Air Force Base and several other Air Force bases lie within the state. California's other military bases include Camp Pendleton and Naval Base Coronado. The military bases are an especially important part of the economy of the San Diego area.

Transportation and communication ranks fifth among service industries. Several railroad companies are based in the San Francisco area. Many shipping and trucking companies also operate in California. The airports in San Francisco and Los Angeles are among the world's busiest. More information about transportation and communication appears later in this section.

Manufacturing. Goods manufactured in California have a *value added by manufacture* of about $220 billion yearly. Value added by manufacture represents the increase in value of raw materials after they become finished products.

Computer and electronic equipment is California's leading manufactured product in terms of value added by manufacture. More than 40 states have a total value-added figure lower than that of California's electronics industry alone. Computers, computer microchips, military communication equipment, and telephone equipment are the leading types of electronic products made in the state. Electronic systems for aircraft and missiles are important products. The San Jose area is the nation's leader in the manufacture of electronic equipment. Silicon Valley, the leading computer-manufacturing region of the United States, is in this area. Apple Computer, Hewlett-Packard, and hundreds of other computer and electronics companies are headquartered there. Facto-

Economy of California

This map shows the economic uses of land in California and where the state's leading farm, mineral, and forest products are produced. Major manufacturing centers are shown in red.

Mostly cropland

Cropland mixed with grazing land

Mostly grazing land

Mostly forest land

Generally unproductive land

Urban area

Manufacturing center

Mineral deposit

WORLD BOOK map

David R. Frazier

Farmworkers plant lettuce on a California vegetable farm. California leads the states in the production of lettuce and several other vegetables. It is the nation's leading agricultural state.

ries in Los Angeles, San Diego, Oakland, and Orange County also produce large amounts of these goods.

Food processing is the second-ranking manufacturing activity. The main food products are baked goods, beverages, and canned fruits and vegetables. Large bakeries operate in many parts of the state. California produces some of the world's finest wines. Soft-drink bottling also provides much income. The San Jose and Stockton areas have numerous canneries. The processing of meats, milk and other dairy products, and sauces is also important in California.

Chemicals rank third among California's manufactured goods. Pharmaceuticals are California's leading chemical product, followed by cleaning compounds and paint. Other leading chemical products include adhesives, fertilizer, and printing ink.

Transportation equipment ranks fourth among California's manufactured products. Aircraft are the state's

Casks of wine are inspected at a winery in the Napa Valley, a major California wine-producing region. California leads all other states in the production of wine.

© John Elk III

most important type of transportation equipment. Southern California is a leading aircraft assembly center in the United States. California's largest aircraft manufacturers include the Boeing Company and Northrop Grumman Corporation. Other types of transportation equipment made in the state include motor vehicles.

Fabricated metal products rank fifth. Machine shops and bolt, nut, and screw manufacturers are among the key parts of this sector.

Other manufactured products of California include clothing, furniture, machinery, plastic and rubber products, printed materials, refined petroleum, and many other kinds of goods.

Agriculture. California leads the states in farm income. Fresno, Monterey, and Tulare counties are the nation's top-ranking counties in agricultural production. California has about 79,000 farms. Many Californians call farms *ranches,* even if the farms raise crops rather than livestock.

The wide range of climate and of soil and water conditions enables California farmers to grow over 300 different crops. Several of these crops are grown commercially nowhere else in the nation. Most California farms are highly specialized. Many specialize in fruits or nuts. Almost all crop production takes place on farmlands that receive irrigation water.

Fruits and nuts account for more than 25 percent of California's farm income. Grapes rank first in value, followed by almonds, strawberries, oranges, and walnuts. The grape crop includes table grapes, wine grapes, and raisin grapes. California produces almost all of the nation's almonds, dates, figs, kiwi fruit, nectarines, olives, pistachios, pomegranates, prunes, and walnuts. California also leads all states in the production of avocados, grapes, lemons, peaches, plums, and strawberries. Only Florida produces more oranges.

Various regions of California specialize in fruits and nuts for which their soil and climate are best suited. For example, the San Joaquin Valley grows almonds, apricots, cantaloupes, grapes, kiwi fruit, nectarines, olives, oranges, peaches, pistachios, plums, and walnuts. The Sacramento Valley yields honeydew melons, prunes, and pears. Southern coastal counties lead in the production of avocados and honeydew melons, and have a heavy production of strawberries. Farms in the Imperial Valley yield dates, grapefruits, and melons.

Livestock and livestock products account for about 25 percent of California's agricultural income. Milk is the state's leading agricultural product. California leads the states in milk production. Beef cattle are another leading agricultural product in the state. Tulare and Fresno counties in the San Joaquin Valley produce the most beef cattle. Many beef cattle also come from Imperial County and other southern counties. California ranks among the leaders in egg production, and in raising sheep and turkeys. California has more bee colonies and produces more honey than any other state.

Vegetables earn nearly 25 percent of the state's farm income. Tomatoes and lettuce are the most important vegetable crops in the state. California ranks first in the production of both tomatoes and lettuce. The most important tomato-growing regions are the northern part of the San Joaquin Valley and the southern part of the Sacramento Valley. Lettuce is cultivated primarily in the southeastern corner of the state and in the regions that lie west of Fresno and southeast of Monterey. Broccoli and carrots rank next in importance. California leads the nation in the production of asparagus, cauliflower, celery, garlic, mushrooms, onions, and spinach.

Field crops provide about 10 percent of the state's agricultural income. Hay is California's leading field crop. Hay is grown throughout the state, but especially in areas that raise large numbers of cattle. Cotton is the second most valuable field crop. California's San Joaquin Valley is a major cotton-growing region. Farmers grow rice in the Sacramento Valley. Other leading field crops include potatoes, sugar beets, and wheat.

Greenhouse and nursery products account for about 10 percent of the state's agricultural income. California leads all states in the production of cut flowers, potted flowering plants, and flower bulbs. It is an important producer of indoor foliage plants and seedlings. Most greenhouse and nursery products are grown in coastal areas from San Francisco to San Diego.

Mining. Petroleum is California's most valuable mined product. Most of the oil wells are in the southern part of the San Joaquin Valley and along the coast near Long Beach, Los Angeles, and Santa Barbara. Much natural gas comes from the petroleum-producing regions and from the Sacramento Valley.

California leads the nation in nonfuel mineral production. California mines yield all of the boron that is produced in the United States. Boron comes from Inyo, Kern, and San Bernardino counties. It is used in boric acid, an antiseptic; in borax, a cleaning agent; and in making glass fibers for such products as insulation and textiles. California is also the leading U.S. producer of diatomite, portland cement, and sand and gravel. California is among the leading states in the production of gemstones, gold, gypsum, magnesium compounds, perlite, and pumice.

Fishing industry. California ranks among the leading states in commercial fishing. Its annual catch is valued at more than $130 million. Crabs are the most valuable catch. Squids are the second most valuable fisheries catch in the state, and California has a larger squid catch than any other state. Other commercially important catches include lobster, sablefish, salmon, sardine, sea urchins, shrimp, swordfish, and tuna. Catches also include halibut, herring, mackerel, oysters, rockfish, shark, and sole.

Electric power and utilities. California's utilities provide electric, gas, and water service. Nearly half of California's electric power comes from plants that burn natural gas. About 20 percent comes from nuclear plants, and about 15 percent comes from hydroelectric plants. Hoover, Davis, Glen Canyon, and Parker dams on the Colorado River supply power to California as well as to other Southwestern states. Power companies also generate power from many dams on rivers in northern California.

The Geysers Geothermal Field near Healdsburg is one of the nation's few commercial electric plants that is powered by *geothermal steam*—steam created by heat deep in the earth. In 1983, what was then the world's largest solar power plant began operation near San Luis Obispo. It produced electric power from sunlight.

Transportation. California's first highway, El Camino Real, began as a path connecting the Spanish missions along the coast during the 1700's. The state's first major freeway, the Arroyo Seco Parkway (now Pasadena Freeway) between Pasadena and Los Angeles, was completed in 1940. Today, complicated freeway systems, with underpasses, overpasses, and cloverleafs, are a familiar symbol of California's urban areas. The state has about 170,000 miles (274,000 kilometers) of roads and highways.

San Francisco Bay has two of the world's most famous bridges. These are the Golden Gate Bridge between San Francisco and Marin County and the San Francisco-

Richard Hewett, Shooting Star

Hollywood, a district of Los Angeles, has been considered the motion-picture capital of the world since the early days of movies. Many television programs are also filmed in Hollywood studios.

Oakland Bay Bridge. Another important bridge, the Richmond-San Rafael Bridge, crosses a northern section of San Francisco Bay.

The international airports at Los Angeles and San Francisco are among the world's busiest. Other major airports include those in Oakland, Orange County, Sacramento, San Diego, San Jose.

California's first railway, completed in 1856, ran 22 miles (35 kilometers) between Sacramento and Folsom. Today, two major rail lines provide freight service on about 7,500 miles (12,100 kilometers) of track. Passenger trains serve about 150 of California's cities.

Southern California has major ports at Los Angeles (San Pedro), Long Beach, and San Diego. The San Francisco Bay area has several deepwater ports that ship millions of tons of goods each year. Besides San Francisco itself, these ports include Oakland, Redwood City, and Richmond. Sacramento and Stockton are important inland ports. They handle shipments of agricultural and mineral products from the Sacramento and San Joaquin valleys. Deepwater channels connect the Sacramento and Stockton ports with San Francisco Bay.

Communication. California's first newspaper, the *Californian,* began publication in Monterey in 1846. Today, the state has about 570 newspapers, including about 100 dailies. The leading newspapers in California include the *Contra Costa Times,* the *Los Angeles Times,* the *Orange County Register, The Sacramento Bee, The San Diego Union-Tribune,* the *San Francisco Chronicle,* and the *San Jose Mercury News.*

In 1909, David Herrold began operating a radio station in connection with a radio school in San Jose. This occurred three years before the Congress of the United States established radio licensing requirements. In 1913, Herrold adopted the call letters SJN. The station's letters were changed to KQW in 1921, and to KCBS in 1949. California's first commercial radio station, KQL in Los Angeles, was licensed in 1921. KWG in Stockton was also licensed in 1921 and is still broadcasting. California's first commercial television station, KTLA in Los Angeles, began operations in 1947. Today, California has about 640 radio stations and about 95 television stations. Cable TV systems and Internet providers serve many communities.

Government

Constitution. California's first Constitution was adopted by the territorial government in 1849. The present Constitution was adopted in 1879. It has been *amended* (changed) hundreds of times. A proposed amendment must be placed on the ballot in a regular statewide election. It may be proposed and placed on the ballot in any of three ways: (1) The Legislature may propose it by a two-thirds majority vote in each house. (2) A group of citizens may propose an amendment by submitting a petition. The petition must be signed by at least 8 percent as many people as voted for governor in the last election. (3) A constitutional convention, approved by two-thirds of the Legislature, may propose an amendment. To become law, an amendment must be approved by a majority of the voters.

Executive. Voters elect California's governor to a four-year term. The governor can serve only two terms.

Other top state officials include the lieutenant governor, secretary of state, attorney general, treasurer, controller, insurance commissioner, and superintendent of public instruction. Voters also elect the five-member State Board of Equalization, which administers several important tax laws. All these officials are elected to four-year terms and may serve no more than two terms in the same office.

Legislature consists of a Senate of 40 members and an Assembly of 80 members. Each senator and each Assembly member represents one senatorial or Assembly district. Senators are elected to four-year terms and may serve only two terms. Members of the Assembly are elected to two-year terms and may serve no more than three terms.

Regular sessions of the Legislature run about two years. They begin on the first Monday in December of each even-numbered year and end on November 30 of the next even-numbered year.

The governor may call special sessions at which the Legislature can deal only with subjects specified by the governor. There is no time limit on special sessions of the Legislature.

California citizens can pass laws directly, through their power of *initiative.* To do so, a proposed law must be favored by at least 5 percent of the people who voted for governor in the last election. This number of people must sign a petition in favor of a measure. Then they can put the measure on the ballot in the next state election. If the voters approve the measure, it becomes law.

In a process called the *referendum,* Californians also have the right to challenge most kinds of laws passed by the Legislature. If 5 percent of the people who voted for governor in the most recent election challenge a new law, the law will not go into effect unless the people approve it in an election.

Courts. The highest court in California is the state Supreme Court. It has a chief justice and six associate justices. The state has six district courts of appeal. Justices of the Supreme Court and of the district courts of appeal are appointed by the governor to 12-year terms, subject to voter approval.

Each county has one superior court. The number of judges for each superior court is fixed by the Legislature. The voters elect superior court judges to six-year terms.

Local government. California has about 450 incorporated cities. The state Constitution gives cities of 3,500 or more people the right to draw up and adopt their own charters. This right is often called *home rule.* About 80 California cities operate under local charters.

Most cities in California have council-manager governments. The others have mayor-council governments.

California has 58 counties. Most of the counties have a form of government specified by the laws of the state. This form of government includes a five-member board of supervisors and a number of elected executive officials. The elected officials include an assessor, auditor, clerk, coroner, district attorney, sheriff, superintendent

© John Elk III

The California Senate meets in chambers in the State Capitol in Sacramento. The 40 members are elected to four-year terms.

of schools, and treasurer. The California constitution provides for county home rule. But only 11 counties have adopted charters under the home-rule law. Most of these counties chose a form of government similar to that of the general-law counties.

Revenue. Taxation provides about 55 percent of the state's *general revenue* (income). Most of the rest of its revenue comes from federal government grants. The largest state tax revenue sources are a personal income tax and a general sales tax. Other tax revenue sources include taxes on corporate profits, motor fuels, and property, and licenses for businesses and motor vehicles.

Politics. Until 1959, California did not require political candidates to declare their party affiliation. For example, they could run as candidates of both the Democratic and Republican parties. This practice, known as *cross-filing*, kept many voters from being loyal to one particular party. As a result, political disagreements between various parts of the state tended to be stronger than disagreements among the parties themselves. Major political conflicts still occur between northern and southern California. For California's electoral votes and voting record in presidential elections, see **Electoral College** (table).

The governors of California

	Party	Term		Party	Term
Peter H. Burnett	Democratic	1849-1851	**Henry T. Gage**	Republican	1899-1903
John McDougal	Democratic	1851-1852	**George C. Pardee**	Republican	1903-1907
John Bigler	Democratic	1852-1856	**James N. Gillett**	Republican	1907-1911
John Neely Johnson	Know-Nothing	1856-1858	**Hiram W. Johnson**	Republican	1911-1917
John B. Weller	Democratic	1858-1860	**William D. Stephens**	Republican	1917-1923
Milton S. Latham	Democratic	1860	**Friend William Richardson**	Republican	1923-1927
John G. Downey	Democratic	1860-1862	**Clement C. Young**	Republican	1927-1931
Leland Stanford	Republican	1862-1863	**James Rolph, Jr.**	Republican	1931-1934
Frederick F. Low	Union	1863-1867	**Frank F. Merriam**	Republican	1934-1939
Henry H. Haight	Democratic	1867-1871	**Culbert L. Olson**	Democratic	1939-1943
Newton Booth	Republican	1871-1875	**Earl Warren**	Republican	1943-1953
Romualdo Pacheco	Republican	1875	**Goodwin J. Knight**	Republican	1953-1959
William Irwin	Democratic	1875-1880	**Edmund G. Brown**	Democratic	1959-1967
George C. Perkins	Republican	1880-1883	**Ronald Reagan**	Republican	1967-1975
George Stoneman	Democratic	1883-1887	**Edmund G. Brown, Jr.**	Democratic	1975-1983
Washington Bartlett	Democratic	1887	**George Deukmejian**	Republican	1983-1991
Robert W. Waterman	Republican	1887-1891	**Pete Wilson**	Republican	1991-1999
Henry H. Markham	Republican	1891-1895	**Gray Davis**	Democratic	1999-2003
James H. Budd	Democratic	1895-1899	**Arnold Schwarzenegger**	Republican	2003-

Early days. As many as 300,000 Indians lived in the fertile parts of the California region before Europeans came. There were many tribes, and they spoke different languages. Deserts and high mountains often separated the California Indian groups from each other and from the tribes farther east. The Hupa Indians lived in the far northwestern part of what is now California. The Maidu lived in the central section, and the Quechan lived in the south. The Pomo Indians occupied the territory that now makes up Lake, Mendocino, and Sonoma counties north of San Francisco. Other Indian groups in the California region included the Miwok, Modoc, and Mojave tribes.

Spanish and English exploration. Juan Rodríguez Cabrillo, a Portuguese explorer employed by Spain, was the first European to see the coast of what is now California. In 1542, Cabrillo sailed north from New Spain (present-day Mexico) along the Pacific Coast. He hoped to find rich cities and a water passage between the Pacific and Atlantic oceans. He discovered San Diego Bay and stopped there before sailing farther north. He died in 1543, but his men continued the voyage. Some historians believe Cabrillo's expedition sailed along the entire California coast, as far north as present-day Oregon.

In 1579, Francis Drake, an English sea captain, followed a route along the California coast during his famous voyage around the world. He claimed the land for England and named it *New Albion.* The Spaniards then sent several exploring parties along the coast, partly because they feared they might lose California to the English. In 1602, Sebastián Vizcaíno led one of these expeditions. He named many landmarks along the coast and sent an enthusiastic report to the king of Spain. In the report, Vizcaíno urged that Spain colonize California.

Spanish and Russian settlement. Beginning in 1697, the Spaniards established missions and other settlements in Baja (Lower) California, the Mexican peninsula south of present-day California. Captain Gaspar de Portolá, governor of Baja California, led an expedition that established the first *presidio* (military fort) at San Diego in 1769. He also established one at Monterey in 1770. In 1776, a group of Spanish settlers arrived at the site of what is now San Francisco. The settlers founded a presidio and a mission there. Later, other groups of settlers sent by Spain established some *pueblos* (villages) near the coast.

However, Spain did not have a strong hold on the California region. Russia had fur-trading interests in Alaska and wanted to search for furs farther south along the Pacific Coast. In 1812, the Russians established Fort Ross on the northern California coast. Russian activity in California was one reason for the Monroe Doctrine, proclaimed in 1823. In the Monroe Doctrine, the United States declared that North and South America should be considered closed to European colonization. In 1824, Russia agreed to limit its settlements to Alaska. However, the Russians did not actually leave the California region until the early 1840's.

The California missions. Franciscan friars of the Roman Catholic Church played an important part in the Spanish settlement of California. In 1769, during the Portolá expedition, Junípero Serra established the first California mission. This mission was San Diego de Alcalá, originally established in what is now San Diego. By 1823, the Franciscans had built a chain of 21 missions. Each mission was about a day's walk from the next. Many Indians who lived near the missions were forced to farm, weave, and perform other tasks for the friars and the local communities. A number of Indians were exposed to new diseases. Many became ill and died.

Many people in California and Mexico wanted the missions broken up. In the early 1830's, the government began giving mission land to private citizens. By 1846, almost all the mission property had been given away. During this period, the government gave or sold many large estates, called *ranchos,* to private landowners, called *rancheros.* Some rancheros became wealthy by raising cattle for hides and *tallow* (fat used in making candles, soap, and other products).

Mexican rule. California became a province of Mexico in 1822, after Mexico won its independence from Spain. The province set up its own legislature and established a military force. But, beginning in 1825, Mexico sent a series of governors to California. Many Californians rebelled against having their affairs dictated by these outsiders. Manuel Victoria, who became governor in 1831, ruled with a strong hand and was especially resented by the Californians. A group led by Pío Pico and others clashed with Mexican government troops in 1831. This fighting was not severe. But the continuing opposition forced Victoria to give up the governorship and return to Mexico City. After that, Mexico's control over the region remained weak.

American settlement. The *Otter,* the first American sailing vessel to reach the coast from the East, appeared in California waters in 1796. After that, American skippers made many trading trips to harbors along the coast of California.

The first American explorer to reach California by land was Jedediah Strong Smith, a trapper who crossed the southwestern deserts in 1826. Other trappers and explorers followed Smith. They included Kit Carson, Joseph Reddeford Walker, and Ewing Young.

In 1841, the first organized group of American settlers came to California by land. These settlers were led by John Bidwell, a schoolteacher, and John Bartleson, a wagon master and land speculator. Soon other overland pioneers arrived to settle in the Mexican territory. They drove long wagon trains through the mountain passes. The new settlers wanted California to become a part of the United States. The United States offered to buy the land from Mexico, but Mexico refused to sell.

The Mexican War. Between 1844 and 1846, the military explorer John C. Frémont led two surveying parties into California. The Mexicans did not trust Frémont because his parties were made up of U.S. soldiers. In March 1846, they ordered Frémont to withdraw his troops, who were camped near Monterey. Instead, Frémont raised the U.S. flag over Hawk's Peak, about 25 miles (40 kilometers) from Monterey. He began to build a fort there. Fighting was avoided when Frémont withdrew to the north under cover of darkness. On May 13, 1846, the United States and Mexico went to war.

In June 1846, without knowing that war had been declared, a band of American settlers took over Sonoma, Mexico's headquarters in northern California. The group was led by frontiersman Ezekiel Merritt. After capturing the fort, the settlers unfurled a homemade flag bearing a star, a grizzly bear, and the words *California Republic.*

Historic California

Fort Ross was established by Russian fur traders on the northern California coast in 1812. Russians did not leave the California region until the 1840's.

The gold rush of 1849 began after James W. Marshall found gold at Sutter's Mill in 1848. He found the first gold in the American River.

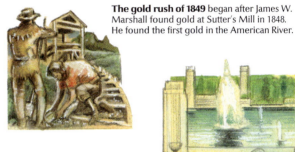

The Golden Gate International Exposition was held on Treasure Island in San Francisco Bay in 1939 and 1940.

The first California mission, San Diego de Alcalá, was founded in 1769 by Junípero Serra. By 1823, Franciscan priests had built a chain of 21 missions in California.

The Central Pacific Railroad, completed in 1869, was the first railroad to connect California with the rest of the United States.

WORLD BOOK illustrations by Kevin Chadwick

Important dates in California

1542 Juan Rodríguez Cabrillo explored San Diego Bay.

1579 Francis Drake sailed along the coast and claimed California for England.

1602 Sebastián Vizcaíno urged that Spain colonize California.

1769 Gaspar de Portolá led a land expedition up the California coast. Junípero Serra established the first Franciscan mission in California, in what is now the city of San Diego.

1776 Spanish settlers from New Spain (Mexico) reached the site of what is now San Francisco.

1812 Russian fur traders built Fort Ross.

1822 California became part of Mexico, which had just won its independence from Spain in 1821.

1841 The Bidwell-Bartleson party became the first organized group of American settlers to travel to California by land.

1846 American rebels raised the "Bear Flag" of the California Republic over Sonoma. United States forces conquered California in the Mexican War (1846-1848).

1848 James W. Marshall discovered gold at Sutter's Mill. The discovery led to the California gold rush. The United States defeated Mexico in the Mexican War and acquired California in the Treaty of Guadalupe Hidalgo.

1850 California became the 31st state on September 9.

1880's A population boom occurred as a result of a railroad and real estate publicity campaign that brought thousands of people to California.

1906 An earthquake and fire destroyed much of San Francisco.

1915 Expositions were begun at San Diego and San Francisco to mark the opening of the Panama Canal.

1963 California became the state with the largest population in the United States.

1978 California voters approved a $7-billion cutback in state property taxes.

1989 A strong earthquake struck the San Francisco-Oakland-San Jose area.

1994 A strong earthquake struck Los Angeles.

2003 Voters recalled Governor Gray Davis and elected motion-picture star Arnold Schwarzenegger to replace him.

California State Library

Gold prospectors were lured to California after the discovery of gold at Sutter's Mill in 1848. Thousands of adventurers, such as these panning for gold near Auburn in 1852, rushed in from many parts of the world.

This action became known as the Bear Flag Revolt.

The real conquest of California was carried out by U.S. soldiers, sailors, and marines. They were led by Frémont, Commodore Robert F. Stockton, and General Stephen W. Kearny. After the United States won the Mexican War in 1848, Mexico surrendered California in the Treaty of Guadalupe Hidalgo. California then became part of the United States.

The gold rush. In 1848, just before the United States and Mexico signed the peace treaty, gold was discovered in California. John A. Sutter, a pioneer trader, had received a large land grant in the Sacramento Valley in 1839. He hired James W. Marshall, a carpenter, to help build a sawmill on the American River. There, at Sutter's Mill, Marshall found the first gold nuggets. News of his discovery spread. People rushed to establish claims. These "Forty-Niners," as they were called, poured in from all parts of the world. Between early 1848 and the end of 1849, California's population increased from about 15,000 to more than 100,000. The free spending by the miners who found gold made such communities as San Francisco and Sacramento into flourishing towns. Some miners who were not so lucky in the gold fields became farmers and ranchers in the Central Valley.

Early statehood. California became the 31st state on Sept. 9, 1850. Peter H. Burnett, a Democrat, was the first state governor. Thousands of settlers went west after the American Civil War ended in 1865. They sought the high wages paid in California and a chance to buy land at low prices. In 1869, the first transcontinental railroad system linked Sacramento with the eastern United States. Part of this system, the Central Pacific Railroad, later became part of the Southern Pacific, owned by Charles Crocker, Mark Hopkins, Collis P. Huntington, and Leland Stanford. These men were known as California's "Big Four." They brought many Chinese laborers to California in the 1860's to work on the railroads.

By 1870, California's population had risen to about 560,000. During the next 10 years, a depression caused widespread unemployment and bank failures. Many unemployed workers blamed their troubles on Chinese laborers, who were willing to work for low wages. Anti-Chinese riots took place in Los Angeles in 1871 and in San Francisco in 1877. During the 1880's, a great publicity campaign brought thousands of people to California. So many came to southern California in 1887 that a land boom occurred. Agriculture and industry flourished as the population increased.

In 1906, a terrible earthquake in San Francisco destroyed about 28,000 buildings and killed more than 3,000 people. However, the city was soon rebuilt.

Progress as a state. During the early 1900's, California grew rapidly in population and in the development of natural resources. Mexican immigration soared after a revolution in Mexico in 1910. Farming in California increased greatly after irrigation turned many desert areas into fertile land. Development of oil and natural gas was accompanied by the growth of new industries. Other minerals besides gold were found, and mining became more important. By 1920, Hollywood had become the motion-picture capital of the world.

In 1910, Californians elected Hiram W. Johnson as governor. Two years later, Johnson joined Theodore Roosevelt in a revolt against the Republican Party. Johnson ran for U.S. vice president under Roosevelt in 1912 on the unsuccessful Progressive Party ticket.

In 1914, the completion of the Panama Canal shortened the important sea route between California and the East. To show the value of the canal to California, the state sponsored the Panama-Pacific International Exposition in San Francisco in 1915 and the Panama-California Exposition in San Diego in 1915 and 1916.

After the United States entered World War I in 1917, shipyards, rubber plants, and other factories were established in California. After the war ended in 1918, interest turned to control of the Colorado River. This mighty river had caused serious flood damage for many years. Between 1905 and 1907, floodwaters from the Colorado had even formed the 450-square-mile (1,165-square-kilometer) Salton Sea in southeastern California. In 1928, Congress authorized a huge dam at Boulder Canyon on the Arizona-Nevada border. The dam was completed in 1936. It controls floods and provides water for irrigation and power in southern California and neighboring states (see **Hoover Dam**).

During the Great Depression of the 1930's, hundreds of people without homes or jobs drifted into California. The state passed laws to close its borders to poor people. But this legislation was later declared unconstitutional by the Supreme Court of the United States. Many Californians blamed the Depression on Mexican Americans, and the state deported hundreds of thousands of Mexican Americans to Mexico.

In 1935 and 1936, the California-Pacific International Exposition was held in San Diego. This fair honored the Pacific Ocean and the countries that border it. The Golden Gate International Exposition was held in 1939 and 1940 on Treasure Island in San Francisco Bay. The Golden Gate Bridge across the entrance of the bay had been completed in 1937.

The mid-1900's. During World War II (1939-1945), California produced airplanes, ships, and weapons. It became the nation's aircraft center. After Japan attacked Pearl Harbor in 1941, the government forcibly moved thousands of Japanese Americans from California to detention camps (see **World War II** [On the home front]). In 1945, representatives of 50 nations approved the United Nations Charter at the San Francisco Conference.

Many people who had come to California as mem-

Granger Collection

The San Francisco earthquake of 1906 destroyed about 28,000 buildings and killed at least 3,000 people. But the city was soon rebuilt.

bers of the armed forces or to work in defense plants settled there after the war. The population soared. Farm centers became metropolitan areas with a variety of industries. Rows of ranch-style houses appeared on former orchards and pastures. New freeways linked smaller cities with Los Angeles and San Francisco.

The population growth boosted California's economy, but it also created problems. The state had to provide more schools and highways. Smog became a serious problem in Los Angeles and other cities as more automobiles and industries discharged fumes and smoke.

Changes in U.S. immigration laws in 1965, which ended quotas based on nationality, led to another increase in California's population. Hundreds of thousands of people from Asian countries settled in the state.

Controlling and distributing water resources remained California's biggest problem during the 1960's. Most of the state's rain and snow falls in the northern mountains. But most of California's people live in southern California, where rainfall does not supply enough water. In the 1960's and early 1970's, the state built a system of canals, dams, reservoirs, and power and pumping plants to store and distribute northern California's excess water to the drier areas. A number of additions to the system have been completed since the 1970's.

In the 1950's and 1960's, African Americans, Asian Americans, and Mexican Americans began to demand equal rights. Racial tensions worsened in 1964 after California voters passed a referendum that overturned a 1963 law guaranteeing equal access to housing. In 1965, racial violence erupted in Watts, a black section of Los Angeles. Rioting broke out after a Los Angeles police officer arrested a black motorist. It resulted in 34 deaths and millions of dollars of damage.

By the end of the 1960's, California had greatly increased its number of state universities and colleges. The state's schools became the center of various student movements. The nation's first major college demonstration, organized by the Free Speech Movement, occurred in 1964 at the University of California in Berkeley.

Richard M. Nixon, born in Yorba Linda, was elected president of the United States in 1968 and was reelected in 1972. He resigned from the office in 1974 because of his involvement in the Watergate political scandal.

Motion-picture stars gained popularity with California voters in the 1960's. George L. Murphy won election to the U.S. Senate in 1964, and Ronald Reagan became governor in 1967. Reagan was elected president of the United States in 1980 and was reelected in 1984.

The late 1900's. In the early 1970's, sharp cuts in federal military spending in California caused a rise in unemployment. In 1978, California voters approved a referendum—known as Proposition 13—that called for a $7-billion reduction in state property taxes. School districts and local government suffered revenue losses.

By the early 1980's, however, California's economy was again thriving, and education and other services benefited from the state's increased revenues. New federal military contracts helped bring prosperity to California's aerospace industry. In addition, Santa Clara County became a world leader in the production of high-technology electronic equipment. It earned the name Silicon Valley. The breakup of the Soviet Union in 1991 and other developments again led to a decrease of federal military spending in California. These events and other factors helped cause a recession in the state in the early 1990's. But growth of service industries and other economic activities improved the economy.

On Oct. 17, 1989, a strong earthquake struck the San Francisco-Oakland-San Jose area. It caused 63 deaths and extensive property damage. Most deaths were caused by the collapse of a section of the Nimitz Freeway in Oakland. In 1991, a major brush fire struck Oakland and surrounding areas. It caused 25 deaths and destroyed much property. In January 1994, another extremely destructive earthquake struck Los Angeles. It caused 57 deaths and much property damage.

In 1992, four police officers who were accused of a 1991 beating of a black motorist, Rodney G. King, were acquitted of criminal charges. The verdict set off several days of rioting, mainly in black areas of South Los Angeles (then called South-Central Los Angeles). The rioting resulted in 53 deaths and over $1 billion in damage.

The state's population continued to grow rapidly, partly because of the large numbers of immigrants from Europe, Asia, and especially Central America and Mexico. In 1986, California voters approved a referendum to make English the state's official language. In 1994, the voters passed a referendum to prohibit illegal immigrants from receiving public education, free nonemergency medical care, and other social services. But implementation was blocked by a number of lawsuits. In 1999, the state abandoned the proposition. Governor Gray Davis said that much of the intent of the proposition was covered by federal immigration laws passed in 1996 that deny certain social services to illegal immigrants.

The beginning of the 2000's. Power outages, called "rolling blackouts," became common across the state in 2001. The energy crisis stemmed in part from actions taken in 1996, when the state had approved legislation to deregulate its utility industry. Government officials had believed the action would result in increased competition among electric companies and lower rates for customers. But by 2000, the state's electric companies faced financial ruin. They had to pay increasingly high wholesale costs for electric power, but the deregulation law prevented them from raising the costs to customers.

In mid-2001, the state stepped in to buy power for the financially weakened utilities. The state also sought federal controls on wholesale electric power costs. California's long-term energy plans called for construction of additional power stations.

In 2002, Gray Davis was elected by a slim margin to a second term as governor. By that time, the state government's expenses so greatly exceeded income that budget *deficits* (shortages) were reaching record levels. A number of Californians blamed Davis for the state's worsening economic problems, and they were successful in petitioning for a *recall election*—that is, a vote to decide whether Davis should be removed from office. On Oct. 7, 2003, California voters recalled Davis and elected motion-picture star Arnold Schwarzenegger governor. Davis became the state's first governor to be recalled. William A. Bowen and Clark Davis

Related articles in *World Book* include:

Biographies

Bradley, Thomas
Brown, Edmund G., Jr.
Burbank, Luther
Carson, Kit
Chavez, Cesar E.
Christopher, Warren M.
Disney, Walt
Drake, Sir Francis
Feinstein, Dianne
Frémont, John C.
Hayakawa, S. I.
Hearst, William R.
Huerta, Dolores Fernandez
Johnson, Hiram W.
Joyner-Kersee, Jackie
Kearny, Stephen W.
King, Thomas S.
London, Jack
Mahony, Roger Michael
McPherson, Aimee S.
Murieta, Joaquín
Nixon, Richard M.
Pauling, Linus C.
Pelosi, Nancy
Reagan, Ronald W.
Ride, Sally K.
Saroyan, William
Schwarzenegger, Arnold
Serra, Junípero
Smith, Jedediah S.
Stanford, Leland
Steinbeck, John
Temple, Shirley
Warren, Earl
Woods, Tiger

Cities

Anaheim
Berkeley
Beverly Hills
Burbank
Carmel
Fresno
Hollywood
Long Beach
Los Angeles
Monterey
Oakland
Palm Springs
Palo Alto
Pasadena
Sacramento
San Bernardino
San Diego
San Francisco
San Jose
San Juan Capistrano
Santa Barbara

History

Compromise of 1850
El Camino Real
Forty-Niners
Gold rush
Guadalupe Hidalgo, Treaty of
Hispanic Americans
Mexican War
Mission life in America
Pony express
Townsend Plan
Western frontier life in America

Indian tribes

Chumash Indians
Miwok Indians
Modoc Indians
Mohave Indians
Quechan Indians
Washoe Indians
Wintun Indians
Yokuts Indians
Yurok Indians

Military installations

Camp Pendleton
Edwards Air Force Base
San Diego Marine Corps Recruit Depot
San Diego Naval Base
Vandenberg Air Force Base

National parks and monuments

Channel Islands National Park
Death Valley National Park
Joshua Tree National Park
Kings Canyon National Park
Lassen Volcanic National Park
Lava Beds National Monument
Muir Woods National Monument
Redwood National Park
Sequoia National Park
Yosemite National Park

Physical features

Cascade Range
Coast Ranges
Colorado Desert
Colorado River
Death Valley
Donner party
Great Basin
Imperial Valley
Lake Tahoe
Lassen Peak
Mojave Desert
Mount Shasta
Mount Whitney
Ribbon Falls
Sacramento River
Salton Sea
San Andreas Fault
San Joaquin River
Sierra Nevada
Sonoran Desert
Yosemite Falls

Other related articles

Alcatraz
Beach Boys
Getty Center
Golden Gate Bridge
La Brea tar pits
Monkey puzzle tree
Motion picture
Oroville Dam
Petrified forest
San Quentin

Outline

I. People
A. Population
B. Schools
C. Libraries
D. Museums

II. Visitor's guide
A. Places to visit
B. Annual events

III. Land and climate
A. Land regions
B. Coastline
C. Rivers, waterfalls, and lakes
D. Plant and animal life
E. Climate

IV. Economy
A. Natural resources
B. Service industries
C. Manufacturing
D. Agriculture
E. Mining
F. Fishing industry
G. Electric power and utilities
H. Transportation
I. Communication

V. Government
A. Constitution
B. Executive
C. Legislature
D. Courts

E. Local government
F. Revenue
G. Politics

VI. History

Questions

What point in California is the lowest point in North America?
Who was the first European to see California?
What was California's first highway?
How did the United States obtain California?
What museum in California exhibits fossils from the La Brea tar pits?
What California trees are the world's oldest living things?
Who were California's "Big Four"?
What are the two major river systems in the Central Valley of California?
Why was Sutter's Mill important in California's history?
Where did California's first newspaper begin publication?

Additional resources

Level I

Heinrichs, Ann. *California.* Children's Pr., 1998.
Margolin, Malcolm, and Montijo, Yolanda, eds. *Native Ways: California Indian Stories and Memories.* Heyday, 1995.
Pelta, Kathy. *California.* 2nd ed. Lerner, 2001.
Schanzer, Rosalyn. *Gold Fever!* National Geographic Soc., 1999.
Van Steenwyk, Elizabeth. *The California Missions.* Watts, 1995.

Level II

Grodin, Joseph R., and others. *The California State Constitution: A Reference Guide.* Greenwood, 1993.
Holliday, J. S. *Rush for Riches: Gold Fever and the Making of California.* Univ. of Calif. Pr., 1999.
Rolle, Andrew F. *California: A History.* 5th ed. Harlan Davidson, 1997.
Schoenherr, Allan A. *A Natural History of California.* 1992. Reprint. Univ. of Calif. Pr., 1995.

California, University of, is a state-supported coeducational institution with 10 campuses. Nine campuses grant bachelor's, master's, and doctor's degrees. The San Francisco campus offers only master's and doctor's degrees. The university's administrative offices are in Oakland.

The university has numerous research centers and laboratories. It operates three laboratories for the U.S. government: the Lawrence Berkeley National Laboratory in Berkeley, the Lawrence Livermore National Laboratory in Livermore, California, and the Los Alamos National Laboratory in Los Alamos, New Mexico. See the separate articles in *World Book* on these laboratories.

The university also administers a cooperative extension program, five teaching hospitals, and a number of public service programs.

The University of California was chartered in 1868. It held its first classes in 1869 in Oakland and moved to Berkeley in 1873.

The Berkeley campus offers programs in business administration, chemistry, education, engineering, environmental design, information management and systems, journalism, law, letters and science, natural resources, optometry, public health, public policy, and social welfare.

The Davis campus has programs in agricultural and environmental sciences, education, engineering, law, letters and science, management, medicine, and veterinary medicine. Its research facilities include the California Primate Research Center and a nuclear laboratory.

The Irvine campus has programs in administration, biological sciences, engineering, fine arts, humanities, medicine, physical sciences, and social sciences. It operates a medical center and has research centers in developmental biology, transportation, and other fields.

The Los Angeles campus is often called UCLA. It offers courses in arts and architecture, dentistry, education and information studies, engineering and applied sciences, law, letters and science, management, medicine, nursing, public affairs, and public health.

The Merced campus offers programs in engineering, natural sciences, social sciences, humanities, and the arts. It also has centers for research on world cultures and environmental issues.

The Riverside campus has programs in administration, engineering, humanities and social sciences, and natural and agricultural sciences. The campus also has centers for research on air pollution and on citrus and dry lands.

The San Diego and Santa Cruz campuses consist of several small liberal arts colleges. They have programs in the humanities, natural and physical sciences, and other fields. The San Diego campus has a medical school and several research centers, including the Scripps Institution of Oceanography (see **Scripps Institution of Oceanography**). The Santa Cruz campus includes a center for coastal marine studies and the headquarters and laboratories of the Lick Observatory (see **Lick Observatory**).

The San Francisco campus, devoted entirely to the health sciences, has schools of dentistry, medicine, nursing, and pharmacy. Scientists in the research centers of the campus study AIDS, arthritis, cancer, and tropical diseases.

The Santa Barbara campus provides programs in creative studies, education, engineering, environmental science and management, and letters and science. It is the only college in California that has an undergraduate program in nuclear engineering.

Critically reviewed by the University of California

California Institute of Technology is a private coeducational university in Pasadena, California. It has divisions of biology; chemistry and chemical engineering; engineering and applied science; geological and planetary sciences; humanities and social sciences; and physics, mathematics, and astronomy.

The institute, often called *Caltech,* was founded in 1891. It operates the Jet Propulsion Laboratory, the Seismological Laboratory, a marine biological laboratory in Corona del Mar, and a radio astronomy observatory near Bishop. It operates the Palomar Observatory near San Diego and is affiliated with the Big Bear Solar Observatory at Big Bear Lake. In addition, Caltech and the University of California operate the W. M. Keck Observatory on Mauna Kea, a volcano on the island of Hawaii.

Critically reviewed by California Institute of Technology

See also **Jet Propulsion Laboratory**.

California State University is the largest state-supported system of four-year and graduate-level higher education in the United States. This coeducational system consists of 23 campuses. It was established in 1960 as the California State Colleges and received its present name in 1982.

The name of each of 15 of the system's 23 campuses is California State University (CSU), followed by the location of the campus. For example, the campus in Long Beach is known as California State University, Long Beach; or CSU, Long Beach.

The 23 campuses are CSU, Bakersfield; CSU, Channel Islands; CSU, Chico; CSU, Dominguez Hills (in Carson); CSU, East Bay (in Hayward); CSU, Fresno; CSU, Fullerton; Humboldt State University (in Arcata); CSU, Long Beach; CSU, Los Angeles; CSU, Monterey Bay (in Seaside); CSU, Northridge; CSU, Sacramento; CSU, San Bernardino; San Diego State University; San Francisco State University; San Jose State University; CSU, San Marcos; Sonoma State University (in Rohnert Park); CSU, Stanislaus (in Turlock); California Maritime Academy, Vallejo; California Polytechnic State University, San Luis Obispo; and California State Polytechnic University, Pomona.

The California Maritime Academy grants bachelor's degrees. Each of the other campuses grants bachelor's and master's degrees. The campuses in Fresno, Long Beach, Los Angeles, San Diego, and San Francisco also grant some doctor's degrees in association with other universities. Instruction is offered in the liberal arts and sciences; the humanities; and the professions, including teaching, business administration, computer science, and engineering.

The system also has an International Programs section, which offers instruction in foreign countries for students enrolled at any of the system's campuses. Several of the system's campuses conduct classes in marine studies at the Moss Landing Marine Laboratory in Monterey Bay and at the Ocean Studies Institute in Long Beach. Several of the campuses also operate the Desert Studies Center near Baker. The system has its administrative offices in Long Beach.

Critically reviewed by the California State University

Californium is an artificially produced radioactive element. Its chemical symbol is Cf, and its *atomic number* (number of protons in its nucleus) is 98. Californium has 20 known *isotopes,* forms with the same number of protons but different numbers of neutrons. The most stable isotope has an *atomic mass number* (total number of neutrons and protons) of 251. That isotope has a *half-life* of 900 years—that is, due to radioactive decay, only half the atoms in a sample of californium 251 would still be atoms of that isotope after 900 years. Another isotope, californium 252, decays partly by *nuclear fission,* the splitting of the nucleus into two nearly equal parts. During fission, the nucleus releases neutrons and much energy. Because californium 252 can undergo fission, it has found uses in industry and medicine.

Californium was named after the University of California in Berkeley, where it was discovered in 1950. Four United States scientists—Stanley G. Thompson, Kenneth Street, Jr., Albert Ghiorso, and Glenn T. Seaborg—first produced californium by bombarding the element curium with helium *ions* (electrically charged atoms). Even though californium is artificially produced, scientists know many of its compounds. Richard L. Hahn

See also **Element, Chemical; Fission.**

Caligula, *kuh LIHG yuh luh* (A.D. 12-41), was a Roman emperor. He was the great-grandson of the Emperor Augustus. His parents were the Roman general Germanicus, nephew of the Emperor Tiberius; and Agrippina the Elder, granddaughter of Augustus. Caligula was born Gaius Caesar Augustus Germanicus on Aug. 31, A.D. 12, in Antium, near Rome. As a child, he wore military boots, and his father's soldiers nicknamed him *Caligula* (Little Boot).

Caligula succeeded Tiberius as emperor in A.D. 37. At first, he was a popular ruler. But after a serious illness early in his reign, his strange and brutal behavior led people to believe he was insane. Caligula spent money extravagantly, quarreled with the Roman Senate, and banished or executed many senators. He planned to invade Britain but abandoned the campaign on the way there. Caligula worshiped his sister Drusilla as a goddess after her death. He was especially hostile to Jews and ordered that a statue of himself be placed in the Jewish Temple in Jerusalem. On Jan. 24, A.D. 41, he was killed in a conspiracy led by the commander of his bodyguard. Robert Gurval

Caliper, *KAL uh puhr,* is an instrument much like a geometry compass. It is used to take small measurements. The legs, usually curved, are joined at one end by a rivet or screw that can open and close them. *Outside calipers* measure the outside of pipes, boards, and

Types of calipers

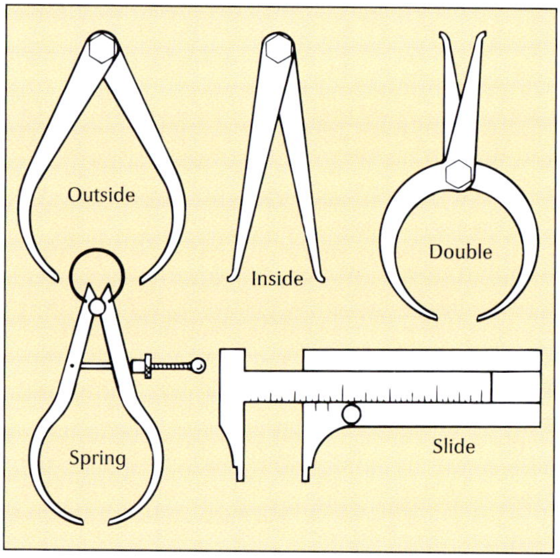

other objects. The open ends are fitted against the object. The legs curve inward so they can circle round objects. *Inside calipers* measure the inside of pipes and other open objects. The legs curve outward. A *double caliper* combines the inside and outside calipers as shown in the accompanying illustration. *Spring calipers* have a spring to automatically open their legs. A *micrometer caliper* is a type of *slide caliper* that has a fine, threaded micrometer screw and can measure to $\frac{1}{10,000}$ inch (0.00254 millimeter). See also **Micrometer; Vernier.**

Todd I. Blue

Calisthenics, *KAL uhs THEHN ihks,* are exercises that help strengthen and stretch body muscles. Most calisthenics involve slow, rhythmic movements and can be performed without special equipment.

Calla, *KAL uh,* is a flowerlike herb with a white, yellow, or pink leaf shaped like a funnel or bell. The large, beautiful leaf is often mistaken for the flower. But the real flowers are tiny blossoms inside the flowerlike leaf. The North American calla is called *marsh calla,* or *water*

WORLD BOOK illustration by Christabel King

The calla has a large white, yellow, or pink leaf often mistaken for the flower. The true flowers are inside the leaf.

arum. This little plant has heart-shaped leaves about 2 inches (5 centimeters) long. It is closely related to the jack-in-the-pulpit. The marsh calla grows wild in marshy places. The plant is also cultivated as a crop along the edges of ponds. In Lapland, the people grind up the root of the marsh calla to make flour for bread.

The most common tropical calla comes from the banks of the Nile River in Egypt. It is called *calla lily, Ethiopian lily,* or *common calla.* It has a 10-inch (25-centimeter) white leaf. The calla lily causes a burning irritation to the mouth and stomach if eaten. David A. Francko

Scientific classification. The calla is in the arum family, Araceae. The common calla is *Zantedeschia aethiopica.* The water arum is *Calla palustris.*

See also **Arum; Jack-in-the-pulpit.**

Callaghan, *KAL uh huhn,* **James** (1912-2005), served as prime minister of the United Kingdom from 1976 to 1979. He succeeded Harold Wilson as prime minister and Labour Party leader after Wilson resigned. During Callaghan's term as prime minister, the United Kingdom faced inflation and major labor strikes. In 1979, the Conservative Party defeated the Labour Party in a general parliamentary election, and Conservative Party leader Margaret Thatcher replaced Callaghan as prime minister. Callaghan resigned as Labour Party leader in 1980.

Leonard James Callaghan was born on March 27, 1912, in Portsmouth, England. In 1945, he was elected to Parliament from Cardiff, Wales. From 1964 until 1967, he served as chancellor of the exchequer, the head of the British Treasury. From 1967 to 1970, he was in charge of the Home Office and responsible for British policy toward Northern Ireland. He was foreign secretary from 1974 until he became prime minister. He retired from Parliament in 1985. Callaghan died on March 26, 2005. Richard Rose

Callaghan, *KAL uh han,* **Morley** (1903-1990), was a Canadian novelist. His works deal mainly with ethical issues and have an urban setting, usually in Montreal or Toronto. His strongest characters are social outcasts who have great moral insight.

Callaghan's first novel, *Strange Fugitive,* was published in 1928. His novels of the 1930's, set against the Great Depression, are his best known, including *Such Is My Beloved* (1934), *They Shall Inherit the Earth* (1935), and *More Joy in Heaven* (1937). In 1951, Callaghan won the Governor General's Award for *The Loved and the Lost,* a novel that explores the relationship between innocence and guilt. Callaghan's later novels include *The Many Colored Coat* (1960), *A Fine and Private Place* (1975), *A Time for Judas* (1983), and *A Wild Old Man on the Road* (1988). *That Summer in Paris* (1963) describes his life in Paris in the late 1920's, and his association with the writers Ernest Hemingway and F. Scott Fitzgerald. He was born in Toronto on Sept. 22, 1903. Laurie R. Ricou

Callao, *kah YAH oh* (pop. 640,000), is one of the largest cities of Peru and the country's chief port. About three-fourths of Peru's imports and one-fourth of its exports pass through Callao's harbor. Callao lies on the Pacific Ocean, about 8 miles (13 kilometers) west of Lima. For location, see **Peru** (political map). Callao and Lima are part of a large metropolitan area that includes more than half of Peru's industries. Callao's chief industries are shipbuilding and fish processing.

The Spaniards founded Callao in 1537. Through the years, earthquakes have severely damaged the city, but the people have always rebuilt it. During the middle and late 1900's, many migrants built crude houses outside the city. Peru's government encouraged construction of improved housing in this area. David J. Robinson

Callas, *KAL uhs,* **Maria** (1923-1977), became one of the world's best-known opera sopranos. She gained world fame for her vocal virtuosity, dramatic intensity, and fiery temperament.

Wide World

Maria Callas

Callas was born in New York City of Greek parents on Dec. 2, 1923, making her both a U.S. and Greek citizen. Her full name was Cecilia Sophia Anna Maria Kalogeropoulos. At 13, she returned with her parents to Greece, and won a scholarship at the Royal Conservatory in Athens. At 17, she her made professional debut at the Athens Opera in *Tosca.* After major triumphs in Italian opera houses, she made her U.S. debut in Chicago in 1954. Callas sang the leading role in Vincenzo Bellini's *Norma* and was a great success. The operas she recorded included *Norma, I Puritani, Tosca, La Bohème,* and *La Traviata.* She gave up her U.S. citizenship in 1966. She died on Sept. 16, 1977. Martin Bernheimer

Calley, William L., Jr. See **My Lai Massacre.**

Calligraphy, *kuh LIHG ruh fee,* is the art of beautiful writing. In every literate culture, handwriting has been used to preserve sacred texts for future generations.

Distinctive variations of calligraphy were developed in different regions and periods of time. The shapes of the letters depended on the tools that were used to make them. In Europe and the Near East, scribes wrote with quills and reeds cut to a chisellike shape. Writing was done on prepared animal skins until paper was in-

Calligraphy is the art of beautiful handwriting. Chinese calligraphy is closely related to Chinese painting. The same type of brush is used in both art forms. The calligraphy pictured here shows Chinese characters that correspond to the words *The World Book Dictionary.*

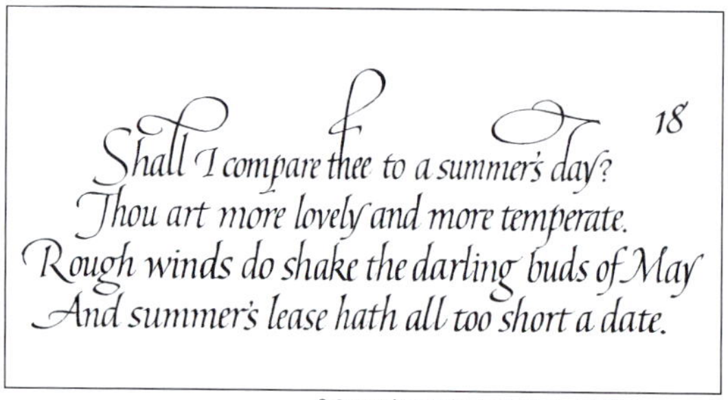
18
Shall I compare thee to a summer's day?
Thou art more lovely and more temperate.
Rough winds do shake the darling buds of May
And summer's lease hath all too short a date.

Styles of calligraphy range from the traditional writing style shown above to the more modern style shown below.

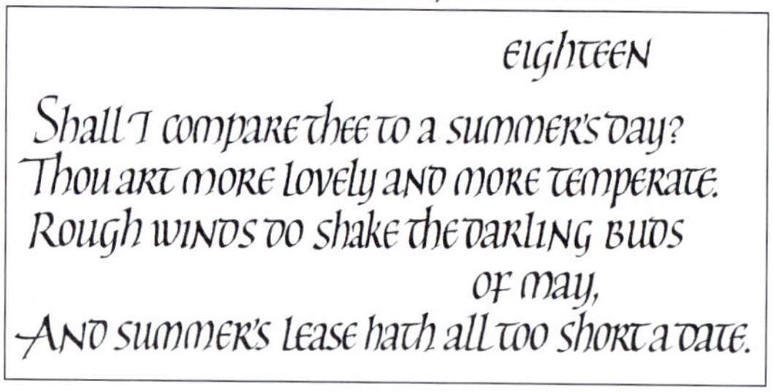
EIGHTEEN
Shall I compare thee to a summer's day?
Thou art more lovely and more temperate.
Rough winds do shake the darling buds
of may,
And summer's lease hath all too short a date.

troduced from Asia. In later periods, manuscripts were adorned with decorated initials in gold and *luminous* (glowing) colors, leading to the term *illuminated manuscript.*

In Asia, calligraphers wrote with a brush on paper, the shapes of the forms depending on the pressure and movement of the brush. Arabic calligraphy has been influenced by Islam, which considers the copying of the holy book, the Qur'ān, a sacred activity. In Western countries, calligraphy changed after movable type was invented in the mid-1400's. By the 1500's, printers had assumed many of the tasks of book production formerly done by hand. Scribes worked closely with printers to make type faces.

Modern calligraphers work at many levels. Some are professionals who create custom lettering for advertising, book jackets, magazines, greeting cards, and television. Others interpret poems or prose and create books prized by collectors. Many amateur calligraphers enjoy calligraphy as a hobby, creating mementos for family and friends. Societies for calligraphy provide workshops, plan exhibits, and present educational programs.

Annie Cicale

Related articles. See **Alphabet** and the articles on each letter of the alphabet. See also:

Book (History)
China (Painting; picture: Fine handwriting)
Handwriting
Hieroglyphics (pictures)
Illuminated manuscript
Islamic art (Calligraphy; picture: Islamic painting)
Library (History)
Manuscript
Painting (Asian painting)

Calliope, in mythology. See **Muses.**

Calliope is a musical instrument that consists of a set of tuned whistles controlled by either a keyboard or a mechanical playing system like that of a player piano. The whistles are sounded by the release of either steam or compressed air, in the manner of an organ pipe. The calliope produces loud music and is generally associated with excursion boats and circuses. Decorated wagons housed calliopes in circus parades. Joshua C. Stoddard, an American inventor, patented the first practical calliope in 1855. He built the first instrument in 1856.

Circus people pronounce the word *KAL ee ohp.*

Tom Kinney

A calliope has a set of tuned whistles that produce loud music. Decorated wagons housed the calliope in circus parades.

Others usually say *kuh LY uh pee,* as in the name of Calliope, the goddess of epic poetry in Greek mythology.

Fred Dahlinger, Jr.

Callisto, *kuh LIHS toh,* is a large moon of Jupiter. It is almost as large as the planet Mercury. It is one of the most heavily cratered bodies in the solar system. Its surface is covered with craters of all sizes caused by the impact of asteroids and comets.

More than 4 billion years of bombardment have darkened Callisto's icy surface. The biggest impacts cracked the surface to form huge bull's-eye patterns. The surface is blanketed by dark dirt that accumulated when icy crater rims and cliffs crumbled away.

Callisto is about half rock and half ice by weight. However, it may not have a distinct rocky core. As Callisto formed and evolved, it may not have became hot enough to melt the ice so that gravity could completely

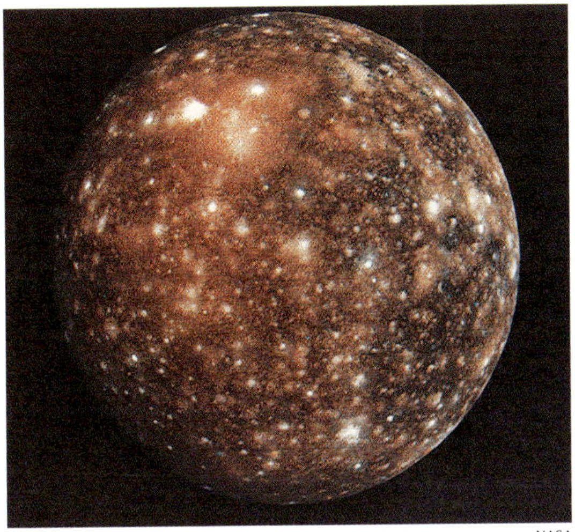

NASA

Callisto, a moon of Jupiter, is covered with craters produced when asteroids and comets struck its icy surface. Beneath the surface may be an ocean of salty liquid water.

separate the rock into a core. The satellite has a carbon dioxide atmosphere that is only slightly denser than the near-vacuum of outer space.

Magnetic measurements taken by spacecraft indicate that Callisto acts as if it is covered by a shell that is *conducting* (carrying) electric current. Scientists suspect that the "shell" is actually an ocean of salty liquid water beneath the surface. Scientists are trying to determine how such an ocean could have formed and why it would not have frozen by now.

Callisto has a diameter of 2,996 miles (4,821 kilometers). It orbits Jupiter every 16.7 days at a distance of 1,170,000 miles (1,883,000 kilometers). The Italian astronomer Galileo discovered Callisto in 1610.

William B. McKinnon

See also **Jupiter** (Galilean satellites); **Satellite** (Inert satellites; picture: Callisto).

Callot, *ka LOH,* **Jacques,** *zhahk* (1592-1635), was a major French printmaker. He made over 1,400 etchings of beggars, court festivals, landscapes, theater performances, battle scenes, religious subjects, and fashionable aristocrats. Many of his etchings are crowded with tiny figures and amusing details. Callot also made important improvements in the technique of etching.

Callot was born in Nancy, in the historical province of Lorraine, and studied etching in Italy. In 1614, he became an artist for the famous Medici family of Florence (see **Medici**). Callot returned to Lorraine in 1621, during the Thirty Years' War between Protestants and Roman Catholics. He made a series of 18 etchings that showed the effects of the war on the province. These etchings make up one of his most famous works, *The Miseries and Misfortunes of War* (1633).

Elizabeth Broun

National Gallery of Art, Washington, D.C., Rosenwald Collection

A Callot etching shows the artist's skill in portraying subjects in great detail. This 1621 etching shows two characters in a type of comic Italian drama called *commedia dell'arte.*

Callus, *KAL uhs,* is a hardening and thickening of the skin. It often forms on the feet and hands. Poorly fitted shoes can cause calluses on the heels and soles of the feet. A *corn* is a special kind of callus that is usually found on the feet (see **Corn**). Hand calluses result from prolonged rubbing on a hard object, such as a rake or a tennis racket. Many calluses can be treated by soaking them in water and then applying a salicylic-acid solution or other softening preparation. Rubbing calluses with scratchy pads or sponges also helps.

A substance called a *callus* forms around broken bones when they begin to mend. This substance is different from a skin callus.

Paul R. Bergstresser

Calms, Regions of, are places in the atmosphere which usually have little or no wind. Several areas of the earth's surface are known as regions of frequent calms. These regions of calms include the northern and southern *horse latitudes,* the northern and southern *subpolar regions,* and the equatorial *doldrums.* All of these calms regions may be disrupted by sudden storms.

The horse latitudes are regions of calms that lie at about 30° north latitude and 30° south latitude, between the oceanic belts of winds called the *prevailing westerlies* and the *trade winds* (see **Prevailing westerly; Trade wind**). In these areas, the air is gently sinking from high altitudes toward the earth's surface. The sinking of the air results in areas of high barometric pressure and weak winds. These areas shift farther north when it is summer in the Northern Hemisphere. They shift farther south when it is summer in the Southern Hemisphere.

The horse latitudes coincide with the *subtropical maritime anticyclones,* or *subtropical highs.* Subtropical highs are large high-pressure areas that occur over the oceans. Changes in their size, shape, position, or direction influence weather conditions throughout the world.

Subpolar regions. The general circulation of air causes cold air over the North and South poles to sink, forming high-pressure areas known as the *polar anticyclones.* But since this cold region has frequent storms, periods of calms are not so persistent as in warmer regions of calms.

The doldrums are ocean regions centered slightly north of the equator. One area of doldrums lies in the Pacific Ocean extending westward from Central America and South America to the Philippines. The other area of equatorial doldrums lies in the Atlantic Ocean between South America and Africa. The trade winds that blow from both the northeast and the southeast toward these areas of doldrums bring masses of air into the regions. The air masses are forced upward after being heated in the tropics. This causes a belt of low pressure to form. Tropical storms may occur at the edges of this belt. This belt moves north and south with the sun as the horse latitudes do.

During the days of sailing ships, sea captains avoided the doldrums areas because of the uncertain winds and heavy downpours. Sailing ships might lie becalmed in these regions for weeks. Mark A. Cane

See also **Horse latitudes; Weather** (Weather systems).

Calorie is a unit that is used to measure heat energy in the metric system of measurement. A calorie is the amount of energy that is needed to raise the temperature of one gram of water by one Celsius degree. The word *calorie* comes from a Latin word that means *heat.* A *kilocalorie,* also called a *kilogram calorie,* is equal to 1,000 calories.

Many chemical *reactions* (changes) produce heat. Scientists measure the amount of heat produced with an instrument called a *calorimeter.* One of the most important uses of the calorimeter is to measure the amount of heat given off by different foods when they burn. This measurement tells how much energy a certain food yields when it is completely used by the body. Food scientists measure the heat produced in the calorimeter in kilogram calories, but they report the measurements as calories.

Another metric unit that is used to measure heat energy is the *joule.* One joule equals 0.239 calorie. The *British thermal unit* (Btu) is used to measure heat in the inch-pound system of measurement, which is customarily used in the United States. One Btu equals 251.996 calories.

Heating engineers make their estimates in calories or Btu's when designing furnaces, boilers, steam turbines, and other machinery. Air-conditioning and refrigeration engineers also use calories or Btu's when designing cooling systems. Gregory Benford

See also **British thermal unit; Heat; Joule; Nutrition.**

Calumet. See **Peace pipe.**

Calvary, called Golgotha in Hebrew, is the spot outside ancient Jerusalem where Jesus Christ was crucified. No one knows the actual site, but tradition places it where the Church of the Holy Sepulcher now stands.

Stanley K. Stowers

See also **Jerusalem** (Holy places).

Calvert, Cecilius (1605?-1675), also called Cecil Calvert, was an Englishman who founded the colony of Maryland. He was also known as the second Lord Baltimore. Calvert inherited the proprietorship of Maryland and the right to the colony's charter from his father, George Calvert, who died in 1632.

The charter granted Calvert "kingly" powers in the colony, but it required him to consult with a colonial assembly. Although the majority of Maryland's people were Protestants, Calvert was a Roman Catholic. Calvert drafted a law to grant religious freedom to all people in the colony, and Maryland's Assembly passed the law in 1649. The law became the first statute for religious freedom in the American Colonies.

Calvert was born in the county of Kent in England. He never visited Maryland. But his brother, Leonard Calvert, lived in the colony, and Cecilius appointed him as the colony's governor. Edward C. Papenfuse

See also **Maryland** (History).

Calvert, Charles (1637-1715), the third Lord Baltimore, was an Englishman who became proprietor of the colony of Maryland. He served as governor of the colony from 1661 to 1675. That year, he succeeded his father, Cecilius Calvert, as the colony's proprietor. Because Charles Calvert was a Roman Catholic, the Protestants in Maryland were suspicious of his rule, and Calvert quarreled with the Maryland Assembly over the extent of his powers. In 1691, Maryland became a royal colony, and the English Crown began to appoint the colony's governors. But Calvert kept his property rights until his death. In 1715, the Crown returned the charter to the Calvert family but retained the right to approve nominations for governor. Edward C. Papenfuse

Calvert, George (1580?-1632), the first Lord Baltimore, was an Englishman who played an important part in establishing the colony of Maryland. He was a member of the Virginia Company from 1609 to 1620 and received a large proprietary grant in Newfoundland in 1620. However, his colony there did not prosper because of the climate, and in 1629 he appealed to King Charles I for land farther south. Calvert had been converted to Roman Catholicism in 1625 and wanted to provide a refuge for English Catholics. In 1632, Charles granted him the proprietorship of Maryland, but he died before the king signed the charter. The charter rights passed to his son, Cecilius (see **Calvert, Cecilius**).

Calvert was born in Kipling, in Yorkshire, England. He served King James I as secretary of state and in the Privy Council. He was also a member of Parliament. Calvert was made Lord Baltimore in 1625. Edward C. Papenfuse

Calvin, John (1509-1564), was one of the chief leaders of the Protestant Reformation. Calvin's brilliant mind, powerful preaching, many books and large correspondence, and capacity for organization and administration made him a dominant figure of the Reformation. He was especially influential in Switzerland, England, Scotland, and colonial North America.

His life. Calvin was born in Noyon, France, near Compiègne. His father was a lawyer for the Roman Catholic Church. Calvin was educated in Paris, Orléans, and Bourges. After his father's death in 1531, he studied Greek and Latin at the University of Paris. Thus, Calvin's education reflected the influence of the liberal and humanistic Renaissance. Unlike several other Reformation leaders, Calvin was probably never ordained a priest.

By 1533, Calvin had declared himself a Protestant. In 1534, he settled in Basel, Switzerland. There, he published the first edition of his *Institutes of the Christian Religion* (1536). This book achieved immediate recognition for Calvin, and he expanded it throughout his life. The book sets forth Calvin's basic ideas on religion and is a masterpiece of Reformation thought.

In 1536, Calvin was persuaded to become a leader of Geneva's first group of Protestant pastors. In 1538, Geneva's leaders reacted against the strict doctrines

Detail of a portrait by an unknown painter of the 1500's; Bibliothèques Municipales, Geneva, Switzerland

John Calvin

of the Protestant pastors, and Calvin and several other clergymen were banished. Later that year, Calvin became pastor of a French refugee Protestant church in Strasbourg, Germany. He was deeply influenced by the older German Protestant leaders of Strasbourg, especially Martin Bucer. Calvin adapted Bucer's ideas on church government and worship.

Geneva lacked able religious and political leadership. The Geneva city council begged Calvin to return, and he did so in 1541. From then until his death, Calvin was the dominant personality in Geneva.

Calvinism. From its beginning in 1517, the Reformation brought religious and political opposition from the Catholic church and from civil rulers. By 1546, many Protestants in Germany, Switzerland, and France were insisting that the people—not just kings and bishops—should share in political and religious policymaking. This idea influenced Calvin and his followers in France, England, Scotland, and the Netherlands. Calvin's French followers were called *Huguenots.* English Protestants who were influenced by his teaching were called *Puritans.*

The Calvinists developed political theories that supported constitutional government, representative government, the right of people to change their government, and the separation of civil government from church government. Calvinists of the 1500's intended these ideas to apply only to the aristocracy. But during the 1600's, more democratic concepts arose, especially in England and later in colonial America.

Calvin agreed with other early Reformation leaders on such basic religious teachings as the superiority of faith over good works, the Bible as the basis of all Christian teachings, and the universal priesthood of all believers. According to the concept of universal priesthood, all believers were considered priests. Catholic priests were set apart from lay people by their power to perform the sacraments.

Calvin also declared that people were saved solely by the grace of God, and that only people called the *Elect* would be saved. Only God knew for sure who the Elect were. For Calvin, however, those who believed in his teachings and were not public sinners were accepted as church members in Geneva. Calvin expanded the idea that Christianity was intended to reform all of society. He lectured and wrote on politics, social problems, and international issues as part of Christian responsibility.

Many of Calvin's ideas were controversial, but no other reformer did so much to force people to think about Christian social ethics. From this ethical concern and Bucer's ideas, Calvin developed the pattern of church government that today is called *presbyterian.* Calvin organized the church government distinct from civil government, though the two governments often cooperated with each other. He was the first Protestant leader in Europe to gain partial church independence from the state. Peter W. Williams

Related articles in *World Book* include:

Foreordination	Presbyterians
Huguenots	Protestantism (History)
Hymn (History)	Puritans
Predestination	Reformation

Additional resources

Cottret, Bernard. *Calvin: A Biography.* Eerdmans, 2000.
Naphy, William G. *Calvin and the Consolidation of the Genevan Reformation.* 1994. Reprint. Westminster John Knox, 2003.

Calypso, *kuh LIHP soh,* is a type of music that originated on the island of Trinidad, in the Caribbean Sea. It is also popular in other Caribbean countries. Calypso combines features of African music, Spanish musical styles, and American jazz and rhythm and blues. The origin of the term *calypso* is uncertain.

Characteristics. Calypso songs are in 2/4 or 4/4 time, with strong accents off the beat. They are usually accompanied by a *steel band,* a group of drums made from steel oil containers and played with sticks. Guitars, flutes, saxophones, and drums may also be used.

Most calypso songs are improvisations based on standard melodic types. The lyrics of a calypso song are extremely important. Expert calypso singers are clever at choosing words and making up rhymes on the spot. The lyrics may express a personal philosophy or comment on local or world events, social conditions, or gossip. Women are a favorite subject.

Development. Calypso originated in singing competitions held by African slaves during annual carnivals. After the United Kingdom abolished slavery in Trinidad in the 1830's, the competitions expanded and became more popular. Calypso was originally sung in a French-Creole dialect called *patois* (pronounced *PAT wah*). Singers began using English during the early 1900's. Singers may adopt colorful names. A performer called the Mighty Sparrow became one of the most popular calypso singers of the middle and late 1900's.

Calypso has become known outside the Caribbean since the 1920's and 1930's, when record companies recorded many calypso singers. Such songs as "Day-O" or "Banana Boat Song" and "Mary Ann" became popular in the United States. Valerie Woodring Goertzen

Camacho, Manuel Ávila. See Ávila Camacho, Manuel.

Cambodia, *kam BOH dee uh,* is a country in Southeast Asia. It is sometimes called Kampuchea. Most Cambodians live on the fertile plains created by the floodwaters of the Mekong River, or near the Tonle Sap (Great Lake) and Tonle Sap River northwest of Phnom Penh. Phnom Penh is Cambodia's capital.

Cambodia is chiefly a farming nation. Its relatively flat land, plentiful water, and tropical climate are ideal for growing rice. By Western standards, its farms are small, and the farmers have few modern tools. The country has few factories and imports most of the manufactured goods it needs.

About a thousand years ago, Cambodia was the center of a great empire of the Khmer people, who controlled much of the Southeast Asian mainland. The ruins of Angkor, the capital of the Khmer empire, feature magnificent sculpture and architecture.

Government. Cambodia is a monarchy with a king as head of state. But the king has only ceremonial powers. A prime minister heads the government. Cambodia's legislature consists of a 122-member National Assembly and a 61-member Senate. The voters elect the Assembly members. Party leaders and the king appointed the first members of the Senate, which was established in 1999.

People. Most of Cambodia's people are Khmer, one of the oldest ethnic groups in Southeast Asia. They speak the Khmer language, which has its own alphabet.

Most Khmer are farmers, laborers, or soldiers. Vietnamese make up the second largest ethnic group in Cambodia. A majority of Cambodians are Buddhists.

Most Cambodians live in villages of 100 to 400 people and work on rice fields near the villages. Rice and fish are the main foods. About one quarter of Cambodian men and half of the women cannot read or write. Some parts of the country do not have schools.

Land. Low mountains border Cambodia, except in the southeast and along part of the coast. The great Mekong River flows south from Laos through Cambodia and enters the South China Sea through Vietnam. Fertile plains cover about a third of the land, and forests cover much of the rest. During the dry season, the Tonle Sap River flows southeast from the shallow Tonle Sap and joins the Mekong at Phnom Penh. During the *monsoon* (rainy) season, the river flows in the opposite direction. The river does this because floods and melted snow from the Mekong's source in Tibet make the river rise to a level higher than that of the lake.

The temperature of Phnom Penh averages about 85 °F (29 °C) throughout the year. The rainy season lasts from May to November. The coast receives nearly 200 inches (510 centimeters) of rainfall a year, but Phnom Penh gets less than 60 inches (150 centimeters).

Economy. Historically, Cambodia's economy has been based on agriculture. Today, agriculture remains important, and most of Cambodia's people are farmers. However, since the mid-1990's, a large percentage of

Cambodia

WORLD BOOK maps

Facts in brief

Capital: Phnom Penh.
Official language: Khmer.
Official name: Kingdom of Cambodia.
Area: 69,898 mi² (181,035 km²). *Greatest distances*—east-west, 350 mi (563 km); north-south, 280 mi (451 km). *Coastline*—220 mi. (354 km).
Population: *Estimated 2006 population*—13,698,000; density, 196 per mi² (76 per km²); distribution, 84 percent rural, 16 percent urban. *1998 census*—11,437,656.
Chief products: *Agriculture*—rice, rubber, soybeans. *Manufacturing and processing*—cement, plywood, processed rice and fish, textiles.
Flag: Horizontal stripes of blue, red, and blue. A white temple appears on the red stripe. See **Flag** (Flags of Asia and the Pacific).
National anthem: "Our Country."
Money: *Basic unit*—riel.

Cambodia's income has come from garment manufacturing. Tourism also has grown in importance. Still, the country relies heavily on foreign aid.

Until the 1970's, Cambodia's farm production was usually high enough to provide food for the Cambodian people and also exports to other countries. Corn and rice were the main crops. Large quantities of rubber also were produced. Many farms and rubber plantations were destroyed during the Vietnam War and civil wars in Cambodia. The country did not regain the ability to produce enough rice for its own needs until the 1990's.

In the 1950's, Cambodia developed industries that make cement, paper, plywood, processed foods, rubber tires, and textiles. However, the wars crippled many of these industries. Since the mid-1990's, the production of many of these goods, especially textiles, has grown considerably. But Cambodia still lacks money for industrial development.

Cambodia's only deepwater port, Kompong Som, handles most of the foreign trade. Fighting in Cambodia badly damaged the roads. The railroad system links Phnom Penh with Kompong Som and Battambang. Phnom Penh, Siem Reap, and Battambang have airports.

History. Cambodia has been a monarchy during most of its history. About A.D. 100, people in the southern part of what is now Cambodia established the kingdom of Funan. This kingdom became one of the greatest early powers of Southeast Asia. Funan gradually lost its influence. By A.D. 600 a new power, Chenla, had arisen north of Funan. The kingdom of Chenla broke up in the 700's.

From the 800's to the 1400's, the Khmer controlled a great Hindu-Buddhist kingdom in Cambodia. Its capital was Angkor. The Khmer built hundreds of beautiful stone temples at Angkor and elsewhere in the empire. They also built hospitals, irrigation canals, reservoirs, and roads. The Khmer empire reached its peak during the 1100's, when it took over much of the land that is now Laos, Thailand, and Vietnam. Costly construction projects, changing trade routes, quarrels within the royal family, and wars with the Thai weakened the Khmer empire. Thai forces captured Angkor in 1431, and the Khmer abandoned the city. But an independent Khmer kingdom, with its capital near what is now Phnom Penh, survived another 400 years.

In the middle to late 1800's, France took control of Vietnam and Cambodia. The region became known as

Bruce Coleman Inc.

A Cambodian village consists of thatch houses built on stilts to provide protection from rising waters. Frequent floods occur during the rainy season, from May to November.

French Indochina. Thai and Japanese forces occupied Cambodia from 1941 to 1945, during World War II. After the war, Cambodia moved toward independence. France recognized Cambodia's independence in 1953.

In 1955, King Norodom Sihanouk gave up the throne to take a more active role in politics. He took the title of prince, and became prime minister in 1955 and head of state in 1960.

In March 1970, two members of Sihanouk's government—Lieutenant General Lon Nol and Prince Sisowath Sirik Matak—overthrew Sihanouk while he was out of the country. In October 1970, the government of Prime Minister Lon Nol abolished the monarchy and proclaimed Cambodia a republic. Lon Nol dissolved the legislature in 1971. The next year, he made himself president and assumed full control of the government.

During the 1950's and 1960's, Cambodia had declared itself neutral in the struggle between Communist and non-Communist nations. But the United States and South Vietnam charged that North Vietnam had troops and supplies in Cambodia for use in the Vietnam War. In 1969, U.S. planes began to bomb Communist targets in Cambodia. In April 1970, after Sihanouk was overthrown, U.S. and South Vietnamese troops entered Cambodia to search for the Communist supply bases (see **Vietnam War**). The U.S. troops left Cambodia at the end of June, but the Vietnamese Communists had withdrawn deeper into Cambodia. By the end of 1970, all of Cambodia was at war. Government forces fought the Communists with the help of South Vietnamese troops and U.S. military aid. The U.S. bombers ended their raids in August 1973, but ground fighting continued.

Meanwhile, Cambodian Communists called Khmer Rouge (Red Khmers) were engaging in full-scale warfare against the country's non-Communist government. In April 1975, they took control of Cambodia. Neighboring South Vietnam and Laos fell to Communist forces the same year. Soon after, North and South Vietnam reunited into the single nation of Vietnam.

The Khmer Rouge Communists, led by Pol Pot, took control of the government and renamed the country Democratic Kampuchea. They forced most people in cities and towns to move to supervised work camps in rural areas. They abolished religion and the use of money. The government took over all businesses and farms. It killed large numbers of Cambodians, including many former government officials and educated people. In addition, a sharp decline in Cambodia's agricultural production caused severe food shortages. More than 1 ½ million Cambodians died as a result of execution, starvation, disease, or hard labor under the Khmer Rouge. Many others fled to Thailand and other countries.

In 1977, disputes led to fighting between Cambodia and Vietnam. In January 1979, Vietnamese troops and allied Cambodian Communists won control of most of Cambodia and overthrew the Khmer Rouge government. The victorious Cambodians renamed the country the People's Republic of Kampuchea. The Vietnamese supported the new government and gained much influence in the country. Strict control of the lives of the people continued under the new government.

The Khmer Rouge continued to fight the Vietnamese and their Cambodian allies. Non-Communist groups also joined in the fighting. In 1982, the non-Communists and the Khmer Rouge formed a coalition. Norodom Sihanouk became head of the coalition. The fighting forced hundreds of thousands of Cambodians into refugee camps during the 1980's.

In the late 1980's, the government took steps to reduce its control of the economy. These included allowing Cambodians to own small businesses and farms. Vietnam gradually withdrew its troops from Cambodia and said in 1989 that it had completed the withdrawal.

Also in 1989, Cambodia's government and opposition

Photoreporters, Inc.

Khmer Rouge Communists entered Phnom Penh in 1975, *shown here.* They seized the capital and took control of the government after defeating the non-Communists in a war.

groups began negotiations to resolve the war. In October 1991, they signed a United Nations-sponsored peace treaty. Under the treaty, the United Nations (UN) supervised the Cambodian government through a transition to democracy. The UN worked with a 12-member Supreme National Council made up of members of the former government and the three opposition groups.

In May 1993, democratic, multiparty elections were held for a 120-member assembly. A transitional government was formed by the parties that won the most seats. It governed until a constitution was put into effect in September 1993. A new democratically elected government headed by two prime ministers was established. The office of king was restored as a ceremonial position. Sihanouk, who had been head of state in the transitional government, became king.

The Khmer Rouge, though it had signed the UN peace treaty, boycotted the elections and did not join the new government. By the late 1990's, most of the group's leaders surrendered or were arrested. Pol Pot died in 1998. By 1999, the Khmer Rouge movement ended.

Relations between Hun Sen and Prince Norodom Ranariddh, the two prime ministers, were strained. In July 1997, Hun Sen forced Ranariddh from office.

Elections for the National Assembly were held in July 1998. Hun Sen's Cambodian People's Party won the most seats, and he remained prime minister. In 1999, Cambodia established a new Senate. In National Assembly elections in 2003, the Cambodian People's Party again won the most seats, but not enough seats to govern alone. In 2004, after months of political struggle, the parties of Hun Sen and Norodom Ranariddh agreed to a power-sharing government, with Hun Sen as prime minister.

Also in 2004, King Sihanouk gave up the throne because of poor health. He was replaced by his son Norodom Sihamoni. In 2006, King Sihamoni appointed Cambodian and international judges to a special court, backed by the UN, to try surviving Khmer Rouge leaders.

Judy L. Ledgerwood

Related articles in *World Book* include:

Angkor	Lon Nol	Phnom Penh
Hun Sen	Mekong River	Pol Pot
Indochina	Norodom	
Khmer Rouge	Sihanouk	

Additional resources

Gottesman, Evan R. *Cambodia After the Khmer Rouge.* Yale, 2002.
Green, Robert. *Cambodia.* Lucent Bks., 2003. Younger readers.

Cambrian Period was a time in Earth's history that lasted from about 543 million to 490 million years ago. Geologists first identified rocks of this age in Wales (once called Cambria) in the early 1800's. The Cambrian Period marks the start of the Paleozoic Era, a time when prehistoric life left behind an abundance of fossils.

The oldest fossils of animals date from the Ediacaran Period, the time just before the Cambrian. Creatures of the Ediacaran Period were mostly simple, soft-bodied animals. Eventually, more complex animals began burrowing deep into *sediments* (accumulated small bits of dirt and rock) on the sea floor. The earliest evidence of this activity marks the start of the Cambrian Period.

Many major types of animals first appear in fossils from the early Cambrian Period. Scientists often refer to this sudden, dramatic increase in the variety of animal fossils as the *Cambrian Explosion.* During the Cambrian Explosion, animals *evolved* (developed gradually) into many new forms and spread throughout all of Earth's oceans. They also began interacting with one another and their environment in more complex ways. Animals began eating other animals, growing skeletons for protection, and burrowing into sea-floor sediments for food and shelter. The first reefs, built by early sponges and bacteria, also formed.

Marine life dominated in the Cambrian Period. No fossil evidence indicates that plants or animals lived outside of the oceans at this time. But genetic studies have suggested that certain plants and fungi lived on land. *Trilobites,* sea animals related to modern crabs, lobsters, and insects, rank as the most abundant Cambrian fossil. Trilobites flourished throughout the Cambrian Period.

During the Cambrian Period, most of Earth's land lay in the Southern Hemisphere. The land consisted mainly of several large continents formed earlier in the breakup of a giant land mass called Rodinia. These continents continued to spread apart, and what is now North America drifted northward, crossing the equator in parts. Global sea levels rose through the Cambrian Period until most of the land was covered by oceans. The climate was generally warm, and ice probably did not cover Earth's poles as it does today.

The extinction of certain species of trilobites and other animals marks the end of the Cambrian Period. No major animal groups disappeared, however, and there was no widespread global extinction like those that mark the end of many other periods in Earth's history.

Stephen Q. Dornbos

Cambridge, *KAYM brihj* (pop. 108,879), is a city in England and the home of Cambridge University. Cambridge lies on the River Cam, about 50 miles (80 kilometers) north of London. It has rapidly growing manufacturing industries on its outskirts, many of them closely associated with the university's famous scientific laboratories.

Cambridge was a fort in Roman times, and Roman ruins still stand there. In the 1200's, monks from Ely established the nucleus of the present university. Cambridge University is noted for scholarship in modern literature and science, especially nuclear physics and astronomy (see **Cambridge University**).

The university's buildings are noted for their fine architecture. The city has many open spaces, gardens, and old bridges. The Cambridge American Cemetery, where United States World War II military casualties are buried, is just west of Cambridge. Peter R. Mounfield

Cambridge, *KAYM brihj,* Massachusetts (pop. 101,355), stands on the Charles River, opposite Boston (see **Massachusetts** [political map]). The city is famous for its educational, historical, literary, and scientific contributions. The presence of Harvard University, Massachusetts Institute of Technology, and Lesley University has given Cambridge the name *University City.*

Cambridge's factories once made such products as furniture, glass, office equipment, books, cameras, candy, and radios. Since the mid-1900's, Cambridge has become a center of research in such fields as electronics, computers, software, space, and biotechnology.

Puritans founded Newtowne in 1630 as the first capital of the Colony of Massachusetts Bay. Harvard College was established in 1636. In 1638, the town's present name was adopted in honor of Cambridge, England.

Cambridge became an armed camp at the outbreak of the Revolutionary War in America. Minutemen gathered on Cambridge Common after the April 1775 battles of Lexington and Concord. On July 3, George Washington took command of the soldiers and formed them into the Continental Army. From 1779 to 1780, a convention drew up Massachusetts's state Constitution in Cambridge.

The city contributed to the great literary movement of the mid-1800's. Authors who lived and wrote in the city included Richard Henry Dana, Jr., Thomas Wentworth Higginson, Margaret Fuller, William Dean Howells, Henry Wadsworth Longfellow, and James Russell Lowell.

Cambridge became a city in 1846. It has a council-manager form of government. Charles M. Sullivan

Cambridge University is a world-famous British university. Cambridge probably originated in 1209, when some scholars left Oxford University after several disturbances there between students and townspeople. A number of these scholars moved to the city of Cambridge, about 50 miles (80 kilometers) north of London, where a new university grew up.

Cambridge University has about 12,500 students. Each student is a member of one of the university's 31 colleges, of which 3 are for women and 28 are for both men and women. Three colleges admit only graduate students. The first college, Peterhouse, was founded in 1284 by Hugo de Balsham, Bishop of Ely. Other noted colleges are Churchill, Christ's, Corpus Christi, Girton, Jesus, King's, Pembroke, Queens', and Trinity Hall.

Each college is an independent, self-governing corporation, though it must obey the laws of the university. Every college owns its own property, has its own income, and admits its own students. The colleges provide lodging, instruction, and social and sporting facilities. The university provides some library and laboratory facilities. The Cambridge University Library has more than 4 million books and manuscripts.

Cambridge grants bachelor's, master's, and doctor's degrees. It first granted degrees to women in 1948.
P. A. McGinley

Camcorder is a portable, battery-powered video camera with a built-in recording mechanism. This mechanism can be a videotape recorder, a DVD recorder, or a hard drive similar to that of a computer. A camcorder captures images and sound and converts them into electronic signals for viewing on television, through some computer systems, or through the camcorder itself. A movie shot using a camcorder can be viewed immediately. A camcorder can also record over material that was recorded earlier. Many people enjoy making home movies with camcorders.

Types of camcorders include *analog* and *digital* camcorders. Analog camcorders represent images and sounds using signals that vary continuously in voltage or current. Digital camcorders represent all information as a numeric code from two distinct voltage signals.

Analog camcorders record images and sound on videotape housed in a cartridge known as a *videocassette.* The size and weight of the camcorder depends mainly on the size of the videocassette used.

A full-size VHS camcorder uses the same size videocassette used in most videocassette recorders (VCR's). The recorded cassette can be played in a standard VCR. Camcorders that use a compact VHS videocassette known as VHS-C are smaller and lighter than full-sized VHS camcorders. VHS-C videocassettes must be placed in a special case called an *adapter* for playback in a VCR. Another type of compact analog camcorder uses a cassette with 8-millimeter videotape instead of VHS tape. This cassette is played back in the camcorder. Often, a cable links the camcorder to the TV set, where the picture appears. Some camcorders send an infrared signal to a receiver that is attached to a TV set, allowing the recording to be viewed without a cable connection.

Digital camcorders may be about the size of a paperback novel, or even smaller. Some use 6.35-millimeter tape in videocassettes in a format called *DV* or *MiniDV.* Others use a 3.8-millimeter format called *MicroMV.* Still others store sound and image information on a hard disk like that used in a computer, or on a special record-

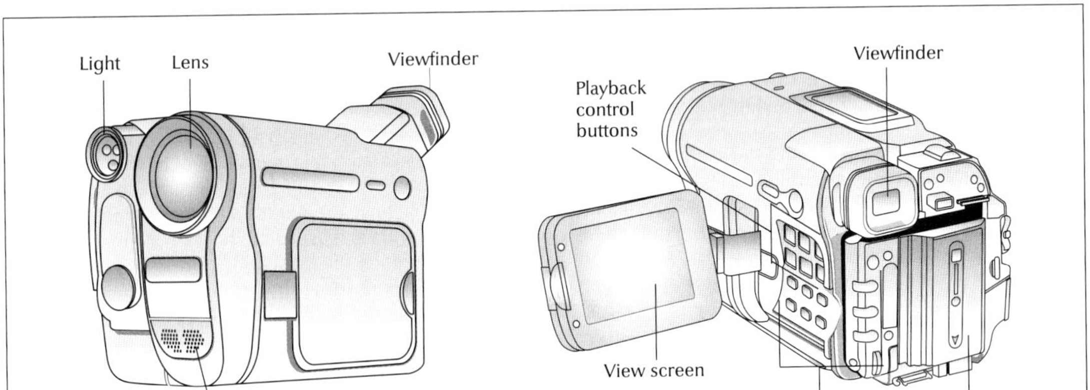

WORLD BOOK illustrations by Jay E. Bensen

A camcorder captures images and sound for viewing on television, through some computer systems, or through the camcorder itself. A tiny television screen inside the viewfinder and a larger view screen at the side of the camcorder display the image being recorded. Control buttons provide such features as titling and image fade-out, and enable the user to play back a recorded scene.

able DVD, a disk that stores digital data. Digital camcorders can be attached to a personal computer, enabling people to use pictures recorded with the camcorder as graphics on the computer.

How a camcorder works. In a typical camcorder, the user selects a scene to record by viewing it through the eyepiece of a viewfinder. The viewfinder is a miniature television screen with a magnifying lens. Most camcorders also include a display monitor measuring about 3 inches (8 centimeters) diagonally. The user adjusts the size of the image on the screen with a zoom lens. The zoom lens focuses light from the scene onto a light-sensitive component called a *charge-coupled device* (CCD). The CCD, along with a special optical filter, separates the light into colors and produces electrical signals that represent the image. Camcorders have a microphone that picks up sound from the scene. Circuits convert the sound into electronic audio signals. In a digital camcorder, electronic components convert the video and audio signals to a numeric code.

If the recording device uses videotape, the video and audio signals are recorded and played back in the same way as by a VCR. For information on how these devices record and play back, see **Videotape recorder** (How videotape recorders work).

In digital camcorders that save information on a DVD, a laser and other devices store the numeric code on the disk in a spiral track. The DVD can be played back on a television set using a DVD player. In camcorders that use hard disks, devices called *read/write heads* store data on circular tracks. Such camcorders can be connected to a television for playback.

The development of camcorders resulted from a gradual miniaturizing of videotape equipment. Beginning in the 1950's, television studios used large videotape recorders with video cameras to tape TV shows. Manufacturers gradually developed miniature electronic circuits and smaller mechanical parts for videotape recorders. By the early 1980's, the videotape recorder had become small enough to be combined with a video camera in one unit—the camcorder. The Eastman Kodak Company of the United States introduced the first 8-millimeter camcorder in 1984. Manufacturers introduced the first digital camcorders for home use in 1995.

Jesse Ben-Harosh

See also **DVD; Videotape recorder**.

Camden (pop. 79,904) is an industrial city in southern New Jersey. It lies on the Delaware River opposite Philadelphia (see **New Jersey** [political map]). Shipping and manufacturing are among the city's economic activities. The products made in Camden include fabricated metal products and communications equipment.

Rutgers, the State University of New Jersey has a branch campus and a law school in Camden. The city's museums include the home in which Walt Whitman, the great American poet, lived from 1884 until his death in 1892. Camden's transportation facilities include the Lindenwold High-Speed Line, a high-speed railway.

African Americans make up about 53 percent of the population. Hispanics, mostly of Puerto Rican ancestry, make up about 39 percent.

Camden has a mayor-council government. Delaware Indians lived in what is now the Camden area before European settlers arrived. In 1681, an English Quaker named William Cooper settled in the area. He began operating ferryboats across the Delaware. A settlement called Cooper's Ferry grew up around the ferry landing. In 1828, it was incorporated and changed its name to Camden for the Earl of Camden, a British political leader who had been sympathetic to the American Colonies.

The arrival of the railroad in 1834 spurred Camden's development. By the end of the 1800's, the city had become a leading center of industry. In the early 1900's, it became one of the nation's top shipbuilding centers. During World War I (1914-1918) and World War II (1939-1945), jobs in the shipyards brought thousands of workers to Camden. But in the mid-1900's, Camden, like many industrial cities in the northeastern United States, began to lose jobs and population. Camden's shipyards began massive layoffs and closed down in 1967. Many other industries moved out of the city, and there was a severe drop in the number of jobs. Also, many middle-income families moved to the suburbs.

By the end of the 1990's, Camden had become the poorest city in the state and was approaching bankruptcy. In mid-2000, the New Jersey governor proposed that the state take over the job of governing Camden. The state appointed a business administrator to oversee the city's finances. Robert M. Hordon

Camel is a large, strong desert animal. Camels can travel great distances across hot, dry deserts with little food or water. They walk easily on soft sand where trucks would get stuck, and carry people and heavy loads to places that have no roads. Camels also serve the people of the desert in many other ways.

A camel carries a built-in food supply on its back in the form of a hump. The hump is a large lump of fat that provides energy for the animal if food is scarce.

There are two chief kinds of camels: (1) the Arabian camel, also called *dromedary,* which has one hump, and (2) the Bactrian camel, which has two humps. In the past, *hybrids* (crossbreeds) of the two species were used widely in Asia. These hybrid camels had one extra-long hump and were larger and stronger than either parent.

Camels have been domesticated by people for thousands of years. Arabian camels may once have lived wild in Arabia, but none are wild today. There are several million Arabian camels, and most of them live with the desert people of Africa and Asia. The first Bactrian camels probably lived in Mongolia and in Turkestan, which was called Bactria in ancient times. A few hundred wild Bactrian camels may still roam parts of Mongolia, and over a million domesticated ones live in Asia.

Scientists believe members of the camel family lived in North America at least 40 million years ago. Before the Pleistocene Epoch, from about 2 million years ago to about 11,500 years ago, camels had developed into a distinct species and had moved west across Alaska to

Facts in brief

Names: *Male,* bull; *female,* cow; *young,* calf, foal; *group,* herd.
Gestation period: About 13 months.
Number of young: Usually 1.
Length of life: Up to 40 years.
Where found: Africa and Asia.
Scientific classification: Camels belong to the camel family, Camelidae. They are in the genus *Camelus.* The Arabian camel is *C. dromedarius.* The Bactrian camel is *C. bactrianus.*

George Holton, Photo Researchers

Herds of Bactrian camels graze in the Gobi Desert. These sturdy animals, whose ancestors roamed wild, can carry heavy packs for long distances over rocky mountain trails.

western Asia. In Asia, two groups separated and gradually became the two chief kinds of camels known today. Meanwhile, smaller members of the camel family had moved southward from North to South America. Today, four members of the camel family live in South America: (1) alpacas, (2) guanacos, (3) llamas, and (4) vicuñas. By the time Europeans came to North America, no members of the camel family had lived there for many thousands of years. No one knows why they disappeared.

During the 1850's, the U.S. Army brought about 120 camels from Africa and Asia to carry cargo from Texas to California. But the railroads, which were growing rapidly, could carry more goods faster and cheaper than the camels could. The Army sold the animals, most of them to circuses and zoos. A few camels escaped and lived wild in Arizona until at least 1905. Beginning about 1840, people in Australia used camels to help them explore and settle that continent. About 15,000 camels still roam wild in the central Australian deserts.

People and camels

Millions of people who live in Africa and Asia depend on camels to supply most of their needs. In lands at the edge of the deserts, camels pull plows, turn water wheels to irrigate fields, and carry grain to market. Deep in the deserts, camels are almost the only source of transportation, food, clothing, and shelter. In turn, camels need people to draw water for them from wells if they are to survive the hot summers.

Camels work hard for people, but their behavior is unpredictable. Bactrian camels may spit, and all camels can kick. Camels may groan and bawl when they are loaded and have to rise. But they routinely carry loads of up to 330 pounds (150 kilograms) for eight hours. They can carry more but do so unwillingly. Usually, camels work only six months of the year. If too much is demanded of them, they will die from overexertion.

Camels are an important source of food in the desert. People eat the meat of young camels, though it can be very tough. They melt fat from the animal's hump and use it for butter. People drink camel's milk and also make cheese from it.

The camel also supplies wool and leather for clothing and shelter. Camel owners weave the animal's soft, woolly fur into fine cloth and warm blankets. The long fur of the Bactrian camel is especially good for weaving into cloth. Arabs use the cloth for much of their clothing and for tents. Camel's hair cloth is sold in many parts of the world for making blankets, coats, and suits. The strong, tough skin of the camel provides leather for shoes, water bags, and packsaddles. Dried camel bones can be carved like ivory for jewelry or utensils. Camel droppings are dried and used for fuel.

The body of a camel

A camel stands from 6 to 7 feet (1.8 to 2.1 meters) tall at the shoulders, and weighs from 550 to 1,500 pounds (250 to 680 kilograms). Its ropelike tail may be almost 21 inches (53 centimeters) long. Camels seem larger than they are because of their thick, woolly fur, which may be all shades of brown, from nearly white to almost black. An Arabian camel's fur is short and helps protect its body from the heat. A Bactrian camel's fur is longer. It may grow about 10 inches (25 centimeters) long on the animal's head, neck, and humps.

All camels lose their fur in spring and grow a new coat. The fur comes off so fast that it hangs in large pieces, making the animal appear ragged. A camel looks sleek and slender for several weeks after losing its coat, but a thick coat of new fur grows by autumn.

Camels have calluslike bare spots on their chests and on their leg joints. These spots look as though the hair had been rubbed off, but they are natural and not signs of wear. Even young camels have them. Thick, leathery skin grows there and becomes tough when the animal is about five months old.

The head. A camel has large eyes on the sides of its head. Each eye is protected by long, curly eyelashes that keep out sand. In the daytime, when the sun is high, the eyes do not allow excessive light in. Glands supply the eyes with a great deal of water to keep them moist. Thick eyebrows shield the eyes from the desert sun.

The camel's small, rounded ears are located far back on its head. The ears are covered with hair, even on the inside. The hair helps keep out sand or dust that might blow into the animal's ears. A camel can hear well, but, like the donkey, it often pays no attention to commands.

The camel has a large mouth and 34 strong, sharp teeth. It can use the teeth as weapons. A camel owner may cover the animal's mouth with a muzzle to keep it from biting. A working camel cannot wear a bit and bridle, as a horse does, because its mouth must be free to chew *cud* (regurgitated food). Instead, a rope for leading the animal is fastened through a hole near the nose.

The hump of a camel is mostly a lump of fat. Bands of strong tissue hold pads of fat together, forming the hump above the backbone. The hump of a healthy, well-fed camel may weigh 80 pounds (36 kilograms) or more.

Most kinds of animals store fat in their bodies, but only camels keep most of their fat in a lump. If food is hard to find, the fat in the hump provides energy. If a camel is starving, its hump shrinks. The hump may even slip off the animal's back and hang down on its side. After the camel has had a few weeks' rest and food, its hump is firm and plump again. The hump is not a storage place for water, as many people believe.

The legs and feet. Camels have long, strong legs. Powerful muscles in the upper part of the legs allow the animals to carry heavy loads for long distances. A camel can carry as much as 1,000 pounds (450 kilograms), but the usual load weighs about 330 pounds (150 kilograms). While working, the animals typically travel about 25 miles (40 kilometers) a day, at a speed of 3 miles (5 kilometers) an hour. Camels usually walk, especially if it is hot, but when they must go faster they either gallop or *pace.* The pace is a medium-speed movement in which both legs on the same side lift and come down together. This leg action produces a swaying, rocking motion that makes some riders "seasick." Camels are sometimes called "ships of the desert."

The tough, leathery skin pads on a camel's legs act as cushions when the animal kneels to rest. The camel bends its front legs and drops to its knees. Then it folds its hind legs and sinks to the ground. To get up, the camel straightens its hind legs and then jerks up its front legs. A camel can lie down and get up again even with a heavy load on its back.

Camels have two toes on each foot. A hoof that looks like a toenail grows at the front of each toe. Cows, horses, and many other animals walk on their hoofs. But a camel walks on a broad pad that connects its two long toes. This cushionlike pad spreads when the camel steps on it. The pad supports the animal on loose sand in much the same way that a snowshoe helps a person walk on snow. The camel's cushioned feet make almost no sound when the animal walks or runs.

The life of a camel

Young. A female camel carries a single young, called a *calf,* inside her body for about 13 months before giving birth. The calf's eyes are open at birth, and a thick, woolly coat covers its body. The calf can run when it is only a few hours old, and it calls to its mother with a soft "baa" somewhat like that of a lamb. The young camel and its mother live together for several years unless they are forcibly kept apart.

Ernst A. Weber, Photo Researchers

A dromedary can be bred and trained for riding and racing. It can run about 10 miles (16 kilometers) per hour, and can travel as far as 100 miles (160 kilometers) in a day.

P. J. Holloway, Photo Researchers

A week-old camel calf, *shown here,* rests beside its mother. Calves can run soon after birth, but stay with their mothers for several years.

Russ Kinne, Photo Researchers

A camel's thick eyebrows, *shown here,* help shade its eyes from the sun. The animal can shut its nostrils and lips tightly to keep out blowing sand.

The skeleton of a camel

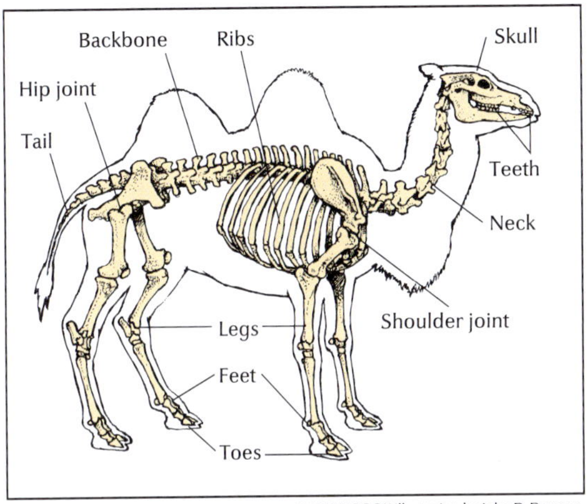

WORLD BOOK illustration by John D. Dawson

When a calf is about a year old, its owner begins to teach it to stand and kneel on command. The young camel also learns to carry a saddle or small, light packs. The size and weight of the packs are gradually increased as the camel grows older. A 5-year-old camel can carry a full load.

Food. Camels can go for days or even weeks with little or no food or water. Desert people feed their camels dates, grass, and such grains as wheat and oats. In zoos, the animals eat hay and dry grains—about 8 pounds (3.6 kilograms) of each every day. When a camel travels across the desert, food may be hard to find. The animal may have to live on dried leaves, seeds, and whatever desert plants it can find. A camel can eat a thorny twig without hurting its mouth. The lining of the mouth is so tough that the sharp thorns cannot push through the skin. If food is very scarce, a camel will eat anything—bones, fish, meat, leather, and even its owner's tent.

A camel does not chew its food well before swallowing it. The animal's stomach has three sections, one of which stores the poorly chewed food. This food, or cud, is later returned to the mouth in a ball-like glob, and the camel chews it. The chewed food is then swallowed and goes to the other parts of the stomach to be completely digested. Camels, deer, cattle, and other kinds of animals that digest their food in this way are called *ruminants* (see **Ruminant**).

Water. A camel can go without water for days or even months. The amount of water a camel drinks varies with the time of year and with the weather. Camels need less water in winter when the weather is cool and the plants they eat contain more moisture than in summer. Camels that graze in the Sahara can go all winter without water and may refuse to drink if water is offered to them. But in very hot weather, a large, thirsty camel can drink up to 53 gallons (200 liters) a day. This water is not stored in the camel's body but replaces water previously used up.

A camel needs little water each day because it gets some moisture from its food. Also, it keeps most of the water that is in its body. Most animals sweat when hot, and the evaporation of the water from their skin keeps them cool. But camels do not sweat much. Instead, their body temperature rises by as much as 11 Fahrenheit degrees (6 Celsius degrees) during the heat of the day and then cools down at night. In people, an increase of only one or two degrees is a sign of illness.

On extremely hot days, a camel keeps as cool as possible by resting rather than feeding. It may lie down in a shady place or face the sun so that only a small part of its body receives the sun's rays. A group of camels may fight off heat by pressing against each other, because the body temperatures of the camels may be lower than the air temperature. Anne Innis Dagg

Related articles in *World Book* include:

Alpaca	Dromedary	Llama
Arabs	Ethiopia (picture)	Sahara (picture)
Asia (pictures)	Guanaco	Vicuña
Camel's-hair cloth		

Camellia, *kuh MEEL yuh* or *kuh MEE lee uh,* is a group of about 80 evergreen trees or shrubs native to eastern Asia. This group includes three well-known plants that are cultivated in warm regions of the United States: the *common camellia,* the *sasanqua,* and the *tea plant.* Camellias have shiny, leathery, dark green leaves. Most varieties bear large, showy blossoms that may be red, white, pink, or spotted.

© David Cain, Photo Researchers

Camellias

Camellias thrive in partial shade and well-drained, fertile soil. Gardeners usually raise the plants from cuttings or by grafting. The common camellia blooms in winter and spring. The sasanqua and the tea plant bloom in autumn.

Camellias were introduced into Europe perhaps as early as 1550. The tea plant, used for making tea for centuries in China, was introduced into Japan before 1000. See **Tea**. J. Massey

Scientific classification. Camellias are in the family Theaceae. The scientific name for the common camellia is *Camellia japonica.* The sasanqua is *C. sasanqua,* and the tea plant is *C. sinensis.*

Camelot, *KAM uh laht,* was the most famous castle in the medieval legends about King Arthur of Britain. Camelot was Arthur's favorite dwelling and the starting point of the Quest for the Holy Grail (see **Holy Grail**). Camelot also came to symbolize the glories of Arthurian civilization.

By the 1200's, Camelot served as the symbolic center of the Arthurian world, but its location is not clear. In his *Le Morte Darthur* (about 1470), Sir Thomas Malory placed the castle in Winchester. Some writers favored Caerleon Castle in Wales as described in Geoffrey of Monmouth's *History of the Kings of Britain* (about 1136). Modern attempts have been made to identify Camelot with ruins of Cadbury Castle in Somerset that were excavated in 1966. However, Camelot is perhaps best viewed not as a particular place but as a state of mind or a reflection of a lost ideal. Edmund Reiss

Camel's-hair cloth is a soft, medium-weight woolen cloth made from the fur of the Bactrian camel. In spring, the camel loses its winter coat and grows a new one. The fur comes off in large pieces, which are gathered and processed.

Camel fur consists of long, coarse hairs that yield poor fibers, and short, fine hairs that produce a soft, warm cloth. The cloth is used to make blankets, coats, shawls, and suits. Keith Slater

See also **Camel** (People and camels).

Cameo, *KAM ee oh,* is an engraved gem. Most cameos are made of stones or shells that are *stratified*—that is, they are formed in layers. Artists cut a design into the top layer to produce a beautiful color contrast with the next layer. Thus, a cameo is actually a miniature bas-relief sculpture. See **Relief** (Low relief).

The most commonly used materials for cameos are

Onyx brooch (mid-1800's), probably by L. Saulini; sardonyx ring (early 1800's) by Niccolò Amastini. The Metropolitan Museum of Art, New York City, the Milton Weil Collection, gift of Mrs. Ethel Weil Worgelt, 1940

Cameos often feature subjects from classical mythology. The brooch on the left shows the head of Medusa, a monster in Greek myths who had snakes for hair. The ring on the right has a scene from the education of Bacchus, the Roman god of wine.

shell, coral, and a variety of quartz called chalcedony (see **Chalcedony**). Imitation cameos are most often made from glass or plastics. Cameos were introduced during the Hellenistic Age in Greece (about 323 to 100 B.C.). The Romans also produced excellent cameos. Today, most cameos are produced in Italy, Germany, and Japan. John S. Lizzadro

Camera is an instrument used for taking photographs, making motion pictures, or transmitting images. The word *camera* comes from a Latin term meaning *chamber.* A camera is a *light-tight box*—that is, a chamber sealed from exterior light. Light transmitted or reflected from the scene being photographed usually enters the camera through a front-mounted lens. The camera holds a light-sensitive electronic device or piece of film that the light exposes to make a picture.

This article explains how a camera takes pictures and discusses various types of cameras. For a discussion of the history and parts of a camera and how to take pictures, see the *World Book* article on **Photography.** For information on making movies, see the articles on **Motion picture** and **Camcorder.** For information on television cameras, see **Television** (The television camera).

How a camera works

All cameras use the same basic principles. Light from the scene being photographed strikes the lens of the camera. The light passes through the lens, bends to come to a point of focus, and forms an *inverted* (upside-down) image on the film or electronic chip at the back of the camera. The photographer usually focuses the image by making fine adjustments in the distance between the lens and the film or chip. Many cameras have a focusing mechanism that the photographer controls. Some focus the image automatically. In addition, most cameras have a *viewfinder,* a sighting instrument that the photographer looks through to frame the subject.

Cameras that use rolled film have a *film advance* that moves unexposed film into position to receive focused light. After an exposure has been taken, the film advance moves the exposed film out of the way. The film advances automatically in many cameras. Some cameras for professional use require individual sheets of film to be loaded and unloaded for each exposure.

Controlling the light. Two devices control the exposure: (1) the *shutter,* a movable set of blades in the lens in most cameras, or a curtain device at the back of the camera, and (2) the *aperture* (also called the *diaphragm),* an adjustable irislike opening in the lens through which light enters. The speed of the shutter's opening and closing determines how long the chip or film is exposed. The size of the aperture determines how much light reaches the chip or film while the shutter remains open. Aperture size is referred to in numbers called *f-stops,* which represent a ratio of the lens *focal length* to the diameter of the aperture. Focal length is the distance from the center of the lens to the point at which incoming light rays focus. Many cameras have adjustable shutter speeds, ranging from 1 second or slower to $\frac{1}{1,000}$ of a second or faster.

The settings for shutter speed and aperture are interrelated. To "freeze" a fast-moving object, you would need a fast shutter speed—in other words, a short exposure time—to avoid blurring the image. To let in enough light during this brief time, you would need a large aperture. Now, suppose you wanted to photograph a sweeping landscape. To bring into sharp focus all parts of the scene at various distances from the camera, you would need a small aperture. To let in enough light through this narrow opening for proper exposure, you would need a slower shutter speed.

Providing additional light. Many cameras have a built-in or attachable electronic flash unit that provides additional light to make an adequate exposure in dim light. The flash unit provides a short burst of light synchronized with the opening of the shutter.

Automatic controls. Many cameras also have built-in devices that perform various parts of the picture-taking process automatically. A tiny built-in computer called a *central processing unit* (CPU) or *microprocessor* determines the correct settings for picture taking. Sensors inside the camera provide the CPU with information that it needs to focus the lens and make a correct exposure. This information includes the brightness of the light, the distance between the subject and the lens, and the light sensitivity of the chip or film.

The CPU processes this information and either adjusts the camera settings itself or displays the information so that the photographer can set the camera manually.

The two chief automatic features are (1) automatic exposure control and (2) automatic focusing.

Automatic exposure control, also called *autoexposure,* helps ensure proper exposure of the chip or film. A feature called *aperture-priority mode* enables the photographer to manually set the aperture, while the camera chooses the shutter speed appropriate for the chosen aperture. *Shutter-priority mode* lets the photographer select the shutter speed, while the camera sets the aperture for proper exposure. Many cameras offer *program mode,* in which the camera chooses both the shutter speed and the aperture.

All automatic exposure systems rely on readings from a built-in light meter. The CPU interprets these readings according to a *metering pattern,* a set of instructions that tells the CPU how to react to different amounts of brightness in specific parts of the scene. Such a system can compensate for much unevenness in lighting, such as a scene with a bright background behind a dark subject. Some cameras offer a choice of metering patterns.

Automatic focusing, also called *autofocus,* adjusts the lens focus automatically to take sharp photographs. There are two chief types of automatic focusing systems: (1) active and (2) passive.

Most active autofocus systems bounce an *infrared* (heat) ray or an ultrasound wave off the subject being photographed. Sensors measure the angle at which the infrared beam returns to the camera or how long it

How a camera uses light

A camera is a dark box with a light-sensitive electronic chip or piece of film at one end and a small *aperture* (hole) at the other. Light passes through the aperture and forms an image on the chip or film. You can see how this process works by shining flashlights through a pinhole in the side of a box.

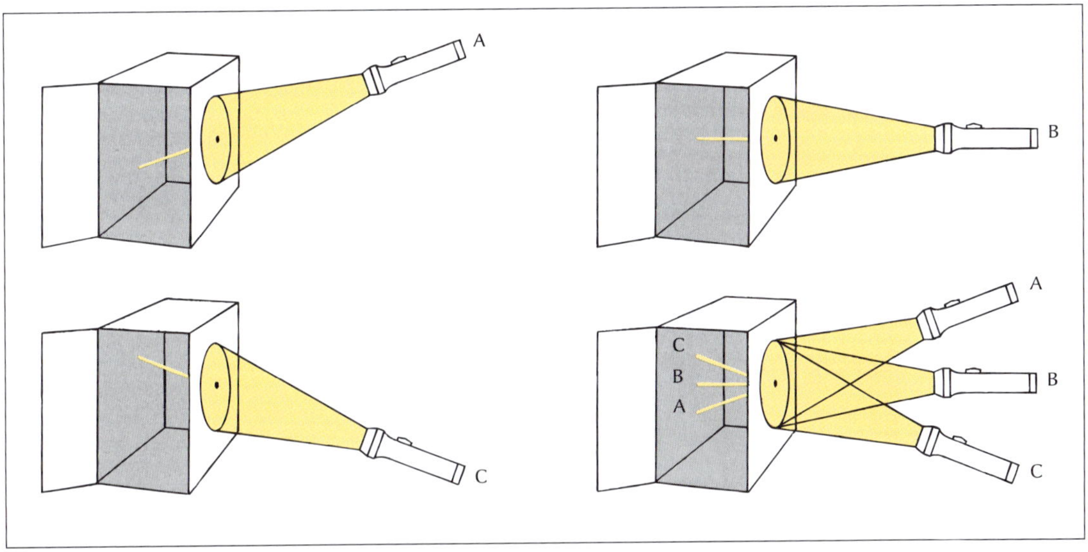

Light passes through the aperture and strikes the opposite side of the box. Light rays travel in a straight line, and so the light reaches the inside wall from the same direction as it entered the box. Light from flashlight A passes downward through the aperture, light from B goes straight across, and light from C travels upward. Light rays coming from all three directions at once cross as they pass through the aperture. As a result, they reverse positions and strike the inside wall at points C, B, and A. Thus, the images formed by light inside a camera are always upside down.

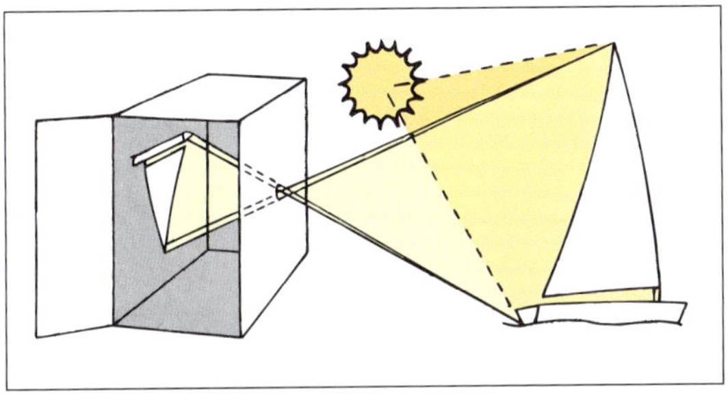

A pinhole allows sunlight reflected from a sailboat to expose a piece of film in the back of the box, thereby creating a picture of the boat. A pinhole aperture admits only a small amount of light. For this reason, it may take several seconds for enough light to enter the box to expose the film.

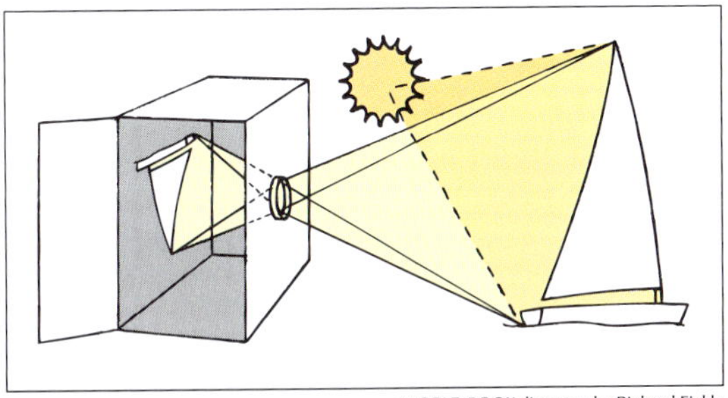

WORLD BOOK diagrams by Richard Fickle

A lens increases the amount of light that enters the box. A picture of a sailboat can be recorded on the film in a fraction of a second by covering the aperture with a lens. A lens also improves the quality of the picture because it focuses the incoming light rays into a sharp image on the film.

takes the beam or ultrasound wave to return. The system uses the measurement to determine how far away the subject is and decide where the lens should focus.

A passive autofocus system analyzes the sharpness of the image entering the lens. In most systems, sensors behind the lens measure the contrast of lines or edges in the subject. This contrast is highest when the camera is sharply focused on the subject. The system adjusts the focus to achieve the maximum contrast.

Some autofocus systems can sense if a subject is moving. These systems make adjustments so that the subject remains in focus during the instant the shutter is open.

Types of cameras

Fixed-focus cameras, the most basic of all cameras, have a nonadjustable fixed lens. Most models have a single aperture setting and only one or two shutter speeds. Most fixed-focus film cameras use 35-millimeter film. A few use Advanced Photo System (APS) film. APS film has a width of 24 millimeters. It includes a magnetic coating that stores printing instructions for each photograph.

In general, a fixed-focus camera can take satisfactory photographs in both ordinary daylight and dim light. The camera may produce a blurred picture if the subject is less than 6 feet (1.8 meters) away. Many fixed-focus cameras include a built-in automatic flash.

Single-use cameras are a type of fixed-focus camera that combines a plastic lens, a shutter, film, and often a flash unit in one small box. Some can take pictures underwater. After the user exposes the film, he or she takes the entire camera to a photo developing laboratory. The lab removes the film for processing and returns the camera to the manufacturer for reuse or recycling.

Point-and-shoot cameras are popular with photography hobbyists. These cameras are simple to operate and have many automatic features. Point-and-shoot cameras usually have a built-in lens and automatic focus and exposure control. Usually, the lens is a *zoom lens* that can be adjusted to make a subject appear closer or farther away with no loss of focus. Point-and-shoot cameras come in both digital and film models. The film models usually use 35-millimeter film.

Single-lens reflex (SLR) cameras appeal to skilled amateur photographers and to professional photographers. The camera's name refers to its viewing system. The photographer views the subject as imaged by the camera lens rather than through a separate viewing lens. A mirror between the lens and the chip or film reflects the image to the viewfinder. When the photographer presses the shutter release, the mirror lifts out of the way to allow the light to expose the chip or film. Thus,

Parts of a single-lens reflex film camera

A single-lens reflex camera enables photographers to see their subject through the lens. Light from the subject passes through the lens and is transmitted by a mirror and a prism to the viewfinder. When the shutter release button is pressed, the mirror lifts so the light will expose the film.

Nikon, Inc.

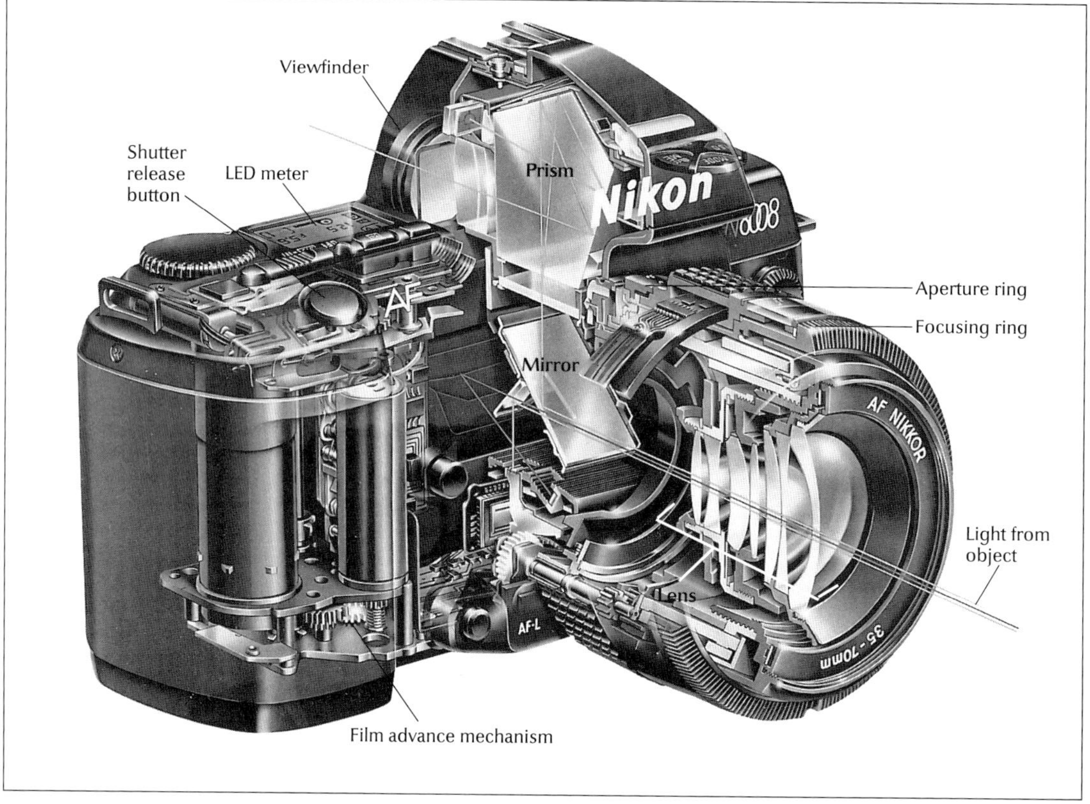

Some kinds of cameras

Eastman Kodak Company

An Advanced Photo System (APS) camera is a special kind of film camera. APS cameras are small and lightweight. Film used in these cameras has a magnetic coating, on which the camera stores instructions for the processing of each picture.

Polaroid Corporation

An instant camera produces a print almost immediately after a picture is taken. The film used in these cameras contains chemicals that develop and print pictures automatically. Some types of film for instant cameras also provide reusable negatives.

WORLD BOOK photo by Ralph Brunke

A view camera is the largest and most adjustable type of camera. The lens end and the back end of this camera can be moved forward or backward and tilted at different angles to produce a variety of artistic effects.

WORLD BOOK photo by Ralph Brunke

A motion-picture camera takes pictures that re-create the movement of subjects when the film is projected on a screen. Many amateur moviemakers use an 8-millimeter camera, like the one shown above.

the photographer sees almost the exact image that the camera records. Like point-and-shoot cameras, SLR's come in both digital and film models. The digital models are often referred to as DSLR's. Most of the film models use 35-millimeter film. With an SLR, a photographer can adjust the focus, select the shutter speed, and control the aperture size. Many SLR's have autofocus and automatic exposure control.

Lenses on SLR cameras are interchangeable. The standard lens of an SLR camera can be replaced by special lenses that change the size and depth relationship of objects in a scene. These lenses include *wide-angle lenses, telephoto lenses,* and *macro lenses.* A wide-angle lens provides a wider view of a scene than a standard lens does. A telephoto lens makes distant objects appear closer. A macro lens focuses on objects close to the lens. Many SLR's use zoom lenses that cover a range of focal lengths, often from wide-angle to telephoto.

View cameras are the largest and most adjustable type of camera. A view camera has a front *standard* (support), upon which a lens is mounted, and a rear standard, which holds the film or electronic sensor. Between the standards is a light-tight bellows. In most cameras, both the shutter and aperture are in the lens and are manually adjustable. A photographer focuses a view camera by moving either standard forward or backward to produce a sharp image on the viewing screen. By changing the angles of the standards, a photographer can control image shape and sharpness. Many professional photographers use view cameras for portraits, architectural images, and product photography. View camera operators use light meters that are not built into the camera.

Instant cameras use special film that does not require developing at a photo lab. The film contains all the chemicals needed for developing. The camera can thus provide a print soon after exposure. The time required to produce a print varies according to the camera and the type of film. Instant cameras provide prints ranging in size from $2\frac{7}{8}$ by $3\frac{5}{8}$ inches (73 by 92 millimeters) to 20 by 24 inches (508 by 610 millimeters). Some instant cameras can take flash pictures and focus automatically.

Digital cameras create pictures that can be instantly viewed on a screen on the camera or on a television screen, or that can be transferred to a computer. Most digital cameras focus light on a reusable light-sensitive sensor called a *charge-coupled device* (CCD). The captured light patterns are converted into a *digital* (numeric) code and transferred as an image file to the camera's storage device, usually a small, removable card. The user can delete images from the camera and use the digital storage space again. He or she can use computer software to manipulate the digital images. The user can also print the images or transfer them over the Internet.

Motion-picture cameras take series of pictures that re-create the motion of a subject. Professional moviemakers generally use large cameras that take 70-, 35-, or 16-millimeter film. Many amateur moviemakers use portable video cameras called *camcorders.* These cameras convert light reflected by the subject into electronic signals that are recorded on magnetic tape. Digital camcorders may record on videotape, a memory card, or a miniature hard disk. Sound for professional movies is recorded separately and later merged onto the film track. Camcorders can record both sound and images at the same time. Most camcorders also have a zoom lens.

Stereo cameras produce images that seem to have a three dimensional quality. One kind of stereo camera has two identical lens systems with matched shutters. This camera takes two pictures of the same subject at the same time—one picture through each lens system—but from slightly different angles. When viewed through special glasses or a device called a *stereoscope,* the two pictures blend into one image, producing the illusion of three dimensions. Stephen J. Diehl

Related articles in *World Book* include:

Astronomy (Optical astronomy)
Camcorder
Camera lucida
Camera obscura
Charge-coupled device
Eastman, George
Fairchild, Sherman M.
Land, Edwin Herbert
Lens
Light meter
Motion picture (The camera)
Photography
Stereoscope

Additional resources

Goldberg, Norman. *Camera Technology: The Dark Side of the Lens.* Academic Pr., 1992.

Wallace, Joseph E. *The Camera.* Atheneum, 2000. Younger readers.

Camera lucida, *LOO suh duh,* is a sketching device that consists of a four-sided prism and a magnifying glass, both attached to a frame. The term means *light chamber.* The device produces a virtual image of the object or scene on the paper where the sketch is made, as in the illustration. Another form uses a right-angled prism with a sheet of glass for a reflector. Artists have used the camera lucida to make accurate drawings of architectural scenes and landscapes, to reduce large drawings, and to transpose sketches. The reflected image's size is controlled by the distance from the object or scene. See also **Prism.** Robert A. Sobieszek

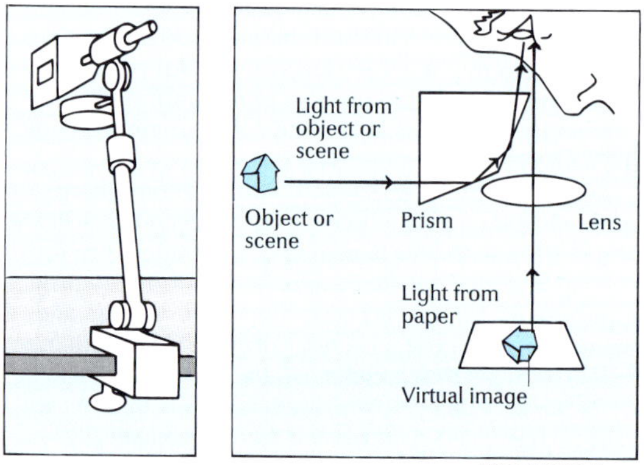

WORLD BOOK diagram

The camera lucida is a device used in sketching.

Camera obscura, *ahb SKYUR uh,* is a box used for sketching large objects or scenes. The term means *dark chamber.* The box contains a mirror set at a 45° angle. Mounted in the front end of the box is a double-convex lens like that in a photographic camera. Light from the object or scene is transmitted through the lens. The mirror reflects this light upward to a ground-glass screen on the top of the box. There, the light forms an image of the object or scene that can be sketched easily. See also **Lens; Photography** (History). Robert A. Sobieszek

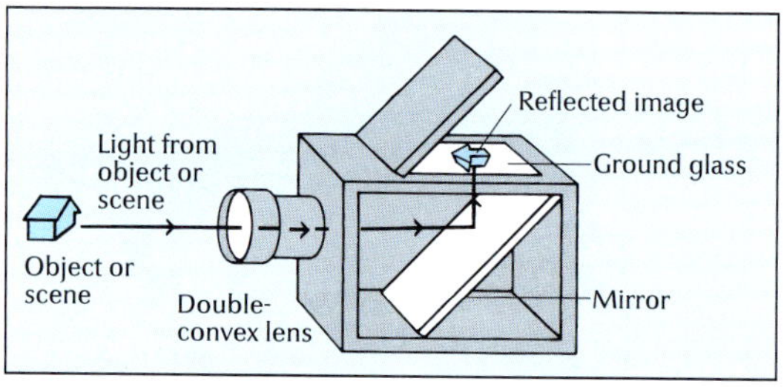

WORLD BOOK diagram

The camera obscura was used by artists to reproduce objects or scenes before photographic cameras became common.

Cameron, *KAM uhr uhn,* **Julia Margaret** (1815-1879), a British photographer, pioneered in the field of artistic photography. She was especially noted for dramatic close-up portraits, but her works also include photographs that portray religious scenes or illustrate poems. She photographed many leading British figures of the 1860's and 1870's.

Cameron did not share the widely held belief that a photograph should be a detailed, visually precise representation of a person or scene. Instead, she tried to capture the character and spirit of her subjects. To achieve this effect, she experimented with lighting and composition. She valued expressiveness over technical quality, and so many of her photographs were blurred or out of focus. These technical flaws made her work controversial. Cameron was born on June 11, 1815, in Calcutta (now Kolkata), India, and moved to England in 1848. She died on Jan. 26, 1879. Charles Hagen

Photography (picture: Portraits by Julia Margaret Cameron).

Cameroon, *KAM uh ROON,* is a country on the west coast of Africa. It has a varied landscape, including mountains in the west, grasslands in the north, and tropical lowlands in the south. The people of Cameroon belong to about 200 ethnic groups. Yaoundé is the country's capital, and Douala is its largest city.

Government. A president, elected by the people to a seven-year term, is Cameroon's head of state. The president also ranks as the most powerful official in the

WORLD BOOK maps

government. A 180-member National Assembly makes the country's laws. The people elect Assembly members to five-year terms. The president appoints the prime minister, Cabinet members, and other officials to help carry out the functions of the government. Cameroon's chief political party is the Cameroon People's Democratic Movement. Cameroon is divided into 10 provinces, each headed by a governor appointed by the president.

People. Cameroon's largest ethnic groups are the Bamiléké, who live in the western region, and the Fulani, who live in the north. The Douala, the Ewondo, and the Fang inhabit the southern and central regions of Cameroon. English and French are Cameroon's official languages, but most Cameroonians speak one of the country's 54 African languages. About 45 percent of the people practice traditional African religions. About 35 percent are Christians. About 20 percent are Muslims.

Most of Cameroon's rural people are farmers, but some are herders. The majority of the rural people live in villages or small towns. Manufacturing and service industries provide jobs in Cameroon's urban areas. Each year, large numbers of rural people move to urban areas to seek jobs. Douala and Yaoundé, the chief cities in Cameroon, have elegant hotels, fine office buildings, and fashionable modern houses. But these cities also have areas in which many people live in slumlike conditions. The cities face the problem of accommodating the many rural people who move to the cities.

Most houses in the northern towns and villages are round clay huts or rectangular brick houses. Northern herders, who move from place to place, build light shelters from poles and woven mats. Most houses in the western mountainous region are square brick structures. Typical homes in the southern forest region are rectangular houses made of wood, palm leaves, and clay. Along the coast, people build wooden houses covered with tree bark or with sheets of metal. In the larger cities, many people live in modern houses and apartment buildings. But others in the cities live in shacks.

The government operates free public schools and universities, and gives financial aid to private schools. But Cameroon has shortages of schools and teachers, and many children do not attend school. More than half of the nation's adults can read and write. For Cameroon's literacy rate, see **Literacy** (table: Literacy rates for selected countries).

Artists in Cameroon are known for their woodcarving and brass masks. Some of the finest Cameroonian art is produced by the Bamiléké and Bamoun peoples, who live in the Western Highlands.

Land and climate. Mountains and hills lie along Cameroon's western border, from Lake Chad in the north to Mount Cameroon in the south near the coast. Mount Cameroon, at 13,353 feet (4,070 meters), is the country's highest point. A forested plateau in central Cameroon separates a *savanna* (grassland with scattered trees) in the north from tropical lowlands along the coast of the Gulf of Guinea in the south. Waza National Park in the north preserves an area of savanna inhabited by many animals, including elephants, giraffes, monkeys, and antelope. Cameroon has three main rivers, the Benue, the Wouri, and the Sanaga.

Facts in brief

Capital: Yaoundé.
Official languages: English and French.
Official name: République du Cameroun (Republic of Cameroon).
Area: 183,569 mi² (475,442 km²). *Greatest distances*—north-south, 770 mi (1,239 km); east-west, 450 mi (724 km). *Coastline*—250 mi (400 km).
Elevation: *Highest*—Mount Cameroon, 13,353 ft (4,070 m) above sea level. *Lowest*—sea level, along the coast.
Population: *Estimated 2006 population*—16,798,000; density, 92 per mi² (35 per km²); distribution, 52 percent rural, 48 percent urban. *1987 census*—10,493,655.
Chief products: *Agriculture and forestry*—bananas, cacao beans, coffee, cotton, palm oil, root crops, rubber, timber. *Manufacturing*—aluminum, beer, cocoa, petroleum products, shoes, soap. *Mining*—petroleum.
National anthem: "O Cameroon, Thou Cradle of Our Fathers."
Flag: The flag has green, red, and yellow vertical stripes, with a yellow star in the center of the red stripe. See **Flag** (picture: Flags of Africa).
Money: *Basic unit*—CFA franc. CFA stands for Coopération Financière en Afrique Centrale (Financial Cooperation in Central Africa).

Yaoundé is the capital of the African nation of Cameroon. The city is a commercial and transportation center. Its shopping district includes this large, three-story open-air market.

Shostal

Cameroon's northern savanna region is hot and dry most of the year. The average temperature is about 82 °F (28 °C), but daytime temperatures sometimes reach 120 °F (49 °C). The central plateau is cooler, with an average temperature of about 75 °F (24 °C). The coastal region is hot and humid. Some places there receive up to 200 inches (500 centimeters) of rain a year, and the average temperature is about 80 °F (27 °C).

Economy. The economy of Cameroon depends primarily on agriculture. About 75 percent of the labor force works in agriculture. Farmers raise such crops as cassava, corn, millet, yams, and sweet potatoes mainly for their own food. Cash crops include bananas, cacao beans, coffee, cotton, and peanuts.

Petroleum is Cameroon's most important natural resource. Bauxite, which is used to make aluminum, is also important. Trees in the country provide palm oil, rubber, and timber. Cameroon has few large manufacturing and processing industries. The industries include the processing of agricultural raw materials, and the manufacture of aluminum products, beer, cigarettes, petroleum products, shoes, soap, and soft drinks.

In the 1970's, Cameroon began pumping petroleum from the Gulf of Guinea. The petroleum trade has helped meet the country's energy needs and aided the economy. Petroleum, cocoa, aluminum, cotton, timber, and coffee are Cameroon's main exports. Imports include machinery and transportation equipment. Cameroon's chief trading partners are France and other members of the European Union, and the United States.

Most of Cameroon's roads are unpaved. Railroads link the country's larger cities and towns. International airports are located at Douala, Garoua, and Yaoundé.

Cameroon has one daily newspaper. Radio and television are controlled by the government.

History. Stone tools and rock carvings found in Cameroon indicate that prehistoric people lived in the area. Bantu-speaking people were one of the earliest identified groups to settle in Cameroon. They lived in the northern highlands hundreds of years before Christ. A state called Kanem that existed from about the A.D. 700's extended into present-day Cameroon.

In the late 1400's, Portuguese explorers became the first Europeans to reach Cameroon. The country's name comes from *camarões,* the Portuguese word for *shrimp.* The Portuguese had found small crayfish resembling shrimp in the Wouri River. From the late 1400's to the late 1800's, other Europeans flocked to the area. Many went to Cameroon to participate in the flourishing slave trade there. In 1807, the United Kingdom abolished its slave trade, as did many other European nations in the early 1800's. Ivory and palm oil became the major trade products after the slave trade ended. In 1858, British missionaries founded Victoria, Cameroon's first permanent European settlement, at Mount Cameroon's base.

In the late 1800's, three European countries—the United Kingdom, France, and Germany—struggled for control of Cameroon. In 1884, two local Douala chiefs signed a treaty with Germany that made Cameroon a German *protectorate*—that is, a territory under partial German control. Germany lost control of Cameroon to the United Kingdom and France during World War I (1914-1918). In 1922, the British and French divided Cameroon into two sections. The British section included two separated parts along the western border. Called British Cameroons, the sections made up about one-fifth of Cameroon. The other four-fifths came under the control of France and was called French Cameroun. Each section was governed according to the laws of the ruling country and adopted the ruling country's language as the official one. In 1946, the United Kingdom and France pledged to eventually give their parts of Cameroon self-government or independence.

On Jan. 1, 1960, French Cameroun became the independent Republic of Cameroon. Ahmadou Ahidjo became the new nation's president. In an election in February 1961, the people in the two parts of British Cameroons were given the choice of joining their territory with the new Republic of Cameroon or with neighboring Nigeria. Voters in the northern part chose to join Nigeria, and their area became part of that country on June 1, 1961. Voters in the southern part chose to join the Republic of Cameroon. This union took place on Oct. 1, 1961. From then until early 1972, Cameroon operated as a federation of two states—East Cameroon and West Cameroon. Then in May 1972, Cameroon adopted a new constitution that united the two separate states.

Ahidjo resigned as president in 1982. His prime minister, Paul Biya, became president. Until 1991, Biya's political party—the Cameroon People's Democratic Movement (CPDM)—was the only one allowed in Cameroon. In 1991, other political parties were legalized. In 1992, Cameroon held its first multiparty elections. Biya was elected president, and the CPDM won a majority in the National Assembly. Biya was reelected president in 1997 and 2004. The CPDM remained in power after legislative elections in 1997 and 2002.

Dennis D. Cordell

See also **Douala; Fulani; Pygmies; Yaoundé.**

Camomile, *KAM uh myl* or *KAM uh meel,* is a group of small plants that are sometimes used in folk medicine. The name is often spelled *chamomile.* The most commonly cultivated camomile grows in the eastern and central regions of the United States, where it was brought from Europe. It is called the *common,* or *corn, camomile,* and sometimes the *English,* or *Roman, camomile.* A perennial, it grows about 12 inches (30 centimeters) high and has a slender, trailing stem and many branches. The flowers look much like daisies. The flowers and leaves smell sweet, but taste bitter. They are sometimes applied as a *poultice* (warm, moist mass) to treat toothaches, or made into a tonic. *German camomile* may grow as high as 2 feet (61 centimeters). Its flower heads can be used in folk medicine. Camomile is related to *mayweed,* a common plant in the Western states. Margaret R. Bolick

WORLD BOOK illustration by Lorraine Epstein

Camomile

Scientific classification. Camomiles belong to the family Compositae. The common camomile is *Anthemis nobilis.* German camomile is *Matricaria chamomilla.*

Camouflage, *KAM uh FLAHZH,* is the art of disguising or hiding military equipment and troops from an enemy. People borrowed the idea of camouflage from nature. Many animals can blend into their natural background for protection. The fur of some small animals of northern countries turns white in winter, to blend with the snow. The fur of these animals is brown in summer, to enable them to hide from enemies in woods or brush.

Camouflage has always been used in war, but it first became a recognized technique in World War I (1914-1918), when the airplane greatly expanded the possibility of observation by an enemy. During World War II (1939-1945), camouflage was applied to nearly every military activity. Camouflage ranged from using white uniforms in Arctic regions and mottled green uniforms in the jungle to concealing cities using smoke screens.

U.S. Army

For camouflage in the desert, soldiers use sand-colored uniforms and equipment. Camouflaged troops in Saudi Arabia , *shown here,* prepare to fire a cannon during the Persian Gulf War of 1991. The war was fought chiefly in desert lands.

The purpose of most camouflage is to conceal forces and equipment from air observation. Roofs of earth and branches can hide gun emplacements from enemy pilots. Troop movements can be concealed by parking trucks and pitching tents in the shadows of trees. An airfield runway can be painted to look like an area of fields and roads from the air. The sides and roof of a building can be painted to appear as part of a road. War plants have been camouflaged to look like golf courses from the air. People employed to play golf on the roofs can aid the deception. Fleets of ships have been hidden by stretching camouflaged nets over a harbor.

Warships of World War I were painted with zigzag lines of many colors to hide them from submarines and enemy ships. This arrangement of colors was called "dazzle paint." World War II ships were painted in softer tones in irregular patterns that blended with sky and sea and made the ships even more difficult to detect.

Most camouflage can be detected by aerial photography. Until the late 1950's, an object painted green to blend with a forest showed up when photographed with infrared film. Military intelligence officers detect many kinds of camouflage from such photographs. In 1957, the United States Navy developed a paint that was effective against infrared film. Ann Alexander Warren

See also **Animal** (Camouflage); **Protective coloration.**

Camp. See **Camping** (The campsite).

Camp David is the official retreat of the president of the United States. It lies in a heavily wooded area of Catoctin Mountain in Maryland, about 70 miles (113 kilometers) from Washington, D.C.

Camp David has an office for the president, and living quarters for the first family, staff, and guests. The camp includes a pitch-and-putt golf green, a swimming pool, and facilities for other sports.

Camp David is administered by the Military Office of the White House and is operated by the United States Navy. Armed guards from the U.S. Marine Corps patrol the area and permit no unauthorized person to enter.

President Franklin D. Roosevelt established the camp

in 1942, as a retreat where he could escape the summer heat of Washington. He chose the site because its elevation made it cool in summer and the isolated high location provided adequate security.

Roosevelt called the camp *Shangri-La,* the name of a perfect mountain kingdom in *Lost Horizon,* a famous novel by English author James Hilton. In 1945, President Harry S. Truman made Shangri-La the official presidential retreat. President Dwight D. Eisenhower renamed the camp in 1953 for his grandson, David Eisenhower. President Eisenhower also added the golf green.

Presidents have conducted their regular business at the retreat, and several have held important conferences there. In 1943, during World War II, Roosevelt met at the camp with Prime Minister Winston Churchill of Britain. Eisenhower conferred at Camp David with Premier Nikita S. Khrushchev of the Soviet Union in 1959.

In 1978, President Jimmy Carter used Camp David to host peace talks between President Anwar el-Sadat of Egypt and Prime Minister Menachem Begin of Israel. The peace talks resulted in a major agreement, called the Camp David Accords. For details on the Camp David Accords, see **Arab-Israeli conflict** (The Camp David Accords). Critically reviewed by the White House Military Office

See also **President of the United States** (picture: Camp David).

Camp Fire USA is a youth development organization in the United States. It seeks to build confidence in children and teen-agers, to provide leadership experiences, and to improve the conditions in society that affect young people. Camp Fire USA designs its programs to meet five main goals: (1) The programs are youth-centered. (2) They engage the entire family. (3) They are welcoming and inclusive. (4) They build partnerships between young people and adults. (5) They provide service to others.

Camp Fire USA has councils throughout the United States. Young members of Camp Fire USA range from infants 6 weeks old in child care programs to adults 21 years of age. However, the majority of young people in Camp Fire USA programs are between 5 and 18 years old. Adult members include people who serve as small-group leaders and program leaders. The organization also has both paid and volunteer staff.

Camp Fire USA programs

Camp Fire USA activities are administered under six types of programs: (1) traditional small-group programs, (2) Community Family Club, (3) Teens in Action, (4) camping and environmental education programs, (5) service learning programs, and (6) self-reliance courses.

Small group programs focus on the individual development of each member. Each small group consists of children who meet regularly—usually after school—and is led by a trained adult leader. The groups provide an environment in which members can grow into responsible adults.

Camp Fire USA has four program levels for small groups. These levels are (1) Starflight, (2) Adventure, (3) Discovery, and (4) Horizon.

Starflight members are kindergartners, first-graders, and second-graders. They participate in enjoyable activities while working with others and learning about the world. Starflight members play games, tell stories, learn crafts, and visit interesting places near their homes. They take part in service projects and in programs that build self-confidence. They also learn to help their parents by taking on responsibilities at home.

Adventure members are third- through fifth-graders. They develop decision-making skills through activities involving business, citizenship, creative arts, games and sports, science, and the outdoors. Adventure members also take part in neighborhood cleanups, collect food and other items for the needy, plant trees, and volunteer for other local service activities.

Discovery members are sixth- through eighth-graders. They take part in a wide variety of activities, including camping, outdoor sports, cooking, music, and the arts. They also participate in community service.

Horizon members are high school students with a strong desire to pursue their interests, abilities, and goals. They study career choices, educational options, and the many directions their lives can take. Horizon members guide younger Camp Fire USA members, vol-

Camp Fire USA

Camp Fire USA

Camp Fire USA offers programs that serve children in age groups from kindergarten through high school. Uniforms differ by club level. The picture at left shows Starflight members in their red vests and Adventure members in their blue vests. Each Discovery and Horizon club chooses its own uniform.

Camp Fire USA, Metropolitan Chicago Council

Camping gives Camp Fire USA members the opportunity to live and work with others in the outdoors. The members, *shown here,* are enjoying a hot drink around a campfire.

unteer at hospitals, assist in community conservation projects, and tutor children. They may also serve on Camp Fire USA council boards and committees.

Horizon members are eligible to receive the *Wohelo Award* for work that contributes to society, betters the individual, and develops valuable skills. The name of the award comes from the first two letters of the words *work, health,* and *love.*

Community Family Club activities focus on interaction between young people and adults. Young people, families, and adult volunteers participate in field trips, community meals, special events, and informal projects. Children and teen-agers may work to develop new skills and improve their academic abilities. Adults may take parenting classes, learn first aid skills, or participate in other activities.

Teens in Action offers opportunities for teen-agers to work toward common goals and to take on leadership roles. The program encourages teen-agers to make productive use of their own strategies, talents, and ideas.

Members of Teens in Action identify social issues that affect their lives. Such issues may include drunken driving, youth violence, or homelessness. The members then address the issues through community projects. In addition, teens may participate in a national youth leadership conference and serve on local and national Camp Fire USA committees. Teens in Action members are also eligible to receive the Wohelo Award.

Camping and environmental education programs are designed to develop the whole child—that is, to help the child use camp experiences to learn about living. Camping and environmental education programs offer opportunities for work, recreation, and decision making. All Camp Fire USA outdoor programs emphasize ecology, conservation, and the relationships between living things.

Service learning programs allow members to learn through activities that help others. A six-week program called *A Gift of Giving* helps children—from kindergarten to eighth grade—identify community needs, design projects to address those needs, and carry out those projects.

Self-reliance courses seek to develop confidence, character, and responsibility in young people. Children in self-reliance courses learn how to resolve conflicts, manage anger, and respond to emergency situations. Teen-agers learn other practical skills, such as how to play with and care for infants and toddlers.

Organization

A board of trustees manages Camp Fire USA. The board establishes national policies, sets up organizational requirements and standards, and charters local councils and community partners. Community partners include companies, schools, faith-based groups, and other organizations that help carry out Camp Fire USA programs.

Local councils and community partners serve cities, metropolitan areas, regions, and states throughout the country. All local councils and partners must be committed to the Camp Fire USA mission and follow the policies and standards of Camp Fire USA. Charters issued by the national organization allow the councils and partners to organize and supervise Camp Fire USA programs. The councils and partners also train leaders and establish membership dues and program fees. Professional staff members work with community volunteers to provide services through the local councils.

Local boards of trustees organize the local councils and elect council officers. Local councils elect delegates in proportion to their membership to represent them at the Camp Fire USA National Convention. The National Convention meets in odd-numbered years to discuss matters of national policy.

Teen-age members of Camp Fire USA serve on local council boards and committees and as voting delegates to national meetings. Some also are members of national committees, boards, and task forces. Adult volunteers commonly serve as small group program leaders. Qualified high school students who are members of a special training program may also lead programs for younger members.

Parents, teachers, neighbors, and civic organizations may sponsor Camp Fire USA groups. Sponsors help the group leaders with special projects and activities and make sure the groups have places to meet. Common meeting places include homes, churches, synagogues,

Camp Fire USA

Adventure members take part in many creative activities. This group is working with a leader on a craft project.

schools, and civic buildings.

Camp Fire USA receives funding from a variety of sources. These sources include candy sales and other fund-raising projects by local councils and community partners, contributions from individuals, grants from government agencies and private foundations, and funds from the United Way of America.

The corporate headquarters and the council development division of Camp Fire USA are in Kansas City, Missouri. The corporate office supports Camp Fire USA programs and provides such services as marketing, merchandising, and training. The council development division provides consultation and other services for local councils.

History

The founders of Camp Fire USA were Luther Halsey Gulick, a physician and national leader in recreational programs, and his wife, Charlotte Vetter Gulick. In 1909, the Gulicks opened Camp Sebago-Wohelo, one of the first girls' camps in the United States, in South Casco, Maine. There, girls took part in swimming, canoeing, and other activities on the shores of Sebago Lake.

Luther Halsey Gulick helped found the Boy Scouts of America in 1910. Soon, the Gulicks began receiving letters calling for a similar organization for girls. In response to the letters, the Gulicks established the Camp Fire Girls that same year. In the following years, the Gulicks—in cooperation with other workers in the fields of education and recreation—organized Camp Fire groups throughout the United States. The groups offered a wide variety of programs and activities, including child development, group camping, outdoor programs, and social action.

Originally, only girls could join Camp Fire groups. But in 1975, Camp Fire began admitting boys at all program levels. In 1979, the organization changed its official name from Camp Fire Girls, Inc., to Camp Fire, Inc. The organization became known as Camp Fire USA in 2001.

Critically reviewed by Camp Fire USA

See also **Camping; Gulick, Luther Halsey.**

Camp H. M. Smith, Hawaii, serves as headquarters of the United States Pacific Command. This unified command controls American military forces from the Arctic Ocean to the South Pole, and from the west coast of the United States to the Indian Ocean. The camp covers about 500 acres (200 hectares), and lies on Aiea Heights, 12 miles (19 kilometers) northwest of Honolulu's chief urban area.

The camp was established in 1942 as a naval hospital and depot. In 1955, it was named for General Holland M. Smith. W. W. Reid

Camp Lejeune, North Carolina, serves as home base and training center for a combat division and a force service support group of the United States Fleet Marine Forces, Atlantic. It covers 110,000 acres (45,000 hectares), extending 1 mile (1.6 kilometers) from the center of Jacksonville to the Atlantic Ocean.

The Marines conduct amphibious training along a 14-mile (23-kilometer) oceanfront. During the summer, 10,000 reservists take part in the training. Major commands at the camp include the Marine Corps base and the largest naval hospital in the southern United States. The 2,700-acre (1,100-hectare) Marine Corps Air Station at nearby New River is controlled by the Marine Corps Air Station at Cherry Point (see **Cherry Point Marine Corps Air Station**).

The Marines established the camp in 1941 and named it for Lieutenant General John A. Lejeune. Lejeune was a Marine Corps commandant from 1920 to 1929.

Critically reviewed by the United States Marine Corps

Camp meeting was an outdoor religious gathering held in the United States, chiefly in the 1800's. Meetings lasted several days and featured daily open-air services. The meetings were intended to revive the spirit of religion but not take the place of regular church functions. Baptist, Methodist, and Presbyterian ministers often preached at the same series of meetings. The participants lived in tents or temporary houses in large clearings. The first camp meeting is said to have taken place in Logan County, Kentucky, in 1800. See also **Pioneer life in America** (Religion); **Revivalism.** Henry Warner Bowden

Camp Pendleton, California, houses a combat division and other units of the United States Marine Corps. It covers 125,000 acres (50,590 hectares) and lies 30 miles (48 kilometers) north of San Diego. It was once the site of a Spanish ranch and mission. The Marines established the camp in 1942 and named it for Major General Joseph H. Pendleton. It was the world's largest Marine installation until 1957, when the Marine Corps commissioned the 596,000-acre (241,000-hectare) Twentynine Palms Marine Corps Base in the California desert.

Critically reviewed by the United States Marine Corps

Campaign. See **Election campaign.**

Campanile, *kam puh NEE lay,* is a bell tower. The term comes from the Italian word that means *bell.* Most cam-

SCALA/Art Resource

A campanile with alternating bands of black and white marble rises from the roof of the Siena Cathedral in Italy, *shown here.* Construction of the bell tower began in 1313.

paniles are in Italy. The towers are usually square, but some are round. Most are built as separate structures, but they can be attached to a church, where their bells serve to call people to prayer. Campaniles also have been attached to town halls, where they once were lookout posts and symbols of civic pride.

The first campaniles were built beside churches in the A.D. 500's. Two of the earliest surviving campaniles were built with the churches of Sant' Apollinare Nuovo and Sant' Apollinare in Classe, both in Ravenna, Italy. The Leaning Tower of Pisa, started in 1173, is a famous campanile. The great Italian artist Giotto designed the campanile of the Cathedral of Florence. Construction began in the 1330's, after Giotto's death. The campanile of the Basilica of St. Mark in Venice is among the tallest at 322 feet (98 meters). Campaniles are still built, but their popularity has declined. William J. Hennessey

See also **Leaning Tower of Pisa; Bell; Tower; Venice** (picture).

Campanula, *kam PAN yuh luh,* or *little bell,* is a group of slender plants that grow wild in Europe, Asia, and North America. There are about 300 species, and many are cultivated as garden plants. The flowers can be white, blue, or purple.

James S. Miller

Scientific classification. Campanulas are members of the bellflower family, Campanulaceae. They make up the genus *Campanula.*

See also **Bellflower; Bluebell; Canterbury bell.**

WORLD BOOK illustration by Robert Hynes

Campanula

Campbell, Ben Nighthorse (1933-), a Northern Cheyenne Indian chief, was a member of the United States Senate from 1993 to 2005. Campbell, who represented Colorado, was the first American Indian since the late 1920's to hold a U.S. Senate seat. Charles Curtis, whose mother was part Indian, served in the Senate from 1907 to 1913 and again from 1915 to 1929. Campbell was a Democrat when he was first elected to the Senate, but he switched to the Republican Party in 1995.

Campbell was born April 13, 1933, in Auburn, California. His father was a Northern Cheyenne Indian. His mother was Portuguese. Campbell served in the U.S. Air Force from 1951 to 1953. He earned a bachelor's degree from San Jose State University in 1957. He also attended Meiji University in Tokyo. Campbell became a judo expert and was a member of the U.S. judo team in the 1964 Olympic Games. In the late 1960's and the 1970's, he built a successful business as a jewelry designer and jewelry maker and moved to Colorado. He served in the Colorado House of Representatives from 1983 until 1986, when he was elected to the U.S. House of Representatives. He won reelection to the U.S. House in 1988 and 1990. Michael Barone

U.S. Senate

Ben Nighthorse Campbell

Campbell, Donald (1921-1967), became the first speedboat racer to exceed 200 mph (320 kph) and live to tell about it. Campbell was born in Povey Cross, Surrey, England. His father, Sir Malcolm Campbell, held the water speed record of 141 mph (227 kph) when he died in 1949. When Stanley Sayres of Seattle set a new mark at 178.497 mph (287.263 kph) in 1952, Donald decided to return the record to the Campbell family. In 1955, Campbell broke the 200-mph (320-kph) speed barrier with a mark of 202.32 mph (325.602 kph). He drove the speedboat *Bluebird II* at a record of 276.34 mph (444.726 kph) in 1964. He died in a speedboat accident. Fred Farley

Campbell, John Douglas Sutherland. See **Lorne, Marquess of.**

Campbell, Joseph (1904-1987), was a famous American authority on mythology. Campbell developed the idea that myths provide ways in which all human cultures express their ideas about themselves and about the natural and supernatural forces they cannot control.

Campbell became particularly interested in the myths that tell of an individual, usually a man, who leaves the ordinary world and enters the supernatural world. There he learns of his heroic destiny and receives charms or magical weapons. The man defeats the forces that oppose him and returns with new knowledge and new powers to the society from which he came. Campbell called this story the "monomyth" of the hero, because he found versions of it in nearly every culture.

Campbell wrote many books about mythology, notably the four-volume *The Masks of God.* It consists of *Primitive Mythology* (1959), *Oriental Mythology* (1962), *Occidental Mythology* (1964), and *Creative Mythology* (1968). He was born in New York City. David H. Richter

Kim Campbell

Prime Minister of Canada
1993

Mulroney
1984-1993

Campbell
1993

Chrétien
1993-2003

Canapress

Campbell, Kim (1947-), served as prime minister of Canada in 1993, the first woman ever to hold that office. She became prime minister in June after being elected leader of Canada's ruling party, the Progressive Conservative Party. Campbell replaced Brian Mulroney, who had resigned. But Campbell served only about four months in office. On Oct. 25, 1993, the Progressive Conservatives finished behind several parties in a general election. Liberal Party leader Jean Chrétien succeeded Campbell as prime minister on Nov. 4, 1993.

Campbell rose quickly in Canadian politics. She began her political career in 1980, when she became a member of the Vancouver school board in Vancouver, B.C. In 1986, she won a seat in the provincial legislature of British Columbia, the Legislative Assembly. In 1988, she was elected to the Canadian House of Commons in Ottawa, Ont. There, Campbell rose quickly in Prime Minister Mulroney's government. Mulroney appointed her attorney general and justice minister of Canada in 1990. In 1993, Campbell was appointed Canada's minister of national defence and minister of veterans affairs. She was the first woman to hold these Cabinet positions.

In February 1993, Mulroney announced his resignation as prime minister and leader of the Progressive Conservatives. He called a party convention for June to choose his replacement. Campbell won the party leadership. She became prime minister on June 25.

When Campbell became prime minister, Canada's economy was struggling to recover from a recession that started in 1990. Campbell also faced the challenge of uniting Canada under a revised constitution. The revised constitution had been adopted in 1982, when it was approved by the legislatures of every province except Quebec. Many Quebecers feared the constitution would not provide sufficient protection for Quebec's French-Canadian society. In 1987 and again in 1992, the Canadian government had agreed on a plan to amend the constitution in an effort to win Quebec's approval. However, neither proposal was adopted, and Quebec still refused to sign the constitution.

Shortly after Campbell became prime minister, she called for a general election. However, many Canadians disapproved of the Progressive Conservatives. They associated the party with the recession and high rates of unemployment that occurred while it was in power. This disapproval was among the reasons why Campbell's party lost the general election. In addition, Campbell failed to maintain a *coalition* (partnership) that Mulroney had built between voters in French-speaking Quebec and conservative western Canada.

Graham Fraser, the contributor of this article, is Parlimentary Correspondent for The Globe and Mail.

Early life

Childhood. Campbell was born on March 10, 1947, in Port Alberni, B.C. She and her older sister, Alix, were the

Important dates in Campbell's life

1947	(March 10) Born in Port Alberni, B.C.
1983	Received a law degree from the University of British Columbia.
1986	Won a seat in British Columbia's Legislative Assembly.
1988	Elected to the Canadian House of Commons.
1990	Appointed first woman minister of justice and attorney general of Canada.
1993	(Jan. 9) Named first woman defence minister of Canada.
1993	(June 25) Became first woman prime minister of Canada.
1993	(Oct. 25) Progressive Conservatives defeated in a general election.

only children of George T. Campbell, a lawyer, and Phyllis (or Lissa) Cook Campbell, a secretary. Kim's given name was Avril Phaedra Campbell. However, she began using the name Kim when she was 12 years old.

Kim excelled at school and studied music and dancing. She attended high school at Prince of Wales Secondary School in Vancouver, where she was student council president. She also wrote music and poetry, and played the piano and guitar. In 1964, Campbell graduated at the top of her high school class.

Education and entry into political life. In 1969, Campbell earned a bachelor's degree in political science from the University of British Columbia. She served as a vice president of the student government at the university. In 1970, after winning a *fellowship* (grant of money), Campbell studied for a Ph.D. degree at the London School of Economics and Political Science. In 1972, during her stay in London, she married Nathan J. Divinsky, a mathematics professor from the University of British Columbia. Campbell moved back to Canada with her husband in 1973, without finishing her Ph.D. program. From 1975 to 1981, she taught political science at the University of British Columbia and Vancouver Community College.

In 1980, Campbell was admitted to the University of British Columbia's law school. That year, she also became a trustee on the Vancouver school board, her first political office. Campbell served as chairman of the school board in 1983. Also that year, she received her law degree and joined the Vancouver law firm of Ladner Downs as a student intern. In 1984, she was admitted to the bar and resigned from the school board. In 1982, she and Divinsky divorced.

Political career

Provincial legislator. In 1985, Campbell was hired as executive director in the office of William R. Bennett, premier of British Columbia. In 1986, Bennett resigned as premier and as leader of the Social Credit Party, the major conservative party in British Columbia. Campbell campaigned for the party leadership. William N. Vander Zalm won the leadership job and became premier. However, Campbell won a seat in British Columbia's Legislative Assembly from the *riding* (district) of Vancouver/Point Grey. She represented the Social Credit Party. In the Legislative Assembly, Campbell chaired the committee that reviewed bills on labor, justice, and intergovernmental relations. She often disagreed with Vander Zalm's policies, though she and the premier belonged to the same party. Campbell particularly opposed Vander Zalm when he tried to suspend public funds for abortions.

In 1986, Campbell married a second time. Her new husband was Howard Eddy, a lawyer for the attorney general of British Columbia.

Member of Parliament. In 1988, Campbell ran for a seat in Canada's House of Commons. She campaigned as a Progressive Conservative candidate from the riding of Vancouver Centre. Campbell won the election over her main opponent, New Democratic Party candidate Johanna den Hertog.

After arriving in Ottawa, Campbell quickly became part of Prime Minister Mulroney's government. In 1989, Mulroney named her minister of state for Indian affairs and northern development. Campbell also served on a key Cabinet committee that approved all federal appointments and regulations.

In 1990, Mulroney appointed Campbell to be Canada's first woman minister of justice and attorney general. As justice minister, Campbell guided 26 bills through Parliament. One of these bills was an important piece of gun control legislation. The legislation made buying firearms in Canada more difficult. Another bill that Campbell helped pass into law set guidelines for court cases involving rape. The law limited the presentation of a rape victim's sexual history in court.

Canapress

Young Kim Campbell, shown at about the age of 6, smiled in the arms of her father, George T. Campbell. Kim spent her childhood in Vancouver, B.C., where her father was a lawyer.

Canapress

Justice Minister Campbell discussed gun control legislation with a Department of Justice official. As a justice minister, Campbell helped pass 26 bills into law, including a gun control bill.

Campbell experienced another marital setback during her first years in Ottawa. In 1991, she and her second husband separated. In 1993, they divorced.

In January 1993, Mulroney appointed Campbell to be Canada's first woman minister of national defence and minister of veterans affairs. As defence minister, Campbell supported the purchase of EH-101 military helicopters. She also defended the renewal of an agreement permitting United States cruise missile tests in Canada.

Some of Campbell's political opponents criticized these policies, arguing that they were inappropriate in a world without the Cold War. The Cold War, an intense rivalry between Communist nations, led by the Soviet Union, and non-Communist nations, including Canada, had recently ended.

Prime minister. After Mulroney announced his resignation as prime minister and party leader, Campbell immediately became the leading candidate to replace him. However, Jean Charest, Canada's minister of the environment, became an important challenger. Charest received support from many delegates to the Progressive Conservative Party convention, and he quickly reduced Campbell's lead in the race. Despite Charest's challenge, Campbell won the election for head of the party. She was sworn in as prime minister on June 25, 1993.

The 1993 election. After becoming prime minister, Campbell called a general election for October 1993. In the campaign that followed, Campbell led the Progressive Conservatives against the Liberal Party, led by Jean Chrétien, and the Bloc Québécois, led by Lucien Bouchard; the Reform Party, led by Preston Manning; and the New Democratic Party, led by Audrey M. McLaughlin. During the campaign, Campbell focused on economic issues. She said she would try to cut Canada's large budget deficit. Campbell also promised to reduce the size of the government. After becoming prime minister, she appointed 24 ministers to her Cabinet, 10 fewer than in Mulroney's Cabinet.

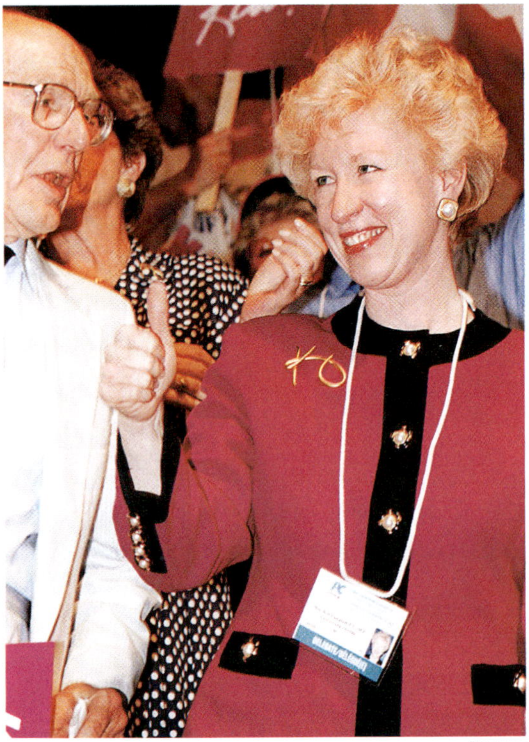

Canapress

Campbell gave the thumbs up sign at the Progressive Conservative Party's convention in June 1993. She became prime minister by being elected party leader at the convention.

Campbell and her party supported the North American Free Trade Agreement (NAFTA). The agreement, signed by leaders of Canada, the United States, and Mexico in 1992, would gradually eliminate *tariffs* (taxes on imports) and other trade barriers among the three countries. But NAFTA required approval of the legislatures of all three countries before it would take effect. Campbell believed that NAFTA, by opening up more markets for Canadian businesses, would create jobs.

Campbell also faced the question of revising the Canadian constitution. The constitutional question had divided the people of Canada since the early 1980's, when Quebec refused to accept the Constitution Act of 1982. Many Quebecers feared that the act, which made changes in Canada's constitution, did not adequately protect their province's French-Canadian character. Prime Minister Mulroney and the 10 provincial premiers had twice agreed on a plan to revise the constitution in an effort to overcome Quebec's objections. The first plan, called the Meech Lake accord, failed in 1990 when the legislatures of two provinces refused to approve it. The second attempt, known as the Charlottetown accord, was rejected by Canadian voters in 1992. The failure of these two agreements strengthened the position of Quebec nationalists, who argued that Quebec should declare its independence from Canada.

Canadian voters were unhappy with the economic recession in Canada that had begun in 1990. Many voters associated the Progressive Conservatives with this recession and high rates of unemployment that accompanied it. These factors hurt Campbell's party. In the 1993 general election, the Progressive Conservatives suffered a stunning defeat. The party, which held 154 seats in the House of Commons before the general election, won only 2 seats in that election. Jean Chrétien replaced Campbell as prime minister. Campbell also lost her seat in the House of Commons. On Dec. 13, 1993, she resigned as leader of the Progressive Conservatives.

Later years. After the 1993 election, Campbell held several university positions. In 1996, she completed *Time and Chance,* in which she wrote about her time as prime minister. From 1996 to 2000, she served as Canadian consul general in Los Angeles. In 1997, Campbell joined the Council of Women World Leaders. Also in 1997, she co-wrote a musical play titled *Noah's Ark* with the Canadian composer Hershey Felder, her third husband. In 2004, she became secretary-general of the Club of Madrid, an organization that supports democracy around the world. Graham Fraser

Related articles in *World Book* include:

Canada, History of
Charest, Jean
Chrétien, Jean
Mulroney, Brian
Prime minister of Canada
Progressive Conservative Party

Campbell, Mrs. Patrick (1865-1940), was a British stage actress. She was a witty, temperamental performer, who specialized in playing women with a socially improper past. In 1886, Campbell made her stage debut in London and established her career in 1893 as the title character in Sir Arthur Wing Pinero's *The Second Mrs. Tanqueray.* She also starred in Pinero's *The Notorious Mrs. Ebbsmith* (1895). She acted in Shakespearean roles with the famous British actor Sir Johnston Forbes-Robertson. George Bernard Shaw wrote the part of Eliza Doolittle in *Pygmalion* especially for her. Selections of Campbell's correspondence with Shaw were published in *Bernard Shaw and Mrs. Patrick Campbell: Their Correspondence* (1952).

Beatrice Stella Tanner was born on Feb. 9, 1865, in London. She married Patrick Campbell in 1884. She wrote an autobiography, *My Life and Some Letters* (1922). Mrs. Campbell died on April 9, 1940. J. P. Wearing

Campbell, William Wallace (1862-1938), an American astronomer, was director of the Lick Observatory in California from 1901 to 1923. He became known for his work in *spectroscopy,* the examination and analysis of spectra of light. He also made important measurements of the motion of stars. During a solar eclipse in 1922, he observed the deflection of starlight by the sun's gravitational field. This observation, first made by Arthur Eddington, supported Albert Einstein's theory of general relativity. Campbell was born on April 16, 1862, in Hancock County, Ohio. He died on June 14, 1938.

Michael J. Crowe

Campbell-Bannerman, Sir Henry (1836-1908), served as the United Kingdom's prime minister from 1905 to 1908. His conciliatory attitude toward the Boers during and after the Anglo-Boer War of 1899-1902 helped prepare for the formation of the Union of South Africa in 1910. He was born on Sept. 7, 1836, in Glasgow, Scotland. He graduated from Trinity College, Cambridge. A Liberal, he served in Parliament for nearly 40 years. He died on April 2, 1908. Keith Robbins

Camphor, *KAM fuhr* (chemical formula $C_{10}H_{16}O$), is a substance that comes from the camphor tree. The trees grow tall and have white flowers. Most grow in Japan, China, and the island of Taiwan. Camphor trees are also grown in southern California and the Southern States.

Camphor is produced by steaming wood chips from the camphor tree. In this process, camphor collects in an oily layer on the chips. The oily substance is drained and pressed to remove the oil and water. Camphor is left in the form of whitish, almost transparent crystals. The crystals are usually purified by *sublimation,* a process by which the camphor changes directly from a solid into a vapor, leaving behind impurities. Today, chemists produce synthetic camphor in laboratories.

WORLD BOOK illustration by John D. Dawson

The camphor tree is the source of camphor.

Camphor is used in cosmetics, lacquers, and pharmaceuticals. *Spirits of camphor*—a mixture of 10 parts camphor, 70 parts alcohol, and 20 parts water—is a mild antiseptic. Camphor is also combined with another compound to make *camphorated parachlorophenol,* a germ-killing drug sometimes used in dental work. Chemists use camphor to denature ethyl alcohol, the alcohol used in alcoholic beverages. Denatured alcohol is ethyl alcohol that has been made unfit for drinking but has other uses. Large doses of camphor are poisonous and will cause delirium and convulsions. David S. Seigler

Scientific classification. The camphor tree is a member of the laurel family, Lauraceae. It is *Cinnamomum camphora.*

Campin, *KAHM pihn,* **Robert** (1375?-1444), was an important painter of altarpieces and portraits in northern Europe. His style appealed to the rising middle class, which admired the artist's depictions of everyday settings and the detailed descriptions of objects. Campin's figures typically have a sculptural solidity expressed by folds of drapery.

Center panel of an altarpiece (about 1425); the Metropolitan Museum of Art, New York City, the Cloisters Collection

Campin's *Annunciation* shows the angel Gabriel telling the Virgin Mary that she will be the mother of Jesus. Campin's realism and attention to detail influenced painters of the 1400's.

Campin's paintings employ what has been called *disguised symbolism.* Realistic objects convey symbolism beyond their identity as recognizable elements of an everyday scene. For example, in his *Annunciation,* a snuffed-out candle may refer to Jesus's life, which was extinguished on the cross. A hanging basin and towel may refer to the purity of the Virgin Mary. In his use of disguised symbolism, Campin influenced the artist Rogier van der Weyden, one of his assistants.

Little is known of Campin's life. He has been called the Master of Flémalle because four paintings attributed to him were mistakenly thought to have hung in an abbey in Flémalle, Belgium, near Liège. Linda Stone-Ferrier

Porterfield-Chickering, Photo Researchers

A family camping vacation can provide an opportunity for water sports and other outdoor recreational activities. But many people go camping simply to relax and enjoy the beauties of nature. National parks, such as Acadia National Park in Maine, above, are popular camping sites.

Camping

Camping is a popular form of outdoor recreation. Various types of camping provide opportunities throughout the year for people to share low-cost outdoor experiences in a natural environment. Camping trips range from spending the night in a tent in one's backyard to passing several weeks in the wilderness. Campers may visit forests, deserts, lakes, or mountains.

Some campers remain at one campsite for their entire trip. From this site they visit tourist attractions, participate in water sports, or just relax. They may also spend time in such popular outdoor activities as bird watching, fishing, rock collecting, photography, and hiking.

Many campers prefer to move from place to place each day in motor vehicles. They usually start early in the morning and select a new campsite by early afternoon. Such campers often tour state or provincial parks, national parks, national monuments, and historic sites.

Some campers prefer to "travel light," carrying all their equipment in backpacks, in canoes, or on bicycles. Usually these campers travel fewer miles than other campers, but enjoy a closer relationship with areas they visit. Most of their activities consist of getting from place to place, enjoying the area, and preparing meals.

Types of camping

Tent camping is the most popular type of camping and also one of the least expensive. Tents come in many sizes, shapes, and colors. Some tents can hold only one person while several people can live comfortably in a large tent. Modern tents are made of lightweight materials and are easy to erect, even by beginning campers. The light weight of many modern tents allows campers to carry them almost anywhere.

Recreational vehicle camping. A recreational vehicle (RV) is a motor vehicle that provides living quarters for campers. RV's range from small, collapsible trailers to large motor homes with most of the conveniences of permanent homes. For example, many recreational vehicles provide refrigerators and stoves for easy food preparation, showers, and restroom facilities. Most RV's also contain storage tanks for wastewater and sewage.

Numerous North American campgrounds provide electricity and water hookups to serve RV's. Many campers use their RV as a base camp while they explore the countryside by foot, bicycle, motorcycle, or automobile. They return to the RV for meals and to sleep.

Planning a camping trip

Campers should plan trips far enough in advance to research campgrounds and make reservations if necessary. Bookstores and sporting goods stores sell guides that list campgrounds, and reference sources in libraries contain information about places to camp. State and provincial tourism bureaus and local chambers of commerce provide maps and other camping information. Local park and recreation agencies usually have information about nearby campgrounds.

At campgrounds that operate on a first-come, first-served basis, it is best to arrive in the morning. But many campgrounds require reservations, especially during

William R. Ruskin, the contributor of this article, is Assistant Director, Office of Economic Development, City of Colorado Springs.

Recreational vehicles provide many of the conveniences of home during a camping trip. A large number of campgrounds supply hookups for electric power and water for such vehicles. Campers can take all-day outings and return to the recreational vehicle at night to sleep.

Artstreet

the vacation season. Most campgrounds charge a small fee for the use of the site. There are additional charges for sites with extra facilities such as electrical hookups and showers. Permits are required to camp in remote parts of national parks or wilderness areas. Campers can obtain permits from the area's ranger.

The information in the following sections refers to tent camping, but it generally applies to most other types of camping.

Camping equipment and food

There is a broad range of equipment available, but people need not take a large amount of gear to have an enjoyable camping trip. Beginners often make the mistake of taking more equipment than they need. New campers should start out with a few essential items of high quality. They will learn from experience which additional items would be useful.

Tents today are usually made of canvas, nylon, or cotton. These fabrics supply strength, fireproofing, waterproofing, and adequate ventilation. Modern tents come in different styles designed to serve specific purposes. For example, backpackers need a small and lightweight single-person tent. Such tents may weigh as little as 2.5 pounds (1.1 kilograms). For family camping, tents must be roomy enough to provide comfortable shelter for a group. Some large tents include dining areas and have storage pockets in the walls. This kind of tent is heavier and more difficult to set up.

Before buying a tent, ask for a demonstration to make sure it is easy to erect. Also make sure the tent is well-constructed, and that all the parts are included.

Sleeping bags are warmer and easier to carry than blankets. A sleeping bag provides efficient insulation to keep campers warm. Goose or duck *down* (soft feathers) is an effective, lightweight insulating material that compresses easily. Several synthetic fabrics insulate nearly as well as down. They also cost less and last longer. In addition, synthetic insulation is easier to clean, and it dries faster than down. The insulation is enclosed in outside coverings made of strong, lightweight fabrics.

Sleeping bags come in three shapes: (1) mummy, which hugs the body and becomes narrow at the bottom, (2) tapered, which is similar to the mummy shape

Richard Rowan, Photo Researchers

Backpackers carry all of their equipment as they hike from site to site. Backpacking allows people to enjoy wilderness areas that cannot be reached by vehicle.

but wider, and (3) rectangular. *Mummy bags* furnish the most warmth, but they limit movement. This lightweight type, often insulated with down, is probably best for backpacking. Mummy bags are also popular for winter camping, and camping at high elevations. *Tapered bags* are designed mainly for the same uses as mummy bags. Tapered bags usually do not provide enough heat for extremely cold temperatures, but they allow more movement. *Rectangular bags* do not insulate as effectively as the other two, but they are the most comfortable. A rectangular bag with synthetic insulation is probably the best choice for the average camper.

Regardless of the style or quality of a sleeping bag, a camper needs additional insulation between the bag and the ground. A *tarpaulin* (piece of canvas or plastic) serves this purpose. Campers also use it as a wrap for gear, a windbreak, or a shelter. A foam pad or inflatable air mattress can provide insulation and comfort.

Clothing for camping trips should protect against wind, rain, sun, cold, and insects. The clothing must be sturdy enough to withstand hard wear and weather extremes. The amount needed depends on the length of the trip and whether the clothing will be laundered.

For warm weather, pack at least two pairs of lightweight trousers, as well as comfortable shorts, shirts, and a hat with a wide brim. A warm shirt or jacket should be included for cool evenings, and on visits to high elevations. For colder weather, bring wool shirts and trousers. Wet blue jeans take a long time to dry and do not provide insulation when wet, so avoid wearing them in snowy or rainy weather. A down vest and windproof outer parka provide protection against cold wind without restricting movement. Always carry a hooded, cloak-type raincoat called a *poncho.*

Hiking boots are recommended for hikes in rough terrain. Lightweight nylon boots have generally replaced heavy leather boots in popularity. Any hiking boot should be worn with two pairs of socks—a thin cotton pair under a heavier pair of wool or a wool and cotton blend. Comfortable sports shoes can be worn for relaxing around the campsite. Bring lightweight work gloves for such activities as cooking and chopping wood.

Food and water. Campers can prepare a great variety of food with the help of portable stoves and ovens and insulated coolers. Each person should bring a complete mess kit, which includes eating utensils. Many campers bring freeze-dried foods, which are prepared with boiling water, for fast cooking. Some plan meals in advance and organize the food in labeled plastic bags.

It is important to select nutritional foods from the basic food groups—vegetables; fruits; breads, cereals, rice, and pasta; milk, yogurt, and cheese; and meats, poultry, fish, dry beans and peas, eggs, and nuts. Some good foods for camping include peanut butter, cheese, pancakes, bacon, nuts, and popcorn. Buy canned and freeze-dried foods before the trip. When possible, buy fresh and frozen foods during the trip.

If you are not sure the water will be safe to drink, bring water from home. Additional water should come from an approved source, such as a campground well. Lakes and streams may look, smell, and taste clean, but still be contaminated with disease-causing microscopic organisms. If water must be taken from a questionable source, boil the water for at least five minutes before using it. Carry fresh water in canteens or water bottles.

Keith Gunnar, West Stock

Putting out a campfire is an important part of camping safety. The camper should extinguish the coals with water and spread them out to make sure there are no burning embers.

Other camp supplies are necessary for most camping trips. They include a small ax for splitting firewood and such basic tools as a hammer, screwdriver, pliers, flashlight, spade, hunting knife, rope, paper towels, matches in a waterproof container, and extra batteries. In addition, at least one camper in the group should carry a complete first-aid kit. Maps are also important, especially for the first visit to an area. Carry a compass at all times, no matter how familiar the area. A large backpack is necessary for overnight hikes away from the base camp. For shorter hikes, use a smaller pack to carry such items as food, maps, and a camera. Duffel bags can also hold clothing and other equipment.

The campsite

Selecting a location. Many campgrounds rent reserved campsites. Such campsites normally include a picnic table, charcoal grill or fireplace, and a suitable place for a tent. Some campgrounds have tenting areas with rest rooms and a convenient water supply.

Other locations, such as wilderness areas and forest preserves, do not have reserved campsites. Campers should follow a number of rules in selecting their sites. Look for a site on high, level ground that is uncluttered and sheltered from the wind. The campsite should be at least 200 feet (50 meters) from hiking trails, scenic attractions, and water. This helps preserve the area's beauty and the water's purity. Also, land next to water is usually low, damp, and a breeding place for insects. The tent should be pitched on sandy soil that is firm enough to hold the stakes securely but still provide good drainage. Always try to avoid disturbing or damaging plant life. Rangers can usually suggest locations to set up camp.

Building a campfire. Natural wood supplies are being rapidly used up in many areas, so some camp-

Camping equipment

Campers should select suitable food, clothing, shelter, and other equipment for a safe and comfortable camping trip. The equipment should be both durable and easy to carry. Factors that guide campers in the selection of equipment include the duration of the trip, the season, and the surface features of the land in the camping area.

WORLD BOOK illustrations by David Cunningham

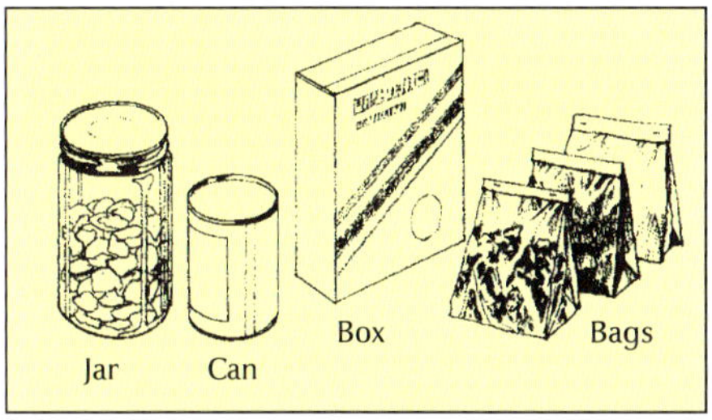

Food should be kept in sanitary containers. Campers can carry lightweight bags and boxes on hikes. Heavier jars and cans should be stored at the campsite.

Clothing should provide protection against insects, bad weather, and the sun. Clothes must also be able to withstand rough use. Campers should carry a change of clothing in case the clothes they are wearing get wet.

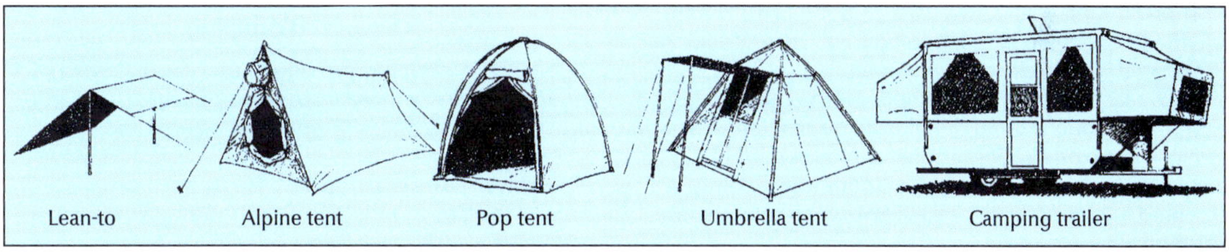

Shelters come in many sizes and styles. The lean-to and the alpine and pop tents can be folded and carried in a pack. The umbrella tent can be collapsed and stored in a car trunk. The camping trailer, which offers many conveniences, must be pulled to a campsite by a car or truck.

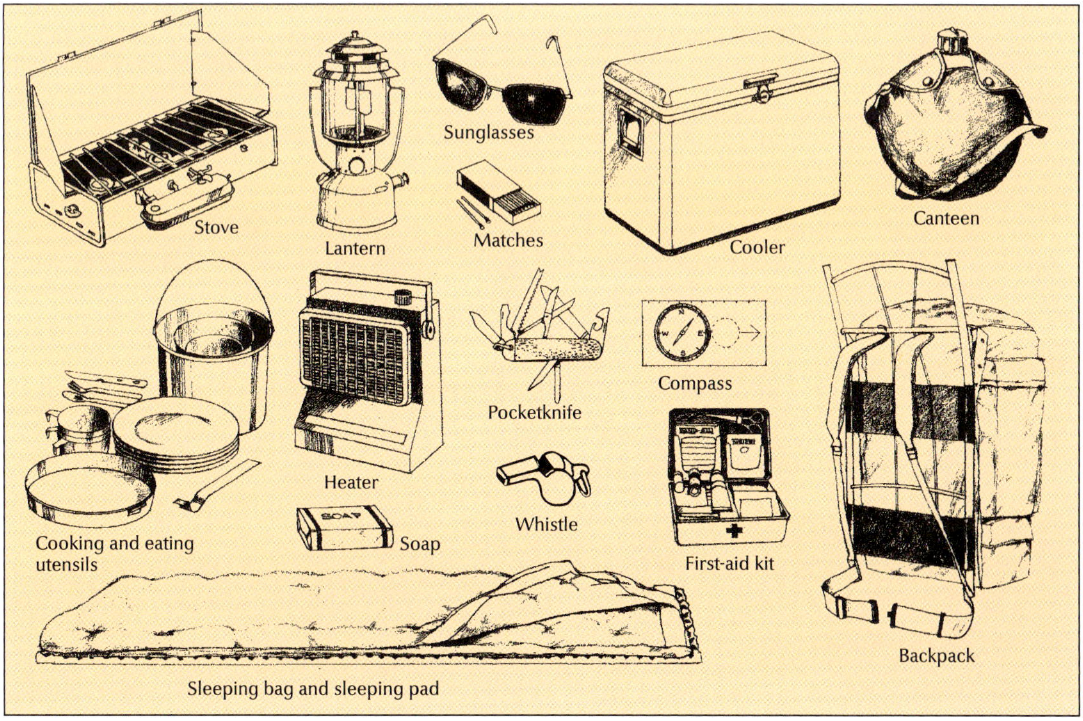

Other equipment. Heaters, stoves, and lanterns are available in small sizes for hikers and in larger sizes for campers who travel in cars and trailers. Hikers carry most of their supplies in a backpack. Perhaps the single most important item of camping equipment is a first-aid kit.

grounds sell firewood, and some campers bring wood with them. Regulations in some areas prohibit open fires, and other areas require permits to build them.

Before building a fire, make certain it will not harm the surroundings. Make pits large enough to keep a fire from spreading. Avoid building fires on windy days. Keep fires small, regularly removing ashes. Someone should be responsible for watching the fire at all times. A bucket of water and a small shovel should be available to control a fire that threatens to spread.

Three types of materials are needed to build a campfire: (1) tinder, (2) kindling, and (3) firewood. Tinder includes dry twigs, pine needles, leaves, and similar materials that ignite quickly. Kindling consists of larger pieces of wood that burn easily and rapidly. Softwoods, such as cedar or pine, make effective kindling. Firewood consists of woods that burn slowly and evenly and produce a bed of long-lasting coals. Hickory, oak, and sugar maple are examples of woods suitable for campfires.

There are many effective ways to build fires. The following method can be used to build a fire for cooking, for warmth, or simply for enjoyment.

First, place a small pile of tinder on the ground and arrange kindling around it in the shape of a tepee. Then enclose the tepee with four pieces of firewood that form a square. Soon after lighting the tinder, the kindling will begin to burn. Gradually, add firewood to keep the fire burning.

To start a fire in wet weather, find dry materials. Paper milk cartons and wadded paper can serve as tinder, and dry wood can sometimes be found under logs and trees. Damp logs should be split, because the inside of a log stays dry longer in wet weather.

Make sure a fire is out before leaving the campsite. To extinguish a fire, first spread the coals out until they lose their red glow. Then sprinkle water on the dead coals and dump soil over them. Next, stir the mixture, scatter it on the ground, and cover it with fresh topsoil. In areas without designated fire pits, no trace of the campfire should remain.

Camping safety and courtesy

Safety. Common sense can prevent most camping injuries. For example, children should never be allowed to use axes or knives, and anyone who is cooking should use gloves and potholders. However, campers must take special precautions to protect against such hazards as poisonous plants, improper food storage, lightning storms, and hiking emergencies.

Poisonous plants. Because many camping trips take place in the forest, campers should learn to identify poison sumac, poison oak, and poison ivy. If contact occurs, wash the affected skin immediately with soap and water. Then apply a lotion that soothes itching.

Improper food storage. Food poisoning can result from lack of refrigeration. Some campers avoid this danger by carrying only freeze-dried foods. Others store all their food in large coolers. Campers with small coolers often pack nonperishable foods separately in airtight containers. The smell of food can attract animals, so never leave food carelessly out in the open or store it in a tent.

Lightning storms occur more frequently than other types of dangerous weather, and they can take place in any sort of climate or terrain. Immediately seek shelter during a lightning storm. If shelter is not available, sit under trees of similar height. Avoid tall trees in open areas and exposed slopes and hilltops. In addition, get out of water and onto land at the first sign of lightning.

Hiking safety. Before leaving, tell your destination and expected length of a hike to someone who will not be hiking. If the terrain is unfamiliar, do not hike alone. Carry emergency supplies, such as waterproof matches. If you get lost, keep calm, remain in one place, and wait for a search party to arrive. At night, build a fire for warmth, protection, and to signal others. Leave the area only as a last resort.

Courtesy. While camping, always try to preserve the natural environment. Besides eliminating campfire remains and leaving wildlife undisturbed, save trash until it can be properly discarded. Bury human waste if no rest rooms are available. Out of respect for animals and neighboring campers, keep as quiet as possible.

Organized camping

Organized camping provides supervised activities for groups. There are three main types of organized camping: (1) summer camps, (2) specialty camps, and (3) school camping.

Summer camps are sponsored by such organizations as the Boy Scouts, Girl Scouts, Camp Fire USA, Young Men's Christian Association (YMCA), and Young Women's Christian Association (YWCA). There are also hundreds of private summer camps throughout the United States and Canada. Almost every summer camp has a lake for swimming, boating, and fishing. In addition, summer camps offer such activities as nature hikes, overnight backpacking trips, crafts, horseback riding, and archery. Campers usually sleep in cabins and eat in dining halls.

Specialty camps combine camping activities with a special activity, such as tennis, music, or computer instruction. There are also specialty camps designed for certain groups, such as people with disabilities, elderly people, and underprivileged children.

School camping combines educational programs with camping during the school year. A group of students spend several days, normally at a private camp, learning about the outdoors. Attendance at school camps is usually voluntary, and the school district pays part of the cost of the trip. William R. Ruskin

Related articles in ***World Book*** include:

Boy Scouts
Camp Fire USA
Canoeing
Girl Scouts
Hiking
Mountain climbing
National Park System (Visiting the parklands)
Outward Bound
Poison ivy
Recreational vehicle
Scouts Canada
Tent

Additional resources

Callan, Kevin. *The Happy Camper: An Essential Guide to Life Outdoors.* Boston Mills Pr., 2005.

Drake, Jane, and Love, Ann. *The Kids Campfire Book.* Kids Can Pr., 1998. Younger readers.

Rutter, Michael. *Camping Made Easy.* 2nd ed. Globe Pequot, 2001.

Camptosaurus, *KAMP tuh sawr uhs,* was a large plant-eating dinosaur from what are now North America and Europe. It lived about 154 million to 150 million years ago, during the Late Jurassic Period. *Camptosaurus* belonged to a group of dinosaurs known as *ornithopods,* meaning *bird-footed ones.* The animal weighed between 1 and 2 tons (0.9 and 1.8 metric tons). It measured about 20 feet (6 meters) in length and stood about 3 to 4 feet (0.9 to 1.2 meters) tall at the hips.

Camptosaurus may have traveled primarily upright on its two powerful hind legs. However, its smaller forelimbs had strong bony wrists, suggesting the animal may also have walked on all fours. This posture inspired the animal's name, which comes from the Greek words for *bent* and *lizard.* The five-fingered hands and four-toed feet of *Camptosaurus* ended in hooflike nails.

Camptosaurus had large jaws and a horny beak that it used to snap off pieces of plants. The front of its beak was toothless, but long rows of ridged, close-packed *cheek teeth* in the sides of its jaws helped it grind up plant food. A long snout enabled *Camptosaurus* to graze selectively. It could push the end of its snout into a plant and bite off the part that it wanted.

Camptosaurus fossils were first uncovered in Wyoming in the United States. The American scientist Othniel C. Marsh, a pioneer in *paleontology* (the study of prehistoric life), named the dinosaur in 1885.

Kenneth Carpenter

Campus school. See **Laboratory school.**

Campylobacter, *KAM pih loh BAK tuhr,* are a kind of bacteria that can cause a form of food poisoning. The illness, called *campylobacteriosis,* is usually caused by the bacterium *Campylobacter jejuni.* The bacterium occurs in unclean water and also in many types of livestock, including chickens, turkeys, and pigs. Scientists did not recognize *Campylobacter* as a cause of food-borne illness until the 1970's. However, health officials now believe that campylobacteriosis is the most common form of bacterial food poisoning in the United States.

The *Campylobacter* bacterium enters the digestive tract either through unclean water or improperly cooked and prepared foods. It passes through the stomach and enters the intestines. The bacterium then attaches to the lining of the intestine and grows. People first have symptoms of campylobacteriosis 2 to 10 days after swallowing the bacterium. A common symptom is diarrhea. The illness is generally mild, and people usually recover within days. In severe cases, however, the bacterium can destroy some of the lining of the intestine, causing intestinal bleeding. People with severe illness may require hospitalization.

To avoid campylobacteriosis, cook meats thoroughly and do not drink untreated water. It is also important to wash hands, cooking utensils, and surfaces thoroughly after using them to prepare raw meat. *Campylobacter* often occur in the juices of raw meats and may remain on a cutting board or knife used to cut up meat and then spread to other foods. James S. Dickson

See also **Food poisoning.**

Camus, *ka MOO,* **Albert,** *al BEHR* (1913-1960), was a French journalist, essayist, philosopher, novelist, and playwright who was associated with the Existentialist movement (see **Existentialism**). He won the 1957 Nobel Prize for literature. Camus wrote moving essays about his native northern Africa and set much of his fiction there. But his writing transcends its setting because it deals with moral problems of universal importance.

Camus was concerned with the freedom and responsibility of the individual, the alienation of the individual from society, and the difficulty of facing life without the comfort of believing in God or in absolute moral standards. These themes appear in his novels *The Stranger* (1942), *The Plague* (1947), and *The Fall* (1957); and in his play *Caligula* (1945).

Camus wrote two widely discussed philosophical essays. In *The Myth of Sisyphus* (1942), he said, "There is but one truly serious philosophical problem and that is suicide." He argued that people hang on to life even though life has no meaning or purpose to justify it and is thus "absurd." *The Rebel* (1951) is a critical examination of the forms of human rebellion.

Camus was born on Nov. 7, 1913, in Algeria and went to France for the first time in 1939. In 1942, he joined the French resistance against the Nazis and edited its underground newspaper, *Combat.* Ivan Soll

Can. See **Food preservation** (Canning); **Tin can.**

Canaan dog is the native dog of Israel. It is descended from the pariah dog, which lives throughout the Middle East and North Africa.

The Canaan dog has a triangular, wedge-shaped head with pointed ears. Its athletic body includes a level back and a well tucked-up belly. The plumed tail is set moderately high and carried curled over the back when the animal is excited. The dog's outer coat lies flat and grows $\frac{1}{2}$ to $1\frac{1}{2}$ inches (1.3 to 3.8 centimeters) thick. Its undercoat varies in thickness depending on the climate. The male should have a noticeable ruff around its neck. The color of the coat ranges from sandy to reddish brown or black and can include white markings. Gray, black-and-tan, or solid white coloring is undesirable for this breed.

Male Canaan dogs should stand 20 to 24 inches (50 to 60 centimeters) high at the shoulders and weigh 45 to 55 pounds (20 to 25 kilograms). Females should stand 19 to 23 inches (48 to 58 centimeters) high at the shoulders and weigh 35 to 45 pounds (16 to 20 kilograms). Canaan dogs are intelligent and may make excellent pets.

Critically reviewed by the Canaan Dog Club of America, Inc.

See also **Dog** (picture: Herding dogs).

Canaanites, *KAY nuh nyts,* were a people mentioned in the Hebrew Bible, or Old Testament. Most of their land, called Canaan, later became known as Palestine. The Canaanites may have settled in the region about 2000 B.C. They were its chief inhabitants until about 1200 B.C. The Bible says that the Israelites conquered Canaan at that time. However, archaeology and some Biblical passages indicate that the Israelites only gradually became the area's dominant people. Archaeology also indicates that many Canaanite cities were destroyed by the Sea Peoples in the 1100's B.C. The Sea Peoples may have migrated to Canaan from the area around the Aegean Sea.

The Canaanites were a Semitic people related to the Arabs, Assyrians, and Israelites. The Canaanites had an advanced civilization. Their main political unit was the *city-state,* which consisted of a city or town and the surrounding villages and land. The chief Canaanite gods were El (a creator god) and Baal (a storm god). The main goddesses were Anat, Asherah, and Astarte.

Some Canaanites settled northwest of Palestine. They became known as Phoenicians. Carole R. Fontaine

See also **Palestine; Phoenicia.**

© Cathy Melloan

Gleaming Vancouver is the largest city in the province of British Columbia in western Canada. The city's natural harbor helps make Vancouver the busiest port in Canada.

Canada

Canada is the second largest country in the world in area. Only Russia covers more land. Canada extends across the continent of North America, from the province of Newfoundland and Labrador on the Atlantic coast to the province of British Columbia on the Pacific coast. Canada is slightly larger than the United States, its southern neighbor, but has only about a tenth as many people. About 75 percent of Canada's people live within 100 miles (150 kilometers) of the southern border. Much of the rest of Canada is uninhabited or thinly populated because the country has rugged terrain and a severe climate. Ottawa is the capital of Canada, and Toronto is the largest city. Both cities are in the province of Ontario.

Canada is a land of great variety. Towering mountains, clear lakes, and lush forests make Canada's far west a region of great natural beauty. Farther inland, fields of wheat and other grains cover vast prairies. These fertile farmlands contrast vividly with the Arctic wastelands to the north. Most of the nation's largest population centers and industrial areas are near the Great Lakes and the St. Lawrence River in central Canada. In the east, fishing villages and sandy beaches dot the Atlantic coast.

Like Canada's landscape, the country's people are also varied. Nearly half of all Canadians have ancestors who came from England, Ireland, Scotland, or Wales. About a fourth have some French ancestry. The Canadian government recognizes both English and French as official languages. French Canadians, most of whom live in the province of Quebec, have kept the language and many customs of their ancestors. Other large ethnic groups include German, Italian, Ukrainian, and Chinese people.

David Jay Bercuson, the contributor of this article, is Professor of History and Director of the Centre for Military and Strategic Studies at the University of Calgary.

Large numbers of Asians live in Western Canada and Ontario. Native peoples—American Indians and Inuit—make up a small percentage of the nation's population.

A wealth of natural resources is Canada's greatest possession. European settlers first came to Canada to fish in its coastal waters and to trap the fur-bearing animals in its forests. Later, the forests became sources of timber for shipbuilding and other construction. Today, pulpwood from these forests enables Canada to lead the world in the production of *newsprint* (paper for newspapers). Fertile soil helps Canada rank among the world's leading wheat producers. Thanks to power plants on its rivers, Canada is a leader in the generation of hydroelectric power. Plentiful resources of petroleum, iron ore, and other minerals provide raw materials that help make Canada a top manufacturing nation.

Canada is a *federation* (union) of 10 provinces and 3 territories. The nation's name probably comes from *kanata-kon,* an Iroquois Indian word that means *to the village* or *to the small houses.* Maintaining a sense of community is one of Canada's major problems because of differences among the provinces and territories. Many Canadians in eastern and western areas think the federal government does not pay enough attention to their particular problems and interests. French Canadians make up about 80 percent of the population of Quebec. Many of these people believe their province should receive special recognition in the Canadian constitution. Quebec has passed legislation aimed at making French the only official language of provincial government.

Canada is an independent, self-governing nation. But the Constitution Act of 1982 recognizes the British monarch, Queen Elizabeth II, as queen of Canada. This position symbolizes the country's historic ties to the United Kingdom. The United Kingdom ruled Canada completely until 1848, when Canada began to gain control of its domestic affairs. But the United Kingdom continued to govern Canada's foreign affairs. In 1931, Canada gained full independence.

George Hunter

Fertile farmlands cover the vast plains of Canada's Prairie Provinces—Alberta, Saskatchewan, and Manitoba.

© Randy Duchaine, The Stock Market

Picturesque Quebec, Canada's oldest city, was founded by the French explorer Samuel de Champlain in 1608.

Eberhard E. Otto, Miller Services

Tiny fishing villages dot the Atlantic coast of Canada. The Atlantic Provinces of Newfoundland and Labrador, New Brunswick, Nova Scotia, and Prince Edward Island provide most of Canada's fish catch.

Canada and the United States have had a relationship of cooperation and friendship since the 1800's. But the United States—because of its larger population and greater economic power—has tended to dominate Canada both culturally and economically. The people of Canada today are striving to maintain control of their economy and to safeguard their Canadian identity.

This article chiefly discusses the people of Canada and their way of life as well as the geography and economy of the country. For more information on the government of Canada and the country's history, see **Canada, Government of,** and **Canada, History of.** For population and other key statistics, see the *Canada in brief* feature that appears in this article.

The nation

Canada has six cultural and economic regions. They are (1) the Atlantic Provinces, (2) Quebec, (3) Ontario, (4) the Prairie Provinces, (5) British Columbia, and (6) the territories.

Canada in brief

Capital: Ottawa.
Official languages: English and French.
National anthem: "O Canada."
National symbols: Maple leaf and beaver.
Largest cities: (2001 census)

Toronto (2,481,494)	Winnipeg (619,544)
Montreal (1,039,534)	Mississauga (612,925)
Calgary (878,866)	Vancouver (545,671)
Ottawa (774,072)	Hamilton (490,268)
Edmonton (666,104)	Halifax (359,111)

Symbols of Canada. The flag of Canada features a red, 11-pointed maple leaf, a national symbol of the country. It became the official flag in 1965. The Canadian coat of arms includes three red maple leaves below the royal arms of England, Scotland, Ireland, and France.

Land and climate

Land: Canada lies in northern North America. It borders the United States and the Atlantic, Pacific, and Arctic oceans. Canada is mountainous in the west, where the Coastal and Rocky Mountains stand. The country is mostly flat or gently rolling from the eastern edge of the Rockies to the low Laurentian Mountains in Quebec. Several low mountain ranges rise in the east. Canada shares four of the five Great Lakes (all but Lake Michigan) with the United States. Its chief rivers include the Churchill, Fraser, Mackenzie, Nelson, and Saint Lawrence rivers.

Area: 3,849,674 mi² (9,970,610 km²), including 291,577 mi² (755,180 km²) of inland water. *Greatest distances*—east-west, 3,223 mi (5,187 km), from Cape Spear, Newfoundland and Labrador, to Mount St. Elias, Yukon; north-south, 2,875 mi (4,627 km), from Cape Columbia on Ellesmere Island to Middle Island in Lake Erie. *Coastline*—151,485 mi (243,791 km), including mainland and islands. *Shoreline*—Great Lakes, 5,251 mi (8,452 km).
Elevation: *Highest*—Mount Logan, 19,551 feet (5,959 meters) above sea level. *Lowest*—sea level.
Climate: Canada is extremely frigid in the north and generally cold elsewhere. However, warmer temperatures occur along the west coast and in the far southeast. The west coast has mild summers and cool winters, with temperatures rarely falling much below freezing. The west coast also has abundant precipitation. Central Canada has short, mild to warm summers and bitterly cold winters. Far southeastern Canada (southeastern Ontario and the Atlantic coast) has warm summers and cool to cold winters.

Government

Form of government: Constitutional monarchy.
Head of state: Queen Elizabeth II of the United Kingdom is queen of Canada. The queen, on the recommendation of Canada's prime minister, appoints a governor general to represent her.
Head of government: Prime minister.
Parliament: *Senate*—105 members, appointed by the governor general on the recommendation of the prime minister. *House of Commons*—308 members elected by the people.
Political subdivisions: 10 provinces, 3 territories.

People

Population: *Estimated 2006 population*—32,229,000. *2001 census*—30,007,094.
Population density: 8 per mi² (3 per km²).
Population distribution: 78 percent urban, 22 percent rural.
Major ethnic/national groups: 79 percent of European descent (chiefly British, Irish, and French, but also some Germans, Italians, Ukrainians, and other ethnic groups), 11 percent Asian (mostly Chinese, with Filipino, Indian, Vietnamese, and others), 4 percent American Indians and Inuit.
Major religions: 43 percent Roman Catholic, 29 percent Protestant. Other groups include Buddhists, Eastern Orthodox, Hindus, Jews, Muslims, and Sikhs.

Population trend

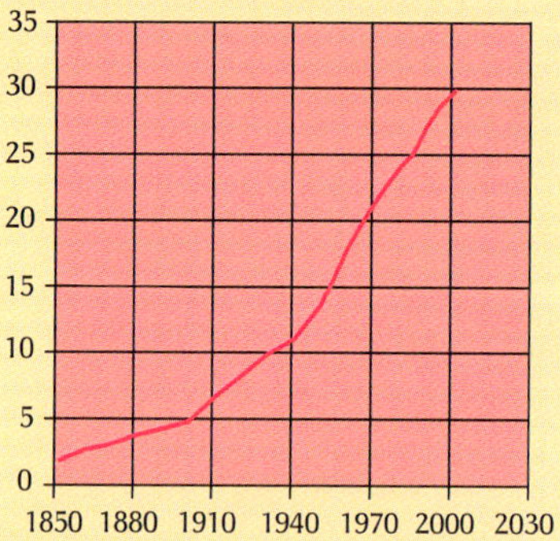

Year	Population
1851	2,436,297
1861	3,229,633
1871	3,689,257
1881	4,324,810
1891	4,833,239
1901	5,371,315
1911	7,206,643
1921	8,787,949
1931	10,376,786
1941	11,506,655
1951	14,009,429
1961	18,238,247
1966	20,014,880
1971	21,568,311
1976	22,992,604
1981	24,343,181
1986	25,354,064
1991	27,296,859
1996	28,846,761
2001	30,007,094

Economy

Chief products: *Agriculture*—beef cattle, canola, chickens, corn, eggs, hogs, milk, nursery products, wheat. *Fishing industry*—crab, lobster, shrimp. *Forestry*—fir, pine, spruce. *Manufacturing*—aluminum, steel, and other metals; chemicals; fabricated metal products; machinery; motor vehicles and parts; paper products; processed foods and beverages; wood products. *Mining*—coal, copper, gold, iron ore, natural gas, nickel, petroleum, potash, uranium, zinc.
Money: *Basic unit*—Canadian dollar (100 cents equal one dollar).
International trade: *Major exports*—motor vehicles and parts; petroleum; precious metals; wheat; wood, newsprint, and wood pulp. *Major imports*—computers, fruits and vegetables, machinery, motor vehicles and parts, scientific equipment. *Major trading partners*—The United States is Canada's most important trading partner. Other major commercial partners of Canada include China, France, Germany, Japan, Mexico, and the United Kingdom.

The Atlantic Provinces lie on the Atlantic Ocean. These four provinces—Newfoundland and Labrador, New Brunswick, Prince Edward Island, and Nova Scotia—make up about 5 percent of Canada's land area. Most of the people are of British descent. New Brunswick, Nova Scotia, and Prince Edward Island are also called the *Maritime Provinces.*

The Atlantic Provinces have long been an important fishing center. The four provinces still provide most of Canada's fish catch, but the fishing industry employs only a small percentage of their workers. *Service industries,* which include such activities as banking, health care, advertising, and shipping, employ most of the region's workers. Agriculture, manufacturing, and mining are also important. Newfoundland and Labrador's offshore Hibernia oil field, which began production in 1997, is a major employer.

A drastic drop in cod stocks has led the federal government to ban nearly all cod fishing off the Atlantic coast. As a result, thousands of people who earned their living in the fishing industry lost their jobs. Despite the addition of other jobs, such as those connected with petroleum production, the region has overall a lower standard of living, lower wages, and a higher rate of unemployment than any other part of Canada.

Quebec differs greatly from the rest of Canada because of its French language and culture. The French explorer Samuel de Champlain founded Quebec City, the first permanent European settlement in Canada, in 1608. Quebec remained a French colony until Britain gained control of it in 1763. Today, about 80 percent of Quebec's people are of French descent. French is the official language of Quebec.

In the past, the Roman Catholic Church dominated Quebec's politics and daily life. Today, the church generally has a less important role in the lives of the people of Quebec. For example, the feast day of Saint Jean Baptiste (Saint John the Baptist) in June is now celebrated largely as a *secular* (nonreligious) holiday. It serves as an occasion for the French-speaking people of Quebec to display their pride in their province.

Quebec is the largest province in area and the second largest in population. Only Ontario has more people. Montreal, Quebec's largest city, is the hub of the province's economic and cultural life. The largest industries in the Quebec region are service industries and manufacturing. Other important economic activities include agriculture, mining, forestry, and fishing.

Ontario is home to more people than any other province. Fur traders explored Ontario during the 1600's, but major European settlement did not begin until the late 1700's. About half of Ontario's people have some English ancestry. The province also has many people of Scottish, Irish, and French descent. Also, Ontario has more American Indians than any other province.

The southern boundary of Ontario passes through four of the five Great Lakes—Superior, Huron, Erie, and Ontario. The province's principal manufacturing area, sometimes called the *Golden Horseshoe,* lies on the western shore of Lake Ontario. The area's cities include Toronto, Hamilton, and St. Catharines. Ontario produces about half of Canada's manufactured goods and also ranks as the leading agricultural province. Toronto, the capital of Ontario and the largest city in Canada, is the most important manufacturing, financial, cultural, and communications center in English-speaking Canada.

The Prairie Provinces are Alberta, Saskatchewan, and Manitoba. These three provinces make up about a fifth of Canada's land area. The southern part of the region has many grain farms and cattle ranches. Lakes and evergreen forests cover its northern area.

Until 1885, the Prairie Provinces remained isolated from eastern Canada, and the fur trade was the region's only important economic activity. After the completion of Canada's first transcontinental railroad in 1885, travelers could reach the region more easily. Hundreds of thousands of people settled on the fertile Canadian prairies in the late 1800's and early 1900's. Most of them

The provinces and territories of Canada

Provinces

Province	Capital	Area In mi²	Area In km²	Rank in area	Population (2001 census)	Rank in pop.	Population density In mi²	Population density In km²	Date became province	Postal abbr.
Alberta	Edmonton	255,287	661,190	4	2,974,807	4	12	4	1905	AB
British Columbia	Victoria	365,900	947,800	3	3,907,738	3	11	4	1871	BC
Manitoba	Winnipeg	250,947	649,950	6	1,119,583	5	4	2	1870	MB
New Brunswick	Fredericton	28,355	73,440	8	729,498	8	26	10	1867	NB
Newfoundland and Labrador	St. John's	156,649	405,720	7	512,930	9	3	1	1949	NL
Nova Scotia	Halifax	21,423	55,490	9	908,007	7	42	16	1867	NS
Ontario	Toronto	412,581	1,068,580	2	11,410,046	1	28	11	1867	ON
Prince Edward Island	Charlottetown	2,185	5,660	10	135,294	10	62	24	1873	PE
Quebec	Quebec	594,860	1,540,680	1	7,237,479	2	12	5	1867	QC
Saskatchewan	Regina	251,866	652,330	5	978,933	6	4	2	1905	SK

Territories

Territory	Capital	Area In mi²	Area In km²	Population (2001 census)	Population density In mi²	Population density In km²	Date became territory	Postal abbr.
Northwest Territories	Yellowknife	501,570	1,299,070	37,360	0.07	0.03	1870	NT
Nunavut	Iqaluit	805,185	2,093,190	26,745	0.03	0.01	1999	NU
Yukon	Whitehorse	186,661	483,450	28,674	0.15	0.06	1898	YT

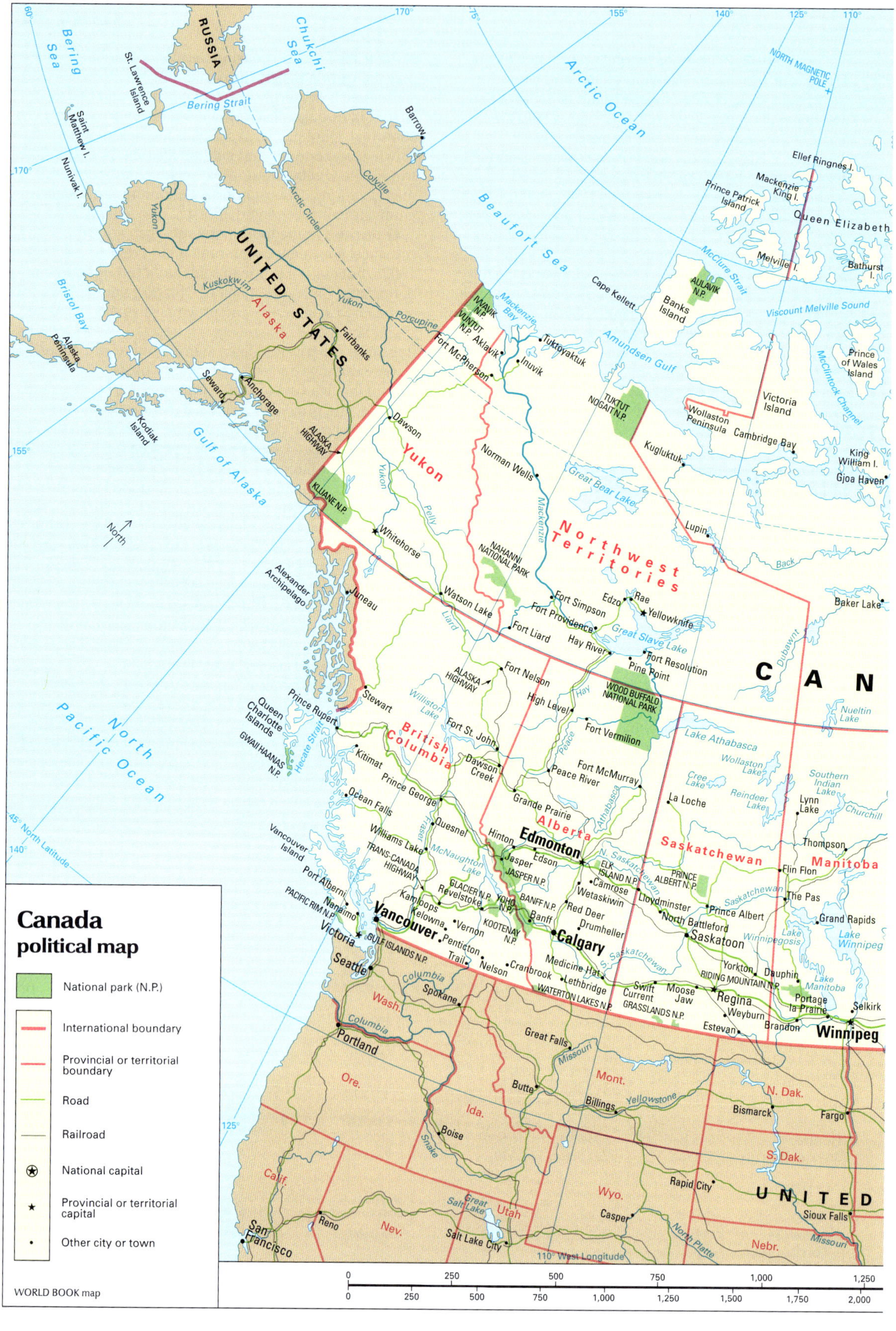

Canada political map

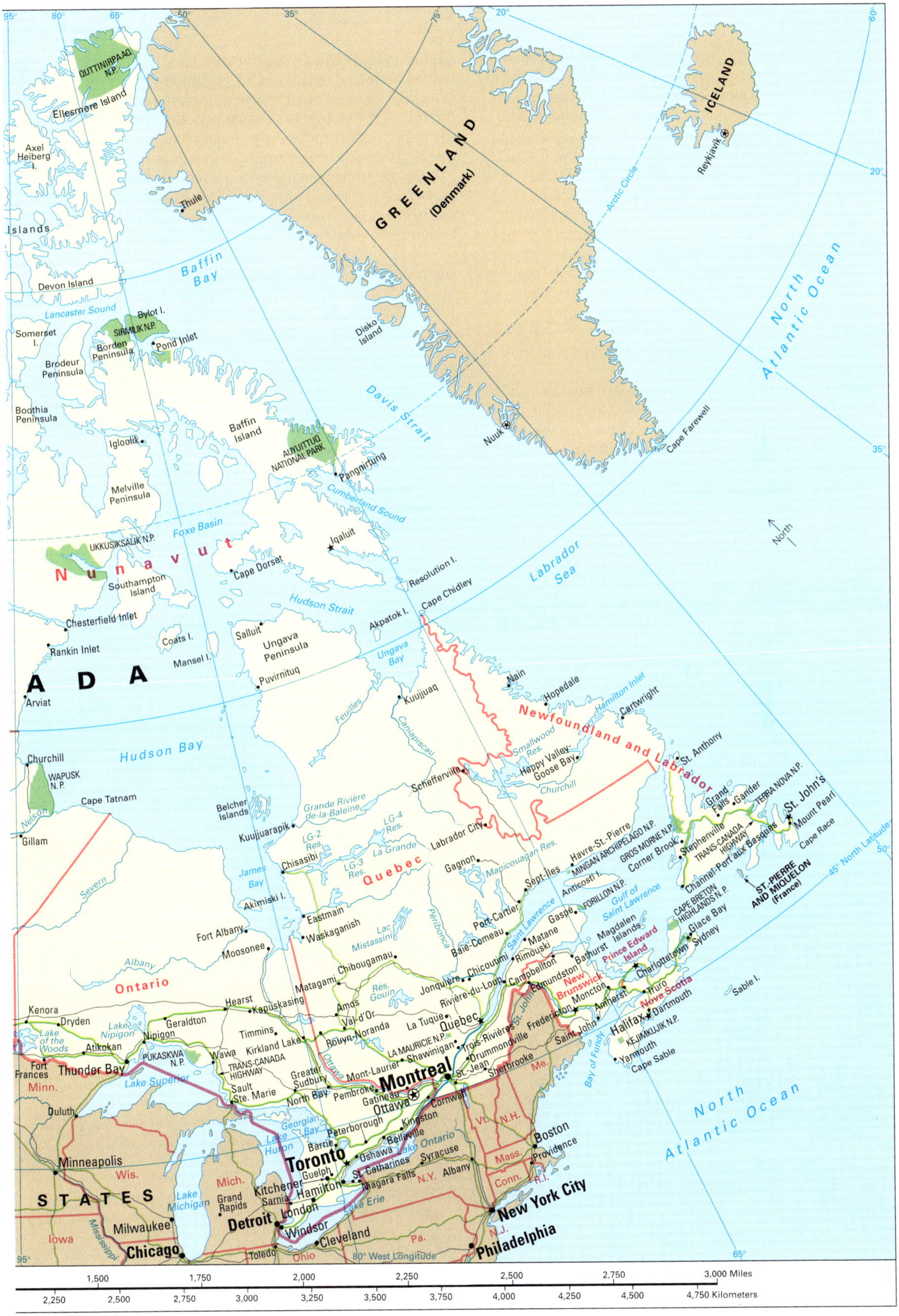

QUTTINIRPAAQ N.P.
Ellesmere Island
Axel Heiberg I.
Islands
Devon Island
Lancaster Sound
Bylot I.
SIRMILIK N.P.
Pond Inlet
Somerset I.
Borden Peninsula
Brodeur Peninsula
Boothia Peninsula
Igloolik
Melville Peninsula
Baffin Island
AUYUITTUQ NATIONAL PARK
Pangnirtung
Cumberland Sound
Foxe Basin
UKKUSIKSALIK N.P.
Nunavut
Iqaluit
Cape Dorset
Southampton Island
Resolution I.
Hudson Strait
Cape Chidley
Chesterfield Inlet
Rankin Inlet
Coats I.
Mansel I.
Salluit
Ungava Peninsula
Akpatok I.
Ungava Bay
Puvirnituq
ADA
Arviat
Thule
Baffin Bay
GREENLAND
(Denmark)
Disko Island
Davis Strait
Nuuk
Cape Farewell
Arctic Circle
ICELAND
Reykjavík
North Atlantic Ocean
Labrador Sea
North
Nain
Hopedale
Hamilton Inlet
Cartwright
Newfoundland and Labrador
Kuujjuaq
Feuilles
Caniapiscau
Smallwood Res.
Happy Valley-Goose Bay
Churchill
St. Anthony
Schefferville
Hudson Bay
Churchill
WAPUSK N.P.
Cape Tatnam
Nelson
Gillam
Belcher Islands
Grande Rivière de-la-Baleine
Kuujjuarapik
LG-2 Res.
LG-3 Res.
LG-4 Res.
La Grande
Chisasibi
Labrador City
Gagnon
Manicouagan Res.
Quebec
James Bay
Akimiski I.
Eastmain
Waskaganish
Lac Mistassini
Péribonca
Severn
Fort Albany
Moosonee
Albany
Ontario
Chibougamau
Rés. Gouin
Matagami
Sept-Îles
Havre-St.-Pierre
MINGAN ARCHIPELAGO N.P.
GROS MORNE N.P.
Anticosti I.
Port-Cartier
Baie-Comeau
Saint Lawrence
Gulf of Saint Lawrence
FORILLON N.P.
Gaspé
Matane
Rimouski
Chicoutimi
Jonquière
Rivière-du-Loup
Campbellton
Edmundston
Bathurst
Magdalen Islands
Prince Edward Island
Charlottetown
New Brunswick
Moncton
Amherst
Truro
Nova Scotia
Dartmouth
Halifax
Sable I.
CAPE BRETON HIGHLANDS N.P.
Glace Bay
Sydney
Grand Falls
Gander
TERRA NOVA N.P.
St. John's
Mount Pearl
Cape Race
Stephenville
Corner Brook
TRANS-CANADA HIGHWAY
Channel-Port aux Basques
ST.-PIERRE AND MIQUELON (France)
Kenora
Dryden
Lake of the Woods
Lake Nipigon
Nipigon
Geraldton
Hearst
Kapuskasing
Timmins
Amos
Val-d'Or
Rouyn-Noranda
Kirkland Lake
La Tuque
Quebec
Trois-Rivières
LA MAURICIE N.P.
Shawinigan
Drummondville
St.-Jean
Sherbrooke
Saint John
Fredericton
St. John
Bay of Fundy
KEJIMKUJIK N.P.
Yarmouth
Cape Sable
Atikokan
Fort Frances
Thunder Bay
PUKASKWA N.P.
Wawa
TRANS-CANADA HIGHWAY
Lake Superior
Sault Ste. Marie
Greater Sudbury
North Bay
Mont-Laurier
Ottawa
Montreal
Pembroke
Gatineau
Ottawa
Cornwall
Kingston
Minn.
Duluth
Georgian Bay
Lake Huron
Barrie
Peterborough
Belleville
Oshawa
Toronto
Lake Ontario
Syracuse
Guelph
Kitchener
Hamilton
St. Catharines
Niagara Falls
Sarnia
London
Lake Erie
Windsor
Detroit
Cleveland
Toledo
Minneapolis
Wis.
Mich.
Grand Rapids
Lake Michigan
STATES
Milwaukee
Chicago
Iowa
Mississippi
Ohio
Pa.
N.Y.
Albany
Vt.
N.H.
Me.
Mass.
Boston
Providence
R.I.
Conn.
N.J.
New York City
Philadelphia
80° West Longitude
45° North Latitude
1,500
1,750
2,000
2,250
2,500
2,750
3,000 Miles
2,250
2,500
2,750
3,000
3,250
3,500
3,750
4,000
4,250
4,500
4,750 Kilometers

came from eastern Canada, the United States, Germany, Italy, the Netherlands, Poland, Ukraine, and the Scandinavian countries—Denmark, Norway, and Sweden.

For years, the economy of the Prairie Provinces was based on agriculture. The region still produces most of Canada's grain and cattle. In the late 1940's, the discovery of petroleum and natural gas in the area provided a new source of wealth and formed the basis for further changes in the economies of the Prairie Provinces. For example, Manitoba is now a major manufacturer of buses, automobile parts, and aircraft parts. Saskatchewan is one of the world's leading producers of potash-based fertilizers. Calgary, Alberta, is now home to the headquarters of more Canadian corporations than any other city in Canada except Toronto. The largest cities in the Prairie Provinces, besides Calgary, are Edmonton in Alberta and Winnipeg in Manitoba.

British Columbia is Canada's westernmost province and its third largest in both area and population. The province lies on the Pacific Ocean. British Columbia's largest city, Vancouver, has Canada's busiest port. The beauty of the province's rugged coastline and lofty mountains attracts many tourists. Southern British Columbia has Canada's mildest climate, and large numbers of older Canadians move there after they retire.

About two-thirds of the province's people have some British or Irish ancestry. Other large ethnic groups include German and French. British Columbia has a higher percentage of Asians than any other province. Asians make up about a third of the population of the Vancouver area.

Evergreen forests cover much of British Columbia, and many of the province's people work in the logging and wood-processing industries. Other major economic activities include agriculture, fishing, and mining.

The territories. The Yukon Territory, the Northwest Territories, and Nunavut make up more than a third of Canada's land area. However, because of the remote location and severe climate of the territories, few of the nation's people live there. The terrain in the Yukon and in the southwestern part of the Northwest Territories consists mainly of forest-covered mountains. Most of the rest of the region is a frozen wasteland for much of the year. The territories have rich mineral deposits, and mining is the chief economic activity.

Inuit and Indians made up almost the entire population of the territories until the region's great mineral wealth was discovered during the late 1800's and the early 1900's. Whitehorse, the capital of the Yukon Territory, was founded during the Klondike gold rush of the late 1890's. Yellowknife, the capital of the Northwest Territories, was established during another gold rush in the 1930's. On the other hand, Iqaluit, the capital of Nunavut, was already used as a seasonal Inuit fishing camp when Europeans arrived in the area in 1576. Iqaluit's population still remains mostly Inuit, as does the population of Nunavut as a whole.

People

Population. Canada's population has grown dramatically since the late 1800's. The increase in population has resulted from heavy immigration and a high birth rate.

Over the years, the many immigrants to Canada have greatly influenced the ethnic makeup of the country. From the early 1900's until World War I began in 1914, most immigrants were from the United Kingdom and Ireland or the United States. European Jews and others from Europe, including Italians, Poles and Ukrainians, also came in large numbers. In the years after World War II ended in 1945, immigrants entering Canada were mainly British, German, Italian, or Dutch. Many of these people had lost their homes in the war. Today, more immigrants to Canada come from China, India, the Philippines, and other countries of Asia than from any other area of the world. Many also have come from Africa, Central and South America, and the Caribbean.

Ancestry. Most Canadians are of European descent. People of Indian and Inuit descent make up about 3 per-

David Burnett, DeWys, Inc.

Inuit children attend elementary school in their own communities. They can continue their education at high schools or vocational schools in larger towns.

Camilla Smith, Rainbow

The Indians of Canada's Pacific coast are famous for their fine woodcarvings. The skilled Indian craftsman shown here is using traditional techniques to carve ceremonial wooden masks.

cent of the nation's population. About half of Canada's people have some ancestors who came from Ireland or the United Kingdom, which includes England, Scotland, and Wales. About a fourth have some French ancestry. Other large ethnic groups include Chinese, Germans, Italians, and Ukrainians.

Europeans. People of British and Irish ancestry make up the majority of the population of every province except Quebec. Many are descendants of Scottish settlers who began arriving in Canada during the late 1700's. The ancestors of many others were English and Irish settlers who flocked to Canada during the 1800's. Still others are descendants of United Empire Loyalists—people who moved from the United States to Canada during and after the Revolutionary War in America (1775-1783). See **United Empire Loyalists.**

About 65,000 French colonists lived in Quebec when France lost that region to the British in 1763. Since that time, the number of Canadians with French ancestry has grown to more than 5 million. Most live in Quebec, but Ontario and New Brunswick also have large numbers of people with French backgrounds. The rest of Canada also has a few areas that are largely French.

About 10 percent of Canadians have some German ancestry, 4 percent have Italian ancestry, and 4 percent have Ukrainian ancestry. Most German Canadians live in Ontario, the Prairie Provinces, and British Columbia. Italian immigrants live chiefly in the cities, particularly Toronto and Montreal. Most Canadians of Ukrainian origin live in the Prairie Provinces. Many other Canadians are of Dutch, Greek, Hungarian, Polish, Portuguese, or Scandinavian origin.

Indians and Inuit had been living in what became Canada for thousands of years when Europeans first arrived. Today, about 700,000 Canadians are registered as Indians by the Canadian Department of Indian Affairs and Northern Development. About 45,000 Canadians are Inuit. The word *Inuit* means *people.* The Inuit of Canada were once called *Eskimos.*

About half of the Inuit live in the Northwest Territories and Nunavut, and most of the rest live in northern areas of the provinces of Newfoundland and Labrador, Ontario, and Quebec. Indians in Canada are often classified by their traditional languages. The major Indian languages of Canada include Cree, Chippewa (also called Ojibwa), Montagnais-Naskapi, Micmac, Dakota/Sioux, and Blackfoot (also called Blackfeet). About half of Canada's Indians live on about 2,700 *reserves* (reservations).

Other Canadians include Chinese, people from India and Pakistan, and other Asians, who make up about 18 percent of the population of British Columbia. Many im-

© Bob Riha, Jr., Liaison Agency

People of Asian descent make up a growing segment of Canada's population. Many immigrants from China have settled in Vancouver's Chinatown, *shown here.*

Where Canadians live

Most Canadians live near the nation's southern border in an area that covers only about a tenth of the country. Canada's vast northern regions are thinly populated because they have such a severe climate and rugged terrain.

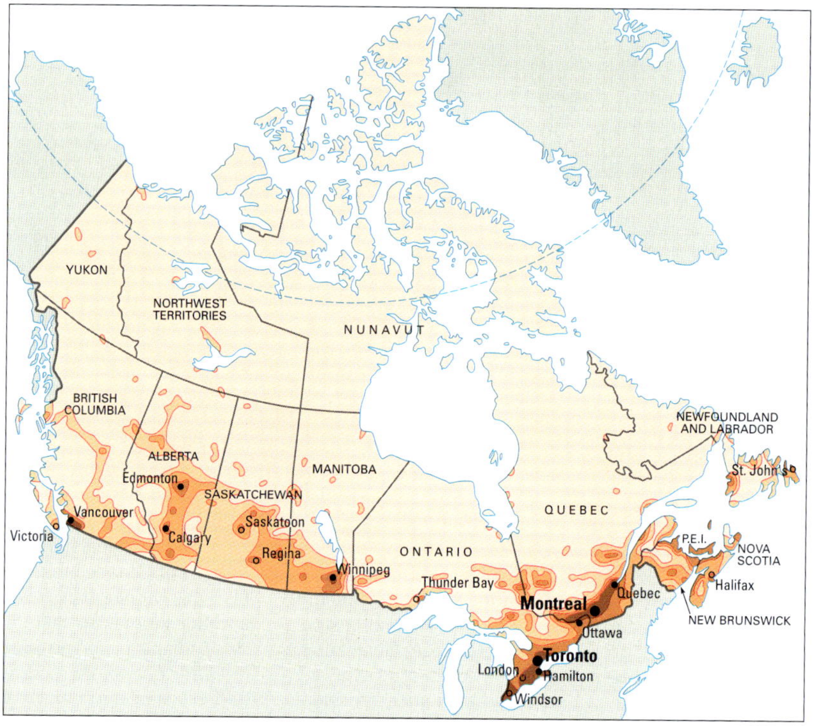

Major Urban Centers

- ● More than 2 million inhabitants
- • 500,000 to 2 million inhabitants
- ○ Less than 500,000 inhabitants

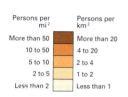

Persons per mi²	Persons per km²
More than 50	More than 20
10 to 50	4 to 20
5 to 10	2 to 4
2 to 5	1 to 2
Less than 2	Less than 1

WORLD BOOK map; adapted from *The National Atlas of Canada*, 4th edition

migrants from China, the Indian subcontinent, and the West Indies have settled in Toronto and Vancouver. Blacks make up about 2 percent of Canada's population. Many black Canadians are of West Indian descent, both from English-speaking islands and from French-speaking Haiti.

Languages. Canada has two official languages, English and French. The Official Languages Act of 1969 guarantees all Canadians the right to communicate with the national government in either French or English. About 59 percent of the Canadian people speak mainly English at home, and about 23 percent speak mainly French. About 18 percent speak other languages, which include Chinese, Italian, German, Punjabi, and Spanish.

Many of Canada's Inuit and Indians use their own traditional languages at home, though they may speak other languages as well. About 50 Indian and Inuit languages are spoken in Canada.

Significant numbers of French-speaking people live in New Brunswick and Ontario. However, most of the French-speaking Canadians live in Quebec, and French is the official language of the province. Quebec's French-speaking citizens, called *Québécois (kay beh KWAH),* consider themselves the guardians of the French language and culture in Canada.

The role of the French language and culture in Quebec has been controversial both within the province and within Canada as a whole. Quebec's legislature has passed a number of laws dealing with the uses of French and English in the province. In the 1970's, for example, the legislature passed laws that made French the language of government and business. Among other provisions, the laws banned the use of English on commercial signs. English-speaking citizens of Quebec opposed these laws. Through a series of court rulings and legislation, the laws were eventually changed. Today, bilingual advertising—in French and English—is allowed to appear on commercial signs as long as the French lettering is larger than the English.

Way of life

City life. Canada began as a nation with a largely rural population. But today, a large majority of the people live in urban areas. This population shift occurred mainly as a result of the rapid development since the 1940's of manufacturing and service industries in urban areas. Skyscrapers have risen in Canada's cities, and expressway systems have been constructed to link the cities with the many suburbs that have sprung up.

Canadian cities, in spite of their rapid growth, have not suffered from social problems as much as have many cities in the United States and some other countries. But there have been signs of future problems. Some of Canada's cities have faced reductions in transportation and welfare funds. Tension among ethnic groups has appeared with the immigration to the cities by people from many nations. In addition, the spread of suburbs into valuable farmland has caused many Canadians to oppose the unlimited growth of urban areas.

Most Canadian city dwellers work for the federal or provincial government, in the retail trades and other service industries, or in manufacturing. Occupations vary widely from city to city. In Vancouver, for example, many jobs are tied to the forest industry. In Toronto and other places in southern Ontario, automobile production is the main manufacturing industry. In Winnipeg and Montreal, construction of aircraft and aircraft parts is important. Halifax and Vancouver are major ports.

Rural life. A small percentage of Canada's rural people live on farms. Others work in such industries as fishing, mining, and lumbering. A small but growing number of Canadians live in rural communities and commute to jobs in the cities.

In Canada, most farmers own their own farms, and farming is largely a family activity. Modern machinery enables a family to do nearly all the work on their farm themselves. The largest Canadian farms are in the Prairie Provinces and cover an average of 1,075 acres (435 hectares). Farms in central and eastern Canada are much smaller, averaging about 180 to 300 acres (73 to 120 hectares).

Farm life has changed greatly since the early 1900's, especially in the Prairie Provinces. The once extensive network of prairie railroad branch lines, with their wooden country grain elevators and small towns, are rapidly disappearing. Large, concrete and steel inland grain terminals are being built to replace the country elevators. Many farmers now drive much farther than they once did to sell their grain at these inland terminals. Larger towns, with modern shopping malls and warehouse outlets, are growing around these terminals. On the farms themselves, satellite dishes and computers connect rural families to the rest of the world.

Arctic life. Canada's vast Arctic region is thinly populated. Inuit and Indians have lived there for thousands of years, and today they form about 40 percent of the region's population.

Many Inuit and Indians still follow their traditional occupations—fishing, hunting, and trapping. In general, however, the old ways of life in the Arctic have ended. The people live in wooden houses rather than tents or snowhouses. They wear modern clothing and eat food bought in stores. Snowmobiles and motorboats have largely replaced dog sleds and kayaks as their chief means of transportation.

The end of the traditional ways of life has brought many social problems to the Inuit. They have high rates of alcoholism, crime, unemployment, and suicide. The future may bring improved economic conditions as the result of petroleum and other resource developments in the Arctic region. Today, managers of large corporations setting up operations in the north to extract oil and gas or to build new mines routinely meet with Inuit leaders. Corporate and Inuit leaders work together to establish vocational training for Inuit young people in an effort to provide them with a fair share of the better-paying jobs.

Education. Religious groups operated the earliest schools in Canada. In 1867, the British North America Act made education a responsibility of the provincial governments. Today, each province and territory in Canada has its own school system. Every system is supervised by the provincial or territorial department of education. A cabinet minister heads each department of education and reports to the legislature of the province or territory. The federal government is responsible for directing the education of children on Indian reserves, the children of members of the Canadian armed forces, and the inmates of federal penitentiaries. See **Education** (Development of Canadian education).

The school systems of most of the provinces have 12 grades. The system of Quebec has 11 grades, and that of Ontario has 13. In some provinces, the law provides for the public school system to include separate schools for certain religious groups. Communities in Alberta, Ontario, Saskatchewan, and the territories have separate schools for Roman Catholics in addition to public schools that are open to all students. The school system of Quebec consists of schools that teach in French and in English. All immigrant children in Quebec are educated in schools that teach in French.

In all universities in Quebec except for three, classes are taught in French. The exceptions are McGill University, Concordia University, and Bishop's University, where English is used. In the other nine provinces, most universities use English as the language of instruction. At the University of Moncton in New Brunswick and Ste. Anne University in Nova Scotia, instruction is in French. Some universities in provinces other than Quebec teach in both English and French. The largest of these bilingual institutions is the University of Ottawa in Ontario.

The major English-language universities in Canada include McGill University; the universities of Alberta, British Columbia, Toronto, and Western Ontario; and York University. The most important French-language institutions are Laval University, the University of Montreal, and the University of Quebec.

The province of Quebec has *collèges d'enseignement général et professionel* (colleges of general and profes-

© Marco Cristofori, The Stock Market

Toronto Eaton Centre is a popular place to shop in Canada's largest city and commercial center. The huge Eaton Centre complex includes about 300 stores and three office buildings.

© Chris Schwarz, Tony Stone Images

Saint Jean Baptiste Day, formerly only a religious holiday, has become an occasion for French-speaking people of Quebec to display their pride in their province. Many of the people in this celebration in Montreal are carrying the blue-and-white provincial flag of Quebec.

sional instruction). They offer a two-year course that high school graduates must complete before enrolling in a Quebec university. In addition, these colleges provide three-year technical and commercial courses. The other provinces also have two-year or three-year institutions of higher learning. Most of these schools are called *community colleges.*

The federal and provincial governments of Canada provide some funds for university education. Canadian students pay from 30 to 50 percent of the cost of their education through their fees. Costs for foreign students attending Canadian universities are much higher.

Canada has an extensive system of public libraries. The National Library of Canada in Ottawa was established in 1953. It publishes *Canadiana,* a monthly and annual listing of new books, pamphlets, and music published in Canada. The Canada Institute for Scientific and Technical Information operates a science library in Ottawa. See **Library** (Canadian government libraries).

Canada has a variety of museums and art galleries. National museums in Ottawa include the National Gallery of Canada, the Canadian Museum of Civilization, the Canadian War Museum, the Canadian Museum of Nature, and the Canada Science and Technology Museum. Another outstanding museum is the Royal Ontario Museum in Toronto. It is known for its exhibits in such fields as archaeology, geology, and zoology. The Royal Tyrrell Museum of Palaeontology in Drumheller, Alberta, is one of the world's leading dinosaur museums. Notable Canadian art galleries include the Art Gallery of Ontario, the Vancouver Art Gallery, and the Winnipeg Art Gallery.

Religion. The early French settlers brought the Roman Catholic faith to Canada, and Catholics are the nation's largest religious group today. Most other Canadians belong to Protestant churches. The largest Protestant denominations are the United Church of Canada and the Anglican Church of Canada. Other major Protestant groups in Canada include Presbyterians, Lutherans, and Baptists. The country's other religious groups include Buddhists, Hindus, Jews, Muslims, and Sikhs.

Recreation and sports. Canadians take part in a wide variety of recreational activities. During the long winters, many people enjoy both downhill and cross-country skiing, snowboarding, skating, and tobogganing. Popular summer sports include swimming, canoeing, fishing, hiking, tennis, and golf.

Canada's extensive national park system includes areas ideal for many recreational activities. The park system began in 1885 with the establishment of Hot Springs Reservation (now Banff National Park) in Alberta. Today, all the provinces and territories have at least one national park. Each province also has its own park system. For information on the national parks, park reserves, marine parks, conservation areas, and national historic sites of Canada, see the tables with this article.

Canada's first national game was lacrosse, which the Indians played before the arrival of the Europeans in North America. Today, hockey is by far the most popular sport in Canada. Young Canadian players begin to compete in amateur hockey leagues when they are 7 years old. Professional teams from Canada and the United States compete in the National Hockey League (NHL), the highest professional hockey league. Most players in the National Hockey League are Canadians. Such stars as Wayne Gretzky, Gordie Howe, Guy Lafleur, and Bobby Orr became national heroes in Canada.

Other popular professional sports in Canada include football, baseball, basketball, and soccer. Teams from eight Canadian cities compete in the Canadian Football League. The Toronto Blue Jays attract major league baseball fans from throughout Canada. The Toronto Raptors play in the National Basketball Association (NBA).

Food. Canadians eat more beef, including steaks and roast beef, than any other meat. They also eat chicken, lamb, pork, and fish. Bread is eaten at most meals, and potatoes are also common. Favorite vegetables, besides

Denis Brodeur

Hockey is Canada's most popular sport. Professional hockey games draw huge crowds, and thousands of Canadians start to play in amateur leagues at the age of 7.

© Michael Philip Manheim

Breathtaking ski slopes, such as this one near Lake Louise, Alberta, attract thousands of skiers to the Canadian Rockies yearly. Skiing is a favorite sport in many areas of Canada.

potatoes, include beans, carrots, lettuce, and peas. Citrus fruits, apples, and bananas are popular fruits.

Hot soup is common with lunch and dinner. Coffee, tea, milk, soft drinks, beer, and wine are popular beverages. Favorite desserts include ice cream and fruit pies—especially apple, blueberry, peach, and rhubarb pies.

Turkey is the most popular special dish at Thanksgiving, Christmas, and New Year's. On Christmas, many French Canadians eat a meat pie called *tourtière.*

Many Canadians eat out often. Both sophisticated restaurants that offer fine cuisine and fast-food restaurants that provide quick service are popular. Specialty restaurants, once common only in major cities, are now also found in smaller cities throughout the country. These include seafood restaurants and ethnic restaurants, such as those that serve French, Italian, Greek, Indian, Chinese, Japanese, Thai, or Vietnamese food.

The arts

Government support has played a vital role in the development of the arts in Canada. In 1957, the Canadian government set up the Canada Council to promote the advancement of the arts, humanities, and social sciences. The council provides financial assistance to individual artists and to orchestras, theaters, and other organizations. Every province except Prince Edward Island supports the arts through grants to individuals and groups.

In 1969, the federal government opened the National Arts Centre in Ottawa. The Arts Centre presents drama, music, opera, ballet, and motion pictures. The National Gallery, also in Ottawa, has an excellent collection of European art and a large number of Canadian works.

Literature. Canada has two great literatures, one written in French and the other in English. For a discussion of Canadian writers and their works, see **Canadian literature.**

Painting and sculpture. The works of most early Canadian painters followed European trends. During the mid-1800's, Cornelius Krieghoff, a Dutch-born artist in Quebec, painted scenes of the life of the *habitants* (French Canadian farmers). At about the same time, the Canadian artist Paul Kane painted pictures of Indian life in western Canada.

A group of landscape painters called the Group of Seven developed the first distinctively Canadian style of painting. Tom Thomson, one of Canada's best-known painters, inspired the group. However, he died three years before the group's first exhibition in 1920. All these artists painted large, brilliantly colored scenes of the Canadian wilderness. See **Group of Seven.**

Canadian painters have developed a wide range of styles in addition to that of the Group of Seven. Emily Carr, for example, became famous for depicting the totem poles of British Columbia. Other noted painters have included the landscape artist David Milne and the abstract painters Jean-Paul Riopelle and Harold Town.

The finest works of Canadian sculpture include woodcarvings of the Haida, Kwakiutl, and other Indians of Canada's northwest coast and some ivory and soapstone carvings by Inuit artists. Bill Reid, for example, used his Haida heritage as a source of design for his totem poles and other sculptures.

Theater. Canada's best-known theatrical event is the Stratford Festival, held annually in Stratford, Ontario, from May to October or November. Famous performers appear in the plays of William Shakespeare and other noted dramatists. Another major annual drama festival is the Shaw Festival. This is held in Niagara-on-the-Lake, Ontario, and features works by the Irish-born British playwright George Bernard Shaw and other dramatists of his time. The leading theater group in French-speaking Canada is Le Théâtre du Nouveau Monde in Montreal. Canada also has many regional theater companies.

Music. Canada's outstanding orchestras are the Montreal Symphony Orchestra, the National Arts Centre Orchestra, the Toronto Symphony Orchestra, and the Vancouver Symphony Orchestra. Solo performers who have gained fame include the pianists Janina Fialkowska, Glenn Gould, and Jon Kimura Parker; the cellists Ofra Harnoy and Shauna Rolston; and the singers Maureen Forrester, Ben Heppner, Lois Marshall, Louis Quilico, and Jon Vickers. Canadian stars in popular music include the singers Bryan Adams, Céline Dion, Gordon Lightfoot, Joni Mitchell, Alanis Morissette, Anne Murray, and Shania Twain.

Ballet and opera. Canada has three professional ballet companies. The oldest, the Royal Winnipeg Ballet, was founded in 1938 and is known for its performances of original Canadian works. The National Ballet of Canada in Toronto and Les Grands Ballets Canadiens in Montreal both tour extensively. The National Ballet has featured many international stars in addition to outstanding Canadian dancers, such as Frank Augustyn, Rex Harrington, Karen Kain, Martine Lamy, and Veronica Tennant. The Canadian Opera Company in Toronto performs six operas during a season that lasts from September to May. Several other Canadian cities have their own opera companies.

Oil painting on canvas (1915); Hart House Permanent Collection, University of Toronto

The Canadian wilderness was a favorite subject of landscape painter Tom Thomson and the artists known as the Group of Seven. Thomson's *The Pointers* (1915), *shown here,* is a fine example of his use of brilliant colors.

© R. Watts, First Light

Canada's Indian heritage appears in the sculpture of Bill Reid, whose *Spirit of Haida Gwaii* shows creatures from Haida mythology.

Oil painting on canvas (1854); The National Gallery of Canada

Scenes from the life of French Canadian farmers, known as the *habitants,* were a favorite subject of the Dutch-born artist Cornelius Krieghoff, who lived in Quebec during the mid-1800's. This painting is called *The Habitant Farm.*

Motion pictures. The Canadian motion-picture industry began in 1939 with the founding of the National Film Board. The board, a government-sponsored organization, has won hundreds of awards for documentaries and animated films. In 1967, the government set up the Canadian Film Development Corporation, which helped establish the country's feature-length film industry. Known today as Telefilm Canada, the organization administers funds for both motion pictures and television programs.

Thousands of Canadians have obtained jobs and training in the motion-picture industry because many Hollywood movies, or parts of them, are filmed in Canada. Many movie companies find it less expensive to film in Canada than in the United States. Calgary, Montreal, Toronto, and Vancouver are often used as "American" cities, and many Western movies are shot in southern Alberta.

Architecture. Familiar examples of traditional architecture in Canada include the French-style homes of Quebec and the neo-Gothic Parliament buildings in Ottawa. Modern Canadian architecture is international in style. The Toronto Dominion Centre in Toronto, designed by German-born architect Mies van der Rohe,

Stratford Festival, Canada from Miller Services

The Stratford Festival in Stratford, Ontario, is Canada's best-known theatrical event. This scene is from a Stratford production of William Shakespeare's *A Midsummer Night's Dream*.

Théâtre du Nouveau Monde, Montreal

Le Théâtre du Nouveau Monde in Montreal is a leading French-language theater group in Canada. This scene is from *Les Rustres,* a comedy by the Italian playwright Carlo Goldoni.

© Ezra Stoller, ESTO

Modern Canadian architecture includes works by Arthur Erickson. The provincial law courts in Vancouver, British Columbia, *shown here,* display Erickson's dramatic use of geometric forms.

and Place Ville Marie in Montreal, by Chinese-born architect I. M. Pei, reflect the sleek, uncluttered glass-and-steel style of the mid-1900's. The Toronto City Hall, one of the most impressive structures in Canada, was designed by Viljo Revell of Finland (see **Toronto** [picture]).

Arthur Erickson, a famous Canadian architect, designed many buildings in or near Vancouver, British Columbia. Erickson is best known for designs that dramatically harmonize with the landscape. Moshe Safdie, an Israeli-born Canadian, first came to public attention with his housing project known as Habitat. This apartment complex, built for the Montreal World's Fair in 1967, consists of arrangements of prefabricated cubes. Douglas Cardinal, a Native American born in Alberta, used smooth, rounded forms for the Canadian Museum of Civilization in Gatineau, Quebec, near Ottawa.

The land

Canada covers most of the northern half of North America. It borders Alaska on the northwest and the rest of the continental United States on the south. From east to west, Canada extends 3,223 miles (5,187 kilometers) from the rocky coast of Newfoundland and Labrador to the St. Elias Mountains in Yukon. Canada has six

AP/Wide World

Canadian performers have achieved wide success in popular music. Céline Dion, *shown here,* became one of Canada's best-known singers.

National Film Board of Canada

Motion pictures produced by the National Film Board of Canada include dramas, documentaries, and animated films. The board's productions have won hundreds of awards. This National Film Board crew is shooting on location.

time zones. At noon in Vancouver, the time in St. John's, Newfoundland and Labrador, is 4:30 p.m. From its southernmost point, Middle Island in Lake Erie, Canada extends 2,875 miles (4,627 kilometers) north to Cape Columbia on Ellesmere Island. Of all the world's land areas, only the northern tip of Greenland is nearer the North Pole than is Cape Columbia.

Canada has one of the longest coastlines of any country—151,488 miles (243,797 kilometers), including island coasts. Canada faces the Pacific Ocean on the west, the Arctic Ocean on the north, and the Atlantic Ocean on the east. Hudson Bay, Hudson Strait, and James Bay form a great inland sea in Canada. Hudson Bay remains frozen for about eight months of the year. But in the summer, it provides a waterway to Canada's vast interior regions.

Forests cover almost half of the land area of Canada, and mountains and Arctic areas make up 41 percent of the land. Most Canadians live in southern agricultural areas and along the Atlantic and Pacific coasts.

Land regions. Canada has eight major land regions. They are (1) the Pacific Ranges and Lowlands, (2) the Rocky Mountains, (3) the Arctic Islands, (4) the Interior Plains, (5) the Canadian Shield, (6) the Hudson Bay Lowlands, (7) the St. Lawrence Lowlands, and (8) the Appalachian Region.

The Pacific Ranges and Lowlands form Canada's westernmost land region. They make up most of British Columbia and the southwestern part of Yukon. The region includes the Queen Charlotte Islands and Vancouver Island. All these islands are the upper portions of a mountain range that is partly covered by the Pacific Ocean. The Coast Mountains rise along the coast of British Columbia. The St. Elias Mountains in Yukon include Canada's highest peak, Mount Logan, near the Alaskan border. It towers 19,551 feet (5,959 meters) above sea level. Glaciers cover many of the higher slopes in the St. Elias Mountains.

Because the Coast Mountains are on the seashore, the coastline of British Columbia has many long, narrow inlets called *fiords.* The fiords provide a water route to Canada's most valuable forests. These dense forests consist of tall redcedars, hemlocks, and other evergreen trees that grow on the lower slopes of the mountains. Black bears, foxes, and a variety of other fur-bearing animals live in the forests.

The Interior Plateau, an area of plains, river valleys, and smaller mountains, lies east of the Coast Mountains. This area has valuable mineral resources, including Canada's largest deposits of the metals bismuth and molybdenum. The southern part of the Interior Plateau has many farms and orchards as well as large grasslands where cattle graze. Forests grow in the northern part of the plateau area.

The Rocky Mountains rise east of the Pacific Ranges and Lowlands. These two regions together are part of the Cordillera, an immense group of mountain ranges that extends from Alaska through Mexico. In Canada, the snowcapped Rockies vary in height from 7,000 to more than 12,000 feet (2,100 to 3,660 meters) above sea level. The tallest peak, Mount Robson in eastern British Columbia, is 12,972 feet (3,954 meters) high. Thousands of people visit the Rockies every year to view the magnificent scenery and to enjoy such recreational activities as camping, hiking, and skiing.

The Rocky Mountain Chain extends for more than 3,000 miles (4,800 kilometers) from New Mexico to northern Alaska. The Canadian portion of the chain includes several separate ranges. The major range, the Canadian Rockies, stretches from Canada's southern border to the Liard River in northern British Columbia. Railroads and highways cross the Canadian Rockies at Crowsnest, Kicking Horse, Vermillion, and Yellowhead passes. Between the Liard River and the Alaskan border are several other ranges, including the Selwyn Moun-

(Text continued on page 115.)

National Park System of Canada

Canada's park system includes 41 national parks and park reserves, 2 national marine conservation areas, and 154 national historic sites. These areas preserve and protect Canada's natural heritage. All the national parks and marine conservation areas and many of the national historic sites are described below and on pages 114 and 115.

National parks and national park reserves

Name	Area In acres	Area In hectares	Location	Outstanding features
Aulavik	3,014,686	1,220,000	Northwest Territories	Deep river canyons; rough desertlike badlands
Auyuittuq	4,716,995	1,908,900	Nunavut	Massive icecap and valley glaciers; fiords
***Banff**	1,641,027	664,100	Alberta	Rocky Mountain scenery with glaciers and hot springs; Banff and Lake Louise resorts
Bruce Peninsula	38,054	15,400	Ontario	Rock pillars, caves, limestone cliffs; orchids and other flowers
Cape Breton Highlands	234,256	94,800	Nova Scotia	Rugged coastline and forested hills; seascapes from Cabot Trail
Elk Island	47,938	19,400	Alberta	Rolling meadows with aspen and spruce forests and many lakes; beaver, buffalo, deer, and elk
Forillon	59,404	24,040	Quebec	Scenic tip of Gaspé Peninsula that juts into Gulf of St. Lawrence; whales, seals, and sea birds
Fundy	50,879	20,590	New Brunswick	Rugged Bay of Fundy shoreline with coves and cliffs; some of the world's highest tides
Georgian Bay Islands	6,326	2,560	Ontario	Glacier-scraped islands; pine trees deformed by wind
Glacier	333,419	134,930	British Columbia	Alpine region in Selkirk Mountains with snow-capped peaks and more than 100 glaciers
Grasslands	223,976	90,640	Saskatchewan	Short-grass prairie; pronghorns, prairie dogs
Gros Morne	446,025	180,500	Newfoundland and Labrador	Scenic Long Range Mountains; fiordlike lakes, waterfalls, and rugged seacoast
Gulf Islands	8,500	3,440	British Columbia	Dramatic coastlines; marine wildlife, including whales, dolphins, porpoises, seals, and sea lions
Gwaii Haanas	369,423	149,500	British Columbia	Forested islands with rare plant and animal life
Ivvavik	2,409,278	975,000	Yukon	Caribou migration route; bears, wolves, and waterfowl
***Jasper**	2,688,013	1,087,800	Alberta	Rocky Mountain landscape with hot springs and lakes; Jasper resort area
Kejimkujik	99,756	40,370	Nova Scotia	Gently rolling landscape with many islands and lakes; Indian rock etchings
Kluane	5,451,392	2,206,100	Yukon	Mount Logan in St. Elias Mountains; large glacier system; caribou, Dall's sheep, grizzly bears
Kootenay	347,529	140,640	British Columbia	Rocky Mountain scenery with broad valleys, glaciers, deep canyons, and hot springs
Kouchibouguac	59,108	23,920	New Brunswick	Salt marshes, lagoons, sand dunes; offshore sandbars and islands
La Mauricie	132,473	53,610	Quebec	Section of Laurentian Mountains with hardwood forests and numerous lakes
Mingan Archipelago	37,239	15,070	Quebec	Chain of islands in Jacques Cartier Passage; unusual rock formations; whales and sea birds
Mount Revelstoke	64,173	25,970	British Columbia	Transition from rain forests to alpine meadows and lakes
Nahanni	1,177,704	476,600	Northwest Territories	Deep canyons; hot springs; Virginia Falls and Hell's Gate on South Nahanni River
Pacific Rim	126,221	51,080	British Columbia	Long Beach, West Coast Trail, Broken Group Islands
Point Pelee	3,756	1,520	Ontario	Southernmost point in Canada; bird and butterfly migrations; freshwater marsh
Prince Albert	957,360	387,430	Saskatchewan	Transition between northern forests and prairie grasslands; lakes and streams
Prince Edward Island	6,672	2,700	Prince Edward Island	Beaches, cliffs, dunes, and salt marshes
Pukaskwa	464,015	187,780	Ontario	Many lakes and rivers, dense forests, and a variety of wildlife in wilderness area on Lake Superior
Quttinirpaaq	9,334,406	3,777,500	Nunavut	Ellesmere Island, the northernmost part of Canada; glaciers; fiords; Arctic wildlife
Riding Mountain	733,656	296,900	Manitoba	Forests, grasslands, and lakes on summit of Manitoba Escarpment
St. Lawrence Islands	2,051	830	Ontario	Scenic islands on St. Lawrence River
Sirmilik	5,485,740	2,220,000	Nunavut	Sea cliffs, glaciers, and fiords; a marine wildlife sanctuary
Terra Nova	98,027	39,670	Newfoundland and Labrador	Spruce forest and bogs along rugged coastline; icebergs offshore in spring
Tuktut Nogait	4,037,702	1,634,000	Northwest Territories	Calving ground for the Bluenose caribou herd
Ukkusiksalik	5,079,993	2,055,800	Nunavut	Eskers, mudflats, cliffs, rolling tundra banks, and coastal areas
Vuntut	1,073,673	434,500	Yukon	Arctic wilderness with large population of musk oxen
Wapusk	2,835,534	1,147,500	Manitoba	Lowlands with polar bear habitat

*Has an article in *World Book*.

National parks and national park reserves (continued)

Waterton Lakes	124,788	50,500	Alberta	Waterton-Glacier International Peace Park
Wood Buffalo	11,070,816	4,480,200	Alberta, Northwest Territories	Largest buffalo herd in North America and nesting grounds of rare whooping crane
Yoho	324,474	131,310	British Columbia	Rocky Mountain scenery with lakes, waterfalls, natural stone bridge, and Yoho Valley

National marine conservation areas

Name	Area In acres	In hectares	Location	Outstanding features
Fathom Five	24,875	10,030	Ontario	Rugged islands with coves and limestone pillars; shipwrecks accessible to scuba divers
Saguenay–St. Lawrence	281,206	113,800	Quebec	Rugged shorelines; beaches; marine life, including whales

National historic sites

Name	Location	Outstanding features
Alexander Graham Bell	Nova Scotia	Museum with models of Bell's experiments
Ardgowan	Prince Edward Island	Home of William Henry Pope, one of the Fathers of Confederation
Banff Park Museum	Alberta	Natural history museum built in 1903
Batoche	Saskatchewan	Métis village; site of Métis defeat by Canadian troops during North West Rebellion in 1885
Battle of the Châteauguay	Quebec	Site of War of 1812 battle
Battle of the Restigouche	Quebec	Site of French and Indian War battle
Beaubears Island Shipbuilding	New Brunswick	Site of Acadian settlement, 1756-1759
Bellevue House	Ontario	Home of first prime minister of Canada, Sir John A. Macdonald, 1848-1849
Bethune Memorial House	Ontario	Birthplace of Canadian surgeon Henry Norman Bethune
Bois Blanc Island Lighthouse	Ontario	Site of defense post for Fort Malden during Rebellion of 1837-1838
Carillon Barracks	Quebec	Military barracks used during Rebellion of 1837-1838; museum
Carleton Martello Tower	New Brunswick	Defense post built during War of 1812
Cartier-Brébeuf	Quebec	Winter camp of French navigator Jacques Cartier in 1535-1536
Castle Hill	Newfoundland and Labrador	French and British fortifications of 1700's
Chilkoot Trail	British Columbia	Main route to the Yukon region in Klondike Gold Rush of 1897-1898
Coteau-du-Lac	Quebec	Site of British military post; historic canal
Dawson Historical Complex	Yukon	Commemorates Gold Rush of 1897-1898; features restored buildings
Fisgard Lighthouse	British Columbia	First permanent lighthouse on Canada's Pacific coast, built 1859-1860
Forges du Saint-Maurice	Quebec	Remains of the first industrial village in Canada
Forks, The	Manitoba	Junction of the Red and Assiniboine rivers; original site of Winnipeg
Fort Anne	Nova Scotia	Site of French fort dating from 1695
Fort Battleford	Saskatchewan	Fort of North-West Mounted Police during North West Rebellion of 1885
Fort Beauséjour	New Brunswick	Site of French fort built in 1750's
Fort Chambly	Quebec	Site of French fort of early 1700's; museum
Fort Edward	Nova Scotia	Oldest blockhouse in Canada, built in 1750
Fort George	Ontario	Reconstructed British fort from War of 1812
Fort Langley	British Columbia	Reconstruction of Hudson's Bay Company post
Fort Lennox	Quebec	Site of British fort built during the early 1800's
Fort Malden	Ontario	Defense post built between 1797 and 1799
Fort Pelly	Saskatchewan	Remains of Hudson's Bay Company fur trade post
Fort Rodd Hill	British Columbia	Gun batteries built in 1890's overlook harbor
Fort St. James	British Columbia	Trading post built in 1806
Fort St. Joseph	Ontario	Trading post built in 1796; most westerly British fort
Fort Témiscamingue	Quebec	Last of a series of posts built by fur traders
Fort Walsh	Saskatchewan	Early post of North-West Mounted Police
Fort Wellington	Ontario	British fort of the late 1830's
Fortifications of Quebec	Quebec	Fortifications built by French and British from 1690 to 1830
Fortress of Louisbourg	Nova Scotia	Reconstruction of largest French fort in Canada
Frenchman Butte	Saskatchewan	Site of 1885 battle between the Cree and the Dominion government
Grand-Pré	Nova Scotia	Acadian site; home of Evangeline, heroine of Henry Wadsworth Longfellow's poem
Halifax Citadel	Nova Scotia	Restored British stone fort built in 1800's
L. M. Montgomery's Cavendish	Prince Edward Island	Includes the childhood home of author Lucy Maud Montgomery and the historical setting for her novel *Anne of Green Gables* (1908)
Lachine Canal	Quebec	Canal built in early 1800's along St. Lawrence River
L'Anse aux Meadows	Newfoundland and Labrador	Authenticated Viking remains
Laurier House	Ontario	Home of Canadian prime ministers Sir Wilfrid Laurier, 1897-1919; and William Lyon Mackenzie King, 1921-1950
Lévis Forts	Quebec	Fortifications built by British, begun in 1865
Louis S. St. Laurent	Quebec	Birthplace of Canadian Prime Minister Louis S. St. Laurent

Photri

The Rocky Mountains of western Canada offer some of the world's most beautiful scenery. Maligne Lake and Spirit Island, *shown here,* are in Jasper National Park in western Alberta.

Lower Fort Garry	Manitoba	Hudson's Bay Company fort built in 1830's and 1840's
Manoir Papineau	Quebec	Home of Patriot leader Louis-Joseph Papineau
Marconi	Nova Scotia	Site of Canada's first wireless telegraph station, 1902-1904
Nan Sdins	British Columbia	Remains of Haida longhouses and totem poles
Point Clark Lighthouse	Ontario	Navigation aid built in 1859 on Lake Huron
Pointe-au-Père Lighthouse	Quebec	Important navigation aid on St. Lawrence River
Port au Choix	Newfoundland and Labrador	Site of prehistoric Indian burial grounds and Inuit settlements
Port-la-Joye—Fort Amherst	Prince Edward Island	Ruins of British fort built in 1758
Port-Royal	Nova Scotia	Reconstruction of French fur-trading settlement of the early 1600's
Prince of Wales Fort	Manitoba	Fort built by Hudson's Bay Company, 1732-1772
Province House	Prince Edward Island	Birthplace of Confederation in 1864
Queenston Heights	Ontario	Site of major British victory in War of 1812
Riel House	Manitoba	Home of Métis leader Louis Riel
Rocky Mountain House	Alberta	Site of rival North West Company and Hudson's Bay Company trading posts
S.S. Klondike	Yukon	Site of the largest and last Yukon commercial steamboat
St. Andrews Blockhouse	New Brunswick	Restored wooden blockhouse built at start of War of 1812
St.-Ours Canal	Quebec	Canal built along Richelieu River in mid-1800's
Sault Ste. Marie Canal	Ontario	First canal with electric locks
Signal Hill	Newfoundland and Labrador	Site of last battle of French and Indian War (1754-1763); reception of first transatlantic wireless telegraph message in 1901
Sir George-Étienne Cartier	Quebec	Home of Sir George-Étienne Cartier, one of the Fathers of Confederation
Woodside	Ontario	Boyhood home of William Lyon Mackenzie King, Canada's prime minister for 21 years
York Redoubt	Nova Scotia	Defense post dating from 1793

tains and the Mackenzie Mountains. The Columbia Mountains in southern British Columbia are separated from the Canadian Rockies to the east by a long, narrow valley called the Rocky Mountain Trench.

The Rockies contain deposits of coal, lead, silver, zinc, and other minerals. Forests of juniper and pine trees grow on the lower slopes. Firs and spruces thrive at higher elevations. Bears, deer, minks, mountain lions, squirrels, and other animals roam forests on the upper slopes. Rocky Mountain goats and bighorn sheep live above the *timber line,* the elevation above which trees cannot grow. Rainbow trout, cutthroat trout, grayling, and other fishes swim in the mountain streams.

The Arctic Islands lie almost entirely within the Arctic Circle. They include about a dozen large islands and hundreds of smaller ones. All the islands are barren, and most remain unexplored. Two of the largest islands, Baffin Island and Ellesmere Island, have many glaciers, tall mountains, and deep fiords. Victoria Island and the other western islands are extremely flat. The seas surrounding the islands remain frozen most of the year.

The Arctic Islands are *tundras,* which are places too cold and dry for trees to grow. The subsoil of the islands is permanently frozen, and only a thin surface lay-

er of soil thaws during the brief, cool summers. Only simple organisms called *lichens* grow on the northernmost islands. The other islands have lichens, mosses, grasses, and grasslike plants known as *sedges.* Herds of caribou and musk oxen graze on the tundras. Other wildlife includes Arctic foxes and hares, lemmings, polar bears, ptarmigans, seals, walruses, and whales. Insects thrive on the Arctic Islands during the summer.

Deposits of petroleum and natural gas, as well as such minerals as lead and zinc, have been discovered in the western Arctic Islands. However, little of this mineral wealth has yet been tapped because of the high production costs and the difficulty of transporting the products to distant markets.

The Interior Plains include the northeastern corner of British Columbia, much of Alberta and Saskatchewan, and the southwestern part of Manitoba. The region extends north through the Northwest Territories to the Arctic Ocean.

Grasslands form the natural cover of the vast prairies in the southern Interior Plains. Farmers have plowed most of the grasslands to grow wheat and other grains in the fertile black soil. Ranchers graze cattle on the remaining grasslands in the drier areas of southern Alber-

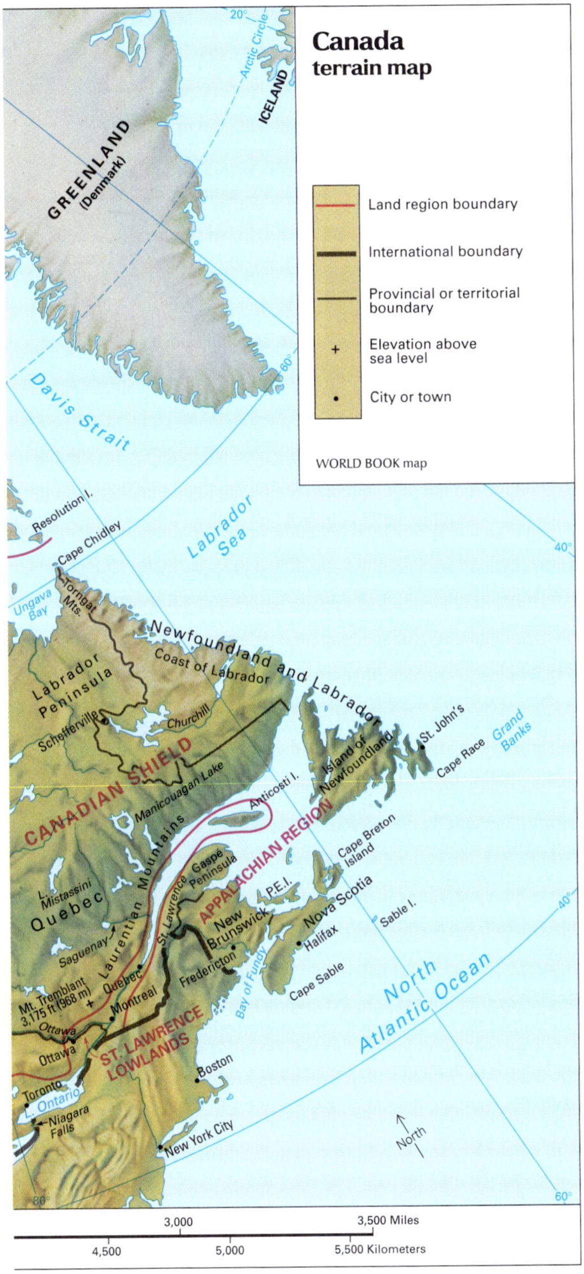

ta. Farther north, evergreen forests form part of the great northern forest that sweeps across Canada from Alaska to Labrador's coast. White spruces and jack pines are the most common trees in these forests. Moose, elk, deer, and many kinds of fur-bearing animals live there. Near the Arctic Ocean, the forests gradually give way to tundras covered by snow for more than half the year.

The Interior Plains have many mineral resources. Large deposits of petroleum, natural gas, and coal have made Alberta a major mining area. One of the world's largest known deposits of *bituminous sands* or *tar sands* (sands that contain oil) lies along the Athabasca River in Alberta. Saskatchewan has important deposits of petroleum and uranium, and the largest potash deposits in the world lie mainly in southern Saskatchewan. The Northwest Territories has petroleum and deposits of diamonds, lead, and zinc.

The Canadian Shield is a vast, horseshoe-shaped region. It curves around Hudson Bay from the Arctic coast of Nunavut to the coast of Labrador, the mainland part of the province of Newfoundland and Labrador. The Canadian Shield covers about half of Canada and is made up of extremely ancient rock. Much of the region lies from 600 to 1,200 feet (180 to 370 meters) above sea level. The eastern part of the region is called the Great Laurentian Uplands north of the St. Lawrence River.

The Canadian Shield consists largely of low hills and thousands of lakes. These lakes are the sources of rivers that break into great rapids and waterfalls at the edge of the region. Many of these rivers have hydroelectric plants, which provide power for pulp and paper mills and other industries as well as towns and cities of Quebec, Ontario, and Manitoba.

Relatively few people live in the Canadian Shield because of its poor soil and cold climate. Only a few areas near the southern edge of the region have soil that is good enough for farming. But the southern part of the Canadian Shield is close to Toronto, Ottawa, and Montreal. Many people of these cities have vacation houses near lakes or ski slopes in the southern part. The northern areas of the Canadian Shield are tundras, and the plant and animal life there resembles that of the Arctic Islands. Valuable evergreen forests cover most of the rest of the Canadian Shield. Deer, elk, moose, wolves, and many smaller animals live in the forests.

The Canadian Shield has much of Canada's mineral wealth. The border between Quebec and the province of Newfoundland and Labrador has huge deposits of iron ore. Deposits of cobalt, copper, gold, nickel, and uranium are mined near Greater Sudbury, Ontario, a major smelting center. The Canadian Shield also contains valuable deposits of platinum, silver, zinc, and other metals.

The Hudson Bay Lowlands form a flat, swampy region between the Canadian Shield and the southwestern coast of Hudson Bay. The lowlands extend about 800 miles (1,300 kilometers) from the Churchill River in Manitoba to the Nottaway River in Quebec. Much of the region is covered by poor-quality forests and huge deposits of decayed vegetable matter called *peat.* The only permanent settlements are several small villages, a few old trading posts and forts, and the ports of Churchill, Manitoba, and Moosonee, Ontario.

The St. Lawrence Lowlands make up the smallest Canadian land region, but more than half of the nation's people live there. This region includes the flat-to-rolling countryside along the St. Lawrence River and the peninsula of southern Ontario. Another part of the region, Anticosti Island at the mouth of the St. Lawrence, remains a wilderness because of its isolation and colder climate. Southern Ontario has Canada's only major *deciduous forests,* which consist of trees that shed their leaves every autumn. The most plentiful trees in these forests include beeches, hickories, maples, oaks, and walnuts. Foxes, rabbits, raccoons, squirrels, and other small animals inhabit the forests.

NFB Photothèque

The Interior Plains are the major grain-producing region of Canada. Small towns like this one in southern Saskatchewan dot the region's broad, fertile prairies. The tall buildings in the picture are grain elevators, where farmers store grain until it can be shipped to market.

The St. Lawrence Lowlands have excellent transportation facilities and lie near markets in the eastern and central United States. These features help make the region the manufacturing center of Canada. Because of the region's rapid industrial growth, however, Ontario and Quebec have had to limit the spread of urban development into farm areas. Fertile soil and a relatively mild climate enable farmers in the St. Lawrence Lowlands to produce about a third of Canada's agricultural output. The most important crops include barley, corn, oats, soybeans, and a wide variety of fruits and vegetables. The region also has a large number of dairy farms.

The Appalachian Region includes southeastern Quebec and all of the Atlantic Provinces region except Labrador. The region forms part of an ancient mountain chain that extends from the island of Newfoundland south to Alabama. The terrain of the Appalachian Region varies but is generally hilly. The effects of glaciers and erosion have rounded the mountains. The Shickshock Mountains on the Gaspé Peninsula of Quebec have the region's highest peaks, which reach just over 4,000 feet (1,220 meters).

Most residents of the Appalachian Region live along the coast, where hundreds of bays and inlets provide excellent harbors for fishing fleets. In most areas, the land rises gradually from the Atlantic Ocean, but parts of Nova Scotia and the island of Newfoundland have steep, rocky coasts. The Bay of Fundy, between New Brunswick and Nova Scotia, is famous for its high tides, which reach more than 50 feet (15 meters) in some areas.

Mixed evergreen and deciduous forests cover much of the Appalachian Region. Valuable farmland lies on the plains of Prince Edward Island and along the St. John River in New Brunswick and the Annapolis River in Nova Scotia. The area around the town of Thetford Mines in Quebec has some of the world's richest deposits of asbestos. Nova Scotia has important coal and gypsum deposits. Copper, lead, zinc, and other minerals are mined in New Brunswick and the island of Newfoundland.

Rivers, waterfalls, and lakes. Large numbers of rivers, waterfalls, and lakes add to the scenic beauty of the Canadian countryside. Until the first railroads were built during the 1800's, the rivers and lakes also provided the only means of reaching Canada's vast interior. Many of these waterways still serve as major transportation routes. In addition, they have great economic importance as sources of hydroelectric power and, in the western provinces, for irrigation.

The water from each of Canada's lakes and rivers eventually drains into one of four major bodies of water. Therefore, the country has four major drainage areas or basins: (1) the Atlantic Basin, (2) the Hudson Bay and Hudson Strait Basin, (3) the Arctic Basin, and (4) the Pacific Basin.

The Atlantic Basin covers about 678,000 square miles (1,756,000 square kilometers) in eastern Canada. The most important waterway in this drainage area is the Great Lakes-St. Lawrence River system. The Great Lakes, the largest group of freshwater lakes in the world, cover 94,230 square miles (244,060 square kilometers). Lake Michigan lies entirely within the United States, but the border between Canada and the United States passes through the other four Great Lakes and the rivers that connect them. These rivers are the Saint Marys, the Detroit, the St. Clair, and the Niagara. Between Lake Erie and Lake Ontario, the Niagara River plunges over a rocky ledge and forms Niagara Falls, a world-famous tourist attraction.

The St. Lawrence River flows about 800 miles (1,300 kilometers) from Lake Ontario to the Gulf of St. Lawrence, an arm of the Atlantic Ocean. The St. Lawrence is sometimes called the *Mother of Canada* because it was the chief route of the European explorers, fur traders, and colonists who came to Canada several hundred years ago. Today, the St. Lawrence forms part of the St. Lawrence Seaway and carries more freight than any other Canadian river. The St. Lawrence Seaway enables oceangoing ships to travel between the Atlantic and such Great Lakes ports as Toronto and Chicago. The Thousand Islands, which lie in the St. Lawrence River near Lake Ontario, are a popular resort area.

Dams on the major tributaries of the St. Lawrence provide much hydroelectric power for Quebec. Generating stations have been built on the Ottawa, Bersimis, Outardes, and Manicouagan rivers. Many other rivers have the potential for hydroelectric power. Such tributaries as the Ottawa, the St. Maurice, and the Saguenay are important to loggers, who float wood to pulp and paper plants downstream.

The Montmorency River plunges 251 feet (77 meters) near Quebec City to form Montmorency Falls. Churchill Falls, on the Churchill River in Labrador, is the site of one of the largest hydroelectric generating stations in the Western Hemisphere. New Brunswick is famous for its Reversing Falls at the mouth of the St. John River. Twice each day, high tides from the Bay of Fundy force the river backward through the falls. See **Reversing Falls of Saint John.**

The Hudson Bay and Hudson Strait Basin covers about a third of mainland Canada. The chief river in this basin is the Nelson, which flows from Lake Winnipeg to Hudson Bay. During the 1700's and 1800's, the Nelson served as an important transportation route for the Hudson's Bay Company. Today, the river is used mainly as a source of hydroelectric power. The Nelson's principal tributaries—the Assiniboine, the North and South Saskatchewan, the Red, and the Winnipeg rivers—flow into Lake Winnipeg rather than directly into the Nelson. The headwaters of the South Saskatchewan provide water for irrigating dry farmlands in southern Alberta. Hydroelectric generating stations on the Winnipeg River supply some electric power for the city of Winnipeg.

Other major rivers that flow into Hudson Bay include the Churchill and Hayes in Manitoba, the Severn and Winisk in Ontario, and the Thelon in the Northwest Territories and Nunavut. Several rivers empty into James Bay. Among them are the Albany and Moose in Ontario, and the Eastmain, Nottaway, and Rupert in Quebec. La Grande River has four large hydroelectric generating stations. Together these stations form one of the world's most important power projects.

The Arctic Basin includes parts of British Columbia, the Prairie Provinces, and the territories. The Mackenzie River system drains about half the basin. The sources of

Eberhard E. Otto, Miller Services

The St. Lawrence Lowlands include large areas of rolling farmland. Fertile soil and a relatively mild climate help this region rank high in Canadian agricultural production.

Photo Librarium, Canada

The Appalachian Region consists primarily of forests and farmland. The forests of this region are a mixture of evergreens and trees that shed their leaves each autumn.

© James Balog, Tony Stone Images

An icebreaker clears a path for a commercial vessel near Newfoundland and Labrador. Canada has a generally cold climate, and in the winter, Arctic air covers most of the country.

this river system, Canada's longest, are high in the Rocky Mountains, where the Peace and Athabasca rivers begin. These two rivers flow into the Slave River, which in turn empties into Great Slave Lake. The Mackenzie River itself flows northwest from Great Slave Lake for 1,100 miles (1,770 kilometers) to the Arctic Ocean. Along the way, the Mackenzie River receives water from many tributaries, the largest of which is the Liard River. The Great Bear River flows into the Mackenzie from Great Bear Lake, the largest lake that lies entirely in Canada.

Barges carry cargo over much of the Mackenzie River system. The main route extends for 1,122 miles (1,805 kilometers) between the Northwest Territories towns of Tuktoyaktuk on the Arctic Ocean and Hay River on Great Slave Lake. Some stretches of the Slave and Athabasca rivers are navigated by barges that provide service to local settlements.

The Pacific Basin covers much of British Columbia and the Yukon Territory. The northern third of the region is drained by the Yukon River. This river rises from a series of lakes in northwest British Columbia and flows west through the Yukon Territory and Alaska to the Pacific Ocean. During the gold rush of the late 1890's, riverboats brought thousands of prospectors up the river to Dawson, a boom town near the Klondike gold fields.

The longest river in the southern part of the Pacific Basin is the Fraser. It flows through a deep valley from the Canadian Rockies to Vancouver, where it empties into the Pacific. The Columbia River rises in the mountains of southeastern British Columbia and flows south into the United States. Hydroelectric plants operate at several points on the Columbia. The Columbia goes through Upper Arrow Lake and Lower Arrow Lake, two long, narrow lakes in the interior valleys. Other important rivers of the Pacific Basin include the Kootenay, Skeena, Stikine, and Thompson.

Climate

Canada's northern location gives the country a generally cold climate, but conditions vary considerably from region to region. During the winter, westerly winds bring frigid Arctic air to most of Canada. Average January temperatures are below 0 °F (−18 °C) in more than two-thirds of the country. January temperatures average above freezing only along the coast of British Columbia. This area has a moderate climate because of mild winds from the Pacific Ocean.

Northern Canada has short, cool summers. In the northern Arctic Islands, July temperatures average below 40 °F (4 °C). Permanent icecaps cover parts of Baffin, Devon, and Ellesmere islands. Southern Canada has summers that are long enough and warm enough for raising crops. Summer winds from the Gulf of Mexico often bring hot weather to southern Ontario and the St. Lawrence River Valley. Southern Ontario has average July temperatures above 70 °F (21 °C) and a frost-free growing season nearly six months long.

Some coastal areas of British Columbia get over 100 inches (250 centimeters) of precipitation annually. Most of it falls during the autumn and winter. The Canadian prairies have from 10 to 20 inches (25 to 50 centimeters) of precipitation a year. Little snow falls there, and most of the rain comes during the summer. These conditions help make the prairies ideal for growing grain.

Southeastern Canada has a humid climate. The average annual precipitation ranges from about 30 inches (76 centimeters) in southern Ontario to about 60 inches (150 centimeters) on the coasts of the province of Newfoundland and Labrador and the province of Nova Scotia. Heavy snow covers eastern Canada in winter. More than 100 inches (250 centimeters) of snow falls annually on large areas of New Brunswick, Newfoundland and Labrador, Quebec, and Ontario.

Economy

In colonial times, most Canadians earned a living by farming, fishing, logging, or fur trapping. Today, these industries still serve the needs of some of Canada's people and produce valuable exports. But the main economic activities in Canada are service industries and manufacturing. Canada's *gross domestic product* (GDP) —the total value of all goods and services produced within the country—is among the top 10 in the world.

The Canadian economy is based on private enterprise. But the national and provincial governments play an active role in many economic activities. For example, they provide free health services to all Canadians. The federal and provincial governments also own broadcasting companies, transportation firms, and utilities.

Average January temperatures

Most of Canada has long, cold winters. January temperatures average below 0 °F (−18 °C) in more than two-thirds of the country. Only the coastal areas of British Columbia have average January temperatures above 32 °F (0 °C).

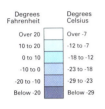

Degrees Fahrenheit	Degrees Celsius
Over 20	Over -7
10 to 20	-12 to -7
0 to 10	-18 to -12
-10 to 0	-23 to -18
-20 to -10	-29 to -23
Below -20	Below -29

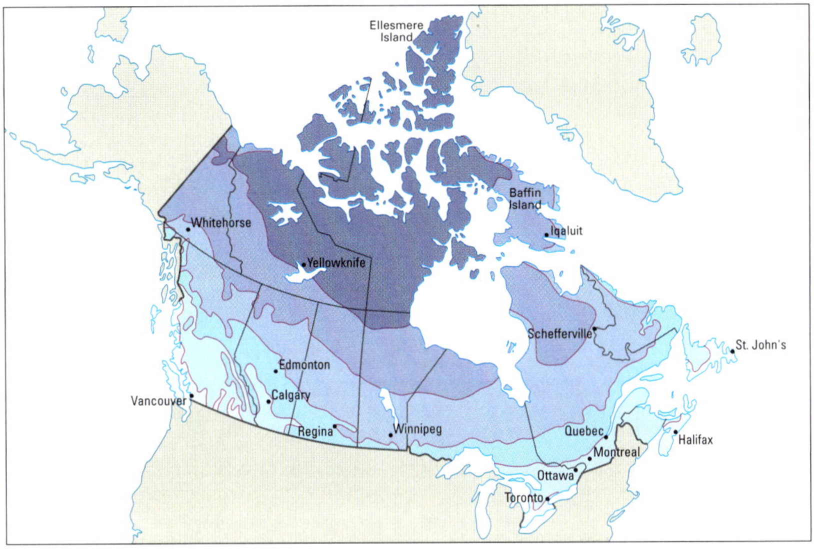

Average July temperatures

Summers are cool in northern Canada but warm enough for farming in the southern areas of the country. Average July temperatures range from approximately 40 °F (4 °C) in the northern Arctic Islands to more than 70 °F (21 °C) in southern Ontario.

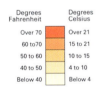

Degrees Fahrenheit	Degrees Celsius
Over 70	Over 21
60 to70	15 to 21
50 to 60	10 to 15
40 to 50	4 to 10
Below 40	Below 4

Average yearly precipitation

Precipitation in Canada is heaviest along the Pacific coast, where it averages over 80 inches (200 centimeters) per year. The Prairie Provinces receive only 8 to 20 inches (20 to 50 centimeters), most of which falls in summer.

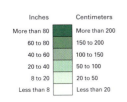

Inches	Centimeters
More than 80	More than 200
60 to 80	150 to 200
40 to 60	100 to 150
20 to 40	50 to 100
8 to 20	20 to 50
Less than 8	Less than 20

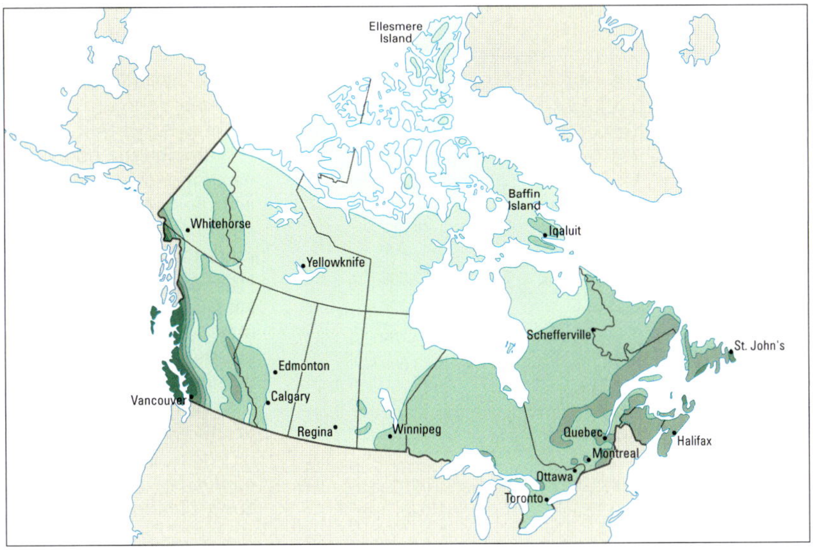

WORLD BOOK maps

Canadian steel mills produce millions of tons of steel annually. The plant shown here is in Hamilton, Ontario, the center of the nation's steel industry.

George Hunter

Canada's gross domestic product

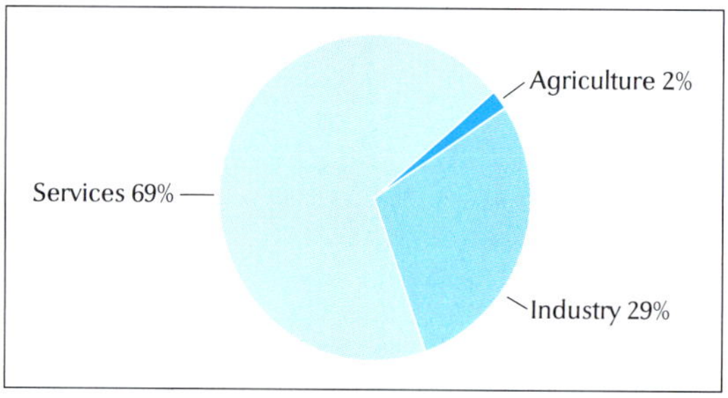

Canada's gross domestic product (GDP) was $994,073,000,000 (U.S. dollars) in 2004. The GDP is the total value of goods and services produced within a country in a year. *Services* include community, business, and personal services; finance, insurance, and real estate; government; trade, restaurants, and hotels; and transportation and communication. *Industry* includes construction, manufacturing, mining, and utilities. *Agriculture* includes agriculture, fishing, and forestry.

Production and workers by economic activities

Economic activities	Percent of GDP produced	Employed workers: Number of people	Percent of total
Community, business, & personal services	20	5,120,400*	32*
Finance, insurance, & real estate	20*	955,000	6
Manufacturing	17	2,297,000	14
Trade, restaurants, & hotels	14	3,510,400	22
Transportation & communication	9	1,542,000	10
Construction	6	952,800	6
Government	5	829,200	5
Mining†	4	285,700	2
Utilities	2	133,000	1
Agriculture, forestry, & fishing	2	324,100	2
Total‡	100	15,949,600	100

*Includes figures from establishments that manage other companies.
†Employment figures include forestry and fishing.
‡Figures may not add up to 100 percent due to rounding.
Figures are for 2004.
Source: Statistics Canada.

Foreign investment and ownership—chiefly from the United States—strongly influence Canada's economy. Japan and countries of the European Union also have large investments in Canada. A free trade agreement with the United States took effect in 1989. The agreement called for the elimination of all *tariffs* (taxes on imports) between the two countries. In 1994, Canada joined with the United States and Mexico in the North American Free Trade Agreement (NAFTA), which built upon the previous pact between Canada and the United States. See **North American Free Trade Agreement.**

Service industries account for the largest portion of Canada's gross domestic product. They are especially important in metropolitan areas. Ranking first among Canada's service industries are (1) community, business, and personal services and (2) finance, insurance, and real estate. These groups each contribute a roughly equal amount to the gross domestic product.

Community, business, and personal services employs more people than any other industry group in Canada. This group includes a great variety of activities, such as education and health care, data processing and legal services, and the operation of recreational facilities.

Toronto and Montreal are the leading financial centers in Canada. The main Canadian stock exchange is in Toronto.

Other service industries include government; trade, restaurants, and hotels; and transportation and communication. Government services, which include military activities, are centered in Ottawa, the nation's capital, and in the provincial capitals and major cities. Restaurants and hotels benefit from the millions of people who visit Canada each year. Retail trade, which consists of such establishments as automobile dealerships, department stores, and supermarkets, employs many people in cities. International trade, transportation, and communication are discussed later in this section.

Manufacturing. Factories in Ontario and Quebec produce more than three-fourths of the value of Canada's manufactured goods. In terms of *value added by manufacture,* transportation equipment ranks as the nation's leading manufactured product, followed by proc-

© Joe Sohm, Photo Researchers

Oil refining is carried out at processing plants such as this one in Sarnia, Ontario. Petroleum production is a major economic activity in Canada, which is one of the world's leading oil refiners.

essed foods and beverages. Value added by manufacture is the difference between the value of raw materials and the value of finished products made from them. The manufacture of motor vehicles and parts dominates the transportation equipment industry. Japanese and U.S. motor vehicle manufacturers operate plants in Ontario. About 2 ½ million vehicles roll off the assembly lines of these plants each year. This figure is split almost evenly between the production of cars and trucks, which include pickups and minivans. Aircraft and aerospace equipment production is a fast-growing part of this industry. Bombardier Aerospace in Quebec is one of the world's largest civil aircraft manufacturers.

Processed meat and poultry are the leading products of Canada's food and beverage industry. Toronto is a major meat-packing center. Other leading processed foods and beverages include dairy products; flour, cereals, and livestock feed; fish products; canned and frozen fruits and vegetables; baked goods; soft drinks; and beer, wine, and liquor.

Other important manufacturing industries in Canada produce chemicals, fabricated metal products, machinery, paper products, primary metals, and wood products. Important chemical products include industrial

The economy of Canada

The Canadian economy is based on a wealth of natural resources. This map shows some of the major products of each region of Canada. It also indicates how the land is used and points out the nation's chief manufacturing centers.

Wheat farming

Mixed cropland and dairy farming

Grain farming and cattle grazing

Cattle grazing

Forest

Generally unproductive land

Fishing

Tree line

Manufacturing center

Mineral deposit

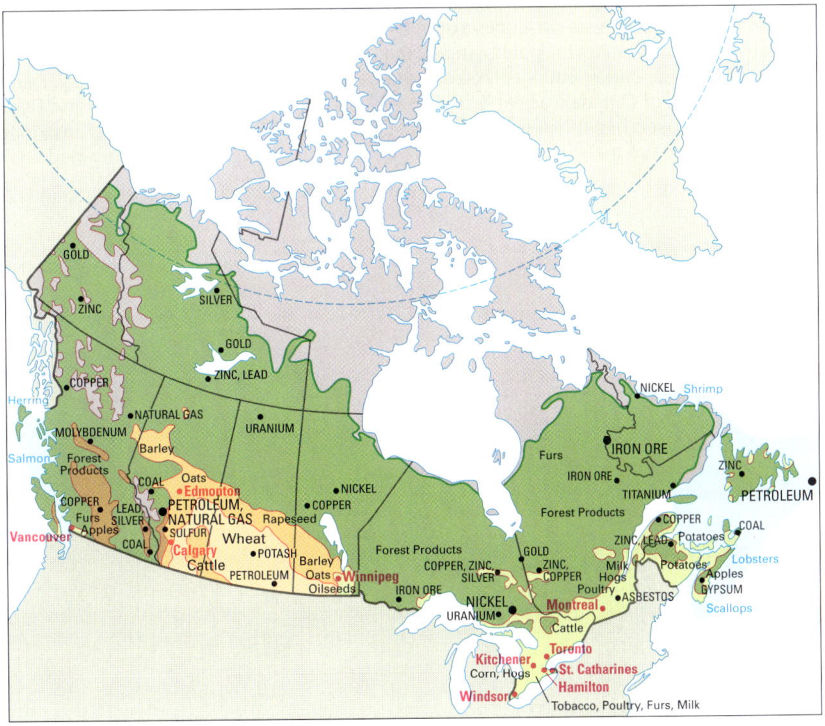

WORLD BOOK map; adapted from *The National Atlas of Canada,* 4th edition

chemicals, pharmaceuticals, paints and varnishes, and cleaning solutions. Canada's fabricated metal production is centered on machine shops and factories that make structural metals. Canada's leading machinery products include those used for agriculture and heavy industry. Quebec is one of the world's leading paper-producing regions. Basic aluminum and steel products are produced at Canada's smelters and refineries. Quebec leads in aluminum production, and Ontario produces the most steel. Sawmills produce most of the nation's wood products.

Mining. Canada is among the major producers of a wide variety of minerals, including copper, gold, iron ore, nickel, potash, uranium, and zinc. The country is also one of the world's leading exporters of minerals.

Canada's two most important mined products are petroleum and natural gas. Alberta is the leading producer of both Canada's petroleum and its natural gas. Valuable amounts of sulfur are obtained from processing Alberta's natural gas. Saskatchewan is a major source of uranium and potash.

Ontario is Canada's leading producer of metal ores. Much of the world's nickel comes from Ontario. Ontario also mines large amounts of gold and copper, as does British Columbia. Quebec is notable for its large iron ore and gold production, but Newfoundland and Labrador leads the provinces in iron ore production. New Brunswick and Quebec are the leading zinc-mining provinces. Canada's other mined products include coal, diamonds, platinum, salt, sand and gravel, and silver.

Agriculture. Farmland covers about 7 percent of Canada's land area. Beef cattle, dairy products, hogs, and wheat combine to account for about half of the total farm income. Other leading products include barley, canola, chickens and eggs, and corn.

About 80 percent of Canada's farmland is in the Prairie Provinces. Saskatchewan produces about half of Canada's wheat, and farmers in Alberta and Manitoba raise most of the rest. Barley, canola, flaxseed, and oats grow in a belt north of Canada's wheat-growing areas. Barley and oats are used mainly for livestock feed. Flaxseed and canola are used to make cooking oils and lubricants.

Farms in Alberta produce most of the nation's beef cattle. Farmers in the Prairie Provinces also raise dairy cattle, hogs, and poultry.

The St. Lawrence Lowlands form Canada's other major agricultural region. Farmers there produce a variety of products, including beef cattle, grains, milk, and vegetables. Southern Ontario's warm summers and long growing season enable farmers to grow a variety of specialty crops, including corn, fruits, vegetables, and tobacco. Quebec leads the provinces in the production of milk, and Ontario ranks second. Quebec's farmers also raise apples, beef cattle, hogs, poultry, and vegetables.

Potato farming and dairying are the chief agricultural activities in the Atlantic Provinces. Farmers from the interior of British Columbia and Vancouver Island produce eggs, livestock, milk, poultry, and tree fruits. British Columbia and Ontario are Canada's leading growers of nursery products and ornamental plants and flowers. Not coincidentally, British Columbia and Ontario are also the provinces with the most area under greenhouses. The production of greenhouse plants is one of Canada's fastest-growing agricultural activities.

Government marketing agencies establish production quotas and price supports to protect Canadian farmers from the effects of changing prices. The federal and provincial governments also provide credit, as well as technical and management assistance, to farmers. In many areas, farmers have formed cooperatives. These organizations market the farmers' products and supply goods and services needed in farming.

Forestry. Canada is a leading timber-producing nation. The federal and provincial governments own most of the forests and lease them to private companies. British Columbia, Ontario, and Quebec lead the provinces in timber production. Loggers cut down cedars, firs, hemlocks, pines, spruce, and many other kinds of trees. Mills process the logs into lumber, paper, plywood, and wood pulp.

Fishing industry. Fishing is Canada's oldest economic activity. The Grand Banks, off the coast of the island of Newfoundland, ranks among the world's best fishing areas. It has attracted fishing crews since the 1500's.

© Bryce Flynn, Picture Group

Herds of beef cattle graze on the grasslands of southern Alberta, where cattle ranching is the chief agricultural activity. Ontario and Saskatchewan are also leading producers of beef cattle.

George Hunter

Workers prepare salmon for canning. Salmon is Canada's leading fish catch from the Pacific Ocean. Other catches from the Pacific include halibut and herring.

Today, the major products of Canada's Atlantic waters include crab, haddock, herring, lobster, redfish, scallops, and shrimp. Cod were once plentiful in the Atlantic coastal waters, but they have nearly disappeared due to overfishing. The population of certain other fishes has also declined. As a result, the government has banned almost all cod fishing and placed restrictions on other fishing in Canada's Atlantic waters.

Fishing crews take halibut, herring, salmon, and shellfish from the Pacific waters of Canada. Fishing fleets catch most of the salmon near the mouths of rivers in British Columbia. The salmon fishing industry is, however, in danger. Salmon stocks have fallen due to overfishing by fishing crews from British Columbia, Alaska and Washington in the United States, and other countries. In 1998, the Canadian government ordered a halt to fishing for some types of salmon. Today, British Columbia has a large number of fish farms that raise salmon.

Canada's lakes provide fish chiefly for the central part of the country and the United States. The principal lake fish include perch, pickerel, and whitefish.

Energy sources. Canada uses energy at a high rate per person. This rate results largely from the huge quantities needed for certain uses. These uses include providing heat in the severe winters, transporting goods and people between distant regions of the country, and processing natural resources. Canada has vast energy resources, but energy conservation is essential. Conservation helps slow the depletion of nonrenewable energy sources, such as petroleum and natural gas. Reducing fuel consumption through conservation also lessens the amount of pollution released into the environment.

Much of the petroleum used in Canada is in the form of gasoline. More than half of Canada's electric power comes from hydroelectric sources. Plants powered by natural gas, oil, or coal provide about a fourth of Canada's power. Other power sources include nuclear energy and renewable sources such as wind or biomass.

International trade. Canada ranks among the leading countries in the world in international trade. The nation's exports total hundreds of billions of dollars annually. About three-fourths of Canada's trade, both exports and imports, is with the United States. Automobiles and automobile parts, chemicals, and various kinds of machinery are exported and imported by both countries.

Other leading exports include aluminum, lumber, precious metals and metal ores, natural gas, newsprint, petroleum, wheat, and wood pulp. Canada's other major imports include computers, fruits and vegetables, and scientific instruments. Canada's chief trading partners, besides the United States, include China, France, Germany, Japan, Mexico, and the United Kingdom.

Transportation. Canada's landscape has many features that are barriers to travel, including mountains, forests, and bodies of water. In spite of these problems, Canadians have built an outstanding system of railroad,

Koos Dykstra, Image Finders

Logging is an important industry in many regions of Canada. This photograph shows a logging operation on the coast of British Columbia, Canada's leading wood-producing province.

Port of Quebec

The St. Lawrence Seaway forms one of the world's major inland waterways. The seaway enables oceangoing ships to sail between the Atlantic Ocean and the Great Lakes. It consists of the St. Lawrence River, several lakes, and a system of canals and locks. This photograph shows vessels on the St. Lawrence River near Quebec City.

highway, water, and air transportation.

Railroads. Canada's railroad system has about 30,000 miles (49,000 kilometers) of mainline track. Canada's two main railroads are the Canadian National Railway and the Canadian Pacific Railway. Both railroads are privately owned. A government-owned corporation called VIA Rail Canada provides the only trans-Canada passenger rail service. Other passenger rail services operate within some provinces, and commuter systems serve a number of urban areas.

Toronto and Montreal have modern subway systems. Calgary, Edmonton, Ottawa, and Vancouver have light rail transit systems, which use electrically powered cars that run on tracks.

Roads and highways. Southern Canada has one of the world's finest highway systems. The Trans-Canada Highway extends about 5,000 miles (8,000 kilometers) between Victoria, British Columbia, and St. John's, Newfoundland and Labrador. Paved two- and four-lane highways link Canada's major cities and extend south to U.S. cities. Northern Canada has few highways. Many roads there are unpaved. Ferries link roads on Vancouver Island and the island of Newfoundland with roads on the mainland and other islands. Confederation Bridge joins Prince Edward Island to New Brunswick on the mainland. Buses provide public transportation in Canadian cities. Buses also link cities with outlying towns and other cities.

Waterways and ports. The Great Lakes and the St. Lawrence Seaway form one of the world's greatest inland waterways. The seaway enables oceangoing ships to sail between the Atlantic Ocean and Great Lakes ports. These ships transport coal, iron ore, wheat, and other bulk cargoes. Other vessels, called *lakers,* transport cargo between ports on the Great Lakes and the St. Lawrence River. For example, lakers carry iron ore from ports on the river to steel mills on the Great Lakes.

The port of Vancouver, including the facilities at nearby Roberts Bank, is Canada's busiest port. Prince Rupert is also an important Pacific port. Major ports on the St. Lawrence River include Montreal, Port-Cartier, Quebec City, and Sept-Îles in Quebec. The main Great Lakes ports are Hamilton, Nanticoke, and Thunder Bay in Ontario. Canada's busiest Atlantic Ocean ports are Come By Chance, Newfoundland and Labrador; Halifax, Nova Scotia; and Saint John, New Brunswick.

Air travel. Air Canada is by far Canada's largest airline. It provides both domestic and international service. WestJet provides service mainly in western Canada, but also serves cities in eastern Canada. Lester B. Pearson International Airport, outside Toronto, is the busiest terminal, followed by Vancouver International Airport.

Communication plays a vital role in linking the various parts of a nation as vast as Canada. Canadians have one of the world's most advanced communication systems, including telephone and Internet service, television and radio, mail service, and publishing.

Telephone and Internet service. A variety of telecommunications companies provide Internet and local and long distance phone service to customers throughout Canada. Deregulation of the industry during the 1990's led to increased competition as well as mergers among telephone service providers.

Bell Canada Enterprises is the country's largest communications company. It provides telephone, Internet, satellite television, and other services to many homes and businesses. Canada's telecommunications systems are linked by cable and satellite to most other countries.

Television and radio. The Canadian Broadcasting Corporation (CBC) operates national television and radio networks in both English and French. The CBC, though financed largely by the government, functions independently in its programming. Canada's satellite communications system enables CBC broadcasts to reach nearly all the population. Canada's other national TV networks are CTV Television Network and Global Television Network, which are privately owned. Commercial networks serve all major metropolitan areas. Many of the nation's households subscribe to cable TV systems, which offer a wide variety of Canadian and U.S. programs. See **Canadian Broadcasting Corporation.**

The Canadian Radio-television and Telecommunications Commission (CRTC), a government agency, regulates all electronic communication systems in Canada. The CRTC issues licenses to radio and television stations and makes sure that certain percentages of their programs have Canadian content. These Canadian content quotas are intended to help maintain a Canadian cultural identity in the face of overwhelming U.S. influence. They also create jobs in Canada by encouraging production there of TV and radio shows.

Publishing. Canada has about 95 daily newspapers that are printed in English and about 10 in French. The leading English-language dailies include *The Toronto Star, The Globe and Mail, The National Post,* and *The Toronto Sun* of Toronto; *The Sun* of Vancouver; *The Gazette* of Montreal; and the *Ottawa Citizen.* The leading French-language dailies are *Le Journal de Montreal* and *La Presse* of Montreal. About 1,000 weekly and biweekly newspapers are also published in Canada.

About 2,000 magazines are published in Canada, the best known of which include *Chatelaine, Maclean's,* and *L'Actualité.* Magazines from the United States are also widely read in Canada, and magazines from France have many readers in Quebec. Major Canadian publishing houses bring out about 16,000 new titles annually. Many U.S., British, and French publications are printed in Canada at the same time as in their own country.

David Jay Bercuson

Related articles in *World Book.* See **Canada, Government of; Canada, History of;** and the separate articles on the provinces and territories with their lists of *Related articles.* See also the following articles:

Physical features

See **Lake; Mountain;** and **River** with their lists of *Related articles.* See also:

Anticosti
Baffin Island
Bay of Fundy
Boothia Peninsula
Canadian Shield
Cape Breton Island
Ellesmere Island
Gaspé Peninsula
Georgian Bay
Grand Banks
Hudson Bay
James Bay
Labrador
Manitoulin Island
Melville Island
Niagara Falls
Queen Charlotte Islands
Reversing Falls of Saint John
Sable Island
Southampton Island
Thousand Islands
Vancouver Island

Other related articles

Alaska Highway
Alcan Inc.
Atlantic Provinces
Bank (Canada)
Bank of Canada
Canada Day
Canadian Armed Forces
Canadian Education Association
Canadian Library Association
Canadian literature
Conservation (Canada)
Education (Education in Canada)
Flag (History of the Canadian flag; picture: Flags of Canada)
Hockey
Inuit
Labor movement (In Canada)
Library
McConnell Family Foundation
Medicine (In Canada)
Museum (Early Canadian museums)
National park (Canada)
O Canada
Postal services (Canadian mail service)
Railroad (In Canada; History)
Remembrance Day
Rideau Canal
Ringette
Royal Canadian Legion
Royal Society of Canada
Saint Lawrence Seaway
Scouts Canada
Soo Canals
Television (In Canada)
Theater (Canada)
Trans-Canada Highway
United Church of Canada
Welland Ship Canal

Outline

I. **The nation**
  A. The Atlantic Provinces
  B. Quebec
  C. Ontario
  D. The Prairie Provinces
  E. British Columbia
  F. The territories
II. **People**
  A. Population
  B. Ancestry
  C. Languages
III. **Way of life**
  A. City life
  B Rural life
  C. Arctic life
  D. Education
  E. Religion
  F. Recreation and sports
  G. Food
IV. **The arts**
  A. Literature
  B. Painting and sculpture
  C. Theater
  D. Music
  E. Ballet and opera
  F. Motion pictures
  G. Architecture
V. **The land**
  A. Land regions
  B. Rivers, waterfalls, and lakes
VI. **Climate**
VII. **Economy**
  A. Service industries
  B. Manufacturing
  C. Mining
  D. Agriculture
  E. Forestry
  F. Fishing industry
  G. Energy sources
  H. International trade
  I. Transportation
  J. Communication

Additional resources

Level I

Bowers, Vivien. *Only in Canada!* Owl Bks., 2002. *That's Very Canadian!* Maple Tree Pr., 2004. *Wow, Canada!* Owl Bks., 1999.
Desaulniers, Kristi L. *Canada.* Chelsea Hse., 2003.
Gall, Timothy L. and Susan B., eds. *Junior Worldmark Encyclopedia of the Canadian Provinces.* 4th ed. UXL, 2004.
Moore, Christopher. *The Big Book of Canada.* Tundra, 2002.
Pang, Guek-Cheng. *Canada.* 2nd ed. Benchmark Bks., 2004.

Level II

Bumsted, J. M. *Canada's Diverse Peoples.* ABC-CLIO, 2003.
Marsh, James H., ed. *The Canadian Encyclopedia.* Rev. ed. McClelland, 1999.
Schulte-Peevers, Andrea. *Canada.* 9th ed. Lonely Planet, 2005.
Statistics Canada. *Canada Year Book.* Minister of Industry (Canada), published annually.
Thompson, Wayne C. *Canada.* Stryker-Post, published annually.

Questions

In which province do most French-speaking Canadians live?
What is Canada's rank in terms of land area compared to other countries of the world?
What is the *Golden Horseshoe?* Where is it?
Which group developed the first distinctively Canadian style of painting?
What plants and animals live on Canada's Arctic Islands?
Which province produces most of Canada's petroleum?
What is the most popular sport in Canada?
Why is the St. Lawrence River sometimes called the *Mother of Canada?*
What percentage of Canadians live in rural areas?
Which nations are Canada's main trading partners?

Canada, Armed Forces of. See Canadian Armed Forces.

National Capital Commission

The Canadian Parliament buildings in Ottawa, Ontario, include chambers of the House of Commons and the Senate. The central tower, called the Peace Tower, houses a set of 53 bells.

Canada, Government of

Canada, Government of. Canada combines a federal form of government with a cabinet system. The federal form of government was originally patterned on that of the United States, and the cabinet system on that of the United Kingdom (also called Britain).

As a federation, Canada is made up of 10 provinces and 3 territories. The country works out its national problems through its central government in Ottawa, which represents all the people of Canada. Each province has its own government. The territories are self-governing, but the federal government plays a large role in their administration.

The cabinet system of Canada unites the legislative and executive branches of the government. The prime minister and all members of the Cabinet are usually members of the House of Commons. Occasionally, a senator may be in the Cabinet. Ministers are responsible for all their actions to the House of Commons, which is elected by the people. If the House of Commons defeats a piece of important government-supported legislation, or if it passes a vote of no confidence in the government, the prime minister must either resign or request that the governor general call a general election.

Queen Elizabeth II of the United Kingdom is queen of Canada. She is the official head of state, but a governor general acts as her representative. However, the governor general performs only certain formal and symbolic tasks. The prime minister directs the government.

The people of Canada elect members of the House of Commons. To vote in national elections, a person must be at least 18 years old and a Canadian citizen. Each

The contributor of this article, J. L. Granatstein, is Professor of History at York University.

Canada's flag features a red maple leaf, the country's national symbol. It became Canada's official flag in 1965.

Canada's coat of arms has three maple leaves below the royal arms of England, Scotland, Ireland, and France.

Facts in brief

Form of government: Constitutional monarchy.
Capital: Ottawa.
Divisions: 10 provinces, 3 territories.
Head of state: Elizabeth II of the United Kingdom is queen of Canada. The queen, on the recommendation of Canada's prime minister, appoints a governor general to represent her.
Head of government: Prime minister, leader of the majority party in the House of Commons.
Parliament: *Senate*—105 members appointed by the governor general. *House of Commons*—308 members elected by the people.
Coat of arms (shown on preceding page): The shield bears the royal arms of England (upper left); Scotland (upper right); Ireland (lower left); and France (lower right). A British lion holds the Union Jack. A unicorn holds the fleur-de-lis of France. The coat of arms is based on a version adopted by Canada in 1921.
Anthems: "O Canada" (national); "God Save the Queen" (royal).
National motto: *A Mari Usque ad Mare* (From Sea to Sea).
Flag (shown on preceding page): A red, 11-pointed maple leaf appears on a white field. At each end is a broad, vertical red stripe. The maple leaf is a national emblem. This flag became Canada's official flag on Feb. 15, 1965.

province sets its own voting requirements for provincial elections. A voter must be at least 19 in British Columbia and at least 18 in other provinces.

Canada is a member of the Commonwealth of Nations, but it is not a dependency of the United Kingdom. Canada is independent, self-governing, and equal in rank to the United Kingdom and all other nations.

The constitution

Canada's constitution is partly unwritten and partly written. The unwritten part consists mainly of usage and customs, including the cabinet system of government. The basic written section is the Constitution Act of 1982. It includes the British North America Act, which was the basic document governing Canada's federal system from 1867 to 1982. Other written parts include ordinary laws and judicial decisions.

The founding fathers of the Canadian confederation wanted a strong central government. Thus, in the British North America Act, the provincial governments received only 16 powers then considered to be of minor importance. The federal government got all other powers. It also received power to *disallow* (reject) any provincial laws it believed undesirable.

However, powers given to the provinces—over such matters as education, health, and natural resources—became more important. Provinces became stronger and richer, and debates on the divisions of power between federal and provincial governments increased.

The Constitution Act of 1982 ended formal British control over amendments to Canada's constitution. Previously, the British Parliament had to approve many of the amendments.

Today, amendments must be approved by Canada's House of Commons; the provinces of Quebec and Ontario; two of the four Atlantic Provinces, representing at least half the region's population; and two of the four Western Provinces, representing at least half of that region's people. The Atlantic Provinces are New Brunswick, Newfoundland and Labrador, Nova Scotia, and Prince Edward Island. The Western Provinces are Alberta, British Columbia, Manitoba, and Saskatchewan. A province is considered to have approved an amendment when a majority of its voters have voted for it. The Canadian Senate also votes on amendments, but its rejection can only delay passage for 180 days.

Executive offices

The governor general. Canada's prime minister recommends a candidate for this office. The queen appoints the governor general as her representative, usually for five years. Until 1952, the governor general came from the United Kingdom. In 1952, Vincent Massey became the first Canadian-born governor general.

The governor general originally had far-reaching powers. But these powers gradually dwindled. Today, the governor general follows the directions and advice of the Cabinet.

BGM Photo Centre Ltd.

The Canadian Senate meets in the Parliament buildings in Ottawa. Senators are appointed by the governor general on the prime minister's recommendation. The Senate can introduce bills that do not involve the spending of money. It can also recommend amendments to any bill. Senate sessions are open to the public.

The prime minister is the actual head of the government. As leader of the majority in the House of Commons, the prime minister is indirectly elected by the people. No law establishes this office. The office is simply a necessity, worked out long ago in England. No government could carry on without Parliament's support. The leader of the majority in the House gradually became the *prime* (first) minister of the Cabinet.

The prime minister is appointed by the governor general, who follows the wishes of the majority in the House. The prime minister holds office only with the backing of this majority. A prime minister who loses this backing must resign, request that the governor general call a new general election, or suggest that the governor general find a new leader with the support of a majority of the House.

Parliament can control the actions of the prime minister by giving or withholding support. However, the prime minister also has control over the actions of the House of Commons. The prime minister may request that the governor general dissolve the House of Commons and call a new general election. See **Prime minister of Canada**.

The Cabinet helps the prime minister direct the government. The Cabinet consists of about 25 ministers chosen by the prime minister, usually from the majority party in the House, and appointed by the governor general. Ministers usually head government departments. In some cases, a single minister can lead more than one ministry at a time. Ministers lose their positions if the government resigns. Ministers may also lose their posts if the Cabinet changes. A deputy minister serves as the permanent head of each government department and reports to the department's minister. Deputy ministers are civil servants.

The Parliament

The Parliament is the national legislature of Canada. It has two houses—an upper house called the Senate and a lower house called the House of Commons. In a strict legal sense, Parliament includes the Crown, represented by the governor general. However, the term *Parliament* is also used to refer to just the Senate and House of Commons.

The Senate normally has 105 members. The governor general appoints the senators and the speaker, the Senate's presiding officer, on the prime minister's recommendation. A new prime minister usually recommends a new speaker. Senators must retire when they reach age 75.

The Atlantic Provinces—Prince Edward Island, New Brunswick, Newfoundland and Labrador, and Nova Scotia—send a total of 30 members to the Senate. The Western Provinces—Alberta, British Columbia, Manitoba, and Saskatchewan—send 24. Quebec and Ontario each send 24 members. The Northwest Territories, Nunavut, and Yukon each have 1 senator.

The Senate has less power than the House of Commons. Since 1982, amendments to Canada's constitution have required approval from the House and a required number—usually seven—of the provincial assemblies. The Senate votes on amendments, but its rejection can only delay passage of an otherwise approved amendment for 180 days. The Senate cannot introduce bills that involve the spending of money.

The House of Commons consists of members elected by the people for five-year terms, unless an election is called earlier. A House rarely lasts for five years without a new election. The number of members for each province is determined after each Canadian census. For

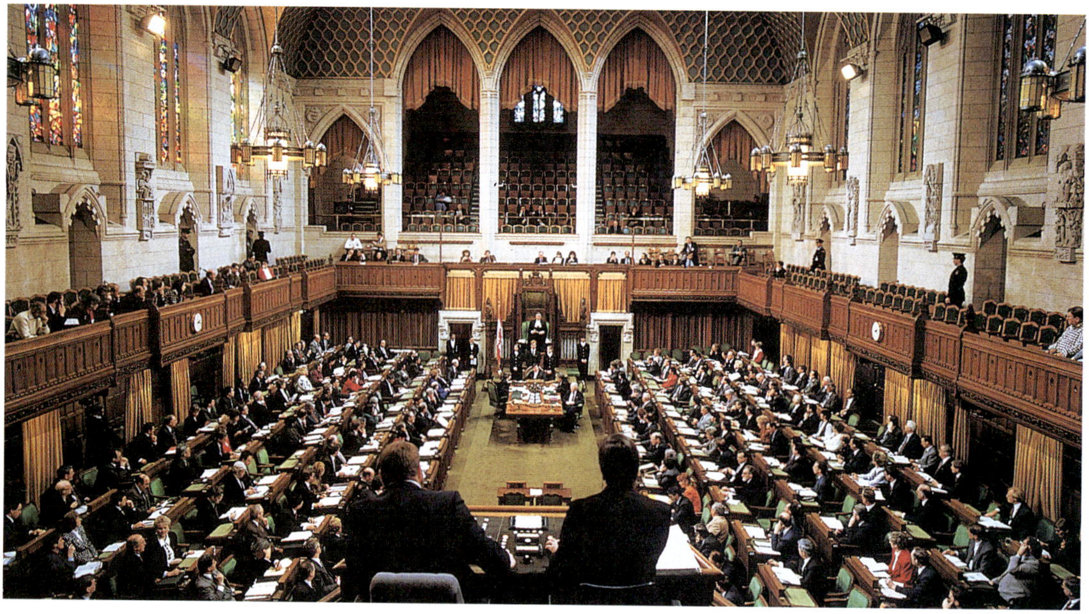

BGM Photo Centre Ltd.

The House of Commons meets in its chamber in the Parliament buildings. Most of the important bills that are introduced in the Canadian Parliament start in the House. The public may observe sessions of the House from galleries.

Canadian province symbols

Designs cut into stone on the curving walls of the Canadian House of Commons at Ottawa show important industries of each of the 10 provinces. William Oosterhoff created the designs.

Alberta

A cowboy and his horse symbolize the ranches along the eastern slopes of the Rockies.

British Columbia

An airplane shows the growth of transportation and industry on the west coast.

Manitoba

A farmer with hayfork and spade stands for farming on Manitoba's prairies.

New Brunswick

A sailing ship represents the province's water transportation and fishing.

Newfoundland and Labrador

A lumberman and his ax represent forest resources.

Nova Scotia

A sailor and a pair of anchors show the importance of shipping in "The Old Colony."

All photos by Malak from Shostal

Ontario

A miner represents the province that is among the nation's leaders in mining.

Prince Edward Island

A fisherman hauling nets suggests the wealth taken from seas near the island.

Quebec

A turbine pictures the province that produces the most hydroelectric power.

Saskatchewan

A farmer and his tractor tell of agricultural plenty from "Canada's Breadbasket."

How a bill becomes law in Canada

The Canadian Parliament considers two general types of bills—*public bills,* which concern the entire nation, and *private bills,* most of which concern a person or a small group. All bills go through three readings in the House of Commons, three in the Senate, and acceptance by the governor general. Most bills can begin in either the House or the Senate. All bills dealing with expenses or taxes must start in the House. The Senate cannot reject these bills, but it can delay them.

WORLD BOOK illustrations by David Cunningham

Action begins on most public bills when a Cabinet minister gives formal notice of the bill to the House of Commons. This notice appears in the *Notice Paper.* But a bill to adopt a tax or spend money starts as a recommendation from the governor general to a Cabinet minister. Actually, the Cabinet decides what expenses and taxes to call for.

Introduction of the bill. The Cabinet minister seeks permission to introduce the bill for the first reading. The minister's motion includes the bill's title and an explanation of the bill's purpose. The House then grants permission.

The Senate reviews the bill during the third reading. Amendments may be offered and put to a vote. If the Senate passes the bill without any amendments, the bill goes to the governor general. If the bill is defeated, it goes back for another first reading in the Senate. If the bill is amended, it is sent to the House of Commons.

One of 10 standing committees in the Senate reviews the House-passed bill and submits a report on it. The committee may suggest reductions—but not increases—for a money bill. It also may recommend amendments.

House-Senate action. If the House of Commons does not accept the Senate's amendments, representatives from both houses meet and try to reach a compromise. If their compromise includes more changes, the revised bill must be given three readings in each house. If the representatives cannot reach a compromise, the bill is killed.

The governor general receives the bill after it has been passed by both houses and, by tradition, accepts it. The bill, now a law, takes effect immediately or when the Cabinet proclaims it.

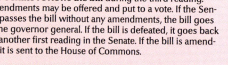

First and second readings. The bill is read for the first time. No debate is allowed, and no amendments may be considered. During the second reading, the most important stage, the House debates the bill's chief purpose but not its details. The bill may be passed or defeated. If passed, it goes to a standing or special committee.

One of 19 standing committees discusses the bill in detail and submits a report on it to the House. Each of these committees deals with a separate activity, such as agriculture. A special committee may be formed to obtain more information for the standing committee. The standing committee may suggest amendments to the bill.

The House of Commons discusses the bill after the committee review. It decides whether to accept the committee's report or to return the bill to the committee for another report. Amendments may be debated and put to a vote. After these proceedings have been completed, the bill goes through a third reading. Some debate is allowed at this time, and other amendments may be put to a vote. If the House passes the bill, it goes to the Senate.

Senate action follows the same pattern, starting with a first reading. If the bill begins in the Senate, the first reading occurs at once. Senate permission is not required to introduce bills. During the second reading, the Senate debates the bill's purpose. If passed, the bill goes to a committee.

The prime minister, the leader of Canada's national government, guides the topics of debate in the House of Commons. This picture shows Prime Minister Stephen J. Harper, *center,* addressing the House in 2006.

Government of Canada

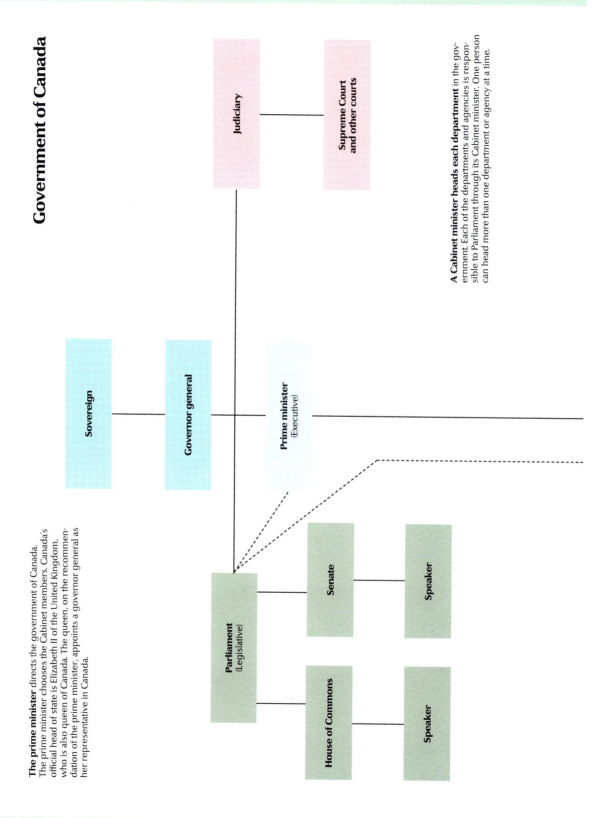

The prime minister directs the government of Canada. The prime minister chooses the Cabinet members. Canada's official head of state is Elizabeth II of the United Kingdom, who is also queen of Canada. The queen, on the recommendation of the prime minister, appoints a governor general as her representative in Canada.

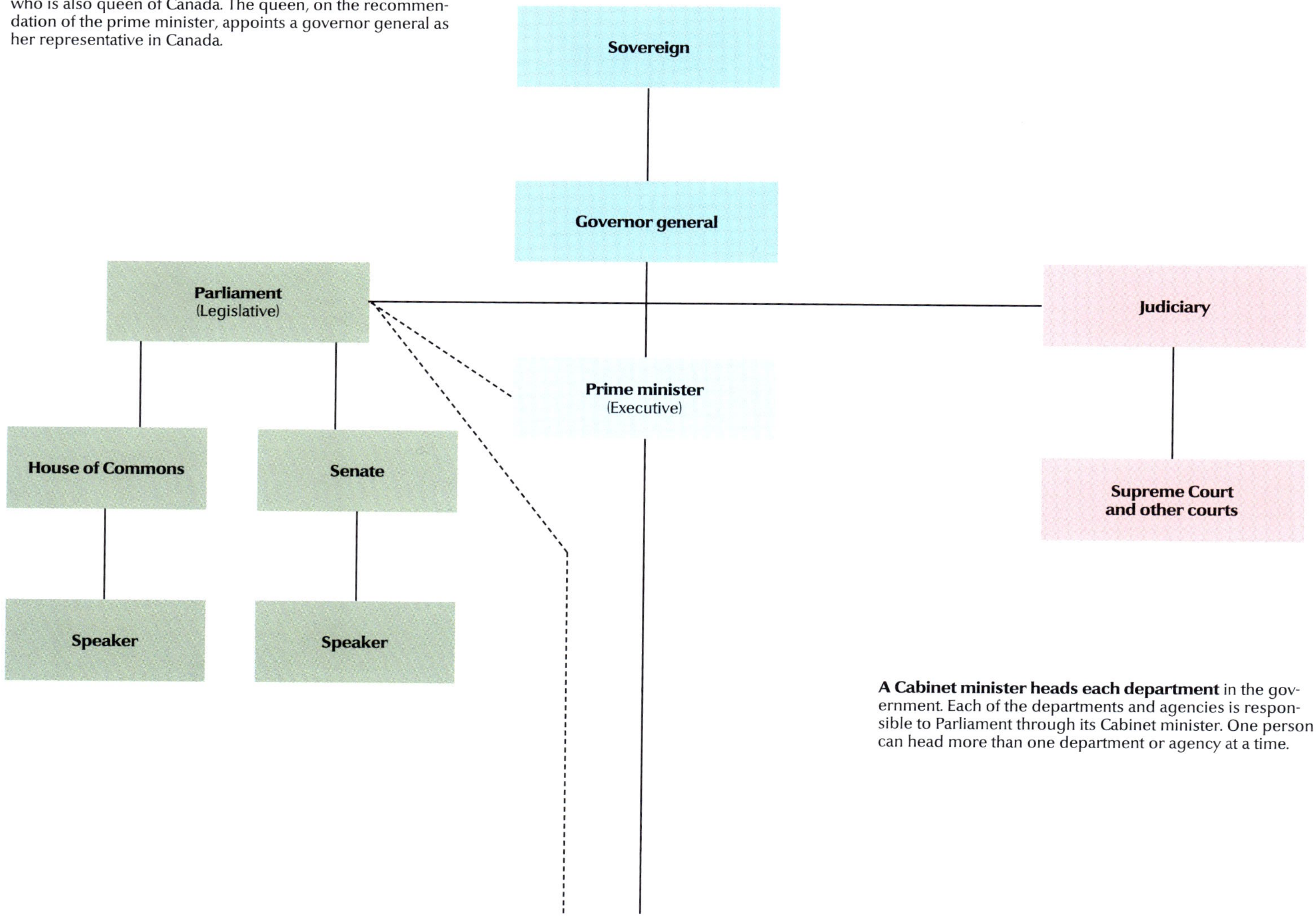

A Cabinet minister heads each department in the government. Each of the departments and agencies is responsible to Parliament through its Cabinet minister. One person can head more than one department or agency at a time.

Cabinet

Leader of the government in the House of Commons and minister for democratic reform

Minister of international trade and minister for the Pacific Gateway and the Vancouver-Whistler Olympics

Minister of labor and minister of the Economic Development Agency of Canada for the regions of Quebec

Minister of veterans affairs

Leader of the government in the Senate

Minister of citizenship and immigration

Minister of agriculture and agri-food and minister for the Canadian Wheat Board

Minister of natural resources

Minister of foreign affairs and minister of the Atlantic Canada Opportunities Agency

Minister of fisheries and oceans

Minister of public safety

Minister of national revenue and minister of western economic diversification

Minister of justice and attorney general of Canada

Minister of the environment

President of the Queen's Privy Council for Canada, minister of intergovernmental affairs, and minister for sport

Minister of human resources and social development

Minister of national defence

Minister of Canadian heritage and status of women

Minister of Indian affairs and northern development and federal interlocutor for Métis and non-status Indians

President of the Treasury Board

Minister of industry

Minister of transport, infrastructure, and communities

Minister of health and minister for the Federal Economic Development Initiative for northern Ontario

Minister of finance

Minister of international cooperation and minister for la Francophonie and official languages

Minister of public works and government services

Departments and agencies

the number of members of Parliament for each province, see the *table* in each province article.

Each House member represents a *constituency* (district) of a province. Members do not have to live in the constituency, or in the province, they represent. The House elects a speaker to preside over meetings. The speaker holds the position until general elections are called.

The courts

The highest courts of Canada are the Supreme Court of Canada and the Federal Court of Canada. There are various other federal courts, and each province and territory has its own court system. Judges of the two highest federal courts and of some provincial and territorial courts are appointed by the *governor general in council.* The governor general in council is the governor general of Canada acting with the advice and consent of the Cabinet. Appointments of chief justices and associate chief justices are made on the recommendation of the prime minister. The other federal appointments are on the recommendation of the minister of justice, with Cabinet approval. The retirement age for federally appointed judges is 70 or 75, depending on their court.

The Supreme Court of Canada is the highest court of appeal in Canada. It has the chief justice of Canada and eight associate judges, called *puisne* (pronounced *PYOO nee)* judges. *Puisne* means *junior,* or *associate.* The Supreme Court hears appeals in civil and criminal cases.

The Federal Court of Canada has a trial division and an appeals division, both of which are under jurisdiction of a single chief justice. The trial division hears all claims against or affecting Canada's government. It consists of an associate chief justice and 13 puisne judges. The appeals division mainly hears appeals from the trial division. It consists of the Federal Court's chief justice and 10 puisne judges.

Other courts. In the provinces and territories, the superior, county, and district courts decide cases that involve federal, provincial, or territorial law. The federal government appoints judges of these courts. Provinces and territories also have lower courts.

Money and taxation

Only the federal government can coin money. Coins are made at the Royal Canadian Mint in Ottawa and in Winnipeg. The Bank of Canada, a central bank that controls credit and currency, issues all of Canada's paper money.

The taxation powers of the Canadian government are unlimited. Provincial governments may impose *direct taxes,* which include income and property taxes. They may also impose provincial sales taxes. The federal and provincial governments levy individual and corporate income taxes.

Provincial and territorial governments

The 10 provinces. Each province has a lieutenant governor who is appointed by the governor general in council. The lieutenant governor once served the federal government as the governor general once served the British, but now holds an honorary position much like the governor general. A premier actually heads the government of each province. Each premier leads the majority party in the legislature. Each province has an elected one-chamber legislature. This body is called the *Legislative Assembly* except in Quebec, where it is called the *National Assembly;* and Newfoundland and Labrador, where it is called the *House of Assembly.*

Each province controls such matters as education, administration of justice, municipal institutions, property, and civil rights. The federal government has the power to *disallow* (reject) any law passed by a provincial legislature. But the federal government has disallowed only about 100 of the thousands of bills adopted by the provinces.

The three territories have separate governments with much less power than those of the provinces. Generally, the territorial governments provide for law enforcement, medical services, and schools in the towns. All three of the territories are governed by a government leader, an executive council, and a Legislative Assembly. In the Northwest Territories and Nunavut, the government leader is known as the *premier.* In all three territories, the government leader and the Assembly are elected by the people. Council members are chosen by the Assembly. Each of the territories has a *commissioner*—an honorary head of government appointed by the federal government. Yukon's Assembly has 17 members. The Assembly for the Northwest Territories has 19. Nunavut's also has 19. Each of the three territories sends one representative to the House of Commons in Ottawa.

Local government

The provinces and territories regulate local government. Each has a different system. Generally, each province is divided into counties or districts. These counties or districts are divided into cities, towns, villages, and townships. Elected councils govern the municipalities. The head of the local government is usually a mayor, reeve, warden, or overseer. Other council members are called controllers, aldermen, or councillors. Municipal governments direct such activities as road repair, water supply, and police and fire protection. They gain much of their revenue from property taxes.

Political parties

The two most prominent parties in Canada are the Liberal Party of Canada and the Conservative Party of Canada. The Conservative Party of Canada was created in December 2003 by a merger of the Progressive Conservative Party and the Canadian Alliance.

Traditionally, the Liberals have favored the expansion of social programs and provincial rights. The Conservative Party of Canada has supported better access to health care, controlled government spending, lower taxes, and increased support of the military.

When the Conservative Party of Canada was created, the Liberals and the Progressive Conservatives historically had been the strongest national parties. Both could trace their origins to before 1867, when the British North America Act established the Dominion of Canada. The Progressive Conservative Party was officially known as the Conservative Party until 1942.

The New Democratic Party and the Bloc Québécois are two other important federal parties. The New Democratic Party was formed in 1961 by trade unions, a socialist party called the Co-operative Commonwealth Federation (CCF), and independent left-wing Canadians. The party favors social welfare measures. It opposes Canadian participation in such military alliances as the North Atlantic Treaty Organization (NATO) and the North American Aerospace Defense Command (NORAD).

The Bloc Québécois was formed in 1990 by a handful of members of Parliament from Quebec. The party advocates the creation of a sovereign Quebec, and it quickly gained support among French-speaking Quebecers. The Bloc won more than 70 percent of Quebec's seats in Parliament in the 2004 and 2006 national elections, giving it an influence in national politics despite its regional base.

International relations

Canada has been completely free since the Statute of Westminster in 1931 ended the last British controls over Canada. Canada now conducts its foreign relations with the United Kingdom and other Commonwealth nations in the same way that it conducts its relations with other nations.

Relations with the United States. Canada's closest economic and social ties are with the United States. The two nations share over 4,000 miles (6,400 kilometers) of common border, and their relations are friendly. The International Joint Commission settles boundary problems (see **International Joint Commission**). Canadians have become increasingly concerned about U.S. ownership of Canadian businesses and U.S. control of parts of Canada's economy. Many Canadians criticize the foreign policy of the United States and oppose Canada's role in NORAD.

Relations with other countries. Canada conducted relations with other foreign countries through the British diplomatic service until the 1920's. After that, Canada sent its own diplomatic representatives to foreign countries, and received their representatives in return. The first exchange of representatives was with the United States, in 1927. Canada became a charter member of the UN in 1945 and of NATO in 1949.

Armed forces

Until 1968, Canada had an army, navy, and air force that were separate from one another. But in that year, all Canadian military forces were merged into one unit called the Canadian Armed Forces. The chief of the defence staff directs the armed forces and reports to the minister of national defence. Canada and the United States formed the Permanent Joint Board on Defence in 1940 to cooperate in North American defense.

Canada has three professional military colleges—the Royal Military College of Canada in Kingston, Ontario; Royal Roads Military College near Victoria, British Columbia; and Collège militaire royal de Saint-Jean in Saint-Jean, Quebec. The Canadian Armed Forces also maintains staff colleges, cadet corps, and officer-training programs in colleges and universities. J. L. Granatstein

Related articles in *World Book* include:

Attorney general
Bank of Canada
Bill of rights (Canada's constitution; Canadian Charter of Rights and Freedoms)
Bloc Québécois
British North America Act
Canadian Alliance
Canadian Armed Forces
Citizenship (Canadian citizenship)
Civil service (Civil service in other lands)
Commonwealth of Nations
Conservative Party of Canada
Governor general
Health insurance, National
Liberal Party of Canada
New Democratic Party
Parti Québécois
Political party (Political parties in Canada)
Postal services (Canadian mail service)
Prime minister of Canada
Privy Council
Progressive Conservative Party
Reform Party
Royal Canadian Mounted Police
Social security (Social security in Canada)
Supreme Court of Canada
Welfare (Welfare around the world)

Outline

I. The constitution
II. Executive offices
A. The governor general
B. The prime minister
C. The Cabinet
III. The Parliament
A. The Senate
B. The House of Commons
IV. The courts
A. The Supreme Court of Canada
B. The Federal Court of Canada
C. Other courts
V. Money and taxation
VI. Provincial and territorial governments
A. The 10 provinces
B. The three territories
VII. Local government
VIII. Political parties
IX. International relations
A. Relations with the United States
B. Relations with other countries
X. Armed forces

Questions

Who is the Canadian head of state?
Who is the head of the government of Canada?
How does the Canadian Senate differ from the United States Senate?
How can Parliament control the actions of the prime minister?
How can the prime minister control the actions of Parliament?
What is the International Joint Commission?
What did the British North America Act do?
How long does the prime minister remain in office?
How do voting requirements differ in Canada and the United States?
Who directs the armed forces of Canada?

Additional resources

Ajzenstat, Janet, and others, eds. *Canada's Founding Debates.* Stoddart, 1999.
Brooks, Stephen. *Canadian Democracy.* 3rd ed. Oxford, 2000. *Public Policy in Canada.* 3rd ed. 1998.
Brownsey, Keith, and Howlett, Michael, eds. *The Provincial State in Canada.* Broadview Pr., 2001.
Canadian Parliamentary Guide. Gale Group, published annually.
Eagles, Munroe, and others. *The Almanac of Canadian Politics.* 2nd ed. Oxford, 1995.
Savoie, Donald J. *Governing from the Centre: The Concentration of Power in Canadian Politics.* Univ. of Toronto Pr., 1999.
Whittington, Michael, and Williams, Glen, eds. *Canadian Politics in the 21st Century.* 5th ed. Nelson Thomson Learning, 2000.

Champlain in Huronia (1967), detail of an oil painting on canvas by Rex Woods; Confederation Life Collection

Trading Ceremony at York Factory 1780's (about 1955), an oil painting on canvas by Adam Sherriff Scott; Hudson's Bay Company

The European settlement of Canada was led by the French and English. In 1608, French explorer Samuel de Champlain, *left center,* founded Quebec and made friends with nearby Indians. Hudson's Bay Company, an English firm formed in 1670, built fur-trading posts, *right.*

History of Canada

Canada, History of. Canada's history is an exciting story that traces the development of a vast wilderness into a great nation. Most experts believe the first people to live in what is now Canada came from Asia at least 15,000 years ago. They arrived by way of a land bridge that once connected Asia and North America at what is now Alaska. Their descendants became known as Indians. The ancestors of the Inuit (sometimes called Eskimos) came to Alaska over the land bridge after the Indians. They first settled in the Arctic region of Canada, probably coming about 5,000 years ago. For details of the first Americans, see **Indian, American; Inuit.**

In 1497, John Cabot, an Italian navigator in the service of England, found rich fishing grounds off Canada's southeast coast. In time, his discovery led to the European exploration of Canada. France took the lead in exploring the country and set up a colony in eastern Canada in the early 1600's. Daring French fur traders traveled westward and came upon many of Canada's sparkling lakes, rushing rivers, and majestic, snow-capped mountains. The United Kingdom gained control of the country in 1763, and thousands of British immigrants began to join the French who remained in Canada. In 1867, the French- and English-speaking Canadians helped create a united colony called the Dominion of Canada. The two groups worked together to settle the country from coast to coast and to develop its great mineral deposits and other natural resources.

David Jay Bercuson, the contributor of this article, is Professor of History and Director of the Centre for Military and Strategic Studies at the University of Calgary

Canada gained its independence from the United Kingdom in 1931. During the mid-1900's, hard-working Canadians turned their country into an economic giant. Today, huge harvests from western Canada make the nation a leading producer of wheat, oats, and barley. Canada also ranks among the world's top manufacturing nations, and it is a major producer of electric power.

Throughout its history, Canada has often been troubled by a lack of unity among its people. French Canadians, mostly from Quebec, have struggled to preserve their French culture. They have long been angered by Canadian policies based on British traditions, and many of them support a movement to make Quebec a separate nation. People in Canada's nine other provinces often favor local needs over national interests.

Canada and the United States have generally enjoyed a long history of cooperation. They have worked together in the defense of North America and have strong economic ties. Canada has tried to develop independently of its southern neighbor. But its economy is so closely linked to the U.S. economy that severe U.S. business slumps usually cause hard times in Canada. In addition, the popularity of U.S. culture in Canada has challenged the efforts of Canadian leaders to establish a separate identity for their country.

This article traces the history of Canada from European exploration to the present. For information on the people, economy, and government of Canada today, see the articles **Canada;** and **Canada, Government of.**

Early European exploration

About A.D. 1000, Vikings from Iceland and Greenland became the first known Europeans to reach North

Fathers of Confederation (1969), an oil painting on canvas by Rex Woods; Confederation Life Collection

The Fathers of Confederation were Canadian leaders who planned the union of the United Kingdom's Canadian colonies under one government. Their plan led to the creation of the Dominion of Canada in 1867. John A. Macdonald, *standing center,* became the Dominion's first prime minister.

America. The Vikings, led by Leif Eriksson, landed somewhere on the northeast coast, a region the explorer called Vinland. The Vikings established a colony in Vinland, but they lived there only a short time. Some historians believe that Vinland was in what is now Maine or Massachusetts. Others think it was in what is now the province of Newfoundland and Labrador. Ruins of a Viking settlement have been found at L'Anse aux Meadows, on the northern tip of the island of Newfoundland. See **Leif Eriksson; Vikings; Vinland.**

Lasting contact between Europe and America began with the voyage of Christopher Columbus in 1492. Columbus sailed west from Spain to find a short sea route to the Indies, as Europeans called eastern Asia. This region was known for its jewels, silks, spices, and other luxury goods. When Columbus landed in America, he thought he had reached the Indies.

In 1497, King Henry VII of England hired an Italian navigator, John Cabot, to cross the Atlantic Ocean in search of a shorter route to Asia than the one Columbus had taken. No one knows exactly where Cabot landed. Most historians say he may have landed somewhere between what are now Newfoundland and Nova Scotia. Cabot claimed the area for England. He found no such luxuries as jewels or spices. But he saw an enormous amount of cod and other fishes in the waters southeast of Newfoundland. Reports of the rich fishing soon brought large European fishing fleets to Canada.

By the early 1500's, some Europeans realized that Columbus had reached an unknown land, which they called the New World. In 1534, King Francis I of France sent Jacques Cartier, a French navigator, to the New World to look for gold and other valuable metals. Cartier sailed into the Gulf of St. Lawrence. He landed on the Gaspé Peninsula and claimed it for France. In 1535, on a second trip, Cartier became the first European to reach the interior of Canada. He sailed up the St. Lawrence River to the site of present-day Montreal. In 1541, on a third visit, Cartier joined a French expedition that hoped to establish a permanent settlement in Canada. But the colony lasted only until 1543.

The development of New France (1604-1688)

French fishing crews helped develop a thriving fishing industry off Canada's east coast. But they played an even greater role in Canada's growth by establishing the fur trade. The fur trade led to the development of a French colonial empire in North America. This empire, called New France, lasted about 150 years and established the French culture and heritage in Canada.

Period facts in brief (1604-1688)

Important dates

1604	Sieur de Monts of France founded Acadia.
1608	Samuel de Champlain of France founded the city of Quebec.
1610	Henry Hudson of England sailed into Hudson Bay.
1642	French missionaries founded Montreal.
1673	Louis Jolliet and Jacques Marquette sailed down the Mississippi River to its junction with the Arkansas River.
1682	Sieur de La Salle sailed to the mouth of the Mississippi River and claimed all the land drained by the river and its branches for France.

Population

1688	About 10,000

Encampment on River Winnipeg (mid-1800's), an oil painting on canvas by Paul Kane; Royal Ontario Museum, Toronto

The fur trade in Canada began during the 1500's as an exchange of furs for manufactured goods between Indians and Europeans. The Europeans gave the Indians such items as tools, weapons, and kettles in exchange for beaver, fox, mink, and other pelts. Much of the trading took place at camps like the one at the left.

Start of the fur trade. The French fishermen who came to Canada landed on the coast to preserve their catches by drying them in the sun. They met Indians who wanted to trade furs for fishhooks, kettles, knives, and other European goods. A brisk trade soon developed. During the second half of the 1500's, felt hats made from beaver fur became tremendously popular in Europe. As a result, the value of Canadian beaver pelts soared. During the late 1500's, more and more French ships sailed to Canada to pick up beaver fur. Traders also supplied such furs as fox, marten, mink, and otter. See **Fur trade**.

Meanwhile, English explorers searched for a water passage to Asia through northern Canada. During the late 1500's, these explorers included Humphrey Gilbert, Martin Frobisher, and John Davis. In 1610, an English sea captain named Henry Hudson sailed into Hudson Bay in his search for the passage. England later based its claim to the vast Hudson Bay region on this voyage.

Early settlements. In 1603, King Henry IV of France completed plans to organize the fur trade and to set up a colony in Canada. The next year, a French explorer named Pierre du Gua (or du Guast), Sieur de Monts, led a small group of settlers to a site near the mouth of the St. Croix River in what is now the province of New Brunswick. In 1605, the settlers left that spot and founded Port Royal (now Annapolis Royal in Nova Scotia). The French called their colony Acadia. See **Acadia**.

In 1608, another French explorer, Samuel de Champlain, founded a settlement along the St. Lawrence River. He named the village Quebec. Champlain made friends with the Algonquin and Huron Indians living nearby and began to trade with them for furs. The two tribes also wanted French help in wars against their main enemy, the powerful Iroquois Indians. In 1609, Champlain and two other French fur traders helped their Indian friends defeat the Iroquois in battle. After this battle, the Iroquois were also enemies of the French.

The Huron lived in an area the French called Huronia. Champlain persuaded the Huron to allow Roman Catholic missionaries to work among them and introduce them to Christianity. The missionaries, especially an order known as the Jesuits, explored much of what is now southern Ontario.

Threats to expansion. Champlain hoped Quebec would become a large settlement, but it remained only a small trading post for many years. By 1625, about 60 people lived there.

New France failed to attract settlers partly because of threats from English colonists as well as from the Iroquois. Like France, England claimed much of what is now eastern Canada. England based its claims on explorations dating from Cabot's landing in 1497. During the early 1600's, many English colonists settled along the east coast of North America south of New France. Numerous disputes over fur-trading rights broke out between the French and the English. In 1629, English forces captured the town of Quebec. The French regained the town in 1632.

During the late 1640's, the Iroquois conquered Huronia and killed most of the French missionaries. The Algonquin and Huron fled, leaving the French to fight the Iroquois alone. During the next 10 years, the Iroquois increased their attacks on the French. A large number of settlers were killed, and the French fur trade was destroyed.

The royal province. In 1663, King Louis XIV made New France a *royal province* (colony) of France. He sent troops to Canada to fight the Iroquois and appointed administrators to govern and develop the colony. The chief official was the governor. A bishop directed the church and missionary work, and a person called an *intendant* managed most other local affairs. The French troops mounted attacks on Iroquois country, forcing some tribes to make peace with the French in the late 1660's. Afterward, frontiersmen known as *coureurs de bois* again developed the fur trade into the chief economic activity of New France (see **Coureurs de bois**).

Louis XIV also promoted the *seigneurial system* to encourage farming in New France. Under this system, the king gave land in the colony to several groups, includ-

A World Book special feature

Canada

The growth of a nation

Canada has long been a land of challenging frontiers and boundless opportunity. Its early pioneers included many daring French and British explorers and fur traders. Arriving in what is now eastern Canada, they found a vast wilderness and began pushing the frontier westward. Hardy and courageous settlers followed them across the continent and turned the wilderness into fertile farms and bustling cities. In time, other energetic Canadians developed canals, railroads, and industries that helped their country become strong and independent. Today, Canada ranks among the world's most important nations. This special feature illustrates major stages in the growth of Canada. It includes maps that help show the way the country expanded.

Detail of *Champlain in Huronia,* an oil painting (1967) by Rex Woods, The Confederation Life Collection; Canapress; Detail of *Canada's First Railway,* an oil painting on canvas (1943) by J. D. Kelly. The Confederation Life Collection.

1600's to 1763

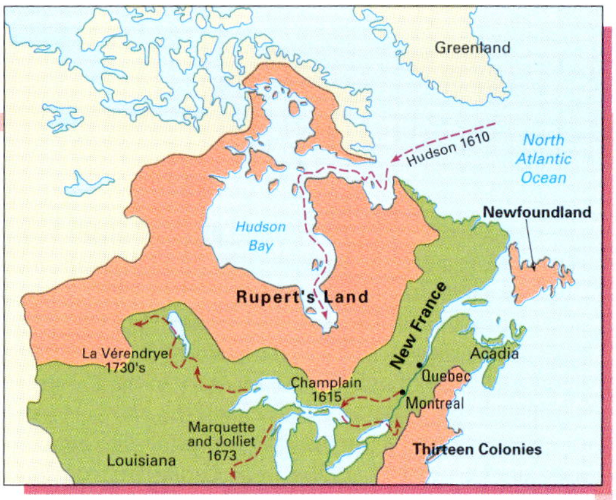

WORLD BOOK map

Beginning in the early 1600's, explorers pushed deep into Canada's wilderness. New France, France's colony in North America, spread across the eastern part of the country. The Hudson's Bay Company, an English fur-trading company, controlled a huge area that extended around Hudson Bay. British colonists settled in this area, called Rupert's Land, and on the east coast of Canada. Rivalries between the French and British colonists grew. By the mid-1700's, the United Kingdom's North American colonies contained about 1 $\frac{1}{2}$ million people. The French colonial population was only about 80,000. Fighting broke out between the French and British colonists, ending with a British victory in 1763. France lost most of its Canadian holdings.

Quebec was the first permanent settlement of New France. The French explorer Samuel de Champlain founded Quebec in 1608 along the St. Lawrence River. This painting shows him returning to his Quebec settlement, called *Habitation*.

An oil painting (1977) by Allan Daniel from *Heritage of Canada* © 1978; The Reader's Digest (Canada) Ltd.

Public Archives of Canada

The Hudson's Bay Company was founded in London in 1670 to establish a fur trade in what is now Canada. Fort York, *shown here,* was built on Hudson Bay in 1684 by Pierre Esprit Radisson, a French fur trader hired by the company. The fort was later called York Factory, and it became the most important fur-trading center on the bay after 1713.

Detail of an engraving (1760) by an unknown artist; The Granger Collection

The Battle of Quebec in 1759 led to the end of New France. British forces approached Quebec City from the St. Lawrence River, *shown here,* and defeated the French on the Plains of Abraham. The peace treaty was signed in 1763.

ing French military officers and merchants. The landholders, called *seigneurs,* brought farmers from France and rented them large sections of the land. Most of the farmers, called habitants, became prosperous. The population of New France grew from about 3,000 in 1666 to about 6,700 in 1673. See **Seigneurial system.**

The boundaries of New France expanded rapidly to the west and south after Louis de Buade, Comte de Frontenac, became governor in 1672. The loss of the Huron fur trade forced the French to go farther inland to get new sources. As a result, Frontenac sent explorers to scout the Great Lakes and the Ohio and Mississippi river valleys.

In 1673, Louis Jolliet, a French-Canadian fur trader, and Jacques Marquette, a French missionary, sailed down the Mississippi River to its junction with the Arkansas River. The French soon built forts and fur-trading posts along the Great Lakes and along the Illinois and Mississippi rivers. In 1682, Rene-Robert Cavelier, Sieur de La Salle, reached the mouth of the Mississippi at the Gulf of Mexico. He claimed all the land drained by the river and its branches for France.

The growing French-English rivalry. The boundaries of English colonies south of New France also expanded during the late 1600's. Settlers poured into the English colonies and pushed the frontier westward, nearer New France. In 1670, an English firm called the Hudson's Bay Company opened fur-trading posts north of New France on the shores of Hudson Bay.

Clashes between England and France in Europe contributed to their rivalry in North America. Other factors also created tension between the English and French colonists. For example, most of the French were Roman Catholics, and the majority of the English were Protestants. Most of the French wanted land for fur trading. The English wanted it for farming. In addition, French and English fur traders competed against each other.

During the 1730's, French-Canadian fur traders traveled farther inland and claimed more land for France. By 1738, Pierre Gaultier de Varennes, Sieur de La Verendrye, had established a chain of fur-trading posts between Montreal and what is now Saskatchewan.

For details on life in New France, see **New France.**

British conquest and rule (1689-1815)

The French and English colonists fought each other in four wars between 1689 and 1763. These conflicts led to the United Kingdom's conquest of New France. The British government then worked hard to win the support of its new French-Canadian subjects. During the late 1700's and early 1800's, Canadian explorers pushed westward across the continent.

The colonial wars. The first three of the four wars between the French and English colonists broke out in Europe before spreading to America. These wars in America were King William's War (1689-1697), Queen Anne's War (1702-1713), and King George's War (1744-1748). Only after the second war did either side gain territory. In 1713, under the Treaty of Utrecht, France gave the United Kingdom Newfoundland, the mainland Nova Scotia region of Acadia, and the Hudson Bay territory.

The fourth war began in the Ohio River Valley in 1754 and lasted until 1763. It spread to Europe in 1756 and became known as the Seven Years' War there and in Canada. The conflict, which is called the French and Indian War in the United States, marked the final chapter in the struggle between the French and British colonists in America. The British had a number of advantages during the war. For example, there were more than a million British colonists compared with about 65,000 French settlers. The British colonies also received greater military support from the United Kingdom than New France did from France. In addition, the British had the help of the Iroquois, the strongest Indian group in the east.

The French did well at first, but the tide of battle slowly turned against them. British armies, backed by the British Royal Navy, captured Quebec City in 1759. Both opposing generals, the Marquis de Montcalm of France and James Wolfe of the United Kingdom, were fatally wounded in the battle (see **Quebec, Battle of**). The British seized Montreal in 1760, and the fighting in America ended. In the Peace of Paris, signed in 1763, France surrendered most of New France to the United Kingdom. See **French and Indian wars.**

The Quebec Act. The United Kingdom gave the name Quebec to the area that made up most of its new

Period facts in brief (1689-1815)

Important dates

- **1689-1763** A series of wars between British and French colonists ended with Britain in control of New France, the French empire in America.
- **1774** The Quebec Act gave French Canadians political and religious rights.
- **1775-1783** During the Revolutionary War in America, an American invasion of Canada in 1775 failed.
- **1784** The colony of New Brunswick was established.
- **1791** The Constitutional Act split Quebec into the colonies of Upper Canada and Lower Canada.
- **1812-1815** During the War of 1812, British and Canadian troops turned back two major invasion attempts of Canada by the United States.

Population

1698	15,355
1812	75,000

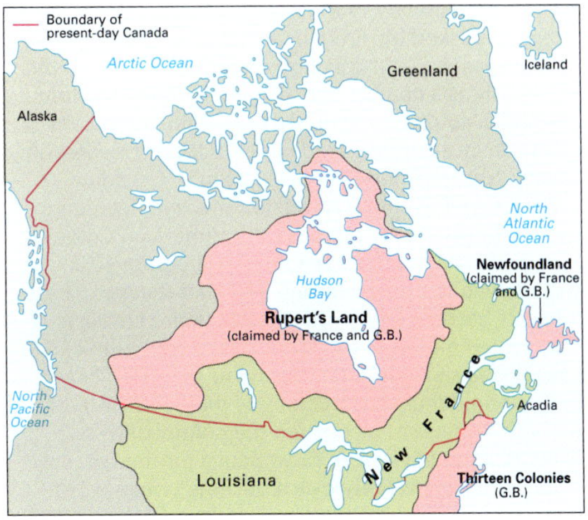

WORLD BOOK map

During the early 1700's, France and Great Britain dominated eastern North America. The French colonial empire on the continent was known as New France. France also claimed the mostly British-held areas of Rupert's Land and Newfoundland.

Detail of an engraving by Hervey Smyth from a painting (late 1700's) by Francis Swaine; Picture Division, Public Archives of Canada, Ottawa

In the Battle of Quebec in 1759, British troops defeated the French forces at Quebec City. The British approached Quebec from the St. Lawrence River, *shown here.* Their victory enabled the United Kingdom to take over France's empire in Canada at the end of the Seven Years' War (1756-1763).

territory in Canada. It added some of the new territory to Nova Scotia and Newfoundland. At first, the British governed Quebec under British laws, which denied Catholics the rights to vote, to be elected, or to hold public office. This policy affected nearly all the colony's French Canadians. Quebec's first two British governors, Generals James Murray and Guy Carleton, opposed the policy because they wanted the United Kingdom to gain the loyalty of the French. Carleton also was aware of discontent in the 13 colonies to the south, then known as the American Colonies. He knew that the British would need the support of the French Canadians if a rebellion broke out.

In 1774, Carleton persuaded the British Parliament to pass the Quebec Act. This act recognized French civil and religious rights. It also preserved the seigneurial landholding system and extended Quebec to include much of what is now Quebec, Ontario, and the Midwestern United States. See **Quebec Act**.

The Revolutionary War in America began in 1775. The Americans asked the French Canadians to join their rebellion against the British. But the French regarded the war mainly as a conflict between the United Kingdom and British colonies and chose to remain neutral. An American invasion of Canada in 1775 failed. See **Revolutionary War in America** (The invasion of Canada).

The United Empire Loyalists. After the Revolutionary War began, many people in the American Colonies remained loyal to the United Kingdom. About 40,000 of them moved to Canada during and after the war. These colonists became known as United Empire Loyalists. They settled mainly in western parts of the colonies of Nova Scotia and Quebec. Those who moved to Nova Scotia soon demanded a colony of their own. In 1784, the British government created the colony of New Brunswick out of western Nova Scotia for the Loyalists.

The Loyalists in Quebec also became unhappy. The Quebec Act gave the Catholic Church a special position in the colony. But most Loyalists were Protestants. In addition, the act did not permit the colony to have its own elected legislature. The Loyalists demanded a government like the one they had before the revolution—one that allowed them to choose their own public officials.

The British solution was the Constitutional Act of 1791. This act divided Quebec into two colonies, Lower Canada and Upper Canada. Lower Canada occupied the area along the lower St. Lawrence River. Upper Canada covered the area near the Great Lakes and the upper St. Lawrence. Each colony had its own elected assembly, though the legislatures had little real power. Each colony also had a lieutenant governor and a Legislative Council. The lieutenant governor and council members, who were appointed by the British, controlled the gov-

Color print (late 1800's) by Henry Sandham; Public Archives of Canada, Ottawa (C168)

The United Empire Loyalists were American colonists who, because of their loyalty to the United Kingdom, moved to Canada during and after the Revolutionary War (1775-1783).

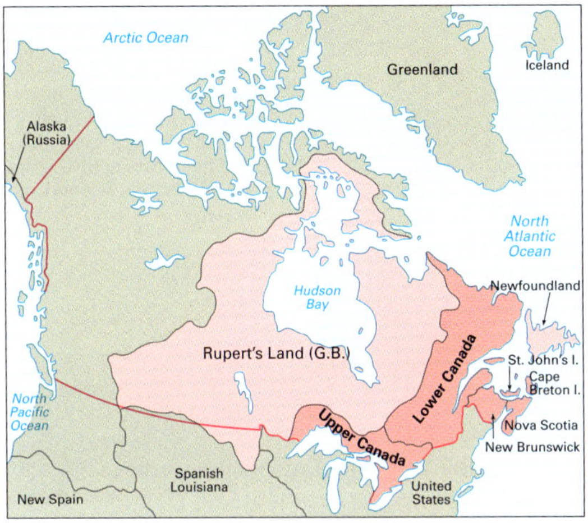

WORLD BOOK map

In 1791, the British government created the colonies of Upper and Lower Canada. The British had gained eastern Canada from France in the Seven Years' War (1756-1763). The British also won undisputed control of Newfoundland and Rupert's Land.

ernment. French Canadians formed the vast majority of the population in Lower Canada. The government there was based on principles of French civil law, Catholicism, and the seigneurial system. English-speaking Canadians made up the majority in Upper Canada. Local officials followed the traditions of English law and property systems. See **United Empire Loyalists.**

Exploration of the West. The Revolutionary War in America led to major developments in the Canadian fur trade. After the United Kingdom gained control of New France in 1763, hundreds of British merchants settled in Montreal and soon took over the French fur trade. Like the French, they obtained most of their furs from Indians in the Ohio and Mississippi river valleys. But most of this area became part of the United States after the Revolutionary War. British merchants in Montreal thus had to look elsewhere for furs. By 1784, they had formed a firm called the North West Company to trade north and west of the Great Lakes. The Hudson's Bay Company already had trading posts in that territory, and a great rivalry developed between the two companies.

In its search for new and better fur-trading areas, the North West Company sent explorers across the unknown western lands. Alexander Mackenzie reached the Mackenzie River in 1789 and the Pacific Ocean in 1793. Simon Fraser followed the Fraser River to the Pacific in 1808. David Thompson mapped the west and navigated the full length of the Columbia River in 1811.

In 1811, Lord Selkirk, a Scottish colonizer, sent a group of Scottish and Irish immigrants to establish a settlement on the Red River in what is now Manitoba. The settlement became known as the Red River Colony. In 1821, the Hudson's Bay Company took over the North West Company and gained control of nearly all Canadian territory west of the Great Lakes.

The War of 1812 developed out of fighting between the United Kingdom and France in Europe. During this conflict, the British set up a naval blockade of France and so interfered with U.S. ships bound for French ports. They also stopped American ships and seized sailors of British birth on them. As a result of these actions, the United States declared war on the United Kingdom on June 18, 1812. American troops tried to capture Upper and Lower Canada during the war, but British and Canadian troops defeated two major invasion attempts. The war ended in 1815. The Canadian and British forces claimed victory because they had held off much larger American forces. Neither side actually won, but the war promoted a sense of unity and patriotism in Canada. See War of 1812.

The struggle for responsible government (1816-1867)

Canada's population began to soar during the early 1800's as thousands of immigrants came from the United Kingdom. During the 1840's, leaders in some Canadian colonies pushed for *responsible government* (self-government) in local affairs. In a system of responsible government, the executive is *responsible* (answerable) to an elected assembly. The United Kingdom gradually granted all the colonies such government. During the mid-1860's, some colonial leaders argued that Canada needed a strong central government to deal with domestic matters. They started a movement for a *confederation* (union) of the Canadian colonies. This movement led to the formation of the Dominion of Canada in 1867.

Growing discontent. After the War of 1812, Canada began to attract large numbers of immigrants from England, Ireland, and Scotland. French Canadians resented the flood of English-speaking newcomers. Many of the French believed that the British government wanted to destroy the French heritage in Canada.

By the 1820's, most French Canadians had become very bitter toward the English-speaking Canadians in Lower Canada. The French controlled the legislature, but the English controlled the Legislative Council. The council, in turn, ran the government. It spent much of the colony's tax money on projects to benefit commerce. French Canadians owned few businesses, however, and so opposed these expenses. The French also feared that the council intended to help English-speaking Canadians take over French-Canadian farms.

Upper Canada also faced serious political problems during the early 1800's. Church leaders, merchants, and landowners there formed a group known as the Family Compact. This group controlled the colonial government. It often cooperated with the lieutenant governor to block the demands of the farmers in the assembly.

Period facts in brief (1816-1867)

Important dates

- **1837** Revolts broke out in Upper and Lower Canada.
- **1841** The Act of Union joined Upper and Lower Canada into the Province of Canada.
- **1848** The Province of Canada and Nova Scotia gained self-government.
- **1858** The colony of British Columbia was established.
- **1864** Conferences in Charlottetown and Quebec City planned for the *confederation* (union) of the Canadian colonies.
- **1867** The British North America Act established the Dominion of Canada.

Population

1824	151,000
1867	3,463,000

Attack on St. Charles, a lithograph (mid-1800's) by Nathaniel Hartnell from a sketch by Lord Charles Beauclerk; Public Archives of Canada, Ottawa (C393)

Short-lived revolts against the government broke out in Lower and Upper Canada in 1837. Rebels in both colonies fought to end harsh British rule. British troops easily defeated the rebels at St. Charles in Lower Canada, *left,* and at other sites.

The Family Compact also used tax money to support Church of England schools, though many Upper Canadians belonged to other religious groups.

The uprisings of 1837. By the late 1830's, many people in Upper and Lower Canada had lost faith in their colonial governments. In November 1837, a revolt broke out in Lower Canada. It was headed by Louis Joseph Papineau, a fiery French Canadian who was a leader in the assembly. Papineau's followers briefly controlled parts of Lower Canada. But the seigneurs and the high church officials remained loyal to the United Kingdom. British troops and colonial militia quickly crushed the revolt, and the rebel leaders fled to the United States.

News of the fighting in Lower Canada triggered a rebellion in Upper Canada in December 1837. William Lyon Mackenzie, a member of the Reform Party in the assembly, led the revolt. The colonial militia defeated the rebels in a brief battle, and Mackenzie escaped to the United States. See **Rebellions of 1837**.

Lord Durham's report. The rebellions in Upper and Lower Canada convinced the British government that it had serious problems in Canada. In 1838, Queen Victoria sent Lord Durham, a British diplomat, to investigate the causes of the uprisings. Durham finished his report in 1839. He recommended that Upper and Lower Canada be united. He also recommended that the Canadian colonies be allowed to handle their local affairs. Both of these ideas had been suggested earlier, and Durham's report did little to influence their eventual adoption by the British government. In 1840, the British Parliament passed the Act of Union. This law, which took effect in 1841, united the two Canadas into one colony, the Province of Canada. See **Union, Act of.**

The beginning of self-government. During the 1840's, several colonial leaders fought for responsible government. These leaders included Robert Baldwin and Louis H. LaFontaine in the Province of Canada and Joseph Howe in Nova Scotia. Many British officials had come to regard the colonies more as a burden than as a benefit, and they supported the self-government movement. The Province of Canada and Nova Scotia gained responsible government in 1848. Nearly all the other Canadian colonies received it soon afterward.

During the mid-1800's, the Canadian colonies expanded trade with the United States. Railways linked more and more towns in the colonies, and new canals became busy transportation routes. These developments and the rapid growth of the fishing, flour-milling, lumber, and textile industries brought prosperity to the Canadian colonies. The American Civil War (1861-1865) also greatly increased demands for Canadian goods.

In spite of responsible government, political problems still troubled the Province of Canada. The main opposing political parties had nearly equal representation in the legislature. As a result, no party could gain a majority of seats or direct the government for long. By the early 1860's, some political leaders had suggested that the colony's problems could be solved only by splitting it again and creating a confederation of the two colonies. The union would give French- and English-speaking Canadians the same central government but would allow them to control their own local affairs.

Confederation. The fear of United States expansion into Canada helped attract support for a Canadian confederation. Many Canadians felt certain that the United States wanted to control all North America and would invade Canada after the Civil War ended.

John A. Macdonald, George Étienne Cartier, and other leaders from the Province of Canada headed the campaign for a federal union. In September 1864, they attended a conference of leaders from the Atlantic colonies who were meeting in Charlottetown, Prince Edward Island, to plan a union of their own. The Canadians persuaded them to abandon their plan in favor of a larger union. Another conference was held in Quebec City. The final details for confederation were worked out there in October (see **Quebec Conference**).

In 1865, the Province of Canada approved the confederation plan. However, Newfoundland and Prince Edward Island rejected it, fearing that they would lose control over local affairs. New Brunswick and Nova Scotia adopted the plan in 1866. Later that same year, officials from Canada, New Brunswick, and Nova Scotia went to London, where they presented the plan to the British government.

In March 1867, the British Parliament passed the British North America Act. This act established the Dominion of Canada. The Dominion used the British parliamentary form of government. It had an elected House of Commons and an appointed Senate, each with almost equal power. A prime minister, usually the leader of the political party with the most seats in the House of Commons, headed the new federal government. The United Kingdom continued to handle the colony's foreign affairs, and the British monarch served as head of state.

The British North America Act took effect on July 1,

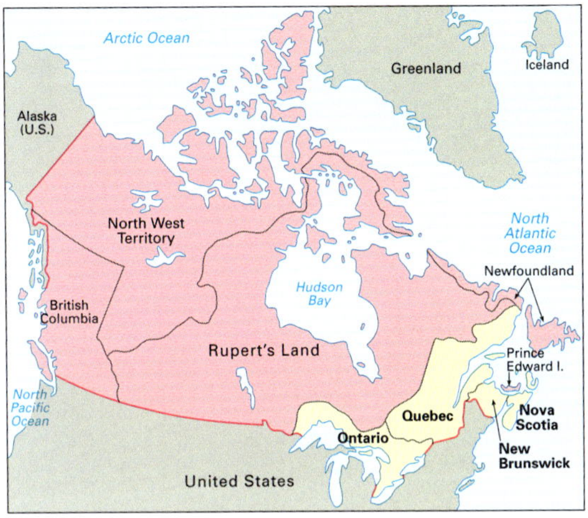

In 1867, a union of British North American colonies led to the formation of the Dominion of Canada. The Dominion had four provinces—New Brunswick, Nova Scotia, Ontario, and Quebec. Britain ruled its other Canadian territories separately.

1867. The new Dominion had four provinces—New Brunswick, Nova Scotia, Ontario, and Quebec. Quebec had formerly been Lower Canada, and Ontario had been Upper Canada. The British North America Act provided that other provinces could join the Dominion. Macdonald, leader of the Liberal-Conservative Party, became the country's first prime minister. See **British North America Act; Confederation of Canada.**

Growth of the Dominion (1868-1913)

The young Dominion of Canada developed rapidly during the late 1800's. A railway connected western and eastern Canada, and courageous pioneers spread across the west. By the early 1900's, the Dominion had nine provinces spanning the continent. Huge wheat crops, rich mines, and new industries brought further economic expansion in this period. In addition, Canada became increasingly involved in international affairs.

New provinces. Macdonald's chief goal as prime minister was to extend the Dominion to the west coast. He immediately turned his attention to the vast, largely unsettled northwest. This territory, called Rupert's Land, was owned by the Hudson's Bay Company. Macdonald worked out an agreement to buy the region in 1869.

About 12,000 people lived in or near the settlement of Red River in Rupert's Land. Most of them were *Métis* (people of mixed white and Indian ancestry). The Métis feared that the transfer of the area to Canada would bring a flood of white settlers who would take their lands. In 1869, Louis Riel, a settler of French and Indian descent, led the Métis in a revolt against the Canadian government. British and Canadian troops easily put down the rebellion (see **Red River Rebellion**).

In 1870, the Dominion took possession of Rupert's Land. At the same time, it acquired the North West Territory from the United Kingdom. This vast territory lay north, west, and south of Rupert's Land. The government combined these two new possessions into the North West Territories, which later became the Northwest Territories. Later in 1870, the government created Manitoba, Canada's fifth province, from part of Rupert's Land. The government also set aside 1,400,000 acres (567,000 hectares) in Manitoba for the Métis.

In 1871, the Pacific coast colony of British Columbia became Canada's sixth province. It agreed to join the Dominion in return for construction of a railway to the Pacific coast. In 1873, the eastern colony of Prince Edward Island became Canada's seventh province.

The Pacific Scandal. Macdonald led the Conservative Party to victory in the election of 1872. Afterward, the government chose a company headed by Sir Hugh Allan to build the railway wanted by British Columbia to the Pacific coast. But the so-called Pacific Scandal stalled the project. The scandal broke out in 1873, when it was revealed that the Conservative Party had accepted a campaign contribution of about $300,000 from Allan in 1872. Leaders of the opposing Liberal Party charged that Allan's group got the railroad contract because of its campaign gift. Macdonald did not use any of the money for his own election, but he resigned as prime minister. In November 1873, Alexander Mackenzie, leader of the Liberal Party, became prime minister.

The return of Macdonald. Mackenzie's government promoted honest and efficient elections by introducing the secret ballot and the one-day national election. It also won the United Kingdom's approval of a policy limiting the authority of the governor general—the British monarch's representative in Canada. The new policy required the governor general to respect decisions made by Canadian officials in the country's internal affairs. In 1875, Mackenzie established the Supreme Court of Canada. The court lessened British control over Canada's legal matters.

The Mackenzie government became increasingly unpopular after 1875, when a worldwide depression caused a severe business slump in Canada. Mackenzie

Period facts in brief (1868-1913)

Prime ministers (with parties, dates of service)
- Sir John A. Macdonald, Conservative, 1867-1873
- Alexander Mackenzie, Liberal, 1873-1878
- Sir John A. Macdonald, Conservative, 1878-1891
- Sir John J. C. Abbott, Conservative, 1891-1892
- Sir John S. D. Thompson, Conservative, 1892-1894
- Sir Mackenzie Bowell, Conservative, 1894-1896
- Sir Charles Tupper, Conservative, 1896
- Sir Wilfrid Laurier, Liberal, 1896-1911
- Sir Robert L. Borden, Conservative, 1911-1917

Provinces in the Dominion
New Brunswick (1867), Nova Scotia (1867), Ontario (1867), Quebec (1867), Manitoba (1870), British Columbia (1871), Prince Edward Island (1873), Alberta (1905), Saskatchewan (1905)

Important dates
- **1869** Louis Riel led the Métis in the Red River Rebellion in Manitoba.
- **1870** The North West Territories (now Northwest Territories) was established.
- **1885** Riel led a Métis revolt in Saskatchewan. The Canadian Pacific Railway spanned Canada.
- **1898** The Yukon area became a territory of Canada.

Population
- 1871 3,700,000
- 1911 7,200,000

had little success in reversing the decline, and Macdonald led the Conservatives to victory in the election of 1878.

In 1879, Macdonald began the National Policy, a program calling for high *tariffs* (taxes) on imported goods. The program was designed to help Canada's industries grow. The National Policy raised the cost of foreign products and made Canadian products less costly by comparison. Macdonald was also determined to complete the stalled coast-to-coast railroad. In 1880, the government gave the Canadian Pacific Railway a contract to finish the job.

The North West Rebellion. During the 1870's, many of the Métis in Manitoba moved westward into what is now Saskatchewan. But they again began to fear the loss of their land during the mid-1880's because of the near completion of the transcontinental railroad and government plans to attract settlers to the prairies.

In March 1885, Riel led another Métis uprising, the North West Rebellion. More than 7,000 government troops ended the rebellion within three months. Riel was found guilty of treason and was hanged on Nov. 16, 1885. See **North West Rebellion**.

Progress under Laurier. Workers laid the final stretch of Canadian Pacific Railway tracks in 1885. Regularly scheduled passenger service began the next year. The transcontinental railroad in time led to a great rush to settle Canada's fertile western prairies. This activity contributed to a major period of progress that began after the Liberal Party won the election of 1896. Wilfrid Laurier, the Liberal Party leader and a Quebec Catholic, became Canada's first French-Canadian prime minister.

Canada's population soared during Laurier's administration. More than 2 million immigrants, most of them from Europe, flocked to Canada between 1896 and 1911. Many settled in such cities as Montreal, Toronto, and Winnipeg. But hundreds of thousands of others took up farming on the prairies. In 1905, the government created two new provinces out of the prairies, Alberta and Saskatchewan.

Canada's economy flourished under Laurier. Farmers in the Prairie Provinces produced huge wheat harvests, and Europe became a great market for Canadian wheat. Aided by the continuing high tariffs, Canada's flour-milling, steel, and textile industries grew quickly. Nova Scotia coal mines thrived, and mining areas opened or expanded in Ontario, British Columbia, and the Klondike region of northern Canada. New hydroelectric power plants and two new transcontinental railroads, the Grand Trunk Pacific and the Canadian Northern, helped make the early 1900's Canada's most prosperous period since 1867.

WORLD BOOK map

By 1905, Canada consisted of nine provinces and two territories. The dates indicate when each new province and territory joined Canada. The rapidly growing country spanned the continent, but Newfoundland remained a separate British colony.

Foreign relations. Canada's role in the British Empire became an issue when the Anglo-Boer War of 1899-1902 broke out between the British and the Boers in southern Africa. Many Canadians had great pride in the empire and wanted Canada to send troops to help the British forces. But a large number of French Canadians opposed Canada's participation in foreign wars. Laurier compromised by deciding to equip and transport volunteers but not to send the Canadian Army.

In 1910, a controversy developed over a trade treaty between Canada and the United States. The treaty allowed each country to export numerous products to the other without paying high tariffs. But many Canadian business executives feared the trade agreement would destroy industries in Canada aided by the tariffs.

Another dispute involving Canada's obligations to the empire arose in 1910. The United Kingdom faced the threat of war with Germany and asked Canada to supply ships and sailors for the British Royal Navy. Laurier responded by announcing a plan to build a separate Canadian navy that could be lent to the United Kingdom in time of war. But English-speaking Canadians insisted

Public Archives of Canada, Ottawa (C14464)

Coast-to-coast rail service for passengers began in Canada in 1886. The first passenger train to cross the country from the Atlantic coast to the Pacific coast is shown at the left at a stop in Port Arthur, Ont. The service was provided by the Canadian Pacific Railway.

European immigrants rushed to Canada during the late 1800's and early 1900's. Many of them settled in such big eastern cities as Toronto and Montreal. But hundreds of thousands of others headed west and took up farming on the prairies. The immigrants at the left settled in Alberta in 1906.

Provincial Archives of Alberta, E. Brown Collection

that Canada contribute directly to the Royal Navy. Many French Canadians also opposed Laurier's plan, charging that it would involve Canada in foreign wars.

Opposition to the trade agreement and the naval plan led to the defeat of Laurier's party in the election of 1911. Robert L. Borden, head of the victorious Conservative Party, became prime minister.

World War I and independence (1914-1931)

Canada entered World War I (1914-1918) to aid the United Kingdom and its allies. Canada's participation in the war enabled it to act more freely in establishing its own foreign policies. In 1931, the Dominion won complete independence from the United Kingdom.

World War I. The United Kingdom's declaration of war on Germany on Aug. 4, 1914, created a tremendous burst of patriotism in Canada. Thousands of Canadians rushed to volunteer for military duty. Canadian troops first saw combat in April 1915. They helped halt the first German gas attack of the war during the Second Battle of Ypres in Belgium. The greatest Canadian triumph came in the Battle of Vimy Ridge in France on April 9, 1917. In the battle, about 100,000 Canadian troops captured the strong German positions on a hill called Vimy Ridge (see **Vimy Ridge, Battle of**). Billy Bishop, a Canadian flier, shot down 72 German planes during the war and became one of its most famous combat pilots (see **Bishop, Billy**). Over 600,000 Canadians served in the armed forces during World War I, and about 60,000 died.

World War I contributed enormously to Canada's industrial strength. The country's steel industry thrived through the sale of ships, artillery shells, and other equipment to the United Kingdom. Wartime demand also greatly expanded agricultural output, especially the production of beef cattle and wheat.

The conscription issue. When World War I began, Borden promised that Canada would not *conscript* (draft) men for overseas military service. He knew that French Canadians bitterly opposed conscription. Early in the war, large numbers of volunteers made a draft needless. By early 1917, however, Canadian forces had suffered high casualties, and the number of volunteers had dropped sharply. As a result, Borden established conscription in July 1917. He received strong support from English-speaking Canadians, but French Canadians strongly objected.

To make conscription work, Borden decided to form a *coalition* (joint) Conservative-Liberal government, which he called the Union government. Borden tried to bring Wilfrid Laurier and other Liberal Party leaders into the coalition. But Laurier opposed conscription and refused to join. The Liberals then split into two groups. One group, the Unionist Liberals, backed conscription. The other group remained loyal to Laurier. Borden appointed a number of Unionist Liberals to his government and called for an election in December 1917. The Unionists won every province except Quebec.

A larger role in the empire's affairs. Borden became increasingly dissatisfied with Canada's colonial status in view of its major contribution to the British war effort. In 1917, Borden and the leaders of other domin-

Period facts in brief (1914-1931)

Prime ministers (with parties, dates of service)
Sir Robert L. Borden, Conservative, 1911-1917
Sir Robert L. Borden, Unionist, 1917-1920
Arthur Meighen, Unionist, 1920-1921
W. L. Mackenzie King, Liberal, 1921-1926
Arthur Meighen, Conservative, 1926
W. L. Mackenzie King, Liberal, 1926-1930
Richard B. Bennett, Conservative, 1930-1935

Provinces of Canada
Number at start of period: 9
Provinces added during the period: none

Important dates
1914-1918 More than 600,000 Canadians served in World War I.
1920 Canada became a member of the League of Nations.
1931 The Statute of Westminster made Canada an independent nation.

Population
1914 7,879,000
1929 10,029,000

ions in the British Empire began to demand greater participation in developing foreign and defense policies. The British needed soldiers and weapons from the dominions and so agreed to their demands.

After World War I, Borden and the other dominion prime ministers were members of the British Empire's peace delegation in Paris in 1919. They signed the Treaty of Versailles, which officially ended the war with Germany. In addition, all the dominions became original members of the League of Nations, an international peacekeeping agency formed in 1920.

Labor and farm unrest. While Borden attended the peace conference in Paris, trouble mounted at home. Workers throughout Canada demanded higher wages, better working conditions, and recognition of their unions. Farmers wanted relief from low crop prices and urged reductions in freight rates. Dissatisfied farmers formed political parties in almost every province. Farmer parties won control of the provincial government in Ontario in 1919 and in Alberta in 1921. In the national election of 1921, the Liberal Party gained a majority of the seats in the House of Commons, and William Lyon Mackenzie King became prime minister.

In 1921, Agnes Macphail became the first woman to serve in the Canadian House of Commons. She was elected to represent the United Farmers of Ontario.

Independence. King was determined to establish Canada's independence in foreign affairs. In 1922, he refused to support the United Kingdom in a possible war with Turkey and rejected a request for Canadian troops. On King's insistence, Canada for the first time signed a treaty alone with another nation in 1923. The treaty, with the United States, regulated halibut fishing in the Pacific Ocean.

In 1926, King and representatives from the other dominions met with British representatives at an Imperial Conference in London. At the conference, King joined a successful fight for dominion independence. The dominion and British representatives declared the dominions to be independent members of the British Commonwealth of Nations, as the British Empire then became known. In 1931, the British Parliament passed the Statute of Westminster, which legalized the declaration. This act thus officially recognized Canada and the other self-governing dominions as independent nations.

Period facts in brief (1932-1957)

Prime ministers (with parties, dates of service)
- Richard B. Bennett, Conservative, 1930-1935
- W. L. Mackenzie King, Liberal, 1935-1948
- Louis S. St. Laurent, Liberal, 1948-1957
- John G. Diefenbaker, Progressive Conservative, 1957-1963

Provinces of Canada
- Number at start of period: 9
- Number at end of period: 10
- Province added during the period: Newfoundland (1949)

Important dates
- **1930's** Canada suffered through the Great Depression.
- **1934** The Bank of Canada was established.
- **1939-1945** More than a million Canadians served in World War II.
- **1940** A social security system was started.
- **1945** Canada joined the United Nations (UN).
- **1949** Canada signed a treaty that set up the North Atlantic Treaty Organization (NATO).

Population
- **1932** 10,510,000
- **1957** 16,610,000

The young nation (1932-1957)

During the 1930's, the young Canadian nation suffered through the Great Depression. The hard economic times ended when production rose during World War II (1939-1945). After the war, an industrial boom at home helped make Canada a major economic power. The nation also became greatly involved in world affairs.

The Great Depression began in 1929 with the stock market crash in the United States and spread throughout the world. The depression caused a sharp drop in foreign trade and especially hurt the demand for Canadian food products, lumber, and minerals. The decline in export income forced thousands of Canadian factories and stores, plus many coal mines, to close. Hundreds of thousands of Canadians lost their jobs and homes. A rapid fall in grain prices and a severe drought worsened the depression in the Prairie Provinces.

Unemployment was the chief issue in the election of 1930. King's government was defeated, and the Conservatives came to power under Richard B. Bennett. Bennett's government established more than 200 relief camps for single, unemployed men and spent hundreds of millions of dollars to aid the needy.

Bennett dealt harshly with strikers and demonstrators and earned the nickname "Iron Heel Bennett." But he also saw the need for reform. His government created a number of important federal agencies, including the Canadian Radio Broadcasting Commission in 1932, the Bank of Canada in 1934, and the Canadian Wheat Board in 1935. Canada's economic problems continued, however, and many Canadians blamed Bennett for failing to ease the hard times. Bennett's unpopularity led to the formation of new political parties, which included the Co-operative Commonwealth Federation in 1932 and the Social Credit Party in 1935. In the election of 1935, the Liberal Party regained control of the House of Commons. King then began his third term as prime minister. See **Great Depression** (Effects in Canada).

World War II. Canada declared war on Germany on Sept. 10, 1939. It declared war on Japan on Dec. 8, 1941, the day after Japan attacked United States bases at Pearl Harbor in Hawaii. The Canadian Army first saw action in December 1941, when it participated in the unsuccessful attempt to defend Hong Kong against a Japanese invasion. In August 1942, the Army suffered heavy losses in the Allied assault on the French port of Dieppe.

Canadian troops also took part in the Allied invasion of Sicily in 1943 and in the battle for Italy. The Third Canadian Division participated in the Allied landing at Normandy in France on June 6, 1944. The First Canadian Army, commanded by General H. D. G. Crerar, fought its way through the Netherlands and advanced into northern Germany. The Royal Canadian Air Force aided the Allies, and the Canadian Navy helped protect Allied ships in the Atlantic Ocean. By the end of the war, over a million Canadian men and women had served in the armed forces. Over 90,000 had been killed or wounded.

The Canadian government lent billions of dollars to the war cause. It sent the British people large quantities

Public Archives of Canada, Ottawa (PA 122765)

During World War II, the Third Canadian Division took part in the Allied landing at Normandy in France on June 6, 1944, *shown here.* By the end of the war in 1945, over a million Canadian men and women had served in the armed forces.

of food during the Battle of Britain. Canadian factories built thousands of planes, ships, and weapons.

When World War II began, King pledged to keep recruiting voluntary for overseas service. In 1942, however, the government asked Canadian voters to release it from a pledge not to send draftees abroad. The vast majority of voters approved the request, though many French Canadians opposed it. However, no Canadian draftees went overseas until November 1944.

The war was especially tragic for Canadians of Japanese descent and for newly arrived immigrants from Japan. Japanese Canadians came under widespread distrust after Japan attacked Pearl Harbor. In February 1942, the Canadian government began to place about 21,000 of them in camps and isolated towns in Alberta, British Columbia, Manitoba, and Ontario. Their rights were not restored until 1949. Most of the Japanese Canadians lost their homes and businesses.

The government adopted several important social programs during the war. It established the beginning of a social security system by introducing unemployment insurance in 1940. In 1944, it adopted a program that assisted families by providing financial aid for children. As the war ended, the government began a vast benefits program to help veterans return to civilian life.

The postwar boom. Canada's economy thrived after World War II. Canadians spent their wartime savings on appliances and other household goods. A great demand for housing created a construction boom. The development of Canada's incredibly rich mineral deposits also flourished. The country became a major producer of asbestos, copper, iron ore, nickel, oil, uranium, and other minerals. Foreign investors, mainly from the United States, helped finance the development of many new industries. By the late 1950's, Canada had changed from a chiefly agricultural country to a leading industrial nation.

Meanwhile, Canada experienced another great wave of immigration. From 1945 to 1956, more than a million people from Germany, Italy, and other war-torn European countries moved to Canada. Many of the immigrants settled in Toronto, Montreal, and other large cities. Suburbs grew rapidly outside the central cities.

Increasing foreign involvement. King retired as prime minister in November 1948. Louis St. Laurent, the new Liberal Party leader, became Canada's second French-Canadian prime minister. One of the first highlights of his administration occurred in March 1949, when Newfoundland (now Newfoundland and Labrador) became Canada's 10th province. Under St. Laurent, Canada played an ever-larger role in international affairs.

Canada's prestige and economic strength after World War II convinced many Canadians that their nation's interests required active involvement in foreign affairs. In 1945, Canada became an original member of the United Nations (UN). In 1949, it signed the treaty that set up the North Atlantic Treaty Organization (NATO). NATO was the first military alliance Canada had joined in peacetime.

During the Korean War (1950-1953), Canada contributed about 22,000 soldiers to the UN forces fighting North Korea's invasion of South Korea. Canada helped bring about peace in the Middle East after the United Kingdom, France, and Israel invaded Egypt in 1956. Lester B. Pearson, Canada's secretary of state for external affairs, won the 1957 Nobel Peace Prize for organizing a UN peacekeeping force for the troubled area.

The end of liberal rule. Canadians took pride in the government's accomplishments in foreign affairs. But they were stunned in 1956, when the government broke the rules of Parliament to push through a bill to finance construction of a natural gas pipeline. John G. Diefenbaker, leader of the Progressive Conservative Party, charged that St. Laurent's government had abused its authority and insulted Parliament. Many voters agreed. In the election of 1957, Diefenbaker thus led his party to a narrow victory and ended 22 years of Liberal rule.

Challenges of the 1960's

Major economic and social problems troubled Canada in the 1960's. A business slump struck the country, and unemployment rose sharply. French Canadians began a movement to increase their political power. In Quebec, many French Canadians began to support a campaign to make their province a separate nation.

The new Conservative government. Diefenbaker hoped to broaden his support in Parliament and called an election in 1958. The Progressive Conservatives won 208 of the 265 seats in the House of Commons, the largest majority in Canadian history. In 1959, Diefenbaker joined Queen Elizabeth II of the United Kingdom and U.S. President Dwight D. Eisenhower at the opening of the St. Lawrence Seaway. The seaway enables large commercial ships to sail between the Atlantic Ocean and the Great Lakes by way of the St. Lawrence River.

Diefenbaker faced a major political problem in 1959 when his government chose to buy American-made Bomarc missiles for defense at home instead of the more expensive Canadian-built Avro Arrow fighter planes. The government also bought United States fighters for Canada's contribution to NATO forces. The rejection of the Avro Arrow planes resulted in heavy criticism.

In 1960, a sagging economy challenged the Diefenbaker government. The government responded by trying to increase foreign trade. It developed new markets for Canadian wheat in China and the Communist countries of Eastern Europe. In 1962, during an election campaign, the government tried to boost the economy by lowering the value of the Canadian dollar. In the June election, the Conservatives won the most seats in the House of Commons but not a majority. The Diefenbaker government was able to stay in power only with the aid of the Social Credit Party, which had won 30 seats.

The Quebec separatist movement. Diefenbaker also faced rising discontent in Quebec. In 1960, the Quebec Liberal Party gained control of the provincial government. Led by Jean Lesage, the new government started the Quiet Revolution, a movement to defend French-Canadian rights throughout the country. Many French Canadians believed they were barred from jobs in government and some large corporations because they spoke French. They also wanted English Canadians to recognize and respect Quebec's French heritage. Lesage also worked to increase Quebec's control over its own economy and to reduce such control by the federal government.

The Quiet Revolution awakened deep feelings of French-Canadian nationalism. In Quebec, it influenced the rise of *separatism,* the demand that the province separate from Canada and become an independent nation. In the early 1960's, several separatist groups entered candidates in provincial elections. Other groups, especially the Front de Libération du Québec (FLQ), used terrorism to promote separatism. In 1963, the FLQ began to bomb federal buildings and symbols of Canada that reflected the country's British traditions.

The return of the Liberals. Early in 1963, a controversy developed over whether Canada had agreed in 1959 to accept nuclear warheads for its Bomarc missiles. The missiles were effective only with such warheads. Diefenbaker had refused to accept the weapons because some members of his Cabinet opposed the use of nuclear arms. The Liberals in Parliament argued that Canada had agreed to take the warheads for use in the defense of North America. Lester B. Pearson, the Liberal leader, accused the government of failing to show leadership. In February, the House of Commons gave Diefenbaker's government a vote of no confidence. Diefenbaker was then forced to call a general election.

In the election of 1963, the Liberals won the most seats in the House but not a majority. Pearson became prime minister with support from several small opposition parties. His government accepted the nuclear warheads. It also expanded social welfare programs, introducing a national pension plan in 1964 and a national health insurance program in 1965.

Pearson achieved a personal goal when Canada adopted a new national flag. The country had long used the British Red Ensign with a coat of arms representing Canada's provinces. The Conservatives wanted to keep the Red Ensign as a symbol of Canada's British heritage. But in 1964, Parliament approved a design that featured a red maple leaf, a symbol of Canada. On Feb. 15, 1965, Canada's new flag flew for the first time.

Canada marked the 100th anniversary of Confederation in 1967 with national celebrations. A highlight was Expo 67, a world's fair held in Montreal.

In April 1968, Pearson resigned as prime minister. His successor, Pierre Elliott Trudeau, became Canada's third French-Canadian prime minister. Trudeau called a national election for June 25. The campaign was marked by widespread enthusiasm that became known as "Trudeaumania." Canadians seemed to be madly in love with Trudeau, a dashing 48-year-old bachelor, and gave his party a majority of the seats in the House.

Period facts in brief (1958-1969)

Prime ministers (with parties, dates of service)
John G. Diefenbaker, Progressive Conservative, 1957-1963
Lester B. Pearson, Liberal, 1963-1968
Pierre Trudeau, Liberal, 1968-1979

Important dates
- **1958** The Progressive Conservatives won the largest majority in the House of Commons in Canadian history.
- **1959** The St. Lawrence Seaway, a joint U.S.-Canadian project, opened.
- **1962** The Trans-Canada Highway, the country's first ocean-to-ocean road, was completed.
- **1964** A national pension plan was introduced.
- **1965** A new official Canadian flag flew for the first time on February 15.
- **1967** Canadians celebrated the 100th anniversary of Confederation with Expo 67, a world's fair in Montreal.
- **1969** The Official Languages Act required federal facilities in Canada to provide service in both French and English if 10 percent of the people in a particular area speak either language.

Population
1958 17,080,000
1969 21,001,000

Canada under Trudeau

Trudeau served as Canada's prime minister almost continuously until 1984. Under Trudeau, Canada at first had high hopes for economic expansion. But sharply rising prices and high unemployment caused problems. Canadian national unity was still threatened by the Quebec separatist movement. Canada also revised its constitution during this period.

Foreign affairs. During the early 1970's, Canada broadened its relations with the two leading Communist nations, China and the Soviet Union. In 1970, Canada and China agreed to resume diplomatic relations, which had ended when the Communists gained control of China in 1949. In 1971, Trudeau and Soviet Premier Aleksei N. Kosygin exchanged visits. Canada increased trade with both China and the Soviet Union.

Relations between the Canadian and U.S. governments, however, became increasingly strained during the 1970's. The U.S. government disapproved of Canada's willingness to accept American men who crossed the border to avoid being drafted in the Vietnam War (1957-1975). The United States also objected to new policies that limited foreign ownership and financing of Canadian industries. In 1973, the Canadian Parliament established the Foreign Investment Review Agency to end conditions that had enabled U.S. companies to gain control of over half of Canada's manufacturing plants.

Canadians, in turn, became upset by threats to their environment from the United States. Trudeau objected to the Garrison Diversion Project in North Dakota, which threatened to pollute Canadian rivers. He also protested the polluting of Canadian waters by acid rain resulting from chemicals released into the air by U.S. industries. Control of fishing waters and other offshore resources in the northeast Pacific and northwest Atlantic also became an issue between Canada and the United States.

The separatist threat. To curb the Quebec separatist movement, Trudeau pledged to create equal opportunities for French- and English-speaking Canadians. His first important move toward this goal was winning Parliament's approval of the Official Languages Act in 1969. This act requires federal facilities to provide service in French in areas where at least 10 percent of the people speak French. It also requires service in English in areas where at least 10 percent of the people speak English. The law brought major changes to the government. But it had little effect on the growing separatist movement.

Canada experienced one of its most serious political crises in October 1970, when the FLQ kidnapped two officials in Montreal. The officials were James R. Cross, the British trade commissioner in Montreal; and Pierre Laporte, Quebec's labor minister. The terrorists offered to exchange the two men for $500,000 and the release of 23 jailed FLQ members.

Trudeau rejected the offer. Instead, he put Canada's War Measures Act into effect. This act allows the government to suspend the civil liberties of people judged dangerous during wartime. The law had never been applied during peacetime. Police used the act to arrest hundreds of FLQ sympathizers during their search for the kidnapped officials. FLQ members murdered Laporte. They released Cross in December, when the government permitted the kidnappers to go to Cuba.

FLQ terrorism ended, but the separatist movement continued. The Parti Québécois, organized as a separatist political party in 1968, won control of the government of Quebec in 1976. René Lévesque, a member of the Quebec legislature and the party's leader, became premier of the province. In 1980, Lévesque's government held a provincewide vote on a proposal to give provincial leaders authority to negotiate with the Canadian federal government for independence. About 60 percent of Quebec's voters rejected the proposal.

Economic developments. During the early 1970's, Canada's economy did not expand fast enough to keep pace with increases in the labor force. The country's difficulties grew after a recession and rapid inflation developed in the mid-1970's. During the 1970's, however, the energy-rich provinces of Alberta, Saskatchewan, and British Columbia began to benefit from a boom in the production of petroleum and natural gas. Their populations grew rapidly, and numerous corporations shifted their head offices from eastern to western Canada.

Trudeau's popularity declined during the mid-1970's. The Liberals lost the election of 1979 to the Progressive Conservatives, and Joe Clark became prime minister. Later that year, Clark announced a plan to conserve energy by raising fuel taxes. But strong opposition to the plan led the House of Commons to give the government a vote of no confidence. Clark then called a general election for February 1980. The Liberals won a majority in the House, and Trudeau returned as prime minister.

Canada's economic problems worsened in the early 1980's, when another recession struck. By March 1983, 14 percent of Canada's workers had no jobs—the highest unemployment rate since the Great Depression.

Constitutional changes. In 1981, Trudeau won approval of proposed changes in Canada's constitution from nine of the provincial heads. The changes became part of the Constitution Act of 1982, passed by the British Parliament in March. The act eliminated the need for British approval of Canadian constitutional amendments. It included a new bill of rights called the Canadian Charter of Rights and Freedoms (see **Bill of Rights** [Canada's constitution]). The revised constitution took effect on April 17, 1982. It replaced the British North America Act as the basic governing document of Canada.

Trudeau resigned in June 1984 and was succeeded by John N. Turner. The Progressive Conservatives, led by Brian Mulroney, won the general election in September 1984. Mulroney succeeded Turner as prime minister.

Canada under Mulroney

Foreign affairs. In 1988, Mulroney and U.S. President Ronald Reagan signed a major free-trade agreement. It called for elimination of all tariffs and many nontariff trade barriers between the two countries. It went into effect on Jan. 1, 1989.

Also during the early 1990's, Canada negotiated the

Period facts in brief (since 1970)

Prime ministers (with parties, dates of service)
- Pierre Trudeau, Liberal, 1968-1979
- Joe Clark, Progressive Conservative, 1979-1980
- Pierre Trudeau, Liberal, 1980-1984
- John N. Turner, Liberal, 1984
- Brian Mulroney, Progressive Conservative, 1984-1993
- Kim Campbell, Progressive Conservative, 1993
- Jean Chrétien, Liberal, 1993-2003
- Paul Martin, Liberal, 2003-2006
- Stephen Harper, Conservative, 2006-

Important dates
- **1970** Separatists in Quebec kidnapped two government officials and murdered one of them.
- **1980** Voters in Quebec rejected a proposal to give provincial leaders authority to negotiate with the federal government for political independence.
- **1982** The Constitution Act ended British control over amendments to Canada's constitution. The act included a new bill of rights.
- **1999** Nunavut became the third territory of Canada.

Population

1970	21,297,000
2001	30,007,094

North American Free Trade Agreement (NAFTA) with the United States and Mexico. The agreement called for the gradual elimination of tariffs and other trade barriers between the three countries. NAFTA took effect in 1994.

During the Persian Gulf War of 1991, the Canadian Armed Forces flew bombing missions over Iraq and Kuwait. It was the first time Canadian forces had been at war since the Korean War ended in 1953.

The constitutional crisis. On April 30, 1987, Mulroney and the premiers of the 10 provinces tentatively agreed to a far-reaching constitutional amendment at Meech Lake, Quebec. They formally approved the accord in Ottawa on June 3. The agreement stated that Quebec was to be recognized as a distinct society in Canada.

To go into effect, the Meech Lake accord had to be ratified by all 10 provinces by June 23, 1990. But Manitoba and Newfoundland withheld their support. Many opponents of the accord thought it granted Quebec's government too much power, especially over the rights of Quebec's English-speaking minority. After the accord failed, many Quebecers began to demand increased independence for Quebec from the rest of Canada.

In August 1992, in Charlottetown, Prince Edward Island, the premiers agreed to a new plan to revise the constitution. The plan called for recognition of Quebec as a distinct society, the replacement of Canada's appointed Senate with an elected one, self-government for native peoples, and the transfer of some federal powers to the provinces. A national referendum on the Charlottetown accord was held in October, and most Canadians, including a majority in Quebec, voted against it.

The 1993 national election. Mulroney resigned in June 1993 and was succeeded by Kim Campbell. In October of that year, Jean Chrétien led the Liberal Party to victory in a general election. He became prime minister in November. The ruling Progressive Conservative Party suffered one of the worst defeats in Canadian history, losing all but 2 of its 154 seats. Two regional parties became the second and third most powerful parties in the House. One of them, the Bloc Québécois, favors sovereignty for Quebec. The other, the Reform Party, was an Alberta-based conservative party.

WORLD BOOK map

In 1949, Newfoundland (now Newfoundland and Labrador) became Canada's 10th province. Newfoundland had gained control of Labrador in the settlement of a boundary dispute with Quebec in 1927. In 1999, the territory of Nunavut came into being.

Canapress Photo Service

The Constitution Act, signed by Queen Elizabeth II on April 17, 1982, *shown here,* gave Canada the sole power to amend its constitution. Canadian Prime Minister Pierre Trudeau looked on.

Liberal Party rule

Quebec referendum. In 1994, the separatist Parti Québécois again gained control of the government of Quebec. In October 1995, Quebec voters narrowly defeated a referendum that called for independence for Quebec. The province remained part of Canada.

The 1997 and 2000 national elections. Chrétien called an election for June 1997. The Liberals again won a majority of seats in the House of Commons, and Chrétien remained prime minister. The Reform Party came in second and replaced the Bloc Québécois as the official opposition. In 2000, Reform Party members voted to join the newly created Canadian Reform Conservative Alliance. The new party, commonly called the Canadian Alliance, became the official opposition in the House.

In 2000, Chrétien called an early election for November. The Liberal Party increased its majority in the House of Commons, and Chrétien continued as prime minister. The Canadian Alliance remained the official opposition.

Territorial and provincial changes. A new territory called Nunavut came into being in 1999. Nunavut was carved out of the eastern Northwest Territories. The new territory provides more self-government for the Inuit, who make up most of its population. In 2001, Canada's Parliament changed the name of the province of Newfoundland to Newfoundland and Labrador.

Recent developments. In November 2003, former finance minister Paul Martin was elected Liberal Party leader. On December 12, he replaced Chrétien as prime minister. That same month, the Progressive Conservative Party and the Canadian Alliance merged to form the Conservative Party of Canada, which then became the official opposition in the House of Commons.

In February 2004, Canada's auditor general reported that the Chrétien government had misused public funds as part of a program to promote national unity in the late 1990's and early 2000's. A commission of inquiry was expected to disclose its findings on the matter in late 2005. In a June 2004 election, the Liberal Party won enough seats to form a *minority government,* and Martin continued as prime minister. In a minority government, the ruling party holds the most, but not a majority of, seats in the House. The new Conservative Party placed second and remained the official opposition.

In 2005, a commission of inquiry confirmed that the Liberals had misused public funds for their own benefit. The opposition parties in the House passed a vote of no confidence in the government, forcing new elections in January 2006. Stephen Harper led the Conservatives to victory in the election. The Conservatives won the most seats in Parliament but not a majority. Harper was sworn in as prime minister of a minority government in February 2006. David Jay Bercuson

Related articles in *World Book*. See the *History* section of the province articles. See also:

Early Canada

Acadia
Bienville, Sieur de
Brulé, Étienne
Cadillac, Antoine de Lamothe
Cartier, Jacques
Champlain, Samuel de
Cornwallis, Edward
Coureurs de bois
French and Indian wars
Frontenac, Comte de
Groseilliers, Sieur des
Iberville, Sieur d'
Jolliet, Louis
La Salle, Sieur de
Laval de Montmorency, François Xavier de
La Vérendrye, Sieur de
Le Moyne, Charles
Louisbourg
Marquette, Jacques
McTavish, Simon
Money (The development of paper money; picture)
Montcalm, Marquis de
Monts, Sieur de
New France
Poutrincourt, Jean de Biencourt de
Quebec, Battle of
Radisson, Pierre E.
Roberval, Sieur de
Seigneurial system
Simcoe, John Graves
Talon, Jean Baptiste
Verchères, Marie Madeleine Jarret de
Wolfe, James
Youville, Saint Marguerite d'

British rule

Amherst, Lord Jeffery
Baldwin, Robert
Brock, Sir Isaac
Carleton, Sir Guy
Cartier, Sir George É.
Douglas, Sir James
Dumont, Gabriel
Durham, Earl of
Elgin, Earl of
Fraser, Simon
Hearne, Samuel
Henry, Alexander
Hincks, Sir Francis
Lafontaine, Sir Louis H.
Mackenzie, Sir Alexander
Mackenzie, Roderick
Mackenzie, William L.
McGillivray, William
Metcalfe, Charles Theophilus
Murray, James
North West Company
Papineau, Louis J.
Quebec Act
Quebec Conference
Rebellions of 1837
Secord, Laura I.
Selkirk, Earl of
Simpson, Sir George
Sydenham, Baron
Taché, Sir Étienne-P.
Thompson, David
Union, Act of
United Empire Loyalists
War of 1812
Webster-Ashburton Treaty

Confederation and after

There is a separate biography of each governor general listed in the table with the **Governor general** article. There is also a separate biography of each prime minister listed in the table with the **Prime minister of Canada** article. See also:

Assiniboia
Bloc Québécois
Bourassa, Henri
British North America Act
Brown, George
Confederation of Canada
Conservative Party of Canada
Crowfoot
Day, Stockwell
Duff, Sir Lyman P.
Foster, Sir George E.
Galt, Sir Alexander T.
Howe, Joseph
Lévesque, René
Liberal Party of Canada
Macdonald, John S.
Macphail, Agnes C.
Manning, Preston
McLaughlin, Audrey Marlene
Métis
Mowat, Sir Oliver
Murphy, Emily G.
North American Free Trade Agreement
North West Rebellion
Parti Québécois
Poundmaker
Progressive Conservative Party
Prohibition (Prohibition in Canada)
Red River Rebellion
Reform Party
Richards, Sir William B.
Riel, Louis
Rose, Sir John
Stanfield, Robert L.
Strathcona and Mount Royal, Baron of
Tilley, Sir Samuel L.
Vimy Ridge, Battle of
Woodsworth, James Shaver

Other related articles

Canada Day
Hudson's Bay Company
Indian, American
Northwest Passage
Remembrance Day
Victoria Day

Outline

I. Early European exploration

II. The development of New France (1604-1688)
A. Start of the fur trade
B. Early settlements
C. Threats to expansion
D. The royal province
E. The growing French-English rivalry

III. British conquest and rule (1689-1815)
A. The colonial wars
B. The Quebec Act
C. The United Empire Loyalists
D. Exploration of the West
E. The War of 1812

IV. The struggle for responsible government (1816-1867)
A. Growing discontent
B. The uprisings of 1837
C. Lord Durham's report
D. The beginning of self-government
E. Confederation

V. Growth of the Dominion (1868-1913)
A. New provinces
B. The Pacific Scandal
C. The return of Macdonald
D. The North West Rebellion
E. Progress under Laurier
F. Foreign relations

VI. World War I and independence (1914-1931)
A. World War I
B. The conscription issue
C. A larger role in the empire's affairs
D. Labor and farm unrest
E. Independence

VII. The young nation (1932-1957)
A. The Great Depression
B. World War II
C. The postwar boom
D. Increasing foreign involvement
E. The end of Liberal rule

VIII. Challenges of the 1960's
A. The new Conservative government
B. The Quebec separatist movement
C. The return of the Liberals

IX. Canada under Trudeau
A. Foreign affairs
B. The separatist threat
C. Economic developments
D. Constitutional changes
X. Canada under Mulroney
A. Foreign affairs
B. The constitutional crisis
C. The 1993 national election
XI. Liberal Party rule
A. Quebec referendum
B. The 1997 and 2000 national elections
C. Territorial and provincial changes
D. Recent developments

Questions

Who were the United Empire Loyalists?
What were some effects of the Quiet Revolution?
What was the Pacific Scandal?
What was the aim of the Official Languages Act?
What led to the start of the fur trade in Canada?
Why was the Peace of Paris important in Canadian history?
How many provinces formed the Dominion of Canada in 1867?
When did Canada become an independent nation?
What serious political crisis did Canada face in 1970?
How did Pierre Elliott Trudeau try to strengthen national unity in Canada?

Additional resources

Level I
Caswell, Maryanne. *Pioneer Girl.* Tundra, 2001.
Grabowski, John F. *Canada.* Lucent Bks., 1998.
Hughes, Susan. *Let's Call It Canada: Amazing Stories of Canadian Place Names.* Maple Tree Pr., 2003.
Morton, Desmond. *Shaping a Nation: A Short History of Canada's Constitution.* Rev. ed. Umbrella Pr., 1996.

Level II
Brown, Craig, ed. *The Illustrated History of Canada.* 4th ed. Key Porter, 2003.
Bumsted, J. M. *The Peoples of Canada.* 2 vols. 2nd ed. Oxford, 2003.
Dickason, Olive P. *Canada's First Nations.* 3rd ed. Oxford, 2001.
Historical Atlas of Canada. 3 vols. Univ. of Toronto Pr., 1987-1993.
Morton, Desmond. *A Military History of Canada.* 4th ed. McClelland, 1999. *A Short History of Canada.* 5th ed., 2001.

Canada Day, one of Canada's most important national holidays, is celebrated on July 1 of each year. It honors the day that the British colonies of New Brunswick, Nova Scotia, and the Province of Canada were united in one country, called the Dominion of Canada. On July 1, 1867, the Dominion of Canada was created by terms of the British North America Act. The national holiday, called *Dominion Day* until 1982, is a time for patriotic programs and events. David Jay Bercuson

Canada goose is the common wild goose of North America. It grows 22 to 43 inches (55 to 110 centimeters) long. It has a black neck and head and white cheeks. Its tail and wings are black, its back and chest are grayish-brown, and its belly and rump are white. About 10 kinds of Canada geese exist. They weigh from about 3 pounds (1.4 kilograms) to about 15 pounds (7 kilograms).

Canada geese spend the spring and summer from Alaska and far northern Canada to the northern half of the United States. In the fall, many of the geese migrate to warmer regions as far south as northern Mexico. Canada geese have been introduced into New Zealand, Norway, Sweden, and the United Kingdom.

Canada geese breed in the spring. They make nests of branches, twigs, grass, and weeds, often in marshes or ponds. The female usually lays from four to six dull-white eggs. The young live with their parents for about a year after hatching and then begin to look for a mate. They keep the same mates for life. Family members often continue to live together, forming extended families of related geese. Canada geese eat marsh grasses and crop plants, especially corn, wheat, and other grains.

Since the mid-1950's, the overall population of Canada geese has increased greatly in North America. This increase has occurred largely because of a rise in the amount of acreage used for corn production and the establishment of numerous wildlife refuges. Today, many nonmigratory populations of Canada geese live year-round in suburban and rural areas of the northern United States. These geese sometimes damage crops, and their droppings can be a nuisance. Robert L. Jarvis

Scientific classification. The Canada goose belongs to the family Anatidae. It is *Branta canadensis.*

See also **Bird** (picture: Birds of the Arctic); **Goose.**

Canada thistle, also known as *creeping thistle,* is one of the most troublesome of weeds. It is native to Europe and Asia but now grows across most of the northern United States and southern Canada. The thistle has prickly leaves and small pink, purple, or white flowers. It grows in cultivated areas and wasteland and is hard to control. It spreads easily because new plants can grow from bits of the roots of old plants. If a plant is only partly uprooted, several plants can still grow from its remaining roots. One way to destroy the plant is to kill its roots through starvation. The leaves supply the food that keeps the roots alive. This food supply can be cut off by cutting down the green stems of the plant when they appear. This method can be combined with the growing of crops, such as corn, that require cultivation between rows. Cultivation brings the thistle seeds nearer the surface so they may start growing. Later, the stems are cut down. Chemical weedkillers are also used to destroy the plant. Margaret R. Bolick

Scientific classification. The Canada thistle belongs to the composite family, Compositae. It is *Cirsium arvense.*

See also **Thistle; Weed.**

Canadian Alliance was a right-wing political party in Canada. The party was officially called the Canadian Reform Conservative Alliance. It supported smaller government, balanced budgets, tax reform, and increased consultation with the public through *referendums* (direct votes by the people) on important issues.

The Canadian Alliance grew out of efforts to unite conservatives in Canadian politics. In the 1997 federal election, the Reform Party, a conservative party based in Alberta, became the official opposition in the Canadian House of Commons. However, the party did not win a single seat outside western Canada. Many Reform members believed that the failure of the party to gain nationwide support was the result of the conservative vote being split between the Reform and the Progressive Conservative parties. They argued that what was needed to defeat the ruling Liberal Party was a new party that united members of the nation's two conservative parties.

The Canadian Alliance was founded in January 2000. In March, Reform Party members voted to join the new Alliance. The new party then became the official opposition. It remained the official opposition after a national election held in November. In 2003, Alliance members voted to merge with the Progressive Conservative Party to form the Conservative Party of Canada. David Taras

See also **Day, Stockwell; Harper, Stephen Joseph.**

Canadian Armed Forces defend Canada and its interests throughout the world. They maintain the equipment, weapons, and troops necessary to protect Canada and to provide humanitarian and civil assistance in Canada and worldwide. In addition, the forces contribute to international peacekeeping and security operations through alliances with other countries. The forces are formally named the Canadian Armed Forces, but they are commonly called the Canadian Forces.

Organization. An officer called the *chief of the defence staff* commands the Canadian Forces. The chief of the defence staff also advises the Canadian government on military matters. The prime minister and the Cabinet appoint the chief.

The Canadian Forces consists of the Regular Forces, who are always on active duty, and the Reserve Forces, who supplement the Regular Forces when necessary. The Canadian Forces includes three large defense organizations: (1) the Land Force, (2) the Maritime Command, (3) and the Air Command.

Land Force is Canada's army. Land Force's primary tasks are to protect Canada and to defend North America in cooperation with the United States. The Canadian Army also participates in overseas operations, antiterrorist operations, and peacekeeping missions. It aids provincial and territorial authorities in dealing with such natural disasters as earthquakes, floods, and forest fires. It maintains three regular combat mechanized brigade groups and more than 12 reserve combat brigade groups. The Canadian Rangers, who serve in the far northern regions of Canada, are members of the Reserve Forces.

Maritime Command (MARCOM), commonly called the Navy, protects Canada's coastline and works with Canada's allies to defend North America. The Navy defends Canadian waters against illegal fishing and environmental damage. Canada's Navy also supports international peacekeeping missions and humanitarian assistance projects. In addition, the Navy maintains security through the North Atlantic Treaty Organization (NATO),

Canadian Forces rank and grade insignia

These insignia are worn on sleeves or shoulder straps.

a military alliance consisting of Canada, the United States, and most European nations. The operations of MARCOM are conducted from two major bases, in Halifax, Nova Scotia; and Esquimalt, British Columbia. MARCOM's activities are assisted by the Naval Reserves.

Air Command (AIRCOM), commonly called the Air Force, is charged with surveillance and control of Canadian airspace. It shares in the joint defense of North American airspace with United States forces through the North American Aerospace Defense Command (NORAD). AIRCOM provides air support to MARCOM and the Land Force, and it transports Canadian Forces personnel and equipment throughout the world. AIRCOM is made up of 13 *wings.* A wing is a group of operational and support units under a single tactical commander. AIRCOM's activities are assisted by the Air Reserves.

Support organizations under the control of the Department of National Defence aid the Canadian Forces. Defence Research and Development Canada provides the Department of Defence and the Canadian Forces with technical and scientific services. The Communications Security Establishment works to keep telecommunications, electronic communications, and computer ized systems secure. The National Search and Rescue Secretariat coordinates the activities of government, private, and volunteer organizations that provide search and rescue services.

Weapons and equipment. Armored vehicles of the Land Force include Leopard tanks and Grizzly and other armored personnel carriers. The force's artillery includes self-propelled howitzers, field guns, antitank weapons, handheld surface-to-air missiles, and air defense missiles.

MARCOM operates frigates, diesel-electric submarines, and supply ships. The Navy also has many smaller vessels and training ships.

AIRCOM flies CF-18 Hornet fighter-bombers, CP-140 Aurora patrol aircraft, and a variety of smaller training aircraft. Transport craft include the CC-115 Buffalo, CC-130 Hercules, and the CC-144 Challenger. The Air Force's helicopters include the CH-124 Sea King, used for antisubmarine warfare, and the CH-113 Labrador and CH-149 Cormorant, used for search and rescue.

Recruitment and training. Officers in the Canadian Armed Forces may receive their commissions in one of three ways. The first is to enter as a direct-entry officer. This type of officer enters the Canadian Forces after graduating from a university and agreeing to active service for three years. The second way is to complete the Officer Candidate Training Program. The program requires a minimum of a 12th-grade education with advanced standing in English, mathematics, and sciences. The candidate must agree to serve for three years. The third method is the Regular Officer Training Program. The candidate receives four years of free education at one of three Canadian military colleges or a civilian university. After completing a degree program, candidates must serve for a minimum of five years.

Noncommissioned recruits must have at least a 10th-grade education and enlist for three years. Basic training for recruits lasts 10 weeks and is followed by occupational training courses. A Canadian citizen must be older than 17 to enlist.

History. During colonial days, Canada's defense was the responsibility of the governments of France and Britain (now the United Kingdom). However, during the mid-1800's, Canada began to move toward independence and to assume responsibility for its own defense. In 1871, the Canadian Army was first organized. The Royal Canadian Navy was formed in 1910, and the Royal Canadian Air Force in 1924.

Canada's military forces fought under British command in the Anglo-Boer War of 1899-1902. During World War I (1914-1918), Canadians fought with the Allied forces under British command. More than 1 million Canadians served with the Allied forces during World War II (1939-1945). Canadian troops fought with the United Nations (UN) in the Korean War (1950-1953) and the Persian Gulf War of 1991. Canadian troops have served in many of the UN's peacekeeping operations since the first one in 1947.

Critically reviewed by National Defence Headquarters

Related articles in *World Book* include:

Bishop, Billy
Canada, History of (The young nation)
McNaughton, Andrew G. L.
NORAD
Royal Canadian Legion
Royal Canadian Mounted Police
Royal Military College of Canada

Canadian Broadcasting Corporation (CBC) is the national public broadcasting service in Canada. The CBC, known as Société Radio-Canada in French, operates radio and television networks and produces information, general interest, special interest, music, and cultural programs. It owns nearly 100 television and radio stations, and it supplies programming to more than 25 affiliate stations. The CBC owns most of its more than 1,400 *rebroadcasters,* low-power stations that receive and retransmit radio or television signals.

The CBC operates two AM radio networks, one of which broadcasts in English and the other in French. It also operates two FM radio networks. Through the corporation's Web site, www.cbc.ca, Internet users can listen to CBC radio broadcasts. The CBC furnishes special radio service to northern Canada in eight languages and dialects of the Indians and Inuit. Radio Canada International, a short-wave radio service of CBC, broadcasts in seven languages. The CBC offers a 30-channel, commercial-free digital radio service by subscription.

The CBC operates two television networks. One broadcasts in English, and the other in French. The CBC also operates two cable television news networks.

The Canadian government finances the majority of the CBC's programming. Other funds come primarily from television advertising. Parliament created the CBC in 1936. Its headquarters are in Ottawa, Ontario.

Critically reviewed by the Canadian Broadcasting Corporation

Canadian Education Association is a national association of education authorities in Canada. It is supported by grants from provincial and territorial departments of education and by about 120 school systems. The association collects and distributes information on public education. It was organized in 1891 as the Dominion Educational Association. Its headquarters are in Toronto. Critically reviewed by the Canadian Education Association

Canadian Library Association (CLA) is a national organization that provides leadership in library and information services in Canada. Its members include librarians, library trustees, workers, and suppliers.

The association provides educational programs and promotes issues and legislation on behalf of libraries. it also offers library school scholarships and presents awards. It publishes a national magazine called *Feliciter.* It also maintains microfilms of early Canadian newspapers. The association was founded in 1946. Its headquarters are in Ottawa, Ontario.

Critically reviewed by the Canadian Library Association

Canadian literature reflects the varied background of Canada's people and the diverse geography and regions of the country. In the late 1600's and 1700's, colonists from both France and England established the first permanent European settlements in Canada. Since then, most Canadian literature has been written in French or English—the nation's two official languages. Canadian literature written in French is called *Québécois literature,* after the French-speaking province of Quebec.

Characteristics of Canadian literature

One of the central themes of Canadian writers is the "idea of North." Images of Canada's awe-inspiring northern landscape dominate its literary history. These images appeared as early as the travel narratives of the mid-1500's and continue in Canadian writing today.

The sense of moving east, west, or north and of making human contact in the face of an indifferent nature also shapes Canadian writing. The literature helps link the vast nation of urban centers and small towns. It also sends people from the prairies on voyages of discovery farther west to the Pacific coast.

Like many nations with colonial beginnings, Canada has struggled to create its own identity. This struggle appears in a long tradition of writers who have developed Canadian voices to express the experience of being in Canada. Their books enable Canadians to understand who they are and to interpret themselves to the world. A Canadian voice began to emerge slowly in Canadian literature in the 1800's and blossomed after the end of World War II in 1945. The publication of literature in languages other than English and French and the emergence of *First Nations* (aboriginal) writers are signs of a growing, distinct Canadian voice.

The notion of Canada as a nation of *duality* (two parts) also characterizes its literature. Canadians focus on both their central government and their distinctive regions. They have two official languages. In addition, Canadians have conflicting feelings about the United States—a country with which they have much in common, but against which they define themselves. Author Margaret Atwood has said that to live in Canada is to choose a "violent duality." This duality is a constant theme and challenge for Canadian writers.

Beginnings of Canadian literature

The earliest writing in Canada was travel literature—journals, diaries, reports, letters, and autobiographies written by explorers and missionaries. In 1535, the French navigator Jacques Cartier led the first European expedition up the St. Lawrence River. His trip is described in *Bref récit de la navigation de Canada* (1545). Others who wrote about life in Canada during the 1600's and 1700's include the explorer Samuel de Champlain; Marie de l'Incarnation, who founded the Ursuline religious order in Canada; and the Jesuit missionary Jean de Brébeuf.

England and France fought a series of wars between 1689 and 1763. As a result of these conflicts, England took over the French empire in America. After the English conquest, such explorers as Alexander Henry, David Thompson, and Samuel Hearne produced narratives describing the new territory and its peoples. Of special note is Hearne's *A Journey from Prince of Wales's Fort, in Hudson's Bay, to the Northern Ocean* (1795).

Early Québécois literature. As a result of the English conquest, French-speaking Canadians concentrated on preserving their unique culture. During the early 1800's, historical works written in French flourished. F.-X. Garneau published his *Histoire du Canada* from 1845 to 1848. Such historical works gave rise to the popular romances of the mid-1800's known as "novels of the soil." These works celebrate the Québécois sense of *patrie* (home) and the traditional religious values of an agricultural society. Notable examples include *Les Anciens Canadiens* (1863) by Philippe Aubert de Gaspé and *Jean Rivard* (1862, 1864) by Antoine Gérin-Lajoie.

Early English-Canadian literature, like Québécois writing, often expressed an optimistic, pioneering attitude toward the new country. Frances Brooke wrote the first Canadian novel, *The History of Emily Montague* (1769). Oliver Goldsmith—grandnephew of the English writer of the same name—wrote *The Rising Village* (1825) to celebrate the future of the new British colony. Susanna Moodie, who emigrated from England, eventually came to feel a genuine love and respect for her new home. She described her experiences in her autobiographical work, *Roughing It in the Bush* (1852). Jonathan Odell and Joseph Stansbury were *United Empire Loyalists,* American colonists who remained loyal to Britain. Both lived in Canada for a period, and their writings express their rejection of the new United States.

John Richardson and Thomas Chandler Haliburton were among the earliest writers born and raised in Canada. Richardson wrote *Wacousta* (1832), a popular historical romance. He set the novel in 1763, at the time of an uprising led by the Indian chief Pontiac against the British. Haliburton ridiculed a sly American peddler in his narrative *The Clockmaker; or, The Sayings and Doings of Sam Slick of Slickville* (1836). This book was the first imaginative representation of Canada's vision of Americans. Haliburton's mix of humor and political satire influenced the work of such later Canadian humorists as Stephen Leacock and Robertson Davies.

Confederation to World War I

The next period of Canadian literature began in the mid-1800's, shortly before the Confederation of Canada. Confederation was the union of British colonies that formed the Dominion of Canada in 1867. This literary period lasted until the end of World War I in 1918.

Poetry: 1850-1918. Even before Confederation, Canadian poetry was flourishing in French and English. About 1855, Octave Crémazie began to publish religious and patriotic verse in *Le Journal de Québec.* Together with the poet Alfred Garneau, Crémazie had an important influence on a group of poets that arose during the 1860's. This group—called the *School of Quebec*—included León-Pamphile Lemay and Louis-Honoré Fréchette. For these poets, the romantic treatment of nature coincided with the expression of patriotic themes.

The first English Canadian to be considered a national poet was Charles Sangster. His poem "The St. Lawrence and the Saguenay" (1856) celebrates the beauty of the Canadian landscape.

By 1888, a group of young poets called the *Confederation poets* began to publish. They included Duncan Campbell Scott, Sir Charles G. D. Roberts, Archibald Lampman, Bliss Carman, and Wilfred Campbell. These writers described nature and regional scenes using forms and rhythms that showed a growing freedom from European styles. Scott, in particular, became well known for his poetic narratives about native peoples. Among his best-known poems on this theme is "The Forsaken" (1905). Pauline Johnson was known for her poetry about Indian life. Her father was a Mohawk Indian chief, and her mother was English. Isabella Valancy Crawford gained fame for a single volume of narrative poems published in 1884, including "Malcolm's Katie."

Émile Nelligan's use of romantic images and symbols also profoundly influenced Canadian poetry of this period. Nelligan and the poet Albert Lozeau were part of the School of Montreal, a group that came together about 1895. This group rejected the patriotic verse that was popular in Quebec at the time.

Fiction: 1850-1918. Important novelists of this period included Laure Conan (the pen name of Marie-Louise-Félicité Angers), Quebec's first female novelist. She combined letters, narrative, and diary in *Angèline de Montbrun* (1881-1882), a psychological examination of disappointed love. Most Québécois novels of the period, however, glorified rural life and religious values. Typical of these works is *La Terre* (1916) by Ernest Choquette. More interesting today are such novels as *Marie Calumet* (1904) by Rodolphe Girard and *La Scouine* (1918) by Albert Laberge. Both are realistic portrayals of Quebec society.

Most English-Canadian novelists of the period wrote historical romances. Some were historical romances modeled on the fiction of the Scottish novelist Sir Walter Scott, such as William Kirby's *The Golden Dog* (1877) and Sir Gilbert Parker's *The Seats of the Mighty* (1896). Some novelists produced sentimental romances or romances with mysterious or supernatural overtones. James De Mille wrote the philosophical fantasy *A Strange Manuscript Found in a Copper Cylinder* (published in 1888, after his death). Rosanna Leprohon's *Antoinette de Mirecourt* (1864) and Sara Jeannette Duncan's *The Imperialist* (1904) describe conflicts faced by characters of different cultural and religious backgrounds.

In the late 1800's and early 1900's, Ralph Connor (the pen name of Charles W. Gordon) and Lucy Maud Mont-

Canadian literature

Two literary traditions have flourished in Canada. One developed from the culture of England, and the other from France. But both traditions reflect the history of Canada and the experience of being a Canadian. The authors in each category of the table are listed in chronological order.

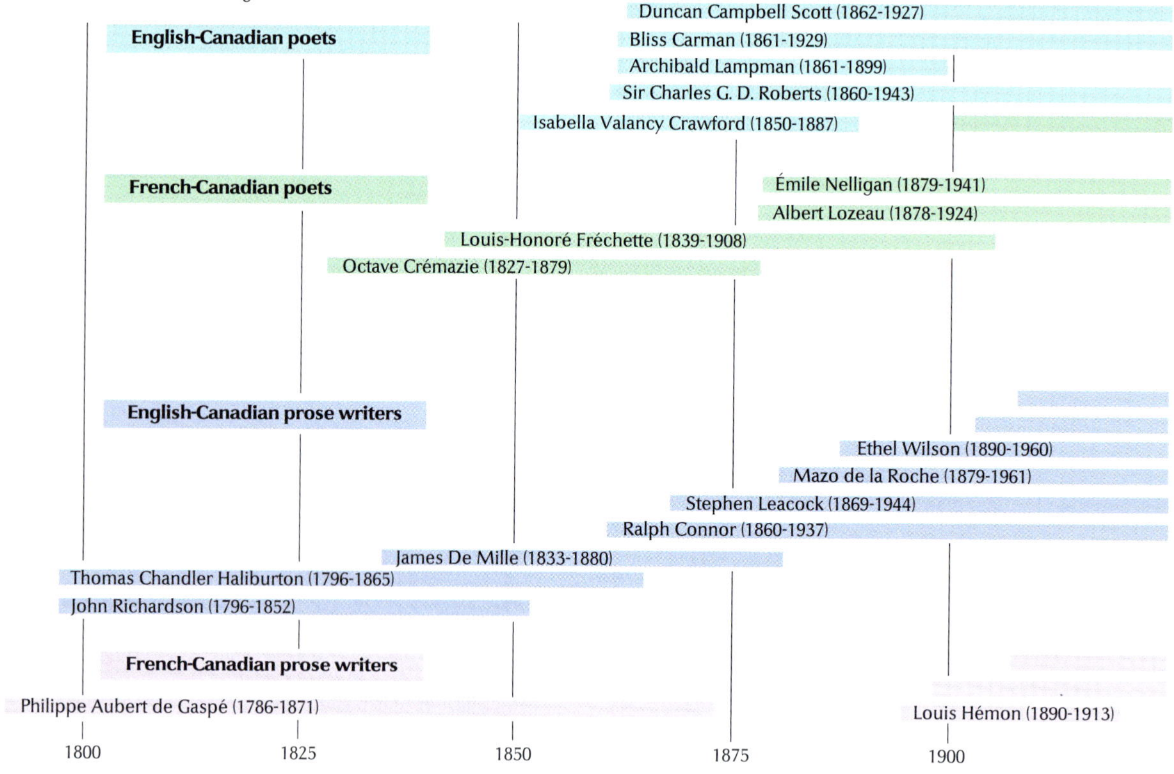

gomery began to publish and quickly gained wide popularity. Connor was the first novelist to write about the Canadian West. In addition, he wrote a series of novels that includes *The Man from Glengarry* (1901), a vivid portrait of pioneer settlements in Connor's native Ontario. In 1908, Montgomery published *Anne of Green Gables,* one of the most beloved Canadian novels. The novel earned Montgomery an international reputation.

Other literature of the period includes short stories, travel and nature sketches, and autobiographies by such writers as Isabella Valancy Crawford, Anna Brownell Jameson, and Catharine Parr Traill. Stephen Leacock wrote *Sunshine Sketches of a Little Town* (1912), a humorous work that remains a Canadian classic.

Literature between the world wars

Modern literary styles were slow to come to Canada. Such writers as Connor, Crémazie, and Mazo de la Roche enjoyed wide popularity well into the 1900's with their traditional fiction. De la Roche wrote 16 novels about the Whiteoak family, beginning with *Jalna* (1927). But new voices were also beginning to be heard.

In Quebec, Louis Hémon expressed the typical romantic view of rural life in *Maria Chapdelaine* (1914). A more realistic novel, *Trente Arpents* (1938), written by Ringuet (pen name of Philippe Panneton), criticized the hardships of rural life. The School of Montreal poets continued to be important. In addition, some younger poets produced complex psychological verse that gained influence after the end of World War II. Hector de Saint-Denys Garneau, Alain Grandbois, and Anne Hébert rank as the most significant of these poets.

Canadian dramatists wrote few works during the period immediately after the war. One limiting factor on playwrights in Quebec was the involvement of the Roman Catholic Church. The church opposed the performance of plays that it considered antifamily or antivirtue. The influence of the church restrained the activity of playwrights and performers. Traveling theater companies from Europe and the United States dominated Canadian stages.

Many English-Canadian writers were influenced by the painters known as the *Group of Seven.* This group inspired a break from empty traditional forms and themes, especially narrow nationalism and the sentimental treatment of nature. Poets who turned to modern themes were E. J. Pratt, F. R. Scott, A. J. M. Smith, Dorothy Livesay, A. M. Klein, and Earle Birney.

Pratt is best known for his long narrative poems written in traditional verse forms. They include his epic poem, *Brébeuf and His Brethren* (1940). The other poets produced more experimental works. In 1927, Scott satirized the conservative poetry establishment in "The Canadian Authors Meet." Smith used free verse in his

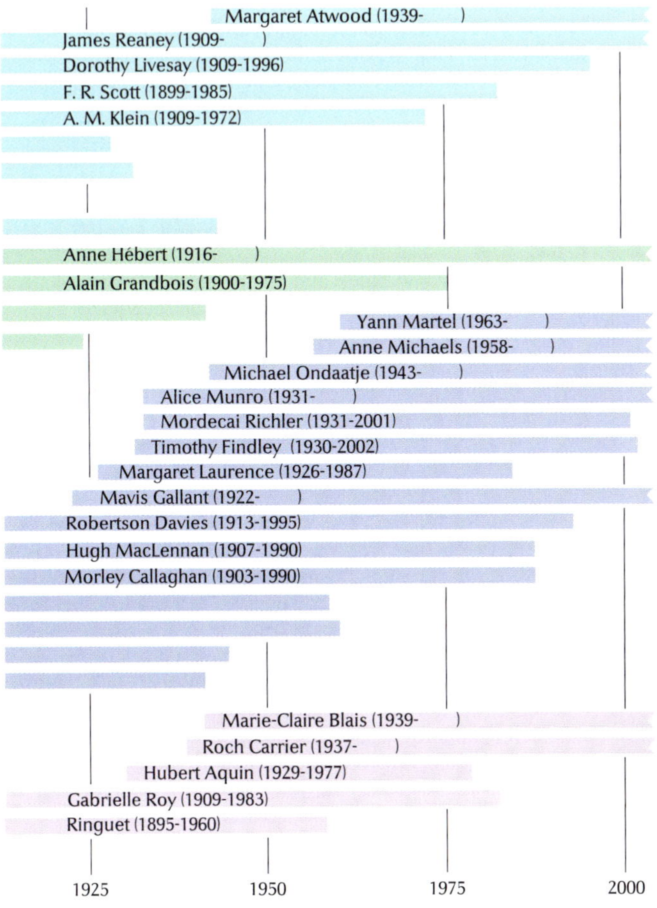

Wacousta **(1832) by John Richardson**

Whiteoaks of Jalna **(1929) by Mazo de la Roche**

WORLD BOOK illustrations by Anthony Saris

poem "The Lonely Land" (1926). Livesay expressed her socialist political views in "Day and Night" (1935), an expressionistic work that celebrates brotherhood. Klein was a learned writer with a knowledge of the cultural traditions of English Canada, French Canada, and Judaism. *The Rocking Chair and Other Poems* (1948) includes Klein's best poetry. Birney became known for technically skillful, experimental poetry in such works as *David* (1942).

Three important novels appeared in the mid-1920's. They were *Settlers of the Marsh* (1925) by Frederick Philip Grove, *Wild Geese* (1925) by Martha Ostenso, and *Grain* (1926) by Robert Stead. These works signaled a trend toward greater realism in Canadian novels. The remarkable novel *As for Me and My House* (1941) by Sinclair Ross used the diary form. It provided a complex, subtle, and moving exploration of the human mind.

Drama was represented later in this period by the works of such playwrights as Herman Voaden, Gwen Pharis Ringwood, and Merrill Denison. Voaden became known for the innovative staging of his expressionist theater. Ringwood's more realistic *Still Stands the House* (1939) explores the alienation of prairie life. Denison's plays include satires and historical romances. The year 1933 marked the beginning of the Dominion Drama Festival and the opening of the Banff School of the Theatre. Together, the festival and the school established a firm base for Canadian theater and playwriting.

Modern literature: 1945 to the present

Since 1945, Québécois fiction has rapidly expanded into an intense and experimental body of writing. Gabrielle Roy's *Bonheur d'occasion* (1945) is a celebrated study of life among Montreal's poor French-speaking Canadians. Hubert Aquin wrote powerful, disturbing fiction. His works include *Prochain épisode* (1965), a detective story and political allegory; *L'Antiphonaire* (1969); and *Neige noire* (1974), cast in the form of a film script. Réjean Ducharme's *L'Avalée des avalés* (1966) describes a young woman's rebellion.

Other important Québécois fiction includes Marie-Claire Blais's novel about Quebec society, *Une Saison dans la vie d'Emmanuel* (1965). Roch Carrier's trilogy on Quebec life begins with *La Guerre, Yes Sir!* (1968). Victor-Lévy Beaulieu wrote *Monsieur Melville* (1978), a three-volume work. Anne Hébert based her novels *Kamouraska* (1970) and *Les Fous de Bassan* (1982) on actual cases of murder and rape.

Modern English-Canadian fiction generally has been less experimental than Québécois writing. Hugh MacLennan's novel *Two Solitudes* (1945) explores conflicts between Canada's English and French cultures. *The Double Hook* (1959) by Sheila Watson is a poetic, symbolic treatment of violence and rebirth in an isolated community.

© Karsh from Rapho Guillumette

Robertson Davies

Several major authors wrote well-crafted novels about life in different regions of Canada. Among Ethel Wilson's best-known works is *Swamp Angel* (1954), set in British Columbia. Margaret Laurence set *The Stone Angel* (1964) and *The Diviners* (1974) in the fictional town of Manawaka, Manitoba. Robertson Davies set many novels in Ontario towns. He first gained fame for his Deptford trilogy—*Fifth Business* (1970), *The Manticore* (1972), and *World of Wonders* (1975). Jack Hodgins wrote about Vancouver Island in *The Honorary Patron* (1987) and other novels. Mordecai Richler wrote a Canadian epic in *Solomon Gursky Was Here* (1989).

Several modern novelists are also poets. They include Margaret Atwood, George Bowering, Robert Kroetsch, and Michael Ondaatje. Such novels as *Surfacing* (1972), *Cat's Eye* (1988), and *Amazing Grace* (1997) earned Atwood an international reputation. Kroetsch wrote *The Studhorse Man* (1969) and *Badlands* (1975), two boisterous, comical tales about the West. Bowering's fiction, especially *Burning Water* (1980), is an ironic combination of history and fiction. Ondaatje gained international acclaim with his novel *The English Patient* (1992).

Rudy Wiebe traced the struggles of First Nations peoples—Canada's Indians, Inuit, and other native peoples—in such novels as *The Temptations of Big Bear* (1973). He turned his attention to the Canadian Arctic in *A Discovery of Strangers* (1994). Joy Kogawa explored the treatment of Japanese Canadians during World War II in *Obasan* (1981). Masterful short-story writers include Clark Blaise, Timothy Findley, Mavis Gallant, Jack Hodgins, Hugh Hood, Alice Munro, and Audrey Thomas. Significant First Nations authors include fiction writers Beatrice Culleton, Tom King, and Ruby Slipperjack, and playwright Tomson Highway. During the late 1900's, a number of new novelists emerged who represented the cultural diversity of Canada. They included Rohinton Mistry, Aritha van Herk, Carol Shields, Anne Michaels, Wayson Choy, Sky Lee, and Guy Vanderhaeghe.

Modern Canadian poets include Margaret Avison, P. K. Page, and Phyllis Webb. Their handling of language and complex psychological and philosophical themes challenges readers. Al Purdy employs casual, everyday language, which masks his passionate concern for modern society. D. G. Jones, Irving Layton, and Eli Mandel have expanded the boundaries of poetry. The next generation of Canadian poets included Atwood, Bowering, Dennis Lee, Gwendolyn MacEwen, and Barrie Phillip Nichol, who wrote as bp Nichol. Nichol finished the first two books of his best-known poem, *The Martyrology,* in 1972. He had expanded the work into six published books by his death in 1988. By 2000, several new poets had emerged, notably Stephanie Bolster, Dionne Brand, Robert Bringhurst, George Elliott Clarke, Lorna Crozier, Kristjana Gunnars, M. Nourbese Philip, Armand Garnet Ruffo, Sharon Thesen, Jim Wong-Chu, and Jan Zwicky. Inuk writer and artist Alootook Ipellie united these elements in *Arctic Dreams and Nightmares* (1993).

In Quebec, the years after World War II marked a new burst of energy associated with poet Gaston Miron and the Hexagone Press. A group called the *Hexagone Poets* was indebted to such Quebec surrealist painters as Paul-Émile Borduas. Borduas and a group of associates rejected the past in *Refus global* (1948), a declaration foreshadowing the Quebec nationalist movement.

The 1960's brought the Quiet Revolution, a movement

Canapress
Margaret Atwood

Canapress
Michel Tremblay

to defend Québécois rights. Some people called for Quebec to separate from the rest of Canada. The movement inspired such Quebec poets as Paul Chamberland, Gérald Godin, and Michèle Lalonde to new heights of political protest poetry. By the mid-1970's, such poets as Louky Bersianik, Nicole Brossard, Madeleine Gagnon, and Yolande Villemaire began writing feminist works. They used humor in attacking attitudes of male superiority. Gagnon's *Lueur* (1979) combines poetry and fiction with the historical and philosophical essay. Other important Québécois writers include France Théoret, Raoul Dugay, François Charron, and Yves Boisvert.

Modern Canadian drama has become a vital and varied form of expression since the mid-1900's. Michel Tremblay became the best-known Québécois playwright. His works include two plays about life in poor sections of Montreal, *Les Belles-soeurs* (1968) and *À toi pour toujours, ta Marie-Lou* (1973). Other notable Québécois playwrights include Robert Gurik, Robert Lepage, and Michel Marc Bouchard. Gurik wrote important experimental plays on political themes. Lepage became known for such multimedia plays as *The Dragons' Trilogy* (1986), *Polygraph* (1988), and *Needles and Opium* (1992). Bouchard wrote about family struggles in *The Orphan Muses* (1989).

Two significant English-Canadian plays in 1967 were John Herbert's *Fortune and Men's Eyes* and George Ryga's *The Ecstasy of Rita Joe.* Both are violent but deeply moving plays about society's misfits and outsiders—reformatory inmates in Herbert's play and Indians in Vancouver in Ryga's drama. Canadian poet James Reaney began writing lyrical and symbolic dramas in the 1960's.

During the 1970's, many theater companies, including an experimental group in Toronto called Theatre Passe Muraille, devoted themselves to performing Canadian plays. Some companies performed *collective creations,* plays developed by a group of actors, along with a director and, sometimes, a playwright. The best-known collective creations include *The Farm Show* (1976), *Paper Wheat* (1978), and Rick Salutin's lively treatment of Canadian history, *1837: The Farmers' Revolt* (1976).

The leading English-Canadian playwrights are Sharon Pollock and George F. Walker. Pollock creates complex psychological feminist plays about family life and plays that explore issues of racism based on historical events. Walker's work is characterized by his flair for spectacle and satire. Other important playwrights include Michael Cook, David French, Wendy Lill, Joan MacLeod, Mansel Robinson, and Judith Thompson. Sherrill E. Grace

Related articles in *World Book* include:

Atwood, Margaret
Berton, Pierre
Brooke, Frances
Buchan, John
Callaghan, Morley
Carman, Bliss
Carr, Emily
Cohen, Leonard
Davies, Robertson
De la Roche, Mazo
Drummond, William Henry
Frye, Northrop
Gallant, Mavis
Governor General's Literary Awards
Grey Owl
Group of Seven
Grove, Frederick P.
Hémon, Louis
Johnson, Pauline
Klein, A. M.
Lampman, Archibald
Laurence, Margaret
Layton, Irving
Leacock, Stephen Butler
Lemelin, Roger
Lowry, Malcolm
MacLennan, Hugh
Mair, Charles
McCrae, John
McLuhan, Marshall
Montgomery, Lucy Maud
Moodie, Susanna
Mowat, Farley
Munro, Alice
Pratt, E. J.
Reaney, James
Richler, Mordecai
Roberts, Charles G. D.
Roy, Gabrielle
Sangster, Charles
Scott, Duncan Campbell
Scott, F. R.
Service, Robert William
Souster, Raymond
Wilson, Ethel

Additional resources

Benson, Eugene, and Toye, William, eds. *The Oxford Companion to Canadian Literature.* 2nd ed. Oxford, 1997.
Kroeller, Eva-Marie, ed. *The Cambridge Companion to Canadian Literature.* Cambridge, 2004.
Lecker, Robert, and others, eds. *Canadian Writers and Their Works.* 22 vols. ECW Pr., 1982-1992.
New, W. H. *Encyclopedia of Literature in Canada.* Univ. of Toronto Pr., 2002. *A History of Canadian Literature.* 2nd ed. McGill-Queen's Univ. Pr., 2003.

Canadian Mounted Police. See Royal Canadian Mounted Police.

Canadian Reform Conservative Alliance. See Canadian Alliance.

Canadian Shield is a huge, rocky region that curves around Hudson Bay like a giant horseshoe. The Shield covers half the land area of Canada. It includes most of Baffin Island, all of Labrador, nine-tenths of Quebec, over half of Ontario and Manitoba, and large areas in Saskatchewan, Nunavut, and the Northwest Territories. About 95 percent of the Shield's 1,864,000-square-mile (4,827,738-square-kilometer) area lies in Canada.

The Shield also dips into the United States to form the Adirondack Mountains of New York and the Superior Uplands of Michigan, Wisconsin, and Minnesota. The Canadian Shield is also called the *Laurentian Plateau,* after the Laurentian Mountains of southern Quebec. See **Canada** (The Canadian Shield).

Geologists estimate that the rock formations that make up most of the Canadian Shield range in age from about 600 million years to the age of Earth itself—about 4.6 billion years. Most of the rocks have undergone one or more periods of mountain-building. During these periods, extreme heat and pressure produced high mountains of granite, diorite, and other crystalline rocks. Weathering and erosion wore down the mountains.

Today, much of the Canadian Shield's central and northwestern part is low and flat. Mountains in the northeastern part of the Shield rise as high as 8,500 feet (2,590 meters). Relatively few people live in the region. Only small areas are suitable for agriculture. The Shield is dotted with lakes, some of which have become famous resorts. Large forests in the southern section rank among Canada's most important natural resources. The Canadian Shield is also rich in copper, gold, iron, nickel, uranium, and other minerals. Roger Nadeau

See also **Earth** (picture: Precambrian rocks).

Travel Bureau, Michigan Department of Commerce

Emil Schulthess, Black Star

Canals have been used to transport goods, people, and water for thousands of years. The modern Soo Canals on the United States-Canadian border, *left*, link Lakes Superior and Huron. The centuries-old Grand Canal, *right*, extends for over 1,000 miles (1,600 kilometers) through China.

Canal is a waterway dug across land. Canals have served as important means of transporting goods and water for thousands of years. Canals are usually used for shipping large quantities of goods when the speed of movement is not important. In such cases, canals are cheaper than such alternatives as railroads or trucks.

There are two major types of canals: *navigation canals* and *water conveyance canals.* Navigation canals link bodies of water, enabling vessels to travel between them. Water conveyance canals, which include irrigation canals and drainage canals, carry water from one place to another and are often referred to as *aqueducts* or *irrigation structures.* This article deals mainly with navigation canals.

Navigation canals may connect two similar bodies of water, such as two lakes, or two different waterways, such as a lake and a river. Navigation canals also link oceans with seaports that lie near, but not directly on, the oceans. In addition, many navigation canals are parts of *canalized rivers*—that is, rivers whose navigable stretches are connected by a series of dams and locks. These structures enable vessels to travel an entire river by avoiding waterfalls, shallow areas, and other navigation hazards. Such major inland waterways as the Mississippi and Ohio rivers in the United States and the Rhine River in Europe are canalized rivers.

Early canals were ditches 3 to 5 feet (0.9 to 1.5 meters) deep and 15 to 40 feet (4.6 to 12 meters) wide. Through the years, boats and canals have become larger. The Panama Canal, opened in 1914, is about 40 feet (12.2 meters) deep and about 500 feet (152.4 meters) wide. Its locks are about 110 feet (33.5 meters) wide.

Most navigation canals are built and operated by government agencies. The Corps of Engineers designs, builds, and maintains the navigation canals of the United States. These waterways are used by industry and by private citizens. But many water conveyance canals are privately owned. They are used by such agencies and businesses as irrigation districts and public utilities.

Planning and building a canal

When planning a canal, engineers study the terrain to determine the course of a canal and to decide whether it will need locks. The width and depth of a canal are based on the size of the vessels it will handle. Environmental specialists also consider how a canal will affect surrounding plant and animal life. For example, a canal might disrupt the migration of certain animals and alter their food supply. Water conveyance canals sometimes have crossover bridges to allow for animal migration. However, such bridges may be impractical for large ship navigation canals.

The construction of a canal primarily involves the digging and moving of earth and rock. Such materials as clay or crushed rock may be added to a canal to reduce leakage and prevent erosion. Some canals are lined with asphalt or concrete.

Canal locks

Canal locks are rectangular chambers that enable ships to move from one water level to another by varying the amount of water in the lock. Most locks are made of concrete and have watertight gates at each end. Water flows in and out of locks by gravity, and so no pumps are needed. Locks do, however, require a supply of water at the upper level of the canal. As a result, some locks have special reservoirs and auxiliary canals to ensure an adequate water supply when the normal supply runs low.

Locks are used to overcome changes of elevation along the course of a canal and variations in tide level near a seacoast. To move a vessel upstream, where the water level is higher, the water level in the lock is lowered to that of the water just downstream. The downstream gates are opened and the ship moves slowly into the lock. After the ship is secured to posts, the gates close and the valves open to fill the lock with water from upstream. The flow of water is carefully controlled to prevent the ship from colliding with another vessel or from ramming the gates. As the lock fills, the ship rises to the level of the water upstream. The upstream gates are then opened and the ship passes through. To move a ship downstream, the process is reversed. After a ship enters the lock, the water is drained out and the ship is lowered to the downstream level.

Major canals of the world

The Panama and Suez canals are the most important canals in the world. Both of them provide valuable navigation shortcuts and have figured prominently in military affairs and international politics.

The Panama Canal links the Atlantic and Pacific oceans. It extends from Limón Bay on the Atlantic to the Bay of Panama on the Pacific, a distance of about 51 miles (82 kilometers). It is the busiest canal in the world. About 12,000 ships pass through it annually.

The Panama Canal reduces the sea route between New York City and San Francisco by more than 7,800 miles (12,600 kilometers). Without the canal, ships traveling between the two cities would have to pass around the southern tip of South America. The Panama Canal played a strategic role during World War II (1939-1945) by enabling United States naval forces to move quickly and easily between the Atlantic and Pacific oceans.

The Suez Canal extends for about 118 miles (190 kilometers), including entrance channels at both ends, between Port Said, Egypt, and the Gulf of Suez, an arm of the Red Sea. It allows ships to move directly between the Mediterranean and Red seas and serves as a major water link between Europe and Asia. For example, the canal shortens sea voyages between Britain and India by about 6,000 miles (9,700 kilometers). Without the canal, ships traveling between the two countries would have to pass around the southern coast of Africa. The Suez Canal was blocked by sunken ships in 1967, during the Arab-Israeli War, and sea traffic between Asia and Europe was disrupted. Egypt reopened the canal in 1975.

Major canals in the United States and Canada include the Soo Canals, the Chicago Sanitary and Ship Canal, and the All-American Canal. Canals also form an important part of the St. Lawrence Seaway and other major waterways.

The Soo Canals, on the United States-Canadian border, connect Lakes Superior and Huron. The Chicago Sanitary and Ship Canal enables ships to travel between Lake Michigan and the Mississippi River via the Chicago, Des Plaines, and Illinois rivers. The All-American Waterway, in southern California, carries water from the Colorado River to the Imperial and Coachella valleys, important agricultural areas.

The St. Lawrence Seaway consists of a system of canals and locks, the St. Lawrence River, and several lakes. It extends for about 450 miles (724 kilometers) from the eastern end of Lake Erie to Montreal, Quebec, and includes the Welland Ship Canal. It links the Great Lakes and the Atlantic Ocean.

How a ship moves through a canal lock

To move upstream, a vessel enters a lock in which the water level has been lowered to that of the water just downstream. The downstream gates are then closed, and the lock is filled with water. After the water level in the lock reaches that of the water upstream, the upstream gates are opened, and the ship passes through. To move a ship downstream, the process is reversed.

WORLD BOOK diagram by George Suyeoka

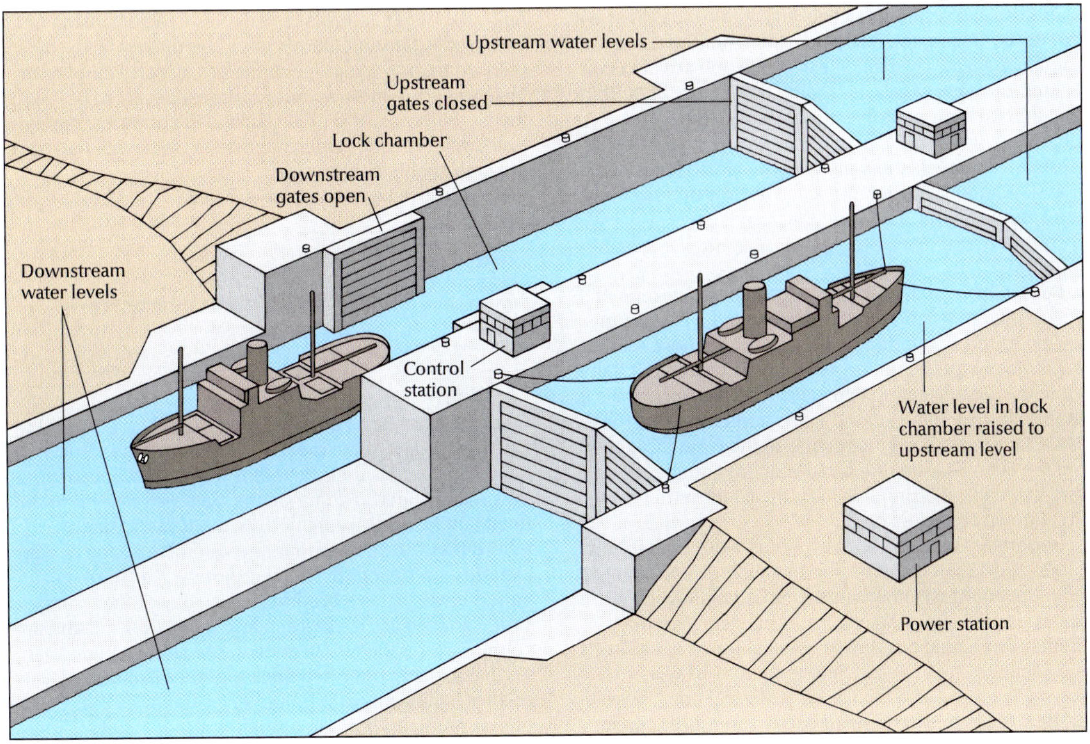

Important ship canals of the world

Canal	Location	Length In mi	Length In km	Minimum width In ft	Minimum width In m	Minimum depth In ft	Minimum depth In m	Number of locks	Year opened
Albert	Belgium	80.8	130	335	102	15	4.5	6	1939
Amsterdam-Rhine	Netherlands	45	72.4	246	75	7.2	2.2	4	1952
Cape Cod	Massachusetts	17.5	28.2	500	152	32	10	0	1914
Chesapeake and Delaware	Delaware, Maryland	46	74	450	137	35	10.7	0	1829
Chicago Sanitary and Ship	Illinois	30.6	49.2	175	53.3	9	2.7	1	1900
Corinth	Greece	3.9	6.3	81	24.6	26	8	0	1893
Erie Canal	New York	363	584	120	36.6	12	3.7	57	1825
Grand Canal	China	1000	1609	100	30.5	2	0.6	24	610
Kiel (Nord-Ostsee)	Germany	61.3	98.6	336	102.5	36	11	8	1895
Manchester Ship	England	36	58	120	36.6	22	6.7	5	1894
McClellan-Kerr Arkansas River System	Arkansas, Oklahoma	445	716	150	45.7	9	2.7	17	1970
Moscow	Russia	80	128	98	30	18	5.5	7	1937
North Sea	Netherlands	15.3	24.7	525	160	49.5	15.1	4	1876
Panama	Panama	50.7	81.6	550	168	45	13.7	12	1914
Sabine-Neches Waterway	Texas	93.7	150.8	200	61	30	9.1	0	1916
Saint Lawrence Seaway*	Canada, New York	182	293	200	61	27	8.2	7	1959
Soo (Sault Sainte Marie)	Canada	1.4	2.2	61	18.6	19	5.8	1	1895
Soo (St. Marys Falls Canal and Locks)	Michigan	1.8	2.9	300	91.4	25.5	7.8	4	1855
Suez†	Egypt	117.9	189.7	741	226	64	19.5	0	1869
Tennessee-Tombigbee Waterway	Alabama, Mississippi	234	377	300	91.4	9	2.7	10	1985
Volga-Baltic	Russia	528	850	70	21.4	11	3.5	7	1964
Welland Ship	Canada	26	42	200	61	27	8.2	8	1932
White Sea-Baltic	Russia	138	222	46	14	10	3.2	19	1933

*Excludes passage through Lake Ontario and Welland Ship Canal.
†Includes entrance channels at both ends.
Sources: Canal officials; U.S. Army Corps of Engineers; Transport Canada; *Soviet Geography.*

Major canals in other countries include the Grand Canal in China and several canals in Russia and in Western Europe. The Grand Canal is a system of canals and navigable sections of the Yangtze and Huai rivers and the Huang He (Yellow River). It extends 1,000 miles (1,609 kilometers) through China. It is the world's longest artificially created waterway.

In Russia, a system of canals links the Volga River with the Arctic Ocean, the Baltic Sea, the Don River, and Moscow. Major rivers in Western Europe are also connected by many canals, including the Amsterdam-Rhine Canal in the Netherlands and the Albert Canal and Charleroi-Brussels Canal in Belgium. The Kiel Canal in Germany connects the Baltic and the North seas. Germany's Rhine-Main-Danube canal links waterway systems between the North and Black seas.

History

People have built and used canals for thousands of years. The ancient Egyptians constructed a navigation canal around a waterfall on the Nile River more than 4,000 years ago. About the same time, the ancient Babylonians built navigation and water conveyance canals in the fertile area between the Tigris and Euphrates rivers. The Chinese began construction of the Grand Canal during the 500's B.C., but the canal was not completed until the A.D. 1200's. During the 900's, the Chinese built the first known canal locks.

Important European canal systems were built in the 1100's and 1200's in the region that includes present-day Belgium and the Netherlands. The Canal du Midi, completed in 1681, became an important waterway in France. The Canal du Midi enabled ships to travel from the Mediterranean Sea at Sète to the Bay of Biscay by way of Toulouse and the Garonne River. Today, however, its size permits only small barge and tourist traffic.

The first U.S. ship canal was built in 1793 on the Connecticut River in Massachusetts. The Erie Canal in New York, completed in 1825, opened up the Great Lakes region to ships from the Atlantic Ocean. It also helped make New York City the nation's financial center.

The success of the Erie Canal also led to a great burst of canal building in the United States. But in the 1830's, railroads began to replace canals as a major means of transporting goods. Goods could be moved faster by railroad than by canal. Nevertheless, canals still play an important role in shipping goods, especially in Belgium, the Netherlands, and other European countries. Today, tourism has brought increased traffic to canals that pass through scenic countryside. Paul D. Trotta

Related articles in *World Book* include:

Aqueduct
Atlantic Intracoastal Waterway
Chesapeake and Ohio Canal
Corinth Canal
Erie Canal
Inland waterway
Irrigation
Kiel Canal
Netherlands (Transportation)
New York State Canal System
Ohio River
Panama Canal
Saint Lawrence Seaway
Soo Canals
Suez Canal
Welland Ship Canal

Canal Zone. See Panama Canal Zone.

Canary is one of the most popular bird pets. People keep canaries for their beautiful songs, and because they make cheerful companions. Canaries belong to the finch family. They are named for the Canary Islands, where they are still found in the wild. The songs of wild canaries are not nearly so melodious as those of the tamed birds that are bred for the quality of their song. Wild canaries are dark green and olive-colored, and are seldom over 8 inches (20 centimeters) long. Wild canaries live in pairs, but often flock together like their distant relatives, the American goldfinches. Canaries build nests of dry moss and grass in branches about 10 feet (3 me-

WORLD BOOK illustration by Trevor Boyer, Linden Artists Ltd.

Canaries are popular pets because of their lively song. A wild canary, *left,* has darker markings than a tame one, *right.*

ters) from the ground. A canary lays four or five eggs.

Most tame canaries are bright yellow, but some are pale yellow. If fed red peppers, canaries may be bright orange.

During the late 1400's, canaries were brought to Spain from the Canary Islands. English, French, Scottish, and Belgian canary breeders have developed many varieties with strange appearances. Some tame canaries bred in Lancashire, England, grow 8 inches (20 centimeters) long. Scottish canaries are long, thin birds with tails that curl between their legs. Belgian canaries have such long necks that their heads droop. French canaries have curly patterns of feathers all over their bodies.

The best singing canaries, such as the St. Andreasburg variety, are bred in the Harz Mountains of Germany. Different kinds of singing canaries are named for the qualities of their songs. *Rollers,* for example, have a rolling, gurgling song.

Canaries should be kept in clean cages that are large enough to let the birds fly for exercise. Although canaries eat canary seed, they also need green food. In addition, canaries should be given water for drinking and bathing.

Because canaries are more sensitive to poisonous gases than human beings, canaries have been used to detect such gases on battlefields and in coal mines. Each year, canaries selectively replace some of their songs with different songs. As a result, canaries have become important laboratory subjects for studies of selective forgetting and learning.

In North America, the name *wild canary* is often given to the American goldfinch and the yellow warbler, both of which look much like the tame canary.

Edward H. Burtt, Jr.

Scientific classification. Canaries belong to the finch family, Fringillidae. The common canary is *Serinus canaria.*

See also **Bird** (picture: Birds as pets); **Goldfinch.**

Canary, Martha Jane. See **Calamity Jane.**

The Canary Islands lie off the northwest coast of the mainland of Africa. The islands are part of Spain and are divided into two provinces.

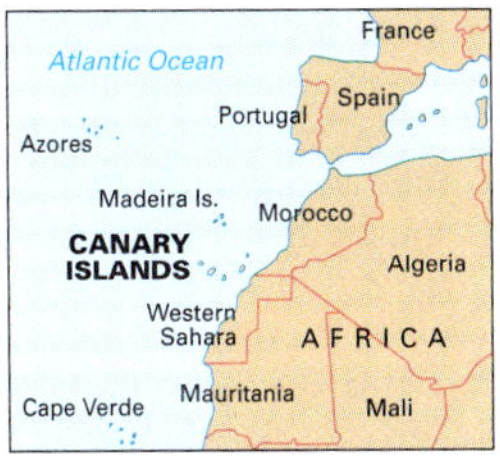

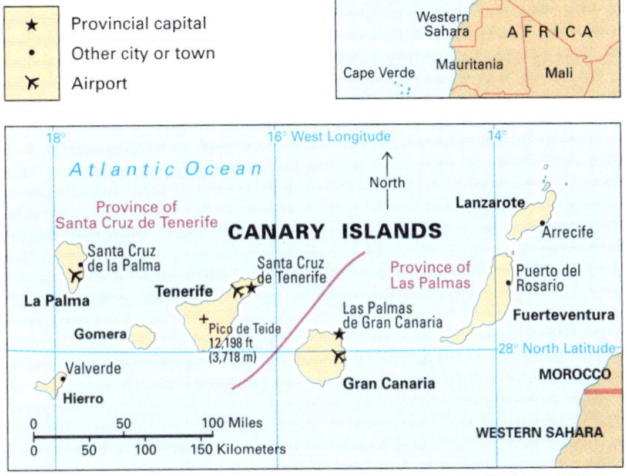

WORLD BOOK maps

Canary Islands make up two provinces of Spain. This group of 13 islands lies in the Atlantic Ocean, about 60 miles (97 kilometers) off the northwest coast of the mainland of Africa. The islands cover 2,796 square miles (7,242 square kilometers) and have 626 miles (1,007 kilometers) of coastline. Seven are inhabited. They have a population of about 1 ⅔ million. Ships going down the West African coast can stop there to refuel.

The islands were divided into two provinces in 1927. The province of Santa Cruz de Tenerife includes the islands of Tenerife, La Palma, Gomera, and Hierro. The capital also is called Santa Cruz de Tenerife. Las Palmas province includes Gran Canaria, Lanzarote, and Fuerteventura. Its capital is Las Palmas de Gran Canaria. The largest island in the Canaries is Tenerife, which has the port of Santa Cruz de Tenerife.

The Canaries are mountainous, and many of the mountains are volcanic. The highest peak is 12,198-foot (3,718-meter) Pico de Teide. The islands have fertile soil and a mild and healthful climate. Crops include grain,

Hutchison Library

A sunny beach at Las Palmas in the Canary Islands attracts many vacationers who enjoy the city's mild climate.

fruit, vegetables, and flowers. The people are of Spanish descent, mixed with the Guanches, a blond-haired people who originally lived there. The inhabitants of Gomera communicate over distances with a whistled language that imitates spoken Spanish.

Sailors in ancient times named the Canary Islands *Canaria* from the Latin word *canis* (dog) because they found large, fierce dogs there. Canary birds are so called because they were first found on the Canary Islands. The islands once belonged to Queen Catherine of Castile, and later to the Portuguese prince, Henry the Navigator. In 1479, they were returned to Spain.

Hartmut S. Walter

See also **Africa** (terrain map); **Columbus, Christopher**.

Canasta, *kuh NAS tuh,* is the name of a high-scoring card game that originated in Uruguay. It is a variation of rummy and may be played by two to six people who form two opposing partnerships. The object of canasta is to score points by forming *melds* of three or more cards of the same rank, including at least one meld of seven cards. A player cannot build sequences of numbers as in other rummy games. A seven-card meld is called a *canasta,* which is Spanish for *basket.*

Canasta is played with two decks of cards and four jokers. The jokers and twos are "wild" cards, and can be used as substitutes for other cards in forming melds. The object of the game is to score 5,000 points.

R. Wayne Schmittberger

Canberra, *KAN behr uh* or *KAN buhr uh* (pop. 311,518), is the capital of Australia and the nation's leading example of large-scale city planning. The city lies within the Australian Capital Territory in southeastern Australia. For location, see **Australia** (political map).

The city is built around several hills and ridges on rolling plains. The Molonglo River flows through Canberra. A dam on the river forms Lake Burley Griffin in the central part of the city. The lake divides Canberra into northern and southern sections. The northern section includes the commercial center of Canberra, the city hall, the Australian National University, and the University of Canberra. The southern section, built around Capital Hill, includes the meeting place of Australia's Parliament, most of the other principal national government buildings, the Australian National Gallery, the National Library, and about 75 embassies.

National Capitol Development Commission

Canberra is Australia's capital. Australia's National Library stands along Lake Burley Griffin in the center of the city.

Residential areas of bungalows and apartment buildings extend north and south of the center of Canberra. Some small industrial plants operate near the center of the city, but most industrial activity is in the suburbs. Several new towns have been developed north and south of Canberra. These projects began during the 1960's. The towns have their own commercial centers.

Economy. The national government employs about half of the city's workers. Other leading economic activities include construction, retail and wholesale trade, and tourism. Buses provide public transportation in Canberra. The streets have special lanes reserved for buses. An airport and railroad station serve the city.

History. Aborigines, the earliest inhabitants of Australia, lived in the Canberra area at least 21,000 years ago. In 1820, British explorers became the first white people to reach the area. White settlers soon established ranches and farms there. In 1901, when the Commonwealth of Australia was established, Canberra was still a small rural community. But in 1908, the government selected the general area as the site for a national capital. The following year, Charles R. Scrivener, a New South Wales district surveyor, recommended the city's present site. In 1912, a city plan by the Chicago architect Walter Burley Griffin was chosen for the capital.

Construction of the capital began in 1913. In 1927, the Australian Parliament met in Canberra for the first time. Canberra grew slowly until the late 1950's. Since then, its population has increased from about 40,000 to about 310,000. In 1988, a new Parliament House was built.

The federal government administered Canberra until 1989. Then the Australian Capital Territory gained the same powers of self-government as Australia's states. Voters in the territory elected a parliament called the Legislative Assembly, which became responsible for the administration of Canberra. Alan Fitzgerald

See also **Australia** (picture); **Australian Capital Territory**.

Cancellation is a method of shortening mathematical problems by striking out terms or factors. To multiply the fractions $\frac{3}{10}$ and $\frac{4}{3}$, a person would get 12, or 4 times 3, for the numerator, and 30, or 10 times 3, for the denominator. The fraction $\frac{12}{30}$ may be reduced by dividing the 12 and 30 by the common factors of 3 and 2. But it is easier to do the divisions before multiplying, rather than after. This is done by cancellation, or by striking out the old terms and replacing them with new ones. The 3's can be divided by 3, and 10 and 4 can be divided by 2:

$$\frac{\overset{1}{\cancel{3}}}{\underset{5}{\cancel{10}}} \times \frac{\overset{2}{\cancel{4}}}{\underset{1}{\cancel{3}}} = \frac{2}{5}$$

To calculate the value of the expression $26 + 7 + 4 - 7$, you can cancel the 7's to avoid the work of adding and subtracting them. In an equation, you can cancel factors or divisors common to both sides, or equal terms that are added to or subtracted from both sides. For example, in the equation $x^2 + y^2 + x - 2 = x^2 + y^2 + 4$, you could cancel the x^2 and y^2 terms by subtracting them from each side of the equation. Robert M. Vancko

See also **Fraction** (Multiplication).

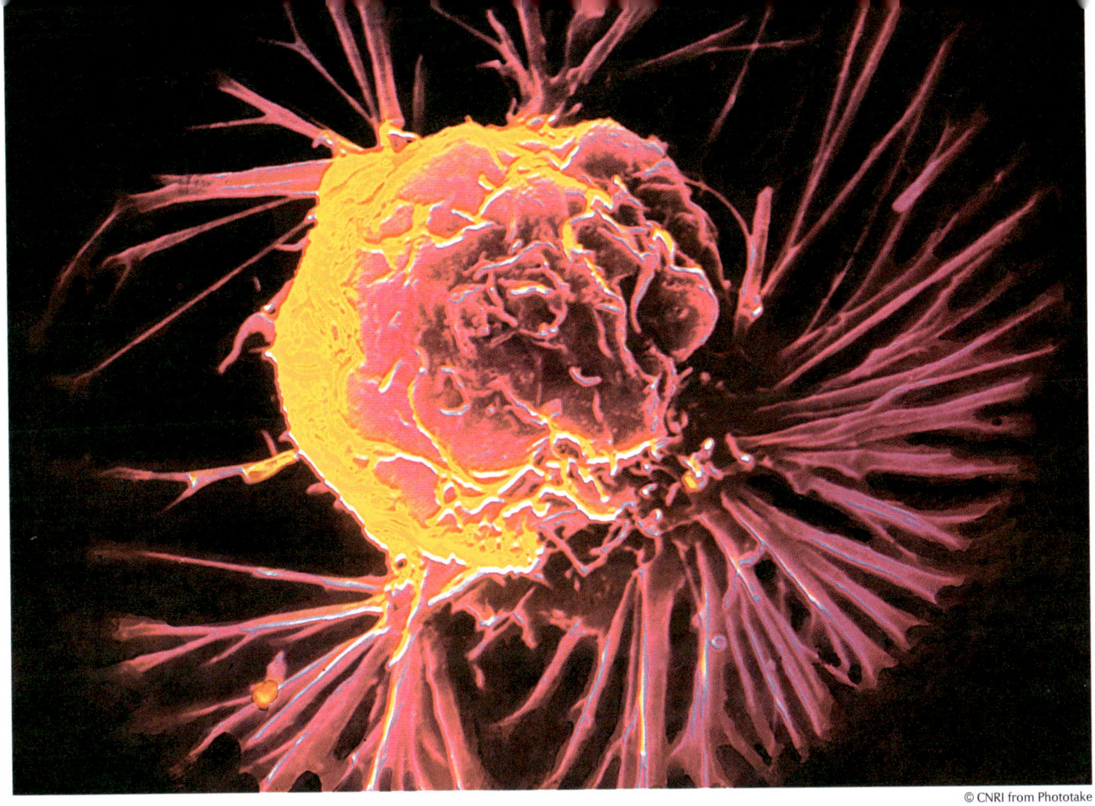

© CNRI from Phototake

Cancer begins in a single cell, as seen in this false-color image of a malignant breast cell, when damaged genes lead to uncontrolled growth and division. The term *cancer* comes from the Latin word for *crab.* The term describes the crablike appearance of advanced cancer tumors.

Cancer

Cancer is a disease in which cells multiply wildly, destroy healthy tissue, and endanger life. About 100 kinds of cancer attack people. Cancer strikes people of all ages but is most common in the middle-aged and the elderly. The disease is a leading cause of death in many countries. Cancer occurs about equally in males and females. The disease can attack any part of the body and may spread to other parts. Cancer occurs in most other animals as well as in people.

The study of the development, treatment, and prevention of cancer is called *oncology.* It includes both research and clinical care. Physicians who specialize in oncology are known as *oncologists.*

Scientists have greatly increased their knowledge of how cancer develops. The cells of all living things contain genes that direct cell growth and reproduction. Cancer arises when these genes become damaged and cells multiply without control. The damaged genes may instruct the cell to divide in an abnormal fashion. Other genes may lose the ability to instruct the cell that it can no longer function and must die. Some damaged genes are changed in ways that enable cancer cells to invade healthy tissue, grow new blood vessels, or spread to other parts of the body.

Some types of abnormalities in genes are inherited. Substances in the environment can also damage genes. A substance that damages genes in a way that can lead to cancer is called a *carcinogen.* Many substances found in nature, both natural and artificial, are carcinogens.

Without treatment, most kinds of cancer are fatal. But methods of diagnosing and treating the disease have improved greatly. About half of all cancer patients now survive at least five years after treatment. People who remain free of cancer during that time have a good chance of remaining permanently free of the disease.

This article discusses major kinds of cancer, causes of the disease, and the main methods of diagnosis and treatment. The article also discusses cancer research.

Marc B. Garnick, the contributor of this article, is Clinical Professor of Medicine at Beth Israel Deaconess Medical Center, Harvard Medical School.

Major types of cancer

Cancers that affect human beings are classified in two ways: (1) by *primary body site*—that is, the part of the body where cancer first develops; and (2) by the type of tissue in which the cancer originates.

Classification by primary body site. Cancer first appears most often in the skin, the female breasts, and the organs of the digestive, respiratory, reproductive, blood-forming, lymphatic, and urinary systems. The number of cases of cancer in these sites varies from country to country. Cancer of the stomach, for example, is much more common in Japan than in the United States or India. Rates of breast cancer are high in the United States and the United Kingdom, but much lower in India and many Asian countries. The following discussion deals with the kinds of cancer that occur most often in many countries.

Skin cancer is the most common type of cancer in the world. Most skin cancers grow slowly and do not spread to other parts of the body. As a result, these can-

How lung cancer develops

Lung cancer, like all other forms of cancer, results from uncontrolled cell growth. Most cases of lung cancer start in the tissue that lines the *bronchi*—that is, the tubes that supply the lungs with air, *below left.* The four pairs of drawings at the right illustrate various stages in the development of such a cancer. The drawings across the top show changes in a portion of the affected tissue. The bottom drawings show, greatly enlarged, changes in the cells that make up the tissue.

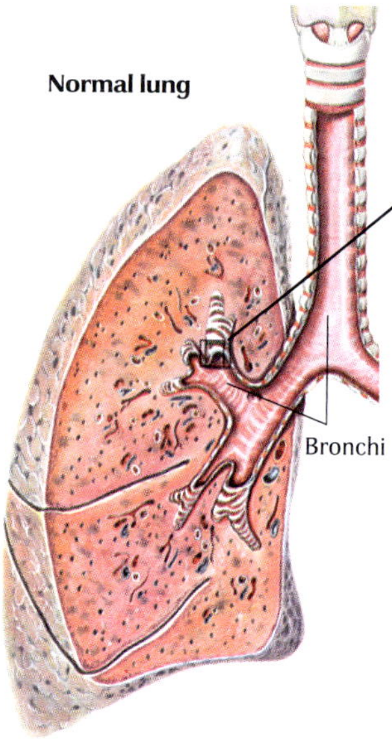

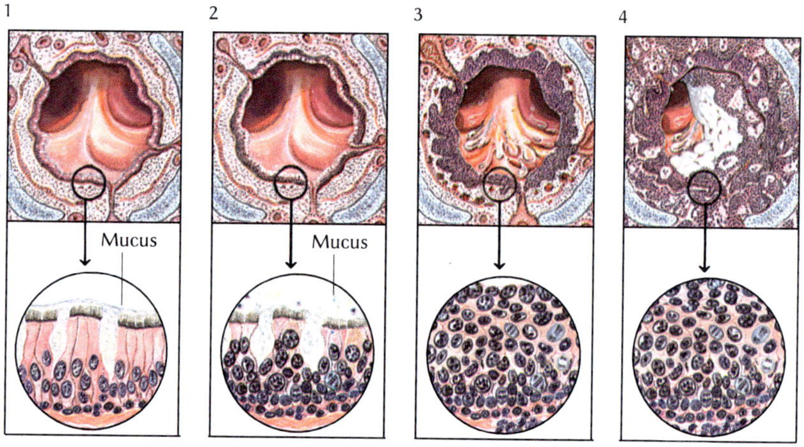

WORLD BOOK illustration by Ernest W. Beck

(1) The lining of a normal bronchus is composed of various kinds of cells. Each kind has a different function. One of the functions is to eliminate mucus from the lung. (2) Cancer begins to develop when certain cells in the lining start to reproduce at a rate faster than normal. As these cells accumulate, they interfere with the elimination of mucus. (3) Some of the rapidly multiplying cells turn into cancer cells. These cells serve no useful purpose but instead crowd out and destroy most neighboring normal cells. Mucus becomes trapped in the lung. (4) The cancer cells form a mass, or *tumor,* that partly blocks the bronchus. Unless surgeons can remove the tumor completely, cancer cells will spread to other sites in the body and eventually cause death.

cers are among the easiest to cure. Most people treated for skin cancer recover completely. However, one form of skin cancer called *malignant melanoma* is particularly dangerous. This type of cancer begins in the skin's pigment cells. If not detected and treated early, it can spread rapidly to other parts of the body.

Breast cancer occurs in both sexes, but it attacks women about 100 times more often than it strikes men. Most of these cancers occur in women over 40 years of age. Female breast cancer patients whose disease is found and treated before it has spread beyond the breast have good long-term survival rates.

Cancers of the digestive organs most commonly affect the parts of the large intestine called the *colon* and the *rectum.* About half of all people treated for cancer of the colon or rectum survive five years or longer after treatment with no return of the disease. Other digestive organs commonly affected by cancer include the esophagus, liver, pancreas, and stomach.

Cancers of the respiratory system involve the larynx and lungs. In most industrial countries, lung cancer kills more people each year than any other kind of cancer. The death rate is high because many lung cancers have spread to other body sites before they are detected.

Cancers of the reproductive system are relatively common among both men and women. The male organ most often affected is a small gland called the *prostate.* Most cases occur in men over 50 years old. Proper treatment can cure the disease in its early stages and control more advanced prostate cancer for many years.

The most common cancers of the female reproductive system affect the *uterus,* the organ in which babies develop. Some cancers arise in the main part of the uterus. Cancer may also affect the lower, necklike part of the organ called the *cervix.* Cancer of the cervix strikes younger women than do other cancers of the uterus.

Cancers of the blood-forming and lymphatic systems. Cancer of the bone marrow and other blood-forming organs is called *leukemia.* In leukemia, immature white blood cells multiply wildly and interfere with production of other vital blood elements.

Cancer may also arise in tissues of the lymphatic system. This system is a network of vessels that returns fluids to the bloodstream and helps fight disease. Lymphatic cancer is called *lymphoma.* A well-known form of lymphoma is *Hodgkin's disease,* named after Thomas Hodgkin, the English physician who first described the disorder. Hodgkin's disease affects both young adults and older individuals. The most common lymphatic cancer is *non-Hodgkin's lymphoma.* Cases of non-Hodgkin's lymphoma have risen steadily since the mid-1900's. Many people with AIDS develop this type of cancer.

Cancers of the urinary system . The bladder is the urinary organ most commonly affected by cancer. The majority of bladder cancer patients are men, and most survive five years. Many such cancers are detected early because they arise in the inner layer of the bladder and cause bleeding in the urine.

Classification by tissue. Scientists group cancers based on the body tissue in which tumors begin. *Car-*

cinomas develop in *epithelial tissue,* which forms the outer layer of skin and lines internal body surfaces and organs. Many organs, including the breast, colon, and lung, also contain glands. Cancers that arise in gland tissue, called *adenocarcinomas,* are among the most common cancers.

Cancers that develop in connective tissue are called *sarcomas.* Connective tissue forms the body's supporting structures, such as bones and cartilage. Sarcomas also form in the breast, digestive system, respiratory system, and reproductive system, but far less often than carcinomas.

Cancer in children, called *pediatric cancer,* differs from adult cancer in several ways. Cancers common in adults, such as those that occur in the lungs, breasts, prostate, or colon, do not usually occur in children. The common types of cancer that strike children include *neuroblastoma,* which arises in nervous tissue; *retinoblastoma,* which develops in the eyes; *nephroblastoma,* also called *Wilm's tumor,* which occurs in the kidneys; *rhabdomyosarcoma,* which arises from soft tissues; and *Ewing's sarcoma,* which develops in the bones. These cancers are extremely rare in adults.

The emotional impact on the family and physical and emotional consequences to the child are important considerations in the treatment of pediatric cancer. Fortunately, many of these cancers and leukemias are highly curable, and many children survive to lead normal lives following treatment. However, the treatment of pediatric cancer may have long-term consequences for patients. For example, radiation therapy and chemotherapy can actually cause secondary cancers, including leukemia, years after treatment has been completed. Other long-term consequences of cancer treatment may include stunted growth and infertility later in life.

Scientists have found that the cells of pediatric cancers often show specific genetic abnormalities. These abnormalities have given researchers a better understanding of the genetic difference between normal cells and cancer cells.

How damaged genes cause cancer

Every person begins life as a single fertilized egg cell. Through a complicated process of growth, division, and specialization, the egg multiplies into the trillions of cells in a healthy body. Every cell contains complex instructions that direct this process. The instructions are chemically coded in long coils of a substance called DNA (*d*eoxyribo*n*ucleic *a*cid). Particular sections of DNA make up genes that control specific cell functions. DNA even contains genes that enable the molecule to repair itself. But as people grow older, damage can build up and destroy DNA's ability to repair itself.

Cancer often results from damage to the genes that control cell growth and division. Two important classes of these genes are called *proto-oncogenes* and *suppressor genes.* Proto-oncogenes promote cell growth or division. Damage to a proto-oncogene may transform it into an overactive form called an *oncogene.* Oncogenes can lead to cancer by directing a cell to multiply excessively. Scientists have identified dozens of oncogenes that contribute to cancers in many sites, including the bladder, breasts, liver, lungs, and colon.

Suppressor genes limit cell growth or division. Damage to a suppressor gene can lead to cancer by destroying that gene's ability to stop cell multiplication.

Scientists think most cancers involve transformation of many proto-oncogenes into oncogenes and inactivation of a number of suppressor genes. In most cases, genetic damage must accumulate for years before a cell becomes cancerous. Once cancer occurs, the disorganized, rapidly dividing cells gradually build up into a mass that compresses and destroys nearby tissue. As the cancer grows, cells can break away and travel through blood or *lymph* (fluid from body tissues) to invade other parts of the body. This spread of cancer to other sites is called *metastasis.* The likelihood of curing cancer drops sharply after the tumor has spread.

People acquire the genetic damage that can lead to cancer in two main ways: (1) by inheriting damaged

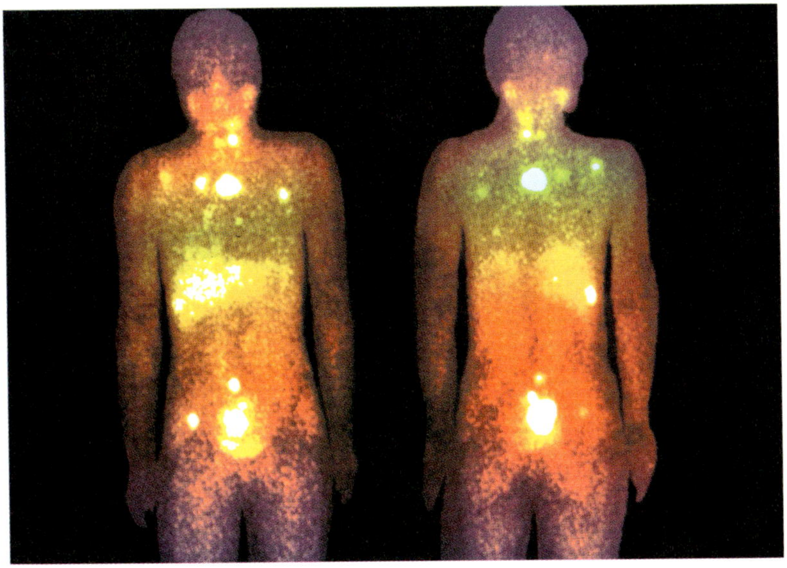

Cancer spreads when cancer cells break away from the primary tumor and travel to other body sites. The bright spots on these images are cancer tumors that have spread throughout the body. After cancer has spread, the chances for a successful cure drop sharply.

genes; and (2) through exposure to substances in the environment that damage genes.

Inheriting damaged genes. Scientists have long known that the risk of some cancers increases for people with close relatives who also have the disease. This increased risk occurs because some types of genetic damage involved in cancer can be passed from parents to children. But most cancers require multiple injuries to DNA. Inherited damage to one gene thus raises risk but does not guarantee that any particular individual will develop cancer. Scientists have identified the inheritable genetic damage involved in certain forms of breast, colon, and other cancers. Researchers are working to learn much more about inherited cancer genetics. They hope their knowledge will lead to new strategies for preventing and treating cancer.

Genes damaged by substances in the environment. Most people who develop cancer do not have inherited genetic abnormalities. Their genes are damaged after birth by carcinogens in their environment.

Scientists identify carcinogens by investigating unusually high cancer rates in groups of unrelated people. For example, scientists might notice that people in a particular job tend to get a certain type of cancer. Experts would then study the ability of chemicals or other substances encountered in that job to cause cancer in laboratory animals. If a high percentage of the animals develop cancer, researchers strongly suspect that the agent may also cause cancer in people.

Once a carcinogen damages a cell's DNA, the damage can be passed on to new cells that arise from division of the damaged cell. The changes are thus passed on to all the cell's descendants. Meanwhile, the descendant cells can acquire additional DNA damage that is also passed along. Experts think many cancers arise from such combined effects of several carcinogens.

Three classes of carcinogens in human beings are (1) chemicals, (2) certain forms of radiation, and (3) viruses.

Chemicals. Scientists have identified many chemicals that can cause cancer in animals. These chemicals may also pose a cancer hazard to human beings. For example, cigarette smoke contains more than 4,000 chemical substances, of which dozens have been identified by scientists as carcinogens.

Some industrial chemicals create a cancer hazard for people who work with them. Such chemicals include aniline dyes, arsenic, asbestos, benzene, chromium, nickel, vinyl chloride, and certain products of coal, lignite, oil shale, and petroleum.

Some substances that are added or applied to foods are also suspected of causing cancer in human beings. These substances include some chemicals used to control weeds and some that are used to kill insects. Government agencies regulate many of these substances, and, in some cases, prohibit their use. Molds that sometimes develop on such food crops as corn and peanuts may also contain carcinogens. The mold can be controlled through proper storage and handling of crops.

Radiation. Certain kinds of radiation can disrupt DNA and lead to cancer. X rays are a cancer hazard in large doses. However, doctors do not believe that routine medical and dental X rays pose a significant danger. A form of nuclear radiation known as *ionizing radiation* can also cause cancer. For example, in 1986, when Ukraine was part of the Soviet Union, a nuclear reactor at a power plant in Chernobyl exploded. Children who were exposed to radioactive fallout from that explosion have experienced an increased rate of thyroid cancer.

Major kinds of cancer in the United States

Primary body site	New cases each year*	Deaths each year*	Signs and symptoms	Precautionary measures
Prostate	232,090	30,350	Difficulty in urinating.	Regular medical checkup, including a rectal examination.
Breast	212,930	40,870	Lump or thickening in the breast.	Monthly self-examination of the breasts; regular medical checkup.
Lung	172,570	163,510	Persistent cough or long-lasting respiratory ailment.	Avoidance of cigarette smoking; regular medical checkup.
Colon and rectum	145,290	56,290	Change in bowel habits; bleeding from the rectum; blood in the stool.	Regular medical checkup, including examination of the colon and rectum.
Urinary organs	101,880	26,590	Difficulty in urinating; blood in the urine.	Regular medical checkup, including analysis of the urine.
Lymph tissues	63,740	20,610	Enlarged lymph nodes.	Regular medical checkup.
Skin‡	59,580	7,770	Sore that does not heal; change in a wart or mole.	Avoidance of excessive sunbathing; regular medical checkup.
Uterus†	51,250	11,020	Unusual bleeding or discharge from the vagina.	Regular medical checkup, including a Pap test.
Blood and blood forming tissue§	50,790	33,870	Anemia; frequent infections.	Regular medical checkup.
Pancreas	32,180	31,800	Yellowing of skin and eyes; abdominal pain.	Regular medical checkup.
Mouth and pharynx	29,370	7,320	Sore that does not heal; difficulty in swallowing.	Regular medical and dental checkup.
Ovary	22,220	16,210	Abdominal discomfort or pain; weight loss.	Regular medical checkup.
Stomach	21,860	11,550	Persistent indigestion.	Regular medical checkup.

*2005 estimates.
†Excludes cases where cells of uterus show changes but are not yet cancer cells.
‡Includes only melanoma, which arises in the skin's pigment cells.
§Includes all leukemias and multiple myeloma, a disease of bone marrow.
Source: American Cancer Society.

Viruses. Experiments have shown that certain kinds of viruses cause cancer in animals. Some viruses can also cause cancer in people. For example, the *human papilloma virus* causes most cases of cervical cancer. However, most experts feel that viruses are not a major cause of human cancers.

Reducing the risk of cancer

Scientists know that many cancers have a genetic cause which limits their ability to prevent the disease. However, scientists have identified several factors that can increase a person's chances of developing cancer. They have also discovered substances that may protect DNA and keep cancer from developing. Many scientists believe that people can decrease their overall chances of developing cancer by adopting a healthy lifestyle and avoiding contact with known carcinogens.

Avoiding carcinogens. Smoking is one of the most widespread and avoidable environmental causes of cancer. Scientists think that smoking causes about one-third of all cases of cancer, including most lung cancers. Smoking also causes many cancers of the mouth, larynx, trachea, esophagus, pancreas, kidney, bladder, and cervix. Cigarette smoke can even cause cancer in nonsmokers who live or work closely with smokers. Smokers who quit can significantly reduce their chance of developing lung cancer.

People can also reduce their risk of developing skin cancer. The sun is one of the most important sources of cancer-causing radiation. Most cases of skin cancer—including deadly melanoma—are caused by an invisible portion of the sun's radiation called *ultraviolet rays.* Physicians advise against sunbathing and recommend that people who work outdoors wear protective clothing or apply sunscreens that block ultraviolet rays.

Nutrition. Some chemicals naturally present in food may become a cancer threat if consumed in large quantities. Diets high in fats, for example, have been associated with cancers of the breast, colon, and prostate gland. Some studies have linked eating large amounts of salt-cured, salt-pickled, and smoked foods to cancers of the digestive system. Excessive alcohol consumption has been linked to cancer of the mouth, pharynx, larynx, esophagus, and liver.

Many scientists believe that certain foods contain substances, called *phytochemicals,* that may help prevent cancers in people. Such foods include broccoli, cauliflower, cabbage, spinach, onions, tomatoes, carrots, fruits, and whole-grain breads or cereals.

Cancer detection and diagnosis

Only a doctor can diagnose cancer. But in many cases, people consult a doctor only after the disease is far advanced. A person should therefore be alert to any physical change that may be a symptom of cancer. Detecting cancer while a tumor is small and confined to one location greatly increases the chances of a cure.

Cancer checkups. Many cancers cause no symptoms in their early stages. To detect early cancers, the American Cancer Society recommends that people aged 20 to 40 have a cancer-related checkup by a physician every 3 years. People aged 40 or older should have a checkup every year. A cancer-related checkup usually includes a physical examination. Physicians watch carefully for any visible signs of cancer when they perform physical examinations.

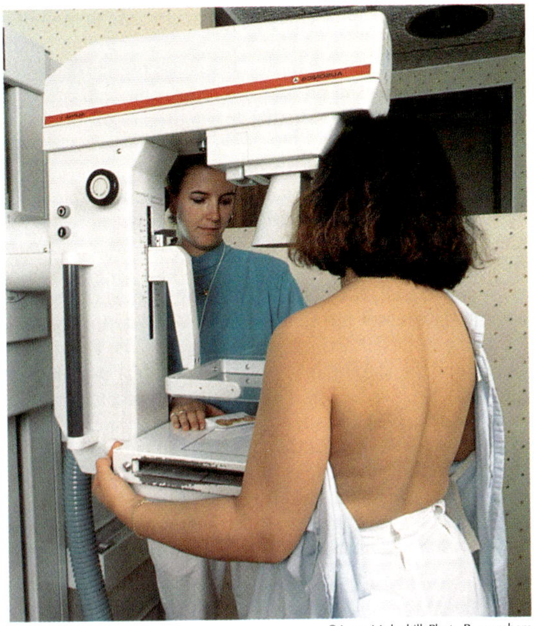

© Larry Mulvehill, Photo Researchers

Detection of breast cancer in an early stage is possible through an X-ray technique called *mammography.* Early detection of certain cancers may increase chances for a cure.

Depending on the patient, *screening tests* for specific types of cancer may also be performed. Screening tests may include a breast X ray called a *mammogram* to detect breast cancer in women. A mammogram can detect some breast cancers before any lumps can be felt.

Physicians recommend that, beginning at age 50, patients have routine tests for colon cancer. In one such test, called a *fecal occult blood test* (FOBT), the patient uses a special kit to collect tiny samples of *stool* (solid body wastes). Laboratories test the samples for microscopic amounts of blood, which may indicate cancer.

The *Pap test,* another recommended yearly test for women, has greatly reduced the death rate from cancer of the uterus. In the Pap test, experts examine cells scraped from the cervix under a microscope. Microscopic signs of cancer can be seen 5 to 10 years before symptoms appear. See **Pap test.**

Preliminary diagnosis identifies a suspicious mass or other change in the body that requires further investigation. Some symptoms must be evaluated with special X rays and other advanced imaging techniques. One X-ray technique, called *computed tomography* or *CT scan,* can reveal suspicious masses in such internal organs as the brain and the lungs. A technique called *magnetic resonance imaging* (MRI) uses magnetic fields and radio waves to produce images of internal organs. These imaging techniques allow physicians to determine the exact location, size, and shape of cancer tumors and determine whether the cancer has spread.

Conclusive diagnosis. The various methods of preliminary diagnosis may reveal the presence of a tumor. But not all tumors are cancerous. Most lumps in the breast, for example, are *benign* (noncancerous). Doctors need to perform a test called a *biopsy* to make a definite diagnosis of cancer. In a biopsy, doctors remove a small piece of tissue from the tumor. In suspected cases of leukemia, they take a blood sample or remove tissue from a blood-forming organ. Experts then examine the tissue under a microscope to check for cancer cells.

Staging. Physicians use a process called *staging* to describe how a particular cancer in a patient has advanced. Staging is important in helping physicians decide which treatments are most likely to be successful in treating the cancer. The most common staging method is known as the *TNM system.* This system describes the tumor (T), whether the cancer has invaded lymph nodes (N), and whether there are any metastases (M). Physicians determine the staging level through physical examination, X rays, CT scans , and other specialized tests.

Since each type of cancer is different, there are different staging categories for each cancer. If cancer is discovered in the early stages, the cancer treatment may be successful. Advanced stage cancers are more difficult to treat. If tests show that the cancer has spread, patients may need to undergo additional treatments.

Cancer treatment

Cancer has a highly emotional impact on the patient who is diagnosed with the disease and his or her family. Most health care providers in the United States try to provide substantial medical and nonmedical support for both the patient and family.

Methods for treating cancer include surgery; radiation therapy; and drug therapy. Most cancer treatment plans combine several or all of these methods in a technique called *multimodality therapy.* Physicians may use *biological response modifiers* to enhance a patient's ability to fight cancer. However, some cancer patients seek nontraditional or alternative treatments.

Surgery is the main method of treating most types of cancer. Cancer surgery chiefly involves taking out the tumor while minimizing the removal of healthy surrounding tissue. Surgeons work closely with a *pathologist* (expert on tissue changes) who can examine tissue during the surgery to determine if the tumor has been completely removed.

Surgeons may also cut out additional tissue that appears healthy. For example, breast cancer may be treated with a *lumpectomy,* an operation that removes the cancerous lump and a margin of the normal tissue surrounding it. Neighboring lymph nodes may also be removed and examined for signs of cancer. Although these nodes may appear normal, they might contain cancer cells that could travel to other parts of the body.

Radiation therapy, also called *radiotherapy,* attacks cancer cells with X rays or other high energy particles from radioactive substances. Radiotherapy is often used to treat cancers of the bladder, prostate, head, and neck. Radiation kills cancer cells, but it also kills normal cells.

One type of radiotherapy, called *external beam radiotherapy,* sends X rays into the target tissue to destroy cancer cells. Machines called *linear accelerators* produce the X rays at increasingly greater energy. The higher the energy of the X rays, the deeper the beam can penetrate into the body to reach cancer tumors.

Physicians use CT scans and MRI to determine the exact size and shape of a cancerous tumor. In a technique called *three-dimensional conformal radiation therapy,* the radiation beam is shaped to exactly match the cancerous tumor. Physicians can then deliver a high dose of radiation to the tumor with little radiation exposure to healthy tissue.

A technique called *stereotactic radiosurgery* is often used to treat cancerous tumors in the brain that cannot be removed through conventional surgery. This technique uses a concentrated dose of *gamma rays*—a form of high energy radiation—from a radioactive source. With stereotactic radiosurgery, a total of 201 radiation beams intersect on a target area of cancer cells within the body. This precise technique destroys the cancer cells while sparing adjacent healthy tissue.

Brachytherapy is often used to treat cancers of the prostate and brain. In this type of radiotherapy, radiation comes from small capsules, called *seeds,* of radioactive material implanted close to, or within, the tumor. The radiation only penetrates a short distance, so nearby healthy tissue is unharmed while cancer cells are killed.

Drug therapy, also called *chemotherapy,* is used against a wide variety of cancers. Chemotherapy has proved especially effective in treating leukemia, lymphoma, and testicular cancer. Cancer cells divide much more rapidly than normal cells. Therefore, many cancer drugs are designed to interfere with cell division.

Chemotherapy causes side effects by injuring the normal body cells, especially those that divide most rapidly. Rapidly dividing normal cells include blood-forming cells, cells that line the intestines, and hair-forming cells. Damage to blood-forming cells may increase a patient's risk of developing anemia or an infection. Injury to intestinal cells may cause nausea and vomiting. Disruption of hair-forming cells can cause hair loss.

Effective chemotherapy usually involves combinations of drugs. Doctors combine drugs that have different methods of acting on cancer cells and that produce different side effects. Combination therapy reduces the chance that cancer cells will develop resistance to the drugs. It also helps avoid serious side effects from large doses of a single drug.

Multimodality therapy involves some combination of surgery, radiotherapy, and drug therapy. In the most common multimodality therapy, doctors prescribe drug therapy to follow surgery, radiotherapy, or both of those treatments. Such follow-up treatment is called *adjuvant drug therapy.* Because the drugs reach all parts of the body, they may destroy cancer cells that have spread undetected to distant organs. Adjuvant drug therapy is used to treat some colon and breast cancers as well as some bone cancers.

Biological response modifiers increase a person's ability to fight cancer by strengthening natural body processes. Some biological modifiers are *immunotherapies*—that is, they stimulate the body's immune system to attack cancer cells. Other biological modifiers improve the body's ability to withstand aggressive drug therapy. The body makes small quantities of many biological response modifiers. Scientists can now produce some of them in laboratories in large quantities using techniques of molecular biology.

Monoclonal antibodies are an important type of immunotherapy. They are designed to recognize certain proteins that are found on the surface of some cancer

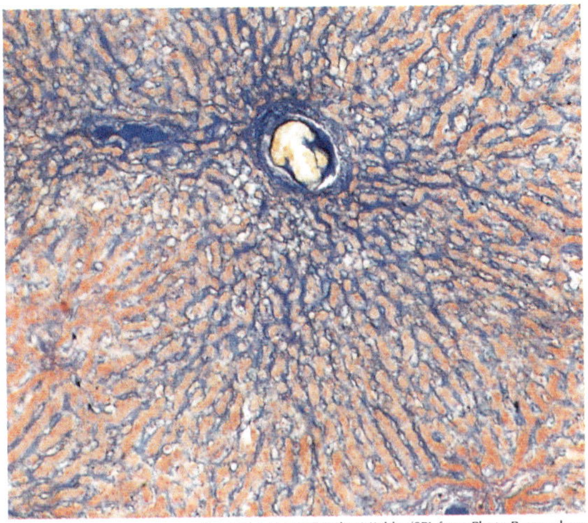

Normal liver cells, seen in this magnification, appear well ordered and healthy. However, many types of cancers can spread, or *metastasize,* to the liver through the bloodstream.

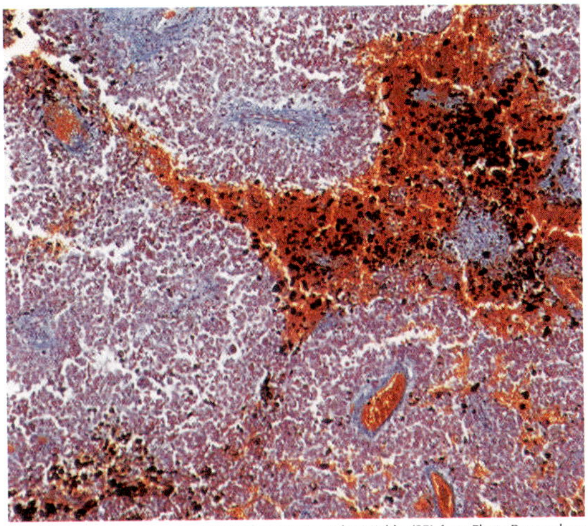

Liver cells with metastasized cancer appear disordered and abnormal. The magnified cancer cells, seen here in dark red, spread from a deadly type of skin cancer called *melanoma.*

cells. The monoclonal antibody then binds onto the protein. This action triggers the body's immune system to attack the cancer cells and can also cause the cells to destroy themselves. For example, about one-third of breast cancer patients have high levels of a protein called *HER2* on the surface of the cancer cells. Scientists have developed a monoclonal antibody that binds onto this protein and stops the cancer cell from growing and dividing. The antibody also causes the body's immune system to attack the cancer cells.

Some experiments are investigating the ability of monoclonal antibodies to deliver microscopic doses of drugs or radiation directly to tumor cells. Scientists are working to make use of tumor-surface *antigens* to produce vaccines against certain kinds of cancer. Antigens are viruses or other foreign substances in the body that trigger the immune response.

Erythropoietin, another biological response modifier, increases a cancer patient's production of red blood cells. Many kinds of chemotherapy cause *anemia* by killing red blood cells. In an anemic person, the blood cannot provide the tissues with enough oxygen, causing the patient to feel weak or tired. Erythropoietin helps cancer patients withstand the stress of chemotherapy and maintain an active life.

Alternative medicine. Many people diagnosed with cancer use alternative or other forms of nontraditional medicine. These treatments may include acupuncture, herbal medicine, homeopathy, vitamins, or various dietary supplements. Most of these alternative treatments have not been tested scientifically. Most physicians doubt the validity of claims that alternative treatments are beneficial, and many believe that they are harmful. See **Acupuncture; Herbal medicine; Homeopathy.**

Cancer research

Cancer research includes a wide range of projects, from identifying carcinogens to developing improved anticancer drugs. Advances in some areas have raised hopes of finding better methods of treatment and prevention. Scientists have made especially rapid progress in the fields of genetics and molecular medicine. These fields involve the development of treatments to target the specific abnormal gene or abnormal function of the gene that is associated with a particular type of cancer. New cancer treatments are tested in clinical trials.

Genetics. Scientists are working to better understand the role of oncogenes and suppressor genes in the development of cancer. This knowledge could lead to new ways of controlling cancer cells. Scientists have developed tests that show if individuals have certain defective genes. But experts disagree about when such tests should be offered. In most cases, doctors cannot yet use these tests to treat or prevent cancer. Some experts question the value of telling people that they have a damaged gene when this knowledge carries little benefit. But researchers hope that genetic tests may one day make it possible to prevent cancer or to detect the disease in its earliest stages.

Molecular medicine involves the development of specific treatments or medicines to interfere with a specific abnormal gene or abnormal function of a gene. Highly targeted molecular medicine can be directed at killing cancer cells without harming healthy cells.

Biologists are investigating a process called *apoptosis* (pronounced *AH pahp TOH sihs*). Apoptosis is also known as *programmed cell death* or *"cell suicide."* In apoptosis, various genes activate mechanisms of self-destruction when cells become damaged or are no longer needed. Techniques that bring on apoptosis in cancer cells may one day offer new treatments.

Another active area of research focuses on preventing blood vessels from growing to nourish cancers. To grow beyond a small, harmless size, every cancer must develop its own blood supply. Development of blood vessels is called *angiogenesis* (pronounced *AN jee oh JEHN uh sihs*). Many experts feel that substances that prevent angiogenesis, called *angiogenesis inhibitors,* can be developed into cancer-fighting drugs.

Researchers are also working to develop drugs that interfere with *signal transduction,* the process by which growth signals are transmitted to cells. Several types of cancer secrete too much growth factor. These factors drive proliferation of the cancer cells. Drugs that interfere with signal transduction would stop the uncontrolled cell growth characteristic of cancer cells.

Clinical trials. Despite advances in cancer treatment, many cancers are not fully curable. Scientists continue to develop new treatments that are tested through clinical trials. In a clinical trial, a group of cancer patients is treated with standard available treatments while another group with the same disease receives a new treatment that is being evaluated. Unfortunately, only a small number of patients who are eligible to participate in clinical trials actually enter these programs. Patients who are interested in participating in a clinical trial should discuss the possibility with their physician. Marc B. Garnick

See **Clinical trial.**

Related articles in *World Book* include:

Kinds of cancer

Breast cancer	Leukemia	Prostate cancer
Cervical cancer	Lung cancer	Skin cancer
Colon cancer	Ovarian cancer	Testicular cancer
Hodgkin's disease		

Other related articles

Antibiotic (Other kinds of antibiotics)	American	Pap test
	Chemotherapy	Radiation (In medicine)
	Disease (graph)	
Angiogenesis	Epithelioma	Radium
Apoptosis	Malignancy	Radon
Biopsy	Mammography	Smoking
Bone marrow transplant	Mastectomy	Tamoxifen
	Nutrition (Cancer)	Taxol
Cancer Society,	Oncology	Tumor

Outline

I. Major types of cancer
- A. Classification by primary body site
- B. Classification by tissue
- C Cancer in children

II. How damaged genes cause cancer
- A. Inheriting damaged genes
- B. Genes damaged by substances in the environment

III. Reducing the risk of cancer
- A. Avoiding carcinogens
- B. Nutrition

IV. Cancer detection and diagnosis
- A. Cancer checkups
- B. Preliminary diagnosis
- C. Conclusive diagnosis
- D. Staging

V. Cancer treatment
- A. Surgery
- B. Radiation therapy
- C. Drug therapy
- D. Multimodality therapy
- E. Biological response modifiers
- F. Alternative medicine

VI. Cancer research
- A. Genetics
- B. Molecular medicine
- C. Clinical trials

Questions

What are the main methods of treating cancer?
What are the most common types of cancer?
What are *carcinogens?*
How are genes that control cell division involved in cancer?
How is pediatric cancer different from cancer in adults?
How do scientists decide if a substance can cause cancer?
What is *staging?*
What are *monoclonal antibodies?*
What is responsible for most cases of lung cancer?
How can people reduce their chances of getting cancer?

Additional resources

Bellenir, Karen, ed. *Cancer Sourcebook.* 4th ed. Omnigraphics, 2003.
Bertino, Joseph R., ed. *Encyclopedia of Cancer.* 2nd ed. Academic Pr., 2002.
Eyre, Harmon J., and others, eds. *Informed Decisions: The Complete Book of Cancer Diagnosis, Treatment, and Recovery.* 2nd ed. Am. Cancer Soc., 2002.
Thackery, Ellen, ed. *The Gale Encyclopedia of Cancer.* Gale Group, 2002.

Cancer is the fourth sign of the zodiac. Cancer, a water sign, is symbolized by a crab. The ancient Egyptians, however, represented this sign with a *scarab,* a sacred beetle. Astrologers believe that the moon rules Cancer.

Astrologers regard people born under the sign of Cancer, from June 21 to July 22, as intuitive and artistic. Characteristics associated with the sign reflect its connection to the moon. Just as the moon has phases, those born under this sign are said to be changeable. They can be emotional and their moods change quickly.

Cancer—The Crab

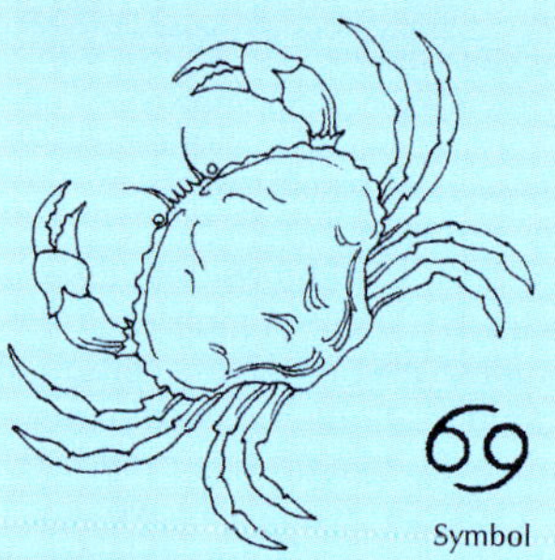

Symbol

Birth dates: June 21-July 22.
Group: Water.
Characteristics: Artistic, emotional, home-loving, instinctive, patriotic, shy.

WORLD BOOK illustration by Robert Keys

Signs of the Zodiac

Aries
March 21-April 19
Taurus
April 20-May 20
Gemini
May 21-June 20
Cancer
June 21-July 22
Leo
July 23-Aug. 22
Virgo
Aug. 23-Sept. 22
Libra
Sept. 23-Oct. 22
Scorpio
Oct. 23-Nov. 21
Sagittarius
Nov. 22-Dec. 21
Capricorn
Dec. 22-Jan. 19
Aquarius
Jan. 20-Feb. 18
Pisces
Feb. 19-March 20

Cancerians may seem shy, but they are often hiding feelings that are easily hurt. Their sensitivity can make them successful in business as they are aware of people's needs. Cancerians can seem selfish since they often prefer to dwell on their own dreams. Charles W. Clark

See also **Astrology; Horoscope; Zodiac.**

Cancer, Tropic of. See Tropic of Cancer.

Cancer Society, American, is a voluntary health organization dedicated to the control and elimination of cancer. It supports research through grants to individuals and institutions. The organization also supports service and rehabilitation programs for cancer patients and their families. It develops and directs educational programs for the public and for health professionals.

The society is governed by a national board of volunteer directors. Half the directors are laypersons, and half are doctors and scientists. Most society funds are raised in its annual community crusade during April, designated as Cancer Control Month by the United States Congress in 1938.

Critically reviewed by the American Cancer Society, Inc.

Cancún, *kan KOON,* is one of Mexico's most popular resorts. The area's warm, sunny climate and white sandy beaches attract about 2 million visitors annually. Cancún lies along the Caribbean coast of the Yucatán Peninsula. For location, see **Mexico** (political map).

Cancún consists of a mainland city and an island resort. Bridges connect the mainland and the island. Cancún City is home to resort employees. The island, often called the "hotel zone," features hotels, a convention center, shopping malls, restaurants, and nightclubs.

The area where Cancún now stands had long been poor and thinly populated. In the late 1960's, the Mexican government decided to build a new resort in the region in an effort to create economic growth and boost tourism. Construction of Cancún began in the early 1970's, and the first tourists arrived in 1974.

Klaus J. Meyer-Arendt

Candela, *kan DEHL uh* or *kan DEE luh,* is the unit of measurement of *luminous intensity,* the amount of light produced in a certain direction by a glowing object. The more luminous intensity a light has, the brighter the light appears. Luminous intensity is sometimes called *candle power.*

The candela is one of seven base units in the metric system. Its abbreviation is *cd.* One candela is now defined as the luminous intensity from a source producing light at a specific frequency and intensity in a given direction. The frequency of the light is 540,000,000,000,000 hertz, and its intensity is $\frac{1}{683}$ watt in a solid angle called a *steradian.* To understand a steradian, imagine a small, uniform light placed at the center of a hollow sphere with a radius of 1 foot (30 centimeters). Beams of light spread uniformly in all directions and illuminate the inside surface of the sphere. If the area illuminated on the inside of the sphere equals 1 square foot (930 square centimeters), then the angle of the light measured near the center of the sphere equals one steradian.

The candela is used to calculate other units of light measurement. These units include *lumens* and *foot-candles.* The unit of measurement for luminous intensity was once the candle, the amount of light produced by a certain kind of candle. But scientists found this unit too difficult to standardize. In 1948, the International Commission on Illumination adopted the candela as a standard unit of measure. One candela is slightly less than 1 candle. Ronald N. Helms

See also **Foot-candle; Light** (The brightness of light; diagram: Basic units of light measurement).

Candle is an object made of wax or a similar material that is burned to give light. When a candle is lighted, wax melted by the flame is drawn up an embedded wick made of cotton, paper, or a combination of the two. This liquid wax *vaporizes* (changes to a gas). The gas then burns, producing light (see **Combustion**). Candles are made in many colors, scents, shapes, and sizes.

Candles have been used since prehistoric times. People have created candles out of many substances, including bayberry wax, beeswax, paraffin, spermaceti, stearin, and tallow. People make candles by hand by (1) dipping the wick repeatedly into liquid wax, (2) pouring liquid wax into a mold that contains a suspended wick, or (3) rolling sheets of softened wax around the wick. Candle manufacturers use machines that produce several dozen to several hundred candles at a time.

Before electric lighting became common in the early 1900's, people used candles as one source of artificial light. Today, candles are used for such purposes as birthday celebrations, holiday and home decorations, and for religious services. Many people enjoy candle making as a hobby. Kirk Lee Zehnder

WORLD BOOK photo

Candles are made in a variety of colors, shapes, and sizes. This photograph shows some of the many types of candles available.

Related articles in *World Book* include:

Beeswax	Easter (Candles)	Paraffin
Christmas (Religious practices)	Eulachon	Tallowtree
	Hanukkah	

Candlefish. See **Eulachon.**

Candlemas Day, *KAN duhl muhs,* is a Christian festival observed on February 2. It celebrates what is now called the Presentation of the Lord, when the infant Jesus was taken to the Temple by His parents according to Jewish custom. Candlemas Day occurs 40 days after Christmas and marks the end of the Christmas cycle.

The name *Candlemas* comes from the traditional observance of blessing candles and distributing the candles to worshipers. The candles recall the lights of Christmas. They also symbolize Simeon's words to Mary and Joseph in Luke 2:32 that Jesus would be "a light to lighten the Gentiles, and the glory of thy people Israel."

Candlemas Day formerly honored Mary's purification after the birth of Jesus. However, modern observances have shifted the emphasis of the day to Jesus.

David G. Truemper

Candy is a popular sweet-tasting food. Candy is also called *confection.* The main ingredient in most candies is sugar, but some candies are made with saccharin and other artificial sweeteners. Candies may also include a variety of other ingredients. These ingredients include eggs, flour, fruits, milk, nuts, and natural or artificial flavorings.

Candy is sold in a variety of forms and packages, including bars, bags of wrapped candies, boxes of assortments, rolls, and single pieces.

Types of candies

Candies vary in their ingredients and the way they are made. There are four major types of candies: (1) chocolate candies, (2) hard candies, (3) chewy candies, and

WORLD BOOK photo

The many varieties of candy differ in shape, texture, and taste. Some popular types, such as chocolates, caramels, and mints, are shown here. *Marzipan, lower left,* is an almond paste that is molded into various shapes.

(4) whipped candies. Candies also may be *grained* or *nongrained.* Grained candies, such as creams and fudges, have fine sugar crystals. Nongrained candies have no crystals. They include caramels and some types of hard candies.

Sugar is the main ingredient in most candies. The most commonly used sugar is *sucrose,* which comes from sugar cane and sugar beets. Manufacturers also sweeten candy with corn syrup, honey, and *invert sugar.* Invert sugar contains the sugars fructose and glucose. Some candies also contain cereals, fats, flour, fruits, milk products, nuts, and peanut butter. Such natural ingredients as cocoa, peppermint, and vanilla give the flavor and color of many confections. But some candies contain artificial dyes and flavorings.

Chocolate candies are the best-selling confections. Solid chocolate and chocolate-covered bars are the most popular. Chocolate consists mainly of cacao butter, sugar, and *chocolate liquor.* Chocolate liquor is made by grinding *cocoa nibs* (shelled cocoa seeds) with *cocoa butter,* the natural fat of the cocoa bean. In making chocolate candies, additional cocoa butter, sugar, and chocolate liquor are mixed and ground into fine particles.

To form chocolate bars, melted chocolate is poured into molds and left to harden. A process called *enrobing* is used to make many chocolate-covered candies. In this process, pieces of candy or cookie are placed on a screenlike conveyor belt, and melted chocolate is poured over them. Chocolate candies with liquid centers are made by *shell molding.* In this process, molds are partly filled with melted chocolate, which then cools to form chocolate shells. Then the shells are filled with syrup and sealed with a layer of chocolate.

Hard candies include fruit drops, mints, and sticks. They are made from a solution of sugar, corn syrup, and a small amount of water. This mixture is boiled and forms a hot syrup, to which flavoring and color are added. After the syrup cools somewhat, it becomes easy to shape. The candy is then pulled into long, thin cords and cut into various shapes.

Butterscotch and brittles are hard candies made with butter or a vegetable fat. Most brittles contain peanuts or some other kind of nut. Some include milk.

Candy canes are peppermint-flavored hard candies that are shaped like a shepherd's crook. They are made from two separate syrups, one of which has been colored red and the other white. When the slightly cooled syrups become easy to shape, they are placed together and pushed through a circular hole, forming a striped rod. The rod is cut into sticks, which are then bent into the crook shape and allowed to harden.

Chewy candies include caramels, toffees, jellies, and gums. Caramels and toffees contain milk cooked with sugars and vegetable fats. The cooked mixture is flavored, cooled, and cut into pieces.

Jellies and gums are made with a solution of sugars and a jelling agent, such as gelatin or starch. The solution is boiled, and the jelling agent, color, and flavoring are added. The mixture is then poured into molds and allowed to set.

Whipped candies, such as nougats and marshmallows, are *aerated* (mixed with air) to produce a smooth texture and to increase their volume. Most whipped candies are concentrated syrups that contain a whipping agent, which makes them easier to aerate. Whipping agents include gelatin and egg whites.

In one method of producing whipped candy, air is beaten into the hot syrup with a *vertical whisk.* This device resembles an electric food mixer. In another method, the syrup is aerated inside a closed mixing chamber and then poured into molds or onto sheets and allowed to set.

Other candies. *Cotton candy* is made from sugar crystals that are melted and spun in a heated whirling device called a *centrifuge* and then wound on a stick. *Marzipan* is produced by grinding almonds and sugars into a paste.

Licorice contains wheat flour dough that has been sweetened, dyed, and flavored. Its flavoring comes from the roots of the licorice herb (see **Licorice**).

Jellybeans, malted milk balls, and sugared or chocolate-covered nuts are known as *panned candies.* The center of the candy is placed in a rotating pan and sprayed with chocolate or syrup. Repeated coatings form the outer shell.

History

The earliest records of candy making date back 3,000 years to ancient Egypt, where confections were made by mixing fruits and nuts with honey. People in ancient India made the first candy with sugar cane. Candy making remained a fairly small industry until the 1800's, when advances in technology enabled large quantities of candy to be produced cheaply.

During the 1900's, candy making developed from a craft involving much handwork to a chiefly automated, computer-controlled industry. Modern candy factories have long production lines, on which machines perform such tasks as measuring and mixing ingredients and packing shipping cases.

During the 1970's, the rising costs of raw materials, particularly cacao beans and sugar, led to the development of new candies. For example, many candy makers began to substitute carob beans and imitation cacao butter for cacao beans in chocolate candies (see **Carob**). Reduced-calorie candies also were developed for people who want to limit the amount of sugar or fat they eat.

Rhona S. Applebaum

See also **Chocolate; Hershey, Milton Snavely; Sugar.**

Candytuft is the name of about 30 species of plants native to southern Europe, northern Africa, and western Asia. Many are cultivated as garden flowers. One such species, the *edging candytuft,* is a shrubby evergreen that grows about 12 inches (30 centimeters) high. It has narrow leaves and clusters of fragrant white flowers. Another popular garden species, the *globe candytuft,* may reach a height of 16 inches (41 centimeters). Its lavender, pink, or red blossoms grow in dense clusters.

WORLD BOOK illustration by Christabel King

Candytuft

Theodore R. Dudley

Scientific classification. Candytufts belong to the mustard family, Brassicaceae or Cruciferae. The scientific name for the edging candytuft is *Iberis sempervirens.* The globe candytuft is *I. umbellata.*

Cane sugar. See **Sugar** (Making cane sugar).

Cane toad is one of the largest toads. Cane toads measure about 9 inches (23 centimeters) long. They are found chiefly in tropical America. The cane toad is also called *marine toad* and *giant toad.*

The cane toad feeds mainly on insects but will eat almost any kind of small animal, including frogs, lizards, snakes, mice, and birds. The toad reproduces by laying eggs and can produce up to 20,000 eggs at one time. A pair of large *parotoid glands* on top of the toad's head secrete substances that are bad tasting and, in some cases, poisonous. These secretions can ward off or even kill animals that prey on the cane toad.

The cane toad has become a serious pest in Australia. The toads were brought there in 1935 to help control beetles that attack sugar cane. Since then, the cane toad population in Australia has increased dramatically. Conservationists are concerned that certain small animals native to Australia may become extinct because cane toads eat so many of them. Laurie J. Vitt

Scientific classification. The cane toad belongs to the toad family, Bufonidae. Its scientific name is *Bufo marinus.*

Canine. See **Dog; Teeth** (Permanent teeth).

Canine parvovirus, *KAY nyn* PAHR *voh VY ruhs,* also called *parvovirus,* is a contagious disease that affects dogs. Its symptoms include diarrhea, vomiting, and fever. Dogs with parvovirus also lose their appetite, become dehydrated, and appear listless. The disease can result in death, especially among puppies.

Canine parvovirus is caused by a virus belonging to a group of viruses called *parvoviruses.* Other members of this group produce diseases in people, cats, cattle, pigs, rodents, and other animals. A dog may get canine parvovirus by consuming food or water that has been contaminated by the *feces* (solid body wastes) of a dog infected with the disease.

There is no cure for canine parvovirus. However, certain treatments can help. A veterinarian may inject fluid into the dog's body to replace fluid loss caused by diarrhea and vomiting. Antibiotics, such as ampicillin or gentamicin, may be given to prevent additional infections.

Dogs that have recovered from parvovirus develop a long-lasting immunity to it. Vaccines that prevent canine parvovirus are available. Most veterinarians recommend yearly vaccination against the disease.

A major outbreak of canine parvovirus occurred in the United States in 1978. Since then, canine parvovirus has occurred throughout the world. Yuan Chung Zee

Canis Major. See **Sirius.**

Canisius, *kuh NIHSH ee uhs,* **Saint Peter** (1524-1597), was the founder of the first German house of Jesuits, and the foremost promoter of the reform of the Roman Catholic Church in south German lands. Saint Ignatius Loyola, founder of the Jesuits, sent him as a missionary to help check the spread of Lutheranism in Germany. There Saint Canisius founded Jesuit colleges to meet the need for educated Roman Catholics.

His most effective tool in strengthening the Roman Catholic faith was his *Summa Doctrinae Christianae* (1555), a catechism with more than 200 editions in 12 languages. His teaching and preaching contributed greatly to halting the spread of Protestantism in Germany, Austria, and Bohemia. Canisius was born on May 8, 1524, in Nijmegen, now in the Netherlands. He died on Dec. 21, 1597. He was canonized in 1925. His feast day is April 27.

Marvin R. O'Connell

Canker sore is a small, painful sore on the tongue or inside the mouth. The sores begin as red swellings and open into grayish-white ulcers with a red border. The medical terms for canker sores include *aphthous stomatitis (AF thuhs* STOH *muh TY tihs)* and *aphthous ulcers.*

The cause of canker sores is not known. Many experts think they occur chiefly because of a flaw or imbalance in the body's disease-fighting immune system. People vary in their likelihood of getting canker sores, and some people have repeated outbreaks. A tendency to develop the sores runs in some families.

Canker sores are rarely serious except in people with AIDS or other conditions that weaken the immune system. Doctors may sometimes order tests for canker sore patients to rule out more serious disorders. Treatment aims at reducing the pain, duration, and frequency of attacks. Measures that may offer relief include avoiding spicy or irritating foods; applying medicated ointments or pastes to the sores; and using mouth rinses that fight bacteria or inflammation. Anne C. O'Connell

Cankerworm is the *larva* (caterpillar) of a moth. It is a *measuring worm* and crawls by humping its back and bringing its hind feet up to its forefeet to make a loop of its body (see **Measuring worm**). Two kinds of cankerworms damage orchards and shade trees. They are the *spring cankerworm* and the *fall cankerworm.* The adult

E. R. Degginger, Animals Animals

The spring cankerworm is an insect pest that eats the leaves of trees. Cankerworms can strip an orchard in a few days.

females of both these insects have no wings. They climb trees to lay their eggs. The spring cankerworm hatches about the time the elm leaves grow, and eats the leaves. The fall cankerworm usually comes from eggs laid by adults that have appeared from their cocoons the autumn before. It hatches in early spring as the leaves unfold.

These caterpillars can strip an orchard or a grove of shade trees in a few days. When they are molested, they drop from the leaves and hang in the air by silken threads. Bands of cloth or paper that have been smeared with a sticky substance and wrapped around bases of the tree trunks will keep the females from laying eggs in the trees. Spraying the trees with arsenate of lead or carbaryl kills the caterpillars. Charles V. Covell, Jr.

Scientific classification. Cankerworms are caterpillars of moths in the measuring worm moth family, Geometridae. The spring cankerworm is *Paleacrita vernata.* The fall cankerworm is *Alsophila pometaria.*

See also **Moth** (pictures).

Canna, *KAN uh,* is a tall ornamental plant with brilliantly colored flowers. The *Indian-shot canna* grows wild in the United States. It may be 4 feet (1.2 meters) high and bears bright red flowers tipped with orange. It has large leaves that sometimes grow 2 feet (61 centimeters) long and 8 inches (20 centimeters) wide.

Florists sell many hybrid varieties of cannas. These plants often grow from $2\frac{1}{2}$ to 10 feet (76 to 300 centimeters) high, and have green, yellow-green, or bronze foliage. The leaves grow densely on stout stems. The blossoms of the hybrid plants contain various colors and markings. Two to five petallike stamens make up the flower.

Cannas can be grown easily, and are widely cultivated as garden plants in all parts of the United States. They grow best in rich, warm soil, and need plenty of moisture. In cold regions, the plant's big root must be dug up and kept in a warm, dry place during the winter to prevent freezing. W. Dennis Clark

Scientific classification. Cannas make up the canna family, Cannaceae. The Indian-shot canna is classified as *Canna indica.*

See also **Flower** (picture: Garden perennials).

Cannabis. See **Marijuana.**

Cannes, *kan* (pop. 68,214), is a luxurious resort city on the French Riviera in southeastern France (see **France** [political map]). Cannes is famous for its annual film festival, which features movies from many countries around the world.

Cannes lies on the Gulf of Napoule, an arm of the Mediterranean Sea. The city is noted for its mild, dry climate and its broad, treelined boulevards. The best-known boulevard in Cannes is the Promenade de la Croisette, which runs along the shore and has elegant hotels and casinos. Other interesting features of Cannes include the Hôtel de Ville (City Hall); the nearby Lérins Islands; and a castle called the Chateau des Abbés de Lérins on Mont Chevalier, a hill overlooking the Gulf of Napoule.

Tourism is Cannes's leading economic activity. Other activities include perfume and soap manufacturing, metalworking, and fishing.

The first settlement at what is now Cannes was a fortress built on Mont Chevalier by an ancient Italian people called *Ligurians.* It was probably established about the 700's B.C. Mark Kesselman

Cannibal is a person who eats human flesh. Throughout history, many individuals and societies in all parts of the world have committed acts of cannibalism. Archaeologists have found evidence of cannibalism that occurred more than 500,000 years ago. Today, cannibalism no longer exists in the world except perhaps among some societies in isolated areas of Africa, Asia, and the Pacific Islands.

Cannibalism may also be practiced today by people who can obtain no food except human flesh. Survivors of a plane crash in the Andes Mountains in 1972 ate their dead companions to survive.

Through the centuries, most cases of cannibalism have been connected with religious or other traditional beliefs. Most cannibals ate only the parts of the body that they considered important. For example, some cannibals believed that the heart contained such qualities as courage and wisdom. They ate the hearts of the dead in

WORLD BOOK illustration by Robert Hynes

A canna produces large, showy blossoms. The largest variety of this tall plant grows up to 10 feet (3 meters) high.

order to acquire those qualities themselves. The inhabitants of ancient Gaul (now mainly France) thought that eating parts of another human being cured diseases.

Some cannibals showed respect to dead relatives and friends by eating them. Central Australia's Aborigines thought this practice strengthened the ties between dead family members and the living ones. Some mothers ate their dead babies to get back the strength they thought they had given the infants in pregnancy.

Some societies thought eating the corpses of enemies prevented the souls of the slain foes from seeking revenge. The Maori of New Zealand felt they insulted their enemies by cooking and eating them. Some cultures in southern Africa believed their members gained courage and wisdom by eating the enemies they had killed.

The word *cannibal* comes from *Carib,* the name of a warlike people who lived on islands in the Caribbean Sea when the Italian navigator Christopher Columbus sailed there in the late 1400's. Neighboring native groups told Columbus that the Carib people ate human flesh. However, some historians and anthropologists doubt this claim. Columbus called the Caribs *Canibales* by mistake. The term *cannibal* also refers to any animal that eats others of its own kind. Wade C. Pendleton

Canning. See **Food preservation** (Canning).

Cannizzaro, *KAN uh ZAH roh* or *KAHN need DZAH roh,* **Stanislao,** *STAH neez LAH oh* (1826-1910), was an Italian chemist who helped define important chemical principles. In 1858, Cannizzaro proposed that measurable amounts of gases could be used to determine the weight of molecules or atoms in those gases. This led to a unified understanding of the composition of chemical compounds and the use of standard chemical formulas.

Cannizzaro was born on July 13, 1826, in Palermo, Sicily. He died on May 10, 1910. Melvyn C. Usselman

Cannon is a weapon of over 1 inch (2.5 centimeters) in caliber that has a barrel, breech, and firing mechanism. The big guns now classed as artillery and the larger guns fired from airplanes during World War II (1939-1945) were once called *cannon. Cannon* comes from the Latin word *canna,* meaning *a tube* or *reed.* Large cannons were first used in warfare about 1350. Cannons of that time were cast of bronze and of wrought iron. Cannons firing heavy balls were used extensively in the American Civil War (1861-1865). Frances M. Lussier

See also **Artillery; Civil War, American** (picture); **Gun.**

Cannon, Annie Jump (1863-1941), was considered the leading American female astronomer of her generation. In 1896, she joined the staff of the Harvard Observatory. Working with other astronomers there, Cannon developed a system of classifying stars by the spectra of their light and applied the system to over 350,000 stars. She discovered 300 variable stars, five *novae* (types of exploding stars), and a binary star. In 1925, Cannon became the first woman awarded an honorary doctorate of science by Oxford University.

Cannon was born on Dec. 11, 1863, in Dover, Delaware. She died on April 13, 1941. Peggy Aldrich Kidwell

Cannon, Joseph Gurney (1836-1926), an Illinois Republican, served in the United States House of Representatives for 46 years of the 50 years from 1873 to 1923. He was speaker of the House from 1903 to 1911. As speaker, Cannon accumulated so much authority that the House voted to reduce the powers of the office.

Cannon was a leader of congressional conservatives called Stalwarts. The Stalwarts opposed liberal legislation sought by progressives, including Republican President Theodore Roosevelt and both Republicans and Democrats in Congress. During Cannon's time, the speaker served as chairman of the House Rules Committee, which determined when proposed legislation would be taken up by the House. The speaker also appointed many of the members of other House committees. Cannon used these powers of the office to block progressive legislation. Discontent over Cannon's control of the House arose. In 1910, the House members voted to strip the speaker of his membership in the Rules Committee and further reduced the power of the office of speaker by ending its role of appointing committee members.

Cannon was born on May 7, 1836, in Guilford County, North Carolina, and grew up in Indiana. He settled in Illinois in 1858. He began his political career as state's attorney of Illinois, from 1861 to 1868. Cannon served in the U.S. House from 1873 to 1891, from 1893 to 1913, and from 1915 to 1923, when he retired. From 1872 to 1920, he won election to the House 23 times and lost only twice. Cannon was nicknamed "Uncle Joe." He died on Nov. 12, 1926.

Cannon-ball tree is a South American tree that bears large, round fruits that resemble cannonballs. The fruits are reddish-brown and grow to 9 inches (23 centime-

Culver

An early giant cannon, the *Dulle Griete,* fired 700-pound (320-kilogram) balls at the Battle of Ghent in 1411.

WORLD BOOK illustration by John D. Dawson

The cannon-ball tree is a South American tree with pink or reddish flowers. A sweet drink is made from its round fruits.

ters) in diameter. They have thin, woody shells filled with soft pulp that has a disagreeable odor. Many seeds lie in the pulp. The tree can shed its leaves several times a year in response to dry weather. It bears fragrant yellow or reddish flowers in clusters directly on the trunk or on short, tangled branches along the trunk. The flowers are about 2 inches (5 centimeters) wide and have four to six curved petals. The cannon-ball tree is related to the Brazil-nut tree. George Yatskievych

Scientific classification. The cannon-ball tree belongs to the monkey pot family, Lecythidaceae. Its scientific name is *Couroupita guianensis.*

See also **Brazil nut.**

Canoeing is a popular sport in which one or more people paddle a light, narrow boat called a canoe. Many people take canoes on camping, fishing, or hunting trips deep into wilderness areas. Others enjoy a peaceful canoe trip across a lake, or an exciting canoe race down a river.

Canoes are easy to operate, maintain, store, and transport. They also cost less than other kinds of boats. However, canoeing can be dangerous. A canoeist should learn proper technique and basic safety rules from a qualified instructor.

Canoeing equipment

A canoeist needs only two basic pieces of equipment—a canoe and a paddle. Many canoeists also use a variety of other equipment. In addition, each person in a canoe should always wear a flotation device, such as a life jacket.

Canoes. Most canoes measure from 11 to 20 feet (3.4 to 6.1 meters) long. They range from 35 to 40 inches (89 to 102 centimeters) in *beam,* the width at the widest point. Their depth varies from 12 to 14 inches (30 to 36 centimeters). Canoes can be made of aluminum, a synthetic fiber called Kevlar, fiberglass, plastic, inflatable rubber, or wood and canvas.

Most canoes are open boats—that is, they have no deck. Some have an enclosed deck with a cockpit where the canoeist kneels. Decked canoes closely resemble kayaks and are used in rough water where an open canoe would quickly fill with water. Other canoes have one square end to which a small motor can be attached. Still other craft, called *sailing canoes,* have a mast and a sail but can also be paddled.

The design of a canoe reflects two opposing principles. *Maneuverability* is the ease with which a canoe can be operated. *Stability* is the quality that prevents it from turning over. In highly maneuverable canoes, the ends may be raised out of the water. The degree to which the ends are raised is called *rocker.* The more rocker a canoe has, the more easily it can spin and turn to miss obstacles. But it cannot travel in a straight line as well as a boat with less rocker. Stable canoes have flat bottoms. Some canoes even have a flat piece of metal or wood called a *keel* that extends into the water from the bottom of the hull. Such canoes hold a straight course easily but are difficult to maneuver on a river.

Paddles. Most canoe paddles are made of wood, but some are made of aluminum, carbon fiber, fiberglass, or plastic. Wood paddles must be examined yearly for splits. The other types are more durable and require less maintenance. Paddles vary in length. A canoeist should select a paddle that extends from the ground to eye level.

The type of paddle blade depends on a person's needs and experience. A wide blade provides a powerful stroke but requires strength and skill to use. A narrow blade requires less strength but does not provide so much power. One popular type, the *beaver tail blade,* measures from 6 to 8 inches (15 to 20 centimeters) wide.

Other equipment includes a *bailer,* which may be a coffee can or a small pump, to empty water from the canoe. Many canoes are fitted with a device called a *yoke* for carrying the craft. When canoeing in cold water, a person may wear a tight-fitting garment called a *wet suit* for protection. A backrest and kneeling pad may be used for comfort.

Canoeists should keep food, clothing, and camping equipment in waterproof storage bags. If the boat overturns, equipment in waterproof bags will float and can be recovered after the boat is righted. Equipment should not be strapped to the exterior of the boat because its weight could make an overturned canoe too heavy to right. However, equipment can be strapped inside the canoe to prevent the loss of items.

Handling a canoe

A skilled canoeist follows certain procedures in handling a canoe safely and efficiently. The most important one involves maintaining balance in the canoe so it re-

© Knud Nielsen, Shutterstock

A canoe ride across a lake is a relaxing form of recreation and exercise for the entire family. Canoes are also used for camping, fishing, and hunting trips. In addition, canoe racing is a popular sport.

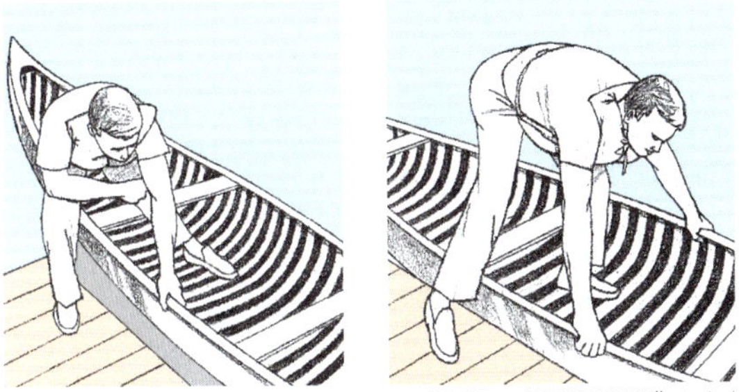

American National Red Cross (WORLD BOOK illustration)

To enter a canoe, a canoeist grips the near rim and places one foot in the middle of the craft, *left.* He then shifts his weight onto the foot in the canoe and grips the far rim, *right.*

mains *trim* (level). This is done by evenly distributing the weight of the people and equipment in the craft, and by keeping the weight low in the canoe. The easiest way to do this is to kneel. Other procedures include (1) entering and leaving a canoe, (2) paddling and steering, and (3) *portaging* (carrying) a canoe.

Entering and leaving a canoe. When entering a canoe, the canoeist faces the bow of the canoe, grips the near *gunwale* (rim of the craft), and puts one foot in the middle of the canoe. Then, with one hand on the near gunwale, the canoeist reaches for the far gunwale with the other hand. At the same time, the canoeist shifts weight onto the foot in the canoe and lifts the other foot aboard. When two canoeists are entering, the first on board sits in the stern and steadies the canoe for the second, who sits in the bow. When leaving a canoe, a canoeist follows the same procedure in reverse. If two persons are leaving, the one in the bow goes first.

Paddling and steering. A canoeist should take a comfortable paddling position, either kneeling or sitting. Whatever position is used, the canoe must be kept trim at all times. When two canoeists are paddling, the one in the stern may use a slightly longer paddle, which enables the craft to be steered more easily. The two canoeists should paddle from opposite sides of the canoe, coordinating their strokes to move through the water efficiently and safely.

Canoeists use several kinds of paddle strokes. The most basic one is the *forward stroke,* which moves the canoe forward. The canoeist holds the paddle with one hand near the *grip* (top) and the other hand near the blade. The hands should be about as far apart as the width of the shoulders. The paddle is planted in the water, and the boat is pulled forward by the rotation of the canoeist's torso.

Each bow stroke turns the canoe away from the side on which the stroke is made. Therefore, various strokes must be used to hold a straight course. One such stroke is the *J-stroke,* in which the top hand rotates downward so the thumb points toward the water and the paddle blade is pushed away from the boat. Other strokes maneuver the canoe backward or sideways. A canoe can be stopped by pushing the paddle forward in the water.

Portaging a canoe. On some canoe trips, the canoe may have to be carried overland. On a river trip, for example, canoeists may want to avoid such obstacles as rapids or falls. Or the canoeists may want to reach a lake that lies several miles from the river. When portaging a canoe, the canoeists may use a padded yoke, which enables the canoe to be carried upside down on their shoulders.

Canoe racing

Canoe racing provides challenge and excitement. The several kinds of competition include (1) marathon racing, (2) white-water racing, (3) flat water, or sprint, racing, and (4) poling and sailing.

Marathon racing can take place on any large body of water. The contestants speed over a course that can extend 20 miles (32 kilometers) or longer. The winner is determined by the fastest time. Men, women, and children compete in separate events.

White-water racing was named for the rough, rapid water on which the race takes place. Open or decked canoes compete in these races. The winner is determined by the fastest time. There are two types of white-water racing, *wildwater* and *slalom.* A wildwater race is based on the endurance, skill, and strength of the racers.

AP/Wide World

Flat water racing takes place on the smooth water of a lake or a lagoon. This exciting form of canoeing requires a great deal of experience as well as endurance, strength, and skill.

A reed canoe is poled by an Indian who lives in a village along the shores of Lake Titicaca on the border between Peru and Bolivia. Indians make the canoes themselves. They have used them for centuries as a convenient means of transportation.

A slalom race features precise maneuvering of canoes through a series of poles called *gates,* which hang over the water.

Flat water racing, also called *sprint racing,* an event of the Summer Olympic Games, takes place on smooth water in a lake or lagoon. One, two, or four racers paddle each canoe over a course of 500 to 10,000 meters.

Poling and sailing are special types of canoe racing. In poling racing, a canoeist propels the craft with a pole that measures from 12 to 14 feet (3.4 to 4.3 meters) long. Contestants in poling races maneuver upstream and downstream and around floating markers called *buoys.* Races are held in several classes of competition.

Canoe camping

Canoe camping became increasingly popular during the early 1970's. Many people found they could use canoes to reach quiet, scenic sites far from crowded campgrounds. Canoe camping includes long trips through wilderness areas, as well as quiet weekends on a local lake or river. Information on the many campsites in North America may be obtained from state agencies or from the American Canoe Association in Newington, Virginia. The equipment that is taken on a canoe trip depends on such factors as the season, the amount of cargo space in the canoe, and the amount of portaging involved. For a discussion of camping equipment, see the *World Book* article on **Camping** (Camping equipment and food).

History

The canoe developed from the seagoing dugouts of the Carib Indians of the Caribbean islands. These dugouts were made from large tree trunks, which had been shaped and then hollowed out. The word *canoe* comes from *kanu,* the Carib term for such a dugout.

The early Indians of North America made canoes by fastening bark, mostly birchbark, to a wooden frame or by hollowing out the trunks of trees. These light, swift canoes were ideal for the lakes, rivers, and streams of the continent.

During the 1600's, canoes played an important part in the exploration of North America. In 1673, Louis Joliet, a French-Canadian explorer, and Father Jacques Marquette, a French missionary, traveled the Mississippi River in birchbark canoes.

Critically reviewed by the American Canoe Association

See also **Indian, American** (Transportation); **Kayaking; Olympic Games** (table).

Additional resources

Arima, Eugene Y., and Jennings, John. *The Canoe.* Firefly Bks., 2002.
Gordon, I. Herbert. *The Complete Book of Canoeing.* 3rd ed. Globe Pequot, 2001.
Kalman, Bobbie. *A Canoe Trip.* Crabtree Pub. Co., 1995. Younger readers.
Kuhne, Cecil. *Canoeing.* Stackpole, 1998.

Canola oil is a vegetable oil made from the seeds of the canola plant. It is used mainly as a cooking and salad oil and in such foods as margarine and shortening. Canola oil has a pale yellow color and is almost tasteless. Canola oil is popular with health-conscious consumers because it contains low levels of saturated fats, which have been linked to heart disease, and because it contains high levels of essential fatty acids, which are necessary for good nutrition.

Canadian plant breeders developed the canola plant in 1974. It is a variety of the rape plant (see **Rape**). Rapeseed is a traditional source of cooking oil in China, India, and northern Europe. Unlike rapeseed oil, canola oil has little *erucic acid,* a fatty substance thought to contribute to heart disease.

Canola seeds consist of about 45 percent oil. To extract it, producers squeeze the seeds with a machine and then soak them in a liquid that draws out the remaining oil. The material that is left, called *canola meal,* is fed to animals. Canada and Europe are the leading producers of canola oil. Levente L. Diosady

Cañon. See Canyon.

Canon, *KAN uhn,* is a musical composition in which two or more voices or instruments repeat a melody. One begins the melody and one or more others imitate it. The additional voices or instruments join in at slightly different times and overlap as a result. Songs that are called *rounds* are the simplest kind of canon. The song "Row, Row, Row Your Boat" is a popular example of a round. Rounds are called *perpetual canons* because they can go on indefinitely. A canon is a type of counterpoint (see **Counterpoint**). A canon is one of the most difficult types of counterpoint to compose because the voice or instrument can enter at any interval or on any rhythmic beat.

The earliest known canons date from the 1200's. Johann Sebastian Bach of Germany was perhaps the greatest composer of canons. Bach's finest canons appear in the *Goldberg Variations* (1742), *Musical Offering* (1747), and other collections. R. M. Longyear

Canonization is a proclamation in the Roman Catholic Church by which a person famous for holiness is understood to be in heaven. That person is given the title of *saint.* Respect is shown for a saint through prayers, festivals, and art connected with the individual. The church encourages imitation of the saint's life.

The church conducts a strict examination and inquiry into the person's life and virtue before issuing the proclamation of canonization. The examination may require several miracles attributed to the person. The individual can then be proposed as an example of how to live a dedicated spiritual life. Only certain people are declared saints through canonization. However, the church does not imply that a deceased person is not a saint or in heaven if canonization has not occurred.

In the early church, apostles and some martyrs were *venerated* (honored) as saints by popular acclaim. By the 300's, holy people in certain regions were considered saints, often leading to their acceptance as saints by the entire church. Gradually, canonization became more formal. The first solemn canonization honored Saint Ulric of Augsburg in 993. Richard L. Schebera

See also **Saint; All Saints' Day**.

Canova, *kuh NOH vuh,* **Antonio** (1757-1822), was one of the most famous and influential European sculptors of the Napoleonic period. Canova's sculpture is usually

Marble sculpture (1805-1808); Villa Borghese, Rome (SCALA/Art Resource)

A Canova statue shows the artist's neoclassical style in its reference to ancient Greek and Roman themes. The work was commissioned by Napoleon I. It portrays Napoleon's sister Pauline Borghese reclining as Venus, the Roman goddess of love.

called "neoclassical" because it shows the strong influence of classical Greek and Roman work. Many of his statues represent the gods and heroes of ancient times. Even when portraying Napoleon and other people of his own time, Canova usually presented them as though they were ancient Romans. Canova's greatness lies in his ability to fill these forms from another time with a distinct grace and vitality. His ability to carve pure white Italian marble has seldom been equaled.

Canova was born on Nov. 1, 1757, in Possagno in northern Italy and spent much of his life in Rome. But he was known and admired all over Europe. Most of his statues are in European collections, but the Metropolitan Museum of Art in New York City owns important works, including *Perseus* and *Cupid and Psyche.*

Douglas K. S. Hyland

Cantaloupe. See **Muskmelon.**

Cantata, *kuhn TAH tuh,* is a form of dramatic vocal music. A cantata may be composed for a single solo voice or for several solo voices and a chorus. The texts may have either religious or nonreligious themes. Accompaniment varies from full orchestra to a small ensemble consisting of a keyboard instrument and wind or stringed instruments. A cantata is similar to a short oratorio or to a brief opera without acting or scenery.

Cantatas originated in Italy during the early 1600's. This style served as the basis for the form in other countries. After 1700, the Italian cantata followed a standard format: two or three songlike sections called *arias* connected by speechlike passages called *recitatives.*

In Germany, the emphasis was on church cantatas. During the 1600's and 1700's, the cantata became the most important musical component in Lutheran church services. These cantatas tended to be more serious, dramatic, and elaborate than Italian *secular* (nonreligious) cantatas. Most have Biblical texts or poetic paraphrases of such texts. During the early 1700's, the German composer Johann Sebastian Bach wrote nearly 300 cantatas, of which about 195 survive today. Many are chorale cantatas—that is, a cantata based on a specific Lutheran chorale melody. Katherine K. Preston

See also **Bach, Johann Sebastian.**

Canterbury is the ancient religious center of Britain. It is the chief town in the district of Canterbury, which has a population of 135,287. Canterbury lies in southeastern England in the county of Kent (see **England** [political map]). The town is a regional service center and has light industries. Canterbury is the home of the University of Kent. Canterbury's history and architecture attract many tourists. The archbishop of Canterbury is the spiritual head of the Church of England. Canterbury's main attraction is its huge Gothic cathedral, which was begun in the 1000's. Canterbury attracted many pilgrims during the Middle Ages. It was the destination of Geoffrey Chaucer's travelers in his famous *Canterbury Tales.* See also **England** (picture: Canterbury Cathedral); **Cathedral** (picture). D. A. Pinder

Canterbury bell is a type of flowering plant with blue, pink, or white bell-shaped flowers. The plants grow as tall as 3 feet (91 centimeters). The flowers measure 2 to 3 inches (5 to 8 centimeters) long and are widely spaced on a single, flowering stem. Canterbury bells have hairy, oval leaves. The leaves at the base of the plant grow up to 10 inches (25 centimeters) long. The leaves on the flowering stem are shorter.

Canterbury bells are biennials—that is, they live for two years and then die. They do not flower until the second summer.They grow wild in woods and stony places, and they are also grown in gardens. Canterbury bells are native to southern Europe. Margaret R. Bolick

Scientific classification. Canterbury bells are in the family Campanulaceae. They are *Campanula medium.*

Canterbury Tales is a group of stories by the English poet Geoffrey Chaucer. Scholars consider it the outstanding work in Middle English, the form of English used from about 1100 to about 1485. Chaucer worked on *The Canterbury Tales* from about 1386 until his death

Illustration from an English manuscript; the British Museum, London (Granger Collection)

The Canterbury Tales is a collection of stories by the English author Geoffrey Chaucer. A group of pilgrims tell the stories as they travel from the Tabard Inn near London to a religious shrine in Canterbury. This illustration dates from the early 1400's, when the tales were first widely circulated.

in 1400. He did not quite complete the work, but his plan is suggested in the general prologue. He gathered 29 pilgrims at the Tabard Inn in Southwark, across the River Thames from London, for a pilgrimage to Canterbury. Each pilgrim agreed to tell two tales going and two tales returning.

Chaucer wrote only 24 tales, and four of these are incomplete. The pilgrims approach Canterbury on the fourth day. There is no return journey. Many critics believe this one-way pilgrimage actually represents Chaucer's intended plan—a pilgrimage of human life that suggests the journey from earth to heaven.

Chaucer introduced the pilgrims in the prologue. The knight, the parson, and the plowman are idealized portraits representing the medieval *three estates*—aristocracy, clergy, and workers. Other pilgrims are drawn mainly from the English middle class of the 1300's.

Chaucer provided much detail about the characters' appearance and private lives. Like their tellers, the tales display diverse subjects and styles. Most tales reflect the personalities of the pilgrims who tell them. For example, the nun tells a story about a saint. Some are arranged in groups and give different viewpoints on a subject. Love, marriage, and domestic harmony are the most common themes. Paul Strohm

See also **Chaucer, Geoffrey**.

Canticles. See **Song of Solomon**.

Cantilever, *KAN tuh LEE vuhr,* is a structure that is supported at one end by a downward force. The other end projects into space without support. Many canopies, theater balconies, and some construction cranes are built as cantilevers. They eliminate the need for supporting columns. A cantilever bridge commonly has two towers, or *piers,* on opposite sides of the river. Each pier supports part of a roadway anchored on the bank at one end. The rest of both roadways project out to the middle of the river, where they are joined. Each half of the bridge is an independent cantilever, standing without support from the other. William J. Hennessey

See also **Architecture** (Architectural terms; picture); **Bridge** (Cantilever bridges; picture).

Canton. See **Guangzhou**.

Canton (pop. 80,806; met. area pop. 406,934) is an industrial and trading center in northeastern Ohio. The city lies about 60 miles (97 kilometers) south of Cleveland (see **Ohio** [political map]).

About 350 companies in the Canton metropolitan area produce such products as alloy and specialty steel, tapered bearings, and vacuum cleaners. Other products include cans and lids, diesel engines, gasoline and other petroleum products, household and cooking wares, meats, metal forgings and castings, rubber gloves, shelving, steel lockers, and wall tile.

Canton lies in a shrinking agricultural area. Much of the surrounding farmland has been developed for commercial and residential use. Dairying is the main farm industry. Pascal celery and other vegetables also flourish there. In addition, the region has important deposits of bituminous coal, clay, and limestone.

Canton's chief tourist attractions are the Pro Football Hall of Fame and the McKinley National Memorial. The annual Pro Football Hall of Fame Festival in July and August includes a ceremony honoring new Hall of Fame members and the first preseason game of the National Football League. The McKinley monument honors United States President William McKinley. He and his wife lived in Canton and are buried at the memorial. Other attractions include the McKinley Museum of History, Science and Industry and the National First Ladies Library.

Canton is the home of Malone College and Walsh University. Canton's Cultural Center for the Arts houses the Art Institute and hosts performances of Canton's opera, drama, symphony, and ballet companies.

Canton was founded in 1805 and became the seat of Stark County in 1809. It was incorporated as a village in 1822 and became a city in 1854. Canton has a mayor-council form of government. Rick Senften

Canute, *kuh NOOT* or *kuh NYOOT* (994?-1035), also spelled *Cnut,* became king of England in 1016. That year, he completed the Danish conquest of England that his father, Sweyn Forkbeard, had begun. Canute divided England into military districts ruled by earls. In 1019, he succeeded his brother as king of Denmark. He acquired Norway in 1028, thus uniting a great Scandinavian empire that centered around the North Sea. In England, Canute ruled wisely and enjoyed strong support from the church. His code of laws restored and enforced Anglo-Saxon customs. He was the first Norse ruler to be accepted as a civilized Christian king. Joel T. Rosenthal

See also **England** (The Anglo-Saxon period).

Canvas is a strong, coarse cloth. The name comes from a Latin word meaning *hemp,* which was originally used to make canvas. Most canvas is made of cotton and is called *duck.* More expensive canvas fabrics are made from synthetic fibers. Artists paint oil pictures on cotton or linen canvas. Canvas is also used for clothing and tennis shoes. Heavy grades of canvas are used for conveyor belts, sails, tents, awnings, and coverings called *tarpaulins.* O. Frank Hunter

Canvasback is a large duck that lives in North America. The duck is named for the male's grayish-white back

© S. Nielsen, Bruce Coleman Inc.

The male canvasback has a reddish-brown head and a black breast. The grayish-white color of its back and sides resembles the color of canvas, giving the duck its name.

and sides, which resemble the color of canvas. The male also has a reddish-brown head and neck and a black breast. The female is gray and brown. Canvasbacks are about 21 inches (53 centimeters) long and weigh 2 to 3 pounds (0.9 to 1.4 kilograms). They dive underwater to feed on wild celery, clams, and other plants and animals that live on the bottom of lakes and marshes.

Canvasbacks breed in marshes on the Canadian prairies and in Alaska. The birds usually build nests in clumps of cattails or bulrushes. The female canvasback lays seven to nine greenish eggs. Another kind of duck, the *redhead,* often lays its eggs in canvasback nests.

Canvasbacks spend the winter in Chesapeake Bay, San Francisco Bay, and other areas on the Atlantic and Pacific coasts of the United States and Mexico. Many hunters prize the duck as a game bird. Eric G. Bolen

Scientific classification. The canvasback belongs to the family Anatidae. It is *Aythya valisineria.*

Canyon, also spelled *cañon,* is a deep valley with steep sides. A narrow canyon with nearly vertical walls or cliffs is called a *gorge, ravine,* or *chasm.*

Most canyons have been formed by rivers or streams. One of the most spectacular examples, the Grand Canyon, in Arizona, was cut by the Colorado River over millions of years. The Grand Canyon has an average depth of 1 mile (1.6 kilometers). Glaciers also have shaped canyons in mountainous regions. Such canyons usually have a U shape. Stream-cut canyons typically have a V shape. Narrow bays called *fiords* have formed on coastlines where the sea level has risen to flood canyons that were cut by glaciers. Canyons also may form as a result of *faulting* (shifts in Earth's crust). Faulting has created many of the large canyons on the ocean floor. Richard G. Reider

See also **Bryce Canyon National Park; Erosion; Grand Canyon; Royal Gorge; Yellowstone National Park.**

Canyon de Chelly National Monument, *duh SHAY,* is located in northeastern Arizona. It features huge, colorful, steep-walled canyons. The canyons once sheltered ancient Indians called *Anasazi.* Many ruins from these Indians remain nestled below towering cliffs or perched on high ledges. The homes of Navajo Indians are scattered along the canyon floors. The monument was authorized in 1931. For the area of the monument, see **National Park System** (table: National monuments).

Critically reviewed by the National Park Service

See also **Canyon** (picture).

Canyonlands National Park lies in southeast Utah. It is near Moab, Utah, and is centered at the junction of the Green and Colorado rivers. This scenic area has red rock canyons, sandstone spires, and series of canyons called the Maze. The region became a national park in 1964. For the area of the park, see **National Park System** (table: National parks).

Critically reviewed by the National Park Service

Canzoniere. See **Petrarch.**

Cap-Haïtien, *kayp HAY shuhn* (pop. 64,406), is the second largest city of Haiti. However, it has less than 10 percent as many people as Port-au-Prince, Haiti's largest city. Cap-Haïtien lies on Haiti's north coast. The city is an

H. Ross, FPG

Red sandstone canyon walls at Canyon de Chelly National Monument in Arizona tower high above a valley. The ruins of an ancient Indian civilization are preserved within the national monument.

important seaport. For the location of Cap-Haïtien, see **Haiti** (map).

The city hall and a large cathedral stand on opposite sides of the Place d'Armes, Cap-Haïtien's central square. Most of the people are poor and live in shacks or huts in slums outside the city's center.

In 1492, Christopher Columbus founded a settlement near Cap-Haïtien, which lasted only a few months. The French gained control of Haiti during the 1600's. They founded Cap-Haïtien in 1670 and named it Cap-Français. The city became an administrative center and a market center for nearby plantation products. It was renamed Cap-Haïtien after Haiti gained independence from France in 1804. Gary Brana-Shute

Capacitor, *kuh PAS uh tuhr,* is a device that can store electric charge. One main use of capacitors is a smoothing out of *alternating current* produced by electric generators. Alternating current regularly reverses its direction of flow, and equipment that uses alternating current operates most efficiently if the reversals occur smoothly. Capacitors also store data in computer chips, work with other components to tune radios and television sets, and supply bursts of electric energy to certain lasers.

The simplest capacitor consists of two metal plates that are held parallel to each other with a small space between them. Occupying this space is a substance called the *dielectric medium.* This substance can be any *electric insulator* (material that blocks the flow of electric current). Examples include oil, paper, glass, ceramics, mica, plastic, and even air.

In a modification of this design, two sets of metal sheets are alternately stacked together, with dielectric medium between all the sheets. The order of stacking is: sheet in Set A, dielectric medium, sheet in Set B, dielectric medium, sheet in set A, dielectric medium, and so on. All the sheets in Set A are then electrically connected to one another, and all the sheets in Set B are electrically connected to one another. Each set of sheets is therefore electrically equivalent to one plate of a two-plate capacitor. But each sheet has a much smaller area than that of an equivalent plate. Thus, a stacked capacitor can store a large amount of charge in a small area.

A wound capacitor can store the most charge in a given volume of space. This kind of capacitor consists of two metal foils and two plastic sheets that are alternately stacked and then wound together to form a cylinder.

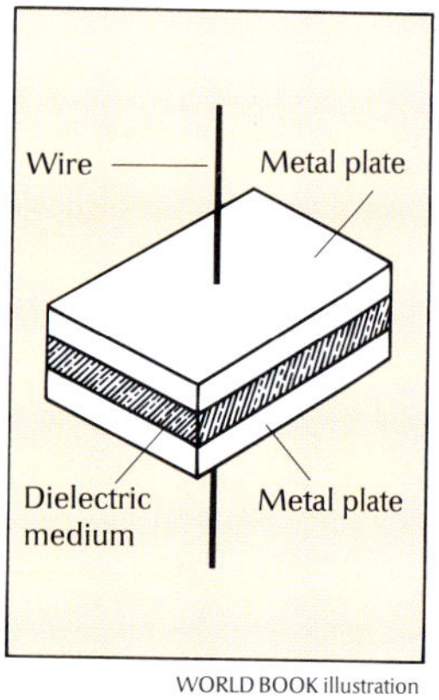

WORLD BOOK illustration

Parts of a capacitor

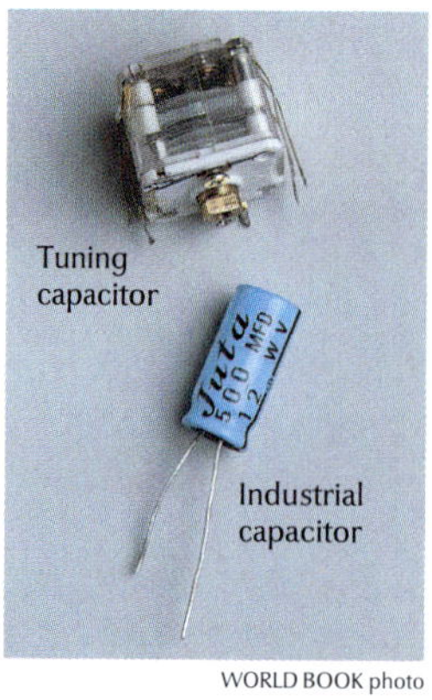

WORLD BOOK photo

Some kinds of capacitors

The foils function as capacitor plates, and the plastic sheets are the dielectric medium.

Capacitors come in various sizes. A capacitor used with a gas laser has two square sheets of metal, each 16 inches (40 centimeters) on a side. Capacitors in computer chips are microscopic. One square centimeter of chip area can contain several million capacitors.

How capacitors work. In an electric circuit, two wires connect the capacitor plates to the opposite terminals of a power source. Charges of equal strength but opposite sign—positive and negative—build up on the plates. The medium prevents current from flowing easily between the plates, though some leakage does occur.

If the power supply is a battery, a voltage builds up between the plates that is equal to the battery voltage. The battery also supplies energy to the capacitor—the energy necessary to charge the capacitor minus losses due to leakage of current between the plates.

A separate pair of wires and an electric switch enable the capacitor to deliver this energy to a device, such as a laser or an electronic flash on a camera. One of these wires connects a capacitor plate to an electric terminal on the device. The second wire connects the device's other terminal to the switch, which is also connected to the capacitor's opposite plate. Normally, the switch is open, so no current flows through the device and no energy is delivered. Closing the switch delivers the energy.

A capacitor can "pass" alternating current almost as if the capacitor were a conductor, even though charge does not flow between the plates. Charge surges into and out of each plate as the current reverses direction. The amount of charge on the plates increases and decreases smoothly, even when the alternating current does not reverse direction smoothly. Thus, a capacitor can smooth out alternating current.

Capacitance is a measure of a capacitor's ability to store charge. The unit of capacitance is the *farad,* which is named after English chemist and physicist Michael Faraday. But 1 farad is a huge amount of capacitance. Most capacitors have capacitances measured in *microfarads* or *picofarads.* One microfarad equals one-millionth of a farad. One picofarad equals one-millionth of a microfarad. Capacitance is defined as the charge on either plate divided by the voltage between the plates. The standard unit of charge is the *coulomb,* and so 1 farad equals 1 coulomb per volt. Peter Bohdan Kosel

See also **Coulomb; Electric current; Farad; Insulator, Electric.**

Cape is a body of land that extends prominently into a lake, sea, or ocean. Capes often form at the tips of islands and continents and are also called *headlands, promontories,* or *points.* The water surrounding capes is often rough, making navigation difficult.

Capes are formed in two chief ways—by erosion and by the build-up of deposits. In erosion, waves and currents wash away parts of the coast. More resistant land, such as volcanic rock, remains and forms a cape. Heceta Head and Cape Foulweather, both on the Oregon coast, are examples of capes that were formed by erosion.

Capes that are created by deposits form when currents and waves dump sandy materials or gravel in coastal waters, or onto sandbars. These deposits eventually form a body of land. Cape Canaveral in Florida is an example of a cape created this way.

Henry D. Meyer, Berg & Associates

A cape is land that projects into a body of water. Lighthouses are often built on capes. The cape that is shown at the left extends from the Oregon coast at Newport into the North Pacific Ocean.

Some capes, such as Cape Cod in Massachusetts, are shaped by both erosion and deposits. Erosion has left a line of cliffs along the Atlantic coast of Cape Cod. Along Cape Cod Bay, however, deposits have built up sandy beaches. Anthony J. Lewis

Cape Breton Island, *BREHT uhn* or *BRIHT uhn,* is a large island off the Atlantic coast of Canada. It forms part of the province of Nova Scotia and covers 3,981 square miles (10,311 square kilometers). A saltwater lake called Bras d'Or Lake occupies about a sixth of the island.

Cape Breton Island has a rugged coastline with many inlets. A highway called the Cabot Trail winds along the northern part of the island, skirting the scenic coastal fringe of Cape Breton Highlands National Park. A stone causeway built in 1955 provides a road and railroad link between Cape Breton and mainland Nova Scotia.

People. About three-fourths of Cape Breton Island's 147,000 residents live in the Cape Breton Regional Municipality. The municipality includes the communities of Dominion, Glace Bay, Louisbourg, New Waterford, North Sydney, Sydney, and Sydney Mines, as well as the surrounding rural areas. Almost half of Cape Breton Island's population is of Scottish descent. There are also many ethnic minorities, including French-speaking Acadians and Native Americans.

Industry. Rich coal fields beneath Cape Breton Island once made it the center of coal and steel production in the four Atlantic Provinces—New Brunswick, Newfoundland and Labrador, Nova Scotia, and Prince Edward Island. That industry declined sharply just after World War II (1939-1945). Chief sources of income today are pulp and paper manufacturing, fishing, tourism, and agriculture.

History. Basque fishermen from Europe visited Cape Breton Island in the early 1500's. The French took control of the island in the early 1600's. In 1763, Britain gained control of Cape Breton Island and made it part of its colony of Nova Scotia. The island became a separate British colony in 1784. In 1820, it reunited with Nova Scotia. Thousands of people, most from Scotland, settled on the island between the 1790's and the 1830's. The coal and steel industries began to thrive in the early 1900's. During the 1970's, many new industries opened in the Sydney area. D. A. Sutherland

See also **Louisbourg; Nova Scotia** (picture: The Northern Highlands region).

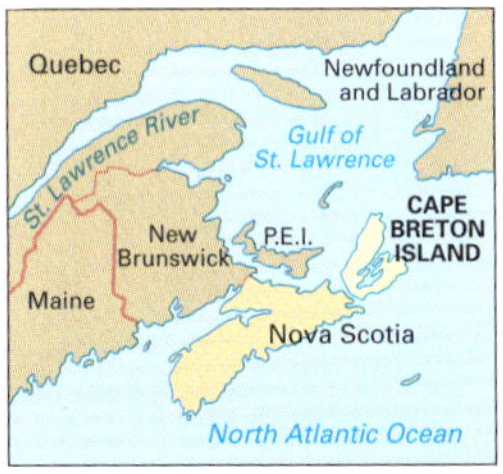

Cape Breton Island lies off the eastern coast of Canada. The island forms the northeastern part of the province of Nova Scotia.

WORLD BOOK maps

Cape buffalo. See **Buffalo** (animal).

Cape Canaveral is a point of land that juts into the Atlantic Ocean from the east coast of Florida. It is the site of Cape Canaveral Air Station, where rockets are launched. People often use the name *Cape Canaveral* to refer to the John F. Kennedy Space Center, the site where the National Aeronautics and Space Administration (NASA) launches all its manned space flights. The center used Air Force facilities on Cape Canaveral until 1964. That year, the center moved to Merritt Island, just west of the cape. *Cape Canaveral* is also the name of a town on the southern end of the cape.

Until 1963, the cape had its present name, and the station was named Cape Canaveral Air Force Station. In 1963, they were renamed Cape Kennedy and Cape Kennedy Air Force Station, respectively. In 1973, the names of the cape and the station were changed back. The word *Force* was dropped from the name of the station in 1994. Roger E. Bilstein

See also **Kennedy Space Center.**

Cape Cod is a hook-shaped peninsula on the coast of Massachusetts. It received its name because of the codfish caught off its shores. Cape Cod Bay lies in the hooked arm of Cape Cod. The islands of Martha's Vineyard and Nantucket are just south of the cape, which is about 65 miles (105 kilometers) long and from 1 to 20 miles (1.6 to 32 kilometers) wide. The cape covers Barnstable County, which has a population of about 220,000.

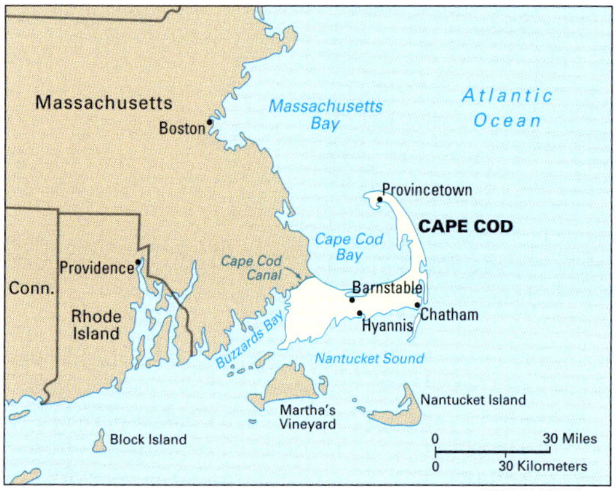

WORLD BOOK map

Location of Cape Cod

The town of Barnstable is the county seat. Sandy beaches, sailing opportunities, and the beautiful shoreline and upland landscape features of Cape Cod National Seashore help make the cape a popular tourist area. Popular destinations on Cape Cod include Hyannis and Provincetown.

Bartholomew Gosnold, an Englishman who sailed around Cape Cod in 1602, is usually credited as the first European to sight it. However, some historians believe that Basque and Norse fishing crews visited the cape long before Gosnold's voyage. Cape Cod was a center of the whaling industry in the 1800's. Laurence A. Lewis

Cape Cod Canal is one of the world's widest artificial waterways. It ranges from 450 to 700 feet (137 to 213 meters) in width. It cuts through the strip of land that joins Cape Cod to the rest of Massachusetts. The canal decreases the sea route between Boston and New York City by 70 miles (110 kilometers), and enables ships to avoid the dangerous shoals off Cape Cod. The total length of the canal is 17 ½ miles (28.2 kilometers).

Cape Colony was a European colony in southern Africa. It occupied the western and southern parts of what is now the country of South Africa. The Cape Colony was sometimes called the Cape of Good Hope, which is the name of the peninsula on the southern coast of Africa where the colony originated. The colony grew in size and eventually covered 276,686 square miles (716,613 square kilometers).

Dutch settlers founded the Cape Colony in 1652 at the present site of Cape Town. The colony gradually annexed lands farther inland. The British took over the colony in 1795. They gave it back to the Dutch in 1803 and regained it in 1806. Many Boers (descendants of Dutch, German, and French settlers) resented British rule and left the colony in the 1830's to settle in what became the Orange Free State and the Transvaal. Boers from these regions invaded the Cape Colony during the Anglo-Boer War of 1899-1902. Many Boers who lived in the colony joined the invading Boer forces. But the Boers lost the war. In 1910, the Cape Colony, Natal, the Orange Free State, and the Transvaal became provinces in the Union of South Africa (later called the Republic of South Africa). The Cape Colony became known as Cape Province.

In 1994, after South Africa's black African majority gained control of the South African government, Cape Province was split into three separate provinces: Eastern Cape, Western Cape, and Northern Cape. In addition, a northeastern section of Cape Province became part of the new province of North West. Bruce Fetter

See also **Anglo-Boer Wars; Cape of Good Hope; Cape Town; Kimberley; Port Elizabeth.**

Cape Hatteras, *HAT uhr uhs,* is a scenic promontory at the southeastern tip of Hatteras Island, which is part of the Outer Banks. It lies over 30 miles (48 kilometers) east of the North Carolina coast (see **North Carolina** [physical map]). The nearby Diamond Shoals are dangerous for ships, and so the area was nicknamed *Graveyard of the Atlantic.* Lighthouses and an offshore light station warn ships away. Cape Hatteras National Seashore is there. Stephen S. Birdsall

Cape Horn is the most southerly part of South America. It lies at the southern tip of Horn Island in Chile. Willem Schouten, a Dutch sailor, named it in 1616 for his native town of Hoorn. The cape runs far into the sea. It has steep sides that rise 500 to 600 feet (150 to 180 meters) in some places. Plant life is sparse on Cape Horn because of the cold climate. The region is so stormy that sailors have dreaded "rounding the Horn." Many ships now use the Panama Canal. Jerry R. Williams

Cape Jasmine. See **Gardenia.**

Cape Kennedy. See **Cape Canaveral.**

Cape of Good Hope is a peninsula in South Africa that lies about 100 miles (160 kilometers) northwest of Cape Agulhas, the southern tip of Africa. It extends south from Table Mountain and is part of the city of Cape Town. South Africans call this peninsula *Cape Peninsula.* They call the peninsula's southern tip *Cape Point.* The peninsula forms the west side of False Bay. The cape is famous for its fine roads and beaches. Much of

Cape Horn is the southernmost tip of South America. The cape lies at the southern end of Horn Island, which belongs to Chile.

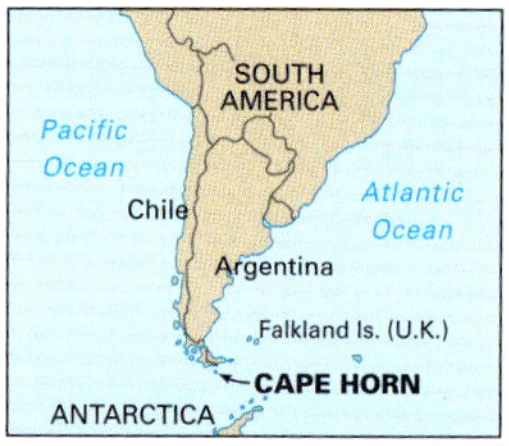

WORLD BOOK maps

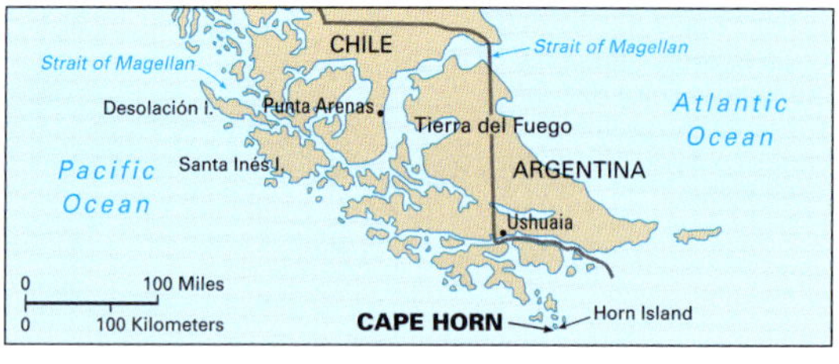

the peninsula lies in Table Mountain National Park.

The Portuguese explorer Bartolomeo Dias is said to have named the Cape of Good Hope when he discovered it in 1488 because he believed his discovery might lead to a sea route to India. The Portuguese explorer Vasco da Gama proved this hope a fact. He sailed around the cape in November 1497, and reached Kozhikode (also known as Calicut), India, in May 1498.

Michael L. McNulty

See also **Da Gama, Vasco; Dias, Bartolomeu.**

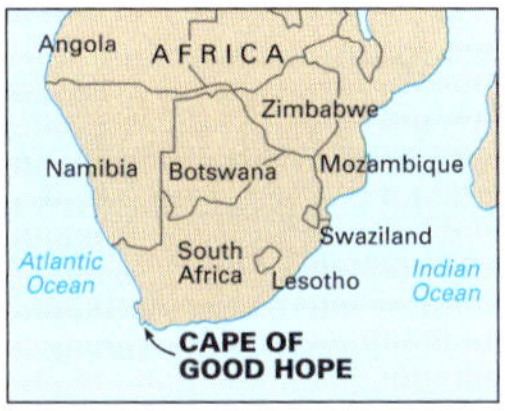

The Cape of Good Hope is a peninsula in South Africa. It lies northwest of Cape Agulhas, the southernmost tip of Africa, and forms the west side of False Bay.

WORLD BOOK maps

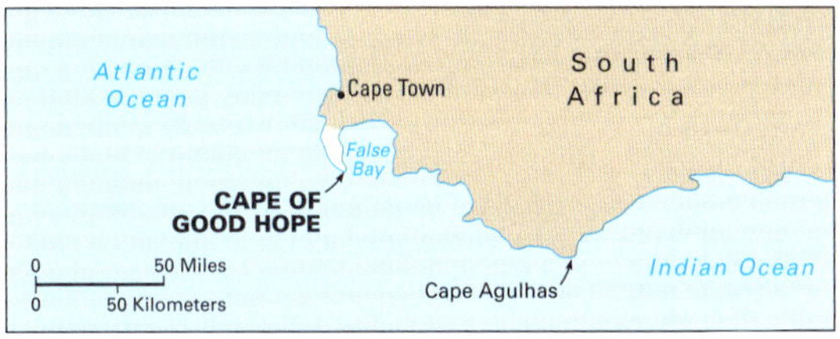

Cape Town (pop. 2,893,251) is the legislative capital of South Africa and one of the country's largest cities. Parliament meets in Cape Town. Pretoria is South Africa's administrative capital, and Bloemfontein is its judicial capital. Cape Town is also the capital of the province of Western Cape. The city lies near the southwestern tip of Africa, close to one of the world's main shipping routes. Cape Town's natural beauty, sandy beaches, and sunny climate make it one of the world's major tourist destinations. For location, see **South Africa** (political map).

Coloureds, who are of mixed African, European, and Asian ancestry, make up nearly half the city's population. About 30 percent of the people are of African descent. Most of them belong to the Xhosa ethnic group. About 20 percent of the people are of European descent.

Table Mountain overlooks the Cape Town city center. The city has many fine buildings, including the Houses of Parliament and several museums, cathedrals, and *mosques* (Muslim houses of worship). Many Cape Town houses reflect the city's early European settlers. The houses feature such elements as Dutch-style rounded gables and British-style Victorian ornaments. The University of Cape Town and the University of the Western Cape are in the municipal area.

Cape Town's excellent docks and harbor make the city an important shipping and trading center. An international airport and South Africa's only nuclear power station are in the Cape Town municipal area.

Cape Town is often called "the mother city" because it was the first place in South Africa to be settled by Europeans. The Dutch East India Company, a trading firm, founded Cape Town in 1652. The British first gained control of the city in 1795. In 1840, Cape Town was declared a municipality. Since the end of South Africa's policy of *apartheid* (racial segregation) in the mid-1990's, the city's boundaries have been extended. Today, Cape Town occupies the entire Cape Peninsula, also called the Cape of Good Hope, and much of the surrounding area (see **Cape of Good Hope**). Grant Saff

Cape Verde, *kayp VURD,* is an African country that consists of 10 main islands and 5 tiny islands. It lies in the Atlantic Ocean, about 400 miles (640 kilometers) west of Dakar, Senegal, on the African mainland.

Cape Verde has a total land area of 1,557 square miles (4,033 square kilometers). São Tiago, also called Santiago, is the largest island. It covers 383 square miles (991 square kilometers). Santo Antão is the second largest island, followed by Boa Vista, Fogo, São Nicolau, Maio, São Vicente, Sal, Brava, and Santa Luzia. Santa Luzia and the five islets are uninhabited.

Praia, the capital and largest city, is on São Tiago. It has a population of about 95,000 and is a major seaport and trading center. Portugal ruled the islands from the 1460's until they gained independence in 1975. The country's official name in Portuguese, the official language, is Republica de Cabo Verde.

Government. Cape Verde is a republic. The people

Silvio Fiore, Shostal

Downtown Cape Town has many modern buildings. The city is the legislative capital of South Africa. The Cape Town city center lies at the foot of Table Mountain, *background.*

Cape Verde

WORLD BOOK maps

elect a 79-member legislature called the People's Assembly, which selects a prime minister. The prime minister is the government head and appoints a cabinet of 10 ministers, upon the Assembly's approval. The people elect a president, who is chief of state. Assembly members, the prime minister, and the president all serve 5-year terms. Cape Verde has two major political parties, the Movement for Democracy (MPD) and the African Party for the Independence of Cape Verde (PAICV).

People. A majority of Cape Verde's people have mixed black African and Portuguese ancestry. Most of the rest of the people are black Africans.

Cape Verde has an extremely low standard of living because many of its people cannot find work. The country's chief industries, farming and fishing, provide workers with only a bare income. Famines have occurred frequently through the years, and many of the people are undernourished. Since the mid-1900's, hundreds of thousands of Cape Verdeans have immigrated to Brazil, Portugal, the United States, and other countries.

The official language of Cape Verde is Portuguese. But most Cape Verdeans speak the national language, Crioulo. Crioulo is a local dialect based on Portuguese and various African languages. Most Cape Verdeans are Roman Catholics, but many practice *animism,* the belief that everything in nature has a soul.

The law requires children from ages 7 through 13 to attend school. About two-thirds of the people 15 years of age or older can read and write.

Land and climate. The islands of Cape Verde were formed by volcanic eruptions 2 ½ million to 65 million years ago. The only remaining active volcano is on Fogo Island. Most of the islands have rugged, mountainous land, with tall cliffs along the coastlines.

Cape Verde has a warm, dry climate, with average annual temperatures that range from 68 to 77 °F (20 to 25 °C). A continual shortage of rain makes most of the land too dry to support plant life.

Economy of Cape Verde is underdeveloped. Agriculture is the country's major industry, but most of the land is too dry to farm. Since the late 1960's, drought has caused about a 90 percent drop in agricultural production and the deaths of most of the country's livestock. Cape Verde's chief crops include coffee beans; sugar cane; bananas and other fruits; and such vegetables as beans, corn, and tomatoes.

During the mid-1900's, Cape Verde worked to develop its fishing industry. Lobsters and tuna are the main catches. The country's mining industry produces salt and *pozzuolana,* a volcanic rock used by the cement industry. Both these products are exported.

Before Cape Verde became independent in 1975, it relied almost entirely on Portugal for economic support. Since then, it has received food aid from the United Nations and financial aid from various countries.

Cape Verde has three radio stations and two newspapers. The islands have about 920 miles (1,480 kilometers) of roads. There are no railroads. Boats operate among the islands infrequently. All of the inhabited islands except Brava have airports.

History. Portuguese explorers discovered the islands of Cape Verde during the late 1450's and early 1460's. The islands were uninhabited, and the Portuguese began to settle there almost immediately. They planted cotton, fruit trees, and sugar, and brought slaves from Africa to work the land.

Slave trading became Cape Verde's most important commercial activity during the 1500's and 1600's, and the islands prospered. Slaves learned how to work on plantations there before being shipped elsewhere. The slave trade declined in the late 1600's, and the prosperity ended. Economic conditions improved slightly in the mid-1800's, when Mindelo became an important refueling port for ships crossing the Atlantic.

Portugal ruled Cape Verde and what is now Guinea-Bissau as a single province from 1576 until 1879, when each became a separate Portuguese province. Guinea-Bissau lies southeast of Cape Verde. In 1869, Portugal

Facts in brief

Capital: Praia.
Official language: Portuguese.
Total land area: 1,557 mi^2 (4,033 km^2). *Coastline*—517 mi (966 km).
Elevation: *Highest*—Pico, 9,281 ft (2,829 m). *Lowest*—sea level.
Population: *Estimated 2006 population*—486,000; density, 312 per mi^2 (121 per km^2); distribution, 53 percent urban, 47 percent rural. *2000 census*—434,812.
Chief products: Bananas, salt, sugar cane.
Flag: The flag has five horizontal stripes of blue, white, red, white, and blue. A ring of 10 yellow, five-pointed stars overlaps all five stripes. It is set toward the lower left part of the flag. See **Flag** (picture: Flags of Africa).
Money: *Basic unit*—Cape Verdean escudo.

Shostal

Mindelo, Cape Verde's second largest city, lies on the island of São Vicente. Volcanic ash covers most of the country's rugged, mountainous land, making it difficult to raise crops.

granted the provincial government greater *autonomy* (self-rule). A nationalist group called the African Party for the Independence of Guinea and Cape Verde, a forerunner of the PAICV, formed in 1956. It fought to overthrow Portuguese rule until 1975, when Cape Verde became independent. Until 1990, the PAICV was the country's only legal political party. That year, the Constitution was amended to allow a multiparty system. After elections in 1991, the MPD became the ruling party. It retained power after elections in 1995. The PAICV, however, regained control after elections in 2001. It remained in power after 2006 elections. Clement Henry Moore

Cape York is a mountainous, ice-covered point of land that extends into Baffin Bay. The cape is on the northwest coast of Greenland at 76° north latitude, well north of the Arctic Circle (see **Arctic Ocean** [map]). Admiral Robert E. Peary used it as a base for many of his explorations around the North Pole. Peary's party discovered huge meteorites there, the largest weighing about 34 tons (31 metric tons). M. Donald Hancock

Čapek, *CHAH pehk,* **Karel,** *KAR uhl* (1890-1938), a Czech author, became famous for introducing the word *robot* into the modern vocabulary. In his play *R.U.R.* (1921), Čapek criticized scientific progress and social conformity by creating a race of manufactured men and women who take over the world. He called them robots, a variation of a Czech word for *slaves.*

Čapek's play *The Insect Comedy* (1922) is a fantasy in which he presents insect behavior as a satire of human society. In *The Makropoulos Secret* (1922), a woman who can live forever finds life unbearably boring. Čapek's best-known novel is *The War of the Newts* (1936). He wrote many of his works with his brother Josef, though Karel is often given sole credit. Karel Čapek was born on Jan. 9, 1890, in Bohemia. Gerald M. Berkowitz

See also **Science fiction** (The early 1900's).

Capelin, *KAP uh lihn* or *KAYP lin,* is a small, silvery saltwater fish that lives in the cold seas around the North Pole. Also spelled *capelan,* it is a popular food fish.

Each year during the warmer months, many capelin swim up onto gravel beaches. Females lay their eggs, and the males fertilize them with sperm. The capelin are washed back into the sea by waves, and most die after spawning. The eggs stick to the gravel and are buried by waves. They hatch in two to four weeks. The young capelin leave the gravel when warmer water is driven onshore by the wind. They eat microscopic animals called *zooplankton.* They become mature enough to produce offspring in about two years and grow to full size, almost 8 inches (20 centimeters), after about three years.

Capelin provide food for seals, whales, and many fishes and birds. People eat capelin and use them to make fish meal and oil. David W. Greenfield

Scientific classification. The capelin belongs to the smelt family, Osmeridae. It is *Mallotus villosus.*

Caper, *KAY puhr,* is a pickled flower bud used as a seasoning in salads and in sauces, including tartar sauce. The buds come from a low, trailing shrub called the *caper bush* that grows primarily in the Mediterranean countries. The caper bush blooms early in summer and has pinkish-white flowers with four petals. The unopened buds are pickled in salt and vinegar to make the seasoning. Lyle E. Craker

WORLD BOOK illustration by Robert Hynes

The caper bush

Scientific classification. The caper bush belongs to the caper family, Capparidaceae. Its scientific name is *Capparis spinosa.*

Capet, Hugh. See **Hugh Capet.**

Capetian dynasty, *kuh PEE shuhn,* is the name given to a long line of kings that ruled France from 987 to 1328. Between 987 and 1316, son followed father without a break in the royal succession. Many Capetian kings had very long reigns. Several of them, notably Philip II (Augustus), Louis IX (Saint Louis), and Philip IV (The Fair), were men of considerable administrative ability. Hugh Capet, the first of the line, ruled a small territory around Paris and was surrounded by feudal lords much more powerful than he. Later Capetians enlarged the royal holdings, increased the powers of the rulers, and gave France a strong centralized government. After the Capetian dynasty, France was ruled by two branches of the Capetian family—the Valois family and the Bourbon family. Valois kings ruled France from 1328 to 1589. Bourbons ruled from 1589 to 1792, and again from 1814 to 1848. See **Hugh Capet; Louis IX; Philip II** (of France); **Philip IV** (of France). Joel T. Rosenthal

Capillarity, *KAP uh LAR uh tee,* is the tendency of liquids to move into or out of tiny, hairlike passageways. These passageways, called *capillaries,* occur within slender tubes or as fine pores in solid materials. A paper towel, for example, has millions of capillaries between its fibers. The passageways absorb water by capillarity.

Capillarity occurs whenever liquid in a capillary is in contact with the air. Capillarity depends on *surface tension*—that is, the attraction of the molecules at a liquid's surface for each other (see **Surface tension**). Surface tension will draw liquid into a capillary if the nearby capillary walls strongly attract the molecules of the liquid's surface. On the other hand, surface tension will *repel* (push out) liquid from a capillary if the liquid molecules are more strongly attracted to each other than to the capillary walls. The narrower the capillary, the greater is its ability to absorb or repel a liquid. The most effective capillaries are visible only with a microscope. Most capillaries are irregular in size and shape, which reduces their effectiveness.

Capillarity has many benefits. It draws water through soil to the roots of plants. The capillarity of clothing keeps people comfortable by absorbing moisture. Advances in capillary engineering are improving products by making capillaries more uniform. For example, precisely shaped capillaries in some diapers help keep the skin dry. Capillaries in rainwear repel water yet let in air for greater comfort. Hugh A. Thompson

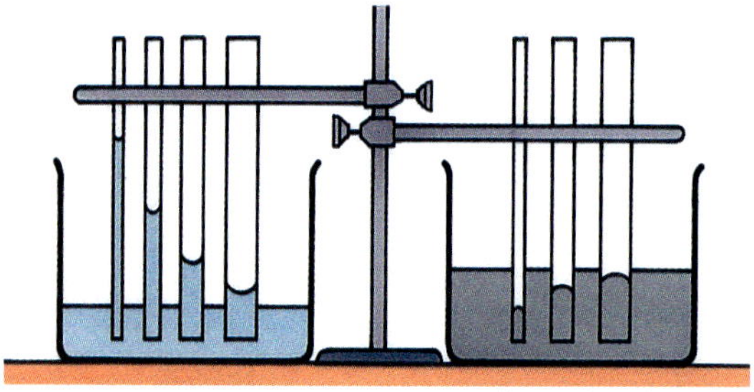

WORLD BOOK illustration by Sarah Woodward

How capillarity works. Glass tubes of different widths are placed in a bowl of water, *left,* and of mercury, *right.* Water rises in the tubes, and rises highest in the narrowest tube. The water is pulled up because its molecules are more attracted to the walls of the tube than to each other. But mercury molecules are more attracted to each other than to the walls of the tubes, and so the level of the mercury in the tubes drops.

Capillary, *KAP uh lehr ee,* is the smallest blood vessel in the body. It can be seen only under the microscope. Most capillaries are so small that only one blood cell can pass through them at a time. Capillaries connect the smallest arteries with the smallest veins. They make up a network of blood vessels throughout the body. The largest capillaries are in the bone marrow and skin. The smallest are located in the brain and lining of the intestine.

Capillaries have thin walls. Foods that are carried in the bloodstream are able to pass through their walls into the tissues. Waste materials from the tissues also pass into the bloodstream through capillary walls. In the capillaries of the lungs, oxygen goes through the walls into the blood, and carbon dioxide goes out. Other waste products pass through tiny capillary walls into the kidneys, intestine, and skin. Dominick Sabatino

See also **Blood; Circulatory system; Vein.**

Capital. See **Column; Capitol.**

Capital refers to anything that produces a "stream of income" over time for individuals or communities. That is how the Scottish economist Adam Smith defined *capital* in his book *The Wealth of Nations* (1776). Economists still use the word in this sense, even though the definition makes little distinction between the various means of production—such as machines and factories—and the money used to purchase them.

There are three principal kinds of capital: (1) physical capital, (2) human capital, and (3) financial capital.

Physical capital refers to inputs that are applied directly to production and that are themselves produced. They include equipment and certain other assets but exclude labor and land.

Human capital refers to the productive skills of workers. According to some estimates, at least half of the total capital in the world consists of human capital. Investments in human capital take the form of education, job training, or work experience. Economists consider these investments an important source of economic growth. To limit confusion, economists often use the word *capital* to refer to physical capital, human capital, or both, but not to financial capital.

Financial capital consists of the funds that firms spend to purchase or rent equipment and land and to hire labor.

There are several other common uses of the word *capital.* For example, the term *capital markets* refers to markets in which various financial assets, such as stocks and bonds, are traded. Likewise, financial economists often use the *capital asset pricing model* to explain the risk-and-reward trade-offs that are reflected in stock prices.

International purchases and sales of various financial assets are recorded in a country's *capital account,* one of two principal categories in the country's balance of payments. The other, the *current account,* reflects the country's international purchases and sales of goods and services. Peter Hans Matthews

Related articles in *World Book* include:

Bank	Economics	Industry (Capital; Management)
Business	Industrial Revolution (The role of capital)	Interest
Capitalism		
Corporation		

Capital gains tax is a tax on income from the sale of capital assets, which include stocks, bonds, real estate, and partnerships. Most countries treat capital gains more favorably than ordinary income, such as wages, interest, and dividends. The favorable treatment may consist of a lower tax rate or of an exclusion of some of the income from the tax.

The United States imposes a tax of up to 20 percent on income from the sale of capital assets owned by an individual for over a year. By contrast, the top tax rate on the ordinary income of individuals is 39.6 percent. Corporations in the United States pay tax on capital gains at the same rate they do on other income. That rate ranges from 15 to 35 percent. The United States and many other countries, including Canada, India, and the United Kingdom, typically do not tax gains from the sale of a home. Most U.S. states treat capital gains the same as ordinary income.

People disagree over whether capital gains should be taxed at a lower rate than ordinary income. Some favor a lower rate as a means of encouraging savings, investment, and the sale of capital assets—and to make up for artificial "gains" in an asset's value due to inflation. Opponents of lower rates stress that such rates benefit primarily higher-income people. They also say that adjustments for inflation can be made in the measurement of income from the sale of capital assets. Some people fear that low capital gains tax rates result in lower government revenues. But low rates may increase revenues by encouraging the sale of capital assets. Emil M. Sunley

Capital punishment is punishment by death for committing a crime. Capital punishment—often called the *death penalty*—is most commonly used in convictions for murder. But it has also been imposed for such crimes as armed robbery, kidnapping, rape, and treason. About 80 countries—including the United States and many African and Asian nations—permit capital punishment. Canada, Australia, and most European and Latin American nations have abolished it.

Throughout history, governments have executed criminals by a variety of methods, including hanging, crucifixion, stoning, beheading, and poisoning. Since the 1600's, shooting—often by firing squads—has been a common method of execution in many countries. Some countries execute criminals using electrocution or deadly gas. The most commonly used method in the United States is *lethal injection.* Lethal injection involves the use of drugs that stop the person's breathing and heartbeat.

History of capital punishment. Governments have used capital punishment since ancient times. In 399 B.C., the Greek philosopher Socrates was forced to drink *hemlock,* a poison the Athenians used for the death penalty. Between the A.D. 400's and 1400's, thousands of people in Europe were executed—usually by hanging or beheading—for crimes against the state and church. During the French Revolution (1789-1799), the revolutionary government executed around 40,000 people. One method of execution in France was the *guillotine,* a beheading machine.

The use of capital punishment in many parts of the world declined during the 1900's. The United Kingdom abolished capital punishment in 1969. Canada did so in 1976. About 100 other nations have formally abolished capital punishment or stopped using it. Many less developed countries continue to impose the death penalty. The United States is the only Western industrialized nation where executions still take place. In the United States, the death penalty may be imposed under federal law, military law, or the laws of 38 states.

The decision of the Supreme Court of the United States in *Furman v. Georgia* (1972) greatly influenced the use of capital punishment in the United States. The court held that the death penalty, as administered at the time, constituted "cruel and unusual punishment" and thus violated the 8th and 14th amendments to the Constitution. However, the court left open the possibility that the death penalty could be constitutional if administered differently. The court stated that death penalty laws must be limited to certain crimes and applied according to fair standards. Following the decision, many states passed new laws to satisfy the court's requirements.

In *Gregg v. Georgia* (1976), the Supreme Court upheld the use of capital punishment for people sentenced under new laws in Florida, Georgia, and Texas. The court ruled that the death penalty itself and the standards developed by the states were constitutional. Later in the 1970's, the court struck down laws that made the death penalty *mandatory* (required) for certain crimes. It also abolished the death penalty as a punishment for rape.

Hundreds of people have been executed in the United States since the Supreme Court upheld the death penalty in 1976. Thousands more are imprisoned on *death row*—that is, they have been sentenced to death but have not yet been executed. Many are awaiting the outcome of legal appeals.

In 2002, the Supreme Court ruled that juries, not judges, must decide sentences in capital punishment cases. That same year, the court ruled that it was unconstitutional to execute people who have mental retardation. In 2005, the court banned the use of capital punishment in cases where the offender was under 18 years of

Capital punishment in the United States

State	Method of execution
Alabama	Lethal injection, electrocution
Alaska	No capital punishment
Arizona	Lethal injection, gas chamber
Arkansas	Lethal injection, electrocution
California	Lethal injection, gas chamber
Colorado	Lethal injection
Connecticut	Lethal injection
Delaware	Lethal injection, hanging
Florida	Lethal injection, electrocution
Georgia	Lethal injection
Hawaii	No capital punishment
Idaho	Lethal injection, firing squad
Illinois	Lethal injection
Indiana	Lethal injection
Iowa	No capital punishment
Kansas	Lethal injection
Kentucky	Lethal injection, electrocution
Louisiana	Lethal injection
Maine	No capital punishment
Maryland	Lethal injection, gas chamber
Massachusetts	No capital punishment
Michigan	No capital punishment
Minnesota	No capital punishment
Mississippi	Lethal injection
Missouri	Lethal injection, gas chamber
Montana	Lethal injection
Nebraska	Electrocution
Nevada	Lethal injection
New Hampshire	Lethal injection, hanging
New Jersey	Lethal injection
New Mexico	Lethal injection
New York	Lethal injection
North Carolina	Lethal injection
North Dakota	No capital punishment
Ohio	Lethal injection
Oklahoma	Lethal injection, electrocution, firing squad
Oregon	Lethal injection
Pennsylvania	Lethal injection
Rhode Island	No capital punishment
South Carolina	Lethal injection, electrocution
South Dakota	Lethal injection
Tennessee	Lethal injection, electrocution
Texas	Lethal injection
Utah	Lethal injection, firing squad
Vermont	No capital punishment
Virginia	Lethal injection, electrocution
Washington	Lethal injection, hanging
West Virginia	No capital punishment
Wisconsin	No capital punishment
Wyoming	Lethal injection, gas chamber

Sources: Death Penalty Information Center; state departments of corrections.

age when the crime was committed.

In the early 2000's, some U.S. states reexamined their capital punishment systems after evidence showed that some prisoners on death row were innocent or had been tried unfairly. For example, in 2001, Illinois declared a *moratorium* (temporary halt) on capital punishment while a commission reviewed the fairness of the system. The panel found many flaws in the system, and Illinois continued its moratorium. In 2003, Illinois Governor George Ryan *commuted* (reduced) the sentences of all prisoners then on death row in the state. He changed most of the sentences to life in prison without parole.

The debate over capital punishment. People often disagree about whether capital punishment is a moral and effective way of dealing with crime. Many people oppose the death penalty because they believe it is cruel and not consistent with the ideals of modern society. Critics also warn that innocent people could be executed if they are mistakenly convicted or unfairly sentenced. Most critics favor life imprisonment as an alternative to capital punishment.

Supporters of capital punishment believe that, in certain circumstances, a person who takes a human life deserves to lose his or her own life. Supporters also argue that the threat of capital punishment *deters* (discourages) people from committing serious crimes. However, studies have not consistently shown that the death penalty has a greater deterrent effect than life imprisonment. Robert W. Taylor

Related articles in *World Book* include:

Drowning	Gas chamber	Hanging
Electrocution	Guillotine	Lethal injection
Garrote		

Additional resources

Banner, Stuart. *The Death Penalty: An American History.* Harvard Univ. Pr., 2002.
Henderson, Harry. *Capital Punishment.* Rev. ed. Facts on File, 2000.
Mitchell, Hayley R., ed. *The Death Penalty.* Greenhaven, 2001.
Palmer, Louis J., Jr. *Encyclopedia of Capital Punishment in the United States.* McFarland, 2001.

Capital stock. See Stock.

Capitalism is an economic model that calls for control of the economy by individual households and privately owned businesses. It is one of two main economic models. The other is *central planning,* which calls for government control of the economy.

No purely capitalist or completely centrally planned economy has ever existed. The economic systems of all nations use some government control and some private choice. But economies that rely mostly on private decisions are usually described as capitalist. Such economies include those of the United States and Canada. The former Soviet Union and many nations of Eastern Europe once relied heavily on central planning. Such economies are sometimes called *socialist* or *Communist.* Many other nations rely less on capitalism than the United States does but more than the Soviet Union did.

How capitalism differs from central planning

In basically capitalist systems, private decision-makers determine how resources will be used, what mix of goods and services will be produced, and how goods and services will be distributed among the members of society. Capitalism is often known as *free enterprise* or *modified free enterprise* because it permits people to engage in economic activities largely free from government control. Other names sometimes applied to basically capitalist systems are *free market systems, laissez faire systems,* and *entrepreneurial systems.* In systems based on central planning, the government makes most major economic decisions. Government planners tell managers what to produce, whom to sell it to, and what price to charge. Centrally planned economies are often called *command economies.*

The root of the word *capitalism* is *capital.* Capital has several meanings in economics and business. In business, it refers to the money needed to hire workers, buy materials, and pay bills. In economics, capital includes buildings, equipment, machinery, roads, and other assets used to produce things. In basically capitalist systems, most land, factories, and other capital is privately owned. In systems based on central planning, the government owns most of the capital used in production.

Capitalism in its ideal form

The Scottish economist Adam Smith, in a landmark book called *The Wealth of Nations* (1776), laid out the basic argument for capitalism. Smith argued that a government should not interfere with a nation's economy but instead should let individuals act as "free agents" who pursue their own self-interest. Such free agents, he said, would naturally act in ways that would bring the greatest good for society "as if guided by an invisible hand."

Private choices. An example of how an ideal capitalist economy would work is an arrangement called *perfect competition,* also known as *pure competition.* In perfect competition, privately owned businesses, driven by a desire for profits, decide what goods or services to produce, how much to produce, and what methods to employ in production. These choices determine how much labor and capital a business will need. In other words, private firms "supply" goods and services and "demand" labor and capital.

Each household chooses what to buy, based on prices, household income, and individual preferences. Each household also decides how much to work—in other words, how much labor to supply. Workers take jobs only when employers offer them wages that adequately compensate them for their time and effort.

Each household also chooses how much to save out of its income. These savings provide capital for businesses. When a household deposits money in a savings account, for example, the bank may loan the funds to businesses. Besides borrowing from banks, most corporations issue stocks and bonds that they sell to investors to raise needed capital. Thus, households "demand" goods and services and "supply" labor and capital.

Markets. Businesses and households exchange labor, capital, and goods and services in markets. A *market* is a place or situation in which people buy and sell things. In a capitalist economy, the prices of labor, capital, and goods and services are determined mainly by the market forces of *supply* and *demand.* Supply is the amount of a good or service that is offered for sale. Demand is the amount of a good or service that users can and would like to buy at alternative prices. Generally, the market will force prices to fall when supply exceeds demand and to rise when demand exceeds supply.

Another important feature of markets is *competition.* Competition exists when many suppliers try to sell the same kinds of things to the same buyers. A supplier who charges lower prices or improves the quality of his or her products can take buyers away from competitors.

Competition among employers for workers and among workers for jobs helps set wage rates. Businesses need to pay wages high enough to attract the workers they need. When jobs are scarce, however, workers may accept lower wages than they would when jobs are plentiful. Similar competition helps determine *interest rates*—that is, the cost of borrowing money.

In theory, pure competition would, with no government involvement, produce exactly the right combination of goods and services to match the tastes and buying power of the consumers. In addition, perfect competition would lead firms to adopt the most economical methods and technologies, and prices would drop to the lowest levels permitted by the cost of production. Inefficient firms would lose money and be driven out of business by better-managed firms.

Capitalism as it exists

Capitalism as it exists today differs in significant ways from the ideal of pure competition. All societies have governments, and all governments make economic decisions. For example, governments tax households and businesses, and use those taxes to purchase goods and services and to transfer income to the needy. The chief areas of government involvement in a capitalist economy include (1) ensuring competition, (2) protecting the public interest, (3) stabilizing the economy, and (4) equalizing the distribution of wealth.

Ensuring competition. For vigorous competition to exist, an industry must consist of numerous producers, none of which controls much of the market. In many industries, however, a few big firms have *market power,* the influence that results from their large share of sales. Market power enables them to limit competition and to raise prices above competitive levels. Firms with market power often erect obstacles called *entry barriers* that prevent new firms from getting started in an industry. For example, a firm may control the supply of raw materials needed to make a product or own patents covering the manufacturing process.

The most extreme market power occurs in a *monopoly.* In a monopoly, a single firm or a cooperating group of firms controls the supply of a product or service for which no close substitute exists. In the United States, huge monopolies dominated many industries in the late 1800's. In response, the government passed the Sherman Antitrust Act of 1890, which outlawed "combinations ... in restraint of trade." In 1914, the Clayton Antitrust Act outlawed a number of business practices that large firms had used to eliminate smaller rivals. Today, the Antitrust Division of the U.S. Department of Justice and the Federal Trade Commission oversee American business to curb unfair methods of competition.

Protecting the public interest. Business leaders in unregulated industries often do not consider costs to society in making their decisions. For example, a factory may dispose of toxic waste cheaply by pouring it into a river. But the resulting pollution may harm people downriver, kill fish, and destroy other valuable natural resources. In most capitalist economies, the government tries to ensure that social costs and environmental impacts are considered in business decisions. The U.S. Environmental Protection Agency, for example, helps enforce clean water and clean air legislation.

Governments also protect the public interest by providing or preserving goods and services called *public goods.* Public goods include law enforcement, national defense, and clean air. Anyone can benefit from whatever public goods are provided, even someone who does not pay for them. Public goods thus differ from most goods and services sold under capitalism, which can be withheld for nonpayment. Private firms seldom find it profitable to preserve or produce public goods. For this and other reasons, such goods are often protected or provided by governments through the use of tax dollars.

Stabilizing the economy. Market economies are naturally unstable, with economic output alternately rising and falling in a pattern called the *business cycle.* Most economists consider a nation's economy to be in a recession if the output of goods and services has fallen for six consecutive months. During recessions, firms are less profitable, unemployment rises, and poverty increases. Recessions hurt many people, especially the workers who lose jobs. Periods of economic growth, on the other hand, often bring a general increase in prices, called *inflation.* Inflation hurts people whose income does not keep pace with prices.

Some economists believe the government should work to stabilize the economy and ease the natural fluctuations of the business cycle. To end a recession, a government may boost its own spending or reduce taxes. It may also lower interest rates so loans will be cheaper and easier to get. These measures tend to increase the demand for goods and services and to create more jobs.

Other economists believe that the government should not intervene to try to stabilize the economy. They believe that economic cycles are self-correcting and that government intervention is ineffective or even may make the fluctuations worse.

Equalizing the distribution of wealth. Some people in capitalist nations are rich and can afford many luxuries. Others lack basic food, clothing, and shelter. This inequality results in part from capitalism's emphasis on economic freedom. To a great extent, people in a capitalist economy are free to profit from—or suffer from—their own economic decisions. People will likely prosper if they have ambition and a willingness to work and take risks. But some people are handicapped by factors beyond their control. These factors include racial, ethnic, and sex discrimination; differences in education; and variations in inherited ability or wealth.

Many government programs exist to correct some of the inequality in capitalist nations. For example, households with higher incomes are required to pay taxes at higher rates, and some needy families get cash benefits.

History of capitalism

From the 1400's to the 1700's, the major European trading nations used an economic system known as *mercantilism.* Under this system, governments regulated their economic affairs to ensure that exports exceeded imports. They placed high tariffs on imported goods to make them cost more at home, and gave financial aid to local farms and industries so they could lower the prices of their exports. Nations enriched their treasuries by selling more goods than they bought.

The development of capitalism. During the mid-1700's, a group of French economists known as *physiocrats* urged governments to stop interfering in foreign trade. Their policy, called *laissez faire*—a French phrase meaning *allow to do*—demanded an end to tariffs and other trade restrictions.

Adam Smith also argued that a nation could increase its wealth most rapidly by allowing free trade. He believed people who followed their economic best interests would automatically act in the economic best interest of society. In *The Wealth of Nations,* Smith described how laissez faire should work. His ideas first became influential during the early 1800's. During that period, the British government began to remove its mercantilist controls and to develop the first capitalist economy. Capitalism soon spread to other major trading nations.

Changing attitudes toward capitalism began to develop in the 1800's, when new technology in industrialized nations helped create many new products. The increased production brought prosperity to many businesses. But problems also developed. Several depressions occurred. In addition, many workers earned low wages and labored under bad conditions.

As a result of these developments, the German social philosopher Karl Marx claimed that laissez-faire capitalism would be destroyed. He predicted that owners of businesses would become wealthier while their workers grew poorer. Finally, the workers would overthrow the capitalist system. Marx was wrong in predicting that workers in capitalist economies would not share in rising standards of living. However, his ideas influenced the revolutions that led to the introduction of Communism in Russia in 1917 and in China in 1949.

Capitalism faced its most serious challenge during the Great Depression, a worldwide business slump that began in 1929. During the 1930's, many banks, factories, and stores closed. Millions of people lost their jobs, homes, and savings. Many also lost faith in capitalism, and political leaders sought new economic theories. As a result, the British economist John Maynard Keynes gained notice. In his book *The General Theory of Employment, Interest and Money* (1936), Keynes, though neither a socialist nor a Communist, rejected the traditional capitalists' belief that government should keep out of economic affairs. He said a nation's level of economic activity depends on the total spending of consumers, business, and government. Keynes urged increased government spending to fight the Depression. The Great Depression lasted until the early 1940's, when huge amounts of government military spending for World War II (1939-1945) finally stimulated the world economy.

Capitalism in former Communist nations. Communist governments were established in much of Eastern Europe after World War II. But in the 1980's, the centrally planned economies of Eastern Europe and the Soviet Union began to crumble. In 1989, non-Communist governments came to power in several Eastern European lands. In 1991, the Soviet Union broke apart.

During the 1990's, Russia and the other formerly Communist lands struggled to build capitalist institutions. They worked to lift government price controls, to increase private ownership of business, and to shift economic decision-making from the government to households and private companies. Karl E. Case

Related articles in *World Book* include:

Business (Business in a free enterprise system)	Marx, Karl
Capital	Monopoly and competition
Communism (The ideas of Marx)	Price
Deflation	Protestant ethic
Economics (The U.S. economy)	Recession
Government regulation	Smith, Adam
Industrial Revolution	Socialism
Inflation	Supply and demand
Investment	Trade (Trade in the United States)
Laissez faire	Weber, Max
	Welfare state

Additional resources

Downing, David. *Capitalism.* Heinemann Lib., 2003. Younger readers.

Greider, William. *The Soul of Capitalism.* Simon & Schuster, 2003.

Hussain, Syed B. *Encyclopedia of Capitalism.* Facts on File, 2004.

Rajan, Raghuram G., and Zingales, Luigi. *Saving Capitalism from the Capitalists.* Crown Business, 2003.

Capitalization means the use of *capital* (large) letters in writing. Capital letters are usually used at the beginnings of certain words. There are many capitalization rules in the English language.

The first word of a sentence or direct quotation is capitalized, as in *The boy asked, "Do you think I should go?"* The first word in each line of most poems or in each part of an outline is capitalized.

Proper nouns and words used as proper nouns are capitalized. This includes names of persons *(Mary Smith),* animals *(my dog, Rover),* places *(416 Maple Street, Cincinnati, Ohio),* and particular things *(White House).* Proper nouns include the specific names of rivers, mountains, buildings, business organizations, schools, and commercial products.

Names of special political, social, or religious groups are capitalized, such as *Common Cause* or the *Lutheran Church.* The collective name of members of a group is also capitalized, as in *Democrats* or *Lutherans.* Holidays *(Fourth of July),* days of the week *(Monday),* and months *(September)* are capitalized, but not names of seasons *(autumn).* Geographical regions are capitalized *(the West),* but not the names of geographical directions *(going west).* Names of special events in history *(Battle of the Bulge)* are capitalized, as well as names of meetings *(the Yalta Conference),* congresses (the *Seventy-Fourth Congress*), alliances *(the Holy Alliance),* and expositions *(the Golden Gate Exposition).* Periods in history are capitalized, as in the *Restoration.* Nationalities and languages are capitalized, as in *Nigerian* and *Norwegian.* Names of school studies are capitalized when they refer to a specific subject *(Mathematics 2).*

Titles of persons are capitalized in certain uses. Titles that precede a name are capitalized, as in *President Woodrow Wilson.* Titles that immediately follow a name or take the place of a name are sometimes capitalized when they show high distinction, as in *Woodrow Wilson, President.* Words that modify a proper noun and are usually used as part of that name are capitalized, as in Frederick the Great. Names of the Deity are always capitalized, as in God or Jehovah.

All important words in a title are capitalized, including the first word *(All Quiet on the Western Front).*

Adjectives taken from proper nouns are capitalized, such as *French* or *Jeffersonian.* When a prefix is used, the prefix is not capitalized, as in *pro-French.*

Personification means treating an object that is not human as a human being. A personified noun is capitalized, as in *When Fortune flatters, she does it to betray.*

Formal statements begin with capital letters, as in *Resolved: That this club meet on the first day of every month.*

O and I are always capitalized when used as words.

Many abbreviations are capitalized, especially abbreviations referring to proper names, such as *U.S.A.* for *United States of America.* See **Abbreviation.**

Susan M. Gass

Capitals of the states. See **United States** (table: Facts in brief about the states).

Capitals of the United States. See **United States capitals.**

Capitol is the government building where a legislature makes laws. The name *Capitol* comes from the *Capitolium,* the ancient temple of Jupiter in Rome. For a description of the United States Capitol, see **Capitol, United States.** See also the pictures of state capitols with the articles on U.S. states, such as **Alabama.**

Capitol, United States, is the building where Congress meets. It stands on Capitol Hill in Washington, D.C. Besides serving as a government office building, the Capitol is a symbol of the United States. Each year, about 10 million people visit the Capitol. Rooms open to the public include the chambers where the House of Representatives and the Senate meet.

The Capitol was built in the Neoclassical style, derived from the architecture of ancient Rome. The building consists of two wings that extend north and south of a central section. A huge cast-iron dome rests on the central section of the building. The dome's white-painted surface blends with the white marble exterior of most of the rest of the Capitol. On top of the dome stands the Statue of Freedom. The statue is 19 ½ feet (5.9 meters) high. It is the figure of a woman wearing a headdress of eagle feathers and holding a sword and shield. The distance from the top of the statue to the ground is almost 300 feet (91 meters).

The Capitol has 540 rooms, including offices and reception rooms. Many rooms hold mementos of U.S. history as well as paintings and sculptures by some of the country's greatest artists. The grand Rotunda, the center of the Capitol, consists of the circular area under the dome. The Rotunda is more than 95 feet (29 meters) in diameter and over 183 feet (56 meters) high. The focal point of the Rotunda is the ceiling under the dome, which is decorated by the fresco *The Apotheosis of George Washington* (1865), by the Italian painter Constantino Brumidi. State funerals for famous U.S. citizens have taken place in the Capitol Rotunda. Presidents Abraham Lincoln and John F. Kennedy were honored in this way.

The Senate wing of the Capitol extends north of the Rotunda. This wing houses the Senate Chamber, the room in which the Senate meets. The chamber has galleries where visitors may watch the Senate in session. Another room in this wing, the President's Room, is one of the most richly decorated rooms. It contains a huge bronze chandelier and portraits of George Washington and his first Cabinet. The Senate side of the Capitol's central section includes the old Supreme Court chamber, where the court met from 1810 to 1860. This room has been restored to look as it did in 1859.

The House of Representatives wing of the Capitol extends south of the Rotunda. The House wing includes the House Chamber, the room in which the House meets. The House Chamber also has galleries for visitors. The House side of the Capitol's central section includes Statuary Hall, which exhibits statues of outstanding Americans (see **Statuary Hall**).

In 1792, the government held a contest for a Capitol design. William Thornton, an American doctor and amateur architect, submitted the winning entry. President George Washington laid the building's cornerstone in 1793. Congress first met in the Capitol in 1800. In 1814, during the War of 1812, British troops set fire to the Capitol. Congress began meeting in the Capitol again in 1819. Workers then began building the center part and finished it, except for the dome, in 1829. The House wing was occupied in 1857, and the Senate wing in 1859. The dome was finished in 1865. In 1962, builders completed a 32 ½-foot (9.9-meter) eastward extension of the Capitol's central section.

Critically reviewed by the Office of the Architect of the Capitol

See also **Congress of the United States** (diagram: Capitol floor plan); **House of Representatives; Senate; Washington, D.C.** (pictures; map).

Capitol Hill. See **Washington, D.C.** (A visitor's guide; map).

Capitol Reef National Park lies near Torrey, Utah. It includes a ridge 20 miles (32 kilometers) long and is topped by a white sandstone formation that resembles a capitol dome. The park also includes the Waterpocket Fold. This feature, 100 miles (160 kilometers) long, is a fold in Earth's crust with shallow depressions that collect and hold water. The area was set up as a national monument in 1937 and became a national park in 1971. For area, see **National Park System** (table: National parks).

Critically reviewed by the National Park Service

Capone, *kuh POHN,* **Al** (1899-1947), was one of the most famous and powerful gangsters in United States history. In the 1920's, he built a criminal empire in Chicago that became the model for present-day organized-crime operations. He was known as *Scarface* because his left cheek was slashed in a fight. Despite his reputation, he was treated as a celebrity. He was often seen riding in an armored limousine to theaters and sports arenas, where he entertained guests in private boxes.

Wide World

Al Capone

Alphonse Capone was born on Jan. 17, 1899, in Brooklyn, New York, to poor Italian immigrants. The original family name was sometimes spelled Caponi. He came to Chicago to work for a racketeer about 1920. A series of gangland shootings soon left the violent and clever Capone in control of much of the city's large-scale criminal activities. His gang dominated prostitution, liquor, and gambling rackets. It fought rival gangs with submachine guns, and corrupted police and politicians with bribes.

Gunmen in Capone's gang were blamed for the murder of seven members of the Bugs Moran gang in the St. Valentine's Day Massacre of 1929, but this charge was never proved. In 1931, a federal jury convicted Capone of income tax evasion. After eight years in prison, Capone retired to his mansion near Miami, Florida. He died in Florida on Jan. 25, 1947, from complications due to syphilis. See also **Ness, Eliot.** William J. Helmer

Additional resources

Bergreen, Laurence. *Capone.* 1994. Reprint. Simon & Schuster, 1996.

Yancey, Diane. *A Travel Guide to Al Capone's Chicago.* Lucent, 2003.

Capote, *kuh POH tee,* **Truman** (1924-1984), was an American author known for his distinctive, polished style. He was also a leading celebrity of his day, and his friendships with rich and famous people were widely reported. His best-known work is *In Cold Blood* (1966). It combines facts with fiction to tell about two drifters who murder a Kansas farm family.

Capote was born on Sept. 30, 1924, in New Orleans. His real name was Truman Streckfus Persons. Many of his works have Southern settings. *Other Voices, Other Rooms* (1948) tells of a boy's bittersweet upbringing in the rural South. *A Tree of Night, and Other Stories* (1949) and the novel *The Grass Harp* (1951) present eccentric characters and unusual situations. The short novel *Breakfast at Tiffany's* (1958) depicts a light-hearted playgirl in New York City. Capote wrote the book and lyrics for *House of Flowers* (1954), a musical set in the West Indies. An unfinished novel, *Answered Prayers* (1986), and *The Complete Short Stories of Truman Capote* (2004) were published after his death on Aug. 25, 1984.

Capote wrote much nonfiction. *The Muses Are Heard* (1956) describes his trip to the Soviet Union with the cast of the opera *Porgy and Bess. Music for Chameleons* (1980) mixes fiction, reporting, and memoirs.

Barbara M. Perkins

Capp, Al (1909-1979), was an American cartoonist who created the comic strip "Li'l Abner." The strip, which ran from 1934 to 1977, made Capp one of the best-known cartoonists of his era. "Li'l Abner" centered around the antics of Li'l Abner Yokum, his family, and other inhabitants of a fictional hillbilly town called "Dogpatch U.S.A." The comic strip was one of the first to treat modern society and politics satirically. It often parodied other popular comic strips, including "Dick Tracy" and "Peanuts."

Capp was born in New Haven, Connecticut, on Sept. 28, 1909. His given and family name was Alfred Gerald Caplin. He joined the Associated Press as a cartoonist in 1932 and served briefly as an assistant to cartoonist Ham Fisher, creator of "Joe Palooka." Capp also created the comic strips "Abbie an' Slats" in 1937 and "Long Sam" in 1954. Capp died on Nov. 5, 1979. Charles P. Green

Capra, *KAP ruh,* **Frank** (1897-1991), was an American motion-picture director. He became noted for his comedy-dramas dealing with a "little man" standing up against corruption in society. These films include *Mr. Deeds Goes to Town* (1936), *You Can't Take It with You* (1938), *Mr. Smith Goes to Washington* (1939), and *Meet John Doe* (1941). Capra won Academy Awards for his direction of *Mr. Deeds Goes to Town, You Can't Take It with You,* and *It Happened One Night* (1934). His other films include *Lost Horizon* (1937), *It's a Wonderful Life* (1946), and *State of the Union* (1948). During World War II (1939-1945), he produced the *Why We Fight* series for the United States Army.

Capra was born in Palermo, Sicily, on May 18, 1897, and moved to the United States at the age of 6. He studied chemical engineering in California before entering the motion-picture industry in 1922. Capra directed several of comedian Harry Langdon's silent films, including *The Strong Man* (1926) and *Long Pants* (1927). His autobiography, *The Name Above the Title,* was published in 1971. He died on Sept. 3, 1991. Robert Sklar

Capri, *KAH pree* or *kuh PREE* (pop. 12,400), is an Italian island in the Tyrrhenian Sea, at the entrance of the Gulf of Naples (see **Italy** [terrain map]). Its climate and scenery attract thousands of visitors. Capri's famous Blue Grotto is a wave-cut cave that is filled with a sapphire-blue coloring when the sun shines through its waters.

The island covers about 4 square miles (10 square kilometers). Mount Solaro (1,932 feet, or 589 meters) is the highest point of the island. The capital, also named Capri, lies in the eastern part of the island. The town of Anacapri, in the western portion, is 738 feet (225 meters) above sea level. Products of Capri include wine, olive oil, and fruits.

In Greek mythology, Capri was the home of the lovely maidens called the Sirens, whose music enchanted Odysseus (Ulysses in Latin) and his sailors. The Roman emperors Augustus and Tiberius built splendid *villas* (mansions) on Capri. Anthony James Joes

Capricorn, *KAP ruh kawrn,* is the 10th sign of the zodiac. Its symbol is a goat. Astrologers believe the planet Saturn rules Capricorn. They consider Saturn to have a stern influence. Capricorn is an earth sign.

According to astrologers, people born under the sign of Capricorn, from December 22 to January 19, take life seriously and do not have much of a sense of humor. They overcome hardship well and enjoy the challenge

WORLD BOOK illustration by Robert Keys

Capricorn—The Goat

Birth dates: Dec. 22-Jan. 19.
Group: Earth.
Characteristics: Ambitious, cautious, dignified, patient, persistent, practical.

Signs of the Zodiac
Aries
Mar. 21-Apr. 19
Taurus
Apr. 20-May 20
Gemini
May 21-June 20
Cancer
June 21-July 22
Leo
July 23-Aug. 22
Virgo
Aug. 23-Sept. 22
Libra
Sept. 23-Oct. 22
Scorpio
Oct. 23-Nov. 21
Sagittarius
Nov. 22-Dec. 21
Capricorn
Dec. 22-Jan. 19
Aquarius
Jan. 20-Feb. 18
Pisces
Feb. 19-Mar. 20

of difficult problems. Capricorns do not rush into friendships, but they remain loyal after their confidence has been gained. They behave with dignity and do not like to hurry. Their stubbornness often leads them to insist that their opinions are right. Capricorns can sometimes be too stern. Christopher McIntosh

See also **Astrology; Horoscope; Zodiac** (diagram: The signs of the zodiac).

Capricorn, Tropic of. See **Tropic of Capricorn.**

Caps and gowns are the official and traditional costumes for students in many nations. In most cases, students wear caps and gowns only at graduation exercises and on special occasions. A student wears a full-flowing robe and a skullcap attached to a stiff square piece called a *mortarboard.* A tassel dangles from the center of the mortarboard. In addition to the cap and gown, a college graduate wears an academic hood that is lined with colored satin and trimmed with velvet.

Most collegiate caps, gowns, and hoods are black. The trimming and the cut of the robe and sleeves indicate various academic degrees. The color of the hood's satin lining indicates the school that conferred the degree. The velvet trim on the hood indicates the graduate's field of study. The tassel may be black or the color that represents the field, and a doctor's cap may have a gold tassel. Some schools have graduates change their tassel from the right side to the left after receiving their diplomas. In the United States, the Intercollegiate Commission set the standards for academic costume in 1894.

Doctor's degree. A doctor wears a gown with full, round sleeves. The gown shows velvet facings on the front. Three velvet bars decorate the sleeves. The color of the velvet trim indicates the doctor's field of study. A doctor wears a 4-foot (122-centimeter) hood with velvet trim that is 5 inches (13 centimeters) wide.

Master's degree. A master wears a gown with full-length square sleeves. A crescent-shaped panel hangs down from each sleeve. The gown has no velvet trim. The 3 ½-foot (107-centimeter) hood has velvet trim that is 3 inches (8 centimeters) wide.

Bachelor's degree. A bachelor wears a gown with pointed sleeves. It has no velvet trim. Women wear white collars. Bachelors wear hoods 3 feet (91 centimeters) long, with velvet trim 2 inches (5 centimeters) wide.

History. During the 1100's, men and women wore gowns and hoods as everyday clothing on campus grounds. Styles have changed over the years, but some universities, such as Oxford University, still have their students wear gowns and hoods. The costume implies that they are individuals of learning, dignity, and maturity, not affected by passing fads and changing tastes.

Early American colleges and universities followed the same customs in regard to dress. American students liked caps and gowns as a simple, dignified, and economical dress for graduation ceremonies. Since 1900, caps and gowns have increased in popularity for use at high school and grammar school graduations. High school caps and gowns are available in many colors. Girls sometimes wear white gowns. Arthur Schankin

Charles Gupton, The Stock Market

High school graduates of many schools wear caps and gowns to add special dignity to their commencement ceremonies.

Capsicum. See **Pepper.**

Captain Jack (1837-1873) was a leader of the Modoc Indians. He led his tribe against the United States Army during the Modoc War (1872-1873).

The tribe lived mainly in the Lost River Valley and around Tule Lake, on the California-Oregon border. In 1864, the government moved the Modoc to the Klamath Reservation in Oregon, but they could not support themselves there. Captain Jack led part of his tribe back to the Lost River Valley in 1872.

Smithsonian Institution National Anthropological Archives, Washington, D.C.

Captain Jack

Fighting broke out when the Army tried to force the Modoc to return to the reservation. The Indians fled to an area near Tule Lake in California. At a peace council, Captain Jack killed General E. R. S. Canby when the general said he could not withdraw his troops from the area. Captain Jack fled, but the Army captured and hanged him on Oct. 3, 1873.

Captain Jack was born near what is now Tulelake, California. His Indian name was *Kintpuash.* W. Jean Hurtado

Captain Kidd. See **Kidd, William.**

Capuchin, *KAP yu chihn* or *KAP yu shihn,* also called *sapajou,* is the name of four species of monkeys that are found in Central and South America. Some zoologists believe that capuchins are the most intelligent New World monkeys. Capuchins got their name because they have a dark patch of hair that resembles a *capuche* (monk's hood) on the top of the head.

Capuchins are black or brown, with white or beige hair on the face. Three species also have white or beige

K. Wothe, Bruce Coleman Ltd.
A capuchin spends most of its time in trees.

hair on the chest and upper arms. The fourth species, the *black-capped capuchin,* has tufts of black hair on the top of the head. A capuchin measures about 17 inches (43 centimeters) in length, not including the tail, which is about 18 inches (46 centimeters) long. It weighs about 5 pounds (2.2 kilograms).

Capuchins live in tropical forests from Honduras to southern Brazil. They spend most of their time in trees but may come to the ground during the day. The monkeys use their tails to hang from branches while gathering food or playing. They eat fruit, seeds, insects, and occasionally small backboned animals, such as lizards, young birds, and young squirrels.

Capuchins live in groups of 5 to 30 or more monkeys. Each group has about the same number of young and adults, with two or three times as many adult females as adult males. A female capuchin gives birth about six months after mating. She has one baby every one or two years. Young capuchins form social ties with one another while playing. The adults, especially the females, spend much time grooming one another's fur. Capuchins enjoy this contact, and it helps preserve social ties among the adult members. John R. Oppenheimer

Scientific classification. Capuchins make up the genus *Cebus* in the New World monkey family, Cebidae. The scientific name for the black-capped capuchin is *C. apella.* The other species are *C. capucinus, C. albifrons,* and *C. nigrivittatus.*

See also **Monkey**.

Capuchins, *KAP yu chihnz,* are members of the Order of Friars Minor Capuchin, a Roman Catholic religious order. They form an independent branch of the Franciscans (see **Franciscans**). Their name comes from the *capuche,* a long pointed hood they wear. The Capuchin ministry includes teaching, preaching, and social work.

Friar Matteo da Bascio founded the Capuchins in 1525 to follow more closely the ideas of poverty and simplicity taught by Saint Francis of Assisi. From its beginning, the order served the poor. It also played a major role in the Catholic renewal movement called the Counter Reformation. A women's order called the Poor Clares joined the Capuchins in 1538. David G. Schultenover

See also **Friar**.

Capulin Volcano National Monument, *KAP yuh luhn,* is in northeastern New Mexico. Capulin Volcano is a *scoria cone,* a cone-shaped mountain of cinder that formed during an explosive volcanic eruption. It rises 8,215 feet (2,504 meters) above sea level and 1,500 feet (457 meters) above the surrounding plain. It has a rim diameter of 1,450 feet (442 meters). The monument was established in 1916. For area, see **National Park System** (table: National monuments).

Critically reviewed by the National Park Service

Capybara, *KAP uh BAHR uh,* is the largest of all rodents. It grows up to 4 feet (1.2 meters) long and may weigh over 100 pounds (45 kilograms). It lives in eastern Panama and in South America east of the Andes.

The capybara looks like a small pig or a large guinea pig. Its thick body is covered with coarse hair that is reddish-brown or gray on its upper parts and yellowish-brown on its underparts. The animal has a large head with a blunt, square muzzle, and a short tail. Its hind legs are somewhat longer than its front legs. It has webbed toes and swims well. It grazes near lakes and rivers, and plunges into the water at any sign of danger. Some people call the capybara a *water pig* or *water hog.*

© Giuseppe Mazza
The capybara, the world's largest rodent, lives in Central and South America. It may weigh over 100 pounds (45 kilograms).

In prehistoric times, capybaras lived in southeastern North America. They are a favorite food of jaguars, alligators, and human beings. C. Richard Taylor

Scientific classification. Capybaras are in the capybara family, Hydrochoeridae. They are *Hydrochoerus hydrochaeris.*

Car. See **Automobile; Cable car; Railroad** (Passenger and freight cars; pictures); **Streetcar**.

Carabao. See **Water buffalo; Buffalo.**

Caracal, *KAR uh kal,* is a member of the cat family related to the lynxes. It lives in dry regions and is found in India and in many places throughout Africa. Like the lynxes, the caracal has tufts of long hair on the tips of its ears. The lynx has brown tufts, but the caracal's are black. The caracal has reddish-brown fur. It is one of the *Carnivora,* a group that eats meat and hunts other animals. Its fur should not be confused with *caracul,* a com-

Peter Steyn, ARDEA

The caracal, a relative of the lynx, lives in India and Africa. Like the lynx, the caracal has tufts of long hair on its ears.

monly used fur that comes from the Karakul, a breed of Asiatic sheep. Elizabeth S. Frank

Scientific classification. The caracal is in the cat family, Felidae. Its scientific name is *Felis caracal.*

See also **Lynx.**

Caracara, *KAHR uh KAHR uh,* is the name given to several large birds of South and Central America and the southern United States. They often eat dead animals as vultures do, but they also capture and kill small animals. They have long legs, and some caracaras can run faster than most other birds. The *crested caracara* of the southern United States and Central and South America has a black crest and a bare red face. This bird is shown on the national emblem of Mexico, where it is called the *Mexican eagle.* Richard D. Brown

Scientific classification. Caracaras belong to the family Falconidae. The scientific name for the crested caracara is *Polyborus plancus.*

WORLD BOOK illustration by John F. Eggert

The crested caracara is a large meat-eating bird. It feeds on the flesh of dead animals and may also catch and kill live prey.

Caracas, *kuh RAH kuhs* (pop. 1,975,787), is the capital, largest city, and economic center of Venezuela. It lies in a valley in northern Venezuela, about 7 miles (11 kilometers) inland from La Guaira, a Caribbean Sea port (see **Venezuela** [political map]).

The city. Caracas is one of the most modern cities in Latin America. Since the 1950's, many new high-rise office and apartment buildings have been erected. This construction boom and a rapidly growing population have changed Caracas from a quiet colonial city to a crowded, busy urban center. Traffic jams occur often.

Caracas has a few districts with buildings dating from its colonial period, which lasted from the 1500's to the 1800's. Many of these historic structures are national landmarks, museums, or homes of the wealthy. The center of the city, near a park called the Plaza Bolívar, is especially rich in history. Old buildings in this area include the gold-domed Venezuelan Capitol, a historic cathedral, and City Hall. A few blocks from the plaza is the Miraflores Palace, a beautifully decorated old building that houses the offices of the president and top presidential advisers. The city has an active cultural life. The Central University of Venezuela has more than 50,000 students. There are numerous theaters and museums, and a botanical garden.

Many of Caracas's middle-class residents live in high-rise apartment buildings. Some wealthy families live in suburbs or in downtown condominium complexes that also include supermarkets, restaurants, and other facilities. About half the population lives in shacks called *ranchos* on the slopes surrounding the city.

Economy. The commercial life of Caracas is based on the activities of the Venezuelan government. Most of the people of Caracas work for government agencies or in the government-owned oil industry. Caracas produces such products as beer, cement, paper, and textiles.

In 1983, the city opened the first segment of a subway system. The system is expanding and has helped to ease traffic problems. The *Autopista,* or Caracas-La Guaira Expressway, winds through steep mountains and connects Caracas with La Guaira, its port.

History. Caracas was founded as Santiago de León de Caracas in 1567 by settlers from Spain. The settlers were looking for gold but stayed to develop the area's agricultural wealth. Caracas became the capital of Venezuela in 1829. Since the 1950's, the national government has used oil profits to make Caracas a modern city and to provide services for its rapidly growing population.

Nathan A. Haverstock

See also **Venezuela** (pictures).

Caracul. See **Karakul.**

Caramanlis, *kahr uh MAHN lees,* **Constantine** (1907-1998), also spelled *Karamanlis,* was a Greek political leader. Caramanlis served as prime minister of Greece from 1955 to 1963 and from 1974 to 1980. He was president of Greece from 1980 to 1985 and from 1990 to 1995. The prime minister heads the government. The president of Greece has less involvement in government operations than does the prime minister. During Caramanlis's terms as prime minister, Greece maintained close ties with the United States. His first term as prime minister was a period of political stability that brought much economic development to Greece. Caramanlis was born on Feb. 23, 1907, in Prote, near Serrai, and received a law degree from Athens University in 1932. He won election to the Greek parliament in every election from 1935 to 1963.

In 1963, following a minor dispute with King Paul of Greece, Caramanlis resigned as prime minister. He went into voluntary exile after his political party lost the election that year. He returned from exile and became prime minister in 1974 after Greek military leaders asked him to form a civilian government. The military government had resigned following the Turkish invasion of Cyprus. In 1980, Caramanlis resigned as prime minister and was elected president. He resigned in 1985. He served again as president from 1990 to 1995. Keith R. Legg

Carat, *KAR uht,* is a measure used by jewelers in weighing precious stones. The term is derived from the Arabic *carat,* meaning a *bean* or *seed.* In ancient times, the seeds of coral and carob trees were used as weights for precious stones. The stones were described to be of so many "beans' weight" or "carats." The metric carat weighs 200 milligrams, or 0.2 gram. It equals 3.086 troy grains, or 0.00705 avoirdupois ounce.

The term is also used to express the amount of gold in an alloy. In this sense, the word is spelled *karat* in most Western countries except the United Kingdom. A karat is $\frac{1}{24}$ of the total weight of the alloy. For example, an 18-karat gold ring has 18 parts gold and 6 parts alloy. Pure gold is 24 karats. E. G. Straus

See also **Alloy; Diamond; Gold.**

Caravaggio, *KAR uh VAH joh,* **Michelangelo Merisi da,** *MY kuhl AN juh LOH muh REE zee dah* (1573-1610), was an Italian painter known for the powerful realism of his religious pictures. Caravaggio refused to idealize his religious figures in the tradition of earlier European art. He supposedly used peasants and people from the streets as models for his unorthodox interpretations of Biblical stories.

In most of his paintings, Caravaggio grouped his figures against a plain, dark background and spotlighted them with an intense, revealing light. An example of his style, *Conversion of Saint Paul,* is reproduced in the **Painting** article. Caravaggio's realistic approach influenced such artists as Peter Paul Rubens and Diego Velázquez and helped establish the baroque movement in European art (see **Baroque**).

Caravaggio's real name was Michelangelo Merisi. He named himself after his birthplace, the northern Italian town of Caravaggio. David Summers

See also **Painting** (The 1600's and 1700's).

Caravan is a long train of people and pack animals that travel together for safety through difficult or dangerous country. The name comes from the Persian word for *people* or *army.* Among the animals used for caravans are camels, mules, and llamas. Caravans of as many as 5,000 camels once brought goods to ports in Persia, China, and India. John H. White, Jr.

Caravel, *KAR uh vehl,* was a type of ship used for trading on the Mediterranean Sea from the 1300's through the 1600's. Columbus sailed on caravels during his first voyage across the Atlantic, and Spanish and Portuguese sailors used such vessels for ocean exploration and trade during the 1500's and 1600's. Some caravels, used for fishing and coastal shipping, weighed about 10 long tons (10.2 metric tons). Those designed for ocean voyages weighed about 50 long tons (51 metric tons).

The caravel was smaller, lighter, and easier to maneuver than the *galleon,* another commonly used ship of the time (see **Galleon**). The ocean caravel had a high structure at the bow called the *forecastle.* A higher structure of two decks at the stern was called the *sterncastle.* The true caravel had four masts. The foremast carried square sails, and the other three carried *lateen,* or triangular sails. Three-masted caravels like Columbus's *Niña* and *Pinta* usually had square sails on the first two masts and lateen sails on the rear mast. Columbus's flagship, the

The Louvre, Paris

Caravaggio's paintings are noted for realism and emphasis on light and shadow. *The Fortune Teller,* shown here, was one of his early works, completed in the mid-1590's. In his later paintings, Caravaggio concentrated on religious subjects.

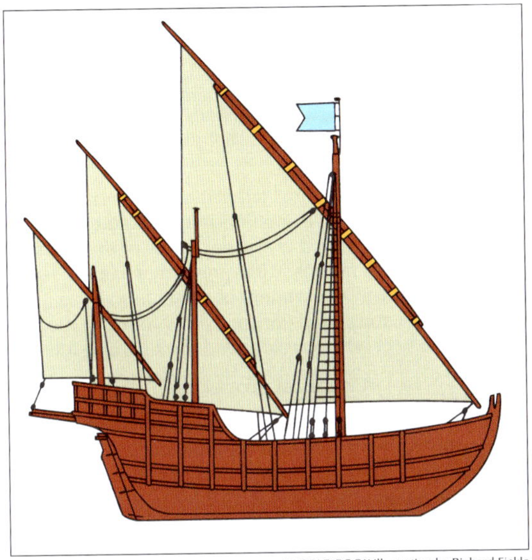

WORLD BOOK illustration by Richard Fickle

A caravel with a two-deck structure at its stern

Santa María, was larger than a caravel and had a deck amidships. It was called a *nao* (ship). See also **Columbus, Christopher**; **Exploration** (picture). James C. Bradford

Caraway, *KAR uh way,* is an herb with spicy seeds. The seeds are used to flavor breads, soups, cheeses, and other foods. The plants grow in Europe, Asia, and the northern United States. See also **Herb** (picture).

Lyle E. Craker

Scientific classification. Caraway belongs to the parsley family, Apiaceae or Umbelliferae. It is *Carum carvi.*

Caraway, *KAR uh way,* **Hattie Ophelia Wyatt,** *HAT tee oh FEEL yuh WY uht* (1878-1950), was the first woman elected to the United States Senate. Caraway, a Democrat, was also the first woman to head a Senate committee. In 1943, she became the first woman to preside over a Senate session.

Hattie Wyatt was born on Feb. 1, 1878, and raised on a farm near Bakersville, Tennessee, southwest of Waverly. She received a B.A. degree from Dickson Normal School. In 1920, her husband, Thaddeus Caraway, a lawyer, was elected to the U.S. Senate from Arkansas. He died in 1931, and Governor Harvey Parnell of Arkansas appointed Hattie Caraway to replace her husband. In a special election in January 1932, she was elected to serve the remaining year of the term. In November 1932, she was reelected to a full six-year term.

Caraway served in the Senate from 1931 to 1945. She was defeated in the primary election for her Senate seat in 1944. She died on Dec. 21, 1950. June Sochen

Carbide, *KAHR byd,* is a chemical compound made up of carbon and a metal. Iron carbide consists of carbon and iron. Different amounts of carbon in iron change the properties of the iron. Pig iron, wrought iron, and steel contain different amounts of carbon. Calcium carbide is the source of such industrially important products as acetylene and calcium cyanamide. Silicon carbide, also called *Carborundum,* is used as an abrasive and to form the cutting edges of tools. Harriet V. Taylor

See also **Carbon**.

Carbine, *KAHR byn* or *KAHR been,* is a short, lightweight version of the United States Army's M16 rifle. It weighs about 7 pounds (3.2 kilograms), or about 3 pounds (1.4 kilograms) less than the M16. Carbines shoot much farther and more accurately than a pistol, but not as far as an M16. Carbines are used by soldiers who must fight from tanks, personnel carriers, or similar cramped spaces. The early carbines were short muskets. Carbines used during World War II (1939-1945) were gas-operated semiautomatic weapons similar to the Garand rifle (see **Garand rifle**). Frances M. Lussier

Carbohydrate, *KAHR boh HY drayt,* is one of the three main classes of nutrients that provide energy to the body. The others are fats and proteins. Carbohydrates include all sugars and starches and also some other substances, such as cellulose and glycogen. They are the main source of energy for animals and plants.

Carbohydrates are made during *photosynthesis,* the process by which green plants make food. Animals obtain carbohydrates by eating these plants or other animals. Animals and plants also store carbohydrates for future use. All carbohydrates consist of the chemical elements carbon, hydrogen, and oxygen.

Carbohydrates make up 55 percent or more of the total number of calories in a well-balanced diet. Foods high in carbohydrate content include bananas, bread, corn, macaroni, potatoes, and rice. Some sources of carbohydrates, such as fruits, vegetables, and whole cereal grains, also contain important amounts of vitamins and minerals. Most candy and soft drinks have a high sugar content. However, they serve only as a source of energy for the body and so do not provide the health benefits of other carbohydrate foods.

Kinds of carbohydrates. There are two kinds of carbohydrates, *simple* and *complex.* Simple carbohydrates have a simple molecular structure. Complex carbohydrates have a complicated molecular structure that consists of simple carbohydrates joined in long chains.

Simple carbohydrates. There are two kinds of simple carbohydrates, *monosaccharides* and *disaccharides,* and all are sugars. Monosaccharides are simple sugars. A disaccharide consists of two monosaccharides.

The principal monosaccharides include *glucose, fructose,* and *galactose.* Glucose, a mildly sweet sugar, is the most important carbohydrate in the blood. It is also called *blood sugar.* Fructose, an extremely sweet sugar, comes from fruits and vegetables. Large amounts of glucose and fructose are in honey. Galactose occurs in food only as part of a disaccharide called lactose.

Among the most important disaccharides are *sucrose, lactose,* and *maltose.* Sucrose is table sugar. A molecule of sucrose consists of a molecule of glucose linked to a molecule of fructose. Much sucrose comes from sugar cane and the juices of the sugar beet plant. Pure sucrose has an extremely sweet taste and almost no odor. Lactose, also called *milk sugar,* makes up about 5 percent of cow's milk. A molecule of lactose consists of a molecule of glucose and a molecule of galactose. Maltose, or *malt sugar,* remains after the brewing process. It is used to flavor some candy. A molecule of maltose consists of two molecules of glucose.

Complex carbohydrates, also called *polysaccharides,* are made up of many monosaccharides. Polysaccharides include *starch, cellulose,* and *glycogen.* A molecule of

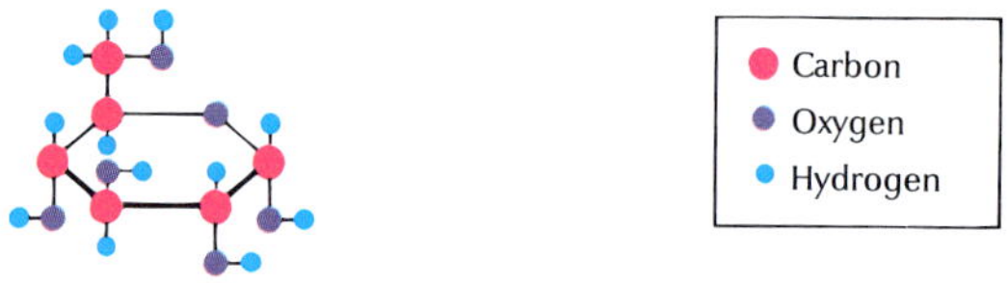

A monosaccharide molecule of glucose

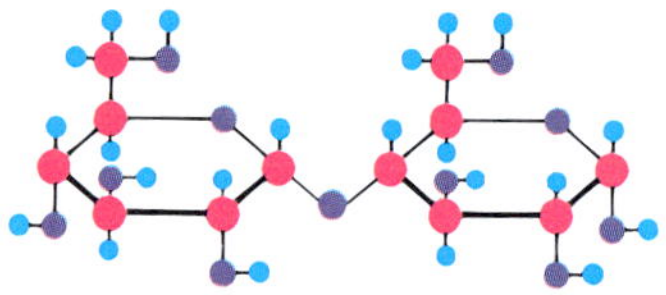

A disaccharide molecule of maltose

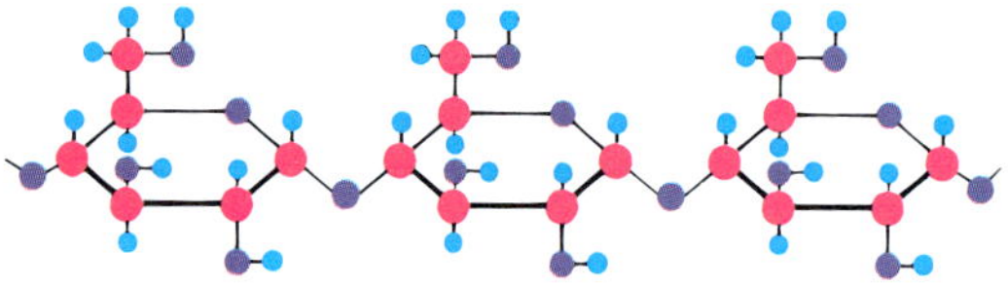

Part of a polysaccharide molecule of starch

WORLD BOOK diagram

Carbohydrates consist of carbon, oxygen, and hydrogen atoms arranged in "building blocks" called *saccharides.* A *monosaccharide* consists of only one saccharide. A *disaccharide* is made up of two saccharides, and a *polysaccharide* has hundreds or more.

starch consists of hundreds or even thousands of glucose molecules joined end to end. It is the chief form of carbohydrate stored by plants. Starch occurs in such foods as beans, corn, potatoes, and wheat. Molecules of cellulose and glycogen, like those of starch, consist of many glucose molecules. Cellulose makes up much of the cell walls of plants. Glycogen, or *animal starch,* is the chief form of stored carbohydrate in animals.

How the body uses carbohydrates. Carbohydrates are used by the body as fuel. However, only monosaccharides can enter the bloodstream directly from the digestive system. Disaccharides and starch must be digested in the small intestine before the body can use them. For example, sucrose must first be broken down into glucose and fructose. Lactose must be broken down into glucose and galactose. Starch has to be broken down first into maltose and then into glucose.

After carbohydrates have been broken down into simple sugars in the small intestine, the blood transports them to the liver. The liver changes fructose and galactose into glucose, which is carried by the blood to all the cells of the body. The cells use glucose as fuel for the muscles and nerves and to build and repair body tissues. The liver changes excess glucose into glycogen and stores it. When the level of sugar in the blood is low, the liver changes glycogen back into glucose and releases it into the blood. Glycogen is also stored in the muscles as an emergency reserve of energy. Some of this glycogen is changed back into glucose when the body needs energy quickly.

Cellulose, unlike most other carbohydrates, cannot be digested by the human body and has no food value. But certain amounts of it are useful. It helps maintain the health and tone of the intestines and thus aids digestion. Cattle, goats, and many other animals that eat plants have bacteria in their digestive systems that break down cellulose. The bodies of such animals use the digested cellulose as fuel. Richard A. Ahrens

Related articles in *World Book* include:

Bread	Glucose	Nutrition (Carbohydrates)	Starch
Cellulose	Glycogen	Saccharides	Sucrose
Dextrose			Sugar

Carbon is one of the most familiar and important chemical elements. All living things are based on carbon, and industry uses it in a wide variety of products. Yet carbon makes up only 0.032 percent of Earth's crust. Carbon is the main component of such fuels as coal, petroleum, and natural gas. Carbon is also found in most plastics, many of which are derived from carbon fuels.

Chemical properties

Carbon has the chemical symbol C. Pure carbon does not react readily with other chemicals at room temperature. Most naturally occurring forms of carbon, such as diamond and graphite, do not dissolve in acid or any other common solvent. Carbon solids are stable up to very high temperatures in the absence of oxygen. At reduced pressures, some forms of carbon *sublime* (change from a solid to a vapor without melting).

Carbon's *atomic number* (number of protons in its nucleus) is 6. The most abundant *isotope* of carbon is carbon 12. The isotopes of an element have the same number of protons but different numbers of neutrons.

Carbon 12 is the international standard for a measurement known as the *relative atomic mass* of an isotope or an element. By agreement, carbon 12 has a *mass* (amount of matter) of exactly 12 *unified atomic mass units* (u). The mass of any other isotope or element is expressed in terms of these units. For example, the mass of copper is expressed as 63.55 u. An element's relative atomic mass is represented by the same number that represents its mass in unified atomic mass units, but the relative atomic mass does not include the "u." Thus, the relative atomic mass of copper is 63.55. The relative atomic mass of an element with two or more natural isotopes is an average value based on the proportions in which the isotopes occur in nature. For this reason, the relative atomic mass of carbon is not precisely 12, but 12.0107.

Carbon atoms are unusual because they can form strong chemical bonds with two, three, or four other atoms. These atoms can be carbon atoms or atoms of other chemical elements. Carbon atoms can link together to form long chains, rings, or combinations of chains and rings. This unique linking ability enables carbon to form the complex molecules that make up living things. Carbon atoms also combine to form balls and tubes.

Carbon compounds

Much of the carbon on Earth exists in combination with other elements. There are more than 1 million known carbon compounds, the largest number of compounds formed by any element except hydrogen. The most abundant carbon compounds are the gas carbon dioxide, which is part of the atmosphere; the carbonate minerals, such as limestone (also known as calcium carbonate) and marble; and the *hydrocarbons,* compounds of carbon and hydrogen that are the chief ingredients of the fuels petroleum and natural gas.

Carbon compounds make up the living tissues of all plants and animals. Organic chemistry—the study of compounds made by and derived from living things—is primarily the study of carbon compounds. Most organic compounds consist mainly of carbon combined with hydrogen, nitrogen, and oxygen in various proportions.

Forms of carbon

Pure carbon occurs in four forms: (1) diamond, (2) graphite, (3) amorphous carbons, and (4) fullerenes. The four forms have different *crystalline structures*—that is, their atoms are arranged differently. The various forms of carbon differ greatly in hardness and other properties, depending on how their atoms are arranged.

Diamond is the hardest naturally occurring substance and one of the most valuable. Natural diamonds form in the rock beneath Earth's crust, where high temperature and pressure cause carbon atoms to make strong bonds with four other carbon atoms each and to crystallize. Volcanic activity then forces the diamonds to the surface. Manufacturers produce artificial diamonds by heating and compressing pure carbon, usually graphite. Scientists grow synthetic diamond coatings by placing the object to be coated in a special chamber where a carbon-rich gas separates chemically and deposits a carbon film on the surface of the object.

The atoms in a diamond are arranged in a pyramid-shaped pattern called a *tetrahedron* that makes the structure extremely rigid. As a result, diamonds are the hardest known substance. The density of diamond is 3.5 grams per cubic centimeter.

Only a small percentage of natural diamonds are pure and perfect enough to become gemstones. Most diamonds, whether natural or synthetic, are used for industrial purposes. Because of diamonds' hardness, manufacturers use them to shape, cut, grind, and polish hard materials. Diamonds have another unique pair of properties—they are good conductors of heat but do not conduct electrical current. Diamond films are thus used in high-power electronic devices to remove excess heat without affecting the device's electrical characteristics.

The crystalline structure of diamond is the same as that of silicon, the chief material used in transistors. As a result, transistors can also be made from diamond. Diamond transistors can be safely used under much harsher conditions, such as extremely high temperatures, than ordinary silicon transistors can.

Graphite is a soft, steel-gray or black mineral that feels slick to the touch. Like diamond, natural graphite forms beneath Earth's surface. Perfect graphite crystals are rare and hard to find, but low-grade graphite is plentiful. Industry produces synthetic graphite by heating *coke,* a solid fuel that contains about 90 percent carbon.

Graphite consists of carbon atoms arranged in flat, parallel layers. The layers slide easily over one another, making the graphite soft and slippery. Graphite is much less dense than diamond, with a density of only 2.2 grams per cubic centimeter.

Because graphite is slick and soft, it is used in powdered lubricants and for the "lead" in some pencils. Unlike diamond, graphite is a good electrical conductor. As a result, it is used to make the contacts in electric

Forms of carbon

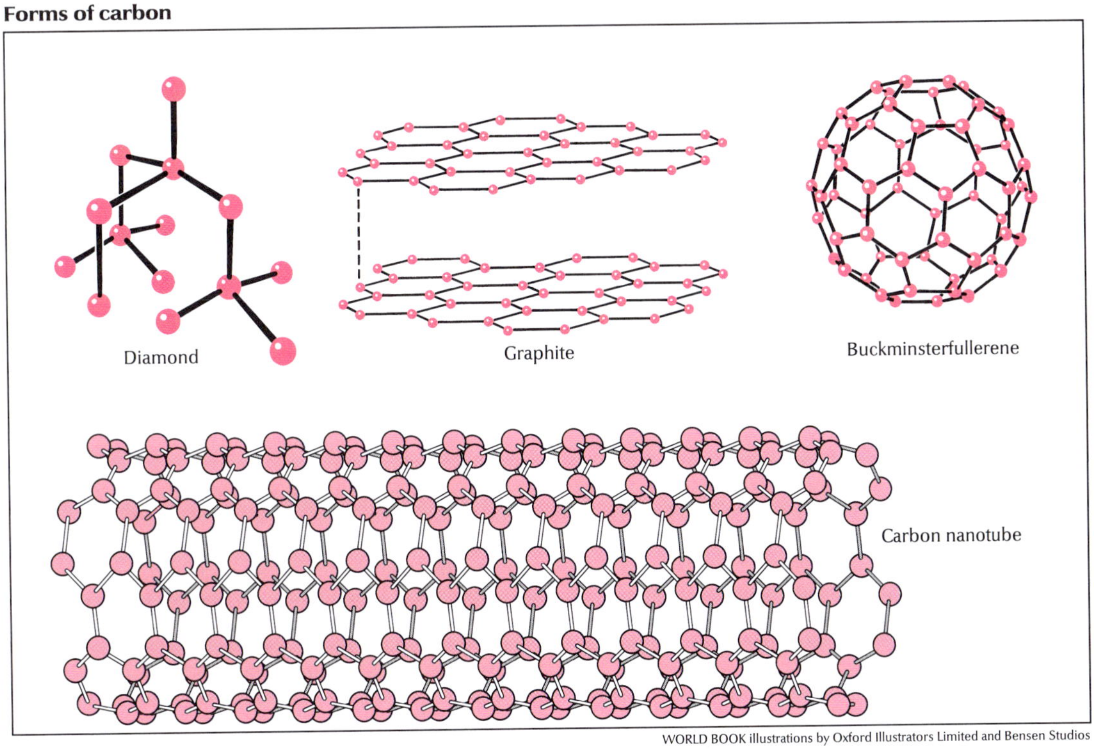

WORLD BOOK illustrations by Oxford Illustrators Limited and Bensen Studios

Pure, solid carbon occurs in three crystalline forms—rigid, pyramid-shaped diamond; flat layers of graphite; and large, hollow fullerenes. Two kinds of fullerenes are shown here: buckminsterfullerene, also known as a *buckyball;* and a carbon nanotube, sometimes called a *buckytube.*

motors and other machinery. Because graphite fibers are strong, they are used to reinforce plastic. Graphite and plastic form a strong, lightweight composite material that is used to make dish antennas, tennis rackets, fishing rods, bicycle frames, and spacecraft parts.

Amorphous carbons, also called *glassy carbons,* are made of tiny, irregularly arranged particles of graphite with no regular crystalline structure. Familiar amorphous carbons include the fuels charcoal and coke.

Amorphous carbons form, along with ash, when carbon-rich substances are heated or burned in an airtight furnace without enough oxygen to convert all the carbon to carbon dioxide. Charcoal, for example, is obtained by burning wood in the absence of air. A powdery soot called *carbon black* forms when natural gas or a petroleum-based fuel, such as kerosene, is burned in the same way. Carbon black is used as the black pigment in automobile tires and printing inks. A similar process using coal or petroleum produces coke and a tarry residue called *pitch.* Coke is an essential raw material in converting iron to steel.

Amorphous carbons have a wide range of properties. They have low densities and are quite porous. *Carbon aerogels,* also called "frozen smoke," are among the world's lightest solids, with densities as low as 0.04 gram per cubic centimeter. The plentiful pores in charcoal trap many substances effectively, so charcoal is used to filter impurities from liquids and the air. The pores also enable oxygen to penetrate rapidly inside the charcoal, making it a good fuel. Amorphous carbons are also hard, resistant to high temperatures, and chemically *inert*—that is, they do not react with most other chemicals. Because of their heat resistance, they are used for shields to protect missiles and spacecraft from getting too hot when they reenter the earth's atmosphere.

Fullerenes are hollow molecules made up of a large, even number of carbon atoms, 32 or more. The best known of these molecules are *buckminsterfullerenes,* also known as C_{60}'s or *buckyballs.* Each buckminsterfullerene consists of 60 carbon atoms bonded together in the shape of a soccer ball. Small amounts of fullerenes occur naturally in rock and in sooty flames, such as those of candles, but scientists make almost all fullerenes in the laboratory.

A fullerene with 70 atoms is shaped somewhat like a rugby ball. Fullerenes with more than 70 atoms can be ball-shaped or tubular. The tubes can have open or closed ends. Tubular fullerenes are sometimes called *buckytubes* or *carbon nanotubes.*

Fullerenes were first produced in 1985 by chemists Harold W. Kroto of the United Kingdom, Richard E. Smalley and Robert F. Curl, Jr., of the United States, and two of Smalley's students. Kroto, Smalley, and Curl won the 1996 Nobel Prize in chemistry for their major contributions to the discovery. The scientists vaporized graphite with a laser, producing clusters of 60 and 70 carbon atoms each. They named the C_{60} molecule *buckminsterfullerene* because its structure resembles a *geodesic dome,* a type of structure designed by American engineer R. Buckminster Fuller. They named the entire group of hollow carbon molecules *fullerenes.*

Buckytubes and ball-shaped fullerenes have a number of properties that may prove to be of commercial value. Filled with metal atoms, for example, buckytubes form the smallest wire imaginable. The buckyball (C_{60}) can be chemically modified to block a key step in the reproduction of the human immunodeficiency virus (HIV), which causes AIDS. Fullerenes can also be made into superconductors, substances that conduct electric current with no resistance at extremely low temperatures.

John E. Fischer

Related articles in *World Book* include:

Bitumen	Carbon tetrachloride	Coal	Organic chemistry
Carbide	Carbonate	Coal tar	Petroleum coke
Carbohydrate	Charcoal	Coke	Pitch
Carbon dioxide	Chemistry	Diamond	Radiocarbon
Carbon monoxide	Chlorofluorocarbon	Graphite	Soot
		Hydrocarbon	

Carbon 14. See **Radiocarbon.**

Carbon black. See **Carbon.**

Carbon dating. See **Radiocarbon** (Radiocarbon dating; diagram: Radiocarbon dating).

Carbon dioxide is a colorless, odorless gas. It occurs in the atmospheres of many planets, including that of Earth. On Earth, all green plants must get carbon dioxide from the atmosphere to live and grow. Animals produce the gas when their bodies convert food into energy and living tissue. Animals release carbon dioxide into the atmosphere. Carbon dioxide is also created by the burning of any substance that contains carbon. Such substances include coal, gasoline, and wood. Fermentation and the decay of plants and animals also produce carbon dioxide (see **Fermentation**). Carbon dioxide makes up less than 1 percent of Earth's atmosphere.

The carbon dioxide in Earth's atmosphere helps regulate the planet's temperature. When sunlight reaches Earth, some of it is converted into heat. Carbon dioxide absorbs some of the heat and so helps keep it near Earth's surface. If all the heat from sunlight escaped into outer space, Earth would become very cold. The amount of carbon dioxide in the atmosphere has been increasing since about the early to middle 1800's, chiefly as a result of the burning of fuels that contain carbon. This increase has caused a slight rise in Earth's average temperature. See **Greenhouse effect.**

Carbon dioxide has important uses in the home and in industry. For example, carbon dioxide released by baking powder or yeast makes cake batter rise. Carbon dioxide in soft drinks, beer, and sparkling wines gives the beverages their fizz. Some fire extinguishers use carbon dioxide because it does not burn and because pure carbon dioxide is heavier than air. Carbon dioxide's heaviness enables it to blanket a fire and prevent oxygen in the air from reaching the fire. Fires need oxygen to continue burning.

The gas becomes a solid at −109.3 °F (−78.5 °C). Solid carbon dioxide is commonly called *dry ice* because, at normal pressures, it does not become a liquid as its temperature rises. Instead, it *sublimes*—that is, it changes from a solid directly into a gas. Carbon dioxide molecules consist of one carbon atom and two oxygen atoms. Carbon dioxide has the chemical formula CO_2. The gas was first identified in the 1750's by Joseph Black, a Scottish chemist and physician. Emily Jane Rose

See also **Climate** (Changes in CO_2 concentration; Human activity); **Dry ice; Fire extinguisher; Gasoline engine** (Air pollution controls); **Photosynthesis.**

Carbon monoxide is a colorless, odorless, tasteless,

Carbon dioxide in the air

Plants absorb carbon dioxide exhaled by people and animals, and give off oxygen. People and animals inhale that oxygen and exhale carbon dioxide, which is produced by burning food in their bodies. Through this cycle, the supply of oxygen and carbon dioxide stays fairly stable.

WORLD BOOK diagram by Sarah Woodward

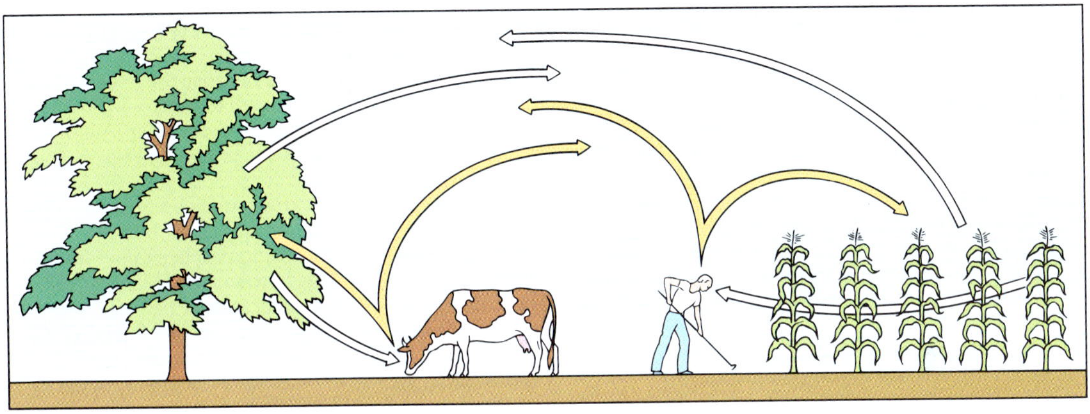

and extremely poisonous gas. Because it has no odor or color, people breathing it usually fall asleep without realizing they are being poisoned. Carbon monoxide prevents *hemoglobin* (the oxygen-carrying substance in the blood) from supplying oxygen to the body. Without oxygen, people and animals soon die.

Carbon monoxide is produced when substances containing carbon—such as coal, wood, oil, or gasoline—are *oxidized* (burned) without enough oxygen present. However, most carbon monoxide in the atmosphere comes from natural sources. For example, the decay of swamp gas and other organic materials in the absence of oxygen produces carbon monoxide. Some reactions in soil and in the atmosphere remove carbon monoxide, thereby keeping the total amount of the gas nearly constant. But car engines also produce carbon monoxide. United States automakers are required to equip vehicles with devices that convert carbon monoxide to carbon dioxide. Cigarette smoke also has a small amount of carbon monoxide. Even this small quantity can be harmful.

Industry burns carbon monoxide for heat in manufacturing processes. The carbon monoxide is usually in a fuel gas such as water gas or producer gas. These gases are sometimes used to heat homes and to cook food. Carbon monoxide is also used to separate metals such as iron and nickel from their ores and to purify them.

The chemical formula of carbon monoxide is CO. The gas was first prepared in the laboratory in 1776 by J. M. F. de Lassone, a French chemist. Its composition was identified in 1800 by William Cruikshank, an English chemist. Emily Jane Rose

See also **Carbon-monoxide detector; Hyperbaric oxygen therapy.**

Carbon-monoxide detector, also called a *CO detector,* is a device designed to monitor levels of carbon monoxide inside homes. The device makes a loud, piercing sound when carbon monoxide reaches potentially unhealthy levels.

There are three types of CO detectors, *biomimetic, semiconductor,* and *electrochemical.* A biomimetic detector contains a light source that shines through a chemically treated disk called a *gel cell.* The cell absorbs carbon monoxide, which causes it to darken. When the cell darkens enough so that light cannot pass through it, an alarm sounds.

In semiconductor and electrochemical detectors, a computer chip monitors the flow of electric current through a substance. This substance is a solid in semiconductor types and a liquid in electrochemical types. When the substance reacts with carbon monoxide, its resistance to the current changes. The computer chip detects the change and causes the alarm to sound.

Manufacturers began making residential CO detectors in the early 1990's. CO detectors are produced as battery-operated or plug-in models. Safety experts recommend the installation of at least one detector near the bedrooms in all homes. Lawrence S. Curran

See also **Carbon monoxide.**

Carbon tetrachloride, *TEHT ruh KLAWR eyed,* is a clear, colorless liquid that does not burn. Industries use it to dissolve oils and rubber, to manufacture refrigerants, and to produce propellants that make liquids spray from containers. The liquid was once widely used as a cleaning fluid. But inhaling its fumes can cause severe illness or death. Carbon tetrachloride will not mix with water, but it changes into poisonous gases when heated. In 1970, the United States government banned the use of carbon tetrachloride in household products.

Manufacturers make carbon tetrachloride by passing chlorine through glowing coke, or by combining chlorine with carbon disulfide or methane. Carbon tetrachloride has the chemical formula CCl_4. Barry Zimmerman

Carbonate, *KAHR buh nayt,* is any compound that contains the carbonate *ion.* An ion is an atom or a group of atoms with an electric charge. The carbonate ion has two negative charges and consists of one carbon atom and three oxygen atoms. Its chemical formula is $CO_3{=}$. Chalk, marble, and other limestones are examples of a naturally abundant carbonate, calcium carbonate. Animal bones and teeth as well as egg and oyster shells have large amounts of calcium carbonate.

Carbonate ions combined with metal ions form the most common carbonates, including calcium carbonate. These metal carbonates can be produced by allowing a water solution of a chemical base, such as sodium hydroxide, to combine with carbon dioxide. The reaction produces a *bicarbonate* (carbonate that includes a hydrogen ion, HCO_3-). A carbonate compound results from heating a bicarbonate compound. For example, common washing soda (sodium carbonate, Na_2CO_3) results from heating baking soda (sodium bicarbonate, $NaHCO_3$). Roger D. Barry

See also **Calcium carbonate; Soda.**

Carboniferous Period, *KAHR buh NIHF uhr uhs,* was a time in Earth's history that lasted from about 359 million to 299 million years ago. The word *carboniferous* is Latin for *coal-bearing.* Rocks of this age from the United States, Europe, and much of Asia contain abundant coal deposits. Carboniferous Period coals fueled the Industrial Revolution, the rapid rise of industrialization that began during the late 1700's. Carboniferous rocks remain an important source of energy because many petroleum deposits formed in them.

Carboniferous rocks from Europe and North America appear similar because the two continents formed a single land mass at the time. Toward the end of the period, this land mass collided with another mass consisting mainly of what are now South America and Africa. Most of the world's land had begun to form a single vast continent called Pangaea. The southern reaches of this continent lay in the cold region around the South Pole. Evidence suggests that a major ice sheet began to form in this area during the end of the Carboniferous Period. This occurrence marked the beginning of one of the longest *glacial epochs* in Earth's history. A glacial epoch is a global cooling period marked by the gradual growth of glaciers. The glacial epoch that began in the Carboniferous Period lasted tens of millions of years, eventually coming to an end in the middle of the following Permian Period.

During the Carboniferous Period, life flourished in a vast expanse of swamps that stretched for great distances along the equator. Various types of trees, many related to modern ferns, grew in these swamps. The compressed remains of the swamps' plant material form the Carboniferous Period coal deposits. The swamps housed the earliest winged insects, the first creatures to fly. Amphibians, many of which resembled crocodiles in both size and appearance, also lived in the swamps. The first reptiles appeared during the Carboniferous Period. Their major innovation, the ability to lay watertight eggs, enabled them to live away from the swamps. However, reptiles did not move to dry land in large numbers until after the Carboniferous Period.

Geologists sometimes divide the Carboniferous Period into two shorter periods. The earlier period, called the Mississippian Period, produced limestone deposits found in North America, Europe, and much of Asia. The later period, the Pennsylvanian, produced equally widespread deposits of coal-bearing rocks. P. B. Wignall

See also **Club moss; Forest** (The first forests); **Plant** (Early plants); **Prehistoric animal** (The move onto land).

Carborundum. See **Gem** (Cutting and polishing).

Carbuncle, *KAHR buhng kuhl,* is a painful infection of the skin and tissues just under the skin. A carbuncle is a warm, tender, dark red lump. Carbuncles most often develop on the back of the neck. They usually break through the skin in several places and discharge pus.

Carbuncles are caused by bacteria called *staphylococci.* The bacteria enter through the opening around a hair or through a break in the skin. They multiply and move into deeper tissues. Carbuncles are most common in elderly or malnourished individuals. They also affect people who suffer from diabetes and certain other *chronic* (long-term) diseases.

Carbuncles are dangerous because the infection can spread through the bloodstream to other parts of the body. They should be treated by a physician. Antibiotics can cure most carbuncles. Yelva Liptzin Lynfield

See also **Abscess; Boil.**

Carburetor is a part of an internal-combustion engine that delivers a mixture of fuel and air for burning. Carburetors were widely used in automobile engines for many years. By the 1980's, however, an electronically controlled device called a *fuel injector* had replaced the carburetor in most automobiles (see **Fuel injection**). Carburetors are still used in smaller, less expensive engines, such as those of motorcycles and lawn mowers.

The main part of a carburetor is an hourglass-shaped device called a *venturi tube.* The piston motion of an engine draws air through the venturi tube, and then through a pipe called the *intake manifold.* As the air enters the narrow part of the venturi, its speed increases and its pressure decreases because of a law of physics called Bernoulli's principle.

A tube called the *fuel nozzle* is located in the narrow part of the venturi tube. There, the low pressure creates a vacuum that draws fuel from a *fuel reservoir* through the nozzle and into the venturi. The fuel reservoir is a small fuel storage tank. Its fuel level is maintained by a flow from the fuel tank through a *fuel line.* The fuel mixes with the air as it leaves the carburetor and travels through the intake manifold and into the combustion chamber, where the mixture of air and fuel burns. Heat from the engine vaporizes part of the liquid gasoline in the manifold and the rest in the combustion chamber.

A carburetor adjusts naturally to the fuel flow for different operating conditions. For example, an engine operating at a high speed requires a high fuel flow rate. As the airflow through the carburetor increases, the lower pressure at the nozzle results in a higher fuel flow from the fuel reservoir.

A disc called a *throttle valve* controls the quantity of fuel-air mixture leaving the venturi and entering the intake manifold. The throttle can be adjusted to fit the needs of the operating device. For example, a person using a lawn mower may use a control to open the throttle as wide as possible when mowing a thick lawn.

The *choke valve,* a disc at the other end of the venturi, controls the amount of air that enters the carburetor. In some engines, the choke is controlled automatically by the temperature of the engine. A cold engine requires more fuel and less air to start than a warm engine does. Thus, when the engine is cold, the choke is partially closed, reducing the amount of air flowing through the carburetor. David E. Foster

Carcassonne, *kahr kah SAWN* (pop. 46,216), is a city in southern France that includes one of the finest examples in Europe of a medieval walled town. The walled town lies southeast of the rest of the city. For location, see **France** (political map). Two walls, both including towers, surround the southeastern section. Landmarks within the walls include the Cathedral of St.-Nazaire, which dates from the 1000's, and the Château Comtal, a castle built in the 1100's. Many tourists visit Carcassonne to see its medieval structures. Carcassonne serves as the capital of the Aude *department* (administrative district). It is a center of the wine trade of its region. Other economic activities include oil refining and the manufacture of furniture, plastics, and rubber products.

Roman soldiers built a walled town at what is now Carcassonne in the last 100 years before Christ. To keep out invaders, the people of Carcassonne rebuilt the walls and towers in the A.D. 600's and enlarged them in the 1100's and 1200's. The area outside the walls began to develop in the 1200's. It became the city's main commercial and residential district. In the late 1800's, most of the walls and towers were repaired or rebuilt for historical preservation purposes. Mark Kesselman

Carcinogen. See Cancer (Genes damaged by substances in the environment).

Carcinoma. See Cancer (Classification by tissue).

Card game is a game of chance or skill played with oblong pieces of thin cardboard. Each piece, or card, has certain *spots* and figures. Hundreds of games can be played with cards. Various numbers of players take part, depending on the game. *Solitaire,* or *patience,* as it used to be called, provides entertainment for one person. *Casino* is usually played by two people. Two, three, or four may play *cribbage* or *pinochle.* Four people play *bridge* or *whist.* The game of *canasta* calls for from two to six players. *Poker* can be played by as many as 10.

Other popular card games include *gin rummy, hearts, euchre, skat, blackjack, five hundred, red dog,* and *piquet.* Each game has its own set of rules.

Playing cards. There are 52 playing cards in a set, also called a *deck* or *pack.* The 52 cards are divided into four *suits* of 13 cards each. There are two black suits (*spades* and *clubs*) and two red suits (*hearts* and *diamonds*). Each suit includes 10 *spot cards* that range from 1 (*ace*) through 10. Each suit also has three *face* (picture) cards: *jack* (knave), *queen,* and *king.* These cards do not picture modern royalty but are stylized drawings that probably originated during the Middle Ages. Some games, such as pinochle and canasta, use parts of two decks, or a combination of decks.

History. Playing cards probably originated in China or in Hindustan about A.D. 800. How they came to Europe is not certain, but they had appeared in Italy by the late 1200's. Soon after, cards spread to Germany, France, and Spain. The four suits originated in France in the 1500's. An object shaped like a clover leaf marked the suit called *trèfle,* now known as the *club* suit. The tip of a pike marked the *pique* suit, now called the *spade.* The third suit was called *coeur,* the French word for *heart.* The name of the fourth suit, *carreau,* means square, but the suit is called *diamond* because of its diamond-shaped spot. R. Wayne Schmittberger

Related articles in *World Book* include:

Bridge	Cribbage	Pinochle
Canasta	Hoyle, Edmond	Poker

Playing cards through history

Cards from the 1800's include an Indian disk card, *above left,* and an American card used as an invitation, *above right.* A German card made of painted silk, *below left,* and a French king of hearts, *below right,* both date from the 1700's.

From the collection of the Playing Card Museum, United States Playing Card Co.

Cardamom, *KAHR duh muhm,* is the fruit of several plants in the ginger family. The fruit and seeds grow in a small shell about ¾ inch (19 millimeters) long. The seeds give an oil that is used in medicine as a stimulant. American and English medicine recognize only the cardamom which grows in Malabar, India, as the *true,* or *official, cardamom.* This kind of cardamom also grows in Jamaica. It reaches a height of 10 feet (3 meters) and has white flowers with blue stripes and a yellow margin. Other forms of cardamom grow in the East Indies, the Bengal region, and Sri Lanka. People in some countries use the fruit of the cardamom to season sauces, curries, and cordials. In Scandinavia and Germany, baked goods are flavored with cardamom. W. Dennis Clark

Scientific classification. Cardamom is in the ginger family, Zingiberaceae. Official cardamom is *Elettaria cardamomum.* Cardamom from Sri Lanka is *E. cardamomum,* variety *major.* East Indian cardamom is *Amomum cardamomum.* Cardamom from Bengal is *A. subulatum.*

Cardboard is a popular name for any stiff paper or paperboard that is more than 0.012 inch (0.3048 millimeter) thick. Papermakers use various names for different kinds of cardboard. The name may be based on the raw material used, such as *newsboard,* a coarse cardboard made from newspaper pulp. It may indicate useful characteristics, such as *bending board.* Or it may designate the final use, such as *poster board* or *shoe board.* A familiar type of cardboard, called *bristol board,* is used for such products as index cards and postal cards. Manufacturers make cardboard by pasting several layers of paper together or by pressing layers of wet pulp together. They often coat cardboard for decoration or to improve the surface of the cardboard for printing. Larry L. Graham

Cárdenas, *KAHR day nahs,* **Lázaro,** *LAH sah ROH* (1895-1970), served as president of Mexico from 1934 to 1940. More than any other president since the beginning of the Mexican Revolution in 1910, he carried out the revolution's reform aims. He established a program that gave land to the poor. In addition, he promoted the construction of schools and brought foreign-owned oil companies under government control. Cárdenas also greatly reduced the influence of the nation's rich landowners and of its military. The vast power of these groups was left over from premodern Mexico. By reducing their influence, Cárdenas helped pave the way for the development of agricultural and commercial capitalism in Mexico. Cárdenas was born on May 21, 1895, in Jiquilpan, Michoacán. He joined the revolutionary army in 1913 and took part in many of its military and political developments. He died on Oct. 19, 1970. See also **Mexico** (Economic and social changes). W. Dirk Raat

Cardiac. See **Heart**.

Cardiff, *KAHR dihf* (pop. 305,340), is the capital and largest city of Wales, a division of the United Kingdom. It is also the chief economic, industrial, and cultural center of Wales. Cardiff lies on the southeast coast of Wales. It borders the Bristol Channel, an arm of the Atlantic Ocean (see **Wales** [map]).

Three rivers—the Taff, the Ely, and the Rhymney—flow through Cardiff into the Bristol Channel. A number of docks line the coast, and many factories are nearby.

A large area of parkland lies near the center of Cardiff. The Civic Center and many of the city's major commercial buildings are clustered around Cathays Park in this area. The Civic Center includes the Law Courts, City Hall, National Museum of Wales, and the University College. Nearby are the National Sports Center, National School of Medicine, many fashionable shops and modern hotels, and Cardiff Castle. The castle was built in 1090. Cardiff is also the home of the medieval Llandaff Cathedral, the Welsh Industrial and Maritime Museum, and the Welsh Folk Museum.

Factories in Cardiff produce automobile parts, chemicals, electronics equipment, engineering products, and processed food and tobacco. The city is a busy shipping center. Modern railroad and highway systems connect Cardiff with the rest of the United Kingdom. Cardiff-Wales International Airport lies outside the city.

About A.D. 75, Roman soldiers built a fort on the site of what is now Cardiff. The name *Cardiff* means *fort on the Taff.* Normans settled the area in the late 1000's. They built Cardiff Castle on the site of the old Roman fort. A walled town grew up around the castle and served as a market and port for Welsh farm products.

By the early 1800's, Cardiff was still a small town. Then, Wales became a major center of coal mining and iron and steel production. Cardiff was the shipping center for these products and grew rapidly. By 1890, it had become known as the *Coal Metropolis of the World.*

Cardiff coal trade declined after World War I ended in 1918, and the city soon developed new industries. Since the mid-1940's, Cardiff has grown steadily as the administrative and commercial center of Wales. In 1955, it became the capital of Wales. D. Q. Bowen

Cardigan Welsh corgi, *KAWR gee,* is a small, strong breed of dog that was first raised in Cardiganshire, Wales. Since about A.D. 1000, Cardigans have been used to herd cattle, nipping the feet of the cattle to drive them. Cardigans also are excellent watchdogs.

Walter Chandoha

The Cardigan Welsh corgi has a long foxlike tail.

Cardigan Welsh corgis measure about 12 inches (30 centimeters) tall at the shoulder and weigh from 26 to 34 pounds (12 to 15 kilograms). They are foxlike in appearance, with large ears and a long furry tail. Their short, rough coat may be almost any color or combination of colors, usually with white markings.

The Cardigan Welsh corgi resembles the Pembroke Welsh corgi. However, the Cardigan has a slightly longer body, bigger ears, a coarser coat, and a long foxlike tail. The word *corgi* comes from two Welsh words meaning *dwarf dog.*

Critically reviewed by the Cardigan Welsh Corgi Club of America

See also **Pembroke Welsh corgi.**

Cardinal is one of a group of Roman Catholic clergymen who serve as counselors to the pope and rank next to him within the church. The cardinals as a group form the Sacred College of Cardinals. Their most important responsibility, as a body, is to elect a new pope upon the death of the previous pope. For information about how cardinals elect a pope, see **Pope** (The election of a pope).

Many cardinals head Catholic dioceses throughout the world. Other cardinals help govern the church from the Vatican in Rome. Individual cardinals have no lawmaking power. However, their rank gives them great influence in church affairs. Since 1059, the Sacred College of Cardinals has elected every pope. In 1970, Pope Paul VI ruled that no cardinal past the age of 80 could vote for a new pope.

The pope appoints all cardinals. For hundreds of years, a pope could make any Roman Catholic a cardinal, and some popes even appointed laypersons to the office. In 1917, the church adopted a rule that went into effect in 1918 providing that cardinals must be at least priests. In 1962, Pope John XXIII declared that all cardinals must be bishops. Cardinals who were not bishops were ordained bishops.

In 1586, Pope Sixtus V set the number of cardinals at 70. After 1959 Pope John XXIII and Pope Paul VI increased the number several times to provide a wider international representation.

Canadian cardinals

Cardinal	Life dates	Elevated	Archdiocese
*Ambrozic, Aloysius M.	1930-	1998	Toronto
Bégin, Louis N.	1840-1925	1914	Quebec
Carter, Gerald E.	1912-2003	1979	Toronto
*Flahiff, George B.	1905-1989	1969	Winnipeg
*Gregoire, Paul	1911-1993	1988	Montreal
Léger, Paul-Émile	1904-1991	1953	Montreal
McGuigan, James C.	1894-1974	1946	Toronto
Ouellet, Marc	1944-	2003	Quebec
Rouleau, Félix R.	1866-1931	1927	Quebec
Roy, Maurice	1905-1985	1965	Quebec
Taschereau, Elzéar A.	1820-1898	1886	Quebec
Turcotte, Jean-Claude	1936-	1994	Montreal
Villeneuve, Jean M.	1883-1947	1933	Quebec

American cardinals

Cardinal	Life dates	Elevated	Archdiocese
*Aponte Martinez, Luis	1922-	1973	San Juan, P.R.
*Baum, William W.	1926-	1976	†
*Bernardin, Joseph L.	1928-1996	1983	Chicago
*Bevilacqua, Anthony J.	1923-	1991	Philadelphia
Brennan, Francis J.	1894-1968	1967	†
Carberry, John J.	1904-1998	1969	St. Louis
Cody, John P.	1907-1982	1967	Chicago
*Cooke, Terence J.	1921-1983	1969	New York
Cushing, Richard	1895-1970	1958	Boston
Dearden, John F.	1907-1988	1969	Detroit
Dougherty, Dennis J.	1865-1951	1921	Philadelphia
Dulles, Avery R.	1918-	2001	‡
Egan, Edward M.	1932-	2001	New York
Farley, John M.	1842-1918	1911	New York
*George, Francis E.	1937-	1998	Chicago
Gibbons, James	1834-1921	1886	Baltimore
Glennon, John J.	1862-1946	1946	St. Louis
Hayes, Patrick J.	1867-1938	1924	New York
Hickey, James A.	1920-2004	1988	Washington, D.C.
Keeler, William H.	1931-	1994	Baltimore
Krol, John J.	1910-1996	1967	Philadelphia
*Law, Bernard F.	1931-	1985	Boston
*Mahony, Roger M.	1936-	1991	Los Angeles
Maida, Adam J.	1930-	1994	Detroit
Manning, Timothy	1909-1989	1973	Los Angeles
McCarrick, Theodore E.	1930-	2001	Washington, D.C.
*McCloskey, John	1810-1885	1875	New York
McIntyre, James F.	1886-1979	1953	Los Angeles
*Medeiros, Humberto S.	1915-1983	1973	Boston
Meyer, Albert G.	1903-1965	1959	Chicago
Mooney, Edward F.	1882-1958	1946	Detroit
Muench, Aloisius J.	1889-1962	1959	†
Mundelein, George W.	1872-1939	1924	Chicago
O'Boyle, Patrick A.	1896-1987	1967	Washington, D.C.
O'Connell, William H.	1859-1944	1911	Boston
*O'Connor, John J.	1920-2000	1985	New York
O'Hara, John F.	1888-1960	1958	Philadelphia
Rigali, Justin	1935-	2003	Philadelphia
Ritter, Joseph E.	1892-1967	1961	St. Louis
*Shehan, Lawrence J.	1898-1984	1965	Baltimore
*Spellman, Francis J.	1889-1967	1946	New York
Stafford, James F.	1932-	1998	†
Stritch, Samuel A.	1887-1958	1946	Chicago
*Szoka, Edmund C.	1927-	1988	Detroit
Wright, John J.	1909-1979	1969	†

*Has a separate biography in *World Book*. †Member of the Roman Curia at the Vatican. ‡Theologian.

No one really knows the origin of the term *cardinal.* Today, many scholars believe the title originated from the fact that some bishops were *incardinated*—that is, named to serve a diocese other than the one in which they had been ordained. Robert P. Imbelli

Related articles in *World Book* include:

Address, Forms of (Cardinal)
Bellarmine, Saint Robert Francis
Langton, Stephen
Mazarin, Jules
Mercier, Désire Joseph
Mindszenty, József
Newman, John Henry
Pope
Rampolla del Tindaro, Mariano
Richelieu, Cardinal
Roman Catholic Church (Church organization)
Vatican Council II
Wolsey, Thomas
Wyszyński, Stefan

Cardinal is a bird common throughout the eastern half of North America. It is sometimes called *redbird.* Cardinals live from southeastern North Dakota, central Minnesota, southern Ontario, and central Maine south to Florida, the Gulf of Mexico, Mexico, and Belize.

The cardinal measures about 7 to 9 inches (18 to 23 centimeters) long. It has a crest of feathers on its head that can be raised to threaten an enemy. Male cardinals are red with some gray on the back. A distinctive black marking around the eyes and at the base of the red-orange bill may reduce glare from the bill. Females are a brownish color with red in the wings, tail, and crest.

The female cardinal usually builds her nest 4 to 5 feet (1.2 to 1.5 meters) above the ground in dense shrubbery, tangles of vines, saplings, or small trees. The nest is made of weed stems, twigs, bark, leaves, and paper. The female typically lays three or four eggs, which are grayish-white with brown spots and many speckles. The female sits on the eggs, and the male finds food. The

Dan Sudia, Photo Researchers

The cardinal is a popular songbird of North America. The female, *left,* is dull brown, and the male, *right,* is bright red.

eggs hatch in 12 to 13 days. At first, both sexes feed the young. The male takes over the feeding entirely when the female builds a new nest for the next brood. Young cardinals leave the nest in about 10 days. The male continues to care for them for another 10 days. Cardinals may have up to four broods from April through August each year.

Cardinals feed on weed seeds, wild fruit, grain, worms, and beetles and other insects. In winter, they often seek food at feeders provided by people. Cardinals prefer sunflower seeds but also eat raisins, pieces of apple, bread, and millet. Young cardinals eat insects, including boll worms, cotton worms, codling moths, and potato beetles.

Both male and female cardinals have a wide variety of cheerful, flutelike songs. The birds were once trapped and sold as songbirds, and their brilliant feathers were used to decorate women's hats. Cardinals are now protected by law. Edward H. Burtt, Jr.

Scientific classification. The cardinal belongs to the family Emberizidae. It is *Cardinalis cardinalis.*

See also **Bird** (table: State and provincial birds; pictures: Birds of urban areas; Birds' eggs).

Cardinal flower is a tall plant that grows in wet or moist soil along springs and in meadows, marshes, and roadside areas. The plant is found chiefly in the eastern and central parts of the United States. It grows 2 to 5 feet (61 to 150 centimeters) high and bears cardinal-red flowers. The plant is a *perennial*—that is, it can live for two years or more. David A. Francko

Scientific classification. The cardinal flower is in the lobelia family, Lobeliaceae. Its scientific name is *Lobelia cardinalis.*

See also **Lobelia.**

Cardinal number. See **Number and numeral.**

Cardinal points. See **Compass.**

Carding. See **Cotton** (Cleaning; picture); **Wool** (Processing of wool; picture).

Cardiology, *KAHR dee AHL uh jee,* is a branch of medicine that deals with the diagnosis and treatment of disorders of the heart. Doctors who specialize in cardiology are called *cardiologists.*

Cardiologists interview and examine patients for possible heart disease. First, the cardiologist asks if the patient has experienced symptoms that suggest heart disease, such as chest pain, shortness of breath, and ankle swelling. The cardiologist then examines the patient by checking the blood pressure, by feeling the beat of the heart on the chest, and by listening with a stethoscope to the sounds produced by the heart.

Following this examination, the cardiologist may order various laboratory tests to help confirm or deny the presence of heart disease. One such test is done with an *electrocardiograph,* a recording device that shows the electrical activity of the heart. The patient may be asked to walk on a *treadmill* (moving platform) while being monitored on the electrocardiograph (see **Electrocardiograph**). The cardiologist may use X rays or sound waves to produce images of the patient's heart. In a technique called *catheterization,* tubes are inserted into the chambers of the heart to measure blood pressure and flow within it and to inject dye for X-ray imaging. If a diagnosis of heart disease is made, the cardiologist will recommend specific therapy, such as medication or surgery. Bruce F. Waller

See also **Heart.**

Cardiopulmonary resuscitation (CPR) is an emergency first-aid procedure used to deliver oxygen-carrying blood to the heart and brain in a person whose breathing and heartbeat have stopped. CPR is most often needed following a heart attack that has caused a person's heart to stop beating, a condition called *cardiac arrest.* People may also go into cardiac arrest and require CPR after serious injury, near drowning, or drug overdose. CPR must begin within minutes after the victim's breathing and heartbeat have stopped.

To administer CPR, the rescuer first checks to see if the victim is responsive by gently shaking the person and asking, "Are you OK?" If the victim does not re-

The basic steps of CPR

Open the airway. The trained rescuer first tilts the victim's head back. Placing his ear near the victim's nose and mouth, he listens and feels for breathing.

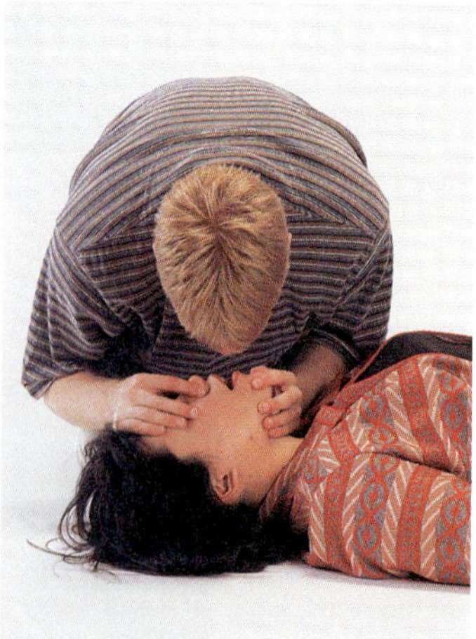

Restore breathing. The rescuer pinches the victim's nostrils shut and takes a deep breath. Then he blows into the victim's mouth to inflate the lungs.

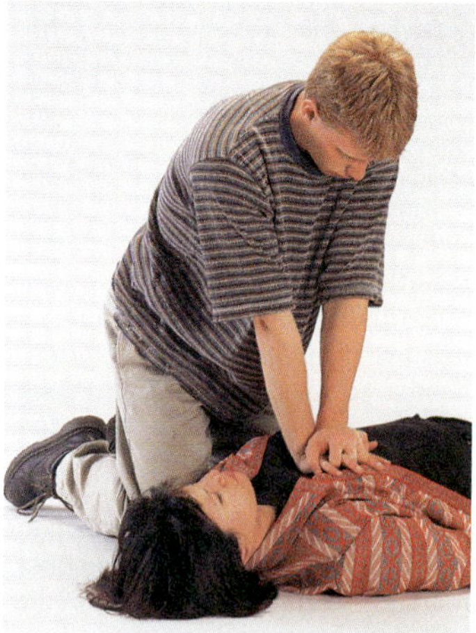

WORLD BOOK photos by Bill Goes

Chest compressions help maintain the victim's heartbeat. The rescuer presses down on the lower part of the victim's breastbone, then releases the pressure.

spond, the rescuer should shout for help and send someone to telephone for an ambulance. Next, the rescuer places the victim flat and face up. The rescuer must then open the victim's airway. If no neck injury is suspected, the rescuer presses down on the victim's forehead and lifts the bony part of the chin. This action opens the victim's airway by lifting the tongue and jaw. In an unconscious person, the tongue often blocks the upper airway. When the rescuer opens the airway, the victim may resume breathing.

If the victim does not begin breathing normally, the rescuer pinches the victim's nostrils shut, takes a deep breath, and places his or her mouth over the victim's mouth. The rescuer blows slowly into the victim's mouth to inflate the lungs and then releases the nose to allow the victim to breathe out. The rescuer gives the victim two breaths in this way.

Next, the rescuer checks for signs of circulation, including normal breathing, coughing, or movement. If the victim has no signs of circulation after two breaths, the rescuer should begin chest compressions.

The rescuer places both hands—one on top of the other—on the lower part of the victim's *sternum* (breastbone) and presses down about 1 ½ to 2 inches (4 to 5 centimeters). This action forces blood to flow from the heart to other parts of the body. The pressure is then released to allow the heart to fill with blood. After every 30 chest compressions, the rescuer gives the victim two full breaths. This procedure should be performed continuously until the victim's heartbeat and breathing resume or until help arrives.

Anyone can learn to perform CPR. The American Heart Association, American Red Cross, and many other organizations offer training courses. People should take a course every year or two to refresh their skills and learn any changes in the CPR procedure. Even people with no training can be "coached" through the steps over the telephone by an Emergency Medical Services dispatcher. Critically reviewed by the American Heart Association

See also **First aid** (Heart attack).

Cardozo, *kahr DOH zoh,* **Benjamin Nathan** (1870-1938), served as an associate justice of the Supreme Court of the United States from 1932 until his death on July 9, 1938. He became a leading member of the court's liberal wing, and wrote the court's opinion upholding the federal Social Security Act in 1937.

Cardozo was born on May 24, 1870, in New York City. He graduated from Columbia University. In 1914, Cardozo became a member of the New York Court of Appeals, and he was selected as chief judge of the court in 1926. President Herbert Hoover appointed him to the Supreme Court in 1932 to succeed Oliver Wendell Holmes. Richard Polenberg

Cards. See **Card game.**

Carducci, *kahr DOOT chee,* **Giosuè,** *jaw SWEH* (1835-1907), an Italian poet, scholar, and literary critic, won the 1906 Nobel Prize in literature. His verse is variously lyrical, political, and historical. Carducci's poetry shows his political liberalism, and his belief in the ideals of Classicism and opposition to Romanticism. The poetry was greatly influenced by his familiarity with European literature, especially Greek, Latin, and Italian works. His major collections include *New Verses* (1887) and *Barbarian Odes* (1877-1889). His critical works had a strong influence on Italian attitudes toward literature.

Carducci was born on July 27, 1835, in Tuscany. He served as professor of Italian literature at the University of Bologna from 1860 to 1904. In 1890, he was named a senator by the Italian government. Carducci died on Feb. 16, 1907. Richard H. Lansing

CARE is a private, nonprofit agency founded in 1945 by 22 leading cooperative, labor, relief, and religious organizations. Its letters mean the *C*ooperative for *A*merican *R*elief *E*verywhere. Originally, CARE supplied packages of food and clothing to needy people in Europe. Later, it extended its service to people in Africa, Asia, and Latin America. CARE provides development projects that include health care, food production, water supply, income generation, and conservation of natural resources. CARE also provides emergency assistance to refugees and disaster victims.

Donors may select the type of aid and the countries to which they wish their gifts sent, or they may let CARE decide. The agency is registered with the United States government's Advisory Committee on Voluntary Foreign Aid. CARE has headquarters in Atlanta, Georgia.

Critically reviewed by CARE

Career education is instruction intended to help young people identify, choose, and prepare for a career. Such instruction may focus on a person's role in work, leisure, or family life. Career education differs from *vocational education,* which is designed to teach specific occupational skills.

Career education includes the formal and informal learning that occurs in the family, in the community, and in schools. In school, career education consists of instructive activities included in many courses. These activities are designed to improve the attitudes, knowledge, and skills important for work roles. For example, a science class might investigate careers in environmental fields, health, and marine sciences. Career education helps students develop self-understanding and use it to plan their education and working life.

A complete career education program in school begins in kindergarten and continues at least through high school. Many colleges and universities also offer career education through their counseling programs. In kindergarten and elementary school, youngsters learn about different types of work. In middle school or junior high school, children begin to explore the occupations and leisure activities that interest them most. School counselors and teachers help children find educational and occupational opportunities that match their abilities and interests. In high school, students get more specific information about occupations and life styles. They learn how to make career decisions. They also should obtain the skills they need for further study or for a job after graduation. Counselors provide information on such matters as how to locate and apply for jobs and how to be successful in interviews.

Teachers and counselors use a variety of methods to provide career education, including films about occupations or industries. Children may invite parents or other adults to come to school and describe their jobs. A student may accompany a worker on the job. *Cooperative education* combines classroom study with practical work experience. David A. Jepsen

See also **Careers; Cooperative education.**

Choosing a career is an important decision that will affect a person's life in many ways. A person should choose a career that suits his or her abilities, interests, and values. Attending job fairs like the one shown here can help a jobseeker learn about career fields and employment opportunities.

Careers

Careers are the patterns of work and work-related activities that people develop throughout a lifetime. A career includes the job or series of jobs a person has until retirement. Careers vary greatly in the type of work involved and in the ways they influence a person's life.

Almost every adult has a career of some kind. Most people build a career to help them satisfy certain goals. Such goals might include earning a living or helping society. The best-known career pattern develops around work for pay. Most workers in such a career hold a job to support themselves and their family. However, some people build a career around activities for which they receive no money. For example, many people's careers are caring for their families and their homes. Others volunteer their time to help others.

The kind of career you have can affect your life in many ways. For example, it can determine where you live, the friends you make, and the amount of money you earn. Your career can also affect how you feel about yourself and the way other people act toward you. By making wise decisions concerning your career, you can help yourself build the life you want.

Duane Brown, the contributor of this article, is Professor of Education at the University of North Carolina at Chapel Hill. He is the coauthor of the books Career Choice and Development *and* Career Counseling Techniques.

Important career decisions include choosing a career field and deciding how you want your career to develop. Other decisions involve selecting the educational and job opportunities that will advance your career. Knowing your abilities, interests, values, and goals gives you a foundation on which to base your career decisions. Also, a broad knowledge of the world of work can help you discover career possibilities that you did not know existed.

This article discusses careers based on work for pay. It provides information that can help you choose and plan a career. It also describes skills that can be useful in getting a job. In addition, the article discusses major career fields and many occupations within each field.

Choosing and planning a career

To make wise career decisions and plans, you need as much information as possible. The more you know about yourself and career opportunities, the better able you will be to choose a satisfying career.

Discovering the world of work. Most people begin to discover the world of work in early childhood. Even before children enter school, they become aware that people work in various occupations. Most children also start to form ideas about life and about themselves as individuals. A realistic view of themselves and the world of work can help children prepare to make successful career choices.

Adults can help children discover the world of work in many ways. For example, parents and teachers can encourage children to notice and talk about different jobs in the community. They might also read and discuss stories that deal with different kinds of workers.

Teachers can ask students to select an occupation and give a report on it. Students may watch workers perform their duties during field trips. Teachers may also invite workers into the classroom to discuss their jobs.

Learning about oneself. Students should begin to explore career fields when they are in middle or junior high school. High school students should become involved in activities that relate to their career interests.

At the high school level, students should think about their life and career goals. To do this, students should determine their (1) aptitudes, (2) interests, (3) personal characteristics, and (4) values. Most workers are happiest and most successful when their jobs match their strengths, personality, and beliefs.

Aptitudes are a person's natural talents. Aptitudes indicate how easily a person can acquire certain skills or be trained for a specific career. An aptitude is sometimes known as an *ability*. However, the term *ability* can also refer to a skill—such as reading or speaking a foreign language—that a person has learned.

One of the most important aptitudes is *scholastic aptitude*. People who have high scholastic aptitude tend to succeed more easily in school than those who do not. Scholastic aptitude plays a major role in determining a person's career choice.

Many special aptitudes besides scholastic aptitude are related to success in various jobs. For example, people with *numerical reasoning aptitude* can easily become skilled in using numbers to solve mathematical problems. *Spatial relations aptitude* can help you imagine objects in two and three dimensions. *Mechanical reasoning aptitude* can help you understand mechanical concepts that relate to repairing and assembling machines. Thinking and reasoning with words involves *verbal reasoning aptitude*. *Abstract reasoning aptitude* can help you reason with symbols other than words and numbers.

Before you make a career choice, you should determine if performing that job requires any special aptitudes. To succeed in engineering, for example, you should have aptitudes for verbal reasoning, numerical reasoning, and spatial relations.

Aptitude tests can predict your ability to learn certain skills. How well you do in recreational activities, such as playing computer games or building model cars, and in various school subjects may also indicate aptitude.

You should remember, however, two important factors about aptitudes. First, people may not realize they have certain aptitudes unless they get an opportunity to develop them. Second, if you have relatively low aptitude in a given area, you can still develop the skills and abilities needed to perform successfully in that area. For example, people with low mechanical aptitude can learn to skillfully perform mechanical tasks. However, they may have more difficulty in learning mechanical skills and concepts than they would if they had more aptitude.

Interests are likes or preferences. The subjects that you like in school and the leisure activities you prefer are indications of your interests. Many people have interests in artistic, mechanical, outdoor, or scientific activities. Other interests include collecting various objects, such as rocks or stamps, or reading books.

Many people base their career choices on their interests. For many workers, job performance and job satisfaction depend on how much their work relates to their interests. It is therefore helpful to identify your strongest interests before you select a career field. To find out what your interests are, examine the kinds of school subjects and activities you have enjoyed. Such activities might include clubs, hobbies, and sports. The activities you enjoy most may represent your strongest interests.

Personal characteristics can contribute to success in a career. They may even be essential elements of some careers. Many employers look for workers who are ambitious, reliable, and trustworthy. In addition, your personality can help you decide what kind of job you want. If you are independent, you might be happiest in a job where you work alone, not as a member of a team. These kinds of characteristics are difficult to measure. However, a serious look at your past behavior can help you find out your qualities.

Values are deeply held beliefs that influence the way people think, act, and feel. They reflect what people consider to be important and greatly affect the goals people set for themselves. Each person has many values, which vary in strength. For example, money is the strongest value for some people—that is, wealth is more important to them than anything else. As a result, they focus their thoughts, behavior, and emotions on the goal of earning a high income. Other values include devotion to religion and helping others. People should understand their values prior to making a career decision.

You can develop an understanding of your values by asking yourself what is most important to you and by examining your beliefs. For example, if it is important to you to spend time with your family, you should find a job that requires little travel or overtime work.

What to look for in career fields. For most workers, job satisfaction depends on how well the various characteristics of a job satisfy their interests and values. In exploring an occupation, you should therefore consider the following job characteristics.

The nature of the work. Some jobs chiefly involve working with things, and others mainly require dealing with people or information. Most jobs combine a variety of work activities. You should look for an occupation that involves activities you enjoy and can do well.

Working conditions mean the environment in which a particular job is performed. A work environment might be indoors or outdoors. Some jobs involve high levels of dust or noise, physical hazards, or mental stress. Other conditions to consider include the number of hours employees work each week and whether employees work alone or in groups.

Special abilities required. Some jobs call for more mechanical aptitude, artistic talent, or other abilities than most people possess. You should therefore be aware of any special requirements in the jobs you consider.

Physical demands. Some occupations make special physical demands on workers. For example, jobs that involve carrying or lifting objects require strength. Some occupations require workers to perform repetitive tasks. Other occupations might require workers who have keen vision or who can stand for long periods. When you consider a job, be sure that you can meet any physical demands the work might make on you.

Preparation needed. The amount of preparation required to enter an occupation varies from job to job. It can range from a few hours of training to more than 10 years of education beyond high school. In addition, workers in many occupations must continue their education to keep their jobs or to advance in them. Some occupations require several years of experience and preparation at lower-level jobs. You should thus consider how much time and money you might have to invest in the careers that interest you.

Chances for employment. Before you choose a career field, you should consider your chances for getting a job in that field. In businesses and industries with steady or decreasing employment, workers are hired only to replace employees who have left their jobs. In growing businesses and industries, however, additional workers are needed. The introduction of new products and advanced technologies affect employment opportunities. Government spending and economic conditions also alter job opportunities.

Probable earnings. In exploring an occupation, you will want to know how much money you can expect to earn. Government, professional, and trade publications supply information on probable earnings for various occupations. Pay scales vary with location and employers, however. Union agreements and the amount of experience and education required also affect salaries and wages. Many employers provide insurance coverage, paid vacations, and other such *fringe benefits,* which you should consider in addition to probable earnings.

Chances for advancement. In exploring various occupations, you should examine possible patterns of promotion, known as *career ladders* or *career paths.* In some occupations, workers are promoted to higher positions based on their ability and experience. However,

Average salaries for selected occupations

This graph shows the average annual salaries for a selection of occupations in the United States. Pay scales vary greatly, depending on location, employer, and other factors.

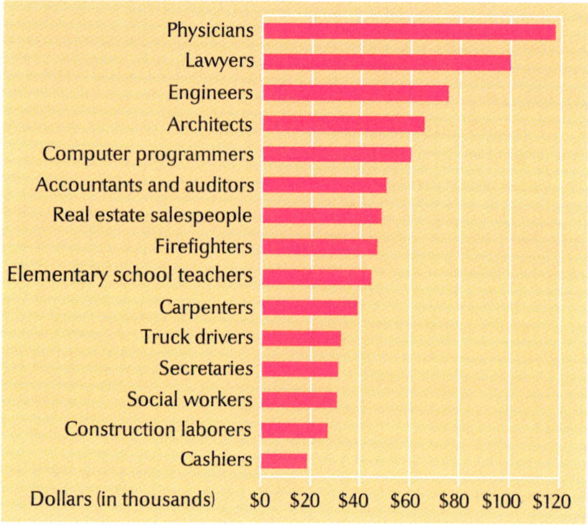

Figures are for 2003.
Source: *World Book* estimates based on data from the U.S. Bureau of Labor Statistics.

some employers hire people from outside the company to fill high-level openings. If employers consistently do this, workers can advance only by changing jobs. Some occupations allow only limited advancement. Workers in such fields must obtain additional education or training or change occupations if they wish to advance.

Social status is a person's position or rank in society. Many people believe that certain jobs have higher social status than others do. Some people who value status seek it through choosing highly regarded occupations. You must decide for yourself how important social status is in making your career choices.

Sources of information. A number of sources supply information that can help you explore career fields. Government agencies, industries, professional organizations, and many employers maintain Web sites and publish materials that describe various occupations.

Many schools offer career courses and clubs to help students learn about job opportunities. Teachers often supplement class discussions with interactive career guidance software available on personal computers.

Career information is also available from career and guidance counselors. These experts work in high schools, community agencies, employment offices, and college career development and placement centers. Counselors can help you identify your immediate and future career goals. They can also administer tests that identify the qualities you have to offer an employer. Counselors can then assist you in determining the right occupation for you. They can also advise you on how to prepare for and obtain a job in your chosen field.

You can learn about individual jobs by interviewing workers in those positions. In addition, you can gain firsthand information about an occupation through part-time jobs and volunteer work. For example, a person considering a career in medicine might volunteer at a hospital. *Job shadowing*—that is, observing a worker performing his or her job for a few hours or a day—can also give you firsthand career information.

Preparing for a career. Career preparation involves learning a variety of skills. Some skills, such as being able to accept supervision and knowing how to get along with others, are learned though everyday experiences in school and in the community. Others require specialized training.

High school courses and experiences are the most important preparations for some careers. In high school, students develop basic verbal and numerical skills, study habits, and other practical abilities. These skills provide the foundation for future learning.

Some people begin specialized career preparation in high school. Business and vocational courses prepare high school students to enter an occupation immediately after graduation. These courses teach skills used in such fields as business, construction, and manufacturing. Most high schools also offer college preparatory courses for students who plan to go to college. Many high schools offer *cooperative education programs* or *school-to-work programs* that help students prepare to enter the work force. Under these programs, students continue their classroom education while they experience the world of work through an internship, volunteer work, or a part-time job.

Certain occupations require only a high school education. But most jobs call for additional training. This section briefly describes the major kinds of career preparation programs.

On-the-job training means that a worker is taught job skills after being hired. In most cases, an experienced worker trains and supervises the beginner. The training may last a few hours or many months.

Apprenticeships are structured programs of training that combine classroom instruction and on-the-job training. They require two or more years of job experience and instruction. Every apprenticeship is based on a written agreement between the employer and the apprentice. Most apprenticeships train workers for skilled occupations in construction and production.

Vocational schools, also called *trade schools,* offer courses in restaurant cooking, automobile repair, and many other skills. Some trade schools specialize in training such workers as dental assistants, hairstylists, and travel agents. Courses range from several months to two years. Most vocational schools prepare students to meet any licensing requirements needed to enter a trade or profession. Many also award certificates to graduates.

Armed forces schools provide career education opportunities for people in military service. These opportunities range from on-the-job training and short courses to college and graduate school. In most cases, the training is designed for jobs in military career fields. However, many skills used in military occupations can be applied to civilian jobs.

Distance learning programs enable people to learn skills anywhere at anytime. Instructors may give lectures on television, or present lessons on the Internet, a global network of computers. Students can also listen to or watch lectures on audiotapes or videocassettes when it is convenient for them. They can also communicate with other students in forums on the Internet called *chat rooms.* Students receive assignments, course materials, study guides, and examinations through the mail, by e-mail (electronic mail), or by fax transmission. They return the completed work to the instructor for grading.

Technical institutes provide advanced, specialized training in such areas as electronics, engineering, computer science, and metalworking. Many graduates of these schools become *technicians*—that is, workers who assist engineers, scientists, and other highly trained specialists. Most technical institutes have two- or three-year programs, and many are associated with a hospital, university, or other institution.

Community colleges provide two years of college-level education. They prepare some students to transfer to a four-year college. They train other students for jobs as technicians and for such occupations as nursing, office management, and law enforcement.

Colleges and universities offer four-year programs that lead to a bachelor's degree. For the first two years, students study a variety of subjects. For the last two, most students take courses in their chosen career fields. College students learn skills for a range of professions, such as architecture, journalism, science, and teaching.

Professional and graduate schools. Such professions as dentistry, law, and medicine require education beyond college at a professional school. In addition, many students in business, education, science, and other fields attend graduate school for advanced study in their subject areas. Most professional and graduate schools are part of large universities.

Getting a job

The first step in advancing a career plan is writing a good *résumé* (pronounced *REHZ u MAY* or *REHZ uh may*), a document that describes your background and qualifications. You must also find job openings, apply for them, and convince employers that you are the best applicant. An employer can tell a lot about potential employees by the way they present their qualifications and apply for a job. Therefore, you should know how to contact employers, how to complete job applications, and how to make a good impression in interviews. All these skills can improve your chances for employment. However, do not be discouraged if you are not offered the first job you apply for. Most employers consider several applicants for each opening, and many people apply for numerous jobs before they are hired.

Writing a résumé. A résumé can be a paper or an electronic document. A good résumé is neat, well organized, and easy to read.

All résumés should include the same basic information. Begin your résumé with your name, address, and telephone number. You could also include your e-mail address if you have one. Most jobseekers include an objective, or career goal, on their résumé. Next list your employment history, starting with the most recent job. Give the names and locations of past employers, dates of employment, job titles, and a description of your duties. You can also include any related volunteer work if you are a recent graduate or have not held many jobs.

Next, list the names and locations of all schools and training programs you have attended since high school. Include your attendance dates and major subjects plus any degrees, diplomas, certificates, and honors you received. You can also list any special skills, such as languages you speak or computer programs you can use, that would relate to the job you are seeking. Some jobseekers list their education and skills before their employment history. Some jobhunters also list their hobbies, travel experience, or awards on their résumé.

Finally, many employers ask for the names and addresses of *personal references*—that is, people the employer may contact to learn more about you.

Finding job opportunities. One of the most common ways to learn about job opportunities is by word-of-mouth. Many jobs are filled by people who have heard of the job opening from professional associates, friends, relatives, teachers, and acquaintances. You should tell the people you know and meet that you are looking for certain kinds of job opportunities. This process is known as *networking.*

Another common way to locate job opportunities is through the help-wanted section of newspapers. Many professional and union newsletters, journals, and other trade publications also carry advertisements for job openings. Most help-wanted ads briefly describe the job responsibilities and provide other information that can help you decide to apply for the position.

Increasingly, people find job opportunities on the Internet. Jobseekers may search the databases of career-related Web sites for job openings and apply for the positions online. They may also *post* (enter) résumés at

Jerry Williams

123 Oak Street
Chicago, Illinois 60123
312/123-4567
jwilliams@mymailbox.com

OBJECTIVE:	To obtain an editorial position where I can apply my talents and experience in a challenging and progressive environment.
EDUCATION:	**Northern Illinois University**, De Kalb, Illinois Bachelor of Arts in Communication, May 1998 Major GPA: 3.8/4.0
SKILLS:	Adobe PageMaker, Adobe Photoshop, Microsoft Word, Netscape Communicator, QuarkXPress
EMPLOYMENT: 1999 to present	**Acme Publishing Company**, Chicago, Illinois *Assistant Editor* Responsibilities include copy editing manuscripts for company s line of children s books. Coordinate work for in-house and free-lance typesetters and free-lance proofreaders. Proofreading as required.
1998 to 1999	**Jacobs Company,** Chicago, Illinois *Corporate Communications Intern* Wrote, designed, and produced Jacobs Company s monthly employee newsletter.
ACTIVITIES AND AWARDS:	Golden Key National Honor Society Member of Society for Professional Journalists Member of Illinois Newspaper Association Northern Illinois Newspaper Association Scholarship Recipient Volunteer for United Way/Crusade of Mercy, Inc.
REFERENCES:	Available upon request.

WORLD BOOK illustration

A traditional résumé describes a jobseeker's work experience and education. It can be mailed or faxed to potential employers.

```
Jerry Williams
123 Oak Street
Chicago, Illinois 60123
312/123-4567
jwilliams@mymailbox.com

OBJECTIVE:
To obtain an editorial position where I can apply my tal-
ents and experience in a challenging and progressive
environment.

EDUCATION:
Northern Illinois University, De Kalb, Illinois
Bachelor of Arts in Communication, May 1998
Major GPA: 3.8/4.0

SKILLS:
Adobe PageMaker, Adobe Photoshop, Microsoft Word, Netscape
Communicator, QuarkXPress

EMPLOYMENT:
Acme Publishing Company, Chicago, Illinois
1999 to present, Assistant Editor
Responsibilities include copy editing manuscripts for comp-
any's line of children's books. Coordinate work for in-
house and free-lance typesetters and free-lance proofreaders.
Proofreading as required.

Jacobs Company, Chicago, Illinois
1998 to 1999, Corporate Communications Intern
Wrote, designed, and produced Jacobs Company's monthly
employee newsletter.

ACTIVITIES AND AWARDS:
Golden Key National Honor Society
Member of Society for Professional Journalists
Member of Illinois Newspaper Association
Northern Illinois Newspaper Association Scholarship
Recipient
Volunteer for United Way/Crusade of Mercy, Inc.

REFERENCES:
Available upon request.
```

WORLD BOOK illustration

An electronic résumé can be sent to employers by e-mail. It provides the same type of information as a traditional résumé.

many of these sites for potential employers to review. In addition, companies and organizations often announce job opportunities on their Web sites.

Information about job openings is also available from employment agencies. Public employment agencies are run by the government and their services are free. Private agencies charge jobseekers or employers a fee if a person is hired as a result of their efforts. Many high schools, colleges, and other schools have *placement offices,* which help students and graduates find jobs.

Jobseekers may also contact employers to learn about openings. Telephone directories and other publications list the names, addresses, and phone numbers of employers in various fields.

Contacting employers. Your first contact with an employer will be either to apply for a known job opening or to find out if any jobs are available. The most common ways of contacting employers are by mail or fax transmission, by e-mail, by telephone, and by personal visit to an employer's office.

If jobseekers contact employers by mail or fax, they should write a letter to an employer, called a *cover letter.* This type of letter introduces the applicant to the employer. If you are responding to a known opening, indicate the position you are applying for and how you became aware of the opening. Briefly indicate your qualifications and accomplishments that would benefit the employer. Finally, state when you would be available for an interview or when you will call the employer to discuss your qualifications. Be sure to include your mailing address, e-mail address, and telephone number so that the employer can reach you. A résumé should be faxed or mailed with the cover letter.

If you contact an employer by e-mail, provide the same information that you would include in a cover letter. If possible, include an ASCII (American Standard Code for Information Interchange) or text-only version of your résumé in the body of the e-mail, or as a separate text file. These formats ensure that employers will be able to read your résumé.

Some jobseekers contact employers by telephone. These applicants may be responding to help-wanted ads. Others call employers to find out if there are any jobs available. In any situation, you should briefly state your qualifications and try to arrange an interview.

Completing job applications. Most employers ask applicants to fill out an application. Applications help employers find out about your qualifications. Most applications request the same kinds of information. Much of the information will already appear on your résumé.

Many companies ask applicants to complete paper application forms. Other employers prefer applicants to complete electronic applications. Applicants may enter their information using computer terminals in a company's office or online at a company's Web site. Some businesses use automated telephone systems that enable applicants to apply for jobs over the phone.

All types of applications ask for your address, telephone number, and the title of the job for which you are applying. In many countries, applications request an identification number, such as a social security or other national insurance number, or a national identification number. Most applications also ask about your previous employment, including employers' and supervisors' names, the dates of your employment, your duties, and your wages. Applications also request that you list the schools you attended, the dates you attended them, and any degrees, diplomas, and certificates you received. Many applications request additional information, such as your military experience or hobbies. They may also ask for personal references. Many companies check the accuracy of information included on job applications.

Being interviewed. If your résumé or application indicates you are qualified, the employer may request an interview. The interview enables you to learn more about the job opening. It also helps the employer find out if you are the best person to hire for the job.

Many people prepare for an interview by learning about the employer's business. They find out about the kinds of products the company manufactures or the services it provides. You can find such information in an organization's annual report or on its Web site. This kind of knowledge can help you ask intelligent questions during your interview. It also shows the interviewer that you are interested in the employer's business.

Most interviewers pay close attention to the way an applicant acts, dresses, and answers questions. You can make a good impression by arriving on time and by being confident, prepared, and well organized. Your clothing should be clean, comfortable, and professional. Wear the kinds of clothes appropriate to the company, unless the workers wear uniforms.

The interviewer will probably ask about your interests, your work experience, and your goals. Common questions also include your reasons for applying for the job and what you believe you can contribute to the success of the employer's business. Answer all questions briefly. You might find it helpful to think out your answers to such questions before an interview. You should also prepare questions to ask the interviewer about the company and the position you are seeking.

Send a follow-up letter to everyone who interviewed you no later than two days after the interview. In the letter, thank the interviewer for the time spent discussing the position with you. Let the interviewer know if you are still interested in the job.

The world of work

The world of work is vast and constantly changing. Scientific advances and other developments constantly eliminate some jobs and create new ones. Anyone selecting a career should explore all the possibilities. People who research a variety of jobs may find that they are interested in a career they may not have considered.

Teachers and career counselors use a variety of sources to help jobseekers learn about occupations. Many of these sources use different classification systems to arrange career information. However, each system groups career fields that are similar in some way. This article divides many of the most common occupations into 17 career groups. These groups are (1) administrative support; (2) art, design, and communications; (3) community and social services; (4) construction, maintenance, and repair; (5) farming, fishing, and forestry; (6) health care; (7) law; (8) life, physical, and social sciences; (9) management; (10) personal services; (11) production; (12) sales; (13) sports and entertainment; (14) teaching; (15) technical and mathematical occupations; (16) tourism and hospitality; and (17) transportation. Occupations within each group have similar interests and job duties.

The following sections contain the characteristics of the occupations of each group. They describe what the workers do, the working conditions, and the training required to perform the occupations. However, these examples provide only a general guide. Responsibilities, working conditions, and preparation requirements vary.

Administrative support. Businesses, governments, industries, and other organizations need workers to help them run smoothly and efficiently. Almost every organization employs workers to perform such tasks as filing, answering telephones, operating office machines, receiving payments, and distributing mail. They also need employees to produce, organize, and analyze documents, letters, reports, and other records.

Secretaries and administrative assistants provide support for managers or executives. They may keep records; compose and edit documents, letters, and reports; schedule meetings; and supervise other office-support workers. Data entry operators process information. They may use computers or scanners to record data, such as information about a customer.

Specialists in the area of records systems gather and analyze information. Bookkeeping clerks record the financial transactions of a business or organization. Accounting clerks assist accountants by performing calculations and preparing other information needed for financial reports. Auditing clerks verify an organization's financial records. Billing clerks prepare customers' bills for various goods or services. Timekeeping clerks review employee timecards and calculate how many hours each employee has worked. Payroll clerks calculate employees' pay and prepare paychecks.

Many administrative and office support workers work directly with customers. Telephone operators assist callers with telephone calls. They may search for phone numbers, handle emergency calls, and transfer calls. Customer service representatives answer customers' questions, help them solve problems, and resolve com-

WORLD BOOK photo by Steven Spicer

Customer service representatives spend most of their workday on the telephone. They help answer customers' questions, solve problems, take customers' orders, and resolve complaints.

plaints. Receptionists greet an organization's visitors. They may also answer telephones and provide information about the organization. Bank tellers assist customers with their banking transactions. They may cash customers' checks or take their deposits or payments.

Other workers are concerned with the delivery of letters, packages, and other items. Shipping clerks keep records of all shipments that leave an organization. They may prepare items for shipment by calculating the shipping costs and making mailing labels. Receiving clerks keep records of all shipments that an organization receives. They verify the contents of each shipment and make sure the items were not damaged during delivery. Postal service clerks perform many duties, such as selling stamps, sorting mail, and checking items for correct postage. Mail carriers deliver mail on assigned routes.

Working conditions. Many workers in this group work in an office. They may sit for long periods at a desk, often repeating the same kinds of tasks. Mail carriers often work outdoors in all kinds of weather. Shipping and receiving clerks may work in warehouses or stockrooms and often lift or carry heavy packages.

Training and education. Most administrative support workers have a high school education, but many employers prefer to hire candidates with some college experience. Many business and vocational schools and community colleges offer training classes.

Art, design, and communications occupations deal with the expression of ideas, feelings, and thoughts. Some workers in this group express themselves while adding beauty to people's lives. Others express thoughts and ideas by processing and delivering information.

Artists express themselves through various creative activities. Such artists as painters, photographers, and sculptors create original pieces of work. They may sell their artwork to clients or display it in galleries or museums. Illustrators produce pictures for books, posters, and other products. Multimedia artists use computers to create animation, special effects, and other images for advertisements, movies, and video games.

Designers help clients express their own ideas and style. Fashion designers study colors, fabrics, and trends before they develop a collection of clothing and accessories. Interior designers plan and furnish indoor areas of homes, hotels, offices, and other buildings. Graphic designers use color, image, and text elements to create art that communicates a message. They may design a company's logo, a layout for a magazine, or a store display for a new product. Industrial designers use product research and their artistic ability to develop or redesign products, such as automobiles, furniture, and toys.

Communications workers deliver ideas to the public. Authors write such materials as articles and novels. Reporters use interviews, investigative techniques, and research to gather information for their stories. Editors review and revise material and prepare it for publication or broadcast. Radio announcers select and introduce music, read the news and weather, and interview guests. Television anchors present news stories and introduce live or taped reports from reporters. Public relations specialists provide information to the public about their clients. Translators and interpreters convert speech and written text from one language to another.

Working conditions differ for various occupations in the art, design, and communications group. Many workers perform their duties in offices or studios. Most journalists work long hours to meet their deadlines. Artists may work at their own pace.

Education and training. Most artists and designers have natural artistic abilities. Some artists have not had

WORLD BOOK photo by Steven Spicer

Workers in the art, design, and communications field often work with one another. The graphic designer shown here is discussing her proposed layout of a children's book with the editor who wrote the text.

any formal training, but others have a degree in fine arts from a college, university, or school of art. Most designers have a college degree. Most employers in the communications field require employees to have a bachelor's or master's degree.

Community and social services workers provide assistance to society. People depend on these workers to help meet their needs and improve the quality of life in their community.

Some workers in this group help individuals, groups, and families solve problems. Counselors help people identify their problems and find solutions. They may help people discover their career interests, work out problems in their marriage, or recover from mental illnesses. Social workers provide counseling, support, guidance, and other services to people in need. For example, they may help people with disabilities, the homeless, or the unemployed.

Members of the clergy, such as ministers, priests, rabbis, and imams, lead religious services and perform rituals. These people also provide counseling to their congregation and participate in community activities.

Other workers in the community and social services group are concerned with the organization and preservation of ideas. Librarians provide information. They may select the materials, such as books and magazines, found in libraries; organize and maintain the materials; and help people with research or questions. Curators oversee museum collections. They plan collections, acquire the items, and prepare them for display.

Some workers in this group safeguard citizens and their possessions. Police officers enforce the law, maintain order, and protect life and property. Police detectives work to solve or prevent crimes. Firefighters put out fires and help people in other emergency situations. They also teach fire prevention.

Military personnel also protect citizens. They stand ready to defend their country. Armored vehicle crew members drive tanks and other armored vehicles. Infantry soldiers fight enemy forces on land. They may use such handheld weapons as grenades, rifles, and machine guns to seize, occupy, and defend land areas. Artillery personnel support the infantry. They aim and fire such heavy weapons as cannons and missiles.

Some employees in the community and social services group work with people who break the law. Parole officers supervise people who have received an early release from prison. Correctional officers guard people who are waiting for a trial or prisoners in jail.

Working conditions. Counselors and social workers may be called at any time to handle emergencies. Members of the clergy work long hours, often on weekends and on holidays. Librarians and curators usually work in quiet settings. Firefighters, police and corrections officers, and military personnel often work in dangerous situations.

Education and training. All branches of the armed forces and most police departments, fire stations, and correctional institutions require applicants to have at least a high school education. Most social workers and parole officers have at least a bachelor's degree. Members of the clergy generally study at a seminary after going to college. Most counselors, librarians, and curators have a master's degree.

WORLD BOOK photo by Mark Downey

A Roman Catholic priest gives Holy Communion, a sacred ceremony, to a boy in the Philippines. Members of the clergy also lead religious services and counsel their congregations.

Construction, maintenance, and repair. Workers in construction build, modernize, and repair bridges, factories, highways, houses, and other buildings and structures. Maintenance workers help keep buildings and homes in good condition. Mechanics and technicians maintain automobiles, computers, and other machinery and fix them when they do not work properly.

Most construction workers specialize in certain building materials. For example, carpenters use wood to construct the framework of buildings and such features as hardwood floors, cabinets, and stairways. Bricklayers use bricks and other similar materials to build arches,

AP/Wide World

Construction workers build, modernize, and repair buildings and other structures. They often work outdoors in dangerous situations, such as these workers installing the roof of a building.

walls, fireplaces, and other structures. Concrete masons build sidewalks, roads, and other structures made of concrete. Electricians install wiring and electrical fixtures that supply light, heat, air conditioning, refrigeration, and communications systems. Plumbers install water, gas, and sewer systems. They can also install such fixtures as bathtubs and sinks, and unclog drains. Roofers cover the roofs of buildings with such materials as shingles, tar, rubber, or metal.

Some construction workers do the finishing work on a building. Carpet installers lay down padding and carpet on floors. Tile and marble setters apply decorative tile or marble to walls, floors, and other surfaces. Painters prepare surfaces, such as walls and ceilings, to be painted and then apply paint to the surfaces.

Maintenance workers care for apartment and office buildings, houses, and other types of buildings and properties. Janitors make sure that buildings are clean and in working order. They may wash floors, empty the garbage, or perform minor repairs. Maids and housekeepers clean such places as houses, hotels, and hospitals. They may dust, vacuum, or make beds. Exterminators make sure that houses and buildings are free from insects or other pests. They set traps or spray chemicals to kill the pests. Landscape workers and groundskeepers care for the lawns of houses, grounds of offices and parks, and other outdoor areas. They may mow grass, trim bushes and shrubs, and plant flowers.

Repair workers, such as mechanics and technicians, make sure that machines and other items work as they should. If equipment is not operating properly, these workers will fix it. Most repairers specialize in one area. Computer and office machine technicians install, repair, and maintain computers and electronic office machines, such as fax and photocopying machines. Aircraft mechanics work on all types of aircraft. Some aircraft mechanics perform regular maintenance after a plane has flown a certain distance. Others may inspect aircraft before a flight. Automobile mechanics maintain and repair automobiles. They may perform routine maintenance or diagnose and fix a problem. Locksmiths install, repair, and open locks. They may also make keys and change locks. Other repair workers include those that fix electronic equipment; heating, air conditioning, and refrigeration systems; household appliances; and telephones.

Working conditions. Many construction workers perform their jobs outdoors or in partly completed buildings. Construction workers are more likely to be injured on the job than are most other kinds of workers. Janitors, housekeepers, and exterminators usually work indoors. Mechanics and technicians may need to lift heavy parts and work in awkward positions to make repairs.

Education and training. Most workers in this group have a high school education. Many construction workers learn their trade through apprenticeship programs. Many repair workers complete training programs offered by their employers or at vocational or technical schools or community colleges. Most maintenance workers learn their skills through on-the-job training.

Farming, fishing, and forestry. Workers in this group help to produce our basic needs. They raise much of the food we eat and many of the materials used to make our clothes and build our homes.

Farmers oversee the entire operation of a farm. They may decide which crops to plant; raise and market livestock; hire, train, and supervise farmworkers; and keep track of the farm's finances.

Farmworkers help farmers. Farmworkers may plant, care for, and harvest crops. They may plow and fertilize the soil, spray the crops with *pesticides* (chemicals that kill insects and other pests), and pack the harvested crops for shipment to markets. Other workers may feed farm animals, clean their living areas, and give medications. Agricultural equipment operators run a variety of farm equipment. They may drive tractors to plant, fertilize, and cultivate crops. Some operate balers to gather and tie hay.

Animal breeders work to improve the quality of livestock by selecting superior animals for reproduction. For example, they may choose to breed animals that produce large quantities of eggs, meat, or milk. Animal breeders also keep records of such information as an animal's *pedigree* (list of ancestors) and *heat cycles* (times when a female animal is sexually receptive).

Agricultural inspectors make sure farm products meet certain standards. They give products a grade after

© Jim Foster, The Stock Market

Farmers produce much of the food we eat. Members of a family, such as the father and son harvesting corn in this photo, often own and operate their own farms.

AP/Wide World

Foresters manage and protect forests, woodlands, and parks. This forester is talking to visitors in a recreational area of a national park.

they check certain characteristics, such as color, condition, and size. Some inspectors also ensure that agricultural workers are following health and safety regulations.

Fishing crews use a variety of equipment, such as nets, hooks, and harpoons, to catch fish. Fish farmers raise fish in ponds, lakes, or artificial enclosures.

Forestry workers include foresters, forest technicians, fallers, and log graders. Foresters manage and protect forests and woodlands. They may decide which trees should be cut for timber, direct the planting of new trees, and protect forests from diseases and pests. Forest technicians work under the direction of foresters. They may gather data on such characteristics as the size and condition of various forest resources, maintain campsites and recreation areas within a forest, and train and supervise other forest workers. Fallers cut down trees with axes or chainsaws. Log graders evaluate logs cut from trees. They give each log a grade after they have calculated its size and looked for defects.

Working conditions. Most workers in this group work outdoors. Many of the jobs are physically demanding. Some of the work is dangerous. Some fishing crews are away from home for weeks or months.

Education and training. There are no formal educational requirements for many occupations in this group. Many of these workers learn their skills on the job. Animal breeders, log graders, and farmers need at least a high school education. Most foresters and agricultural inspectors have a bachelor's degree.

Health care. Workers in this group help people live healthier and happier lives. The services they provide range from teaching children how to brush their teeth to performing a kidney transplant.

Physicians diagnose, treat, and prevent diseases and conditions. Primary care physicians treat general medical problems, but many physicians specialize in one area of medicine. For example, dermatologists diagnose and treat diseases and disorders of the skin, hair, and nails; and surgeons perform operations.

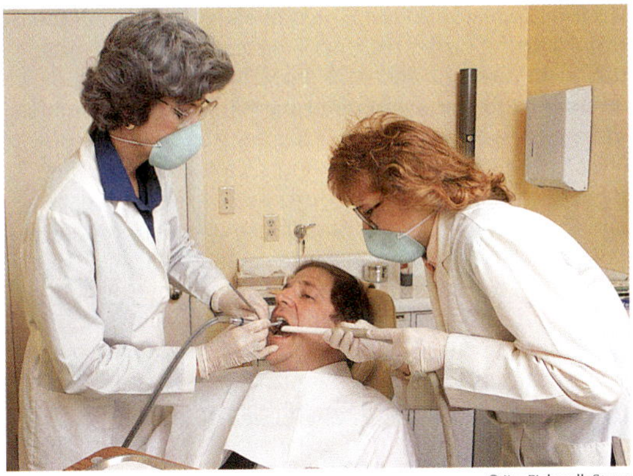

© Jim Pickerell, Stone

A dentist, *left,* uses a drill to remove decay from her patient's tooth before filling a cavity. A trained dental assistant, *right,* helps the dentist during the procedure.

WORLD BOOK photo

A veterinarian cares for family pets, livestock, and other animals. These doctors prevent, diagnose, and treat illnesses in animals. This veterinarian is examining the eyes of a dog.

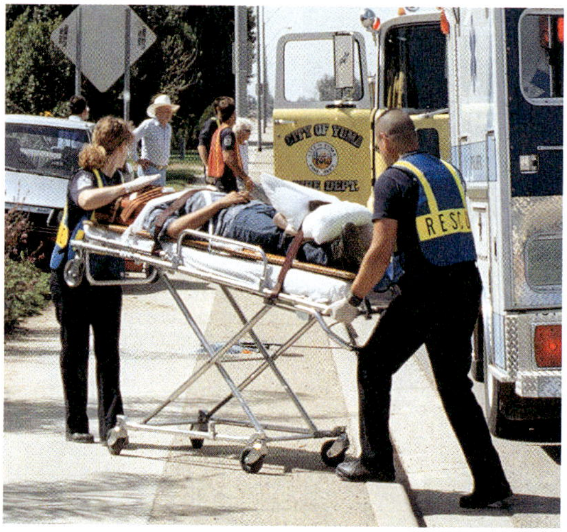

© Tony Freeman, PhotoEdit

Emergency medical technicians provide emergency care to critically ill or injured people. These technicians are preparing to transport a patient to a medical facility for further treatment.

Other types of doctors include chiropractors, dentists, optometrists, podiatrists, and veterinarians. Chiropractors treat diseases and conditions by manipulating or adjusting the spine and other parts of the body. Dentists diagnose, treat, and prevent diseases and other problems of the teeth, jaws, and gums. Optometrists diagnose vision problems and diseases. They may prescribe and fit eyeglasses and contact lenses. Podiatrists diagnose, treat, and prevent diseases and conditions of the foot and lower leg. Veterinarians treat animals.

Other health care professionals also provide medical care. Physician assistants provide basic medical care under the supervision of a physician. They may examine patients or order tests. Some physician assistants prescribe medication. Nurses take care of sick and injured people and people with disabilities. They also help healthy people stay well. Registered nurses may assist physicians during treatments and examinations, monitor patients' conditions, give medications and vaccinations, and keep patients' medical records up to date. Advanced practice nurses, such as nurse practitioners and certified nurse midwives, are registered nurses who have completed specialized training. Licensed practical nurses, also called licensed vocational nurses, assist registered nurses by providing routine patient care.

Some health care professionals provide treatments recommended by physicians. Dietitians, also called nutritionists, plan balanced diets for individuals or groups. Pharmacists fill prescriptions written by physicians and other health practitioners. They also provide patients with instructions on how to take the medication and inform them of possible side effects. Speech-language pathologists work with people with speech and language problems, such as stuttering. They identify a patient's problem and organize a treatment plan. Audiologists detect and diagnose hearing problems. They may also fit patients for hearing aids. Occupational therapists work with people with disabilities or illnesses. They plan a program of activities that help their patients recover, develop, or maintain practical skills. Physical therapists use such rehabilitation treatments as heat, cold, and exercise to relieve pain or correct injuries or diseases.

Many health care workers perform tests and procedures that help doctors diagnose and treat diseases and conditions. Cardiovascular technologists conduct or assist in tests and procedures to diagnose disorders of the heart and blood vessels. Medical laboratory technicians perform tests on patients' blood and other body fluids or tissues. Radiologic technologists prepare patients for imaging procedures, such as X rays. They also operate the equipment used during the procedures. Dental hygienists help patients maintain good oral health. They clean and polish teeth, examine the mouth for signs of disease, and take X rays of the teeth and jaws. They may also teach their patients how to properly brush and floss their teeth.

© Hank Morgan/Science Source from Photo Researchers

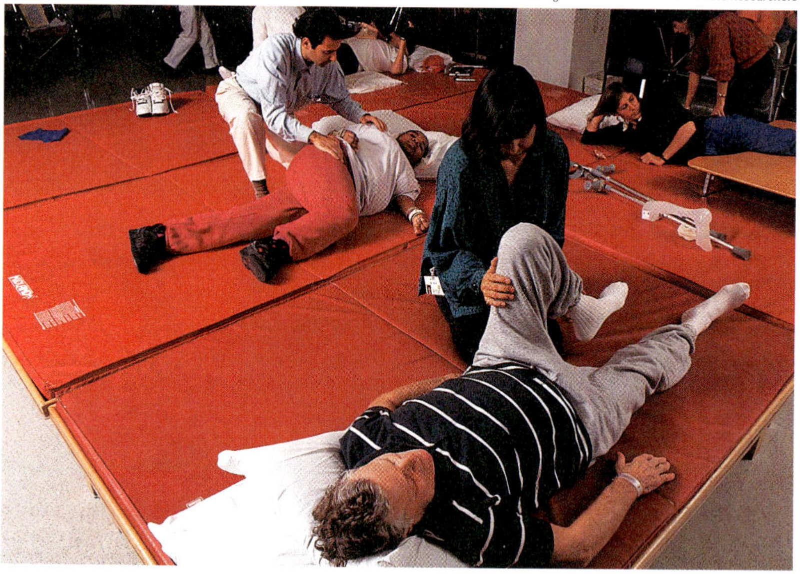

Physical therapists and patients work together to improve the patients' health. Physical therapists use rehabilitation treatments, such as exercise, to help patients relieve pain or correct injuries or disease.

© Robert E. Daemmrich, Stone

A lawyer protects and preserves the rights and freedoms of clients. A lawyer also offers advice on legal matters and represents clients in courts of law.

Other workers play an important role in patient care. Emergency medical technicians drive ambulances or fly specially equipped helicopters to the scenes of accidents or other emergencies. They provide urgent medical care to critically ill or injured people and transport them to medical facilities. Medical records technicians organize, file, and track patients' health information.

Working conditions. Many health care professionals work weekend, evening, or late-night shifts. Some deal with seriously ill or injured patients and may be exposed to various diseases. Many of these workers may be called in to work at any time to handle emergencies. However, taking care of sick people can be rewarding.

Education and training. Preparing for a health care career can take many years of study. Most chiropractors, dentists, optometrists, physicians, podiatrists, and veterinarians earn a bachelor's degree before they begin their medical training. Audiologists, physical therapists, and speech-language pathologists must have at least a master's degree. Dietitians, medical technicians and technologists, occupational therapists, pharmacists, and most physician assistants have a bachelor's degree. Other health care workers usually need an associate's degree.

Law. Legal occupations are important in every society. Workers in this field help people protect and preserve their rights and freedoms.

Lawyers, also called attorneys, represent clients in a court of law. They also advise their clients on legal matters and draw up legal documents, such as wills or divorce agreements. Judges are public officials that preside over law courts. They may advise lawyers, give instructions to a jury, or determine the punishment for people found guilty of a crime.

Paralegals, also called legal assistants, perform routine legal tasks under a lawyer's supervision. Paralegals may do preparatory work for lawyers, conduct legal research, and assist lawyers during trials. Court reporters document all words spoken during trials, hearings, and other official proceedings.

Working conditions. Most workers in legal occupations work in courtrooms, offices, and law libraries. Many lawyers and paralegals work long hours while they prepare for a case.

Education and training. Most lawyers have a college education and a degree from a law school. Most judges have been lawyers. Paralegals usually have an associate's or a bachelor's degree and have completed a paralegal training program. Employers often require court reporters to complete a training program offered by many technical and vocational schools.

Life, physical, and social sciences. Workers in this group, called scientists, explore the workings of the world. Their discoveries can range from developing new drugs to finding better ways to prevent pollution.

Life scientists study living matter. Specialists in the life sciences include agricultural scientists, biochemists, microbiologists, zoologists, and epidemiologists.

Agricultural scientists study the relationship of animals and crops to their environment. They develop ways to improve the quality and quantity of crops and the breeding and raising of livestock. Some agricultural scientists specialize in farm animals. They may research animal nutrition and how it affects the quality of meat and other animal products. Other scientists may specialize in soil and plants. They may study how to make crops resistant to pests or how to improve soil conditions.

Biochemists study the chemical processes of living things. They examine the composition and function of molecules in cells and tissues. Biochemists may use this information to solve biological problems, such as determining the effectiveness of new medications.

Microbiologists study microscopic organisms, often called microbes. Many microbiologists investigate the relationships between microbes and human beings, animals, and plants. Medical microbiologists analyze the relationship between microbes and disease and search for cures. Others may specialize in agricultural, environmental, food, and industrial microbiology.

Zoologists study animals. They may investigate how animals *evolved* (changed over long periods), how they interact with human beings and other animals, and the characteristics that many animals have in common. Most

A cultural anthropologist might travel the world to study the origin and development of human cultures. This cultural anthropologist is learning about a community in Indonesia by living with the people and participating in their daily lives.

© Arne Hodalic, Saola from Liaison Agency

zoologists specialize in a certain type of animal. For example, entomologists study insects.

Epidemiologists study outbreaks of diseases. They first try to figure out what caused the outbreak. They then try to control the disease and prevent its spread.

Physical scientists study nonliving matter. Specialists in the physical sciences include astronomers, physicists, chemists, geoscientists, meteorologists, and environmental scientists.

Astronomers study the universe and comets, planets, stars, and other celestial bodies. They investigate the size, composition, shape, position, and movement of objects in the universe. Their findings help us to understand the origins of the universe and predict future events. They also help plan space missions. Astronauts may conduct experiments and do research in space. Their work may focus on a particular area of science, such as astronomy or biology.

Physicists study the properties and behavior of matter and energy. Some physicists perform experiments. Based on what they observe, these physicists develop laws and theories. Other physicists use this knowledge to solve problems in other fields.

Chemists investigate the characteristics of substances. They study how substances behave under different conditions. Many chemists work to improve and create new products, such as medications and artificial fibers.

Geoscientists, also called geologists and geophysicists, study the composition, structure, and history of the earth. Geologists research how the earth was formed and how it changes. They may study fossils, rocks, and soils or explore the earth for oil, gas, coal, ground water, and other natural resources. Geophysicists use physics to research the earth's physical properties and processes. They may study earthquakes and tremors, glaciers, volcanoes, oceans, and mountains.

Meteorologists study the earth's atmosphere and the conditions that produce weather. Weather satellites and balloons, radar, and computers measure the wind, temperature, air pressure, and other conditions. Meteorologists use this information to predict the weather.

Environmental scientists work to protect the environment. They perform research to determine the causes of air, water, soil, and noise pollution. They investigate possible ways to prevent and control these problems.

Social scientists study human society. Specialists in the social sciences include anthropologists, economists, psychologists, sociologists, and political scientists.

Anthropologists active in *cultural anthropology* study the origin and development of human cultures. They compare the arts, beliefs, customs, daily life, inventions, languages, social relationships, and values of cultures throughout the world. Another type of anthropology, *physical anthropology,* studies changes and variations in the human body.

Economists study how people produce, distribute, and use goods and services. They conduct research and analyze data on economic trends and issues. Economists can then determine how various economic systems work and predict how changes will affect the systems.

Psychologists study mental processes and behavior. They observe people and groups, perform experiments, conduct interviews, and administer tests. The information they obtain helps psychologists understand why people act, think, and feel as they do. Many psychologists provide counseling to individuals, couples, and groups.

Sociologists study behavior in groups. They observe groups and other social institutions. They study how groups are formed, how people interact in groups, and how groups influence the behavior of their members.

Political scientists study political systems. They research the origin and operation of various forms of government. Political scientists study political parties, elections, public policies, and other political activities. They also measure peoples' opinions about political topics.

Working conditions. Some life, physical, and social scientists work long hours. Many scientists work in an office or in a laboratory. Some scientists, however, such as soil and plant scientists and anthropologists, may do

NASA

An astronaut works in Spacelab, a laboratory carried by a space shuttle. Astronauts often conduct scientific experiments in space. Many astronauts have degrees in biological or physical sciences.

much of their work outdoors. Some workers, including chemists, must take safety precautions while they work.

Education and training. Life, physical, and social scientists who plan to do research or teach at a four-year college or university must have a doctor's degree. Graduates with a bachelor's degree can teach at elementary, middle, and high schools. Employers may hire applicants with a bachelor's degree for some entry-level positions. Workers with a master's degree may teach at community or junior colleges or assist with research.

Management workers, called managers, are the leaders of organizations and businesses. All businesses and organizations need managers to plan and administer activities and policies and to train and supervise other employees. Mayors of cities, governors, state representatives, presidents of countries, and other elected officials are also managers. They develop laws and direct government activities.

A business or organization usually has three levels of managers. Each level has a different amount of authority or responsibility. Upper managers, such as chief executive officers and presidents or vice presidents of a company, have the most authority. They usually determine company policies and the long-term strategies for an organization. Middle managers may be in charge of a specific department in an organization, such as accounting. They report to upper managers and are responsible for making decisions about how the company should operate over the short term. Supervisory managers, such as foremen and forewomen in a factory, have the least authority. They may make decisions that relate to the daily operation of an organization.

Managers work in all fields. They may have worked in a certain field for a time before they were promoted to a managerial position. For example, a publisher of an encyclopedia may have begun his or her career as an editor or a writer. A principal probably started as a teacher.

© David R. Frazier

A plant foreman, *center,* discusses a project with workers in a factory. Foremen and forewomen supervise groups of workers. They may monitor rates of production and train new employees.

Managers may perform different duties that are specific to their industry. Managers have many responsibilities in common, however. Managers make plans, such as setting long- and short-term goals for their business or organization. They make sure that employees use their skills effectively. Managers also make sure that the organization's goals are being met. They let their employees know how well they are doing their job. They should also make their employees' jobs rewarding.

Human resources, also called personnel management, is a special field of management. Managers in this field may interview and recommend applicants to fill job openings. They may also coordinate employee benefits, such as health insurance and retirement savings programs, evaluate compensation programs, direct training programs, and help solve work-related problems.

Businesses and organizations hire management analysts and consultants when they have a problem. For example, a company may want to cut costs. Analysts and consultants evaluate the problem and suggest solutions.

Working conditions. Many managers work long hours in an office setting. Some managers may feel stress if they are asked to meet specific goals within a short time. Management analysts and consultants frequently travel to their clients' offices.

Education and training. Most managers, elected officials, and management analysts and consultants are college graduates, and many have advanced degrees. Courses in business administration are helpful. Many elected officials have been lawyers. Some organizations offer formal training programs for their managers.

Personal services. Workers in this category perform personal tasks for people. Many personal services include tasks that most people could do themselves. But some people have workers do these tasks because the jobs may be difficult or time consuming. Some personal services require special skills that many people lack.

Some workers in this field help people to look and feel their best. Cosmetologists take care of the hair and skin. Some, known as hairdressers, shampoo, cut, style, and apply color to women's hair. Some give facials and head and neck massages and remove unwanted hair from a client's face or body. Others, called manicurists and pedicurists, clip, shape, and polish their client's nails. Barbers usually work on men's hair and may also shave or trim beards and mustaches. Fitness trainers teach people how to exercise. They may design individual workout programs and show their clients how to use proper techniques while they exercise.

Other personal services workers provide care for family members. Child-care workers and nannies take care of children while their parents are at work or away from home. They feed and dress the children and organize play activities. Home-care aides help elderly or disabled adults with personal care and household chores. They may make beds, clean house, or help their client bathe and dress. Some workers take care of people after they have died. Embalmers prepare bodies for funerals. Funeral directors help families plan and arrange funeral services. Some people also need workers to care for their pets. Animal trainers teach animals to obey commands. They also prepare animals for competitions. Animal caretakers feed, groom, and exercise pets.

Flight attendants look after the safety of airline passengers. They teach the passengers emergency procedures and make sure they are comfortable during the flight.

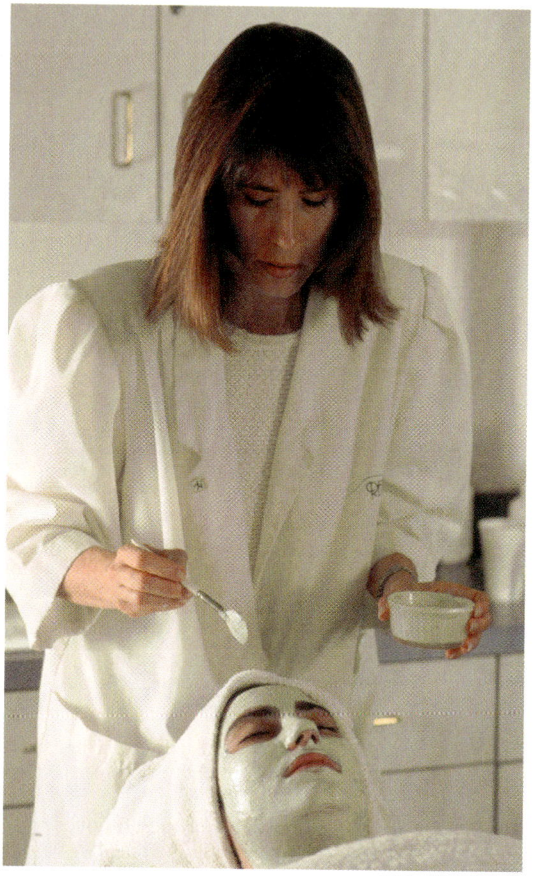

© Patrick Bennett, Corbis

A cosmetologist helps people look and feel their best. This cosmetologist is giving her client a facial treatment. Many cosmetologists also provide hair care services and give massages.

Concierges arrange personal services for such clients as hotel guests, apartment residents, and office tenants. They may make dinner and theater reservations, arrange leisure activities, or run errands.

Working conditions. Many cosmetologists and barbers work on weekends and spend much of their time standing. Nannies, child-care workers, and home-care aides usually work in their employer's home. Funeral directors may be called into work at any time. Pets sometimes bite or scratch animal trainers and caretakers. Flight attendants travel to other cities and countries and may spend time away from home between flights. Concierges may work with many people in busy lobbies or independently with personal clients.

Education and training. Some employers in this field require that applicants have at least a high school education. Cosmetologists and barbers must graduate from a cosmetology or barber school. Other workers, including animal trainers and caretakers, receive on-the-job training. Requirements vary for nannies, child-care workers, and home-care aides. Some employers require these workers to have formal training.

Many airlines prefer to hire flight attendants who

have a college degree. A majority of flight attendants receive specialized training in safety procedures and customer service. Funeral directors and embalmers usually need an associate's or bachelor's degree.

Production. Workers in this group are involved in making or preparing goods by hand or machine. These products range from simple wooden objects, such as tables and chairs, to complex computer parts.

Some production workers are involved in food processing. Bakers produce bread, pies, cakes, and pastries. Meat dressers kill animals, such as cattle and hogs, and prepare the meat. After they have slaughtered the animal, they use knives and other equipment to divide the meat into large cuts. Butchers cut and trim these cuts into meal-sized portions and sell them to consumers.

Apparel, textile, and upholstery workers make clothes, fabrics, and furniture. Tailors and dressmakers take a person's measurements and make clothing to fit. They also repair or alter clothing. Textile machinery operators run machines that manufacture a variety of fabrics. Upholsterers make new upholstered furniture or replace the worn coverings on existing furniture.

Assemblers put together parts to make finished products, such as automobiles and radios. Precision assemblers construct particularly complex goods, such as aerospace and computer equipment.

Other production occupations deal with metals. Machinists operate the power-driven machines, called *machine tools,* that are used to shape or cut metal. Tool-and-die makers are skilled machinists. They produce the precision parts and devices used by machine tools. Welders operate a variety of equipment that uses heat, pressure, or both to permanently join pieces of metal.

© David R. Frazier

A baker in a large commercial bakery follows recipes to produce bread, cakes, pastries, pies, and other baked goods in large quantities. This baker is making loaves of bread.

Other occupations in this group are in the printing industry. Prepress workers prepare materials for printing. Their responsibilities may include typesetting text, making negatives of illustrations, or preparing customer-supplied computer files for printing. Printing press operators run printing presses that reproduce words and images on paper and other materials. Bindery workers operate machinery that transforms printed materials into finished products. The machines may fold paper into pamphlets or fasten loose pages into books.

Woodworkers make various items out of wood. Some woodworkers operate machines that cut logs into boards. Others run machinery that cuts and shapes wood into parts that are later assembled to form such products as tables and chairs.

Jewelers make jewelry from precious metals, such as gold, silver, and gemstones. Jewelers may also repair and *appraise* (determine the value of) jewelry.

Mine workers are also included in the production group. Mining machine operators use specialized machines to cut coal and minerals, such as copper, iron, and silver, from the earth.

Working conditions. Most employees in the production industry work in factories or shops. Common working conditions include high levels of dust, heat, or noise. Some factory jobs require great strength or standing for long periods. Other jobs involve repetitive tasks.

Education and training. Most employers in this group prefer to hire workers with at least a high school education. Most bakers, meat dressers, butchers, bindery workers, and woodworkers receive on-the-job training. Other workers, such as tool-and-die makers, participate in apprenticeship programs or study at college or at vocational or technical schools.

Sales. Workers in sales inform people about products or services and persuade them to buy. Most sales workers sell their products in stores, but others may sell over the telephone or inside people's homes.

Retail salespeople work in retail stores, such as department, discount, or grocery stores, and sell merchandise directly to the consumer. Retail salespeople may help consumers find what they are looking for, demonstrate how a product works, or answer questions.

Many workers in this group are sales representatives. Wholesalers buy large quantities of an item from several manufacturers. Sales representatives for wholesalers then try to sell smaller amounts of that item to retail stores. Manufacturers' representatives sell goods to other manufacturers, to wholesalers, or to retail stores.

Other sales representatives sell services. Insurance sales agents sell various types of insurance policies, including automobile, health, and life insurance. Stockbrokers buy and sell *securities* (stocks and bonds). They determine their clients' investment goals and then advise them about which securities to buy or sell. Financial services sales representatives sell banking services, such as certificates of deposit and financial planning. Real estate agents help their clients buy, sell, or rent buildings and land. They may determine the value of a property a client wants to sell and prepare advertise-

© Paul Barton, The Stock Market

A real estate agent discusses the features of a house for sale with prospective home buyers. Real estate agents help their clients buy, sell, or rent buildings and land.

© David R. Frazier

Athletes competing in team sports may draw large crowds of fans. Jobs in the sports field often require both natural talent and many hours of practice and can be physically demanding.

ments describing the house, building, or land. Advertising sales representatives sell advertising time for commercials on TV or radio or advertising space in newspapers or magazines. They may also sell ad space on Web sites on the Internet, on the sides of buses and buildings, or on outdoor facilities, including billboards and benches.

Other types of sales workers include telemarketers and fashion models. Telemarketers call customers over the telephone and persuade them to buy goods or services. Models promote the sale of clothing and accessories. They may wear these items at fashion shows or may pose for photographs that appear in advertisements on TV or in catalogs, magazines, and newspapers.

Working conditions. Many workers in this group work long hours, often in the evening or on weekends. Some travel to meet with potential customers and may be away from home for some time. Other sales workers have flexible hours and work when they want. Some sales workers feel stress because they are expected to sell a certain amount of product in a specified time.

Education and training. Most employers prefer retail sales workers to have at least a high school education. They usually receive on-the-job training or participate in formal training programs. Real estate agents must have at least a high school education. Some models have taken courses from modeling schools. Most insurance sales agents, stockbrokers, and financial services sales representatives have a college education. Employers also prefer to hire wholesale and manufacturing sales representatives who have a college degree.

Sports and entertainment. Workers in sports and entertainment perform in activities that amuse or interest audiences. Millions of people watch sporting events and enjoy the excitement of the competition. Others like the beauty of a ballet, concert, or other performance.

Workers in the sports field participate in organized athletic activities. Athletes compete in individual sporting events or team sports. Coaches instruct individual athletes or teams. They help to improve the athletes' techniques and plan strategies for competition. Scouts observe athletes during practice and competition and evaluate their performance. They then try to recruit talented athletes to play for their team. Umpires, referees,

© Dan Nelken, Liaison Agency

Performing artists work to entertain audiences. This singer, *left,* and composer, *right,* are working in a recording studio to make an album of music for listeners to enjoy.

and other sports officials make sure the athletes follow the rules of the sport. They must know the rules, watch for violations, and determine the correct penalties.

Many workers in the entertainment field participate in the performing arts. Actors and actresses pretend to be characters in stage plays and movies and on television and radio. Dancers perform dances. They use their bodies to express emotions, tell a story, or set a mood. Instrumental musicians play such instruments as piano, drums, or guitar. They often perform alone or in groups, including rock bands or orchestras. Some musicians record their music. Singers are musicians who produce musical tones using their voices. Conductors direct musical groups, such as orchestras and choirs.

Other workers in the performing arts work behind the scenes. Producers are the business managers of a production. They may select scripts, raise money to finance the production, and set a budget. Directors make creative decisions for a production, such as interpreting the script, casting and rehearsing performers, and working with set and costume designers. Choreographers create new dance routines and teach them to dancers. Composers write music for musicians to play.

Working conditions. Many workers in this group, such as actors, musicians, and singers, work long hours. They may have difficulty finding steady work. Others, including producers and directors, may need to work under deadlines. Dancers and athletes must practice many hours. Their work is physically demanding. Coaches need to make quick decisions during competitions.

Training and education. There are no specific educational requirements for many careers in the sports and entertainment group. Almost all workers in this field have natural talent and must practice or train many hours every day. However, many athletes earn a degree while they compete in college athletic programs. Many coaches and sports officials begin their careers as athletes. Singers, dancers, musicians, and actors and actresses may have studied with private teachers for years. Others have attended schools for the performing arts. Almost all choreographers begin as dancers. Composers and conductors may have attended a *conservatory* (specialized music school) or studied music at a college or university.

Teaching. Workers in this group help other people learn. They teach many kinds of skills and transmit cultural values to students of all ages.

Preschool teachers use a variety of play activities to develop the intellectual, physical, and social skills of children up to 6 years old. Teachers may read stories, create learning opportunities, and care for children.

Kindergarten teachers prepare children who are 4 to 6 years old for elementary school. They use activities, such as group discussion, games, and storytelling, to teach basic subjects. Some kindergarten teachers offer instruction in reading and writing.

Elementary school teachers teach basic academic and social skills to students from ages 5 or 6 to age 12, 13, or 14. They usually teach many subjects to one class of students who are the same age. These teachers also emphasize communication and mathematical skills and personal development.

Middle school teachers teach basic subjects to students in sixth, seventh, and eighth grade. They prepare their students for high school. Middle school teachers also help young people understand the physical, social, and emotional changes they are going through.

High school teachers cover subjects in more detail than what was taught in elementary school. They prepare students for college or for a job after graduation.

Special education teachers provide instruction for disabled or gifted children. They use special equipment or programs to help children with physical or mental disabilities learn. They coach gifted children and help them develop their talents.

College and university faculty teach advanced courses. They specialize in one area, such as business or English, and teach a variety of courses in that field. Most college and university teachers also conduct research.

Many kinds of teachers hold classes for adults. Some teachers may provide remedial education courses in basic skills, such as reading and writing. Continuing education teachers lead classes for adults who want to continue to learn. They may teach personal interest courses, such as cooking or photography, or help people learn new job skills. Vocational education teachers prepare students for occupations that do not require a college degree, such as automobile repair.

Teachers use a variety of methods to help their students learn. This teacher helps her student master new skills by using a computer to tap into information resources on the Internet.

Teacher aides work under the supervision of teachers. They help with classroom activities. Aides may also grade tests and homework, provide individual attention to students, and help answer parents' questions.

Working conditions. Working with students and watching them learn new skills can be rewarding. But teachers may experience stress if classrooms become overcrowded. Many teachers work only during the school year. Long summer vacations enable them to travel, take continuing education classes, or pursue other interests.

Education and training. Almost all teachers need a bachelor's degree. Most also need to complete a professional training program before they can teach. Some preschool teachers and teacher aides do not need a degree. Many high school teachers and most college and university faculty have advanced degrees.

Technical and mathematical occupations. Workers in this group use technology and mathematics to prepare or analyze a variety of complicated procedures. Businesses and other organizations could not function efficiently without these workers.

Some workers in this group are computer specialists. Computer hardware engineers design *hardware* (the physical parts of computer systems), such as memory chips and microprocessors. Computer software engineers design *software* (programs, or sets of computer instructions and information). They may create *specifications* (detailed plans) for programs for general use or customize programs for clients.

Computer systems analysts design or modify computer systems to meet the needs of an organization. Analysts first evaluate an organization's requirements. They then prepare detailed specifications, which may include modifying software or hardware.

Computer programmers write programs. They break down the program specifications into logical steps. They then write these steps into instructions the computer can follow using various computer languages. They may work with systems analysts and software engineers to create new programs or modify existing programs. Some programmers also design Web sites.

Computer network administrators maintain an organization's *network* (system of two or more computers connected by communications lines). They also maintain the network's software and hardware. Database administrators use special software to manage *databases* (large, searchable bodies of information). They supervise the operation of databases and make sure the information is kept up to date. Computer support specialists help computer users. They may answer users' questions about hardware, such as printers, or software, such as word processing applications.

Some workers in this group are mathematics specialists. They use their knowledge to conduct research, develop new theories, or predict future developments. Mathematicians may develop new mathematical theories, relationships, and principles. Other mathematicians use existing techniques to solve problems in other fields. Statisticians use statistical methods to collect, organize, analyze, and interpret data. Their findings provide information that enables others to draw conclusions and make decisions. For example, a statistician may predict the change in population for a specific area.

© David R. Frazier

A computer programmer writes sets of coded computer instructions called *programs* using various programming languages. This programmer is checking his code for errors.

Actuaries are mathematicians who calculate future risk. Some actuaries work for insurance companies. They analyze data to calculate the probability of such occurrences as accidents and death. They then help design policies, calculate premium rates, and determine insurance company reserves to ensure payment of claims.

Financial specialists use mathematics to keep track of money. Accountants gather, analyze, and summarize their clients' financial information. They prepare statements and reports and provide advice to help their clients make decisions and plan for the future. They also design systems and procedures to track financial information. Budget analysts prepare an organization's financial plan that determines how money will be spent.

Specialized occupations in the technical and mathematical group include cartographers, architects, drafters, and surveyors. Cartographers use such information as statistical data, photographs taken from airplanes, and satellite images to produce maps. Architects design buildings and other structures. They prepare plans for every detail of the structure, such as plumbing and air-conditioning systems. They must make sure the structure meets safety and design regulations. Drafters prepare technical drawings and plans. These drawings and plans provide precise information on how to build products and structures. Surveyors take measurements to determine land, air space, and water boundaries. They may also gather information about such character-

© Lawrence Manning, Stone

Architects combine artistic and engineering skills in designing offices, museums, churches, houses, and other buildings. These architects are examining a model of a part of a structure.

© Frank Cezus, Stone

A surveyor uses special equipment to take measurements of various boundaries. Many surveyors work at construction sites to check the positioning of a wall or other architectural feature.

istics of land features as elevation and shape.

Other professionals in the technical and mathematical group have careers in engineering. Engineers use scientific knowledge to solve practical problems. They specialize in a particular field of engineering, including aerospace, biomedical, chemical, civil, electrical, industrial, materials, mechanical, nuclear, mining and geological, and petroleum engineering.

Aerospace engineers design, produce, and test aircraft, guided missiles, and spacecraft. Biomedical engineers use engineering methods to solve medical problems. For example, they may design artificial limbs or hearing aids. Chemical engineers design chemical factories and equipment used to process chemicals and chemical products for industrial and consumer uses. Civil engineers plan and supervise the construction and maintenance of large structures and facilities, such as bridges, dams, highways, and sewer systems.

Electrical engineers develop, produce, and test electrical devices and equipment. For example, they may design the equipment used to generate and transmit power for electric companies. Electronics engineers specialize in designing electronic equipment, such as communications gear. Industrial engineers determine the most economic and efficient ways to use people, machines, and materials to produce goods and services.

Materials engineers work with various materials, such as metals, ceramics, and plastics. They evaluate the properties, structure, and production methods of materials. They then work to develop new materials or new uses for existing materials.

Mechanical engineers plan, design, and test all kinds of machines that produce and use power, such as air-conditioning equipment, elevators, engines, and machine tools. Nuclear engineers study the production and use of nuclear energy and radiation. Most nuclear engineers design, develop, and operate nuclear power plants that generate electric power.

Mining engineers find deposits of minerals, such as copper and tin, and determine the best way to remove the *ore* (mineral-bearing material). They design mines, supervise the construction of shafts and tunnels, and select the mining machinery. Petroleum engineers locate petroleum and natural gas deposits and develop methods to drill and recover the oil and gas from the earth.

Working conditions. Most workers in the technical and mathematical group work in offices, laboratories, or industrial plants. Other workers, such as surveyors and mining and petroleum engineers, perform some or all of their duties outdoors. Many workers in this group need to work extra hours to meet deadlines. Some workers, especially computer specialists, can *telecommute*—that is, use computers to do some or all of their work from home.

Education and training. Employers prefer to hire drafters who have a high school education and have completed training programs offered at technical institutes, community colleges, and universities. Computer programmers, architects, surveyors, and cartographers need a bachelor's degree. Most other occupations in the technical and mathematical group require at least a bachelor's degree. Many of these workers have advanced degrees. Workers who want to participate in research or teach at an institution of higher education should have a doctor's degree.

Tourism and hospitality. Workers in the field of tourism and hospitality provide services that help people enjoy their leisure time. Some plan activities, while others make sure that their guests are happy and enjoying the service and surroundings.

Travel agents help people plan vacations and business trips. They help their clients decide on a destination and provide information about restaurants, transportation, and hotels and other accommodations. They also make airline and hotel reservations and other travel arrangements. Tour guides take tourists on sightseeing excursions or to places of interest. They also help tourists learn about the areas they visit.

© Michael Newman, PhotoEdit

A travel agent shows her client brochures and helps him decide on a destination. Travel agents handle hotel and transportation reservations. Most agents get discounts on their own travel.

© Nik Wheeler, Corbis

A chef adds a decorative touch to a dish while he teaches students how to prepare fish. Most chefs plan menus and cook food, but one of their main duties is to supervise cooks.

When people are away from home, many kinds of workers help make them comfortable. These workers include employees who provide lodging in hotels, motels, and similar establishments. Front desk clerks greet guests and assign them rooms to sleep in. They also take and confirm room reservations and help guests check out when they are ready to leave.

Other workers prepare or serve food and drinks in restaurants and bars. Restaurant hosts and hostesses greet guests, seat them at tables, and give them menus. Waiters and waitresses take guests' orders and serve their food and drinks. Bartenders prepare drinks. Cooks prepare meals. Chefs supervise the cooks and other kitchen workers, plan the menu, and order supplies. They may also prepare and cook food.

Working conditions. Many workers in the tourism and hospitality group work evenings, weekends, and on holidays. Travel agents do most of their work on computers. Chefs and cooks work long hours near hot ovens and grills. Waiters and waitresses spend many hours standing and often carry heavy trays of food.

Education and training. Most tourism and hospitality workers need at least a high school education. Many employers prefer to hire travel agents who have com-

AP/Wide World

A tour guide takes visitors to places of interest. This guide leads tourists in a ceremony at the grave of President George Washington. She wears clothing from the 1700's to help visitors learn about the history of the site.

pleted travel courses at vocational schools, community colleges, or universities. Some bartenders receive training at bartending, vocational, or technical schools. Many cooks and chefs learn their skills through vocational and apprenticeship programs or take college courses.

Transportation. Industrialized societies need fast, safe, and dependable methods for moving people and goods from one place to another. Workers in the transportation field help passengers and goods travel by air, land, and water.

Pilots and air traffic controllers are two of the best-known air transportation workers. Pilots operate and navigate aircraft and are responsible for the safety of their aircraft, passengers, crew, and cargo. Air traffic controllers help provide safe air transportation. They direct the movement of aircraft preparing to take off or land. They also make sure that all aircraft are clear from other traffic in the air.

Land transportation workers can be divided into two groups: (1) road and highway and (2) rail. Road and highway transportation moves goods and people by automobile, bus, or truck. Taxi drivers and chauffeurs operate such motor vehicles as automobiles, vans, and limousines and take passengers wherever they need to go. Bus drivers operate buses, usually on a fixed route. They may provide transportation for passengers traveling from one city to another or within a city. Other bus drivers carry students to and from school. Truckdrivers operate trucks to pick up, transport, or deliver packages and other goods. They may drive short distances within a specific area or long distances across many states.

AP/Wide World

A truckdriver uses a truck to transport packages and other goods. This truckdriver works for a package delivery service. He drives a short distance each day on a specific route.

Rail transportation moves freight and passengers by trains, streetcars, and subways. Locomotive engineers operate trains. Conductors supervise the crew on passenger and freight trains. On passenger trains, they may collect tickets and inform the engineer when it is safe to leave a station after a stop. On freight trains, they may check the contents of each car and make sure the appropriate cars are removed or added at each stop.

Water transportation involves barges, general cargo ships, passenger liners, riverboats, tankers, and a wide variety of other vessels. Captains are the top officers on ships. They are responsible for their ship, passengers, crew, and cargo. Officers called mates assist the captain. They navigate the ship and supervise other crew members. Marine engineers design ships and their machinery. They also make sure the machinery is working properly and make any needed repairs. Pilots guide ships through harbors and difficult waters.

Working conditions. Most transportation workers travel as a part of their job. Workers assigned to long-distance trips may be away from their homes for long periods. Some transportation employers, such as airlines, allow employees to travel at no cost or at reduced fares.

Education and training. Employers prefer to hire road and highway transportation workers who have a high school education. These workers often receive on-the-job training. Railroad conductors must have at least a high school education. Locomotive engineers usually participate in a formal training program. Many airlines prefer to hire pilots who have a bachelor's degree. All pilots, however, must have attended a flight school or received armed forces training. Air traffic controllers receive formal and on-the-job training. Many also have a college degree. Many water transportation workers have a bachelor's degree from a nautical school or marine academy. Duane Brown

Related articles in ***World Book*** include:

Career opportunities

The following articles contain information helpful to a general understanding of a career area. Many of the articles include a *Careers* section and give qualifications and sources of further information.

Accounting	Automobile	City planning
Advertising	Aviation	Clothing
Agriculture	Ballet	Coal
Air conditioning	Bank	Coast Guard, U.S.
Air Force, U.S.	Biology	Commercial art
Anesthesiology	Bookkeeping	Computer
Anthropology	Botany	Conservation
Archaeology	Building trade	Crime laboratory
Architecture	Business	Criminology
Army, U.S.	Cardiology	Dental hygiene
Astronomy	Chemistry	Dentistry
Audiology	Chiropractic	Dermatology

Disability
Economics
Electronics
Embalming
Engineering
Entomology
Family and consumer sciences
Federal Bureau of Investigation
Fire department
Forestry
Gardening
Geography
Geology
Government
Hairdressing
Hospital
Hotel
Industrial design
Insurance
Interior design
Iron and steel
Journalism
Law
Library
Marine Corps, U.S.
Mathematics
Mechanical drawing
Medical examiner
Medicine
Merchant marine
Metallurgy
Meteorology
Mining
Modeling
Motion picture
Museum
Music
Navy, U.S.
Neonatology
Neurology
Nuclear energy
Nursing
Nutrition
Obstetrics and gynecology
Occupational medicine
Occupational therapy
Ocean
Office work
Oncology
Ophthalmology
Optometry
Orthopedics
Osteopathic medicine
Paramedic
Pediatrics
Personnel management
Petroleum
Pharmacy
Photography
Physical education
Physical therapy
Physics
Plastics
Podiatry
Police
Psychiatry
Psychology
Public relations
Publishing
Radio
Railroad
Real estate
Recording industry
Religious education
Restaurant
Retailing
Sales
Science
Secretarial work
Social work
Sociology
Speech therapy
Surveying
Taxidermy
Teaching
Telephone
Television
Theater
Toolmaking
Travel agency
Truck
Veterinary medicine
Vocational rehabilitation
Writing
Zoology

Other related articles

Adolescent (Career planning)
Apprentice
Career education
Civil service
Community college
Correspondence school
Employment agency
Fellowship
Foreign Service
Guidance
Job Corps
Letter writing
Peace Corps
Retirement
Scholarship
Service industries
Universities and colleges
Vocational education
Women's movement (Impact of women's movements)

Outline

I. Choosing and planning a career
A. Discovering the world of work
B. Learning about oneself
C. What to look for in career fields
D. Sources of information
E. Preparing for a career

II. Getting a job
A. Writing a resume
B. Finding job opportunities
C. Contacting employers
D. Completing job applications
E. Being interviewed

III. The world of work
A. Administrative support
B. Art, design, and communications
C. Community and social services
D. Construction, maintenance, and repair
E. Farming, fishing, and forestry
F. Health care
G. Law
H. Life, physical, and social sciences
I. Management
J. Personal services
K. Production
L. Sales
M. Sports and entertainment
N. Teaching
O. Technical and mathematical occupations
P. Tourism and hospitality
Q. Transportation

Questions

How can you prepare for an interview?
Why is it important to learn about yourself before choosing a career field?
In what ways can a person learn about job openings?
What are some job characteristics to consider when you explore an occupation?
In what ways can the career you have affect your life?
What is a cover letter? A resume? A thank-you letter? Why are they used?
How can high schools help students prepare for a career?
What are some sources of information that can help you explore a career field?
How can aptitudes influence a person's career choice?
What is *job shadowing*?

Additional resources

Bolles, Richard N. *What Color Is Your Parachute? A Practical Manual for Job-Hunters & Career Changers.* Ten Speed, revised annually.
Career Discovery Encyclopedia. 8 vols. 5th ed. Ferguson Pub. Co., 2003. Younger readers.
Citrin, James M., and Smith, R. A. *The Five Patterns of Extraordinary Careers.* Crown Business, 2003.
Dowd, Karen O., and Taguchi, S. G. *The Ultimate Guide to Getting the Career You Want: And What to Do Once You Have It.* McGraw, 2004.
Levitt, Julie G. *Your Career: How to Make It Happen.* 5th ed. South-Western, 2003.
Maltz, Susan, and Grahn, Barbara. *A Fork in the Road: A Career Planning Guide for Young Adults.* Impact Pubns., 2003.
Morkes, Andrew, ed. *Encyclopedia of Careers and Vocational Guidance.* 4 vols. 12th ed. Ferguson Pub. Co., 2003.
Phifer, Paul. *College Majors and Careers.* 5th ed. Ferguson Pub. Co., 2003.
Richardson, Bradley. *Career Comeback.* Broadway Bks., 2004. A guide for dealing with a major career setback.

Cargo. See **Airplane; Airport** (Cargo handling; Airport terms; picture); **Aviation; Ship** (Classification of cargo ships; General cargo ships; pictures).

Carib Indians, *KAR ihb,* were a warlike group of South American tribes who lived mainly in the Amazon River Valley and the Guiana lowlands. These fierce Indians ate their war captives. Our word *cannibal* comes from the Spanish name for these Indians. About 1300, the Carib moved from northeastern South America to islands in the Caribbean Sea now known as the Windward Islands. They captured these islands from the Arawak Indians (see **Arawak Indians**).

The Carib were farmers and raised *cassava,* a root crop. They also fished, hunted, and gathered wild plants for food. They lived in small, independent villages. The people had no tribal chiefs or permanent village chiefs, but followed special leaders in time of war. The Carib, especially those who lived on the islands, were expert canoeists. They used large, planked dugouts. They hunted with traps, javelins, and clubs, and shot fish with poison arrows. The Carib are said to have valued personal independence so highly that they looked down on Spaniards who took orders from others.

Like other aggressive tribes, the Carib trained their sons for war from childhood. A boy had to prove his endurance and skill with weapons when he came of age. If he passed the tests, the tribe accepted him as a warrior and gave him a new name. Most of the Carib died from warfare and disease soon after the Spanish invasion. Today, hundreds of Carib live on the islands, in the Guianas, and in the Amazon Valley. Samuel M. Wilson

Caribbean Sea, *KAR uh BEE uhn* or *kuh RIHB ee uhn,* is a part of the Atlantic Ocean between the West Indies and Central and South America. It is about 1,700 miles (2,740 kilometers) long from west to east and between 500 and 800 miles (800 and 1,300 kilometers) wide from north to south. Its greatest depth is 24,720 feet (7,535 meters). The widest entrance is the Yucatán Channel, between Mexico and Cuba. Ships sail the Caribbean carrying sugar from the West Indies; petroleum from Venezuela and Colombia; coffee from Colombia, Costa Rica, and Guatemala; and bananas from Panama, Costa Rica,

WORLD BOOK map

Location of Caribbean Sea

Honduras, and El Salvador. The United States has military bases in Panama and Puerto Rico. In the 1500's and 1600's, many pirates and privateers sailed the Caribbean, plundering cargo ships on the Spanish Main. See also **South America** (map); **Spanish Main.** Gustavo A. Antonini

Caribou, *KAR uh boo,* is a large deer from Greenland and northern North America. Caribou and reindeer make up a single *species* (type) of deer, but scientists break up this species into *subspecies.* Reindeer subspecies are native to northernmost Europe and Asia.

A *bull* (male) caribou weighs from 250 to 700 pounds (113 to 320 kilograms), stands 4 to 5 feet (1.2 to 1.5 meters) tall, and measures 6 to 8 feet (1.8 to 2.4 meters) long. A *cow* (female) grows smaller than a bull. Cows give birth to one calf in late spring.

Caribou have broad hoofs to support them in deep snow and spongy tundra. For most caribou, their heavy coat is predominantly brownish or grayish in color. The animals possess broad antlers, and the male's antlers grow much larger than the female's. Female caribou and reindeer are the only female deer with antlers.

There are two main kinds of caribou—*barren ground* and *woodland.* Barren-ground caribou spend the summer in the Arctic tundra and the winter in the evergreen forests south of the tundra. They may occur from western Alaska to northeastern Greenland. In the western part of their range, they live in large herds. Woodland caribou grow slightly larger and darker than barren-ground caribou. They inhabit forests from the Canadian province of Newfoundland and Labrador to Canada's Northwest Territories and down through British Columbia, northern Idaho, and northeastern Washington.

Roaming barren-ground caribou cover the land for days at a time. They do not overgraze their range because they keep moving from place to place. In summer, they eat mostly grass and shrub leaves. In winter, they live mainly on plantlike organisms called *lichens.* Some caribou migrate more than 3,000 miles (4,800 kilometers) from summer range to winter range, the longest known migration for any land mammal. Kenneth J. Raedeke

Scientific classification. Caribou belong to the deer family, Cervidae. They are subspecies of *Rangifer tarandus.*

See also **Animal** (picture: Animals of the polar regions); **Mammal** (picture); **Reindeer; Tundra.**

Caricature, *KAR uh kuh chur,* in art, is a picture that exaggerates or distorts the physical features or peculiarities of a person or object. The term comes from an Italian word that means *overload* or *exaggerate.* Artists create caricatures to make fun of their subjects. Many caricatures ridicule famous individuals. Others poke fun at certain groups, such as politicians or lawyers.

The first important caricatures appeared in Europe during the 1500's. Many of them attacked either the Protestant or Roman Catholic side during the religious revolution called the Reformation. Britain produced a number of outstanding caricaturists during the 1700's and 1800's. William Hogarth became famous for his caricatures that satirized various classes of English society. George Cruikshank, James Gillray, and Thomas Rowlandson created hundreds of biting caricatures on English politics and government.

Perhaps the most famous artist to make caricatures was Honoré Daumier of France. During the early 1800's, Daumier ridiculed political figures. He drew the fat King Louis Philippe as a giant pear. The king had Daumier imprisoned briefly. After his release, Daumier turned to caricatures of the rising middle class in France. He satirized their fashions, taste in art, and manners.

In the United States, most caricatures have appeared as political cartoons in newspapers. Thomas Nast gained fame for caricatures published from 1869 to 1872 that at-

Len Rue, Jr., Tom Stack & Assoc.

The caribou lives in the North American tundra. The male, *shown here,* has larger antlers than does the female.

Lithograph by James Gilray; Bibliothèque Nationale, Paris

Ink drawing by David Levine; reprinted with permission from *The New York Review of Books,* © 1969 *The New York Review*

Drawing by Oscar Berger

Caricatures may exaggerate physical characteristics or something associated with a person. The above caricature, created in 1806, portrays Napoleon I in his military uniform and exaggerates his hat. A drawing of the German philosopher Karl Marx, *upper right,* emphasizes his thick hair and beard. A caricature of the English statesman Sir Winston Churchill, *right,* highlights his cigar.

tacked political corruption in New York City. Leading American caricaturists today include cartoonists Patrick Oliphant and David Levine. Elizabeth Broun

See also **Beerbohm, Max; Cartoon; Cruikshank, George; Daumier, Honoré; Hogarth, William; Nast, Thomas; Oliphant, Patrick B.**

Caries. See **Teeth** (Diseases and defects).

Carillon, *KAR uh lahn,* is a set of 23 or more stationary bells arranged to play music. The bells vary in size from a diameter of $3\frac{1}{2}$ inches (9 centimeters) and a weight of 7 pounds (3.2 kilograms) to a diameter of $10\frac{1}{4}$ feet (3.1 meters) and a weight of 20 tons (18 metric tons). A carillon has a range of two to six octaves. Most carillons are located in bell towers in Europe and North America. American carillons have from 23 to 77 bells.

A carillon may be played either manually or mechanically. When a carillon is played manually, the musician usually sits at a keyboard below the bells. The keyboard consists of rounded wooden keys for the hands and short pedals for the feet. The keys and pedals are connected to metal *clappers.* By pushing down on the keys and pedals, the musician moves the clappers, which strike the sides of the bells to produce sound. A mechanical carillon has a rotating barrel with projecting

Frank Muth, Shostal

Carillon bells hang in a stationary position, usually inside large bell towers. A carillon may have dozens of bells of various sizes, which produce different musical notes.

Frank Muth, Shostal

A carillon keyboard consists of wooden keys and pedals connected to metal clappers inside a set of bells. Pressing down on the keys and pedals causes the clappers to strike the bells.

pegs that automatically cause the clappers to strike.

The carillon originated in the Netherlands, Belgium, and northern France in the 1500's. Some modern electronic devices try to reproduce bell sounds through loudspeakers, but they are not true carillons.

William De Turk

See also **Campanile**.

Carl XVI Gustaf, *GUHS tahv* (1946-), became king of Sweden in 1973. Carl Gustaf succeeded his grandfather, Gustaf VI Adolf. His father died in 1947, when Carl Gustaf was less than a year old.

Carl Gustaf Folke Hubertus was born near Stockholm. After his great-grandfather, Gustaf V, died in 1950, his grandfather became king, and Carl Gustaf became crown prince. He received his early education from tutors and then entered a private school in Sigtuna. He graduated in 1966. For the next two years, Carl Gustaf served in the Swedish armed forces. He then attended Uppsala University for a year.

Carl Gustaf worked in several Swedish government agencies from 1969 to 1971. In 1976, he married Silvia Renate Sommerlath, the daughter of a West German businessman. M. Donald Hancock

Carleton, *KAHRL tuhn,* **Sir Guy** (1724-1808), was a British general and governor in Canada. He tried to gain the support of French Canadians for British rule in the colony of Quebec. France had yielded Quebec to Britain in 1763. Carleton helped frame the Quebec Act of 1774, which granted greater freedom to the French Canadians. See **Quebec Act**.

Carleton was born in Strabane in what is now Northern Ireland. He began a military career in Britain and was named governor of Quebec in 1768. He held that post 10 years. In 1775, during the Revolutionary War in America, Carleton defended Quebec against an American invasion. For his success, he was knighted. In 1782, Carleton became British commander-in-chief in North America. In 1786, he was given separate commissions as governor of the colonies of Quebec, Nova Scotia, and New Brunswick. Carleton also received the title Baron Dorchester. During his administration, the Constitutional Act of 1791 divided Quebec into the colonies of Upper and Lower Canada and gave Canadians representative government. In 1796, Carleton returned to England.

Cornelius J. Jaenen

Carlos, Juan. See **Juan Carlos I**.

Carlota, Empress. See **Maximilian**.

Carlsbad. See **Karlovy Vary**.

Carlsbad Caverns National Park, in southeastern New Mexico, is famous for its many caverns, or caves. The largest of these caverns is Carlsbad Caverns, one of the biggest underground caverns in the world. In the chambers of Carlsbad Caverns, stalactites and stalagmites form shapes that resemble Chinese temples, heavy pillars, and lacy icicles (see **Stalactite; Stalagmite**). One large chamber, called the Big Room, is 1,800 feet (550 meters) long and 1,100 feet (335 meters) wide. At one point, the ceiling is 255 feet (78 meters) high. Such animals as foxes, gophers, jack rabbits, mule deer, and rattlesnakes live in the park. The national park was established in 1930. For its area, see **National Park System** (table: National parks).

Most passages in Carlsbad Caverns have been explored, but unexplored areas still exist. Two levels, at 750 feet (229 meters) and 829 feet (253 meters) underground, may be reached by trail from the natural entrance, or by elevator. One part of the caverns contains hundreds of thousands of bats. Paintings on the wall of the entrance to Carlsbad Caverns show that Indians visited the mouth of the caverns.

James P. Rowan

Carlsbad Caverns National Park in New Mexico is famous for its spectacular underground landscape of stalactites and stalagmites. The caves are made of hollowed-out limestone.

Carlsbad Caverns is part of a huge limestone formation. Geologists believe the caverns formed 60 to 70 million years ago when movements in the earth caused cracks to open up in the limestone. Ground water flowed through the cracks, hollowing out caverns. About 3 million years ago, earth movements lifted the region, and the ground water drained away. The stalactites and stalagmites in the caverns developed when water seeped through cracks in the limestone and deposited dissolved minerals.

Critically reviewed by the National Park Service

See also **Cave** (table); **New Mexico** (picture: Stalactites and stalagmites in Carlsbad Caverns).

Carlyle, Thomas (1795-1881), was a Scottish essayist and historian. He once was considered the greatest social philosopher of Victorian England. Carlyle's reputation declined in the 1900's, but his works are still read for his distinctive ideas on democracy, heroism, and revolution.

Early career. Carlyle was born in Ecclefechan, near Dumfries, Scotland. In 1819, he moved to Edinburgh and began writing articles on science and literature for the city's leading magazines and encyclopedias. In 1826, he married Jane Welsh, the daughter of a Scottish physician. Two years later, the couple moved to Craigenputtock, Jane Carlyle's farm near Dumfries.

At Craigenputtock, Carlyle wrote *Sartor Resartus,* which was published in 1833 and 1834. This work brought him fame and is still considered his most original and enduring achievement. The book is an elaborate work of fiction about a German professor. Through this character, Carlyle poured out his own ideas and experiences. He thus made *Sartor Resartus* one of the greatest—and one of the most incomprehensible—autobiographies in literary history. The work introduced readers to *Carlylese,* a writing style that used a rich vocabulary and complex sentence structures.

Carlyle moved to London in 1834 and began writing a history of the French Revolution. He lent the completed manuscript of the first volume to the philosopher John Stuart Mill, and it was accidentally burned by a housemaid. Carlyle then rewrote *The French Revolution* largely from memory, and it was published in 1837. In *The French Revolution,* Carlyle discussed both the dangers and the promise of revolution. He also delivered many public lectures, including a series he published as *On Heroes, Hero-Worship, and the Heroic in History* (1841). In *On Heroes and Hero-Worship,* as the book is often called, he stated that the main cause of social progress is a strong, heroic leader.

Detail of an oil portrait by Sir John Everett Millais; National Portrait Gallery, London

Thomas Carlyle

Later career. In the 1840's, Carlyle turned to what he called "the condition-of-England question"—the problem of mass poverty existing alongside increasing middle-class wealth. In *Past and Present* (1843), he attacked political and social conditions. He called for a revival of certain medieval ways of life before the development of machines. The book inspired many people in Victorian England to try to correct the social ills. He then wrote *Oliver Cromwell's Letters and Speeches, with Elucidations* (1845), a study of Oliver Cromwell, England's strongest leader at the time of the English Civil War of the 1640's. Carlyle discussed his ideas on the need for a hero to lead social change and solve the United Kingdom's problems.

In 1848, the United Kingdom stood on the brink of revolution because of *Chartism,* a movement to extend the vote to workers (see **Chartism**). The prospect of violence over electoral reform turned Carlyle and other formerly progressive intellectuals into conservatives on social issues. Carlyle wrote against electoral reform and the possibility of a society dominated by the working class in *Latter-Day Pamphlets* (1850) and the biography *Frederick the Great,* published from 1858 to 1865. Many readers agreed with Carlyle's conservative views. But others disliked the extremism of his later writings. These works contributed to the decline of his reputation.

In his later years, Carlyle received many public honors, and his writings were widely read. But he remained uneasy over the continuing growth of democracy in the United Kingdom. Avrom Fleishman

Additional resources

Heffer, Simon. *Moral Desperado: A Life of Thomas Carlyle.* Weidenfeld & Nicolson, 1995.

Jessop, Ralph. *Carlyle and Scottish Thought.* St. Martin's, 1997.

Carman, Bliss (1861-1929), was a Canadian poet whose verse praises the beauty and power he saw in nature. Carman's descriptions of the landscape suggest images of death and lost love. Much of his verse expresses a sense of yearning for the beauty of scenes from his past. His poetry also praises the carefree life of a wanderer. Carman was influenced by the religious and philosophical movement called *Transcendentalism,* and by the American poets Ralph Waldo Emerson and Walt Whitman (see **Transcendentalism**).

Carman's first book of verse, *Low Tide on Grand Pré,* was published in 1893. It contained some of his best-known lyrics on nature. Perhaps Carman's most popular books were the Vagabondia series, written with the American poet Richard Hovey. These books include *Songs from Vagabondia* (1895), *More Songs from Vagabondia* (1896), and *Last Songs from Vagabondia* (1901). Carman later won praise for his love poems in *From the Book of Myths* (1902), *Songs of the Sea Children* (1904), and *Sappho* (1904). He also wrote a number of essays.

William Bliss Carman was born in Fredericton, New Brunswick. After attending Oxford and Harvard universities, he began his career as a journalist in New York City.

Rosemary Sullivan

Carmel, California (pop. 4,081), is a seaside community on the Monterey Peninsula, south of San Francisco (see **California** [political map]). Its official name is Carmel-by-the-Sea. The town's mild climate, rugged coastline, and white sand beaches attract many visitors.

In 1771, Spanish missionaries relocated Mission San Carlos Borromeo to the area from Monterey. A group of American artists and writers settled the town in the early 1900's. They wished to keep the community simple and rural, and for many years it had no paved streets and no gas or electric service. Carmel still has no jail or neon signs, nor does it have street lights, sidewalks, or street numbers in its residential area. Mail delivery is limited to a small portion of its residential area. Carmel was incorporated in 1916. The town has a mayor-council form of government, with an administrator. James J. Rawls

Carmelites, *KAHR muh lyts,* are members of several Roman Catholic orders of men and women. The Carmelites originated in the 1100's with a group of men living on Mount Carmel in what is now Israel. About 1209, the men adopted a *rule* (program of life) emphasizing solitude, penance, and prayer. They called themselves the Order of Our Lady of Mount Carmel. In time, the Carmelites moved to Europe and adapted their rule to include preaching, teaching, and missionary work. Communities of women emerged in the 1200's. Reform under Saint Teresa and Saint John of the Cross in the 1500's led to the founding of independent branches for women and men who desired to return to the original rule. These branches are called *discalced* (barefoot) because of their custom of wearing sandals.

David G. Schultenover

See also **Teresa, Saint.**

Carmichael, Hoagy (1899-1981), was an American composer of popular songs. He is best known for the ballad "Star Dust" (1929), which became a popular classic after Mitchell Parish added lyrics to the music. His song "Georgia on My Mind" (1930) was adopted as the state song of Georgia. His other notable songs include "Rockin' Chair" (1930), "Lazybones" (1933), "Two Sleepy People" (1938), and "The Nearness of You" (1940). From 1944 to 1955, Carmichael appeared in about 10 motion pictures, usually playing a folksy pianist and performing his own songs. He shared a 1951 Academy Award with Johnny Mercer for the song "In the Cool, Cool, Cool of the Evening," from *Here Comes the Groom.*

Carmichael was born in Bloomington, Indiana. His full name was Hoagland Howard Carmichael. He earned a degree in law at Indiana University but decided to become a composer instead of a lawyer. He wrote his first song, "Riverboat Shuffle," in 1925. Gerald Bordman

Carmichael, Stokely (1941-1998), became a spokesman for the doctrine of Black Power. This doctrine urges black Americans to gain political and economic control of their own communities. It also urges them to form their own standards and reject the values of white America. It rejects complete nonviolence, and calls for blacks to meet violence with violence.

Carmichael was born in Trinidad, in the West Indies. He grew up in Harlem, a New York City ghetto, and graduated from Howard University in 1964. While in college, he led protests and helped teach blacks in the South how to register and vote. In 1966, he became chairman of the Student Nonviolent Coordinating Committee (SNCC), a civil rights group he had helped form. Under his leadership, SNCC moved toward Black Power ideals. Carmichael left SNCC in 1968, and became prime minister of the Black Panther Party, a militant Black Power group. He resigned in 1969. He and Charles Hamilton wrote *Black Power* (1967). In 1969, Carmichael moved to the African nation of Guinea. In 1979, he changed his name to Kwame Ture. C. Eric Lincoln

See also **Student Nonviolent Coordinating Committee**.

Carnation is a tall, colorful flower with many blossoms. It is related to a group of flowers called *pinks.* Carnations are from 1 to 3 feet (30 to 91 centimeters) high, and may be pink, purple, red, white, or yellow.

Carnations originally came from southern Europe, but several varieties are grown in the United States, both outdoors and in greenhouses. The carnation may bloom throughout the year, depending on its cultivation and the climate. Carnations are usually raised by planting young shoots from the stems of mature plants, or by bending one of the stems into the ground again so that it forms a new root. Carnations require a rich, loamy soil, manure, leaf mold, and some sand.

Gardeners have raised carnations since ancient times. The flower is used in bouquets and as a lapel flower. It is one of the special flowers of January. The scarlet carnation is the state flower of Ohio. James S. Miller

WORLD BOOK illustration by Robert Hynes

Carnations are tall, hardy flowers with a spicy fragrance. They grow well both outdoors and in greenhouses.

Scientific classification. The carnation belongs to the pink family, Caryophyllaceae. It is classified as *Dianthus caryophyllus.*

See also **Pink; Sweet William**.

Carnauba wax, *kahr NOW buh,* is a vegetable wax. It is obtained from the leaves of the carnauba palm, which is native to Brazil. The leaves are dried until their waxy coating turns to a flourlike dust. This dust is melted, cooled, and formed into cakes for shipment. It is the hardest natural wax. It is used in polishes, plastics, varnishes, and other products. Richard F. Blewitt

Carneades, *kahr NEE uh DEEZ* (213?-129? B.C.), was a Greek philosopher. He argued against the dogmatic schools of philosophy of his time, stating that there is no standard of truth and thus no knowledge of reality. Carneades was famous for his ability to present persuasive arguments both for and against any given philosophical thesis. The goal of such arguments was to show how insecure and unstable the arguments were for any philosophic position and the necessity for suspending judgment. Carneades claimed we should not agree to any sense impressions because we cannot be certain of their truth. We can still act on "convincing" impressions, which come in three degrees. First are those that simply appear true. Second are those that appear true and are not contradicted by the associated impressions we have at the same time as the main impression. Third are those that have the attributes of the second but after we have explored the associated impressions.

Carneades was born in North Africa. He became head of the Academy, the philosophical school founded by the Greek philosopher Plato. Carl A. Huffman

See also **Skepticism**.

Carnegie, *kahr NAY gee* or *KAHR nuh gee,* **Andrew** (1835-1919), a Scottish-born American, was a leading steel manufacturer and one of the wealthiest individuals of his time. He used his huge fortune to establish many cultural, educational, and scientific institutions.

Early life. Carnegie was born in Dunfermline, Scotland. His father was a weaver. After power looms began to replace handweaving, the family immigrated to the United States for new opportunities. Andrew was then 12 years old. The family settled in Allegheny City, Pennsylvania, now part of Pittsburgh. Andrew worked in a cotton mill and later became a telegraph messenger. He taught himself to send telegraph messages, and became a telegraph operator when he was 17.

In 1853, he got a job as a clerk and telegraph operator for the Pennsylvania Railroad. He later became a secretary for one of the railroad's division superintendents, Thomas A. Scott. With Scott's help, Carnegie advanced in the firm and eventually succeeded Scott as superintendent. During the Civil War (1861-1865), Carnegie helped organize telegraph services for the Union Army.

Rise to wealth. While working for the Pennsylvania Railroad, Carnegie invested in several iron companies. One was the Keystone Bridge Company, which built iron railroad bridges. He also bought stock in an oil company and in the Woodruff Sleeping Car Company, which made railroad sleeping cars. Carnegie left the Pennsylvania Railroad in 1865 to run his businesses.

In 1872, Carnegie traveled to Europe to sell bonds to European investors. During his travels, he realized that the demand for steel would increase in the years ahead and decided to enter the steel industry. In 1873, he and several partners bought land near Pittsburgh and established the J. Edgar Thomson Works, which became the largest and most modern steel mill of its time.

A nationwide business slump occurred in the United States from 1873 to 1879. Despite the slump, Carnegie expanded his steel company. During the early 1880's, business revived, and the demand for steel increased. Carnegie's mills earned millions of dollars. Another business slump began in 1883. Most steel companies suffered, but Carnegie's firm continued to expand. In 1883, Carnegie purchased the Homestead Works, one of the largest competing steel mills. He also bought a majority of the stock in a coke company established by Henry Clay Frick, an American industrialist, and made Frick one of his partners.

In 1892, Carnegie combined three of his companies and formed the Carnegie Steel Company. Frick became chairman of the new firm and took responsibility for its daily operation. Carnegie handled the company's investments and long-range planning.

Carnegie's financial success resulted partly from his sales ability. He also outbid his competitors and created a talented management team. Also, he expanded during periods of economic decline, when most of his competitors cut back their investments. Carnegie thus enlarged his facilities inexpensively and could meet the increased demand for steel during years of economic growth.

The Homestead Strike. In 1892, steelworkers at Carnegie's Homestead plant went on strike because they had received a wage cut. Carnegie was vacationing in Scotland at the time, and Frick refused to bargain with union leaders. Frick reopened the plant by force. He hired guards from the Pinkerton Detective Agency to protect nonunion workers from the strikers. Fighting broke out between the guards and the strikers, and several people were killed. The state militia restored order and reopened the plant. Most of the strikers quit the union and returned to work. The strike ended in failure.

Throughout the Homestead incident, Carnegie remained silent. Previously, he had claimed to support labor unions and oppose the use of force to end a strike. He thus kept his reputation as a supporter of workers' rights. Later, many people criticized his silence, which they interpreted as approval of Frick's actions.

Retirement. In 1901, Carnegie sold the Carnegie Steel Company for $480 million to J. P. Morgan, an American banker, and retired. "Mr. Carnegie," Morgan said, "I want to congratulate you on being the richest man in the world." Carnegie's fortune was estimated at $500 million. Morgan and other manufacturers later combined their companies to form the United States Steel Corporation.

U&U
Andrew Carnegie

After Carnegie retired, he devoted his time largely to writing and to promoting worthy causes. In an essay called "Wealth," published in 1889, he outlined his ideas on using large fortunes for the improvement of society. Carnegie also wrote the books *Triumphant Democracy* (1886), *The Empire of Business* (1902), *Problems of Today* (1908), and *Autobiography of Andrew Carnegie* (1920).

Carnegie's contributions to society. Carnegie believed that people could improve themselves through hard work. He also thought wealthy individuals should use their fortunes to aid society. He opposed charity but believed in helping others to help themselves, chiefly by providing educational opportunities.

Carnegie donated about $350 million to various causes. With this money, he established over 2,500 public libraries throughout the world. He also financed the construction of Carnegie Hall, a famous concert hall in New York City. A group of technical schools founded by Carnegie now form part of Carnegie Mellon University in Pittsburgh. The Carnegie Institution of Washington was established to encourage research in the biological and physical sciences.

The Carnegie Hero Fund Commission gives rewards for bravery. The Carnegie Foundation for the Advancement of Teaching provides pensions for college professors. The Endowment for International Peace works to end war. The Carnegie Corporation of New York provides funds to educational institutions and to organizations that conduct research on education and public affairs. Robert Sobel

Related articles in *World Book* include:

Carnegie Corporation of New York
Carnegie Foundation for the Advancement of Teaching
Foundations (History)
Homestead Strike
Iron and steel (Growth of the steel industry)
Library (Libraries in the United States)

Additional resources

Kent, Zachary. *Andrew Carnegie.* Enslow, 1999. Younger readers.
Krass, Peter. *Carnegie.* Wiley, 2002.
Meltzer, Milton. *Many Lives of Andrew Carnegie.* Watts, 1997.
Wall, Joseph F. *Andrew Carnegie.* 1970. Reprint. Univ. of Pittsburgh Pr., 1989.

Carnegie, Dale (1888-1955), was a pioneer in public speaking and personality development. He became famous by showing others how to become successful. His book *How to Win Friends and Influence People* (1936) has sold more than 10 million copies and has been translated into many languages. His books became popular because of his illustrative stories and simple, well-phrased rules. Two of his most famous maxims are, "Believe that you will succeed, and you will," and "Learn to love, respect and enjoy other people." His other books include *How to Stop Worrying and Start Living* (1948). Toward the beginning of his career, Carnegie wrote *Public Speaking and Influencing Men in Business* (1931), which became a standard text.

Carnegie attended Warrensburg (Missouri) State Teachers College. He became a salesman for Armour and Company. Later, Carnegie taught public speaking to businessmen. He was born on Nov. 22, 1888, in Maryville, Missouri. Carnegie died on Nov. 1, 1955.

Carl Niemeyer

Carnegie Corporation of New York is a philanthropic foundation dedicated to "the advancement and diffusion of knowledge and understanding." The foundation issues grants for such purposes as education, international development, international peace and security, and the strengthening of democracy. The Carnegie Corporation primarily seeks to help the people of the United States. However, a small portion of the corporation's funds may be used in countries that are or have been members of the Commonwealth of Nations. The American industrialist Andrew Carnegie established the foundation in 1911 with an endowment of about $135 million. The organization's offices are in New York City. For assets, see **Foundations** (table: Leading United States foundations).

Critically reviewed by the Carnegie Corporation of New York

Carnegie Foundation for the Advancement of Teaching is an organization that seeks to promote the cause of education and the dignity of the teaching profession. It conducts research and presents reports on problems and issues in education. Its studies have had much influence on all levels of education in America.

The American industrialist Andrew Carnegie established the foundation in 1905 with an endowment of $15 million. With the Carnegie Corporation of New York, the foundation established the Teachers Insurance and Annuity Association in 1918. Headquarters are in Stanford, California. Critically reviewed by the Carnegie Foundation for the Advancement of Teaching

Carnelian, *kahr NEEL yuhn,* is an orange to reddish-brown variety of quartz that can be cut and polished as a jewel. This gem is sometimes called a *cornelian.* Most carnelian comes from India, South America, and Japan. It is used in rings, bracelets, and other jewelry. Imitations are made by staining gray or white chalcedony. The carnelian was one of the first stones to be used as a decoration. People of ancient times believed the carnelian had special powers that would protect its wearer from weapons and evil spirits. Muhammad wore a ring that had a carnelian stone to seal his important papers. See also **Chalcedony; Gem.** Willis Hames

Carnival is a traditional form of outdoor amusement that consists of exhibits, games, rides, and shows. Most carnivals today are small and are held in towns and small cities, setting up their attractions in streets and parking lots. The term *carnival* also can refer to feasting and merrymaking just before Lent. The Mardi Gras in New Orleans is a famous American carnival of this type (see **Easter** (Carnivals).

A carnival is arranged around a main street called a *midway.* The area near the entrance is called the *front end* and includes the games and refreshment and souvenir stands. The rear area, called the *back end,* usually consists of the rides and shows. The most popular rides include the Ferris wheel and merry-go-round (see **Ferris wheel; Merry-go-round**). Side shows that displayed unusual exhibits and acts were once a main attraction of carnivals, but they have become rare.

Carnivals developed from traditional festivals in Europe dating back hundreds of years. The traveling carnival in America began in the late 1800's as a result of improved transportation and technology. The success of the 1893 World's Columbian Exposition in Chicago stimulated people to take special attractions to other cities. Today, there are about 500 carnivals that travel across the United States. But they are not as elaborate as earlier carnivals. Modern amusement parks include rides and other features of the traditional carnival. Don B. Wilmeth

See also **Brazil** (Recreation; picture).

Carnivore, *KAHR nuh vawr,* is any animal that eats chiefly meat. Most such animals prey on *herbivores* (plant-eating animals). Carnivores thus help regulate the number of herbivores and preserve the balance of nature (see **Balance of nature**). The term *carnivore* also refers to an *order* (group) of mammals. This article discusses such mammals, which include cats and dogs.

All mammals classified as carnivores have well-developed canine teeth. Most of them have one pair of blade-like shearing teeth on each side of the jaw. They also have a heavy skull and strong jaw muscles. Most carnivores hunt and kill their own prey. Some carnivores, such as bears and raccoons, also eat fruits and berries. Others, such as hyenas and jackals, are scavengers and usually eat animals that they find dead.

Carnivores live in all parts of the world except Antarctica and some islands. Most dwell on land, but some, such as otters and polar bears, spend much time in water. Most carnivores live alone or in family groups. Some, such as lions and wolves, live in larger groups. Carnivores range in size from the least weasel, which weighs about 2 ounces (57 grams), to the brown bear, which may weigh over 1,500 pounds (680 kilograms).

Most carnivores mate once a year. The number of young born at one time varies among the species. A weasel, for example, may have as many as eight young at a time, but some kinds of bears have only one.

Some carnivores, such as foxes and minks, are sources of valuable fur. People sometimes kill other carnivores, such as coyotes and lions, for sport or because the animals kill livestock. James L. Patton

Scientific classification. Carnivores make up the order Carnivora in the class Mammalia and the phylum Chordata. To learn where this order fits into the animal kingdom, see **Animal** (table: A classification of the animal kingdom).

See also **Mammal** (illustration: The teeth of mammals) and the separate articles in *World Book* on the carnivores mentioned in this article.

Carnivorous plant, *kahr NIHV uhr uhs,* is any plant that traps insects for food. Such plants are also called *insectivorous plants.* Carnivorous plants usually live in moist places where they get little or no nitrogen from the soil. The plants must obtain nitrogen from the insects that they trap. Carnivorous plants have special organs with which to capture insects, and glands that give off a digestive fluid to help them make use of their food. Some carnivorous plants have flowers colored or scented in such a way as to appear or smell at a distance like decaying meat. This attracts insects.

Various devices have been developed by carnivorous plants as traps. For example, pitcher plants have tube-shaped leaves that hold rain water in which the insects drown. Rosettes of leaves provided with sticky, hairlike parts are borne by the sundews. When an insect is caught by the hairlike parts, the leaf margins curl around it, trapping it inside. Venus's-flytrap has leaves that work like a steel trap. They close tightly about an insect, holding it inside. Norman L. Christensen, Jr.

Related articles in *World Book* include:

Bladderwort
Butterwort
Pitcher plant
Plant (Insect-eating plants; pictures)
Sundew
Venus's-flytrap

Carnotite, *KAHR nuh tyt,* is a yellow mineral. It is a source of uranium and vanadium. Its chemical formula is $K_2(UO_2)_2(VO_4)_2{\cdot}3H_2O$. Most carnotite occurs as a powder, but some is found as tiny, flat crystals. Geologists believe carnotite forms by the action of surface water on uraninite, a type of uranium oxide. For this reason, they call carnotite a *secondary* mineral. Carnotite often appears with similarly formed minerals. In the 1940's, important deposits of carnotite were discovered in the United States in the region where Colorado, Utah, New Mexico, and Arizona meet. Robert B. Cook

Carob, *KAR uhb,* is a dark evergreen tree that grows in countries along the Mediterranean Sea. Some carobs are found in warm regions of the United States, especially the Southwest. The carob has brown, leathery pods that produce a gum. The gum, also called *carob,* has a taste similar to chocolate. After being roasted and ground, it can be substituted for chocolate.

Carob provides a chocolate flavor in many dishes and in such products as beverages and candy bars. During the 1970's, large numbers of consumers and manufacturers began to use carob because of the increasingly high cost of chocolate. Some people prefer carob because they are allergic to chocolate.

The carob tree grows as tall as 50 feet (15 meters) and has small red flowers. Its pods range from 4 to 10 inches (10 to 25 centimeters) long. Daniel F. Austin

Scientific classification. Carob is in the pea family, Fabaceae or Leguminosae. Its scientific name is *Ceratonia siliqua.*

Carol. See **Christmas** (Christmas carols).

Carol I (1839-1914) ruled Romania from 1866 until his death on Oct. 10, 1914. Under his rule, Romania won its independence from the Ottoman Empire in 1878.

Carol was born on April 20, 1839, in Sigmaringen, east of Freiburg (now in southwestern Germany). He was a prince of the Hohenzollern family, a famous royal family that then ruled Prussia. In 1866, Romania's parliament chose him to rule their country as Prince Carol I.

The Ottoman Empire had controlled Romania since about 1500. Carol sent 38,000 soldiers to fight the empire in the Russo-Turkish War of 1877-1878. The Ottomans lost the war, and the Congress of Berlin granted Romania its independence. See **Berlin, Congress of.**

In 1881, Romania became a kingdom, and Carol was crowned king. He built a railroad network and helped develop industry and the Romanian army. Maria Bucur

Carol II (1893-1953) was king of Romania from 1930 to 1940. He tried to prevent Germany from dominating Romania before World War II (1939-1945), but failed.

Carol was born in Sinaia, Romania, on Oct. 15, 1893. In 1925, he gave up his right to the throne because of his love for a commoner, Magda Lupescu. In 1930, the government repealed the law that kept Carol from the throne, and he became Romania's king.

The Iron Guard, a *fascist* (extremely patriotic and militarist) movement, charged that Carol's rule was corrupt. Carol had its leader assassinated and, in 1938, made himself dictator. He outlawed the Iron Guard and all political parties. In 1940, Germany forced Carol to give parts of Romania to Bulgaria, Hungary, and the Soviet Union. The Iron Guard helped to force Carol from the throne. His son, Michael, succeeded him. Carol died on April 4, 1953. Maria Bucur

Carolina. See **North Carolina; South Carolina.**

Caroline Islands (pop. 137,000) are an archipelago of more than 930 islands in the Pacific Ocean. They lie just north of the equator, between the Marshall Islands and the Philippines (see **Pacific Islands** [map]). The island group extends more than 2,000 miles (3,200 kilometers), but the combined land area of the Carolines is only 463 square miles (1,199 square kilometers). There are five large islands or island groups: Kosrae Island, Pohnpei Island, the Truk Islands, the Yap Islands, and the Palau Islands. There are also 32 atolls and some isolated islets. The Carolines are part of an island group called *Micronesia,* which means *small islands. Copra* (dried coconut meat) is the chief export.

The Yap and Palau islands were among the first island groups to be settled in Micronesia. Archaeologists believe that people from Asia moved to those islands thousands of years ago. Kosrae, Pohnpei, and the Truk Islands were later settled by people from Asia.

In the 1500's, Spanish explorers became the first Europeans to reach the Caroline Islands. Spain formally claimed the islands in 1885 and sold them to Germany in 1899.

Japan captured the Caroline Islands during World War I (1914-1918). After the war ended, the League of Nations gave them to Japan as mandates. Japan fortified some of the islands. During World War II, United States forces captured some of the islands, including Peleliu. In 1947, two years after the war ended, the United Nations made the United States trustee of the Carolines as part of the Trust Territory of the Pacific Islands.

In 1978, the United States agreed to give the Carolines self-government. The agreement divided the islands into two groups—the Palau Islands and the Federated States of Micronesia. The federated states consist of the Truk Islands, the Yap Islands, and the islands of Kosrae and Pohnpei. In 1979, the federated states adopted their own constitution. In 1986, they gained independence in free association with the United States.

In October 1994, the Palau Islands, renamed Palau, also became an independent nation in free association with the United States. Under free association, the people of Palau and the Federated States of Micronesia control their internal and foreign affairs. But the United States must defend the islands in emergencies.

Robert C. Kiste

See also **Micronesia, Federated States of; Pacific Islands; Palau; Truk Islands; Yap Islands.**

Carolingian art was a style of art created in the late 700's and the 800's in France and western Germany. It is named for Charlemagne, who was king of the Franks from 768 to 814. Carolingian architects made major contributions to church design and monastic planning. Carolingian scribes created a new type of handwriting. In previous centuries, artists had emphasized abstract geometric patterns and fantastic animals. Carolingian painters, sculptors, and artisans reintroduced the human figure in a natural setting into the visual arts.

Carolingian architects claimed they were copying early Christian buildings, but they changed their models to suit their needs. These architects followed the plan of the early Christian church called the *basilica,* but they added chapels, elaborate crypts, and high towers. They also invented a *westwork,* an entrance that included a porch, chapels, two towers enclosing stairways, and, in an imperial church, a throne room. Carolingian abbots developed a monastic plan in which covered walks joined the church, the library, and the living quarters.

Carolingian scribes developed a beautiful, legible script, which they used in copying the Bible and other books. Painters added illustrations, such as narrative scenes and a portrait of the ruler. Marilyn Stokstad

See also **Charlemagne; Architecture** (Carolingian).

Carolingian Empire. See **Middle Ages** (The Carolingian Empire).

Carotene. See **Vitamin** (Vitamin A).

Carp is the name of several large, hardy fish native to rivers and other inland waters of Europe and Asia. The *common carp,* also called *German Carp,* was introduced into the United States from Germany in the late 1870's. Since then, it has become the dominant fish in many bodies of water in the United States. The word *carp* also refers to a family of about 2,000 species of fish. In addition to the species known as carp, this family includes barbs, danios, goldfish, and minnows.

Carp range in color from olive to yellow-green on the back, with sides that are lighter than the back. The fins are gray-green, brown, or sometimes reddish. Most common carp measure from about 12 to 30 inches (30 to 76 centimeters) in length and weigh from 2 to 10 pounds (0.9 to 4.5 kilograms). Some grow to 40 inches (102 centimeters) and weigh up to 60 pounds (27 kilograms). Other species are generally smaller.

Carp live in all types of freshwater environments. They prefer lakes or slow-moving streams and rivers with much vegetation and can thrive in polluted water.

Tempera painting (about 870) by an unknown French artist; Abbey of S. Paolo fuori le Mura, Rome (Istituto Poligrafico e Zecca Dello Stato)

Carolingian art included beautifully painted book illustrations. The painting above portrays episodes from the life of Saint Paul and is from the Bible of Charles I of France.

WORLD BOOK illustration by John F. Eggert

The grass carp is a hardy fish that eats water plants.

They tend to avoid clear, fast-flowing streams and rivers.

Carp are *omnivores*—that is, they eat both animals and plants. They feed mainly by sucking and rooting insects and plants off the bottom of the water. A female carp can produce 35,000 to 2,000,000 eggs each year. Carp grow rapidly, reaching 8 inches (20 centimeters) in the first year. They live 15 to 18 years. Carp are popular food fish in Europe and Asia.

In the United States, many fishery managers and fishing enthusiasts consider common carp a nuisance. When carp root food from the water bottom, they stir silt and debris and muddy the water. This hinders the ability of other species of fish to feed and reproduce. Common carp also eat the eggs of other fish and compete with the fish for food and space. Because of these problems, fish-removal programs have been conducted in many bodies of water to reduce the numbers of common carp. Such programs include selective netting, commercial fishing, and even killing with poisons.

In 1963, the *grass carp* was brought to the United States from Asia to help control the overgrowth of certain water plants. But the species has grown so successfully that scientists are concerned about its effect on other freshwater fish. Robert D. Hoyt

Scientific classification. Carp belong to the family Cyprinidae. The scientific name for the common carp is *Cyprinus carpio.*

Carpal tunnel syndrome is a common disorder that causes pain and interferes with the use of the hand. Carpel tunnel syndrome is caused by pressure on the *median nerve* as the nerve passes through a canal formed by the bones and ligaments in the wrist. This canal is known as the *carpal tunnel.* A variety of conditions can cause the carpal tunnel to narrow and put pressure on the median nerve. These include injuries, such as wrist fractures; arthritis complicated by swelling of the tendons in the carpal tunnel; pregnancy, which may cause the *synovium* (membrane) around the tendons to thicken; and glandular abnormalities, such as diabetes and thyroid disorders. Repetitive wrist motions also may cause the disorder.

Symptoms of carpal tunnel syndrome include pain and numbness in the thumb and in the index, middle, and ring fingers. Many people are awakened at night with these symptoms. Some sufferers experience weakness of certain hand muscles and may drop objects. Symptoms often occur with the wrist in certain posi-

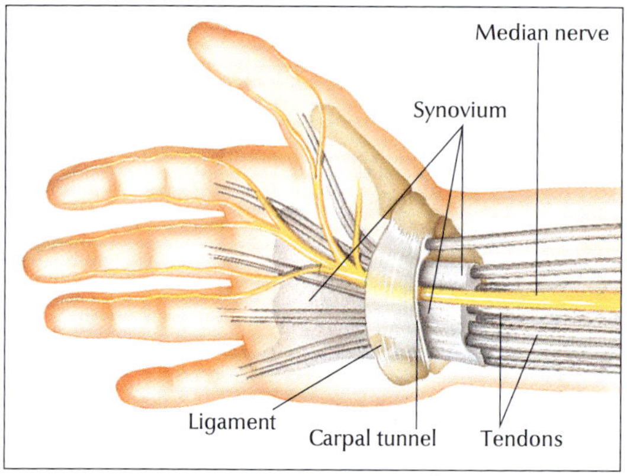

WORLD BOOK illustration by Charles Wellek

Carpal tunnel syndrome is caused by pressure on the median nerve as it passes through the *carpal tunnel,* a canal formed by bones and ligaments in the wrist. Various conditions, including thickening of the *synovium* (membrane) around the tendons, can cause the tunnel to narrow and put pressure on the nerve.

tions, such as while driving an automobile or while holding a book for reading.

Doctors treat carpal tunnel syndrome by attempting to improve the underlying condition. In many cases, doctors apply a splint to the wrist and prescribe anti-inflammatory medications. In some cases, surgery to enlarge the carpal tunnel is performed to relieve symptoms and to prevent permanent damage to the median nerve. Gordon H. Derman

Carpathian Mountains, *kahr PAY thee uhn,* are part of the great mountain system of central Europe. The Carpathians extend for about 900 miles (1,400 kilometers) along the Slovakia-Poland border and into Ukraine and Romania. Most of them lie in Slovakia and Romania. For location, see **Europe** (physical map). The highest elevation is Gerlachovský Štít (8,711 feet, or 2,655 meters) in Slovakia's Tatra Mountains.

The Carpathians are an extension of the mountain range that includes the Alps. But the Carpathian peaks are generally lower than the Alps and have fewer lakes, glaciers, and waterfalls. The Carpathians contain several mineral resources, including deposits of coal, natural gas, oil, and salt. Large quantities of timber come from the fir, oak, and beech forests that cover the lower slopes of the mountains. Wolves, lynx, and bears roam through these forests. Many fertile farms lie in the valleys of the Carpathian Mountains, especially in the region of Transylvania in Romania. People cross the mountains by using any of the narrow passes. Leslie Dienes

See also **Galicia.**

Carpenter, M. Scott (1925-), one of the first United States astronauts, was the second American to circle the earth in a spacecraft. John Glenn was the first. During Carpenter's three-orbit flight in the *Aurora 7* spacecraft on May 24, 1962, he conducted a number of experiments, made observations on the atmosphere, and photographed the earth. His trip ended dramatically when his spacecraft landed more than 200 miles (320 kilometers) beyond the intended landing area. He was out of contact with the recovery forces for almost an hour before a search plane spotted him.

Malcolm Scott Carpenter was born in Boulder, Colorado. He served in the Navy during World War II (1939-1945) and then studied aeronautical engineering at the University of Colorado. Carpenter served as a Navy pilot during the Korean War (1950-1953) and became a test pilot in 1954. In 1959, the National Aeronautics and Space Administration (NASA) selected him to be an astronaut in the Mercury program. In 1965, Carpenter took a leave of absence from NASA to be an aquanaut in the Navy's Man-in-the-Sea program. In 1966, he became branch chief for advanced programs for NASA. He resigned from NASA in 1967 to do deep-sea research for the Navy. Leg injuries ended his deep-diving career in 1969. He retired from the Navy that year. James R. Hansen

See also **Astronaut; Space exploration.**

Carpenters and Joiners of America, United Brotherhood of, is one of the unions of the American Federation of Labor and Congress of Industrial Organizations. Its membership includes workers in wood, construction, and other industries that require carpentry or similar skills. The brotherhood has *locals* (branches) in the United States, Canada, and Puerto Rico.

The union was organized in Chicago in 1881, and it combined with the Amalgamated Wood Workers of America in 1912. Workers in logging and lumber camps became part of the brotherhood in 1935. Some logging and lumber workers' locals broke away from the brotherhood in 1937 and formed the International Woodworkers of America. In 1979, the Wood, Wire, and Metal Lathers' International Union joined the brotherhood.

The brotherhood holds a convention every five years. It has headquarters at 101 Constitution Ave. NW, Washington, DC 20001. For total membership, see **Labor movement** (table). Critically reviewed by the United Brotherhood of Carpenters and Joiners of America

Carpentry is the building and repairing of structures. It involves all types of work done by carpenters, including the construction of buildings and parts of buildings. Carpentry also includes the design and assembly of cabinets, furniture, and other items. Most carpenters work chiefly with wood, but some also work with such materials as metals and plastics.

Carpenters must have a thorough knowledge of construction materials and methods. This knowledge includes the ability to understand technical literature and follow the instructions of a blueprint or scale drawing. Carpenters also must know how to use various hand tools, including chisels, hammers, and planes, and such power tools as drills and power saws. Some carpenters use *pneumatic tools,* which operate by compressed air. These tools include air drills and pneumatic nailers.

There are two types of carpentry, *rough carpentry* and *finish carpentry.* Rough carpenters assemble the frameworks of buildings and then place coverings called *sheathing* and *siding* on the structures. They also apply shingles and do other exterior work. After the rough carpentry has been completed, finish carpenters do various types of interior work. Their jobs include hanging doors and windows, applying wood trim, installing paneling, and laying floors.

Some finish carpenters are specialists. For example, *cabinetmakers* design, shape, and assemble cabinets, furniture, and other items. Many cabinetmakers are employed by furniture manufacturers, and many work for companies that produce *millwork,* such as doors, windows, and moldings. Specialists called *joiners* cut, fit, and join wood to make stairs, tabletops, and other items. Joiners do especially precise, complicated work.

Some carpenters learn their trade through on-the-job training, and others attend a technical or vocational school. Still others receive instruction in a four-year apprenticeship program. Alva H. Jared

See also **House** (Building a house); **Woodworking.**

Carpet. See **Rugs and carpets.**

Carpet beetle is a common insect pest. Its *larvae* (young) live on carpets made of natural fibers. Carpet beetles also enter closets and eat woolens, feathers, and furs. In spring, adult beetles may be found around infested houses. They are brownish-black or marked with red or yellowish-white spots. Protective measures against carpet beetles include good housekeeping and spraying with various insecticides.

David J. Shetlar

Scientific classification. The carpet beetle belongs to the order Coleoptera. It is a member of the skin beetle family, Dermestidae. The scientific name for the carpet beetle is *Anthrenus scrophulariae.*

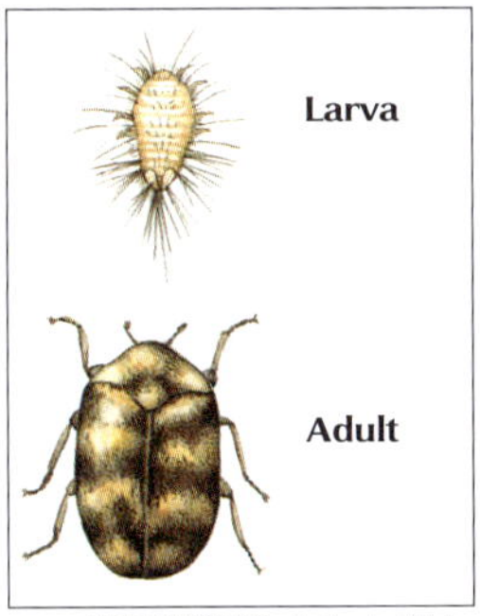

WORLD BOOK illustration by Shirley Hooper, Oxford Illustrators Limited

Carpet beetle

See also **Beetle; Larva.**

Carpetbaggers was a term of scorn and hostility used by white Southerners to describe Northerners active in the Republican Party in the South after the Civil War. Northern Republicans were influential in the South following the war, during the period known as Reconstruction (1865-1877). During Reconstruction, the Republican Party, which was based in the North, extended its organization to the South. The party gained control of Southern state governments and granted civil rights to blacks, including the right to vote. It also worked to establish public schools and to increase opportunities for ordinary Southern whites.

The traditional leaders of the South feared that these policies would further reduce their power and change their way of life. These leaders charged that the Northerners were people of little ability and lowly origins whose personal possessions were so small that each had carried them south in a single carpetbag. Carpetbags, suitcases made of carpet material, were widely used at the time.

Southern Democrats used the term *carpetbagger* as part of a propaganda campaign to convince other Southerners that the Republican Party was non-Southern and undesirable. The Democrats also excluded the Republicans from social affairs and used violence against them. They even had some assassinated. By the early 1870's, this treatment made it difficult for most Northerners to remain in Southern politics or even to remain in the South.

Some of the people known as carpetbaggers were unprincipled and corrupt. However, most were not, and many came to the South for honorable reasons. Some were Union soldiers who after the war decided to stay

Culver

The carpetbaggers' trek to the South after the Civil War was satirized in this caricature by the famed cartoonist Thomas Nast.

in the South to begin a new life as farmers or as operators of small businesses. Others worked in the South for the Freedmen's Bureau, a federal agency that aided former slaves. Another group consisted of people experienced in Northern politics who felt that they could be useful and influential in the Republican Party in the South.

The people known as carpetbaggers played an important role in the Republican Party as well as in the progressive Southern state governments the party controlled during Reconstruction. Many of these people served as governors, state legislators, or members of Congress. Today, the term *carpetbagger* is still used to describe outsiders who try to exert influence where they are not wanted. Michael Perman

See also **Reconstruction.**

Carr, Emily (1871-1945), was a noted Canadian painter and writer. She painted for most of her life and began her writing career only a few years before her death in 1945.

Carr was born on Dec. 13, 1871, in Victoria, British Columbia. In 1904, she made the first of many visits to Indian villages in British Columbia. Most of Carr's early paintings portray the Indian culture that she encountered there. These works received little favorable attention, and so Carr gave up painting almost completely in 1913.

In 1927, an exhibit of Carr's paintings at the National Gallery in Ottawa, Ontario, brought her to the attention of the Group of Seven. The members of this group were nationally known Canadian landscape painters. They and their works inspired Carr to resume painting and encouraged her interest in landscapes. Most of her later paintings reflect her desire to capture the spirit of the vast forests of Canada's west coast. Carr's first book, *Klee Wyck* (1941), is a collection of stories about her experiences among the Indians. She also wrote six other books. Rosemary Sullivan

Carrageen. See **Irish moss.**

Carranza, *kahr RAHN sah* or *kuh RAN zuh,* **Venustiano,** *VAY noos TYAH noh* (1859-1920), became Mexico's "First Chief" in 1914, after leading a revolt against the government of Victoriano Huerta. Carranza became president of Mexico in 1915. As the nation's leader, Carranza called a congress to prepare Mexico's present constitution, which was adopted in 1917. In 1920, Carranza was killed during a revolt led by General Álvaro Obregón.

Carranza was born in Cuatrociénegas, in the Mexican state of Coahuila. Before he became president, he served in the Mexican Senate and as governor of Coahuila. He supported rebel leader Francisco Madero in the Mexican Revolution, which began in 1910.

W. Dirk Raat

See also **Mexico** (The Constitution of 1917).

Carriage is a horse-drawn vehicle used for the transportation of people. It developed in the early 1700's from the slow, heavy wagons and coaches used for passenger travel. Better roads permitted the use of the more graceful and speedy carriage.

The carriage was characterized by its light weight, flexibility, and elegant design. The running gear was usually made of strong, springy wood such as oak, ash, or hickory. Wrought iron brackets and fittings braced the slender wooden parts of the carriage. Early wheels were usually made of hickory and fitted with iron tires, but solid rubber tires came into use after 1875.

The first carriages were imported into America from England and France. Carriages were not manufactured in America until about 1740, but by 1880 the United States produced more horse-drawn vehicles than any other country in the world. Popular carriages built in America included the *buckboard,* the *buggy,* the *chaise,* and the *rockaway.* People of wealth and social standing used fashionable carriages called *landaus* and *victorias.*

Use of the carriage reached a peak in 1905 when about 8,000 builders produced more than 930,000 vehicles. The introduction of the automobile at this time brought the end of the carriage. By World War I, it was no longer an important private carrier.

John H. White, Jr.

See also **Transportation** (pictures).

Carrier pigeon is a bird originally bred from pigeons used to carry messages from one place to another. Through the years, however, the carrier pigeon has lost most of its homing instinct. Today, it is bred as a show bird. The carrier pigeon may be blue, black, white, grayish-brown, or yellow. It is larger than other types of pigeons, and it carries itself stiffly erect. The bird has strong wings and feet. It has large, fleshy growths around its big yellow eyes and on its bill. The growths may cover the nose of an old bird. See also **Homing pigeon; Pigeon.** Edward H. Burtt, Jr.

WORLD BOOK illustration by Colin Newman, Bernard Thornton Artists

Carrier pigeon

Scientific classification. The carrier pigeon is in the pigeon and dove family, Columbidae. Its scientific name is *Columba livia.*

Carroll was the family name of three early American leaders, two brothers and their cousin.

Daniel Carroll (1730-1796) signed both the Articles of Confederation and the United States Constitution. He favored a strong central government and opposed election of the president by Congress. He first favored direct election by the people, but later urged the Electoral College system. He served in the first Maryland state Senate in 1777, and was president of the Senate in 1783. In 1789, he was elected to the first House of Representatives under the U.S. Constitution. From 1791 to 1795, he was a commissioner of the District of Columbia. He was born in Prince George's County, Maryland. He is usually called "Daniel Carroll of Rock Creek," to distinguish him from relatives of the same name.

John Carroll (1735-1815), brother of Daniel, became the first Roman Catholic bishop in the United States. American priests elected him bishop in 1789, and he took office in 1790. Bishop Carroll founded Georgetown University in 1789 and helped establish other Catholic colleges. Under his leadership, the Basilica of the Assumption, the first major Catholic cathedral in the United States, was built in Baltimore. In 1808, he was elevated to archbishop. He was born in Upper Marlboro, Maryland, and was ordained in 1769.

Charles Carroll (1737-1832) was the last surviving signer of the Declaration of Independence. He always signed his name "Charles Carroll of Carrollton" to distinguish himself from several others who had the same name. Carroll went to Canada in 1776 with his cousin John Carroll, Samuel Chase, and Benjamin Franklin to ask Canadians to help America in the Revolutionary War. Their mission failed.

Carroll was elected to Maryland's first state Senate in 1777. He served there until 1801. From 1776 to 1778, he was a member of the Continental Congress, where he signed the Declaration of Independence. He was a U.S. senator from Maryland between 1789 and 1792. Carroll retired from politics in 1801, and he devoted the rest of his life to private affairs. A statue of Carroll represents Maryland in the U.S. Capitol in Washington, D.C. Carroll was born in Annapolis, Maryland. Joan R. Gundersen

Carroll, Lewis, was the pen name of Charles Lutwidge Dodgson (1832-1898), an English author. Carroll wrote two of the most famous books in English literature—*Alice's Adventures in Wonderland* and its continuation, *Through the Looking-Glass and What Alice Found There.* People throughout the world read these books. *Alice in Wonderland,* as the first book is usually called, has been translated into more than 30 languages, including Arabic and Chinese.

Carroll wrote both books to give pleasure to children. But adults also enjoy the humor, fantastic characters, and adventures in the stories. Scholars study the books to find meanings in what seems to be nonsense.

Brown Brothers
Lewis Carroll

Life. Carroll was born in Daresbury, in northwest England. He graduated from Christ Church College, Oxford University, in 1854. Carroll began teaching mathematics at Christ Church in 1855 and spent most of his life at the school. He became a *deacon* (officer) in the Church of England in 1861.

The *Alice* books. Carroll enjoyed being with children. He created the character of Alice to amuse a little girl named Alice Liddell, the daughter of the dean of Christ Church. On July 4, 1862, Carroll went rowing on the River Isis with Alice Liddell and two of her sisters. He began to tell the story of Alice that day. Later, he wrote the story down, and called it "Alice's Adventures Underground." Carroll en-

The British Library (Copyright by University Microfilms, Inc., 1964)
Alice's Adventures in Wonderland was written by Lewis Carroll in the early 1860's. The author decorated his original text with pictures illustrating the story. In this picture, Carroll showed Alice arguing with the bad-tempered Queen of Hearts.

larged the story into its present book-length version, which was published in 1865.

Alice in Wonderland tells about the adventures of a little girl in a make-believe world under the ground. Alice lands in this "wonderland" after she falls down a hole while following a rabbit. She meets many strange characters, including the Cheshire Cat, the Mad Hatter, the Queen of Hearts, and the Mock Turtle. *Alice in Wonderland* became so well known that the names of some of its characters are part of everyday speech. For example, we hear about people who "grin like a Cheshire Cat" or who are as "mad as a March Hare."

Through the Looking-Glass (1871) introduced new characters, including the frightening Jabberwock dragon, the silly twins Tweedledum and Tweedledee, and the Walrus and the Carpenter. Sir John Tenniel illustrated both books. His pictures became nearly as famous as the stories. See **Tenniel, Sir John.**

Other works. Carroll also wrote *Sylvie and Bruno,* a fairy tale in verse and prose (two parts, 1889 and 1893). The poem "The Hunting of the Snark" (1876) tells the story of the Banker, Baker, Beaver, Bellman, and other amusing characters in search of a Snark, an animal that does not exist. Carroll wrote many works on mathematics under his real name. They include "Notes on the First Two Books of Euclid" (1860) and *Curiosa Mathematica* (two parts, 1888 and 1894). Carroll also was a fine photographer. Carol Tecla Christ

See also **Literature for children** (picture: *Through the Looking-Glass*).

Additional resources

Carpenter, Angelica S. *Lewis Carroll.* Lerner, 2003.
Carroll, Lewis. *The Annotated Alice.* Ed. by Martin Gardner. Norton, 1999.
Cohen, Morton N. *Lewis Carroll.* 1995. Reprint. Vintage Bks., 1996.

Carrot is a plant with an orange root that is eaten as a vegetable. Carrots contain vitamin B_1, and small amounts of vitamins B_2 and C. Carrots also contain *carotene,* a substance that is used by the human body to produce vitamin A. In addition, carrots are rich in sugar and potassium.

People eat raw carrots alone or in salads. They also eat boiled carrots, sometimes prepared with soups and stews. In some parts of the world, carrots have been roasted, ground, and used as a substitute for coffee. The plant's thick, lacy leaves and long stems are also edible and may be chopped up and sprinkled on meats.

Three types of carrots are grown commercially: (1) fresh market carrots, such as the Imperator and Nantes varieties; (2) processing or dicing carrots, such as the Danvers and Chantaney varieties; and (3) baby carrots. They differ in size and use. Imperator carrots measure about 9 inches (23 centimeters) long. They are sold fresh in grocery stores. Dicing carrots are wider than Imperators and about 7 to 8 inches (18 to 20 centimeters) long. They are cut up and sold frozen or canned. Baby carrots

WORLD BOOK illustration by Kate Lloyd-Jones, Linden Artists Ltd.
The carrot is a popular, nutritious vegetable grown throughout the world. The stems and fernlike leaves are also edible.

grow about 3 inches (8 centimeters) long and are sold as a novelty or gourmet vegetable.

Carrots grow from tiny seeds that are planted in rows about ½ inch (1.3 centimeters) deep. The rows of seeds are spaced from 1 foot (30 centimeters) to more than 2 feet (60 centimeters) apart, depending on the type of carrot. Carrots grow best in deep, rich soils that contain sand or muck. A crop takes about 100 days to grow. Large crops are usually harvested mechanically, several rows at a time. Carrots are grown in the summer in the northern United States and southern Canada. They can be grown in winter in Florida and southern California.

Carrots are native to the Mediterranean region. The ancient Greeks and Romans grew carrots that had thin, tough roots. They used the plants as a medicine but not as a food. Carrots resembling modern types were later developed in France and were common in Europe by the 1200's. Today, leading carrot-producing countries include China, Japan, Poland, the United Kingdom, and the United States. Albert Liptay

Scientific classification. Carrots belong to the parsley family, Apiaceae or Umbelliferae. Their scientific name is *Daucus carota,* variety *sativus.*

See also **Vitamin** (Vitamin A); **Wild carrot.**

Carrousel. See **Merry-go-round.**

Carson, Johnny (1925-2005), a popular American entertainer, became famous as host of "The Tonight Show" on television. He appeared as a guest host on "The Tonight Show" in 1958 and was the regular host from 1962 to 1992. Carson became noted for his quick sense of humor and natural performing style.

Carson was born on Oct. 23, 1925, in Corning, Iowa, and grew up in Norfolk, Nebraska. He began his career in Lincoln, Nebraska, as a radio announcer in the late 1940's. During the early 1950's, Carson worked as a writer and performer in radio and television in Los Angeles. In 1955, he starred in "The Johnny Carson Show," a weekly TV program. From 1957 to 1962, Carson hosted a daytime game show originally called "Do You Trust Your Wife?" but soon renamed "Who Do You Trust?" Carson died on Jan. 23, 2005. Joe Robinowitz

Carson, Kit (1809-1868), was a famous American frontiersman. He became known as a skillful and daring hunter, guide, and soldier.

Early life. Carson, whose real first name was Christopher, was born in Madison County, Kentucky, on Dec. 24, 1809. His family moved to Boon's Lick, Missouri, near Arrow Rock, when he was 1 year old. At the age of 14 or 15, Kit was sent to work for a saddlemaker. He hated the job and ran away in 1826 to join a group of traders headed for Santa Fe, now in New Mexico. From 1829 to 1841, Carson worked in the fur trade. He trapped beavers in Arizona, California, Idaho, Wyoming, and the Rocky Mountains and took part in many fights with Indians.

Culver

Kit Carson

Rise to prominence. John C. Frémont, who became a famous government explorer, hired Carson in 1842 to guide his party along the Oregon Trail to South Pass in the Rockies in Wyoming. They passed safely through the rugged mountains. Frémont praised Carson in his official reports, which helped make Carson well known. In 1843 and 1844, Carson helped guide Frémont's second expedition, which included a survey of Great Salt Lake in Utah and part of the Oregon Trail. In 1845, Carson guided the explorer's third expedition from Colorado to California and north into Oregon.

The Mexican War broke out in 1846, and Frémont and his group returned to California. They joined the American settlers there in a revolt against the Mexicans who controlled the region. The Americans defeated the Mexicans, and Frémont sent Carson to Washington, D.C., with messages, including news of the victory. But at Socorro, New Mexico, General Stephen W. Kearny ordered Carson to guide him to California. Kearny's troops were attacked by Mexicans at San Pasqual, California, near Escondido. Carson and two others slipped through the enemy lines to seek help from American forces in San Diego. They had to walk or crawl for about 30 miles (48 kilometers), but Kearny's troops were rescued.

Military career. After the American Civil War began in 1861, Carson became colonel of the New Mexico Volunteer Regiment. In 1862, he fought Confederate forces in a battle at Valverde, New Mexico, near Socorro. Carson later led a campaign against the Apache Indians to force them to live on a reservation. In the fall of 1862, Carson gathered about 400 Apache and placed them on a reservation near Fort Sumner, New Mexico.

Carson then led a campaign against the Navajo Indians. By destroying their crops and animals, he forced about 8,000 Navajo to accept reservation life (see **Navajo Indians**). In November 1864, Carson fought the Kiowas, Comanches, and other Plains Indians at Adobe Walls, an abandoned trading post in Texas. His force of about 400 men retreated after being attacked by 1,500 to 3,000 Indians. Carson was made a brigadier general in 1865 and took command of Fort Garland in Colorado the following year. He resigned from the Army in 1867 because of illness and died on May 23, 1868. Howard R. Lamar

See also **Frémont, John C.; Kearny, Stephen W.**

Additional resources

Boraas, Tracey. *Kit Carson.* Bridgestone, 2003. Younger readers.
Dunlay, Thomas W. *Kit Carson and the Indians.* Bison Bks., 2000.
Roberts, David. *A Newer World: Kit Carson, John C. Frémont, and the Claiming of the American West.* Touchstone, 2001.

Carson, Rachel (1907-1964), was an American marine biologist and science writer. She wrote several books that reflect her lifelong interest in the life of the seas and the seashores.

In her writings, Carson stressed the interrelation of all living things and the dependence of human welfare on natural processes. *The Sea Around Us* (1951) describes the biology, chemistry, geography, and history of the sea. *Silent Spring* (1962) called public attention to the wasteful and destructive use of pesticides.

Carson warned that pesticides poison the food supply of animals and kill many birds and fish. She pointed out that pesticides could also contaminate human food supplies. Her arguments helped lead to restrictions on the use of pesticides in many parts of the world.

Rachel Louise Carson was born in Springdale, Pennsylvania, on May 27, 1907. She graduated from the Penn-

sylvania College for Women in 1929 and received a master's degree from Johns Hopkins University in 1932. She worked for the United States Fish and Wildlife Service for most of her adult life. Carson died on April 14, 1964.
Sheldon M. Novick

Carson City (pop. 52,457) is the capital of Nevada and a tourist center. It lies at the eastern base of the Sierra Nevada, near the Nevada-California border. For the location of Carson City, see **Nevada** (political map).

The Carson City area has many places of historical interest. About 30 houses in the city date from the mining days of the 1800's. The Nevada State Museum building in Carson City once housed a United States mint that coined gold and silver from 1870 to 1893.

Land speculator Abraham Curry founded Carson City in 1858. He named it after the famous frontier scout Kit Carson. In 1859, prospectors discovered a rich deposit of silver ore, the Comstock Lode, near Carson City (see **Comstock Lode**). The town grew quickly as a mining supply center. Carson City became the capital of the Nevada Territory in 1861 and the state capital in 1864.

Carson City served as the seat of Ormsby County until 1969, when the city and county merged and became the independent city of Carson City. It is now considered both a city and a county. A board of supervisors and a city manager head the government.

During the late 1900's, Carson City grew rapidly. Its population rose from 32,022 in 1980 to about 40,500 in 1990, an increase of 26 percent. By 2000, Carson City had 52,457 people, a 30 percent increase. Kurtis R. Hildebrand

See also **Nevada** (picture: The State Capitol).

Cartagena, *KAHR tah HAY nah* (pop. 184,686), stands on a beautiful bay of the Mediterranean Sea in southeastern Spain. For Cartagena's location, see **Spain** (political map). The city has a large harbor and is the site of one of Spain's most important naval bases. It exports agricultural products and lead and iron ore. Factories there produce cordage, canvas, and chemicals.

The mines near Cartagena attracted the Carthaginians, who founded the city about 225 B.C. The city's people were among the first to rise against Napoleon after he conquered Spain in 1808. Cartagena served as headquarters of the Republican fleet during the Spanish Civil War (1936-1939). Stanley G. Payne

Cartel, *kahr TEHL* or *KAHR tuhl,* is an association formed among producers in a particular industry to control the market for their product. Cartels raise the selling price of their product by restricting the available supply. A cartel may consist of privately owned companies in one country or several countries. A cartel also may be formed among governments.

To succeed, a cartel should have relatively few members. However, the cartel must include all or most producers in the industry and so have a monopoly or near monopoly on the product. The product must have no close substitutes, and new supplies must be scarce.

A cartel sets a relatively high selling price for its product. To obtain this price, the cartel limits the output of each member. It also assigns each member a share of the market. The cartel will likely fail if too many members cheat on these arrangements.

Until the late 1930's, international cartels existed among firms in such industries as drugs and steel. Since 1960, some cartels have been formed among governments of countries that produce oil or other natural resource products. The best known of these is the Organization of the Petroleum Exporting Countries (OPEC).

Cartels within the United States are illegal. But in certain circumstances, American firms may join international cartels to sell export goods. Robert B. Carson

See also **Monopoly and competition**.

Carter, Don (1926-), an American, was voted the greatest bowler of all time in 1970 in a poll of bowling writers. He was the first to achieve a *grand slam* by winning the four major bowling titles of his day. They were the World Invitational, All-Star, Professional Bowlers Association (PBA) National, and American Bowling Conference (ABC) Masters championships. Carter helped make bowling a popular television sport in the 1950's.

Donald James Carter was born on July 29, 1926, in St. Louis, Missouri. He won the World Invitational in 1957, 1959, 1960, 1961, and 1962. He also won the Bowling Proprietor's Association of America All-Star Championship (now the United States Open) in 1953, 1954, 1957, and 1958; the PBA National in 1960; and the ABC Masters in 1961. He was elected to the ABC Hall of Fame in 1970 and the PBA Hall of Fame in 1975. He was a founding member and first president of the PBA. Nelson Burton, Jr.

Carter, Elliott (1908-), is one of the leading American composers of the 1900's. His music is extremely intricate, and its performance requires highly skillful musicianship. Carter is especially noted for his chamber music. He won two Pulitzer Prizes for his String Quartets No. 2 (1959) and No. 3 (1973), which take novel approaches to the traditional quartet. For example, in String Quartet No. 3, Carter divides the group into two duos (violin I and viola, violin II and cello). Original in form and detail, Carter's music also shows the influence of the modern composers Charles Ives of the United States, Arnold Schoenberg of Austria, and Igor Stravinsky of Russia.

Carter's first important compositions were the ballet suite *Pocahontas* (1939) and the choral work *The Defense of Corinth* (1941). In his works since the late 1940's, he has used complicated rhythmic patterns, which he calls *metrical modulations.* Carter has also composed several major works for orchestra. They include *Variations for Orchestra* (1955), *Double Concerto for Piano with Harpsichord and Two Chamber Orchestras* (1961), *Piano Concerto* (1967), *Concerto for Orchestra* (1970), and *A Symphony of Three Orchestras* (1976). Elliott Cook Carter, Jr., was born Dec. 11, 1908, in New York City. Stephen Jaffe

Carter, Howard (1874-1939), was an English archaeologist who excavated and documented ancient Egyptian temples and tombs. His most famous discovery was the tomb of king Tutankhamun in 1922 (see **Tutankhamun**).

In 1899, after working in Egypt for many years, Carter became chief inspector of archaeological sites for the Egyptian government. In 1905, he returned to private work as an artist and excavator. From 1917 to 1922, Carter and his patron Lord Carnarvon searched the Valley of the Kings for the tomb of Tutankhamun.

Carter was born May 9, 1874, in Swaffham, England. Much of his early training came from the famous archaeologist Sir Flinders Petrie. Carter first went to Egypt in 1890 as a member of an expedition headed by Petrie. His most famous publication was the three-volume *The Tomb of Tut·ankh·amen* (1923-1933). Carter died on March 2, 1939. Emily Teeter

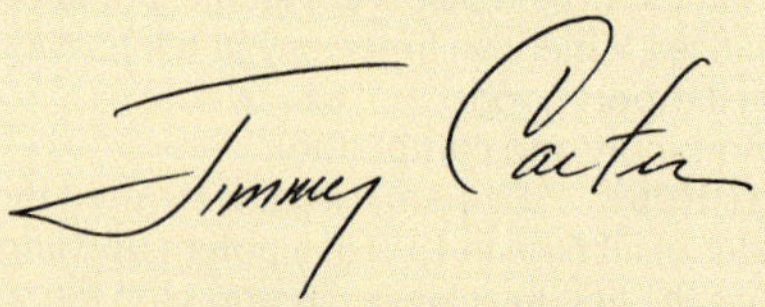

39th president of the United States 1977-1981

Ford
38th president
1974-1977
Republican

Carter
39th president
1977-1981
Democrat

Reagan
40th president
1981-1989
Republican

Bill Fitz-Patrick, The White House

Walter F. Mondale
Vice president
1977-1981

Carter, Jimmy (1924-), was elected president of the United States in 1976, climaxing a remarkable rise to national fame. Carter had been governor of Georgia from 1971 to 1975 and was little known elsewhere at the beginning of 1976. But then he won 18 primary elections and became the Democratic candidate for president. Carter defeated President Gerald R. Ford in the 1976 election. In 1980, Carter was defeated in his bid for a second term by former Governor Ronald Reagan of California, his Republican opponent.

Before Carter won election as governor, he served in the Georgia Senate. He had managed his family peanut warehouse business and farm before entering politics. Carter also had been an officer in the United States Navy. He was the first graduate of the U.S. Naval Academy to become chief executive.

During Carter's presidency, the United States faced problems both at home and abroad. At home, the economy suffered from unemployment and severe inflation. Abroad, relations between the United States and the Soviet Union plunged to their lowest point in several years following a Soviet invasion of Afghanistan. In Iran, a group of Americans were held hostage by revolutionaries who had taken over the U.S. Embassy in Tehran. The revolutionaries had seized the hostages to protest U.S. support for the deposed shah of Iran. Despite these problems, Carter won praise for some achievements in foreign affairs. He helped establish diplomatic relations between the United States and China. He also helped bring about a peace treaty between Egypt and Israel.

After leaving the presidency, Carter continued working to find peaceful solutions to international conflicts. He received the Nobel Peace Prize in 2002.

A reserved and soft-spoken person, Carter was known to his friends as a man of great warmth and charm. His political aides said he demanded hard work and set high standards but pushed himself the hardest.

Hugh S. Sidey, the contributor of this article, is Washington Contributing Editor of Time *magazine.*

Early life

Boyhood. James Earl Carter, Jr., was born on Oct. 1, 1924, in Plains, Georgia. Throughout his life, he has been known by the nickname Jimmy. He had two sisters, Gloria (1926-1990) and Ruth (1929-1983), and a brother, William Alton III (1937-1988), usually called Billy.

Carter's father, a farmer and businessman, ran a farm products store on the family farm in the rural community of Archery, a few miles west of Plains. Carter's mother, Lillian Gordy Carter, was a registered nurse.

The Carters lived in Plains when Jimmy was born. Four years later, they moved to the farm in Archery. Jimmy grew up there and helped with the farm chores during his boyhood. He also developed an early interest in business. When the sandy-haired boy was about 5 years old, he began to sell boiled peanuts on the streets of Plains. He earned about $1 a day on weekdays and about $5 on Saturdays. At the age of 9, Jimmy bought five huge bales of cotton for 5 cents a pound. He stored the cotton and sold it a few years later, when the price had more than tripled.

Education. Jimmy went to public school in Plains. He shared his mother's love of reading and received good grades. A schoolmate later remembered that Jimmy "was always the smartest in the class." The boy's favorite subjects included history, literature, and music. As a teen-ager, he played on the high school basketball team.

In 1941, following graduation from high school, Car-

© Romano Cagnoni, Black Star; Simonet, Gamma/Liaison

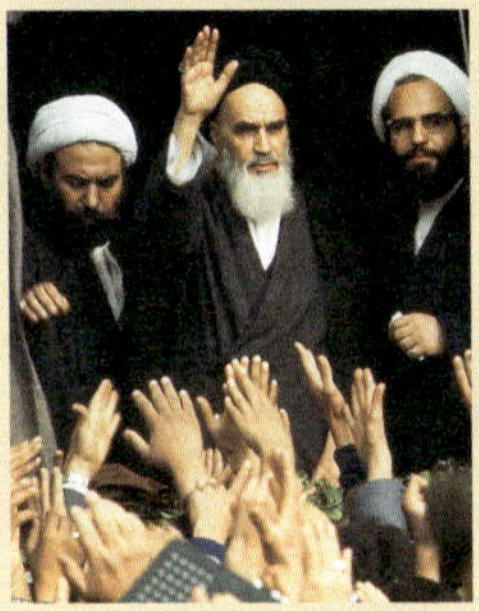

Important events during Carter's term included the Soviet invasion of Afghanistan, *above,* and the rise to power of Ayatollah Ruhollah Khomeini in Iran, *left.* Carter urged a U.S. boycott of the 1980 Summer Olympics in Moscow to protest the invasion. In Iran, revolutionaries took over the U.S. embassy and held a group of Americans hostage for 444 days.

The world of President Carter

The television drama "Roots" attracted one of the largest audiences in television history when it was presented in 1977. The eight-part program, based on a book by Alex Haley, traced the 200-year history of a black family in America, from slavery to freedom.

Space exploration made impressive gains in the late 1970's with the launching of the Pioneer and Voyager space probes. The Pioneer probes reached Venus in 1978 and sent back data and radar photographs of the planet. The Voyager spacecraft relayed pictures and other information about Jupiter and Saturn, beginning in 1979.

An accident at Three Mile Island, a nuclear power plant near Harrisburg, Pennsylvania., triggered widespread concern in 1979. Many people questioned the safety of nuclear energy.

Gasoline shortages in 1979 resulted in long lines at service stations in many parts of the country. People shopping for automobiles took new interest in small, fuel-efficient models.

Thousands of immigrants from Vietnam and other Southeast Asian nations poured into the United States in the late 1970's. Many were "boat people," who had traveled in small boats on the open seas to escape persecution.

A peace treaty between Egypt and Israel was worked out in 1979 by Carter and heads of the two Middle Eastern nations.

The eruption of Mount Saint Helens, a volcano in the Cascade Mountains south of Seattle, Washington, caused extensive damage and about 60 deaths in 1980.

ter entered Georgia Southwestern College in nearby Americus. In 1942, a boyhood dream came true when he got an appointment to the United States Naval Academy in Annapolis, Maryland. "Even as a grammar school child, I read books about the Navy and Annapolis," Carter recalled. However, he lacked the mathematics courses required for admission to the academy and enrolled at Georgia Institute of Technology to fulfill this requirement. Carter entered the academy in 1943. He did especially well in electronics, gunnery, and naval tactics and graduated in 1946, ranking 59th in a class of 820.

Carter's family. In 1945, Carter had started to date Rosalynn Smith (Aug. 18, 1927-) of Plains. She was the best friend of his sister Ruth. Rosalynn's father, a garage mechanic, died when she was 13 years old. She took a part-time job as cleaning girl in a beauty shop to help pay the family's expenses.

Jimmy and Rosalynn were married July 7, 1946, about a month after he graduated from Annapolis. They had four children: John William (1947-); James Earl III (1950-); Donnel Jeffrey (1952-); and Amy Lynn (1967-).

Naval career. Carter spent his first two years in the Navy chiefly as an electronics instructor. He served first on the U.S.S. *Wyoming* and later on the U.S.S. *Mississippi.* These battleships were being used to test new equipment. Near the end of his period on the *Mississippi,* Carter volunteered for submarine duty. He graduated from submarine-training school in 1948, ranking third in a class of 52. Carter was then assigned to the submarine U.S.S. *Pomfret* and, in 1950, to the U.S.S. *K-1,* a submarine designed for antisubmarine warfare.

In 1952, Carter joined a select group of officers who were developing the world's first nuclear-powered submarines. He became engineering officer of the nuclear submarine *Sea Wolf.* Carter served under Captain Hyman G. Rickover, who pioneered the nuclear project. Carter later wrote that Rickover "had a profound effect on my life—perhaps more than anyone except my own

Important dates in Carter's life

1924	(Oct. 1) Born in Plains, Georgia.
1946	Graduated from the United States Naval Academy.
1946	(July 7) Married Rosalynn Smith.
1946-1953	Served in the United States Navy.
1962	Elected to the Georgia Senate.
1964	Reelected to the Georgia Senate.
1970	Elected governor of Georgia.
1976	Elected president of the United States.
1980	Lost presidential election to Ronald Reagan.
2002	Received the Nobel Peace Prize.

Lawrence Smith, *The Ledger-Enquirer*

Carter's boyhood home was this wooden clapboard house on a farm in Archery, Georgia. He was born in nearby Plains, and his family moved to the farm when he was 4 years old.

parents. ... He expected the maximum from us, but he always contributed more."

A turning point in Carter's life occurred in 1953, when his father died of cancer. Carter felt he was needed in Plains to manage the family business. But Rosalynn had no desire to return to Plains, and she argued against his leaving the Navy. Carter later called their disagreement "the first really serious argument in our marriage." He resigned from the Navy that year with the rank of lieutenant senior grade.

Return to Plains

Businessman and civic leader. Soon after Carter returned to Plains, he took over the family farm and a peanut warehouse that his father had established in the town. He studied modern farming techniques at the Agricultural Experiment Station in Tifton, Georgia. During the late 1950's and the 1960's, Carter expanded the warehouse and bought new machinery for the farm. The family businesses thrived under his management.

Carter devoted much time to civic affairs. He served on the Sumter County Board of Education from 1955 to 1962, the last two years as chairman. Carter also became a deacon and Sunday-school teacher of the Plains Baptist Church and a member of the local hospital and library boards.

Carter was widely respected in Plains. But his views on racial issues often differed from those of most of his neighbors. He disapproved of the segregation laws that separated blacks and whites in schools and other public facilities throughout the South. During the 1950's, these laws came under increasing attack by federal courts and civil rights workers. Many Southerners formed local chapters of the White Citizens' Council, an organization designed to help preserve segregation. A chapter was established in Plains in 1955, and Carter was asked to join. He refused to do so and declared that he would rather move from Plains.

In 1965, Carter's church considered a proposal to ban blacks from Sunday services. At that time, black civil rights workers were trying to integrate various Southern churches. Carter urged his congregation to defeat the measure, but only his family and one other church member voted against it.

State senator. In 1962, Carter ran for the Georgia Senate. He received a stormy introduction to state politics. On the day of the Georgia primary election, Carter saw voters marking their ballots openly in front of the election supervisor in the town of Georgetown. He charged that this action violated voting laws. But the election supervisor, who was the political boss of the area and a supporter of Carter's opponent, ignored the protest.

The results of the primary election showed that Carter had lost by only a few votes. He angrily challenged the results in court. Just three days before the general election, he was declared to be the Democratic nominee. Carter beat his Republican opponent by about 1,000 votes. He was reelected to the Senate in 1964. As a state senator, Carter worked hard for reforms in education.

Steps to the governorship. In 1966, Carter became a candidate for the Democratic nomination for governor of Georgia. He was defeated in the primary election. But Carter, determined to win the governorship, decided later that year to run for the office again in 1970. From 1966 to 1970, he worked to increase his understanding of Georgia's problems and made about 1,800 speeches throughout the state.

Carter Family Album from *Chicago Sun-Times*

At the age of 13, Carter posed for this picture while attending a summer camp near Covington, Georgia. Back home, he helped with farm chores and attended school in Plains.

In 1970, political experts gave Carter little chance of winning the Democratic nomination for governor. The heavily favored candidate was Carl E. Sanders, a liberal who had served as governor from 1963 to 1967. During the campaign, Carter opposed the busing of students to achieve racial balance in schools. He also took other stands that were important to Georgia's rural, conservative voters. Carter's critics charged he was appealing for the support of segregationists. Carter won the nomination. In the general election, he defeated his Republican opponent, Hal Suit, an Atlanta television newscaster, by about 200,000 votes.

Governor of Georgia

Carter began his term as governor in January 1971 and quickly made clear that he would work to aid all needy Georgians. In his inaugural address, he declared: "I say to you quite frankly that the time for racial discrimination is over. No poor, rural, weak, or black person should ever have to bear the additional burden of being deprived of the opportunity of an education, a job, or simple justice." This speech brought Carter his first nationwide attention.

Political reformer. During Carter's campaign for the governorship, he had promised to make the state government more efficient. Soon after he took office, he set up task forces of leaders from education, industry, and state government to study every state agency. One task force member later recalled that the new governor "was right there with us, working just as hard, digging just as deep into every little problem. It was his program and he worked on it as hard as anybody, and the final product was distinctly his." As a result of this detailed study, Carter merged about 300 state agencies and boards into about 30 agencies.

Carter also pushed a series of reforms through the legislature. One of the most important was a law to provide equal state aid to schools in the wealthy and poor areas of Georgia. Other reforms set up community centers for children with mental retardation and increased educational programs for convicts. At Carter's urging, the legislature passed laws to protect the environment, preserve historic sites, and decrease secrecy in government. Carter took pride in a program he introduced for the appointment of judges and state government officials. Under this program, all such appointments were based on merit, rather than political influence.

Concern for blacks. Carter opened many job opportunities for blacks in the Georgia state government. During his administration, the number of black appointees on major state boards and agencies increased from 3 to 53. The number of black state employees rose by about 40 percent.

Carter also established a project to honor notable black Georgians. In 1973, he appointed a committee to nominate blacks for the portrait galleries in the State Capitol. Pictures of many prominent Georgia men and women hung there, but none were of blacks. The committee's first choice was Martin Luther King, Jr. A portrait of the famous civil rights leader was hung in the Capitol in 1974.

Plans for the presidency. While serving as governor, Carter became increasingly active in national activities of the Democratic Party. He headed the 1972 Democratic Governors' Campaign Committee, which worked to help elect the party's candidates for governor. He also served as chairman of the Democratic National Campaign Committee in 1974.

At about the middle of his term as governor, Carter began to consider running for president in 1976. Georgia law prohibited a governor from serving two consecutive terms. But Carter also saw no heavy favorite for the Democratic presidential nomination. In addition, he believed that voters would support a leader from outside Washington, D.C., who offered bold, new solutions to the nation's problems.

Carter's mother later recalled that she learned in September 1973 of his plan to seek the presidency. She asked him what he intended to do after leaving the governorship, and Carter replied, "I'm going to run for president." She asked, "President of what?", and he answered: "Momma, I'm going to run for president of the United States, and I'm going to win."

In December 1974, a month before his term as governor expired, Carter announced his candidacy for the 1976 Democratic presidential nomination. He was still little known outside Georgia.

Presidential candidate

Rise to prominence. Carter began to work full time for the presidential nomination soon after leaving office as governor in January 1975. He campaigned outside Georgia for about 250 days that year, but his campaign attracted little public attention. In October 1975, a public opinion poll that ranked possible contenders for the Democratic presidential nomination did not even mention Carter.

In January 1976, Carter began a whirlwind rise to national prominence. That month, he received the most votes in an Iowa caucus, the first contest to elect delegates to the 1976 Democratic National Convention. In

Library of Congress

As a naval officer, Carter, *seated third from left,* first served aboard the battleship U.S.S. *Wyoming.* He had graduated from the U.S. Naval Academy at Annapolis, Maryland, in 1946.

Johnson Publishing Co.

As governor of Georgia, Carter established a project to honor black Georgians by hanging their portraits in the State Capitol. In 1974, the portrait of civil rights leader Martin Luther King, Jr., became the first to be hung. Carter joined Mrs. King, *left,* in unveiling the portrait.

February, Carter won the year's first presidential primary election, in New Hampshire. By then, 10 other Democrats were seeking the nomination. Carter's chief opponents were Senator Henry M. Jackson of Washington, Representative Morris K. Udall of Arizona, and Governor George C. Wallace of Alabama. In March, Carter beat Wallace in the Florida primary election. Soon afterward, a public opinion poll showed that Carter was the top choice of Democrats for the presidential nomination.

Many voters liked Carter largely because he had not served in Washington, D.C. He became a symbol of their desire for a leader without ties to various interest groups in the nation's capital. Carter also attracted much support with his vow to restore moral leadership to the presidency. Public confidence in government had been shaken by the Watergate scandal, which led to the resignation of President Richard M. Nixon (see **Watergate**). Vice President Gerald R. Ford succeeded Nixon as president. But Ford's popularity fell sharply after he pardoned Nixon for any federal crimes Nixon may have committed as president.

Carter easily won the nomination for president on the first ballot at the Democratic National Convention in New York City. At his request, Senator Walter F. Mondale of Minnesota was nominated for vice president. The Republicans nominated Ford and his vice presidential choice, Senator Robert J. Dole of Kansas.

The 1976 election. Many political observers believed that Carter's nomination would unite the Democratic Party. Since 1964, millions of conservative Democrats in the South had supported Republican presidential candidates. But in 1976, most of these men and women were expected to vote for Carter.

In the presidential campaign, Carter charged that Ford had failed to deal effectively with high unemployment. During the autumn of 1976, about 8 percent of the nation's workers had no jobs. Carter promised to help create more jobs by increasing federal spending and encouraging business expansion. Ford argued that Carter's plans would lead to rapid inflation. Carter also pledged to consider pardons for Vietnam War draft evaders, to reorganize the federal government, and to develop a national energy policy.

In the 1976 presidential election, Carter defeated Ford by 1,682,970 popular votes, 40,830,763 to 39,147,793. Other candidates received about 1,580,000 votes. Carter won 297 electoral votes and Ford won 240 electoral votes. Former Governor Ronald Reagan of California re-

National Archives

As the Democratic nominee for president in 1976, Carter shared the spotlight at the national party convention with his running mate, Senator Walter F. Mondale of Minnesota.

Carter's election

Place of nominating convention	New York City
Ballot on which nominated	1st
Republican opponent	Gerald R. Ford
Electoral vote*	297 (Carter) to 240 (Ford) and 1 (Reagan)
Popular vote	40,830,763 (Carter) to 39,147,793 (Ford)
Age at inauguration	52

*For votes by states, see **Electoral College** (table).

ceived 1 electoral vote. For the electoral vote by states, see **Electoral College** (table).

Carter's administration (1977-1981)

Early programs. Carter's first major decision as president was to pardon draft evaders of the Vietnam War period. Later in 1977, he approved a plan to review and possibly upgrade the less-than-honorable discharges of deserters and other military law violators of the Vietnam era. These actions fulfilled one of Carter's most controversial campaign pledges.

The president succeeded in winning quick congressional passage of several major measures. In March 1977, Congress approved his request for the authority to eliminate or consolidate federal agencies that he felt duplicated services. Soon afterward, Carter won congressional passage of legislation to lower federal income taxes. In August 1977, Congress adopted the president's proposal to establish a new executive department—the Department of Energy.

During the 1976 presidential campaign, Carter had often charged that the program to produce B-1 bombers was "wasteful." The cost of the program was estimated at over $25 billion. Many military officials and members of Congress had argued that the U.S. Air Force needed about 245 of these bombers. But in June 1977, Carter halted manufacture of the B-1 and instead supported development of the *cruise missile.* Cruise missiles can be launched from airplanes or submarines and can be directed to avoid enemy defenses.

The national scene. During Carter's first year as president, the nation's economy improved and unemployment fell. But in 1978, inflation became a major problem. In an attempt to fight inflation, Carter urged businesses to avoid big price increases and asked labor leaders to hold down wage demands. But these steps had little effect on inflation.

In 1978, Carter won congressional approval of a national energy program. The energy legislation was designed largely to reduce U.S. oil imports. The legislation included tax penalties for owners of automobiles that used excessive amounts of gasoline. But despite this legislation, oil imports remained at a high level. Inflation grew steadily worse. In 1979, continuing high inflation and gasoline shortages contributed to a sharp drop in Carter's performance rating in public opinion polls.

In July 1979, the president asked his entire Cabinet to submit their resignations for his consideration. Carter then made six Cabinet changes in hopes of strengthening his administration. Carter also named Hamilton Jordan, one of his presidential assistants, to the newly created position of White House chief of staff.

In September 1979, Congress adopted Carter's proposal to establish a Cabinet-level Department of Education. The Department of Health, Education, and Welfare was renamed the Department of Health and Human Services.

In March 1980, Carter announced a new program to fight inflation. The program included cuts in federal spending, a tax on imported oil, and voluntary restraints on wages and prices. Carter also ordered restrictions on credit cards and certain other types of consumer credit. Despite these measures, prices continued to rise. The rate of inflation soared to about 15 percent for the first half of 1980. In 1976, the year before Carter took office, the inflation rate had been less than 6 percent. In July 1980, a public opinion poll showed that only 21 percent of Americans approved of Carter's performance, the lowest score on record for any president.

Foreign affairs. Carter attracted worldwide attention in 1977 when he strongly supported the struggle for human rights in the Soviet Union and other nations. Carter limited or completely banned U.S. aid and exports to some nations whose governments he believed to be violating human rights. Most of these nations were in Africa, Asia, and Latin America.

The president achieved one of his major foreign policy goals in 1978. In that year, the U.S. Senate ratified two treaties concerning the Panama Canal, which the United States had controlled since its construction in the early 1900's. One treaty specified that Panama would gain control of the canal on Dec. 31, 1999. The other treaty gave the United States the right to defend the canal's neutrality.

Also in 1978, Carter strengthened official ties between the United States and the Communist government of China. The two nations established full diplomatic relations with one another in 1979.

The president received much praise for his efforts in bringing about a peace treaty between Egypt and Israel.

Vice president and Cabinet

Vice president	*Walter F. Mondale
Secretary of state	*Cyrus R. Vance *Edmund S. Muskie (1980)
Secretary of the treasury	W. Michael Blumenthal G. William Miller (1979)
Secretary of defense	Harold Brown
Attorney general	Griffin B. Bell Benjamin R. Civiletti (1979)
Secretary of the interior	Cecil D. Andrus
Secretary of agriculture	Robert S. Bergland
Secretary of commerce	*Juanita M. Kreps Philip M. Klutznick (1980)
Secretary of labor	Ray Marshall
Secretary of health, education, and welfare	*Joseph A. Califano, Jr. *Patricia R. Harris (1979)
Secretary of health and human services†	*Patricia R. Harris
Secretary of housing and urban development	*Patricia R. Harris Moon Landrieu (1979)
Secretary of transportation	Brock Adams Neil E. Goldschmidt (1979)
Secretary of energy	James R. Schlesinger Charles W. Duncan, Jr. (1979)
Secretary of education	*Shirley M. Hufstedler

*Has a biography in *World Book.*
†The Department of Health, Education, and Welfare was renamed the Department of Health and Human Services in 1979, when Congress created a separate Department of Education.

Middle East leaders met with President Carter at Camp David, Maryland, in 1978 to discuss ways to bring peace to their war-torn region. President Anwar el-Sadat of Egypt, *left,* and Prime Minister Menachem Begin of Israel, *right,* reached an agreement that eventually led to a peace treaty between their two nations.

Karl Schumacher, The White House

In 1978, he arranged meetings in the United States between himself and President Anwar el-Sadat of Egypt and Prime Minister Menachem Begin of Israel. Carter helped work out a major agreement that included a call for the creation of a peace treaty between Egypt and Israel. The two nations adopted the treaty in 1979. See **Middle East** (The 1970's and 1980's).

Also in 1979, the Carter administration and Soviet officials negotiated a treaty to limit the use of nuclear weapons by the United States and the Soviet Union. The treaty, called SALT II, resulted from the second round of Strategic Arms Limitations Talks. It would not take effect unless it was approved by the U.S. Senate. Opponents of SALT II argued that it would weaken the U.S. defense system. Supporters believed the treaty was necessary to slow the arms race.

In late 1979 and early 1980, the Soviet Union invaded Afghanistan, and Soviet-American relations plunged to their lowest point in several years. At Carter's urging, the United States and many other nations refused to participate in the 1980 Summer Olympic Games in Moscow as a protest against the invasion. Carter also asked the U.S. Senate to postpone consideration of the SALT II treaty.

The Iranian crisis. In February 1979, a movement led by Ayatollah Ruhollah Khomeini, a Muslim religious leader, overthrew the government of the shah of Iran. The shah, Mohammad Reza Pahlavi, had left Iran in Janu-

Jack Kightlinger, The White House

The Panama Canal treaties settled disputes between the United States and Panama over control of the Canal Zone. In a ceremony in 1977 at the Organization of American States, President Carter, *seated left,* and Panamanian leader Omar Torrijos Herrera, *seated right,* signed the documents.

Jimmy Carter Library

President Carter sat with his wife, Rosalynn Smith Carter, and their daughter, Amy, for this portrait in front of the White House. The Carters also have three sons, John, James, and Jeffrey.

ary. In October, Carter allowed the deposed shah to enter the United States for medical treatment. The next month, Iranian revolutionaries took over the United States Embassy in Tehran, the capital of Iran. They seized a group of U.S. citizens, most of whom were embassy employees, and held them as hostages. They demanded that the United States return the shah to Iran for trial in exchange for the prisoners.

Carter denounced the Iranians' action as a violation of international law, and he refused to meet their demands. He soon banned imports from Iran and cut diplomatic relations between the United States and Iran.

In April 1980, Carter authorized an armed rescue mission to attempt to free the hostages. The mission ended in failure after three of its eight helicopters broke down while flying through a sandstorm. After the project had been canceled, a fourth helicopter crashed into a transport plane. Both aircraft exploded, killing eight men. Secretary of State Cyrus R. Vance, who had opposed the rescue attempt, resigned. In July, the former shah died in Egypt, but the Iranian revolutionaries continued to hold the hostages to protest U.S. policies toward their country. They finally released the Americans on Jan. 20, 1981, the day Carter left office.

Life in the White House. Carter ended much of the ceremony and pageantry that had marked official receptions in the White House. For example, he eliminated the practice of having trumpeteers announce the presidential family and of having a color guard precede it. Most state dinners ended about 11 p.m., far earlier than those of most previous presidents. Carter conducted official business during some state functions in the White House and worked after others.

The Carters' daughter, Amy, was 9 years old when her father became president. She attended public schools near the White House. Amy often enlivened the White House by bringing classmates there to play.

Rosalynn Carter became an active representative of Carter's administration. In 1977, she led a U.S. delegation on a tour of Latin America. She also worked to help women gain equal rights and to improve care for the elderly and the mentally ill.

The 1980 election. Senator Edward M. Kennedy of Massachusetts challenged Carter for the 1980 Democratic presidential nomination. In August 1979, polls showed that Democrats preferred Kennedy over Carter by a huge margin. But Carter regained popularity during late 1979 and early 1980, partly for his handling of the Iranian crisis. He won enough delegates in primary elections to gain renomination on the first ballot at the Democratic National Convention in New York City. Mondale again became his running mate. The Republicans chose former Governor Ronald Reagan of California for president and George H. W. Bush, former U.S. ambassador to the United Nations (UN), for vice president. Representative John B. Anderson of Illinois and his running mate, former Governor Patrick J. Lucey of Wisconsin, ran as independent candidates.

In the presidential campaign, Carter stressed such achievements as his energy program and the Egyptian-Israeli peace treaty. Reagan charged that Carter had failed to deal effectively with inflation and high unemployment. Carter lost the 1980 election by a wide margin. He received about 35 million popular votes to about 44 million for Reagan, but he got only 49 electoral votes to Reagan's 489. Carter carried six states and the District of Columbia. Reagan carried 44 states. For the vote by states, see **Electoral College** (table).

Later years

Carter returned to Plains after leaving the White House. In 1982, he founded the Carter Center of Emory University as a forum for the discussion of national and international issues. Since the mid-1980's, Carter has worked as a volunteer carpenter on projects for Habitat for Humanity, a nonprofit organization that builds houses for the poor. The Carter Presidential Center was completed in Atlanta in 1986. It includes the Carter Center of Emory University and the Jimmy Carter Library.

Carter wrote several books after leaving the presidency, including *Keeping Faith: Memoirs of a President* (1982) and *An Hour Before Daylight: Memories of a Rural Boyhood* (2000). He wrote *Everything to Gain: Making the Most of the Rest of Your Life* (1987) with his wife, Rosalynn.

In 1991, Carter founded the International Negotiation Network Council. The council consists of former heads of state and other prominent people willing to conduct peace negotiations or monitor elections. Also in 1991, Carter launched the Atlanta Project to coordinate government and private efforts to solve social problems that affect poor families. In 1994, he traveled to North Korea to help reduce tensions between that country and the United States over North Korea's suspected development of nuclear weapons. Carter helped bring about negotiations. Also in 1994, Carter went to Haiti and helped convince military leaders who had taken control of the government in 1991 to return the president to office. In December 1999, Carter represented the United States in Panama at a ceremony marking the turning over of control of the Panama Canal to Panama.

In May 2002, Carter made a historic trip to Cuba at the invitation of President Fidel Castro in an attempt to improve relations between the United States and Cuba. He urged the Cuban government to adopt democratic reforms and called on the United States to end its embargo on trade with Cuba. In 2002, Carter was awarded the Nobel Peace Prize for his efforts to find peaceful solutions to international conflicts and to advance democracy and human rights. Hugh S. Sidey

See also **Democratic Party; Ford, Gerald R.; Mondale, Walter F.; President of the United States.**

Outline

I. Early life
- A. Boyhood
- B. Education
- C. Carter's family
- D. Naval career

II. Return to Plains
- A. Businessman and civic leader
- B. State senator
- C. Steps to the governorship

III. Governor of Georgia
- A. Political reformer
- B. Concern for blacks
- C. Plans for the presidency

IV. Presidential candidate
- A. Rise to prominence
- B. The 1976 election

V. Carter's administration (1977-1981)
- A. Early programs
- B. The national scene
- C. Foreign affairs
- D. The Iranian crisis
- E. Life in the White House
- F. The 1980 election

VI. Later years

Questions

What boyhood dream came true for Carter in 1942?
How did Carter receive a stormy start to Georgia politics?
What special project did Carter join in the Navy?
Why did Carter decide to seek the presidency?
How did Carter first gain nationwide attention?
How did Carter help bring about a peace treaty between Egypt and Israel after he became president?
Why was Carter's nomination for president expected to unite the Democratic Party in the 1976 election?
What were some ways Carter earned money as a boy?
How did Carter change life in the White House?

Additional resources

Brinkley, Douglas. *The Unfinished Presidency: Jimmy Carter's Journey Beyond the White House.* 1998. Reprint. Penguin, 1999.
Carter, Jimmy. *An Hour Before Daylight: Memories of a Rural Boyhood.* Simon & Schuster, 2001.
Fink, Gary M., and Graham, H. D., eds. *The Carter Presidency.* Univ. Pr. of Kans., 1998.
Richardson, Don, ed. *Conversations with Carter.* Rienner, 1998.

Carter Family was probably the most popular and influential group in the early history of country music in the United States. Family members influenced the development of country music in the 1920's through their original compositions, reworkings of folk songs, and performances of older popular and sentimental songs.

In 1915, A. P. (Alvin Pleasant) Carter married Sara Dougherty, a singer who accompanied herself on guitar, banjo, and autoharp. A. P. also sang and the two began performing together at local functions. In 1926, Sara's cousin, Maybelle Addington, married Ezra Carter, A. P.'s younger brother. Maybelle was a talented instrumentalist as well as a singer, and began performing with A. P. and Sara as the Carter Family.

The Carter Family made their first recordings in 1927. During their career, they recorded more than 250 songs. Many became standards of country music, including "Wildwood Flower," "Will the Circle Be Unbroken," "I'm Thinking Tonight of My Blue Eyes," "Keep on the Sunny Side," and "Wabash Cannonball." Maybelle was influential as an instrumentalist because she was among the first guitarists in country music to play melody instead of just chords to accompany singers.

The Carters were never full-time musicians. However, they made many personal appearances, mostly in the mid-South. From 1938 to 1941, they lived in Del Rio, Texas, and performed on the powerful radio station that operated across the border in Mexico. These broadcasts carried the family's music to much of North America.

The original Carter Family broke up in 1943. Maybelle continued to perform with her daughters Helen, June, and Anita. June Carter became the best known of the second generation of Carters. In 1968, she married country singer Johnny Cash and often performed and recorded with him. A. P. and Sara, who divorced in 1932, recorded with their children Joe and Janette in the 1950's. Sara and Maybelle reunited briefly in 1967 to record one album. Paul F. Wells

Carthage, *KAHR thihj,* was one of the greatest cities of ancient times. A wealthy trading center, it stood on a peninsula in Northern Africa, near the present city of Tunis, Tunisia. Carthage was one of the colonies founded by Phoenician merchant seamen as a trade and shipping outpost. The Phoenician name for Carthage is *Karthadasht,* meaning *new capital* or *new city.* Legend says that Dido, daughter of a king of Tyre, a city in Phoenicia, founded Carthage. The story of her tragic love for Aeneas, a Trojan prince whose family founded Rome hundreds of years later, is sung in Virgil's poem, the *Aeneid.*

Importance. Carthage grew quickly because of its location on a peninsula and its two excellent harbors. One harbor was inside the city walls and was large enough to shelter hundreds of military vessels. The city was well protected. A wall about 40 feet (12 meters) high and 30 feet (9 meters) wide stretched across the peninsula. Another wall enclosed the Byrsa, an inner fortress. Carthage was probably the first city-state to conquer and control an empire. It ruled much of western North Africa, southern Spain, Sardinia, Corsica, and western Sicily.

History. According to tradition, colonists from Tyre founded Carthage in 814 B.C. But archaeologists who have searched the ruins of Carthage have found no remains from earlier than about 750 B.C.

Tyre and other Phoenician cities weakened during a period of Assyrian and Babylonian control from the mid-800's to the 500's B.C. But the colony of Carthage grew

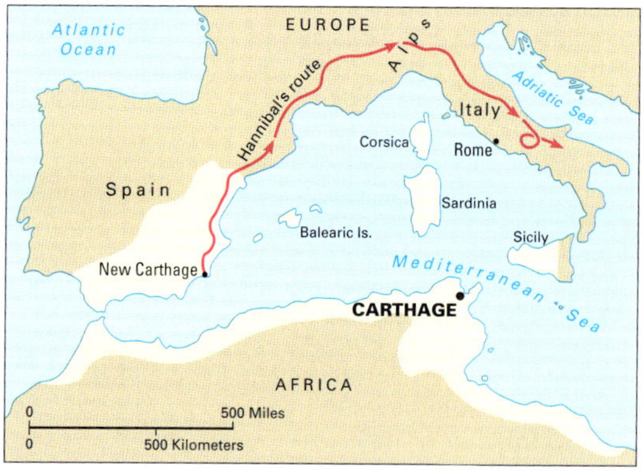

WORLD BOOK map

Carthage was an ancient city in North Africa. It controlled large areas on the Mediterranean Sea.

DPI

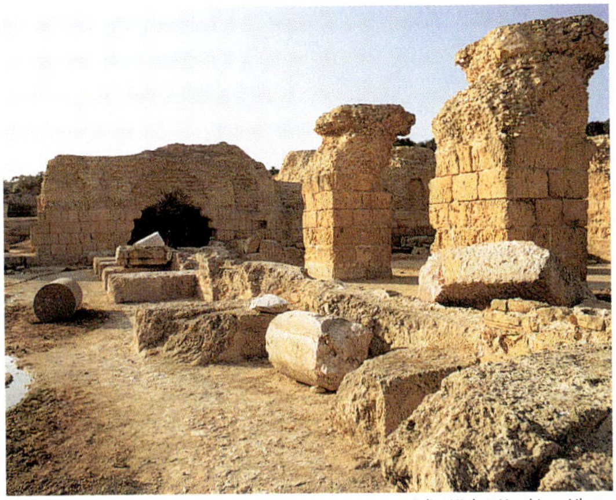
Juliet Highet, Hutchison Library

Ruins of Carthage include cave houses, *left,* outside present-day Tunis, and remnants of buildings, *right,* constructed by the Romans after they conquered Carthage in the 100's B.C.

stronger and more independent. When the Phoenician cities fell to the Persians in the 500's B.C., Carthage became the leader of the western Phoenician territories.

Carthage often fought with Greek forces on Sicily. The city made an alliance with the Etruscans, a people who lived in central Italy. But Etruscan power declined as Roman power rose after 500 B.C. In 480 B.C., the Greeks crushed a Carthaginian army at Himera, in Sicily. Carthage could not get help from eastern Phoenicians, who lost many ships to the Athenians while taking part in the Persian invasion of Greece.

Carthage then went through a period of isolation and decline. The government system changed from a one-man rule to an *oligarchy* (rule by a few). There was an assembly of citizens, but the real power lay with the *sufets* (magistrates), the generals, and a council of nobles.

Carthage expanded in Sicily again about 410 B.C., and ruled much of Sicily at times. After 265 B.C., the Romans also wanted Sicily. Carthage fought and lost three wars called the Punic Wars with Rome, from 264 to 241, from 218 to 201, and from 149 to 146 B.C. The genius of Hannibal, a Carthaginian general, nearly won the second war for Carthage. But the Romans destroyed Carthage in the third war. Carthage later became an important city and a center of Christianity in the Roman Empire. St. Augustine was one of its famous inhabitants. Carthage was overrun by a Germanic people called the Vandals around A.D. 430. The city's final destruction came in A.D. 698, during the Arab conquest of North Africa. John F. Robertson

Related articles in *World Book* include:

Aeneid	Dido	Phoenicia
Cato, Marcus Porcius, the Elder	Hamilcar Barca	Punic Wars
	Hannibal	

Carthusians, *kahr THOO zhuhnz,* are members of a Roman Catholic order of monks, nuns, and lay brothers and sisters. Saint Bruno of Cologne founded the order in 1084 in the valley of Chartreuse in the French Alps. The order takes its name from the Latin form of the French word *Chartreuse.*

The Carthusian order is *contemplative*—that is, its members devote themselves to group prayer, study, meditation, and manual labor. Each monk must live in a hermitage, eat no meat, chant the church's *office* (prayers), and observe silence except during weekly walks of three to four hours. Nuns live similar, though slightly less solitary, lives. The material needs of the monks and nuns are met by lay brothers and sisters. The famous Chartreuse liqueur is made by monks from the founding monastery of La Grande Chartreuse near Grenoble, France. David G. Schultenover

Cartier, *kahr TYAY,* **Sir George Étienne,** *zhawrzh ay TYEHN* (1814-1873), was a French-Canadian political leader. He was one of the Fathers of Confederation, the men whose plan for a union of British North American colonies led to the formation of the Dominion of Canada in 1867. He played the key role in winning French-Canadian support for the dominion.

Cartier was born on Sept. 6, 1814, at St.-Antoine-sur-Richelieu in Lower Canada (now Quebec). As a young man, he became a critic of British rule in Canada. In 1837, he joined a rebellion against the government and was forced to flee to the United States. Later pardoned, he became a member of the Legislative Assembly and a cabinet minister in the government of the Province of Canada. From 1857 to 1862, he served as joint prime minister of the province with John A. Macdonald.

From 1867 to 1873, Cartier served as minister of militia in the first cabinet of the Dominion of Canada. He strongly supported westward expansion and arranged the government's purchase of Rupert's Land, a vast territory in the northwest owned by the Hudson's Bay Company. Cartier also encouraged the construction of a Canadian transcontinental railroad. He was made a baronet of the United Kingdom in 1868. He died on May 20, 1873. Andrée Désilets

Cartier, *kahr TYAY,* **Jacques,** *zhahk* (1491?-1557), was a French navigator. His explorations established the basis for France's claims to territory in what is now Canada. In 1535, he led the first European expedition up the St. Lawrence River.

Cartier was born in the seaport of St.-Malo and studied navigation in Dieppe, a French center for navigators. He may have sailed to Newfoundland with a fishing fleet in the early 1500's. Some historians believe he was with the Italian navigator Giovanni da Verrazzano on French expeditions to the New World during the 1520's.

Cartier landed in Canada in 1534. This map of the 1540's shows Cartier, *center,* wearing a red hat and short black coat, surrounded by members of his expedition. Cartier explored the Gulf of St. Lawrence and claimed the region for France.

Engraving from the *Vallard Atlas* (1546); the Huntington Library, San Marino, Calif.

Exploration of Canada. In 1534, King Francis I of France sent Cartier to North America to search for gold and other precious metals. Cartier left St.-Malo in April with two ships. The expedition sailed into what is now the Gulf of St. Lawrence and landed on the Gaspé Peninsula, which Cartier claimed for France.

Cartier met a group of Iroquois Indians, who told him that precious jewels and metals could be found farther northwest. The French gave gifts to the Indians and established friendly relations with them. Their chief let two of his sons sail to France with Cartier in August. Cartier's men brought a supply of corn that was probably the first corn ever seen in northern Europe.

In May 1535, the king sent Cartier on a second expedition to Canada. The two Indian boys returned home on this voyage. On August 10, Cartier reached the northern coast of the Gaspé Peninsula and entered a nearby bay. He named the bay for Saint Lawrence because the expedition had arrived there on the saint's feast day. Cartier then saw the mouth of the great river that also became known for Saint Lawrence. Cartier sailed up the river to the foot of a mountain, which he named Mont Réal (Mount Royal). It became the site of the city of Montreal. Cartier sailed back to what is now Quebec City for the winter. The expedition returned to France the next summer.

Attempts at colonization. In 1541, the king organized an expedition to establish a permanent settlement in Canada. He appointed a nobleman named Jean-François de La Rocque, Sieur de Roberval, in command over Cartier. However, Cartier sailed in May before Roberval had completed plans for his own voyage.

Cartier sailed up the St. Lawrence River to what is now Cap Rouge, near Quebec City. Some of his men remained there and built a settlement. Cartier and the others continued to search for gold. They sailed to Mont Réal and traveled farther west on foot but found no precious metals. Cartier then returned to the settlement.

During the winter, the Iroquois attacked and killed several Frenchmen. Roberval had not arrived by spring, and Cartier decided to sail back to France.

On his return voyage, Cartier met Roberval in Newfoundland. Roberval ordered Cartier to remain in Canada, but Cartier refused and warned the nobleman about the Indians. Cartier then returned to France. He was pardoned for disobeying Roberval and lived the rest of his life in and around St.-Malo. Franklin L. Ford

See also **New Brunswick** (Exploration and settlement); **Roberval, Sieur de.**

Additional resources

Blashfield, Jean F. *Cartier.* Compass Point, 2001. Younger readers.
Cartier, Jacques. *The Voyages of Jacques Cartier.* Ed. by Henry P. Biggar and Ramsay Cook. Univ. of Toronto Pr., 1993.
Donaldson-Forbes, Jeff. *Jacques Cartier.* PowerKids Pr., 2002. Younger readers.

Cartier-Bresson, *kah TYAY breh SAWN,* **Henri,** *ahn REE* (1908-2004), was a French photographer known for his ability to capture the significance of an event by the arrangement of people and objects in a scene. Cartier-Bresson's photographs often combine a unique moment with geometric patterns or shapes.

Cartier-Bresson was born in Chanteloup, near Paris, on Aug. 22, 1908. He became a photographer in 1930, after studying painting and literature. He photographed news events throughout the world for newspapers and magazines. In 1947, Cartier-Bresson helped found Magnum, an agency that provides publishers with photos.

Cartier-Bresson worked with a small, handheld camera. He chiefly used black-and-white film because he believed color took attention from a photograph's subject. He rarely used filters or flash equipment, preferring natural light to illuminate his subjects. Books featuring his

© 1930 Henri Cartier-Bresson/Magnum

Hyères, France, 1930, a photograph by Henri Cartier-Bresson, captures the elements of the scene in a lively visual balance.

photos include studies of Asia, Europe, and the United States. In the 1970's, he withdrew from photography and turned to painting and drawing. Cartier-Bresson died on Aug. 3, 2004. John G. Freeman

Cartilage, *KAHR tuh lihj,* commonly called *gristle,* is a bluish-white rubbery tissue found in human beings and animals that have backbones. It is found at the ends of long bones, between the *vertebrae* (bones) of the spine, and in the ears, nose, and internal respiratory passages. Cartilage cushions long bones against shock and prevents them from rubbing against one another. For example, the *meniscus cartilage* acts as a cushion at the knee joint. Injury to this tissue is often called *torn cartilage.* Cartilage also makes an elastic but firm framework for the ear and respiratory passages, ensuring that these openings do not collapse. *Vertebrates* (animals with backbones) have skeletons of cartilage before they are born. Some vertebrates, such as sharks, lampreys, and hagfishes, retain this skeleton throughout their lives. However in all other vertebrates, bone gradually replaces the cartilage as the animal grows. Cartilage cells are round and are enclosed in capsules. Groups of cartilage cells lie embedded in a noncellular framework called a *matrix.* Bruce Reider

See also **Bone; Knee; Larynx.**

Cartography is the making and study of maps. See **Map.**

Cartoon is a drawing or series of drawings that tells a story or expresses a message. Cartoonists simplify pictures to increase their power of communication. Cartoonists use a visual language much like writers use words. A few lines in a cartoon may carry a wealth of information. By leaving out certain details, the cartoonist can focus attention on other more important aspects of the people, places, and things that the pictures portray.

People worldwide enjoy cartoons. They appear as animated motion pictures in movie theaters and on television. They also appear in comic strips and comic books, advertisements, and a wide variety of merchandise. Cartoons are particularly popular in children's entertainment. Children respond to cartoons and are able to recognize them and produce their own simple cartoons at an early age. Though many cartoons are directed at young people, some are intended specifically for adults.

The term *cartoon* first described a simple preliminary drawing that an artist in the mid-1600's prepared as a plan for a painting, tapestry, or other work of art. Centuries later, the word was used to describe the completed, though simple, illustrations in European and American humor magazines. Cartoon art use in animated films is so common that such films are often called *cartoons.*

Comic strips and comic books use cartoon pictures, arranged in a sequence to tell stories and jokes or to communicate ideas. Comic-strip art in particular tends toward cartoon stylization. Such comics characters as Snoopy in Charles Schulz's "Peanuts" are often nothing more than a few curved lines. In many comic books, especially those with heroic fantasy themes, the art tends to be more realistic than in comic strips.

Kinds of cartoons

There are several kinds of cartoons, including (1) editorial, (2) single panel, (3) illustration, and (4) advertising. For information on motion-picture cartoons, see **Animation.** For information on cartoons in comic strips and comic books, see **Comics.**

Editorial cartoons accomplish in pictures what editorials do in words. An editorial cartoon encourages

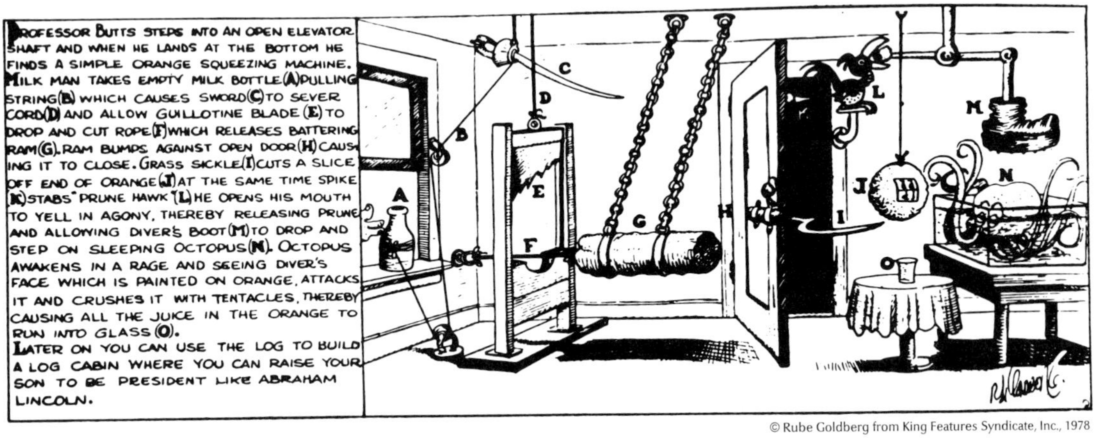

© Rube Goldberg from King Features Syndicate, Inc., 1978

Rube Goldberg's cartoons were a popular feature in many American newspapers during the early 1900's. Goldberg drew ridiculously complicated contraptions that were designed to accomplish simple tasks. In this cartoon, he explained how his orange-juice squeezer worked.

Drawing by Jeff MacNelly, Reprinted by permission of Tribune Media Services.

An editorial cartoon comments in a striking manner on important events or problems. Most editorial cartoons appear on a newspaper's editorial page as a single panel. The cartoon may or may not have captions or titles.

THE FAR SIDE By GARY LARSON

A panel comic consists of a single panel. Panel comics appear as regular features in newspapers and magazines. "The Far Side," *left,* drawn by Gary Larson, gained popularity for its unusual approach to humor.

"Krazy Kat" was a popular cartoon drawn from 1910 to 1944 by George Herriman. The cartoon followed the adventures of Krazy Kat, *center,* who loved the mouse Ignatz. The cartoon gained fame for the originality of its language and its bizarre scenes.

© 1986 The New Yorker Magazine, Inc.

A gag cartoon is a popular type of humorous single-panel cartoon published primarily in magazines. Charles Addams gained fame for gag cartoons that treat mysterious subjects in a comic or offbeat manner.

a reader to develop an opinion about someone or something prominent in the news. Most editorial cartoons appear as single panels on the editorial pages of newspapers. Some have captions or titles. Others consist only of a drawing. Editorial cartoons may support an editorial of the day, or they may deal with a news event. Many editorial cartoonists use an exaggerated form of drawing called a *caricature* to poke fun at well-known people (see **Caricature**).

Editorial cartoons have been an important part of newspapers and magazines since the mid-1800's. In 1841, editorial cartoons began appearing in the British comic magazine *Punch.* Weekly magazines in the United States started to feature them in the 1850's. Influential cartoonists included Thomas Nast in *Harper's Weekly* and Joseph Keppler in *Puck.* Nast introduced the elephant as the symbol of the Republican Party and the donkey as a symbol of the Democrats. For examples of Nast's cartoons, see **Democratic Party** and **Republican Party.**

In the late 1800's, editorial cartoons became regular features in daily newspapers. Newspaper cartoonists used less detail and a looser style than magazine cartoonists. The use of editorial cartoons in magazines has declined because cartoons in daily newspapers can comment on news more quickly.

The Pulitzer Prizes awarded each year include a cartoon category. For a list of winners, see **Pulitzer Prizes.**

Single panel cartoons, like editorial cartoons, have been popular since the mid-1800's. This type of cartoon remained popular in magazines after most editorial cartoons had migrated to newspapers.

New York Public Library

"You are free to speak" (1835), a lithograph by Honoré Daumier; collection of Howard P. Vincent

Many early cartoons dealt with political issues. In 1754, Benjamin Franklin urged the American Colonies to unite against the French and the Indians in his cartoon, "Join, or Die," *above.* In an 1835 cartoon, *right,* the French artist Honoré Daumier attacked what he considered to be the French government's restriction of free speech.

How a cartoonist tells a story

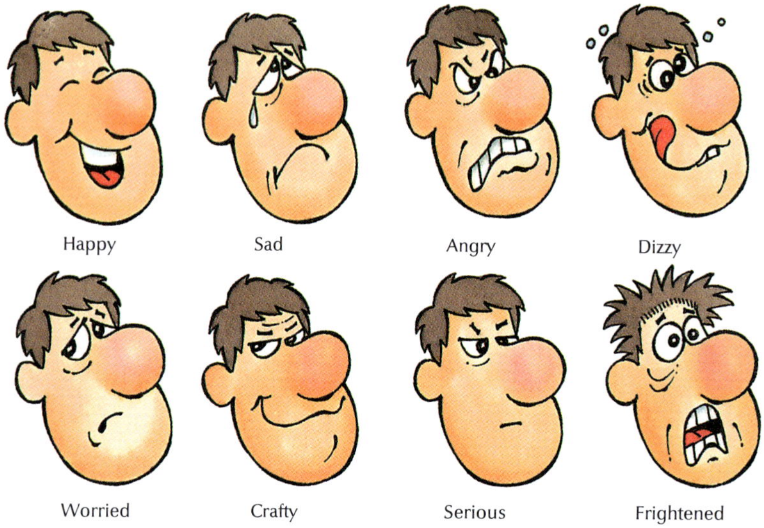

Facial expressions tell a reader immediately how a cartoon character feels. A cartoonist can illustrate almost any mood by drawing a character's eyes and mouth in a certain way.

WORLD BOOK illustrations by Rich Incrocci

The senses are illustrated by lines, symbols, and words. The lines and stars around the thumb suggest pain. The words "snif snif" and the lines leading from the dog's nose represent smell.

Movement is illustrated largely through the use of lines of different sizes. For example, long thin lines trailing a running horse show speed. Short broken lines indicate a jumping frog.

The humorous *gag cartoon* is the most common single panel cartoon. It is often accompanied by a caption consisting of words spoken by a character in the panel.

In *The New Yorker* magazine, such cartoonists as James Thurber, Charles Addams, and Peter Arno turned the gag cartoon into a powerful tool for sophisticated social commentary. Others, such as Saul Steinberg and William Steig, explored cartooning as an art form in *The New Yorker.* In newspapers, single panel cartoons usually appear next to the daily comic strips.

Illustration. Cartoons are an important part of children's book illustration. Many children's authors, including Dr. Seuss and Maurice Sendak, have successfully combined cartooning with book illustration.

Cartoons are occasionally used as book illustration for adult audiences, generally for lighter works such as collections of jokes or humorous stories. Instructional manuals and some nonfiction books may use diagrams containing cartoons. Cartoons are often used in a diagram because they eliminate much of the distracting detail that would be included in photographs.

Advertising makes frequent use of the cartoon's ability to clarify the messages of the service or product being sold. Many companies use popular cartoon characters to endorse their products.

Creating a cartoon

Developing the idea. Cartoonists develop ideas for their drawings in several ways. Most editorial cartoonists meet with their editors to discuss the day's news and decide which events deserve editorial comment. Then the cartoonist sketches several ideas, and the editor of the editorial page selects one to be completed. Some top editorial cartoonists have considerable control in the selection of material to be used.

Drawing a comic strip

Cartoons consisting of several related drawings are called comic strips. In creating a comic strip, the cartoonist must present the action so that the reader can easily follow the story from drawing to drawing. Most strips go through three major stages before they are finished. These stages are illustrated below in the development of an episode for "B.C.," a comic strip by Johnny Hart.

In the first stage, the cartoonist determines the content of each drawing in the strip. Using a pencil, the cartoonist draws the strip's basic elements—dialogue, figures, and major objects.

During the second stage, the cartoonist adds backgrounds and strengthens the lines. Minor changes also may be made to improve the content of the cartoon.

Finally, the cartoonist applies ink over the pencil lines. Textures and tones are added to indicate the surfaces of clothes, objects, and skin. The cartoonist also erases any unwanted pencil marks.

By permission of John Hart and Field Enterprises, Inc.

Gag cartoonists may develop their own ideas or work with the ideas of writers. Comic-strip and comic-book artists may also team with a writer.

Cartoonists who draw illustrative and advertising cartoons work from manuscripts supplied by writers or editors. These cartoonists must create cartoons that emphasize or clarify key points of the text.

Producing the finished cartoon. Depending on his or her own style—and the editor's requirements—a cartoonist may take from 30 minutes to a day to create a gag cartoon or comic strip. A comic-book page requires one-half to three days of work to fully write and draw.

Most cartoonists begin with a penciled outline. They go over the outline with a pen or brush dipped in India ink or with a felt- or nylon-tip marker.

The cartoonist may draw parts of the cartoon over and over again and then piece the parts together. This piecing does not show in the printed version.

Shaded areas and areas of solid black help to create contrast in a cartoon. Traditional methods of shading include drawing a series of thin lines close together or pasting down pieces of thin plastic on which a pattern of dots or lines has been printed.

In another traditional method, editorial cartoonists draw with a brush on rough-textured paper or on chemically treated paper with preprinted patterns. They then shade with a grease crayon. For information on how cartoons are reproduced for publication, see **Printing.**

Increasingly, cartoonists in all fields are turning to computer graphics programs to handle lettering, coloring, and rendering. Some cartoonists have begun to use computers for all aspects of cartoon art. Scott McCloud

Related articles in ***World Book*** include:

Adams, Scott	Darling, Ding	Pop Art
Addams, Charles	Daumier, Honoré	Public opinion (The press)
Animation	Disney, Walt	Ripley, Robert L.
Beerbohm, Max	Held, John, Jr.	Schulz, Charles M.
Block, Herbert L.	Hogarth, William	Sendak, Maurice
Capp, Al	Larson, Gary	Seuss, Dr.
Carpetbaggers (picture)	Mauldin, Bill	Steinberg, Saul
Computer graphics	Nast, Thomas	Tenniel, Sir John
Cruikshank, George	Oliphant, Patrick B.	Thurber, James
	Outcault, Richard F.	Trudeau, Garry

Additional resources

Amara, Philip. *So, You Wanna Be a Comic Book Artist?* Beyond Words, 2001. Younger readers.

Horn, Maurice, ed. *The World Encyclopedia of Comics.* 7 vols. Rev. ed. Chelsea Hse., 1999.

McCloud, Scott. *Reinventing Comics.* HarperPerennial, 2000. *Understanding Comics.* Kitchen Sink Pr., 1993.

Walker, Brian. *The Comics.* 2 vols. Abrams, 2002, 2004.

Cartouche, *kahr TOOSH,* in architecture, is an ornament shaped like a scroll with rolled-up ends. Architects also use the term for an inscribed tablet shaped like a partly unrolled scroll.

In Egyptian archaeology, a cartouche is an oval

frame with the name or symbol of a ruler inscribed on it. In heraldry, the term refers to an oval shield used by popes and churchmen of noble descent to display their coats of arms (see **Heraldry**). The word also means a map title drawn in the form of a scroll.

The word *cartouche* comes from the Italian word *cartoccio* (roll of paper). It first referred to the wadded roll of parchment or paper containing the explosive charge of a firearm. The word *cartridge* originally came from this Italian term.

Whitney Smith

SCALA/Art Resource

A cartouche representing Tutankhamen, king of Egypt, was inscribed on this vase.

Cartridge is a metal or paper case that holds a charge of explosive powder and a bullet or a charge of shot. The cartridge used in rifles and machine guns is a metal cylinder with a percussion cap at the base. The explosive is placed in the cartridge and the bullet is placed on top of it. The metal is *crimped* (pressed) against the bullet to hold it firmly in place. When the gun is fired, the charge ignites and the resulting explosion propels the bullet down the barrel.

Cartridges for shotguns usually consist of several thicknesses of stout paper with a brass base to give additional strength and to hold the percussion cap. A *blank cartridge* contains a charge of explosive, but no ball or shot. Cartridges made of paper were first used in muskets in 1585. Frances M. Lussier

See also **Ammunition** (Small-arms ammunition); **Bullet**; **Cartouche**.

Cartwright, Alexander. See **Baseball** (Alexander Cartwright; table: National Baseball Hall of Fame).

Cartwright, Edmund (1743-1823), was a British inventor and clergyman. He developed a steam-powered loom for weaving cotton that led to the invention of more effective power looms and to the development of the modern weaving industry.

Cartwright was born on April 24, 1743, at Marnham, in Nottinghamshire. He graduated from Oxford University and became pastor of a rural parish in Leicestershire. In 1784, Cartwright learned of the need for a weaving machine that could make cloth faster than the hand loom. He became convinced that he could make a power loom even though he had never seen a loom in operation. Cartwright's first weaving machine, patented in 1785, required two strong people to operate it for a short time and was not much more effective than a hand loom. But in 1786, Cartwright invented a steam-powered loom, and the next year he used the loom in a spinning and weaving factory that he opened at Doncaster.

In 1791, a mill at Manchester ordered 400 of Cartwright's looms. But the factory was burned down by workers who feared the new power machinery would eliminate their jobs. A few other manufacturers tried to use Cartwright's loom, but their efforts failed and Cartwright closed his mill in 1793. Although Cartwright's looms were never fully practical, Parliament recognized his pioneering work in 1809 by awarding him the equivalent of $50,000.

Cartwright also invented a wool-combing machine and a grain-cutting machine for farmers. But neither invention brought him much money. Monte A. Calvert

Caruso, *kuh ROO soh,* **Enrico,** *ehn REE koh* (1873-1921), an Italian tenor, was one of the greatest opera stars of the 1900's. He became famous for his powerful voice, his ringing high notes, and his extraordinary breath control. Caruso performed mainly in French and Italian operas. His most famous roles included Canio in *Pagliacci* and Radames in *Aida*. Caruso was one of the first opera singers to record extensively.

Caruso was born into a poor family in Naples on Feb. 25, 1873. He received little formal education, and less musical training than most opera stars. Caruso made his debut in 1894, in Naples in *L'Amico Francesco*.

In 1902, he acquired international fame with a successful appearance at Covent Garden in London. In 1903, Caruso made his debut at the Metropolitan Opera in New York City. He became closely associated with the Metropolitan Opera, regularly appearing there from 1903 to 1920. Thomas Bauman

Additional resources

Caruso, Enrico, Jr., and Farkas, Andrew. *Enrico Caruso: My Father and My Family.* Abridged ed. Amadeus Pr., 1997.
Greenfeld, Howard. *Caruso.* Putnam, 1983.
Scott, Michael. *The Great Caruso.* Knopf, 1988.

Carver, George Washington (1864?-1943), was an African American scientist who won international fame for his agricultural research. He was especially noted for his work with peanuts. Carver made more than 300 products from peanuts, including a milk substitute, face powder, printer's ink, and soap. He also created more than 75 products from pecans and more than 100 products from sweet potatoes, including flour, shoe polish, and candy. He developed a type of synthetic marble made from wood shavings and many other products.

Carver's achievements with these crops persuaded many Southern farmers to grow them in place of cotton. This shift provided farmers with new sources of income. Carver also helped promote the interests of black people and improve relations between blacks and whites.

Early years. Carver was born a slave on a farm near Diamond, Missouri. Shortly after Carver's birth, his father was killed in an accident and his mother was kidnapped. He was reared by Moses and Susan Carver, his owners until slavery was abolished in 1865. As a young boy, George showed a keen interest in plants and a great desire to learn. The Carvers taught him to read and write. When he was about 11 years old, he moved to Neosho, Missouri, to attend a school for black children.

For the next 20 years, Carver worked at various jobs to support himself and pay for his education. In 1890, he entered Simpson College in Indianola, Iowa. He showed promise as a painter but decided to pursue a career in agriculture instead. Carver believed such a career would enable him to help African Americans in the South, many of whom worked on farms. In 1891, he transferred to Iowa State Agricultural College (now Iowa State University) in Ames. Carver received a bachelor's degree in agriculture in 1894 and a master's degree in 1896.

Tuskegee instructor and researcher. In 1896, Carver moved to Alabama to join the faculty of the Tuskegee Institute (now Tuskegee University), an industrial and agricultural school for African Americans. Carver became head of the Tuskegee agricultural department and director of a state agricultural station.

At Tuskegee, Carver began to direct his attention toward soil conservation and other ways to improve crop production. He wrote pamphlets and bulletins on applied agriculture and distributed them to farmers in Alabama and other states. Carver also sought to teach more productive agricultural practices to Southern farmers—particularly black farmers—through conferences, traveling exhibits, demonstrations, and lectures.

In 1910, Carver became head of Tuskegee's newly created Department of Research. After 1914, he began to focus his research on peanuts. He received national attention in 1921, when he testified before a committee of Congress in support of a *tariff* (tax) on imported peanuts. He later gave lectures on peanuts throughout much of the country. Carver also worked to improve race relations. He was especially active in his work for the Commission on Inter-Racial Cooperation and the Young Men's Christian Association (YMCA).

Carver never married. In 1940, he gave his life savings of $33,000 to the Tuskegee Institute. The money was used to establish the George Washington Carver Research Foundation for agricultural research there. Carver died on Jan. 5, 1943.

Brown Bros.

George Washington Carver worked many long hours in his laboratory to improve agricultural methods in the South.

Awards and honors. Carver received many awards for his accomplishments. In 1916, he was named a fellow of the Royal Society of Arts of London. In 1923, the National Association for the Advancement of Colored People (NAACP) awarded him the Spingarn Medal for distinguished service in agricultural chemistry. In 1939, Carver received the Theodore Roosevelt Medal for his valuable contributions to science. In 1951, the George Washington Carver National Monument was established on 210 acres (85 hectares) of the Missouri farm where Carver was born. Gary R. Kremer

See also **George Washington Carver National Monument; Sweet potato; Tuskegee University.**

Additional resources

Carey, Charles W. *George Washington Carver.* Child's World, 1999. Younger readers.

Carter, Andy, and Saller, Carol. *George Washington Carver.* Carolrhoda, 2001. Younger readers.

Carver, John (1576?-1621), became the first governor of Plymouth Colony immediately after the signing of the Mayflower Compact in 1620. As governor, he made a peace treaty with the Indian chief Massasoit that lasted many years. Carver's piety and wisdom greatly aided the colonists during a difficult period of adjustment after they arrived in America. Carver was born in Nottinghamshire, England. He became a merchant before joining the Pilgrim church in Leiden, Holland, about 1610. A few years later, he became a deacon in the church and helped negotiate with the merchants who financed the Pilgrim voyage. Four months after he arrived in Massachusetts, Carver died of sunstroke while working in the fields. See also **Massasoit; Plymouth Colony** (The founding of Plymouth Colony). James Axtell

Carver, Raymond (1938-1988), was an American author known for his short stories. Carver's stories portray alienated and economically struggling working class characters who battle to keep their families together and their meager dreams alive.

Carver became the leading author of "minimalist fiction," a style of extreme realism prominent in the 1970's and 1980's. The style features a flat tone, an obsession with drabness, and inarticulate characters. Carver's technique has been praised for its readability and its sensitivity to the problems of ordinary people.

Carver's reputation for stylistic restraint and bleak outlook is largely based on his story collections *Will You Please Be Quiet, Please?* (1976), *Furious Seasons* (1977), and *What We Talk About When We Talk About Love* (1981). He showed more optimism and a less severe technique in the later collection *Cathedral* (1983). A collection covering Carver's entire career was published as *Where I'm Calling From* (1988). Carver's poetry was collected in *All of Us* (published in 1998, after his death).

Carver was born on May 25, 1938, in Clatskanie, Oregon. He worked low-paying jobs, experienced financial and family difficulties, and suffered from alcoholism. These painful experiences dominate his fiction.

Arthur M. Saltzman

Carving. See **Ivory** (Ivory carvings; pictures); **Woodcarving.**

Cary, Joyce (1888-1957), ranks among the leading British novelists of the mid-1900's. Cary combined great verbal gifts, humor, and striking realism with his lively style. The view of life he showed in his novels was full-blooded and sometimes heartwarming. His many energetic characters owe more to the comic spirit of earlier British fiction than to experimental modern works.

Cary's major works are two *trilogies* (groups of three related novels). The first trilogy consists of *Herself Surprised* (1941), *To Be a Pilgrim* (1942), and *The Horse's Mouth* (1944). The second consists of *Prisoner of Grace* (1952), *Except the Lord* (1953), and *Not Honour More* (1955). All six novels deal with the traditional literary themes of conflict between the generations, between the rich and the poor, the individual and society, the artist and the middle class, and freedom and authority.

Cary was born on Dec. 7, 1888, in Londonderry, Northern Ireland. He studied art at the University of Edinburgh and in Paris. He worked in Africa as a member of the Nigerian Political Service from 1913 to 1920. Cary's early novels are about Africa and Africans. He died on March 29, 1957. Michael Seidel

Cary, Mary Ann Shadd (1823-1893), was an American teacher and journalist known for helping fugitive slaves living in Canada. She was the first black woman in North America to establish and edit a weekly newspaper. In 1853, she helped found the *Provincial Freeman,* a weekly paper in Windsor, Ontario, for blacks in Canada.

Mary Ann Shadd was born in Wilmington, Delaware, on Oct. 9, 1823. From 1839 to 1851, she taught in and established schools for blacks in Delaware, New York, and Pennsylvania. She moved to Windsor in 1851. She worked to help slaves who escaped to Canada after the United States Congress passed the Fugitive Slave Act of 1850. This law provided for the return of slaves who escaped from one state to another. She married Thomas F. Cary, a Toronto barber, in 1856.

In 1869, Cary moved to Washington, D.C., where she taught school for the next 15 years. She also worked for women's voting rights. Cary studied law at Howard University and received an LL.B. degree in 1883. She was one of the first black female lawyers in the United States. Cary died on June 5, 1893. Robert A. Pratt

Casa Grande Ruins National Monument, *KAH sah GRAHN day,* in southern Arizona, includes the ruins of a four-story *casa grande* (big house) built by Indians who irrigated and farmed the land in the Gila Valley 600 years ago. The adobe building was discovered in 1694. The monument was established in 1892. For its area, see **National Park System** (table: National monuments).

Critically reviewed by the National Park Service

Casaba, *kuh SAH buh,* is a type of muskmelon sometimes called *winter melon.* Casaba melons are round or oval in shape with a pointed stem end. The casaba has a yellow, wrinkled *rind* (hard outer skin) and a juicy, edible flesh. The rind has many shallow grooves and turns from green to golden-yellow during ripening. A ripe casaba has white or green flesh. The flesh is sweet and lacks the strong musk odor of other muskmelons. It is rich in vitamin C and potassium and is eaten raw as a dessert.

Casaba melons grow on vines. These melons require a long growing season and ripen in late autumn. Casabas are called winter melons because they are available in many supermarkets during the winter.

Casabas were introduced into the United States about 1871 from Kasaba, a town in southwestern Turkey. Most casabas eaten in the United States are grown in California and the Southwest. Gary W. Elmstrom

WORLD BOOK illustration by Lorraine Epstein

Casabas ripen in autumn and have a juicy flesh.

Scientific classification. The casaba plant belongs to the gourd family, Cucurbitaceae. Its scientific name is *Cucumis melo,* variety *inodorus.*

Casablanca, *KAS uh BLANG kuh* or *KAH suh BLAHNK kuh* (pop. 2,949,805), is the largest city in Morocco and a major port in North Africa. About 70 percent of Morocco's trade passes through this port. For location, see **Morocco** (map). Casablanca is Morocco's manufacturing center. An automobile manufacturing plant, a sugar refinery, textile mills, brickworks, and canneries are among the factories there. The city is also the center of Morocco's banking and insurance industries. Spanish merchants named the city *Casa Blanca* (Spanish for *white house)* because of the whitewash used on its houses. The name later became *Casablanca.*

Casablanca has a modern business section with shops and tall buildings. The city's oldest section is the Old Medina. Casablanca developed around this small, crowded neighborhood. The New Medina, a second densely populated area, was built in the 1920's to house the city's growing population. Many poor people live in shacks on the outskirts of the city. Casablanca also has suburban communities with large homes and modern apartment buildings.

The Portuguese founded Casablanca on the site of a small fishing village in 1575. The town was rebuilt after an earthquake in 1755. Casablanca was the site of a meeting between United States President Franklin D. Roosevelt and British Prime Minister Winston Churchill in January 1943. The two leaders met there to decide the course of World War II (1939-1945). Kenneth J. Perkins

Casals, *kah SAHLS,* **Pablo,** *PAH bloh* (1876-1973), a Spanish cellist, was one of the greatest musicians of his time. He was also a conductor, composer, and teacher. Casals modernized cello technique, broadened the range of music that cellos could play, and established the cello firmly as a concert instrument.

Casals was born on Dec. 29, 1876, in Vendrell, Spain. He made his debut as a cellist in Paris in 1898. In 1919, he founded the Orquestra Pau Casals in Barcelona and directed it until 1936, when the Spanish Civil War broke out. Casals was outraged by the overthrow of the Spanish republic by Francisco Franco. In protest, he went into exile in Prades, France, in 1939. Beginning with World War II (1939-1945), Casals spent much of his time helping Spanish refugees.

Karsh, Ottawa
Pablo Casals

In 1950, Casals established a music festival in Prades. In 1956, he moved to Puerto Rico, his mother's birthplace. He relocated his festival there and continued as its director. Casals remained active in music until the end of his long life. But he believed he was most important as a champion of freedom and peace for Spain and all humanity.

Casals wrote a memoir, *Joys and Sorrows* (1970). He died on Oct. 23, 1973.

Abram Loft

Casanova, *kaz uh NOH vuh,* **Giacomo,** *JAH koh moh* (1725-1798), was an Italian adventurer and author. Casanova was a man of many interests and a strong intelligence, but he is known chiefly for his numerous love affairs. He not only seduced women, but he also celebrated his adventures in his writings. Casanova's most important work is his autobiography, *The History of My Life,* or *Memoirs,* written in French and published after his death. In these memoirs, he relates his conquests as a lover and narrates many tales of adventure.

Detail of a portrait (1775) by Alessandro Longhi; The Toledo Museum of Art, Toledo, Ohio. Gift of Edward Drummond Libbey, 1965
Giacomo Casanova

Casanova was born on April 2, 1725, in Venice. He studied law at Padua, served as a secretary to a cardinal, and even played the violin in a Venetian theater. In addition to writing many books, he was a spy and a gambler.

Casanova's adventures got him into trouble with the authorities, and he often had to flee from one European country to another. Casanova was arrested and imprisoned in Venice in 1755. He made a daring escape a year later, which increased his fame as an adventurer. He died on June 4, 1798. Richard H. Lansing

Cascade Range is a chain of mountains that extends between Lassen Peak in northern California and the Fraser River in southern British Columbia. The range is about 700 miles (1,100 kilometers) long. It lies approximately 100 to 150 miles (160 to 240 kilometers) inland from the Pacific Coast (see **North America** [terrain map]).

The most famous mountains in the Cascades are volcanoes. Two of them erupted in the 1900's. Mount St. Helens, in Washington, erupted frequently between 1980 and 1986. Lassen Peak, in California, last erupted in 1917. Volcanoes also make up the highest peaks in the range. The two highest peaks are Mount Rainier (14,410 feet or 4,392 meters), in west-central Washington; and Mount Shasta (14,162 feet or 4,317 meters), in northern California. These peaks are also among the highest in the United States. The Cascades began forming about 240 million years ago and have been further uplifted within the past 63 million years.

Rainfall is heavy in the Cascade Range. Some parts of the western slope average more than 100 inches (250 centimeters) of precipitation a year. Streams have cut deep valleys, which are covered with heavy fir and pine forests. The gorge of the Columbia River, which in places measures over 4,000 feet (1,200 meters) deep, cuts through the Cascades on the border of Washington and Oregon. The range takes its name from the spectacular cascades occurring along the gorge. Several long railroad tunnels have been built through the mountains.

Jois C. Child

See also **Lassen Peak; Mount Rainier; Mount Saint Helens; Mount Shasta; Oregon** (pictures).

Cascara sagrada, *kas KAIR uh suh GRAY duh* or *kas KAHR uh suh GRAH duh,* is an important medicinal plant found in the northwestern United States. It grows as a shrub or a small tree, reaches about 25 feet (7.6 meters) high, and thrives in rich, moist soil. The plant's oval leaves may be 3 to 6 inches (8 to 15 centimeters) long. The small, green flowers form black, berrylike fruits.

WORLD BOOK illustration by John D. Dawson

The cascara sagrada has oval leaves and black, berrylike fruit. Substances from the plant's bark are used to make medicine.

The Spanish term *cascara sagrada* means *sacred bark.* Substances from the bark are used in medicines as a laxative. The bark is peeled from the trunk and branches. Then the tree dies. If it is cut down and the stump left with its bark whole, the roots send up new shoots. Cascara sagrada can be grown from seed. Frank Welsch

Scientific classification. Cascara sagrada belongs to the buckthorn family, Rhamnaceae. Its scientific name is *Rhamnus purshiana.*

Case is a feature of nouns and pronouns that helps show their relation to other parts of speech in a sentence. The case of a noun is shown by the inflectional ending attached to it. For instance, in some languages a noun may have one ending when it is the subject of a verb, another when it is the direct object, a third when it is the indirect object, and so on.

Languages differ widely in the number of cases they have. Old English nouns have five cases, but modern English nouns have only two. Latin has six. Some languages, such as Hungarian, have as many as 25 or 30 cases.

Cases in Latin

Latin provides a good example of a case system. The Latin word *servus,* which means *slave,* has the following forms in the singular:

nominative	*servus*
vocative	*serve*
genitive	*servi*
dative	*servo*
accusative	*servum*
ablative	*servo*

The *nominative* form occurred when the word was the subject of a verb: "The slave was waiting." The *vocative* was used when a person called or addressed someone else: "Get me my toga, slave." The *genitive* resembled the English possessive, and denoted possession or origin: "The slave's clothes," "A child of the slave." The *dative* corresponded to the English indirect object: "He gave the slave his freedom." The *accusative* was used when the word was the object of a verb: "I saw the slave." The *ablative* followed certain prepositions: "He went with the slave." The ablative and dative are listed as separate cases, although the forms for this particular noun are the same, because some nouns had different forms. For example, the word for *foot (pes)* is *pedi* in the dative and *pede* in the ablative.

Cases in English

Nouns. Over a period of about 1,000 years, the case forms of English nouns were reduced from five to two —*common* and *possessive.* The common, or all-purpose, case is the base form of the noun used in either the subject or object position. The possessive case is the base form, plus, in writing, *'s.* For example, the common case nouns *girl, boy,* and *monkey* become *girl's, boy's,* and *monkey's* in the possessive case. If the form is both plural and possessive, an apostrophe follows the plural ending: *girls', boys', monkeys'.* In speech, the possessive ending is identical with the plural ending. The following pairs are pronounced alike: *boy's* and *boys, rat's* and *rats, witch's* and *witches.*

As the name suggests, the possessive ending usually indicates that the noun names a possessor or owner of something else: "the boy's car," "the rat's nest." Often, however, the possessive indicates meanings other than physical possession. Thus we have the possessive in "the boy's picture," though the boy may not own the portrait of himself. Other examples showing the varied meaning of the possessive are "a day's work," "land's end," and "a stone's throw." Notice that the expression "Shakespeare's plays" has two meanings: plays owned by Shakespeare and plays written by Shakespeare.

Proper nouns ending in *s* are sometimes written in the possessive with just the apostrophe and no additional *s.* For example, either "Keats's poems" or "Keats' poems" is correct. Common nouns ending in *s* are generally written *'s* (the waitress's husband), though the ending may sometimes drop out in speech.

An interesting feature in English is illustrated by the expression "the king of Spain's hat." The possessive ending is attached to *Spain,* not to *king,* although the hat belongs to the king, not to Spain. The possessive always follows the whole possessive phrase occurring just before the noun modified by the possessive: "someone else's hat," "the man in the back row's remark."

Pronouns. Some English personal pronouns and the relative pronoun *who* retain three case forms instead of two. The subject forms are *I, he, she, we, they,* and *who.* These pronouns are said to be in the *subjective,* or *nominative,* case. The object forms are *me, him, her, us, them,* and *whom.* These pronouns are in the *objective* case. The pronouns *you* and *it* have a common case form for subject and object positions. All pronouns show a possessive form *(my, your, his, her, its, their, whose).* Most have a variant form of the possessive *(mine, yours, hers, ours, theirs).* This form is used for special positions ("*my* book," but "The book is *mine*" and "*Mine* is lost").

Generally, the subject form is used when the pronoun is the subject of a verb ("*She* sang") or when it is a complement after the verb *to be* ("This is *she*"). The object form is used when the pronoun is the object of a verb ("The light blinded *her*"), the indirect object of a verb ("John did *her* a favor"), or the object of a preposition ("The class gave special recognition to *her*"). The possessive forms are often used as modifiers ("*their* house," "This is *his*"). They also serve in the subject position ("*Hers* has been destroyed") or the object position ("I bought *mine*").

Informal usage often interferes with the orderly use of case forms. For example, many people use *who* in a question like "*Who* are you going with?" because *who* occupies what is ordinarily a subject position, even though it is the object of the preposition *with.* Despite such trends in usage, many writers still maintain careful case distinctions. They prefer "*Whom* are you going with?" or "With *whom* are you going?" Patricia A. Moody

Case method, in law schools, is a system of learning the law through the study of actual cases. Law students read these decisions and discuss the reasoning by which they were reached. For nearly a hundred years before 1870, law schools in the United States had taught by lectures and individual reading of the few law books available. In that year, Christopher C. Langdell, a professor at the Harvard Law School, introduced the case method of study. Langdell collected decisions, or cases decided by appellate courts, in a *case book.* Law students studied these decisions and discussed the cases in class. By the early 1900's, most law schools had adopted the case method. Students now study statutes and administrative regulations in addition to cases. The case method is also used in other social sciences. See also **Law** (Common-law systems). Jean Appleman

Casein, *KAY seen* or *KAY see ihn,* is the chief protein in milk. It is also the main ingredient in cheese. Casein separates as curd when milk sours, or when acid is added. It also separates from sweet milk when the enzyme rennin is added. Casein contains carbon, hydrogen, nitrogen, oxygen, phosphorus, and sulfur. Pure casein is a tasteless, odorless, white solid. Cow milk contains about 3 percent casein. See **Cheese; Milk.**

Casein is produced commercially from skim milk. The curd is washed, dried, and ground. Commercially prepared casein is pale yellow and has a pleasant odor. It is widely used in medicines, cosmetics, and as a *sizing* (coating) for paper. Casein is also used in waterproof glues, casein paints, and certain plastic articles such as buttons. Michael F. Hutjens

Cash, Johnny (1932-2003), was an American singer, guitarist, and composer. His style mixed traditional country music with folk, gospel, blues, and rock 'n' roll. Most of his songs deal compassionately with the hard lives of poor rural people. Many describe outsiders, such as gamblers, hobos, and convicts. Cash had a rich, distinctive baritone voice. He wrote many songs, including "Hey Porter" (1955), "Folsom Prison Blues" (1956), "I Walk the Line" (1956), and "Don't Take Your Guns to Town" (1959).

John R. Cash was born on Feb. 26, 1932, in Kingsland, Arkansas, to a poor sharecropper family. He taught himself to play the guitar and began to compose his own songs. He made his first record in 1955. In 1968, Cash married June Carter, a member of a famous family of country performers. Cash discussed his life in two autobiographies, *Man in Black* (1975) and *Cash* (1997). In 2001, Cash won the Grammy award for best male country vocalist. He died on Sept. 12, 2003. Lydia Dixon Harden

See also **Country music** (picture: The "outlaws").

Cash register is a device that records and displays information about the sale of goods or services. Most cash registers have a printer to create receipts and a cash drawer to hold cash, checks, and credit card slips. A cash register may be mechanical, or an electronic or computerized device.

In many businesses, computer terminals are connected to a store's main computer to form a *point-of-sale,* or *POS, system.* Each terminal includes a device called a *scanner* that "reads" a *bar code* (pattern of lines and bars) printed on or attached to an item and interprets it as a sequence of numbers. The sequence refers to a record in the main computer in which price and other product information are stored. Store managers can use the information collected by a POS system to perform such tasks as tracking earnings and identifying which items have been sold and which remain in stock. A small business may use a single personal computer with a scanner and other devices to form a simple POS system.

James Ritty, an American restaurant owner, invented the mechanical cash register in 1879. To help reduce theft, his machine featured a bell that rang each time the cash drawer was opened. Later cash registers kept a printed record of the amount of money received each time a sale was "rung up." At the end of the day, the store manager could compare the cash register record with the amount of money in the cash drawer to make sure the two were equal. Michael F. Koehler

See also **Bar coding; Ritty, James.**

Cashew, *KASH oo,* is a bean-shaped nut that grows on a tropical evergreen tree. Cashew nuts are delicious when roasted and are a popular food in the United States. India, Brazil, and several African countries produce most of the world's cashew nuts. The cashew tree is related to poison ivy, and the shell of the cashew nut contains an irritating poison. People who touch the shell sometimes develop skin blisters. But roasting removes all poison from the nuts.

The cashew tree is native to Central America and other tropical regions. The first cashew trees in India were brought from South America. In the United States,

WORLD BOOK illustration by Stuart Lafford, Linden Artists Ltd.

Cashews grow in bean-shaped shells attached to fruitlike cashew apples. The nut grows at the end opposite the stem.

WORLD BOOK photo by Jeff Guerrant

A computerized cash register system links checkout terminals with a main computer. At the checkout counter, a clerk passes each purchase over a scanner, which "reads" a bar code. The main computer relays the price and a short description of the product to the terminal for display on a screen and printing on a paper sales slip. The main computer records all purchases in order to track the store's stock of each item.

cashew trees grow mostly in Florida.

The trees sometimes reach a height of 40 feet (12 meters). They have large, leathery, green leaves up to 6 inches (15 centimeters) long and 4 inches (10 centimeters) wide. Each fruit of the cashew contains one nut. In addition to the nut, people eat the fleshy red or yellow base of the fruit, called the cashew apple. The apple may be eaten raw or made into a preserve. Cashew trees also yield a gum used in varnishes. Richard A. Jaynes

Scientific classification. Cashew trees belong to the cashew family, Anacardiaceae. The scientific name for the most important kind is *Anacardium occidentale*.

Cashmere, *KASH mihr,* is a fiber made from the soft undercoat of Cashmere goats. The term *cashmere* also refers to soft, fine wool fabric with a *twill* (diagonal) weave, and to some similar fabrics. Cashmere is used to make such garments as sweaters, dresses, and scarves. See also **Cashmere goat**. Keith Slater

Cashmere goat, *KASH mihr,* is a long-haired goat, famous for its fine, silky wool. Cashmere goats live in Tibet and India. Some have also been raised in France and in Germany. The Cashmere goat is a medium-sized animal. It has drooping ears and spirally twisted horns. The goats from the high plateaus and mountains are colored deep yellow. Goats that do not live in such high places

ARDEA

Cashmere goats have soft fleece underneath their top coat of hair. The fleece is used to produce cashmere, a fine wool.

are lighter colored, and those that live in the valleys and plains below the mountains are pure white. The goats that live in cold places have the heaviest fleece. The meat can be eaten, and the milk is rich. See also **Cashmere; Goat**. William L. Franklin

Casper (pop. 49,644; met. area pop. 66,533) is the second largest city in Wyoming. Only Cheyenne has more people. Casper serves as a production center for oil and gas companies and as a supply center for mining equipment. Many tourists visit Casper to enjoy camping, fishing, hunting, and winter sports and to see the city's historic sites. Casper lies on the North Platte River in east-central Wyoming. See **Wyoming** (political map).

Casper began as a river-crossing point on the Oregon and Mormon trails. In 1858, a military post called Platte Bridge Station was established to guard the bridge and ferry crossings. In 1865, the name was changed to Caspar to honor Caspar W. Collins, a soldier who died there fighting Cheyenne and other Indians. A clerical error probably caused the spelling change to Casper. In 1889, oil was discovered about 30 miles (50 kilometers) north of Casper. The city grew as oil wells developed in the area. Casper has a council-manager government and is the seat of Natrona County. Dan Neal

Caspian Sea, *KAS pee uhn,* a great salt lake below sea level, is the largest inland body of water in the world. It lies between Europe and Asia east of the Caucasus Mountains. The Caspian Sea is bordered by Kazakhstan on the north and northeast, Turkmenistan on the southeast, Iran on the south, Azerbaijan on the southwest, and Russia on the west and northwest.

The Caspian Sea covers 143,250 square miles (371,000 square kilometers). It is about 750 miles (1,210 kilometers) long at its greatest extent, and varies from 130 to 300 miles (209 to 483 kilometers) in width. During the past several centuries, the Caspian has been shrinking in size because the rivers that empty into it bring less water than it loses by evaporation. Irrigation projects in the Caspian Basin drain off much water from these rivers. Important rivers that empty into the Caspian include the Volga, Ural, Emba, Terek, and Kur. The Volga-Don Canal links the Caspian Sea to the Black Sea.

Caspian Sea

Area: 143,250 sq. mi. (371,000 km²)

Elevation: 92 ft. (28 m) below sea level

Deepest point: • 3,363 ft. (1,025 m)

International boundary

Railroad

Major oil field

City or town

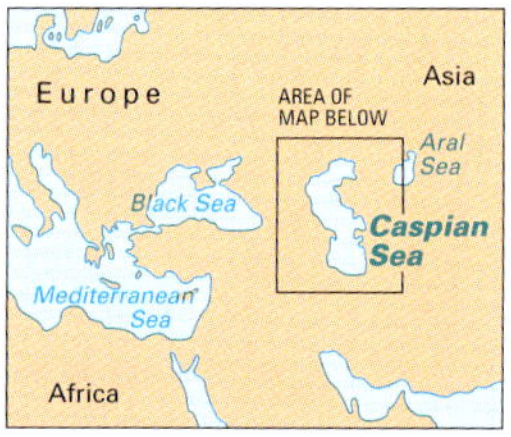

WORLD BOOK maps

The Caspian Sea lies 92 feet (28 meters) below sea level. No natural outlets drain water from the Caspian Sea into any ocean. Caspian waters are less salty than ocean waters and abound with freshwater and saltwater fish. The Caspian Sea has no tides. About 50 small islands scattered in the lake have a combined area of about 135 square miles (350 square kilometers).

The rivers that flow into the Caspian Sea yield most of the annual Russian harvest of sturgeon. The Caspian Sea is an important source of petroleum and natural gas. Major Caspian ports include Krasnovodsk in Turkmenistan, Bandar-e Torkeman and Bandar-e Anzali in Iran, Baku in Azerbaijan, and Astrakhan and Makhachkala in Russia. Leszek A. Kosinski

Cass, Lewis (1782-1866), was the Democratic candidate for president in 1848, but he lost the election to Zachary Taylor. Cass was a leading supporter of the doctrine of *popular sovereignty,* which held that the people who lived in a territory should decide whether or not to permit slavery there (see **Popular sovereignty**). His nomination angered many antislavery Democrats, who broke away and joined the Free Soil Party.

Cass served as a brigadier general in the War of 1812, as governor of the Territory of Michigan from 1813 to 1831, as secretary of war for President Andrew Jackson from 1831 to 1836, and as minister to France from 1836 to 1842. He represented Michigan in the United States Senate from 1845 to 1848. After resigning to run for president, he was returned to the Senate and served from 1849 to 1857. As a senator, Cass helped pass the Compromise of 1850, which applied popular sovereignty to territories in the West. From 1857 to 1860, he served as President James Buchanan's secretary of state. A statue of Cass represents Michigan in Statuary Hall in the United States Capitol. Cass was born on Oct. 9, 1782, in Exeter, New Hampshire. Michael F. Holt

Cassandra *kuh SAN druh,* was the daughter of Priam and Hecuba, king and queen of Troy in Greek and Roman mythology. According to Homer, her beauty was so great that Apollo fell in love with her and gave her the power to foretell the future. But she would not love him in return. Apollo angrily punished her by ordering that no one should ever believe her prophecies.

Cassandra warned the Trojans to return Helen to the Greeks and to beware of the Trojan Horse. But they paid no attention. Cassandra was praying at the altar of Athena when Troy fell (see **Troy**). Agamemnon took her to Mycenae as a slave. There Clytemnestra and Aegisthus murdered her.

The story of Cassandra has been told often in literature. She is a major character in two ancient Greek tragedies, *Agamemnon* by Aeschylus and *The Trojan Women* by Euripides. Cassandra also appears in William Shakespeare's play *Troilus and Cressida* and many modern poems. Cassandra's name has come to stand for any prophet of doom. Justin M. Glenn

Cassatt, *kuh SAT,* **Mary** (1844-1926), was an American painter who spent much of her career in France. She was a member of the French impressionist movement of the late 1800's. Like her French impressionist friends, Cassatt used light, bright colors and sketchy brushstrokes to create the effect of what the eye sees at a glance.

Cassatt painted scenes of people engaged in ordinary daily activities. She became particularly well known for her paintings of peaceful, loving moments shared by mothers and their young children. Cassatt also painted scenes showing women drinking tea, quietly reading, or writing letters. See **Impressionism.**

Cassatt was born on May 25, 1844, in Allegheny City (now part of Pittsburgh), Pennsylvania. She studied at the Pennsylvania Academy of Fine Arts from 1861 to 1865. She settled in France in 1866 and lived there the rest of her life. Cassatt began painting in the impressionist style in the late 1870's and first exhibited with the group in 1879. Cassatt's closest friend among the impressionist painters was Edgar Degas, who strongly influenced her style. Like Degas, Cassatt often arranged her compositions asymmetrically, in order to make them seem lifelike and informal (see **Degas, Edgar**).

In the 1890's, Cassatt created a series of beautiful

Oil painting (about 1892) by Mary Cassatt; The Art Institute of Chicago, Robert A. Waller Fund

Mary Cassatt became famous for her paintings of mothers and children in everyday situations. *The Bath, above,* shows how she used flat, delicate colors and strong, clear lines. The French painter Edgar Degas, a friend of Cassatt's, painted her portrait, *left.*

A detail of an oil portrait by Edgar Degas; collection of André Meyer, New York City (WORLD BOOK photo by Robert Crandall)

prints. In their strong outlines and flattened, simplified shapes, these prints show the influence of woodcuts by Japanese artists. In addition to her importance as a painter, Cassatt played a major role in advising American collectors to buy Impressionist art. Cassatt died on June 14, 1926. Sarah Burns

Cassava, *kuh SAH vuh,* is a type of small shrub with thick roots that are eaten like potatoes or used to make tapioca. The cassava is native to South America. It is grown in the southern part of the United States and in other warm areas. Cassava is also called *manioc, mandioca,* and *yuca.*

Cassava roots are an important food in wet, tropical lowlands where potatoes cannot be grown. The roots may be left in the ground as a food reserve. There are two main varieties of cassava—bitter and sweet. Bitter cassava may be poisonous and must be washed and cooked before it is eaten. Cassava is an important source of starch but contains little protein. Unless the roots are eaten as part of a balanced diet, malnutrition may occur. William C. Burger

Scientific classification. Cassava is in the spurge family, Euphorbiaceae. Bitter and sweet varieties of cassavas belong to the same species, *Manihot esculenta.*

See also **Tapioca.**

Prato, Bruce Coleman Ltd.

Cassava plants, *above,* grow in warm climates. Roots from a sweet cassava, *left,* are prepared and eaten like potatoes.

Dr. Nigel Smith, Earth Scenes

Cassette. See **Tape recorder; Television** (Video entertainment systems); **Videotape recorder.**

Cassia, *KASH uh* or *KAS ee uh,* is the name of a group of plants found mainly in warm and tropical regions. Some botanists place more than 500 species in this group. Cassias range from low herbs to trees more than 50 feet (15 meters) high. Most cassias have showy yellow flowers.

Many species of cassias are cultivated for their leaves and fruits, which contain medicinal compounds. The dried leaves of various species, cultivated chiefly in Africa and India, supply *senna,* used as a laxative. The seed pods of certain species are dried and used like senna.

The name *cassia* also refers to a tree of the laurel family. The bark of this tree is used like cinnamon. See **Cinnamon.** Michael J. Tanabe

Scientific classification. Cassias belong to the pea family, Fabaceae or Leguminosae. They make up the genus *Cassia.*

Cassini is a spacecraft sent to Saturn to study the planet and its rings and satellites. The United States National Aeronautics and Space Administration (NASA) launched Cassini on Oct. 15, 1997. The craft began orbiting Saturn on July 1, 2004. Cassini has also studied Saturn's *magnetosphere,* a zone of strong *magnetic fields* originating in Saturn. A magnetic field is the influence that a magnet—in this case, the planet—creates in the region around it.

Engineers and scientists at NASA's Jet Propulsion Laboratory built Cassini. The Italian Space Agency provided a large antenna and several other elements of the spacecraft. The craft was named for the Italian-born French astronomer Giovanni Domenico Cassini, who made major discoveries about Saturn in the late 1600's.

Cassini carried a probe called Huygens. The European Space Agency designed and built Huygens to drop into the atmosphere of Titan, Saturn's largest satellite. Huygens was equipped with six instruments to study Titan's atmosphere and surface. The probe was named for the Dutch physicist, astronomer, and mathematician Christiaan Huygens, who discovered Titan in 1655.

Cassini's primary mission called for 45 close fly-bys of Titan and visits to the satellites Dione, Enceladus, Hyperion, Iapetus, Phoebe, Rhea, and Tethys. Cassini also made distant observations of those moons and others.

NASA

The Cassini probe began orbiting Saturn in 2004. Cassini was designed to study Saturn, its rings, and its moons and to drop a probe called Huygens into the atmosphere of the moon Titan.

Some of Cassini's studies have focused on Saturn's atmosphere and interior. Cassini has also investigated the rings and smaller moons to help scientists understand the origin and evolution of the ring system. In 2006, Cassini found evidence of tiny "moonlets" about 300 feet (100 meters) in diameter orbiting inside the rings.

Cassini and Huygens have studied Titan closely for two reasons: (1) it is one of the largest satellites in the solar system, and (2) it has the thickest atmosphere of any moon. Titan's atmosphere consists mostly of nitrogen and has a thick, smoglike haze. Visible light cannot pass through the haze, so Cassini carries a radar that can penetrate the atmosphere. The spacecraft also has cameras equipped with filters that enable them to photograph Titan's surface.

On Dec. 25, 2004, Cassini released Huygens. Huygens arrived at Titan's atmosphere on Jan. 14, 2005. For 2 ½ hours, the probe analyzed chemicals, recorded sounds, and measured winds as it parachuted toward the moon's surface. Titan's haze cleared at an altitude of about 20 miles (30 kilometers), enabling the probe's cameras to capture photographs of Titan's surface. The images revealed a landscape that appeared to have been carved by rains of liquid methane. Huygens touched down in a soft mixture of water ice and hydrocarbon ice, becoming the first craft to land on a satellite of a planet other than Earth. William S. Kurth

See also **Saturn; Titan.**

Cassini, Giovanni Domenico (1625-1712), was an Italian-born French astronomer who discovered four moons of Saturn and a large gap in Saturn's ring system. The gap is now known as the *Cassini division.* Cassini is also known by the French name Jean Dominique Cassini. Because of his discoveries pertaining to Saturn, a space probe that the United States launched in 1997 to investigate Saturn was named for him.

Cassini was born on June 8, 1625, in Perinaldo, in what is now northern Italy. In 1650, he became a professor of astronomy at the University of Bologna. He went to Paris in 1669 and soon became the first director of the Paris Observatory. He became a French citizen in 1673.

Cassini's tables of the sun, published in 1662, established his reputation as an astronomer. He had precisely measured the sun's apparent motion through the sky. Later, he closely approximated the distance from Earth to the sun.

Cassini's observations of Jupiter were so precise that he could distinguish between shadows cast by moons of Jupiter and fixed shadows on Jupiter's surface. Cassini used the moon shadows to create tables of the motions of the moons. He used the fixed shadows to determine the length of Jupiter's day. Cassini died in Paris on Sept. 14, 1712. Roger Ariew

Cassiopeia, *KAS ee uh PEE uh,* is an easily seen constellation of the Northern Hemisphere. It is on the side of the North Star opposite the Big Dipper, about the same distance away. It lies directly north of the constellation Andromeda. In Greek mythology, Cassiopeia was the mother of Andromeda. Five of the brightest stars in Cassiopeia form a large, irregular letter W. In 1572, the Danish astronomer Tycho Brahe observed a *supernova* (exploding star) in this constellation. Sumner Starrfield

Cassiterite, *kuh SIHT uh ryt* (chemical formula, SnO_2), is the only important ore mineral of tin. It is sometimes called *tinstone.* Cassiterite usually has a slight metallic luster, with a brown or black color. It usually occurs in veins associated with quartz, and it is found either in or near granite rocks. Countries that are major producers of cassiterite include Brazil, Bolivia, China, Indonesia, Malaysia, and Thailand. Robert B. Cook

See also **Tin.**

Cassius Longinus, *KASH ih uhs lahn JY nuhs,* **Gaius,** *GAY uhs* (? -42 B.C.), was a Roman general and statesman who, with Marcus Junius Brutus, led the conspiracy against Julius Caesar. During the civil war between Caesar and Pompey, Cassius commanded a fleet for Pompey. Caesar won the war, pardoned Cassius, and made him *praetor* (administrator of the courts) in 44 B.C. But Cassius helped murder Caesar later that year. Cassius and his brother-in-law Brutus fled east and raised a large army. Mark Antony and Octavian defeated them at Philippi. Cassius committed suicide when his camp was taken. Arthur M. Eckstein

See also **Caesar, Julius.**

Cassowary, *KAS uh WEHR ee,* is a large, shy bird that lives in thick forests in Australia, New Guinea, and nearby islands. Cassowaries cannot fly. All three species of this bird have a massive body, long legs, and a featherless but brightly colored neck and head. A bony helmet, used to butt through undergrowth, covers the head.

WORLD BOOK illustration by John Rignall, Linden Artists Ltd.

The cassowary is a large bird that lives in the forests of Australia, New Guinea, and nearby Pacific islands. Although it cannot fly, it can sprint as fast as 40 miles (64 kilometers) per hour.

The largest species, the single-wattled cassowary of New Guinea, stands about 5 feet (1.5 meters) tall and weighs about 120 pounds (54 kilograms). Its wings and tail are small and almost hidden. Brownish-black, bristlelike feathers cover the body. Each foot has three toes armed with sharp claws. These claws are deadly weapons in a fight. John W. Fitzpatrick

Scientific classification. Cassowaries make up the cassowary family, Casuariidae. The single-wattled cassowary is *Casuarius unappendiculatus.*

See also **Emu.**

Cast and casting. Casting is a method of shaping an object by pouring a liquid into a mold and letting it harden. The shaped object is called either a *cast* or a

Sand casting

Sand casting is one of the methods used to make castings. Some of the steps in sand casting are shown here. The mold for a casting is made by pressing a pattern into two beds of damp sand, *below left.* Each bed contains half a mold. The beds are matched and locked together. A worker pours molten metal into the mold, *below right.* After the metal cools, the mold and casting are emptied onto a screen. The screen vibrates and the sand mold is shaken from the cast.

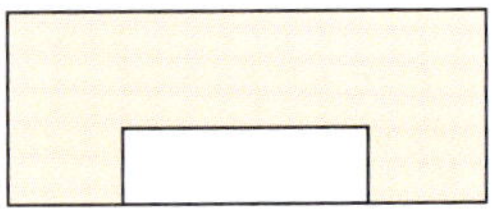

A sand mold is made from a pattern of the object to be cast. Damp sand is packed around the pattern in a wooden or metal box.

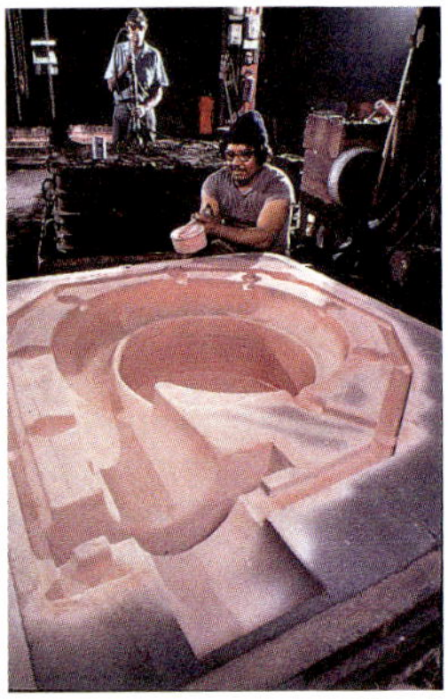

Jim Pickerell

Jim Pickerell

The drag is the bottom half of the mold. It has a pouring gate and mold cavity, which will be filled with metal.

The cope is the top half of the mold. It has a pouring basin and a *sprue* (channel for pouring metal).

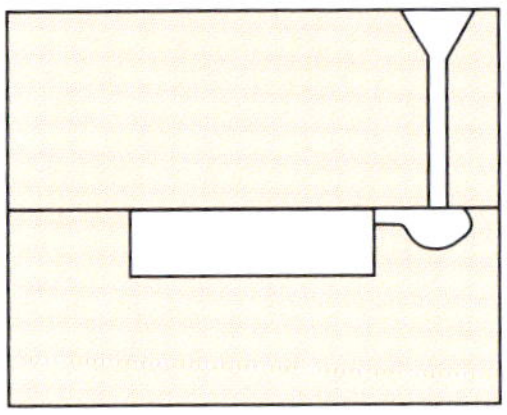

The flask consists of the cope and the drag, which are fastened together. Molten metal is poured into the mold.

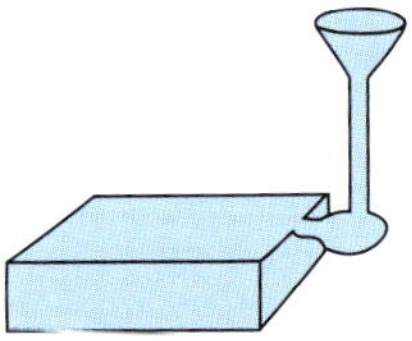

WORLD BOOK illustrations

The casting has the same shape as the original pattern. The sprue is later removed from the casting.

casting. Casting is used to make thousands of articles, including tools, machine parts, toys, and art objects such as statues. The Egyptians cast bronze in molds more than 3,500 years ago. Today, plastics, iron, steel, aluminum, ceramics, and numerous other materials are used in casting.

Patterns for casting. Before materials are cast, workers make a wood or metal pattern of the article to be cast. These patterns are later used to make the molds from which the actual castings are made. Patterns may be made in a number of ways, depending on the size of the article and on how many times the mold will be used. Solid, or one-piece, patterns are called *loose patterns.* Such patterns are generally used when the object is extremely large and when only a few pieces of the object will be needed. A *match-plate* pattern is made by splitting the pattern in two halves. A *split pattern* consists of two halves that can be fitted and held together with pins.

Types of molds. Most metals are cast in *green sand,* which is a mixture of sand, clay, water, and a binder to hold the sand grains together. A *dry sand* mold makes a smoother casting surface. It contains a special binder. The surfaces of a dry sand mold are dried with an open flame before the mold is poured. *Permanent molds,* made of metal, are used for special types of castings.

How castings are made. Metal is usually cast in a sand mold. If an object, such as an iron dumbbell, is to be cast from a split pattern, one half of the pattern is placed on a board, with its flat side down. The board is surrounded by two loose-fitting wooden or metal boxes. Together, these boxes make up a *flask.* Damp sand is packed firmly around the pattern to fill the space between the pattern and the sides of the flask. The board is removed, and the other half of the pattern is fitted to the first half. Sand is then packed around it.

The top half of the flask with its sand is called the *cope.* The bottom half is called the *drag.* The cope and the drag of the mold are fitted together after the pattern has been removed from the sand. A small opening called a *gate* is formed to each end of the cope so the metal can be poured into the mold. A cavity can be made in a casting by suspending a hard sand object called a *core* in the mold. When the metal is poured into the mold, it cools quickly and forms a solid. The sand is then broken away.

Other types of casting. In *pit molding,* extremely large castings are molded in a deep pit. It takes several days or even a week to make a mold and complete the casting in a pit mold. In *centrifugal casting,* molds are rotated rapidly while the metal is being poured. The centrifugal force of the rotation forces the metal to the inner surface of the mold.

Three processes are used to make *precision castings:* (1) shell molding, (2) die casting, and (3) the lost wax process. In *shell molding,* the copes and drags are from $\frac{1}{4}$ to $\frac{1}{2}$ inch (6 to 13 millimeters) thick, and are held in place by clamps or weights. The pattern is heated and placed in the molding material. This material consists of fine sand and a plastic substance that holds the sand together when heat is applied. In *die casting,* the melted metal is forced into a permanent metal mold called the *die,* and the castings are removed when they cool. A machine can perform the entire process. In the *lost wax process,* moist plaster of Paris is placed around a wax pattern. The mold is heated or baked, and the wax runs out, leaving a precise mold. This process is used to make dental plates and to shape metals that cannot be shaped by the usual factory methods. James A. Clum

Related articles in *World Book* include:

Aluminum (Casting)
Cast iron
Die and diemaking
Foundry
Glass (How glass is shaped; pictures)
Iron and steel (Cast iron; Shaping and finishing steel)
Plastics
Pottery
Sculpture (The sculptor at work)
Silver (pictures)

Cast iron is a hard, brittle form of iron made by *casting.* Casting is a process in which metal that has been melted is poured into molds and allowed to harden. Cast iron is often made by remelting a form of iron called pig iron. Solid cast iron is inexpensive and easy to make. It is known for its strength, density, and ability to absorb shock and vibration. All these qualities make cast iron especially useful in producing engine blocks, machinery frames, pipes, fire hydrants, and construction materials.

Cast iron is an *alloy* (mixture of metals) that contains about 90 percent iron, 2 to 4 percent carbon, 1 to 3 percent silicon, and smaller amounts of manganese, phosphorus, and sulfur. The high carbon content of cast iron contributes to its brittleness. This condition makes cast iron impossible to shape at any temperature below its melting point and requires the use of molds.

James A. Clum

Castanets, *KAS tuh NEHTS,* are a small percussion instrument of indefinite pitch. Each castanet is a spoon-shaped clapper made of a hard wood. In the original Spanish form, two castanets are tied together in pairs. A dancer carries a pair of castanets in each hand and clicks them together to add a rhythmic accompaniment. For orchestral use, castanets are tied on both sides of a small wooden paddle, and the performer uses only one pair. The instrument is ancient and characteristically Spanish.

John H. Beck

Paul Robert Perry

Castanets are so called because they look like chestnuts, the Latin word for which is *castanea.*

Caste, *kast,* is a social class to which a person belongs by birth. Within a caste, most people share the same culture or occupation, belong to the same religious *sect* (group), or enjoy the same level of wealth. The term *caste* is most often applied to the closed groups into which the people of India are divided. This article discusses India's caste system.

There are as many as 3,000 castes, or *jatis,* in India. Each caste has its own customs and rituals. To maintain ritual purity, members of each caste neither marry nor dine with members of other castes.

Castes may have existed in India before the arrival of Aryans from central Asia about 1500 B.C. Eventually, Aryan religious leaders and scholars called *Brahmans* developed a system for ranking the castes. It consisted of four ranked categories called *varnas* (colors).

The top varna was *white* and was occupied by Brahmans. The next varna was *red* and consisted of *Kshatriyas*—that is, rulers, nobles, and warriors. Then came the *yellow* varna. People in this category engaged in banking and other kinds of business and were known as Vaisyas. The *black* varna was next, and it included Sudras—artisans and laborers.

Besides the four varnas developed by the Brahmans, there was also a fifth category. People of the castes in this category were sometimes called *panchamas* (fifths) or *outcastes.* Today, panchamas are also known as *untouchables.* About a fifth of India's people belong to untouchable castes.

India's caste system has rarely matched the one outlined above. Through the centuries, however, the actual system became increasingly rigid and elaborate. Many attempts have been made to eliminate the system, but all have failed. India's 1950 Constitution outlaws untouchability and grants equal status to all peoples. But laws and modern urban life have weakened the system only somewhat. Caste prejudice remains an important factor interfering with India's social integration and economic progress. Robert Eric Frykenberg

See also **Buddhism; Gandhi, Mohandas K.; Hinduism; India** (Social structure); **Mythology** (Mythology and society).

Castiglione, *KAHS tee LYOH nay,* **Baldassare,** *BAHL dahs SAH ray* (1478-1529), was a writer of the Italian Renaissance. He is best known for *The Book of the Courtier* (1528), in which he set forth standards of conduct for the perfect courtier. This work is in the form of dialogues and has four sections. The first two sections describe the qualities and virtues of the ideal courtier. The third deals with the court lady and her role in her husband's achievement of excellence. The fourth section relates this excellence to the courtier's responsibility to his prince. Translations of Castiglione's book became guides to social refinement in Spain, France, and England.

Castiglione was born near Mantua. He spent much time in the courts of Milan and Urbino. The Urbino court was the setting for *The Book of the Courtier.*

Richard H. Lansing

Castile and Aragon, *kas TEEL, AR uh gahn,* were two separate and powerful kingdoms of Spain. They were united in 1479 under the rule of Ferdinand and Isabella, the monarchs who later earned a place in American history through their ties to Christopher Columbus. The combined territories formed the heart of the modern kingdom of Spain. Aragon extended over the northeastern part of the peninsula, and Castile occupied the greater part of present-day Spain, ranging from the Bay of Biscay southward. Both kingdoms were formed as a result of Christian victories over the Moors, who had taken control of most of Spain in the A.D. 700's. The strength gained from the union of Castile with Aragon made possible the death blow to Moorish dominion in

Europe (see **Moors**). Today, Castilian Spanish is the official language of Spain, though such languages as Basque, Catalan, and Galician have official status in certain regions. James W. Brodman

See also **Ferdinand V; Isabella I; Madrid; Spain** (History).

Castilla, *kahs TEE yah,* **Ramón,** *rah MAWN* (1797?-1867), one of Peru's great statesmen, was president of Peru from 1845 to 1851 and from 1855 to 1862. A nationalist and a liberal, he gave Peru its first period of peace and stability. He encouraged the guano and nitrate industries, docks, railroads, and the telegraph. He freed Peru's last slaves, extended voting rights, and ended forced payments from Indian workers to their employers. Castilla was born in Tarapacá, Peru (now part of Chile). In 1821, he joined the independence forces led by General José de San Martín. See also **Peru** (The early republic). Michael L. Conniff

Castillo de San Marcos National Monument, *kas TEE yoh duh san MAHRK uhs,* is in St. Augustine, Florida. It includes the oldest masonry fort in the continental United States. The Spaniards started its construction in 1672. The monument was established in 1924. It was formerly called Fort Marion National Monument. For area, see **National Park System** (table: National monuments). Critically reviewed by the National Park Service

Casting. See **Cast and casting.**

Casting, in fishing. See **Fishing** (Reels).

Castle was the home and fortress of a monarch or noble. Castles became important in western Europe in the late A.D. 900's and the 1000's. They played a central role in the political and military system called *feudalism.* In the Middle Ages, which lasted from the A.D. 400's to 1500, Europe was divided into many small states, and local conflicts were common. Under feudalism, kings in western Europe often granted land to nobles called *vassals* in exchange for military and other services. A castle helped the king or vassal defend the land where the castle stood. It also provided a home for the monarch or noble's family and servants. In addition, a castle served as a barracks, prison, storehouse, armory, treasure house, and center of local government.

The word *castle* comes from a Latin word meaning *fortress.* European castles developed from fortified camps built by the ancient Romans and from fenced villages of prehistoric Europeans. People in the Middle East and Japan also built castles. This article deals chiefly with castles built in Europe between A.D. 1000 and 1400.

Structure. Before the 1100's, most castles were made of timber and earth. A majority of them had a natural or artificially created hill called a *motte.* A tower called a *keep* or *donjon* often stood on the flat top of the motte. The keep, typically made of wood, was the castle's best-protected building and served as its last defense. In some cases, the castle holder's family and guards lived in the keep. A *palisade* (wooden wall) enclosed the top of the motte. In most cases, one or more *baileys* (fortified courtyards) lay at the foot of the motte.

Deep ditches called *moats* surrounded the motte and each bailey. Earth dug from a bailey's moat was piled up to form a barrier just inside the moat. In many cases, a palisade topped each barrier. Enemies attacking a castle had to break through the defenses of one or more baileys before they could reach the motte's defenses.

In the 1100's, Europeans began to build more and more castles out of stone. Stone castles provided better protection from enemy attacks, fires, and weather. In the late 1200's, strong stone walls and towers began to replace the keep as the castle's main defenses. Some stone castles had an inner courtyard called the *inner bailey* or *inner ward.* This courtyard was surrounded by high stone walls, which, in turn, were protected by additional encircling walls. The areas between the walls also were known as *baileys* or *wards.*

Preventing an enemy from reaching the walls of a castle was one of the best ways to defend it. Moats were often used for this purpose. In many cases, the moat was filled with water. A drawbridge lay across the moat in front of the castle entrance and could be raised when an enemy approached. Some people built castles on the banks of lakes or rivers and channeled the water into the moat. Others built castles on mountaintops or steep hillsides.

The walls of stone castles could be up to 33 feet (10 meters) thick. In most cases, round towers stood at the corners of the walls and along the lengths of the walls. Guards walked along the tops of the walls and towers, where they were protected by defensive structures called *battlements.* The battlements consisted of stone uprights known as *merlons* and open spaces called *crenels.* The merlons shielded the guards from enemy missiles. Through the crenels, the guards could shoot arrows or drop rocks on attackers.

Many stone castles were entered through a structure called a *gatehouse.* Typically, the gatehouse consisted of two large towers—one on each side of the entrance—and one or more rooms above the entrance. From inside the gatehouse, people could open and close huge doors that stood at the entrance. They could also raise and lower one or more *portcullises,* heavy metal gratings that blocked the entrance. The drawbridge also could be operated from inside the gatehouse.

Uses. During feudal times in Europe, monarchs and nobles depended on castles to provide safety and de-

Bob and Ira Spring from West Stock

Château Queyras stands in the French Alps near the boundary between France and Italy. This castle was originally built during the Middle Ages.

WORLD BOOK illustration by Linden Artists Ltd.

A stone castle of the Middle Ages had high, strong walls and was protected by a wide moat. A typical castle included living quarters for the lord and his family, their servants, and soldiers.

fense for themselves, their families, and their lands. Strong castles were very difficult to capture. The huge walls and the well-protected entrance withstood most first attacks. A *siege* might be more successful. In a siege, enemy forces repeatedly attacked a castle while cutting off all food, water, and help from outside. But it could take months to starve out a castle's defenders, and few attackers could mount and maintain a long siege.

Castles also helped feudal lords maintain their rule over the lands around the castle. A monarch or noble could control a river crossing, mountain pass, or sea harbor by building a castle there. When a king wished to spread his power to new lands, he often built castles there to help control the new territory.

The castle served as a center for local government. Peasants who farmed the land around the castle became tenants of the noble who lived in the castle. The peasants paid rents and performed services that helped support the castle. The noble protected the peasants during wartime. The lord of a castle held a court of law to settle disputes among the peasants.

A castle was also a social center for the nobility. Lords and ladies gathered for great feasts at which they danced and listened to *minstrels* (wandering singers). On special occasions, the lord held a tournament in a field outside the castle, with *jousting* (armed fights on horseback) and feasting.

Life in a castle. A castle could house a noble's family, their servants and staff, priests, a company of soldiers, and horses, pigs, and other animals. Most castles had a *great hall,* in which castle life centered; a kitchen; a chapel; toilets (called *garderobes*); and places to sleep. Heat was provided by fires in the middle of the hall and, later, by fireplaces. Candles and torches provided light. For nobles, living in a castle could be exciting at times. But there were also long periods during which they had no communication with people from the outside. In addition, castles could be uncomfortable. In winter, the stone walls became damp and cold, and the rooms were drafty.

Decline of castles. By 1500, castles had become much less important in Europe. Gunpowder and can-

© Steve Elmore, West Stock

Spanish castles, such as this impressive fortress in Segovia, were called *alcazars.* Kings of Castile and Leon in Spain lived in this turreted castle during the Middle Ages.

nons came into common use during the 1400's, and they were more effective against castles than the old methods of attack. Cannons could fire stone or iron balls against castles until they knocked down the tall towers and thick walls. Also, many nobles sought more comfortable housing. In addition, the monarchs of France, England, and other western European countries began discouraging the construction and use of castles. In this way, they hoped to reduce the power of local feudal lords. Lon R. Shelby

Related articles in *World Book* include:

Pictures of castles

The following articles have pictures of castles:

Citadel	Germany	Spain
Crusades	Moravia	Teutonic Knights
Edinburgh	Rhine River	Windsor Castle
England		

Other related articles

Camelot	Middle Ages

Additional resources

Kennedy, Hugh. *Crusader Castles.* 1994. Reprint. Cambridge, 2001.
Pounds, Norman J. G. *The Medieval Castle in England and Wales.* Cambridge, 1990.
Steele, Philip. *Castles.* 1995. Reprint. Kingfisher, 1999. Younger readers.

Castle Clinton National Monument is in New York City. It was originally a fort that was built to defend New York City during the War of 1812. The fort served as military headquarters for the U.S. Army in New York during the war. In 1815, the fort was named Castle Clinton in honor of De Witt Clinton, then mayor of New York City. It was later named Castle Garden and used as an entertainment center. From 1855 until 1890, it was an immigration station, and from 1896 until 1941, it was the site of the New York Aquarium (now Aquarium for Wildlife Conservation). The monument was established in 1946. For its area, see **National Park System** (table: National monuments). Critically reviewed by the National Park Service

Castlereagh, *KAS uhl ray,* **Viscount** (1769-1822), was a noted British statesman at the time of the Napoleonic Wars. He was born on June 18, 1769, in Dublin, Ireland. His given name was Robert Stewart.

In 1790, Castlereagh was elected to the Irish Parliament. In 1800, he persuaded the Irish Parliament to pass the Act of Union, which joined Ireland and Great Britain to form the United Kingdom.

Castlereagh served in the Parliament of the United Kingdom from 1801 until his death. He served as war secretary in 1805 and from 1807 to 1809. In 1809, he wounded Foreign Secretary George Canning in a duel over war policy and resigned from office temporarily.

Castlereagh served as both foreign secretary and leader of the House of Commons from 1812 to 1822. He worked out many of the peace settlements at the Congress of Vienna in 1815. Castlereagh committed suicide on Aug. 12, 1822. Marjorie Bloy

Castor and Pollux were twin heroes in Greek mythology. Pollux is also called *Polydeuces.* Castor and Pollux are often called the *Dioscuri,* which means *the sons of Zeus.* Zeus was king of the gods. But it was said that only Pollux was Zeus's son and that Castor was the son of Tyndareus, the husband of their mother, Leda. The sisters of Castor and Pollux were Helen of Troy and Clytemnestra, the wife of Agamemnon, who was king of Mycenae (or Argos). The two brothers were good companions and became, as gods, patrons of athletes and protectors of sailors at sea. Castor and Pollux had power over winds and waves.

Castor and Pollux quarreled with their cousins, Idas and Lynceus. Idas killed Castor. Then Pollux and Zeus killed Idas and Lynceus. Pollux, an immortal as the son of Zeus, begged to share his immortality with Castor. As a result, the brothers spent every second day on Mount Olympus—the home of the gods—and the rest of the time in Hades, the land of the dead. According to another version of the story, they were placed together in the sky as the constellation *Gemini,* or *The Twins.*

William F. Hansen

Castor oil is a colorless oil that is used as a laxative. When fresh, it is clear and sticky. Castor oil gently irritates the walls of the intestines and causes them to function. If used too frequently, it may cause constipation. Castor oil is used as a medicine, but most of the world's supply is used in industrial processes.

The castor tree grows in many tropical countries, especially Brazil and India. The plant grows up to 40 feet (12 meters) high in tropical climates. In colder climates, it grows as an annual no more than 15 feet (4.6 meters) high. The spiny *capsules* (fruits) contain the beanlike seeds. The seed is poisonous if eaten. A deadly poison called *ricin* can be extracted from castor seeds. Castor oil for medicinal use is obtained from the seed, leaving the poison in residue, by a process called *cold pressing.* Further processing of the poisonous residue by *solvent extraction* yields more oil for industrial use. Industry uses castor oil in the manufacture of paints, varnishes, and dyes. The oil is also used as a lubricant for boat and airplane engines. Daniel R. Sullivan

WORLD BOOK illustration by John D. Dawson

Castor-oil plants bear spiny fruits that contain the oil-producing beans. Much castor oil comes from Brazil and India.

Scientific classification. The castor tree belongs to the spurge family, Euphorbiaceae. It is *Ricinus communis.*

See also **Vegetable oil** (production).

Castration. See **Cat** (Birth control); **Dog** (Social and moral responsibilities); **Pet** (Birth control).

Castries, *ka STREE* or *KAHS trees* (pop. 52,868), is the capital and largest city of St. Lucia, an island country in the Caribbean Sea. The city borders a well-protected harbor on the northwest coast of the country (see **Saint Lucia** [map]). Castries has a busy port, which handles most of the nation's trade and serves cruise ships. Fires in 1948 and 1951 destroyed many of Castries's buildings, which were made of wood. Today, modern glass and concrete buildings line the streets of the city's business and government district.

French settlers founded Castries in 1651. From the 1600's to 1814, control of St. Lucia alternated many times between England (later part of the United Kingdom) and France. The United Kingdom governed the island from 1814 to 1979, when St. Lucia became an independent nation. Gerald R. Showalter

Castro, *KAS troh,* **Fidel,** *fih DEHL* (1926-), has ruled Cuba since 1959, when he overthrew the military dictatorship of Fulgencio Batista. Castro established a dictatorship and made Cuba the first Communist state in the Western Hemisphere. He became famous for his fiery, anti-American speeches.

Castro was born on Aug. 13, 1926, in Birán, near Mayarí, Cuba. His full name was Fidel Castro Ruz. His father was a Spanish immigrant who owned a small plantation. Castro graduated from the University of Havana in 1950 with a law degree. Afterward, Castro opened a law office in Havana. In 1952, he ran for election to the Cuban House of Representatives. But troops led by Batista halted the election and ended democracy in Cuba.

As a result of Batista's actions, Castro tried to start a revolution against the Batista dictatorship. On July 26, 1953, Castro's forces attacked the Moncada army barracks in the city of Santiago de Cuba. Castro was captured and sentenced to 15 years in prison. But Batista released him in 1955. Castro then formed the *26th of July Movement,* a group of revolutionaries named after the date of his first revolt. He then went into exile in Mexico. Castro's forces landed in Cuba in December 1956. Many rebels were killed, and Castro and other survivors fled to the Sierra Maestra, a mountain range in southeast Cuba. People from the surrounding countryside joined the rebellion. Batista fled from Cuba on Jan. 1, 1959, and Castro took control of the government.

Castro seized property owned by Americans and other foreigners as well as Cubans. In 1960, the Castro government took over U.S. oil refineries in Cuba. The United States then stopped buying Cuban sugar. Castro responded by taking over all U.S. businesses in Cuba.

Castro has supported a number of revolutionary movements in South America, Central America, and Africa. The Castro government has provided improved education and health facilities for many Cubans. But the economy has often been troubled. In the early 1960's, Cuba began depending heavily on the Soviet Union for economic support. This support ended in 1991, when the Soviet Union was dissolved. Castro vowed that Cuba would remain a Communist country. But in the early 1990's, Cuba undertook limited reforms that loosened state control over parts of the country's economy.

Patrick Durand, Sygma

Fidel Castro

Castro has been closely assisted by his brother Raúl. He has named Raúl as his eventual successor.

Jaime Suchlicki

See also **Cuba** (The Castro revolution); **Cuban missile crisis; Kennedy, John Fitzgerald** (Foreign affairs).

Additional resources

Balfour, Sebastian. *Castro.* 2nd ed. 1995. Reprint. Longman Pub. Group, 2000.
Foss, Clive. *Fidel Castro.* Sutton, 2000.

Castro, *KAS troh,* **Raul Hector,** *rah OOL* (1916-), served as governor of Arizona from 1975 to 1977. Castro, a Democrat, was the first Mexican American to hold that office. In 1977, President Jimmy Carter appointed him to serve as United States ambassador to Argentina. Castro held that office until 1980.

Markow Photography

Raul H. Castro

Castro was born on June 12, 1916, in Cananea, Mexico. His family moved to Pirtleville, Arizona, in 1926, and Castro became a U.S. citizen in 1939. He graduated from Arizona State Teachers' College (now Northern Arizona University) and earned a law degree from the University of Arizona.

From 1949 to 1955, Castro practiced law in Tucson, Arizona, and served as an assistant attorney for Pima County. He became county attorney in 1955 and was judge of the Pima County Superior Court from 1959 to 1964.

Castro served as ambassador to El Salvador from 1964 to 1968 and to Bolivia in 1968 and 1969. He practiced law in Arizona from 1970 until he became governor and again after he returned from Argentina. Guy Halverson

Caswell, *KAZ wehl,* **Hollis Leland,** *HAHL ihs LEE luhnd* (1901-1988), an American educator, became an authority on curriculum planning in schools. Caswell directed surveys of curriculum practices in a number of school systems. He wrote several books on the subject.

Caswell was born on Oct. 22, 1901, in Woodruff, Kansas. He graduated from the University of Nebraska and Teachers College, Columbia University. He taught and conducted research at George Peabody College for Teachers from 1929 to 1937. He joined the staff at Teachers College in 1937 and served as its president from 1954 to 1962. Caswell became a member of the editorial advisory board of *The World Book Encyclopedia* in 1936. Caswell served as chairman of the advisory board from 1948 to 1966. He died on Nov. 22, 1988. Amy E. Wells

Fabian Bachrach

Hollis L. Caswell

Hediye Kerman

A kitten staring curiously at a vase

Pete Pearson, Van Cleve Photography

A cat hunting in a field

© Hans Reinhard

A tabby clawing at a tree

© Hans Reinhard

A cat washing itself

Cat

Cat is a favorite pet of people around the world. Cats are intelligent and have an independent nature. These small animals can also be playful and entertaining. Many cats make affectionate, loyal pets, providing companionship for people of all ages. Tens of millions of cats are kept as pets worldwide.

The word *cat* also refers to a family of meat-eating animals that includes tigers, lions, and leopards. This family also includes *domestic cats*—that is, those that people keep as pets. Domestic cats and their wild relatives share many characteristics. All these animals have long, powerful bodies and somewhat rounded heads. They have short, strong jaws and 30 sharp teeth. Cats are also skillful hunters. They are able to catch other animals by approaching them swiftly and quietly on padded feet. Or they may wait motionless until an animal comes close and then spring upon it suddenly.

This article deals with domestic cats. These animals have many special physical abilities. They see better in dim light than people do. They can climb trees, run at a high speed, and leap long distances. Cats also have a keen sense of balance and can easily walk along the tops of narrow fences or along narrow ledges. When cats fall, they almost always land on their feet.

Cats vary in personality and in certain physical features, such as the length and color of their coats. There

---

Terri McGinnis, the contributor of this article, is a veterinarian and the author of The Well Cat Book. *She has written a magazine column on pets and has hosted a pet health radio show.*

Why cats do the things they do

WORLD BOOK illustrations by Tim Gray

A cat licks its fur to clean it and to remove fleas and other parasites. A cat's tongue is covered with tiny hooklike projections called *papillae*. The papillae act like small combs, collecting and removing foreign material and loose hair.

Playing with a toy develops a kitten's hunting skills. Kittens instinctively stalk, paw, pounce upon, and wrestle with toys. Even adult cats that have no need to hunt seem to enjoy engaging in these motions.

A cat arches its back and fluffs up its fur when frightened. These actions make the cat's body look larger, which may help to frighten away whatever is scaring the cat.

Rubbing against legs is a familiar way for cats to greet people. The rubbing releases scent from special glands on the cat's head, face, and tail. Marking a person with its own scent makes the cat more comfortable with the person.

The skeleton of a cat

The body of a cat includes about 250 bones. The exact number of bones varies, depending on the length of a cat's tail. The skeleton supports and protects the tissues and organs of the body.

WORLD BOOK illustration by James Teason and John D. Dawson

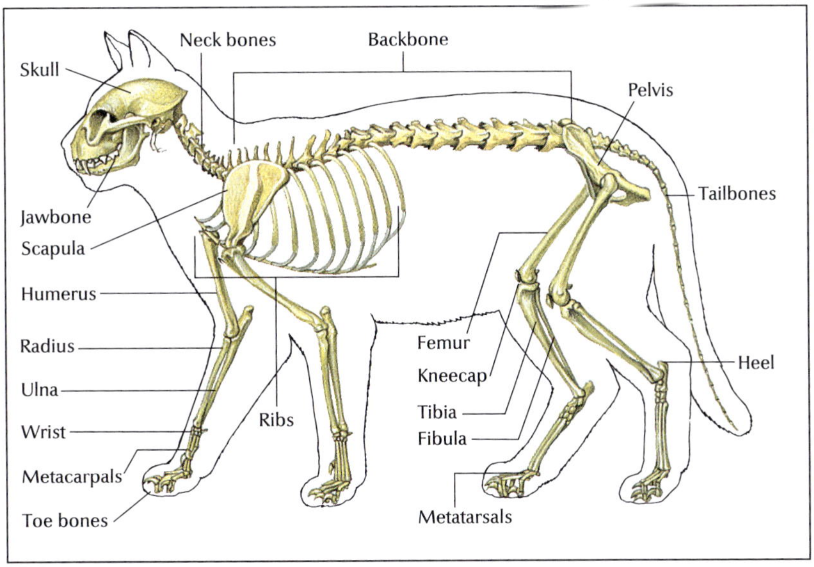

The paws of a cat

Spongy footpads, *right,* enable a cat to walk quietly. Each of a cat's toes ends in a sharp, hooked claw. When retracted, *below left,* the claws are held under the skin by ligaments. The claws extend when muscles tighten the tendons, *below right.*

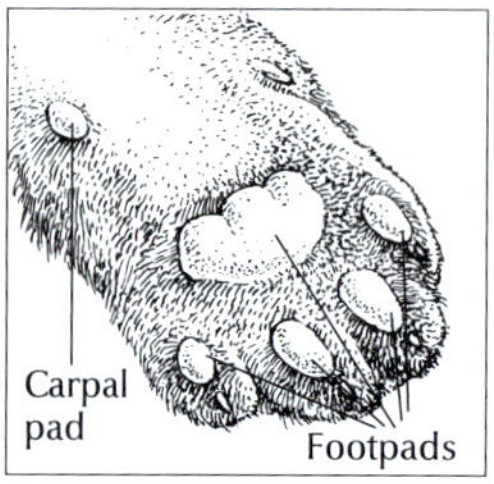

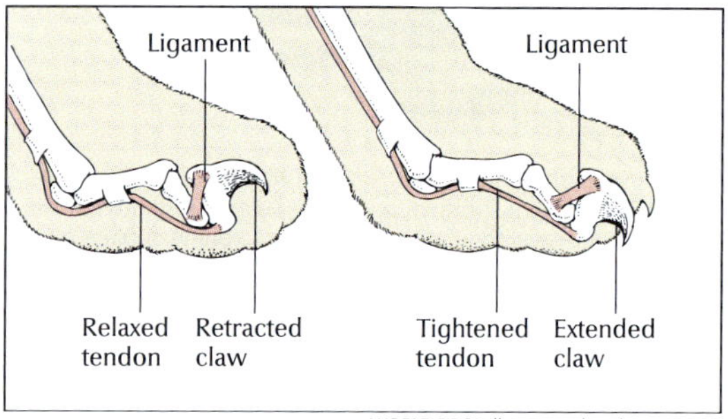

WORLD BOOK illustrations by John D. Dawson

are many breeds of cats. Special characteristics set each breed apart from all others. Among the favorite breeds are the Siamese and the Persian.

No one knows exactly when the first cats were tamed. But some authorities believe cats were tamed about 5,000 years ago. Throughout history, people have valued cats for their skill at hunting and killing mice, rats, and snakes. Cats help keep farms, homes, and businesses free of these animals. The ancient Egyptians considered cats sacred. Today, people in many societies believe cats bring good fortune. But some people associate cats with bad luck and so fear them. Many people find cats mysterious because they move swiftly and silently and because their eyes seem to glow in the dark.

The grace and beauty of cats have made them favorite subjects of artists throughout history. Cats have also been featured in almost every type of literature. They appear in the mythology of ancient Greece and Rome. Hundreds of years ago, Asian writers praised cats in their stories and poems. Cats are also commonly mentioned in the fairy tales, folklore, and legends of many countries. In modern times, books, comic strips, motion pictures, and television programs have featured cats.

The eyes of a cat

The illustrations below show some of the special features of a cat's eyes. Cats can see well in normal and dim light.

Narrowing of the pupils in bright light allows less light into the eyes.

Widening of the pupils in dim light permits more light to enter the eyes.

A third eyelid, in the inner corner of each eye, protects and lubricates the eyes.

WORLD BOOK illustrations by Keith Freeman

Irises of different colors are a feature of *odd-eyed* cats. The cats have normal vision.

The body of a cat

Body size and structure. Adult cats average about 8 to 10 inches (20 to 25 centimeters) tall at the shoulder. Most weigh from 6 to 15 pounds (2.7 to 7 kilograms). But some cats weigh more than 20 pounds (9 kilograms), and some weigh less than 5 pounds (2.3 kilograms).

Cats have the same basic skeleton and internal organs as human beings and other meat-eating mammals. The skeleton of a cat has about 250 bones. The exact number of bones varies, depending on the length of the cat's tail. The skeleton serves as a framework that supports and protects the tissues and organs of a cat's body. Most of the cat's muscles are long, thin, and flexible. They enable a cat to move with great ease and speed. Cats can run about 30 miles (48 kilometers) per hour.

The arrangement of the bones and the joints that connect them permits a cat to perform a variety of movements. Unlike many animals, a cat walks by moving the front and rear legs on one side of its body at the same time, and then the legs on the other side. As a result, a cat seems to glide. Its hip joint enables a cat to leap easily. Other special joints allow a cat to turn its head to reach most parts of its body.

A cat has five toes on each forepaw, including a thumblike inner toe that is helpful in catching prey. Each hindpaw has four toes. Some cats have extra toes. Each of a cat's toes ends in a sharp, hooklike claw. The claws usually are *retracted* (held back) under the skin by elastic ligaments, which are a type of connective tissue. However, when the claws are needed, certain muscles quickly pull the *tendons* (cordlike tissues) connected to the claws. This action extends the claws. A cat uses its claws in climbing, in catching prey, and in defending itself. Several spongy pads of thick skin cover the bottoms of a cat's feet. The pads cushion the paws and enable a cat to move quietly.

A cat's tail is an extension of its backbone. The flexible tail helps a cat keep its balance. When a cat falls, it whips the tail and twists its body to land on its feet.

Head. A cat's head is small and has short, powerful jaws. Kittens have about 26 needlelike temporary teeth, which they shed by about 6 months of age. Adult cats have 30 teeth, which are used for grasping, cutting, and shredding food. Unlike human beings, cats have no teeth for grinding food. But a cat's stomach and intestines can digest chunks of unchewed food. Tiny hooklike projections called *papillae* cover a cat's tongue, making it rough. The rough surface of the tongue helps a cat lick meat from bones and groom its coat.

A cat has a small, wedge-shaped nose. The tip is covered by a tough layer of skin called *nose leather.* The nose leather may be various colors. It is usually moist and cool. A sick cat may have a warm, dry nose.

The colored part of a cat's eyes, called the *iris,* may be shades of green, yellow, orange, copper, blue, or lavender. *Odd-eyed* cats have irises of different colors. For example, one eye may be green and the other blue.

At the back of each eye, a cat has a special mirrorlike structure called the *tapetum lucidum.* It reflects light and so helps a cat see in dim light. It also produces *eyeshine* , the glow a person sees when light strikes the eyes of a cat at night. Each of a cat's eyes has a third eyelid at the inner corner. This structure, called the *nictitating membrane,* protects and lubricates the eyes.

A cat's ears are near the top of its skull. Each ear can move independently. A cat can aim the cup of its ears in the direction from which a sound is coming and so improve its hearing.

Coat. A cat's coat protects its skin and provides insulation. Most coats have two types of hairs. The outer part of the coat is made up of long, stiff *primary,* or *guard,* hairs. The undercoat consists of softer and shorter *secondary,* or *down,* hairs. The color, length, and texture of the coat vary greatly among cats. The Sphinx breed of cat, in fact, may have no hair. Terms commonly used to describe the color of a cat's coat are *solid* or *self, smoke, shaded, tabby, parti-color,* and *colorpoint.*

Solid, or *self,* coats have only one color. The solid colors are black, *blue* (dark gray), brown, *cream* (tan), *lilac* (light gray), *red* (shades of orange), and white.

Smoke coats consist of a white undercoat covered by guard hairs of a dark color. In most cases, the guard hairs are black, blue, or red.

Shaded coats are similar to smoke coats except that the dark color is limited to the tips of the guard hairs. A *chinchilla* coat has a sparkling appearance because only the extreme tips of the guard hairs are dark. Red chinchilla coats are sometimes called *shell cameos.*

Tabby coats are symmetrically patterned with stripes and blotches of a dark color on a lighter background. The patterns are formed by bands of a dark color on individual hairs. Tabby colors include blue, brown, cream, red, and silver. *Mackerel* tabbies have narrow markings.

Parti-color coats have two or more clearly defined colors, such as black and white or blue and cream. *Tortoiseshell* coats are black, red, and cream. *Calico* coats have patches of white, black, red, and cream.

Colorpoint coats consist of a solid color over the trunk of the body and a contrasting color on the *points.* The points include the face, ears, feet, and tail.

Senses. A cat's vision is not as keen as that of a human being. Cats probably see most colors as various shades of gray. However, they can detect the slightest motion, which is helpful in hunting. They see well in dim light but cannot see in total darkness.

Cats have a highly developed sense of smell. Newborn kittens, for example, are able to recognize their

The coats of cats The coats of cats vary in color and pattern, as shown in the illustrations below. Most cats have an undercoat of short, soft *down* hairs and an outer coat of longer, stiffer *guard* hairs.

WORLD BOOK illustrations by Keith Freeman

A solid coat has only one color, such as the red coat above. Other common solid colors are black, cream, and white.

A smoke coat consists of a white undercoat covered by dark guard hairs. This cat has a blue smoke coat.

A shaded coat is white with a dark color on the tips of the guard hairs. This cat has a silver chinchilla coat.

Tabby coat has patterns of dark stripes and blotches on a lighter ground color. A brown tabby is shown above.

A parti-color coat has two or more clearly defined colors. This calico cat has white, black, red, and cream patches.

A colorpoint coat has a solid color on the trunk of the body and a contrasting color on the face, ears, feet, and tail.

Short-haired breeds

These pictures show some of the most common short-haired breeds of cats. The breeds differ in a number of ways. For example, the Siamese has a wedge-shaped head, slender body, and tapering tail; and a short-haired type of Manx has a round head, muscular body, and no tail.

All photos on this page, unless otherwise credited, are WORLD BOOK photos by Alice Su.

Devon rex

Russian blue

Burmese

Havana brown

WORLD BOOK photo

Korat

Siamese

Manx (short-haired)

WORLD BOOK photo

Abyssinian

Long-haired breeds

These pictures show some of the most common long-haired breeds of cats. The breeds vary in body size and shape. The large, muscular Maine coon has an almost rectangular shape. The Persian is a stocky animal. The Turkish Angora has a long, slender body.

All photos on this page, unless otherwise credited, are WORLD BOOK photos by Alice Su.

Maine coon

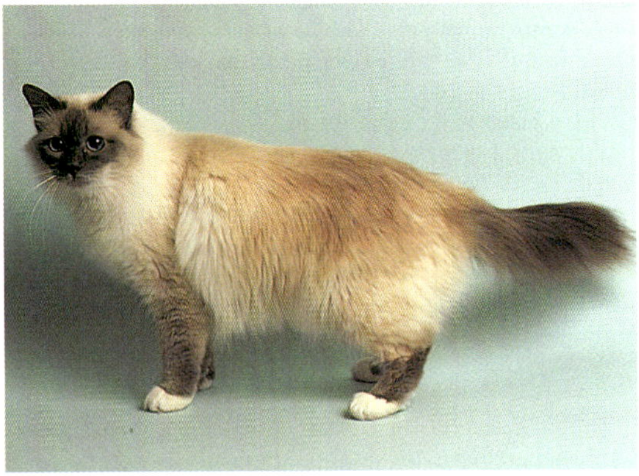

Birman

Persian

Balinese

Somali

© Chanan Photography

Manx (long-haired)

Turkish Angora

nest by scent alone. In addition to its nose, a cat has another sense organ in its mouth that detects scents.

Cats also have a keen sense of hearing. They hear a much broader range of sounds than people do. Deafness is rare among cats. However, it is an inherited defect among some white cats, particularly those with blue or odd-color eyes.

The whiskers of a cat are special hairs that serve as highly sensitive touch organs. These hairs, called *vibrissae* or *tactile hairs,* grow on the chin, at the sides of the face, and above the eyes. The hairs are attached to nerves in the skin, which transmit signals to the brain when the whiskers brush against objects. The whiskers may help a cat protect its eyes, feel its way in the dark, and detect changes in wind direction.

Breeds of cats

The many breeds of cats vary greatly in appearance. Cat breeders have developed numerous breeds by selectively mating animals with certain desirable and distinctive characteristics. These characteristics appear consistently in the offspring of *purebred* cats. A purebred cat is one whose mother and father belong to the same breed. The offspring of cats that have mated randomly are known as *crossbreds* or *alley cats.*

Many people prefer the special features of a certain breed of cats. For example, such purebreds as the Abyssinian and the Birman are among the most beautiful and unusual animals in the world. But crossbreds may be just as beautiful and lovable as purebreds, and they are often healthier.

Certain associations officially recognize cat breeds and establish standards for the ideal characteristics of each breed. However, different cat associations recognize different breeds, and breed standards also vary somewhat. In the United States, cat breeds are commonly divided into two major groups: (1) short-haired breeds and (2) long-haired breeds. Some breeds include both long- and short-haired types.

Short-haired breeds. The Cat Fanciers' Association (CFA), the major U.S. cat association, recognizes numerous short-haired breeds. They include the Abyssinian, American shorthair, American wirehair, Bombay, British shorthair, Burmese, Chartreux, Colorpoint shorthair, Cornish rex, Devon rex, Egyptian Mau, Exotic, Havana brown, Japanese bobtail, Korat, Manx, Ocicat, Oriental, Russian blue, Scottish fold, Selkirk rex, Siamese, Singapura, Sphinx, and Tonkinese.

WORLD BOOK photo

The Japanese bobtail has a short, bushy tail. This cat has been a symbol of good luck in Japan for hundreds of years.

Abyssinian is a slender, muscular, medium-sized cat with a long, tapering tail. *Aby* cats, as they are sometimes called, have a wedge-shaped head and large ears. Their almond-shaped eyes are commonly green, gold, or hazel. These cats are known for their *agouti* coat pattern, which is common in wild animals. Each hair of an Aby's soft coat has two or three bands of alternating light and dark colors. The bands may be a variety of colors, ranging from cream and silver to bluish tones to black and shades of brown and brownish-red.

People once thought the Aby originated in Abyssinia (now called Ethiopia) and descended from the sacred cats of ancient Egypt. Today, some cat experts believe the Aby probably originated in Southeast Asia. Cats resembling the Aby were brought to the United Kingdom from Abyssinia in the mid-1800's.

American shorthair is a muscular, medium- to large-sized animal. Its large head features full cheeks; a broad, squarish muzzle; large, round eyes; and rounded, medium-sized ears. The coat and eyes may be any color. The breed probably developed from cats originally brought to the American Colonies by Europeans.

American wirehair is a medium- to large-sized cat with a rounded head and roundish ears and eyes. It has dense, springy, coarse fur and curly whiskers. The coat may be any color or pattern. This breed originated as a *mutation* (random genetic change) in a litter of upstate New York farm cats in 1966.

Bombay looks somewhat like a miniature black panther. It has a sleek black coat and golden to reddish-brown eyes. This medium-sized breed originated in 1958 in Louisville, Kentucky, as a cross between a black American shorthair and a Burmese.

British shorthair traces its ancestry to domestic cats that lived thousands of years ago in parts of Europe, including what is now the United Kingdom. This medium- to large-sized cat typically has a massive, roundish head; large, round eyes; and ears with rounded tips. It is similar to the American shorthair but has a stockier build and a thicker coat.

Burmese is a medium-sized cat with a muscular body. The cat has round, golden eyes and a short, sleek coat that most commonly is dark brown. This breed was developed from a female cat that was brought to the United States from Burma (now Myanmar) in 1930.

Chartreux is a breed believed to have been brought to France from South Africa by Carthusian monks in the 1600's. This medium- to large-sized cat has a blue-gray coat with a slightly woolly texture. Its eyes may be reddish-brown to golden or brilliant orange. The Chartreux is strong, friendly, and intelligent.

Colorpoint shorthair was developed in England in the early 1900's by crossing Siamese, red British shorthair, and Abyssinian cats. Like the Siamese, this medium-sized breed has a slender body, blue eyes, and a colorpoint coat.

Cornish rex has a short, silky, wavy coat and a greyhoundlike body. The coat, which may be any color, has no guard hairs. This slender, small- to medium-sized cat has a long tail, small head, large ears, and a curved nose. The Cornish rex originated in Cornwall, England, about

WORLD BOOK photo

The Scottish fold has ears that are folded forward. This stocky breed was developed in Scotland during the 1960's.

1950 as a cross between a tortoise-shell cat and a white barn cat.

Devon rex is a strong, medium-sized cat with large eyes, a short muzzle, and huge, low-set ears that give it an elfin appearance. Its soft, wavy coat may be any color. The breed originated in Devonshire, England, in 1960 as a mutation of barn cats.

Egyptian Mau (pronounced *mow*) is one of the oldest breeds of domestic cats, dating back to about 1400 B.C. It has a distinctive coat of dark spots against a lighter background. The spots become bars on the face, legs, and tail. This graceful, medium-sized cat has a rounded head and light green eyes.

Exotic was developed in the United States during the 1950's and 1960's by crossing American shorthair and Persian cats. The Exotic is a stocky, medium-sized cat with a snub nose, large round eyes, and small rounded ears. Its coat, which varies in color and pattern, is short, soft, and thick.

Havana brown is a strong, medium-sized cat with a solid, reddish-brown coat. It has a long head and oval, vivid green eyes. The breed was developed in England during the late 1940's and early 1950's from mating a black British shorthair and a Siamese cat. The Havana brown is friendly to other cats and to people.

Japanese bobtail has a short, rigid tail with bushy hair. This slender, medium-sized animal has been raised in Japan for hundreds of years. Some Japanese believe the bobtail brings good luck. Many works of art portray this cat seated with a paw raised in greeting.

The bobtail has a triangular head with a long nose, slanted eyes, and large ears. It has silky, medium-length fur. Some types of the bobtail have long hair. The coat may be any color. But the traditional "good luck" color of the coat is white with patches of red and black. The playful bobtail has a soft voice and adapts well to other animals and to new surroundings.

Korat is a quiet, gentle animal that originated in Thailand between 1350 and the late 1700's. In Thailand, this breed is believed to bring good luck. It is a muscular, medium-sized cat with a rounded back. The Korat has a heart-shaped face and large, luminous green eyes. Its short, silvery-gray coat lies flat.

Manx is named for the Isle of Man in the Irish Sea, where the breed originated hundreds of years ago. Types of Manx cats include the *rumpy, rumpy-riser, stumpy,* and *longie.* The most common is the rumpy, which is the only kind of cat without a tail. The cat has a notch where the tail would normally be. The rumpy-riser has a short knot at the tail base. The stumpy has an extremely short tail, and the rare longie has a full-length tail. The playful, sweet-natured Manx has a small body with a round head, broad chest, arched back, and high rump. The muscular rear legs are longer than the front legs. The cat runs with a rabbitlike hop. Its coat and eyes may be any color.

This breed also includes a long-haired type. The long-haired Manx used to be called the Cymric.

Ocicat resembles a wild spotted cat. It has a short, sleek, agouti spotted coat and a large, muscular body. Its coat and eye color varies. The breed originated in Michigan in 1964 by crossing Abyssinian, Siamese, and American shorthair cats. Ocicats are easy to train.

Oriental was developed in England as early as 1950 by crossing Siamese, British shorthair, and Abyssinian cats. The Oriental looks like the Siamese except for its coat and eye color. The eyes are green except in white cats, which can have blue eyes. The coat may be any solid or tabby color. This breed also includes a long-haired type, which was developed in Europe and North America during the 1980's. The long-haired Oriental has a fine, feathery tail plume.

Russian blue has short, extremely thick, bluish-gray fur that is unlike the fur of any other cat. The plush coat seems to glitter because the guard hairs are silver-tipped. The Russian blue has a large, muscular body, long legs, and a long tail. The cat's wedge-shaped head features large ears, a flat forehead, and round green eyes. Despite its name, the origin of this breed is unclear. The animal was brought to England from Russia or northern Europe in the 1800's.

Scottish fold is a medium-sized cat with ears that fold toward the face and downward. Its coat may be any color and pattern. Some types of Scottish fold have long fur. This cat has a roundish body and head and large round eyes. The breed was developed from a farm cat found in Scotland in 1961 that had folded ears as a result of a natural mutation. The Scottish fold has a soft voice and is gentle and affectionate.

Selkirk rex is a large cat with curly, plush fur. Its medium-length coat may be any color and pattern. Some types of Selkirk rex have long hair. The breed originated in Montana near the Selkirk Mountains in 1987 from mating an unusual-looking curly cat found in an animal shelter with a Persian cat. Selkirk rex has a round head, large eyes, and full cheeks that give it a sweet expression.

Siamese is the most popular short-haired cat. It is best known for its fine, glossy colorpoint coat. The Siamese is a loving pet that seems less independent than other breeds. Siamese cats often utter loud, mournful meows until they get attention.

The Siamese has a long, slender, medium-sized body

and a thin tail. Its legs are slim, and its paws small. Its long, wedge-shaped head has straight sides and large, pointed ears. Its eyes are almond-shaped and deep blue. The fur on the trunk of its body is a solid light color. The points are one of four colors—blue, chocolate, lilac, or *seal* (dark brown). Siamese kittens are born white but develop their adult color within a year.

The Siamese originated in Thailand (formerly called Siam). There, these cats were royal property and guarded palaces and temples. In 1884, a pair of Siamese were brought to the United Kingdom. Their offspring won many prizes at cat shows, and the breed soon gained worldwide popularity.

Singapura is a small- to medium-sized, muscular cat with strikingly large ears. Its fine, short coat has dark brown marks on a whitish background. The eyes have hazel, green, or yellow coloring. The Singapura originated from three cats found in Singapore during the early 1970's.

Sphinx is a medium-sized cat with large ears and a hairless or nearly hairless body. It can have a variety of skin colors. The Sphinx was developed from a cat born in Canada in 1966.

Tonkinese is a medium-sized cat with almond-shaped, aqua eyes. Its fine, silky fur may be various shades of brown or blue with a colorpoint pattern. The breed originated in the United States around 1930 as a cross between Siamese and Burmese cats.

Long-haired breeds. The long-haired cat breeds recognized by the Cat Fancier's Association include the American curl, Balinese, Birman, Javanese, Maine coon, Norwegian forest cat, Persian, Ragdoll, Siberian, Somali, Turkish Angora, and Turkish van.

American curl is a medium-sized cat with firm, erect ears that curve up and back from the face toward the center of the back of the head. Its fur may be any color or pattern. Some types have short fur. The eyes may be any color. The American curl traces its origin to a black, long-haired female cat that was found in California in 1981. The breed was developed by mating this cat and her offspring to various domestic short- and long-haired cats.

Balinese was developed from the Siamese and has the same body structure and coloring. But the fine, silky fur of the Balinese is about 2 inches (5 centimeters) long and has no undercoat. The hair on its long tail spreads out like a plume. The Balinese became an established breed in the United States during the 1960's.

Birman is a large, long-bodied cat with a bushy tail and short legs. Its head is round with a curved nose, round blue eyes, and rounded ears. The cat's long, silky coat has a colorpoint pattern, except that the large, rounded paws are always white. The Birman is a gentle, affectionate animal. The breed originated in what is now Myanmar, where it is considered sacred.

Javanese was developed during the late 1960's and early 1970's in the United States by crossing the Balinese with the colorpoint shorthair. Javanese cats are identical in appearance to colorpoint shorthair cats except for their long, silky coats.

Maine coon, the largest cat, looks somewhat like a raccoon. Its heavy, silky coat is medium length and may be any color. Its fur falls smoothly over most of the body but is shaggy on the *ruff,* stomach, and tail. A ruff is a fringe of long hairs that circles the neck.

The broad, muscular body of the Maine coon has an almost rectangular shape. Its head features a long nose and large eyes and ears. The cat stands on sturdy, medium-length legs. Tufts of fur cover its large, round paws, which are well suited to running across ice and snow. The breed developed in New England during the 1800's, probably as a result of matings between American shorthairs and long-haired cats brought to Maine by sailors prior to the 1850's.

Norwegian forest cat is an ancient breed that is mentioned in Norwegian mythology. It is a large, muscular cat with a triangular head and large ears with prominent tufts. Its thick fur, which can be any color, has a woolly undercoat and an abundant ruff. Its oval eyes are usually a green-gold color except in white cats, which often have copper or blue eyes or are odd-eyed.

Persian is the most popular breed of long-haired cats. This animal has a stocky, medium- to large-sized body with short, strong legs. Its large, round head includes a snubbed nose; large, wide-set, round eyes; and small, rounded ears. The Persian is admired for its extremely long, fine-textured, glossy coat. Its fur stands out from the body and forms a large ruff and a full, brushlike tail. The coats of Persians vary in color and pattern. Most Persians have copper eyes.

The exact origin of the Persian is unknown. But the breed probably lived in the Middle East more than 3,000 years ago. Persians have been carefully bred for hundreds of years to develop their present distinctive appearance.

Ragdoll, a large-sized cat, gets its name from its limpness. When a ragdoll cat is picked up, it relaxes completely and flops over like a ragdoll. Its thick fur is similar to the Birman's fur in color and pattern except that many ragdolls have white markings on the face, ruff, and stomach. The ragdoll is a fearless and calm animal. The breed originated in the United States in the 1960's.

Siberian, a medium- to large-sized cat, has a moderately long coat of any color. The coat becomes noticeably thicker during cold weather. This Russian breed may have been developed at least 1,000 years ago.

Somali looks like the Abyssinian except for its soft, medium-length double coat, which has blue, reddish, or brown bands. The eye color is gold or green. The breed developed from the offspring of Abyssinian cats that were born in the United Kingdom around 1900.

Turkish Angora is one of the oldest breeds. The cat originated in Turkey and spread throughout Europe during the 1700's and 1800's. Beginning in the early 1900's, Angoras were commonly crossed with Persians. As a result, the pure Angora nearly became extinct. Only a few remained by the early 1960's. Then, cat breeders and officials of the zoo in Ankara, Turkey, established a breeding program that saved these cats.

The Turkish Angora has a medium-sized, long, slender body. Its wedge-shaped head includes a long nose and long, pointed ears. Its silky, medium-length hair forms big tufts on the ears and between the toes. The color of the coat and eyes varies. This affectionate cat is known for its intelligence.

Turkish van is a rare and ancient breed that originated in the Lake Van area of southeastern Turkey, where it is considered a regional treasure. Crusaders brought the animal to Europe during the Middle Ages, from about the A.D. 400's through the 1400's. Turkish van cats are also known as *swimming cats* because they love water. Their cashmerelike, medium-long fur is pure white except for markings on the head and tail. The eyes may be blue, amber, or odd-eyed. The Turkish van's body is similar to the Turkish Angora.

Other breeds. There are many other breeds of cats around the world. Some breeds are extremely rare and unusual. Other breeds are popular in only one country or area. Still others have been developed recently and have not yet gained wide recognition.

The life of a cat

Most healthy cats live from 12 to 15 years. But many reach 18 or 19 years of age, and some have lived longer than 30 years.

Reproduction. A *queen* (female cat) can begin mating when she is between 5 and 9 months old, and a *tom* (male cat) can begin when he is between 7 and 10 months old. Toms can mate at any time. Queens mate only during a period of sexual excitement called *estrus* or *heat.* Estrus usually occurs during the spring and sometimes during the fall. This period is the breeding season. Estrus usually lasts from 6 to 10 days. If a queen is prevented from mating while she is in heat, she will probably come into heat again within 3 weeks. In most cases, this cycle recurs during the breeding season until the queen becomes pregnant.

The pregnancy period among cats lasts about nine weeks. When a queen is ready to give birth, she selects a quiet, safe spot as a nest. On the average, a queen bears from 3 to 5 kittens at a time. However, litters of as many as 14 kittens have been reported. The mother can deliver the kittens herself with no human assistance, unless complications develop.

Most newborn kittens weigh about 3 ½ ounces (99 grams). The mother licks the kittens and so dries them and stimulates their breathing and other body functions. Like other mammals, cats feed their young on milk produced by the mother's body. Newborn kittens cannot see or hear because their eyes and ears are sealed. They depend on their mother to nurse, clean, and protect them. The father plays no role in caring for the kittens.

Growth and development. Healthy kittens show a steady, daily weight gain. Their eyes usually open from 7 to 10 days after birth. Soon afterward, their ears open and the first teeth begin to appear. Kittens start to walk and explore their environment at about 3 weeks of age. But the mother watches over them and retrieves kittens that stray too far from the nest.

By about 5 weeks of age, kittens have most of their temporary teeth. They then begin to eat solid foods and to lap water. The mother usually begins to *wean* (stop nursing) them at about this age. The weaning process lasts several weeks.

When kittens are about 4 weeks old, owners should begin to handle them frequently and play with them gently. Kittens that receive such attention tend to become good pets. They learn faster and have fewer behavior problems than kittens that are ignored or overprotected. A kitten that has contact with a variety of people will be less fearful of strangers and new situations as an adult. Kittens can even learn not to fear dogs if they are allowed to play with a friendly dog.

By about 6 weeks of age, kittens have a fully developed brain and nervous system and can be safely separated from their mother. However, if possible, kittens should remain with their mother and their littermates until they are 9 or 10 weeks of age.

Kittens develop important physical skills by playing with one another. They also learn to get along with other cats in this way. In addition, kittens improve many instinctive skills, especially hunting skills, by watching and imitating their mother. The majority of cats reach their adult body size at about 1 year of age.

Communication. Cats communicate with one another, with other animals, and with human beings in a variety of ways, using sounds, body signals, and scents.

Some experts estimate that a cat can make more than 60 different sounds, ranging from a soft purr to a loud wail, or *caterwaul.* These sounds originate in the *larynx* (voice box) in the throat. Cats can purr on both *inspiration* (breathing in) and *expiration* (breathing out). The sound is produced by air as it vibrates through the space in the larynx called the *glottis.*

The sounds a cat makes may have various meanings. For example, depending on the situation, a meow can be a friendly greeting, or it may express curiosity, hunger, or loneliness. Purring usually means contentment,

Edward O. King, Alpha

A mother cat nurses her kittens until they can eat solid foods. Healthy kittens show a steady weight gain.

© Hans Reinhard

A mother cat carries a kitten back to the nest if it strays too far. Kittens begin to walk at about 3 weeks of age.

but some cats also purr when they are sick. Hisses, growls, and screams indicate anger and fear.

Cats also communicate through various body and tail positions and facial expressions. A contented cat often lies on its chest with its eyes half closed. To invite play or petting, some cats roll over on one side and wave a paw in the air. However, a similar posture accompanied by extended claws, a direct stare, and ears folded back indicates a fearful cat ready to defend itself. A friendly cat may greet someone with its tail raised vertically. It may also bump its head against the person and lick an extended hand. An angry or frightened cat flicks its tail from side to side, arches its back, and puffs up its fur. A submissive cat crouches down, flattens its ears, and avoids direct eye contact.

Cats commonly communicate with one another by means of odors. Cats have scent glands on the forehead, around the mouth, and near the base of the tail. A cat rubs these glands against people and objects and so marks them with its scent. Only cats and a few other animals can smell these odors. A tom sprays urine on objects and so marks his mating territory.

Caring for a cat

Feeding. Cats need a balanced diet. Such a diet supplies the proper amount of various nutrients, which provide energy and are essential for growth and replacement of body tissues. Cats require proteins, fats, vitamins, and minerals in their diet. The easiest way to meet a cat's nutritional needs is to buy high-quality commercial cat food. The label should indicate that the food is "complete and balanced." Cats should not be fed dog food because it does not meet their dietary requirements. A diet of mostly meat is unbalanced.

Cats are not naturally finicky eaters. But owners should give them a variety of commercial foods to prevent them from developing fussy appetites. Cats may occasionally be fed small amounts of such cooked foods as beef liver, eggs, fish, and vegetables. Many cats also enjoy milk, cheese, and other dairy products. However, such foods cause diarrhea in some cats. Owners should provide fresh drinking water at all times. Food and water bowls should be cleaned daily.

Kittens that have been weaned should be fed small amounts four times a day until they are 3 months old. They should eat three times daily until they are 6 months old, and then twice a day until they are full grown. Adult cats require only one meal a day, but many seem happier with two smaller meals. Food may be kept available at all times for a healthy cat that does not overeat. Sick cats, pregnant and nursing queens, and old cats often need special diets.

Grooming. Cats instinctively clean themselves. They do so by licking their fur with their tongue. They also rub and scratch their fur with their paws. At least once a day, a cat licks a paw and washes its face and head with the wet paw. But not all cats groom themselves well.

Owners should brush or comb a cat's fur daily to clean it and to remove loose hairs. In the case of long-haired cats, such care is essential to prevent the coat from tangling and matting. Daily brushing or combing also reduces the amount of loose hairs that cats swallow when they clean themselves. Swallowed hair may wad up and form a *hairball* in the cat's stomach. Hairballs can cause gagging, vomiting, and loss of appetite. If a cat cannot spit up a hairball, surgery may be required to remove it. Owners may feed their cat a small amount of petroleum jelly or a commercial preparation once a week to prevent hairball formation. A veterinarian can suggest safe methods of administering such products. If necessary, owners may clean their cat's ears with a soft cloth and brush their teeth with a cotton-tipped swab or a small toothbrush. Owners may also trim the tips of a cat's claws.

Some cats—especially those allowed outdoors—become so soiled that they need a bath. Most cats dislike bathing. But if cats are bathed about once a month when they are kittens, they will become accustomed to water. Kittens also should be brushed or combed so that they will be easier to care for after they grow older.

Training should begin when a kitten is about 8 weeks old. A cat can learn to respond to its name. Some cats have been trained to walk on a leash and to do such tricks as shaking hands and retrieving a ball.

The most effective way to train a cat is with praise, petting, and food rewards for good behavior. Correct a cat immediately with a sharp "No" if it misbehaves. Always react to a particular action in the same manner so that the cat can learn what to expect. Owners should be patient with their pet and avoid using physical punishment. Squirting a cat with water is a good way to stop undesirable behavior.

Indoor cats should learn to use a litter box. Cats instinctively bury their body wastes, and so training them to use a litter box is easy. Kittens raised with a mother that uses a litter box will usually begin to use it themselves before they are 5 or 6 weeks old.

Any smooth-surfaced plastic or enamel pan can be used as a litter box. Put the pan in a quiet spot. Place a layer of commercial litter or sterilized sand or soil in the bottom. Sift the litter clean with a strainer each day. Clean the pan and change the litter whenever a third of the litter is damp or, at least, every fourth day. Most cats will not use a wet or dirty box.

Dirty litter can spread disease. Cat owners, especially pregnant women, should take care not to directly touch the litter when cleaning the litter box.

Cats that have not learned to use a litter box at an early age must be trained. Place the cat in the box after it eats, when it wakes up, and after play. Praise the cat if it uses the box. The cat will soon learn to go to the box by itself.

Cats should also be trained to claw a scratching post instead of carpeting, draperies, and furniture. Cats naturally scratch at objects to pull off the worn outer layers of their claws and to mark their territory. A bark-covered log or a piece of wood covered with carpeting, cork, or fabric makes a good scratching post. Rub some *catnip,* a strongly scented herb that many cats love to sniff, into the post to attract the cat's interest. Guide the cat's front paws down the post. Whenever the cat begins to claw another object, correct the animal immediately and take it to the post. Some cats cannot be trained to use a post, however, and so some owners take their pet to a veterinarian for *declawing.* Declawing is a surgical procedure in which the claws are removed from the paws. A declawed cat may have difficulty defending itself, and so the animal should not be allowed outdoors unattended.

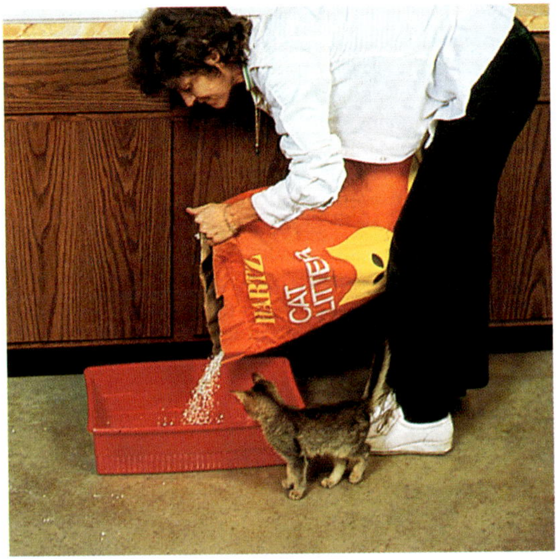

Caring for a cat includes providing a clean litter box. Cats also need fresh water and a balanced diet.

WORLD BOOK photos

Training helps a cat become a good pet. Many cats can learn to claw a scratching post, *shown here,* instead of furniture.

Some cats enjoy chewing plants. But owners can train their cat to leave house plants alone, especially if they provide a pot of grass or oats for the pet.

Veterinary care. A cat that is kept indoors faces fewer health risks than an outdoor cat. Outdoor cats may be struck by automobiles, poisoned by pesticides, or attacked by sick or unfriendly animals. But even indoor cats are not entirely safe. They can fall from open windows and unenclosed balconies. In addition, many cleaning products and certain houseplants, such as ivy and philodendron, are poisonous to cats. Owners should place such items out of the reach of cats.

Kittens should be taken to a veterinarian when they are about 8 to 10 weeks old for a physical examination. They should also receive vaccinations to protect them from common cat diseases. An adult cat should visit a veterinarian once a year for a checkup and additional shots. Veterinary care protects an owner's health as well as a cat's because some animal diseases can be transmitted to people. Such a disease is called a *zoonosis.*

Cat owners should learn to recognize signs of illness in their pet. A healthy cat has clean ears, clear eyes, a moist nose, pink tongue and gums, and a clean, glossy coat. Consult a veterinarian if a cat shows any change in appearance or behavior for more than 24 hours.

The most dangerous cat zoonosis, *rabies,* is an infection of the nervous system. Rabies is commonly transmitted by a bite from an infected animal. All cats permitted outdoors require periodic rabies vaccinations.

One of the most widespread cat diseases is *panleukopenia,* also called *feline enteritis* or *cat distemper.* This highly contagious infection is caused by a virus and is often fatal. Symptoms of panleukopenia include listlessness, loss of appetite, high fever, and severe vomiting and diarrhea. If a cat has several of these symptoms, call a veterinarian at once. All cats should be vaccinated against panleukopenia.

Two other serious diseases of cats are *feline leukemia* and the illness caused by the *feline immunodeficiency virus* (FIV). Feline leukemia is a form of cancer that affects the cat's blood-forming organs and lymph tissues. This fatal disease is caused by a virus that also can cause other, nonfatal ailments in cats. FIV attacks the cat's immune system and causes it to grow steadily weaker. Symptoms of the illness include infections, fevers, enlarged lymph nodes, and loss of appetite. FIV is spread by the bite of infected cats and can cause signs of illness many months or years after infection. Vaccinations exist for both feline leukemia and FIV.

Respiratory infections, ranging from mild colds to pneumonia, are common among cats. Signs of such infections include sneezing, a runny nose, watery eyes, and fever. A veterinarian can give vaccinations to prevent respiratory infections.

Many kinds of parasites may cause health problems in cats. Certain types of worms, including roundworms and tapeworms, can infect a cat's intestines and other organs. Worms may cause listlessness, weight loss, vomiting, and diarrhea. Some other parasites may live on a cat's skin and cause severe itching. Fleas and ear mites are the most common external parasites. Cats may also get *ringworm,* a skin disease caused by a fungus. Owners should remove parasites from cats to improve the pet's health and to prevent the cat from transmitting diseases to people.

Birth control. Each year, millions of unwanted cats are abandoned. Animal shelters must destroy many of these cats. Countless other strays die of starvation, injury, or disease. Because the problem of unwanted cats is so serious, owners should not allow their cats to mate unless a good home can be provided for the kittens.

Owners can try to prevent cats from mating by keeping them indoors. But this method of birth control is difficult. It also does not prevent such undesirable sex-related behavior as the spraying of urine by toms and the howling of queens during estrus.

A veterinarian can permanently prevent a cat from reproducing by *neutering* it—that is, by surgically removing some of the cat's sex organs. Neutering also ends sex-related behavior. The operation is commonly called *spaying* when performed on a female cat, and *castration* when done on a male cat. In an effort to control cat overpopulation, many veterinarians now neuter cats any time after 6 weeks of age. Most cats, however, are neutered just before they reach sexual maturity, around 6 months of age in females and after 6 months in males.

Cat associations and shows

Cat lovers worldwide have formed many associations to promote interest in cats. The largest of these groups, the Cat Fanciers' Association, Incorporated, has member clubs throughout the world. Cat associations *register* purebreds—that is, they record the ancestries of the animals—to ensure the preservation of the breeds. The associations also sponsor cat shows and establish standards for judging each breed. These standards cover such features as the shape of the body and the head, eye color, and coat type and color.

Breeders and pet owners display their finest cats at shows. Cats compete in groups based on such factors as age, sex, and breed. Show judges award points for healthiness, for temperament, and for how closely the animal meets breed standards. Cats that earn enough points may become champions or grand champions.

History

Scientists believe that members of the cat family gradually developed from a small weasellike animal called *Miacis,* which lived more than 50 million years ago. Miacis also was probably the ancestor of such mammals as bears, dogs, and raccoons. Members of the cat family first appeared about 40 million years ago.

No one knows exactly how or where cats were first tamed. But many authorities believe the domestic cat is a direct descendant of an African wildcat that the Egyptians tamed—possibly as early as 3500 B.C. Domesticated wildcats killed mice, rats, and snakes and so prevented these pests from overrunning Egyptian farms and grain storehouses. The cats became pampered pets and were honored in paintings and sculptures.

By about 1500 B.C., the Egyptians had begun to consider cats sacred. They worshiped a goddess of love and fertility called *Bastet,* or *Bast,* who was represented as having the head of a cat and the body of a woman. If a person killed a cat, the punishment was usually death. When a pet cat died, the Egyptians shaved off their eyebrows as a sign of mourning. They made dead cats into mummies. Scientists have found an ancient cat cemetery in Egypt containing over 300,000 cat mummies.

Greek and Phoenician traders probably brought domestic cats to Europe and the Middle East about 1000 B.C. The ancient Greeks and Romans valued cats for their ability to control rodents. In Rome, the cat was a symbol of liberty and was regarded as the guardian spirit of a household.

Domestic cats spread from the Middle East throughout Asia. In the Far East, cats were used to keep rodents from destroying temple manuscripts and from attacking silkworm cocoons, from which silk is made. People of Asia admired the beauty and mystery of the cat. The animal became a favorite subject of artists and writers in China and Japan.

In Europe during the Middle Ages, the cat was considered a symbol of evil. Superstitious people associated the cat with witchcraft and the Devil. For this reason, people killed hundreds of thousands of cats.

Experts believe that the destruction of so many cats led to a huge increase in the rat population of Europe and contributed to the spread of the *Black Death,* an epidemic of plague. This disease is transmitted to people by rat fleas. In the 1300's, it killed from one-fourth to one-half of the people who lived in Europe.

By the 1600's, Europeans had begun to realize once again the importance of cats in controlling rodents. Cats gradually regained popularity. European explorers, colonists, and traders brought domestic cats to the New World during the 1600's and 1700's. Throughout the 1800's, settlers took cats with them as they moved westward. Most cats in the United States and Canada today are descendants of these cats.

The first cat show was held in London in 1871. In 1887, the National Cat Club of the United Kingdom was formed. Interest in breeding and owning cats increased greatly. Today, the cat's ever-growing popularity has produced a billion-dollar industry that provides services and products for cats and their owners. Terri McGinnis

Scientific classification. Cats belong to the cat family, Felidae. Domestic cats are *Felis domesticus.*

Charles Edwin Wilbour Fund, The Brooklyn Museum, New York City

The ancient Egyptians worshiped cats and honored them in works of art. This bronze statue of a standing cat was created more than 2,000 years ago by an unknown Egyptian sculptor.

Related articles in *World Book* include:

Animal (pictures: The cat and its relatives)
Bobcat
Brain (picture: Brains of some vertebrates)
Caracal
Catnip
Cheetah
Distemper
Florida panther
Jaguar

Jaguarundi	Margay	Saber-toothed cat	Tiger
Leopard	Mountain lion	Serval	Toxoplasmosis
Lion	Ocelot	Snow leopard	Wildcat
Lynx	Panther		

Outline

I. The body of a cat
- A. Body size and structure
- B. Head
- C. Coat
- D. Senses

II. Breeds of cats
- A. Short-haired breeds
- B. Long-haired breeds
- C. Other breeds

III. The life of a cat
- A. Reproduction
- B. Growth and development
- C. Communication

IV. Caring for a cat
- A. Feeding
- B. Grooming
- C. Training
- D. Veterinary care
- E. Birth control

V. Cat associations and shows

VI. History

Questions

How long do most healthy cats live?
What is the only kind of cat without a tail?
Why did people kill cats in Europe during the Middle Ages?
How are tabby coats patterned?
How many teeth do adult cats have?
How do cats clean themselves?
What are some serious cat diseases?
What are some of the ways in which cats communicate?
What purpose do the whiskers of a cat serve?

Additional resources

Level I

Edney, Andrew. *ASPCA Complete Cat Care Manual.* D K Pub., 1992.
Gutman, Bill. *Becoming Your Cat's Best Friend.* Millbrook, 1997.
Zeaman, John. *Why the Cat Chose Us.* Watts, 1998.

Level II

McGinnis, Terri. *The Well Cat Book.* 2nd ed. 1993. Reprint. Random Hse., 1996.
Verhoef-Verhallen, Esther J. *The Cat Encyclopedia.* Firefly Bks., 1997.
Wild Discovery Guide to Your Cat. Discovery Bks., 1999.

CAT scan. See **Computed tomography**.

Catacombs, *KAT uh kohmz,* are systems of underground passages or rooms once used as burial places. The most famous catacombs lie on the outskirts of Rome. The early Christians cut them into the soft tufa rock in the 200's and 300's. The catacombs formed a network of connecting corridors and rooms covering about 600 acres (240 hectares). Graves were cut into the walls. Bricks or marble slabs were used to close some of the graves. When more space was needed, additional *galleries* (halls) were dug beneath the first.

The Christians used the catacombs for funeral and memorial services. The fresco paintings on the walls are examples of early Christian art. Such scenes as *Daniel in the Lions' Den* and *Moses Striking the Rock* symbolize God's salvation of people and nations. The paintings also show *orante* (praying) figures of the dead resurrected in Paradise, with their arms raised in adoration.

During times of persecution, Christians took refuge in the catacombs because Roman law held burial places sacred. But the catacombs lost their usefulness when Christianity became the established religion of the Roman Empire. Their existence was forgotten after about 400. The catacombs were rediscovered in 1578.

Catacombs have been found in other Italian cities and in Sicily, Malta, Egypt, North Africa, and Palestine. The burial chapels of some monasteries and nunneries in Europe are sometimes called catacombs. The *catacombs of Paris* are abandoned stone quarries that were first used for burials in 1787. Richard A. Kalish

See also **Bible** (picture: Scenes from Biblical stories); **Rome** (The catacombs).

Catalepsy, *KAT uh LEHP see,* is a condition in which a person temporarily loses the ability to move voluntarily. A person with catalepsy is not paralyzed but simply lacks the will to move. The arms and legs of a cataleptic person can be placed in unusual positions. The person will hold such positions for many minutes. Sometimes the facial muscles become immobile. Catalepsy is often associated with severe cases of a mental illness called *schizophrenia* (see **Schizophrenia**). Catalepsy is often confused with *cataplexy,* the temporary loss of muscle tone. See also **Cataplexy; Hypnotism.** R. Craig Lefebvre

Catalog. See **Mail-order business**.

Catalpa, *kuh TAL puh* or *kuh TAHL puh,* also called *Indian bean,* is the name of a group of trees native to North America and eastern Asia. There are about 10 species of catalpas. The *southern catalpa* grows in the southeastern United States. The *northern catalpa,* also called the *western catalpa,* is found from Indiana to Arkansas. Both are planted as shade trees.

A catalpa has large, heart-shaped leaves. Its trumpet-shaped flowers bloom in the early summer. The flowers occur in large clusters and may be white or yellow. Catalpas also grow long, narrow seed pods that resemble pea pods. The pods, which may be up to 18 inches (46 centimeters) long, fall a few at a time and can become a litter problem on lawns. Harrison L. Flint

Scientific classification. Catalpas belong to the bignonia family, Bignoniaceae. The southern catalpa is *Catalpa bignonioides.* The northern catalpa is *C. speciosa.*

See also **Tree** (Broadleaf and needleleaf trees [picture]).

Catalysis, *kuh TAL uh sihs,* is a process in which a substance increases the speed of a chemical reaction without being consumed by the reaction. Any substance that accelerates a reaction in this way is called a *catalyst.* In industry, catalysts speed up many chemical reactions that otherwise would take place too slowly to be practical. Enzymes serve as catalysts in many complex reactions that occur in all animals and plants (see **Enzyme**).

In most cases, there are several possible sequences of steps by which a reaction can take place. A catalyst participates in some or all of the steps of a particular sequence. By doing so, the catalyst provides a chemical pathway along which the overall reaction can proceed far more rapidly than it otherwise could.

A typical example of catalysis is the effect of nitric oxide (NO) on the decomposition of ozone (O_3) in the upper atmosphere of the earth. An oxygen atom (O) and an ozone molecule combine slowly by themselves and produce two oxygen molecules (O_2). But in the presence of nitric oxide, a catalyst, a rapid two-step reaction takes place instead. First, a nitric oxide molecule combines with an oxygen atom, producing nitrogen dioxide (NO_2). Then the nitrogen dioxide reacts with ozone and forms two molecules of oxygen and one molecule of nitric oxide. The second step of the reaction produces exactly as much nitric oxide as is consumed by the first step. Thus, the amount of nitric oxide does not change.

There are two types of catalysis, *homogeneous* and *heterogeneous.* In homogeneous catalysis, the catalyst and the *reactants* (reacting substances) are in the same physical state. For example, the catalytic decomposition of ozone is homogeneous because nitric oxide, oxygen, and ozone are all gases. On the other hand, heterogeneous catalysis involves two physical states, such as a solid catalyst affecting gaseous reactants.

Heterogeneous catalysts are generally used in industry because they can easily be separated from the products of reactions and then reused. Such catalysts are widely used in refining petroleum (see **Petroleum** [Conversion]). In the production of ammonia, iron catalyzes the reaction of nitrogen with hydrogen. In the manufacture of nitric acid, platinum speeds the oxidation of ammonia. Gary L. Haller

See also **Catalytic converter; Zeolite.**

Catalytic converter is a device that reduces the exhaust pollutants produced by the engine of a motor vehicle. It uses *catalysts,* substances that speed chemical reactions, to convert harmful exhaust pollutants to harmless substances.

The combustion of gasoline and diesel fuels in engines produces three main gaseous pollutants: (1) nitrogen oxides, (2) hydrocarbons, and (3) carbon monoxide. Burned gases, including these harmful compounds, flow through the catalytic converter, which is installed in a vehicle's exhaust system. Most catalytic converters use either *three-way catalysts,* which can remove all three pollutants at the same time, or *oxidation catalysts,* also called *two-way catalysts,* which can remove only hydrocarbons and carbon monoxide.

A typical catalytic converter consists of tiny, honeycomblike passages made of a ceramic or metal *substrate* (underlying material). The substrate is mounted within a stainless steel container. Thin layers of *noble metals,* such as platinum, palladium, and rhodium, coat the substrate and serve as catalysts. Noble metals do not corrode easily. As the exhaust gases flow over the coated passages, an *oxidizing* reaction takes place. Hydrocarbons and carbon monoxide are converted to water vapor and carbon dioxide through the addition of oxygen. In a converter with a three-way catalyst, a *reducing* reaction takes place at the same time. This reaction removes oxygen atoms from the nitrogen oxides, producing nitrogen and oxygen.

Catalytic converters are most effective when complete combustion of the fuel occurs. Sensors monitor the exhaust entering the catalytic converter and relay information to a computer in the engine. The computer directs adjustments of the *fuel injection system* to produce a fuel-air mixture that provides for complete combustion.

Catalytic converters are ineffective at lower temperatures, and they do not begin operating properly until the substrate is warmed to about 570 °F (300 °C). In addition, the presence of lead, phosphorus, or sulfur in the exhaust stream can reduce the effectiveness of the catalysts. Diesel engines use much more air for combustion than gasoline engines do. Abundant oxygen in the exhaust system renders catalytic converters essentially ineffective at reducing nitrogen oxides. For this reason, vehicles with diesel engines usually employ oxidation catalysts instead of three-way catalysts. A. Selamet

See also **Automobile** (Environmental impact); **Gasoline engine** (Air pollution controls).

Catamaran, *KAT uh muh RAN,* is a raftlike boat that has two hulls. In the United States, catamarans are used mainly as pleasure boats. Their light weight and two slim, shallow hulls allow catamarans to slip through the water with little resistance. The design was developed from outrigger boats used by the Polynesians and Malays for thousands of years.

Catamarans can be powered by sail or by motor. Most of the boats are less than 40 feet (12 meters) long. Some racing catamarans, designed for long ocean races, may be more than 70 feet (21 meters) long. They have sailing rigs that may drive them at speeds up to 30 miles (48 kilometers) per hour. Patience Wales

See also **Boating** (picture); **Outrigger.**

Cataplexy, *KAT uh PLEHK see,* is a condition that involves a sudden, temporary loss of muscle tone. It is often caused by extreme emotional states, especially laughter, anger, and excitement. Cataplectic attacks vary in strength and duration. Mild attacks can consist of weakening of the knees or a drop of the jaw or head. Severe attacks can cause sudden paralysis of almost all muscles of the body, causing the person to collapse. A cataplectic attack may last from a few seconds to 20 minutes. The person remains conscious but cannot voluntarily move the affected muscles. Cataplexy is often accompanied by *narcolepsy,* an irresistible urge to sleep (see **Narcolepsy**).

Cataplexy is not a form of epilepsy. It is sometimes confused with *catalepsy,* the temporary loss of voluntary movement (see **Catalepsy**). R. Craig Lefebvre

Catapult, *KAT uh puhlt,* was a war machine that shot such objects as spears or stones or hurled large weights against an enemy's defenses. There were two main types of catapults: *nontorsion* and *torsion.* Nontorsion catapults operated like giant bows and arrows, with the

WORLD BOOK illustration by Tak Murakami

Catapults were used by warriors in ancient times and during the Middle Ages to attack walled cities and castles. The catapult worked like a giant slingshot to hurl heavy stones over the walls and into the city or castle.

shooting power coming from the release of stretched fibers. In torsion catapults, the release of a twisted rope caused a beam to spring forward, heaving heavy stones or weights.

Greek engineers built effective nontorsion catapults early in the 300's B.C. Small nontorsion catapults that could hurl stones weighing as much as 5 pounds (2.3 kilograms) appeared about the same time. Torsion catapults, which were more powerful, were developed around 350 B.C. By A.D. 100, Roman soldiers made these catapults mobile by mounting them on carriages.

Soldiers often used catapults in attacking and defending walled cities. In the Middle Ages, castles with surrounding moats were the usual targets for catapults. Burning materials were sometimes shot from catapults, and eventually cans with gunpowder, dynamite, and poison gas were fired from them. In some cases, soldiers used young trees as catapults. They bent the trees back and loaded them with pockets containing material for bombardment. They then let the trees spring forward, releasing the loaded materials.

In modern naval warfare, a catapult is used to launch airplanes from the decks of aircraft carriers. In this type of catapult, a steam-driven piston propels the plane down the deck until the plane reaches flying speed.

Richard A. Sauers

Cataract, *KAT uh rakt,* is the clouding of the lens of the eye. Its effect on vision depends on the extent of the cloudiness. Small spots in the lens may cause little or no vision loss. However, the spots can spread and make all or part of the lens *opaque* (nontransparent), resulting in blindness. Cataracts may affect either or both eyes.

A normal lens is clear. It lies behind the pupil and iris of the eye and helps the eye focus. Light rays enter the eye through the *cornea,* the transparent tissue that covers the eyeball. The lens bends them and causes them to form an image on the *retina,* the light-sensitive tissue lining the back of the eyeball. The lens focuses light rays by changing shape. It becomes rounder and thicker to focus light that comes from nearby objects. The lens flattens to focus light from distant objects.

Cataracts usually are associated with aging. As a person grows older, the lens becomes less flexible and loses some of its ability to focus light onto the retina. As the lens becomes harder, it tends to become less transparent—that is, it tends to develop cataracts. Cataracts can eventually become milky white and fill the lens.

Cataracts also may result from certain diseases. For example, cataracts often occur in people who have diabetes. Eye inflammation or injuries may cause cataracts. Some babies are born with cataracts. Also, certain drugs and some forms of radiation can cause cataracts.

Doctors do not know how to prevent or cure most types of cataracts. But surgery to remove the diseased lens can improve vision for most cataract patients. After such surgery, some patients must wear strong glasses or contact lenses to see well enough to carry on normal activities. In most cases, however, surgeons replace the diseased lens with a plastic *intraocular lens.* A patient who receives an intraocular lens may or may not need glasses or contact lenses to see well. David E. Eifrig

See also **Blindness; Eye.**

Catbird is a North American songbird related to mockingbirds and thrashers. The best-known species is the *gray catbird.* It is about 9 inches (23 centimeters) long and slate-gray in color. The top of its head is black, and it has a brick-red patch beneath the base of its long tail feathers. The gray catbird breeds in the eastern, central, and southern United States and in southern Canada. It is found as far west as central Washington, Utah, and Arizona. It winters along the Atlantic Coast and in the Gulf States, West Indies, Mexico, and Central America.

© Joe McDonald, Corbis

The gray catbird lives throughout much of North America.

The gray catbird hides its loosely made nest of twigs and rootlets in tangled thickets and thick brush. It lays three to five bluish-green eggs. It sometimes eats strawberries, raspberries, and cherries, but it also eats harmful insects. The gray catbird can imitate the songs of other birds and gets its name from its call, which sounds like a cat's mew.

Another species of catbird, the *black catbird,* has black feathers with some purple and blue-green. It lives in Central America year-round. Martha Hatch Balph

Scientific classification. Catbirds belong to the mockingbird and thrasher family, Mimidae. The gray catbird is *Dumetella carolinensis.* The black catbird is *Melanoptila glabrirostris.*

See also **Bird** (pictures: Birds of brushy areas; Birds' eggs); **Mockingbird.**

Catchup. See **Ketchup.**

Catechism, *KAT uh kihz uhm,* is a summary of basic Christian doctrine used for religious instruction. A catechism is typically presented as a series of questions and answers. The type of written catechisms common today first came into widespread use in the 1500's, though similar teaching manuals had been used earlier.

There are several major catechisms. The Large and Small Catechisms (1529) of Martin Luther are used in Lutheran churches. The Geneva Catechism (1542), the second catechism written by John Calvin, and the Heidelberg Catechism (1563) are used in Reformed churches. The influential Tridentine Catechism was issued by the Roman Catholic Church in 1566. Today, the Roman Catholic Church uses a variety of catechisms. The Shorter and the Larger Westminster Catechisms (1647) are used in Presbyterian churches. Catechisms found in Books of Common Prayer are used in churches of the Anglican Communion. Today, most catechism instruction tries to help people gain deeper insight into their

Christian beliefs rather than simply memorize questions and answers about their religion. Frank C. Senn

Catechu, *KAT uh choo,* also called *black cutch,* is a brown, tarlike or resinlike substance obtained chiefly from the wood of acacia trees. It is rich in tannic acid. Catechu makes rich brown dyes used in coloring leather. Craftworkers use it to dye and print cotton cloth, such as khaki or calico. Fishing crews apply catechu to sails and nets to preserve them. It was once used in certain medicines. To extract catechu, processors cut the *heartwood* (inner wood) of the acacia into pieces and boil them in water. When the extract is partly hardened, it is formed into rough blocks or balls for marketing. See also **Acacia; Tannic acid.** Renzo Shamey

Caterpillar is a wormlike creature that is the second, or *larval,* stage in the life history of butterflies and moths. When a butterfly or moth egg hatches, a tiny caterpillar crawls out and begins to eat. The caterpillar grows, but its skin does not grow with it as does the skin of most animals. Soon the skin becomes too tight, and a split appears near the head end. The caterpillar then wriggles out of the old skin. It now has a new, soft skin that had formed under the old one. This skin, too, is soon outgrown, and the process is repeated a number of times. Eventually, the butterfly or moth caterpillar becomes a *pupa,* the insect's third stage of development. The pupa, in turn, develops into an adult. Most caterpillar stages last from two to four weeks. In very cold climates, some butterflies and moths take two to three years to pass from egg to adult.

WORLD BOOK illustration by Shirley Hooper, Oxford Illustrators Limited

Caterpillar

Appearance. A caterpillar has 13 body segments, not including the head. To each of the first three segments is attached a pair of five-jointed legs. These develop later into the legs of the adult insect. There usually are four or five pairs of fleshy *prolegs* on the abdomen. These are not true legs, and they are absent in the adult. Prolegs may have *crochets* (hooks) on the tips. Caterpillars called *measuring worms* possess only two or three pairs of prolegs on the abdomen, and they move by drawing these hind legs up to the front three pairs. The head of a caterpillar has six simple eyes on each side. It also has a pair of short *antennae* (feelers) that enable the larva to guide itself. A caterpillar's strong, biting jaws differ from the sucking mouthparts of an adult. The larva's body may be naked or covered with bristles, spines, or hairs.

Some caterpillars have glands that secrete an unpleasant fluid. Others have a sickening taste that saves them from being eaten by birds and other animals. A few types are covered with sharp spines that inject stinging fluids if they break off in a person's skin. False eyespots help frighten away attackers of some caterpillars, while long, whiplike appendages on the backs of other larvae are lashed about as a means of defense. But in spite of these devices, very few caterpillars ever reach the adult stage. Larger animals eat them, and tiny, parasitic wasp and fly larvae feed within their bodies and kill them.

Habits. Most caterpillars eat plants. A butterfly or moth does all of its growing during the caterpillar stage. The larva stores up *nutrients* (nourishing substances) that it later uses to become the pupa and eventually the adult insect.

A few larvae, including silkworms, are prized by people, but most are not. When caterpillars become numerous, they may strip the vegetation from fields and the leaves from trees. Cabbage worms, gypsy moth caterpillars, cotton worms, corn earworms, army worms, and cutworms have all become serious pests. E. W. Cupp

Related articles in *World Book* include:

Army worm	Larva	Silk (Raising silkworms)
Butterfly	Measuring worm	Spruce budworm
Cankerworm	Moth	Tent caterpillar
Chrysalis	Rotenone	Woollybear
Jumping bean		

Catfish is the name of a large group of fish that have two to four pairs of whiskers. These whiskers, called *barbels,* resemble the whiskers of a cat. Catfish also differ from most other fish in that they do not have scales. Several species of catfish have sharp spines on their backs and near their gills. These spines give off a poison when they enter the body of another animal and can cause serious wounds. They are probably used mainly as a defense against enemies.

There are more than 2,000 species of catfish. Most live in fresh water and some inhabit the oceans. Most freshwater species live in lakes, ponds, or slow-moving parts of streams. But the *channel catfish* and a few other species live in swift-flowing waters. Catfish feed on a variety of aquatic organisms, including frogs and insects. Larger catfish may also eat other fish.

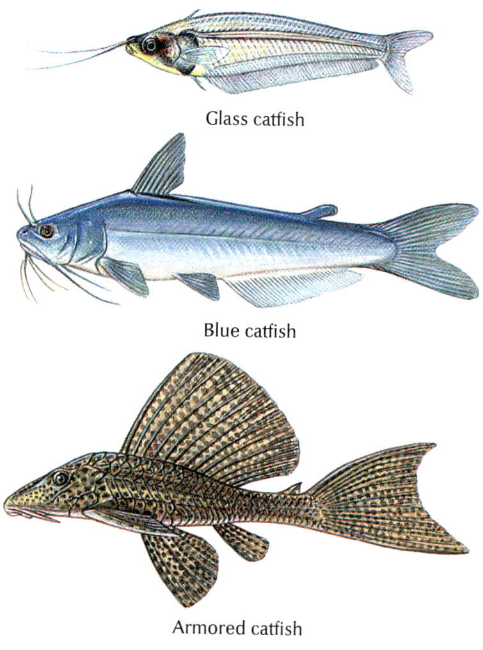

WORLD BOOK illustration by Rod Sutterby, Linden Artists Ltd.

Catfish usually have two to four pairs of whiskers. The small glass catfish is popular in home aquariums. The blue catfish is a food fish found in the Mississippi Valley. The armored catfish is protected from enemies by overlapping bony plates.

Catfish vary in size. The largest species, the *European catfish* or *wels,* may grow more than 10 feet (3 meters) long and may weigh as much as 400 pounds (180 kilograms). The tiny *glass catfish* grows only 4 inches (10 centimeters) long, and many people keep it in home aquariums.

Some kinds of catfish have unusual features or habits. The *upside-down catfish* swims upside down. The *electric catfish* can send out a strong electric shock. The *eelcat* is long and slim and resembles an eel. The *candiru* swims into the gills of larger fish, rips the gills with its sharp spines, and drinks the victim's blood. Among some species of ocean catfish, the male carries the eggs in his mouth and does not eat until they hatch.

The *walking catfish* of tropical Asia can move overland from one body of water to another. It pushes itself along the ground with its tail, using its strong *pectoral fins* (fins behind the gill openings) to lift the front of its body. It has gills, but it also has additional air-breathing organs. Walking catfish often come out on shore at night to feed. In the 1960's, walking catfish were introduced into southern Florida, where they have established large populations in some rivers. They may eventually replace some of the native fishes in these waters.

About 45 species of catfish are native to North America. They include *flathead catfish, channel catfish, bullheads,* and *madtoms.* Flatheads and channel catfish may weigh over 70 pounds (32 kilograms). Most bullheads and madtoms weigh less than 1 pound (0.45 kilogram).

Catfish are raised commercially on fish farms for use as food. Fish farms in the United States produce more than 300 million pounds (140 million kilograms) of catfish—mainly channel catfish—annually. Most of these fish farms are located in Alabama, Arkansas, and Mississippi. Bill A. Simco

Scientific classification. Catfish include many families and genera. Most catfish of North America belong to the family Ictaluridae. The channel catfish is *Ictalurus punctatus.* The walking catfish is *Clarias batrachus.*

See also **Bullhead**.

Catgut is a tough cord made from the intestines of certain animals and used mainly for the strings of musical instruments and for sewing up wounds. Most catgut is made from the intestines of hogs or sheep. The intestine casings are split into ribbons that are cleaned, cured, and spun into string. The string is dried and polished. Catgut is also used on looms, in the controls of artificial limbs, and in the mechanisms of clocks and typewriters. Catgut was once used to string tennis and badminton rackets but has been largely replaced by nylon and other synthetic materials. Despite its name, catgut probably was never made from cat intestines. The *cat* portion of the word *catgut* may come from the word *kit,* an old term for a small violin. Stephen Clapp

Catharsis is a term psychiatrists and psychoanalysts use to describe the way in which psychotherapy helps a person release pent-up emotions. The ancient Greek philosopher Aristotle used the word, which means *purging* or cleaning out, to describe the emotional effect of tragedy on a spectator. In psychotherapy, the therapist brings about catharsis by encouraging the patient to recall memories of painful or *traumatic* (shocking) events. The therapist helps the patient to become aware of unconscious wishes and fears and thus to accept or release the emotions associated with them.

Allen Frances

See also **Aristotle** (Literary criticism).

Cathay, *ka THAY,* is the name Europeans once gave to China, especially the part north of the Yangtze River. The name *Cathay* is derived from *Khitan,* a pre-Mongol people who controlled parts of China from the early A.D. 900's to the early 1100's. The Italian trader Marco Polo called the country Khitai, or Cathay, in his account of his travels to the land of Kublai Khan. His journey there took place in the late 1200's. In Russia and Central Asia, Khitai is still the preferred term for China. Grant Hardy

See also **Kublai Khan; Polo, Marco.**

Cathedral is the church of a bishop of some Christian denominations. It is also the administrative headquarters of a *diocese,* a church district headed by a bishop. The bishop's throne, a symbol of the office, is located in the cathedral. The word *cathedral* comes from the Greek word *kathedra,* meaning *seat.* Only the Anglican, Eastern Orthodox, and Roman Catholic denominations and some Lutheran groups have cathedrals.

Medieval cathedrals, especially in France, were usually located in the middle of town and served as a center of public life. Markets and meetings, as well as daily church services, were held there. Though cathedrals continue to be built today, their importance as centers of town life has declined.

The plan of a cathedral. No church laws specify the design of a cathedral. However, cathedrals in Western

Basil Spence & Partners, Architects

A modern cathedral interior in Coventry, England, conveys a feeling of soaring height. The cathedral was completed in 1962, replacing a 600-year old church that was destroyed in 1940.

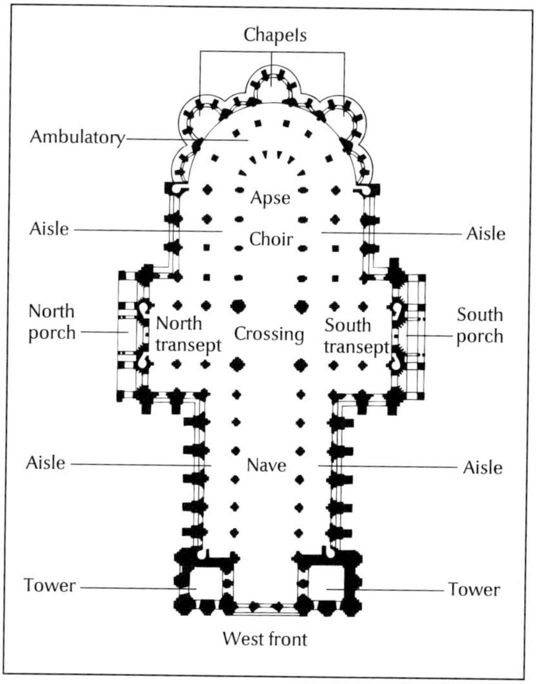

WORLD BOOK diagram

A cathedral is shaped like a cross. The entrance faces west. At the east end, chapels and an aisle called an *ambulatory* are outside a semicircular area known as the *apse.*

religions have traditionally been built according to the general plan of a medieval cathedral. For a description of Eastern Orthodox cathedrals, see **Byzantine art.**

Most cathedrals are built in the shape of a cross. The main entrance is at the west end, at the bottom of the cross. A long central aisle, called the *nave,* and two side aisles extend from the entrance. The two arms of the cross, called the *transepts,* meet the nave at the *crossing.* Worshipers assemble in the nave and transepts.

The altar and the seats for the choir lie at the east end of the nave, in front of a semicircular area called the *apse.* A walkway called the *ambulatory* extends around the apse and may open onto several chapels. The bishop's throne usually stands to one side of the altar.

Through the years, architects have made changes in the basic plan of a cathedral. For example, architects of the 1600's designed cathedrals with extremely short transepts so the entire congregation could see the altar. However, most modern cathedrals have retained major features of the medieval design.

Historical importance of cathedrals. The greatest era of cathedral building occurred in Europe during the Middle Ages from around 1000 to 1500. Medieval cathedrals were often magnificent structures built both to inspire and to teach. Cathedrals were filled with carved sculptures. Their walls were lined with paintings or stained-glass windows that portrayed scenes from the Bible and the lives of the saints. These scenes made up a visual encyclopedia of medieval knowledge for the many worshipers who could not read.

Famous cathedrals. Many cathedrals of western Europe are famous for their great beauty. France is the home of some of the most magnificent cathedrals, including those in Amiens, Chartres, Paris, Reims, and Strasbourg. St. Paul's Cathedral in London and the cathedrals at Canterbury, Salisbury, Lincoln, and York are among the greatest English cathedrals. Other famous European cathedrals include the Cologne Cathedral in Germany and the Milan Cathedral in Italy. The Seville Cathedral in Spain is the largest cathedral in Europe.

A number of North American cathedrals were built in the style of the great European cathedrals. Outstanding U.S. cathedrals include St. John the Divine and St. Patrick's Cathedral, both in New York City. A well-known Canadian cathedral is the Cathedral-Basilica of Mary, Queen of the World, in Montreal. The Metropolitan Cathedral in Mexico City dates from the 1500's and is the oldest in North America. William J. Hennessey

Related articles in *World Book.* Articles with pictures of cathedrals include **England, Lima, Manitoba, Reims, Rouen, Salisbury, Santiago,** and **Strasbourg.** See also:

Architecture (pictures)
Campanile
Chartres Cathedral (picture)
Coventry
Gothic art
Hagia Sophia
Middle Ages (The Christian church)
Milan Cathedral
Notre Dame, Cathedral of
Romanesque architecture
Saint Mark, Basilica of
Saint Patrick's Cathedral
Spire
Stained glass
Washington National Cathedral

Cather, Willa (1873-1947), was one of America's finest novelists. Her reputation rests on her novels about Nebraska and the American Southwest. In them, she expressed a deep love of the land and a strong distaste for the materialism and conformism she saw in modern life. She showed a genuine devotion to traditional values—the importance of family, human dignity, hope, and courage. Cather also questioned customary ways of thinking and feeling, especially by creating strong female characters who have strength and determination of a sort that earlier writers had credited only to men.

Steichen, courtesy Alfred Knopf
Willa Cather

Cather wrote 12 novels, of which *My Ántonia* (1918) and *Death Comes for the Archbishop* (1927) rank as the best. *My Ántonia* describes how an immigrant farm girl triumphs over hardship in pioneer Nebraska. *Death Comes for the Archbishop* is a historical novel about the work of the first Roman Catholic archbishop in the New Mexico Territory. It conveys Cather's sense of the sacred in the archbishop's work and also in the natural world.

Willa Sibert Cather was born on Dec. 7, 1873, near Winchester, Virginia, and moved to Nebraska with her family at the age of 9. In 1905, she published her first collection of stories and was hired by *McClure's Magazine,* one of the leading American magazines. She quickly became managing editor, then a position of unusual power and influence for a woman. In 1912, Cather published her first novel, *Alexander's Bridge.* She then resigned from *McClure's* and devoted the rest of her life to writing fiction. Daniel Mark Fogel

Catherine de Médicis, *MEHD ih chee* or *may dee SEES* (1519-1589), was a powerful woman in France during the reigns of three kings—Francis II, Charles IX, and Henry III. These three monarchs were sons of Catherine and her husband, King Henry II of France. Catherine was the niece of Pope Clement VII and belonged to the famous Medici family of Florence, Italy. The Italian spelling of the family name is de' Medici.

© Corbis/Archivo Iconografico, S.A
Catherine de Médicis

Henry II died in 1559, and Francis II became king at age 15. Francis died the following year, and Charles IX succeeded him at age 10. Charles died in 1574, and Henry III became king at age 22. All three sons relied heavily on their mother's advice.

Catherine's actions showed energy and ability. She sought to shield her sons from the influence of advisers from the powerful Guise family. A Roman Catholic, she also worked for peace between *Huguenots* (French Protestants) and Catholics in France (see **Huguenots**). But, she became jealous of the Huguenot leader Gaspard de Coligny's influence over Charles IX and feared that Coligny's policies would lead to war with Spain. Historians disagree on Catherine's role in the events that began on Aug. 24, 1572, during which Catholics killed Coligny and thousands of other Huguenots in what became known as the Massacre of St. Bartholomew's Day. Traditionally she has been blamed for persuading Charles IX to order the massacre. But many historians now believe that though she may have been involved in a plan to murder Coligny and other Huguenot leaders, she did not intend the large massacre of Huguenots that accompanied Coligny's assassination. Catherine was born on April 13, 1519, in Florence. Donald A. Bailey

See also **Henry II** (of France); **Saint Bartholomew's Day, Massacre of.**

Catherine of Aragon, *AR uh gon or AR uh guhn* (1485-1536), was the first wife of King Henry VIII of England. She was the daughter of King Ferdinand and Queen Isabella of Spain. At age 15, she became the wife of Arthur, Prince of Wales, the oldest son of King Henry VII of England. Arthur died five months later. In 1509, Catherine married Arthur's younger brother, Henry VIII.

Catherine was born on Dec. 16, 1485, near Madrid, Spain. Of her six children, only Mary lived. She later became Queen Mary I. But Henry wanted a male heir. A lady in Catherine's court, Anne Boleyn, enchanted him. In 1531, he separated from Catherine and married Anne in 1533. He broke with the Roman Catholic Church when it refused to *annul* (cancel) his marriage to Catherine. Catherine never saw Henry after 1531. She was loyal to him and the Catholic faith until she died. Richard L. Greaves

Catherine of Siena, *see EHN uh,* **Saint** (1347-1380), was a Christian reformer and *mystic.* A mystic is an individual who has intense spiritual experiences, such as visions. Catherine spent much of her life caring for people who were sick, poor, or spiritually needy. Her book *Dialogue* stresses the love of neighbors as an expression of the love of God. She also expressed her piety and religious ideals in her letters, 400 of which survive.

Catherine devoted a great deal of her energy to religious reform. She campaigned for the return of Pope Gregory XI from Avignon, France, to the papacy's traditional home in Rome. She also worked to end the war the papacy waged against Florence and other Italian city-states, and she urged the start of a Crusade to the Holy Land. Catherine spent her last days trying to end the *schism* (division) within the church caused by the election of two rival popes.

Catherine was born on March 25, 1347, in Siena, Italy. At about age 6, she reportedly received a vision of Jesus Christ. She joined the Third Order of St. Dominic at about age 16. Her feast day is April 29. Marilyn J. Harran

Catherine the Great (1729-1796) ruled as empress of Russia from 1762 until her death. During her reign, Russia expanded greatly. Catherine was born a German princess and promoted European culture in Russia.

Catherine was born on May 2, 1729, in Stettin, Prussia (now Szczecin, Poland). At age 16, she went to St. Petersburg, Russia, and married Peter, the weak and incompetent successor to Russia's throne. In 1762 he became Emperor Peter III but was deposed later that year by Catherine and her allies and was assassinated. Catherine succeeded Peter to the throne as Catherine II. She is considered a Russian ruler of the Romanov line.

Detail of an oil portrait by Johann Baptist Lampi I; Russian State Museum, St. Petersburg (Library of Congress)
Catherine the Great

Catherine was a gifted person, devoted to art, literature, science, and politics. She lived simply and proved to be a conscientious ruler, although she maintained extravagant surroundings. Early in her reign, she grew interested in the liberal ideas of her time, called the Age of Reason because its great thinkers emphasized the use of reason. She built schools and hospitals, encouraged smallpox vaccination, promoted women's education, and extended religious tolerance. Teachers, scientists, writers, actors, and artists from other countries moved to Russia.

But Catherine did little to grant basic civil rights to the majority of the Russian people. She tightened landowners' control over the serfs, and she forcefully put down a peasant revolt. Except for raising the status of nobles and merchants, she carried out few social reforms.

Her achievements consisted mainly in modernizing the administration, though she did little to curb its corruption. She also extended the frontiers of Russia. She acquired most of Ukraine, Lithuania, and Poland through three *partitions* (divisions). Her successful wars on the Ottoman Empire gained the Crimea and lands along the Black Sea for Russia. She also conquered Siberian and central Asian peoples. See also **Russia** (Catherine the Great); **Russo-Turkish wars.** James Cracraft

Catholic Church, Roman. See **Roman Catholic Church.**

Catholic Library Association (CLA) is an organization interested in encouraging good literature and improving libraries in Roman Catholic institutions in the United States and in other countries. Publications include *Catholic Library World, The Catholic Periodical and Literature Index,* and bibliographies on religious subjects. CLA sponsors the Regina Medal, a children's literature award (see **Regina Medal**). CLA was founded in 1921 and has headquarters in Pittsfield, Massachusetts. Critically reviewed by the Catholic Library Association

Catholic Youth Organization (CYO) is the parish youth group of many dioceses of the Roman Catholic Church in the United States. CYO offers social, cultural, spiritual, recreational, and community service activities. It includes athletics, camping, drama, retreats, and service projects to help the aged and the poor. Programs are directed by individual dioceses. The national office, known as the National Federation for Catholic Youth Ministry, provides assistance to the dioceses. CYO was founded in Chicago in 1930.

Critically reviewed by the National Federation for Catholic Youth Ministry

Catiline, *KAT uh LYN* (? -62 B.C.), was a Roman who led an unsuccessful plot against his country's government in 63 B.C. He came from a *patrician* (aristocratic) family. His name in Latin was Lucius Sergius Catilina.

Catiline sought Rome's highest political office, the consulship. He was not allowed to run for consul in 66 B.C. because he faced a trial on charges of misgovernment while he was governor in Africa. In 65 B.C., Catiline plotted the murder of government leaders in Rome, but the plot was not carried out. Catiline lost the election for consul in 64 B.C. to Cicero. When he failed again in 63 B.C., Catiline renewed his plot against the state. He tried to gain the support of discontented Romans by calling for the cancellation of debts.

Cicero publicly denounced Catiline in a famous speech before the Roman Senate, but he lacked proof of Catiline's treason. Catiline fled from Rome. When new evidence about the plot against the government was found, the Senate gave Cicero extraordinary power. Cicero seized and executed the plotters in Rome. Catiline managed to raise a small army in Etruria, in northern Italy. But in 62 B.C., he and his men were killed by Roman troops. Henry C. Boren

Catkin is a tassellike flower cluster that consists of numerous small flowers arranged around a long central axis. Each flower lacks the colored petals that are typical of most familiar wildflowers. For this reason, the grayish- or yellowish-green catkins are rarely thought of as flowers. Each catkin is either *staminate* (male, producing pollen) or *pistillate* (female, producing seeds). The wind pollinates the female catkins. The most familiar catkin is the pussy willow. Catkins appear on the branches of willows, alders, and poplars long before other spring flowers appear. Most catkins are long and drooping. They are also called *aments.* See also **Pollen; Pussy willow.**

Richard C. Schlesinger

Catlin, George (1796-1872), was an American artist known for his paintings and drawings of American Indians. His works rank among the most important studies of North American Indian culture.

Catlin was born on July 26, 1796, in Wilkes-Barre, Pennsylvania. He practiced law but quit in 1823 to become a portrait painter. Later, Catlin said he decided to portray Indians after seeing a group of them traveling to Washington, D.C. He wanted to paint Indian portraits and scenes of their customs to preserve their vanishing culture.

From 1830 to 1836, Catlin spent several summers among various Indian tribes. He painted Indians in St. Louis, along the Missouri River, in present-day Oklahoma, and in the Mississippi River region. By 1837, he had made almost 500 portraits and sketches and had gathered information from almost 50 tribes. He used these materials in an exhibition called "Catlin's Indian Gallery," which he took to major cities in the United States and Europe. From 1852 to 1857, Catlin traveled in South America and in North America west of the Rocky Mountains to paint Indians. Except for those years, he lived in Europe from 1840 to 1870. Catlin died on Dec. 23, 1872. Several of his paintings appear in **Indian, American.** Sarah E. Boehme

Catnip, also called *catmint,* is a strong-smelling plant of the mint family. It grows to a height of 2 or 3 feet (61 to 91 centimeters). Catnip bears little clusters of whitish flowers with small purple dots. The downy, heart-shaped leaves are green above and whitish below. Catnip has been cultivated for centuries and used for medical purposes. A tonic made from the plant is said to be a good remedy for colds. Catnip also provides a seasoning for cooking and is used as an herbal tea. The plants are harvested when in full bloom. Catnip is a common weed in North America and Europe. See also **Mint.** Donna M. Eggers Ware

WORLD BOOK illustration by Robert Hynes

Catnip

Scientific classification. Catnip belongs to the mint family, Lamiaceae or Labiatae. It is *Nepeta cataria.*

Cato, *KAY toh,* **Marcus Porcius,** *MAHR kuhs PAWR shee uhs,* **the Elder** (234-149 B.C.), was a prominent soldier and statesman of ancient Rome. He began his political career under Valerius Flaccus, an influential Roman. Flaccus was impressed with Cato's service in the war against Hannibal of Carthage. Cato was known as a *conservative* because he generally opposed change. For 50 years after the war, Cato fought against the luxury Romans enjoyed as the city's wealth increased. As *censor* (a high administrative official), he tried to restore simplicity to Roman life.

Toward the end of his life, Cato was alarmed by the recovery of Carthage. He is said to have ended every speech with the phrase, "Carthage must be destroyed." His warnings encouraged Rome to fight Carthage again, and the Romans destroyed Carthage in 146 B.C.

Cato opposed the influence of the Greeks, but he learned Greek at the age of 80. He published his speeches and wrote a book on farming that gives a picture of life in ancient Italy. Cato was the great-grandfather of Cato the Younger (see **Cato, Marcus Porcius, the Younger**). Arther Ferrill

Cato, *KAY toh,* **Marcus Porcius,** *MAHR kuhs PAWR shee uhs,* **the Younger** (95-46 B.C.), was a statesman and soldier of ancient Rome. He became a Stoic philosopher and was a stubborn conservative in politics. He often considered principles more important than compromise. In 65 B.C., Cato became *quaestor* (treasurer) and helped reform the treasury. As a *tribune* (elected leader), he backed Cicero against Catiline and opposed the First Triumvirate. In 54 B.C., he became *praetor* (magistrate).

When Pompey and Julius Caesar quarreled, Cato supported Pompey. When the news of Pompey's defeat at Pharsalus in 48 B.C. reached him, Cato fled to North Africa. There he received command of the defense of Utica. After the defeat of Pompey's forces at Thapsus in 46 B.C., Cato committed suicide by stabbing himself. He became a hero to those who idealized the dying Roman Republic. He was the great-grandson of the Roman statesman Cato the Elder. Arthur M. Eckstein

See also **Caesar, Julius; Cato, Marcus Porcius, the Elder.**

Cat's-eye is a gem that produces a thin streak of white light across the top of the stone when the gem is cut a certain way. The streak resembles the pupil of a cat's eye. The streak seems to change position as the stone is moved. This change is known as the *chatoyant effect* and is caused by light reflecting from tiny hollow channels within the stone. Cat's-eyes display shades of yellow, green, red, and brown. They are used in jewelry and for other ornamental purposes. The term *cat's-eye* used by itself describes only a semiprecious stone called *chrysoberyl,* also known as *true cat's-eye* or *precious cat's-eye.* Other types of cat's-eyes have a specific gem name, such as tourmaline cat's-eye. Most true cat's-eyes are found in Sri Lanka. Pansy D. Kraus

See also **Gem** (picture).

Catskill Mountains are a group of mountains west of the Hudson River in New York. They form part of the Appalachian mountain system. The southern edge of the Catskills lies about 40 miles (64 kilometers) northwest of New York City (see **New York** [physical map]). The chain is about 70 miles (110 kilometers) long and 50 miles (80 kilometers) wide. The highest peaks are Slide Mountain (4,204 feet, or 1,281 meters) and Hunter Mountain (4,025 feet, or 1,227 meters).

The Catskill Mountains were carved out by glacial ice sheets thousands of years ago. They make up one of the most beautiful natural regions in New York. The Catskills and the Hudson River Valley became famous in the 1800's as a setting for writers and landscape painters. Catskill State Park was established in 1904 and now covers 705,000 acres (285,000 hectares). Resorts in the mountains offer canoeing, fly fishing, hiking, and skiing. The Schoharie and Ashokan reservoirs in the Catskills supply fresh water to New York City through the Catskill Aqueduct. Ray Bromley

Catsup. See **Ketchup.**

Catt, Carrie Chapman (1859-1947), was an American leader in the campaign for woman suffrage. She served as president of the National American Woman Suffrage Association (NAWSA) from 1900 to 1904, and from 1915 to 1920, when the 19th Amendment to the United States Constitution gave women the right to vote.

Catt began her suffrage work in 1887 with the Iowa Woman Suffrage Association. She was one of the suffrage movement's most effective lobbyists and organizers. As president of NAWSA, she developed her "Winning Plan" for campaigning at the state and national levels. From 1904 to 1923, she served as president of the International Woman Suffrage Alliance. Catt helped found the National League of Women Voters (now the League of Women Voters) in 1920, and she founded the National Committee on the Cause and Cure of War in 1925. She also supported the League of Nations and, later, the United Nations.

Clinedist

Carrie Chapman Catt

Carrie Clinton Lane was born on Jan. 9, 1859, in Ripon, Wisconsin. She attended Iowa State College. Catt taught school and became the first woman superintendent of schools in Mason City, Iowa. She died on March 9, 1947. Melanie S. Gustafson

See also **League of Women Voters; Woman suffrage.**

Cattail is the name of a group of about 14 wild plants that grow in swamps, marshes, and other wetlands throughout most parts of the world. The *broad-leaved cattail* is one of the more common species. It grows throughout temperate parts of the Northern Hemisphere and in some tropical areas of Africa. This plant grows to about 13 feet (4 meters) high. The flowering parts of a cattail plant enlarge and become long, brown spikes. They are sometimes used for winter decorations.

Cattails are used in many ways. The roots of cattails contain starch and are eaten in times of famine in many parts of the world. Cattail pollen can be used like flour. The silky down surrounding the seeds of cattails can be used to stuff life jackets and mattresses. The leaves can be woven into mats and chair seats. Cattails provide shelter and food for wild waterfowl. However, thick growths of cattails can cause problems by blocking drainage ditches. Roy E. Gereau

Scientific classification. Cattails belong to the cattail family, Typhaceae. The scientific name for the broad-leaved cattail is *Typha latifolia.*

See also **Bulrush.**

Stephen Kraseman, DRK Photo

Cattails are wild plants that grow in swamps and marshes.

Grant Heilman

Hereford cattle graze in a pasture.

Cattle

Cattle are among the most important farm animals. We eat the meat of cattle as roast beef, veal, hamburger, and hot dogs. We drink the milk of cattle and use it to make butter, cheese, and ice cream. The hides of cattle provide leather for shoes. Cattle also furnish materials for such useful items as medicines, soap, and glue. In some countries, cattle supply power by pulling plows, carts, and wagons. In some parts of the world, a family's wealth is judged by the number of cattle it owns.

All kinds of cattle have large bodies, long tails, and *cloven* (divided) hoofs. Some cattle have horns. Cattle chew their food two separate times to digest it. After they chew and swallow the food, they bring it up from the stomach and chew it again. This once-swallowed food is called a *cud.*

Cattle are less intelligent than many other domestic animals. People sometimes name them. But cattle rarely learn to respond to their names as horses and dogs do.

Cattle roam and graze in green pastures and on the plains. Their mooing, or *lowing,* often breaks the silence of the countryside. *Beef cattle* are raised for their meat. *Dairy cattle* are raised for their milk. *Dual-purpose* cattle provide both meat and milk.

M. Peter Hoffman, the contributor of this article, is Professor of Animal Science at Iowa State University.

People around the world raise cattle. Cattle live in cold lands, such as Canada and Iceland, and in hot countries, such as Brazil and India. Hindus in India believe cattle are holy animals. They do not kill cattle or eat beef.

The word *cattle* usually means cows, bulls, steers, heifers, and calves. A *cow* is a female, and a *bull* is a male. *Steers* are males that have had some of their reproductive organs removed. A young cow is called a *heifer* until she gives birth to a calf. A *calf* is a young heifer or bull. The mother of a calf is called a *dam,* and the father is a *sire.* A group of cattle is known as a *herd.*

Beef cattle and dairy cattle that can be traced through all their ancestors to the original animals of a breed are called *purebred.* A *registered* animal is one whose family history has been recorded with the appropriate breed association in its register, called a *herdbook.*

Not all purebred cattle are registered. Some farmers and ranchers have no interest in registering their cattle.

The bodies of cattle

Cattle have muscular bodies, especially at *maturity* (full growth). Most cattle reach a height of about 5 feet (1.5 meters). Cows weigh from about 900 to 2,000 pounds (410 to 910 kilograms). Bulls may weigh 2,000 pounds or more.

Many cattle have black, white, or red coats of hair.

Others have coats that are various shades or combinations of shades of these colors. Most cattle have a coat of short hair that grows thicker and somewhat longer during the winter. A few breeds have long hair. The long, shaggy hair of Galloway cattle enables them to survive the extremely cold weather in Scotland, where the breed developed and where most of them are raised. Cattle also have a long tail, which they use to shoo away insects.

Teeth. Adult cattle have 32 teeth—8 in the front of the lower jaw and 12 each in the back of the upper and lower jaws. A cow cannot bite off grass because it does not have cutting teeth in the front of its upper jaw. It must tear the grass by moving its head. Cattle chew their cud with their *molars* (back teeth).

Horns. The horns of cattle are hollow and have no branches, as do those of some other horned animals such as deer. Cattle born without horns are called *polled* cattle. Cattle owners have increased the number of polled animals through selective breeding. They *dehorn* (remove the horns of) most horned cattle to keep them from injuring other cattle or people. The horns are removed with chemicals, a hot iron, or a cutting tool. In most cases, dehorning occurs when a calf is less than 3 weeks old.

Stomach. Cattle have a stomach with four compartments. This kind of stomach enables them to bring swallowed food back into their mouth to be chewed and swallowed again. Animals with such stomachs are called *ruminants* (see **Ruminant**). The compartments are the *rumen,* the *reticulum,* the *omasum,* and the *abomasum.*

When cattle eat, they first chew their food only enough to swallow it. The food goes down the *esophagus* (food pipe) into the rumen. The rumen and the reticulum form a large storage area. In that area, the food is mixed and softened. At the same time, microorganisms

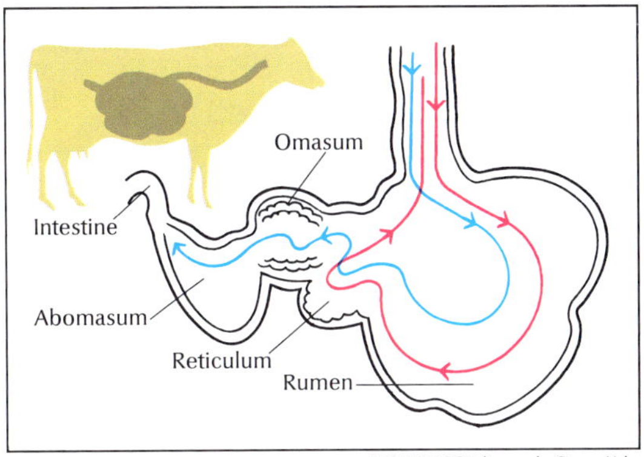

WORLD BOOK diagram by Steven Liska

A cow's stomach has four compartments. Food first enters the two sections shown by the red line. The cow then rechews the food as a *cud,* which follows the path shown by the blue line. In the drawing, the animal's stomach has been stretched out of its actual shape to show how food travels through it.

that grow in the rumen break down complex carbohydrates into simple carbohydrates. Such simple carbohydrates as sugars and starches provide the major source of energy for the animal. The microorganisms also build protein and many B-complex vitamins.

After the solid food has been mixed and softened, stomach muscles send it back up into the animal's mouth. The animal rechews this cud and swallows it. The swallowed cud goes back to the rumen and reticulum, where it undergoes further chemical breakdown. The food and fluids then move down into the omasum, where much of the water is absorbed. The food then enters the abomasum. The walls of the abomasum produce digestive juices. These juices further digest the food. The abomasum is called the *true stomach,* be-

Grant Heilman

A milking parlor on a dairy farm has sanitary equipment that milks cows, such as the Holsteins shown at the left. The milk is stored in a refrigerated tank until it is delivered to a processing plant.

American Angus Association

Aberdeen-Angus

© B. E. Fichte, Rosebud Communications, Inc.

Beefmaster

© Grant Heilman

Charolais

cause it functions in much the same way as the stomach of creatures that are not ruminants. From the stomach, the food goes to the intestine, where digestion and absorption are completed.

Udder. Cows have a suspended organ called an *udder,* which holds their milk. The udder hangs from the cow's body between and in front of the hind legs. The udder has four sections that hold milk. When a farmer milks a cow by hand, pressure causes the cow's milk to squirt out of the udder through large nipples called *teats.*

Today, farmers rarely milk their cows by hand. They use electrically operated milking machines. Milking machines use suction to draw the milk from the cow's udder into a container (see **Milking machine**). Beef cows, which produce milk only for their calves, have smaller udders than dairy cows.

Beef cattle

Most beef cattle graze on large areas of open grassland that are unsuitable for growing crops. This method of feeding enables farmers and ranchers to raise stock without using large numbers of workers and expensive feeds and equipment. Beef cattle have been bred to produce meat under such conditions.

Beef cattle have also been bred to mature earlier than dairy cattle and to produce less milk than dairy cattle. Steers and heifers from dairy breeds also provide excellent beef, however, and contribute to the world's meat supply.

Meat from calves that are less than 3 months old is called *veal.* Meat from older animals is called *beef.* Butchers classify beef into various *cuts,* such as steaks and roasts. People also eat the brains, heart, kidneys, liver, *sweetbread* (pancreas and thymus), tongue, and *tripe* (stomach lining) of cattle.

Among the most numerous breeds of beef cattle are the Aberdeen-Angus, Beefmaster, Charolais, Hereford, Limousin, and Simmental.

Aberdeen-Angus cattle, often called simply Angus, are polled animals with black coats. These cattle mature and *finish* (become ready to market) at lighter weights than most other breeds. Their meat has more *marbling* (fat mixed with lean meat) than that of other breeds. This quality makes the cattle's meat more flavorful. Some cattle raisers believe the breed is not large enough at maturity. A number of breeders crossbreed the Angus with certain larger breeds to produce bigger offspring.

Breeders developed the Angus in the Highlands of Northern Scotland. The Red Angus, a separate breed, was developed in the United States from red calves born to Aberdeen-Angus cattle. Except for their red color, these Angus resemble Aberdeen-Angus.

Beefmaster cattle thrive in hot, humid climates. Beefmaster cattle have horns. They also have short hair and large body surface areas for heat loss that enable them to withstand heat and humidity. The Beefmaster breed has a fleshy hump over its shoulders. Most of these cattle are various shades of red, but some may have other colors. Breeders in the United States developed the Beefmaster by crossing Hereford, Shorthorn, and Brahman cattle.

Charolais cattle are a large, white breed that originated in France. Commercial cattle producers seek Charolais for crossbreeding because of their great size, their heavy muscular system, and the rapid growth of Charolais calves.

Hereford cattle have red bodies and white faces, so they often are called *whitefaces.* They also have white patches on their chests, flanks, lower legs, and on the *switches* (tips) of their tails.

This breed thrives in grasslands because they can survive wide ranges in temperature better than most larger breeds. Herefords also require less care and attention than many large breeds. The Hereford breed was developed in the county of Hereford in England.

Polled Hereford cattle are a *strain* (type) of Herefords. They resemble Herefords but have no horns. Polled Herefords were developed by Warren Gammon, a farmer in St. Marys, Iowa, near Des Moines, in 1900. He produced the strain by crossbreeding Herefords born without horns.

Limousin cattle were developed in France. These golden-colored cattle can be either horned or polled. The breed has a muscular body. Breeders often use the Limousin in crossbreeding programs to enhance the muscle development of less muscular cattle.

Simmental cattle originated in Switzerland. The breed is found in many parts of Europe, where it is raised for beef, milk, and *draft* (pulling loads). In the United States and other countries, the large-bodied Simmental is raised mainly for beef. The cattle range in color. They may be black and white, red and white, or *fawn* (light yellowish-brown) and white. The American Simmental breed has rapidly increased in numbers because of such breeding techniques as *artificial insemination* and *embryo transfer* (see **Breeding**).

Other beef cattle. The Shorthorn was developed in England and became the first imported breed. Shorthorns were brought from England to the United States in 1783. The Polled Shorthorn was developed in 1889 in the United States by breeding hornless Shorthorns. Shorthorns and Polled Shorthorns are used for beef production. The Milking Shorthorn was developed from the original Shorthorn cattle by selecting and breeding the cattle for high milk production. Shorthorns may be white, red, or *roan* (white-red), or a combination of red and white.

Many other breeds remain popular among cattle owners. Numerous U.S. breeds were developed from Zebus, humped cattle native to India. The Brahman was developed almost entirely from Zebus, whereas the Santa Getrudis was bred from Zebus and Shorthorn cattle. Brahman cattle, in turn, were mixed with various cattle to produce still other breeds. The Brangus developed from Brahman and Angus breeds and the Simbrah from Brahman and Simmental.

Popular breeds from other countries include the Chianina, from Italy; the Gelbvieh, from Austria and Germany; and the Tarentaise, from France. Still other kinds of cattle, called *composites,* also contribute to the world's beef production. These cattle, which were developed by crossing various breeds, are not considered true beef breeds.

Dairy cattle

Among the most important breeds of milk cows are the Holstein-Friesian, Jersey, Guernsey, Ayrshire, Brown

Danny Weaver, Agri-Graphic Services

Hereford

© Walt Browarny, Browarny Photographics Ltd.

Limousin

American Simmental Association

Simmental

Danny Weaver, Agri-Graphic Services

Holstein-Friesian

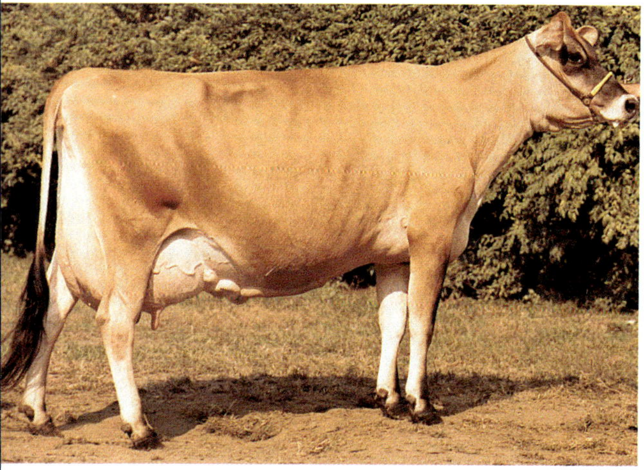

The American Jersey Cattle Club

Jersey

Danny Weaver, Agri-Graphic Services

Guernsey

Swiss, and Milking Shorthorn. All of these breeds are considered good milk producers, but some, such as the Holstein-Friesian, produce more milk than others.

In the past, dairy cows produced less milk than they do today. Dairy farmers increased the milk output, butterfat content, and protein content by improving their cattle herds. The butterfat content is important because people use butterfat to make butter. Protein is important in human diets because it helps the body grow and maintain itself. Since the 1960's, the average annual output of milk per cow in the United States has more than doubled.

Dairy cows normally give milk for about five or six years, but some still give it at the age of 20 or older. When these cows no longer give milk, they usually are sent to a livestock market for processing into beef. Dairy cattle breeds provide about 25 percent of our beef and veal.

Holstein-Friesian cattle, usually called Holsteins, are identified by their black-and-white coats. Some Holsteins are nearly all black or all white in color. A few varieties are red and white. Holsteins rank as the largest dairy cattle. They have broad hips and long, deep body trunks, called *barrels*. Their horns slant forward and curve inward.

Holsteins rank among the most common dairy breeds in the world. Many farmers favor them because a Holstein cow produces more milk than other breeds. The milk contains less butterfat than that of other breeds, however.

Holsteins probably were developed from a strain of black-and-white cattle found in the province of Friesland in the Netherlands. Cattle raisers of the Schleswig-Holstein region of Germany also helped to develop the breed.

Jersey cattle range in color from gray to dark fawn, or reddish-brown. Some appear almost black. The Jersey cow is the smallest of the major dairy breeds. Its broad face is unusually short from its forehead to its nostrils. The small horns curve inward.

Jersey cows produce less milk than the four other major breeds, but their milk contains the most butterfat. A thick mass of cream rises to the top of a container of Jersey milk. Jersey cattle came from the tiny British island of Jersey in the English Channel.

Guernsey cattle are slightly larger than Jerseys. The Guernsey's orange, fawn-colored coat is spotted with white markings. The Guernsey has a long head. A white shield often appears on its broad forehead. The horns curve upward and forward.

Guernseys produce a little more milk than Jerseys. But the rich milk of the Guernsey ranks second to that of the top-ranking Jersey in butterfat content.

Guernseys probably originated on Guernsey, an island in the English Channel. Breeders crossed cattle from two regions in northwestern France, the red brindle cattle of Normandy and the small brown-and-white cattle of Brittany.

Ayrshire cattle are red and white or brown and white. Some are nearly all red or all white. The Ayrshire's long, curving horns give it an impressive appearance. Its body is sturdy but somewhat lean. Production of milk from Ayrshire cattle ranks between Brown Swiss and Guernsey.

Ayrshires came from the hilly country of Ayr in southwest Scotland. They are more rugged than other breeds, and they thrive on land with many hills.

Brown Swiss may be light brown, dark brown, or brownish-gray. A light gray stripe may run along the back. The nose, horn tips, and tail switch are black. Brown Swiss are larger than most dairy cattle. The horns slant forward and upward.

Brown Swiss milk production ranks second only to that of Holsteins. The milk is pure white, and it is rich in nonfat solids, including proteins, minerals, and *lactose* (milk sugar). These qualities make the milk of Brown Swiss cattle excellent for cheese.

Like the Holstein, the Brown Swiss is one of the oldest breeds of dairy cattle. It was first raised in the *canton* (state) of Schwyz in Switzerland.

Milking Shorthorn cattle are white, red, or roan in color and may be either horned or polled. Milking Shorthorns grow larger than most other kinds of dairy cattle, and many cattle experts consider them to be among the hardiest of the dairy breeds. They produce about as much milk as the smaller dairy breeds. The breed was developed in England.

Other dairy cattle. Dutch Belted cattle are black, with a wide belt of white around the middle. Their milk contains about as much butterfat as that of the Brown Swiss and Ayrshire cattle.

French Canadian cattle are a small, dark brown breed, much like the Jersey and the Guernsey. They are raised mostly in Quebec. The milk of these cows is rich in butterfat.

Kerry cattle, a black breed, originated in Ireland. They are closely related to Dexter cattle, which are small and have short legs. Dexters produce about one half Dexter offspring, one fourth Kerry-type offspring, and one fourth abnormal "bulldog" calves that die at birth.

Red Sindhi is a red, Brahman-type of cattle that originated in the province of Sind in Pakistan. It produces more milk than the Brahman. Cattle breeders in the United States have crossed it with other breeds to develop cattle with greater resistance to high temperatures.

Dual-purpose cattle

Some cattle can be raised for beef or kept as dairy cattle. They are called *dual-purpose cattle.* These animals have many of the qualities of beef cattle, but they also are good milk producers. Many farmers raise dual-purpose breeds only for their meat. These breeds produce calves that grow rapidly and can be processed for veal or baby beef sooner than can some beef cattle breeds.

Dairy cattle add to our supply of beef and veal. But they are not classified as dual-purpose cattle, because they are bred and raised chiefly for the production of milk.

The most important dual-purpose breed is the Red Poll. It is a red, hornless cattle. Horned Norfolk cattle were crossed with polled Suffolk to produce Red Polls. The breed originated in the counties of Norfolk and Suffolk in England.

Breeding and care of cattle

Breeding. Cattle breeders select and mate the best types of cattle for a special purpose, such as producing

David Patrick; Agri-Graphics

Ayrshire

© Agri-Graphic Services (Brown Swiss Cattle Breeders' Association)

Brown Swiss

© Lynn M. Stone, Animals Animals

Milking Shorthorn

Danny Weaver, Agri-Graphic Services

Red Poll

large quantities of milk or high-quality beef. Then they mate the best of the offspring until, after several generations, the cattle possess the desired qualities. In this way, beef cattle have been bred to mature earlier. They thus can be sold at a greater profit than they could if they had to be fed over a longer time. Selective breeding has increased milk output and the percentage of butterfat.

Heifers usually are mated when they are about 15 months old. A cow carries her calf in her body for nine months before she gives birth. Cows usually have one calf every year. At birth, calves may normally weigh from 50 to 100 pounds (23 to 45 kilograms). Sometimes twin calves are born. Bulls may start breeding at the age of 1 year. They are most active between 2 and 6 years of age, however.

A cow cannot produce milk unless it has given birth to a calf. Such a cow is known as a "fresh" cow. After the birth of the calf, the cow usually gives milk for about 10 months. A cow that does not give milk is called a "dry cow."

Feeding. Feeding methods have greatly improved the production of both meat and milk. Cattle are hearty eaters. The recommended daily diet for finishing a 1-year-old beef steer includes 25 pounds (11 kilograms) of corn or sorghum silage, 14 pounds (6 kilograms) of corn or ground grain sorghum, and $\frac{1}{2}$ pound (0.2 kilogram) of soybean meal with added vitamins and minerals. The best cattle feeders use the latest scientific methods to make their cattle gain weight rapidly and efficiently and at the lowest cost.

Certain chemicals called *additives* may be added to cattle feed to help the cattle grow more quickly and to make them digest food more efficiently. Cattle owners may also implant additives in the back of the animal's ear. Some farmers and ranchers add antibiotics to cattle feed to increase their animals' weight gains.

A farmer can increase the amount of milk and butterfat produced each year by a cow by giving the animal a proper diet. The average dairy cow eats 3 pounds (1.4 kilograms) of silage or 1 pound (0.45 kilogram) of hay a day for every 100 pounds (45 kilograms) of its body weight. In addition, a dairy cow receives 1 pound of grain or other concentrated feed for every 3 pounds of milk it produces. Both dairy and beef cattle eat large amounts of *forage* (coarse feed), such as corn silage and alfalfa. They turn the feed into meat and milk for people to eat and drink.

Many cattle have been poisoned by eating certain kinds of plants. Weeds that may poison cattle include locoweed, death camas, and some lupines and larkspurs. Cattle owners sometimes destroy these plants with chemicals. See **Locoweed.**

Diseases cost cattle owners millions of dollars each year. The most widespread cattle illnesses infect the animal's respiratory system and digestive system. Other diseases may affect the nervous system, reproductive organs, muscles, liver, eyes, mouth, and skin.

Respiratory diseases occur in cattle of any age. However, they usually infect young animals that are exposed

Six main breeds of beef cattle

Breed	Aberdeen-Angus	Beefmaster	Charolais	Hereford	Limousin	Simmental
Color	Black	Shades of red and other colors	White	Red and white	Golden	Black and white, red and white, or fawn and white
Place of origin	Scotland	United States	France	England	France	Switzerland
Rank in body size	6	4	1	5	3	2
Year brought into United States	1873	—	1936	1817	1968	1967
Rank in number registered in United States	1	4	5	2	3	6
National registry association formed	1883	1924	1957	1881	1968	1968

Grant Heilman

In a feedlot, cattle eat carefully selected feed that makes them gain weight much faster than they would by grazing. Feedlots are an efficient means of fattening cattle before they are sent to a packing house.

to the disease during shipping, periods of extreme temperature, or other stressful circumstances. Many viruses and other organisms can cause respiratory diseases, and veterinarians generally find more than one infectious organism in the lungs of cattle with respiratory illness. Some respiratory diseases can damage the lungs and lower the animal's resistance to other infections. Signs of respiratory disease include coughing, nasal discharge, fever, and difficulty breathing. A veterinarian can give vaccines to prevent some types of disease.

Many digestive disorders are caused by bacteria, viruses, and parasites. Infected cattle usually experience diarrhea and dehydration, which can result in death in severe cases. Cattle suffering from such disorders may eat well but still lose weight. Some animals may be infected but have no symptoms. One of the most common infectious organisms, *Salmonella,* infects both calves and older cattle and can cause severe diarrhea.

Two other common diseases of cattle are *mastitis* and *bloat.* Mastitis likely costs dairy farmers more money each year than any other disease. Cattle obtain this bacteria from other infected cattle or from objects in the environment. The bacteria infect a cow's udder, making it hard, swollen, and painful. Mastitis causes a drop in milk production and quality. Antibiotics can effectively treat the disease. Practicing proper care with cattle, such as good milking techniques, may help prevent mastitis.

Bloat is a noninfectious disease in which gas swells the rumen, causing the animal to stagger and gasp for breath. Cattle may be stricken with bloat when grazing in lush pastures, especially if the grass contains a large concentration of alfalfa or clover. A change in feed when cattle are hungry also may cause them to bloat. Severe bloat may result in sudden death.

Other less common diseases also infect cattle. *Anthrax* is caused by a germ that is usually picked up in the soil. It produces a high fever and often stops the flow of milk. *Blackleg* is one of the deadliest cattle diseases. It causes lameness, convulsions, rapid swelling, and high fever. *Brucellosis,* also called Bang's disease, attacks the lymph

Six main breeds of dairy cattle

Breed	Ayrshire	Brown Swiss	Guernsey	Holstein-Friesian	Jersey	Milking Shorthorn
Color	Red or brown and white	Brownish-gray	Orange, fawn, and white	Black and white	Gray to dark fawn or reddish-brown	White, red, or roan, or red and white
Place of origin	Scotland	Switzerland	Isle of Guernsey	Netherlands and Germany	Isle of Jersey	England
Rank in body size	4	3	5	1	6	2
Average percent butterfat of milk	3.9	4.1	4.5	3.7	4.7	3.6
Average percent protein of milk	3.3	3.6	3.6	3.2	3.8	3.3
Average annual milk yield	15,271 lbs. (6,927 kg)	17,103 lbs. (7,758 kg)	14,249 lbs. (6,463 kg)	20,853 lbs. (9,459 kg)	14,677 lbs. (6,657 kg)	14,116 lbs. (6,403 kg)
Rank in number registered in United States	5	3	4	1	2	6
National registry association formed	1875	1880	1877	1885	1868	1912

glands, udders, and reproductive organs of cows. Cattle pick up the brucellosis germ from infected feed or from other objects. Cows with brucellosis often cannot bear calves. Another illness, called *foot-and-mouth disease,* often results in lameness and reduces milk output. *Mad cow disease* is a rare but serious brain disease that causes odd behavior, difficulty walking, and eventually death. Scientists think the disease arose when cattle were fed parts of sheep infected with *scrapie,* a similar disease.

Parasites are also costly to the cattle industry. They can transmit diseases that reduce cattle growth and milk production, and possibly cause death. *External parasites* include such insects as flies, lice, and mosquitoes and such arachnids as ticks and mites. These parasites bite cattle and may eat their flesh or suck their blood, which can cause cattle much pain. Farmers can control external parasites with *insecticides* (chemicals that kill insects).

Internal parasites include roundworms, tapeworms, and flukes. Farmers often have difficulty detecting cattle infected with these types of parasites. Internal parasites are also hard to eliminate. Providing proper care and medications that expel worms helps reduce the chance of cattle becoming infected.

Raising and marketing cattle

Most beef calves are born in the spring. The young calves spend the summer with cows in fenced pastures, or on an open range. Most calves are *branded* (marked) with a hot iron to show their ownership (see **Ranching** [picture: Famous ranch brands]). In the fall, the calves are *weaned* (taken from their mothers).

Feeder cattle. The farmer or rancher sells the weaned calves to farmers called *feeders.* Such calves, known as *feeder cattle,* are raised in feedlots. A feedlot is an enclosed area where cattle receive special feed to finish them for market. The farmer then sends them to a meat-packing plant for processing. See **Meat packing.**

Ranchers and farmers sometimes send their calves directly to a market instead of selling them to feeders. Farmers, in turn, may buy feeder cattle from a carefully chosen market instead of from a rancher. The farmers feed such calves to a desired weight for market and then sell them to a meat-packing plant at a profit.

A farmer usually feeds feeder cattle for 120 to 240 days. The farmer tries to sell them when market conditions offer the largest profit. A steer is normally ready for processing by the time it reaches 15 to 20 months of age. Cattle grow to their full size in 2 to 3 years. Many cattle are heavy enough to sell before they reach maturity, however.

Some farmers in the East and Midwest breed and raise their own cattle. But most farmers find it more profitable to buy feeder cattle and use their land for growing corn and other livestock feed to give the stock.

Grass-fed cattle. Cattle owners sometimes feed their stock on grass for one or two years, and sell the animals as "grass fattened." Some grass-fattened cattle also receive grain feed for several weeks before they are finished. Farmers in southern coastal areas raise many calves that are sold for early processing or for grazing on richer pastures. Their land is not suitable for raising feeds on which to finish cattle.

Dairy cows. Most dairy cows spend their lives on one farm. Heifers from cows that have produced little milk are sent to market to be processed for veal when only a few weeks old. It is probable that such calves, like their mothers, would be poor milk producers. Most male calves also are sent to market. Dairy farmers save the female calves of the best cows for herd replace-

Leading beef cattle states and provinces

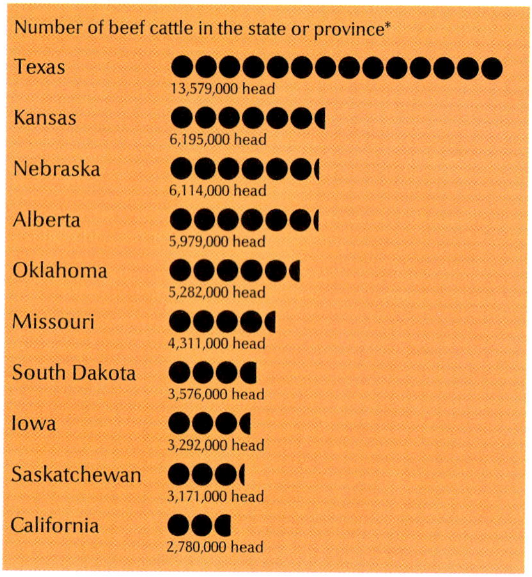

*State figures include all calves under 500 pounds (227 kilograms). Province figures include all calves under 1 year old.
Figures are for Jan. 1, 2003.
Sources: U.S. Department of Agriculture; Statistics Canada.

Leading dairy cattle states and provinces

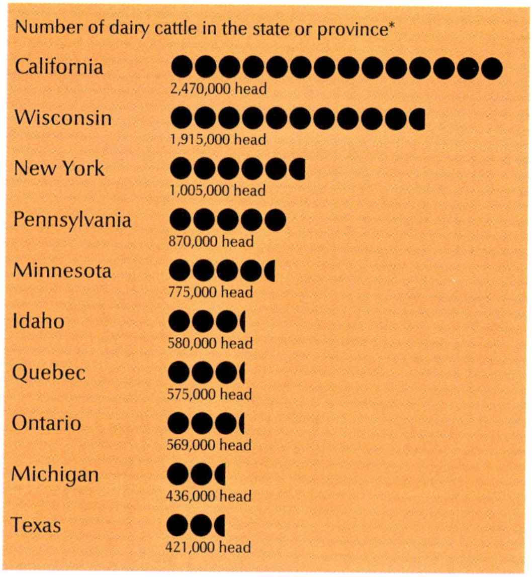

*State figures do not include calves under 500 pounds (227 kilograms). Province figures do not include calves under 1 year old.
Figures are for Jan. 1, 2003.
Sources: U.S. Department of Agriculture; Statistics Canada.

ments. When a cow fails to produce milk economically, it is sent to a livestock market and sold for processing. Such dairy cows produce much of the world's low-grade beef.

Show cattle. Cattle owners exhibit prize animals at local and regional fairs and livestock expositions. A champion dairy cow has a large body, a strong set of feet and legs, and a well-developed udder. In the United States, a blue-ribbon beef animal has a solid, compact body with a rectangular shape. Exhibitors, such as 4-H Club members, start developing show cattle as soon as the calves are weaned. They carefully feed, exercise, and groom the animals.

Nomadic cattle raising. In some parts of the world, farmers still follow the ancient practice of *nomadic cattle raising*—moving with herds of cattle in search of grazing and water. An example is the Maasai people of Kenya. The herds of cattle maintained by nomadic people can be extremely large. Because cattle are a sign of wealth, the people usually consider the quantity of animals more important than their quality.

History

Early cattle. Cattle belong to the genus *Bos.* Modern breeds developed from the early domestic cattle of Europe and Asia. Some scientists consider each group to be a distinct species. They give the name *B. taurus* to European cattle and *B. indicus* to Asian cattle. Others believe both types are only one species, classifying them together as *B. taurus.* Both groups descended from the *aurochs,* or wild oxen, that once roamed Asia, Europe, and northern Africa. The last aurochs died in Poland in 1627.

People have raised cattle for thousands of years. Pictures carved in ancient Egyptian tombs show oxen pulling plows and treading grain.

Cattle raisers once followed their herds from land to land as the cattle searched for grass to eat. Later, some of these herders and their families settled in one place. They fed their cattle grain in addition to grass.

Leading cattle-raising countries

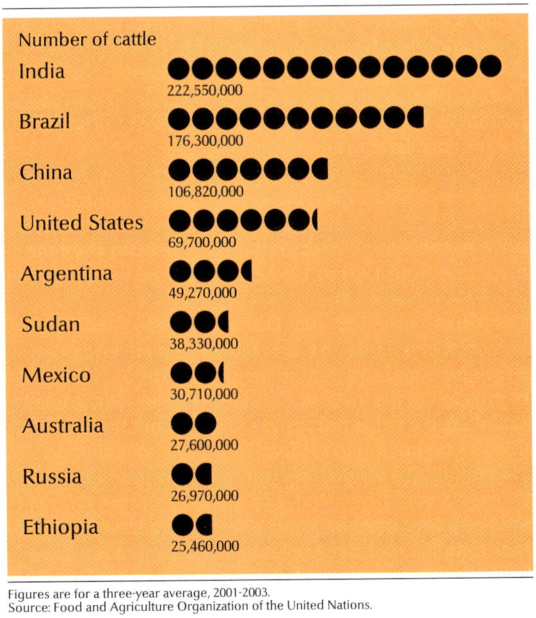

Figures are for a three-year average, 2001-2003.
Source: Food and Agriculture Organization of the United Nations.

Beginning of breeding. The first cattle were used as work animals as well as for producing milk and beef. Gradually, people began to breed cattle either as beef animals or for producing milk. Robert Bakewell, a farmer in Leicestershire, England, was the first person to use modern livestock breeding methods. He began improving his cattle in the late 1700's. He used a breed of cattle called Longhorns (different from Texas longhorns) and tried to develop cattle that would give larger amounts of meat.

American cattle. Some historians believe that cattle were first brought to the Americas by Norwegian Vikings in the early 1000's. In 1493, the Italian explorer Christopher Columbus brought long-horned cattle from Spain to Santo Domingo (now part of the West Indies) on his second voyage to America. Descendants of these cattle later were taken into Mexico and eventually into Texas. They were ancestors of the famous Texas longhorns.

Governor Edward Winslow of Plymouth Colony brought cattle to New England in 1624. Cattle raising spread westward as the pioneers moved across the continent. The pioneers used oxen to pull wagons and plows.

Railroads helped cattle ranchers on the plains by providing transportation to the eastern markets. Refrigerated railroad cars made it possible to ship meat products safely over long distances. Breeders' organizations encouraged the improvement of beef and dairy cattle. Livestock shows spurred interest in breeding prizewinning cattle.

In the West, ranchers came to realize that the Texas longhorn grew more slowly and was less profitable than such breeds as the Hereford and Aberdeen-Angus. The longhorn produced little beef in proportion to its bulk. By the 1920's, the Texas longhorn had nearly disappeared from the Western ranges. The number of Texas longhorns began to increase again during the 1970's, however. Today, a few farmers and ranchers use longhorns chiefly for crossbreeding with other breeds of cattle.

The world supply. There are about 1 $\frac{1}{3}$ billion beef and dairy cattle worldwide. Asia raises about 35 percent of the world's cattle. South America ranks second among the continents in the number of existing cattle.

India has the most cattle of any country in the world. But India's cattle are undernourished and have little work value. There is also little demand for meat in India because Hindus consider the cow sacred. Brazil, the United States, and China rank as the three largest producers of beef and dairy cattle. Cattle farmers in many countries work to improve their breeds and to increase beef and milk production. M. Peter Hoffman

Scientific classification. Domestic cattle belong to the genus *Bos* of the bovid family, Bovidae.

Related articles in *World Book* include:

Kinds of cattle

Aurochs
Buffalo
Kouprey
Musk ox
Ox
Water buffalo
Yak

Diseases and pests

Actinomycosis
Anthrax
Bot fly
Brucellosis
Cattle tick
Face fly
Foot-and-mouth disease
Mad cow disease
Rinderpest
Tsetse fly
Warble fly

Industry

Agriculture
Breeding
Dairying
Livestock
Meat packing
Ranching

Products

Beef
Butter
Casein
Cheese
Gelatin
Leather
Milk
Tallow
Veal

Other related articles

Cowboy
DES
Farm and farming (pictures)
Horn
Ruminant
Ungulate
Western frontier life in America (The cattle drive)

Outline

I. The bodies of cattle
- A. Teeth
- B. Horns
- C. Stomach
- D. Udder

II. Beef cattle
- A. Aberdeen-Angus
- B. Beefmaster
- C. Charolais
- D. Hereford/Polled Hereford
- E. Limousin
- F. Simmental
- G. Other beef cattle

III. Dairy cattle
- A. Holstein-Friesian
- B. Jersey
- C. Guernsey
- D. Ayrshire
- E. Brown Swiss
- F. Milking Shorthorn
- G. Other dairy cattle

IV. Dual-purpose cattle

V. Breeding and care of cattle
- A. Breeding
- B. Feeding
- C. Diseases

VI. Raising and marketing cattle
- A. Feeder cattle
- B. Grass-fed cattle
- C. Dairy cows
- D. Show cattle

VII. History

Questions

What are polled cattle?
What do cattle owners strive for in breeding beef cattle? In breeding dairy cattle?
Why are Charolais cattle popular for crossbreeding?
How can Holsteins be identified? How do they rank in size among the dairy breeds? In milk production?
What was the original meaning of the word *cattle*?
About how many beef and dairy cattle are there in the world?
Why had Texas Longhorns nearly disappeared in the United States by the 1920's?
What are purebred cattle? Are they always registered?
How long do cows usually produce milk?
What country has the most cattle?

Additional resources

Carlson, Laurie W. *Cattle: An Informal Social History.* Ivan R. Dee, 2001.
Thomas, Heather S. *A Guide to Raising Beef Cattle.* Storey Bks., 1998.
Wolfman, Judy. *Life on a Cattle Farm.* Carolrhoda, 2002. Younger readers.

Cattle tick, also called *Texas fever tick,* carries Texas fever, a disease of cattle. The tick is round and chestnut-brown in color. It carries a one-celled organism that causes the disease. The tick injects the one-celled organisms into the cow with its saliva when feeding on the cow's body fluids.

Texas fever is an infectious disease. The one-celled organisms multiply in the cattle's blood and destroy the red blood corpuscles. The disease became serious in the southwestern part of the United States in about the mid-1800's. It once threatened all the cattle in the country but has been brought under control. Today, control measures restrict this tick to extreme southern Texas. But the tick is still common in Mexico.

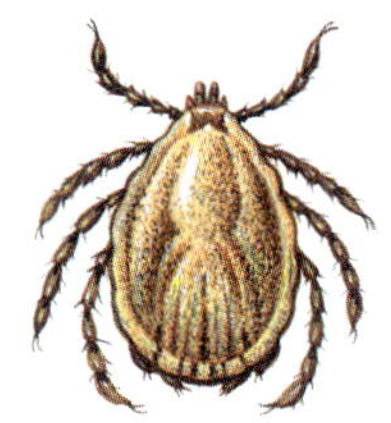
WORLD BOOK illustration by James Teason
Cattle tick

Edwin W. Minch

Scientific classification. The cattle tick belongs to the tick family, Ixodidae. Its scientific name is *Boophilus annulatus.*

See also Tick.

Catton, Bruce (1899-1978), an American historian and journalist, won the Pulitzer Prize in 1954 for *A Stillness at Appomattox* (1953). He wrote many other books about people and events of the American Civil War. These include *Mr. Lincoln's Army* (1951), *Glory Road* (1952), *U. S. Grant and the Military Tradition* (1954), *Grant Moves South* (1960), *The Coming Fury* (1961), *Terrible Swift Sword* (1963), and *Never Call Retreat* (1965). Catton's vivid narratives were the result of a close study of original documents, letters, and diaries.

Catton was born on Oct. 9, 1899, in Petoskey, Michigan. From 1926 to 1941, he was Washington correspondent and special writer for the Newspaper Enterprise Association. He was editor of *American Heritage* magazine from 1954 to 1959 and senior editor from 1959 to 1978. Robert C. Sims

Catullus, *kuh TUHL uhs,* **Gaius Valerius,** *GAY uhs vuh LEER ee uhs* (84? B.C.-54? B.C.), a Roman lyric poet, wrote personal and passionate poetry. His best-known poems tell of his love for Clodia, an aristocratic Roman called Lesbia in his poems. He wrote about the affair from its beginning to his final disillusionment in her.

Catullus also wrote long poems on mythological themes, a wedding hymn, and many epigrams. One of the epigrams attacked Julius Caesar, who later forgave him. Catullus also wrote a famous farewell to his dead brother. His most famous poem is: "I hate and I love. You may ask why I do this. I do not know, but I feel it happen, and am tormented." Catullus was born in Verona, Italy. Anthony A. Barrett

See also **Latin literature** (The age of Cicero).

Caucasoid race. See **Races, Human** (The three-race theory).

Caucasus, *KAW kuh suhs,* is a region that includes Armenia, Azerbaijan, Georgia, and a small portion of southern Russia. The region is divided by the Caucasus Mountains, which extend from the Black Sea to the Caspian Sea. The area north of the Caucasus Mountains is called *Northern Caucasus;* that to the south, *Transcaucasia* or *Transcaucasus.* About 33 million people live in Caucasus. Caucasus is rich in natural resources, including oil, natural gas, coal, and such metals as iron, copper, lead, tungsten, manganese, molybdenum, and zinc.

After the Bolshevik Revolution of 1917, Northern Caucasus became part of the Russian Soviet Federative Socialist Republic. Armenia, Azerbaijan, and Georgia became Communist states under the control of the Russian Communists. When the Soviet Union was formed in 1922, these states were reorganized as the Transcaucasian Soviet Federated Socialist Republic. They were reorganized again in December 1936 as separate Soviet republics. In 1991, the Soviet Union broke apart, and Armenia, Azerbaijan, Georgia, and Russia became independent countries.

Caucasus has experienced much upheaval since the late 1980's. Armenia and Azerbaijan have struggled for control of the Nagorno-Karabakh region. In 1988, Armenia suffered a devastating earthquake. Since the early 1990's, the people of Chechnya in southern Russia have fought for independence. Craig ZumBrunnen

See also **Armenia; Azerbaijan; Georgia.**

Caucasus Mountains, *KAW kuh suhs,* are a great mountain range in Russia, Georgia, and Azerbaijan. They rise between the Black and Caspian seas and extend from northwest to southeast for about 750 miles (1,210 kilometers). For location, see **Russia** (terrain map). The chief peak is Mount Elbrus (18,510 feet, or 5,642 meters, above sea level), which is also the highest spot in Europe. Many geographers consider the Caucasus to be a boundary line between Europe and Asia.

The mountains have a number of passes over 10,000 feet (3,000 meters) high. Roads cross a few passes, but railroads skirt around the mountains. The glaciers of the Caucasus rival those of the Alps in size, but there are almost no lakes. Among the Caucasus's rich mineral resources are the oil fields of Baku, Groznyy (also spelled Grozny), and Maykop; the rich manganese deposits of Georgia; and valuable tungsten and molybdenum reserves. Historically, the mountains have been a barrier to migration, but numerous invasions swept over them in ancient times and in the Middle Ages. Leslie Dienes

See also **Mount Elbrus.**

Caucus is any gathering of individuals to nominate candidates for office or to endorse a policy or program. In many countries, the members of a political party hold a caucus to develop party policy and to nominate candidates for leadership positions. In the United States, for example, the members of each party in Congress traditionally hold a caucus to select congressional leaders.

Another type of caucus, called a *participatory caucus,* is prominent in the United States in presidential election years. The best-known participatory caucuses are those held in Iowa by the Republican and Democratic parties. The Iowa caucuses are the first major events in a series of state caucuses and primary elections that end in the nomination of each party's presidential candidate.

A participatory caucus may be attended by any eligible voter willing to acknowledge association with the party that holds it. People who attend such caucuses in presidential election years help elect delegates to a political convention that covers a larger region, such as a county. Typically, each delegate selected has promised to support a particular candidate at the convention.

During the early history of the United States, small groups of party leaders chose candidates for office in meetings called *party caucuses.* But the party caucus system became unpopular because it gave other party members little voice in the selection of candidates.

Since the 1830's, major U.S. political parties have used national conventions to nominate their candidates for president. During much of the 1800's, delegates to these conventions were selected by party officials at state conventions. These officials were typically selected, in turn, by party officials at local conventions. This arrangement became known as the *party convention system.* In the late 1800's, some Western states began using participatory caucuses instead of conventions at the lowest level of this process, usually in individual voting districts. This change opened local participation to anyone who turned out at the caucus. Other states, including Iowa, eventually adopted this *caucus-convention system.*

The party convention system has been in decline since the early 1900's and the caucus-convention system since the 1960's. Most states now use primary elections instead. Some states still use caucuses to select or endorse candidates for public office at the local or state level. Byron E. Shafer

See also **House of Representatives** (Organization of the U.S. House); **Political convention; Primary election; Senate** (The leaders of the Senate).

Cauliflower is a garden vegetable that is rich in vitamins and minerals. It is most commonly eaten cooked, but it is sometimes eaten pickled or raw.

The white *curd* (head) of the cauliflower is the part

WORLD BOOK illustration by Kate Lloyd-Jones, Linden Artists Ltd.

The cauliflower plant has large leaves that surround the cauliflower head. The plant's clustered white flower buds are eaten.

that is eaten. The curd consists of thick clusters of flower buds. It forms at the top of the plant's stem and is surrounded by large green leaves. Gardeners tie these leaves together over the head as soon as it appears in order to *blanch* it—that is, keep it white.

Most of the cauliflower produced in the United States comes from California. The vegetable grows best in a cool, moist climate. If temperatures are too hot, the plants will not form heads. If temperatures are too cold, the plants may develop a condition called *buttoning,* which results in small, unusable heads. Albert Liptay

Scientific classification. Cauliflower belongs to the mustard family, Brassicaceae or Cruciferae. It is *Brassica oleracea botrytis.*

Cavalier King Charles spaniel is a breed of dog developed in England in the 1920's. It was named after King Charles II of England. The dog resembles its close relative, the English toy spaniel, but it has a longer nose. Its silky coat can be red; black and tan; chestnut and white; or black, tan, and white. Longer fringes of hair grow on the ears, chest, legs, tail, and feet. It weighs 13 to 18 pounds (6 to 8 kilograms) and grows about 1 foot (30 centimeters) high. It makes a gentle, affectionate pet.

Critically reviewed by the American Cavalier King Charles Spaniel Club

Cavalry was a unit of soldiers that fought on horseback. These swift-striking, wide-ranging forces formed an important part of many armies from ancient times until the early 1900's. But by that time, cannons, machine guns, and other high-powered weapons had been developed that could easily destroy entire cavalry units.

Cavalry performed a number of other duties during warfare in addition to fighting on the battlefield. Mounted units carried messages between army camps, provided an armed escort for generals, and scouted enemy positions. They also carried out certain screening maneuvers to confuse or hold back enemy forces.

The ancient Assyrians, Macedonians, Persians, and Scythians relied heavily on cavalry, as did the Roman Army of the late A.D. 300's. The mounted knights of the Middle Ages became famous for their gallantry, dash, valor, and honor. But the heavy armor that protected the horse and rider also limited speed and movement—and thus the effectiveness of a knight in battle.

Cavalry reached the height of its effectiveness during the 1700's and 1800's, with the development of the galloping cavalry charge. This military tactic was used skillfully by European armies of the period, particularly the Prussian Army under Frederick the Great and the French Army under Napoleon I. Through speed and shock, the cavalry charge often broke enemy lines and forced opposing soldiers to flee. In such charges, the cavalry's favorite weapon was the *saber,* a curved sword specially designed for use on horseback.

In the United States, cavalry first became a major factor in warfare during the American Civil War (1861-1865). In this conflict, such Union cavalry leaders as Philip H. Sheridan and George A. Custer clashed with Confederate cavalry led by such officers as Jeb Stuart and Nathan B. Forrest. During the second half of the 1800's, the U.S. cavalry was used extensively in battling Indians on the western frontier. Custer's famous "last stand" at the Battle of the Little Bighorn in Montana Territory in 1876 is probably the best known of the hundreds of battles fought between the U.S. cavalry and Indians.

The widespread use of cannons, machine guns, and similar weapons during World War I (1914-1918) made attacks by mounted troops useless and costly. In 1950, President Harry S. Truman signed a bill that officially abolished the horse cavalry of the U.S. Army. Today, armored and mechanized units often perform military tactics formerly accomplished on horseback. Such units are sometimes called *cavalry.* Robert M. Utley

Cavazos, *kuh VAH sohs,* **Lauro Fred** (1927-), served as United States secretary of education from 1988 to 1990. He was appointed by President Ronald Reagan and remained in office under President George H. W. Bush, until Dec. 15, 1990. Cavazos became the first Hispanic American to hold a U.S. Cabinet post. Before his appointment, he was president of Texas Tech University.

Cavazos was born on Jan. 4, 1927, near Kingsville, Texas. He received a B.A. degree in 1949 and an M.A. degree in 1951 from Texas Tech. In 1954, Cavazos earned a Ph.D. degree in physiology from Iowa State University. From 1954 to 1964, Cavazos taught anatomy at the Medical College of Virginia. He taught at the Tufts University School of Medicine from 1964 to 1980 and served as its

On the Southern Plains (1907), an oil painting on canvas by Frederic Remington; the Metropolitan Museum of Art, New York City, gift of several gentlemen

The cavalry charge was an important military tactic that relied on speed and shock to defeat enemy forces. During the second half of the 1800's, the U.S. cavalry was often used in battling Indians on the western frontier, *shown here.*

dean from 1975 to 1980. Cavazos became president of Texas Tech in 1980. He has written numerous books on the medical sciences as well as several on medical education. Lee Thornton

Cave, also called *cavern,* is a naturally hollow area in the earth that is large enough for a person to enter. Some caves consist of a single chamber only a few yards or meters deep. Other caves are vast networks of passages and chambers. The longest cave ever explored is the Mammoth-Flint Ridge cave system in Kentucky. This cave has about 340 miles (550 kilometers) of explored and mapped passageways, but geologists think that it extends even farther.

The interior of a cave is a dark, damp place where sunlight never enters. However, artificial light supplied by explorers may reveal a strange underground landscape filled with beautiful, oddly shaped mineral deposits called *speleothems.* Many caves also have underground lakes, rivers, and waterfalls.

Some of the most spectacular caves are popular tourist attractions. These caves have been equipped with pathways and electric lights. However, thousands of caves remain in their natural state, and many new caves and passages are discovered each year.

The scientific study of caves is called *speleology.* Scientists who study caves and the organisms that live in them are known as *speleologists.* Many people enjoy *caving,* the hobby of exploring and mapping caves.

How caves are formed. Most caves are formed in limestone or in a related rock, such as marble or dolomite. Such caves, called *solution caves,* form as underground water slowly dissolves the rock. This process takes thousands of years. It begins when surface water trickles down through tiny cracks in the rock to a zone that is saturated with water. The topmost level of this saturated zone is called the *water table.* Water flowing above and below the water table dissolves some of the rock, forming passages, chambers, and pits.

Limestone and similar rock are only slightly soluble in water. But the water that trickles down from the surface contains carbon dioxide, which has been absorbed from the air and soil above the rock. The carbon dioxide forms a mild acid in the water, and this acid helps dissolve the rock.

Eventually, the water table may drop below the level of the cave. Or, the cave may be raised above the water table by a gradual uplifting of the ground. Most of the water then drains out, and air fills the cave. A surface stream may enter the cave and flow through it. The stream continues to dissolve the rock, enlarging the cave. Connections from the cave to the surface may develop in several ways. For example, the rock above part of the cave may collapse, forming a vertical entrance called a *sinkhole.* A horizontal entrance may develop on a hillside or a valley slope, especially at a point where a spring or stream flows from the cave.

Other types of caves include *lava tubes* and *sea caves.* Lava tubes form from molten lava. As lava flows down a slope, its outer surface cools and hardens, but the lava beneath remains molten. The molten lava continues to flow and eventually drains out, forming a cave. Lava caves lie near the surface of the earth and commonly have many openings in their thin roof. *Sea caves* form along rocky shores as the surf wears away weak areas of the rock. Inland, flowing water can carry rock away from weak areas of rock such as granite, forming caves.

Michael Nichols, Magnum

A cave may consist of an enormous chamber filled with oddly shaped rock formations. The Vesuvius Room, *shown,* is one of many such chambers in Lechuguilla Cave in New Mexico.

Speleothems. After most of the water has drained from a cave, water may continue to seep in through cracks in the rock. This water often contains dissolved minerals. As it enters the cave, some of the minerals crystallize and are deposited as speleothems. Although speleothems are commonly white, they may be of many colors, depending on the minerals that form them.

The best-known kinds of speleothems are *stalactites* and *stalagmites.* Stalactites are iciclelike formations that hang from the ceiling of a cave. Stalagmites are pillars that rise from the floor. A stalactite and a stalagmite may join and form a *column.* See **Stalactite; Stalagmite.**

Many other kinds of speleothems also form in caves. *Drapery* consists of thin sheets of rock that hang from the ceiling. *Flowstone* develops where a thin film of water flows over the walls and floor of a cave, depositing sheets of minerals. *Gypsum flowers* are delicate spi-

A sectional view of a solution cave

A solution cave, such as the one shown below, is formed in limestone when water dissolves sections of the rock. Many of the cave's features develop from minerals deposited by the water.

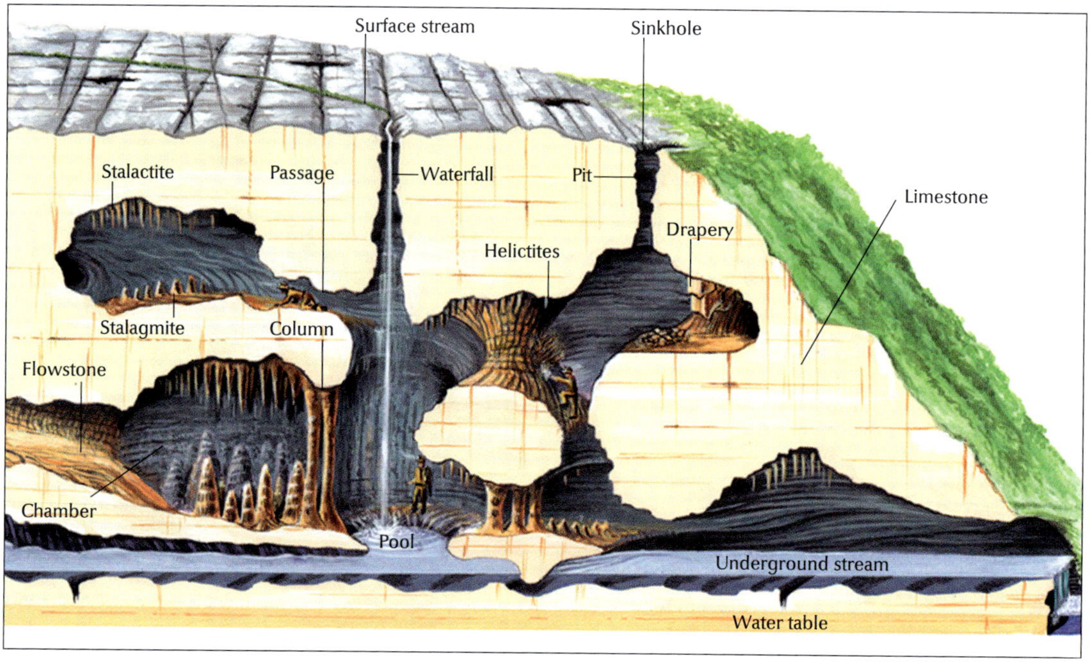

WORLD BOOK diagram by Bruce Kerr

ral crystals that sprout from porous rock. *Helictites* are strangely twisted cylinders that grow from the walls, ceiling, of floor of a cave, or from other formations.

Life in caves. Wall paintings, stone tools, and skeletal remains found in caves show that people lived there thousands of years ago. Today, many kinds of animals, including a small number of human beings, use caves as permanent shelters. See **Cave dwellers.**

Animals that live in caves include birds, crickets, lizards, raccoons, rats, salamanders, and spiders. Large numbers of bats roost in caves during the day and fly out at night to hunt for insects. The *guano* (manure) of bats provides food for the countless beetles, millipedes, flatworms, and other creatures that live in caves.

Interesting caves of the world

Cave or cave area	Location	Outstanding features
Blue Grotto	Isle of Capri, Italy	Sea cave that fills with sapphire-blue light when the sun shines through its waters.
Carlsbad Caverns	Southeastern New Mexico	Contains some of the world's largest and most spectacular stalactites and stalagmites. Includes Lechuguilla Cave, one of the most ornamental caves in the United States.
Lascaux Cave	Southwestern France	Has prehistoric wall paintings believed to be tens of thousands of years old. Closed to the public.
Lava Beds National Monument	Northern California	Includes more than 300 lava caves, as well as other volcanic formations.
Lubang Nasib Bagus	Sarawak, Malaysia	Contains the world's largest cave chamber, Sarawak Chamber, which is about 2,300 feet (700 meters) long, 1,480 feet (450 meters) wide at its widest point, and nowhere less than 230 feet (70 meters) high.
Luray Caverns	Northern Virginia	Contains a large number of exceptionally beautiful and colorful speleothems.
Mammoth-Flint Ridge Cave System	Central Kentucky	Longest cave system ever explored, with about 340 miles (550 kilometers) of interconnected passages and chambers. Has underground lakes and rivers.
Réseau Jean Bernard	Southeastern France	One of the world's deepest caves, measuring about 1 mile (1.6 kilometers) in depth.
Waitomo Cave	North Island, New Zealand	Thousands of tiny glowworms cling to the cave ceiling, resembling stars in the night sky.

K. R. Downey

A lava tube is a cave that has formed from molten lava. As the lava flowed down a slope, its outer surface cooled and hardened. When the molten lava inside eventually drained out, it left a tube, such as Lava River Cave, *shown here,* in Oregon.

Various species of animals known as *troglobites* live in the dark innermost part of most caves, where there is no light, wind, or change in temperature and humidity. Such animals include certain beetles, fish, salamanders, and spiders. Most troglobites are blind and have a thin, colorless skin or shell. They rely on highly developed senses of smell and touch to make up for their lack of sight.

Green plants, such as ferns and mosses, may grow in the outer parts of caves, which receive some sunlight. Only fungi and other organisms that do not require light can live in the dark inner areas.

Caving, also called *spelunking,* is an exciting but somewhat risky hobby. Individuals who wish to explore caves should always do so in groups headed by experienced leaders.

Cavers use some of the techniques and equipment of mountain climbing. For example, they use sturdy ropes to climb up and down steep underground cliffs. In addition, cavers wear hardhats and rugged, heavy clothing for protection against jagged rocks and low temperatures. Cavers should always carry at least three sources of light—a headlamp attached to the hardhat plus two flashlights.

Experienced cavers want a cave to be in the same condition after they explore it as it was before they entered it. Therefore, they neither damage nor remove anything they may find in the cave. Speleothems are fragile and, if broken, cannot be restored. In addition, many cave animals are extremely rare and can be easily harmed. Louise D. Hose

Related articles in *World Book* include:

Alabama (picture)
Carlsbad Caverns National Park
Jewel Cave National Monument
Luray Caverns
Mammoth Cave National Park
Prehistoric people
Sinkhole
Wind Cave National Park

Additional resources

Cooper, Margaret. *Exploring the Ice Age.* Atheneum, 2001. Younger readers.

Gamble, Clive. *The Paleolithic Societies of Europe.* Cambridge, 1999.

Cave dwellers are people who live in caves or in the shelter provided by overhanging rocks at the bottom of cliffs. Prehistoric people are often incorrectly called "cave men," though some did live in caves.

One of the earliest known caves used by people in Europe is located in southern France. About 500,000 years ago, people used stone tools in the cave to kill animals for meat. Another famous cave site is located near Beijing (also spelled Peking), China. Prehistoric people occupied the cave between 500,000 and 250,000 years ago.

By about 100,000 years ago, some Neandertal people lived in caves in Europe and western Asia. Some Cro-Magnon people occupied caves in those regions from about 40,000 years ago until about 10,000 years ago. The Neandertals and Cro-Magnons built tents and other shelters in the cave entrances. They used the dark interiors for ceremonial purposes. The Cro-Magnons painted pictures of animals on the cave walls and probably thought the paintings had magic qualities.

However, relatively few people have ever been cave dwellers. Caves are uncommon in most parts of the world. In addition, people have found most caves too cold, damp, or dark to live in. Such animals as cave bears, cave hyenas, and cave lions also discouraged cave dwelling.

In the New World, some Anasazi Indians lived in cave villages in what is now the Southwestern United States from about A.D. 1000 to 1300 (see **Anasazi**). Today, a few cave dwellers live in parts of Africa, Asia, Europe, and the Near East. In Spain, about 3,000 Roma (sometimes called Gypsies) make their homes in caves near Granada. Their dwellings range from single rooms to caves of about 200 rooms. These Roma also have churches, schools, and stores in caves. Karl W. Butzer

See also **Prehistoric people** (picture: Cave paintings).

Additional resources

Cooper, Margaret. *Exploring the Ice Age.* Atheneum, 2001. Younger readers.

Lewis-Williams, J. David. *The Mind in the Cave.* Thames & Hudson, 2002.

Cave man. See Cave dwellers.

Caveat emptor, *KAH vee aht* or *KAY vee at EHMP tawr,* is a Latin term meaning *let the buyer beware.* Technically, unless a guarantee accompanies goods or services, the buyer assumes any risks of purchase. Since the 1960's, however, a movement to protect consumers has strengthened the buyer's position. Many governments, businesses, and consumer advocates now take a position of *caveat venditor*—that is, "let the seller beware." Jay Diamond

Cavefish is the name of several kinds of small fish that live in waters in and near caves in the eastern United States. Cavefish are also called *blindfish.* These fish spend their entire lives in caves. They have no eyes and no body pigment. They are pink because the blood shows through the flesh. A cavefish has rows of small projections on its body, including the head. These projections provide the fish with a keen sense of touch that helps the fish partially overcome its lack of sight. Cavefish grow no more than 5 inches (13 centimeters) in length.

One of the best-known kinds of cavefish is that found in Mammoth Cave in Kentucky. Scientists think that the ancestors of this fish once had eyes and that the eyes

WORLD BOOK illustration by John F. Eggert

A cavefish is pink because blood shows through its flesh. Cavefish live in waters of caves in the eastern United States.

gradually degenerated through the ages in the cave environment.

In addition to the kinds of sightless fish called *cavefish,* more than 20 other kinds of fish are known to be blind. They live in caves and the deep sea throughout the world. Robert D. Hoyt

Scientific classification. The cavefish of Mammoth Cave and related fish of the United States belong to the cavefish family, Amblyopsidae.

Cavelier, René-Robert. See **La Salle, Sieur de.**

Cavell, *KAV uhl,* **Edith Louisa** (1865-1915), was an English nurse and one of the martyrs of World War I (1914-1918). Cavell was in charge of a hospital in Brussels, Belgium, when German troops occupied the city in 1915. For several months she helped Allied soldiers, about 200 in all, to escape to the Dutch border. Arrested by the Germans, she was sentenced to death. Cavell's last words before a German firing squad shot her were: "Patriotism is not enough. I must have no hatred or bitterness towards anyone." Her body later was taken back to England, and a statue was erected to her memory in London. Cavell was born on Dec. 4, 1865, in Norfolk. Mount Edith Cavell in Jasper National Park, Alberta, Canada, is named for her. Kenneth R. Manning

Cavendish, *KAV uhn dihsh,* **Henry** (1731-1810), an English physicist and chemist, discovered many fundamental laws of electricity. He also conducted important experiments in chemistry and heat. In 1766, Cavendish discovered the properties of hydrogen and identified it as an element, calling it *inflammable air.* Later he showed that water is a compound of hydrogen and oxygen. In 1798, using a torsion-balance type of apparatus, Cavendish measured the density of Earth (see **Torsion balance**). Much of his work in electricity remained unpublished until the late 1800's, when another physicist, James Clerk Maxwell, edited his papers (see **Maxwell, James Clerk**). Cavendish was born on Oct. 10, 1731, in Nice, France. He attended Cambridge University. Richard G. Olson

Caviar, *KAV ee ahr* or *KAH vee ahr,* is the salted eggs of sturgeons, a group of large fish. Caviar is considered a delicacy in many parts of the world. Soon after the eggs are harvested, they are salted, drained, and packaged for sale. Caviar spoils easily and requires refrigeration. It may be pasteurized and vacuum-packed to prevent spoilage during shipping. Iran and Russia produce most of the world's caviar.

Caviar ranges in color from gray to black. The most valuable caviar comes from a kind of sturgeon called *beluga.* Other fine caviar comes from the *osetra* and *sevruga* sturgeons. Pressed caviar is a flavorful and less expensive product made from broken or crushed sturgeon eggs. The eggs of lumpfish, salmon, and whitefish are sometimes marketed as caviar. They cost much less than sturgeon eggs. George J. Flick, Jr.

Cavour, *kah VOOR,* **Count di** (1810-1861), played a decisive role in the unification of Italy. He was born on Aug. 10, 1810, in Turin. He served as prime minister of the Kingdom of Sardinia from 1852 to 1859 and from 1860 to 1861. The kingdom included the island of Sardinia and the Piedmont region of what is now Italy.

In 1859, under Cavour's leadership, Sardinia and France fought a war against Austria. The war ended with Sardinia's annexation of the Austrian province of Lombardy. Inspired by Austria's defeat, patriots in central and southern Italy overthrew their rulers. With Cavour's support, southern Italy and most of central Italy united with Sardinia in 1860. This expanded kingdom became the Kingdom of Italy in 1861. Cavour's given and family name was Camillo Benso. Susan A. Ashley

See also **Italy** (Italy united); **Sardinia, Kingdom of.**

Cavy, *KAY vee,* is the general name for several related South American rodents. Guinea pigs are the best-known cavies. Other cavies include maras, also called Patagonian hares, and mocos. Most cavies have thick bodies, short legs, and short, bristly hair. But maras have long, thin legs. A few kinds of *domesticated* (tamed) guinea pigs have long hair. All cavies are plant eaters.

See also **Guinea pig; Rodent.** Clyde Jones

Scientific classification. Cavies make up the cavy family, Caviidae, of the order Rodentia.

Cawnpore. See **Kanpur.**

Caxton, William (1422?-1492), was the first person to print a book in the English language and to print a book in England. The first book in the language was *The Recuyell of the Historyes of Troy,* Caxton's translation of a popular French adventure tale. Caxton printed this book in Bruges, in what is now Belgium, in about 1475. The first book printed in England was *The Dictes or Sayings of the Philosophers,* produced in 1477. Other important works from his press in England include the first editions of *The Canterbury Tales* by the English poet Geoffrey Chaucer.

Caxton also translated many other French works, as well as Latin and Dutch literature. His translations helped establish the literary form of the English language as Middle English slowly developed into Modern English.

Caxton was born in Kent, England. From 1441 to 1471, he worked as a merchant in Bruges. In 1471, he went to Cologne, in what is now Germany, to learn printing. In 1476, he set up a press in London. Peter M. VanWingen

See also **Advertising** (The impact of printing); **Encyclopedia; English literature** (The beginning of Modern English).

Cayenne, *ky EHN* or *kay EHN* (pop. 38,000), is the capital and largest city of French Guiana, a French possession in South America. The city lies on the coast along the Atlantic Ocean (see **French Guiana** [map]).

Cayenne is a shipping center. Its industries include the production of diamonds, gold, rice, sugar cane, and timber. It has an international airport and two modern hotels. The city also has many old colonial buildings that are used as museums and government offices.

Cayenne was founded by the French in 1643, but it was not permanently settled until 1664. France gained control of what is now French Guiana in 1667. In 1854, France turned French Guiana into a colony for prisoners. The prisons were closed in 1945. Gary Brana-Shute

Cayenne pepper, *ky EHN* or *kay EHN,* is a hot-tasting red powder made from fruits or pods of a kind of capsicum plant. It is used as a food flavoring. It is made by powdering the dried fruits or by grinding and baking them into cakes. The cakes are then ground and sifted. See also **Pepper.** William G. D'Arcy

Scientific classification. Cayenne pepper plants belong to the nightshade family, Solanaceae. Their scientific names are *Capsicum baccatum* and *C. frutescens.*

Cayley, *KAY lee,* **Sir George** (1773-1857), is often called the father of modern aeronautics. He contributed many ideas to the early history of aviation. Cayley wrote about helicopters, parachutes, and streamlining. He conceived the biplane and built a glider that flew 900 feet (270 meters). But Cayley believed that the first attempts at powered flight would be successful only with lighter-than-air craft. He suggested the use of a long, streamlined balloon—such as those used today in blimps—to support such a craft. Cayley was born on Dec. 27, 1773, near Scarborough, England. See also **Airplane** (First human flights); **Glider** (Early days). Roger E. Bilstein

Cayman Islands, *KAY muhn,* an overseas territory of the United Kingdom, lies about 200 miles (320 kilometers) northwest of Jamaica in the Caribbean Sea. The three islands that form the group—Grand Cayman, Little Cayman, and Cayman Brac—cover about 100 square miles (259 square kilometers) and have about 44,000 people. The capital and largest city, George Town, lies on Grand Cayman, the largest island. Taxes are extremely low in the Cayman Islands. As a result, many companies from other lands conduct business there. These businesses and tourism contribute greatly to the economy. Agricultural production is low in the Caymans, and most food must be imported. Gary Brana-Shute

Cayuga Indians, *kay YOO guh* or *ky YOO guh,* are a tribe of Iroquois Indians who once occupied an area near Cayuga Lake in central New York. Today, most of the tribe's approximately 2,000 members live in Canada on the Six Nations Indian Reserve near Brantford, Ontario. Others live in New York and Oklahoma.

The Cayuga, along with the Mohawk, Oneida, Onondaga, and Seneca, formed a federation of tribes known as the *Iroquois League* or the *Five Nations.* The Iroquois established the league sometime between about 1400 and about 1600. About 1722, the Tuscarora joined the league, which then became known as the *Six Nations.*

Like other Iroquois, the Cayuga once lived in large rectangular dwellings called *longhouses.* In most cases, from 6 to 10 related families lived in each house. Villages included from 30 to 150 such dwellings.

Cayuga men hunted deer, bear, and small animals. They also fished in the region's many lakes and rivers. The women grew corn, beans, and squash and collected roots, berries, and nuts. In the spring, the Cayuga tapped trees for syrup, which they used to make sugar.

The Iroquois League broke up during the American Revolutionary War (1775-1783) because of a dispute over which side to support. The Cayuga and three other tribes sided with the British. After the Americans won the war, the Cayuga sold their reservation to New York, and most of them moved to Canada. In the late 1970's, the Cayuga began a legal battle to recover their former land. They claimed the sale took place without approval of the federal government, making it illegal under a 1790 law. Robert E. Powless

See also **Iroquois Indians.**

CCC. See **Civilian Conservation Corps.**

CCC. See **Commodity Credit Corporation.**

CCD. See **Charge-coupled device.**

CD, in banking. See **Certificate of deposit.**

CD, in recording. See **Compact disc.**

Ceauşescu, *chow SHEHS koo,* **Nicolae,** *NEE kaw LY* (1918-1989), ruled Romania from 1965 to 1989 as head of the country's Communist Party. In 1968, he also became head of state. Ceauşescu worked to make Romania independent from the Soviet Union, which was Europe's top Communist power. This policy was supported by the United States. But Ceauşescu was a dictator and placed strict controls on the lives of the people. He also established economic programs that caused severe shortages of consumer goods. Ceauşescu illegally used his power to gain great wealth and put many of his relatives in high government positions. By the late 1980's, the United States had withdrawn its support of Ceauşescu.

In 1989, Ceauşescu refused to follow democratic reforms that had swept through other European Communist countries. Tens of thousands of Romanians protested his rule. Thousands were killed when his security forces tried to crush the demonstrations. After fierce fighting, an antigovernment group overthrew Ceauşescu. Ceauşescu and his wife, Elena, were executed on Dec. 25, 1989, after the new government found them guilty of murder and embezzlement.

Ceauşescu was born on Jan. 26, 1918, in Scorniceşti, near Piteşti. He served in the Union of Communist Youth from 1933 to 1936 and then joined the Communist Party. In 1948, he was elected to the party's Central Committee. He served as a committee secretary from 1954 to 1965. Stuart D. Goldman

Cebu City, *seh BOO* or *say BOO* (pop. 718,821), is one of the largest cities in the Philippines. It is on the east coast of Cebu Island. For location, see **Philippines** (map). Cebu City is an important commercial center. The Spaniards established their first permanent settlement in the Philippines at Cebu City in 1565. David J. Steinberg

Cecil, Robert Arthur Talbot Gascoyne-. See **Salisbury, Marquess of.**

Cecil, William. See **Burghley, Lord.**

Cecilia, *see SIHL ih uh* or *sih SEEL yuh,* **Saint,** is a saint and martyr of the Roman Catholic Church. She is the patroness of music and, according to tradition, invented the organ. Many music societies have been named in her honor. Because she was blind, she is also the patron saint of the blind. According to her legend, which dates from the late A.D. 400's, she was cruelly put to death about 230. Her tomb is in the Church of Saint Cecilia in Rome. Her feast day is November 22.

Many artists have portrayed Saint Cecilia in paintings. She appears in "The Second Nun's Tale" in Geoffrey Chaucer's *The Canterbury Tales.* She also appears in the poems "Alexander's Feast" and "Song for St. Cecilia's

Day" by John Dryden and "Ode for Music on St. Cecilia's Day" by Alexander Pope. Stanley K. Stowers

Cedar is any of a variety of evergreen trees that grow in many parts of the world. There are two major groups of cedars, the *scale-leaved cedars* of the cypress family and the *needle-leaved cedars* of the pine family.

Scale-leaved cedars have small, scalelike leaves that grow flattened against the branches. They also have small cones, most less than ½ inch (1.3 centimeters) long.

Several species of scale-leaved cedars grow in North America. Most of these trees have shallow roots and thrive in moist soil. Four kinds grow in the mountains of western North America from Alaska to northern California. They are the *Alaska-cedar,* the *incense-cedar,* the *Port-Orford-cedar,* and the *western redcedar.* Three other cedars are found in eastern North America. The *northern white-cedar* grows in eastern Canada and the northeastern United States. The *Atlantic white-cedar* is found in the Atlantic and Gulf coastal plains. The *eastern redcedar* grows in the central and eastern United States. The western redcedar and northern white-cedar are sometimes called *arborvitae.* The eastern redcedar belongs to the same group of trees as the juniper.

The wood of North American cedars resists rotting better than many other woods, and it can be easily sawed, planed, and carved. Many clothing chests and closets are lined with cedar because its pleasant odor seems to keep moths away. The wood is used to make boats, pencils, shingles, and telephone poles.

Needle-leaved cedars have tufts of needlelike leaves that measure from ½ to 1 ½ inches (1.3 to 4 centimeters) long. Their cones are 3 to 5 inches (8 to 13 centimeters) long and grow straight up on the branches. There are four species—the *Atlas cedar* of the Atlas Mountains in northern Africa; the *Cyprus cedar* of the island of Cyprus; the *cedar of Lebanon* of the Middle East and Asia Minor; and the *deodar cedar* of the Himalaya.

Some needle-leaved cedars are planted as ornamentals in warm regions of the United States. The cedar of Lebanon, which is the best-known needle-leaved cedar, has attractive, fragrant, durable wood. The people of early Middle East civilizations used it for building palaces, ships, temples, and tombs. Donald B. Zobel

Scientific classification. North American cedars belong to the cypress family, Cupressaceae. The scientific name for the western redcedar is *Thuja plicata,* and the northern white-cedar is *T. occidentalis.* The Port-Orford-cedar is *Chamaecyparis lawsoniana;* the Alaska-cedar, *C. nootkatensis;* the Atlantic white-cedar, *C. thyoides.* The incense-cedar is *Libocedrus decurrens.* Needle-leaved cedars make up the genus *Cedrus* in the pine family, Pinaceae. The cedar of Lebanon is *C. libani.*

See also **Juniper; Pine.**

The main kinds of cedars, scale-leaved and needle-leaved cedars, differ in structure. Scale-leaved species include the Port-Orford-cedar, *above.* The cedar of Lebanon, *below,* is a needle-leaved cedar.

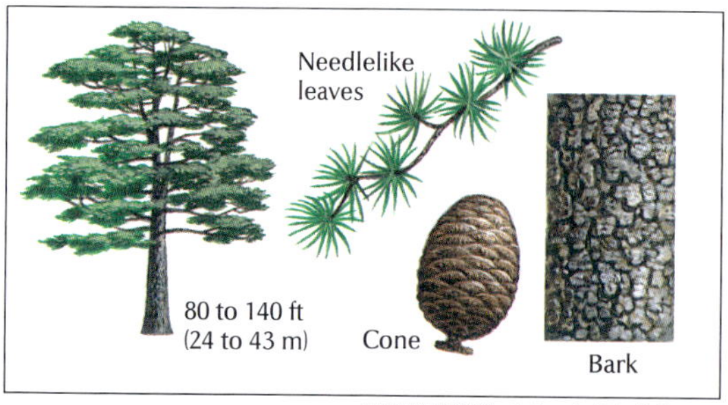

WORLD BOOK illustrations by John D. Dawson

Cedar Rapids (pop. 120,758; met. area pop. 237,230) is the second largest city in Iowa. Only Des Moines is larger. Cedar Rapids is a manufacturing and distributing city. It lies on the Cedar River in Linn County, at the center of a large farming area in east-central Iowa (see **Iowa** [political map]). Oatmeal mills, established in the 1870's, were the start of the city's thriving cereal-processing industry. Other foods processed include corn, meat, and soybeans. Industries in the city produce machinery, flight control equipment, and computer systems. The city is also a center of *telemarketing* (selling by phone).

Cultural attractions in the city include a symphony orchestra, a community theater, and an art museum. Cedar Rapids is the home of Coe College and Mount Mercy College. The Iowa Masonic Library has a large collection of books on Freemasonry.

Cedar Rapids was first settled as Rapids City in 1841 and was incorporated under the present name in 1849. The rapids in the Cedar River inspired both names. The city has a commission form of government, and it is the seat of Linn County. Mark E. Bowden

Celandine, *SEHL uhn dyn,* is an herb commonly used as an ornamental plant in gardens. The plant grows from 12 to 30 inches (30 to 76 centimeters) high. It has grayish-green leaves and yellow flowers. Celandine thrives in rich, damp soil. It occurs throughout the world, though it is native to Europe and Asia.

George Yatskievych

Scientific classification. Celandine is in the poppy family, Papaveraceae. It is *Chelidonium majus.*

WORLD BOOK illustration by James Teason

Celandine leaves and buds

Celebes. See **Indonesia** (The islands).

Celebration. See **Feasts and festivals; Holiday**; and articles for each month of the year.

Celery is a popular vegetable related to carrots and parsley. Celery is eaten raw in salads or with dips. It also is used in soups and as a garnish for other foods.

The celery plant consists of several long stalks with feathery leaves at their tops. The stalks of the celery plant grow from a short base that is called the *mainstem* and measure up to 14 inches (36 centimeters) long. The stalk is the part of the plant that is eaten. The leaves grow from the tops of the stalks and form a circular cluster. Most varieties of celery have a light-green color.

Celery requires a long growing season and moist, fertile soil. It grows best in cool weather. Growers often plant celery seeds in greenhouses or outdoor beds. After the seedlings reach 5 to 6 inches (13 to 15 centimeters) high, they are transplanted to the field. The plant takes two years to complete its life cycle. The stalks grow and are harvested in the first year. The next year, the mainstem forms into a bushy plant 3 to 4 feet (0.9 to 1.2 meters) tall. The seeds of the celery plant form there.

Celery probably originated in areas near the Mediterranean Sea. The plant was first cultivated in 1623 in France. George R. Hughes

WORLD BOOK illustration by Jill Coombs

The celery plant, *left,* consists of stalks that grow directly from the center of the root, *right.* Celery has feathery leaves, *bottom center,* and tiny, greenish-white flowers, *top center.*

Scientific classification. Celery belongs to the family Apiaceae or Umbelliferae. It is *Apium graveolens.*

Celesta, *suh LEHS tuh,* is a pianolike musical instrument that is played by means of a keyboard. Small hammers striking against steel plates instead of strings produce the tone. The plates rest above hollow boxes that *resonate* (increase) the sound.

The celesta makes a clear, sweet sound, and its name comes from a French word meaning *heavenly.* The celesta is used in orchestras but rarely as a solo instrument. Auguste Mustel, a Frenchman, invented the celesta in 1886. F. E. Kirby

Claire Rydell

Celesta

Celiac disease is a disorder characterized by an intolerance to certain proteins, commonly referred to as *gluten,* found in grains such as wheat, barley, and rye. Celiac disease is an *autoimmune* disorder in which the body's immune system attacks and destroys its own tissues. When people with celiac disease eat foods containing gluten, their immune system reacts and causes inflammation in the small intestine. The condition is also referred to as *gluten sensitive enteropathy.*

Inflammation of the small intestine can interfere with digestion and cause *malabsorption* (faulty absorption of nourishing substances of food). Symptoms include diarrhea, weight loss, and malnutrition. Anemia, osteoporosis, and vitamin deficiencies can result from malabsorption of iron, calcium, and other nutrients.

People with celiac disease must avoid foods containing gluten and related proteins for their entire life. A gluten-free diet usually leads to a complete recovery. Eating even small amounts of gluten can cause serious complications. Celiac disease has been associated with intestinal *lymphoma,* a rare type of cancer.

Most patients possess genes that predispose them to celiac disease and other autoimmune diseases. About 10 percent of patients also have a related skin condition called *dermatitis herpetiformis,* which causes an itchy rash. David A. Nelsen, Jr.

See also **Gluten.**

Celibacy, *SEHL uh buh see,* is the state of being unmarried. In particular, the term refers to the custom of refraining from sexual relations, temporarily or permanently, for religious or moral reasons.

Some religions teach that priests must avoid sexual relations for a time to purify themselves before conducting religious ceremonies. Some Christian leaders have taught that celibacy frees individuals from family distractions so they can concentrate on religious duties. Christian and Buddhist monks and nuns practice celibacy as a religious ideal. In addition, all Roman Catholic priests must remain celibate. In Eastern churches, married men can become priests, but bishops must practice celibacy. However, most major religions do not view permanent celibacy as a moral ideal.

In the early Christian church, clergy could marry. By the 400's, however, several church councils and popes had begun to require them to practice celibacy. This requirement was not generally met for several hundred years. Albert J. Raboteau

Céline, *say LEEN,* **Louis-Ferdinand** (1894-1961), was the pen name of Henri-Louis Destouches (pronounced *day TOOSH),* a French novelist. He became best known for two unconventional novels, *Journey to the End of the Night* (1932) and *Death on the Installment Plan* (1936). Ferdinand Bardamu, the autobiographical hero of these pessimistic, rambling works, is a wandering outsider in search of a better life. In both novels, Céline protested against human suffering, especially sickness and death. His emotional, often crude style is filled with slang and obscene expressions. This style influenced many French and American writers.

Céline was born on May 27, 1894, in Courbevoie. In the 1930's, he became anti-Semitic and wrote racist political essays. In 1944, during World War II, he went into exile in Germany and Denmark. Céline returned to France in 1951. His novels *Fable for Another Time* (1952), *Castle to Castle* (1957), and *North* (1960) are bitter, violent accounts of his experiences during the war.

Catharine Savage Brosman

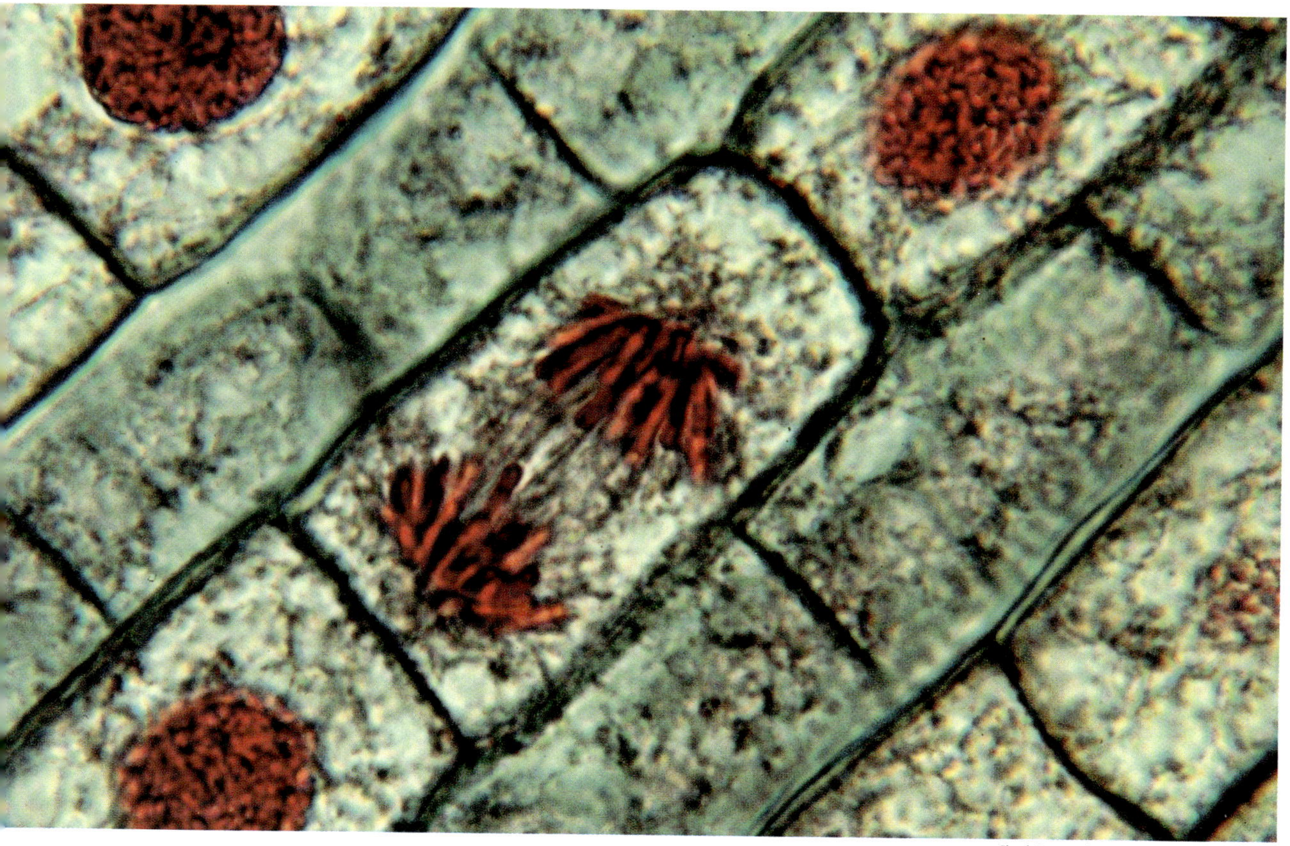

Chuck Brown, Photo Researchers

Cells, the building blocks of all living things, stand out clearly in this photograph of a plant root tip. The cells have been stained and magnified about 400 times. The reddish stains show *chromosomes,* structures that become apparent just before a cell divides and becomes two cells.

Cell

Cell is the basic unit of all life. All living things are made up of cells. Some organisms consist of only one cell. Plants and animals are made up of many cells. The human body has more than 10 trillion (10,000,000,000,000) cells.

Most cells are so small they can be seen only with a microscope. It would take about 40,000 of your red blood cells to fill this letter *O.* It takes millions of cells to make up the skin on the palm of your hand.

Some one-celled organisms lead independent lives. Others live in loosely organized groups. The cells in plants and animals are specialists with particular jobs to do. As you read these words, for example, nerve cells in your eyes are carrying messages of what you are reading to your brain cells. Muscle cells attached to your eyeballs are moving your eyes across the page. Nerve cells, muscle cells, and other specialized cells group together to form *tissues,* such as nerve tissue or muscle tissue. Different kinds of tissues form *organs,* such as the eyes, heart, and lungs. All the specialized cells together form you—or some other complete organism.

All cells have some things in common, whether they are specialized cells or one-celled organisms. A cell is alive—as alive as you are. It "breathes," takes in food, and gets rid of wastes. It also grows and *reproduces* (creates its own kind). And, in time, it dies.

A thin covering called a *membrane* encloses every cell. The complete contents of a cell are called the *protoplasm.* Most cells have a structure called the *nucleus.* The nucleus contains the cell's *genetic program,* the master plan that controls almost everything the cell does. The part of the protoplasm outside the nucleus is called the *cytoplasm.*

Just as all living things are made up of cells, every new cell is produced from an existing cell. Cells reproduce by dividing, so that there are two cells where there once was only one cell. When a cell divides, each of the two newly produced cells gets a copy of the genetic program.

The genetic program is "written" in a chemical sub-

The contributors of this article are Irwin Rubenstein, Professor of Plant Biology at the University of Minnesota, Twin Cities Campus; and Susan M. Wick, Professor of Plant Biology at the University of Minnesota, Twin Cities Campus.

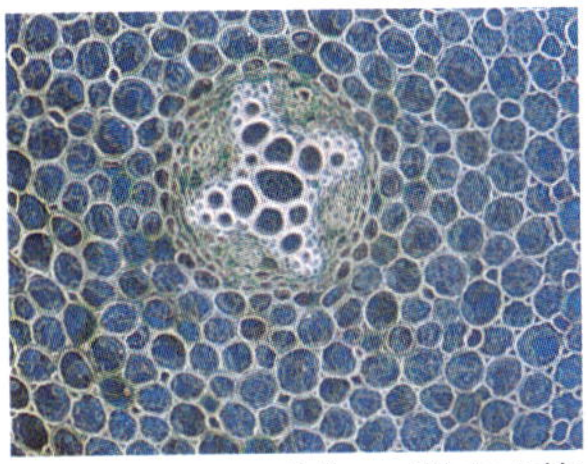

Dr. Roman Vishniac, Publix

Buttercup root cells

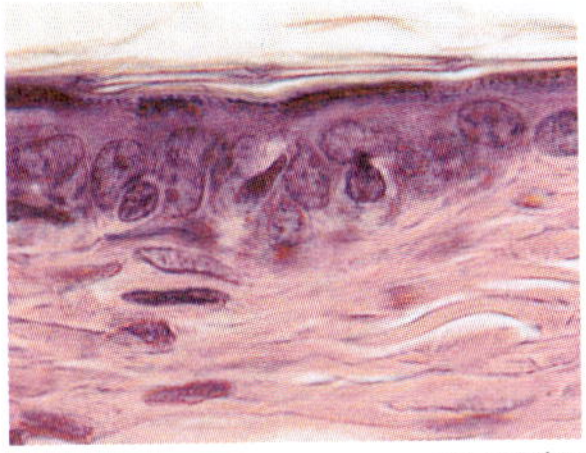

Vories Fisher

Rat skin cells

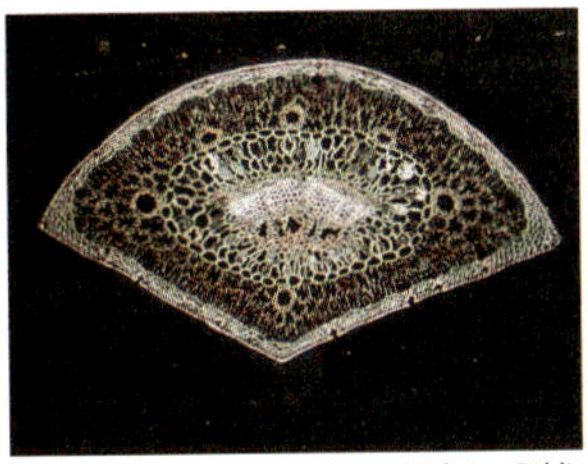

Dr. Roman Vishniac, Publix

Pine needle cells

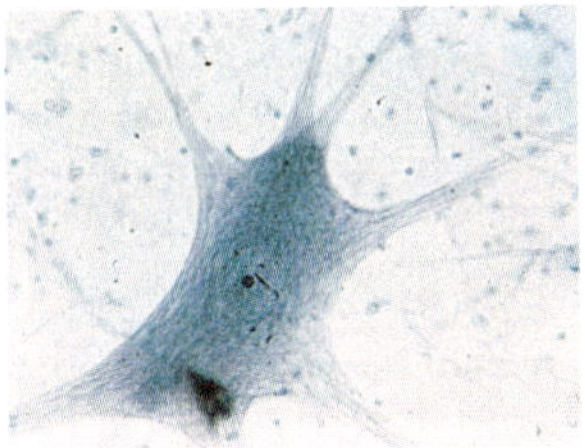

General Biological Supply

WORLD BOOK illustrations by Paul D. Turnbaugh

Ox nerve cell

stance called *DNA* (deoxyribonucleic acid). All DNA looks much alike and is made up of the same building blocks. But the genetic program carried in DNA makes every living thing different from all others. This program makes a dog different from a fish, a zebra different from a rose, and a willow different from a wasp. It makes you different from other people.

Scientists understand much about a cell's genetic program and the chemical code carried by its DNA. They have used this understanding to alter a cell's genetic program so that an organism develops new characteristics. The new traits of such genetically engineered organisms can have commercially important applications. For example, researchers have developed genetically engineered varieties of tomatoes that stay fresh longer than normal varieties. Scientists hope to eventually control cancer and other diseases by correcting mistakes in a cell's genetic program.

This article describes the cell and how it works. For further information, see also the *World Book* articles on **Heredity** and **Life.**

Some terms used in the study of cells

Amino acids are the building blocks of proteins.

ATP (adenosine triphosphate) is a compound produced in a cell that supplies energy for the cell's activities.

Chromosomes are threadlike structures inside each cell. They are made up of *chromatin,* a substance that contains protein and DNA, the cell's hereditary material.

Cytoplasm is all the material inside the cell membrane except the nucleus.

Cytoskeleton is a network of proteins that gives a cell its shape and moves structures in the cell cytoplasm. In some cells, the cytoskeleton helps the whole cell to move.

DNA (deoxyribonucleic acid) is the chemical substance within the chromosomes that carries the cell's hereditary material and genetic program.

Endoplasmic reticulum is a complex network of membranes in the cytoplasm.

Enzymes are molecules that speed up chemical reactions. Most enzymes are proteins.

Eukaryotic cells are cells that have their hereditary material (DNA) in a nucleus that is surrounded by a membrane.

Genes are units of heredity that determine particular characteristics, such as height and hair color. Each gene is a section of a DNA molecule and carries instructions for making all or part of a specific protein.

Meiosis is the process of division in the nucleus of some cells of the sex organs. It reduces the number of chromosomes in sex cells to half the number found in somatic cells.

Mitochondria are a cell's "power plants." They transform chemical energy from food into an energy form the cell can use.

Mitosis is the process of division in the nucleus of a cell in which two identical daughter nuclei are produced, each containing two sets of chromosomes.

Nucleus is the structure in a eukaryotic cell that contains the cell's hereditary material.

Organelles are structures inside the cell that have a specific function. They include the endoplasmic reticulum, mitochondria, nucleus, and ribosomes.

Prokaryotic cells are cells that have hereditary material (DNA) that is not contained in a nucleus.

Proteins are substances made up of amino acids. A cell's structures are built chiefly of proteins. Proteins called enzymes speed up chemical reactions in a cell.

Ribosomes are tiny bodies in a cell that are involved in protein production.

RNA (ribonucleic acid) is a chemical substance similar to DNA. It carries out DNA's instructions for making specific proteins.

Somatic cells are all the cells in a multicellular organism except the sex cells. Somatic cells contain two of each type of chromosome. Mature sex cells contain only one of each type of chromosome.

Looking at a cell

One of the main tools scientists use to study cells is the microscope. An *optical microscope* can magnify a cell up to 2,000 times. An *electron microscope* can magnify a cell by 1 million times. An ant magnified 200,000 times would be more than 2 $\frac{1}{2}$ miles (4 kilometers) long. But even with such tremendous magnification, the detailed structure of some cell parts still cannot be seen.

Scientists also use dyes to study cells. When various parts of a cell are stained with certain dyes, these parts stand out clearly under a microscope.

Another tool used to study cells is the *centrifuge.* This

instrument separates the various substances in a mixture by whirling the mixture at high speeds. Scientists first grind up the cells. Then they put the mixture containing the cellular parts in a tube. The tube is placed in a centrifuge and whirled rapidly to separate the cellular parts. The heaviest parts move to the bottom of the tube, and the lightest remain at the top. After the parts have been separated, scientists can study their chemical content and activity.

Shapes of cells. Cells may be shaped like boxes, coils, corkscrews, cubes, octopuses, rods, saucers, stars, or blobs of jelly. Many *unicellular* (one-celled) organisms look like tiny balls. They include some yeasts and certain algae. The ameba, another unicellular organism, has no particular shape at all. It is a flattened jellylike mass that changes its shape to move about. Bacteria are shaped like balls, rods, or coils. Diatoms are one-celled algae that occur in a wide range of shapes, including cubes, spheres, and pyramids.

Most cells of *multicellular* (many-celled) plants are shaped like cubes or many-sided boxes. The greatest variety in cell shapes occurs in human beings and other multicellular animals. Animal cells may be spherical or flat-sided, or they may have other shapes. Some muscle cells are long, thin, and pointed at each end. Some nerve cells, with their long branches, resemble trees.

A cell's shape is related to its needs or to the job it does. For example, the long, thin muscle cells can contract to do work. The long, many-branched nerve cells relay messages throughout the body.

Sizes of cells. Cells vary widely in size, just as they do in shape. Most cells are about 1/1,000 of an inch (0.0025 centimeter) in diameter. About 500 of these average-sized cells would fit within the period at the end of this sentence.

Bacterial cells are among the smallest of all cells. Certain kinds of bacterial cells are so small that a row of 50,000 of them would measure only 1 inch (2.5 centimeters) long. The largest cells are the yolks of birds' eggs. The largest cell of all is the yolk of an ostrich egg, which is about the size of a baseball.

The size of any organism depends on the total number of cells it has, not on the size of the cells. An elephant is a giant compared with a mouse because it has trillions more cells, not because its cells are larger.

Inside a living cell

Cells differ greatly in size, in shape, and in the special jobs they do. But all cells have certain features, and each cell can be thought of as a tiny chemical factory. It has a control center that tells it what to do and when. It has power plants for generating the energy it needs to function, and it has machinery for making its products or performing its services.

A thin covering called the *cell membrane* or *plasma membrane* encloses the cell and regulates substances that pass through it. Membranes consist of a double layer of fatty substance called *phospholipid* (see **Lipid**). Outside the membrane, many cells have a special covering that helps protect them or hold them to neighboring cells. In plant cells, this covering is called the *cell wall.*

Within the cell membrane, all cells except those of archaea and bacteria have two main parts: (1) the nucleus and (2) the cytoplasm. Cells with a nucleus are called *eukaryotic,* which means *having a true nucleus.* All multicellular animals and plants consist of eukaryotic cells, as do fungi and such unicellular organisms as amebas and diatoms. Archaea and bacteria cells lack a nucleus. They are called *prokaryotic,* which means *before the nucleus.*

Shapes of some types of cells

The shapes of cells vary greatly. A cell's shape is related to its needs or to the job it does. For example, a nerve cell has many branches that receive messages from other nerve cells.

WORLD BOOK illustrations by Charles Wellek

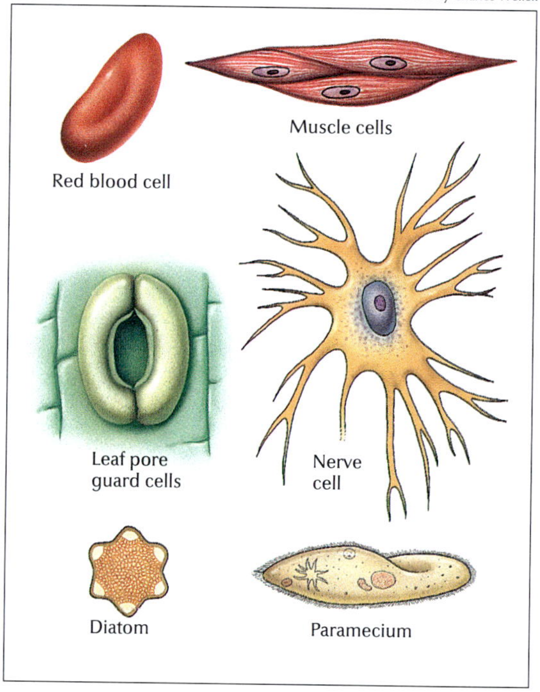

The nucleus is the control center that directs the activities of the cell. A *nuclear membrane* surrounds the nucleus and separates it from the cytoplasm. The nucleus contains two important types of structures, *chromosomes* and *nucleoli.*

Chromosomes are long, threadlike strands of a substance called *chromatin.* Chromatin consists of DNA and certain proteins. DNA makes up the *genes,* the basic units of heredity. Genes control the passing on of characteristics from parents to offspring. Each gene consists of part of a DNA molecule. The chemical structure of the DNA that makes up the genes determines that a dog will give birth to a dog instead of a fish or some other organism. This chemical structure determines your blood type, the color of your eyes, the texture of your hair, and thousands of other characteristics.

DNA works its wonders chiefly by directing the production of complicated proteins. The cell's structures are built mostly of proteins. In addition, certain proteins called *enzymes* speed up chemical reactions in the cell. Without enzymes, these reactions would occur very slowly, and the cell could not function normally (see **Enzyme**). Thus, the kinds of proteins a cell makes help determine the nature of the cell.

Nucleoli are round bodies that form in certain regions of specific chromosomes. Each nucleus may contain one or more nucleoli, though some cells have none. Nucleoli help in the formation of *ribosomes,* the cell's centers of protein production. Nucleoli are made up of proteins and *RNA* (ribonucleic acid). RNA is chemically similar to DNA and plays important roles in making proteins.

The cytoplasm is all the material enclosed by the cell membrane, except for the nucleus. Thus, in prokaryotes, which do not have a nucleus, the cytoplasm includes everything inside the cell membrane. The cytoplasm of all cells contains ribosomes. Proteins manufactured on ribosomes make it possible for the cell to grow, repair itself, and perform the thousands of chemical operations that are required during the cell's lifetime.

The cytoplasm of eukaryotic cells also contains many other small structures called *organelles.* Each organelle has a particular job to do. The organelles include the *mitochondria, endoplasmic reticulum,* and *Golgi complex.* Some cells have other organelles, such as *lysosomes, vacuoles,* or *chloroplasts.* All eukaryotic cells also contain a network of proteins known as the *cytoskeleton.*

Mitochondria are the power plants of the cell. A cell may contain hundreds or even thousands of mitochondria. These structures convert the chemical energy contained in food into a form of energy the cell can use to grow, divide, and do its work.

The endoplasmic reticulum is a complex network of membranes. It forms a system of pouches that store proteins and help channel substances to various parts of the cell. Some parts of the endoplasmic reticulum have a smooth surface. Other parts of the membrane have many ribosomes attached to their surface. Many of the cell's proteins are made on these ribosomes.

The Golgi complex, also known as the *Golgi apparatus,* consists of a stack of flat membrane sacs. These sacs process proteins and other substances produced in the cell. Small spheres called *vesicles* pinch off from the Golgi complex and move some of these substances to the cell membrane. They then may be transported across the membrane to other cells in the body or used to make the cell's covering. Other Golgi vesicles remain inside the cell and fuse with each other to form compartments that store proteins or other substances.

Lysosomes are round bodies containing enzymes that can break down many substances. For example, lysosomes inside white blood cells can destroy harmful bacteria. In plant cells and certain unicellular organisms, large, fluid-filled vacuoles usually perform the same function as lysosomes. In some plant cells, a single vacuole can take up most of the space in the cytoplasm.

Chloroplasts are organelles found in the cells of plants and algae. They contain a green substance called *chlorophyll.* During a process called *photosynthesis,* chlorophyll captures the energy of sunlight. Chloroplasts then use this energy to make sugars that are rich in chemical energy (see **Photosynthesis**). All living things directly or indirectly depend on these sugars for the energy to make all the other chemical substances in cells. For example, animals get energy by eating plants or by eating animals that have eaten plants.

The cytoskeleton consists of several types of protein rods that form a complicated network in the cytoplasm. The position of portions of the network against other portions or the expansion and contraction of parts of the network give a cell its shape, move organelles in the cell, and, in some cells, cause cell movement. Cells that swim do so by means of hairlike structures that extend out from the cell. These structures, called *cilia* or *fla-*

The structures of a cell Cells differ in shape, size, and function, but all cells have many structures in common. The illustrations below show the structures of a typical plant and animal cell.

WORLD BOOK illustrations by Oxford Illustrators Limited

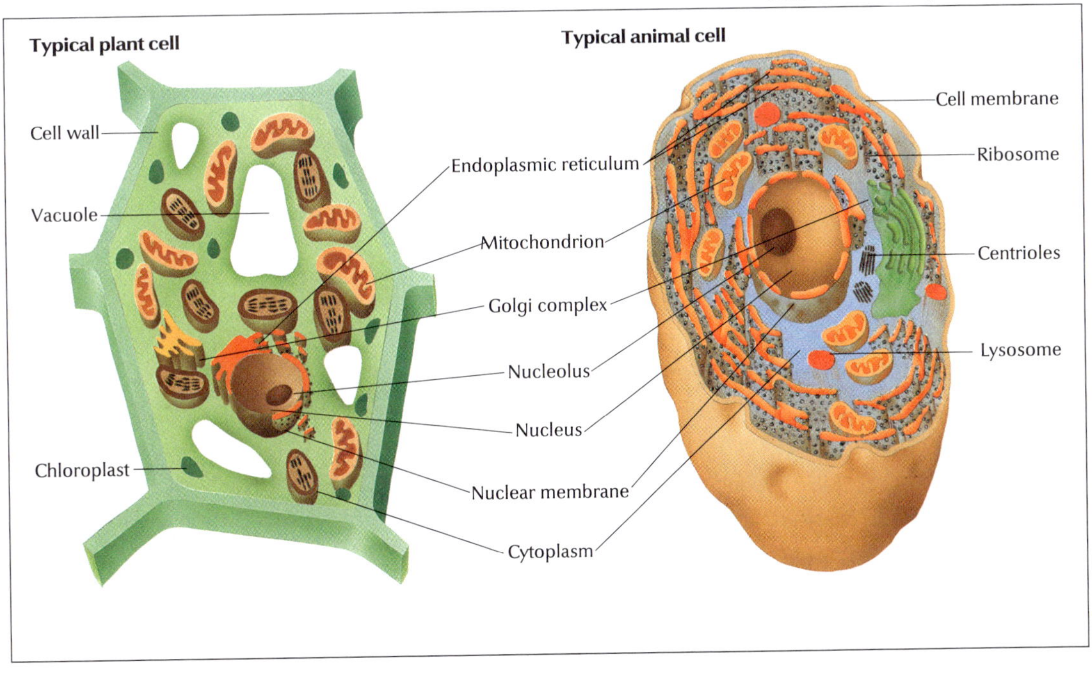

gella, contain a bundle of cytoskeleton rods. In many cells, some of the cytoskeleton is found in the *centrioles,* a pair of short, wide cylinders involved in cell reproduction. Centrioles lie at right angles to each other, usually near the nucleus.

Bacteria are extremely small, single-celled organisms that lack a nucleus. The region inside the bacterial cell that contains DNA is called the *nucleoid.* Bacteria have a single chromosome that consists of a circular DNA molecule. Bacteria do not contain a cytoskeleton or any of the membrane-surrounded organelles found in eukaryotic cells. However, some have extensions of the cell membrane that form folds in the cytoplasm and perform some of the jobs of mitochondria or chloroplasts. Some bacteria also have flagella, but they differ in structure from those of eukaryotic cells. They rotate like the blades of a propeller to make the bacteria move.

Cell division

Every living thing is made up of one or more cells, and each of these cells was produced by an already existing cell. New cells are formed by division, so that there are two cells where there once was only one cell. One-celled organisms begin and complete their lives as single cells.

Human beings and other multicellular organisms also develop from a single cell. After the cell grows to a certain size, it divides and forms two cells. These two cells remain attached to each other. They grow and divide, forming four cells. The cells grow and divide over and over again, and during this process they begin to specialize. A dog, a fish, a human being, or some other multicellular organism finally develops from the single cell.

Cell division involves two processes. In the first process, called *nuclear division,* the nucleus divides. In the second process, called *cytokinesis,* the cytoplasm divides, and the cell splits in half. There are two types of nuclear division: (1) mitosis and (2) meiosis.

Mitosis. Most eukaryotic cells divide their nucleus by mitosis. In this process, the nucleus divides and forms two identical nuclei. Usually, the cytoplasm divides soon after mitosis, producing two daughter cells with identical nuclei. Most one-celled organisms and most of the cells in multicelled organisms reproduce by mitosis.

Mitosis takes place in four stages: (1) prophase, (2) metaphase, (3) anaphase, and (4) telophase. The period between the completion of one nuclear division and the beginning of the next one is called *interphase.* During interphase, the cell grows and carries on its normal activities, and its chromosomes are difficult to see with an optical microscope. Each chromosome and centriole makes a copy of itself at a particular time in interphase. The original chromosome and its copy are called *sister chromatids.* They are joined by a structure called a *centromere.* After duplication of the centrioles and chromosomes, the cell is ready to undergo mitosis.

The first stage of mitosis is called *prophase.* At this time, the chromosomes begin to coil up, condensing into visible threads that become progressively shorter and thicker. As the chromosomes condense, part of the cytoskeleton organizes into a network of fibers extending across the cell. This network is called the *spindle.* The centrioles move apart along the fibers of the spindle until they are at opposite sides of the cell. The centrioles mark the *poles* of the spindle. Toward the end of prophase, the nuclear membrane breaks apart.

In *metaphase,* the second stage of mitosis, the sister chromatids move to the spindle's middle, called the

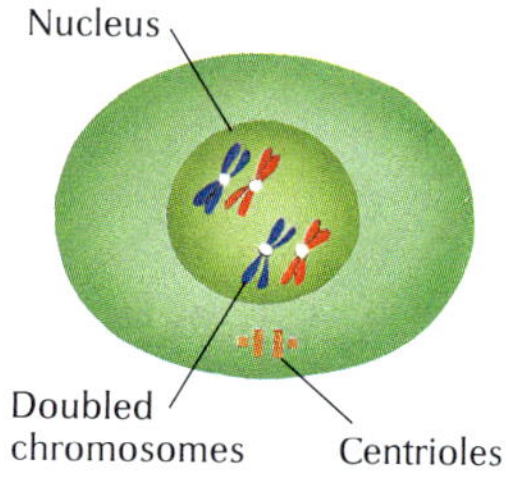

1. This animal cell has two pairs of chromosomes. Before it begins mitosis, chromosomes and centrioles will duplicate.

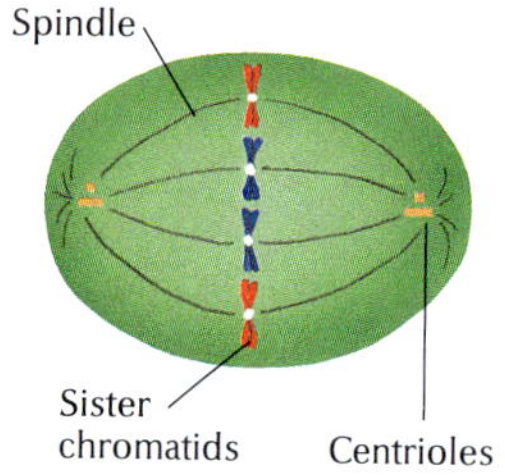

2. Centrioles move to opposite sides, and a spindle forms. *Sister chromatids* (duplicated chromosomes) line up along the middle of the spindle.

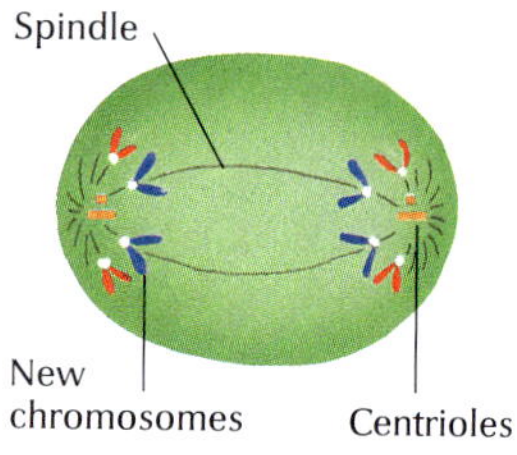

3. Sister chromatids separate and become new chromosomes. The separated chromosomes move to opposite sides of the cell.

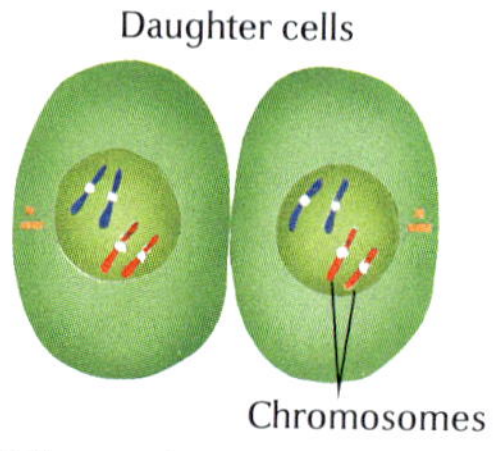

4. The cytoplasm divides, and the cell splits. Each daughter cell receives chromosomes that are duplicates of those of the parent cell.

WORLD BOOK illustrations by Oxford Illustrators Limited

Mitosis

Eukaryotic cells reproduce most often by *mitosis.* In mitosis, the cell nucleus divides to produce two nuclei, each identical to the parent nucleus. Mitosis is followed by *cytokinesis,* the division of the cytoplasm. The drawings at the left show these two processes in an animal cell. The photograph below shows two daughter cells following cytokinesis of the cell of a fish.

Michael Abbey, Science Source from Photo Researchers

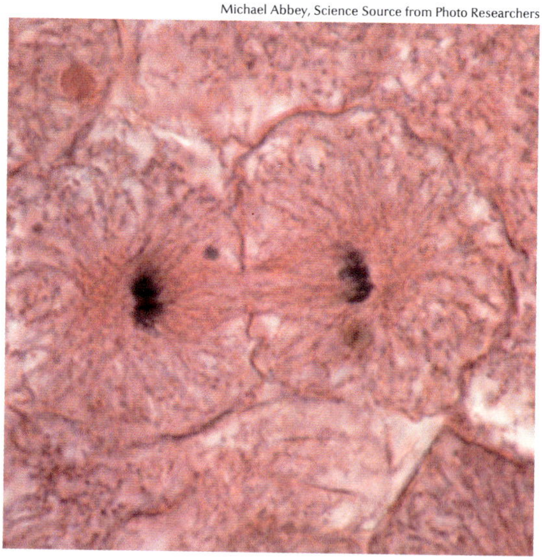

equator. They are still joined, but they line up on opposite sides of the equator. Each sister chromatid is attached at its centromere to at least one spindle fiber. In the third stage, called *anaphase,* the centromeres divide, and each sister chromatid becomes a new chromosome. The new chromosomes separate and move to opposite poles.

In *telophase,* the final stage of mitosis, individual chromosomes uncoil and again become hard to see. A new nuclear membrane forms around each new daughter nucleus. Also, the spindle breaks down, and the proteins from spindle fibers form part of the networks of cytoskeleton in the daughter cells.

Usually, division of the cytoplasm also begins during telophase. In animal cells, cytokinesis occurs when the cell membrane pinches between the two daughter nuclei to form two daughter cells. In plant cells and other cells that have a cell wall, a cell wall grows between the daughter nuclei, forming two cells. In either case, each new cell has as many chromosomes as the original cell and contains the same hereditary information.

Cytokinesis does not always create two identical cells. Sometimes, one of the daughter cells receives more of one kind of organelle than does the other cell. Cytokinesis may also result in two different sized cells. In addition, if mitosis occurs more than once in the same cell without cytokinesis, the cell can have more than one nucleus.

Mitosis in plant cells differs somewhat from that in animal cells. Cells in multicellular plants do not have centrioles, but they do form a spindle similar to that formed in animal cells.

Meiosis. Human beings and many other living things reproduce sexually. A new individual can be created only if a male sex cell, called a *sperm,* unites with a female sex cell, called an *egg.* Sex cells, also called *germ cells,* are produced in special reproductive tissues or organs. At first, new sex cells are produced by mitosis. These cells then go through a special kind of cell division called *meiosis.* To understand why, we must understand something about heredity.

Every species of life has a certain number of chromosomes in each of its *somatic* (body) cells. These chromosomes exist in pairs. For example, human beings have 23 pairs of chromosomes; frogs, 13 pairs; and pea plants, 7 pairs. The members of each pair are similar in size, shape, and hereditary content. Suppose the egg and sperm cells had the same number of chromosomes as all the other cells in an organism. If they united, the somatic cells in the offspring would have twice the number of chromosomes that they should have.

For example, human beings have 46 chromosomes in their somatic cells. If the father's sperm cells and the mother's egg cells also contained 46 chromosomes, their child's somatic cells would have 92 chromosomes. The next generation would have 184, and so on. To prevent this from happening, the sex cells have half the chromosomes found in the somatic cells. This is accomplished by meiosis.

Meiosis consists of two separate nuclear divisions of sex cells. Each chromosome duplicates before the first division. Then each chromosome, which now consists of two joined sister chromatids, lines up side by side with the other chromosomes of its pair. Each pair of doubled chromosomes moves to the equator. The paired chromosomes then separate. One chromosome, still consisting of two chromatids, goes to one pole. The other chromosome moves to the opposite pole. Cytokinesis

Meiosis

Sex cells undergo a type of nuclear division called *meiosis.* It requires two nuclear divisions to reduce the chromosomes in sex cells to half the number found in other cells. When a male and female sex cell unite, the full number of chromosomes is restored. The photo below shows meiosis in a pollen cell of a lily.

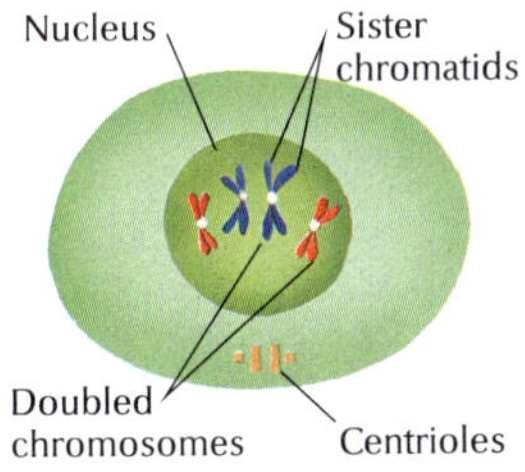

1. Before a cell begins meiosis, its chromosomes and centrioles duplicate. Similar doubled chromosomes, made up of sister chromatids, pair up.

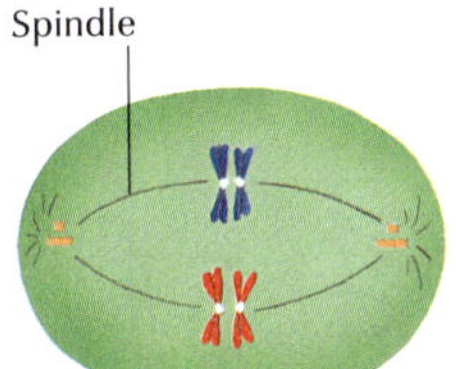

2. The doubled chromosome pairs move to the middle of the spindle. The pairs then separate, and the chromosomes go to opposite sides.

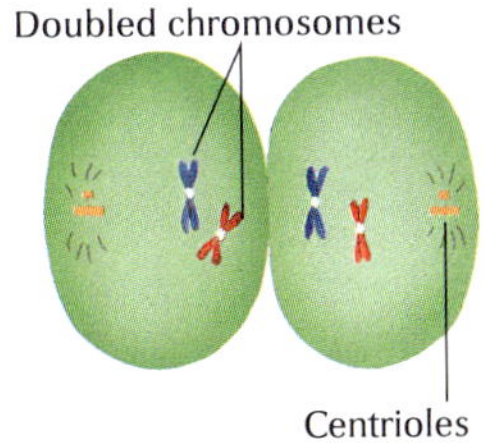

3. After the first division of meiosis, each new cell has one doubled chromosome from each of the original chromosome pairs.

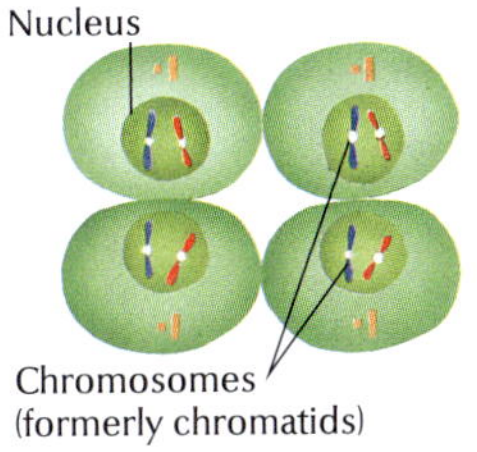

4. After the second division, the sister chromatids split. The four cells each have one chromosome from each of the original doubled pairs.

WORLD BOOK illustrations by Oxford Illustrators Limited

Biological Photo Service

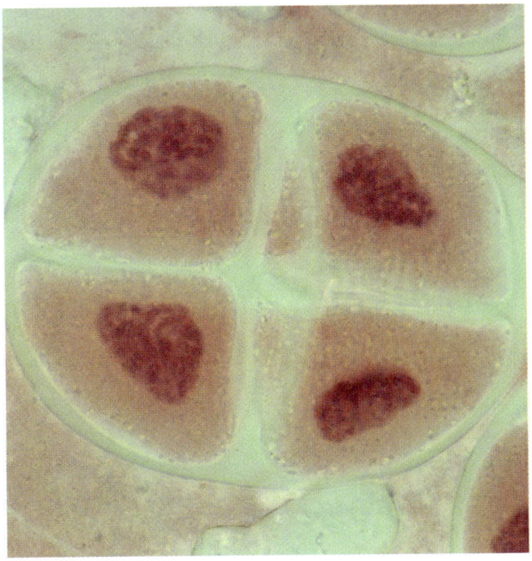

occurs, dividing the cytoplasm into two. Each daughter cell thus receives one chromosome, made up of two sister chromatids, from each of the original pairs. These new cells then divide. In this second division, one of each of the sister chromatids goes to each new daughter cell. Thus, the two divisions of meiosis produce a total of four cells. Each cell contains half the number of chromosomes found in all the other cells of the organism.

Human sperm and egg cells have 23 chromosomes each. When a sperm and an egg combine in a process called *fertilization,* they produce a single cell—the *fertilized egg*—with 46 chromosomes, or 23 similar pairs. A child develops from this egg. See **Heredity** (Sex cells and reproduction).

Growth and specialization are the processes by which a single fertilized egg cell develops into a particular organism. The fertilized egg from which you developed contained all the instructions on how you were to grow. The single cell divided by mitosis and cytokinesis. Then, cell after cell divided. After a large mass of cells had formed, the dividing cells began to *differentiate* (specialize), and became muscle cells, skin cells, nerve cells, and so on. The different cells grouped into tissues. These tissues then formed organs, such as your heart and lungs.

Understanding differentiation is a challenging problem for scientists. Every time a cell divides, it passes on the same heredity material. Scientists think that differentiation occurs when a specific set of genes becomes active in a cell. These genes produce certain proteins, many of which are enzymes, that cause the cell to differentiate. All the cells in an organism have the same genes and the same DNA, so what activates the specific set of genes in one cell type?

Death of a cell. Like all other living things, cells die. Each day, several billion cells in the body die and are replaced by cell division. Dead skin cells flake off. Dead cells from internal organs pass out of the body with waste products. The life span of cells varies. For example, white blood cells live about 13 days; red blood cells live about 120 days; and liver cells live about 18 months. Nerve cells can live about 100 years.

The work of a cell

A cell is intensely active. It carries out life's functions, including growth and reproduction. In addition, cells in multicellular organisms have special jobs. To live and to do its work, a cell must obtain energy. It also must manufacture proteins and other substances needed for the construction of its parts and to speed up the thousands of chemical reactions that occur in the cell.

Producing energy. Most of a body's energy comes from the mitochondria, the power producers of a cell. The mitochondria are like power plants that burn fuel to produce the electric power that runs machines. The food a person eats is the fuel that is "burned" inside the mitochondria. A product of this burning is a compound called *adenosine triphosphate* (ATP). ATP is the "electric power" that runs a cell's activities. It supplies the energy

Producing energy This diagram shows how a human cell produces energy. Most energy is produced in tiny structures called *mitochondria* and is stored in a compound called *ATP.* To produce ATP, mitochondria require fuel. In human beings, this fuel comes from food. The digestive system first breaks down food into amino acids, fatty acids, and simple sugars. The blood carries these substances to the cells. In the cell's cytoplasm, the sugars are broken down into pyruvic acid. Some ATP is also produced. The amino, fatty, and pyruvic acids enter the mitochondria. There, in a series of chemical reactions, ATP is produced while carbon dioxide and water are released as waste products.

WORLD BOOK diagram by Siena Artworks

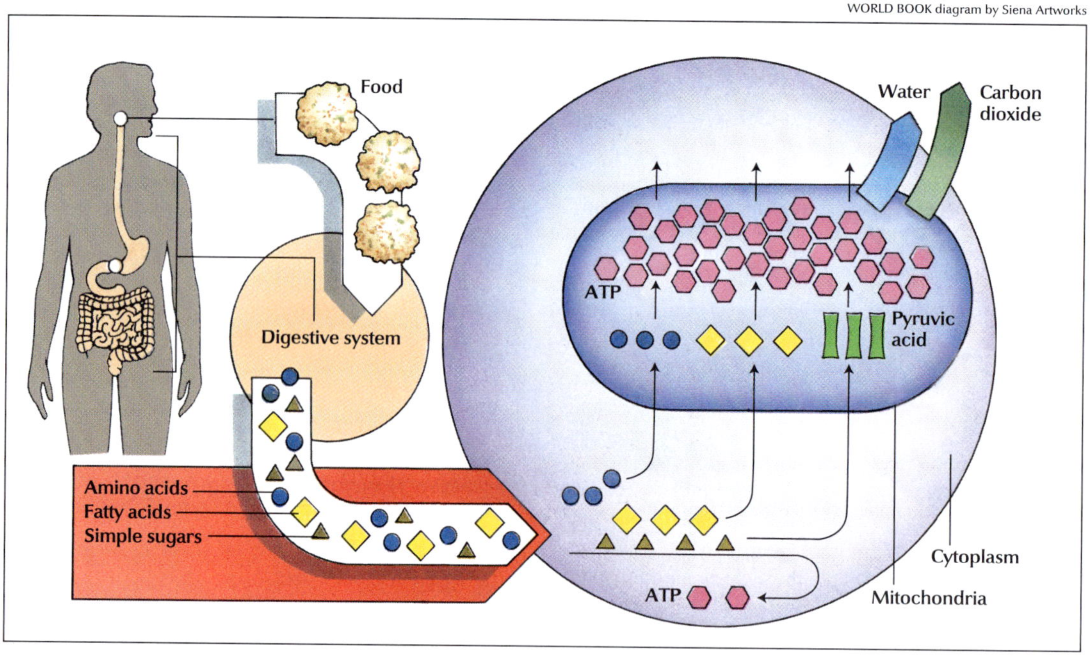

Producing proteins

The form and function of a cell, such as the animal cell shown below, are determined by the proteins it produces. Proteins, in turn, are made up of tiny units called *amino acids.* DNA contains the blueprints for all the proteins made in a cell. These blueprints direct the order in which the amino acids will be linked together to form particular proteins.

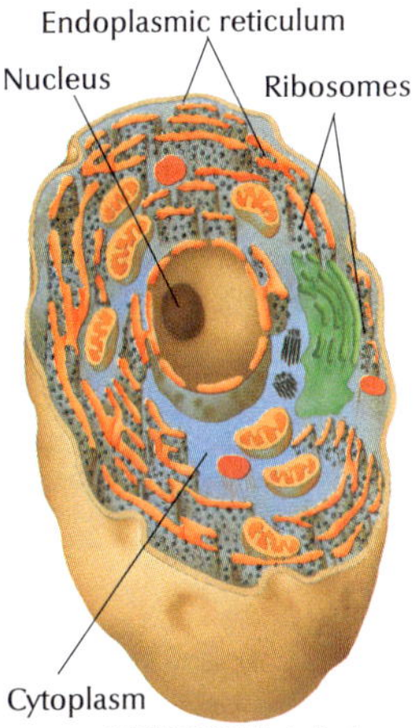

WORLD BOOK illustration by Oxford Illustrators Limited

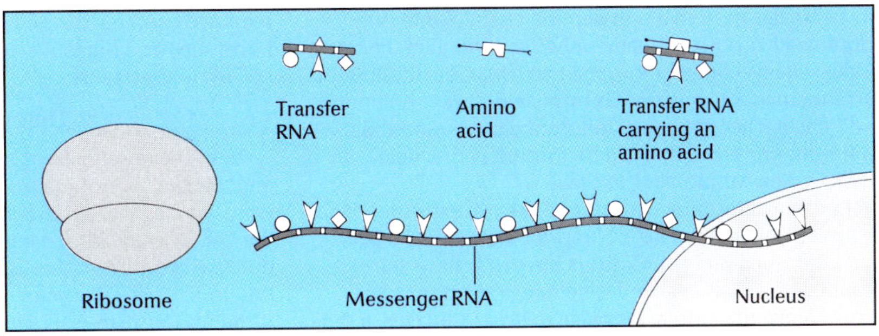

When a particular protein is to be made, an RNA copy of the DNA blueprint for that protein is made in the nucleus. This RNA, called *messenger RNA,* then goes to a ribosome, a tiny body on the surface of the endoplasmic reticulum in the cytoplasm. The messenger RNA lines up amino acids in the proper order. Another type of RNA, *transfer RNA,* collects amino acids in the cytoplasm.

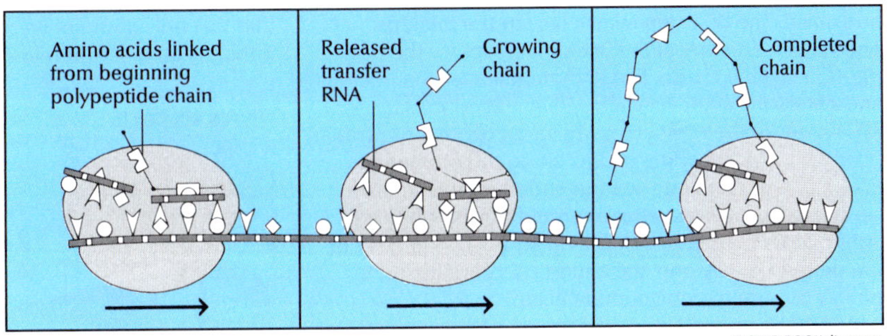

WORLD BOOK diagrams

The ribosome moves along the messenger RNA. The transfer RNA, carrying amino acids, lines up with the messenger RNA in the ribosome. The amino acids link together, and the transfer RNA is released, *left.* As the ribosome moves down the messenger RNA, a polypeptide chain forms, *center.* The final segment of messenger RNA, *right,* signals that the chain is complete.

needed to do work in the cells. For example, ATP supplies the energy to contract a muscle or send a message between nerve cells.

An ATP molecule contains three phosphate groups. *Chemical bonds* (forces that hold atoms together) link the phosphate groups together like railroad cars. The bonds that attach the second and third phosphate groups are especially rich in energy. When the bonds are broken, energy is released that the cell can use.

The source of energy for most living things—directly or indirectly—is the sun. Plant cells produce ATP during photosynthesis, the process by which green plants capture energy from the sun and use it to make sugars. When sunlight strikes a chlorophyll molecule in a chloroplast, it sets off a series of chemical reactions. The ATP produced provides the energy by which a plant then turns carbon dioxide from air and water from soil into sugars and other substances. Some other organisms, including certain bacteria, also produce ATP by photosynthesis. See **Photosynthesis.**

Animal cells obtain their energy from food that the animal eats. The animal's digestive system breaks down the food into basic parts. It breaks fats into fatty acids, sugars and starches into simple sugars, and proteins into chemical units called *amino acids.* The blood carries these substances to cells in the body.

In the cell's cytoplasm, the simple sugars are broken down into pyruvic acid, and a small amount of ATP is produced. The amino, fatty, and pyruvic acids then enter the mitochondria. Enzymes in the mitochondria break down these substances further in a series of chemical reactions. Oxygen must also be present in the mitochondria for these reactions to take place. The reactions produce carbon dioxide, water, and many molecules of ATP. The ATP molecules then leave the mitochondria and provide energy wherever it is needed in the cell. For every job that requires energy, special enzymes break the ATP phosphate bonds and release the energy.

Producing proteins. All living things contain proteins. The structures of a cell are built largely of proteins. The proteins called enzymes speed up the chemical reactions of life. They help digest your food, help produce energy, and assist in building other proteins. A single cell may contain hundreds of different kinds of enzymes. Many *hormones,* the substances that regulate chemical activities throughout your body, are proteins. The body also makes proteins called *antibodies* to fight disease germs.

Proteins are complex, three-dimensional substances composed of one or more long, folded *polypeptide chains.* These chains consist of amino acid units. All amino acids contain carbon, hydrogen, oxygen, and nitrogen, and some also contain sulfur. The amino acids link together in a line to form polypeptide chains. There are 20 kinds of amino acids commonly involved in protein production, and any number of them may be linked in any order to form a polypeptide chain. Some polypeptide chains may contain only 10 amino acid "links." Other chains contain more than 100 links. Each different arrangement of amino acids forms a different polypeptide chain. The number of different chains—and thus, different proteins—that can be formed is practically unlimited. See **Amino acid; Protein.**

DNA contains blueprints for all the proteins made in a cell. Each gene contains a blueprint for a specific polypeptide. Such blueprints direct the order in which amino acids will be linked together to form proteins. Protein manufacture takes place in the cytoplasm of the cell. But the DNA does not leave the nucleus to help make the proteins. This job is done by DNA's chemical cousin, RNA. RNA is made in the nucleus of the cell, and it is present in both the nucleus and the cytoplasm.

To understand how proteins are made, let us trace the production of a protein that consists of one polypeptide chain. The first step takes place in the nucleus. There, an RNA copy of the DNA blueprint for the polypeptide chain is made. The RNA then leaves the nucleus and enters the cytoplasm. This RNA, called *messenger RNA,* goes to the ribosomes, the cell's centers of protein production. A ribosome moves along the messenger RNA, "reading" the information coded on it. The messenger RNA acts as a *template* (mold) to line up the amino acids in the exact order called for by the DNA of the genes. One by one, the amino acids are linked together to form the polypeptide chain.

Another type of RNA, called *transfer RNA,* collects the amino acids in the cytoplasm and brings them to the messenger RNA ribosomes attached to the messenger RNA. There are specific transfer RNA molecules for each kind of amino acid. The specific transfer RNA and the correct amino acid are brought together with the help of ATP and an enzyme.

During the production of a protein, a ribosome is attached to two adjacent coding segments of a messenger RNA molecule. Each coding segment, which consists of three nucleotides, is called a *codon* and specifies one amino acid. The correct transfer RNA, with its amino acid attached, lines up on the first codon of the messenger RNA template. After a second transfer RNA and its amino acid have lined up on the other codon, the two amino acids are linked together. The first transfer RNA is then set free to collect more amino acids.

The second transfer RNA holds the growing polypeptide chain to the ribosome. The ribosome then moves one codon further down the messenger RNA. The appropriate transfer RNA, with its attached amino acid, lines up on this codon. The amino acid is joined to the first two amino acids, and the second transfer DNA is set free. The ribosome moves one position further, covering the next codon on the messenger RNA template. This process continues until the ribosome has passed over the entire length of the messenger RNA, step by step. The last codon on the messenger RNA does not code for an amino acid. It signals that the chain is complete. The finished polypeptide chain is then released. In this case, the protein is complete.

In most proteins that consist of more than one polypeptide chain, the chains are manufactured separately, and then they combine to make the protein. The finished protein then starts to do its particular job. Some proteins are used inside the cell. Other proteins, such as hormones and digestive enzymes, are released from the cell to do their work.

The code of life

As we have seen, DNA controls the life of the cell—and the lives of organisms made up of cells—in two ways. First, DNA determines the form and function of the cell by regulating the kinds of proteins the cell produces. Second, it passes on all the hereditary information from one generation of cells to the next. Thus, DNA is the master plan of all life.

DNA—the wondrous molecule. DNA molecules lie tightly coiled in the chromosomes of a cell. Each chromosome probably contains one extremely long DNA molecule. On the average, a single human chromosome consists of a DNA molecule that is almost 2 inches (5 centimeters) long. But the DNA molecule is a thread so thin that only some of its details can be seen when magnified by an electron microscope. Scientists have deter-

DNA's six parts

A DNA molecule consists of *phosphate,* a sugar called *deoxyribose,* and four bases—*adenine, cytosine, guanine,* and *thymine.*

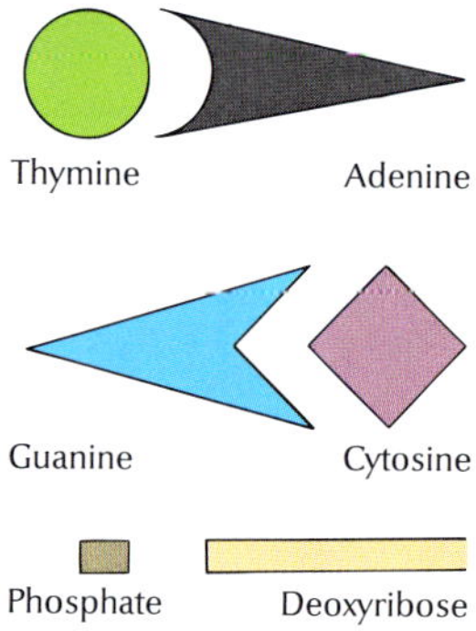

RNA's six parts

RNA differs from DNA in two chief ways. The sugar in RNA is *ribose,* and RNA contains *uracil* instead of thymine.

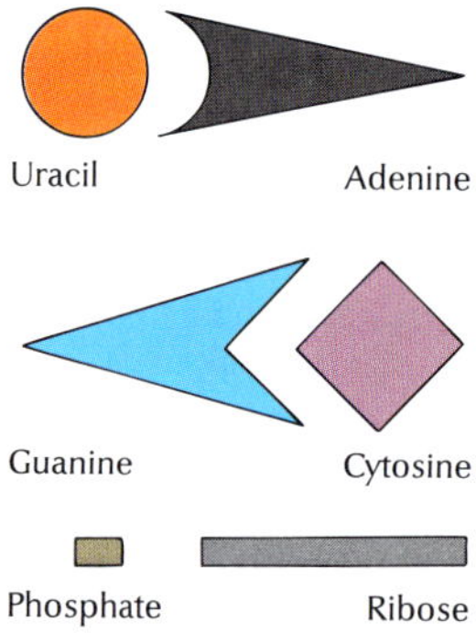

The DNA ladder

DNA's parts link together like a twisted ladder. Each rung consists of two matching bases. The sides are sugar and phosphate.

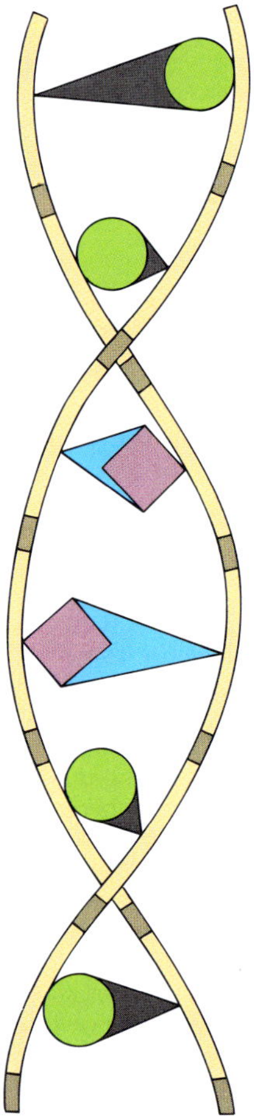

mined the structure of the DNA molecule primarily on the basis of its chemical composition. They have determined the molecule's shape by bouncing X rays off the atoms in the molecule and then studying the patterns the scattered X rays made on photographic plates. The patterns show that the molecule has the shape of a rope ladder that is coiled like a spring. This shape is called a *double helix.* All DNA molecules have this shape.

The DNA ladder contains four building blocks called *nucleotides.* Nucleotides float freely in the cell nucleus. Each nucleotide consists of a sugar called *deoxyribose* joined to a phosphate and one of four compounds called *bases.* The bases are *adenine, cytosine, guanine,* and *thymine* (abbreviated A, C, G, and T). The sides of the ladder contain alternating units of phosphate and sugar. The rungs are made up of bases. The bases are attached to the sugar units of the ladder's side pieces. Each rung consists of two bases: A-T, T-A, C-G, or G-C. No other combination is possible, because only the A-T and C-G pairs are chemically attracted to each other and only these pairs make rungs of the proper length to fit between the ladder's side pieces. Any other combination of bases is too long or too short. The order of the bases in one *strand* (half) of the ladder determines the order of the bases in the other strand. For example, if the bases in one strand of the ladder are ATCGAT, the bases in the opposite strand would be TAGCTA.

Before a cell divides, the DNA duplicates. The ladder splits lengthwise, separating the two bases that make up each rung. Then each half ladder pairs up with unattached nucleotides. But the bases in each half ladder can pair up only with their matching mates. The A's attach to T's, the T's to A's, the G's to C's, and the C's to G's. In this way, each new ladder becomes a duplicate of the original ladder. These duplicate DNA molecules can be seen at mitosis as the two chromatids of a chromosome. When the cell undergoes mitosis and cytokinesis, each new daughter cell receives identical DNA molecules.

RNA—the master copy. RNA, the substance that carries out DNA's instructions for protein production, re-

DNA duplication

1. Before a cell divides, the DNA duplicates. The ladder splits lengthwise, separating the bases of each rung.

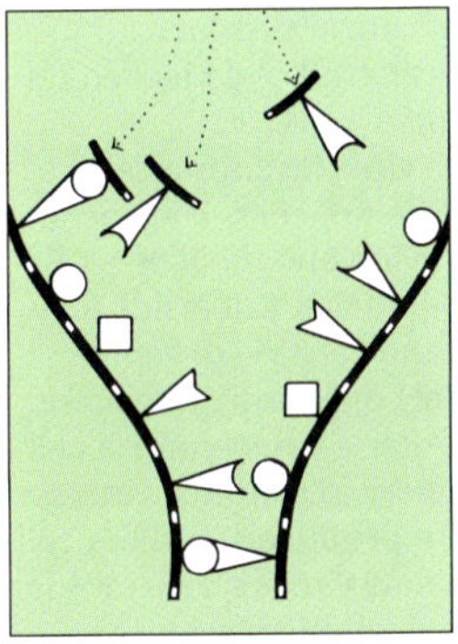

2. Free bases, with sugars and phosphates, attach to bases of each half ladder. Only matching bases pair up.

3. Two ladders are built, each a duplicate of the original. When the cell divides, each new cell gets identical DNA.

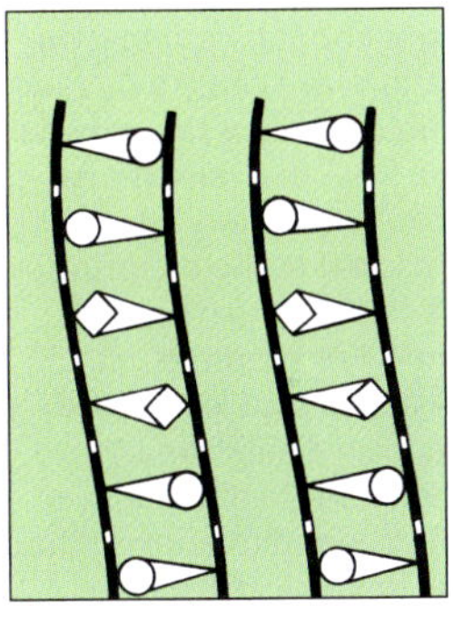

How messenger RNA is formed

1. When RNA copies DNA's blueprint for making a protein, the DNA ladder first splits lengthwise through its bases. Half the ladder serves as a mold to form messenger RNA. Free RNA bases, with their attached sugars and phosphates, match up with the exposed DNA bases. A strand of messenger RNA thus begins to form.

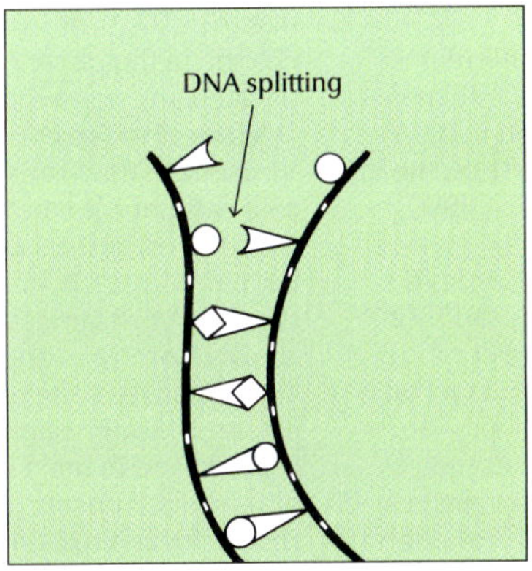

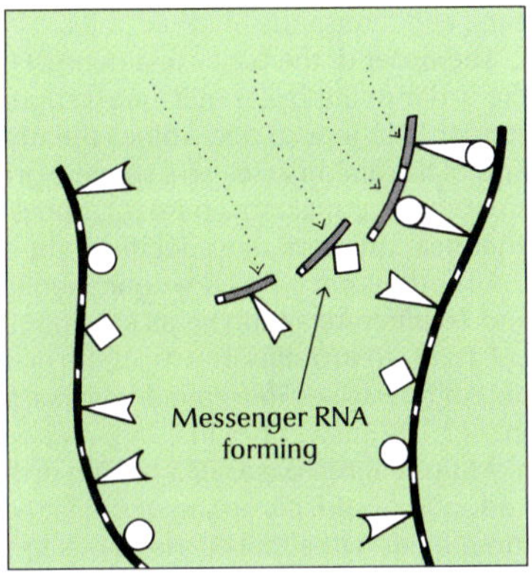

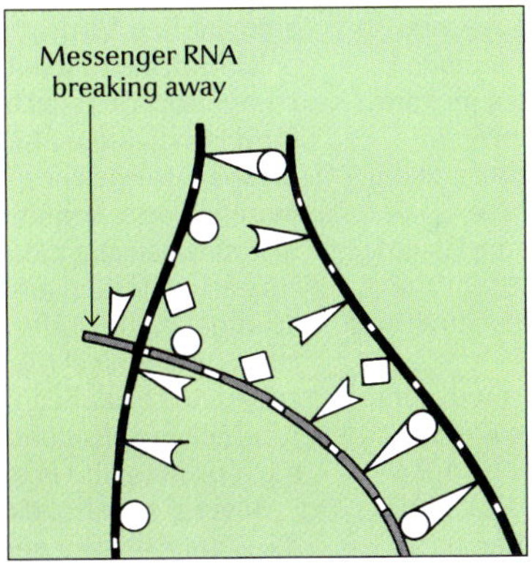

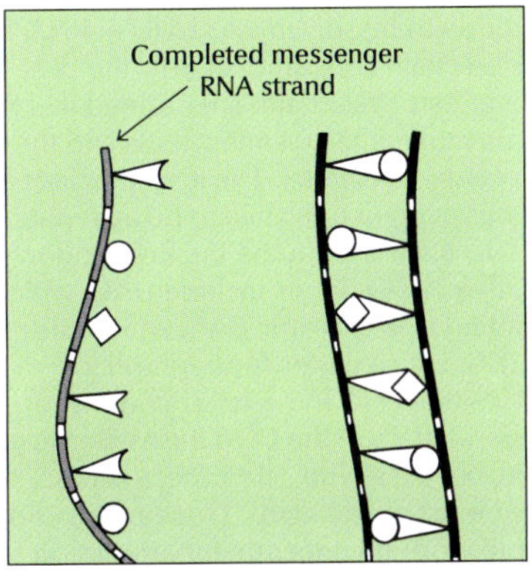

2. As messenger RNA forms, it becomes a reverse copy of the DNA blueprint and begins to peel off the DNA mold. As it breaks away, bases of the ladder start to rejoin.

3. The completed messenger RNA leaves the nucleus and goes to the ribosomes. It will serve as a mold on which amino acids will be linked into a protein chain.

sembles DNA in chemical structure. But there are two major differences. The sugar in RNA is *ribose* instead of deoxyribose, and RNA contains the base *uracil* (abbreviated U) instead of thymine. Like thymine, uracil will pair only with the base adenine. RNA's other three bases—A, C, and G—and the phosphate unit are identical to those in DNA.

How does messenger RNA copy the DNA blueprints for making proteins? First, a part of the DNA molecule unwinds and splits, exposing bases on the ladder's interior. One of the halves then serves as a template for lining up RNA nucleotides. The bases of unattached RNA nucleotides pair up with the exposed DNA bases. For example, the RNA bases AUCGAU pair up with the DNA bases TAGCTA. A strand of messenger RNA thus begins to form. The completed strand of messenger RNA, which may consist of hundreds of bases, peels off the DNA template and carries the instructions for making a protein to the ribosomes on the endoplasmic reticulum. The bases of the DNA molecule rejoin, the ladder rewinds, and the master plan is again locked away.

The genetic code lies in the order of the bases in the DNA molecule. This order of bases is passed on from one generation of cells to the next, and from one generation of an organism to the next. It makes an elephant give birth to an elephant, not a zebra. It is this order that determines the color of your eyes, the shape of your ears, and thousands of other traits.

The order of the bases in a gene's DNA determines the order of the bases in its messenger RNA. The messenger RNA in turn determines the order and composition of the amino acids in a specific protein. Thus, the instructions for making a particular protein lie in the chemical structure of a specific gene.

Four different bases are contained in DNA or RNA and 20 different amino acids are commonly used by a cell to make proteins. How can the order and composition of four bases determine which amino acid will be made? The answer lies in a *triplet code.* In other words, a group of three bases in a certain order forms the codon for a specific amino acid. Each codon is given a three-letter name that corresponds to the abbreviation of the names of its bases.

Scientists have broken the genetic code. The first codon to be solved was UUU of RNA. Scientists used an RNA chain consisting of only the base uracil repeated over and over again. They added this RNA to a mixture containing the 20 amino acids and the cell's protein-making machinery. The RNA produced a protein chain consisting of only the amino acid phenylalanine. So, UUU turned out to be the RNA codon for phenylalanine. Other RNA codons include UAU, which codes for the amino acid tyrosine; CAC, which codes for histidine; and UGG, which codes for tryptophan.

A total of 64 three-letter codons can be formed from the 4 letters of the DNA bases. Because there are only 20, not 64, amino acids, there is more than one codon for most amino acids. Three of the codons, UAA, UAG, and UGA, do not code for any amino acid. They act as signals for the release of the polypeptide from the ribosome, thus stopping the process of making that polypeptide.

The genetic code is nearly universal. The same three-letter codons specify the same amino acids in most organisms that have been studied—from bacteria to human beings. Thus, underlying the vast variety of life is a common unit, the cell, whose activities are directed by a common language—the genetic code written in DNA.

The cell in disease

A cell usually functions perfectly. It grows and reproduces in an orderly fashion and performs its tasks with remarkable efficiency. But sometimes things go wrong. Instead of dividing in an orderly fashion, a cell may go wild and multiply without stopping—and form a tumor. A virus may take over the machinery of the cell for its own purposes and kill it. The genetic code may contain an error, and a needed protein may not be produced, or an abnormal one may be formed.

Cancer is a disease marked by a disorderly growth of cells. It occurs in human beings and other animals. Many cancer cells look like immature cells that have not yet begun to specialize into cells of a particular tissue. In some cancerous tissues, many nuclei are in the process of mitosis. The dividing cells eventually pile up and form a tumor. Cells in the tumor may break away, invade other tissues, and form additional tumors that disrupt the function of the tissue. Many factors, including smoking, exposure to certain chemicals, or excessive exposure to X rays, may cause cells to become cancerous and begin the process of tumor formation. Some scientists believe that the causes of some types of cancer produce a change in the genetic code. The altered code is then duplicated and passed on to daughter cells.

Virus diseases occur when a virus invades a cell. Viruses are tiny parasites. They are not cells. They occupy a twilight zone between the living and the lifeless. By themselves, viruses are lifeless particles. But inside a living cell, viruses become active and capable of reproduction. Most viruses consist only of hereditary material—DNA or RNA—and protein. After a virus enters a cell, it may take over the cell's machinery to produce viruses like itself. Soon, many viruses are produced, and the cell is destroyed in most cases. The new viruses then invade other cells. Viruses that attack human beings cause AIDS, chickenpox, colds, flu, hepatitis, measles, mumps, poliomyelitis, and many other diseases. Scientists have proved that certain viruses cause cancer in laboratory animals. See **Virus.**

Metabolic diseases. *Metabolism* is the sum of the chemical processes by which all living things transform food into living matter and energy. Metabolism depends on specific enzymes, which are made according to the genetic code. Sometimes the code contains an error that may cause a metabolic disease. Many of these errors are inherited and are brought about by a *mutation* (change) in the code. Most mutations are caused by radiation or chemicals, which scramble a part of the genetic code and result in an error. If the DNA in a parent's reproductive cells contains an error in the plans for making a protein, the error may be passed to the offspring.

Several metabolic diseases occur because the code does not call for a needed enzyme. For example, *galactosemia,* a disease of infants, is caused by a lack of the enzyme needed to convert galactose, a milk sugar, to glucose. *Phenylketonuria,* another disease of infants, is caused by the lack of the enzyme needed to convert the amino acid phenylalanine to the amino acid tyrosine.

Both these diseases cause mental retardation and poor physical development.

Some metabolic diseases are caused when the instructions for making a protein are "misspelled" in the genetic code. *Sickle cell anemia,* a frequently fatal human disease, is one such metabolic disease. Normal red blood cells are disk-shaped. But in a sickle cell victim, some red blood cells become twisted into a hooked, or sickle, shape. These deformed cells die quickly, causing severe anemia. Red blood cells contain a protein called hemoglobin, which carries oxygen to the body's tissues. Hemoglobin is made of several hundred amino acids. The deadly sickling occurs when, in only one part of this long chain, the genetic code calls for the amino acid valine instead of glutamic acid.

Cell research

The mystery of the cell has long been a challenge. More than 2,000 years ago, people debated how a human being grew from a single egg cell. Some thought this cell contained a tiny, completely formed human being. Others argued that the heart, legs, arms, and all other parts of the body developed successively. But only with the development of the microscope could scientists begin to solve the mysteries of the cell.

Before 1900. In 1665, Robert Hooke, an English scientist, observed a thin slice of cork under his microscope. He saw that it was composed of neat holes enclosed by walls. He called these holes *cells.* Other scientists also studied cells and tiny living things under the microscope. But for many years, few guessed the significance of the cell.

In 1838, the German botanist Matthias Schleiden stated that the cell was the basic unit of all life. The next year, Theodor Schwann, a German physiologist, advanced the same idea. A number of other scientists had already come to believe that all organisms were made up of cells. But from that time on, biologists regarded the cell as the building block of life.

In the mid-1800's, Gregor Mendel, an Austrian monk, discovered the laws of heredity through experiments with garden peas. Mendel's work, translated into modern terms, suggested that there is a basic unit of heredity—the *gene.* Mendel's work also suggested that the genes in a cell's nucleus usually occurred in pairs, with each parent supplying one member of every pair. In 1865, Mendel published a paper presenting his findings. But his work went unrecognized until 1900.

During the mid- and late 1800's, using microscopes with better lenses, scientists discovered much about cells. They learned that cells reproduced by division. They found that every cell nucleus contained a substance they called chromatin. During cell division, the chromatin condensed into a certain number of visible pairs of chromosomes, depending on the organism. Each somatic daughter cell received the same number of chromosomes that the parent cell had. Egg and sperm cells received only half the number of chromosomes that the somatic cells had.

Near the end of the 1800's, a number of scientists argued that chromosomes must be the basis of heredity. However, this opinion was not yet generally accepted.

The 1900's. Mendel's work was rediscovered on three separate occasions in 1900—by Hugo de Vries of

Highlights in cell research

1838 — Matthias Schleiden called the cell the basic unit of life.

Mid-1800's — Gregor Mendel's research formulated the basic laws of heredity.

Late 1800's — Scientists discovered that cells reproduce by division.

Early 1900's — Thomas Hunt Morgan proved genes the basic units of heredity.

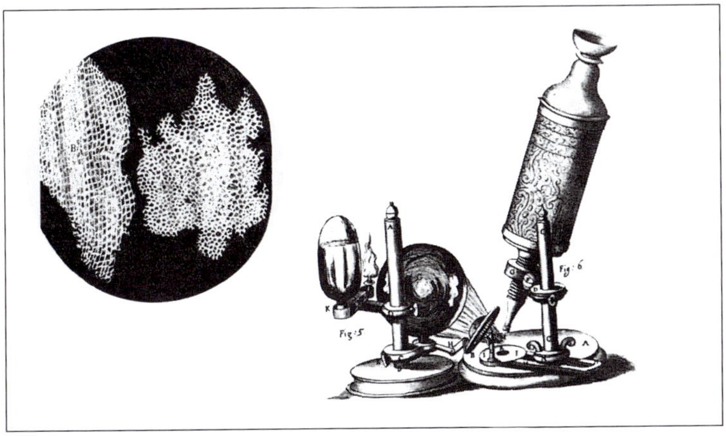

The structure of a piece of cork was observed and drawn in 1665 by Robert Hooke. Looking through a microscope he had built, Hooke saw that the cork was composed of neat holes enclosed by walls. He called the holes *cells.* Most scientists did not realize the significance of cells until many years later.

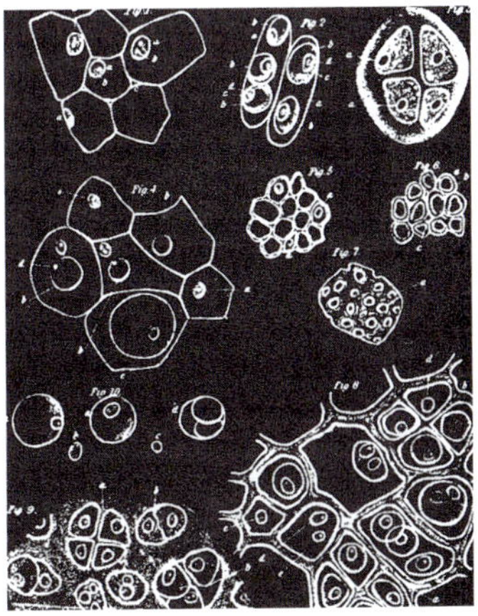

Theodor Schwann's drawings of cells helped prove that all living things consist of cells. He and Matthias Schleiden advanced this idea in the 1830's.

the Netherlands, Carl Correns of Germany, and Erich von Tschermak of Austria. Each of these botanists, working independently on the problem of heredity, came across Mendel's findings. In 1902, Walter S. Sutton, an American scientist, pointed out that during cell division chromosomes behaved as Mendel had believed inherited traits behaved. A few years later at Columbia University, Thomas Hunt Morgan and his associates proved that genes are the units of heredity. They also proved that genes are arranged in a specific order on chromosomes.

The question then became: How do genes determine the structure and behavior of living things? Two American scientists, George W. Beadle and Edward L. Tatum, found part of the answer in the early 1940's. They discovered that some genes control chemical reactions in cells by directing the formation of enzymes. They found that there is a specific gene for each enzyme.

Scientists became increasingly interested in the chemistry of the gene in the 1940's. They knew that chromosomes consisted of DNA and protein. In fact, DNA had been discovered in 1868 by a Swiss biochemist, Friedrich Miescher. But scientists had dismissed DNA as unimportant, knowing how essential proteins were in life processes. The turning point came in 1944, when a team headed by American geneticist Oswald T. Avery found evidence that DNA alone determined heredity.

Scientists knew that the DNA molecule consisted of *phosphate, deoxyribose,* and four *bases*—adenine, cytosine, guanine, and thymine. But they did not know how these units fit together. In 1953, James D. Watson, an American, and Francis H. C. Crick, of the United Kingdom, proposed that the structure of the DNA molecule resembled a twisted ladder. They based this model on the experimental findings of the British scientists Rosalind E. Franklin and Maurice H. F. Wilkins. Experiments have proved their model correct.

In 1957, Arthur Kornberg, an American biochemist, produced DNA in a test tube. He mixed DNA nucleotides with an enzyme and added a chain of natural DNA as a template. The DNA nucleotides linked together into a chain resembling the template DNA. Ten years later, Kornberg manufactured DNA that was *biologically active* (able to reproduce naturally).

Many scientists have worked on unraveling the genetic code, found in the sequence of the bases of DNA. In 1962, Marshall W. Nirenberg, an American biochemist, discovered the code for one amino acid. He and others eventually determined the code for the 20 amino acids involved in protein production. Other scientists discovered how RNA copies of the DNA code are produced.

In the 1970's, scientists discovered techniques for removing genes from one organism and inserting them into another. Today, these techniques are called *recombinant DNA technology.* Experiments with recombinant DNA have helped scientists to learn more about the structure and function of genes and have led to advances in agriculture, medicine, and industry. See **Genetic engineering.**

In the 1980's, scientists began using a powerful microscope called the *scanning tunneling microscope.* This tool provided scientists with detailed images of the structure of DNA. See **Scanning probe microscope.**

In the 1990's, doctors began to use *gene therapy* as treatment for certain diseases. This treatment involves

1944 — Oswald T. Avery discovered that DNA alone determines heredity.

1957 — Arthur Kornberg produced DNA in a test tube.

1970's — Scientists developed methods of recombinant DNA technology.

1990 — Doctors first used gene therapy as a treatment for disease.

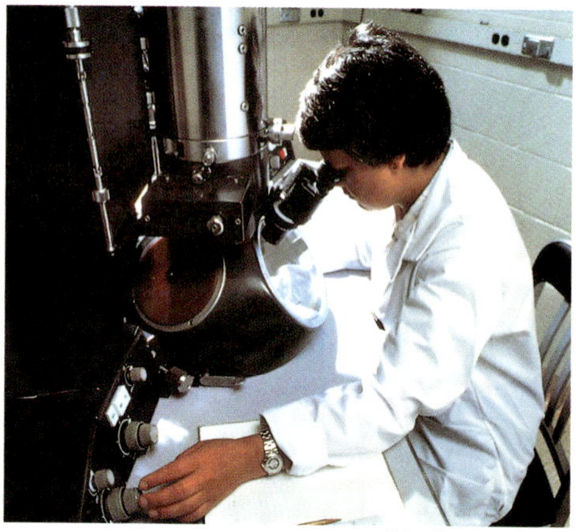

National Institutes of Health

The electron microscope became a vital tool of cell research in the 1950's. With its tremendous magnifying power, it opened a new world to scientists. It revealed that cells contain many elaborate structures.

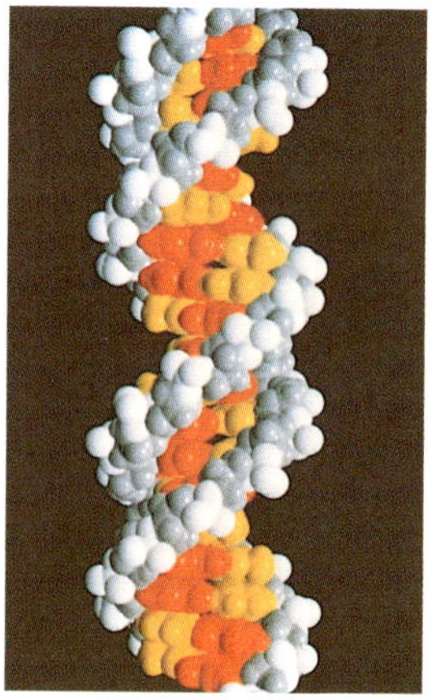

Richard J. Feldman, National Institutes of Health

A model of a DNA molecule resembles a twisted ladder. Scientists first proposed this shape in 1953.

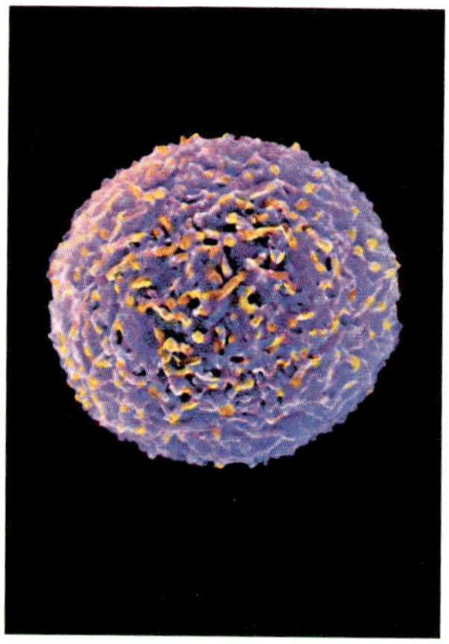

CNRI/SPL from Photo Researchers

A three-dimensional image produced by a scanning electron microscope shows details of the surface of a white blood cell.

inserting a gene into the cells of a patient to correct defects in cell function. See **Gene therapy.**

The future holds enormous challenges and exciting promises for cell research. Tomorrow's medical triumphs will probably be in controlling disorders that arise in the cell. Scientists understand how genes manufacture proteins, but other aspects of how genes operate remain a mystery. Many questions must still be answered, including: What causes a cell to die? Can errors in the genetic code that cause mental and physical disorders be corrected? What makes a cell differentiate?

If scientists can discover what causes a cell to die, they may be able to slow the aging process and increase the span of human life. As scientists learn more about DNA and the genetic code, they may be able to alter the code and erase hundreds of inherited mental and physical defects. They may find how to control cancer. Or perhaps scientists may be able to replace worn-out or diseased tissues. By manipulating hereditary processes, scientists may be able to raise disease-resistant farm crops and livestock and increase agricultural production. Irwin Rubenstein and Susan M. Wick

Related articles in *World Book* include:

Amino acid	Gene	Mutation
Apoptosis	Gene mapping	Nervous system
Beadle, George W.	Genetic engineering	Photosynthesis
Biology	Genetics	Protein
Biosynthesis	Golgi, Camillo	Protoplasm
Biotechnology	Growth	Reproduction
Blood	Heredity	RNA
Cancer	Histology	Sickle cell anemia
Cellulose	Hooke, Robert	Spontaneous generation
Centrifuge	Human body	Stem cell
Chromosome	Life	Tissue
Crick, Francis H. C.	Mendel, Gregor J.	Virus
DNA	Microscope	Watson, James D.
Enzyme	Microtome	Wilkins, Maurice H. F.
Evolution	Microtomy	
Franklin, Rosalind E.	Mitochondria	

Outline

I. Looking at a cell
- A. Shapes of cells
- B. Sizes of cells

II. Inside a living cell
- A. The nucleus
- B. The cytoplasm
- C. Bacteria

III. Cell division
- A. Mitosis
- B. Meiosis
- C. Growth and specialization
- D. Death of a cell

IV. The work of a cell
- A. Producing energy
- B. Producing proteins

V. The code of life
- A. DNA—the wondrous molecule
- B. RNA—the master copy
- C. The genetic code

VI. The cell in disease
- A. Cancer
- B. Virus diseases
- C. Metabolic diseases

VII. Cell research

Questions

What is cytokinesis?
What structures do most cells have in common?
What are the two main types of nuclear division?
How does a cell make proteins?
What is the genetic code?
Why is ATP so important in the life and work of a cell?
How do viruses cause disease?
In what two ways does DNA control the life of a cell?
What is *differentiation?* Why is differentiation such a challenging problem?
What role do *mitochondria* play in cells?

Additional resources

Bolsover, Steven R., and others. *From Genes to Cells.* Wiley-Liss, 1997.
Harold, Franklin M. *The Way of the Cell.* Oxford, 2001.
Rensberger, Boyce. *Life Itself: Exploring the Realm of the Living Cell.* Oxford, 1996.
Wallace, Holly. *Cells and Systems.* Heinemann Lib., 2001. Younger readers.

Cellini, *chuh LEE nee,* **Benvenuto,** *BEHN vuh NOO toh* (1500-1571), was an Italian goldsmith and sculptor. Although regarded as an outstanding sculptor during his lifetime, it is doubtful whether his name would mean much today were it not for his writings. Cellini began writing his *Autobiography* in 1558. The unfinished work follows the bragging, arrogant Cellini through adventures in the courts of Rome, Florence, and Paris.

Kunsthistorisches Museum, Vienna

Cellini's saltcellar is the artist's only major surviving work as a goldsmith. It was created for King Francis I of France. A thief stole the saltcellar from a Vienna museum in 2003, but the police recovered it in 2006.

Cellini's story is instructive and entertaining. It takes the reader through such historical events as the siege of Rome in 1527, and introduces people of his time in such a way that they seem to live again. Cellini vividly describes every step of the casting of his masterpiece, *Perseus,* and says that its completion was hailed with joy throughout Italy. This is typical of his exaggerations. But critics have praised *Perseus* for its expressive outlines and striking *patina* (oxidized surface). A picture of the statue appears in the *World Book* article on **Sculpture.**

Cellini's only identifiable work as a goldsmith, except for some coins and medals, is an elaborate silver and gold table ornament known as the *Saltcellar of Francis I.* It was done in the 1540's. The forced poses, elongated proportions, and rich ornamentation show the influence of both the movement known as Mannerism and of Michelangelo. The same ornamentation appears in Cellini's bronze relief of the goddess Diana, called *Nymph of Fontainebleau* (1543-1544). Cellini was born on Nov. 3, 1500, in Florence. He died on Feb. 13, 1571. Roger Ward

Cello, *CHEHL oh,* is a stringed musical instrument of the violin family that is played with a bow. It is also called *violoncello* (pronounced *VY uh luhn CHEHL oh).* The cello is shaped like a violin but is much larger. The cello measures about 4 feet (1.2 meters) long and about 1 ½ feet (0.5 meter) across its widest part. The cello has four strings and produces full, rich sounds. The cello, supported by an end pin, is held between the knees in an upright position.

The cello probably originated in northern Italy in the 1530's. It was first used as a supporting bass instrument. In the late 1600's, composers began writing music for the cello. The cello became prominent in chamber music groups and symphony orchestras in the 1700's and 1800's. Stephen Clapp

See also **Casals, Pablo; Ma, Yo-Yo; Piatigorsky, Gregor; Rostropovich, Mstislav.**

Northwestern University (WORLD BOOK photo by Ted Nielsen)

The cello, or violoncello, became popular as a solo instrument in the late 1600's. It has a rich, deep tone.

Cellophane is a thin, flexible, synthetic material. It is made from cellulose, a substance in the walls of plant cells (see **Cellulose**). Most cellophane is coated with special chemicals to make it airproof and moisture-resistant. These chemicals also make cellophane heat sealable—that is, they enable cellophane to be sealed to itself and to certain other materials through the application of heat and pressure.

Most cellophane is used to package goods that need protection from air and moisture to stay fresh. Such products include baked goods, candy, and cigars. Most cellophane is transparent and colorless and is about 1/1,000 inch (0.03 millimeter) thick. It is flammable.

How cellophane is made. Cellulose manufacturers begin by chemically removing cellulose from wood pulp and mixing it with sodium hydroxide (also called caustic soda, or lye). This mixture is aged and treated with carbon disulfide to create a thick, sticky liquid called *viscose.* After the viscose has been aged and filtered, manufacturing machinery *extrudes* (pushes) it through a long, narrow slit, forming it into a thin liquid sheet. This sheet is immediately treated with sulfuric acid, which hardens it into cellophane. Various chemical processes remove impurities and make the cellophane flexible. The product is then dried and wound onto rolls.

History. A Swiss chemist named Jacques E. Brandenberger discovered cellophane in 1908, when he sprayed viscose on a tablecloth he was trying to make stain-resistant. He found he could peel the coating from the cloth in the form of a thin, transparent sheet. In 1911, Brandenberger designed a machine to produce the material. In 1927, the DuPont Company developed coatings to make cellophane moisture-resistant and heat-sealable. Since the 1960's, polyesters and other film materials made from petroleum have replaced cellophane for most packaging. Marvis E. Hartman

Cellular telephone is a wireless telephone that transmits and receives messages via radio signals. It enables people to communicate over a wide area by using a network of radio antennas and other equipment arranged in small geographical areas called *cells.* Cells vary in size and number, based on the network's extent. A cellular telephone unit is actually a radio *transceiver*—that is, a transmitter and receiver in one. Many such units enable the user to send and receive text messages and pictures in addition to voice messages. Some units enable the user to send and receive video images. Cellular telephones are often called *cell phones* or *mobile phones,* or simply *cells* or *mobiles.*

How cellular telephones work. Radio waves carry a user's message to an antenna in the cell in which the user is operating the telephone. Typically, the antenna is mounted on a steel tower. Cables connect the antenna to a receiver and transmitter at the tower's base. The base transmitter relays the call to a mobile telephone switching office (MTSO). The MTSO transmits the call to a local phone company, which sends it to the receiving phone or to a long-distance company for completion.

As the caller moves, the network automatically passes the call from one cell to the next without interruption. This transfer of a call from cell to cell is called *handoff* or *handover.* The term *roaming* describes the use of a cellular telephone outside one's local calling area. Communications companies whose cellular networks do not cover a large region often share their networks with one another to offer their customers roaming.

WORLD BOOK illustration by Paul Perrault

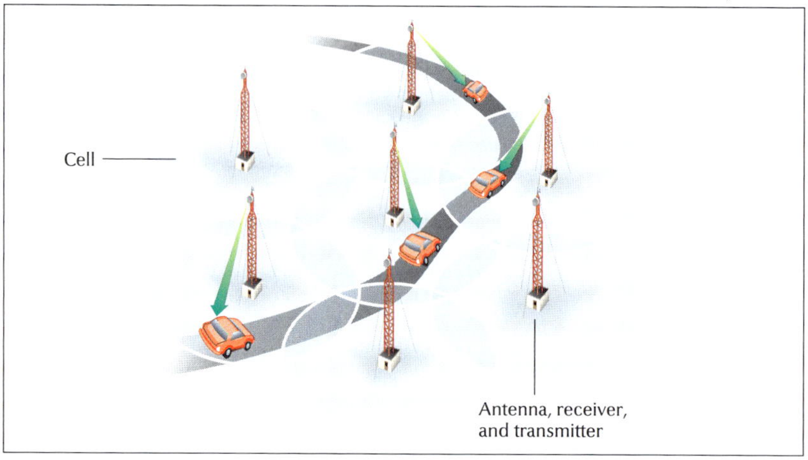

A cellular telephone network is made up of many adjoining geographic areas called *cells.* Each cell has its own antenna connected to a receiver and transmitter. When a person traveling in a car uses a cellular telephone, the network passes the call from one cell to the next cell without interruption. In some U.S. states, it is illegal for a driver of a vehicle to use a cellular telephone not adapted for hands-free operation.

To receive and transmit calls outside the local calling area, a user may need to key a code into the phone. This action automatically notifies the MTSO of the region of cells in which the user can be reached. The MTSO can then deliver a call by directing the transmitters in those cells to signal the desired phone. Often, users can preprogram their roaming preferences into their phones.

Many cellular telephones have *multiple modes* or *multiple bands* that allow the phone to be used on different types of networks or in different parts of the world. A multiple-mode phone can switch back and forth between different technologies used to transmit communication signals. A multiple-band phone can operate within different ranges of radio frequencies. Some cellular phones have a satellite mode, in which messages are sent to and from artificial satellites instead of land-based antennas (see **Communications satellite**).

Features of cellular telephones. Most cellular telephones are portable, battery-powered units small enough to keep in a coat pocket. Many cellular telephones are equipped with other communication or computer features. For example, most phones can store phone numbers, calendar events, or other data. Multipurpose devices called *smartphones* have many of the features of *personal digital assistants* or other handheld computers (see **Handheld computer**). Users may customize such phones by adding a variety of software. Smartphones may include such features as Internet access, digital cameras, digital music players, electronic games, and receivers for Global Positioning System navigation (see **Global Positioning System**).

History. The first commercial cellular system went into operation in 1983 in the United States. Cellular service is now available in much of the world. Many less developed countries have used cellular technology to provide telephone service in remote areas without installing phone lines. David W. Matolak

See also **Communication** (picture: Cellular telephone); **Wireless communication.**

Cellulose, *SEHL yuh lohs,* is a substance that forms a major part of the cell walls of trees, grasses, vegetables, and many other plants. Cellulose is a *carbohydrate*—that is, a substance composed of carbon, hydrogen, and oxygen. All fruits and vegetables contain cellulose. Industries use cellulose in the manufacture of hundreds of products, including paper, textiles, and plastics.

Biological importance. Cellulose fibers strengthen the stems, roots, and leaves of many kinds of plants. Plants make cellulose from glucose, a sugar they first produce from carbon dioxide and water through the process of photosynthesis (see **Photosynthesis**). Cellulose consists of glucose molecules linked in chains called *polymers.* Its chemical structure resembles that of starch, another polymer of glucose. But the glucose molecules of the two polymers are linked differently.

The foods most abundant in cellulose are vegetables that consist of stalks or leaves, such as celery and spinach. The human body cannot digest cellulose. However, cellulose serves as bulk that aids in elimination.

Industrial uses. Cellulose makes up a major part of two important raw materials. Wood, which is used in buildings and in furniture and many other products, is 40 percent cellulose. Cotton, the fiber most widely used in textile manufacturing, contains more than 95 percent cellulose. Paper consists largely of cellulose. The highest quality papers are almost pure cellulose.

Industries use strong acids and alkalis to modify the properties of cellulose for various purposes. For example, textile producers often strengthen cotton fibers by treating them with an alkaline solution, such as sodium hydroxide (also called caustic soda, or lye). This process is called *mercerization.* A solution called *viscose* is made by treating cellulose with sodium hydroxide and carbon disulfide. Manufacturers process viscose to produce cellophane and to produce rayon fibers for use in textiles and tire cord.

Manufacturers produce substances called *cellulose derivatives* by combining cellulose with certain chemicals. The most widely used cellulose derivative is *cellulose acetate,* a plastic made by treating cellulose with acetic anhydride. Products that are made of cellulose acetate include photographic film, magnetic sound-recording tape, electrical insulation, and textile fibers. *Cellulose acetate butyrate,* a tougher and more water-resistant plastic than cellulose acetate, is used in such items as steering wheels and tool handles. Manufacturers cast a plastic called *ethyl cellulose* to produce tough, rigid items, such as luggage and flashlight cases.

Other derivatives include *carboxymethyl cellulose* and *cellulose nitrate.* Carboxymethyl cellulose dissolves in water. It can be used to thicken foods and paints. Cellulose nitrate is used in lacquers and other coatings. It is made by treating cellulose with a mixture of nitric and sulfuric acids. A form of cellulose nitrate called *guncotton* is an explosive used in smokeless gunpowders.

In the late 1940's, synthetic polymers made primarily from petroleum began to replace cellulose in some plastics, fibers, and photographic films. Often, the petroleum-based substances were cheaper and easier to process than cellulose. But some experts believe a rise in oil prices and the ability of cellulose in solid waste to *biodegrade* (break down from the action of bacteria) will lead to more use of cellulose. John Blackwell

See also **Cellophane; Fiber** (Regenerated fibers); **Guncotton; Rayon.**

Cellulose acetate. See **Cellulose; Rayon.**

Celsius, *SEHL see uhs,* **Anders** (1701-1744), a Swedish astronomer, developed the Celsius scale. The scale (sometimes called the centigrade scale) is used to measure temperature in the metric system.

Astronomers in the mid-1700's studied the weather along with stars and planets. In 1742, Celsius developed a new way of marking thermometers. He used the freezing point of water as one end of the scale and the boiling point of water as the other. He divided the range between these points into 100 equal parts or degrees. Celsius's original scale labeled water's boiling point as 0 degrees and its freezing point as 100 degrees. Scientists later reversed the scale. See **Celsius scale.**

In 1736, Celsius joined an expedition to Lapland that helped show that Earth is flattened around the North and South poles. The fame he earned helped him raise money to build an observatory in Uppsala, Sweden. Celsius also first linked *auroras* to disturbances in Earth's *magnetic field.* Auroras are natural displays of light that occur in the sky. Earth's magnetic field is the pattern of magnetic force surrounding the planet.

Anders Celsius was born in Uppsala on Nov. 27, 1701.

Both his father and grandfather were astronomers. He served as a professor of astronomy at the University of Uppsala from 1730 until he died on April 25, 1744.

James S. Sweitzer

Celsius scale, *SEHL see uhs,* is a scale for measuring temperature. It is a part of the metric system of measurement. People in all major countries of the world except the United States use the Celsius scale for everyday temperature measurement. Scientists throughout the world also use this temperature scale.

In the United States, the Fahrenheit scale is generally used for everyday purposes. But the Celsius scale is gradually coming into greater use. Bank thermometers and radio and television weather reports often give temperatures in both Fahrenheit and Celsius degrees.

On the Celsius scale, 0° is the freezing point of water, and 100° is the boiling point. The scale is divided into 100 equal parts between these fixed points. The Celsius scale is sometimes called the *centigrade* scale because this word means *divided into 100 parts.* Other important temperatures on the Celsius scale include 37° (body temperature) and 20° (room temperature). Temperatures below the freezing point of water have a negative sign in front of them.

Sometimes it is necessary to compare a Celsius temperature to a Fahrenheit temperature. To change a Celsius temperature to a Fahrenheit temperature, multiply the Celsius temperature by $\frac{9}{5}$ and then add 32: $°F = \frac{9}{5}(°C) + 32$. To change a Fahrenheit temperature to a Celsius temperature, subtract 32 from the Fahrenheit temperature and then multiply by $\frac{5}{9}$: $°C = \frac{5}{9}(°F - 32)$.

Another way to compare Celsius and Fahrenheit temperatures is to sketch two liquid-in-glass thermometers in vertical side-by-side positions. Label the scale on one C and the scale on the other F. Draw a single horizontal line across the lower parts of the sketches and mark 0 on the Celsius scale and 32 on the Fahrenheit scale. Because 5 Celsius degrees are equal to 9 Fahrenheit degrees, you may mark 41 °F (32 + 9) equal to 5 °C (0 + 5), 50 °F (32 + 18) equal to 10 °C (0 + 10), and so on. Interestingly, as you mark the scale below 0 °C and 32 °F, you will see that -40 °F is equal to -40 °C.

The Celsius scale was originally developed in 1742 by the Swedish astronomer Anders Celsius. It was later changed and improved. The ninth General Conference of Weights and Measures officially named the scale the Celsius scale in 1948. Joseph J. Snoble

See also **Celsius, Anders; Thermometer.**

Celts, *kehlts,* were ancient inhabitants of Europe. The term has also traditionally included the people of Iron Age Great Britain and Ireland. The Celts were a diverse group of peoples connected by a shared language, religion, and material culture. Scholars know of Celtic culture mainly from the writings of the Roman general and statesman Julius Caesar and other ancient authors and through the work of archaeologists.

The earliest evidence of Celtic culture comes from the village of Hallstatt, near Salzburg, Austria. There, archaeologists discovered nearly 2,000 burials dating from about 700 to 500 B.C. The people of Hallstatt were among the first peoples in central Europe to make iron. At its greatest extent, Celtic culture extended from present-day Portugal to the Balkans, and from Austria to the southern coast of France. In continental Europe, Celtic culture spread through the migration of Celtic peoples to new areas. Celtic culture arrived in Great Britain and Ireland sometime after 500 B.C. In these areas, however, the culture spread through contact and trade with the continental Celts rather than through migration.

Celtic peoples were organized into tribes, with some tribes forming loose federations. Celtic society was divided into three social classes. The warrior elite were the nobility. A learned priestly class, called Druids, performed religious rituals and served as oral historians, judges, and advisers to the tribal kings. Commoners, the largest social class, lived on small farms where they grew wheat and barley and kept livestock. Larger settlements, called *oppida* or *hillforts,* sometimes served as tribal capitals. Earthen banks or ditches with *palisades* (wooden walls) for defense enclosed many of these settlements. Commoners gathered at hillforts and oppida to trade and, in times of conflict, to seek protection.

Historians divide Celtic culture into two periods: *Hallstatt* from 800 to 500 B.C. and *La Tène* from after 500 B.C. to about A.D. 100. The Hallstatt period was characterized by hillforts and elaborate burials for the elite. The La Tène period is characterized by coinage and a distinctive style of art called *curvilinear* for the curved lines that make up its designs. By about A.D. 100, the Romans conquered much of Celtic Europe. Celtic culture and languages then declined in many areas outside Great Britain and Ireland.

Musée des Antiquités Nationales, Saint-Germain-en-Laye, France (© Erich Lessing, Art Resource)

A Celtic vase from France shows the distinctive curved line design that originated in the La Tène period about 500 B.C.

Few Celtic languages survive today. A Celtic language, called *Q-Celtic* by scholars, gave rise to modern Irish, Scottish Gaelic, and Manx Gaelic. Modern Breton, Welsh, and Cornish derive from *P-Celtic,* a related language. *Ogham,* a Celtic writing style with distinctive line characters, originated in Ireland, where it was often used on territory markers. Christine Hamlin

See also **Druids; England** (History); **Gaels; Halloween** (Samhain); **Mythology** (Celtic mythology).

Additional resources

Cunliffe, Barry, ed. *The Ancient Celts.* 1997. Reprint. Oxford, 2003.
Haywood, John. *Atlas of the Celtic World.* Thames & Hudson, 2001.

Cement and concrete are among the most important building materials. Cement is a fine, gray powder. It is mixed with water and such materials as sand, gravel, and crushed stone to make concrete. Cement and water form a paste that binds the other materials together as the concrete hardens. People often misuse the words *cement* and *concrete.* A person may speak of "a cement sidewalk." But the sidewalk actually is made of concrete.

Concrete is highly fire-resistant, water-resistant, and comparatively cheap and easy to make. When first mixed, concrete can be molded into almost any shape. It quickly hardens into an extremely strong material that lasts a long time and requires little care.

Nearly all the cement used today is *portland cement,* which is a *hydraulic* cement, or one that hardens under water. This cement was named *portland* because it has the same color as stone quarried on the Isle of Portland, a peninsula on the south coast of England.

Uses of cement and concrete

Nearly all skyscrapers and factories and many homes stand on concrete foundations. These buildings may also have concrete frames, walls, floors, and roofs. Concrete is used to build dams and bridges. Cars and trucks travel on concrete highways, and airplanes land on concrete runways. Concrete tunnels run through mountains and under rivers. Concrete pipe distributes water, carries away sewage, drains farmland, and protects underground telephone and electric-power cables.

Portland cement is used chiefly to make concrete. But it can also be mixed with soil and water to form *soil-cement,* which is used in road paving and dam construction and for lining reservoirs.

Kinds of concrete

There are special ways of strengthening concrete or of making concrete building materials. These include (1) reinforced concrete, (2) prestressed concrete, (3) precast concrete, and (4) concrete masonry. Types of concrete with specialized uses include (1) air-entrained concrete, (2) high-early-strength concrete, (3) lightweight concrete, and (4) polymer concrete.

Reinforced concrete is made by casting concrete around steel rods or bars. The steel strengthens the concrete. Almost all large structures, including skyscrapers and bridges, require this extra-strong concrete.

Prestressed concrete usually is made by casting concrete around steel cables stretched by hydraulic jacks. After the concrete hardens, the jacks are released and the cables compress the concrete. Concrete is strongest when it is compressed. Steel is strong when it is stretched, or in tension. Prestressed concrete combines the two strongest qualities of the two materials. The steel cables can also be bent into an arc, so that they exert a force in any desired direction, such as upward in a bridge. Prestressed concrete beams, roofs, floors, and bridges are often cheaper for some uses than those made of reinforced concrete.

Precast concrete is cast and hardened before being used for construction. Precasting firms make concrete sewer pipes, floor and roof units, wall panels, beams, and girders, and ship them to the building site. Sometimes builders make such pieces at the building site and hoist them into place after they harden. Precasting makes possible the mass production of concrete building materials. Nearly all prestressed concrete is precast.

Concrete masonry includes many shapes and sizes of precast block. It is commonly used to make masonry walls. Some masonry is decorative or resembles brick.

Air-entrained concrete contains microscopic air bubbles. These bubbles are formed by adding soaplike resinous or fatty materials to the cement, or to the concrete when it is mixed (see **Resin**). The bubbles give the water in concrete room to expand as it freezes, and provide resistance to chemicals. For these reasons, air-entrained concrete is a good material for roads and airport runways.

High-early-strength concrete is chiefly used in cold weather. This concrete is made with high-early-strength portland cement and hardens much more quickly than ordinary concrete. It costs more than ordinary concrete. But it is often cheaper to use, because it cuts the amount of time the concrete must be protected in cold weather.

Lightweight concrete weighs less than other kinds of concrete. To make it, builders may use shales, clays, pumice, or other lightweight materials instead of sand, gravel, and rock. Or they may add chemicals that foam to create air spaces in the concrete as it hardens. These spaces are larger than those in air-entrained concrete.

Polymer concrete contains no portland cement. Instead, a *polymer* (synthetic resin) binds the other materials. Polymer concrete is known for its quick curing time, resistance to chemicals, and stability over a wide range of temperatures. It is often used to make precast products, including floor tiles and pipes.

How concrete is made

Materials. Most concrete is a mixture of portland cement, water, and aggregates. *Aggregates* are such materials as sand, gravel, crushed rock, and blast furnace *slag* (waste). The cement and water form a paste that binds the aggregates into a rocklike mass as the paste hardens. Builders generally use both a fine aggregate, such as sand, and a coarse aggregate, such as crushed rock, to make concrete. The aggregates must be free from clay, mud, silt, and other materials that might weaken the concrete. The water used to make concrete should also be free from dirt and other impurities.

Builders may add materials called *admixtures* to concrete to give it special properties. Very fine materials, such as *fly ash,* a product of coal-burning power plants, make fresh concrete more *plastic* (easily shaped). Other admixtures include various fats, sugars, and minerals. These are used to speed up or slow down the hardening of the concrete or to give it color or increased durability and weather resistance.

Mixing. Before concrete is mixed, workers measure the proper amounts of the materials. The strength and durability of concrete depend chiefly on the amount of water used. If too much water is added, the cement paste will be too weak to hold the aggregates together firmly when it hardens. The less water used, within reasonable limits, the stronger the concrete will be.

Concrete can be mixed either by hand or by machine. Machine mixing makes more uniform batches. Proper mixing coats every particle of aggregate and fills all the spaces between them with cement paste. For most home repairs, concrete can be hand mixed.

The methods for mixing concrete by machines vary. The concrete may be mixed by machines at the place where the concrete will be used. *Ready-mix* companies make huge batches of concrete at mixing plants, and haul it to the work site in trucks. Some firms use mixing machines mounted on trucks. These machines mix the concrete as the truck carries it to the building site.

Homeowners can buy prepared mixtures of cement and aggregates for small repair jobs. Only water has to be added to such mixtures.

Placing. Workers place the freshly mixed, wet concrete into forms made of wood, plywood, or steel. The forms hold the concrete in shape until it hardens. The concrete may be dumped directly into the forms, or poured down chutes. Workers use wheelbarrows, two-wheeled carts called *buggies,* small rail cars, trucks, or buckets lifted by cranes. The concrete may also be pumped through steel pipes.

After the concrete is placed, it must be worked into the corners and sides of the forms with wooden spades and *puddling sticks.* The concrete should also be *tamped,* or packed down, to prevent open spaces called *honeycombs.* Sometimes workers stick *vibrators* into the concrete or fasten them to the forms in order to help settle the concrete.

Concrete placed for floors, sidewalks, and driveways should be leveled off with a straight-edged board. Next, it should stand until the film of moisture on its surface has disappeared. Then, the concrete should be smoothed off with a wooden trowel called a *wood float.* The float produces a rough surface that prevents slipping or skidding after the concrete hardens. A smoother surface can be made by using a *steel trowel* after the wood float. Motorized rotary steel floats are often used.

Curing makes concrete harden properly. After the concrete becomes firm enough to resist marring, it should be sprinkled with water, then covered with wet canvas, wet burlap, or wet sand. This cover keeps the concrete from drying too rapidly. A chemical reaction between portland cement and water makes concrete harden. For this reason, the longer concrete remains moist, the stronger it becomes. In hot weather, concrete should be kept moist at least three days. Cold weather slows the rate at which concrete hardens. Hardening concrete must be protected by canvas or straw when the temperature drops near freezing.

Concrete shrinks as it hardens. This results from the loss of moisture as the concrete dries, or from the cooling of the concrete. The chemical reaction of water and portland cement produces heat. When large amounts of concrete are used, as in dams, this heat must be drained away to make the concrete harden properly. This is usually done by running cold water through pipes stuck into the concrete. Cement companies have developed a special portland cement that produces less heat than other cements.

How cement is made

Raw materials. Portland cement contains about 60 percent lime, 25 percent silica, and 5 percent alumina. Iron oxide and gypsum make up the rest of the materials. The gypsum regulates the *setting,* or hardening, time of cement. The lime comes from materials such as limestone, oyster shells, and a type of clay called *marl.* Shale, clay, silica sand, slate, and blast-furnace slag provide the silica and alumina. Iron oxide is supplied by iron ore, pyrite, and other materials.

Most cement plants are located near limestone quarries. They may also be near deposits of clay and other raw materials. Ships, trains, trucks, and conveyer belts haul the limestone and other raw materials to the plants. In the plants, the materials go through a chemical process that consists of three basic steps: (1) crushing and grinding, (2) burning, and (3) finish grinding.

Crushing and grinding. The quarried limestone is dumped into *primary crushers* that can handle pieces as large as an upright piano. This first crushing smashes the rock into pieces about the size of a softball. *Secondary crushers,* or *hammer mills,* then break the rock into pieces about $\frac{3}{4}$ inch (19 millimeters) wide.

Next, the crushed rock and other raw materials are mixed in the right proportions to make portland cement. This mixture is then ground in rotating *ball mills* and *tube mills.* These mills contain thousands of steel balls that grind the mixture into fine particles. The materials can be ground by either a wet or dry method. In the *wet process,* water is added during the grinding until a soupy mixture called a *slurry* forms.

Burning. After the raw materials have been ground, they are fed into a *kiln,* a huge cylindrical furnace made of steel and lined with firebricks. A cement kiln rotates about one turn a minute, and is the largest piece of moving machinery used in any industry. It may be over 25 feet (8 meters) in diameter and 750 feet (229 meters) in length. The kiln is mounted with one end higher than the other. The ground, raw materials are fed into the higher end and slide slowly toward the lower end as the kiln revolves. It takes about four hours for the materials to travel through the kiln. Oil, gas, or powdered coal is burned at the lower end. This produces a flame that heats the materials to 2600 to 3000 °F (1430 to 1600 °C). The heat changes the materials into a substance called *clinker,* in pieces about the size of marbles.

Finish grinding. Large fans cool the clinker after it leaves the kiln. The clinker may be stockpiled for future use, or it may be reground at once in ball or tube mills. A small amount of gypsum is added to the clinker before the regrinding. This final grinding produces powdery portland cement that is finer than flour. The cement is stored in silos until it is shipped.

Shipping. Cement plants ship cement either *in bulk* (unpackaged) or packed in strong paper sacks. Unpackaged cement is shipped by railroad, truck, or barge. Packaged cement is shipped in sacks containing 94 pounds (43 kilograms), or 1 cubic foot (0.03 cubic meter), of cement to the sack.

History

The ancient Romans developed cement and concrete similar to the kinds used today. Their cement had such great durability that some of their buildings, roads, and bridges still exist. To make cement, the Romans mixed *slaked lime* (lime to which water has been added) with a volcanic ash called *pozzuolana.* The ash produced a hydraulic cement that hardened underwater. People lost the art of making cement after the fall of the Roman Empire in the A.D. 400's. In 1756, John Smeaton, a British engineer, again found how to make cement.

Construction of the Erie Canal created the first big demand for cement in the United States. In 1818, Canvass White, an American engineer, discovered rock in Madison County, New York, that made natural hydraulic cement with little processing. Cement made from this rock was used in building the canal.

Joseph Aspdin, a British bricklayer, invented portland cement in 1824 and gave the cement its name. Aspdin made a cement that was superior to natural cement by mixing, grinding, burning, and regrinding amounts of limestone and clay. David O. Saylor probably established the first portland cement plant in the United States at Coplay, Pennsylvania, in 1871.

At first, portland cement manufacturers developed their own formulas. In 1898, manufacturers in the United States used 91 different formulas. In 1917, the National Bureau of Standards (now the National Institute of Standards and Technology) and the American Society for Testing Materials established a standard formula for portland cement produced in the United States. The Portland Cement Association was formed in Chicago in 1916. Its research laboratories perfected air-entrained concrete in the early 1940's.

Joseph Monier, a French gardener, developed reinforced concrete about 1850. In 1927, Eugene Freyssinet, a French engineer, developed prestressed concrete.

The cement and concrete industry

China is by far the world's leading producer of cement. The country produces about a third of the world total. Other important cement producing countries include India, Japan, and the United States. The leading states are California, Pennsylvania, and Texas.

Manufacturers of ready-mixed concrete use a majority of the cement produced in the United States and Canada. The production of ready-mixed concrete ranks as the largest branch of the concrete industry in North America. The second largest branch is the manufacture of precast concrete for construction. Other important concrete products include bricks, blocks, and pipe.

Matthew A. Dettman

Related articles in *World Book* include:

Materials used to make cement and concrete

Alumina	Gravel	Limestone	Silica
Chalk	Gypsum	Sand	Slate
Clay	Lime		

Other related articles

Building construction	Plaster
Dam (Masonry dams)	Road

Cemetery Ridge. See **Civil War, American** (Battle of Gettysburg).

Cenizero. See **Rain tree.**

Cenozoic Era, *SEE nuh ZOH ihk* or *SEHN uh ZOH ihk,* is the most recent era in the geologic time scale of Earth's history. Geologists believe this era began about 65 million years ago. The Cenozoic Era is sometimes called the Age of Mammals. See also **Earth** (The Cenozoic Era; table: Outline of Earth's history); **Mammal** (The Age of Mammals).

Censer, *SEHN suhr,* is a vessel in which incense is burned on charcoal as a sign of honor and prayer during religious ceremonies. The censer is also called a *thurible.* The ancient Jews used censers in their tabernacles and temples. Christians began to use censers in the 300's. Today, censers are used in some services of the Roman Catholic Church, the Anglican Communion, and the Eastern Orthodox Churches.

WORLD BOOK photo by Dan Miller

Censer

Most censers are ornamental. Attached chains are used to swing the vessel back and forth. Holes in the top allow the perfumed smoke to stream out. Richard L. Schebera

Censorship is the control of what people may say or hear, write or read, or see or do. In most cases, this kind of control comes from a government or from various types of private groups. Censorship can affect books, newspapers, magazines, motion pictures, radio and television programs, and speeches. It also may influence music, painting, sculpture, and other arts.

Whenever a government or a private group feels endangered by free expression, it may turn to censorship to protect its basic beliefs. Every society, including democratic ones, has had some kind of censorship when its rulers have felt it would benefit the nation—or themselves. But the strictest control of expression and information occurs in dictatorships and during wartime. The difference between censorship in democracies and in dictatorships is that democracies have ways to limit such action. In the United States, for example, the Bill of Rights and the Supreme Court serve as checks on unlimited censorship.

There are four major types of censorship: (1) moral, (2) military, (3) political, and (4) religious.

Moral censorship is the most common kind of censorship today. Many governments or groups try to preserve their standards of morality by preventing people from learning about or following other standards. Moral censorship may result when some people believe they have the right to force their values on others. It also may result if the majority of the people of a country believe that their government should promote certain moral codes.

Many countries, including the United States, have obscenity laws. But since the 1960's, the definition of obscenity in the United States has narrowed considerably. See **Obscenity and pornography.**

Military censorship. During a war, battle plans, troop movement schedules, weapons data, and other information could help the enemy. The armed forces of every country have *censors* who read the letters written and received by servicemen and servicewomen. The censors snip out or blot out any information that might be valuable to the enemy.

The military also may withhold information from the press for security reasons. In Canada, the United States, and some other countries, the press, radio, and TV voluntarily censor themselves during wartime. Most nations have some military censorship during peacetime as well.

Political censorship is used by governments that fear the free expression of criticism and opposing ideas. It is common in nondemocratic countries, where unapproved forms of expression are forbidden.

Democracies do not officially permit political censorship. But many democratic governments try to discourage the expression of certain radical ideas. In the United States, various laws prohibit speeches or writings that might lead to violence. During wartime, many democratic governments carry on political censorship. They believe that criticism of the government or opposition to the war could aid the enemy.

Religious censorship occurs in some nations where the government is close to one religion or where religious feelings run high. Those in power may censor the ideas and practices of other religions. Throughout much of its history, Spain, almost all of whose people are Roman Catholics, did not allow Protestants or Jews to hold public religious services. The Spanish government dropped this ban in 1967.

Censorship methods. There are two main kinds of censorship methods, *formal* and *informal*. Formal censorship occurs when government officials follow the law to control free expression. Informal censorship takes place if no specific law covers an offense.

Officials may act informally because of pressure from a private group to censor something the group dislikes. Some groups also pressure various companies by threatening not to buy their products. A number of businesses, including the motion-picture and television industries, censor themselves in an effort to avoid public disapproval. But standards have loosened since the 1950's.

Censorship can occur before or after something is released to the public. In checking material before release, officials may approve it, reject it, or approve it with certain changes. Censors may also act against a book, magazine, or motion picture after its release, although they rarely succeed in doing so in the United States. The U.S. Postal Service may refuse to deliver objectionable mail, and the United States Customs Service may prevent the importation of certain materials. Jethro K. Lieberman

Related articles in *World Book* include:

Comstock Law
Freedom
Freedom of religion
Freedom of speech
Freedom of the press
Motion picture (Censorship and self-regulation)

Additional resources

Day, Nancy. *Censorship, or Freedom of Expression?* Lerner, 2000.
Jones, Derek, ed. *Censorship: A World Encyclopedia.* 4 vols. Fitzroy Dearborn, 2001.
Roleff, Tamara L., ed. *Censorship: Opposing Viewpoints.* Greenhaven, 2002.

Census is a survey conducted by a national government to gather information about the society that it governs. Censuses examine such aspects of a nation as population, housing, agriculture, and manufacturing. A population census determines the size of a population and such information as the age, employment, income, race, and sex of people. Other censuses gather such data as the quality of housing or transportation, the level of agricultural or industrial production, or the form of organization of local governments. About 90 percent of the world's nations conduct a population census. Governmental administration of a census helps ensure that the census is accurate and serves the entire society.

In conducting a census, a government first selects topics to be included and prepares questions that are easy to understand and can be answered accurately. Questionnaires are designed to avoid anything that might *bias* (slant) responses. Next, the government publicizes the census to encourage public cooperation. The government prepares maps and lists of all households. Regional and local offices are established, and temporary workers are hired and trained. Then, census takers contact one or more adults in each household by mail, personal visit, or telephone and ask them to provide information about everyone who lives there.

Upon receiving the information, census takers process, tabulate, and organize the results. National, state or provincial, and local governments analyze the data to determine the extent of economic and social problems. The results also help identify resources available to solve such problems. Most national governments make census information available to the public.

The United Nations (UN) encourages all nations to conduct complete periodic censuses. The UN publishes manuals of recommended census procedures and content questions. It also helps arrange technical support. It works to establish standard censuses in order to collect accurate world statistics. The UN publishes summary data for most countries of the world in its annual *Demographic Yearbook.*

United States censuses

The United States collects more varied and complete census information than any other nation. The United States Census Bureau, an agency of the Department of Commerce, conducts all U.S. federal censuses.

The first United States census was a population count that began on Aug. 2, 1790. The results were presented to President George Washington about 13 months later, on Sept. 1, 1791. Fewer than 4 million people lived in the United States at the time, but they were scattered throughout a largely undeveloped country. *Enumerators* (interviewers) on horseback rode through the countryside to count most of the population. The enumerators counted the number of (1) free persons, (2) slaves, and (3) free white males under and over 16 years of age. In addition, they recorded the sex and race of free persons and the names and addresses of heads of families. Many people refused to cooperate because they did not know why the government needed information about them.

Kinds of censuses. The Census Bureau conducts censuses of population, housing, agriculture, govern-

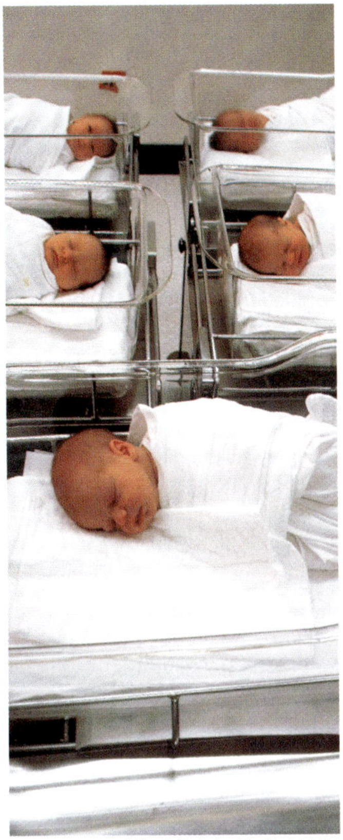

© Randy Duchaine, The Stock Market

© Stephen R. Brown, The Stock Market

© Brent Jones from Marilyn Gartman

© Gabe Palmer, The Stock Market

Population, agriculture, business, and manufacturing are some of the topics covered by censuses. A population census counts the people of a country. Other censuses gather such information as the level of agricultural and industrial production or the value of total retail sales.

ments, and economic activity.

The Census of Population gathers such population data as the total number of people and their age, education, employment, income, marital status, race, and sex. The United States Constitution provides for a count of the population "within three years after the first meeting of the Congress of the United States, and within every subsequent term of ten years...."

The Census of Housing has been conducted along with every Census of Population since 1940. It gathers various information for each housing unit—the year it was built; the number of rooms; the type of plumbing facilities and heating equipment; and the monthly rent or value of the home.

The Census of Agriculture, begun in 1840, is conducted every five years. It gathers such information as the number of farms, the amount of crops harvested during the preceding year, the number of farmworkers, and the amount of irrigated farmland.

The Census of Governments collects information every five years on counties, cities, villages, and other units of local government. This information includes the form of government organization, the number of people employed, and the financial arrangements of the government.

The Census Bureau conducts the economic censuses every five years. These surveys cover construction, manufacturing, mining, retail trade, wholesale trade, service industries, and transportation. They collect data on the output and resources of the various industries. The information includes the form of ownership, the volume of business, the size of the payroll, and the quantity and type of equipment available for use.

Conducting censuses. Planning for a census begins right after the previous census is concluded. The Census Bureau evaluates all phases of the previous census, assesses new technologies, and asks for advice on future needs for information. The bureau must determine census content, prepare field procedures for taking the census, select processing procedures, and set timetables and formats for issuing census information.

Census content. The Federal Reports Act of 1942 established guidelines for census questions. The Census Bureau, with the approval of the Office of Management and Budget and of Congress, determines the content of each census.

Before choosing the topics, the bureau consults many public and private groups that use census information. Agencies at all levels of government—federal, state, and local—have the greatest influence on the choice of topics. Other users of census data, including business executives, educators, and researchers, work with the Census Bureau through advisory committees. These committees meet regularly with bureau specialists to discuss census needs and uses. The bureau also holds public meetings in every region of the country.

After selecting the topics to be covered, the Census Bureau develops questions that will obtain the desired information. The bureau conducts many studies to test whether new questions produce useful responses. For example, every decade it is necessary to redesign questions on race and ethnicity, because of changes in population and in how people refer to their ethnic heritage. For each census, a few questions are added, dropped, or rephrased.

Taking a census of population. Most early censuses were taken by sending enumerators from door to door. But since 1960, the Census Bureau has used a combination of enumerators and *self-enumeration* procedures. In self-enumeration, individuals fill out the census forms for themselves and other members of their household. Since 1970, the forms have been mailed to most households, and individuals have mailed them back. Enumerators are still needed to contact people who do not return their forms on time or who make mistakes in completing the forms.

Enumerators go door to door to find housing units, to leave census forms to be mailed back, and in some cases to collect information. Personal contact is necessary in areas where households do not have standard addresses or do not get mail. Enumerators are also used in areas where language barriers, poverty, distrust of government, or other reasons make the standard mailing procedure ineffective.

The Census Bureau must also contact U.S. citizens who live outside the United States, including military personnel, employees of the federal government, and their families. In addition, the bureau must get information about people in prisons, nursing homes, shelters for the homeless, and other special residences.

Sampling involves surveying a carefully selected portion of the population and then using the findings to estimate information for the total population. Sampling methods can generate a large amount of information while reducing costs and minimizing the burden on the public.

In the 2000 census, for instance, every household was asked to complete a short form that included questions on age, sex, race, Hispanic origin, family relationship, and housing status. In addition, one of every six households was asked to complete a longer form with additional questions. The longer form was a *sample survey* within the census.

Sample surveys are used extensively by the United States and other governments. These surveys provide more detailed information on a wider range of topics than can be included in a census. For a survey of thousands of households, a census bureau can use a highly

How the United States population changed from 1990 to 2000

This map shows how the population of the United States changed from 1990 to 2000. The population of the nation increased by 13.2 percent. The 10-year period was the first since 1900 in which the population of every state increased. The District of Columbia, however, decreased in population.

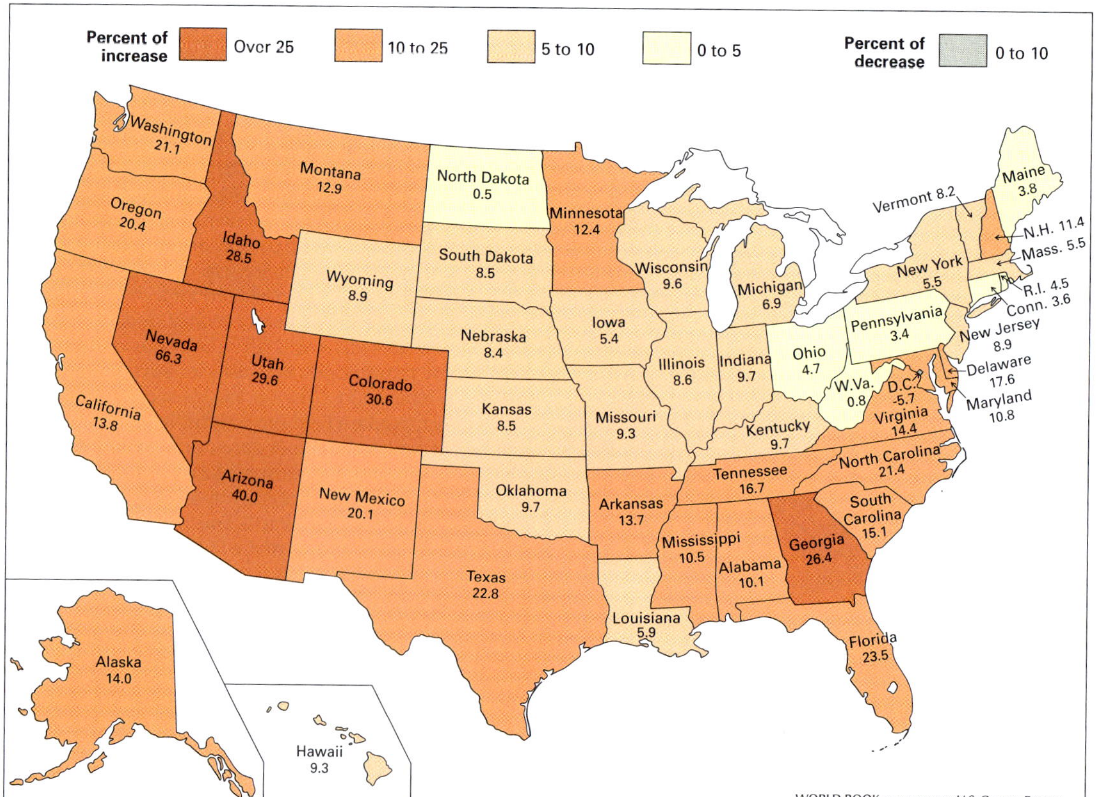

WORLD BOOK map; source: U.S. Census Bureau.

trained staff and maintain tight administrative oversight over all phases of data collection and processing. Using scientific methods for designing a sample and projecting results to the total population, the staff can keep sampling errors small.

Processing the results. The Census Bureau processes all census information, tabulating statistics and organizing them into usable form. The bureau once processed all data by hand. Following the invention of card-sorting equipment around 1890, machines processed increasingly large portions of census information. By 1960, computers processed most of the data gathered by the Census Bureau.

At processing centers, cameralike machines called *scanners* translate the information on completed census forms into numerical form for processing by Census Bureau computers. A computer technique called *optical mark recognition* captures information that is provided by putting an X or a check mark in a box. The computer system also evaluates areas of the census form where handwritten replies are expected. The system uses a technique called *optical character recognition* to "read" the letters. The system gives each letter a rating indicating how sure it is that it recognizes the letter. Words that the system recognizes with a high degree of confidence go directly into the database of census information. Words recognized with less confidence go to a human operator, who reads what is written and keys in the information.

Publishing census information. The government printed the 1790 census results in a single 56-page volume. The amount of published census information increased steadily for nearly two centuries. Basic information for counties, states, and other locales is printed as bulletins or volumes. Tables of census information also appear on the bureau's Internet Web site, with a range of additional data that cannot fit in printed tables. In printed tables, census officials choose the age groups, racial categories, and income ranges used. On the Web site, users can choose their own combinations of subjects and geographical areas. Some of this information is also issued on digitally coded discs called CD-ROM's (*C*ompact *D*isc *R*ead-*O*nly *M*emory) for use on computers.

The bureau follows special procedures to make sure personal records stay confidential. Concern that census taking might invade privacy led the U.S. Congress to guarantee the confidentiality of personal information. The bureau withholds personal identification data, such as names and addresses, when it feeds information into the computers. By law, only bureau employees may examine census records. The bureau cannot share census information on individuals with other government agencies. For instance, census responses may not be used by the Internal Revenue Service for determining taxes or by immigration officials to determine legal status.

Seventy-two years after a census is taken, the names and other confidential facts it includes are made available to the public. *Genealogists* (people who study family trees) and others interested in family and local history find this information helpful.

Uses of census information. Census results are essential to federal, state, and local governments. Census information helps government agencies administer programs, distribute revenues, study social and economic problems, evaluate policies, and plan activities. The statistics provided by a population census affect the assignment of funds for economic development, housing, education, medical care, and social security. Population size determines the number of representatives each state may have in the U.S. House of Representatives. Membership in state legislatures is also determined on the basis of population. Economic censuses tell much about the nation's changing economic condition. The Census of Agriculture provides a picture of the nation's farmers, agricultural production, and resources.

Business leaders study census figures in making such decisions as where to locate new facilities, where to direct their advertising, and how to plan production. The construction industry uses census data to decide where to build new housing. Utility companies determine service requirements on the basis of census data. Nongovernment organizations and community groups use census information to identify problems, track progress, and evaluate programs.

Census statistics also help social scientists analyze economic and social problems and plan solutions. These experts study census statistics on such subjects as marriage and divorce, population movement, geographic locations of older people, and the relationship of education to income and employment.

Controversy over census results. Because census results are used to draw voting districts and to determine the distribution of government aid, many groups are concerned about the accuracy of census figures. Officials of large cities and leaders of minority groups have gone to court, charging that the Census Bureau violated fairness by failing to count many minority residents.

The population censuses have always failed to count some people, especially among the poor and members of minority groups. People with little education or whose native language is not English may have difficulty completing self-enumeration forms. In addition, some people refuse to give the government information about themselves. But over the years, census-taking procedures have been improved to reduce such undercounting.

In 1996, the Census Bureau announced that for the 2000 census, it would use statistical methods to adjust the figures that the bureau obtains by counting. In 1999, however, the Supreme Court of the United States ruled that federal law prohibits the use of statistical methods to determine the number of seats each state should have in the U.S. House of Representatives.

Censuses around the world

Early censuses. In ancient Rome, census takers prepared lists of people and property, chiefly for taxation and the enforcement of military service requirements. The word *census* comes from a Latin word that means *assess* or *estimate.* In 1086, 20 years after William the Conqueror defeated England, his officials made a count of the country's land, people, and property. They listed this information in the Domesday Book (see **Domesday Book**).

During the 1400's and 1500's, various European cities began to count their populations. The first such count took place in Nuremberg, Germany, in 1449. In 1666, a French official named Jean Baptiste Talon completed a census of the people of Canada, then called New France. In 1749, the Swedish government conducted the first national census. It based the census on church records of births, deaths, and migration.

Modern censuses. Countries with long histories of periodic censuses include the United Kingdom (beginning in 1801), France (1836), Belgium (1846), Italy (1861), Germany (1871), Russia (1897), and Japan (1920). In Canada, the Census Division of Statistics Canada conducts censuses of agriculture, housing, and population every five years. China, the world's most populated country, conducts censuses every 10 years.

Nations conducting censuses encounter a great number of technical and practical problems. In Brazil, for example, census takers faced a variety of challenges in different parts of the country. In the Amazon region, census officials had to fly over the jungle in helicopters to search for houses. In some cities, census workers feared gangs and violence. Brazil, like much of the world, has undergone rapid urbanization. This means that the majority of people no longer live in traditional village and household settings. Millions live in *favelas* (shantytowns or slums), where it is hard to locate each residence and determine who lives there.

Turkey's 2000 census was conducted in an unusual single-day effort, in which people were required to stay home while census takers went door to door. The preliminary count from the census was more than expected. Some officials suspected that the results were biased because local governments inflated their counts to gain more aid from the national government.

It is difficult to design and carry out census procedures that avoid undercounting and double counting. Nearly all countries devote a great deal of effort to overcoming these and other problems because they recognize the importance of accurate and up-to-date information. Karl Taeuber

See also **Census Bureau, United States; Population.**

Census Bureau, United States, is an agency of the U.S. Department of Commerce best known for its publication of population and housing statistics. It also conducts censuses of agriculture, business, governments, manufacturers, mineral industries, and transportation. In addition, the agency compiles data on other nations and on U.S. foreign trade. Its publications include the annual *Statistical Abstract of the United States.* The bureau was set up in 1902 as part of the Department of the Interior. It became part of the Department of Commerce and Labor in 1903 and of the Department of Commerce in 1913.

Critically reviewed by the United States Census Bureau

See also **Census.**

Cent is a small United States coin worth one-hundredth of a dollar. Coins of this name were first made in the United States in the 1780's. Similarly named coins were later used in Canada and other countries that based their system of money on the U.S. system.

The name *cent* was first suggested in the 1780's by the American statesman Gouverneur Morris while he was serving as assistant superintendent of finance of the United States. Morris probably adapted the term from a Latin word meaning *a hundred.* People often refer to the cent as a *penny.*

After the American Colonies declared their independence from the United Kingdom in 1776, some of them began to make their own coins. The first cents were minted in 1785 by Connecticut and Vermont. Cents made in Massachusetts beginning in 1787 were the first coins to include the word *cent* as part of their design.

WORLD BOOK photos by James Simek

The U.S. chain, or link, cent, *shown here,* was the first cent issued by the United States Mint. It appeared in 1793.

WORLD BOOK photos by James Simek

The Indian head cent was minted from 1859 to 1909. It had an Indian head on the front and a wreath on the back.

In 1787, the U.S. government hired private companies to produce a limited number of cents. Some experts believe that the design of these copper coins was suggested by the American statesman Benjamin Franklin. The coins were called *Fugio cents* or *Franklin cents.*

In 1792, the United States government set up its own mint to make coins to replace those of the separate states. The mint issued its first cents, which were made of copper, in 1793. Since then, cents have been minted every year except 1815, when the government ran out of copper. The government also issued half cents from 1793 to 1857, two-cent pieces from 1864 to 1873, and three-cent pieces from 1851 to 1889.

The U.S. cent has changed in appearance and composition over the years. Until 1857, it was about as large as a quarter and was made entirely of copper. In that year, the U.S. government introduced cents that were made of a copper alloy and were approximately the size of those used today. Today, cents are made of copper-coated zinc. R. G. Doty

See also **Money** (United States currency today; picture).

Centaur, *SEHN tawr,* was a creature in Greek mythology. In art, the centaur was portrayed with the upper body of a man and the lower body of a horse. Centaurs lived in Thessaly in northern Greece. Most of them were known for their violent, uncivilized behavior. At the wedding feast of the king of the Lapiths, the centaurs became drunk and tried to kidnap the Lapith women. In the following battle, the Lapiths defeated the centaurs.

In several myths, the centaurs fought the Greek hero

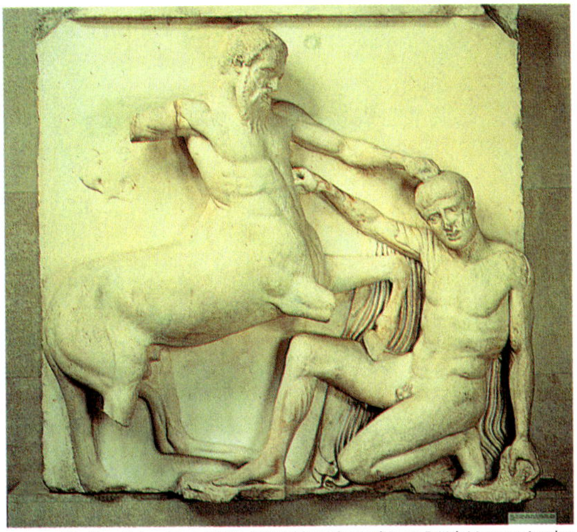

Marble relief sculpture (447 to 432 B.C.) from the Parthenon; British Museum, London (Bridgeman Art Library/Art Resource)

A centaur fights with a guest at the wedding feast of the king of the Lapiths, shown here. According to a Greek myth, a battle began after drunken centaurs tried to kidnap the Lapith women.

Hercules. The centaur Nessus tried to rape Deianira, Hercules's wife. Hercules shot him with a poisoned arrow. See **Hercules** (The death of Hercules).

The most famous centaur was Chiron. Unlike most other centaurs, he was wise and just and famous for his skill in medicine. Chiron taught Achilles, Jason, and other Greek heroes. He was immortal but was accidentally wounded by Hercules. The pain was so great that Chiron begged to become mortal. According to some accounts, the Titan Prometheus agreed to take on Chiron's immortality so the centaur could die. F. Carter Philips

See also **Mythology** (picture: The centaurs).

Center for Science in the Public Interest is an independent, nonprofit organization founded in 1971. The group, often referred to as the CSPI, focuses on nutrition, food safety, alcohol abuse, and scientific honesty. Much of its work educates the public about the health dangers of fats, salt, and other substances in foods. The CSPI gained fame for calling attention to the high fat content of movie theater popcorn. Another well-known effort pointed out the nutritional shortcomings of meals from fast-food and ethnic restaurants. Some critics question whether certain CSPI targets—such as movie popcorn—really pose serious threats to public health.

The group also works to pass laws that support its positions. For example, the CSPI helped pass the Nutrition Labeling and Education Act of 1990. This law requires that all packaged and processed food sold in the United States carry labels with nutritional information. The CSPI also joined a successful campaign to require warning labels on alcoholic beverages. The CSPI's headquarters are in Washington, D.C. Johanna T. Dwyer

Center of gravity. See **Gravity, Center of.**

Centers for Disease Control and Prevention, often referred to as the CDC, is an agency of the Public Health Service and part of the United States Department of Health and Human Services. It works to protect public health by administering national programs for the prevention and control of disease and disability.

The agency provides health information and statistics and conducts research to track down the sources of epidemics. The CDC works with state and local agencies and private organizations to develop immunization services and other programs to eliminate or prevent causes of disease. The CDC also has established programs to ensure a rapid response by federal, state, and local agencies to attacks that involve biological warfare or biological terrorism.

The National Institute for Occupational Safety and Health, a unit of the CDC, develops standards for safe and healthful working conditions. The CDC cooperates with foreign governments and international agencies in a worldwide effort to prevent disease and improve health. The CDC was established in 1946. Its headquarters and many of its laboratories are in Atlanta, Georgia.

Critically reviewed by the Centers for Disease Control and Prevention

Centigrade scale. See **Celsius scale.**

Centimeter, *SEHN tuh MEE tuhr,* also spelled *centimetre,* is a measure of length in the metric system of measurement. A centimeter is $\frac{1}{100}$ meter. There are exactly 2.54 centimeters in 1 inch. To convert centimeters to inches, divide by 2.54, which is the precise conversion factor; or multiply by 0.394, a rounded-off conversion factor. The symbol for the centimeter is *cm.* See **Metric system.**

Richard S. Davis

Centipede, *SEHN tuh peed,* is any of a group of animals that resemble caterpillars. The narrow bodies of centipedes are divided into many *segments* (sections) that lie behind each other. Each section has two legs. Some centipedes have only 15 pairs of legs, while others have more than 180 pairs.

Animals Animals

A centipede has a body divided into many segments, each one with a pair of legs. Centipedes may possess 360 or more legs.

A centipede's head includes two *antennae* (jointed feelers) and a pair of jaws. The first pair of legs behind the head are modified into fangs. Centipedes use these fangs for defense or capturing prey, but not for walking. The fangs are called *poison claws* because a gland in the head fills them with poison. Centipedes hunt at night, usually for mollusks, worms, and insects. The bite of some centipedes can be dangerous to human beings.

There are thousands of kinds of centipedes. The *giant desert centipede* of southern North America can grow to about 8 inches (20 centimeters) long. It may kill and eat such animals as mice or small lizards. Its bite is painful to people, but usually not fatal. Jonathan A. Coddington

Scientific classification. Centipedes make up the class Chilopoda. The giant desert centipede is *Scolopendra heros.*

Central African Republic

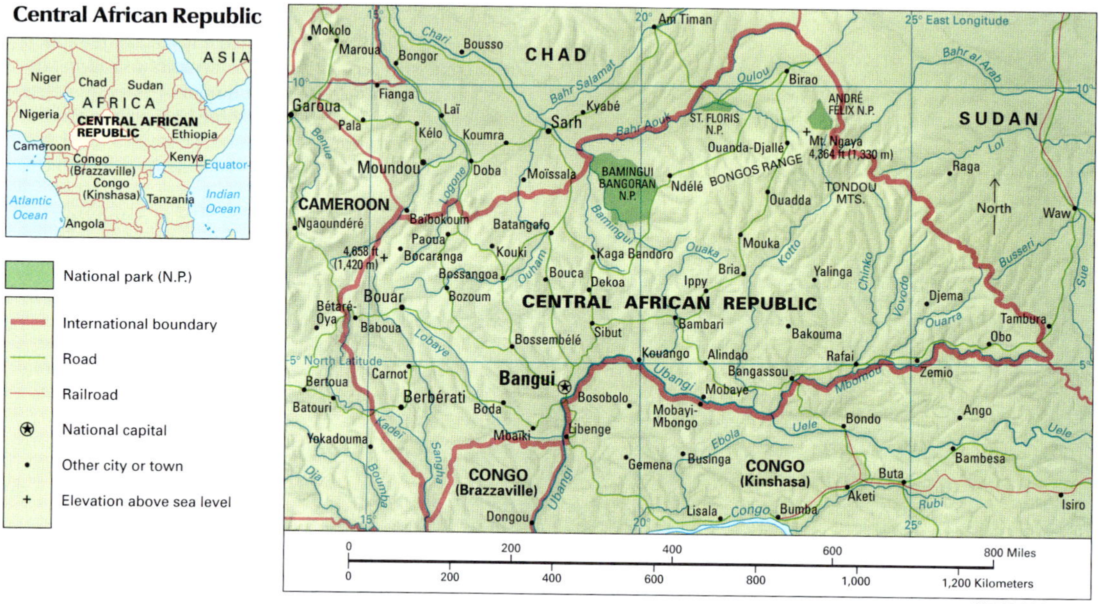

WORLD BOOK maps

Central African Republic is a thinly populated country in the center of Africa. Most of the Central African Republic is a vast, rolling plateau broken by deep river valleys. Grass and scattered trees cover most of the country. Rain forests grow in the southwest, and the extreme northeast is arid. Antelope, buffaloes, elephants, gorillas, lions, rhinoceroses, and other animals live in the Central African Republic.

The Central African Republic is one of the least developed countries in Africa. Most of the people are farmers, and the country has little manufacturing. The country was formerly a territory in French Equatorial Africa called Ubangi-Shari. It became independent in 1960. Bangui, a river port, is the capital and largest city of the Central African Republic.

Government. In 2003, General François Bozize seized control of the Central African Republic's government and declared himself president. He suspended the country's Constitution and dissolved the National Assembly, the country's parliament. In 2004, voters approved a new constitution. Elections for a new president and National Assembly were held in 2005, with Bozize winning the presidential race. Under the Constitution, the people elect the president and the 105 Assembly members to five-year terms.

People. Rural Central Africans hunt, fish, and raise food crops to feed their families. They also raise cattle, goats, pigs, sheep, and poultry.

The people of the Central African Republic belong to many ethnic groups and speak many languages, of which the most common is Sango. About 50 percent of the people are Christians, and about 15 percent are Muslims. The rest of the people practice local African religions. Most of the older people of the Central African Republic cannot read or write. For the country's literacy rate, see **Literacy** (table: Literacy rates). About 60 percent of the children receive an elementary school education. The country also has secondary schools and a university.

Land. The plateau that makes up most of the Central African Republic has an average altitude of about 2,000 feet (600 meters) above sea level. Areas in the northeast and on the country's western border with Cameroon rise more than 4,500 feet (1,370 meters) above sea level.

Many rivers flow through the country. In the north, most are tributaries of the Chari River, which flows north to Lake Chad (see **Lake Chad**). A divide separates these rivers from those that flow south from the central and southern parts of the country to the Congo River Basin. Many of these rivers are tributaries of the Ubangi River, which joins the Congo River. The Ubangi and one of its tributaries, the Mbomou River, form most of the country's southern boundary with Congo (Kinshasa).

The country has a fairly comfortable climate, mainly because of its altitude. The average temperature is 80 °F (27 °C). Each year, the country receives about 31 ½ inches (80 centimeters) of rainfall in the north and about 63 inches (160 centimeters) in the south. The rainy season

Facts in brief

Capital: Bangui.
Official language: French.
Official name: République Centrafricaine (Central African Republic).
Area: 240,535 mi² (622,984 km²).
Population: *Estimated 2006 population*—4,021,000; density, 17 per mi² (6 per km²); distribution, 61 percent rural, 39 percent urban. *1988 census*—2,463,616.
Chief products: *Agriculture*—bananas, coffee, cotton, livestock, palm kernels, peanuts, rubber, sesame, yams. *Forestry*—timber. *Mining*—diamonds, gold.
Flag: Horizontal blue, white, green, and yellow stripes are divided at the center by a red vertical stripe. A yellow star represents the guiding light of the future. Red, white, and blue recall the French flag. Green, yellow, and red are for the people and their unity. See **Flag** (picture: Flags of Africa).
Money: *Basic unit*—CFA franc. CFA stands for Coopération Financière en Afrique Centrale (Financial Cooperation in Central Africa).

extends from June through October in most parts of the Central African Republic. In the southwest, rain may fall throughout the year.

Economy. The Central African Republic is a landlocked country with no railroads and many roads that are impassable during the rainy season. A few plantations raise coffee, cotton, and rubber for export. Diamond mining is the only important mining industry. A few farmers raise livestock in regions where there are no tsetse flies. These insects spread African sleeping sickness (see **Sleeping sickness; Tsetse fly**). There are a few manufacturing plants in the country.

Rivers form the most important transportation routes. Boats can navigate the Ubangi River throughout the year from Bangui to Brazzaville, in Congo (Brazzaville). From Brazzaville, exports are carried by railroad to the port of Pointe Noire. Bangui has an international airport. Bambari, Bouar, and several other towns also have airports.

History. Before the arrival of Europeans in the 1800's, most of the people of what is now the Central African Republic lived in local societies. Slave raids in the 1800's brought turmoil to the region. In 1889, France established an outpost at Bangui. The French created the territory of Ubangi-Shari in 1894. In 1910, they linked it with what are now the countries of Chad, Congo (Brazzaville), and Gabon to form French Equatorial Africa.

The French established a local parliament in Ubangi-Shari in 1946. Elected members represented the country in the French parliament. In 1958, the country gained internal self-government as the Central African Republic. It joined the French Community, an organization that linked France and its overseas territories. The country became fully independent on Aug. 13, 1960.

The first prime minister and leading political figure, Barthélemy Boganda, was killed in an air accident in 1959. His nephew David Dacko succeeded him and became the country's first president in 1960.

The country became a one-party state in 1962 and, in 1964, Dacko was elected to a seven-year term as president. But in 1966, army officers overthrew him. Jean-Bédel Bokassa, head of the army, became president. In 1972, Bokassa was named president for life. In 1976, he declared himself emperor and changed the country's name to the Central African Empire. In 1979, supporters of Dacko overthrew Bokassa, and Dacko again became president. Bokassa went into exile in France. The country's name was changed back to Central African Republic. In March 1981, the country became a multiparty state again, and Dacko was elected president.

In September 1981, army officers overthrew Dacko once more and took control of the government. General André Kolingba was declared president. The new military government banned all political parties. In 1992, it restored a multiparty political system. Multiparty elections were held in 1993 for president and the National Assembly. Ange-Félix Patassé was elected president.

Bokassa had returned to the Central African Republic in 1986. In 1987, a court convicted him of embezzlement and murder, and he was imprisoned. In 1993, he was released from prison.

In the mid-1990's, soldiers staged several revolts against the Patassé government. Hundreds of people were killed and thousands of people were forced from their homes during the fighting. A cease-fire agreement ended the hostilities in mid-1997. Patassé was reelected president in 1999. Rebel uprisings again took place in May 2001 and October 2002. Government forces, aided by Libyan troops, put a stop to the fighting both times.

In March 2003, rebels led by General François Bozize seized control of the government. Bozize suspended the country's Constitution, dissolved the parliament, and declared himself president. In 2004, voters approved a new constitution. In 2005, presidential and parliamentary elections were held under the new Constitution, and Bozize won the presidential race. Dennis D. Cordell

See also **Bangui; Ubangi River**.

Shostal

Bangui, capital city of the Central African Republic, nestles at the foot of a hill on the banks of the Ubangi River. It is the country's largest city and its leading shipping and commercial center.

Central America is the narrow bridge of land at the southern end of North America. It borders Mexico on the north and Colombia on the south. The Pacific Ocean lies to the west, and the Caribbean Sea—an arm of the Atlantic Ocean—lies to the east. Central America consists of seven countries: Belize, Costa Rica, El Salvador, Guatemala, Honduras, Nicaragua, and Panama. The region covers about 201,000 square miles (521,000 square kilometers). Central America has a total population of about 41 million.

On both coasts of Central America, there are lowlands. Inland, rugged mountains crisscross the region. They make transportation and economic development difficult. Many of the mountains are active volcanoes. Severe earthquakes and volcanic eruptions sometimes strike Central America, causing much damage.

Central America has a diverse population. The people of Guatemala are primarily of Indian origin. Most of the people of Honduras and El Salvador are *mestizo* (mixed Indian and European ancestry). Large numbers of blacks live in Belize, Nicaragua, and Panama. Costa Ricans are mainly of European descent.

Spanish is the official language of all the Central American countries except Belize, where the official language is English. Many Indians in Guatemala speak their own tribal languages.

Most people of Central America live in the highlands of mountainous regions, where they earn their living on tiny farms. But Central America's main sources of income traditionally have been large plantations, and forests and mines. Plantations in the highlands produce about 10 percent of the world's coffee. Those in the lowlands produce about 10 percent of the world's bananas.

A small percentage of Central America's people have great wealth, and the region has a growing middle class. However, large numbers of the people live in poverty. A high population growth rate contributes to unemployment, especially among young people.

The constitution of every Central American country provides for the democratic election of representatives.

In the past, however, many governments disregarded their constitutions. Some Central American countries were ruled by military dictators. In the middle and late 1900's, economic problems and civil wars caused widespread suffering in many parts of Central America. Today the civil wars have ended, but the countries of Central America still face widespread poverty and other serious problems.

This article traces the history of Central America. For additional information on the region, see the articles on **Latin America** and **North America**, and the articles on each Central American country.

Early history

Thousands of years ago, the ancestors of today's Central American Indians migrated to Central America from Asia. About 400 B.C., the Maya Indians emerged as the dominant culture of Central America. Their culture especially flourished from about A.D. 250 to 900. The Maya were accomplished engineers and architects, building many magnificent cities. The ruins of hundreds of Maya palaces, pyramids, and temples still stand. The Maya also constructed a vast system of canals that drained swampy fields where they grew corn, beans, and squash. The Maya were skilled astronomers and mathematicians. They developed a solar calendar and a system of hieroglyphic writing. About A.D. 900, the Maya mysteriously abandoned their cities. Today their descendants live in the mountains of Mexico as well as in Central America. Many of these people still wear traditional costumes and speak Maya languages.

The colonial period

In 1501, Rodrigo de Bastidas and Juan de la Cosa of Spain became the first Europeans to explore the Central American coast. In 1502, the Italian explorer Christopher Columbus sailed the Caribbean coast from Honduras to Panama, and claimed the land for Spain, the country sponsoring his voyage. For the next 13 years, Spanish *conquistadors* (conquerors) invaded Central America, fighting the Indians throughout the region. The Spanish completed their conquest in 1525. By then, many Indians had been killed or sent as slaves to plantations in the West Indies.

In 1570, the Spanish established an administrative center, called an *audiencia,* in Guatemala. The Audiencia of Guatemala ruled over all of Central America except Panama. It was a subdivision of the Viceroyalty of New Spain, which governed most of the Spanish colonies in North America from its headquarters in Mexico City.

Spain paid more attention to Mexico and Peru, which had treasures of gold and silver, than it paid to Central America, which had far less mineral wealth. Administrative matters were often handled locally in Central America. Gradually, missionaries established an educational system in Central America and converted most of the Indians to the Roman Catholic religion. Colonists developed a plantation system of agriculture.

Panama owed its early development to its strategic position and to the fact that its land was a narrow isthmus. The Spaniards built a stone road across the isthmus, near the site of the present Panama Canal. Under Spain, Panama became an important shipping route for provisions for colonies on the west coast of South America and for gold and other treasures bound for Spain. Panama also became a center for the distribution of black African slaves in the New World. However, Spain let Panama govern itself in most matters.

Independence

In 1808, Napoleon I of France invaded Spain and forced the Spanish king into exile. As a result, Spain's control over its colonies weakened. In Central America, conservatives remained loyal to Spain. However, liberals resented the taxes and trade restrictions that Spain had imposed. They saw in Spain's conflict with France an opportunity to break away from the mother country. On Sept. 15, 1821, the Audiencia of Guatemala declared its independence, removing from Spanish control all of Central America except what is now Panama. That same year, Panama broke away from Spanish rule and became a province of the newly independent nation of Colombia. The independence movement succeeded throughout Central America with little bloodshed.

What is now Belize had belonged to the Audiencia of Guatemala. But the Spaniards did not establish settlements there and did little to exercise their rule over the area. In 1638, British sailors, who had been shipwrecked off the coast of Belize, established the first known European settlement in the area. The British built other settlements in the area during the next 150 years. In the mid-1800's, they took formal possession of Belize. Britain made it a colony called British Honduras. Belize did not become an independent country until 1981.

During the first years after independence, Central Americans generally favored union with newly independent Mexico because they felt loyalty toward the former seat of the viceroyalty in Mexico City. From January 1822 to March 1823, Costa Rica, El Salvador, Guatemala, Honduras, and Nicaragua were legally part of Mexico. In 1823, these states separated from Mexico and formed a united federation among themselves. They called the federation the United Provinces of Central America. There were disagreements between those who favored states' rights and those who wanted a strong central government. The constitution, which provided for strong states' rights, was completed in November 1824. The federation freed the slaves and ended the special privileges of the powerful landowners and the Roman Catholic Church. The federation began to collapse under various pressures, including efforts by rich landowners and the priests to regain their former privileges. Rivalries also developed between local governments and the federal government. In the late 1830's, the federation broke up and the individual states became independent republics.

In the early 1900's, the United States wanted to build a canal across Panama. With U.S. support, Panama separated itself from Colombia in 1903 and formed an independent nation. Panama granted the United States a strip of land 10 miles (16 kilometers) wide upon which to build the canal. The Panama Canal was completed in 1914. The land returned to Panama's control in 1979, and Panama took over the canal in 1999.

Attempts at unification

Since the early 1800's, various combinations of Central American countries have attempted at least 25 times to achieve political unification. All these unions were short-lived, most lasting only a few months and none more than a few years. In 1907, Costa Rica, El Salvador, Guatemala, Honduras, and Nicaragua set up the Central American Court of Justice. This court handled cases between the nations. It was dissolved in 1918, after Nicaragua had ignored its findings in a dispute over canal-building rights.

Developments since the mid-1900's

All of the Central American countries experienced rapid economic changes during the 1900's, and particularly after World War II ended in 1945. The Great Depression of the 1930's caused tremendous economic hardship and accelerated the growth of the labor movement—and labor unrest—in the region. The powerful landowners saw the labor movement as a threat. They supported civilian dictators who used the military to repress efforts to organize workers. For example, following an uprising by poor mestizos and Indians in El Salvador in 1932, the government killed about 10,000 people.

After World War II, new commercial activities led to increased economic prosperity throughout the region. Cotton plantations began to appear on the Pacific coast, and cattle ranching became increasingly popular due to growing markets for beef abroad. These various economic changes were accompanied by an increase of popular opposition against the wealthy landowners and the Roman Catholic Church.

During the 1940's and 1950's, military dictators took control of a number of Central American countries. The 1940's and early 1950's marked the beginning of the Cold War, an intense rivalry between Communist and non-Communist nations. The United States government opposed the spread of Communist influences in Central America and tended to support the conservative military governments there. Civilian politicians who sought reforms often faced repression and accusations of being Communists. In Guatemala, for example, the U.S. Central Intelligence Agency (CIA) cooperated with local military commanders to overthrow the freely elected civilian government of President Jacobo Arbenz Guzmán in 1954. The U.S. government had feared Communist influences in the Arbenz administration.

The countries of Central America continued to experience economic growth during the 1960's and 1970's. In the 1970's, however, several factors combined to end this growth. The countries of Central America had to pay much higher prices for imported oil and agricultural chemicals, while the prices they received for exports dropped. They had also borrowed billions of dollars at high interest rates to finance their development and began to experience problems in paying back their loans. In addition, a population explosion led to widespread unemployment in the region.

Civil wars broke out in El Salvador, Guatemala, and Nicaragua in the late 1970's. The civil wars began to decrease in intensity during the late 1980's, and the wars in Nicaragua and El Salvador ended in the early 1990's. Peace accords were signed between government and guerrilla forces in Guatemala in 1996.

Although democratically elected civilian governments hold power throughout Central America today, many problems remain. Poverty and unemployment are widespread, economies are weak, and the environment is being seriously damaged by various agricultural and industrial activities.

In 2004, Costa Rica, the Dominican Republic, El Salvador, Guatemala, Honduras, Nicaragua, and the United States signed the Central American-Dominican Republic Free Trade Agreement (CAFTA-DR). This pact was designed to reduce trade barriers among the seven countries. Each country's legislature had to ratify the treaty and adjust its nation's existing trade regulations before the country could participate in CAFTA-DR. In 2006, the treaty went into effect in all but Costa Rica and the Dominican Republic. Steve C. Ropp

Related articles in *World Book* include:

Countries

Belize
Costa Rica
El Salvador
Guatemala
Honduras
Nicaragua
Panama

Other related articles

Flag (picture: Historical flags of the world)
Hispanic Americans (Recent Hispanic immigrants)
Latin America
Maya
North America
Organization of American States
Panama Canal
Panama Canal Zone

Central Intelligence Agency (CIA) is a major United States government agency that gathers information about foreign governments and certain nongovernmental groups, including those that engage in terrorism or organized crime. The information collected by the CIA is political, economic, and military in nature, and much of it is secret. The CIA analyzes the information, which is called *intelligence,* for the president, Congress, and other federal agencies. The CIA also engages in *counterintelligence,* which consists of attempts to identify, neutralize, and manipulate the intelligence activities of other countries. Another important function of the agency is *covert action*—that is, secret efforts to influence events abroad.

Functions. The CIA collects intelligence about the intentions and capabilities of countries that threaten the security of the United States or its citizens. Much of the information is *classified* (secret). Sources include reports from spies, recordings from secret listening devices, and pictures taken from spy satellites in space. News organizations may report what foreign officials say at press conferences, but the CIA also tries to determine what the officials say in private meetings.

CIA analysts try to make world events understandable for United States leaders. They analyze information gathered by the CIA and other United States government agencies—including the Departments of Defense, State, and the Treasury—to tell policymakers who is doing what, when they are doing it, and why. Analysts also identify opportunities for the United States to influence world events.

Counterintelligence protects U.S. secrets from foreign spies. Such secrets include information about U.S. armed forces and military plans. CIA counterintelligence units also try to learn whether a foreign government is giving American spies *disinformation* (false information) intended to deceive the U.S. government.

The CIA's covert actions include propaganda, unofficial military operations, and secret aid to foreign political and military groups that support U.S. interests. During the Cold War, the CIA used propaganda and secret transfers of money and information to limit the Soviet Union's own covert actions in Western Europe. The Cold War was a period of intense U.S.-Soviet rivalry that began after World War II (1939-1945) and lasted until the early 1990's. The U.S. government does not publicly acknowledge its role in covert actions.

The CIA's headquarters are in Langley, Virginia, but many of its officers and agents are stationed in other countries. Sometimes, CIA employees claim to work for other parts of the U.S. government. Some operate under *nonofficial cover,* meaning they pose as private citizens of the United States or of a foreign country.

The CIA is an executive branch agency responsible to the president. The National Security Council, whose members include the president, the vice president, and the secretaries of state and defense, oversees the CIA. The director of the CIA also guides other U.S. foreign intelligence agencies. They include the Defense Intelligence Agency, which gives intelligence to the armed forces, and the National Security Agency/Central Security Service, which specializes in communication and *cryptography* (using and deciphering secret communication). The CIA's Web site at http://www.cia.gov presents information about the CIA.

History. Congress and President Harry S. Truman created the CIA early in the Cold War by approving the National Security Act of 1947. After the war, the CIA's focus shifted toward such problems as terrorism, organized crime, and the spread of weapons of mass destruction.

CIA operations have sometimes created controversy. In the mid-1970's, the CIA was the focus of congressional and other federal investigations of charges that it had abused its powers. The investigators concluded that some charges were false but found others to be true. For example, a commission headed by Vice President Nelson A. Rockefeller reported the CIA had spied on some Americans who opposed U.S. involvement in the Vietnam War. To guard against future abuses, reforms were adopted to make the CIA and other U.S. intelligence agencies more accountable to Congress. Today, the CIA must report major activities to two congressional committees that specialize in intelligence matters.

On Sept. 11, 2001, terrorists crashed hijacked jetliners into the World Trade Center in New York City and the Pentagon Building near Washington, D.C. About 3,000 people were killed. Following the attacks, the CIA and other government agencies received criticism for failing to detect the terrorists' activity before the attacks. The CIA also received criticism for apparent intelligence failures leading up to the Iraq War, which began in 2003. The agency's estimates of Iraq's weapons programs at that time are widely believed to have been inaccurate.

In 2004, Congress passed the Intelligence Reform and Terrorist Prevention Act, which included numerous antiterrorism measures that affected the CIA. The act established the office of the director of national intelligence to oversee the intelligence-gathering operations of the CIA and other agencies. The act also set guidelines for improved cooperation between the CIA and other intelligence services. Roy Godson

See also **Espionage; Intelligence service; Iran-contra affair; National Security Council.**

Additional resources

Doyle, David W. *True Men & Traitors.* Wiley, 2001. Memoir of a former CIA agent.
Kessler, Ronald. *Inside the CIA.* 1992. Reprint. Pocket Bks., 1994.

Centrifugal force, *sehn TRIHF yuh guhl* or *sehn TRIHF uh guhl,* is often incorrectly defined as the force that pulls an object outward when it moves in a circle. Actually, an object moving in a circle is being pulled inward. If no force pulled it inward, it would still move in a straight line with constant speed. Physicists call the force that pulls the object inward *centripetal force.*

If you tie a string to a stone and whirl the stone around, you must exert a centripetal force to keep the stone from moving in a straight line. In the same way, Earth's gravity exerts a centripetal force on a speeding satellite and keeps it from flying into space.

Physicists find the idea of centrifugal force useful in certain situations. When you ride on a merry-go-round, for example, you can feel yourself being thrown away from the center of rotation. If you observe your motion with respect to the merry-go-round, you could say that centrifugal force pulls you away from the center. Physicists would call the merry-go-round *a rotating reference frame.* You do not need the idea of centrifugal force if you observe your motion with respect to the ground instead of to the merry-go-round. You would then say the merry-go-round exerts centripetal force that keeps you from moving in a straight line. Leon N. Cooper

See also **Centripetal force; Inertia; Motion** (Newton's laws of motion).

Centrifuge, *SEHN truh fyooj,* is an instrument used to separate two liquids mixed together, or solid particles that are mixed in a liquid. The centrifuge causes the more dense substance to move to the bottom of the container, leaving the less dense substance on top. A centrifuge usually consists of a large wheel connected to an electric motor. The mixtures to be separated are balanced in containers on each side of the wheel. When

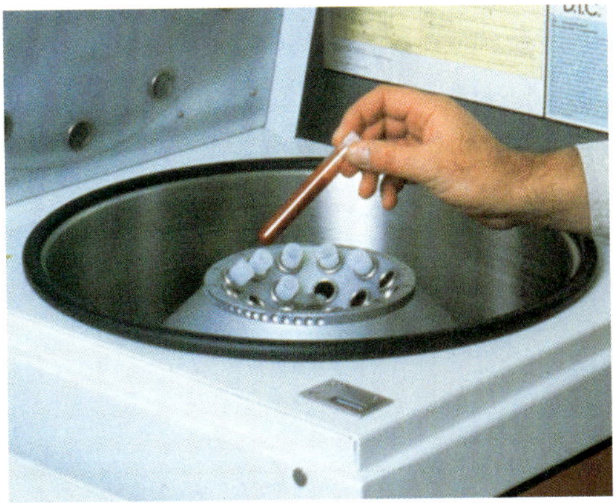

Biophoto Associates from Photo Researchers

The bench-top centrifuge is used to separate liquids in industry, medical clinics, and research laboratories.

the motor is turned on, the wheel rotates rapidly and the containers swing out from the center. A smaller centrifuge consists of a small rotating top in which test tubes of material can be placed at an angle. Centrifuges turn from 800 to 6,000 times per minute.

Centrifuges are commonly used in chemical and biological laboratories. They are used in medicine to prepare serums and plasma. Centrifuges separate the heavier blood cells or blood clot from the blood plasma or serum. They separate heavy bacteria from lighter kinds without destroying them. The cream separator is a centrifuge that takes cream out of whole milk, the cream being lighter than the skim milk that remains.

The *ultracentrifuge* is a newer kind of centrifuge with tremendous speed. It can spin at around 80,000 turns per minute. The rotating part of an ultracentrifuge touches nothing solid. It is balanced on a cushion of air. The ultracentrifuge whirls by means of jets of compressed air that touch the outer surface. Ultracentrifuges are used in the study of viruses. Leon N. Cooper

See also **Plasma.**

Centripetal force, *sehn TRIHP uh tuhl,* is the force that compels a body to move in a circular path. According to the law of inertia, in the absence of forces, an object moves in a straight line at a constant speed. An outside force must act on an object to make it move in a curved path. When you whirl a stone around on a string, you must pull on the string to keep the stone from flying off in a straight line. The force the string applies to the object is the *centripetal force.* The word *centripetal* is from two Latin words meaning *to seek the center.*

Centripetal force acts in other ways. For example, a speeding automobile tends to move in a straight line. Centripetal force must act on the car to make it travel around a curve. This force comes from the friction between the tires and the pavement. If the pavement is wet or icy, this frictional force is reduced. The car may then skid off the road because there is not enough centripetal force to keep it moving in a curved path.

You can use the following formula to calculate the centripetal force, *F,* necessary to make an object travel in a circular path:

$$F = \frac{mv^2}{r}$$

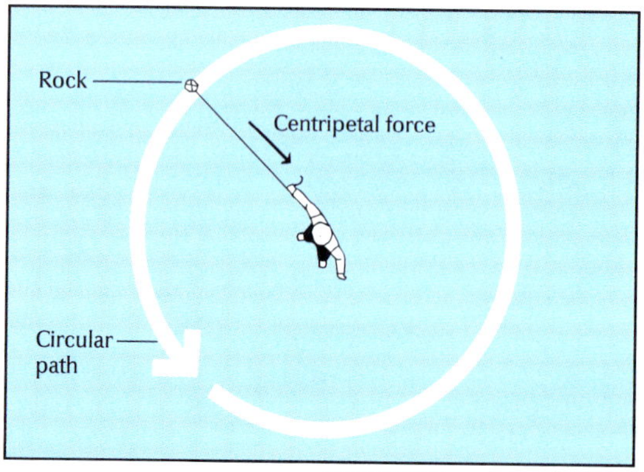

WORLD BOOK diagram by David Cunningham

Centripetal force compels an object to move in a circular path. The person in this illustration exerts a centripetal force on the rock by pulling on the string.

Multiply the object's mass, *m,* by the square of its velocity (the velocity multiplied by itself), v^2, and divide this product by the radius of the circle in which the object moves, *r.* In the metric system, the centripetal force is given in newtons when the object's mass is expressed in kilograms, the velocity in meters per second, and the radius in meters. Leon N. Cooper

See also **Inertia; Motion** (Newton's laws of motion).

Centurion. See **Legion.**

Century ordinarily means 100 years. The word is from the Latin *centuria,* meaning a hundred. The years 1 through 100 after the birth of Christ are called the first century; from 101 through 200 was the second century. The 21st century began Jan. 1, 2001. C. R. O'Dell

Century plant is the name of a group of desert plants that belong to the agave family. It is also called *agave* (pronounced *ah GAH vee* or *ah GAY vee).* The name *century plant* came from the mistaken idea that the American century plant blooms only once in 100 years. Some century plants flower many times. Others bloom only once and then die. But none blooms so rarely as once in 100 years.

The American century plant has thick, fleshy leaves with sharp-spined edges. The white or greenish flowers grow in an open cluster on the upper portion of the stalk. The leaves die after the plant has bloomed. The roots remain alive and produce a new plant. The American century plant is also known as the *American aloe.*

The people of Mexico use the sap of certain agaves to

© Giuseppe Mazza

A century plant reaches its full height—20 to 30 feet (6 to 9 meters)—in one season.

make beverages, such as *pulque, tequila,* and *mescal.* The long, tough fibers of other agaves, such as the sisal and henequen, may be formed into thread, cord, and rope. The green leaves of the plants are used as fodder.

Michael G. Barbour

Scientific classification. Agaves belong to the agave family, Agavaceae. The American century plant is classified as *Agave americana.*

See also **Henequen; Maguey; Sisal.**

Cephalopod. See **Mollusk** (Octopuses and squids).

Cephalosporin, *SEHF uh luh SPAWR ihn,* is any of a group of widely used antibiotics. Doctors use cephalosporins to treat a variety of bacterial infections, including diseases of the respiratory system, urinary tract, bloodstream, and skin. Doctors also use cephalosporins to prevent infections following surgical procedures and to treat certain sexually transmitted diseases. In addition, some cephalosporins are used to treat certain diseases that affect the central nervous system, including some forms of meningitis.

Cephalosporins are chemically similar to penicillins, and the two types of antibiotics have many similar properties. But cephalosporins fight more kinds of bacteria than penicillins do. Doctors occasionally use cephalosporins in treating patients who are allergic to penicillins. In some patients, however, both antibiotics cause allergic reactions. Like penicillins, cephalosporins fight bacteria by preventing the bacteria from making the rigid cell walls that they need to live. Human cells do not have rigid walls and are not damaged by the antibiotics. Also, as with penicillins, bacteria can become resistant to cephalosporins by making enzymes that break down the chemical structure of the drug.

The first cephalosporin was found in 1948. Since then, many cephalosporins have become available. They differ in the bacteria they kill and how they are absorbed by the body. One of the most commonly prescribed kinds is *cephalexin.* Eugene M. Johnson, Jr.

See also **Antibiotic.**

Ceramics, *suh RAM ihks,* are one of the three most important types of engineering materials that are primarily synthetic. The other two are metals and plastics. Ceramics include such everyday materials as brick, cement, glass, and porcelain. They also include unusual materials used in electronics and spacecraft. Most ceramics are hard and can withstand heat and chemicals. These properties give them a variety of uses in industry. Artists also create ceramics. This article discusses the use of ceramics in industry. For information on how artists make ceramics, see **Pottery.**

Properties of ceramics. Manufacturers make common ceramics from such minerals as clay, feldspar, silica, and talc. These minerals, called *silicates,* form most of the earth's crust. Clay is an important silicate. But it is not used in all ceramic materials. Glass, for example, is made from sand. Chemists make materials called *advanced ceramics* in the laboratory from compounds other than silicates. These compounds include alumina, silicon carbide, and barium titanate.

Most ceramic products, like their mineral ingredients, can withstand acids, gases, salts, water, and high temperatures. But not all ceramic products have the same properties. Common ceramics are good *insulators*—that is, they conduct electric current poorly. Certain ceramics, however, lose their electrical resistance and become *superconductors* when they are cooled (see **Superconductivity**). Some ceramic materials are magnetic. Engineers control the properties of ceramics by controlling the proportion and type of materials used.

Kinds of ceramic products. The properties of ceramics make them especially suitable for certain products. Products made of ceramic materials include *abrasives* (materials used for grinding), construction materials, dinnerware, electrical equipment, glass products, and *refractories* (heat-resistant materials).

Abrasives. Manufacturers use some extremely hard ceramic materials for cutting metals and for grinding, sanding, and polishing. These materials include alumina, silicon carbide, and silicon nitride.

Construction materials. Clay and shale are used in making strong, durable bricks and drainpipes for homes and other buildings. Tiles are made of clay and talc. Cement consists chiefly of calcium silicates and is used primarily in making concrete. Gypsum is used to produce plaster for the surfaces of walls and ceilings. Bathtubs, sinks, and toilets are made of porcelain, which consists chiefly of clay, feldspar, and quartz.

Dinnerware. Ceramics make excellent containers for food and drinks. They do not absorb liquids, and they resist acids, salts, detergents, and changes in temperature. Most ceramic dinnerware is made from a mixture of clays, feldspar, and quartz.

Electrical and electronic equipment. Ceramics that do not conduct electric current are used as insulators in automobile spark plugs, on electric power lines, and in television sets. Such ceramics include alumina and porcelain. Another ceramic, barium titanate, is used in making *capacitors,* which store electric charges in electronic equipment. Magnetic ceramics are widely used in cellular telephones and electric motors. Complex electronic circuits are bonded on thin layers of alumina.

Glass products. Glass is one of the most important materials, chiefly because of its transparency. Products made of glass include food containers, light bulbs, windows, and lenses for eyeglasses and telescopes. Fiberglass insulates the walls of many homes. Cables made of glass fibers transmit telephone calls and other information (see **Fiber optics**). The main ingredient in glass is silica. See **Glass.**

A glasslike coating called *porcelain enamel* serves as a protective surface on many metal products. These products include such appliances as refrigerators, stoves, and washing machines. Porcelain enamel also makes outdoor signs weather resistant.

Refractories. The property of heat resistance makes refractories suitable for the manufacture of industrial boilers and furnaces, such as the furnaces used to make steel. Refractories shaped into tiles cover the surface of space shuttles, which must withstand the intense heat created by friction between the speeding shuttle and the air. Ceramics used in making refractories include alumina, magnesium oxide, silica, silicon carbide, and zirconium oxide.

Other products. Ceramic engineers continually develop new uses for ceramics. For example, porcelain is used to make false teeth and alumina to make artificial bone joints. Uranium oxide ceramics serve as fuel elements for nuclear reactors. Cutting tools are made from

WORLD BOOK photo

Ceramics are useful materials that can be tailored to fit many specific purposes. All the products shown here contain ceramics. But the items differ greatly in chemical resistance, heat resistance, durability, strength, and other properties.

Harbison-Walker Refractories

Ceramic brick serves as an excellent lining for steelmaking furnaces because it can withstand extremely high temperatures.

silicon nitride. Refractories made from carbides are used to make parts for aircraft engines. Alumina is used in making certain types of *lasers* (instruments that produce narrow beams of intense light).

Making ceramics. The clays and other minerals used in ceramics are dug from the earth and refined to improve their purity. Machines crush and grind the materials into fine particles. The particles are mixed in the proper proportion, and water or other liquid is added to produce a mixture that can be shaped. A gluelike substance is sometimes added to mixtures that do not contain clay. Glass and some refractory products are made by melting the particles and shaping them when they are molten.

The most common ways of shaping clay ceramics are *slip casting, jiggering, extrusion,* and *pressing.* In slip casting, the liquid mixture is poured into a mold that absorbs water. As the water is absorbed, a layer of ceramic particles is deposited onto the mold, forming such hollow items as teapots and *crucibles* (melting pots). The excess liquid is then poured out of the mold. In jiggering, a machine presses the clay onto a rotating mold. Jiggering is used to make dinnerware. Extrusion shapes items into rods or tubes by forcing ceramic paste through a shaping tool called a *die.* In pressing, ceramic powder is pressed in a steel die or a rubber mold.

After the product has dried, it is strengthened by *firing,* a process that takes place in special furnaces called *kilns.* Ceramics are fired at temperatures ranging from about 1200 to 3000 °F (650 to 1650 °C). Firing hardens the product permanently and gives it strength, durability, and other desired qualities.

Manufacturers cover many ceramic products with a glassy coating called *glaze.* Glaze prevents the item from absorbing liquids and makes it smoother and easier to clean. Glazes are also used for decoration.

History. Fired-clay figurines are the oldest known ceramic objects. Figurines dating back to about 25,000 B.C. have been found in central Europe. The earliest known ceramic pots, found in northern Japan, date from about 14,500 B.C.

Industrial uses of ceramics began in the 1900's. Military requirements of World War II (1939-1945) created a need for high-performance materials and helped speed the development of ceramic science and engineering. During the 1960's and 1970's, advances in electronics, communications, nuclear energy, and space travel required new kinds of ceramics. For example, heat-resistant ceramic tiles were created to help protect spacecraft from the high temperatures generated upon their reentry into Earth's atmosphere. The discovery of ceramic superconductors in the 1980's spurred intense worldwide research to develop superconducting ceramic parts for electronic devices. James S. Reed

Related articles in *World Book* include:

Brick
Cement and concrete
Clay
Enamel
Materials
Porcelain
Tile

Additional resources

Kassinger, Ruth. *Ceramics.* 21st Century Bks., 2003.
Mattison, Steve. *The Complete Potter.* Barron's, 2003.
Scotchie, Virginia. *Setting up Your Ceramic Studio.* Lark Bks., 2003.
Sentence, Bryan. *Ceramics.* Thames & Hudson, 2004.

Cerberus, *SUR buhr uhs,* was a monstrous three-headed dog who guarded the entrance to Hades, the underworld of Greek and Roman mythology. Cerberus was the offspring of the monsters Typhon and Echidna. His mane or tail consisted of snakes.

Cerberus allowed only *shades* (spirits) of the dead to enter Hades and savagely barred their escape. However, three living mortals successfully overcame him. Orpheus used the magical power of his music to charm Cerberus into submission. Hercules used his great strength. Aeneas entered the underworld with the help of an old woman called the sibyl, who lulled Cerberus to sleep with drugged food. Justin M. Glenn

See also **Hercules; Hades; Orpheus.**

Cereal is a food made from such cereal grains as wheat, oats, corn, rice, barley, and buckwheat. The main types of breakfast cereals are *ready-to-eat* and *hot.* Both are usually served with milk or cream.

Ready-to-eat breakfast cereals require no cooking and are more popular than hot cereals. Manufacturers use a variety of processes, including grinding and rolling, to form the grains into flakes, puffs, and other shapes. Sugar or another sweetener is added to some cereals.

Some ready-to-eat cereals contain no artificial substances, such as colorings or preservatives. Most of these *natural cereals* are made up of oats and wheat and may be mixed with honey, nuts, dried fruit, or other ingredients.

Hot cereals, most of which are made of oats or wheat, are manufactured in three main forms—regular, quick-cooking, and instant. Manufacturers make regular hot cereals by steaming the oats or wheat and then rolling the grains into flakes. Wheat grains may also be prepared by exploding them in moist heat. Regular hot cereals take about 15 minutes to prepare at home. The grains for quick-cooking cereals are precooked or are exploded in a vacuum. Such cereals take 3 minutes or less to cook. Instant hot cereals require only the addition of hot water. They are made of grain that has been cut into three or more pieces and pressed into thin flakes.

Hot cereals and *whole-grain* ready-to-eat cereals are made from all parts of the grain, and so they keep their natural nourishing qualities. But many ready-to-eat cereals are made from only parts of the grain. These cereals lose some of their nutrients during their manufacture. In the 1940's, manufacturers began to restore to cereals such important nutrients as iron and the B vitamins *niacin* and *thiamine.* These *restored cereals* contain about the same amount of nutrients as does the whole grain.

Today, manufacturers fortify many ready-to-eat cereals with extra nutrients. Fortified cereals are sprayed with synthetic nutrients, including vitamins A, B_6, C, niacin, riboflavin, and thiamine. Some cereals, called *high-protein cereals,* are strengthened with such protein foods as soy flour and sesame.

Breakfast cereals consist largely of energy-producing carbohydrates and may contain from 5 to 25 percent protein, depending on the ingredients. Adding milk or cream to a cereal provides calcium, protein, vitamins, and other nutrients. Fortified cereals contain significant amounts of vitamins and iron. Cereals that contain bran provide fiber, a natural laxative. Kay Franzen Jamieson

See also **Bran; Ceres; Grain; Nutrition; Oatmeal.**

Cerebellum. See **Brain** (The cerebellum).

Cerebral hemorrhage, *SEHR uh bruhl* or *suh REE bruhl, HEHM uh rihj,* is bleeding that results from a broken blood vessel in the brain. Blood escapes into the brain and destroys or damages the surrounding tissue. In addition, other brain tissue suffers damage because of the interruption of normal circulation. The victim suffers a stroke (see **Stroke**).

Most victims of cerebral hemorrhage suffer from *hypertension* (high blood pressure). In many cases, the victim also has *arteriosclerosis,* or "hardening of the arteries." Arteriosclerosis makes the arteries stiff and more likely to rupture under continued high blood pressure. In other cases, the victim may have a weak spot in the wall of a blood vessel in the brain. Hypertension may cause this weak spot to swell like a bubble. This swollen area, called an *aneurysm,* may eventually burst (see **Aneurysm**). Cerebral hemorrhages can occur at any age but are most common in people over 50 years old.

A cerebral hemorrhage occurs without warning. Within six hours, it can cause unconsciousness and paralysis of the limbs. The presence of blood in the brain after a cerebral hemorrhage occurs is easily detected with an X-ray machine called a *computed tomographic scanner,* also known as a *CT scanner.* Some cerebral hemorrhages cause death. Others leave the victim with various disabilities, depending on what areas of the brain are damaged. The speed and extent of recovery depend on the amount of damage. James N. Davis

See also **Arteriosclerosis; Hypertension.**

Cerebral palsy, *SEHR uh bruhl* or *suh REE bruhl, PAWL zee,* is a general term for a variety of disorders caused by damage to the brain. The damage occurs before or during birth or in the first few years of life. The brain damage may cause severe crippling, or the symptoms may be so mild that they hardly interfere with the patient's activities.

There are several types of cerebral palsy, and all involve lack of muscle control. Common effects of the disorder include a clumsy walk, lack of balance, shaking, jerky movements, and unclear speech. In many patients, the brain damage also causes mental retardation, learning disability, seizures, and problems in sight and hearing. About half of 1 percent of the people in the world have cerebral palsy.

Causes. In most cases, the causes of faulty growth of the brain that result in cerebral palsy cannot be determined. In some cases, however, brain damage may result from illness in the mother during pregnancy. For example, rubella can severely harm an unborn child, even though the mother may have had only mild symptoms or none at all during pregnancy. Cerebral palsy is rarely an inherited trait.

Brain damage can also occur during the birth process, especially in premature births. In babies born after a normal term of pregnancy, brain damage may occur if there is a significant period of *hypoxia* (lack of oxygen), causing brain cells to die.

After birth, a baby may develop cerebral palsy if disease or injury damages the brain. During the first year of life, infections and accidental head injuries are the most frequent causes of the condition. In some cases, child abuse has caused cerebral palsy.

Types. There are four chief types of cerebral palsy. These types are (1) *ataxic,* (2) *athetoid,* (3) *hypotonic,* and

(4) *spastic.* In the ataxic form, the patient's voluntary movements are jerky, and a loss of balance is suffered (see **Ataxia**). In the athetoid type, the person's muscles move continually. These movements prevent or interfere greatly with voluntary actions. A person with hypotonic cerebral palsy appears limp. The person can move little or not at all because the muscles cannot contract. Spastic cerebral palsy patients have stiff muscles and cannot move some body parts (see **Spastic paralysis**). A person with cerebral palsy may have more than one muscle disorder. The person may be only slightly disabled or completely paralyzed.

Cerebral palsy does not worsen progressively but may appear to worsen if it is untreated. A child's *spastic* (tight) muscles become fixed from lack of use. Some patients lose the ability to walk if they gain too much weight.

Treatment of cerebral palsy is aimed at preventing the condition from worsening and also helping the child use his or her abilities to the best possible advantage. Each type of cerebral palsy requires different therapy. Each patient needs individual care. The impact of cerebral palsy on people's lives depends on the extent of their disabilities.

Most people with cerebral palsy can be helped by physical therapy. If possible, the patient learns to maintain balance and to move about unaided. The patient may develop such self-help skills as dressing, eating, and toilet care. See **Occupational therapy** (Helping people with physical disabilities); **Physical therapy**.

A child with cerebral palsy may face the task of conquering problems of speech, sight, and hearing that could interfere with other learning. Speech therapy, glasses, and hearing aids may correct some of these problems. The child can then learn to communicate and so continue an education. Later, the child may receive training that can help in finding a suitable job.

Physicians may prescribe drugs for cerebral palsy patients to relax muscles and to control their convulsions. Braces and other mechanical devices provide support and help the victim walk. In some cases, a surgical operation called *selective posterior rhizotomy* can reduce the rigidity of spastic muscles. In this operation, the surgeon cuts selected nerve fibers in the spinal cord.

Prevention of brain damage before, during, and soon after birth is the most important way of fighting cerebral palsy. Before becoming pregnant, a woman should be vaccinated against any disease that could harm her unborn baby. An expectant mother should only take drugs prescribed by her physician. A woman under the age of 16 or over 40 has a greater chance than other women of giving birth to a premature baby. After birth, a baby can be protected from brain damage by careful handling, proper care, and vaccination against childhood diseases. Marianne Schuelein

Additional resources

Geralis, Elaine, ed. *Children with Cerebral Palsy: A Parents' Guide.* 2nd ed. Woodbine Hse., 1998.
Gray, Susan H. *Living with Cerebral Palsy.* Child's World, 2003. Younger readers.
Miller, Freeman, and others. *Cerebral Palsy.* Johns Hopkins, 1995.

Cerebrospinal fluid, *SEHR uh broh SPY nuhl,* is the liquid in the body that surrounds the entire surface of the brain and the spinal cord. It flows between the *meninges,* or membranes, that cover these nerve centers. The fluid serves as an extra cushion to protect the brain and spine from damage. It also removes wastes produced by cerebral metabolism. Doctors sometimes withdraw a little fluid by inserting a hypodermic needle in the spinal canal. This is called a *spinal tap,* or *lumbar puncture.* Doctors analyze the fluid to diagnose many diseases, including meningitis. Pressure on the brain may be detected from the pressure of the fluid.

Daniel S. Barth

See also **Brain** (How the brain is protected); **Spine.**

Cerebrum. See **Brain** (The cerebrum).

Ceres, *SIHR eez,* was the goddess of grain, the harvest, and agriculture in Roman mythology. The worship of Ceres dates back to early Roman history. The Romans dedicated a temple to her in 493 B.C. She was one of the six children of Saturn and his sister Ops. Ceres came to be identified with the Greek goddess Demeter.

Ceres was worshiped primarily by the common people of Rome and by farmers outside the city. A festival called the *Cerealia* honored her each year from April 12 to April 19. The word *cereal* comes from her name.

The most important story about Ceres tells of her search for her daughter Proserpina, who was called Persephone in Greek mythology. The girl had been kidnapped by Pluto, the Roman god of the dead. For details of this myth, see **Persephone.** Daniel P. Harmon

See also **Demeter; Saturn.**

Ceres, *SIHR eez,* is one of millions of *asteroids* (minor planets) between the orbits of Mars and Jupiter. Ceres, the largest asteroid, was the first one to be discovered. It is shaped like a slightly squashed sphere. Its longest diameter is 960 kilometers (596 miles), and its shortest diameter is 932 kilometers (579 miles). The Italian astronomer Giuseppe Piazzi first saw it by accident, on Jan. 1, 1801, from Palermo, Sicily. He was making routine observations when he noticed an unknown object. Piazzi tracked the object for several weeks until he lost it due to solar glare. In the fall of 1801, the German mathematician Carl Friedrich Gauss predicted the place in the sky where Ceres was found again by astronomers at the end of the year. Ceres is named for the Roman goddess of agriculture. Sumner Starrfield

Cerium, *SIHR ee uhm,* is a soft, gray metal of the rare-earth group of chemical elements. Cerium was discovered in 1803 by the Swedish chemist Jöns Berzelius and the Swedish geologist Wilhelm von Hisinger, and independently by the German chemist Martin Klaproth. It is named for Ceres, which is an *asteroid* (small planet).

Cerium is the most abundant of the rare-earth elements. It is found in a number of minerals and is obtained commercially from the minerals monazite and bastnasite. Radioactive *isotopes* (forms) of cerium occur during the *fission* (nuclear splitting) of uranium, thorium, and plutonium.

Cerium differs from the other rare-earth elements in the ease with which its electron structure may be changed. It is added to alloys to strengthen them. It is also used to remove fission products from melted uranium. Cerium oxide is used in making porcelain and in polishing glass.

The chemical symbol for cerium is Ce. Its *atomic number* (number of protons in its nucleus) is 58. Its *relative atomic mass* is 140.116. An element's relative atomic mass equals its *mass* (amount of matter) divided by 1/12 of the mass of carbon 12, the most abundant isotope of carbon. Cerium has a melting point of 798 °C and a boiling point of 3433 °C. It has a density of 6.773 grams per cubic centimeter at 25 °C. Larry C. Thompson

See also **Element, Chemical; Rare earth.**

Cermet. See **Composite materials.**

CERN is the world's largest research center for the study of subatomic particles. An association of 20 European nations called the European Organization for Nuclear Research finances and operates CERN, which is near Geneva, Switzerland. The name *CERN* comes from the original name of this association in French. The center is known informally as the European Laboratory for Particle Physics.

Activities at CERN center on experiments that use *particle accelerators,* devices that produce beams of subatomic particles of extremely high energies. Scientists used CERN's *super-proton synchrotron* (SPS) for the laboratory's most celebrated achievement—the discovery of the *W particle* and the *Z particle.* These subatomic particles transmit the weak nuclear force, one of four fundamental forces in nature. Physicists Carlo Rubbia of Italy and Simon van der Meer of the Netherlands received the 1984 Nobel Prize in physics for the discovery. CERN's largest accelerator was the LEP2 (*l*arge *e*lectron-*p*ositron) synchrotron, a ring-shaped machine measuring 17 miles (27 kilometers) in circumference. CERN shut down LEP2 in November 2000 so that construction could begin on a more powerful accelerator in the same tunnel.

CERN has a staff of several thousand scientists and other personnel. Thousands of visiting scientists also carry out research at the center. The center also ranks as a leader in the development of research and computer equipment.

CERN members are Austria, Belgium, Bulgaria, the Czech Republic, Denmark, Finland, France, Germany, Greece, Hungary, Italy, the Netherlands, Norway, Poland, Portugal, Slovakia, Spain, Sweden, Switzerland, and the United Kingdom. CERN was founded in 1954.

Critically reviewed by CERN

See also **Particle accelerator.**

Certificate of deposit, also called a CD, is a receipt issued by a bank for money placed in a certain type of savings account. Most CD accounts pay a higher rate of interest than do regular savings accounts. To open a CD account, a person must place a minimum amount of money in it and agree to pay a penalty if any of the money is withdrawn before a given date. The investment period ranges from 30 days to 10 years. Few CD accounts require a minimum deposit of less than $500. In general, the more money invested or the longer the investment period, the higher the interest rate. The rate usually stays the same throughout the investment period. Like other savings accounts, most CD accounts are insured by the federal government. Paul Taubman

Certified public accountant, also called CPA, is an accountant in the United States who has passed the Uniform CPA Examination and has obtained a special license to practice as a CPA. The examination is prepared by the American Institute of Certified Public Accountants, and licenses are granted by the individual states.

CPA's examine and report on the financial records of businesses and individuals. They provide a number of services, including auditing and preparing tax returns. Many CPA's are employed by corporations, government agencies, or other organizations. Some CPA's practice as individuals or for large accounting firms. See also **Accounting; Audit.** Patricia Casey Douglas

Certiorari, *SUR shee uh RAIR ee,* **Writ of,** in its original form, is a written command by a higher court to a lower court, public board, or public officer. It orders them to send up for review the record of a proceedings. The higher court then examines the record and decides whether the decision was according to law. Courts use the writ to review decisions involving rights, but not legislative or executive decisions. State laws have made many changes in the form of the writ of certiorari.

Paul C. Giannelli

Cervantes, *sehr VAHN tays* or *suhr VAN tees,* **Miguel de,** *mih GEHL day* (1547-1616), ranks as the outstanding writer in Spanish literature. Cervantes's masterpiece, *Don Quixote,* is a novel about a middle-aged country landowner who imagines himself a knight in armor and goes into the world to battle injustice. *Don Quixote* ranks among the great works in literature and has been a major influence on the development of the novel. See **Don Quixote.**

His early life. Miguel de Cervantes Saavedra was born in Alcalá de Henares, probably on Sept. 29, 1547. Unlike most writers of his time, he apparently did not attend a university. But he read widely, and his writings show the influence of many other works, including literary theory, pastoral novels, and romances of chivalry.

Cervantes joined the army about 1568. He fought in the naval battle of Lepanto against the Ottoman Turks in 1571. He was wounded in the chest and left hand, thus earning the nickname the *Maimed of Lepanto.* Cervantes was devoted to military life, and he remained in the army, fighting in northern Africa and other Mediterranean lands.

Cervantes sailed for Spain in 1575. But his ship was captured by pirates and he was taken as a slave to Algiers, where he spent the next five years. Cervantes attempted to escape several times before his family and a religious order ransomed him. Incidents from Cervantes's captivity became episodes in *Don Quixote.*

After obtaining his freedom, Cervantes reached Madrid in 1580, seeking employment to repay the cost of his ransom. He hoped to continue his military career. Instead, he obtained a job as a messenger. Shortly after that, Cervantes married and began to write verse and prose. He was finally appointed a grain collector. In his job, Cervantes met many kinds of people as he traveled the highways of southwest Spain. He gained an understanding of human nature that enabled him to ponder in *Don Quixote* and other works the conflict between hope and disillusionment, and dreams and reality.

His literary career. Cervantes's first long work was *La Galatea* (1585), a prose pastoral romance. He wrote many plays during the next 20 years but found few producers who would present them. The publication of the first part of *Don Quixote* in 1605 made him famous. But Cervantes published nothing else for eight years.

Old and lonely, Cervantes became incredibly active during his last three years. *Novelas ejemplares (Exemplary Novels)* appeared in 1613. These stories, some of which had been written years before, rank as Cervantes's major works after *Don Quixote.* The stories vary in style and subject matter, ranging from crude Naturalism to Romanticism. The most popular stories are noted for their realism and satirical flavor.

Journey to Parnassus (1614), a long poem, is of interest chiefly for its critical appraisals of Spanish poets. In 1615, Cervantes finished the second part of *Don Quixote* and *Eight Comedies and Eight Entremeses,* a collection of plays. His *entremeses* (one-act comedies) are among his best works and are superior to his more serious plays.

Cervantes's last work was *Persiles and Sigismunda,* a romantic adventure novel published in 1617 after his death. In the book's eloquent and moving introduction, completed four days before his death, Cervantes foresaw his death and bid farewell to life. He died on April 23, 1616. Harry Sieber

See also **Spanish literature** (The Golden Age).

Cervical cancer is uncontrolled multiplication of cells in a woman's *cervix.* The cervix includes the lower portion and opening of the *uterus,* the hollow, muscular organ in which a baby develops. Throughout the world, cancer of the cervix is an extremely common cancer of the female reproductive system. But it is a cancer that can be diagnosed and cured in its early stages.

Cervical cancer arises in cells of the *epithelium (EHP uh THEE lee uhm),* a type of tissue that covers the cervix. The first phase of the disease is called *cervical intraepithelial neoplasia,* pronounced *SUR vuh kuhl IHN truh EHP uh THEE lee uhl NEE oh PLAY zhuh* and often abbreviated CIN. In CIN, cells of the epithelium look abnormal under a microscope but have not yet become cancerous.

Untreated CIN may progress to a phase known as *preinvasive.* This progression usually occurs over 5 to 10 years but may take less than a year. Preinvasive neoplasia has not yet spread from the epithelium into deeper tissues of the cervix. The preinvasive phase may then progress to *invasive cancer.* Invasive cancer extends into layers of cervical tissue beneath the epithelium. In the most advanced cases, it reaches other organs or even distant parts of the body.

A simple, painless office procedure called a Pap test can detect all stages of cervical cell abnormalities. For a complete description of this procedure, see the **Pap test** article. If a Pap test reveals abnormalities, doctors usually examine the cervix with a type of microscope called a *colposcope (KAHL puh skohp).* Tissue samples from suspicious areas provide a definite diagnosis.

Doctors can treat most cases of CIN or preinvasive neoplasia by removing only the affected cervical tissue. Removal methods include surgery, laser vaporization, and *cryotherapy* (freezing). Women with no future plans to have children may be treated with a *hysterectomy* (removal of the entire uterus).

In most cases, doctors can cure invasive cervical cancer with either a *radical hysterectomy* (surgery that removes the uterus and nearby lymph nodes) or with radiation. Radiation combined with *chemotherapy* (treatment with drugs) can also cure many tumors that extend to nearby organs. Cancer that has spread to distant parts of the body can rarely be cured but may be controlled for some time with chemotherapy.

The most common cause of cervical cancer is infection with *human papilloma virus* (HPV), a virus transmitted during sexual intercourse. Smoking cigarettes or inhaling second-hand smoke increases the risk of infection. Having sex during early adolescence also increases risk, because the cervical epithelium is more easily infected in young women. Having sex with multiple partners raises risk, as does having sex with one partner who has had many other partners. In 2006, the United States Food and Drug Administration (FDA) approved a vaccine that is highly effective against HPV and which may be used to prevent cervical cancer caused by the virus. Barrie Anderson

Cesarean section. See **Childbirth** (The birth process); **Surgery** (Obstetrics and gynecology).

Cesium, *SEE zee uhm,* is a soft, silvery metallic element. Dissolved cesium salts, such as cesium carbonate and cesium chloride, exist in low concentrations in mineral waters and brines. German scientists Robert Bunsen and Gustav Kirchhoff first detected cesium in 1860. In 1882, chemist Carl Setterberg isolated the pure metal.

Cesium has an *atomic number* (number of protons in its nucleus) of 55. Its *relative atomic mass* is 132.90545. An element's relative atomic mass equals its *mass* (amount of matter) divided by $\frac{1}{12}$ of the mass of an atom of carbon 12, the most abundant form of carbon. Cesium's chemical symbol is Cs. The element belongs to the group of elements called *alkali metals* (see **Element, Chemical** [Periodic table of the elements]). It reacts vigorously with air and water. Cesium melts at 28.6 °C and boils at 670 °C. At 20 °C, it has a density of 1.873 grams per cubic centimeter (see **Density**).

Most cesium metal is obtained from cesium chloride. Cesium ionizes readily when heated or struck by light. Because of this property, it is used in *photomultiplier tubes* that measure weak light (see **Photomultiplier tube**). Scientists are studying the use of cesium as a fuel in ion-propulsion engines for space vehicles. They also are experimenting with methods of power generation that involve the ionization of cesium. Duward F. Shriver

Cetacean, *sih TAY shuhn,* is a member of the *order* (group) of mammals made up of whales, dolphins, and porpoises. Cetaceans bear live young, and the babies nurse on the mother's milk. Cetaceans live entirely in water and breathe air through lungs. Their bodies have a thick layer of fat called *blubber* that keeps them warm. Cetaceans have flippers for front limbs. They have no hind limbs and almost no hair. John K. B. Ford

Scientific classification. Cetaceans make up the order Cetacea in the class Mammalia and the phylum Chordata.

See also **Dolphin; Porpoise; River dolphin; Whale.**

Ceylon. See **Sri Lanka.**

Cézanne, *say ZAHN,* **Paul** (1839-1906), a French painter, was one of the most significant painters in modern art. He became noted for his use of color, his way of structuring a painting, and the interaction between depth and flatness in his canvases. Cézanne's style influenced major movements of the 1900's, notably the Fauves, Cubists, and Abstract Expressionists.

Cézanne was born in Aix-en-Provence on Jan. 19, 1839, and lived there most of his life. Largely self-taught, he copied works of the Flemish painter Peter Paul Rubens and the Italian painter Tintoretto in the Louvre in Paris. He also admired the work of France's Gustave Courbet, as reflected in the lumpy modeling, thick paint, and dark

The Art Institute of Chicago,
The Albert Hern Fund

Paul Cézanne was a leader of the Postimpressionism school of painting. The pencil sketch shown here is a self-portrait from one of his notebooks. Cézanne's painting *Mont Sainte-Victoire* shows the feeling for depth and the attention to form that appear in the artist's landscapes.

The Metropolitan Museum of Art, New York City, The H. O. Havemeyer Collection, 1929

colors of Cézanne's early paintings. Many of these early works deal with such grim subjects as murder and rape.

Cézanne's style changed while working with the French Impressionist painter Camille Pissarro from 1872 to 1874. He learned to paint with greater discipline and to lighten his colors. But unlike the Impressionists, Cézanne did not emphasize the effects of light and how light could dissolve forms and change perceptions of color. He wanted to capture color that was not only true to the color of the object being painted, but to the color itself, in its most intense form. Cézanne also began to emphasize the form and structure of objects.

Cézanne is best known for the many landscapes he painted of Mont Ste.-Victoire near his home in Aix-en-Provence. In *Mont Sainte-Victoire,* reproduced with this article, Cézanne challenged the clearly defined foreground, middle ground, background, and perspective of the traditional landscape. While the title of the painting draws the eye to the mountain in the background, the prominent pine tree in the center of the painting pulls the attention back to the foreground. One branch of the tree follows the curve of the river, causing the viewer to see the branch and river as two real forms separated by space, as well as abstract parallel lines on the canvas. The buildings suggest three-dimensional structures. But Cézanne's narrow, parallel brushstrokes dissolve this solidity by uniting the work in a glowing tapestry of color that floats on the surface of the canvas. The use of repeated colors contributes to this unity.

Cézanne often painted such traditional still-life subjects as vases, bowls, napkins, and pieces of fruit, but without using traditional perspective. Flat surfaces appear tilted, and the objects on them are precariously balanced in relation to space and to one another. An example is his *Still Life with Commode,* which is reproduced in the **Painting** article. Ann Friedman

See also **Painting** (Postimpressionism).

Additional resources

Athanassoglou-Kallmyer, Nina M. *Cézanne and Provence.* Univ. of Chicago Pr., 2003.
Cachin, Françoise, and others. *Cézanne.* Abrams, 1996.

CFC. See **Chlorofluorocarbon.**

Chaco Culture National Historical Park, *CHAHK oh,* in northwestern New Mexico, has numerous large, prehistoric ruins of the Anasazi Indians. The best-known ruin, Pueblo Bonito, was an ancient apartment building with about 800 rooms. The area was established as a national monument in 1907 and became a national historical park in 1980. For the area of the park's, see **National Park System** (table: National historical parks).

Critically reviewed by the National Park Service

Chad is a large, thinly populated country in north-central Africa. Chad has no borders on the sea. Most of its people live in the fertile southern part of the country. The northern part is mostly desert. N'Djamena is the capital and largest city. Chad became an independent nation in 1960. It had been ruled by France since 1920.

Since the mid-1960's, much of Chad's history has been marked by ethnic, religious, and political violence. Most conflicts have been between the Muslim peoples of the north and the peoples of the south, many of whom follow traditional African religions or Christianity. This fighting and other factors, such as high energy costs and Chad's landlocked location, have made it one of the world's least developed nations. But Chad began to develop and export its oil resources in the early 2000's.

Government. The president of Chad is the head of state. The people elect the president to a five-year term. The president appoints a prime minister to head the Council of Ministers, which directs the operations of Chad's government. The 155-member National Assembly makes the laws. Assembly members are elected to four-year terms. The Supreme Court is Chad's highest court.

For purposes of local government, Chad is divided into 28 departments plus the capital city of N'Djamena. Local authority rests with traditional chiefs in some areas and with officials appointed by the national government in other areas.

People. The people of Chad, called Chadians, belong to a variety of ethnic groups. French and Arabic are the official languages of the country. But most Chadians speak their own local languages. Most adults in Chad cannot read and write. For the country's literacy rate, see **Literacy** (table: Literacy rates for selected countries).

Most of Chad's people live in the countryside and work as farmers or *nomadic* (wandering) herders. The rest live in N'Djamena and a few other cities. Many of these people also work as farmers nearby.

In northern Chad, most of the people are Arabs or members of the African Toubou ethnic group. Most of these people are cattle traders. They travel through the desert in small bands with herds of livestock. They make tents out of sticks and woven mats. The men of northern Chad usually wear loose gowns and turbans or small skullcaps. Some men also wrap long, white scarves around their faces for protection during sandstorms. The women typically wrap themselves in light blue or black one-piece robes.

Chad

WORLD BOOK maps

Facts in brief

Capital: N'Djamena.
Official languages: French and Arabic.
Official name: République du Tchad (Republic of Chad).
Area: 495,755 mi^2 (1,284,000 km^2). *Greatest distances*—east-west, 640 mi (1,030 km); *north-south,* 1,097 mi (1,765 km).
Elevation: *Highest*—Emi Koussi, 11,204 ft (3,415 m) above sea level. *Lowest*—Lake Chad, 922 ft (281 m) above sea level.
Population: *Estimated 2006 population*—9,382,000; density, 19 per mi^2 (7 per km^2); distribution, 76 percent rural, 24 percent urban. *1993 census*—6,279,931.
Chief products: *Agriculture*—cattle, cotton, millet, peanuts, rice, sorghum. *Manufacturing*—beer, cigarettes, textiles. *Mining*—petroleum.
National anthem: "La Tchadienne" ("The Chadian").
Flag: The flag has vertical blue, yellow, and red stripes. Blue symbolizes the sky and hope. Yellow stands for the sun. Red represents fire and unity. See **Flag** (picture: Flags of Africa).
Money: *Basic unit*—CFA franc. CFA stands for Coopération Financière en Afrique Centrale (Financial Cooperation in Central Africa).

Northern Chadians raise cattle, camels, goats, and sheep. Milk and meat are the basis of their diet. The northerners also eat dates and vegetables that are grown in oases and villages. Arabic is the most common language spoken in northern Chad, and a majority of the people in the region are Muslims. Less than a tenth of the school-age children in the north attend school.

Most of the people in southern Chad are black Africans from various ethnic groups. The largest of these groups, the Sara, live chiefly in the far south.

Most southern Chadians are settled farmers. Their main cash crop is cotton. They live in circular houses made of adobe brick or dried mud covered with a straw roof. Some houses are made entirely of straw. The men usually wear cotton trousers or shorts and loose shirts. Women commonly dress in brightly colored blouses and one-piece skirts. The diet of the people of southern Chad consists mainly of millet, sorghum, and rice. Meals occasionally include vegetables, fish, or meat.

Sara is the most widely spoken language in the south, but there are many others. The majority of southern Chadians follow traditional African religions, but many have converted to Christianity. The missionaries who introduced Christianity in the region also started the school system. Education has helped the south gain a dominant position in Chad. Most of Chad's primary and secondary schools are in areas where the Sara live. Most business people, teachers, traders, and government workers come from that region. The south also contains most of Chad's cities and industries.

The tremendous gap in education and economic development has added to the conflict between residents of the north and south. Northerners feel they lack the opportunity to advance in education, business, and other aspects of life. Religious differences between Muslims and Christians have added to this tension.

Land and climate. Most of the country consists of arid desert land and rocky plateaus. The Tibesti mountain range in northwestern Chad includes the country's highest point, Emi Koussi. This mountain rises 11,204 feet (3,415 meters) above sea level. A flat stretch of *savanna* (grassland with scattered trees) in central Chad separates the vast desert in the north from a small, extremely fertile region in the south.

The area south and southeast of the Chari River was called "Useful Chad" by French colonists because it has all the advantages that northern Chad lacks. Its soil and climate are ideal for cultivating cotton, and it is by far Chad's richest farming region. This tropical forested region also has a rich supply of wild animals, including antelope, elephants, lions, and giraffes. These animals can be seen in Zakouma National Park, northeast of Sarh.

Chad has several rivers, most of them in the south. The largest of these, the Chari and the Logone, meet at N'Djamena and then flow into Lake Chad. The lake's size varies greatly between rainy and dry seasons. Crocodiles, hippopotamuses, and cranes live in the marshy area around the lake.

Temperatures in the northern desert often reach 120 °F (49 °C), and the region receives less than 5 inches (13 centimeters) of rain annually. Central Chad averages 25 inches (64 centimeters) of rain each year, while southern Chad receives about 40 inches (100 centimeters). The average temperature in these two regions is 82 °F (28 °C).

Economy. Chad is one of the poorest countries. Most land north of the Chari is useless for growing crops. But Chad has been working to develop its oil resources. In the early 2000's, the World Bank and the U.S. oil company ExxonMobil Corporation funded construction of a pipeline from southern Chad through Cameroon to the Gulf of Guinea. In return, Chad agreed to use most of the oil revenues for social development projects. Oil exports began in 2003. Chad also has undeveloped deposits of oil and *natron* (a natural salt used as a preservative) near Lake Chad, and uranium in the north.

Traditional agriculture, fishing, and livestock raising employ 90 percent of Chad's workers. Herders in the north who tend livestock make up about 20 percent of these people. Most of the remainder are farmers in the south. The southern farmers grow cotton, Chad's most valuable crop, along with cassava, millet, sorghum, peanuts, rice, and yams. Severe droughts in the late 1960's, early 1970's, and early 1980's destroyed crops and livestock and caused many deaths. Fishing in the Chari and Logone rivers and in Lake Chad is a seasonal activity.

Chad has little industry. A brewery, a textile plant, cigarette factories, soap factories, construction firms, and mills that process peanuts, cotton, and cotton oil are located in N'Djamena and far southern cities. But civil conflicts have interrupted the operations of most of these businesses, and exports have dropped sharply.

Poor transportation and communications facilities are obstacles to Chad's economic development. The country has no railroads, and almost all its roads are unpaved. Less than 1 percent of the people own an automobile. N'Djamena has an international airport. Chad has limited telephone, telegraph, and postal services. The weekly *Al-Watan* and the mimeographed government bulletin *Info-Tchad* are the only newspapers. Chad has an average of about 1 radio for every 4 people. The country averages only about 1 television set for every 850 people.

The country imports most of its goods from France. France and the United States give Chad economic aid.

J. Alex Langley, Aspect Picture Library

A village in southern Chad has circular straw houses. Most of the people in southern Chad are farmers. They raise cotton and a variety of food crops.

Other countries and private organizations concerned about the famines in Chad have also helped. They have donated emergency food and economic aid.

History. Little is known about Chad's earliest history. Remains of prehistoric civilizations have been discovered in the Tibesti, Borkou, and Ennedi regions in northern Chad. Rock engravings and paintings dating back to 5000 B.C. show hunting and herding scenes. Primitive tools found around Lake Chad point to the existence of cattle-raising peoples as early as 500 B.C. Developing trade routes led to the formation of a state called Kanem northeast of Lake Chad about A.D. 700's. A series of kings from the Sefuwa family ruled Kanem for about 1,000 years. Islam was introduced around 1100.

The smaller kingdoms of Baguirmi and Ouaddai developed near Kanem in the 1500's and 1600's. All three kingdoms became powerful and prosperous by trading goods and slaves. Traders from the northern kingdoms often raided the southern tribes to capture slaves. One reason for the conflict in Chad today is that the Sara people remember that northern raiders seized thousands of their people as slaves.

The French claimed and explored Chad during the 1880's and 1890's. Chad became a French colony in 1920 and was part of a region called French Equatorial Africa.

The Sara suffered more than any other group under colonial rule. Many died in battle in World War I (1914-1918) and World War II (1939-1945). Thousands were sent to work on a railway in what is now Congo (Brazzaville), and never returned. But when Chad became independent in 1960, a Sara-dominated government took over. For the Sara, independence meant freedom from the age-old domination by northern slave traders. François Tombalbaye, a Sara, became Chad's first president.

In 1962, a group of northerners formed a rebel organization called the National Liberation Front *(Front de Libération National)*, or *Frolinat.* Most of its leaders were Muslims. Civil war between Frolinat and government troops broke out in the mid-1960's. The government of Chad turned to France for military aid. In 1971, Frolinat began to get military supplies from Libya. Libyan President Mu'ammar Muhammad al-Qadhāfī hoped to make Chad part of Libya. In 1973, Libyan forces occupied the

Aozou Strip along Chad's northern border. This area is believed to contain uranium and other minerals.

Tombalbaye was killed in 1975 by military and police units that overthrew the government. Félix Malloum, a Sara and the head of Chad's army, became president of the new military regime. Fighting continued until the rebels captured almost half the Chadian army in 1978. A new government was then formed with almost equal representation from the north and the south. Hissene Habré, a former Frolinat leader, became prime minister.

Malloum fled in 1979, and two groups within the rebel forces battled for control. One group followed Habré, then minister of defense. The other group was headed by the new president, Goukouni Oueddei. Goukouni received support from Libya. In 1980, the army led by Habré was defeated by Goukouni's troops and Libyans who aided them. Goukouni took control of the government. Libyan troops remained in Chad until late 1981, when Goukouni asked them to leave. A peacekeeping force from the Organization of African Unity (OAU) replaced the Libyan troops.

In June 1982, an army led by Habré overthrew the government of President Goukouni. Goukouni fled the country, and the OAU peacekeeping force withdrew. Habré became president, but Goukouni returned with troops from Libya. In 1983, France sent troops and military equipment to support Habré. Goukouni's forces and Libyan troops occupied the northern part of Chad, while Habré's forces controlled N'Djamena.

In 1986, conflict broke out between Goukouni's troops and their Libyan allies. Goukouni's troops joined with Habré's forces, and Habré launched attacks against the Libyans. By 1987, the Libyans had been driven from all of Chad except the Aozou Strip. The two countries agreed to a truce in late 1987. Libya withdrew its forces from the area in 1994 after the United Nations International Court of Justice ruled that the Aozou Strip belonged to Chad.

In 1990, rebels of the Patriotic Salvation Movement (MPS), led by Idriss Deby, overthrew Habré. In 1993, a national conference of political and other groups set up an interim government. In 1996, Chad adopted a new constitution and held a multiparty presidential election, which Deby won. In 1997, the MPS won legislative elections. Deby was reelected president in 2001.

In 1998, the Movement for Democracy and Justice in Chad, based in Chad, rebelled against the government. The two sides signed pacts in 2002, 2003, and 2005 that ended most of the fighting. Since 2003, a conflict in the Darfur area of western Sudan has driven about 200,000 Sudanese refugees into Chad. In 2006, Chadians reelected Deby as president, but opposition parties boycotted the election. René Lemarchand

See also **Lake Chad; N'Djamena.**

Chad, Lake. See Lake Chad.

Chadwick, Sir James (1891-1974), a British physicist, won the 1935 Nobel Prize in physics for his discovery of the neutron, one of the particles making up the nucleus of an atom. In 1924, Chadwick became assistant director of Cavendish Laboratory in Cambridge, England, where he worked with the physicist Ernest Rutherford. The two scientists bombarded chemical elements with alpha particles (see **Alpha particle**). Chadwick studied how these elements were *transmuted* (changed) into different ones. This work led him to discover the neutron and determine its mass (see **Neutron**). Chadwick was born Oct. 20, 1891, near Manchester, England. He studied at the University of Manchester and in Berlin. Chadwick died on July 24, 1974. Roger H. Stuewer

Chagall, *shah GAHL,* **Marc** (1887-1985), was a Russian-born artist who combined elements of dreams, fantasy, and religion to create paintings with a joyous quality. Chagall was born on July 7, 1887, in the Russian-Jewish village of Vitebsk (now Vitsyebsk, Belarus). He grew up in a deeply religious family in Vitebsk. In 1910, he moved to Paris. There he began to paint in a style that incorporated religious symbols and childhood memories

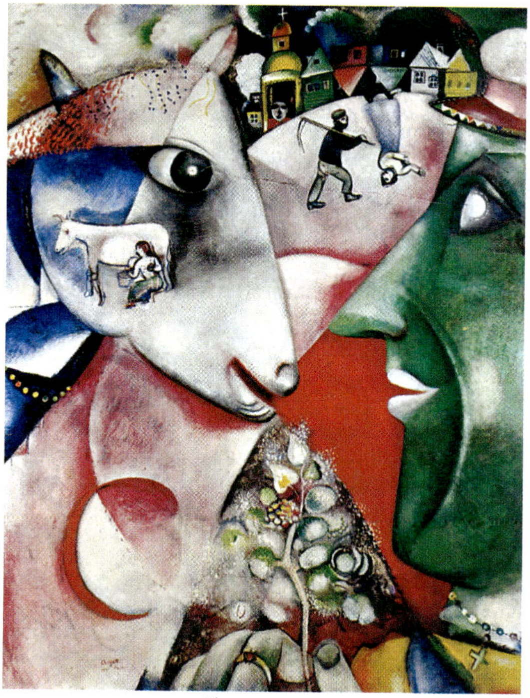

Oil painting on canvas (1911); the Museum of Modern Art, New York City, Mrs. Simon Guggenheim Fund

Chagall's *I and the Village* shows scenes of life in Vitebsk, the village where the artist grew up. The bright colors and topsy-turvy figure are typical of his style. The influence of the Cubist art movement appears in the painting's geometric shapes.

into the colors and structures of French art of the time. The geometric division of Chagall's paintings suggests Cubism. He portrayed objects without concern for realistic scale. Figures, including animals, lovers, and musicians, often float in the air, sometimes upside down. These fantasy aspects relate Chagall's art to the dreamlike style of Surrealism (see **Cubism; Surrealism**).

After 1922, Chagall became a leading lithographer. In 1945, he designed the sets and costumes for a production of the ballet *The Firebird.* During the 1960's, Chagall completed a ceiling painting for the Paris Opera and murals for the Metropolitan Opera in New York City. In 1964, he designed stained glass windows for the Hadassah-Hebrew Medical Center in Jerusalem. Chagall died on March 28, 1985. Pamela A. Ivinski

For examples of Chagall's work, see **Stained glass** and **Opera** *(The Magic Flute).*

Chagnon Foundation, *shah NYAWN,* **Lucie and André,** is a private charitable organization in Canada. The foundation's mission is to help improve people's physical, psychological, social, and spiritual well-being. The foundation funds and manages a variety of projects that seek to reduce poverty and prevent disease. It works to provide support for children and parents, and to promote awareness of various health issues. The foundation carries out much of its work through partnerships with community groups and government agencies. The Chagnon Foundation's headquarters are in Montreal, Quebec.

The Chagnon Foundation was established by the Canadian businessman André Chagnon and his wife, Lucie. It began operations in 2000. For assets, see **Foundations** (table).

Critically reviewed by the Lucie and André Chagnon Foundation

Chagres River, *CHAH grehs,* is a chief source of water for the Panama Canal. The Chagres rises in the mountains of eastern Panama, flows southwest, and empties into Gatun Lake—a part of the Panama Canal route. See also **Panama Canal** (Gatun Lake).

Steve C. Ropp

Chaikovsky, Peter Ilich. See Tchaikovsky, Peter Ilich.

Chain is a flexible length of links or rings joined together. The links of a chain are usually made from metal bent into loops, with the ends of each link joined together inside the loop of the next link.

The size of a chain is measured by the thickness of its links. A half-inch chain has links made from a metal rod ½ inch (13 millimeters) in diameter. Chains vary in size from small ones used in jewelry to huge ones used in heavy machinery. Iron, steel, brass, and plastic are used to make the stronger chains. Ornamental chains may be made from alloys of gold, silver, or other metals.

The links of chains sometimes consist of several pieces. Roller chains, such as those used on bicycles, are made this way. Chains used in conveyor belts and industrial machinery may be made of cast metal or plastic pieces. In some chains, each link has a metal brace called a *stud* to make it stronger. Alva H. Jared

Chain, Ernst Boris (1906-1979), a British biochemist, shared the 1945 Nobel Prize in physiology or medicine with Alexander Fleming and Howard Florey for their research on penicillin. Fleming had discovered that penicillin destroyed many types of disease-causing bacteria. Beginning in 1938, Chain worked with Florey on antibiotic substances produced by various microorganisms. They purified penicillin in a way that made it possible to use the drug as an antibiotic. Chain was born on June 19, 1906, in Berlin, Germany, and died on Aug. 12, 1979.

Daniel J. Kevles

Chain gang is a group of prisoners chained together for labor. They traditionally have worn leg shackles connected by a short chain. A longer chain connects one convict to another. Chain gangs were once used to build roads in the southern United States. Many people consider doing such work as a member of a chain gang to be harsh and brutal punishment. James O. Finckenauer

Chain store is one of a group of retail stores whose activities are supervised or coordinated by a centralized managerial body. The United States Census Bureau defines a chain as being an organization that has 11 or more retail stores. More than half the supermarkets in the United States are chain stores.

Chain stores have several advantages over independent stores. For example, a chain can buy large quantities of goods for all its stores at once, and receive a discount for placing a large order. This system enables the chain to offer lower prices. Chain stores can also share costs in such areas as accounting and advertising.

The Great American Tea Company became the first chain-store company in the United States. This company, now the Great Atlantic and Pacific Tea Company (A&P), was established in 1859. Other early chain-store companies included Montgomery Ward and Company (1872), Woolworth Company (1879), the Kroger Company (1882), and Sears, Roebuck and Co. (1893). Wal-Mart, Inc., is the largest chain-store company in the world.

Today, there are three major types of chain-store companies. These types are (1) corporate, (2) voluntary, and (3) franchise.

Corporate chain stores are owned and operated by a parent company, such as Wal-Mart, Inc., or Limited Brands. A manager who is supervised by the chain's central office controls each store. This office may decide such matters as store hours, advertising, merchandise display, and pricing for each store.

Voluntary chain stores are important in the retailing of groceries and hardware. In voluntary chains, the managers of the stores are also store owners. The owners have agreed or volunteered to adopt methods of operation that are similar to those used by the corporate chains. Owners of stores in voluntary chains agree to buy the same kind of goods from the same wholesale merchants and manufacturers, advertise alike, and display their goods in the same way. IGA food stores and ACE hardware stores are examples of voluntary chains.

Franchise chain stores operate according to business agreements called *franchises.* Under such agreements, a store or other business pays the franchise company a sum of money and promises to give the company a percentage of the store's future profits. In return, the business—or *franchisee*—receives such benefits as managerial aid and advertising assistance. The franchisee also has the right to use the company's name. Most franchise companies have a name that is well known. Examples include McDonald's Corporation and KFC Corporation (Kentucky Fried Chicken). V. Ann Paulins

See also **Department store; Franchise; Restaurant** (Chains and franchises); **Retailing; Wal-Mart Stores, Inc.**

Chair. See **Furniture.**

Chalcedony, *kal SEHD uh nee* or *KAL suh* DOH *nee,* is a mineral that consists chiefly of tiny crystals of quartz with extremely small pores. Common chalcedony, sometimes called *white agate,* is semitransparent and clouded with circles and spots. It has a waxy luster. Other kinds of chalcedony are nearly transparent and may have many colors. They include agate, carnelian, onyx, and sard. The petrified forests of Arizona were formed in part by water depositing chalcedony in the decaying woody fibers of trees.

Chalcedony is used chiefly as a gemstone and for ornamental purposes. A type called *bloodstone* is a birthstone for March. It is green with red spots.

Chalcedony was named for the ancient town of Chalcedon in what is now Turkey, which is near deposits of the mineral. Other deposits of chalcedony occur in Iceland and Scotland, and in California and Colorado.

Robert W. Charles

See also **Agate; Carnelian; Gem; Onyx; Quartz; Sardonyx.**

Chalcocite, *KAL kuh syt,* is a mineral made up of copper and sulfur. It is shiny and lead-gray when freshly broken, but it quickly turns black when exposed to air. Exposure to air also softens chalcocite, so the mineral may make sooty, black streaks when rubbed. Chalcocite is an important source of copper. Its chemical formula is Cu_2S. Its crystal structure is orthorhombic, and the crystals are flat tablets (see **Crystal** [Classifying crystals]). Chalcocite forms when sulfuric acid and copper sulfate solutions interact chemically with rock that contains other copper minerals. This process concentrates copper, thereby helping to form minable deposits of copper ore. Chalcocite occurs in copper deposits throughout the world. Maria Luisa Crawford

Chalcopyrite, *KAL koh PY ryt,* is the most widespread copper ore and one of the chief sources of copper. It is a compound of copper, iron, and sulfur. Its chemical formula is $CuFeS_2$. The ore is a brassy yellow with a metallic luster. It looks like gold but is slightly harder and more brittle. When tarnished, much chalcopyrite displays changing colors like those of the rainbow. The ore has a rare crystal structure called *tetragonal-scalenohedral*—a shape like that of an eight-sided wedge. Chalcopyrite can be scratched with a steel knife. The resulting streak is greenish black. Major deposits of chalcopyrite occur in Canada, Japan, Spain, and the United States. The major U.S. deposits are in Arizona, Montana, Tennessee, and Utah. See also **Copper; Mineral** (picture). David F. Hess

Chaldea, *kal DEE uh,* also spelled *Chaldaea,* was a region of ancient Babylonia, in what is now southeastern Iraq. Chaldean rulers helped develop an impressive civilization in Babylonia.

The Chaldeans were Semites, a group of people who spoke languages related to Aramaic. The Chaldeans migrated to Babylonia from the west between 1100 and 875 B.C. Chaldean kings ruled Babylonia at various times during the 700's B.C. The most important one was Merodach-Baladan II, who reigned from 721 to 710 B.C. and rebelled against the Assyrian Empire.

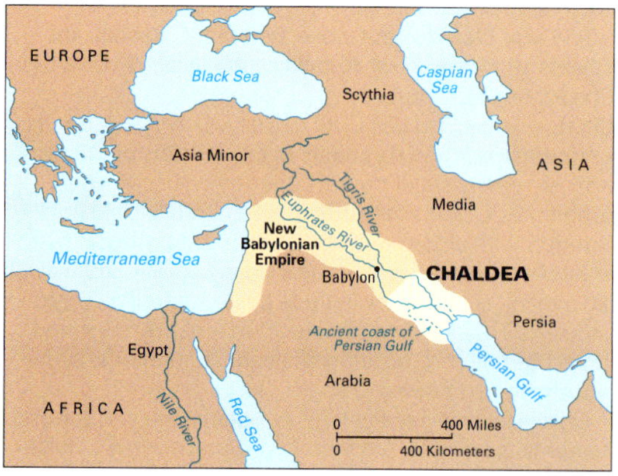

WORLD BOOK map

Chaldea was a region of ancient Babylonia. In 612 B.C., the *New Babylonian Empire* was founded and ruled by a Chaldean king.

In 626 B.C., a ruler of Chaldea named Nabopolassar became king of Babylonia. In 612 B.C., allied armies from Babylonia and nearby Media and Scythia conquered Assyria. Nabopolassar then founded the New Babylonian Empire. This empire has been called the *Chaldean Empire* because Nabopolassar had ruled Chaldea. The New Babylonian Empire gained control of a large part of the present-day Middle East. It reached its height of wealth and power under Nebuchadnezzar II, who ruled from 605 to 562 B.C. and rebuilt the city of Babylon. In 539 B.C., Persia conquered Babylonia.

Babylonian achievements between the 700's and 500's B.C. are often said to be Chaldean, particularly major efforts in astronomy and astrology. Babylonians kept detailed astronomical records and could predict eclipses of the sun and moon. They also calculated the length of a year. Their astrologers became famous for studying the stars and planets to foretell the future. Especially after about 500 B.C., the terms *Chaldean* and *Babylonian* came to mean the same thing. John A. Brinkman

See also **Nebuchadnezzar II.**

Chalk is a soft, fine-grained white limestone. It was formed as a mud on the bottom of an ancient sea. It differs from many pure, fine-grained limestones only in still being soft and easily rubbed off. That is, it did not change into hard rock.

Chalk consists largely of tiny shells and crystals of calcite. Both of these materials are made up of the compound calcium carbonate. The white cliffs of Dover are thick layers of chalk. The color of the cliffs gave the name *Albion* to England. Albion probably means *white land.* Chalk deposits in western Kansas contain the preserved skeletons of extinct sea serpents, flying reptiles, birds, and fishes.

Most deposits formed during the Cretaceous Period of time. The Cretaceous Period got its name from the Latin word for chalk, *creta.*

Chalk is made into *whiting,* a substance used to manufacture rubber goods, paint, putty, soft polishing powders, and tooth powder. Industry also uses chalk, like any other limestone, in making portland cement and as a top dressing for soils. Chalk is also used to make crayons for writing on chalkboard. Robert W. Charles

See also **Calcite; Calcium carbonate.**

Chalkboard is a smooth, dark board usually made of slate, glass, or wood. Crayon or chalk is used to write or draw on the board. The chalkboard is probably the world's most widely used visual aid to education. Instructors use chalkboards to help emphasize classroom lessons. Chalkboards were once black, but many are now green.

The chalkboard grew out of the hornbook of the Middle Ages. It was in fairly common use in Europe by the 1600's, but was not widely used in the United States until the early 1800's. Gerald L. Gutek

See also **Eraser.**

Chamber music is a type of classical music written for small groups of musicians. These groups, called *ensembles,* may vary in size from two to nine performers. Most ensembles consist of three to five musicians who play string or wind instruments. One musician plays each part.

Chamber music is generally classified according to

the number of performers in the ensemble. Music performed by two musicians is called a *duet* or *duo.* Other forms of chamber music include *trios, quartets,* and *quintets.* Chamber music may be further classified by the type of instruments played. For example, a *string quartet* is performed by two violins, a viola, and a cello. A *brass quintet* calls for two trumpets, a French horn, a trombone, and a tuba.

Since about 1750, most great composers have written chamber music. Some of the best works are string quartets written by Joseph Haydn and Wolfgang Amadeus Mozart of Austria, Ludwig van Beethoven and Johannes Brahms of Germany, Béla Bartók of Hungary, and Dimitri Shostakovich of Russia.

The term *chamber music* was first used during the 1500's, when small groups performed in private homes. Until about 1900, musicians played chamber music chiefly for their own enjoyment and for small gatherings of music lovers. Today, many ensembles perform in concert halls before large audiences. R. M. Longyear

See also **Classical music** (pictures: A string quartet; Chamber music).

Chamber of commerce is an association of business people that promotes the interests of its members and of business in general. Chambers of commerce have been organized in towns, cities, regions, and countries. In many European countries, chambers of commerce are official agencies, supported by taxes. Chambers of commerce are sometimes called boards of trade, merchants' associations, or associations of commerce. The International Chamber of Commerce is an organization of business people from many countries. The organization's purpose is to bring about closer international economic ties. In the United States, another organization, the National Retail Federation, works to make retailers aware of trends in retailing.

Chambers of commerce work to bring new industries to their communities. These groups also furnish information about their communities that may help those planning to move there. The first associations of this kind were formed in the Roman Empire. The first group to have the name "Chamber of Commerce" was organized in Marseille, France, in 1599. Jay Diamond

Chamber of Commerce of the United States is the world's largest federation of businesses, trade and professional associations, and state and local chambers of commerce. It has about 3 million members. The chamber's primary purpose is to promote free enterprise. It sets policy according to its members' views and makes these views known to members of Congress and the president to motivate public policy that would benefit business. It is administered by a 62-member board.

The chamber was organized in 1912 at a conference called by President William Howard Taft in Washington, D.C. At that time, many local chambers already existed to satisfy local business needs. Today, the chamber has affiliated U.S. chambers of commerce in dozens of other countries. Its headquarters are in Washington, D.C.

Critically reviewed by the Chamber of Commerce of the United States

Chamberlain, *CHAYM buhr lihn,* **Neville** (1869-1940), served as prime minister of the United Kingdom from 1937 to 1940. Chamberlain was closely associated with the policy of *appeasement* toward Nazi Germany. This policy was based on the belief that war could be prevented by meeting some of the demands of the German dictator Adolf Hitler. The policy led to the United Kingdom's acceptance of the Munich Agreement of 1938, which gave Germany the Sudetenland region of Czechoslovakia. In return, Hitler promised that Germany would claim no additional territory in Czechoslovakia. But in March 1939, Hitler seized the rest of that country. On September 1, Germany invaded Poland. Two days later, Chamberlain's government took the United Kingdom into World War II. British dissatisfaction with Chamberlain's handling of the war led to his resignation in 1940. He died on November 9 of that year.

Arthur Neville Chamberlain was born on March 18, 1869, in Birmingham. In 1918, he was elected to Parliament as a Conservative. He was minister of health from 1924 to 1929 and chancellor of the exchequer from 1931 to 1937.

Other members of the Chamberlain family were also prominent in British politics. Neville's father, Joseph Chamberlain, won election to Parliament in 1876 and was the United Kingdom's colonial secretary from 1895 to 1903. Neville's half brother, Sir Austen Chamberlain, was elected to Parliament in 1892 and served as the United Kingdom's foreign secretary from 1924 to 1929. He helped negotiate the Locarno treaties of 1925 and shared the Nobel Peace Prize that year (see **Locarno Conference**). Keith Robbins

See also **Munich Agreement; World War II** (The failure of appeasement).

Chamberlain, *CHAYM buhr lihn,* **Wilt** (1936-1999), was one of the greatest scorers in National Basketball Association (NBA) history. In his 14-year NBA career, he scored 31,419 points. Only Kareem Abdul-Jabbar, Karl Malone, and Michael Jordan have scored more. Chamberlain, a center, set an NBA record for career rebounds with 23,924. He stood 7 feet 1 inch (216 centimeters) tall.

Chamberlain was born on Aug. 21, 1936, in Philadelphia. He played for the University of Kansas before joining the NBA's Philadelphia (now Golden State) Warriors

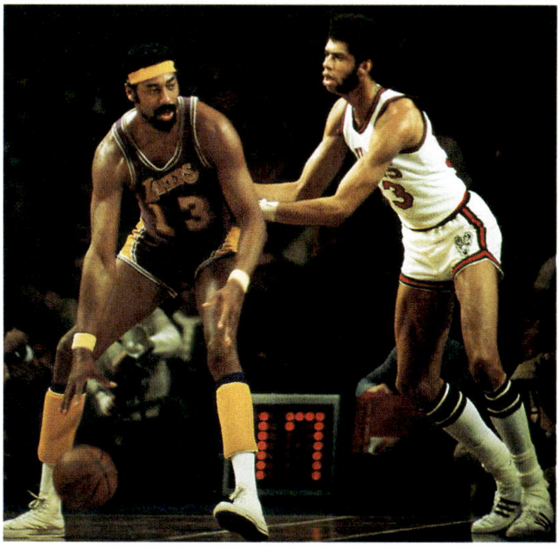

Focus on Sports

Wilt Chamberlain, *left,* was one of the greatest centers in the history of the National Basketball Association. He is shown here playing against another great center, Kareem Abdul-Jabbar.

in 1959. He led the NBA in scoring during his first seven seasons. In the 1961-1962 season, he set league records for average points per game (50.4) and most points in regular-season play (4,029). Chamberlain also set a league record for most points in a single game (100) against the New York Knicks on March 2, 1962.

In 1965, the Warriors traded Chamberlain to the Philadelphia 76ers. In 1966-1967, he helped lead the 76ers to the NBA title. In 1968, Philadelphia traded Chamberlain to the Los Angeles Lakers. He helped lead the Lakers to the NBA title in 1972. Chamberlain coached the San Diego Conquistadors of the American Basketball Association (ABA) during the 1973-1974 season. He died on Oct. 12, 1999. Bob Logan

See also **Basketball** (picture).

Chambers, Whittaker, *HWIHT tuh kuhr* (1901-1961), a confessed spy, was the United States government's chief witness in the 1949 perjury trials of Alger Hiss. Chambers said Hiss, a former Department of State official, was one of several Communists in the United States government who gave him secret government documents. Chambers produced microfilms of secret papers he had hidden in a pumpkin on his farm (see **Hiss, Alger**).

Chambers was born on April 1, 1901, in Philadelphia. He joined the Communist Party in 1925. He was an editor for the Communist *Daily Worker* newspaper until 1929 and a messenger for the Soviet spy system in Washington, D.C., in the 1930's. Disillusioned, he left the Communist Party in 1938. Chambers worked on the editorial staffs of *Time* and *Life* magazines from 1939 to 1948. He died on July 9, 1961. Thomas C. Reeves

Chameleon, *kuh MEE lee uhn,* is any of a large group of lizards. Most chameleons live in the forests of mainland Africa and the African island country of Madagascar. A few kinds live in the Middle East, in southern Asia, and in southern Spain.

Chameleons are known for their ability to change color, but a number of other kinds of lizards also have this ability. A chameleon may be green, yellow, or tan one minute, and the next minute change to brown or black. Chameleons also may become spotted or blotched. These lizards change color to blend in with their surroundings. However, the changes also occur in response to variations in light or temperature, as the result of fright, or to communicate with other chameleons. The chameleon's color is controlled by body chemicals called *hormones.* These chemicals affect pigments in the skin.

Lizards known as *anoles* (pronounced *uh NOH lees)* are closely related to chameleons. The hundreds of anole *species* (kinds) live in South America, Central America, and the southeastern United States. People commonly refer to anoles as *American chameleons.* See **Anole.**

The body of a chameleon is flattened from side to side. Chameleons range from 1 ¼ to 25 inches (3.2 to 63 centimeters) long. As many as three horns may grow from a chameleon's head. The eyes stick out and function independently, so that the animal can look forward and backward at the same time. A chameleon's feet grasp like hands rather than cling with sharp claws, as do those of most other lizards. The chameleon is one of the few lizards that has a *prehensile* (grasping) tail.

Stephen Dalton, Oxford Scientific Films

A chameleon shoots out its tongue to capture an insect. The chameleon's tongue, which is controlled by powerful neck muscles, moves so rapidly that the human eye can hardly see it.

The life of a chameleon. Chameleons move extremely slowly. Most types live in trees and bushes, while some reside on the ground under fallen leaves or other plant materials. Chameleons have a long, sticky tongue with which they capture insects and other small prey. The tongue, which may measure as long as the entire body, is controlled by powerful muscles in the throat. The tongue shoots out so rapidly that the human eye can hardly see it.

Chameleons do not actively fight one another. The males establish feeding territories, which they defend by trying to outbluff their rivals. To scare away other males, they may puff out their throat and the rest of their body to look larger, or they may change color.

In most species of chameleons, the males rarely come to the ground. However, females of many species dig nests in the ground for the 30 to 40 eggs that they lay every year. Females of other species keep the eggs in their bodies until they are ready to hatch.

D. Bruce Means

Scientific classification. Chameleons make up their own family, Chamaeleonidae.

See also **Rain forest** (picture).

Chamois, *SHAM ee,* is a shy animal noted for its swiftness and keen sense of smell. It is often called a *goat antelope,* but it looks a little more like a goat than an antelope. The chamois lives in the high mountains of Europe and western Asia, and was once common in the Swiss Alps. In summer, the chamois lives in alpine meadows and the snowy parts of the mountains. In winter, it goes down to the forests.

The chamois stands about 30 inches (76 centimeters) high at the shoulder and weighs about 80 pounds (36 kilograms). It is reddish-brown with a black tail. The fur changes to a dark brown in the winter. Its head is a pale yellow with a black band around the eyes from the nose to the ears.

Both the males and females have smooth, black horns about 7 inches (18 centimeters) long. The horns grow straight up and curve backward into a sharp hook at the tip. The longest chamois horns ever found were 12 ¾ inches (32.4 centimeters) long.

It is difficult to hunt chamois because the animals are so light and quick that they can easily jump across a

Leonard Lee Rue III, Tom Stack & Associates

The chamois lives in the high mountains of Europe and western Asia. It resembles a goat and has sharp, hooked horns.

wide ravine. Chamois live in bands of about 10 to 15 animals. The flesh of the chamois is good food, but the skin is the animal's most valuable part. The skin is used to make the soft, warm leather called *chamois skin.* Much sheepskin is sold as chamois skin. William L. Franklin

Scientific classification. The chamois is in the bovid family, Bovidae. It is *Rupicapra rupicapra.*

Chamomile. See Camomile.

Chamorro, *chuh MAW roh,* **Violeta Barrios de,** *vee oh LAY tah BAHR ee ohs deh* (1929-), was president of Nicaragua from 1990 to 1997. She succeeded Daniel Ortega after defeating him in a presidential election that year. Ortega represented the Sandinista National Liberation Front, which had governed Nicaragua since the overthrow of dictator Anastasio Somoza Debayle in 1979. Chamorro was supported by 14 anti-Sandinista parties that united in a group known as the National Opposition Union. These political parties, ranging from conservatives to Communists, saw her as a candidate who could unite Nicaragua after years of civil war.

© Brad Markel, Gamma/Liaison

Violeta Chamorro

Chamorro was born Violeta Barrios in Rivas, Nicaragua. She married Pedro Joaquín Chamorro in 1950. He served as editor of the newspaper *La Prensa,* which was highly critical of the Somoza dictatorship. Pedro Chamorro was assassinated in 1978. Then, Violeta began to work with the Sandinistas to overthrow Somoza. When they succeeded, she became one of the five members of the junta that led the Sandinista government. She resigned in 1980 as a protest against government policies that she considered undemocratic. Steve C. Ropp

Champagne, *sham PAYN,* is a sparkling wine. It takes its name from the French province of Champagne, where the wine was first made. In general, only wines produced in that region by a traditional procedure receive the name *champagne.* Thus, sparkling wines from Italy are called *spumante,* those from Germany *Sekt,* and those from Spain *cava.* However, many sparkling wines made in the United States are labeled *champagne.*

Most champagnes are made from a blend of different grapes. They range in flavor from sweet to *dry* (non-sweet). The driest champagnes are labeled *brut.* The bubbles in champagne are produced by carbon dioxide gas. The gas becomes trapped in the wine during a process called *secondary fermentation.* To bring about this fermentation, winemakers add yeast and sugar to wine that has been bottled or placed in a closed tank.

Roger Boulton

Champlain, Lake. See Lake Champlain.

Champlain, *sham PLAYN,* **Samuel de** (1570?-1635), was a French explorer who founded the Canadian city of Quebec. He helped colonize French North America, once known as *New France,* and is often called the *Father of New France.*

Early life. Champlain was born in Brouage, France, near Rochefort. His father, a sea captain, taught him navigation. Champlain joined the French Army at the age of about 20 and served until 1598. The next year, he sailed to the Spanish colonies in America on a French trading ship. From 1599 to 1601, he made several voyages to the West Indies, Mexico, and Panama.

Champlain returned to France in 1601 and wrote a book about his voyages. He described the splendor of Mexico City and was one of the first people to propose the construction of a canal across Panama. Champlain's book interested King Henry IV, who was eager for France to acquire wealth in America. Henry also hoped the French could find a "Northwest Passage"—that is, a waterway through North America to Asia.

In 1603, Champlain sailed to Canada and explored the St. Lawrence River for the king. Champlain also became one of the first Europeans to write about Niagara Falls. He sailed back to Canada in 1604 and then explored the New England coast. In 1605, Champlain helped found the settlement of Port Royal (later moved to the present site of Annapolis Royal, Nova Scotia). In 1605 and 1606, he made two more voyages along the New England coast in search of a better site for the settlement.

The founding of Quebec. Champlain returned to Canada in 1608 to establish a fur-trading post. He chose a site along the St. Lawrence River and named it Quebec. It became the first permanent settlement in New France. Champlain and his men built a fort and storehouse. The first winter was extremely cold, and only 8 of the 24 settlers survived.

Champlain became friendly with the Algonquin and Huron Indians living near Quebec. He believed his friendship could prevent Indian attacks on the settlement and that peaceful relations would make it easier to trade furs with the Indians and to explore the country. In 1609, Champlain and two French companions joined the Algonquin and Huron in a raid on the Iroquois, who lived in what is now New York. Champlain and his friends had muskets and easily defeated the Iroquois, who knew nothing about firearms. On this raid, he became the first European to reach Lake Champlain, which he named for himself. He won the lasting friendship of

Samuel de Champlain founded Quebec, the first permanent settlement in New France. The map shows his explorations of the St. Lawrence River, parts of the North American coast, and the Great Lakes region.

Detail of an oil painting by Theophile Hamel; Public Archives of Canada, Ottawa

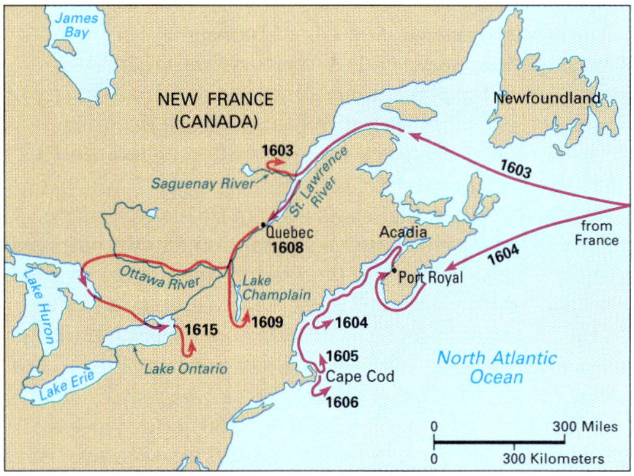

WORLD BOOK map

the Algonquin and the Huron by helping them.

Later life. From 1610 to 1624, Champlain made several trips to France to get aid for Quebec. He also explored Lake Ontario and the Georgian Bay of Lake Huron.

War broke out between France and England in 1626, and the English began to seize French settlements in Canada. In 1628, an English fleet cut off supplies to Quebec and ordered Champlain to surrender the fort. The settlers held out for a year but finally surrendered after they ran out of food. The English took Champlain to England but allowed him to return to France in 1629. In 1632, the Treaty of Saint-Germain-en-Laye returned Quebec to France. Champlain sailed back to Quebec in 1633 and rebuilt the fort, where he lived until his death on Dec. 25, 1635. Franklin L. Ford

See also **Brulé, Étienne; Canada, History of** (Early settlements; picture); **Monts, Sieur de; Nova Scotia** (Exploration and settlement).

Additional resources

Armstrong, Joe C. *Champlain.* Macmillan, 1987.
Jacobs, William J. *Champlain.* Watts, 1994. Younger readers.

Chance music. See **Aleatory music.**

Chancellorsville, Battle of. See **Civil War, American** (Battle of Chancellorsville; table: Major battles).

Chandler, Raymond (1888-1959), was one of the leading writers of the "hard-boiled" school of detective fiction. His stories are noted for their realism, violence, and colorful style. Chandler created the *private eye* (private investigator) Philip Marlowe. Marlowe is a modern knight who roams the Los Angeles area, protecting the helpless and bringing the guilty to justice.

Chandler was born on July 23, 1888, in Chicago. He published his first story in 1933 in *Black Mask,* a detective story magazine. Chandler wrote slowly and carefully. He produced only seven novels. They are *The Big Sleep* (1939), *Farewell, My Lovely* (1940), *The High Window* (1942), *The Lady in the Lake* (1943), *The Little Sister* (1949), *The Long Goodbye* (1953), and *Playback* (1958). A collection called *The Simple Art of Murder* (1950) includes short stories and a famous essay on Chandler's philosophy of detective-story writing. David Geherin

Chandler, Zachariah, *ZAK uh RY uh* (1813-1879), was an early leader of the Republican Party. He began his career as a Whig, but his strong antislavery views led him to call for a new party, the Republican Party. The party was formed in 1854. He was a United States senator from Michigan from 1857 to 1875 and U.S. secretary of the interior from 1875 to 1877. Chandler welcomed the American Civil War (1861-1865) as a chance to destroy slavery. He later favored punishing Southern leaders. Chandler was born on Dec. 10, 1813, in Bedford, New Hampshire. A statue of Chandler represents Michigan in the U.S. Capitol. James E. Sefton

Chandragupta Maurya, *CHUHN druh GUP tuh MAH oor yuh* (?-298? B.C.), founded the Mauryan Empire and ruled in what is now northern India, Pakistan, Bangladesh, and part of Afghanistan from about 324 to 298 B.C. He probably gained power in western India while fighting against Alexander the Great, the king of Macedonia. Chandragupta then conquered Magadha, a kingdom in the fertile Ganges River Valley. He used the kingdom's mineral and agricultural resources to expand his empire.

Chandragupta taxed India's growing commerce, including trade with Greece and Persia, to build a powerful army and effective administration. He provided great economic benefits for his people by improving irrigation canals and roads. He used spies and informers to ensure obedience to his will. Michael H. Fisher

See also **Mauryan Empire.**

Chandrasekhar, *SHAHN druh SAY kahr,* **Subrahmanyan,** *SU brah MAN yuhn* (1910-1995), an American astrophysicist, shared the 1983 Nobel Prize in physics with William A. Fowler for research on the evolution and death of stars. Chandrasekhar is best known for his work on white dwarf stars—the compact final state in the evolution of certain stars.

Chandrasekhar discovered that white dwarfs with a mass 1.4 times greater than the mass of our sun collapse as a result of their own gravitation. Eventually, they become neutron stars—stars with the density of an atomic nucleus—or collapse even further to become *black holes.* A black hole is so dense that not even light can escape from its powerful gravitation. The maximum mass a white dwarf star can have before it begins to collapse is known as the *Chandrasekhar limit.*

Chandrasekhar was born on Oct. 19, 1910, in Lahore in what is now Pakistan. He joined the faculty of the University of Chicago in 1937. In 1953, he became a United States citizen. David N. Schramm

See also **White dwarf.**

Chanel, *shuh NEHL,* **Coco** (1883-1971), was an influential French designer of women's fashions. Her influence came from her sensitivity to the active lives of modern women. Through her choice of fit and fabric, Chanel sought to create designs that allowed freedom of movement. Her designs were noted for simplicity of line that she accented with accessories, often combining real and costume jewelry. The inspiration for her designs came from men's clothing, but her suits and dresses enhanced the elegance and femininity of the wearer.

Gabrielle Bonheur Chanel was born Aug. 19, 1883, in Saumur, France. She began her career in 1910 by opening a hat shop. She opened a fashion house in Paris in 1919 and introduced her famous Chanel No. 5 perfume in 1922. She retired at the outbreak of World War II in 1939. Chanel reopened her business in 1954, regaining her prominence in the fashion world. Jean L. Druesedow

Chang Jiang. See Yangtze River.

Channel bass. See Redfish.

Channel Islands are a group of islands in the English Channel. They are British crown dependencies, but they lie only about 10 to 30 miles (15 to 50 kilometers) off the French coast. The four main islands are Jersey, Guernsey, Alderney, and Sark. The group also includes several smaller islands and a number of tiny, rocky isles.

The Channel Islands have a total land area of 76 square miles (197 square kilometers) and a population of about 150,000. English is the official language. Tourism and financial services are the islands' leading economic activities. The mild climate and fertile soil help make farming important as well. Farmers grow fruit, vegetables, and flowers for export. Jersey, Guernsey, and Alderney have long been famous for their fine breeds of dairy cattle.

England gained control of the Channel Islands during the 1000's, and the islands have remained British territory ever since. However, they have been largely self-governing since the 1200's. The laws of the United Kingdom do not apply to the Channel Islands unless the islands are specifically named in them. Molly Warrington

See also **Guernsey; Jersey; Sark.**

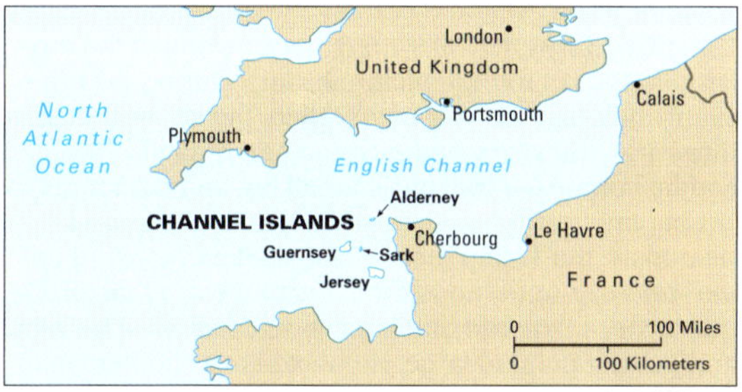

WORLD BOOK map

The Channel Islands lie in the English Channel.

Channel Islands National Park lies off the coast of southern California, west and southwest of Los Angeles. It consists of Anacapa, San Miguel, Santa Barbara, Santa Cruz, and Santa Rosa islands. The islands feature sea lions, nesting sea birds, animal fossils, and archaeological remnants of the islands' first inhabitants, the Chumash Indians. Anacapa and Santa Barbara islands were established as a national monument in 1938. The five islands became a national park in 1980. For the area, see **National Park System** (table: National parks).

Critically reviewed by the National Park Service

Channel Tunnel is a railway tunnel beneath the English Channel. The "Chunnel" links the United Kingdom and France. It opened in 1994. The tunnel was built and is run by the Eurotunnel Group, which operates in both France and the United Kingdom.

The tunnel carries three types of trains: (1) high-speed passenger trains; (2) shuttle trains for automobiles, trucks, buses, and their passengers; and (3) freight trains. Road vehicles are driven on and off the shuttles at terminals near the two entrances. One entrance is near Folkestone, England. The other is in Coquelles, a village near Calais, France. The trip through the tunnel takes about half an hour.

The Channel Tunnel measures nearly 31 miles (50 kilometers) from entrance to entrance, with 23 ½ miles (37.8 kilometers) underwater. The structure consists of three parallel tubes. Two of them are rail tubes that are 25 feet

WORLD BOOK diagram by Terry Hadler, Bernard Thornton Artists

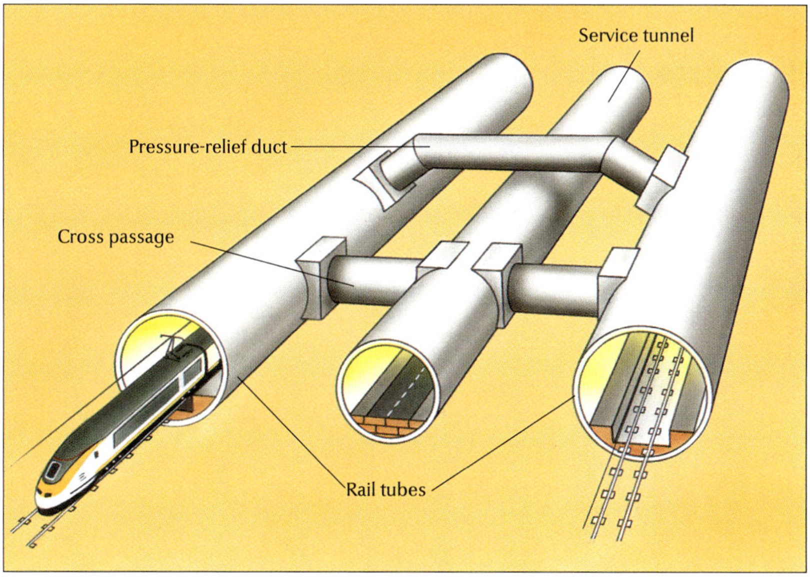

The Channel Tunnel lies beneath the English Channel. It consists of three parallel tubes, two of which carry trains between the United Kingdom and France. The third tube is a service tunnel. This tube supplies fresh air and maintenance access to the rail tubes, and could be used for emergency evacuation. Cross passages link the service tunnel to the rail tubes. Pressure-relief ducts provide an escape for air pressure created by high-speed trains.

(7.6 meters) in diameter. The third tube, a service tunnel, lies between the other two and has a diameter of 16 feet (4.8 meters). This tube supplies fresh air and maintenance access to the rail tubes, and could be used for emergency evacuation.

The three tubes generally lie about 130 feet (40 meters) beneath the seabed. Thick rings of concrete or iron form a continuous lining in the tubes. Passages connect the three tubes, and at two points the rail tubes merge to enable trains to cross from one track to the other.

Since the mid-1700's, there had been interest in building a tunnel beneath the channel. Some digging occurred on both sides of the channel in the 1880's, but the project was abandoned. In 1986, France and the United Kingdom announced that they would permit a tunnel to be built entirely with money from private investors. From 1987 to 1991, 11 boring machines dug the tunnels for the three tubes. Robert L. Mokwa

Chanukah. See Hanukkah.

Chao Tzu-yang. See Zhao Ziyang.

Chaos, *KAY ahs,* is a field of science that deals with complex and irregular processes. Physical processes that are chaotic include the changing of weather patterns, the collision of billiard balls, and the orbital movement of particles in Saturn's rings. Scientists study *chaotic systems,* sets of objects that, as a whole, display chaotic behavior. In the case of a collision of billiard balls, the main objects in the system would be the balls, the playing surface of the table, and the cushions at the sides of the playing surface.

Scientists once thought that, with enough information, they could make exact predictions about chaotic systems. The science of chaos has shown, however, that it is difficult to predict the long-range behavior of such complex systems. There are two reasons for this difficulty: (1) a chaotic system has what scientists call a *sensitive dependence upon initial conditions,* and (2) it is difficult to obtain enough information about those conditions.

Sensitive dependence upon initial conditions means that a tiny difference in starting conditions can lead to much different results. For example, in a complex billiards shot, a small error in the player's aim would cause only a slight change in the cue ball's path at first. With each collision, however, the ball would veer farther from the intended path.

The early parts of the path would be relatively easy to predict. A scientist would measure such factors as the location of each ball, the speed and direction of the cue ball, and the friction between the balls and the playing surface. The scientist would then use these measurements in physics equations. To predict the path after each successive collision would be increasingly difficult, however. The scientist would need more information about the initial conditions. Not only would the measurements have to be more precise, but also more measurements would be needed. For example, the scientist might need to know how level the playing table was.

Suppose there were much less friction between the balls and the playing surface. The cue ball would not slow down as much, more collisions would occur, and the measurements would have to be even more precise and extensive. If the amount of friction were small enough, the prediction would require so much information that it would not be practical to try to obtain all of it.

Although scientists cannot make long-term forecasts of chaotic systems, they can make reasonably accurate short-term predictions. They do this by discovering and applying general patterns of behavior in the systems. For example, *meteorologists* (scientists who study the weather) have analyzed the development of weather patterns in different places over various lengths of time. They have then used their analyses to make useful five-day forecasts available in many parts of the world. See **Weather** (Weather forecasting). Harold M. Hastings

Chaparral, *CHAP uh RAL,* is a region of shrubs and small trees that occurs in areas with mild, moist winters and hot, dry summers. Ecologists regard the chaparral as one of the major *biomes*—that is, natural communities of plants and animals (see **Biome**). Chaparrals are found in the Mediterranean region, from southern California into Baja California in Mexico, and in parts of Chile, southern Australia, and South Africa.

Plants commonly found on North American chaparrals include manzanita, mountain mahogany, scrub oak, and especially the chamise shrub. Most chaparral plants have tough, crooked branches and thick, leathery leaves that do not fall off in winter. Few of the plants grow more than 10 feet (3 meters) tall. In some areas, plants grow so densely that people cannot walk through them. Animals that live on North American chaparrals include coyotes, mule deer, and lizards. Eric G. Bolen

Chaplin, Charlie (1889-1977), became one of the most famous stars in motion-picture history. During the era of silent comedies, he was often called "the funniest man in the world." He wrote and directed nearly all his films, and he composed the music for all his sound pictures.

Chaplin's stardom began in 1914, when he first appeared as "the Tramp" or "the Little Fellow." Looking undersized and undernourished, Chaplin wore a small mustache, a battered derby hat, a coat too small for him, and pants much too large. He walked in a shuffling manner that suggested he had never worn a pair of shoes his own size. But this figure of poverty also wore gloves and carried a bamboo cane that seemed to reflect a spirit that bounces back from the most crushing defeats. The last shot in many of Chaplin's early silent films shows him walking down a road into the distance. The Tramp was homeless and penniless once more, but with hat tilted and cane flourishing, he again was ready for whatever adventure lay around the corner.

In 1919, Chaplin formed the United Artists film corporation with actor Douglas Fairbanks, Sr., actress Mary Pickford, and director D. W. Griffith. He made fewer pictures, and those he made were longer and more serious. He continued to create laughter, but he also seemed to be commenting on why the world of respectability and authority offered so little to the human soul. His films during this time included *The Kid* (1921) and *The Gold Rush* (1925). Chaplin played the Tramp in these films and in his first two sound films, *City Lights* (1931) and *Modern Times* (1936). In *The Great Dictator* (1940), he played two roles, a humble Jewish barber and a tyrant based on the German dictator Adolf Hitler. Chaplin played a murderer in *Monsieur Verdoux* (1947) and an elderly music hall comedian in *Limelight* (1952).

Charles Spencer Chaplin was born on April 16, 1889, into a poor London family. In 1898, he became a variety and music hall performer and began touring the United

States in 1910. He lived in the United States for more than 40 years but never became a citizen. In 1943, Chaplin married Oona O'Neill, daughter of American playwright Eugene O'Neill. It was Chaplin's fourth marriage.

Pictorial Parade
Charlie Chaplin

In the 1940's and early 1950's, Chaplin was a center of controversy. Some people criticized his personal life as immoral and accused him of supporting Communism. In 1952, Chaplin traveled to Europe. The U.S. government announced that Chaplin could not reenter the United States unless hearings were held on his personal life and political views. Chaplin decided not to return, and he and his family settled in Switzerland.

In 1972, Chaplin took part in ceremonies in his honor in New York City and Los Angeles. Chaplin received an honorary Oscar at the annual Academy Award ceremonies in April. The award praised Chaplin "for the incalculable effect he has had in making motion pictures the art form of this century." In 1975, Chaplin was knighted by Queen Elizabeth II. He died on Dec. 25, 1977.

Robert Sklar

Additional resources

Lynn, Kenneth S. *Charlie Chaplin and His Times.* 1997. Reprint. Cooper Square, 2003.
Vance, Jeffrey. *Chaplin.* Abrams, 2003.

Chapman, George (1559?-1634?), was an English poet, playwright, and scholar. He was concerned with both the philosophical and the moral significance of poetry, as well as the importance of classical learning.

Chapman was born in Hertfordshire. His first publication was a philosophical poem, *The Shadow of Night* (1594). As a playwright, Chapman wrote both comedies and tragedies, including the famous tragedy *Bussy D'Ambois* (1604). His tragedies usually center on a great man's relation to his society. They concern ideals of order in each person and in society, and the corruption of these ideals.

In 1616, Chapman published his impressive translation of the *Iliad* and the *Odyssey.* John Keats expressed his awe at the imaginative world opened to him by these translations in his sonnet "On First Looking into Chapman's Homer." Stephen Orgel

Chapman, John. See **Appleseed, Johnny.**

Characin. See Tetra.

Character education is a type of instruction that focuses on values such as honesty, responsibility, respect, caring, and fairness among students. The character education movement encourages schools to develop programs that emphasize ethics and responsibility. Supporters of such programs believe that "good character" can be formed through teaching, the setting of examples, and practice in a supportive school community. The long-term goal of character education is the development of a more responsible and caring society.

Character education begins with the establishment of core ethical values that form the basis for instruction in school and the community. The values are then integrated into school activities and into the general lesson strategies of the teachers. Character education can be presented at any grade level. In early grades, character education usually emphasizes behavioral skills. In later grades, it includes such topics as reducing prejudice and resolving conflicts. *Service learning,* in which students participate in programs that help others, is a central component of character education.

Character education programs are widespread in the United States. A variety of organizations—including nonprofit associations, universities, and school districts—suggest strategies for effectively incorporating character education into the curriculum. A similar emphasis on character education can be found in schools in most developed nations. Lawrence O. Picus

See also **Moral education.**

Charcoal is a black, brittle substance that has a variety of uses. For example, it is used in *pigments* (coloring matter); in filters to remove unwanted colors, flavors, and odors; as a fuel; and as a drawing instrument.

Charcoal consists mainly of *amorphous carbon* and ash. Amorphous carbon is carbon made of tiny, irregularly arranged particles of *graphite* (a form of pure carbon). Charcoal also contains small amounts of impurities, such as sulfur and hydrogen compounds.

Manufacturers produce charcoal by heating carbon-rich plant or animal materials, such as wood or bones, in ovens that contain little or no air. During the heating process, most of the hydrogen, nitrogen, and oxygen in the raw materials escape. The end product is a black, *porous* (full of tiny holes) material, which is charcoal.

Activated charcoal is charcoal from which most of the impurities have been removed. Manufacturers make it by treating ordinary charcoal with steam and air heated to above 600 °F (316 °C).

Uses of charcoal. Wood charcoal is the most widely used kind of charcoal. Small chunks of wood charcoal burn well and are an excellent fuel. Many people burn wood charcoal *briquettes* (small, molded pieces) in outdoor barbecues. Artists draw with small sticks of wood charcoal (see **Drawing** [picture: A charcoal drawing]). In powdered form, wood charcoal is used in filters and as an ingredient in gunpowder.

Manufacturers use bone charcoal in powdered form to make pigments for dyeing leathers and coloring inks and paints. Powdered forms of wood, bone, and activated charcoal are used to *adsorb* (hold on their internal surfaces) unwanted colors, flavors, and odors from gases and liquids. This adsorption process is used in the manufacture of white sugar. Activated charcoal is the best adsorbent, because its spaces give it a large internal surface area. Geoffrey E. Dolbear

Chardin, *shahr DAN,* **Jean Baptiste Siméon** (1699-1779), is now regarded as one of the great French painters of the 1700's. Born on Nov. 2, 1699, in Paris, Chardin lived there all his life, content to paint the common scenes and objects of daily life. *The Cardplayer* (1737) and *Grace Before Meat* (1740) are two excellent examples of Chardin's early style.

Like the Dutch masters of the 1600's, Chardin deals with themes that must attract interest chiefly through the quality of the paintings. He lifts simple people and objects into a painted world of quiet perfection with a sure sense of design, color, and texture. Even the critic Denis Diderot, who thought art should deal with "noble" themes, admired Chardin for his ability to make common things universal through the magic of style. Chardin's intimate subjects show the growing influence of middle-class taste on painting during his time.

Chardin's colors are generally low in key so that the effect is subdued. He applied paint in a mixture of glazes and thick pigment that suggests the textures of his subjects with amazing accuracy. His paintings are carefully composed, and each form or part has a balanced, proportioned place in the final effect. Ann Friedman

Charest, *shah RAY,* **Jean,** *zhahn* (1958-), became premier of Quebec in 2003. He opposes independence for the province. Charest has led the provincial Quebec Liberal Party since 1998. He served as head of the federal Progressive Conservative Party from 1993 to 1998.

Charest was born in Sherbrooke, Quebec, on June 24, 1958. In 1980, he received a law degree from the University of Sherbrooke. He became a member of Canada's House of Commons in 1984. In 1990, he led a committee to settle disagreements over proposed changes in Canada's constitution. From 1991 to 1993, he was minister of the environment under Prime Minister Brian Mulroney.

In February 1993, Mulroney announced his resignation as prime minister and Progressive Conservative Party leader. In June, Charest ran in the party election to replace Mulroney, but he narrowly lost to Kim Campbell. He then served as deputy prime minister in Campbell's government. In October 1993, the Progressive Conservatives, under Campbell, suffered a stunning defeat in a general election. The party had been the majority party in the Commons since 1984. Charest became head of the Progressive Conservatives two months after the election.

In 1998, Charest became the head of the provincial Quebec Liberal Party. That year, the Parti Quebecois (PQ) defeated the Liberal Party in provincial elections. In elections in 2003, the Liberal Party defeated the PQ, and Charest became premier of Quebec. Graham Fraser

Charge-coupled device, abbreviated CCD, is an electronic device that can produce images. A CCD transmits a signal as a succession of "packets" of electric charge from one part of an electric circuit to another. The best-known kinds of CCD's are used in cameras and other instruments that produce still images and motion pictures. CCD's have replaced film in applications ranging from handheld digital cameras to large cameras mounted in astronomers' telescopes. Many television cameras use CCD's instead of vacuum tubes. CCD's are also used in camcorders, photocopiers, fax machines, and medical imaging systems that use ultrasound.

Charge-coupled devices have three advantages over film: (1) They can be reused, (2) they produce electric signals that can be used by computers, and (3) some of them are more sensitive to light than film is. In addition, CCD's are smaller and lighter than vacuum tubes.

Most CCD's used in imaging systems consist of a silicon chip with tiny, square parts called *pixels* arranged in rows and columns on its surface. As light falls on a pixel, an electric charge builds up in the pixel. The amount of charge depends upon the amount of light—the more light, the greater the charge. The CCD thus translates the light from a scene striking the pixel array into an "electronic picture" consisting of the charges in all the pixels.

The CCD then releases the charges, one pixel at a time. The charges flow as an electric current, with variations in the current representing the various parts of the picture. Other devices translate the current into *binary digits*—the 0's and 1's that computers use—then translate the digits into a visible image.

In a CCD used to produce still images, the process of building up and transmitting the charges occurs once for each picture. In a CCD used for motion pictures, the process continually repeats itself.

The number of pixels in a camera's CCD depends upon the intended use. A still camera used mainly by amateur photographers might have an *array* (arrangement) of pixels 1,600 columns wide by 1,200 rows high, for a total of 1,920,000 pixels. Higher quality cameras used by professional photographers have about 5 million pixels. Peter Bohdan Kosel

See also **Camcorder; Telescope** (What telescopes do); **Television** (Creating television signals).

Chariot is a two-wheeled or four-wheeled vehicle, usually drawn by a horse. Chariots were among the earliest wheeled vehicles. They were probably first built in Mesopotamia, a region of the Middle East, more than 4,000 years ago. Two-wheeled chariots were used in battle by many peoples of ancient times, including the Assyrians, Egyptians, Greeks, Persians, and Romans. The wheels of some war chariots were fitted with scythelike blades that could severely injure enemy soldiers or horses. In time, chariot racing became a popular sport, especially in ancient Rome. A light four-wheeled chariot called a *post-chariot* became popular in Europe during the 1700's and early 1800's. The body of a post-chariot was suspended over the wheels on leather straps, and the driver sat in a seat at the front. Post-chariots carried the mail and as many as four passengers.

Charlemagne, *SHAHR luh* MAYN (742-814), or Charles the Great, was the most famous ruler of the Middle Ages and a key figure in European history. He conquered much of western Europe and united it under a great empire. Charlemagne revived the political and cultural life of Europe, which had declined after the fall of the West Roman Empire in the A.D. 400's. His activities laid the foundation for the European civilization that arose during the later Middle Ages.

More is known about Charlemagne than most medieval rulers because of a biography by Einhard, one of the court attendants. This book describes Charlemagne

Detail of a stained glass window (about 1200) in the Strasbourg Cathedral, Strasbourg, France (Ronald Sheridan)

Charlemagne

Empire of Charlemagne

This map shows the growth of Charlemagne's empire. In 768, Charlemagne and his brother Carloman became joint rulers of the Frankish kingdom, shown in yellow. Charlemagne's share of the kingdom consisted of Austrasia, Neustria, and half of Aquitaine. Carloman died in 771, and Charlemagne became king of all the Franks. He enlarged his empire by conquering Saxony, the Kingdom of the Lombards, Bavaria, and other areas, shown in light tan.

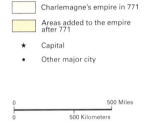

Charlemagne's empire in 771

Areas added to the empire after 771

★ Capital

• Other major city

0 500 Miles

0 500 Kilometers

WORLD BOOK map

as more than 6 feet (183 centimeters) tall, with piercing eyes, fair hair, a thick neck, and a potbelly. He was strong, fond of exercise, and had an alert mind and a forceful personality. Charlemagne could read and speak Latin, the language of educated people of the time. However, he never learned to write it.

Military conquests. Charlemagne was a son of Pepin the Short, who became king of the Franks in 751. After Pepin died in 768, his two sons, Charlemagne and Carloman, shared the Frankish kingdom. The kingdom covered what is now Belgium, France, Luxembourg, the Netherlands, and part of western Germany. Charlemagne became the sole ruler of the Frankish kingdom following Carloman's death in 771.

Charlemagne began to expand his kingdom almost immediately. He conquered the Lombard kingdom and Bavaria and added them to his realm. He took land and treasure from the Avars in eastern Europe.

Charlemagne waged his longest and bitterest campaign against the Saxons, a pagan people in northwestern Germany. He subdued the Saxons after about 30 years of war and forced them to accept Christianity.

Charlemagne also waged war in Spain. He was returning from an expedition there in 778 when a mountain people called the Basques ambushed and wiped out his rear guard. This incident became the subject of the famous epic poem *The Song of Roland.* See **Roland**.

By 800, Charlemagne's realm extended from central Italy north to Denmark and from eastern Germany west to the Atlantic Ocean. Throughout his reign, Charlemagne followed a policy of friendship and cooperation with the Christian church. He protected the church and continually extended its power. In recognition of Charlemagne's vast power, and to strengthen the king's alliance with the church, Pope Leo III crowned him emperor of the Romans on Christmas Day, 800. See **Roman Catholic Church** (Charlemagne).

Administration and influence. In Charlemagne's time, Europe had hardly any towns, trade, or industry. Almost all the people made their living by farming, and they raised barely enough to feed themselves. Few people had much money, and the government and laws of the old Roman Empire had disappeared.

Charlemagne introduced a system to the rest of Europe that his father and grandfather had employed in the Frankish kingdom. He granted large estates to loyal nobles, who, in return, provided military and political services to the king. The nobles also maintained the roads, bridges, and fortifications on their land. This system became the basis for *feudalism,* the political and military system of Europe for the next 400 years (see **Feudalism**). To stimulate trade, Charlemagne coined silver money, encouraged the establishment of markets, and discouraged excessive tolls.

Charlemagne was devoted to justice and good government. He decreed that all courts be held regularly and that judges base their decisions only on accepted law. He divided his realm into districts and appointed efficient officers to administer them. Periodically, Charlemagne sent royal inspectors to carry his orders to the districts and to report on local conditions. In this way, he kept control of the distant parts of his empire.

Charlemagne also improved education and culture by establishing a school at his palace in Aachen. This *palace school* attracted the best teachers and students in Europe. It educated clergymen, thus strengthening the church, and trained teachers for schools throughout the empire. Scholars at the schools collected and copied ancient Roman manuscripts, which otherwise might have been lost forever. They also developed a new style of handwriting, called *Carolingian minuscule.* This style of handwriting later became the model for printing. The revival of learning under Charlemagne is sometimes called the *Carolingian Renaissance.*

After Charlemagne died in 814, his empire gradually fell apart. Attacks by Vikings and other invaders weakened the empire, and in 843, Charlemagne's grandsons divided it into three parts. By the late 800's, the empire had ceased to exist. However, the cultural revival begun by Charlemagne had a lasting effect on European civilization. Charlemagne's empire also inspired later attempts to unite many European nations, including the Holy Roman Empire. Later in the Middle Ages, Charlemagne became a hero of legends and stories that credited him with superhuman wisdom and strength.

Deborah Mauskopf Deliyannis

Related articles in *World Book* include:

Aachen	Holy Roman Empire
Architecture (Carolingian architecture)	Middle Ages (The Carolingian Empire)
Carolingian art	Pepin the Short
Franks	Verdun, Treaty of

Additional resources

Becher, Matthias. *Charlemagne.* Yale, 2003.
Greenblatt, Miriam. *Charlemagne and the Early Middle Ages.* Benchmark Bks., 2002.

Charles I (1887-1922) was the last emperor of Austria and king of Hungary. He was born on Aug. 17, 1887, at Persenbeug Castle, in Austria. In 1916, during World War I (1914-1918), he succeeded to the throne upon the death of his great-uncle, Francis Joseph. Charles secretly tried to make a separate peace between Austria-Hungary and the Allies in 1917. After his country was defeated, he went into exile in Switzerland. He later made two unsuccessful attempts to regain the throne of Hungary. Charles was finally sent with his family to the island of Madeira, where he died on April 1, 1922. John W. Boyer

Charles I (1600-1649) became king of England, Scotland, and Ireland in 1625. Charles supported the *divine right of kings,* the belief that a monarch's right to rule came solely and directly from God. His conflicts with Parliament helped lead to the English Civil War in 1642. Charles was a member of the House of Stuart. He was born in Dunfermline, Scotland, on Nov. 19, 1600.

From 1625 to 1629, Charles called three Parliaments and dissolved each one because the members opposed his political, fiscal, and religious reforms. In 1628, he reluctantly accepted the Petition of Right, a document that was drawn up by Parliament and which insisted that Charles rule by existing laws.

Charles ruled without Parliament from 1629 to 1640. He tried to force Scotland to use English forms of worship, and in 1639 the Scots rebelled. Charles had to call Parliament to obtain money to fight the rebels. He dismissed one Parliament, called the Short Parliament, after three weeks, but he had to summon another. This Parliament, known as the Long Parliament, met from 1640 to 1653 and again briefly in 1660. In 1641, it passed sweeping political and legal reforms.

The king tried to arrest six parliamentary leaders in 1642. This attempt helped lead to civil war later that year. Charles had the support of many members of the upper classes and of the clergy of the Church of England. Numerous merchants and religious reformers called Puritans supported Parliament. Oliver Cromwell, a Puritan and parliamentary general, won key battles. Charles surrendered to Scotland's army, and the fighting ended in 1646. Soon afterward, Scottish leaders turned Charles over to Parliament. He escaped in 1647, leading to a brief return to civil war in 1648. In 1649, a special court created by Parliament convicted Charles of treason, and he was beheaded on January 30. Richard L. Greaves

Related articles in *World Book* include:

Cromwell, Oliver	Painting (The 1600's and 1700's [picture])
Divine right of kings	Petition of Right
England (Civil war; picture: The trial of Charles I)	Rump Parliament
Laud, William	Scotland (History)
Long Parliament	

Charles I (of Spain). See **Charles V** (Holy Roman emperor).

Charles II (1630-1685) became king of England, Scotland, and Ireland in 1660. He had lived in exile after the execution of his father, King Charles I, in 1649. That year, the Scots proclaimed Charles king of Scotland. But the Puritan leader Oliver Cromwell defeated his army in 1651, and Charles fled to France. After Cromwell died in 1658, the English people became increasingly dissatisfied with the government that he had set up. In 1660, Parliament invited Charles to return and declared him king. The important events of his reign included two wars with the Dutch; the Great Plague; the Great Fire of London; and the Rye House Plot, an assassination attempt. Charles was a member of the House of Stuart. He was born May 29, 1630, in London. Richard L. Greaves

See also **Restoration; Rye House Plot.**

Charles II (823-877), or Charles the Bald, ruled the kingdom that later became France. He was a grandson of Charlemagne (Charles I), who had united much of western Europe into an empire. Charles II is called Charles I by historians who do not give Charlemagne that title.

Charles II and his half brothers Louis the German and Lothair fought a series of civil wars over how Charlemagne's empire should be divided. Charles and Louis united and defeated Lothair, bringing about the Treaty of Verdun in 843. This treaty gave Charles the empire's western part, which formed the basis for France.

Charles was born June 13, 823. He spent most of his career fighting Vikings, crushing uprisings of the nobility, and stopping raids from Muslim Spain. He also took over part of the kingdom of Lothair and his descendants, which bordered his own kingdom on the east. In 875, he obtained the title Emperor Charles II. Bernard S. Bachrach

Charles III (879-929), also called Charles the Simple, ruled the kingdom that later became France. Born Sept. 17, 879, he was a descendant of the great ruler Charlemagne. A group of nobles recognized Charles as king in A.D. 893. But Count Odo (also called Eudes) of Paris had been king since 887 and was still alive. Civil war followed between Charles's supporters and Odo's followers. In 898, Odo died. Charles then ruled a state that was troubled by Viking invasions and civil conflict. As king, his most important act was to give, in 911, a group of Vikings the right to settle in much of what is now Normandy. This act provided some stability in the kingdom. But Charles displeased many nobles. They deposed him in 922 and imprisoned him in 923. Bernard S. Bachrach

Charles III (1716-1788) reigned as king of Spain from 1759 until his death. He was a member of the Bourbon family, a French royal family that began to rule Spain in

1700. Charles's reign marked the high point of a period of reforms in Spain that were known as the *Bourbon Reforms.* During this period, Spain greatly developed its economy and modernized its administration.

Charles stimulated the construction of shipyards and the growth of manufacturing. His government liberalized trade, improved the country's transportation system, issued the first Spanish paper money, and conducted the first census of the kingdom. In 1767, the Jesuits, members of a powerful Roman Catholic order, were expelled from Spain and the Spanish Empire.

During the Revolutionary War in America (1775-1783), Charles aided the American Colonies financially and diplomatically. In 1780 and 1781, his forces defeated British troops in the South at Mobile and Pensacola. As a result, Spain officially regained Florida from Britain in 1783. Spain had lost Florida to Britain in 1763.

Charles was born in Madrid. He was the son of King Philip V of Spain. Miguel A. Bretos

Charles V (1338-1380), king of France, was known to his people as The Wise. An able monarch, he ruled during the Hundred Years' War with England (1337-1453).

Charles was born in Vincennes, France. At the age of 18, he began ruling France for his father, King John II. The English had captured John at Poitiers, France, in 1356. In the early years of his rule, Charles had to control rebellious nobles, crush a peasant uprising, and fight off rivals who wanted his throne.

Charles formally became king in 1364 when his father died. As king, Charles used the help of advisers to strengthen the government and reorganize the army. In 1369, Charles resumed the Hundred Years' War, which had been temporarily stopped since 1360. By the time he died, he had regained almost all French land lost to England earlier in the war. Sue Helder Goliber

See also **Hundred Years' War.**

Charles V (1500-1558) of the House of Habsburg (or Hapsburg) became Holy Roman emperor in 1519, succeeding his grandfather Maximilian I. The Holy Roman Empire was a German-based empire in central Europe.

Charles was born in Ghent, Belgium. In 1506, he inherited the Low Countries (now most of Belgium, Luxembourg, and the Netherlands) and Burgundy (now in France) from his father, Philip, Duke of Burgundy. From his grandparents Ferdinand and Isabella of Spain, he got the Spanish throne, becoming King Charles I of Spain in 1516. Charles won lands in Italy from France in the 1520's. But his power was weakened by the Protestant Reformation, which split Germany into rival Protestant and Roman Catholic groups. In 1555 and 1556, he gave up the Low Countries, Spain, and all Spanish lands in Italy and America to his son, Philip II, and the Holy Roman Empire to his brother, Ferdinand I (see **Philip II** [of Spain]). Jonathan W. Zophy

Charles VII (1403-1461) was a king of France who, with the aid of Joan of Arc, won the Hundred Years' War against England (1337-1453). He also strengthened the French military and state.

Charles was born in Paris. His father, King Charles VI, was forced to declare King Henry V of England heir to the French throne in the Treaty of Troyes in 1420. But when Charles VI died in 1422, Charles VII declared himself king. Much of southern France recognized him as ruler. But northern France was controlled by the English, his enemies in the war. Charles could not be crowned because Reims, the city where French kings were crowned, lay in enemy territory.

In 1428, the English began a siege of Orléans, France. Joan of Arc, a young peasant woman, led French troops and ended the siege in 1429. She took Charles through enemy territory to Reims, where he was crowned that year. Joan later became a prisoner of the English, but Charles made no attempt to help her, and she was burned to death as a heretic.

Charles strengthened the French monarchy by creating a standing army and establishing a permanent tax. By 1453, the French had expelled England from all of France except the city of Calais. Sue Helder Goliber

See also **Hundred Years' War; Joan of Arc, Saint.**

Charles VII (1697-1745) was Holy Roman emperor from 1742 to 1745. He was the first Holy Roman emperor in more than 300 years who was not a member of the Habsburg (or Hapsburg) family.

Charles VII was born Charles Albert Wittelsbach in Schleissheim, Bavaria, near Munich in what is now Germany. In 1726, he became the ruler of Bavaria as Elector Charles Albert.

After Holy Roman Emperor Charles VI died in 1740, a dispute arose about who would succeed him. Charles Albert and several other rulers broke a pledge to let Charles VI's daughter Maria Theresa inherit his territories. They took some of her lands in the War of the Austrian Succession (1740-1748). Charles Albert claimed the throne, and with French help, became Holy Roman emperor as Charles VII. Jonathan W. Zophy

See also **Habsburg, House of; Maria Theresa; Succession wars** (The War of the Austrian Succession).

Charles VIII (1470-1498) was king of France from 1483 until his death. He helped introduce the culture of the Italian Renaissance to his country. However, his foreign policy began 65 years of conflict with the Holy Roman Empire over control of Italy.

Charles was born in Amboise, France, near Tours. He succeeded his father, King Louis XI, at the age of 13. Good-natured, romantic, but sickly, Charles showed little ability to rule. His older sister, Anne of Beaujeu, and her husband, Pierre, ruled wisely on his behalf until the early 1490's. In 1494, Charles invaded Italy. He easily defeated the divided and militarily weak Italians. But a coalition that included the Holy Roman Empire, Spain, Venice, Milan, and Pope Alexander VI forced him to withdraw. Charles spent the rest of his rule planning another campaign against Italy. Sue Helder Goliber

Charles IX (1550-1574) of France ruled from 1560 to 1574. The second son of Henry II and Catherine de Médicis, Charles succeeded his brother Francis II at the age of 10. Catherine officially ruled for Charles until 1563. Even after that, she dominated his government. To balance her influence, Charles sought the counsel of Gaspard de Coligny, a leading *Huguenot* (French Protestant). Catherine's jealousy of Coligny and her fear that his policies would result in war with Spain helped lead in 1572 to the killing, by Roman Catholics, of Coligny and thousands of other Huguenots. This event became known as the Massacre of St. Bartholomew's Day. Charles's entire reign was marked by fighting between Catholics and Huguenots, led by nobles who used their religious differences to disguise their struggles for wealth and power. Charles was born on June 27, 1550, at St.-Germain-en-Laye and died on May 30, 1574.

Donald A. Bailey

See also **Catherine de Médicis; Huguenots; Saint Bartholomew's Day, Massacre of.**

Charles X (1757-1836) was king of France from 1824 to 1830. He belonged to the royal Bourbon family of France. Born Oct. 9, 1757, at Versailles, Charles was the younger brother of Kings Louis XVI and Louis XVIII. Near the start of the French Revolution (1789-1799), Charles fled France, and he soon went to Britain. He returned to France in 1814. Charles succeeded Louis XVIII as king in 1824. As king, Charles tried to restore the power of the monarchy and increase the authority of the church and aristocracy in France. His measures drew increasing opposition from French liberals. In 1830, after the enactment of new laws restricting freedom of the press, liberals and artisans in Paris overthrew Charles in an uprising called the July Revolution. The leaders of the revolution replaced him with Louis Philippe, and Charles fled to Britain. He died on Nov. 6, 1836. See also **July Revolution.** Peter N. Stearns

Charles X (1622-1660) of Sweden became king in 1654 when Queen Christina gave up the throne. He was the nephew of King Gustavus Adolphus. While Charles was king, Sweden suffered from serious financial and social problems. But Charles could pay only limited attention to these matters because the country was at war during most of his reign. From 1655 to 1657, he fought a largely indecisive war in Poland. In 1657, Denmark, Poland's ally, declared war on Sweden. Charles quickly defeated Denmark. In 1658 in the Treaty of Roskilde, Denmark gave Sweden territories in what are now Sweden, Denmark, and Norway. This treaty marked the high point of Sweden's Baltic empire. Later in 1658, faced by a coalition of Poland, Russia, Prussia, and Denmark, Charles attacked Denmark again. He died during this conflict, on Feb. 13, 1660, probably of pneumonia. Charles was born on Nov. 8, 1622, in Nyköping, Sweden. Byron J. Nordstrom

Charles XI (1655-1697), king of Sweden, succeeded his father, Charles X, in 1660. Because Charles was only 4 years old when he became king, Sweden was governed for him by a council of nobles until 1672.

From 1674 to 1679, Charles fought a costly and inconclusive war against Prussia and Denmark. After that, he pursued a peaceful foreign policy and attended to Sweden's long-standing economic and social problems. With the support of Sweden's parliament, Charles reduced the power of the nobility and was made an absolute monarch. He introduced a program called the Reduction to reclaim land given to nobles in return for service to the state. The Reduction greatly increased the wealth of the state and provided funds for reform of the army. Charles was an energetic and dedicated king who left a well-run state and a full treasury when he died on April 5, 1697. He was born on Nov. 24, 1655, in Stockholm. Byron J. Nordstrom

Charles XII (1682-1718) became king of Sweden in 1697. He succeeded his father, Charles XI. In 1700, Denmark, Russia, Poland, and Saxony attacked Sweden, beginning the Great Northern War. Charles quickly defeated Denmark and in 1700 won a famous battle against the Russians at Narva, in what is now Estonia. Charles then spent almost seven years defeating Poland and Saxony. In 1708, he turned his attention back to Russia. But he was defeated in 1709 by a Russian army at Poltava, in what is now Ukraine. Charles escaped to the Ottoman Empire and tried to lead Sweden from there. The war continued, and Sweden lost its Baltic empire. In 1714, Charles made his way back to what is now northern Germany to continue fighting. He returned to Sweden in 1715. He was killed on Nov. 30, 1718, observing a siege at what is now Halden, Norway. After his death, Sweden made peace with its enemies, and the nation's absolute monarchy and imperial age ended. Charles was born on June 17, 1682, in Stockholm. Byron J. Nordstrom

Charles, Prince (1948-), is the heir to the British throne. He is the oldest child of Queen Elizabeth II and Prince Philip. His full name and titles are His Royal Highness The Prince Charles Philip Arthur George, Prince of Wales, Duke of Cornwall, Earl of Chester, Duke of Rothesay, Earl of Carrick, Baron Renfrew, Lord of the Isles, Prince and Great Steward of Scotland.

© Tim Graham, Corbis

Prince Charles

Prince Charles was born on Nov. 14, 1948, at Buckingham Palace in London. He was the first heir to the British throne to get most of his education away from the royal palace, rather than having tutors at home. From 1957 to 1962, he went to Cheam, a preparatory school near London. In 1962, he enrolled at Gordonstoun, a school in the Scottish Highlands that his father had attended. He spent six months in 1966 at Timbertop, an Australian school that stresses rugged outdoor activities. Charles graduated from Trinity College at Cambridge University in 1970 with a degree in history.

In 1958, Queen Elizabeth officially named Charles Prince of Wales, the 700-year-old title traditionally given to the heir to the throne. In 1969, she presented the prince to the people of Wales in a ceremony at Caernarfon Castle in Wales. Prince Charles enrolled at the Royal Air Force College in 1971 and graduated from its advanced flying course later that year. He then entered the Royal Navy and served until 1976. In the Navy, his activities included flying helicopters and commanding a ship, the minehunter *Bronington.*

After leaving the Navy, Prince Charles began to handle a full schedule of public duties. He has frequently represented Queen Elizabeth on state visits to foreign countries. Prince Charles has concerned himself with such issues as disadvantaged people, education, and the environment; and he has been a critic of modern architecture. Prince Charles is the founder of two charitable organizations—The Prince's Trust and The Prince's Youth Business Trust. The prince enjoys fishing, gardening, and other outdoor activities.

On July 29, 1981, Prince Charles married Lady Diana Spencer, a British aristocrat. They had two sons—Prince William Arthur Philip Louis, born in 1982, and Prince Henry Charles Albert David, born in 1984. Prince Charles and Diana divorced in 1996. Diana was killed in an automobile accident in 1997.

In February 2005, Prince Charles announced his engagement to Camilla Parker Bowles, a long-time friend. The couple married on April 9, 2005. Richard Rose

See also **Diana, Princess of Wales.**

Charles, Ray (1930-2004), was an American singer, songwriter, bandleader, and pianist. His style was influenced by gospel music, rhythm and blues, and jazz. Charles was best known for his work in popular music. He became famous for singing such standards as "Georgia on My Mind" (recorded in 1960) and "I Can't Stop Loving You" (recorded in 1962). His other hits included "I Got a Woman" (1955), "What'd I Say" (1959), "Hit the Road Jack" (1961), "Busted" (1963), "Crying Time" (1966), "I'll Be Good to You" (1990), and "A Song for You" (1993).

Reuters/Bettmann Newsphotos

Ray Charles

Ray Charles Robinson was born on Sept. 23, 1930, into a poor family in Albany, Georgia. He changed his name to Ray Charles in the early 1950's to avoid confusion with boxer Sugar Ray Robinson. Charles went blind at the age of 7, possibly from glaucoma. He studied music, piano, and braille at the St. Augustine (Florida) School for the Deaf and Blind. In the late 1940's, he began touring with his own jazz groups, developing the personal sound as soul singer and instrumentalist that won him international popularity. Charles died on June 10, 2004. Frank Tirro

Charles Martel (688?-741) ruled northern Gaul from 719 to 741. Gaul was a region in Europe that included what are now France, Germany west of the Rhine River, and Belgium. Charles was not a king but ruled as "mayor of the palace" in the name of several weak kings of the Merovingian *dynasty* (family of rulers). From 714 to 719, he fought to establish his rule in northern Gaul. Later, he brought Burgundy, the southeastern part of present-day France, under his control. He also conquered Frisia in what is now the Netherlands. He helped convert Germany to Christianity by sponsoring Saint Boniface's missionary work. In 732, Charles defeated an invading Muslim army at the Battle of Poitiers, also called the Battle of Tours. The fighting began near Tours, France, and ended near Poitiers. He was later called *Martel,* meaning *the Hammer,* due to his victory over the Muslims.

Charles's son Pepin the Short was the first king in the Carolingian dynasty. Charles's grandson Charlemagne conquered a vast empire. Bernard S. Bachrach

See also **Charlemagne; Franks; Merovingian dynasty; Pepin the Short; Poitiers, Battle of.**

Charles the Bald. See **Charles II** (of France).

Charles the Great. See **Charlemagne.**

Charleston, South Carolina (pop. 96,650; met. area pop. 549,033), is an important Atlantic Coast port and the second largest city in the state. Only Columbia has more people. Charleston lies on a peninsula between the Ashley and Cooper rivers, about midway on the coastline (see **South Carolina** [political map]).

Charleston was founded in 1670 and was named Charles Town for King Charles II of England. The city's people changed the name in 1783. Many houses and other buildings in Charleston date from the 1700's and 1800's. The American Civil War began on the Charleston waterfront in 1861 when Confederate soldiers attacked Union troops at Fort Sumter in the city's harbor.

The city. Charleston is South Carolina's chief port and one of the busiest container ports in the nation. The city's manufactured products include aluminum, chemicals, steel, and transportation equipment. The main sources of employment in the city are the Medical University of South Carolina and the United States Navy.

Charleston's economy also depends heavily on tourism. Many people visit the city's Old and Historic District during the annual Festival of Houses and Gardens in March and April. Many visitors also attend the Spoleto Festival U.S.A., an annual presentation of art, drama, and music, in May and June. The Charleston Museum, founded in 1773, is the oldest museum in the United States. Also popular are gardens that are near Charleston, including Middleton Place Gardens, Magnolia Gardens, and Cypress Gardens. Middleton Place Gardens, established in 1741, are the oldest landscaped gardens in the United States.

The College of Charleston, founded in 1770, is one of the nation's oldest colleges. The University of Charleston, a graduate school, was established as part of it in 1992. Charleston is also the home of Charleston Southern University; the Medical University of South Carolina; and The Citadel, The Military College of South Carolina.

Government and history. Charleston has a mayor-council form of government. The city is the seat of Charleston County.

Kiawah, Sewee, and Wando Indians lived in what is now the Charleston area until the mid-1700's. Most of the first white settlers came from England. Charleston was the capital of South Carolina from 1670 to 1790, when Columbia became the capital. Charleston was the wealthiest city in the South during the early colonial period. Its wealth came chiefly from exports of rice and indigo. Thousands of slaves worked on vast plantations that grew these crops. A deerskin trade with Indians extended to the Ohio and Mississippi rivers and added to

© James Blank, West Stock

Historic Charleston homes date from the 1700's and 1800's. The city's annual Festival of Houses and Gardens, held in March and April, attracts many visitors.

Charleston's wealth. In 1831, the nation's first regularly scheduled train service began in Charleston. The train's locomotive was named *Best Friend of Charleston.*

During the American Civil War (1861-1865), the city suffered great economic loss. After the war ended in 1865, the construction of fertilizer plants and a naval yard helped Charleston recover. Revival of the port encouraged shipping and many other industries to come to the Charleston area. By the late 1930's, the city's factories were manufacturing asbestos, oil, paint, rubber, and other products. Charleston also had a flourishing trade in fruit, lumber, seafood, and vegetables.

During the 1970's, Charleston's port was expanded, and parts of downtown were revitalized. A hotel and convention center, designed to harmonize with the city's historic architecture, was opened in 1986.

A major disaster struck Charleston in September 1989, when Hurricane Hugo tore through the city. The hurricane's wind speed measured 135 miles (217 kilometers) per hour when it hit Charleston. Hurricane Hugo caused 18 deaths and $3 billion in property damage in the Charleston area. Peggy McIntyre

For the monthly weather in Charleston, see **South Carolina** (Climate). See also **Fort Moultrie; Fort Sumter; South Carolina** (pictures).

Charleston, West Virginia (pop. 53,421; met. area pop. 309,635), is the capital and the leading industrial, trade, and transportation center of the state. Charleston lies at the meeting place of the Elk and Kanawha rivers (see **West Virginia** [political map]).

Description. Charleston, the seat of Kanawha County, covers 29 square miles (75 square kilometers). Its metropolitan area occupies 2,531 square miles (6,555 square kilometers) and covers Boone, Clay, Kanawha, Lincoln, and Putnam counties. The State Capitol and the central business district are about 2 miles (3 kilometers) apart on the north bank of the Kanawha River.

Charleston is the home of the University of Charleston. A campus of Marshall University Graduate College is in nearby South Charleston, and West Virginia State University is in nearby Institute. Charleston has a ballet company, a symphony orchestra, a light opera company, and theater groups. The Clay Center for the Arts & Sciences includes a concert hall, a theater, an art museum, a planetarium, and a science museum. The West Virginia Cultural Center at the Capitol features the state museum, the state library, and a theater. City festivals include the Vandalia Gathering, held Memorial Day weekend, and the Sternwheel Regatta, a five-day river festival in the summer.

Economy. Retail and wholesale trade, government, and manufacturing together employ more than half of the city's workers. The Charleston metropolitan area has more than 200 manufacturing plants. The chemical industry provides much of the city's industrial income. It relies heavily on coal, natural gas, petroleum, and salt from the nearby area. Other products include automotive and electrical machinery parts, metal products, plastics, and processed food.

Barge lines and railroad freight lines serve the city. Charleston also has passenger train service. Yeager Airport lies just outside the city.

Government and history. Charleston has a mayor-council form of government. The voters elect a mayor and 26 council members, all to four-year terms.

Shawnee Indians and other tribes hunted in the Kanawha Valley when white settlers first arrived. In 1787, George Clendenin, a Virginia legislator, bought the land where Charleston now stands. In 1788, he and a group of soldiers built Fort Lee to protect the Kanawha Valley.

Settlers soon built cabins near Fort Lee. In 1794, the settlement officially became a town, which Clendenin named Charlestown for his father, Charles Clendenin. During the 1790's, the famous frontiersman Daniel Boone lived near the town and served the area briefly as a representative to the state legislature. The people of Charlestown changed its name to Charleston in 1818.

A road that crossed the Appalachian Mountains was extended to Charleston in the early 1800's. The town became a transportation center where travelers transferred between wagons and riverboats. Its main industry was salt mining and processing. The West Virginia region formed part of Virginia until 1863, when it became a state. Charleston served as the state capital from 1870 to 1875 and became the permanent capital in 1885.

Coal mining in the Charleston area expanded greatly after 1873, when rail lines reached the city. Trains provided a practical way to ship the coal to Eastern cities.

During the early 1900's, Charleston's coal, salt, and other natural resources attracted several chemical companies to the area. These factories created many new jobs, and the city's population grew. But in the 1960's and 1970's, several local industries declined and many families left. Charleston's population decreased from 85,796 to 63,968 during that period. The population decrease continued during the 1980's.

In the early 1980's, much urban renewal took place in the central business district. Projects included restoration of the civic center and construction of office buildings, apartment buildings, hotels, a coliseum, and a shopping mall. In the 1990's, the city's population continued to decrease as people moved to the suburbs. The retail center shifted from a downtown mall to a number of shopping complexes south of the city. In the late 1990's and early 2000's, Charleston's chemical industry faced uncertainty as mergers and labor-force reductions took place. However, automotive-parts manufacturing expanded in the metropolitan area. Rosalie Earle

See also **West Virginia** (Climate; pictures).

Charlotte (pop. 540,828; met. area pop. 1,330,448) is the largest city in North Carolina. It ranks as a major financial center. It is also a transportation and wholesaling center in the Southeast. Uptown Charlotte lies about 15 miles (24 kilometers) north of the North Carolina-South Carolina border (see **North Carolina** [political map]).

Beginning about 1748, Scotch-Irish and German farmers settled in what is now the Charlotte area. The settlers named Charlotte for Queen Charlotte of Mecklenburg-Strelitz, wife of Britain's King George III.

Description. Charlotte is the seat of Mecklenburg County. The city is the home of Central Piedmont Community College, Johnson C. Smith University, Queens University of Charlotte, and a branch of the University of North Carolina.

The Mint Museum of Art and the Charlotte Symphony Orchestra have existed in the city since the 1930's. Other attractions include the Blumenthal Performing Arts Center; the Mint Museum of Craft + Design; Spirit Square, a center for visual arts and art education; and Discovery Place, a science museum. Charlotte is home to the Charlotte Bobcats of the National Basketball Association and the Carolina Panthers of the National Football League.

Economy. Charlotte ranks as one of the largest banking centers in the nation. Headquarters for Bank of America and Wachovia Corporation, a banking company, are in the city. Branches of many leading banks and hundreds of foreign-owned businesses are also there.

The city provides insurance, medical, technological, and wholesaling services for the Piedmont Region, of which it is a part. The Piedmont Region lies between the Appalachian Mountains and the Atlantic Coastal Plain (see **Piedmont Region**). Charlotte is also a trucking center and a manufacturing center. The city's products include electronic equipment, fabricated metals, machinery, processed foods, and textiles. Railroads and Charlotte/Douglas International Airport serve the city.

Government and history. Charlotte has a council-manager government. The voters elect a mayor and the 11 members of the City Council. A number of city agencies, including law enforcement and public education, have merged with county agencies for efficiency.

Catawba Indians lived in what is now the Charlotte area when Scotch-Irish and German farmers began settling there in the 1740's. The fertile soil and the friendliness of the Indians attracted the settlers. The city was incorporated in 1768. On May 31, 1775, Charlotte passed the Mecklenburg Resolves, which declared the county independent of Britain. These resolutions were among the earliest such declarations by the American colonists. Charlotte became a center of gold mining after the discovery of gold in nearby Cabarrus County in 1799. Over 50 mines were being worked in the Piedmont in the early 1800's. A branch of the United States Mint operated in the city from 1837 to 1913.

Industrialization spread in the South after the American Civil War (1861-1865), and Charlotte became the center of the Piedmont's booming textile industry. The railroads expanded, and Charlotte's trucking industry later developed to distribute the products of the textile mills.

In 1970, the Charlotte-Mecklenburg school system began one of the nation's first large-scale programs to integrate schools by busing students. A federal court ordered the countywide system to improve the racial balance in the schools by busing students to schools outside their neighborhood. The Supreme Court of the United States upheld the program in 1971. The Charlotte busing program became a national model.

In 1983, Harvey Gantt became the city's first African American mayor. He served until 1987. Sue Myrick, the city's first female mayor, held office from 1987 to 1991.

In 1992, a system of magnet schools was established to attract students from throughout the area. In 1999, Charlotte discontinued its busing program. A federal judge ruled that busing was no longer necessary because all traces of intentional discrimination had disappeared. In the late 1900's and early 2000's, Charlotte continued to expand as a major center of commerce and finance.

In 2006, Charlotte was selected as the site for the NASCAR Hall of Fame. The hall will honor drivers from NASCAR, the organization that governs the nation's most popular form of stock car automobile racing. Construction of the hall, which will be funded mainly by a Mecklenburg County hotel tax, was scheduled to begin in 2007. Jerry L. Surratt

See also **North Carolina** (Climate; picture).

Charlotte Amalie, *uh MAHL yuh* (pop. 12,331), capital of the United States Virgin Islands, is a harbor city on the Caribbean Sea. It lies on the central coast of the south side of St. Thomas Island. The island is about 40 miles (64 kilometers) east of Puerto Rico. Charlotte Amalie is the chief trading center for the islands and a famous tourist resort. Charlotte Amalie was named for the wife of King Christian V of Denmark. The Danes controlled St. Thomas Island until 1917. See also **Virgin Islands** (map); **Virgin Islands, United States** (pictures).

Gary Brana-Shute

Charlottesville (pop. 45,049; met. area pop. 174,021) is in the Blue Ridge Mountains foothills in Virginia (see **Virginia** [political map]). On one of these hills, overlooking the city, is Monticello, Thomas Jefferson's home. Charlottesville is the home of the University of Virginia, founded by Jefferson in 1819. Near Monticello is Ash Lawn, the home of James Monroe. The city is a marketing center for the area. Charlottesville has a council-manager government. It is the seat of Albemarle County. See also **Monticello.** Robert Ryder Gibson

Charlottetown (pop. 32,245), the capital of Prince Edward Island, is one of Canada's most historic cities. In 1864, representatives from several British North American colonies met in Charlottetown and discussed plans to unite. This meeting led to the formation in 1867 of the Dominion of Canada.

Charlottetown covers 2.7 square miles (7 square kilometers) on the southern coast of Prince Edward Island (see **Prince Edward Island** [political map]). Mi'kmaq Indians lived in the area before European colonists first arrived in the early 1700's. The British founded Charlottetown in 1763 and made it the capital of the island. They named the city after Queen Charlotte of Britain.

Charlottetown has several dairies, construction firms, and small manufacturing plants. Provincial and federal government agencies also provide jobs for many people in the city's work force. The main office of the Canadian Department of Veterans Affairs is in Charlottetown. A convention hotel stands along the city's waterfront.

Charlottetown attracts a number of tourists. Its Confederation Centre of the Arts has three theaters, an art gallery, a public library, a restaurant, and a gift shop. The Confederation Chamber in Province House, where the historic 1864 meeting took place, is known as the Birthplace of Canada. Charlottetown is the home of the University of Prince Edward Island and the Atlantic Veterinary College. The city has a mayor-council government.

Walter MacIntyre

For the monthly weather in Charlottetown, see **Prince Edward Island** (Land and climate). See also **Prince Edward Island** (pictures).

Charon. See **Hades; Styx.**

Charter, called *articles of incorporation* in certain instances, is a written document granted by a government. A charter entitles the holder to certain rights, powers, or liberties, such as the right to engage in business. It may be granted to a person, corporation, or local government. State charters set up the limits within which banks, corporations, and associations must conduct business. See also **Atlantic Charter; Colonial life in America** (Economic reasons); **Corporation; Magna Carta; United Nations** (The charter). Jean Appleman

Charter Oak was a huge tree in Hartford, Connecticut. It became famous because of a tradition that Connecticut's original charter was hidden there to keep the English governor from seizing it.

When James II became king of England in 1685, he appointed Sir Edmund Andros governor of the Dominion of New England. Andros was sent to Hartford in 1687 to seize the Connecticut charter and take control of the colony. He appeared at a legislative meeting to demand the charter. Debate lasted into the night, and candles were lighted. Suddenly, the candles went out. When they were relighted, the charter was gone. According to tradition, Joseph Wadsworth took the charter and hid it in a nearby oak tree.

Andros's rule ended in 1689 after James II fell from power. The charter remained Connecticut's supreme law until a new constitution was adopted in 1818. A windstorm destroyed the Charter Oak in 1856. A granite shaft marks the spot where it stood. Donna J. Spindel

See also **Andros, Sir Edmund.**

Charter school is a public school that operates under a special contract giving it freedom from many of the rules that apply to traditional public schools. The contract—called a *charter*—states how the school will be run, what will be taught, and how success will be measured. The contract is arranged between a group of school organizers and a sponsor. Organizers may include parents, educators, or community leaders. Sponsors are usually local or state boards of education.

Charter schools rank as one of the fastest-growing trends in education. In England and Wales, such schools are called *grant-maintained schools* and have operated since 1988. In the United States, state laws authorize charter schools. Minnesota enacted the first such law in 1991, and many other states soon followed suit.

The terms of school charters differ widely. For example, some charters allow schools to focus on a particular subject, such as science or art. Other charters emphasize teaching methods that use individual learning plans, projects outside the classroom, or other creative approaches. Some charter schools serve special groups, such as gifted students or students experiencing academic difficulties. Many charters require a charter school to achieve certain scores on tests of student achievement. If a school fails to meet these conditions, the sponsor may close the school or take back its charter.

Most U.S. public schools operate under policies set by states and by district boards of education. These policies determine such matters as what subjects should be taught and what qualifications teachers need. Charter schools, however, operate under local control. Supporters of charter schools believe that local control enables the people who know students best to run the schools.

Most school districts assign students to a certain public school, but students must choose to attend a charter school. Critics of the charter school movement fear that it will weaken public education by providing special opportunities for small numbers of students. But supporters believe that competition for students will strengthen all the schools in a system. Priscilla Wohlstetter

See also **Alternative school.**

Charterhouse is a leading English public school. It was founded in London for poor boys in 1611 by Thomas Sutton, a wealthy merchant. Today, the school is located near Godalming in Surrey. Students pay fees, but need- and merit-based scholarships are available. The school has about 700 pupils, most of whom are boarders. P. A. McGinley

Chartism, *CHAR tihz uhm,* was a political movement of the British working class during the early 1800's. It tried to win voting rights for all men and to reform the House of Commons. The movement took its name from its Charter of 1838, which set forth six points: (1) universal manhood suffrage, (2) a secret ballot, (3) no property qualifications for members of Parliament, (4) salaries for members of Parliament, (5) annual elections, and (6) equal electoral districts. The movement did not achieve these points, but all except the fifth were later adopted. In addition, the movement demonstrated that the working class could be organized on a massive scale. See also **Labour Party.** Chris Cook

Chartres, *SHAHR truh* or *shahrt* (pop. 42,059), is a city in north-central France that is famous for its cathedral, which is a masterpiece of Gothic architecture. Chartres is the capital of the Eure-et-Loir *department* (administrative district). For location, see **France** (political map).

Chartres Cathedral, officially called the Cathedral of Notre Dame, stands near the center of Chartres. It features beautiful stained-glass windows and hundreds of sculptured religious figures. It has two bell towers, one 378 feet (115 meters) high and one 350 feet (107 meters).

Chartres lies on a hill that is surrounded by grainfields. The Eure River runs next to the city. Chartres serves as a market for products of the surrounding area. Its other economic activities include flour milling; leatherworking; and the manufacture of electronic equipment, farm machinery, and home appliances. Chartres was founded by the Carnutes, an ancient tribe of Celts whose activities in Chartres were described by Julius Caesar about 50 B.C. The Chartres Cathedral was originally built in the mid-1100's, but most of it was destroyed by fire in 1194. Most of the cathedral was rebuilt between 1194 and 1230. Mark Kesselman

See also **Chartres Cathedral.**

Chartres Cathedral, *SHAHR truh* or *shahrt,* ranks among the most magnificent examples of Gothic architecture. The cathedral stands in the city of Chartres, France. It is also known as the Cathedral of Notre Dame because it is dedicated to the Virgin Mary. Most of the present cathedral was built from 1194 to 1260, when it was consecrated.

Chartres Cathedral was designed like a typical Gothic cathedral (see **Cathedral** [diagram]). From a distance, the most striking features are two giant towers topped by steeples. The south tower was built from about 1140 to 1160. The spire of the north tower was begun in 1507. The main entrance to the cathedral is called the *west facade* (see **Europe** [The arts: picture]). The west facade has three doorways, called the Royal Portal, which are decorated with many sculptures portraying figures from the Bible. Above the Royal Portal is a *rose window* (ornamental circular window) that contains beautiful examples of medieval stained glass.

The interior of the cathedral is dominated by stone *vaults* (arched ceilings) 118 feet (36 meters) above the

© SCALA/Art Resource

Chartres Cathedral is a masterpiece of medieval Gothic architecture. The cathedral is particularly known for its stained glass windows and its two giant towers topped by steeples.

floor. Stained glass windows are set into the lower walls and into upper walls called *clerestories.*

William J. Hennessey

See also **Chartres; Gothic art; Stained glass** (Technical improvements).

Chase, Salmon Portland (1808-1873), was a prominent American statesman and chief justice of the United States. He served as secretary of the treasury under President Abraham Lincoln. Chase is considered one of the greatest secretaries because of his work in the American Civil War (1861-1865). He maintained national credit and raised money to carry on the war. Chase laid the basis of the present national banking system. After he resigned in 1864 because of a policy dispute, Lincoln, who disliked him personally, named him chief justice in recognition of his ability. As chief justice, Chase presided capably over the impeachment trial of President Andrew Johnson.

Chase was born on Jan. 13, 1808, in Cornish, New Hampshire. After studying law in Washington, D.C., he became a lawyer in Cincinnati, Ohio. He was a leader of the antislavery movement and defended many runaway slaves. As a U.S. senator from 1849 to 1855, he opposed the extension of slavery into the new territories. He served as governor of Ohio from 1856 to 1860. In later years, Chase wanted to become president of the United States. A founder of the Republican Party, he sought its presidential nomination several times. In 1872, he tried to get the Democratic nomination. Jerre S. Williams

See also **Emancipation Proclamation** (picture).

Chase, Samuel (1741-1811), was an associate justice of the Supreme Court of the United States. He was appointed to the court in 1796 by President George Washington. Chase and Washington were members of the Federalist Party. In 1804, the U.S. House of Representatives *impeached* (brought charges against) Chase for criticizing Thomas Jefferson, the leader of the Democratic-Republican Party. Chase had criticized Jefferson both before and after Jefferson became president in 1801. The Senate acquitted Chase in 1805. The acquittal helped establish the independence of federal judges by making it less likely that they could be removed from office on largely political grounds. Chase served on the Supreme Court until 1811. He died on June 19, 1811.

Chase was born on April 17, 1741, in Somerset County, Maryland. He was a delegate to the Continental Congress and signed the Declaration of Independence.

Bruce Allen Murphy

See also **Impeachment** (History); **Jefferson, Thomas** (The courts).

Chase, William Merritt (1849-1916), was an American painter and art teacher. In his paintings, Chase combined flowing, spontaneous brushwork with glowing colors and dazzling contrasts to create striking visual effects. One of his favorite subjects was the elaborate interior of his studio in New York City. Chase made many paintings that included stylish women examining the room's exotic ornaments. He also painted sunny coastal landscapes of Long Island, city park scenes, and sophisticated portraits of wealthy people.

Chase was born on Nov. 1, 1849, in Nineveh, Indiana. He studied at the National Academy of Design in New York City and at the Royal Academy in Munich. Chase's early paintings reflect the Munich style and feature dashing brushstrokes, dark tones, and brilliant highlights. In the late 1880's, influenced by French Impressionism, he began using lighter colors. Chase taught in New York City and his own art school on Long Island.

For the Little One (1895), an oil painting on canvas; Metropolitan Museum of Art, New York City, Amelia B. Lazarus Fund, by exchange, 1917

A Chase painting shows the artist's interest in portraying women and interiors in bold brushstrokes and glowing colors. The painting shows the influence of impressionism on Chase.

His students included American painters Charles Sheeler, Edward Hopper, and Georgia O'Keeffe. Chase died on Oct. 25, 1916. Sarah Burns

Château. See **Architecture** (Renaissance architecture); **Castle; France** (Arts).

Chateaubriand, *shah toh bree AHN,* **François-René de,** *frahn SWAH ruh NAY duh* (1768-1848), was one of the most important figures in French Romantic literature. His novel *Atala* (1801) describes a tragic love affair between two North American Indians. The novel is an example of the European Romantic's fascination with primitive and faraway subjects. Chateaubriand's *The Spirit of Christianity* (1802) praises Christianity as a great cultural and moral force. One part of it, called *René,* is the story of a young man whose vague feeling of despair makes him a typical Romantic hero. Chateaubriand's autobiography, *Memoirs from Beyond the Grave,* was published soon after his death on July 4, 1848. It is often called his best work.

Chateaubriand was born on Sept. 4, 1768, in St.-Malo. He held several diplomatic posts, including that of French foreign minister in 1823. Thomas H. Goetz

Châtelet, *SHAH tuh LEH,* **Marquise du** (1706-1749), was a French mathematician, physicist, and science writer. She contributed to the revival of French science by promoting the theories of the English scientist Sir Isaac Newton. She also influenced the work of Voltaire, one of France's leading authors and philosophers, and became his mistress.

Du Châtelet began her interpretations of Newton's work in 1735 with an essay on his discoveries in optics. Voltaire incorporated some of her later writings on Newton in his book *Elements of Newton's Philosophy* (1738). From 1745 to 1749, du Châtelet worked on a translation and analytical review of Newton's most important work, *Principia mathematica* (1687). The translation was published in 1759, after her death.

Du Châtelet was born Gabrielle-Émilie Le Tonnelier de Breteuil in Paris on Dec. 17, 1706. As an aristocrat, she received an excellent education in literature and science. In 1724, she married Florent-Claude, Marquis du Châtelet, the governor of Semur-en-Auxois. She died on Sept. 10, 1749. Romualdas Sviedrys

Chatham, Earl of. See **Pitt, William.**

Chattanooga, *CHAT uh NOO guh* (pop. 155,554; met. area pop. 476,531), is an industrial city in southeastern Tennessee. It was a key city in the American Civil War (1861-1865). Chattanooga lies on both banks of the sharp Moccasin Bend of the Tennessee River, north of the Tennessee-Georgia border (see **Tennessee** [political map]). Part of its metropolitan area lies in Georgia.

Chattanooga is in the Appalachian Ridge and Valley Region at the edge of the Cumberland Plateau. Lookout Mountain stands to the south. Indians are thought to have called this mountain *Chat-to-to-noog-gee,* meaning *mountain rising to a point.* Some of the steep ridges have been cut through for the three interstate highways that intersect in the city. Chattanooga is joined to other cities by railroads, airlines, and river barge lines. The city serves as a U.S. port of entry (see **Port of entry**).

After the Civil War, Chattanooga became one of the chief manufacturing cities of the South. From the 1860's to the 1960's, the city was known for its iron and steel products. Today, the economy of Chattanooga depends heavily on services and on retail and wholesale trade. But the city still has more than 100 factories. Its chief manufactured products include clothing, food products, and plumbing and heating equipment. Chemical plants also operate in the metropolitan area, and factories produce synthetic yarn for the area's carpet industry.

Chickamauga Dam to the east and Nickajack Dam to the west are parts of the Tennessee Valley Authority (TVA). The TVA is a federal corporation that controls floods, generates electric power, and works to develop the Tennessee Valley.

Places of interest in Chattanooga include its Civil War battlefields and the Tennessee Aquarium. The area's natural beauty also draws many tourists. Chattanooga has a civic chorus, symphony orchestra, opera association, theater group, and University of Tennessee campus.

The Chickamauga, a branch of the Cherokee Indians, lived in the Chattanooga area when white settlers first arrived in the 1600's and 1700's. The Indians were conquered in 1794 and were moved west in 1838. During this period, a chief named John Ross operated a trading post called Ross's Landing on the site. Chattanooga received its present name when it was incorporated as a town in 1839. It received its city charter in 1851.

Chattanooga had only 5,545 inhabitants when the Civil War broke out. But it had a strategic location, and metal industries developed to supply the Confederacy. The Battle of Chattanooga took place in November 1863 (see **Civil War, American** [Battle of Chattanooga]). About 1,500 people lived in the city at the end of the war. There were 13,000 by 1880. Chattanooga's most rapid growth began in the 1930's, after the establishment of the TVA.

Chattanooga has a mayor-council form of government. It is the seat of Hamilton County. Charles S. Aiken

Chattanooga, Battle of. See **Civil War, American** (Battle of Chattanooga; table: Major battles of the American Civil War).

Chaucer, *CHAW suhr,* **Geoffrey,** *JEHF rih* (1340?-1400), was the greatest English poet of the Middle Ages. He wrote *The Canterbury Tales,* a group of stories that ranks among the masterpieces of literature.

Life. Chaucer was born in London sometime between 1340 and 1343. He lived most of his life there. He came from a prosperous middle-class family and was trained as a civil servant and diplomat. Chaucer was controller of customs from 1374 to 1386 and clerk of the king's works from 1389 to 1391. He was appointed a justice of the peace in 1385 and to Parliament in 1386. His experiences in all these positions probably developed his fascination with people, his wide knowledge of English life, and the tone of charitable irony in his works.

Chaucer wrote for people in and around the courts of Edward III and, especially, Richard II. Though Chaucer supported Richard II, he also was associated with Richard's rival, the powerful nobleman John of Gaunt. Chaucer viewed the aristocratic fashion called "courtly love" with polite and amused skepticism. In his poetry, he often satirized the fashion's lofty ideals, elaborate etiquette, and literary style. He viewed the corruption he saw in the medieval church with less tolerance than he had for the fashion of courtly love. In *The Canterbury Tales,* he satirized church abuses in his portrayals of the friar, monk, pardoner, and summoner.

Chaucer was one of the most learned men of his age.

He traveled in Flanders, France, Italy, and Spain on diplomatic missions. He was influenced by French and Italian writers, especially Boccaccio, Dante, and Petrarch. Chaucer may have studied law. He was familiar with Latin classics, medieval science, and theology. Chaucer's prose works include a translation of Boethius's *Consolation of Philosophy* and an essay on the astrolabe, an astronomical instrument that was the forerunner of the sextant. Chaucer died on Oct. 25, 1400.

Poetry. Chaucer wrote in Middle English, the form of English used from about 1100 to about 1485. He was the first English poet to use *heroic verse* (rhymed couplets in iambic pentameter).

The Book of the Duchess (1368), one of Chaucer's earliest works, is a graceful elegy on the death of John of Gaunt's first wife. Chaucer modeled it on the French dream-vision form of poetry. He gradually developed his individual style in *The House of Fame* (1379?), *The Parliament of Fowls* (1380?), *The Legend of Good Women* (1387?-1394?), and other shorter lyrics.

Apart from *The Canterbury Tales,* Chaucer's greatest poem is *Troilus and Criseyde* (about 1386). Adapted from a love story by Boccaccio, this poem is both a medieval romance and a philosophical tragedy. Set in ancient Troy just before its fall, it tells of the love of Prince Troilus for Criseyde. In the poem, Chaucer explored the beauty of love, the mysterious workings of fortune, and the sad brevity of earthly joy.

The Canterbury Tales (about 1386-1400) is a collection of stories told by a group of pilgrims on a journey to the shrine of Thomas Becket in Canterbury. One of the pilgrims represents Chaucer himself. Chaucer pictured this pilgrim as a simple fellow who takes everything at face value. This device allowed Chaucer to describe the other pilgrims objectively, while allowing the reader to see the pilgrims' real personalities. For more information, see **Canterbury Tales.** Paul Strohm

Additional resources

Pearsall, Derek. *The Life of Geoffrey Chaucer.* Blackwell, 1992.
Rossignol, Rosalyn. *Chaucer A to Z.* Facts on File, 1999.

Chautauqua, *shuh TAW kwuh,* is a system of summer school and correspondence school education founded at Chautauqua Lake, New York, in 1874. The term also refers to traveling groups, called Tent Chautauquas, which had no connection with the original schools.

The Chautauqua Institution. John H. Vincent, a Methodist clergyman, and Lewis Miller of Akron, Ohio, first conceived the idea of setting up a summer school to give instruction to Sunday-school teachers. The first assembly was held at Chautauqua in August 1874. The movement rapidly expanded to include a school of languages (1878), a summer school for public school teachers (1879), a school of theology (1881), and a series of clubs for young people interested in reading, music, fine arts, physical education, and religion. In 1883, the Chautauqua University was established. The university closed in 1898. But the Chautauqua Institution continues a summer adult education program and makes its facilities available to other interested groups.

The Chautauqua Literary and Scientific Circle is a correspondence school with courses in such fields as history, literature, science, and art. Founded in 1878, it is one of the oldest U.S. correspondence schools. It influenced adult education leaders in many countries.

Tent Chautauquas were traveling groups that operated in the United States from 1903 to 1930. These chautauquas moved from town to town giving lectures, concerts, recitals, and shows in a tent. The popularity of tent chautauquas decreased with the development of radio and other forms of entertainment. Merle L. Borrowman

See also **Lyceum** (organization).

Chávez, *CHAH vehz,* **Carlos** (1899-1978), a Mexican composer, was one of the most important influences on the musical life of Mexico in the 1900's. Many of Chávez's works reflect his interest in Mexican folk music. Some of his other compositions were written in a strong romantic style. The use of complex rhythms became a dominant element in his mature compositions.

Chávez wrote seven symphonies, several ballets, and cantatas, songs, and chamber works. Several of his pieces use native Mexican folk instruments. For example, *Xochipilli Macuilxochitl* (1940) is an orchestral composition that requires traditional Indian drums.

Chávez was born on June 13, 1899, in Mexico City. In 1928, he organized the first permanent symphony orchestra in Mexico and served as its conductor until 1949. He also directed the National Conservatory of Music almost continuously from 1928 to 1934 and the National Institute of Fine Arts from 1947 to 1952. He served as guest conductor for several major United States orchestras. Chávez died on Aug. 2, 1978. Vincent McDermott

Chavez, *SHAH vehz,* **Cesar Estrada** (1927-1993), was a labor union organizer and spokesman for the poor—especially his fellow Mexican American farmworkers. He supported nonviolent action to achieve his aims. Chavez declared that the "truest act of courage ... is to sacrifice ourselves for others in a totally nonviolent struggle for justice."

Chavez began to organize grape pickers in California in 1962, when he established the National Farm Workers Association with activist Dolores Huerta. In 1966, his union merged with another one into the United Farm Workers Organizing Committee (UFWOC). The two earlier unions had been on strike since 1965 against California grape growers. After the merger, California's wine grape growers agreed to accept the UFWOC as the collective bargaining agent for the grape pickers. But the table grape growers refused to do so. Chavez then organized a nationwide boycott of California table grapes. In 1970, most table grape growers agreed to accept the union, and the boycott ended. Later that year, Chavez called for a boycott of lettuce produced by growers without union contracts.

In 1972, the union changed its name to the United Farm Workers of America (UFW). Many grape growers failed to renew their contracts in 1973, and Chavez led a new grape boycott. He ended the boycotts of lettuce and grapes in 1978.

UPI/Bettmann Newsphotos
Cesar Chavez

Chavez was born on a farm near Yuma, Arizona, on March 31, 1927. When he was 10, his parents lost their farm and the family became migrant workers in California. He died on April 23, 1993. Feliciano M. Ribera

See also **Huerta, Dolores Fernandez; Labor movement** (picture); **United Farm Workers of America.**

Additional resources

Etulain, Richard W. *Cesar Chavez: A Brief Biography with Documents.* Palgrave, 2002.

Zannos, Susan. *Cesar Chavez.* Mitchell Lane, 1999. Younger readers.

Chavez, *SHAH vehz,* **Dennis** (1888-1962), a Democrat, became the second Hispanic American to serve in the United States Senate. He represented New Mexico in the Senate from 1935 to 1962. The first Hispanic senator, Octaviano Larrazolo, served in 1928 and 1929. As a U.S. senator, Chavez worked for laws that aided such minorities as Hispanics and American Indians. For example, he was an early supporter of federal fair employment laws.

Chavez was born on April 8, 1888, in Los Chavez, New Mexico, a town south of Albuquerque. He served in the U.S. House of Representatives from 1931 to 1935, when he was appointed to fill out a term in the Senate. He won election to the Senate five times between 1936 and 1958. A statue of Chavez represents New Mexico in the U.S. Capitol in Washington, D.C. Richard A. Bartlett

Chayote, *chah YOH tay,* is a climbing vine grown chiefly for its fruit. Chayote has thick roots, cream-colored flowers, and large leaves with pointed lobes. A single plant may cover a tree 50 feet (15 meters) tall.

Chayote gourds are round to pear-shaped. These fruits grow as long as 6 inches (15 centimeters) and usually weigh from 6 ounces to 2 pounds (170 to 900 grams). They range in color from ivory-white to dark green and contain one large seed. Immature chayote gourds are usually cooked but can be eaten fresh in salads. The roots, leaves, and young shoots are also edible, and the plant is sometimes used as livestock feed.

WORLD BOOK illustration by Stuart Lafford, Linden Artists Ltd.

Chayote fruit ranges from ivory-white to dark green.

Chayote may be native to Mexico, but it now grows throughout Latin America and much of the southern United States. New vines are grown by planting either gourds or cuttings from the stem. Gary W. Elmstrom

Scientific classification. Chayote belongs to the family Cucurbitaceae. Its scientific name is *Sechium edule.*

Chechnya, *CHEHCH nyuh,* is a Russian republic in the northern Caucasus Mountains. It was once part of the Soviet Chechen-Ingush Autonomous Republic. In 1991, Chechnya began a drive for independence from Russia, a goal it has pursued for centuries.

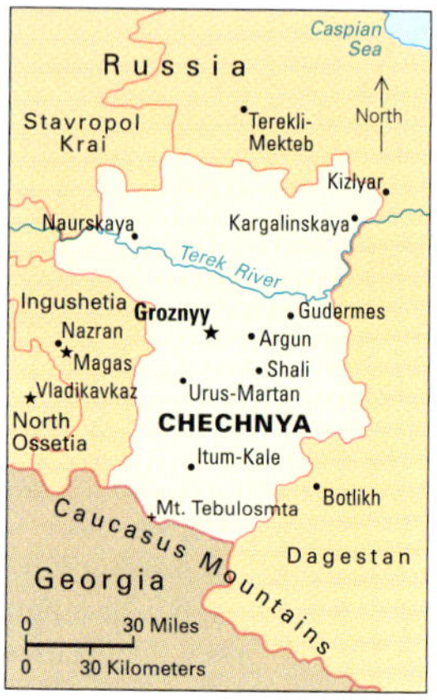

WORLD BOOK map

Chechnya lies along Russia's border with Georgia.

Chechnya covers about 6,000 square miles (15,500 square kilometers). It has about 650,000 people, although thousands more have fled the fighting. Chechens are Muslims. The country's capital and largest city is Groznyy (or Grozny).

In 1991, Chechnya declared independence from Russia. In 1994, Russia sent troops to crush the independence movement. Thousands of civilians were killed, and bombs destroyed much of Groznyy. A cease-fire in 1996 ended the fighting, and in 1997 a peace treaty formalized the truce.

In 1999, Islamic militants tried to unite Chechnya and the neighboring republic of Dagestan. Russia invaded Chechnya to defeat the rebellion and again heavily damaged Chechnya's cities and killed many civilians. Russian forces gained control of Chechnya's main cities by mid-2000. The militants refused to surrender and began making surprise attacks. Chechen terrorists took hostages and bombed Russian civilians. See **Russia** (History).

In 2003, voters in Chechnya approved a new constitution that affirmed the region's ties to Russia. But Russia's government helped write the constitution, and voters included Russian soldiers. Voters then elected a new, Russian-supported president, Akhmad Kadyrov. In 2004, a rebel bomb blast killed Kadyrov. Later that year, Alu Alkhanov was elected president. Conflicts with Chechen rebels continued. Jaroslaw Bilocerkowycz

Check is a written order directing a bank to pay money to a person or organization, or to the bearer. A check may be written by any person or organization with money in a checking account. The bank transfers the amount specified on the check from the *payer's* (check writer's) account to the *payee,* the designated person or organization. The word *check* is spelled *cheque* in Canada, the United Kingdom, and some other countries.

Checks are widely used because they are safer and more convenient than cash. For example, a person who has a checking account does not have to carry large sums of money, which could be lost or stolen. Checks can be sent safely through the mail because only the payees can legally cash them. Used checks, called *canceled* checks, serve as convenient records of payment.

How the checking system works. When a person or organization opens a checking account, the depositor receives a checkbook containing blank checks. The depositor issues a check by writing in the date, the name of the payee, and the amount of money involved. The depositor also signs the check. Every month, the bank sends the depositor a *statement.* This document lists the deposits made into the account, and the amounts of the checks written against it. The statement also shows the *balance,* the amount remaining in the account. Most banks enclose the canceled checks for the month. But some banks hold the checks and issue only a statement.

The payee may *cash* the check—that is, exchange it for cash—or deposit it in a bank account or transfer it to another person or organization. To cash, deposit, or transfer a check, the payee *endorses* it by signing it on the back. The endorser becomes responsible for the payment of the check if the issuer's checking account lacks enough money to cover it.

After a bank has received a check in a deposit, the bank collects its money by returning the check to the bank of the check writer. The check writer's bank then charges the writer's account for the amount involved. If the two banks are in the same community, the check is routed through a clearinghouse. The clearinghouse collects checks and determines how much money the banks owe each other. Most out-of-town checks are collected by a Federal Reserve Bank or other large bank.

Numbers printed on checks with magnetic ink identify the bank and the owner of the checking account. They make possible the electronic sorting of checks.

Special checking services. Some payments require the use of a *certified check* or a *cashier's check.* A certified check is an ordinary check made out by a person or organization and then stamped *Certified* by a bank. The bank sets aside sufficient funds from the check writer's account to pay for a check that it certifies. A cashier's check is the bank's own check, which the bank guarantees. The bank charges its customer's account for the amount. Cashier's checks may also be purchased with cash.

Banks and travel agencies sell blank *traveler's checks* in denominations of $10, $20, $50, and $100. The person who buys the checks signs them immediately at the bank or agency. He or she signs them again to obtain cash or to make purchases. The second signature verifies the person's identity. Traveler's checks can be used throughout the world because the issuing bank or company guarantees payment. The bank or travel agency replaces lost or stolen traveler's checks.

Checks and the economy. Checks serve as the chief method of payment in many parts of the world. For this reason, economists consider *checkbook money* (funds in checking accounts) as part of a nation's money supply. Such funds make up about 75 percent of the total amount of money in circulation in the United States.

Federal law once prohibited U.S. banks from paying interest on money in checking accounts, unlike funds in savings accounts. In 1980, however, Congress lifted the ban on interest-paying checking accounts. It authorized banks to offer *negotiable order of withdrawal accounts,* usually called *NOW accounts.* Like a savings account, a NOW account pays interest. But the depositor can transfer funds to someone else by writing a *negotiable order of withdrawal,* which is like a check.

For many years, checking accounts were offered only by *commercial banks* (banks that offer a full range of banking services). Since the 1970's, however, other institutions have provided accounts that compete with the checking accounts of commercial banks. For example, savings banks and savings and loan associations offer NOW accounts. Banks and other financial institutions also offer special interest-bearing accounts known as *money market accounts,* from which withdrawals may be made by check. Credit unions use *share drafts,* which also are similar to checks. Joanna H. Frodin

See also **Clearinghouse; Negotiable instrument; Traveler's check; Alaska** (picture: A U.S. Treasury warrant).

Check, Traveler's. See Traveler's check.

Checkers is a game played on a checkerboard by two people. It is also called *draughts* (pronounced *drafts*). The checkerboard most often used in the United States has 64 alternating dark and light squares. Each player has 12 round, flat pieces called *men* or *checkers.* In most games, one set is black and the other red or white. The players sit opposite each other, and each arranges his or her men on the first three rows of black squares, one man per square. Two center rows remain open.

The player with the black men starts by moving one black checker diagonally forward toward the red checkers. Then the other player moves a red man toward the black. The men can be moved forward only, and only on the black squares.

The object of the game is to capture or block all the opponent's men. A man captures an opponent's man on an adjacent square by jumping over it and landing on the square immediately beyond, which must be vacant. A man may make more than one capture in a single turn. Usually, a player is required to make a capture if possible. All captured men are removed from the board.

If a man reaches the back line on an opponent's side, it is *crowned* and becomes a *king.* A second checker is placed on top of the king to distinguish it from the other men. A king can move and jump backward or forward.

In many countries, more complicated forms of checkers are played. The most widely played game is international checkers, which uses 20 checkers per player and a 100-square board. In this game, men may jump backward as well as forward, and kings may move and jump any distance. R. Wayne Schmittberger

WORLD BOOK illustration by Sarah Woodward

Setting up the checkerboard, players on opposite sides place 12 men on the first three rows of black squares. A black square must be on the lower left in setting up the board.

Checking account. See Bank (Providing a means of payment); Check.

Checks and balances are limitations on the power of any branch of government, with each branch having some control over the actions of the others. The United States system of government is based on a set of checks and balances, designed to prevent one person or branch of government from becoming too powerful.

The Constitution of the United States divides the powers of the federal government among the president, the Congress, and the federal courts. Each branch has some powers that offset those of the other two. For example, the president can veto bills passed by Congress. But the veto power is balanced by Congress's power to pass bills over a veto. The president influences the federal courts by appointing judges, and such appointments require congressional approval. But the federal courts can restrain both the president and the Congress with their power to declare presidential orders or legislative acts unconstitutional.

The system of checks and balances also works between the two houses of Congress. Before a bill becomes law, both the Senate and the House of Representatives must approve it in identical form. If the Senate and House pass different versions, a conference committee of senators and representatives tries to work out the differences. This system ensures that both houses of Congress will have a voice in making laws.

Many countries have a democratic government without a system of checks and balances or separation of the powers of government. In Australia, Canada, and the United Kingdom, for example, executive power rests with the prime minister and Cabinet, who are members of Parliament, the legislative body. In addition, the courts in certain of these countries, including the United Kingdom and Switzerland, cannot declare an act of the nation's Parliament invalid. Kenneth Janda

See also **Government** (Presidential democracy); **President** (Limited presidency); **United States, Government of the** (Separation of powers).

Cheerleading is a colorful American sports tradition in which people called *cheerleaders* direct spectators in organized cheering during athletic events. School cheerleading programs generally begin about sixth grade and continue through college. Some professional sports teams also have cheerleaders. Professional cheerleaders and some college cheerleaders are paid for their work. Cheerleading began at the University of Minnesota in 1898 and became nationally popular by 1920.

Cheerleaders most often perform at football and basketball games. They lead yells and chants with rhythmic body motions to generate enthusiasm and entertain spectators. They also may dance and perform acrobatic stunts. The International Cheerleading Foundation holds training camps in most states and conducts a worldwide competition for high school cheerleaders.

Randy L. Neil

Cheese is a healthful, tasty food made from milk. For thousands of years, cheese has been one of the most important foods of people throughout the world. Cheese can be eaten alone or it can be served on crackers, in sandwiches, in salads, and in cooked foods.

There are hundreds of kinds of cheeses. They differ in taste, texture, and appearance. Many cheeses spread easily, but others are hard and crumbly. Some kinds taste sweet, and others have a sharp or spicy taste.

Cheese stays fresh longer than milk, and it has much of milk's food value, including proteins, minerals, and vitamins. Cheese contains these nutrients of milk in concentrated form. For example, 8 ounces (227 grams) of Cheddar cheese provide as much protein and calcium as $1\frac{1}{2}$ quarts (1.4 liters) of milk. Cheese, like milk, supplies important amounts of vitamin A and riboflavin.

The United States leads the world in cheese production. Almost every state of the United States makes cheese. Wisconsin and California are the leading cheese-producing states. Together, they account for about half of U.S. cheese production. The U.S. Department of Agriculture grades a large quantity of the cheese produced in the United States as AA, A, B, or C. In addition, some states have their own standards for grading cheese. Most cheese made in Canada comes from the provinces of Quebec and Ontario. The Canadian government has its own standards for grading cheese produced in that country.

Most cheese is produced from cow's milk. People in Europe and Asia frequently make cheese from the milk of such animals as buffaloes, goats, and sheep. But cheese can be made from the milk of any animal. Herders in Lapland use reindeer milk in making cheese. In Tibet, yaks supply milk for cheese. Cheese is also commonly made from the milk of camels, donkeys, horses, and zebras.

Kinds of cheese

There are more than 400 kinds of cheese. They have over 2,000 names because some cheeses are known by two or more names. For example, Swiss cheese is also called Emmentaler. Many cheeses take their names from the country or region where they were first produced. Swiss cheese originally came from Switzerland, and Roquefort cheese is made only near Roquefort, France.

Almost all cheeses belong to one of four main groups: (1) soft, (2) semisoft, (3) hard, and (4) very hard, or grating. The amount of moisture in the cheese determines its classification. The more moisture the cheese contains, the softer it is.

Soft cheese. The two most popular kinds of soft cheese are cottage cheese and cream cheese. Some soft cheeses, including Brie and Camembert, develop a crust. The crust releases enzymes that soften the cheese and develop its flavor.

Semisoft cheese includes such varieties as blue, brick, Limburger, Monterey Jack, mozzarella, Munster, Port du Salut, Roquefort, and Stilton. Blue, Roquefort, and Stilton cheese have streaks of blue mold running through them. The mold, which is added during the cheese-making process, gives these cheeses a special flavor. Blue and Stilton are made with cow's milk, but Roquefort is made only from sheep's milk.

Hard cheese. Cheddar, Edam, Gruyère, and Swiss are popular varieties of hard cheese. Gruyère and Swiss cheese have holes called *eyes.* Cheese makers form the eyes by adding bacteria that produce bubbles of carbon dioxide gas in the cheese. When the cheese is sliced, the bubbles become holes.

Very hard, or grating, cheese includes Asiago, Parmesan, Romano, and sapsago. People usually grind such cheeses and sprinkle them over such foods as soups, vegetables, and pizza.

How cheese is made

Almost all the cheese produced in the United States is made in large factories. The process used involves five basic steps: (1) processing the milk; (2) separating the curd; (3) treating the curd; (4) ripening; and (5) packaging. Slight differences in the process result in the production of several hundred varieties of cheese.

Processing the milk. Cheese makers inspect the milk and remove any solid substances by a process called *clarification.* The milk flows into a pasteurizer that kills harmful bacteria. Pumps force the pasteurized milk into metal tanks or vats that hold from 8,000 to 35,000 pounds (3,600 to 15,900 kilograms). About 10,500 pounds (4,760 kilograms) of milk are used to make 1,000 pounds (450 kilograms) of cheddar cheese.

Separating the curd. After the milk has been processed, it is treated to form a soft, custardlike substance called curd. The curd contains a liquid called *whey,* which must be expelled before cheese can be made. Cheese makers form the curd by first heating the milk to 86 to 96 °F (30 to 36 °C). Then they add a liquid called a starter culture to the milk. This liquid contains bacteria that form acids and turn milk sour. Vegetable dye may also be added to give the cheese a certain color. At the start of the souring process, mechanical paddles stir the starter culture and dye evenly through the milk.

After 15 to 90 minutes, workers add an enzyme that causes the milk to thicken. Cheese makers have long used rennet, a substance from the lining of the stomachs of calves. But a shortage of such rennet has caused them to use other enzymes, including pepsin from the stomachs of hogs and rennets produced by molds. Also, genetically engineered bacteria are expected to become a major source of rennet (see **Genetic engineering**). The paddles blend the enzymes into the milk, which is then left undisturbed for about 30 minutes so curd will form.

Special knives cut the curd into thousands of small cubes, and the whey oozes from them. The paddles stir the curd and whey, and the temperature in the vat is raised to between 102 and 130 °F (39 and 54 °C). The motion and heat force more whey from the curd. The whey is then drained or the curd is lifted from the vat.

Treating the curd. In making most cheeses, the curd is left undisturbed after the whey is drained off. The particles stick together and form a solid mass. The curd is then broken up into small pieces for pressing. To make cottage cheese, workers rinse the curd with water and mix it with cream and salt.

The curd for Cheddar goes through a special step after being formed into a solid mass. Workers cut the curd into large slabs, stack them in the vat, and turn them every 10 minutes. This process, called *cheddaring,* may also be done mechanically in large towers, rotating cylinders, or steel boxes. The slabs of curd pass through a mill, which chops them into small pieces.

The curd for most cheeses is packed into metal hoops or molds for pressing. The containers are put into

Some kinds of cheese

The four main groups of cheese are (1) soft, (2) semisoft, (3) hard, and (4) very hard or grating. The amount of moisture in a cheese determines its classification. The more moisture the cheese has, the softer it is. The drawings below show some popular cheeses in the four groups.

WORLD BOOK illustrations by James Teason

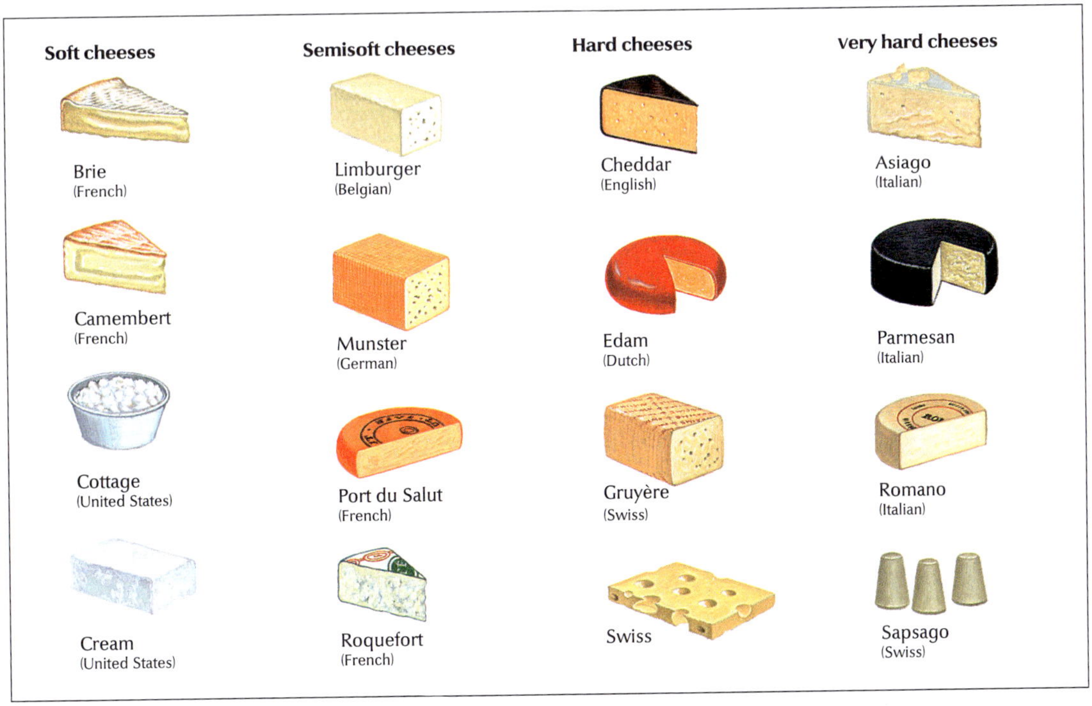

How cheese is made

Cheese manufacturers make cheese from milk. They treat the milk with bacterial starters and rennet to form *curd,* a custardlike substance. The curd contains a liquid called *whey,* which must be removed before the cheese can be made. The photos show the steps in making Swiss cheese.

Separating the curd and whey. After the curd becomes firm, a worker skims off the top layer. The curd is cut into small cubes, mixed, and stirred. After the curd settles, some of the whey is drained.

Hoisting the curd. A worker collects the curd into a large "dipping cloth" and lifts it from the whey. The large bundle of curd hangs over the kettle until the excess whey drains off.

Kunio Owaki, The Stock Market

Pressing the curd. The curd is pressed in a stainless steel mold for 24 hours. Then it is salted and aged in a warm room for several months. The familiar "eyes," or holes, form during this time.

presses that keep the cheese under great pressure for a few hours to a few days. During pressing, more whey drains and the curd is shaped into blocks or wheels. Most cheeses are salted after pressing. But Cheddar and some other cheeses are salted before pressing.

After pressing, workers remove the cheese from the hoops or molds. A crust called a *rind* begins to form on the cheese as it dries. To prevent a rind from forming, most cheeses are sealed in plastic wrap immediately after they are removed from the metal hoops. Most cheeses today are rindless.

Ripening, also called *aging* or *curing,* helps give cheese its flavor and texture. Cheese is aged in storage rooms or warehouses that have a controlled temperature and humidity. Aging times vary for different cheeses. Brick cheese and others need two months to age. Parmesan requires about a year. The longer the curing time, the sharper the cheese's flavor.

Packaging. After being aged, cheese is packaged in a wide variety of shapes and sizes. Some cheeses are sliced at the factory and sealed in foil or plastic. Others are sold whole—in large blocks, wedges, balls called *rounds,* or short cylinders called *wheels.*

Process cheese

Much of the cheese produced in the United States is made into *process cheese,* a blend of natural cheeses. Process cheese keeps better than natural cheeses, and it melts more evenly when used in cooking. Some process cheese is made from two or more kinds of cheese.

Leading cheese-producing countries

Amount of cheese produced in a year

United States	9,114,000,000 pounds (4,134,200,000 kilograms)
France	3,875,000,000 pounds (1,757,800,000 kilograms)
Germany	3,727,000,000 pounds (1,690,400,000 kilograms)
Italy	2,401,000,000 pounds (1,088,900,000 kilograms)
Netherlands	1,466,000,000 pounds (664,800,000 kilograms)
Poland	1,106,000,000 pounds (501,840,000 kilograms)

Figures are for a three-year average, 2000-2002.
Source: Food and Agriculture Organization of the United Nations.

Leading cheese-producing states

Amount of cheese produced in a year

Wisconsin	2,133,200,000 pounds (967,580,000 kilograms)
California	1,619,400,000 pounds (734,540,000 kilograms)
New York	702,750,000 pounds (318,760,000 kilograms)
Minnesota	594,090,000 pounds (269,470,000 kilograms)
Idaho	569,420,000 pounds (258,280,000 kilograms)
Pennsylvania	366,970,000 pounds (166,460,000 kilograms)

Figures are for 2001.
Source: U.S. Department of Agriculture.

Other process cheese is a mixture of batches of the same kind of cheese that differ in taste and texture. The cheeses are ground up and then blended with the aid of heat and chemicals called *emulsifiers.* Process cheese made from only one variety of cheese is named for that cheese. For example, process Swiss cheese is made only from Swiss. However, process cheese labeled Pasteurized Process American Cheese may be made from a combination of cheeses, including Cheddar, Colby, and washed curd cheese. In the United States, all cheeses used in process cheese made from two or more kinds of cheese must be identified on the label.

Process cheese foods and process cheese spreads are made like process cheese. But cream, milk, or whey are added to make them more moist. Fruit, meat, spices, or vegetables may be added for extra flavor. *Cold-pack cheese* is a blend of natural cheeses. Its manufacturing process involves no heat. Much cold-pack cheese includes meat or wine as flavoring.

History

The first cheese was probably made more than 4,000 years ago by nomadic tribes in Asia. Through the years, knowledge of cheese making spread to Europe.

Cheese making began in the American Colonies in 1611. That year, settlers in Jamestown, in the Virginia Colony, imported cows from England. In 1851, an American dairyman named Jesse Williams established the nation's first cheese factory, near Rome, New York.

In 1917, J. L. Kraft, an American businessman, patented a method for making process cheese. His company also developed a method for wrapping individual slices of cheese mechanically.

During the 1970's, scientists developed methods of removing proteins and *lactose* (milk sugar) from whey. Most whey had previously been thrown away. Today, manufacturers add these nutritious substances from whey to baby food, bread, ice cream, and other foods.

Also during the 1970's, European cheese makers began to use a process called *ultrafiltration* for making soft cheeses. In this process, the milk is strained through such a fine filter that only water, lactose, and salts are lost. The remaining liquid contains most of the proteins normally drained off with the whey. By concentrating the milk mixture so highly, ultrafiltration makes it possible to produce more cheese in a vat. The process was first used commercially in the United States in the mid-1980's. Robert T. Marshall

See also **Casein.**

Cheetah is a large cat chiefly found on the grassy plains of eastern and southern Africa. It is the fastest land mammal over short distances. Cheetahs can run at a top speed of 50 to 70 miles (80 to 110 kilometers) per hour. But they can maintain this speed for only a few hundred yards or meters.

Body. The cheetah has a slender body, long legs, and a small head. An adult cheetah stands 30 to 36 inches (75 to 90 centimeters) tall at the shoulder and weighs 77 to 132 pounds (35 to 60 kilograms). The animal measures about 6 to 7 feet (1.8 to 2.1 meters) in length, including the tail. Males generally are larger than females. The cheetah has a yellowish-brown coat with black spots, except for the throat and underparts, which are white to yellowish-white with black spots.

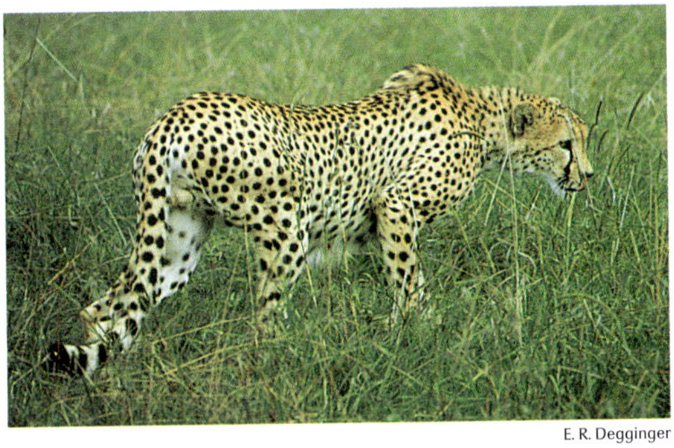

E. R. Degginger

The cheetah hunts by prowling quietly through grass until it nears its prey. Then it swiftly rushes to the kill. It can run as fast as 70 miles (110 kilometers) per hour for short distances.

Life. In eastern Africa, adult female cheetahs usually live alone unless they have cubs. Adult males live alone or with one to three other males, usually brothers. Cheetahs in southern Africa may live in larger groups that contain more than one adult female.

Male and female cheetahs may mate at any time of year. Several males may fight over a potential female mate. After mating, the male remains with the female for a day or two. He then leaves and does not help raise the young.

After a pregnancy of about three months, the female gives birth to an average of three to five cubs. Many cheetah cubs die during their first three months of life. They typically are killed by lions, hyenas, and birds of prey. The surviving cheetah cubs remain with the mother about 14 to 18 months. During this time, they learn to hunt.

Cheetahs usually hunt by day. They commonly attack medium-sized mammals, particularly small or young antelope. The cheetah uses its great speed to run down prey after stalking close to it.

Survival problems. Cheetahs once inhabited grassy plains throughout Africa and across the Middle East into central Asia and India. Since the early 1900's, their numbers have declined rapidly. This decline has occurred chiefly because people have hunted the cheetah for its pelt and have converted much of the animal's grassland habitat into farming and manufacturing areas. Today, the cheetah is an endangered species. Biologists estimate that fewer than 15,000 cheetahs remain in the wild.

Many biologists believe that cheetahs narrowly escaped extinction about 10,000 years ago. Although the species survived, inbreeding among the few remaining individuals may have led to a loss of genetic diversity. Some scientists believe that this lack of diversity affects the cheetah's immune system and makes the animal more vulnerable to disease. Cheetahs are bred in captivity to try to maintain their remaining genetic variation. Biologists hope to eventually release some of these cheetahs into the wild. Nadja Wielebnowski

Scientific classification. The cheetah belongs to the cat family, Felidae. Its scientific name is *Acinonyx jubatus.*

Cheever, John (1912-1982), was an American short-story writer and novelist. Cheever's typical characters are the descendants of genteel old American families, or the inhabitants of comfortable, upper middle-class suburbia. He wrote about these people in a style that is both lyrical and lightly ironic. In his fiction, Cheever balanced the claims of individual freedom and desire against society's values of emotional restraint and good manners. He often created characters who attempt to disrupt their seemingly tranquil lives to pursue some kind of personal satisfaction. Their attempts usually end partly in defeat and partly in success.

In his related novels *The Wapshot Chronicle* (1957) and *The Wapshot Scandal* (1964), Cheever wrote about the modern-day descendants of an old New England seafaring family. The novels reveal how the family's tradition of strong individualism and eccentricity conflicts with the restrictions of an increasingly impersonal American society. Two of Cheever's later novels explore darker themes. *Bullet Park* (1969) tells a story of drug addiction and insanity in a typical suburban setting. *Falconer* (1977) is a story about a college professor who kills his brother, is imprisoned, and escapes. Cheever won the 1979 Pulitzer Prize for fiction for *The Stories of John Cheever* (1978). *The Journals of John Cheever* was published in 1991, after his death. Cheever was born on May 27, 1912, in Quincy, Massachusetts. Marcus Klein

Chekhov, *CHEHK awf,* **Anton,** *ahn TAWN* (1860-1904), was a Russian playwright and short-story writer. His works show the stagnant, helpless quality of Russian society, especially the rural landowners, in the late 1800's. Most of his characters are decent and sensitive. They dream of improving their lives, but most fail, victims of their sense of helplessness and uselessness. Scholars believe Chekhov probably was criticizing the backwardness he saw in Russian social and political life under the czars. But he never preached at his readers or audiences, preferring to present highly individualized characters with specific problems.

Perhaps Chekhov's most famous works are four plays he wrote late in his life—*The Sea Gull* (1896), *Uncle Vanya* (1899), *The Three Sisters* (1901), and *The Cherry Orchard* (1904). These plays have been called gloomy and pessimistic. But they blend poetic atmosphere with sympathetic treatment of characters who are trapped in unfulfilling lives and cannot help themselves.

Chekhov was born on Jan. 29, 1860 (January 17 on the Russian calendar then in use), in Taganrog. In 1879, he moved to Moscow and studied medicine. He began his literary career writing sketches and short humorous stories for popular newspapers and comic sheets to help support his needy family. He graduated from medical school and became a doctor. His experiences as a country doctor and his scientific background contributed to the realism of his mature stories. In 1890, Chekhov studied the Russian state prisons on Sakhalin Island in the Pacific Ocean. He described the terrible living conditions there in *Sakhalin Island* (1893-1894). In 1901, he married Olga Knipper, an actress who played leading roles in many of his plays that the famous Moscow Art Theater staged. He died of tuberculosis. Anna Lisa Crone

Additional resources

Bloom, Harold, ed. *Anton Chekhov.* Chelsea Hse., 1999.
Malcolm, Janet. *Reading Chekhov.* Random Hse., 2001.

Chelation therapy, *kee LAY shuhn,* is medical treatment that involves the use of drugs to remove toxic metal ions from the body. These drugs *chelate* (bind strongly) to the metal ions to form soluble substances removed in the urine. The technique is used to treat lead poisoning and to reduce iron levels in patients with thalassemia or other diseases that require frequent blood transfusions. It is also used for treating overexposure to mercury, zinc, and a variety of other metals. Chelation therapy has been used to treat *arteriosclerosis* (hardening of the arteries), but its effectiveness has never been proven. Some doctors continue to use the treatment, but most medical authorities discourage the use of it to treat arteriosclerosis. Thomas H. Maugh II

Chemical is any of the many substances that make up the world's materials. Many chemicals are naturally occurring substances called *elements.* They include hydrogen, nitrogen, and sulfur. Various elements can be combined to make a variety of chemicals. Ammonia and sulfuric acid are examples of artificially produced chemicals. See also **Chemistry; Element, Chemical.**

Chemical-biological-radiological warfare (CBR) is war waged with chemicals, biological agents, or radioactive materials. CBR includes both the use of CBR weapons and the application of defenses against such weapons. CBR weapons can be designed to kill large numbers of people, temporarily disable them, or destroy their food supplies. The weapons are usually effective without destroying property.

Chemical agents affect the nervous system, respiratory system, skin, eyes, nose, or throat. They include gases, liquids, sprays, and powders. They can be sprayed from airplanes, dropped as bombs, fired by artillery in explosive shells, or dispersed by land mines.

Some chemical agents, called *nerve agents* or *poison gas,* can cause death. They may be colorless, odorless, and tasteless. They can cause death rapidly if the victim inhales them or if they are splashed on bare skin. Chemical agents have not been widely used in warfare since World War I ended in 1918. Other chemical agents are not fatal, but they make their victims unable to fight. Blister agents cause huge blisters on the skin. A blister agent called *mustard gas* caused many casualties during World War I. Other chemical agents can cause temporary blindness or confusion. Gas masks, other protective coverings, and injections of antidotes are used as defenses against chemical agents. See **Gas mask.**

Chemical agents also have nonmilitary uses. Some agents, including *tear gas,* may be used to control rioting crowds. These agents affect the eyes, nose, and throat. They cause blinding tears and often violent coughing. But these effects disappear soon after the victim reaches fresh air. Other chemicals are used to kill harmful insects or to strip leaves from trees.

Biological warfare is the military use of harmful microorganisms, or the *toxins* (poisons) they produce, as weapons against people, animals, or crops. It is sometimes called *germ warfare.* A small number of these microorganisms could kill millions of people if effectively distributed. Biological agents could also be used to make enemy soldiers too sick to fight, or to ruin an enemy's food supply. A biological agent that seriously damaged the enemy country's crops might be a decisive factor in a war. Biological weapons have not played a part in modern warfare. But military strategists must assume that the enemy has such weapons. Thus, much research is devoted to defenses against biological weapons.

In 1969, President Richard M. Nixon stated that the United States would not conduct biological warfare against another nation even if that nation used such warfare against the United States. Nixon ordered U.S. stocks of biological weapons destroyed.

An international treaty banning biological weapons went into effect in 1975. It bars the production, possession, and use of such weapons. More than 140 nations have ratified the treaty.

Radiological agents give off invisible radiation that can damage a person's internal organs and even cause death. Radiation from nuclear *fallout* could be a major factor in any war involving nuclear weapons. Radiological warfare is dangerous for all sides in a war. A nuclear weapon used against an enemy would create fallout that might be carried by winds back to the country or troops that used the weapon. Radioactivity might also make an area temporarily unfit for human life.

History. Radiological warfare became possible with the development of atomic weapons during the 1940's. However, chemical and biological warfare have long histories. The Spartans used pitch and sulfur in a form of chemical warfare during the Peloponnesian War in the 400's B.C. During ancient and medieval times, soldiers sometimes threw bodies of people who died from plague over the walls of besieged cities, or into water wells. During the French and Indian wars (1689-1763), blankets used by smallpox victims were purposefully given to Indians in the hope that the blankets would infect them.

Germany introduced the use of gas in war during World War I. In 1915, the Germans used gas against Allied forces at Ypres, Belgium. Before the end of the war, gases of many types were used by all armies. Gas caused nearly 30 percent of all United States casualties in the war.

Gas warfare proved so destructive that most nations have agreed to avoid the use of poison gas and other chemical weapons. But Iraq used chemical weapons against Iranian troops during the war between Iran and Iraq (1980-1988). This use may have begun in 1983. In 1988, Iraq was also accused of using chemical weapons against its Kurdish citizens, who were seeking independence from Iraq. Frances M. Lussier

See also **Army** (picture: Armies wear protective clothing); **Biological Weapons Convention; Chemical Weapons Convention.**

Chemical element. See **Element, Chemical.**

Chemical equilibrium. See **Equilibrium, Chemical.**

Chemical industry is made up of the industries that use chemistry in the manufacture of a variety of products. These products include fuels, detergents, drugs, and paints. Plastics, synthetic fibers, and synthetic rubber are some important materials developed by the industry.

Related articles in *World Book* include:

Chemistry (History)	Petrochemicals
Drug	Plastics
Fiber	Synthetics
Hazardous wastes	

Chemical Mace. See **Mace.**

Chemical reaction is a process in which one substance is chemically converted to another. All chemical reactions involve the formation or destruction of bonds between atoms. Chemical reactions include the rusting of iron and the digestion of food. Most chemical reactions give off heat. For example, chemical reactions that occur in digestion give off heat that keeps our bodies warm and functioning.

Chemists use *chemical equations* to express what occurs in chemical reactions. Chemical equations consist of chemical formulas and symbols that show the substances involved in chemical changes. For example, an equation for the rusting of iron is as follows:

$$4Fe(s) + 3O_2(g) \rightarrow 2Fe_2O_3(s)$$

This equation shows that four atoms of solid iron (Fe[s]) react with three molecules of oxygen gas (O_2[g]) to form two units of solid rust (Fe_2O_3[s]). Experiments demonstrate that iron and oxygen react in these proportions in air at room temperature. Rust is the *product,* or result, of the reaction. Iron and oxygen are the *reactants.* The reactants are substances that undergo the chemical change.

In a chemical reaction, the total number of atoms and the kinds of atoms do not change, even though one substance disappears while another is formed. In the rust example that is given above, the reactants contain a total of 10 atoms. This total includes the six atoms that make up the three molecules of oxygen gas. The product also contains 10 atoms. But the products of a chemical reaction and their formulas are different from the reactants.

Chemical reactions differ from physical changes and nuclear reactions. In a physical change, such as the melting of ice, the substance undergoing change (ice) has the same formula as the resulting substance (water). In a nuclear reaction, an atom becomes another kind of atom as a result of changes in the composition of its nucleus. Ronald C. Johnson

Chemical Society, American. See **American Chemical Society.**

Chemical warfare. See **Chemical-biological-radiological warfare.**

Chemical Weapons Convention is an international agreement to ban the production and use of chemical weapons. Nations that officially accept the treaty must agree not to produce, possess, or engage in the trade or use of chemical weapons. Chemical weapons are chemical agents used to injure or kill people.

The official name of the treaty is the Convention on the Prohibition of the Development, Production, Stockpiling and Use of Chemical Weapons and on their Destruction. The treaty went into effect in 1997. By 2000, 129 nations had *ratified* (approved) it.

The agreement is a complex one because many of the components used for chemical weapons are also used for peaceful purposes, such as pesticides. The treaty allows international inspection teams to enter a country and inspect all chemical industry facilities that handle or make certain chemicals. The treaty tries to regulate and control the production and use of many chemicals, without imposing excessive costs on the chemical industry.

The treaty created an international organization that carries out the terms of the agreement, including organizing the inspection teams. Most nations with large chemical industries have seats on the organization's executive council. William B. Vogele

See also **Chemical-biological-radiological warfare.**

John Zoinar from Peter Arnold

Monitoring a fermentation process

A. G. E. Fotostock from Peter Arnold

Building a three-dimensional model of a molecule

Dan McCoy, Rainbow

Measuring molecular weights with a mass spectrometer

Research in chemistry attempts to answer questions about the nature of substances. Some chemists, for example, try to understand the chemical changes that substances go through. Others use models or advanced instruments to explore the structure and composition of substances.

Chemistry

Chemistry is the scientific study of substances. Chemists investigate the *properties* (characteristics) of the substances that make up the universe. They study how those substances behave under different conditions. They attempt to explain the behavior of a substance in terms of the substance's structure and composition. Chemists also seek to understand chemical changes. Chemical changes involve alterations in a substance's chemical makeup. The combination of iron with oxygen from the air to form rust is a chemical change. Substances may also go through physical change without altering their chemical makeup. Water changes physically but not chemically when it freezes.

Chemical changes occur constantly in nature and make life on the earth possible. During a thunderstorm, for instance, lightning causes a chemical change in the air. The electrical energy and heat of a lightning bolt cause some of the nitrogen and oxygen in the atmosphere to combine and form gases called *nitrogen oxides.* The nitrogen oxides dissolve in raindrops that fall to the ground. In the soil, they are chemically changed into *nitrates,* substances that serve as fertilizer.

Chemical changes also occur as wood burns and becomes ashes and gases. The food we eat goes through many chemical changes in our bodies.

Chemists have learned much about the chemical substances and processes that occur in nature. In addition, chemical researchers have created many useful substances that do not occur naturally. Products resulting from chemical research include many artificial fibers, drugs, dyes, fertilizers, and plastics. The knowledge gained by chemists and the materials they have produced have greatly improved people's lives.

Melvyn C. Usselman, the contributor of this article, is Associate Professor of Chemistry at the University of Western Ontario.

The work of chemists

Chemistry involves the study of many substances. Substances differ greatly in properties, structure, and composition. The methods chemists use and the questions they attempt to answer also differ greatly. However, all chemists share certain fundamental ideas.

Fundamental ideas of chemistry. The simplest chemical substances are the chemical elements. They

Ray Pfortner from Peter Arnold

Collecting soil samples at a hazardous waste site

Dick Luria, Photo Researchers

Perfecting a formula for a new perfume

Dick Luria, Photo Researchers

Inspecting drug purification equipment

The practical applications of chemistry range from the development of new methods of disposing of hazardous wastes to the discovery of new formulas for perfumes. Cosmetics, drugs, dyes, and synthetic fibers are only a few of the products resulting from chemical research.

are the building blocks of all other substances. Each chemical element is made up of only one kind of atom. The atoms of one element differ from those of all other elements. Chemists use letters of the alphabet as symbols for the elements. The symbols for the elements carbon, hydrogen, oxygen, and iron, for example, are C, H, O, and Fe. There are 91 elements known to exist on Earth. An additional 20 elements have been produced artificially. See **Element, Chemical**.

Electrical forces at the atomic level create chemical bonds that join two or more atoms together, forming molecules. Some molecules consist of atoms of a single element. Oxygen molecules, for example, are made up of two oxygen atoms. Chemists represent the oxygen molecule by the chemical formula O_2. The *2* indicates the number of atoms in the molecule. See **Molecule**.

When atoms of two or more different elements bond together, they form a chemical compound. Water is a compound made up of two hydrogen atoms and one oxygen atom. The chemical formula for a water molecule is H_2O. See **Compound**.

Compounds are formed or broken down by means of chemical reactions. All chemical reactions involve the formation or destruction of chemical bonds. Chemists use *chemical equations* to express what occurs in chemical reactions. Chemical equations consist of chemical formulas and symbols that show the substances involved in chemical changes. For example, the equation

$$C + O_2 \rightarrow CO_2$$

expresses the chemical change that occurs when one carbon atom reacts, or bonds, with an oxygen molecule. The reaction produces one molecule of carbon dioxide, which has the formula CO_2.

The broad range of study. Chemists study substances according to questions they want to answer. Many chemists study special groups of substances, such as compounds containing carbon-to-carbon bonds. Some chemists specialize in techniques that enable them to analyze any substance and identify the elements and compounds it consists of. Other chemists study the forces involved in chemical changes. Much chemical research deals with the atomic and molecular structures of substances. Certain chemists try to predict chemical behavior from theories about the forces at work within the atom. Chemists also work to create new substances and to make synthetic forms of rare but useful natural materials. Their field is called *synthetic chemistry.* A number of chemists apply their knowledge to finding ways of using substances and chemical processes in agriculture, industry, medicine, and other fields.

In some cases, chemistry overlaps such sciences as biology, geology, mathematics, and physics to such an extent that *interdisciplinary sciences* have been established. *Biochemistry,* for example, combines biology and chemistry in studying the chemical processes of living things.

Tools and techniques. Chemists use a wide variety of tools and techniques. Specialized instruments and computers help chemists make accurate measurements. A device called a *mass spectrometer,* for example, enables chemists to determine the *mass* and atomic composition of molecules. Mass is the total quantity of matter that anything contains. Chemists can identify how atoms are arranged in molecules by using instruments that measure the radiation absorbed and given off by the molecules. The measurement technique is called *spectroscopy.* A technique called *chromatography* enables chemists to separate complicated mixtures into their parts and to detect and measure low concentrations of substances, such as pollutants in air and water.

History of chemistry

Beginnings. In prehistoric times, people made many useful discoveries by observing the properties of natural substances and the changes those substances go through. About 1 $\frac{1}{2}$ million years ago, people began to use fire. Fire was the first chemical reaction that human beings learned to produce and control. The use of fire enabled people to change the properties of substances. They used fire for cooking, hardening pottery, and making metal from ores. Fire also enabled them to create new materials. About 3500 B.C., for example, people learned to make bronze by melting together copper and arsenic—and later, copper and tin.

The people of many ancient cultures believed that gods or spirits caused natural events. About 600 B.C., however, some Greek philosophers began to regard nature in a different way. They believed that nature worked according to laws that people could discover by observation and logic.

Several ancient Greek philosophers developed theories about the basic substances that make up the world. Empedocles, who lived during the 400's B.C., argued that there were four primary elements—air, earth, fire, and water—and that they combined in various proportions to form all other substances.

About 400 B.C., a Greek philosopher named Democritus taught that all matter was composed of a single material that existed in the form of tiny, indestructible units called atoms. According to his theory, differences among substances were caused only by differences in the size, shape, and position of their atoms.

The Greek philosopher Aristotle, who lived during the 300's B.C., claimed that each of the four primary elements proposed by Empedocles could be changed into any of the other elements by adding or removing heat and moisture. He stated that such a change—called *transmutation*—occurred whenever a substance was involved in a chemical reaction or changed from one physical state—solid, liquid, or gas—to another. Aristotle believed that water, for example, changed to air when it was heated.

Alchemy. During the first 300 years after the birth of Christ, scholars and craftworkers in Egypt developed a chemical practice that came to be called *alchemy.* They based their work on Aristotle's theory of the transmutation of elements and tried to change lead and other metals into gold. Alchemy began to spread to the Arabian Peninsula in the A.D. 600's and to much of western Europe in the 1100's. Until the 1600's, alchemy was a major source of chemical knowledge.

Despite centuries of experimentation, alchemists failed to produce gold from other materials. They did gain wide knowledge of chemical substances, however,

Major branches of chemistry

Analytical chemistry determines the properties of chemical substances and the structure and composition of compounds and mixtures.
- *Qualitative analysis* identifies the types of elements and compounds that make up substances.
- *Quantitative analysis* measures the amounts of the different chemicals that make up substances.
- *Radiochemistry* involves the identification and production of radioactive elements and their use in the study of chemical processes.

Applied chemistry refers to the practical use of the knowledge of chemical substances and processes.
- *Agricultural chemistry* develops fertilizers and pesticides and studies the chemical processes that occur in the soil and that are involved in crop growth.
- *Environmental chemistry* studies, monitors, and controls chemical processes and other factors in the environment and their relationships to living things.
- *Industrial chemistry* involves the chemical production of raw materials and the development, study, and control of industrial chemical processes and products.

Biochemistry deals with chemical processes of living things.

Inorganic chemistry concerns chemical substances that do not contain carbon-to-carbon bonds.

Organic chemistry is the study of chemical substances that contain carbon-to-carbon bonds.

Physical chemistry interprets chemical processes in terms of physical properties of matter, such as mass, motion, heat, electricity, and radiation.
- *Chemical kinetics* studies the sequence of steps in chemical reactions and the factors that affect the rates at which chemical reactions proceed.
- *Chemical thermodynamics* deals with the energy changes that occur during chemical reactions and how temperature and pressure differences affect reactions.
- *Nuclear chemistry* is the use of chemical techniques in the study of nuclear reactions.
- *Quantum chemistry* analyzes the distribution of electrons in molecules and interprets the chemical behavior of molecules in terms of their electron structure.
- *Radiation chemistry* concerns the chemical effects of high-energy radiation on substances.
- *Solid-state chemistry* deals with the composition of solids and the changes that occur within and between solids.
- *Stereochemistry* studies the arrangement of atoms in molecules and the properties that follow from such arrangements.
- *Surface chemistry* examines the surface characteristics of chemical substances.

Polymer chemistry deals with chainlike molecules formed by linking smaller molecules; and with *plastics,* which consist of chainlike molecules, often combined with other materials.

Synthetic chemistry involves combining chemical elements and compounds to duplicate naturally occurring substances or to produce compounds that do not occur naturally.

and invented many tools and techniques still used by chemists. Alchemists used such laboratory equipment as funnels, strainers, *crucibles* (pots for melting metals), and balance scales for weighing chemicals—that is, for determining their mass. They also discovered new ways of producing chemical changes and learned to make and use various acids and alcohols.

Alchemists also searched for a substance that could cure disease and lengthen life. During the 1500's, some alchemists and physicians began to apply their knowledge of chemistry to the treatment of disease. The medical chemistry of the 1500's and 1600's is called *iatrochemistry* (pronounced *eye AT roh KEHM uh stree*). The prefix comes from *iatros,* the Greek word for *physician.* Iatrochemists made the first studies of the chemical effects of medicines on the human body.

Robert Boyle, an Irish scientist of the 1600's, was one of the first modern chemists. He taught that theories must be supported by careful experiments. Boyle conducted many experiments that showed that air, earth, fire, and water are not true elements. He believed that the best explanation of the properties of matter was provided by an atomistic theory that described substances as composed of tiny particles in motion.

The phlogiston theory (pronounced *floh JIHS tuhn*) was a very successful chemical theory, though it was eventually replaced by a better one. The theory was developed in the early 1700's by a German chemist and physician named Georg Ernst Stahl. Stahl wrote that all flammable materials contained a substance called *phlogiston.* According to his theory, materials gave off phlogiston as they burned. Air was necessary for combustion because it absorbed the phlogiston that was released. Plants, in turn, removed phlogiston from the air. They therefore became rich in the substance and burned when dry. Like all other good chemical theories, the phlogiston theory provided an explanation for the results of a variety of experiments and offered clues to areas of study in which new discoveries could be made. For that reason, the theory was widely accepted in the 1700's and led to many findings in chemistry.

Chemists of the middle and late 1700's developed ways to isolate and study gases. They based their work on the phlogiston theory and made many discoveries. In the 1750's, the Scottish chemist and physician Joseph Black identified carbon dioxide, the first gas recognized to have properties different from those of air. In 1766, Henry Cavendish, an English chemist and physicist, discovered important properties of hydrogen and identified it as an element. Because hydrogen is very flammable, Cavendish believed that hydrogen was pure phlogiston. Oxygen was discovered independently by the Swedish chemist Carl Scheele in the early 1770's and the English chemist Joseph Priestley in 1774. Wood burns stronger in oxygen than in air. Thus, Priestley believed oxygen could absorb great quantities of phlogiston. He called oxygen *dephlogisticated air* (air without phlogiston).

Lavoisier's contributions. Antoine Lavoisier, a French chemist, revolutionized chemistry in the late 1700's. He repeated many of the experiments of earlier chemists but interpreted the results far differently. Lavoisier paid particular attention to the mass of the ingredients involved in chemical reactions and of the products that resulted. He found that the mass of the products of combustion equals that of the original ingredients. His discovery became known as the *law of the conservation of mass* (or *matter*).

Lavoisier noted that the mass of the air in which combustion occurred decreases. He found that the loss of mass results from the burning material combining with and removing a substance in the air. That substance was the same as dephlogisticated air, but Lavoisier renamed it oxygen. Lavoisier's oxygen theory of combustion came to replace the phlogiston theory.

Lavoisier and Pierre Simon Laplace, a French astronomer and mathematician, also carried out experiments demonstrating that respiration in animals is chemically similar to combustion. Their studies of the chemical processes of living organisms were among the first experiments in biochemistry. Lavoisier also helped work out the present-day system of chemical names. He

The Metropolitan Museum of Art, Rogers Fund, 1931

Metal smelting and casting are shown in this Egyptian wall painting from about 1474 B.C. Ancient peoples knew how to use various substances to make many things.

Granger Collection

The alchemist's workshop was the forerunner of the modern chemical laboratory. Alchemists used such laboratory equipment as funnels, strainers, and balance scales.

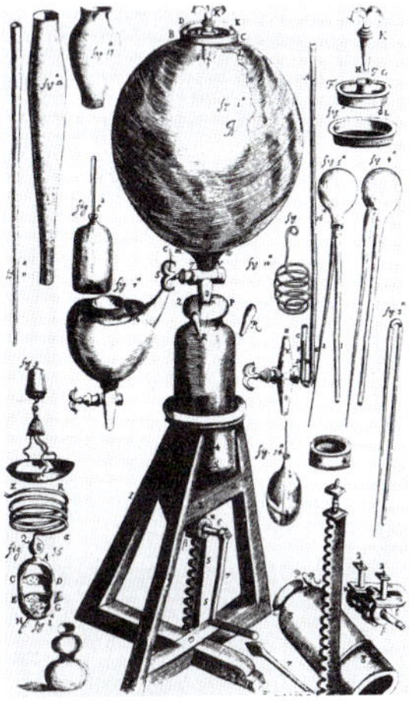

From Boyle's *New Experiments,* 1660

An air pump built by Robert Boyle and Robert Hooke in the mid-1600's was used to investigate vacuums.

Important dates in chemistry

c. 3500 B.C. People learned to make bronze.
c. 400 B.C. Democritus proposed an atomic theory.
A.D. 600's Alchemy began to spread from Egypt to the Arabian Peninsula and reached western Europe in the 1100's.
1600's Robert Boyle taught that theories must be supported by careful experiments.
Early 1700's Georg Ernst Stahl developed the phlogiston theory.
1750's Joseph Black identified carbon dioxide.
1766 Henry Cavendish identified hydrogen as an element.
1770's Carl Scheele and Joseph Priestley discovered oxygen.
Late 1700's Antoine Lavoisier stated the law of the conservation of mass and proposed the oxygen theory of combustion.
1803 John Dalton proposed his atomic theory.
1811 Amedeo Avogadro suggested that equal volumes of all gases at the same temperature and pressure contain equal numbers of particles.
Early 1800's Jöns J. Berzelius calculated the masses of a number of elements.
1828 Friedrich Wöhler made the first synthetic organic substance from inorganic compounds.
1856 Sir William H. Perkin made the first synthetic dye.
1869 Dmitri Mendeleev and Julius Lothar Meyer discovered the periodic law.
1910 Fritz Haber patented a process to produce synthetic ammonia.
1913 Niels Bohr proposed his model of the atom.
1916 Gilbert N. Lewis described electron bonding between atoms.
1950's Biochemists began to discover how such chemicals as *deoxyribonucleic acid* (DNA) and *ribonucleic acid* (RNA) affect heredity.
Early 1980's Chemists began working to develop a solar-powered device that produces hydrogen fuel by means of the chemical breakdown of water.
1985 Richard E. Smalley, Robert F. Curl, Jr., and Harold W. Kroto discover *buckminsterfullerene,* a ball-shaped molecule consisting only of carbon.

published his ideas on combustion, respiration, and the naming of compounds in *Elementary Treatise on Chemistry* (1789), the first modern textbook of chemistry.

Dalton's atomic theory. In 1803, an English chemist named John Dalton developed an atomic theory based on the idea that each chemical element has its own kind of atoms. He believed that all the atoms of a particular element had the same mass and chemical properties. The theory could explain and predict the results of various experiments and was gradually accepted.

According to Dalton's theory, a fixed number of atoms of one substance always combined with a fixed number of atoms of another substance in forming a compound. Dalton realized that substances must combine in the same proportions by mass as the mass proportions of their atoms. Chemists had already observed that pure substances do combine in fixed proportions. They called that finding the *law of definite* (or *constant) proportions.* Dalton's theory explained the law.

Dalton was the first to calculate the relative masses of the atoms of several elements. By 1814, Jöns J. Berzelius, a Swedish chemist, had obtained accurate atomic masses for a number of elements. He also began the system of using letters as symbols for elements.

Formation of the periodic table. In 1869, Russian chemist Dmitri Mendeleev and German chemist Julius Lothar Meyer independently announced their discovery of the *periodic law.* The law is based on their observation that when elements are arranged in a table according to their relative atomic masses, elements with similar properties appear at regular intervals, or *periods,* in the table. The two chemists rearranged the table in columns so that elements with similar properties were grouped together. Such an arrangement became known as the *periodic table.* Both men left gaps in the table, and Mendeleev correctly predicted that elements with certain properties would be discovered to fill the gaps. The modern periodic table serves as a guide to the chemistry of all known elements. See **Element, Chemical** (Periodic table of the elements).

Granger Collection
Antoine Lavoisier studied chemical processes in the 1700's. This engraving shows his experiment proving that water consists of hydrogen and oxygen.

Granger Collection
John Dalton developed an atomic theory in 1803. His theory, based on the idea that each chemical element has its own kind of atoms, gradually won acceptance.

Granger Collection
Friedrich Wöhler made the first organic substance from inorganic chemicals in 1828, showing that living things were not the only source of organic compounds.

A *World Book* science project

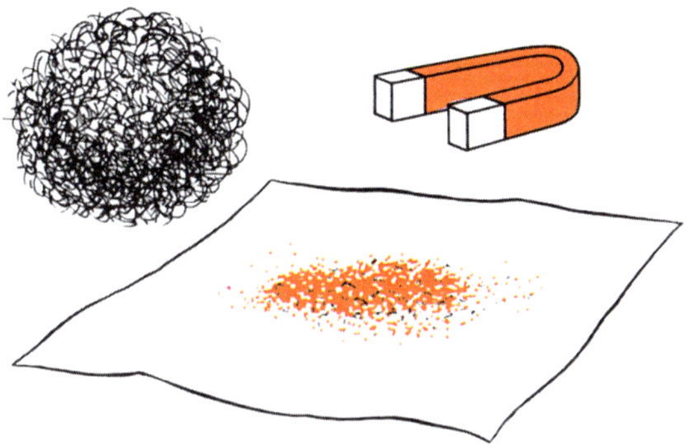

This experiment shows that iron and oxygen can combine in different ways to form two compounds. One compound is a reddish, nonmagnetic powder, and the other is a blue-black magnetic powder.

Materials

Steel wool rusts slowly in water, but quickly in a solution containing hypochlorous acid. You can make such a solution by mixing bleach and vinegar. The hypochlorous acid (HClO) in the solution reacts with the iron (Fe) in steel wool to form hydrated ferric oxide ($Fe_2O_3 \cdot H_2O$). By heating this oxide, you can change it to magnetic oxide of iron (Fe_3O_4).

Two small jars

Small ball of steel wool

Bleach

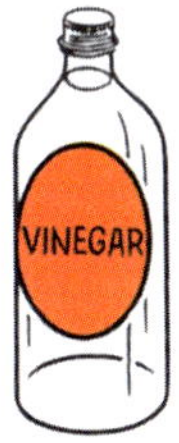

Vinegar

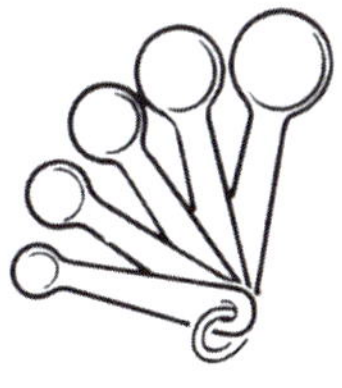

Measuring spoons

Water

Paper napkin

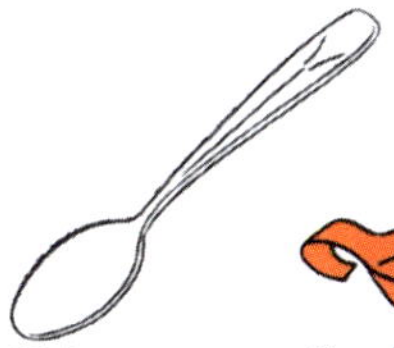

Old spoon

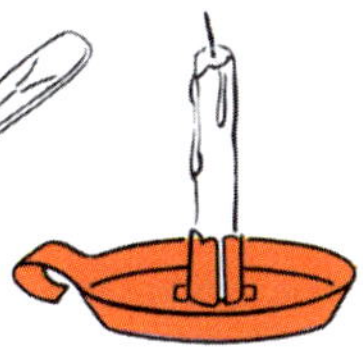

Candle and holder

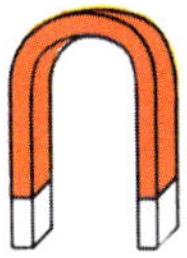

Magnet

WORLD BOOK illustration by Raymond Perlman

Procedure

Place the ball of steel wool into one of the jars and add enough water to cover the ball. You see no change in the steel wool because water affects iron slowly.

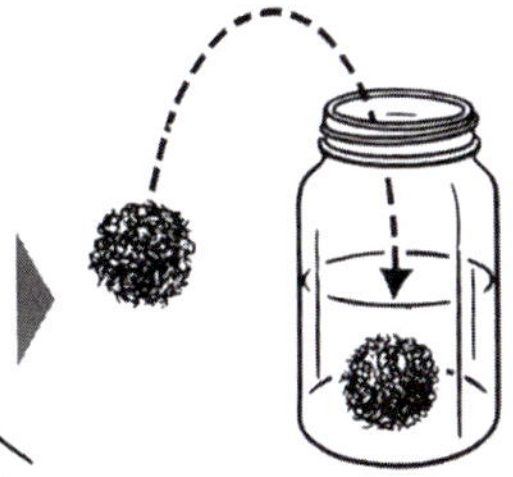

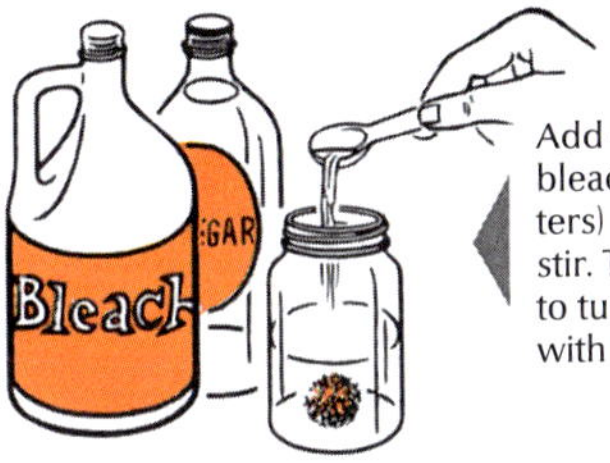

Add 4 teaspoons (20 milliliters) of bleach and 2 teaspoons (10 milliliters) of vinegar to the water and stir. The steel immediately begins to turn red as the iron in it reacts with hypochlorous acid.

In about 5 minutes, the liquid is full of red powder. This powder is hydrated ferric oxide (rust). Remove the steel wool from the jar and wait for the powder to settle.

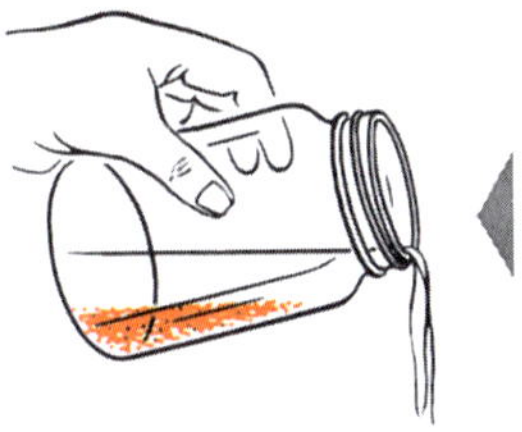

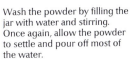

After the powder has settled, carefully pour off the clear solution. The powder and some liquid will stay at the bottom of the jar.

Wash the powder by filling the jar with water and stirring. Once again, allow the powder to settle and pour off most of the water.

Place a paper napkin over the mouth of another jar and pour the mixture of powder and liquid into the napkin. Wait for all the liquid to filter through the paper.

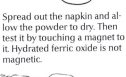

Spread out the napkin and allow the powder to dry. Then test it by touching a magnet to it. Hydrated ferric oxide is not magnetic.

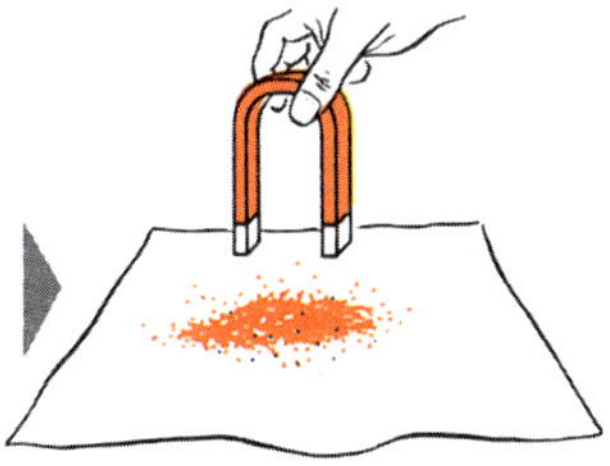

Place the powder on an old spoon and heat it in the flame of a candle. The red powder slowly turns blue-black as it changes to magnetic oxide of iron.

After the color of the powder has changed completely, test it again for magnetism. The blue-black grains will cling to the magnet.

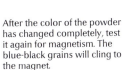

Development of organic chemistry. From the time of the alchemists, researchers had investigated various substances found in plants and animals. Such organic substances, however, proved difficult to analyze.

Most chemists of the early 1800's believed that organic compounds could be produced only with the aid of a *vital force,* a life force present in plants and animals. That belief is called *vitalism.* In 1828, German chemist Friedrich Wöhler mixed two inorganic substances, heated them, and obtained *urea*—an organic compound found in urine. Wöhler thus made the first synthetic organic substance from inorganic materials, proving that no vital force is needed to produce organic compounds.

During the 1800's, chemists isolated many organic substances. They discovered that most organic compounds consist mainly of carbon combined with hydrogen, nitrogen, and oxygen in various proportions. In 1831, German chemist Justus von Liebig published a simple, accurate technique for analyzing organic compounds. About the same time, chemists found that, in certain cases, two organic compounds with different properties are composed of the same elements in the same proportions. Berzelius called such compounds *isomers.* Isomers have the same kinds and numbers of atoms but differ in how the atoms are joined.

In the mid-1800's, chemists developed the *valence theory* to explain how atoms combine and form molecules. Valence refers to the normal number of bonds one atom can form with other atoms. In 1858, a German chemist named Friedrich Kekulé von Stradonitz proposed that carbon atoms can bond to four other atoms and that certain carbon atoms can link to form chains. As a result of his ideas, chemists quickly recognized organic compounds as molecules based on a framework of carbon-to-carbon bonds.

By 1900, the study of organic substances had become a major branch of chemistry. Chemists have since learned how to produce numerous complex organic molecules.

In the mid-1900's, Melvin Calvin, an American chemist, solved many long-standing mysteries of *photosynthesis,* the chemical process by which plants make food. Since the mid-1900's, biochemists have discovered how such complex organic substances as *deoxyribonucleic acid* (DNA) and *ribonucleic acid* (RNA) affect heredity (see **Heredity**; **DNA**; **RNA**).

Development of physical chemistry. During the 1800's, many chemists and physicists investigated the properties of substances and the energy changes that accompany chemical reactions. They based their work on ideas about the structure and behavior of atoms and molecules. Such study is called *physical chemistry.*

One of the first scientists to explore the area of physical chemistry was Amedeo Avogadro, an Italian physicist. In 1811, Avogadro suggested that equal volumes of all gases with the same temperature and pressure contain equal numbers of particles. His idea, now known as *Avogadro's law,* helped chemists calculate relative atomic masses. Later in the 1800's, physical chemists developed the *kinetic theory of gases.* This theory describes gases as clusters of particles that are in constant motion. It explains how the movement of these clusters at high speeds determines the pressure, temperature, and other properties of gases.

During the mid-1800's, physicists formulated the principles involved in the conversion of heat into mechanical energy and vice versa. They thereby laid the foundations for *chemical thermodynamics,* the study of the changes in heat that accompany many reactions.

During the 1870's, an American scientist named Josiah Willard Gibbs developed the *phase rule.* The rule explains the physical relationships among the solid, liquid, and gaseous *phases* (states) of matter. Jacobus van't Hoff, a Dutch chemist, relied on the phase rule in his studies of how crystals form in various solutions. Van't Hoff's work led to the development of *stereochemistry,* the study of the arrangement of atoms in molecules.

In the late 1800's, physical chemists Svante A. Arrhe-

Granger Collection

Sir William H. Perkin discovered the first synthetic dye accidentally in 1856. He produced mauve while trying to make quinine from a coal tar product.

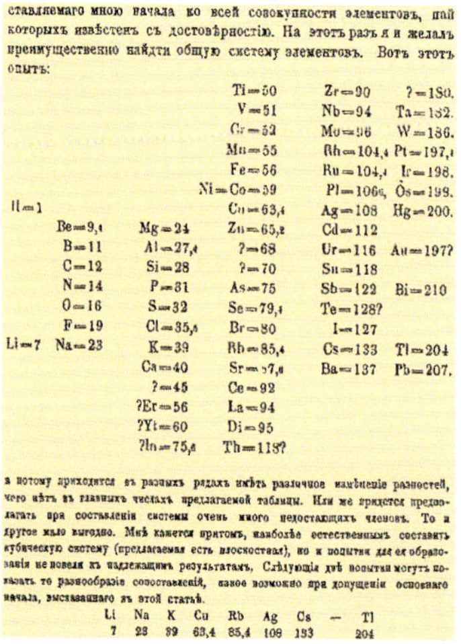

ставляемаго мною начала ко всей совокупности элементовъ, пай которыхъ извѣстенъ съ достовѣрностію. На этотъ разъ я и желалъ преимущественно найти общую систему элементовъ. Вотъ этотъ опытъ:

			Ti=50	Zr=90	?=180.
			V=51	Nb=94	Ta=182.
			Cr=52	Mo=96	W=186.
			Mn=55	Rh=104,4	Pt=197,4
			Fe=56	Ru=104,4	Ir=198.
			Ni=Co=59	Pl=106,6	Os=199.
H=1			Cu=63,4	Ag=108	Hg=200.
	Be=9,4	Mg=24	Zn=65,2	Cd=112	
	B=11	Al=27,4	?=68	Ur=116	Au=197?
	C=12	Si=28	?=70	Sn=118	
	N=14	P=31	As=75	Sb=122	Bi=210
	O=16	S=32	Se=79,4	Te=128?	
	F=19	Cl=35,5	Br=80	I=127	
Li=7	Na=23	K=39	Rb=85,4	Cs=133	Tl=204
		Ca=40	Sr=87,6	Ba=137	Pb=207.
		?=45	Ce=92		
		?Er=56	La=94		
		?Yt=60	Di=95		
		?In=75,6	Th=118?		

а потому приходится въ разныхъ рядахъ имѣть различное измѣненіе разностей, чего нѣтъ въ главныхъ числахъ предлагаемой таблицы. Или же придется предполагать при составленіи системы очень много недостающихъ членовъ. То и другое мало выгодно. Мнѣ кажется притомъ, наиболѣе естественнымъ составить кубическую систему (предлагаемая есть плоскостная), но и попытки для ея образованія не повели къ надлежащимъ результатамъ. Слѣдующія двѣ попытки могутъ показать то разнообразіе сопоставленій, какое возможно при допущеніи основнаго начала, высказаннаго въ этой статьѣ.

Li	Na	K	Cu	Rb	Ag	Cs	—	Tl
7	23	39	63,4	85,4	108	133		204

Granger Collection

A periodic table grouping elements by their *masses*—that is, by the amount of matter their atoms contain— was proposed by Dmitri Mendeleev in 1869.

Lawrence Berkeley National Laboratory

Melvin Calvin, winner of the 1961 Nobel Prize in chemistry, used a radioactive tracer to map the chemical reactions that occur during photosynthesis.

nius of Sweden and Wilhelm Ostwald of Germany proposed that electricity is carried through solutions by charged atoms or molecules called *ions.* Ostwald wrote one of the first textbooks in *electrochemistry,* the study of chemical changes associated with electrical forces.

Since the early 1900's, chemists and physicists have devoted much study to the structure of atoms and molecules. In 1913, a Danish physicist named Niels Bohr suggested a model of the atom in which electrons are arranged in successively larger orbits around a small nucleus of protons and neutrons. He believed many properties of an element depend on the number of electrons in the outer orbit of the atoms of that element.

Bohr's model of the atom also helped explain how atoms interact with light and other forms of radiation. Bohr assumed that the absorption and *emission* (giving off) of light by an atom involve a change in the energy state of an electron and a resulting electron jump from one orbit to another. Chemists have gained much information about the structure of molecules by measuring their absorption and emission of radiation.

In 1916, Gilbert N. Lewis, an American chemist, proposed that the bond between atoms in a molecule consists of a pair of electrons that both atoms share. His idea led to the *electron pair theory,* which explains the bonding characteristics of elements in terms of the arrangement of their electrons. See **Bond** (chemical).

Growth of industrial chemistry. The use of chemical knowledge by manufacturers started with the origins of chemistry itself. During the 1700's, however, manufacturers of such products as acids, alkalis, and soap began to use the knowledge of chemists on a broad scale to improve their products and production methods. During the 1800's, factories turned out huge quantities of such chemicals as sulfuric acid, sodium carbonate, and bleaching powder. In 1856, the English chemist Sir William H. Perkin produced *mauve,* also called *aniline purple*—the first synthetic dye. Its popularity soon led to the synthesis of other dyes for the textile industry.

By 1900, Germany had the most advanced chemical industry in the world. In 1910, a German chemist named Fritz Haber patented a process to produce ammonia from hydrogen and nitrogen. His work led to the large-scale manufacture of chemical agricultural fertilizers. During World War I (1914-1918) and World War II (1939-1945), the chemical industry expanded greatly in several countries to meet the demand for such war materials as explosives, medications, and synthetic rubber.

After World War II, the chemical industry continued to produce a great variety of goods for consumers. The development of new materials resulted in the widespread use of plastics and such synthetic fibers as nylon and polyesters. In addition, further discoveries led to the availability of many new drugs, food preservatives, fertilizers, and pesticides.

Current research. Biochemistry is a particularly active area of scientific research today. New instruments have enabled biochemists to study the action of chemicals within an organism without harming the organism. Biochemists are studying substances suspected of causing cancer or genetic damage to determine what molecular features are responsible for the harmful effects. Other chemists are investigating how chemical pollutants affect the environment and how they break down into other substances.

Synthetic chemistry is another area of active research. Chemists synthesize many thousands of new compounds each year. They have discovered chemical agents that can be used in reactions to add special groups of atoms to specific parts of other molecules. Researchers design new molecules and use such agents in a series of reactions to build the new compounds. Their techniques have led to the creation of many drugs.

The study of the surface properties of chemical compounds—called *surface chemistry*—is another promising field of present-day research. Chemists have learned that surface characteristics are responsible for the ability of certain substances—called *catalysts*—to speed up the rate of chemical reactions. Chemists today are also working to develop a chemical cell that would use the energy of sunlight to break up water molecules into oxygen and hydrogen. The hydrogen thus produced could be used as fuel. Such cells may one day provide a valuable new source of energy.

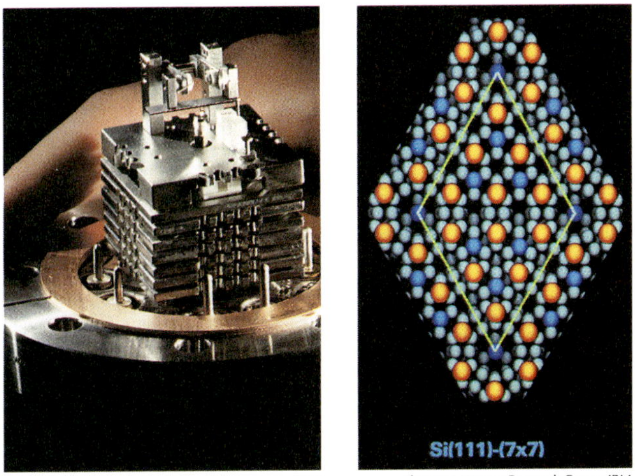

IBM   Thomas J. Watson Research Center, IBM

The scanning tunneling microscope, *above left,* provides chemists with new insights into the surface properties of materials. Its image of a piece of silicon, *above right,* shows the individual atoms on the surface.

The chemical industry

The chemical industry plays a vital role in the production of many manufactured goods. The industry provides a tremendous variety of materials to other manufacturers. It also produces many chemical products that benefit people directly. Major products of the industry include detergents, drugs, dyes, fertilizers, food preservatives and flavorings, glass, metal alloys, paper products, plastics, and synthetic fibers.

Most major chemical products are *basic chemicals* used in the manufacture of other products. Sulfuric acid is the chief basic chemical in the United States and many other countries. It is used to produce fertilizers and numerous other chemicals. Other basic chemicals include chlorine, nitrogen, and oxygen; such alkalis as lime and sodium hydroxide; and chemicals used in plastics.

The production of chemicals has become increasingly concentrated in *multinational companies.* These firms have plants and offices in a number of countries. To help keep costs low, the companies tend to locate their factories in countries where raw materials are readily available. Many basic chemicals are produced in developing countries by factories of multinational firms. But chemicals requiring advanced production methods are made mainly in developed countries.

Most chemical companies have research and development programs. Chemists in those programs work to develop new substances, new uses for known chemicals, and improvements in chemical production techniques.

The success of the chemical industry has been accompanied by environmental and safety problems. For example, the use of huge amounts of pesticides has resulted in soil and water pollution. In addition, the production of some chemicals results in harmful waste products that must be disposed of safely. Many chemical dumps for the storage of such wastes have leaked, threatening the health of people in nearby areas. During the late 1900's, a number of accidents occurred at chemical plants in several countries and resulted in the release of harmful substances.

Chemical companies have had to spend much money in efforts to solve environmental and safety problems. For example, they are working to develop insecticides that will quickly break down into harmless substances in the environment. They are also seeking safer methods of disposing of chemical wastes and of cleaning up chemical dumps. In addition, the companies are increasing safety precautions at chemical plants to guard against accidents.

Careers in chemistry

Chemistry offers a variety of challenging career opportunities in education, industry, and government. High school and college courses helpful to students preparing for a career in chemistry include mathematics and physics as well as classes in chemistry. Many chemical instruments make use of computer technology, and so classes in computer science are also useful. Writing courses help chemists develop their ability to communicate scientific information to others.

A bachelor's or master's degree in chemistry is sufficient for some careers, including teaching chemistry in junior high and high schools. Some chemists with advanced degrees teach at universities or conduct research. A doctor's degree is important for students who wish to pursue *basic research*—that is, the study of fundamental laws and processes of chemistry.

Many university graduates with specialized knowledge in chemistry find employment in industry. They work as plant superintendents, chemical engineers, quality control personnel, and salespeople. In addition, a large number of chemists are hired by government agencies involved in such areas as trade, environmental protection, and public health. Melvyn C. Usselman

Related articles in *World Book*. Each naturally occurring chemical element has a separate article. See **Element, Chemical** for a list of elements and the Periodic table of elements. See also:

American chemists

Baekeland, Leo H.
Bloch, Konrad E.
Harkins, William D.
Julian, Percy L.
Lipmann, Fritz Albert
Mulliken, Robert S.
Pauling, Linus C.
Seaborg, Glenn T.
Silliman, Benjamin
Urey, Harold C.
Wald, George

British chemists

Bragg, Sir William H.
Cavendish, Henry
Chain, Ernst B.
Crookes, Sir William
Dalton, John
Davy, Sir Humphry
Faraday, Michael
Franklin, Rosalind E.
Hodgkin, Dorothy C.
Ingold, Sir Christopher
Kendrew, John Cowdery
Priestley, Joseph
Ramsay, Sir William
Sanger, Frederick
Smithson, James
Soddy, Frederick

French chemists

Curie, Marie S.
Curie, Pierre
Gay-Lussac, Joseph L.
Joliot-Curie, Irene
Lavoisier, Antoine L.
Pasteur, Louis
Proust, Joseph L.

German chemists

Böttger, Johann F.
Bunsen, Robert W.
Hahn, Otto
Krebs, Sir Hans A.
Lynen, Feodor
Meyer, Julius L.
Ostwald, Wilhelm
Strassmann, Fritz
Wöhler, Friedrich

Other chemists

Andrada e Silva, José B. de
Berzelius, Jöns J.
Black, Joseph
Boyle, Robert
Cannizzaro, Stanislao
Debye, Peter J. W.
Mendeleev, Dmitri I.
Nobel, Alfred B.
Oparin, Alexander I.
Weizmann, Chaim

Branches of chemistry

Biochemistry
Electrochemistry
Inorganic chemistry
Organic chemistry
Photochemistry
Physical chemistry
Radiochemistry

Groups of compounds

Acid
Alcohol
Alkali
Alkaloid
Amino acid
Anhydride
Base
Carbide
Carbohydrate
Carbonate
Chloride
Chlorofluorocarbon
Cyanide
Electrolyte
Ester
Glycol
Hydrate
Hydrocarbon
Hydroxide
Nitrate
Nitrite
Oxide
Phosphate
Saccharides
Salt, Chemical
Silicone
Soda
Steroid
Sulfate
Sulfide

Terms

Allotropy
Alloy
Bond (chemical)
Colloid
Compound
Crystal
Density
Electromotive series
Emulsion
Halogen
Ion
Isomers
Isotope
Melting point
Mole
Molecule
Monomer
pH
Physical change
Polymer
Pressure
Radical
Saturation
Solution
Solvent
Suspension
Valence
Viscosity

Processes and tests

Absorption and adsorption
Catalysis
Chemical reaction
Chromatography
Combustion
Corrosion
Decomposition
Diffusion
Distillation
Electrolysis
Equilibrium, Chemical
Evaporation
Fermentation
Flame test
Flotation process
Fluoridation
Haber process
Hydrogenation
Hydrolysis
Litmus
Neutralization
Oxidation
Pasteurization
Phenolphthalein

Reduction
Sublimation
Transmutation of elements

Other related articles

Alchemy
Atom
Boiling point
Centrifuge
Chemical-biological-radiological warfare
Coal tar
Crime laboratory (Analyzing the evidence)
Drug (How drugs are produced and sold)
Electron
Energy
Fluid
Flux
Freezing point
Gas
Geochemistry
Heat (Sources of heat)
Liquid air
Liquid crystal
Mass
Matter
Metal
Neutron
Nobel Prizes
Noble gas
Nutrition
Petroleum
Radiation
Rare earth
Soil (Chemical conditions)
Steam
Transuranium element
Vapor
Water (The chemistry of water)

Outline

I. The work of chemists
A. Fundamental ideas of chemistry
B. The broad range of study
C. Tools and techniques
II. History of chemistry
III. The chemical industry
IV. Careers in chemistry

Questions

What early chemical practice involved trying to turn lead and other metals into gold?
Who proposed that the bond between atoms in a molecule consists of a pair of shared electrons?
What did the phlogiston theory have in common with all other good chemical theories?
Who began the use of letters as symbols for chemical elements?
What are some environmental and safety problems faced by the chemical industry?
What was the first chemical reaction that human beings learned to produce and control?
Whose combustion theory replaced the phlogiston theory?
Why did the chemical industry in several countries expand greatly during World Wars I and II?
Who was the first chemist to make an organic molecule from inorganic substances?
How do physical changes and chemical changes differ?

Additional resources

Lide, David R. *CRC Handbook of Chemistry and Physics.* 84th ed. CRC Pr., 2003.
Masterton, William L., and Hurley, C. N. *Chemistry.* 5th ed. Brooks/Cole, 2003.
Myers, Richard. *The Basics of Chemistry.* Greenwood, 2003.
Parker, Sybil P., ed. *McGraw-Hill Dictionary of Chemistry.* 2nd ed. McGraw, 2003.

Chemnitz, *KEHM nihts* (pop. 252,618), is a manufacturing center on the Chemnitz River in Germany (see **Germany** [political map]). The city has great machine works. Chemnitz lies in the German hill country, which has parks and old castles. The city was renamed Karl-Marx-Stadt in 1953, when Communists controlled it. In 1990, after the end of Communist control, the city's name was changed back to Chemnitz. John W. Boyer

Chemotherapy, *KEE moh THEHR uh pee,* is the treatment of cancers or infections with drugs that have a toxic effect on the cause of the illness. Ideally, chemotherapy is *selectively toxic*—that is, the drugs poison cancer cells or infectious microbes without harming healthy cells. Chemotherapy is most selectively toxic when it attacks diseases through a chemical step that does not occur in healthy cells. The antibiotic penicillin, for example, prevents certain bacteria from building their stiff cell walls. Animal cells do not form cell walls. This difference in chemistry makes penicillin selectively toxic to bacteria.

Cancer cells are chemically similar to the healthy cells from which they develop. This makes it hard for scientists to create selectively toxic cancer drugs. Because cancer cells often divide more rapidly than normal cells, most cancer drugs attack cells as they divide. As a result, cancer drugs often kill rapidly dividing healthy cells, such as those that line the digestive tract and those that form hair. The death of normal cells causes nausea, hair loss, decreased *immunity* (resistance to disease), and other troublesome side effects. Doctors must supervise use of these drugs with great care. N. E. Sladek

See also **Antibiotic; Cancer** (Drug therapy); **Drug** (The drug revolution); **Ehrlich, Paul; Taxol.**

Ch'en Jung. See **Chen Rong.**

Chen Rong, *chuhn rawng* (mid-1200's), was one of the greatest painters of Chinese dragons. His name is also spelled Ch'en Jung. Chen Rong imagined the dragon as a personification of the power of running water and of a storm. He began his paintings in a fit of excitement, splattering ink and spitting out water, or smearing his inky cap over the paper. He later touched up his work, and the blotches became dramatic compositions of writhing dragons, half seen among clouds or rocks. Robert A. Rorex

Cheney, *CHEE nee,* **Richard Bruce** (1941-), became vice president of the United States in 2001 under President George W. Bush. He had served as secretary of defense under Bush's father, President George H. W. Bush, from 1989 to 1993. In that office, Cheney had acted as an adviser on military strategy against Iraq during the Persian Gulf War of 1991. As vice president, Cheney advised on strategy when the United States went to war against Iraq in 2003.

© Reuters/Archive Photos
Richard B. Cheney

Early life. Cheney, often called Dick Cheney, was born on Jan. 30, 1941, in Lincoln, Nebraska. He moved with his parents to Casper, Wyoming, while still a boy. He entered Yale University but returned home after three semesters. He took a job with an electric company, working on power lines. He then attended the University of Wyoming, earning a B.A. in 1965 and an M.A. in 1966, both in political science.

In 1964, Cheney married Lynne Ann Vincent, a graduate student who went on to earn a Ph.D. in English literature. Lynne Cheney became a college teacher, novelist, and magazine editor. She headed the National Endowment for the Humanities from 1986 to 1993. The couple have two daughters, Elizabeth and Mary.

Career. Cheney and his family moved to the Washington, D.C., area after he received a congressional fellowship in 1968. In 1969, he joined the staff of Donald H. Rumsfeld, then director of the Office of Economic Opportunity. Cheney worked for Rumsfeld in various jobs until 1973. In 1974 and 1975, Cheney was a deputy assistant to President Gerald R. Ford. He served as White House chief of staff under Ford from 1975 to 1977.

In 1978, Cheney won election to the U.S. House of Representatives as a Republican from Wyoming. He was reelected five times. As a representative, Cheney was known for his conservative political views. In 1988, he became the Republican *whip* (assistant leader) in the House. He also served on several House committees, including the Select Committee on Intelligence and a committee that investigated the sale of arms by the United States to Iran (see **Reagan, Ronald W.** [The Iran-contra affair]). Cheney gave up his House seat in 1989 after accepting the post of secretary of defense.

After Cheney completed his stint as defense secretary in 1993, he left government service and joined the boards of several corporations. In 1995, he became the president and chief executive officer of Halliburton Company, a Dallas-based oil-field services and construction firm.

In July 2000, Texas Governor George W. Bush, the Republican presidential nominee, asked Cheney to be his running mate. In the 2000 presidential election, Bush and Cheney narrowly defeated their Democratic opponents, Vice President Al Gore and Senator Joseph I. Lieberman. In 2004, they defeated Senators John F. Kerry and John Edwards to win reelection. Lee Thornton

See **Bush, George Walker.**

Chengdu, *chuhng doo* (pop. 4,333,541), also spelled Ch'eng-tu and Chengtu, is a city in south-central China. It serves as the capital of Sichuan Province (see **China** [political map]). Chengdu is a regional center of commerce, finance, technology, and transportation. It also has many educational institutions, including Sichuan University.

An ancient city, Chengdu has been the political center of Sichuan Province since about 300 B.C. It was an old-fashioned walled city before the Communists took control of China in 1949. The Communists modernized the city into an industrial center. Factories and office and apartment buildings were constructed, and most of the city's walls and their towers were torn down. However, Chengdu still has an old section with narrow streets lined by traditional wooden houses and busy markets.

Mingzheng Shi

See also **China** (picture: Bicycles).

Chenille, *shuh NEEL,* is a fuzzy yarn made of cotton, silk, wool, or rayon. The word *chenille* means *caterpillar* in French. Chenille yarn is used to make rugs, fabrics, and fringes and tassels. Cotton bedspreads are often decorated with patterns of colored chenille. Some bathrobes also are made of chenille. O. Frank Hunter

Chennai, *cheh NY* (pop. 4,216,268; met. area pop. 6,424,624), is India's fourth largest city. Only Mumbai, Delhi, and Kolkata have more people. Chennai lies on India's southeast coast. For location, see **India** (political map). Formerly called Madras, Chennai serves as the capital of the state of Tamil Nadu. Chennai is also the state's chief port and commercial city.

A shipping center, Chennai has one of India's busiest harbors. Its industrial plants include a railway coach factory; factories that produce combat vehicles; automobile assembly plants; cotton mills; tanneries; and cement, glass, and iron works. The city's landmarks include old Hindu temples and Christian churches, the University of Madras, and Fort St. George—formerly a British fort. An international airport serves Chennai, and highways and railroads connect it with inland areas.

In 1640, the British—who later became the colonial rulers of India—built Fort St. George near the coast of what is now Chennai. At that time, Chennai was a small village called Madraspatam. Through the years, settlements grew up around the fort, and nearby towns were made part of Chennai. Large industrial, commercial, and residential areas were established, and Chennai grew into a huge urban area. P. P. Karan

Chennault, *shuh NAWLT,* **Claire Lee** (1893-1958), led the *Flying Tigers,* a group of volunteer American aviators who supported China in its war against Japan before the United States entered World War II in 1941. He took command of the U.S. Fourteenth Air Force in China in 1943. He retired in 1945 as a major general and became head of a Chinese airline. He died on July 27, 1958.

Chennault was born on Sept. 6, 1893, in Commerce, Texas. He was principal of a Texas high school until World War I (1914-1918), when he joined the U.S. Army Air Service. He became an expert in precision flying with an exhibition team of air corps pilots. In 1937, he became air adviser to Chiang Kai-shek, the leader of China's Nationalist government. See also **Flying Tigers.**

Alfred Goldberg

Cheops. See **Khufu.**

Cheque. See **Check.**

Cherbourg, *SHAIR boorg* (pop. 26,750), is an industrial city and seaport on the northern coast of France (see **France** [political map]). Its harbor, formed by an artificial barrier called a *breakwater,* provides a protective dock for transatlantic ships. Cherbourg's attractions include a park filled with exotic plant life and a medieval chapel near the city. The city has both a commercial port and a naval port. Its major industries include fishing, shipping, textile production, and the manufacture of electrical equipment and nuclear submarines.

In the 1700's, King Louis XVI of France began the construction of the breakwater that forms Cherbourg's harbor. In 1940, during World War II, German armed forces captured the city and used it as a military base. Allied armies freed Cherbourg in 1944. Mark Kesselman

Cherimoya, *CHER uh MOY uh,* is a small tree that bears an edible fruit. It grows wild in the tropical highlands of the Andes Mountains in South America, and it is cultivated in California and Florida. The oval leaves grow 3 to 6 inches (8 to 15 centimeters) long. The tree bears small, yellow flowers. The egg- or heart-shaped fruit has depressions on its surface and weighs 1 pound (0.5 kilogram) or more. Most cherimoyas contain a few black seeds. The creamy, soft, white pulp of the fruit is eaten fresh and in ice cream and marmalade. Jaime E. Lazarte

Scientific classification. The cherimoya tree belongs to the family Annonaceae. Its scientific name is *Annona cherimola.*

Chernobyl. See **Nuclear energy** (Safety concerns).

Chernomyrdin, *chehr noh MEER duhn,* **Viktor Stepanovich,** *VEEK tuhr stih PAHN uh vihch* (1938-), was prime minister of Russia from 1992 to 1998. In March 1998, while Russia was experiencing severe economic difficulties, President Boris N. Yeltsin abruptly replaced Chernomyrdin with a reform-minded candidate. But in August, Yeltsin dismissed the replacement and renominated Chernomyrdin. However, the Russian par-

Detail of *The Cherokee Trail of Tears, 1838* (1939), an oil mural on canvas by Elizabeth Janes; Oklahoma Historical Society

The Cherokee Indians were forced to move from the Southeast to the Oklahoma area as whites took over their land. Many Indians died on the journey, which took place during the winter of 1838-1839. The trip became known as the *Trail of Tears.*

liament refused to approve Chernomyrdin.

During the mid-1990's, Chernomyrdin was one of Russia's most powerful leaders. Many experts believe he unofficially took charge of the government several times when President Yeltsin was ill but remained in office.

Chernomyrdin was born on April 9, 1938, in the village of Cherny Otrog in southeast Russia. He studied engineering at Russian technical schools and held technical and administrative positions in government energy agencies. From 1985 to 1989, he headed the department that supervised the Soviet natural gas industry. In 1989, he became head of Gazprom, a huge state-run corporation that replaced the gas department.

Stuart D. Goldman

Cherokee Indians, *CHEHR uh kee,* are the largest Indian tribe in the United States, according to the 2000 U.S. census. The census reported that there are about 280,000 Cherokee. About 95,000 Cherokee live in Oklahoma, more than in any other state. Some Cherokee make their homes on a reservation in North Carolina. In the early 1800's, the Cherokee were one of the most prosperous and progressive tribes in the country.

The early Cherokee farmed and hunted in the southern Appalachian region. In the 1750's and 1760's, they fought the colonists who moved into their territory. During the Revolutionary War in America (1775-1783), the Cherokee sided with the British against the colonists.

About 1800, the Cherokee began to adopt the economic and political structure of the white settlers. Some owned large plantations and kept slaves. Others had small-scale farms. The tribe also established a republican form of government called the *Cherokee Nation.* In 1821, a Cherokee named Sequoyah introduced a system of writing for the Cherokee language (see **Sequoyah**).

In the early 1800's, white settlers demanded that the U.S. government move all Indians in the southeastern United States to areas west of the Mississippi River. In 1835, some Cherokee agreed to move in a treaty they signed with the government. But most Cherokee, led by Chief John Ross, opposed the treaty.

During the winter of 1838-1839, U.S. troops forced from 13,000 to 17,000 Cherokee to move to the Indian Territory, in what is now Oklahoma. Thousands of Cherokee died on the way. Their forced march became known as the *Trail of Tears.* About 1,000 Cherokee escaped removal and remained in the Great Smoky Mountains, which form the boundary between Tennessee and North Carolina. They eventually bought land there and the government let them stay. These Indians became known as the *Eastern Band of Cherokee.*

The Cherokee who went west reestablished the Cherokee Nation and set up their own schools and churches. But in the late 1800's, Congress abolished the Cherokee Nation and opened much of the Cherokee land for resettlement by whites. Today, many Cherokee live in northeastern Oklahoma, where they have restored their tribal government.

Raymond D. Fogelson

Related articles in ***World Book*** include:

Five Civilized Tribes
Indian Territory
Jackson, Andrew (The Indian issue)
Ross, John
Trail of Tears
United States, History of the (picture: Eastern Indians)

Additional resources

Anderson, William L., ed. *Cherokee Removal: Before and After.* Univ. of Ga. Pr., 1991.

Long, Cathryn J. *The Cherokee.* Lucent Bks., 2000. Younger readers.

Mails, Thomas E. *The Cherokee People.* 1992. Reprint. Marlowe, 1996.

Cherry is a small round fruit from a tree of the same name. When ripe, cherry fruits vary in color from yellow to red to black. They typically measure less than ¾ inch (2 centimeters) wide. Cherries are *drupes,* fleshy fruits with a hard core called a *pit.* Cherry trees produce clusters of small white to pink blossoms. Growers cultivate the trees for their fruit and as ornamental plants.

Several different kinds of cherry trees come from Asia, Europe, and North America. They grow throughout the *temperate zones*—areas between the polar regions and the tropics. Breeders have developed most cherry tree *cultivars* (varieties) for fruit production from either the *sweet cherry tree* or the *sour cherry tree.* One important cultivar, the *Duke cherry,* was developed by cross-breeding the sweet and sour cherries.

Sweet cherry trees grow tall and stout. Mature trees can measure up to 40 feet (12 meters) high and have a trunk diameter of more than 1 foot (30 centimeters).

Most sweet cherry trees are *self-unfruitful*—that is, they will produce fruit only after they have been pollinated with pollen from a different sweet cherry cultivar.

Cherry Marketing Institute

A mechanical cherry picker shakes the trunk of the cherry tree, knocking fruit from the branches onto the machine.

WORLD BOOK illustrations by Nancy Lee Walter

The main types of cherries include sweet cherries, *top,* and sour cherries, *bottom.* A third variety, Duke cherries, is a hybrid of sweet and sour cherries. Clusters of tiny fragrant blossoms decorate all types of cherry trees in the spring.

Thus, fruit growers typically plant at least two different varieties to ensure fruit production. Honey bees help transfer pollen from one cultivar to another.

Growers sell most sweet cherries as fresh fruit, harvesting them by hand. They use machines to harvest cherries sent to processing plants.

Sour cherry trees grow smaller and tolerate colder, drier climates than do sweet cherry trees. Sour cherries are *self-fruitful* and will produce fruit when pollinated with their own pollen. Growers harvest most sour cherries by using tree-shaking machines. Processors typically use the fruit as pie filling or as maraschino cherries.

Many nurseries cultivate cherry trees as ornamental plants or for their flowers. The nurseries use primarily cultivars developed from species native to Asia and eastern Europe. Plants of Asian origin, sometimes called *Japanese cherry trees,* have abundant delicate blossoms. *Mahaleb cherry trees,* which originated in eastern Europe, serve as landscape trees in many countries.

Growers develop cherry tree cultivars by taking buds of the most desirable fruiting plants and grafting them onto seedling cherry trees called *rootstocks.* The use of rootstocks helps to control tree size, which makes harvesting easier. See **Grafting.**

A number of animals and diseases attack cherry trees. Birds that eat the fruit rank among the most serious pests. Mites, slugs, and such insects as aphids, fruit flies, and scale insects can also damage the crop. Cherry tree diseases include brown rot, verticillium wilt, and leaf spot. Growers control such pests and diseases by planting resistant cultivars and using chemical sprays.

James E. Pollard

Scientific classification. Cherry trees belong to the rose family, Rosaceae. The scientific name for sweet cherry trees is *Prunus avium.* Sour cherry trees are *P. cerasus,* Japanese cherry trees are *P. serrulata,* and Mahaleb cherries are *P. mahaleb.*

Related articles in *World Book* include:

Acerola
Blight
Cherry laurel
Maraschino cherry
Tree (Broadleaf and needleleaf trees [picture])
Washington, D.C. (The Tidal Basin)

Cherry laurel is an evergreen shrub closely related to cherry trees. It is not a true laurel. The cherry laurel is native to the Mediterranean region. It also grows in the United States. Its small, shiny leaves have finely toothed edges. The fragrant white flowers grow in clusters. The fruits are dark purple and have a bitter taste. The leaves and the round stones of the cherry laurel are poisonous. A related plant, also called *cherry laurel,* is common in the Southeastern States.

Walter S. Judd

Scientific classification. The cherry laurel belongs to the rose family, Rosaceae. Its scientific name is *Prunus laurocerasus.*

WORLD BOOK illustration by Robert Hynes

Cherry laurel

Cherry Point Marine Corps Air Station, North Carolina, is the largest air station of the United States Marine Corps. It has overhaul facilities for high-performance aircraft. It is the host installation for Commander Marine Corps Air Bases East and houses a Marine aircraft wing. The Cherry Point Marine Corps Air Station, commissioned in 1942, is in the city of Havelock. It covers about 13,200 acres (5,300 hectares) at the primary complex. It is named after a post office that once served the area.

W. W. Reid

Cherubini, *KAY roo BEE nee,* **Luigi,** *loo EE jee* (1760-1842), was an Italian-born composer, though it was in

Germany that his works were most widely appreciated. He settled in Paris in 1788 and played an important role in Parisian musical life until his death. He composed about 30 operas and 11 masses. The operas are noted for their dramatic music, forceful use of ensembles, and rich orchestration. They include *Lodoïska* (1791), *Elisa* (1794), *Médée* (1797), and *Les Deux Journées* (1800).

After 1809, Cherubini concentrated on composing religious music and on teaching. One of his finest works is the *Requiem in C minor* (1816). He taught at the Paris Conservatory from its founding in 1795 and was director from 1822 to 1841. Maria Luigi Carlo Zenobio Salvatore Cherubini was born in Florence. Stewart L. Ross

Chesapeake, a ship. See **War of 1812** (Impressment of seamen).

Chesapeake and Ohio Canal was a waterway planned to connect the Potomac and Ohio rivers. Construction began in 1828, with generous financial backing from towns along the Potomac River and Chesapeake Bay. These towns hoped to establish a trade route to Ohio River settlements. The waterway began above the falls of the Potomac River at Washington, D.C. When construction was halted by the depression of 1837, the canal extended only about 100 miles (160 kilometers) westward. Half-hearted building continued until 1850. The canal was used until 1924 as far as Cumberland, Maryland, where building ended. It cost $11 million. The Chesapeake and Ohio Canal was 184 miles (296 kilometers) long and 60 feet (18 meters) wide, and it averaged 6 feet (1.8 meters) deep. Today, the canal is a national historical park. Edward C. Papenfuse

Chesapeake Bay is a long, narrow arm of the Atlantic Ocean that runs north from the coast of Virginia, and divides Maryland into two parts. It is 200 miles (320 kilometers) long and from 4 to 40 miles (6 to 64 kilometers) wide. The Indians called this bay the *Great Salt Water.*

The channel at the entrance to Chesapeake Bay is 12 miles (19 kilometers) wide. Seagoing ships can sail almost the entire length of the bay. The shore is cut by smaller bays and by the wide mouths of several rivers. Rivers emptying into the bay include the James, York, Rappahannock, Potomac, and Susquehanna. Important bay ports include Baltimore, Maryland, and Norfolk and

WORLD BOOK map

Location of Chesapeake Bay

Portsmouth, Virginia. The U.S. Naval Academy is at Annapolis on the western shore. Michael P. O'Neill

See also **Maryland** (physical map).

Chesapeake Bay retriever is a hunting dog. Many owners claim that it is the best of all duck retrievers, especially in cold, rough waters. It has a thick, oily coat that sheds water. The dog has unusual endurance and has fine working qualities in water and in the field. Males stand 23 to 26 inches (58 to 66 centimeters) high at the shoulder, and weigh 65 to 80 pounds (29 to 36 kilograms). Most Chesapeakes range from dark brown to pale tan in color. See also **Dog** (pictures: Sporting dogs; A mother nurses her puppies).

WORLD BOOK photo

The Chesapeake Bay retriever is an excellent hunting dog. Its thick, oily coat sheds water, and it is a strong swimmer.

Critically reviewed by the American Chesapeake Club

Chesnutt, Charles Waddell (1858-1932), is considered to have been the first major African American writer of fiction. His first book, *The Conjure Woman* (1899), is written in the style of folk tales and tells about slavery in the South. Chesnutt's other fiction describes racial struggles of African Americans, especially those who have both black and white ancestry. He featured these themes in *The Wife of His Youth and Other Stories of the Color Line* (1899), as well as in his novels, *The House Behind the Cedars* (1900), *The Marrow of Tradition* (1901), and *The Colonel's Dream* (1905).

Chesnutt was born in Cleveland, Ohio. His family moved to Fayetteville, North Carolina, when he was 8 years old. He attended school until he was 13 and later studied with tutors and taught himself. Chesnutt left the South during his 20's. He worked as a court stenographer in Cleveland and passed examinations that permitted him to become a lawyer. In 1928, Chesnutt received the Spingarn Medal, partly for his "pioneer work as a literary artist depicting the life and struggles of Americans of Negro descent." William L. Andrews

Chess is a game of skill in which two players move objects called *men* on a board divided into squares. Players try to *checkmate* (trap) the opponent's principal man, the king, while protecting their own king.

The board and the men. There is no standard size for chessboards, but most boards fit easily on a table. The chessboard is divided into 64 squares that are arranged in 8 rows of 8 squares each. The squares are

Chess tournament games are played within a time limit. The time used by each player is recorded on a special clock, which can be seen behind the chessboard. After making a move, a player presses a button that stops that player's clock and starts the opponent's clock. This photo shows a game between Garry Kasparov, *left,* and Anatoly Karpov, *right,* during the 1986 world chess championships held in London and Leningrad (now St. Petersburg).

A. Nogues, Sygma

alternately light and dark in color. The rows of squares that run across the board are called *ranks.* The rows that run up and down the board are called *files.* The slanting rows are called *diagonals.* Players sit at opposite ends of the board, each with a light-colored square at the right-hand corner.

Each player uses a set of 16 men. One set is light-colored, and the other set is dark-colored. The player who uses the light-colored set is called *White.* The player with the dark-colored set is *Black.* Each player's set includes eight identical men called *pawns.* The other eight men are called *pieces.* The pieces consist of one *king,* one *queen,* two *rooks,* two *bishops,* and two *knights.*

Before a game begins, players arrange their pieces on the rank nearest them. They also place their pawns on the rank in front of the pieces. The rooks occupy the corner squares. The knights stand next to them, and the bishops stand beside the knights. The queen occupies the central square of its own color, and the king stands next to the queen. The opposing kings and queens face each other across the board.

The moves. Each chessman moves in a specific way. But players cannot make any move that would expose their king to capture. In addition, each man but the king is assigned a value according to its degree of mobility. In order of value from greatest to least, they are the queen, rook, bishop, knight, and pawn. A man's value may increase or decrease during a game, depending on its position in relation to the other men.

The queen is the most powerful chessman. It can move in any direction along any rank, file, or diagonal until its path is blocked by another man. The king also moves in any direction, but one square at a time.

A rook can move along any rank or file as far as its path is clear. A bishop can move as far as its path is clear along any diagonal but must stay on the color square it started on. Knights are the only men that can leap over men in their paths. A knight moves in an L shape—one rank up or down and two files left or right, or two ranks up or down and one file left or right. A pawn can ad-

The chessboard and chessmen The diagram at the left shows the three types of rows on a chessboard. The six kinds of chessmen appear below the board. The position of the men at the beginning of a game is shown at the right.

WORLD BOOK illustrations

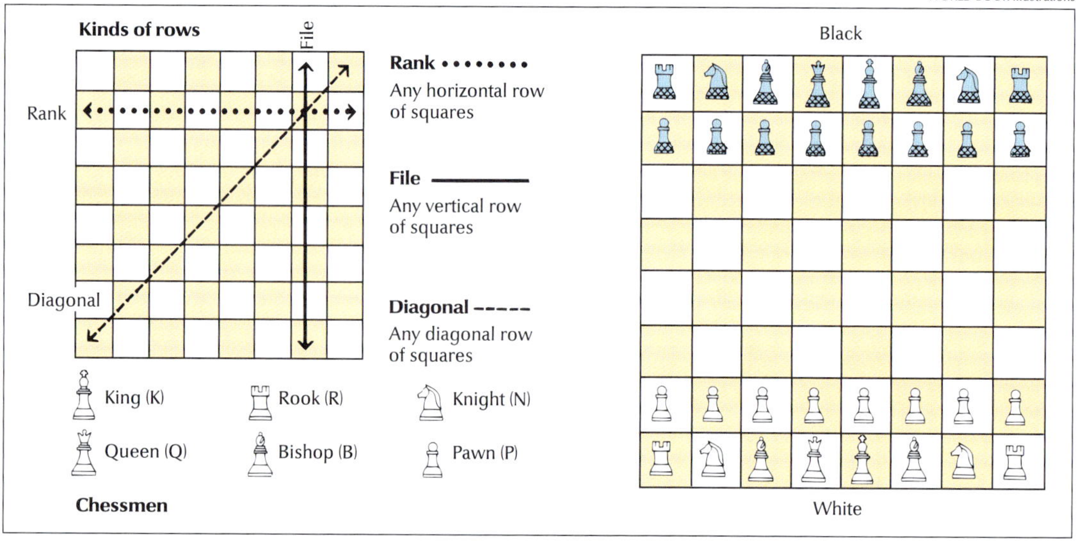

vance only one space at a time, except on its first move, when it can advance either one or two squares.

A piece may *capture* any opposing man that stops its progress. A player makes a *capture* by moving a man to a space occupied by an enemy man. The player removes the captured man from the board and replaces it on the space with his or her capturing man. A man in danger of being captured is *under attack.*

A pawn is the only man that does not capture men straight in its path. Instead, it normally captures a man one square to the left or right of the square in front of the pawn. A pawn may also capture *en passant* (French for "in passing"). This special rule applies only if a player has a pawn on the fifth rank. If an enemy pawn on a neighboring file advances two squares, it can be captured as if it had moved only one square, but it must be captured on the player's next move. When a pawn reaches the rank farthest from its player, it is *promoted* (exchanged) for any piece other than a king. Because players usually exchange pawns for queens, this promotion is often called *queening the pawn.*

How chess is played. White always moves first in a chess game. The players then alternate moves.

Most chess games are played in three stages—(1) the opening, (2) the middle game, and (3) the end game. In the opening, players move their men to positions where they can attack opposing men or hamper their movements. Experts suggest that players move only one or two center pawns at the beginning of the game and that they bring knights into play before bishops.

Players often *castle* during the opening to protect the king. This is the only move during which a player can move two men at the same time. To castle, a player moves the king two squares toward either rook, and places the rook on the square the king passed over. A player may castle only if the king or rook have not previously been moved and if no other pieces stand between them. A player cannot castle if the king is under immediate attack *(check)* or if the square the king crosses or the one it lands on puts it into check.

Much of the excitement in a chess game occurs during the middle game, as players try to gain an advantage in the position of their men in preparation for a direct attack on the enemy king. During the end game, each player concentrates on queening a pawn. Players may use the king as an aggressor during the end game, when most men have been captured and it is safer to bring the king out into the open board.

A player who attacks the enemy king traditionally gives notice by saying "check," though this is not required. A player whose king is in check must move only to rescue the king. The player may capture the attacking man or move the king to a square that is not under attack. A player can also place a man between the king and the attacking man *(interposition).* If none of these moves is possible, the game ends in a checkmate. The attacking player wins. A player can *resign* (surrender) before checkmate if the position appears hopeless.

A chess game may also end in a tie, called a *draw.* Players may agree to a draw if neither one has an advantage that could lead to a victory. Sometimes, players repeat the same sequence of moves. They declare a draw when they have repeated the sequence three times in a row. Players also draw if each has made 50 consecutive

How chessmen move

WORLD BOOK illustrations

The queen and king may both move in any direction. The queen may move any number of squares, but the king can move only one square at a time. The rook may move any number of squares, but only along a rank or file.

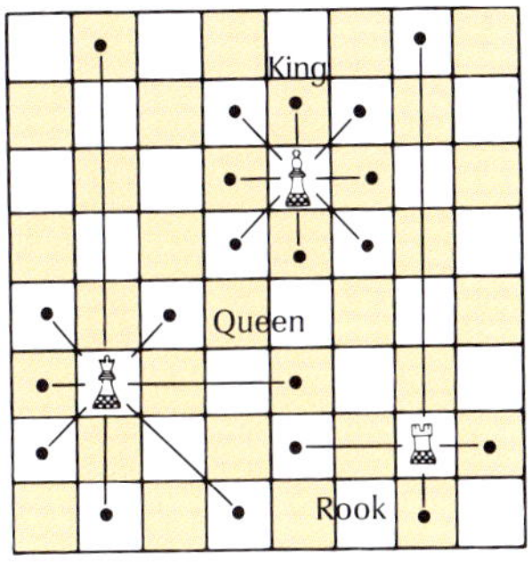

The bishop can move any number of squares, but only along diagonals. The knight moves in an L-shaped route. The pawn can move forward one or two squares on its first move and after that only one square at a time. It captures men by moving diagonally.

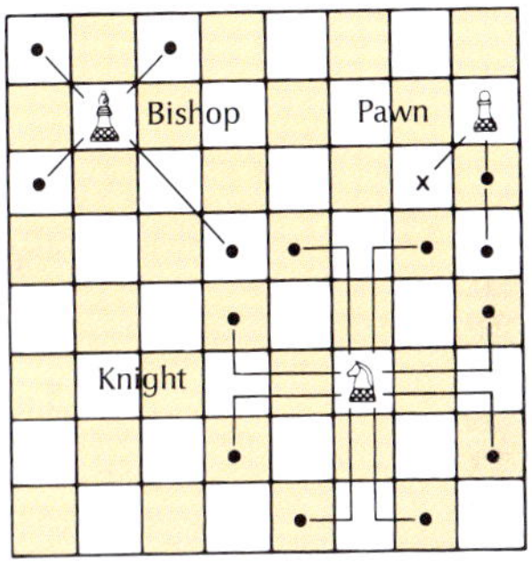

moves without moving a pawn or capturing a man. A kind of draw called a *stalemate* occurs when a player's only move would put his or her king in check.

Chess notation. Most chess players in English-speaking nations use *descriptive notation,* also called *English notation,* to keep a written record of their games. In this system, the pieces beside the king are called the *kingside,* and those beside the queen are called the *queenside.* Pawns are named for the pieces they stand in front of at the beginning of the game. Players record moves by naming the men and the squares they move to. The squares in each file are named for the piece that occupies the first square in that file at the beginning of the game. For example, the squares in the center files are called the *king's file* and the *queen's file.* Players number the ranks from one through eight starting from the ranks nearest them. Letters represent the chess pieces. *K* stands for *King, KB* for *King's Bishop, KN* for *King's Knight,* and *KR* for *King's Rook.* The queen's pieces are indicated in the same way, using *Q* for *Queen. P* stands for *Pawn.* Other symbols used include *x* for *captures,* — for *moves to,* and *ch* or † for *check.*

In a system called *algebraic notation,* the letters *a* through *h* indicate the files, beginning from White's left. The numbers one through eight indicate the ranks, beginning from the rank nearest White. Players record moves of pieces by naming the pieces and the squares they move them to. They record pawn moves by naming only the square the pawn moves to.

Tournament competition. The Fédération Internationale des Échecs (FIDE) governs chess internationally. FIDE holds a match to determine the world chess champion. A challenger is determined in a series of prelimi-

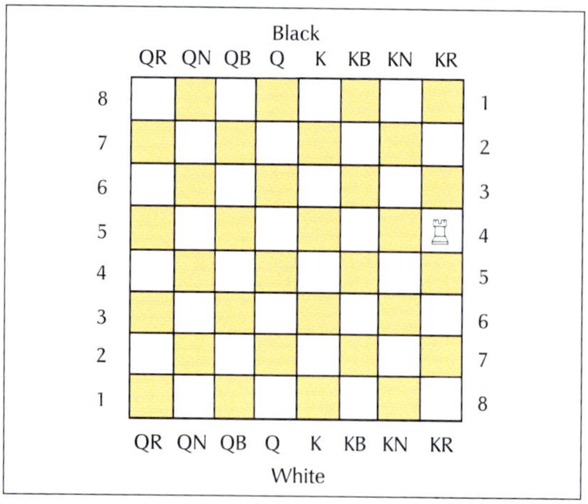

WORLD BOOK diagram

In descriptive notation, each file is named for the piece on the first square of that file at the start of the game. The ranks are numbered from 1 to 8, beginning with the rank nearest each player. The rook is on White's *KR5* and on Black's *KR4.*

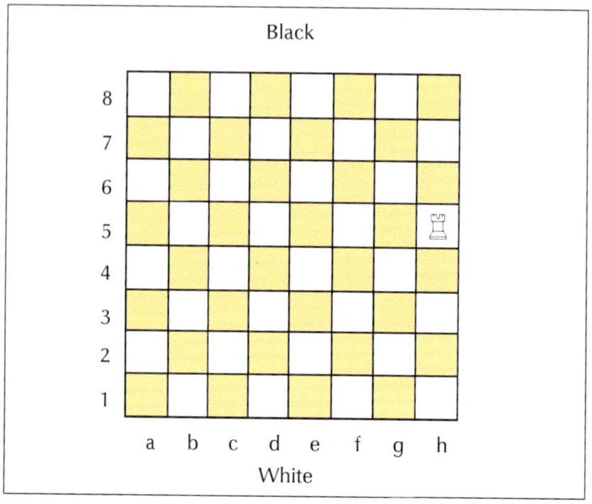

WORLD BOOK diagram

In algebraic notation, files are lettered *a* to *h.* Ranks are numbered 1 to 8, beginning with White's first rank. Every square has a name consisting of its file letter and its rank number. In this diagram, the rook stands on square *h5.*

World chess champions

1866-1894	William Steinitz, Austria
1894-1921	Emanuel Lasker, Germany
1921-1927	José R. Capablanca, Cuba
1927-1935	Alexander A. Alekhine, Soviet Union
1935-1937	Max Euwe, Netherlands
1937-1946	Alexander A. Alekhine, Soviet Union
1947	No champion
1948-1956	Mikhail Botvinnik, Soviet Union
1957-1958	Vassily Smyslov, Soviet Union
1958-1960	Mikhail Botvinnik, Soviet Union
1960-1961	Mikhail Tal, Soviet Union
1961-1963	Mikhail Botvinnik, Soviet Union
1963-1969	Tigran Petrosian, Soviet Union
1969-1972	Boris Spassky, Soviet Union
1972-1975	Bobby Fischer, United States
1975-1985	Anatoly Karpov, Soviet Union
1985-1993	Garry Kasparov, Soviet Union (later Russia)
1993-1999	Anatoly Karpov, Russia*
1999-2000	Alexander Khalifman, Russia*
2000-2002	Viswanathan Anand, India
2002-2004	Ruslan Ponomariov, Ukraine*
2004-2005	Rustam Kasimdzhanov, Uzbekistan*
2005-	Veselin Topalov, Bulgaria*

*FIDE champion. Other organizations have declared other players as world champion.

United States chess champions

1845-1857	Charles Stanley
1857-1871	Paul Morphy
1871-1890	George Mackenzie
1890-1891	Jackson Showalter
1891-1894	Solomon Lipschutz
1894-1895	Albert Hodges
1895-1897	Jackson Showalter
1897-1906	Harry Pillsbury
1906-1909	Jackson Showalter (Pillsbury died in 1906)
1909-1936	Frank Marshall*
1936-1944	Samuel Reshevsky
1944-1946	Arnold Denker
1946-1948	Samuel Reshevsky
1948-1951	Herman Steiner
1951-1954	Larry Evans
1954-1957	Arthur Bisguier
1957-1961	Bobby Fischer
1961-1962	Larry Evans
1962-1968	Bobby Fischer
1968-1969	Larry Evans
1969-1972	Samuel Reshevsky
1972-1973	Robert Byrne
1973-1974	John Grefe and Lubomir Kavalek (tie)
1974-1978	Walter Browne
1978-1980	Lubomir Kavalek
1980-1981	Walter Browne, Larry Christiansen, and Larry Evans (tie)
1981-1983	Walter Browne and Yasser Seirawan (tie)
1983-1984	Walter Browne, Larry Christiansen, and Roman Dzindzichashvili (tie)
1984-1986	Lev Alburt
1986-1987	Yasser Seirawan
1987-1988	Joel Benjamin and Nick DeFirmian (tie)
1988-1989	Michael Wilder
1989-1990	Roman Dzindzichashvili, Stuart Rachels, and Yasser Seirawan (tie)
1990-1991	Lev Alburt
1991-1992	Gata Kamsky
1992-1993	Patrick Wolff
1993-1994	Alexander Shabalov and Alex Yermolinsky (tie)
1994-1995	Boris Gulko
1995-1996	Nick DeFirmian, Alexander Ivanov, and Patrick Wolff (tie)
1996-1997	Alex Yermolinsky
1997-1998	Joel Benjamin
1998-1999	Nick DeFirmian
1999	Boris Gulko
1999-2000	Alex Yermolinsky
2000-2002	Joel Benjamin, Yasser Seirawan, and Alexander Shabalov (tie)
2002-2003	Larry Christiansen and Nick DeFirmian (tie)
2003-2004	Alexander Shabalov
2004-	Hikaru Nakamura

*Until 1936, the United States had a series of unofficial champions. Since that time, tournaments have been held periodically to determine the U.S. champion.

nary rounds. In the championship series, the player who wins the most games out of a possible 24 games wins the title. The champion keeps the title whenever there is a tie. In all tournament games, players are required to make a certain number of moves within a given time period. A match is timed by a double-faced clock.

History. Historians disagree on how old chess is or who invented it. They believe it originated in India in the A.D. 600's, and spread to Persia. Knowledge of the game spread to nearby countries after the Arabs conquered Persia in the 640's. Muslim invaders brought chess to Spain in the early 700's. By 1000, the game had probably spread through Europe as far north as Scandinavia.

The modern era of chess dates from the 1500's, when the moves of the game began to take their present form. Philidor, a Frenchman who played in the 1700's, is widely regarded as the first world champion. In 1972, Bobby Fischer became the first American to win the official world chess championship. FIDE took away Fischer's title in 1975 after he refused to play challenger Anatoly Karpov of the Soviet Union under federation rules. Karpov then became the world champion by default.

FIDE took the world championship title from Garry Kasparov of Russia in 1993 and from Anatoly Karpov of Russia in 1999 after the two champions refused to play in a FIDE tournament for the title. Both players criticized FIDE's handling of the world championship. Kasparov created the Professional Chess Association (PCA) in 1993 and held the PCA title until it dissolved in 1998. Brain Games Network, a British Internet company, sponsored a non-FIDE title match in 2000 in which Vladimir Kramnik of Russia defeated Kasparov. The company went out of business, and an agreement was made in 2002 to unify the championship. Kramnik would play Peter Leko of Hungary and Kasparov would play Ruslan Ponomariov of Ukraine, recognized by FIDE as the world champion. The winners would play for the title. But, neither match was ever held. Now, the world championship is in a state of confusion and there is no agreement as to who is the champion and who is the challenger. See also **Fischer, Bobby; Kasparov, Garry.** Larry Evans

Additional resources

Hooper, David, and Whyld, Kenneth. *The Oxford Companion to Chess.* 2nd ed. 1992. Reprint. Oxford, 1996.

King, Daniel. *Chess: From First Moves to Checkmate.* Kingfisher, 2000. Younger readers.

Chest, also called *thorax,* is the part of the body between the base of the neck and the abdomen. Its sides are formed by the ribs, which are attached to the breastbone in front and to the spine in back. The *diaphragm,* a strong, dome-shaped muscle, forms the base of the chest. A thick, vertical partition called the *mediastinum* or *mediastinal septum* extends down the center of the thorax. Enclosed within this partition are the heart, the large blood vessels, the esophagus, the lower part of the trachea, and various glands and nerves. The lungs and their coverings are suspended on either side of the mediastinum. Mammals, birds, and crocodiles are the only animals that have a separate chest and abdomen. See also **Diaphragm; Heart; Human body** (Trans-Vision color picture); **Lung; Respiration.** Bruce Reider

Chesterfield, Earl of (1694-1773), was an English aristocrat, wit, and political figure. He became known for his worldly, sensible letters to his son.

Chesterfield was born Philip Dormer Stanhope on Sept. 22, 1694, in London. He became fourth Earl of Chesterfield in 1726. About 1732, he fathered an illegitimate son, Philip. When the boy was 5 years old, Chesterfield began writing him letters. The correspondence continued for 30 years. The over 400 letters that survive were intended to educate Philip in the art of being a gentleman—to give him manners, a classical education, and a realistic view of humanity. With sophistication, frankness, and affection, Chesterfield described men as selfish and women as frail creatures to be controlled.

The earl wanted his son to become a diplomat. But Philip, shy and socially crude, failed as a diplomat. He married secretly and died young. His widow sold the earl's letters. Their publication in 1774, soon after the earl's death, made Chesterfield famous. Gary A. Stringer

Chesterton, G. K. (1874-1936), was an English author known for his essays on almost every popular subject of his time. He also wrote biographies, fiction, and poetry.

Chesterton's essays are known for their wit and vigor. However, his detective stories, novels, and literary criticism now rank as his most widely read works. Chesterton's best-known stories include a series of mysteries featuring Father Brown, a Roman Catholic priest, as the detective. In his novel *The Napoleon of Notting Hill* (1904), Chesterton created a fantasy in which an eccentric rules the London of the future. Chesterton also wrote a fantasy called *The Man Who Was Thursday* (1908), which centers on spies and detectives.

Critics consider Chesterton's biographies his finest works. These writings include studies of Robert Browning, Charles Dickens, and other English authors. Chesterton's full name was Gilbert Keith Chesterton. He was born on May 29, 1874, in London. Avrom Fleishman

Chestnut is the name of about 12 species of trees with spreading branches. Chestnut trees grow in parts of North America, Asia, Africa, and Europe. They bear spiny burs that contain edible, starchy nuts. The *Chinese, Japanese,* and *European chestnuts* are grown commercially for the nuts they produce.

The *American chestnut* was once the most important

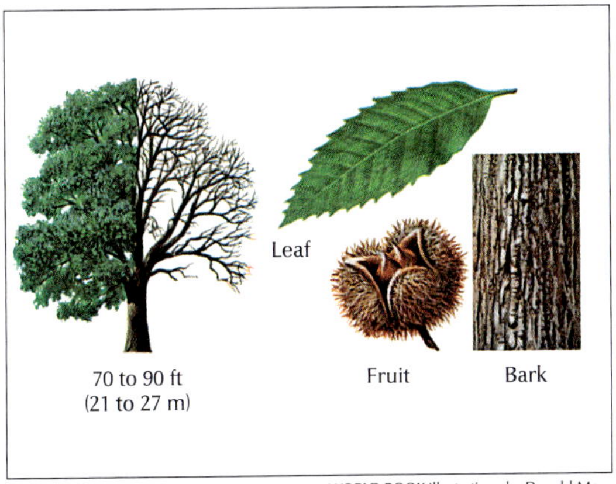

WORLD BOOK illustrations by Donald Moss

The American chestnut has toothed, glossy green leaves. Its nuts develop in a prickly, clinging seedcase called a bur. The wood of the American chestnut is extremely durable.

Muriel and Arthur Norman Orans

The spreading chestnut tree makes an excellent shade tree. The trunk has unusually rough bark. Chestnut wood is durable and is widely used as a building material.

forest tree in the eastern United States. This large tree was found from central Maine, along the Appalachian Mountains, and westward to the Mississippi River. From 1905 to 1940, a fungal disease called *chestnut blight* killed most of these trees in North America. The disease probably entered the United States in the 1890's from China or Japan. American chestnuts grow more than 70 feet (21 meters) tall. In the past, people valued the American chestnut for its decay-resistant wood, the *tannin* (a substance used to tan leather) it supplied, and the nuts it produced. Chestnut wood was widely used for railroad ties, telephone and telegraph poles, fence posts, lumber, furniture, and woodwork. The *chinquapin,* a small tree or shrub related to the American chestnut, grows in Oklahoma and the Southeast. Each bur of this species contains only one small nut. Richard A. Jaynes

Scientific classification. Chestnuts are in the beech family, Fagaceae. The American chestnut is *Castanea dentata.* The chinquapin is *C. pumila.*

See also **Tree** (Broadleaf and needleleaf trees [picture]).

Chevalier, *shuh VAL yay* or *shuh val YAY,* **Maurice,** *maw REES* (1888-1972), was an internationally popular French motion-picture and stage performer. He earned fame both as a singer and actor and became known for his straw hat and his charming, light-hearted manner.

Maurice Auguste Chevalier was born in Paris. He made his professional debut in 1901 as a singing comedian in a Paris music hall. In 1909, he began performing in the *Folies-Bergère,* a famous French revue.

Chevalier made his American motion-picture debut in 1929 in the musical *Innocents of Paris.* Between 1929 and 1935, he starred in 11 other American film musicals. He introduced the songs "Louise" in *Innocents in Paris* and "Mimi" in *Love Me Tonight* (1932). Both songs became identified with him throughout his career. Chevalier's later films include *Gigi* (1958), *Fanny* (1961), and *In Search of the Castaways* (1962). Gerald Bordman

Chevrolet, *SHEHV roh LAY,* **Louis** (1878-1941), helped organize the Chevrolet Motor Company in 1911, and designed its first automobile. He was also a leading figure in automobile racing, and was elected to the automobile racing Hall of Fame in 1952. Chevrolet sold his interest in the motor company in 1915. He then began building racing cars. His *Monroe* won the Indianapolis 500-mile race in 1920. His *Frontenac* won the race in 1921. Chevrolet and his brother Arthur organized the Chevrolet Brothers Aircraft Company in 1929, but it failed. Born near Bern, Switzerland, Chevrolet moved to the United States in 1900. Sylvia Wilkinson

Chevron, *SHEHV ruhn,* consists of two lines joined together at one end to form an angle. Chevrons on the sleeves of military or other types of uniforms indicate the rank of the wearer. In architecture, the word describes the angles formed by roof rafters. Chevrons in heraldry represent the rafters of a house, and signify the accomplishment of a memorable and important work. A chevron often served to symbolize that the bearer had founded a family. Thomas E. Griess

Chewing gum is a type of confection that people chew but do not swallow. It comes in a variety of shapes, including sticks, balls, pellets, and chunks. The most popular flavors of gum are spearmint, peppermint, cinnamon, and fruit flavors. Many people find that gum chewing helps increase concentration and relieve boredom. In addition, studies have shown that gum chewing helps people relax.

Ingredients. Standard chewing gum consists of five basic ingredients: gum base, sugar, corn syrup, softeners, and flavorings. Gum base is the *insoluble* part of the gum—that is, it does not dissolve during chewing. It makes gum chewy and acts as a base for the other ingredients. Gum base is made of various waxes, *resins* (sticky substances from plants and trees), and *latexes* (milky juices found in plants). The gum base in bubble gum is firmer and more elastic than the base in other chewing gum. This stretchier base allows the chewer to blow gum bubbles.

Sugar sweetens the gum. Corn syrup keeps the gum fresh and flexible and helps sweeten it. Softeners, such as vegetable oil products, help blend the ingredients and keep the gum soft by retaining moisture. Flavorings make the gum tasty. They come from spearmint and peppermint plants, fruits, and spices. Some gum is made without sugar or corn syrup. This *sugarfree gum* is made with such natural and artificial sweeteners as sorbitol, mannitol, aspartame, and saccharin.

How gum is made. The manufacturing process for gum varies according to the gum's type and shape. But generally, the ingredients of the gum base are first ground, melted, and purified. All the ingredients are then slowly blended in mixing machines. To make stick gum, the ingredients are passed through a series of rollers that form the gum into a wide sheet. The sheet is lightly covered with finely powdered sugar or sugar substitute to prevent sticking and to provide sweetness. Next, the sheet is *scored* (cut) and broken into sticks. The gum is then cooled and hardened in a room where temperature and humidity are carefully controlled. Finally, high-speed machines wrap and package the gum.

History. The ancient Greeks chewed *mastiche,* a gum they made from a resin found in the bark of the mastic tree. More than 1,000 years ago, the Maya Indians of Mexico chewed *chicle,* a gummy substance made from the latex of the sapodilla tree. Later, Indians in New England taught American colonists to chew the hardened sap from the spruce tree. About 1850, sweetened paraffin wax became more popular than spruce gum.

How chewing gum is made

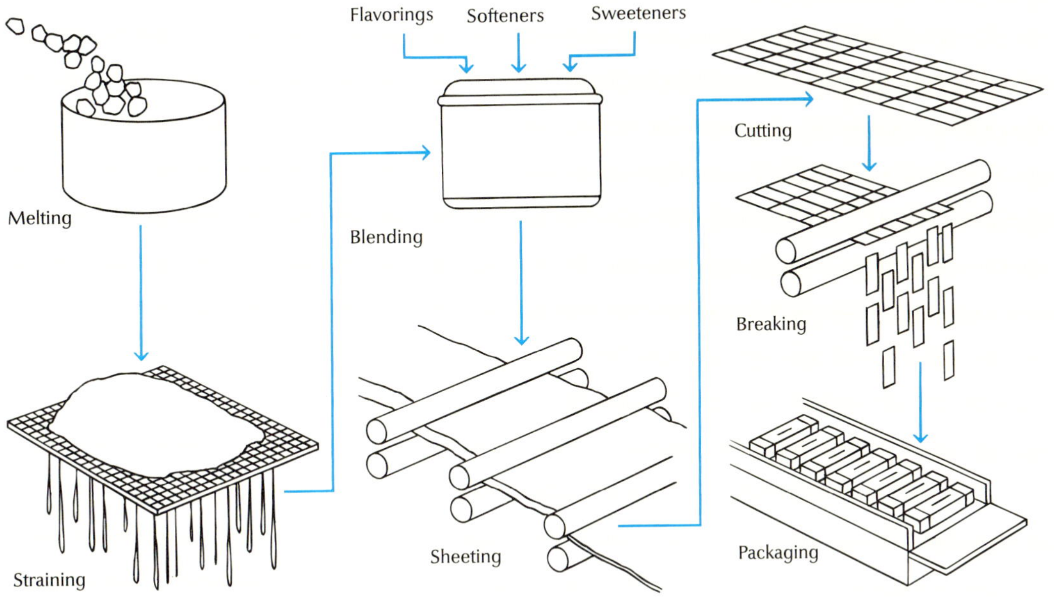

Gum base, the chief ingredient of chewing gum, is made by melting waxes, and certain substances obtained from plants and trees, in kettles. The soft, warm base is strained for purification.

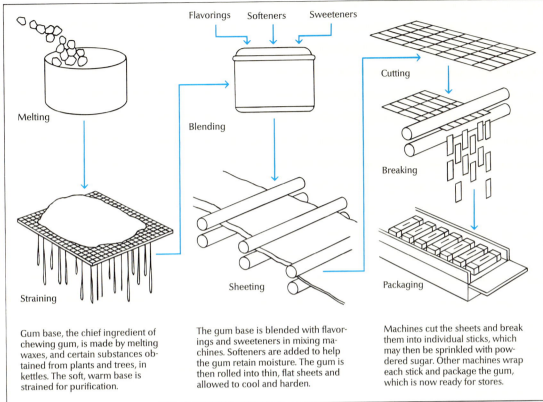

The gum base is blended with flavorings and sweeteners in mixing machines. Softeners are added to help the gum retain moisture. The gum is then rolled into thin, flat sheets and allowed to cool and harden.

Machines cut the sheets and break them into individual sticks, which may then be sprinkled with powdered sugar. Other machines wrap each stick and package the gum, which is now ready for stores.

WORLD BOOK diagram by Dick Fickle

The type of chewing gum known today had its beginnings in the late 1860's. At that time, some chicle was brought to the United States from Mexico to be sold as a type of rubber. A New York City inventor named Thomas Adams, Sr., tried to make chicle into rubber but found that it would not harden. When Adams boiled the chicle, however, he found that it made excellent chewing gum. This kind of gum soon won favor over spruce and paraffin gum. Bubble gum was first produced in 1906, but it was not perfected and marketed until 1928.

In the mid-1960's, chewing gum companies began to manufacture sugarfree gum. Many dentists recommend sugarfree gum because they believe sugar can contribute to tooth decay. But research suggests that the sugar in regular gum separates from the other ingredients, and that the washing effect of saliva produced during chewing lessens the possibility of tooth decay. Chewing gum is not harmful if it is accidentally swallowed.

Today, more than 500 companies in about 100 countries produce chewing gum. The United States ranks as the major producer. Other gum-producing countries include Canada, France, Italy, Japan, and the United Kingdom. Critically reviewed by the National Association of Chewing Gum Manufacturers

See also **Bubble gum; Chicle; Latex; Sapodilla**.

Cheyenne, *SHY ehn* or *shy AN* (pop. 53,011; met. area pop. 81,607), one of the most historic towns of the Old West, is the capital and largest city of Wyoming. It serves as the trade center of a large agricultural area and as a major defense center of the United States. Cheyenne lies near the southeast corner of Wyoming. For location, see **Wyoming** (political map).

Description. Cheyenne, the county seat of Laramie County, covers about 17 square miles (44 square kilometers). Cheyenne's annual Frontier Days celebration, which began in 1897, is one of the nation's most famous rodeos. The State Capitol, completed in 1888, also attracts many tourists. The Wyoming State Museum exhibits historical items of the Old West.

Just outside Cheyenne lies Warren Air Force Base, the site of the control center of one of the world's largest intercontinental ballistic missile networks. The base is the headquarters of a missile unit that controls about 200 missiles. These missiles are spread out over 8,000 square miles (21,000 square kilometers) in the surrounding region of Wyoming, Colorado, and Nebraska.

Nearly a third of Cheyenne's people work for the federal, state, or local government. Oil refining and cattle and sheep ranching also contribute to the economy.

History. Major General Grenville M. Dodge, the chief engineer of the Union Pacific Railroad, founded Cheyenne in 1867. He chose the site as a terminal for the railroad, which was being built westward from Omaha, Nebraska. Dodge named the city after the Cheyenne Indians, who lived in the area.

Shortly after Dodge founded Cheyenne, thousands of people rushed there ahead of the railroad. Cheyenne became a boom town known for lawlessness. Outlaws

Karl Kummels, Shostal

Cheyenne is the capital of Wyoming. Many tourists visit the city each July for Frontier Days celebration. A nationally famous rodeo, *shown here,* is the highlight of Frontier Days.

controlled the town for a short time until vigilante groups restored order.

During the late 1860's, cattlemen drove their animals north via trails from Texas to rangelands in Wyoming. Cheyenne served as a railroad shipping point and, by the early 1880's, was the center of a large cattle-ranching area. The city became the territorial capital in 1869 and the state capital in 1890.

Fort D. A. Russell was built nearby at the same time as Cheyenne. It protected the railroad construction crews from Indian attacks. In 1930, the post was renamed Fort Francis E. Warren in honor of Wyoming's first governor. It became Warren Air Force Base in 1947. In 1963, the base became the headquarters of the 90th Strategic Missile Wing, control center of ballistic missile installations. Cheyenne has a mayor-council form of government.

Ronald E. Beiswenger

For the monthly weather in Cheyenne, see **Wyoming** (Climate). See also **Wyoming** (pictures).

Cheyenne Indians are a group of American Indians separated geographically into two groups, the Northern Cheyenne and the Southern Cheyenne. About 2,700 Northern Cheyenne live on a reservation in Montana, and about 2,200 Southern Cheyenne live in Oklahoma. Many Cheyenne also live and work in cities.

All the Cheyenne once fished and hunted in the region around Lake Superior. After the mid-1700's, they moved to the Great Plains, where they lived in tepees and hunted buffalo. In the early 1830's, the Cheyenne divided into the Northern and Southern groups. Troops of the Colorado militia massacred about 300 peaceful Southern Cheyenne and Arapaho at Sand Creek, Colorado, in 1864. The surviving Indians moved to a reservation in Oklahoma in 1869.

The Northern Cheyenne fought to keep their hunting lands when white settlers tried to take them. In 1876, Northern Cheyenne and Sioux forces defeated Lieutenant Colonel George A. Custer in the Battle of the Little Bighorn in Montana. The government gave the Northern Cheyenne a reservation in Montana in 1884. C. B. Clark

See also **Black Kettle; Indian wars** (Wars on the Plains).

Chiang Ch'ing. See **Jiang Qing.**

Chiang Ching-kuo, *jyahng jihng GWOH* (1910-1988), was the most powerful leader of the Nationalist Chinese government on Taiwan from 1975 until his death in 1988. He came to power after his father, Chiang Kai-shek, died

Photo by Stanley J. Morrow, 1878; Smithsonian Institution, Washington, D.C.

The Cheyenne Indians lived in tepees and hunted buffaloes on the Great Plains. They staked out and dressed the buffalo hides and hung the meat on racks to dry in the sun, *shown here.*

in 1975. Chiang Ching-kuo served as prime minister of the government from 1972 to 1978, when he became Taiwan's president. His involvement with popular organizations gave him a reputation as close to the people.

Chiang was born on March 18, 1910, in Zhejiang Province. He went to the Soviet Union in 1925. There, he graduated from Sun Yat-sen University in 1927 and from a military academy in 1930. Chiang returned to China in 1937 and held a series of government positions of increasing importance. After the Chinese Communists conquered China in 1949, the Nationalists moved their government to the island of Taiwan. Chiang took charge of the Nationalist secret police and directed youth and veterans' organizations. He served as minister of defense from 1965 to 1969, and as deputy prime minister from 1969 to 1972. Chiang died on Jan. 13, 1988. Arif Dirlik

Chiang Kai-shek, *jyahng ky SHEHK* (1887-1975), was the political and military leader of the Nationalist Chinese government on Taiwan from 1949 until his death on April 5, 1975. He took command of the Kuomintang Party in the 1920's. This was the Nationalist Party that had overthrown the Manchu (Qing) dynasty and proclaimed a republic in 1912. Chiang was the decisive power in China from the mid-1920's until 1949, when Communists took control. He then fled to Taiwan and established his government there.

Chiang was born on Oct. 31, 1887, in the Zhejiang Province. He received a military education in China and in Tokyo, Japan. In Tokyo he met Sun Yat-sen, the Chinese revolutionary leader, and joined Sun's revolutionary organization. Sun sent Chiang to the Soviet Union in 1923. When Chiang returned to China, Sun appointed him president of the Whampoa Military Academy. Sun died in 1925, and the next year Chiang took command of the Nationalist Army. See **Sun Yat-sen**.

Nationalist victory. In 1926, Nationalist forces, aided by Communist organizers, left Guangzhou on a campaign against warlords in the north. The warlords were defeated and the Nationalists became the strongest force in China. Soviet advisers tried but failed to seize political power at Hankou and Shanghai. The Soviets were expelled from China. In 1927, Chiang set up a capital at Nanjing. That year, he married Soong Mei-ling (see **Chiang Soong Mei-ling**). He later became a Christian. The National Government of China was created in 1928.

From 1928 to 1937, Chiang improved economic and political institutions in China. However, political consolidations proved difficult. The Japanese military and Chinese Communists continually sabotaged his regime.

The Japanese attack on China in 1937 made it necessary for the Nationalists to form a united front with the Communists. Chiang assumed full military power in this union as generalissimo. After the Japanese captured Nanjing later that year, he made the city of Chongqing his wartime capital. Chiang led China to victory in 1945.

Wide World
Chiang Kai-shek

Communist triumph. Near the end of World War II (1939-1945), when Japanese surrender became inevitable, fighting between the Nationalists and the Communists resumed. Chiang issued a new constitution and called for a popular election. In 1948, Chiang was elected president of China. Li Tsung-jen became vice president. But these popular measures failed to ensure political stability. The Communists were winning the civil war. Chiang's resignation and Li's assumption of the presidency did not save the situation. By the end of 1949, the Communists had driven Chiang and his armies from the Chinese mainland to the island of Taiwan, off China's coast in the South China Sea. See **China** (Civil war).

On Taiwan, Chiang took full military and civil authority. He established Taipei as the capital of his government. He was reelected president in 1954, 1960, 1966, and 1972. Immanuel C. Y. Hsu

Additional resources

Ch'en Chieh-ju. *Chiang Kai-shek's Secret Past: The Memoir of His Second Wife.* Westview, 1993.
Fenby, Jonathan. *Chiang Kai-shek.* Carroll & Graf, 2003.
Lai, Zehan, and others. *A Tragic Beginning: The Taiwan Uprising of February 28, 1947.* Stanford, 1991.

Chiang Soong Mei-ling, *jyahng sung may LIHNG,* or Mayling (1897-2003), the wife of Chiang Kai-shek, was a Chinese social leader. She was born on March 5, 1897, in Shanghai and graduated from Wellesley College in Massachusetts. In 1927, she married Chiang Kai-shek and supported him through difficult crises of his career (see **Chiang Kai-shek**). During the mid-1930's, she was a force in the New Life Movement, an attempt to modernize the Chinese.

Wide World
Chiang Soong Mei-ling

In 1943, Chiang Soong Mei-ling served as her husband's interpreter at the Cairo Conference, when he met with United States President Franklin D. Roosevelt and British Prime Minister Winston Churchill. During World War II (1939-1945) and the civil war in China that followed, she pleaded the Nationalist cause in the United States. She won much sympathy for the Chiang government against the Communists. She died on Oct. 23, 2003. Arif Dirlik

Chibcha Indians, *CHIB chuh,* lived on the high plains of the central Colombian Andes. The only known sources of information about them are archaeology and Spanish records. The Spanish conquered the Chibcha in the 1500's. The Chibcha culture changed quickly, and their language became extinct in the 1700's.

The Chibcha were once classified as a highly advanced civilization, as great as those of the Aztec, Inca, and Maya. They worked gold, drilled emeralds, made pottery and basketry, and wove textiles. But their craftwork was not as highly developed as that of other Indian cultures in Colombia. They did some farming in lowlands and on terraced hillsides. Research shows they had only small villages. Roberto DaMatta

See also **Colombia** (picture: The Raft of El Dorado); **El Dorado.**

Peter J. Schulz, City of Chicago

The skyscrapers of downtown Chicago rise against the backdrop of Lake Michigan. Chicago is the third largest city in the United States and a center of trade, industry, and transportation.

Chicago

Chicago is a huge city in northeastern Illinois that stretches along the southwest shore of Lake Michigan. It is the third largest city in the United States. Only New York City and Los Angeles have more people. Chicago also ranks among the world's leading industrial and transportation centers.

About 3 million people live in this energetic city. The Chicago area manufactures more fabricated metals and food products than any other urban area in the United States. Trucks and railroad cars carry more goods in and out of Chicago than any other city in the country.

The American poet Carl Sandburg called Chicago the "City of the Big Shoulders." And the city does do things in a big way. For example, Chicago has the world's largest grain market, largest concentration of medical facilities, and some of the world's tallest buildings.

Chicago also has one of the world's most beautiful lakefronts. Most of it is public parkland, with broad beaches and lawns stretching far along the shoreline. In addition, the city has an excellent symphony orchestra and fascinating museums. Chicago surprises many of its approximately 25 million annual visitors because its historic image as a hub of business and industry has overshadowed its rich tradition of beauty and culture.

Throughout its history, Chicago has been known for providing good jobs. Young men from Germany and Ireland came to Chicago to dig a shipping canal soon after Chicago became a city in 1837. During the next 100 years, thousands of European families came to work in Chicago's factories, steel mills, and shipping businesses. By the late 1800's, Chicago had become an industrial and commercial giant.

In 1871, the Great Chicago Fire destroyed much of the city. But Chicagoans rebuilt their city with a daring that made it a center of world architecture. During the 1920's, Chicago gained a reputation for crime and violence that it has never lived down. Yet the 1920's was also a creative period in the arts, and the booming industries in Chicago continued to attract new residents.

Since the mid-1900's, most newcomers to Chicago have been blacks and whites from poor areas of the South; Hispanic families from Mexico, Puerto Rico, and Central America; and Asian families. Many of these people have lacked the skills and education needed for today's jobs. Other problems for the city include a high crime rate in poor neighborhoods and a public school system with a high dropout rate.

Suburbs spread out far beyond the city. They provide both living and recreation space, and a growing number of jobs.

The city

Chicago extends about 25 miles (40 kilometers) along the southwest shore of Lake Michigan in northeastern Illinois. It covers 228 square miles (591 square kilometers) and lies on a plain 595 feet (181 meters) above sea level.

The Chicago River flows westward from Lake Michigan near the center of the city. It is famous as *the river that flows backward.* The river flowed into the lake until 1900. That year, engineers reversed the flow to prevent sewage in the river from polluting the lake, which provides Chicago's water supply. About 1 mile (1.6 kilometers) inland from the lake, the river splits into two branches. One branch flows northwest through Chicago. The other flows south into the Chicago Sanitary and Ship Canal, which cuts southwest through the city.

Chicago has four main sections: (1) Downtown, (2) the North Side, (3) the West Side, and (4) the South Side.

Downtown Chicago is known for its spectacular skyscrapers, huge department stores, fashionable shops, and beautiful "front yard," Grant Park. Every workday, hundreds of thousands of people stream into the downtown area to work. Thousands of people live downtown in luxurious, modern high-rise apartment buildings, new single-family row houses, and handsome old office buildings that have been remodeled into apartments.

The main downtown area extends about 16 blocks south and about 7 blocks north of the Chicago River's main stem. It extends about 10 blocks west of Lake Michigan, its eastern border. Within this area, elevated trains run along a rectangular "loop" of tracks 5 blocks wide and 7 blocks long. These tracks give the central downtown area its nickname, the *Loop.* Trains travel between the Loop and many of the suburbs.

The heart of the Loop is the intersection of State and Madison streets. These two streets form the base lines of Chicago's street-numbering system. Madison, which runs east and west, divides the north and south numbers. State, a north-south street, divides east and west numbers. State Street is also a famous shopping area. It includes Macy's at State Street, originally the Marshall Field and Company department store, with its landmark clock that juts out above the pavement; and the original Carson Pirie Scott & Company Building, which houses a department store and was designed by the noted architect Louis Sullivan.

Three blocks west of State Street is LaSalle Street, Chicago's financial district. Along the street stand several major banks, the Chicago Stock Exchange (formerly the Midwest Stock Exchange), and the Chicago Board of Trade, one of the world's largest grain markets. The City Hall-County Building and the striking, blue-tinted James R. Thompson Center also face LaSalle Street.

Wacker Drive, a double-deck boulevard, follows the inside curve of the Chicago River and its south branch. Local traffic uses the upper, street-level deck, and express traffic uses the lower level. The drive connects with 17 of the 19 downtown bridges that cross the river. The Merchandise Mart, one of the world's largest commercial buildings, stands across the river from Wacker Drive. It has more than 4 million square feet (370,000 square meters) of floor space. East of the Mart rises Marina City, two circular, 60-story apartment buildings.

A stunning group of office buildings in airy plazas lines South Wacker Drive and the river. The most impressive is the 110-story Sears Tower. It rises 1,450 feet (442 meters) and was once the world's tallest building.

Two blocks east of State Street in the main downtown area is Michigan Avenue. Fashionable shops, hotels, and tall office buildings line its west side. Grant Park covers about 300 acres (120 hectares) between Michigan Avenue and the lake. Its attractions include Buckingham Memorial Fountain, the John G. Shedd Aquarium, the Field Museum of Natural History, and the world-famous Art Institute of Chicago.

Beautiful Lake Shore Drive runs along the lakefront on Grant Park's east side. It extends from downtown far into the North and South sides. Many modern high-rise apartment buildings have been built along the drive.

North of the Chicago River, Michigan Avenue forms the core of the northern downtown area. This area has been named the *Magnificent Mile* because of its many elegant stores, hotels, restaurants, and office buildings.

East of Michigan Avenue, Navy Pier juts out into Lake Michigan. It includes shops and restaurants, a Ferris wheel, a winter skating rink, the Chicago Children's Museum, and the Chicago Shakespeare Theater.

The Old Water Tower, a Chicago landmark, stands at Michigan and Chicago avenues. The little tower was one of the few structures in the area to survive the Great Chicago Fire. Across Michigan Avenue from the tower is Water Tower Place, a popular indoor shopping mall that also contains a hotel and apartments. The 100-story John Hancock Center rises one block north. It houses stores, offices, and more than 700 apartments.

Hotel Burnham

Chicago's outstanding architecture includes the historic Reliance Building (1894), now a hotel, *shown here.* Its steel frame and terra-cotta covering were an advance in skyscraper design.

WORLD BOOK map

Chicago is in northeastern Illinois.

Chicago
Park, forest preserve, or cemetery
State boundary
County boundary
City boundary
Expressway
Major highway
Other road or street
Railroad
Point of interest
0 5 10 15 Miles
0 5 10 15 20 Kilometers
WORLD BOOK map
North
Lake Michigan
CHICAGO
AREA OF DOWNTOWN MAP
NORTHWESTERN UNIVERSITY
WILLARD HOUSE
CARTER HOUSE
EMIL BACH HOUSE
LOYOLA UNIVERSITY
WILSON AVE. WATER INTAKE
CARTER H. HARRISON WATER INTAKE
FOUR-MILE WATER INTAKE
68TH ST. WATER INTAKE
Morton Grove
Niles
Skokie
Evanston
Des Plaines
Park Ridge
Rosemont
Lincolnwood
Schiller Park
Norridge
Harwood Heights
Bensenville
Franklin Park
River Grove
Elmwood Park
Northlake
Melrose Park
Elmhurst
Bellwood
Berkeley
River Forest
Maywood
Hillside
Oak Park
Forest Park
Westchester
Broadview
Oak Brook
La Grange Park
Brookfield
Riverside
Berwyn
Cicero
Stickney
La Grange
Western Springs
Hinsdale
Summit
Justice
Bedford Park
Bridgeview
Burbank
Hickory Hills
Hometown
Evergreen Park
Oak Lawn
Palos Hills
Chicago Ridge
Worth
Palos Heights
Alsip
Blue Island
Crestwood
Riverdale
Dolton
Orland Park
Midlothian
Calumet City
Edison Park
Norwood Park
Sauganash
North Park
Jefferson Park
Albany Park
Portage Park
Irving Park
Uptown
Rogers Park
Lakeview
Logan Square
Near North Side
Gold Coast
Austin
Loop
South Lawndale
Bridgeport
Brighton Park
Hyde Park
Clearing
Chicago Lawn
Englewood
Woodlawn
South Shore
South Chicago
Chatham
Beverly
Roseland
Pullman
Morgan Park
West Pullman
Hegewisch
ALLSTATE ARENA
CAMPGROUND WOODS
ALGONQUIN WOODS
CAMP FORT DEARBORN
O'HARE INTERNATIONAL AIRPORT
TERMINAL
EDGEBROOK WOODS
ROSEHILL CEMETERY
NORTHEASTERN ILLINOIS UNIV.
HORNER PARK
GRACELAND CEMETERY
HUTCHINSON STREET DISTRICT
GETTY TOMB
ALTA VISTA TERRACE DISTRICT
WRIGLEY FIELD
LINCOLN PARK
READ MENTAL HEALTH CENTER
SCHILLER WOODS
RIIS PARK
SHRINERS HOSPITAL
HANSON PARK
CHILDREN'S MEMORIAL HOSPITAL
McCORMICK ROW HOUSE DISTRICT
ZOO
DE PAUL UNIVERSITY
STEPPENWOLF THEATRE
HUMBOLDT PARK
HOLY TRINITY RUSSIAN ORTHODOX CATHEDRAL
POLISH MUSEUM
JOHN HANCOCK CENTER
MERCHANDISE MART
DALEY CENTER
UNITED CENTER
SEARS TOWER
ART INSTITUTE
CONSERVATORY
GARFIELD PARK
JACKSON BOULEVARD HISTORIC DISTRICT
MEDICAL CENTER DISTRICT
HULL HOUSE
UNIVERSITY OF ILLINOIS AT CHICAGO
FIELD MUSEUM
DOUGLAS PARK
MAYWOOD PARK RACE TRACK
LIZZADRO LAPIDARY ART MUSEUM
TRAILSIDE MUSEUM OF NATURAL HISTORY
DOMINICAN UNIVERSITY
CONCORDIA UNIVERSITY
WRIGHT HOUSE AND STUDIO
DRUMMOND HOUSE
UNITY TEMPLE
COLUMBUS PARK
LOYOLA UNIVERSITY MEDICAL CENTER
MILLER MEADOW
VETERANS ADMINISTRATION HOSPITAL
WESTCHESTER WOODS
BEMIS WOODS
OLD MILL MUSEUM
BROOKFIELD ZOO
RIVERSIDE HISTORIC DISTRICT
CONLEY HOUSE
ROBERT CROWN CENTER FOR HEALTH EDUCATION
SPORTSMAN'S PARK RACE TRACK
HAWTHORNE RACE TRACK
MICHAEL REESE HOSPITAL
ROBERT TAYLOR HOMES
SOUTH COMMONS
ILLINOIS INSTITUTE OF TECHNOLOGY
U.S. CELLULAR FIELD
DOUGLAS TOMB STATE MEMORIAL
MC KINLEY PARK
LAKE MEADOWS
BURNHAM PARK
BALZEKAS MUSEUM
UNION STOCK YARD GATE
CHICAGO PORTAGE NATIONAL HISTORIC SITE
ATRIUM HOUSES
WASHINGTON PARK
WEISS MUSEUM
HYDE PARK REDEVELOPMENT
MUSEUM OF AFRICAN AMERICAN HISTORY
UNIVERSITY OF CHICAGO
MUSEUM OF SCIENCE AND INDUSTRY
BILLINGS HOSPITAL
ROCKEFELLER CHAPEL
ROBIE HOUSE
JACKSON PARK
TO ARGONNE NATIONAL LABORATORY
HALE PARK
TERMINAL
MIDWAY AIRPORT
GAGE PARK
MARQUETTE PARK
OGDEN PARK
BOGAN PARK
SOUTH DISTRICT FILTRATION PLANT
FOSTER PARK
DAN RYAN WOODS
CHICAGO STATE UNIVERSITY
COAST GUARD STATION
CALUMET PARK
ST. XAVIER UNIVERSITY
PULLMAN HISTORIC DISTRICT
FLORENCE HOTEL
TRINITY CHRISTIAN COLLEGE
PORT OF CHICAGO CALUMET HARBOR
POWERS STATE CONSERVATION AREA
BEAUBIEN WOODS
TINLEY CREEK WOODS
CONKEY WOODS
BACHELOR GROVE WOODS
KICKAPOO MEADOWS
Dempster St.
Oakton St.
Touhy Ave.
Devon Ave.
Peterson Ave.
Foster Ave.
Addison St.
Belmont Ave.
Diversey Ave.
Fullerton Ave.
North Ave.
Chicago Ave.
Madison St.
Roosevelt Rd.
Cermak Rd.
Ogden Ave.
Pershing Rd.
47th St.
55th St.
Garfield Blvd.
59th St.
Marquette Rd.
79th St.
87th St.
95th St.
103rd St.
111th St.
127th St.
135th St.
143rd St.
Irving Park Rd.
Grand Ave.
Butterfield Rd.
Archer Ave.
Columbus Ave.
Midlothian Tpk.
Northwest Tollway
Kennedy Expwy.
Edens Expwy.
Eisenhower Expwy.
Stevenson Expwy.
Dan Ryan Expwy.
Bishop Ford Expwy.
Chicago Skyway
Tri-State Tollway
Southwest Hwy.
Caldwell Ave.
Lincoln Ave.
Milwaukee Ave.
Lake Shore Dr.
Clark St.
State St.
Michigan Ave.
Halsted St.
Ashland Ave.
Western Ave.
Kedzie Ave.
Pulaski Rd.
Cicero Ave.
Central Ave.
Harlem Ave.
Narragansett Ave.
Mannheim Rd.
York Rd.
Wolf Rd.
Elmhurst Rd.
Skokie Blvd.
Asbury Ave.
River Rd.
La Grange Rd.
Ridgeland Ave.
Stony Island Ave.
Jeffery Blvd.
Torrence Ave.
North Shore Channel
Chicago River
Des Plaines River
Salt Creek
Chicago Sanitary and Ship Canal
Calumet Sag Channel
Little Calumet River
Calumet River
Lake Calumet
Wolf Lake
DU PAGE COUNTY
COOK COUNTY
LAKE COUNTY
ILLINOIS
INDIANA

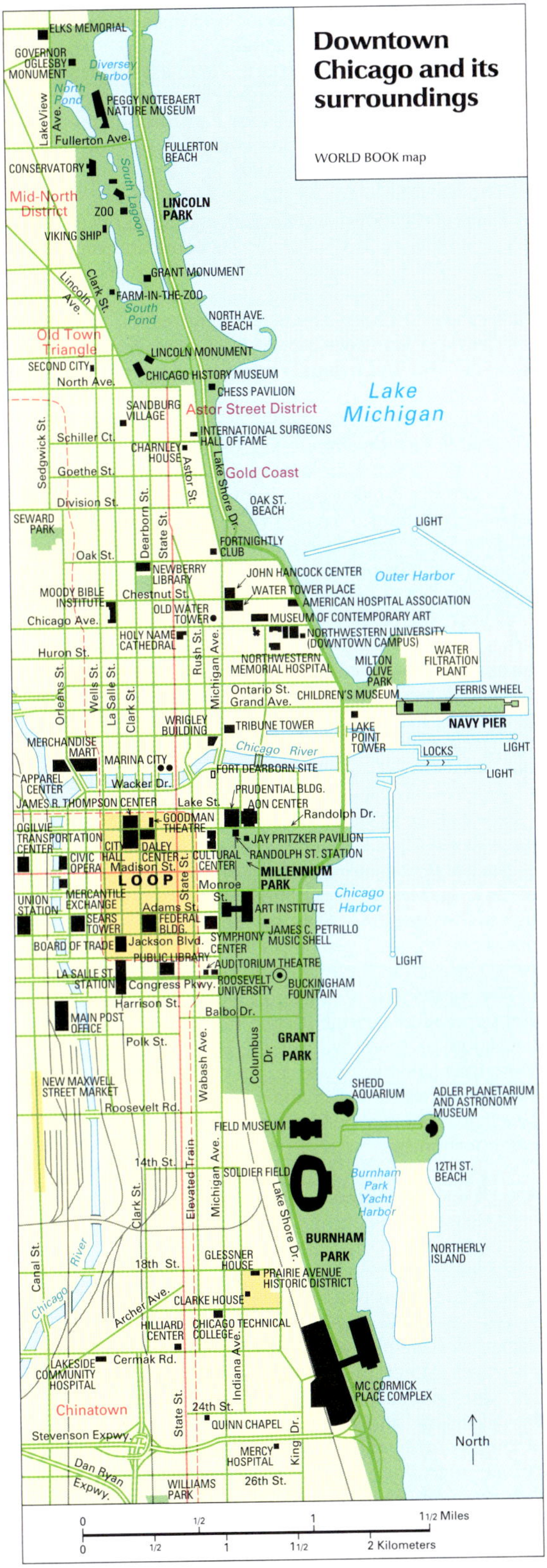

Downtown Chicago and its surroundings

WORLD BOOK map

Facts in brief

Population: *City*—2,896,016. *Metropolitan division*—7,628,412. *Metropolitan statistical area*—9,098,316 (8,272,768 in Illinois, 675,971 in Indiana, and 149,577 in Wisconsin).

Area: 228 mi^2 (591 km^2). *Metropolitan division*—4,616 mi^2 (11,955 km^2). *Metropolitan statistical area*—7,214 mi^2 (18,684 km^2), excluding inland water, consisting of 5,064 mi^2 (13,116 km^2) in Illinois, 1,877 mi^2 (4,861 km^2) in Indiana, and 273 mi^2 (707 km^2) in Wisconsin.

Climate: *Average temperature*—January, 22 °F (−6 °C); July, 73 °F (23 °C). *Average annual precipitation* (rainfall, melted snow, and other forms of moisture)—38 in (97 cm). For the monthly weather in Chicago, see **Illinois** (Climate).

Government: Mayor-council. *Terms*—4 years for the mayor and the 50 council members.

Founded: 1803. Incorporated as a city in 1837.

Largest communities in the Chicago area

Name	Population	Name	Population
Chicago	2,896,016	Elgin	94,487
Aurora	142,990	Kenosha (WI)	90,352
Naperville	128,358	Waukegan	87,901
Joliet	106,221	Cicero	85,616
Gary (IN)	102,746	Hammond (IN)	83,048

Source: 2000 census.

Symbols of Chicago. The city's flag was adopted in 1939. The stars signify Fort Dearborn, the Great Chicago Fire, and the city's two world's fairs. The blue stripes stand for the Chicago River and its two branches. The seal bears the date on which Chicago was incorporated as a city.

The North Side is almost entirely residential. It stretches from downtown north about 9 miles (14.5 kilometers) and northwest about 13 miles (21 kilometers).

The area just north of downtown is called the Near North Side. One famous Near North neighborhood is the Gold Coast, a luxurious residential area that begins at Oak Street. It extends about 10 blocks north along Lake Shore Drive and a few blocks west. The area is a blend of graceful old apartment buildings, Victorian mansions, and expensive skyscraper apartments.

Just west of the Gold Coast stands Carl Sandburg Village, a high-rise apartment complex. Sandburg Village has thousands of residents, many of them people who work downtown. Old Town includes the area west of Sandburg Village. Old Town has many gift shops, nightclubs, restaurants, and renovated old homes. Southwest of Old Town stands the Cabrini-Green public housing project. In the early 2000's, this group of high-rise apartment buildings was being demolished and replaced by low-rise, mixed-income housing.

Kevin O. Mooney, Odyssey Productions

The Gold Coast on Chicago's Near North Side is a luxurious residential area. Expensive high-rise apartment buildings along Lake Michigan overlook popular Oak Street Beach.

Lincoln Park, Chicago's largest and most popular park, begins north of the Gold Coast and marks the end of the Near North Side. The park stretches along almost two-thirds of the North Side lakefront and covers about 1,185 acres (480 hectares). It has beaches, lagoons, and a zoo. A long line of luxury apartment buildings overlooks Lincoln Park and extends along the lakeshore.

The mid-North Side neighborhood west of Lincoln Park, sometimes called New Town, was once old and shabby. Young professional people began to move into the area during the 1960's and repair some of the old houses. Since then, New Town has become a lively community of remodeled apartment buildings, new homes, shops, restaurants, and small theaters that present a variety of plays and musicals.

The rest of the North Side consists largely of middle-class white neighborhoods with three- to six-unit brick apartment buildings and single-family brick bungalows. More expensive homes are in such neighborhoods as Edgebrook and Sauganash on the Far Northwest Side.

To many Chicagoans, the most famous North Side street is Milwaukee Avenue, which was once an Indian trail. It runs diagonally across the North Side and into the northwest suburbs. From the 1860's until the 1940's, many thousands of families from Poland settled along Milwaukee Avenue. As their fortunes improved, they moved to better homes on the Northwest Side. Many of the Polish food stores, bakeries, and restaurants remain and are popular with Chicagoans.

O'Hare International Airport, one of the world's busiest airports, lies in the far northwest corner of the city. The John F. Kennedy Expressway cuts through the North Side and links O'Hare Airport with the Near Northwest Side, just northwest of the Loop.

The West Side lies west of the Loop between Grand Avenue on the north and the Chicago Sanitary and Ship Canal on the south. One of the city's chief industrial districts lies along the canal. This district has many factories, rail yards, truck-loading docks, and warehouses. Since the mid-1900's, however, many leading employers on the West Side have moved their operations to more spacious sites in Chicago's suburbs, taking thousands of jobs from the area.

Large sections of residential neighborhoods in the West Side include abandoned, decaying buildings. High crime rates and unemployment plague the residents. In several areas, however, community groups have undertaken restorations of run-down apartment buildings and houses. These projects are funded by businesses, foundations, and city government.

The Dwight D. Eisenhower Expressway cuts through the West Side between the Loop and the western suburbs. West of downtown, the expressway tunnels through a large building once occupied by the main branch of the Chicago Post Office. In 1996, the post office moved to a new building just across the street to the south. West of the post office complex, the Eisenhower Expressway passes the University of Illinois at Chicago and the West Side Medical Center. The medical center's seven hospitals and two medical schools make it the world's largest concentration of medical facilities.

The medical center and the construction in the 1960's of the university prompted growth in the eastern portion of the West Side. New apartment buildings and single-family houses were built. Old factories were converted into attractive offices and studios for artists.

The South Side is Chicago's biggest section in area and population. It stretches about 16 miles (26 kilometers) south of downtown and the West Side and covers more than half the city's area. The South Side includes industrial areas, an international port, spacious parks, pleasant residential communities, and poverty-stricken neighborhoods.

A large percentage of the South Siders are African Americans. Other ethnic groups include people of German, Hispanic, Irish, and Polish descent. Most blacks and whites live in separate communities.

But the South Side has a few integrated communities. Several large apartment buildings and rows of town houses near downtown have black, white, Asian, and Hispanic residents. Many of these residents work in the Loop area, or nearby at the Illinois Institute of Technology, Mercy Hospital and Medical Center, or Michael Reese Hospital and Medical Center. Hyde Park, the site of the University of Chicago, is an integrated community farther south along the lake. On the Far Southwest Side, the communities of Morgan Park and Beverly have a mix of black and white homeowners.

The Robert Taylor Homes, once Chicago's biggest public housing project, covered about 15 blocks along

South State Street and the Dan Ryan Expressway. By the early 2000's, however, the city had demolished most of the high-rise apartment buildings in this development. The city planned to replace them with low-rise housing that would accommodate people of varied incomes.

The South Side's largest park is Burnham Park. It stretches south from Grant Park and covers 598 acres (242 hectares) along the lakefront. McCormick Place, one of the nation's largest convention and exhibition center complexes, stands in the north end of Burnham Park. The park's southern edge borders Jackson Park, which covers 543 acres (220 hectares) along the lake. About 12 blocks west of Jackson Park, Washington Park occupies 368 acres (149 hectares).

The Chicago Skyway, an elevated toll road, crosses the industrial Far Southeast Side. The skyway runs from the Dan Ryan Expressway, the South Side's major north-south route, to the Indiana border. On the way, it passes steel mills, oil refineries, warehouses, grain elevators, and huge stockpiles of iron ore and limestone. Cargo ships follow the nearby Calumet River inland from Lake Michigan to terminals along Lake Calumet, Chicago's largest harbor.

The Far Southwest Side is one of Chicago's newest communities. It has block after block of neat, single-family homes and only scattered industrial districts. Nearly all the residents are white.

Two well-known neighborhoods of Chicago's Near Southwest Side are Chinatown and Bridgeport. Chinatown has a small residential section, restaurants, food stores, and gift shops. Bridgeport is a community of small bungalows. Many city employees and five Chicago mayors have lived in Bridgeport. The famous Union Stock Yards, which closed in 1971, lie southwest of Bridgeport. The huge stockyards, which once supplied meat to much of the nation, are now an industrial park.

Metropolitan area. The U.S. Census Bureau defines the Chicago-Naperville-Joliet metropolitan division as eight Illinois counties—Cook (which includes all of Chicago proper), DeKalb, Du Page, Grundy, Kane, Kendall, McHenry, and Will counties. The metropolitan division has about 7 ½ million people. About 5 million live in Cook County, the second largest U.S. county in population after Los Angeles County. The metropolitan division covers 4,615 square miles (11,953 square kilometers).

The Census Bureau also defines a metropolitan statistical area, also named Chicago-Naperville-Joliet. It consists of the Chicago-Naperville-Joliet metropolitan division in Illinois, the Gary metropolitan division in Indiana, and the Lake County-Kenosha County metropolitan division in Illinois and Wisconsin, respectively. This area has a population of more than 9 million and covers 7,214 square miles (18,684 square kilometers).

The Chicago metropolitan area has changed dramatically since the 1940's. The suburban population has grown rapidly, while that of Chicago proper has fallen. Many shopping centers, office buildings, and modern industrial complexes have been built in the suburbs.

Northwest Cook County has had the greatest growth. It has so many shopping centers, restaurants, and recreational facilities that many residents rarely visit downtown Chicago. Arlington Heights, the center of the area, grew from 5,700 people in 1940 to over 75,000 in 2000. Most of the area now covered by Schaumburg, Hoffman

© James P. Rowan

Chicago's North Side neighborhoods are mostly residential. Both single-family and multifamily homes line this quiet street in the Jefferson Park area, in the northwestern part of the city.

© Churchill & Klehr Photography

On Chicago's West Side, shops and apartments line a busy street. The Pilsen area, *shown here,* once home to many immigrants from Eastern Europe, has a large Hispanic population.

© Churchill & Klehr Photography

Rows of single-family brick bungalows can be found in many Chicago neighborhoods. About one-fourth of the city's families live in single-family houses. The rest live in apartments.

Estates, and Elk Grove Village was farmland in 1960. By 2000, these communities had a total of about 160,000 residents. In the 1980's and 1990's, striking growth followed the I-88 corridor to the west. High-tech business and research facilities there earned the area the nickname "Silicon Prairie." Naperville, once a farming town, grew from 15,000 people in 1960 to 130,000 in 2000.

The old, elegant towns of Winnetka, Kenilworth, and Wilmette lie along the lake north of the city. Some suburbs have many black and white residents. One of these suburbs is Park Forest, located south of the city. This attractive community was built in the late 1940's. A few towns in the far south metropolitan area have mostly African American residents. But only about 6 percent of the suburban people are African Americans.

People

Chicago has always been known as a city where industrious people could find good jobs. By the 1860's, when Chicago was only 30 years old, its reputation was spreading throughout the poor farmlands and slums of Europe. Thousands of Europeans moved to the booming prairie town, where they settled in separate sections. By the end of the 1800's, the city consisted of many small communities that duplicated the language and customs of such countries as Germany, Italy, Poland, and Ireland.

Most of the old European ethnic communities have faded away. But they have left a rich heritage. Many Chicagoans enjoy visiting the city's numerous ethnic restaurants, food stores, and gift shops. They also take pride in the impressive churches and charming blocks of homes constructed by the hard-working European immigrants who built the city.

Ethnic groups. About 37 percent of the city's people are black and about 31 percent are non-Hispanic white. People of Hispanic descent–who may be white, black, or of mixed ancestry–make up about 26 percent of the population. The expansion of Hispanic communities during the 1990's accounted for a slight increase in the city's total population, halting five decades of decline.

African Americans make up Chicago's largest ethnic group, with about 1,065,000 people. Most live in neighborhoods that are nearly all black. These communities range from the attractive, treelined streets of Avalon Park and South Shore on the South Side to the crumbling slums of the West Side.

As in other U.S. cities, Chicago's blacks have generally suffered from poverty, a lack of education, and discrimination in jobs and housing. However, Chicago also has many successful black business and professional people. Many of them live in recently built downtown apartment buildings and on the Near North Side. Chicago has thousands of businesses owned by blacks.

Hispanics make up Chicago's fastest-growing ethnic group. The city has about 750,000 Hispanics, an increase of about 300 percent since 1970. About 70 percent are Mexican Americans, 15 percent Puerto Ricans, and 1 percent Cubans. The rest trace their ancestry to other Latin American nations or are of mixed Hispanic origin.

Chicago's other large ethnic groups include Poles, Germans, Irish, and Italians. Chicago's Polish immigrants became known for budgeting their money and building homes—chiefly on the Northwest Side—as soon as they had saved enough. They founded some of the city's most pleasant neighborhoods. Thousands of German and Scandinavian immigrants started farms outside the city. They founded a number of today's prosperous suburbs. People of Irish descent have long been a major force in Chicago politics. Many government officials, judges, and police officers are of Irish descent.

Chicago has many different ethnic groups, including Asian Indians, Chinese, English, Filipinos, Greeks,

Brent Jones

Jackson Park, along Lake Michigan on the South Side, is a popular spot for family outings. These boaters are enjoying a leisurely ride on one of the park's lagoons.

Koreans, Russians, Swedes, and Ukrainians.

Housing. About a fourth of all Chicago residents live in single-family houses, and about a third live in buildings with two, three, or four apartments. The rest live in large apartment buildings. Some areas, especially along the lake, have many high-rise apartment buildings. But most areas have a mixture of houses—chiefly bungalows—and small apartment buildings.

Although the city has many pleasant residential areas, housing is one of its worst problems. About two-thirds of the city's 1,150,000 housing units are over 45 years old. In low-income neighborhoods, numerous buildings have been overcrowded and poorly maintained for many years. Many other buildings are unusable and have been abandoned by their owners. The Chicago Housing Authority (CHA) maintains about 28,000 homes for low- and moderate-income people. The CHA is a government agency whose board is appointed by Chicago's mayor. It is funded mainly by the federal government. Many of its dwellings traditionally have been in crowded high-rise projects. In 1999, the CHA began a redevelopment project that included demolishing many of the high-rise buildings, replacing this housing with new mixed-income developments, and restoring existing low-rise family developments.

Education. Chicago has the third largest public school system in the United States, with about 600 schools and 435,000 students. Only New York City and Los Angeles have larger systems.

A seven-member Board of Trustees governs Chicago's public school system. The mayor appoints the members. A local council has authority in each public school. Each council includes the principal and 10 elected members. The elected members include six parents who have children in the school, two community members without children in the school, and two of the school's teachers. High school councils also include one student member who is elected by the school's students. The councils—established in 1989—have the authority to approve budgets, change curriculums, and hire or fire principals.

About 80,000 Chicago students attend Roman Catholic schools. About 25,000 go to other private schools.

Chicago's largest institution of higher education is the University of Illinois at Chicago, with about 25,000 students. Two other state universities—Chicago State and Northeastern Illinois—are also in the city.

Well-known private schools include the University of Chicago, Roosevelt University, and two Catholic institutions—DePaul University and Loyola University Chicago. Northwestern University in suburban Evanston has a downtown Chicago campus, where several of its graduate professional schools are located. The Chicago area has six medical schools and is one of the world's leading centers of medical education and research. Several Chicago institutions have branches in the suburbs, where there are also a number of small private colleges.

Other educational institutions in Chicago include Columbia College, the Illinois Institute of Technology, National-Louis University, the School of the Art Institute of Chicago, the Institute for Clinical Social Work, and several business and law schools. The seven City Colleges of Chicago, which are public community colleges, have about 200,000 enrolled students. This total includes about 50,000 people in overseas courses for the U.S. armed forces and about 50,000 Chicago residents learning to speak English.

Artstreet

Michigan Avenue, an attractive shopping area, features Water Tower Place, an indoor, multilevel shopping mall, *right.* Across the street stands the Old Water Tower, *left,* a historic landmark.

Sports and recreation. Chicagoans enthusiastically support spectator sports, and professional teams represent Chicago in all major U.S. sports. The city has two major league baseball teams, the Chicago Cubs of the National League and the Chicago White Sox of the American League. It is also the home of the Chicago Blackhawks of the National Hockey League, the Chicago Bulls of the National Basketball Association, and the Chicago Bears of the National Football League.

Chicago has more than 560 parks and playgrounds. They total about 7,300 acres (3,000 hectares). The lakefront parkland, which covers about 3,000 acres (1,200 hectares), becomes a huge playground in warm weather. This parkland has beaches, bicycle paths, golf courses, soccer fields, softball diamonds, and tennis courts. It also has several harbors for the thousands of boats that cruise up and down the shoreline in summer.

The Cook County Forest Preserves dot Chicago's outskirts and suburban areas. The various preserves cover about 64,000 acres (25,900 hectares) of woodland. They have picnic grounds, golf courses, bridle paths, swimming pools, nature museums, and toboggan runs.

Social problems. The chief social problems in Chicago, as in most other large cities in the United States, involve poverty and racial discrimination. The Chicago area has one of the lowest unemployment rates in the nation. Yet about one-fifth of all Chicagoans receive some form of public aid.

Chicago's African Americans and Hispanics carry most of the burden of poverty. For example, about a third of all Chicago black families have an annual income below the level considered the "poverty line" by the federal government. The unemployment rate for Chicago's blacks is often twice the city's overall rate.

Family breakdown, crime, and inadequate health care also contribute to poverty in the city. About half of all Chicagoans who receive public aid are women and children with no other means of support. People in black neighborhoods are much more likely to be the victims of a violent crime than people in white areas.

Cultural life and places to visit

Chicago ranks among the greatest cultural centers of the United States. Its cultural life and many other features help attract more than 15 million tourists every year. Another 13 million people visit Chicago annually for business meetings, conventions, and trade shows.

The arts. The world-famous Chicago Symphony Orchestra performs in Orchestra Hall on Michigan Avenue at the Symphony Center for 32 weeks beginning each September. In summer, the orchestra plays outdoors at Ravinia Park in north suburban Highland Park. From late June to the end of August, the Grant Park Symphony Orchestra presents free concerts in the outdoor band shell in Millennium Park, the northwest corner of Grant Park. The Lyric Opera Company of Chicago has an annual fall and winter season in the Civic Opera House on Wacker Drive. The company brings the world's leading opera singers to Chicago. Visiting dance companies, orchestras, and concert stars also perform in the Opera House and in the Auditorium Theatre on Congress Parkway. This theater was designed during the 1880's by noted architects Louis Sullivan and Dankmar Adler. In 1995, the famed Joffrey Ballet moved from New York to Chicago.

WORLD BOOK photo by Steven Spicer

Elevated trains run on tracks above the streets in parts of the city. Downtown, the tracks form a "loop" 5 blocks wide and 7 blocks long. They are a familiar part of the city's architecture.

Chicago city and suburban theaters present a wide range of plays, including popular Broadway shows; classics; experimental and other new works; and plays for children. Nationally known Chicago theaters include the Goodman downtown; the Steppenwolf in the Lincoln Park area; and the Court in Hyde Park on the South Side. The Lincoln Park area is the home of the nationally known Second City comedy club.

Architecture. Chicago has dominated American architecture since the late 1800's. New styles and new construction techniques have first appeared in Chicago and then spread to other cities. Designers and engineers from around the world visit Chicago to study its spectacular buildings.

The city's tradition of architectural pioneering began after the Great Chicago Fire of 1871 destroyed much of the city. Outstanding architects, including William Le Baron Jenney, Daniel H. Burnham, and Louis Sullivan, helped rebuild Chicago. Their work produced a famous style of architecture known as the *Chicago School.*

The great development of the Chicago School was the skyscraper. Architects stripped away the heavy walls of stone and brick that had supported tall buildings. Instead, they designed structures with steel skeletons, which allowed buildings to soar to great heights and yet look light and graceful.

Jenney designed the 10-story Home Insurance Building, often considered the world's first metal-framed skyscraper. Built in downtown Chicago, it was completed in 1885. But this building and some other masterpieces of the Chicago School have been demolished. Many other examples of this type of architecture still stand, however. One of these structures is the Reliance Building, designed by Burnham and John W. Root, at State and Washington streets. Another is Jenney's Sears, Roebuck and Co. store (now an office and retail building called One Congress Center) at State and Van Buren. A third Chicago School masterpiece is the Carson Pirie Scott & Company Building, designed by Sullivan. It curves gracefully around a corner at State and Madison streets. All three of these structures were built in the 1890's.

During the 1920's, downtown Chicago enjoyed a building boom that resulted in a canyonlike LaSalle Street financial district. During the 1940's, the German architect Ludwig Mies van der Rohe, master of the glass-and-steel style, began a second generation of the Chicago School. His Chicago masterpieces include buildings at the Illinois Institute of Technology and apartments on Lake Shore Drive near Chicago Avenue. Other Chicago structures that reflect the influence of Mies include the Chicago Civic Center, the John Hancock Center, and McCormick Place.

Frank Lloyd Wright, who developed the *Prairie School* of architecture, moved to Chicago in the 1880's. He created houses and other buildings that were long, low, and fluid—like the sweep of the Midwestern prairie. Many of Wright's works are in west suburban Oak Park, where his own home and studio still stand. His best-known design in the city is Robie House. This house, built in 1909, is in the University of Chicago area.

Museums. Several of Chicago's finest museums stand in Grant Park. On the park's south end, the Field Museum exhibits mounted animals, life-sized displays of

The Art Institute of Chicago ranks as one of the world's greatest museums. It has fine galleries of many different types of art. The people in this photograph are viewing *Sunday Afternoon on the Island of La Grande Jatte,* a painting by the French artist Georges Seurat.

Kevin O. Mooney, Odyssey Productions

The Shedd Aquarium has more fish and other water animals than any other indoor aquarium in the world. It features an outstanding oceanarium. An audience watches a dolphin performance at the oceanarium, *shown here.*

prehistoric people, and dinosaur skeletons. Across from the Field Museum, the John G. Shedd Aquarium has about 6,000 fish and other water animals. Nearby, the Adler Planetarium and Astronomy Museum depicts the movements of heavenly bodies in its domed theater. The Art Institute of Chicago, on Grant Park's north end, is famous for its collection of French Impressionist art. In addition, the museum has fine galleries of primitive art and Asian art.

Several museums can be found outside of downtown. These include the Museum of Contemporary Art on the Near North Side and the Oriental Institute and the Smart Museum of Art on the University of Chicago campus in Hyde Park. The huge Museum of Science and Industry, one of Chicago's best-known institutions, stands in Jackson Park. Its displays include a space center, a working coal mine, a World War II German submarine, and many exhibits that relate to chemistry and physics.

The Chicago History Museum, in Lincoln Park, traces local history from the end of the ice ages to the present. On the South Side, the Du Sable Museum of African-American History is named after Chicago's first known

WORLD BOOK photo by Steven Spicer

Buckingham Memorial Fountain is a lovely summer attraction. At night, it is lit by a dazzling display of colored lights. Located in Grant Park, it offers fine views of Lake Michigan just east and of downtown skyscrapers in the distance to the north.

settler, Jean Baptiste Point du Sable, a black man. Chicago has many other museums devoted to its different nationalities and ethnic groups.

Libraries. The Chicago Public Library is one of the nation's largest public libraries. It has millions of books, microforms, records, tapes, films, and periodicals. The library has dozens of branches and reading centers. The Great Chicago Fire destroyed the main library downtown in 1871. But the library was restarted the following year when the British people donated 8,000 books to the city. The main public library branch is south of the Loop. It was named the Harold Washington Library Center in honor of Chicago's first African American mayor.

Many private libraries in Chicago specialize in particular subjects, such as history or science. On the Near North Side is the Newberry Library, one of the nation's leading historical research libraries. The John Crerar Library at the University of Chicago has fine collections on science and technology. The Art Institute of Chicago houses the Burnham Library of Architecture and the Ryerson Art Library. The Municipal Reference Library and the Chicago History Museum have fine materials on Chicago history.

Places to visit. Following are descriptions of a few of Chicago's many interesting places to visit. Others are discussed and pictured elsewhere in this article.

Brookfield Zoo, in west suburban Brookfield, covers about 200 acres (81 hectares) and exhibits animals in natural settings. Its Seven Seas Panorama has a dolphin show, and the children's zoo features baby animals.

Buckingham Memorial Fountain, in Grant Park, is one of the world's largest lighted fountains. It operates daily from May 1 through October 1. It contains about 1 ½ million gallons (5.7 million liters) of water and shoots its central spout about 150 feet (45 meters) in the air. Colorful lights illuminate the fountain each evening.

Chicago Board of Trade, at LaSalle and Jackson streets, is one of the world's largest commodity exchanges. In its hectic main hall, hundreds of brokers buy and sell farm products, metals, and foreign currencies for future delivery. Visitors may watch from a gallery.

Dearborn Street plazas, along downtown Dearborn Street, display magnificent works of art. A five-story

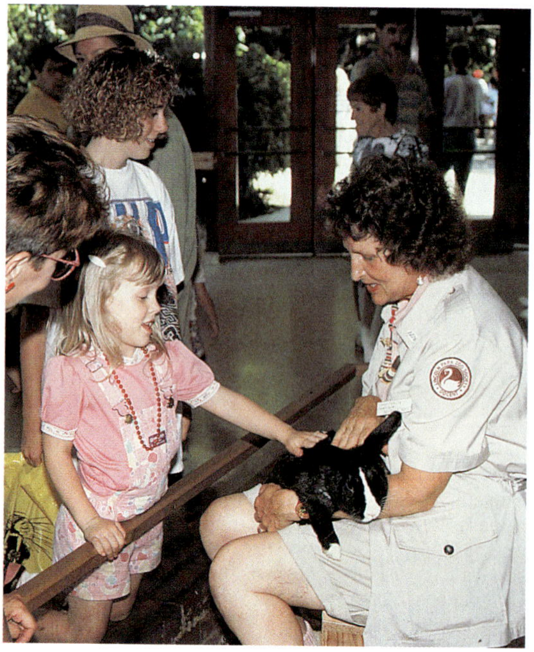

Artstreet

Lincoln Park Zoo, on Chicago's North Side, has many types of birds, mammals, and reptiles. It also has a children's zoo, *shown here,* where youngsters can pet some animals.

WORLD BOOK photo

The Chicago Picasso stands in Richard J. Daley Plaza. The Spanish artist Pablo Picasso designed the steel sculpture. The plaza is a popular gathering place in the downtown area.

sculpture by the Spanish artist Pablo Picasso stands in Richard J. Daley Plaza. Some people think it is a likeness of the artist's pet Afghan hound. Others think the sculpture resembles a woman's head. Alexander Calder, an American artist, designed the tall, red metal sculpture in the Federal Center Plaza. It is titled *Flamingo.* Some people think it resembles a drooping flower. The Russian-born artist Marc Chagall created *The Four Seasons,* a huge mosaic at Dearborn and Monroe streets.

Millennium Park, the northwest corner of Grant Park, is the site of the Pritzker Pavilion, a band shell designed by American architect Frank Gehry. The park includes an ice-skating rink, a fountain, a garden, and a huge stainless-steel sculpture by Indian-born artist Anish Kapoor.

Sears Tower, 110 stories high on Wacker Drive, is the tallest building in the United States. A public observation deck on the 103rd floor gives a spectacular view of Chicago and the Lake Michigan shoreline.

© Tootsie Roll Industries, Inc.

A worker inspects candy moving along conveyor belts at a factory on Chicago's Southwest Side. Chicago is a leading producer of processed foods and a wide range of other products.

Economy

The Chicago metropolitan area ranks among the leading industrial centers of the United States. Chicago is the nation's leading transportation center. The city also serves as the Midwest's financial capital.

About 3 ½ million people work in the Chicago metropolitan area. The number of jobs has grown rapidly since the mid-1900's. But the growth has been in Chicago's suburbs, not in the city itself. In 1950, for example, about 80 percent of all the jobs in the metropolitan area were in the city. Today, only about 40 percent are in Chicago. The large expanses of open land, the relatively low taxes and crime rate, and the ever-increasing population have attracted businesses and industries to the suburbs. Many firms moved to the suburbs from Chicago. Others came from outside Illinois to build headquarters, branch offices, or research plants.

Service industries employ about 80 percent of the workers in the Chicago area. Numerous service industries workers in the Chicago area work in the trade, hotels, and restaurants sector. Many others are employed in community, social, and personal services. This category includes doctors, lawyers, and private-school teachers. It also includes people employed in government; finance, insurance, and real estate; and communications and transportation. Many service industries are discussed after the *Industry* section.

Industry. This sector, which includes manufacturing, construction, mining, and utilities, employs about 20 percent of all workers in the Chicago metropolitan area. The area has about 13,000 industrial plants and is the nation's top producer of food products and fabricated metals. It is a leading U.S. producer of chemicals, electrical and electronic products, machinery, and iron and steel. It is also a major center of the construction industry.

The Chicago area is one of the nation's chief industrial research centers. Its industries operate hundreds of research laboratories. Chicago has been a leader in atomic

Sheraton Chicago Hotel & Towers (WORLD BOOK photo by Bill Goes)

Downtown hotels are an important part of Chicago's thriving trade, hotels, and restaurants economic sector. Each year, millions of people come to the city for conventions, business meetings, and cultural and recreational opportunities. Visitors check into one of the hotels, *left.*

Chicago Mercantile Exchange

The Chicago Mercantile Exchange is one of the world's busiest markets for agricultural goods, foreign currencies, and other commodities. In the background of this photograph, traders shout their bids and offer prices for a variety of products. In the foreground, traders conduct such business electronically, using computers.

research ever since the Italian physicist Enrico Fermi produced the world's first nuclear chain reaction at the University of Chicago in 1942. Argonne National Laboratory in suburban Lemont has pioneered in the development of nuclear reactors for electric power production. About 60 percent of the electric power in the Chicago area and surrounding regions of northern Illinois comes from nuclear power plants. The Fermi National Accelerator Laboratory, which houses one of the world's largest particle accelerators, is in suburban Batavia (see **Fermi National Accelerator Laboratory**).

Chicago was once the world's leading meat-packing center. The poet Carl Sandburg called the city the "Hog Butcher for the World." The city's famous Union Stock Yards processed about 18 million head of livestock yearly. But the yards began to decline in the 1950's with the growth of regional livestock centers, and the Union Stock Yards closed in 1971.

Trade. Chicago is one of the busiest ports in the United States. It is the only place in North America where the Great Lakes connect with the huge Mississippi River system. Chicago became a seaport in 1959 upon the opening of the St. Lawrence Seaway. This inland waterway links the Great Lakes and the Atlantic Ocean. Cargo ships sail to and from Chicago through the seaway and four of the Great Lakes—Ontario, Erie, Huron, and Michigan. The city's port handles about 26 million tons (24 million metric tons) of manufactured goods, raw materials, and produce every year.

Many terminals in the area receive cargo ships and barges. Major facilities on the Chicago Sanitary and Ship Canal and the Chicago River load and unload large amounts of steel, crushed stone, salt, and other products. Facilities on the Illinois River handle shipments of chemicals, coal, grain, and fertilizer. Terminals on Lake Calumet and the Calumet River have huge grain elevators that bulge with wheat and other grains each spring. Ice closes the St. Lawrence Seaway in winter. But early in April, after the ice has thawed, ships from dozens of countries arrive at the Calumet terminals to pick up Midwest grain and carry it to ports throughout the world.

Chicago is a busy port for river barges as well as for oceangoing ships. The barges use the Chicago Sanitary and Ship Canal, which connects with the Mississippi River system. This system links Chicago with the Gulf of Mexico and with ports as far east as Pittsburgh, Pennsylvania, and as far west as Omaha, Nebraska.

The Chicago area also ranks as one of the nation's leading wholesale and retail trading centers. More than 15,000 wholesale companies and about 30,000 retail firms operate in the area. The Sears Holdings Corporation, which owns the retail firms Kmart and Sears, has its corporate headquarters in suburban Hoffman Estates.

Finance. Chicago is the financial capital of the Midwest. The Chicago Stock Exchange (formerly the Midwest Stock Exchange) ranks as the second largest U.S. securities market, after the New York Stock Exchange. The Seventh Federal Reserve District Bank has its head-

Edward Simonek

Dozens of truck trailers, carried piggyback by railroad flatcars, await pickup at a terminal south of downtown Chicago. The city is the leading transportation center of the United States.

quarters in Chicago. Chicago is also home to several large commercial banking firms.

The Chicago Board of Trade, founded in 1848, is the oldest U.S. financial exchange. The Chicago Mercantile Exchange, also known as CME, dates from 1919. The Board of Trade and the Mercantile Exchange account for most of the nation's *futures contracts.* These contracts are agreements between buyers and sellers that arrange for a certain quantity of a product to be delivered at a specified price and date. Futures contracts may involve such commodities as grain, cattle, eggs, crude petroleum, foreign currencies, and U.S. Treasury bonds.

Transportation. Chicago is the nation's biggest transportation center. In no other area of the country do the railroad yards or trucking firms handle as much freight. These yards and firms transport hundreds of millions of tons of freight each year.

Two airports serve the city. O'Hare International Airport, which lies in the northwest corner of Chicago, is one of the busiest airports in the world. In addition to the millions of passengers that pass through the airport, cargo planes carry a large volume of freight through O'Hare. For the numbers of passengers and aircraft that pass through O'Hare each year, see **Airport** (table: World's 25 busiest airports).

Chicago Midway Airport, on the South Side, once ranked as the world's busiest. But it was unable to handle large jet airplanes and the volume of traffic in the Chicago area. By 1970, O'Hare had taken nearly all of its business. In the late 1900's, however, Midway increased its business with flights of smaller jets.

Smaller airports operate in suburban areas of Chicago. Aurora Municipal Airport is southwest of the city. Du Page Airport lies to the west. Palwaukee Municipal Airport and Waukegan Regional Airport lie to the north.

Over 1,000 passenger trains once passed through Chicago's downtown depots. Today, the city remains a major hub for dozens of Amtrak trains that use Union Station. Chicago is also a major connecting point for commercial buses.

About 70 percent of all Chicago area jobholders drive to work. Three major expressways stretch from an interchange near the downtown area through the city and suburbs. The John F. Kennedy Expressway extends northwest, the Dwight D. Eisenhower Expressway runs west, and the Dan Ryan Expressway stretches south. In addition, the Edens Expressway extends from the Kennedy Expressway through the north suburbs, and the Adlai E. Stevenson Expressway runs southwest from Lake Shore Drive.

The publicly owned Chicago Transit Authority (CTA) operates bus lines in the city. It also operates elevated, subway, and ground-level trains in the city and some suburbs. About 1 ½ million passenger rides are taken on CTA buses and trains each weekday. In 1974, Chicago area residents voted to establish a Regional Transportation Authority (RTA) to operate a public transportation system for the area. The CTA became part of the RTA, as did the six commuter railroads that serve the city. These railroad lines between the city and the suburbs carry about 150,000 passengers each workday. The RTA also operates a number of suburban bus companies.

Communications. Chicago has two general daily newspapers. They are the *Chicago Sun-Times* and the *Chicago Tribune.* Both publish morning and early evening editions. The two newspapers have a combined daily circulation of about 1 million copies. Another daily newspaper, the *Chicago Defender,* is directed chiefly at African American readers. This newspaper has a circulation of about 20,000 copies daily. Chicago also has about 30 foreign-language newspapers and about 100 neighborhood and suburban newspapers.

Several national magazines are published in Chicago. Other national magazines and nationally circulated newspapers have branch offices in the city. Chicago also ranks as a leading center of the advertising and book-publishing industries.

The Chicago area has 10 commercial television stations. It also has two nonprofit stations—one associated with the national Corporation for Public Broadcasting and one operated by the City Colleges of Chicago. The area has more than 70 radio stations, several of which feature foreign-language broadcasts. It also has a nonprofit station associated with National Public Radio.

Government

Chicago's government is headed by a mayor and a City Council, which consists of an alderman from each of the city's 50 wards. The voters elect the mayor and the aldermen, as well as a city treasurer and a city clerk, to four-year terms. The mayor appoints the other top officials, including city department heads, the police commissioner, and the fire commissioner.

Unlike most other large U.S. cities, Chicago has a weak-mayor, strong-council form of government. Chicago's mayor must obtain the City Council's approval on many important decisions and on most appointments. Also, some services provided by city governments in other cities are provided by the state and county governments in Chicago. The state, for example, administers most of Chicago's welfare services. Several other important government functions are administered by separate government units, such as the Chicago Park District and the Metropolitan Water Reclamation District.

In spite of the weak-mayor system, Chicago had the most powerful mayor of any major United States city during the third quarter of the 1900's, Richard J. Daley. For details on Daley's power and role as mayor, see *Political developments in the late 1900's* in the *History* section of this article.

By 2005, Chicago had an annual budget of more than $5 billion. Real estate taxes provide about a sixth of the city's revenue. Other taxes include a tax on utilities, a motor vehicle tax, and a city sales tax. Additional sources of revenue include a share of state income and sales taxes and grants from the federal government.

History

American Indians lived in the Chicago area more than 5,000 years ago. During the 1600's, when the first white people arrived, Potawatomi Indians lived near the Chicago River, which they called the *Checagou.* The name *Chicago* comes from that Indian word. The Potawatomi hunted buffalo, deer, and other wildlife. They raised such crops as corn, squash, and pumpkins. They also traded with nearby tribes by traveling the many trails that fanned out from the mouth of the Chicago River.

The river itself was part of another well-traveled route

Chicago in Flames, View from Randolph Street Bridge No. 1 (1871-1872), a color lithograph by an unknown artist; Chicago History Museum

The Great Chicago Fire of 1871 forced thousands of panic-stricken people to flee before the racing flames. The fire killed at least 300 people and destroyed about $200 million in property.

through the area. The Potawatomi paddled canoes down the river to a muddy *portage* (overland route) that led to the Des Plaines River. They then carried their canoes over the portage and followed the Des Plaines to the Illinois River. The Illinois connected with the mighty Mississippi River. The Potawatomi were peaceful and prosperous. When the first whites arrived, the friendly Potawatomi greeted them warmly.

Exploration and early settlement. The first white people to reach the Chicago area were probably the French-Canadian explorer Louis Jolliet and a French Jesuit priest named Jacques Marquette. They arrived at the portage in 1673 on their way north to Canada. During the next 25 years, French fur traders and missionaries frequently used the portage. But then the Fox Indians to the south closed the route to the portage to white men. As a result, little is known about life in the Chicago area from about 1700 to the 1770's.

In the late 1770's, a prosperous fur trader of mixed French and Dominican heritage arrived in the region. He was Jean Baptiste Point du Sable, who established a trading post on the north bank of the Chicago River mouth. His business prospered until his retirement and departure from the region in 1800.

Indian troubles. By the late 1700's, the westward expansion of settlement into what is now the Midwest touched off decades of warfare between the American military and the Indians, though relations in the Chicago area were peaceful. In 1803, the U.S. government built Fort Dearborn, its westernmost post. Soon a small settlement of traders and farmers had formed around the fort.

After the War of 1812 began between the Americans and the British, the United States government feared that unrest among the Indians might lead to violence against the outpost, which would be difficult to defend. On Aug. 15, 1812, about 100 soldiers and settlers left the fort and headed southeast for Fort Wayne in Indiana. They had traveled only about two miles when a raiding party of Indians attacked. Half of the evacuees were killed and the others were captured. The Indians burned Fort Dearborn. The Chicago area remained unsettled until 1816, when American soldiers rebuilt the fort.

Birth of the city. In 1816, several survivors of the attack who were released by the Indians returned to Chicago. Other settlers also moved to the area, and a new community grew up around rebuilt Fort Dearborn. When Illinois became a state in 1818, the Chicago settlement was included within its boundaries. By 1833, Chicago's population had grown to more than 150—large enough to be incorporated as a town.

In 1834 and 1835, U.S. government agents forced the Potawatomi and neighboring tribes to sell their land. In payment, the Indians received a small sum of money and territory west of the Mississippi. More than 3,000 Indians left their homeland for reservations in Kansas. After their departure, the town of Chicago boomed. It grew to about 4,000 people by 1837. On March 4, 1837, Chicago was incorporated as a city.

Growth as a city. Between 1836 and 1848, workers built the Illinois and Michigan Canal. It stretched 75 miles from the old portage to La Salle on the Illinois River. Chicago was thus linked with the Mississippi River system. Transportation soon became the city's major industry. But the canal played only a secondary role.

Chicago's most spectacular achievement between 1848 and 1856 was the growth of its railroads. The city's first railroad, the Galena and Chicago Union, began operation in 1848. By 1856, Chicago had become the hub of 10 main railroad lines with about 3,000 miles (4,800 kilometers) of track. Nearly 100 trains arrived or departed daily. The city had become the world's busiest rail center. It had also become the biggest city in Illinois, with a population of over 100,000.

Chicago boomed during the American Civil War (1861-1865). Cattle from the West streamed into the city's stockyards. The huge Union Stock Yards were completed in 1865. The grain trade thrived, making the Chicago Board of Trade the nation's chief grain market. The city's manufacturing industries also grew rapidly.

After the war, immigrants from Ireland, Germany, and the Scandinavian countries poured into Chicago. Crowded neighborhoods of factory workers living in small wooden cottages sprouted around the city. And Chicago continued to prosper. By 1870, it was the world's largest grain, livestock, and lumber market. Its population had grown to nearly 300,000.

As the world's lumber capital, Chicago was fittingly built almost entirely of wood. Houses, churches, stores, grain elevators, factories, and even streets were nearly all made of wood.

The Great Chicago Fire. The summer of 1871 was unusually dry in Chicago. Only about one-fourth of the normal amount of rain fell between July and October. With all its wooden buildings, Chicago was like kindling. Then on the evening of Oct. 8, 1871, a fire started on the Southwest Side of the city.

Historians believe the fire started in a barn owned by Mrs. Patrick O'Leary. According to legend, a cow kicked over a lighted lantern in the barn. Fanned by strong winds, the flames raced north and east through the city. They leaped across the river and chased panic-stricken families fleeing north toward Lincoln Park. Hundreds of other families fled into the chilly waters of the lake. The fire raged for more than 24 hours. It wiped out the downtown area and most North Side homes. It killed at least 300 people and left 90,000 homeless. The fire also destroyed millions of dollars worth of property.

A city reborn. Chicago rose from the ruins of the fire and became one of the world's great cities. The opportunity to rebuild Chicago attracted many of the nation's finest architects, such as William Le Baron Jenney, Louis Sullivan, Daniel H. Burnham, John W. Root, and the German-born Dankmar Adler. The 10-story Home Insurance Building, often considered the world's first metal-framed skyscraper, was erected in Chicago. The structure, designed by Jenney, was completed in 1885. Chicago became the nation's architectural capital.

Chicago's industry skyrocketed along with its buildings. More and more workers, many of them immigrants, crowded into the city. Many lived in hurriedly constructed, barrackslike housing. Much of it quickly turned into slums. Working conditions were miserable. Factory workers protested, and a wave of strikes erupted. In 1877, Chicago was the center of a violent national railroad strike. In 1886, a riot developed after a bomb exploded during a workers' rally at Haymarket Square, a produce center west of downtown. At least seven policemen and one civilian died. See **Haymarket Riot**.

Many in Chicago began to escape the problems of the city by moving to the suburbs. Others tried to aid the suffering poor. In 1889, Hull House, one of the first settlement houses in the United States, opened in Chicago. Jane Addams and Ellen Starr founded it to help immigrant workers adjust to life in the city. See **Hull House**.

By 1890, Chicago had become the second largest city in the United States. Only New York City had more people. More than a million people lived in Chicago. Nearly 80 percent of them were European immigrants or the children of immigrants.

In 1893, the World's Columbian Exposition opened in Jackson Park. This elaborate fair observed the 400th anniversary of the arrival of Christopher Columbus in the New World. But Chicago also staged the fair to draw attention to the city's accomplishments. The fair's chief architect was Daniel H. Burnham. He produced a comprehensive Plan of Chicago in 1909. His dream of a lakefront protected by artificial islands was only partly realized.

Chicagoans bragged so much about the Columbian Exposition that Charles A. Dana, a New York City newspaper editor, made the *Windy City* a popular nickname for Chicago. The howling gusts that blow across the city from Lake Michigan have helped make the nickname last. In the 1950's, Chicago received the nickname *Second City* because it ranked second to New York City in population and other areas.

The Columbian Exposition also attracted the first of many talented writers who would be drawn to the city in the years before 1920. These included poets Carl Sandburg and Edgar Lee Masters and the writers Hamlin Garland, Theodore Dreiser, and Sherwood Anderson. Harriet Monroe founded *Poetry,* the first magazine devoted entirely to verse. Chicago hosted experimental theater and was home to a thriving movie industry.

Tragedy and racial conflict. The years of civic pride that began with the Columbian Exposition were marred by tragedy. In 1903, a fire in the Iroquois Theater took 575 lives. In 1915, the tour boat *Eastland* sank in the Chicago River, and 812 people drowned.

Chicago History Museum

The World's Columbian Exposition was held in Chicago in 1893 to honor Columbus's arrival in America. Visitors marveled at the fair's pools, fountains, and gleaming white buildings.

During World War I (1914-1918), Chicago's industries expanded to meet wartime needs. Thousands of African Americans from the South moved to Chicago to work in its war industries. Prevented from living in most sections of the city, they crowded into an old run-down area on the South Side. On July 27, 1919, a black youth swimming off the 27th Street beach drifted into waters opposite an unofficially "whites only" part of the beach. When he tried to swim ashore, whites stoned him and he drowned. The incident started the biggest race riot in Chicago history. It raged for four days and left 23 blacks and 15 whites dead. More than 500 other people were injured, and about 1,000 homes were burned.

The Roaring Twenties were years of prosperity that saw working-class families build more than 125,000 bungalow houses. Railroad suburbs expanded greatly. But the decade also produced violence that would stain the city's reputation for many years to come.

The 18th Amendment to the Constitution of the United States, which went into effect in 1920, prohibited the manufacture and sale of alcoholic beverages. But many people drank illegally in clubs called *speakeasies.* Gangsters in Chicago, including Al Capone, took over the illegal distribution of liquor, a practice called *bootlegging.* Gangs fought for control of bootlegging, gambling, and other illegal activities. Gangland murders became common. The violence reached its peak in the St. Valentine's Day Massacre of 1929. Four gangsters disguised as policemen shot down seven members of a rival gang.

But the Roaring Twenties were also creative years. The trumpeter Louis Armstrong and other jazz musicians came from New Orleans. The jazz clarinetist Benny Goodman, who learned to play in Hull House, formed his first band in Chicago. The first of the great blues musicians, who would give voice to the Great Depression, arrived just as the economy was beginning to weaken.

Ending a century of progress. The Great Depression of the 1930's brought business failure and unemployment to Chicago. In spite of these problems, the city opened the Century of Progress Exposition in 1933. Chicago staged the gigantic fair to celebrate the 100th anniversary of its incorporation as a town. The exposition, held on the lakefront, featured outstanding exhibits of science and industry. It brought business to the city during the depths of the Depression.

The mid-1900's. During World War II (1939-1945), Chicago became the site of one of the most important events in world history. On Dec. 2, 1942, the first nuclear chain reaction was set off at the University of Chicago. It led to the development of the atomic bomb and of nuclear energy for peaceful uses.

Many giant public construction projects were started in Chicago after the war, and the civic building boom continued into the early 1970's. New projects included four expressways, two huge water filtration plants, the McCormick Place convention and exposition center, O'Hare Airport, and the Richard J. Daley Civic Center. Urban renewal replaced huge slum areas with a mixture of roads, public housing, and middle-income apartments.

A building boom also took place in the downtown area and along the North Side lakefront. The John Hancock Center, the First National Bank Building, the Sears Tower, the Standard Oil Building (now the Aon Center), and many apartment buildings were erected.

While the downtown area boomed with new construction in the 1960's, many neighborhoods faltered when their residents' paychecks disappeared. Once a leader in virtually every industrial category, Chicago lost thousands of jobs to foreign competition. Many factories moved to areas where land was cheaper. Many workers, who also sought less crime and better schools, left the city. Chicago was left with an increasing proportion of poorly skilled and poorly educated people. Most of these people were minorities who had been attracted by the prospect of work that no longer existed.

The response to these and earlier changes took several forms. From the 1930's to the 1970's, for example, Chicago writers focused on the troubles of everyday people. Writers who gained fame include novelists Nelson Algren, Saul Bellow, James T. Farrell, and Richard Wright; journalists Mike Royko and Studs Terkel; and poet Gwendolyn Brooks.

In the late 1960's, frustration over segregation and the Vietnam War turned to violence. In April 1968, riots broke out on the West Side following the assassination of the black civil rights leader Martin Luther King, Jr. Eleven people were killed, and damage was estimated at $10 million. After the riots, some efforts were begun to improve housing and health services for poor families. But the great difference in income levels and living conditions between most blacks and most whites remained. The 1968 Democratic National Convention was held in Chicago in August. During the convention, clashes between Vietnam War protesters and police focused national attention on the city.

Political developments in the late 1900's. From 1931 to 1979, Chicago was ruled by the Cook County Democratic Organization. The organization was started during the Great Depression by Mayor Anton Cermak and was continued by mayors Edward Kelly, who served from 1933 to 1947, and Martin Kennelly, who served from 1947 to 1955. The organization reached its peak of power under Richard J. Daley, who became its chair in 1953. Elected to the first of his six mayoral terms in 1955, Daley used both offices to control who ran on the Democratic ticket and who was elected to the city council. As head of such a powerful urban political machine, Daley earned the title "last of the big-city bosses."

The organization quickly declined after Daley's death in 1976. A series of federal court decisions and a number of union contracts protecting city employees reduced the mayor's power to hire and fire. Many aldermen no longer felt they had to take direction from Daley's successor, Michael Bilandic.

In 1979, Jane M. Byrne, a former city official and protégé of Daley's, became the first woman mayor of Chicago. Byrne received 82 percent of the vote—the highest percentage ever won in a Chicago mayoral election. But Byrne would serve only one term.

In the 1983 mayoral primary, African American community leaders organized a massive voter registration drive and campaign effort that gave the Democratic nomination to Harold Washington, a black and a member of the United States House of Representatives. Washington narrowly defeated his Republican opponent and became Chicago's first black mayor. The voters reelected Washington in April 1987, but he died of a heart attack in November of that year. The City Council then elected Eugene Sawyer, a black council member, acting mayor.

In 1989, special elections were held to fill out Washington's term. Richard M. Daley, a son of former mayor Richard J. Daley, defeated Sawyer for the Democratic nomination. In the general election, voters elected Daley mayor. Daley was reelected in the regular mayoral elections in 1991, 1995, 1999, and 2003.

Dealing with aging infrastructure. Like all cities, Chicago has had to face the issue of upgrading the older parts of its *infrastructure,* including buildings and transportation systems. In April 1992, millions of gallons of water from the Chicago River poured through a hole in the wall of a 90-year-old freight tunnel system under the Loop. The flooding caused millions of dollars of damage. But the event drew attention to the potential of the tunnels for housing telecommunications lines.

Other developments were more gradual. The Chicago Housing Authority replaced thousands of decaying high-rise public housing units with units in smaller buildings in mixed-income developments. The Chicago Transit Authority also upgraded, replaced, or extended miles of aging elevated and subway lines. In 1993, the CTA added a new line to Midway Airport. The Chicago Public Schools system rebuilt or remodeled hundreds of buildings as part of an effort to upgrade the learning environment of its pupils.

In the private sector, thousands of older apartment buildings have been renovated, and hundreds of old factory buildings have been razed or converted to residential lofts. Many renovated factory buildings hold new companies that are part of Chicago's successful transition from manufacturing to a new service economy based on research, corporate administration, and the convention and tourism business.

New construction. Despite Chicago's problems, developments continue to keep it an appealing, lively, and economically strong city. In 1991, the Harold Washington Library Center was completed at the south end of downtown. In the early 1990's, two modern middle-class residential sections—Printer's Row and Dearborn Park—were completed nearby. The northern downtown area has experienced much development since completion of the popular Water Tower Place shopping mall in 1976. The mall complex, which includes a hotel and apartments, led to the establishment of other retail businesses and hotels in the area. Since the mid-1970's, more than one hundred other major building projects have altered the skyline. They are a testament to the continued attractiveness of the city as a place to live, do business, and seek entertainment and education. Perry R. Duis

Related articles in *World Book* include:

Biographies

Alinsky, Saul David
Burnham, Daniel H.
Byrne, Jane M.
Capone, Al
Daley, Richard J.
Du Sable, Jean Baptiste P.
Field, Marshall, I
Jolliet, Louis
Marquette, Jacques
Ness, Eliot
Palmer, Potter
Sandburg, Carl
Thompson, William H.
Washington, Harold

Buildings and institutions

Art Institute of Chicago
Field Museum
Hull House
Museum of Science and Industry
Sears Tower

History

Fort Dearborn
Haymarket Riot
Jazz (The 1920's)
Ramp

Other related articles

Architecture (Early modern architecture in America)
Illinois (pictures)
Jahn, Helmut (picture)
Skyscraper (with picture)
Taft, Lorado (picture)
Water (illustration: How Chicago treats its water)

Outline

I. The city
A. Downtown Chicago
B. The North Side
C. The West Side
D. The South Side
E. Metropolitan area

II. People
A. Ethnic groups
B. Housing
C. Education
D. Sports and recreation
E. Social problems

III. Cultural life and places to visit
A. The arts
B. Architecture
C. Museums
D. Libraries
E. Places to visit

IV. Economy
A. Service industries
B. Industry
C. Trade
D. Finance
E. Transportation
F. Communications

V. Government

VI. History

Questions

Why is Chicago called the *Windy City?*
What is unusual about the flow of the Chicago River?
How does Chicago rank in population among U.S. cities?
What was the great development of the Chicago School of architecture?
What important event in world history took place at the University of Chicago in 1942?
Where did the Great Chicago Fire start?
How has the economy of the Chicago area changed in recent decades?
What are some of Chicago's major problems?
What kind of reputation did Chicago gain in the 1920's?
What is the Loop? The Gold Coast? The Magnificent Mile?

Additional resources

Miller, Donald L. *City of the Century.* Simon & Schuster, 1996.
Schnedler, Jack, and others. *Chicago.* 3rd ed. Random Hse., 2001.
Stein, R. Conrad. *Chicago.* Children's Pr., 1997. Younger readers.

Chicago, Art Institute of. See **Art Institute of Chicago.**

Chicago, Judy (1939-), is an American sculptor and writer who became a leader in the feminist art movement. Chicago creates large multimedia projects that celebrate the unique qualities she sees in womankind. She is best known for her large sculpture called *The Dinner Party* (1974-1979). The work consists of a triangular dinner table, each side 48 feet (14.6 meters) long. *The Dinner Party* integrates traditional women's crafts, such as weaving and embroidery, with ceramics. On the table are 39 place settings that honor famous women throughout history, both real and mythical. More than 400 artists contributed to the project. See **Sculpture** (The importance of sculpture [picture]).

Chicago has also created other major works. *The Birth Project* (1980-1985) explores the essential female experience of childbirth through images she designed for needlework. *The Holocaust Project* (1984-1993) deals with hatred and violence against Jews. The project consists of various media, including photography, painting, tapestry, and stained glass.

In addition to sculpture, Chicago has advanced her

feminist views through her writings. They include the autobiographies *Through the Flower: My Struggle as a Woman Artist* (1975, revised 1982 and 1993) and *Beyond the Flower: The Autobiography of a Feminist Artist* (1996).

Chicago was born on July 20, 1939, in Chicago. Her original name was Judy Cohen. She changed it legally in 1970 to rid herself "of all names imposed upon her through male social dominance." Joseph F. Lamb

Chicago, University of, is a leading private educational and research institution in Chicago. The university's campus lies on both sides of the Midway Plaisance. This wide street served as one of the main avenues of the World's Columbian Exposition of 1893. Unlike most American universities, the University of Chicago began as a full university. It provided facilities for research and graduate study as well as undergraduate education. The university became famous for its experiments to improve higher education in the United States. It is also known as the birthplace of nuclear energy.

Educational program. The University of Chicago is coeducational. The undergraduate school is called the College. Its students divide their study about equally between specialized courses and general education in broad fields of knowledge. Graduate divisions provide advanced instruction in the biological sciences, humanities, physical sciences, and social sciences. Graduate schools of business, divinity, law, medicine, public policy studies, and social service administration offer professional training. The university also has a continuing education program for adults. Students at the University of Chicago may qualify for B.A., B.S., M.A., M.S., and Ph.D. degrees and for professional degrees.

Research program. The university ranks as a leading research center in the humanities and in the physical, biological, and social sciences. It played an important part in developing the atomic bomb during World War II. Experiments there resulted in the first artificially produced nuclear chain reaction on Dec. 2, 1942. Enrico Fermi, then professor of physics at the university, and a team of scientists conducted this research. After the war, the university established the Enrico Fermi Institute for research in high-energy physics. The university also operates the Argonne National Laboratory near Lemont, Illinois, for the U.S. Department of Energy, and the Yerkes Observatory in Williams Bay, Wisconsin. In 2005, the university announced plans to sell Yerkes Observatory.

The university's medical school, biological science laboratories, hospitals, and clinics have made it an important center for research in biochemistry, cardiology, endocrinology, genetics, pathology, radiology, and virology. University scientists do research on AIDS, cancer, diabetes, and related problems. The John Crerar Library, an independent research library on the campus, owns an excellent collection of books, periodicals, and visual materials on science, engineering, and medicine.

In 1892, Chicago became the first university to establish a department of sociology. Many outstanding American sociologists have taught at the university. Two of them—Albion W. Small and George E. Vincent—wrote the first textbook on sociology in 1894. Sophonisba Breckinridge, a pioneer teacher of social work, taught at the university for 38 years and helped establish its School of Social Service Administration. Leading American economists who have taught at the university include Thorstein Veblen and Milton Friedman. Veblen's book *The Theory of the Leisure Class* (1899) has become required reading for almost every student of economics. Friedman's theories in two of his books, *Capitalism and Freedom* (1962) and *A Monetary History of the United States, 1867-1960* (1963), have sparked widespread debate among economists.

Campus laboratory schools conduct precollegiate education at nursery, elementary, and high school levels. The American philosopher John Dewey established the laboratory schools in 1896. The Oriental Institute, which was founded by James H. Breasted in 1919, conducts research on the ancient Near East.

History. The University of Chicago was founded in 1891 and opened for classes on Oct. 1, 1892. Gifts to the university included $35 million contributed by John D. Rockefeller during his lifetime.

William Rainey Harper, the university's first president, planned it as a model university. His first faculty included eight former college presidents. Harper introduced the quarter system, which divides the calendar year into four academic sessions. He insisted that women receive equal educational and teaching opportunities at the university. Harper established an extension division as a main division of the university and developed the first practical correspondence course in the United States. In 1892, he started the University of Chicago Press, now one of the nation's largest academic publishers.

Critically reviewed by the University of Chicago

Related articles in *World Book* include:

Argonne National Laboratory	Harper, William Rainey
Breasted, James Henry	Hutchins, Robert Maynard
Breckinridge, Sophonisba	Veblen, Thorstein
Friedman, Milton	Yerkes Observatory

Chicago Sanitary and Ship Canal connects Lake Michigan with the Des Plaines River by way of the Chicago River. The canal, sometimes called the Chicago Drainage Canal, carries Chicago's treated sewage into the Des Plaines River, near Lockport, Illinois. The Des Plaines flows southwest and joins the Illinois River.

The Mississippi River receives the Illinois River and carries its waters on to the Gulf of Mexico. Before completion of the canal in 1900, Chicago sewage was dumped into Lake Michigan. This caused pollution of water used in the city water system.

The natural course of the Chicago River is eastward, through downtown Chicago into Lake Michigan. Engineers made the river flow westward through the Drainage Canal. The river is now an outlet instead of an inlet of Lake Michigan. It was the first river in the world to flow away from its mouth.

Chicago's sewage is treated in plants of the Metropolitan Water Reclamation District of Greater Chicago, then turned into the channel. The Chicago Sanitary and Ship Canal is 30 miles (48 kilometers) long, 202 feet (62 meters) wide, and 24 feet (7.3 meters) deep. The rate of flow is controlled by sluice gates at Chicago Harbor and at the Calumet River's O'Brien Lock, and by pumps at Wilmette Harbor.

The canal was built between 1892 and 1900. It forms a link in the Illinois Waterway, a part of the Lakes-to-Gulf Waterway. Critically reviewed by the Metropolitan Water Reclamation District of Greater Chicago

See also **Canal**.

Chicanos. See **Hispanic Americans.**

Chichén Itzá, *chee CHEHN eet SAH,* was the most powerful city of the Maya Indians between about A.D. 900 and about A.D. 1200. It was built on the Yucatán Peninsula in what is now Mexico. For location, see **Maya** (map: The land of the Maya).

Chichén dominated Yucatán through both military strength and control of important trade routes. In the 800's, it replaced Tikal, another Maya city, as a major destination of trade routes that linked Yucatán with central Mexico. Chichén began weakening in the 1000's or 1100's as Mayapán and other nearby Maya cities became more prominent and competitive.

Some scholars believe Chichén was dominated in part by a group of Maya who had adopted some of the cultural characteristics of the Toltec and other Indians of central Mexico. These Maya built an immense plaza at the center of Chichén. They also constructed the largest building there, a tall limestone pyramid with a temple on top. They dedicated the pyramid to Kukulkan, a feathered serpent god called Quetzalcóatl in central Mexico. Other structures on the plaza included raised ceremonial platforms, a public steam bath, and a huge ball court. Chichén also had an observatory from which astronomers studied the stars and other heavenly bodies. Today, the city's ruins are a major archaeological site and tourist attraction. Payson Sheets

Chichester, *CHIHCH ihs tur,* **Sir Francis** (1901-1972), a British adventurer, made long-distance boat and airplane voyages. In August 1966, he sailed alone from England to Australia in his 53-foot (16-meter) yacht, *Gipsy Moth IV.* He returned to England in May 1967, passing through the dangerous seas around Cape Horn.

Chichester's other long-distance journeys included one of the first solo flights from England to Australia, in 1929; and the first east-west flight across the Tasman Sea between New Zealand and Australia, in 1931. He won the first solo sailing race across the Atlantic in 1960. He was born on Sept. 1, 1901, in Shirwell, England.

Chickadee is the name of seven species of small, sociable birds that live in woodlands of North America. Most adult chickadees measure from 4 to 6 inches (10 to 15 centimeters) long.

The most common species, the *black-capped chickadee,* inhabits Canada and the northern United States, including Alaska. It has a black head and throat, white cheeks, and a gray back. The belly is whitish, and the tail is black with white outer feathers. The word *chickadee* comes from the black-capped chickadee's call, which sounds like *chick-a-dee-dee-dee.* The song consists of several whistled notes that descend in pitch. The *Carolina chickadee* looks like the black-capped chickadee but is smaller. It lives chiefly in the southeastern United States. The *boreal chickadee* inhabits New England, Alaska, and Canada. It has a brown head and back.

Most chickadees nest in holes in tree trunks. They line the bottom of the nest with plant fibers, fur, feathers, and other soft materials. These birds feed mainly on insects and spiders. They hang upside down from a branch using their strong legs, and they grab their prey with swift, acrobatic movements. Chickadees also eat some seeds and berries. They often hide their seeds under bark and return later to retrieve them.

Chickadees generally stay in the same area for the

© Leonard Lee Rue III

The black-capped chickadee lives in North America.

winter. Two or more chickadees may keep warm on cold nights by roosting together in an old nest. In the spring, female chickadees usually lay six to eight eggs.

Chickadees are often seen in yards and gardens. They readily make use of birdhouses, nest boxes, and feeding stations provided by people. Sandra L. Vehrencamp

Scientific classification. Chickadees belong to the titmouse family, Paridae. The scientific name of the black-capped chickadee is *Poecile atricapillus.* The Carolina chickadee is *P. carolinensis,* and the boreal chickadee is *P. hudsonicus.*

See also **Bird** (table: State and provincial birds; picture: Birds' eggs); **Titmouse.**

Chickasaw Indians are a tribe that originally lived in the Southern United States. Their territory included northern Mississippi, northwestern Alabama, and western Tennessee and Kentucky. In the 1830's, the U.S. government relocated the tribe in what is now Oklahoma.

The Chickasaw lived in several villages of small, one-room log cabins. Each village was headed by a chief. The people supported themselves by farming, fishing, hunting, and trading with neighboring tribes.

The Spanish explorer Hernando de Soto was the first white person to come into contact with the Chickasaw. He and his group spent the winter of 1540-1541 in one of their villages while searching for gold. Before leaving, de Soto demanded that some of the Chickasaw join him to help carry supplies. The Indians became angry and attacked de Soto's expedition, killing about 12 of his men.

The Chickasaw were fierce warriors. They helped Britain fight France and Spain for control of what is now the Southeastern United States. They also supported the British in the Revolutionary War (1775-1783). In the Civil War (1861-1865), the tribe fought for the Confederacy.

In 1837, the government moved the Chickasaw west to the Indian Territory to make room for more white settlement in the South. Thousands of Indians died on the forced march to the Territory. In 1907, the Chickasaw territory became part of the new state of Oklahoma.

According to the 2000 census, there are about 21,000 Chickasaw. About 12,600 people of Chickasaw descent live in Oklahoma. A tribal government elected by the Chickasaw helps provide for the general welfare of the tribe. Arrell Morgan Gibson

See also **Five Civilized Tribes; Indian Territory.**

J. Mechling

New Hampshire chickens, *shown here,* are kept in small flocks on many farms. These chickens provide farm families with both eggs and meat.

Chicken

Chicken is a bird that is raised for its meat and eggs. There are probably more chickens than any other single kind of bird, and they live throughout the world.

Chickens—like other birds—have feathers and wings. But chickens also have a number of special growths on their bodies that most other birds do not have. These growths include the red *comb* on top of the head and the red *wattles* that hang beneath the beak.

Chicken meat and eggs are a good source of *protein.* Protein is a chemical compound that is necessary for a healthy diet. Chicken meat is also low in fat. However, chicken eggs contain a large amount of a fatty substance called *cholesterol.* Many physicians believe that too much cholesterol in a person's diet may contribute to heart disease (see **Cholesterol**).

Raising chickens for meat and eggs is a major industry in many countries, including Brazil, China, India, Japan, Mexico, and the United States. The world's people eat about 145 billion pounds (66 billion kilograms) of chicken meat each year. Hens produce about 800 billion eggs every year.

Some people raise chickens as a hobby. They breed them for body size, and for the color and color pattern of the feathers. The birds are exhibited at fairs and livestock shows. People sometimes use feathers from the chicken's neck and back to make *flies* (special hooks) for fishing. In addition, scientists may use chickens for research in medicine and other fields. Chicken eggs are used to make many *vaccines,* which protect human beings and animals from diseases.

B. M. Hargis, the contributor of this article, is Director of the Poultry Health Laboratory at the University of Arkansas.

The body of a chicken

Adult chickens range in weight from about 1.1 pounds (0.5 kilogram) to more than 11 pounds (5 kilograms). Feathers cover most of the body of a chicken, except for the *shanks* (lower legs) and feet, which have scales. The feathers help the chicken to keep warm in cold weather. Wings enable chickens to fly. However, they can fly only a few hundred feet or meters at a time. They fly mainly to escape enemies and to reach perches on which to roost at night.

The comb and wattles of chickens are fleshy structures. They are bright red because they have a rich blood supply. Earlobes grow on the sides of the head. They may be red or white, depending on the breed of chicken. The comb, wattles, and earlobes may help individual chickens recognize each other and select mates. They may also help chickens keep cool.

Chickens have claws on their feet. Males also have a bony structure called a *spur* on each leg. Chickens use their claws, spurs, and beak as a defense against enemies, and to dig in the soil for insects and seeds to eat. Chickens have a keen sense of sight and hearing, but their ability to taste and smell is poor compared with that of human beings. People can train chickens to perform certain simple acts in return for food.

Certain internal organs of chickens are specialized. For example, the throat contains a pouch, called a *crop.* The crop stores food and slowly passes it to the stomach for digestion. After the food has been mixed with digestive juices, it enters a muscular part of the stomach called the *gizzard.* The gizzard contains particles of sand or stone that the chicken has swallowed. These particles and the movement of the walls of the gizzard grind the food into fine pieces.

Kinds of chickens

Chickens are grouped according to *class, breed,* and *variety.* Most classes are named for the area where the chickens were first developed. A breed consists of chickens within a class that all have a similar body type. Each variety is made up of chickens within a breed that have a certain combination of features in common. These features include the type of comb, skin color, and feather color and pattern.

There are four basic kinds of combs—the *single comb; pea comb; rose comb;* and *cushion comb,* or *walnut comb.* The single comb is a single blade with several points on top. The pea comb has three rows of points. Both the rose comb and the cushion comb are fairly compact structures that do not have points. Some breeds of chickens have unusual and characteristic combs, such as the *V-shaped, buttercup,* and *strawberry.*

Feathers grow in a variety of colors and patterns. White, *buff* (gold), brown, red, and black are common colors. *Barred* feathers have bars of black separated by white or gold coloring. *Mottled* feathers are black with white tips. *Spangled* feathers are gold or white with dark tips. Some birds have a bunch of feathers on the head, called a *crest.* Certain crested breeds also have a *muff*—a thick growth of feathers on the side of the face—or a *beard*—a bunch of feathers under the throat.

American class chickens have a medium-sized body, red earlobes, and white to yellow skin. All the breeds lay brown eggs, except for the Lamona and Holland, whose eggs are white. Common breeds in the American class include the Plymouth Rock, Rhode Island Red, New Hampshire, and Delaware. Most breeds of the American class were developed during the 1800's or the early 1900's, by crossing chickens from the Mediterranean, English, and Asiatic classes.

Asiatic class chickens are large birds with feathers on their shanks and feet. The three Asiatic breeds—Brahmas, Cochins, and Langshans—have red earlobes and lay eggs with brown eggshells. Cochins and Brahmas have yellow skin. Langshans have white skin. The Asiatic breeds are raised mainly for show purposes.

English class chickens. Most breeds in the English class are hearty birds that were developed for the production of eggs and meat. All breeds of the English class have red earlobes, and all except the Cornish have white skin. Only the Dorking and the Redcap lay white eggs.

Mediterranean class chickens. Most chickens in the Mediterranean class are light in weight. They have white earlobes, and their skin is white or yellow. They are bred for egg production, and all breeds lay white eggs. Some breeds, such as the Minorca, are heavy birds and lay large eggs. The most important breeds of this class originally came from Italy and Spain. The class includes the Leghorn, Ancona, and Buttercup breeds.

Other classes. There are many other classes that include only one or two breeds. Some of the most colorful breeds are the Houdan and Polish, which have crests on top of their heads and mottled feathers. Frizzle fowl have curled feathers. Silkies have long slender feathers and are the only breed with black skin. The Hamburg

Parts of a chicken Chickens, like other birds, have wings and feathers. However, chickens have several body parts that other birds lack. These parts include the fleshy *combs* atop their heads, and the pouchlike *wattles* that hang from their beaks. Males have hard bony growths called *spurs* on their legs.

WORLD BOOK illustrations by Patricia Wynne

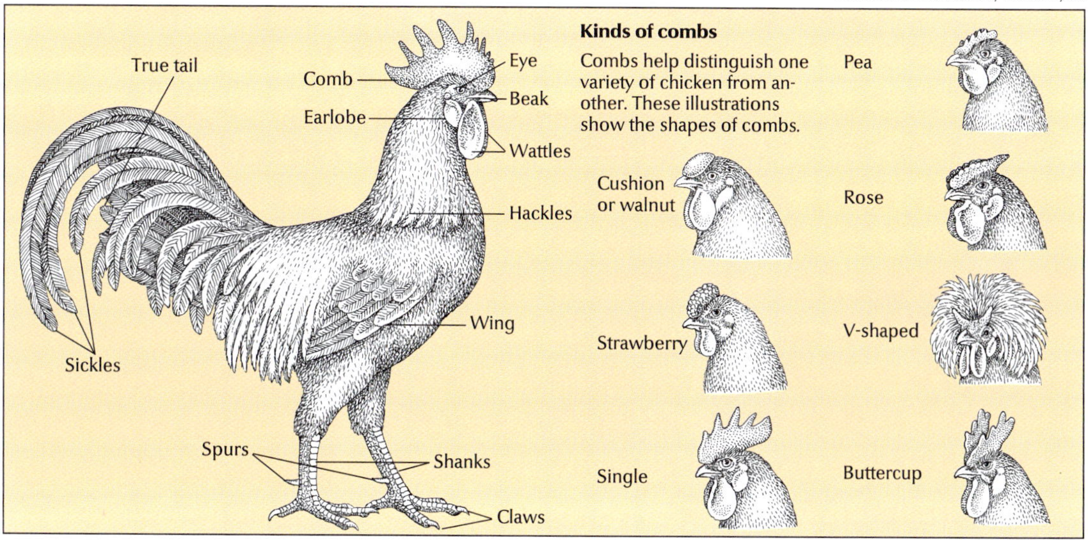

Some kinds of chickens

Grant Heilman

White Leghorn rooster

Grant Heilman

Rhode Island Red hen

Grant Heilman

Barred Plymouth Rock hen

Grant Heilman

Old English black-breasted red game rooster

Poultry World, London

Silver-spangled Hamburg hen

Shostal

Golden Sebright bantam rooster

Grant Heilman

Bearded mille fleur hen

has a rose comb with a long point. Many chickens are also bred in *bantam* (miniature) varieties. They are raised mainly as a hobby or for show purposes.

Chickens in the Game class are slender and stand up straighter than other breeds. They are active birds with strong legs and thighs, and are used in some parts of the world for cockfighting (see **Cockfighting**).

Commercially important breeds. Certain chicken breeds have become especially important for the commercial production of meat and eggs. Generally, chickens selected to produce meat have larger bodies than do chickens selected to produce eggs. Larger birds yield more meat but tend to produce fewer eggs than do smaller birds. The single-comb white Leghorn, from the Mediterranean class, is the most important white-egg producing breed in the world. Many of the breeds used for meat production are derived from a cross between the Plymouth Rock and the Cornish breeds.

The chicken industry

There are more than 16 billion chickens in the world. Some chickens live in small flocks, supplying eggs and meat to farm families or small local markets. However, most chickens are raised on large commercial farms that are specialized to produce either eggs or meat.

Breeding and hatching. On a commercial farm, eggs are removed from the laying house each day. The eggs are taken to other buildings, where they are allowed to develop in an *incubator.* An incubator is a large device in which the temperature, humidity, and air flow are carefully controlled (see **Incubator**).

The *embryo* (unborn chick) develops rapidly inside the eggshell. It uses the egg yolk, egg white, and eggshell as its source of nourishment. After about 18 days of incubation, the eggs are placed on hatching trays in the incubator. The trays allow more room for the chicks to hatch. On the 21st day of incubation, the chicks hatch, using their beaks to break through the eggshell. Their damp bodies dry quickly, leaving them covered with short, fluffy feathers called *down.* Newly hatched chicks can walk, see, eat, and drink.

After hatching, chicks sometimes are sorted according to sex. Then they are vaccinated. For chicks selected to produce eggs, the tip of the beak is removed to keep the chicks from pecking each other. The chicks are then placed in specially designed boxes and shipped to the farms where they will be raised.

Raising chicks. Chicks that will be used for egg production are raised in wire cages or in pens with straw, wood shavings, or other absorbent material on the floor. Chickens raised for meat are kept only in pens. During the first few weeks of life, chicks require a warm environment. The temperature in a chick house may be as high as 95 °F (35 °C) for the first week. The chicks are fed mixed feeds made of ground grains, plant by-products, meat scraps, and vitamin and mineral supplements. They are given vaccines to protect them from diseases.

Producing eggs. Only eggs that have been fertilized by mating produce chicks. However, female chickens do not need to mate to lay eggs.

Hens begin laying at about 20 weeks of age. The exact age depends on the lighting in the laying house, the breed, nutrition, and the occurrence of diseases. Farmers can control when a chicken begins laying eggs by using artificial lighting in the laying house. When lighting is used that imitates long or lengthening days, chickens will begin to lay their eggs at an earlier age. In addition, chickens lay an increased number of eggs when they are exposed to 14 to 16 hours of light per day.

Egg formation is a complicated process. It begins in an organ called the *ovary,* with the development of the yolk. After about nine days, the yolk is released from the ovary and enters a tube called the *oviduct.* The egg white, the *membranes* (thin layers of eggshell lining), and the shell itself are formed around the yolk as it passes through the oviduct. The addition of egg white and eggshell membranes occurs in only a few hours. But shell formation takes at least 20 hours.

Hens are generally kept for one year of egg production. The number of eggs a hen is able to lay decreases slowly during the year until the rate is too low to be profitable. Hens are then slaughtered for meat. In the United States, commercial laying hens produce an average of about 260 eggs each per year.

Some important breeds of chickens

Breeds	Comb	Egg color	Standard weight Cock (Lbs)	(Kg)	Hen (Lbs)	(Kg)
American class						
Buckeye	Pea	Brown	9	(4.1)	6 ½	(2.94)
Chantecler	Cushion	Brown	8 ½	(3.86)	6 ½	(2.94)
Delaware	Single	Brown	8 ½	(3.86)	6 ½	(2.94)
Dominique	Rose	Brown	7	(3.2)	5	(2.3)
Holland	Single	White	8 ½	(3.86)	6 ½	(2.94)
Java	Single	Brown	9 ½	(4.31)	7 ½	(3.40)
Jersey Giant	Single	Brown	13	(5.9)	10	(4.5)
Lamona	Single	White	8	(3.6)	6 ½	(2.94)
New Hampshire	Single	Brown	8 ½	(3.86)	6 ½	(2.94)
Plymouth Rock	Single	Brown	9 ½	(4.31)	7 ½	(3.40)
Rhode Island Red	Single or Rose	Brown	8 ½	(3.86)	6 ½	(2.94)
Rhode Island White	Rose	Brown	8 ½	(3.86)	6 ½	(2.94)
Wyandotte	Rose	Brown	8 ½	(3.86)	6 ½	(2.94)
Asiatic class						
Brahma	Pea	Brown	11 ½	(5.21)	9	(4.1)
Cochin	Single	Brown	11	(5.0)	8 ½	(3.9)
Langshan	Single	Brown	9 ½	(4.31)	7 ½	(3.40)
English class						
Australorp	Single	Tinted	8 ½	(3.86)	6 ½	(2.94)
Cornish	Pea	Brown	10 ½	(4.76)	8	(3.6)
Dorking	Single or Rose	White	8 ½	(3.86)	6 ½	(2.94)
Orpington	Single	Brown	10	(4.5)	8	(3.6)
Redcap	Rose	White	7 ½	(3.40)	6	(2.7)
Sussex	Single	Brown	9	(4.1)	7	(3.2)
Mediterranean class						
Ancona	Single or Rose	White	6	(2.7)	4 ½	(2.04)
Blue Andalusian	Single	White	7	(3.2)	5 ½	(2.49)
Buttercup	Buttercup	White	6 ½	(2.94)	5	(2.3)
Catalanas	Single	White	8	(3.6)	6	(2.7)
Leghorn	Single or Rose	White	6	(2.7)	4 ½	(2.04)
Minorca	Single or Rose	White	8 ½	(3.86)	7	(3.2)
Spanish	Single	White	8	(3.6)	6 ½	(2.94)

The chicken industry

Most commercial chicken farms specialize in producing either eggs or meat. Many are huge, highly automated concerns. Egg-producing farms often have more than 1 million laying hens.

Grant Heilman

John Colwell from Grant Heilman

John Colwell from Grant Heilman

Breeding chickens. Chicks are hatched in large incubators, *above left.* They are sorted by sex and examined for disease, *above center,* before they are shipped in crates to the farms where they will be raised, *above right.*

Grant Heilman

Grant Heilman

Producing eggs. Laying hens are kept in large laying houses, *above left.* The eggs are collected automatically by belts that run below the cages. Before the eggs are sold, workers grade them by viewing them over bright lights, *above right.* This process is called *candling.*

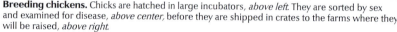

Grant Heilman

John Colwell from Grant Heilman

Charlton Photos

Producing broilers. Newborn chicks are first housed in a *brooder,* which keeps them warm and dry, *above left.* At about 7 weeks of age, broilers are shipped in crates to processing plants, *above center.* There, they are slaughtered, cleaned, and packed for marketing to consumers, *above right.*

Eggs are gathered each day. On farms that have large flocks housed in cages, eggs are collected automatically. Eggs roll down the sloping floors of the cages onto a moving belt that carries them to processing equipment. This equipment organizes the eggs into orderly rows and then washes, rinses, and dries them.

After the eggs have been cleaned, they are rolled over bright lights. The lights shine through the shell, enabling workers to see inside the egg. This process is called *candling.* Candling enables workers to detect eggs that are cracked or have blood spots or other imperfections. Workers also *grade* (rate) eggs by candling. After they have been inspected, the eggs are weighed, separated according to size, and packed in cartons or egg cases for shipping.

Producing meat. Most chicken meat comes from chickens called *broilers.* Broilers are often slaughtered at about 7 weeks of age, when they weigh as much as 4 ½ pounds (2 kilograms). Broilers feed on a rich, high-energy diet that makes them grow fast. Some meat also comes from *roasters* and *fowl.* Roasters grow to a heavier weight than broilers, usually 6 to 8 pounds (2.7 to 3.6 kilograms), before being killed. They usually reach this weight in less than 9 weeks. Fowl consist of breeder chickens that are killed after about a year.

After being slaughtered, the chicken is scalded and the feathers are removed. Then the body is *singed* (lightly burned) with a flame to rid it of tiny hairlike feathers. Shanks, feet, and head are removed, and the internal organs are taken out. Then, a government official inspects the chicken to make sure that it is clean and free from disease. After inspection, the chicken is washed and cooled in ice water or in a refrigeration unit. The chicken may be cut in half or into parts for marketing to consumers. Some poultry are further processed into chicken franks, chicken bologna, batter-dipped chicken pieces, deboned chicken pieces, and many other specialty items.

Leading broiler-producing states

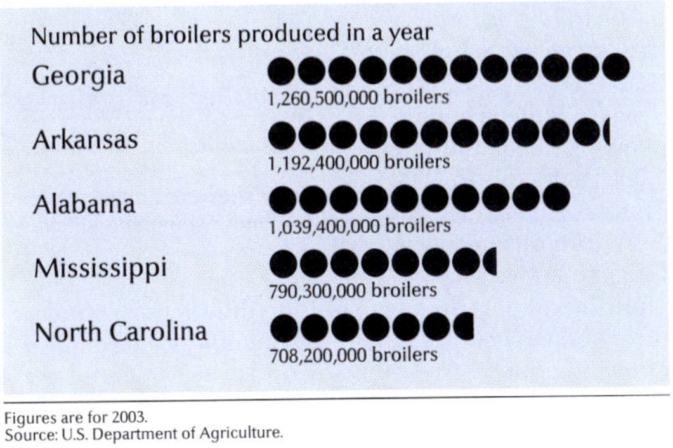

Figures are for 2003.
Source: U.S. Department of Agriculture.

Leading egg-producing states

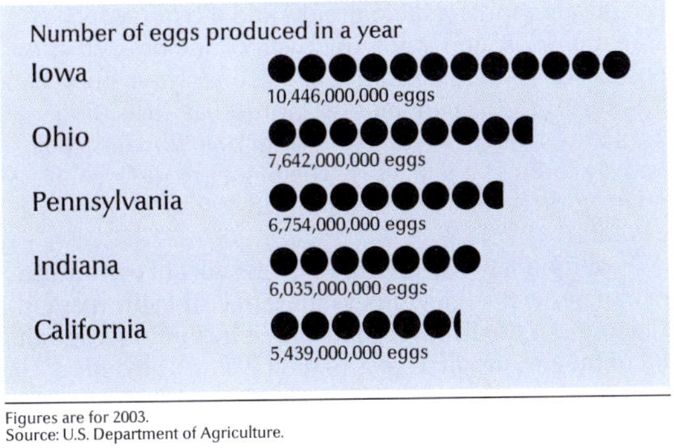

Figures are for 2003.
Source: U.S. Department of Agriculture.

History

Most experts believe that chickens developed from the *red junglefowl,* a species of wild fowl found in Southeast Asia. People probably began to tame the chicken in prehistoric times. They bred chickens for feather color, egg color, body size, and other characteristics. Records from China show that people raised chickens there as early as 1400 B.C. As chickens were brought into Europe, they were bred to produce many varieties.

During the 1500's, chickens were often taken on board ships as a source of food. Spanish explorers brought certain breeds to North America at that time. During the 1600's, English settlers brought English class chickens to North America. Several breeds in the American class were developed during the 1800's. At that time, the chicken industry consisted of small backyard flocks. Nearly all farms had some chickens that served as a source of meat and eggs for the farm family.

The poultry industry became important during the early 1900's. Many improvements were made in breeding techniques. By the mid-1900's, chickens had become the main product on many farms. Smaller farms still combine crop production and chicken or egg production. Most large poultry farms, however, do not raise crops or other animals. B. M. Hargis

Scientific classification. Chickens belong to the family Phasianidae. They are *Gallus domesticus.*

Related articles in *World Book* include:

Bantam	Gizzard
Cockfighting	Junglefowl
Egg	Poultry
Feather	Skeleton (picture)

Outline

I. The body of a chicken
II. Kinds of chickens
A. American class chickens
B. Asiatic class chickens
C. English class chickens
D. Mediterranean class chickens
E. Other classes
F. Commercially important breeds
III. The chicken industry
A. Breeding and hatching
B. Raising chicks
C. Producing eggs
D. Producing meat
IV. History

Questions

How are chickens like other birds? How are they different?
What are chickens raised for besides meat and eggs?
What are the comb and wattles?
What is an incubator?
How old do chickens have to be to lay eggs?
From what type of bird did the chicken originate?
What is the most important white-egg producing breed?
At what age are broiler chickens often slaughtered?

How does artificial lighting affect egg production?
What are the crop and gizzard used for?

Additional resources

Damerow, Gail. *Storey's Guide to Raising Chickens.* Storey Bks., 1995. *Your Chickens: A Kid's Guide to Raising and Showing.* Garden Way, 1993. Younger readers.
Rose, S. P. *Principles of Poultry Science.* CAB International, 1997.
Smith, Page, and Daniel, Charles. *The Chicken Book.* 1975. Reprint. Univ. of Ga. Pr., 2000.

Chickenpox, also called *varicella,* is a common, generally mild, contagious disease of children. The attack may be so mild that it is not recognized. However, chickenpox may kill children receiving radiation or drug treatment for leukemia or other forms of cancer.

The first sign of the disease is a kind of skin rash. Fever and a general feeling of discomfort often accompany the rash. Red blotches appear first on the skin of the back or chest. They change into pimples after a few hours. Then the pimples turn into blisters that enlarge and may become filled with a milky liquid. The blisters dry up in a few days and are covered with *scabs* (dried tissue). The skin rash appears in *crops* (groups). New blotches form while old ones change to blisters and dry up.

The *incubation period* (time between exposure to the disease and the appearance of symptoms) ranges from 11 to 20 days. Chickenpox is caused by the *varicella-zoster virus,* one of the herpesviruses. This same virus causes shingles (see **Shingles**). A child who has had chickenpox before usually does not get the disease again. Adults may get the disease if they did not have it as a child. However, they are more likely to develop shingles. In a small number of patients, secondary infections follow the chickenpox. An uncommon but serious complication is *Reye's syndrome* (see **Reye's syndrome**).

In otherwise healthy children, treatment is limited to relieving the symptoms, especially itching. Also, the patient's fingernails should be kept short and clean to lessen the risk of infection from scratching. Aspirin should not be given to children with chickenpox because of the possible link to Reye's syndrome. In 1995, the United States Food and Drug Administration approved a vaccine for chickenpox. Children should be vaccinated after they reach 12 months of age.

Neil R. Blacklow

See also **Disease** (table: Some communicable diseases).

Chickpea, also called *garbanzo, gar BAHN zoh,* is a plant grown for its nutritious, edible seeds. The chickpea plant is cultivated in India, the Middle East, northern Africa, southern Europe, Central America, and California. The plant grows approximately 1 to 2 feet (30 to 60 centimeters) tall. It bears rectangular pods that contain one or two chickpeas, which may be white, creamy yellow, red, brown, or nearly black.

WORLD BOOK illustrations by John F. Eggert
Chickpea

Chickpeas are high in carbohydrates and are a good source of protein. In India, people eat them roasted as a snack. They also use chickpeas to make a type of split pea soup called *dhal.* People in the Middle East and southern Europe make *hummus* by mashing cooked chickpeas and adding lemon juice, olive oil, garlic, and crushed sesame seeds. This food is used as a spread, dip, or sauce and is eaten with bread. Chickpeas also are used to make small cakes called *felafel,* which are deep-fried in oil. Kanti M. Rawal

Scientific classification. Chickpeas belong to the pea family, Leguminosae, or Fabaceae. They are *Cicer arietinum.*

Chicle, *CHIHK uhl* or *CHEEK lay,* is a naturally occurring latex obtained from the chicle tree, also known as the *sapodilla* or *sapota* tree. The tree is common to certain forests of Mexico, Guatemala, and Belize. Chicle was once widely used to make chewing gum. But today, only a few "natural chewing gum" products contain chicle.

Karl Kummels, Shostal
A worker taps a tree to obtain latex for making chicle.

Workers known as *chicleros* tap chicle trees by using machetes to cut a herringbone pattern in the bark. The latex drains down the cuts overnight and collects in a cloth bag at the tree base. The milky latex is boiled until it is thick. It is then cooled and formed into blocks for export. Chicleros must allow a tree to heal for more than three years before retapping it.

Maya Indians began chewing chicle more than 1,000 years ago. In 1869, Thomas Adams, Sr., an American businessman, began manufacturing chewing gum using chicle. During the 1940's, manufacturers began using synthetic substitutes as a base for chewing gum. Peter W. Alcorn

See also **Chewing gum** (History); **Gum tree; Sapodilla.**

Chicory, *CHIHK uhr ee,* is the name of several species of herbs that are native chiefly to Europe, northern Africa, and western Asia. The *common chicory,* or *succory,* is cultivated for its edible greens and its root, which is sometimes ground and mixed with coffee or used as a coffee substitute. The common chicory grows from 3 to $5\frac{1}{2}$ feet (91 to 168 centimeters) high. It has spreading branches, coarse leaves, and bright blue flower heads, and it produces a milky sap. The plant is widely cultivated in North America. In addition, chicory often grows as a weed.

Pure-food laws in the United States forbid the mixing of chicory with coffee unless the label is plainly marked. Chicory can be discovered in coffee by putting a spoonful of the mixture in a glass of cold water. The coffee will float on the surface. The chicory will separate from the coffee and color the water. David J. Keil

Scientific classification. Chicory plants belong to the composite family, Asteraceae or Compositae. The scientific name for the common chicory is *Cichorium intybus.*

Chief, Indian. See Indian, American.

Chief executive. See **President of the United States.**

Chief justice is the presiding judge of a court that has several judges, such as the Supreme Court of the United States. The chief justice presides over the court, assigns tasks to the members of the court, and is often in charge of general court administration. Although a chief justice has only one vote, the position presents an opportunity for leadership.

The president nominates the chief justice of the United States, and the Senate confirms the nomination. In many state courts, the judge who has served the longest time on the bench is designated as chief justice. In some states, the office is rotated. Jack M. Kress

See also **Supreme Court of the United States.**

Chief of staff. See **Joint Chiefs of Staff.**

Chigger, also called *jigger,* is the common name of two kinds of pests that attack human beings. One is the chigoe flea, and the other is the larva of a harvest mite. Only the latter lives in the United States.

The larva of the harvest mite is a tiny red creature with a body divided into two parts. It creeps into skin pores and hair follicles to inject saliva and to feed, and causes a rash and itching. The female chigoe digs into the flesh, causing a sore.

WORLD BOOK illustration by James Teason

Harvest mite chigger

The harvest mite is merely a nuisance in North America and Europe. But in East Asian countries and many Pacific islands, it is a serious danger because it carries scrub fever, a disease also known as Japanese river fever or *tsutsugamushi.* The parasitic larvae of the harvest mite usually get the disease from infected rodents. The mite keeps the disease during its nymphal and adult stages, and gives it to the larvae of the next generation. The larvae in turn pass it on to human beings. Harvest mites are common in the Midwest and the South. Edwin W. Minch

Scientific classification. The chigoe flea belongs to the jigger and sticktight family, Tungidae. Its scientific name is *Tunga penetrans.* Harvest mites (North American chiggers) make up the family Trombidiidae. They are *Trombicula alfreddugesi.*

See also **Mite.**

Chigoe. See **Chigger.**

Chihuahua, *chee WAH wah* (pop. 670,208), is an important city in northern Mexico and the capital of the state of Chihuahua. It lies about 780 miles (1,260 kilometers) northwest of Mexico City (see **Mexico** [political map]). The city has a mild climate. Large cattle ranches operate around Chihuahua. Facilities in the city process beef, milk, and cheese. Chihuahua also has plants that smelt copper, gold, lead, silver, and zinc mined from nearby mountains. Governor Antonio Deza y Ulloa of Nueva Vizcaya (now Chihuahua state) founded the city as San Francisco Cuellar in 1709. James D. Riley

Chihuahua, *chee WAH wah,* is the largest state in area in Mexico. It covers 94,571 square miles (244,938 square kilometers). Chihuahua shares its northern border with the United States (see **Mexico** [political map]). At the time of the 2000 census, the population was 3,047,867. The city of Chihuahua is the state capital.

Chihuahua is a major agricultural and mining state. Farmers there cultivate apples, cotton, and wheat. Ranchers raise cattle. Beef, cheese, and milk are important products. The state's mines yield copper, gold, silver, and zinc. In the late 1900's, manufacturing became more prominent in Chihuahua. Today, the state's largest city, Juárez, is a major industrial center. James D. Riley

See also **Chihuahua** (city); **Juárez.**

Chihuahua, *chee WAH wah,* is the smallest breed of dogs. Chihuahuas stand about 5 inches (13 centimeters) high at the shoulder and weigh from 1 to 6 pounds (0.5 to 2.7 kilograms). There are two varieties of chihuahuas, the smooth coat and the long coat. Chihuahuas may be almost any color with various markings. The dog is loyal to its owner and makes an ideal pet and companion.

The chihuahua is often referred to as the "royal dog of the Americas." It was developed in Mexico and is named for the Mexican state of Chihuahua. The dog is called a *chihuahueno* in Mexico. Some experts believe the chihuahua originated more than 500 years ago.

Critically reviewed by the Chihuahua Club of America

See also **Dog** (picture: Toy dogs).

WORLD BOOK photo

The chihuahua, like this long-coat variety, stands about 5 inches (13 centimeters) high. The breed developed in Mexico.

Chilblain, *CHIHL blayn,* is a condition in which the skin stings, itches, burns, and sometimes turns red. It affects particularly the skin of the feet. The principal cause is exposure to extreme cold, or to extreme cold and wet. The feet become sensitive to cold after one attack and easily suffer further attacks.

Chilblain usually may be prevented by protecting the feet with warm shoes and heavy socks during cold, wet weather. Regular exercise and massage help to improve the circulation in the area affected by chilblain.

John F. Waller

See also **Frostbite; Immersion foot.**

© Thinkstock/Getty Images

© The Image Bank/Getty Images

Daniel D. Miller, Tom Stack & Assoc.

Children of different ages vary in their social development. A toddler may be content to play alone, *top left*. By the early school years, many youngsters enjoy playing with other children, *right*. During the preteen-age years, friends play a major role in a child's life, *bottom left*.

Child

Child is a person between the ages of about 18 months and 10 to 12 years. Childhood is the period of development between *infancy* and *adolescence*. Infancy extends from birth to about 18 months of age. Adolescence begins at about 10 to 12 years and lasts until young adulthood. For information on development during infancy, see **Baby.** For information on development during adolescence, see **Adolescent.**

Childhood is a period of transformation that involves a variety of physical, psychological, and social processes. These processes largely determine the type of adult that a child will become. During childhood, most boys and girls nearly double in height and quadruple in weight. They also begin to develop sexually. But childhood involves far more than physical growth and development. It involves significant changes in a child's behavior, thought processes, emotions, and attitudes. Parents, *siblings* (brothers and sisters), and other family members traditionally play vital roles in guiding a child's development. But as childhood progresses, boys and girls become increasingly independent and responsible for their own well-being.

Cultures throughout the world differ in their attitudes, beliefs, and traditions relating to childhood. Some cultures, for instance, define *childhood* as the period that lasts from birth until sometime past the age of 20. Some of these cultures do not recognize infancy and adolescence as distinct stages of development. Cultures also differ in the skills, values, and personality traits that they seek to develop in children.

Every child is a unique individual, with his or her own talents, characteristics, personality, and background. Despite these differences, many of the basic stages, experiences, and challenges of childhood are similar throughout the world.

Donald Wertlieb, the contributor of this article, is Professor of Child Development at Tufts University.

The stages of childhood

Experts studying human development have used a variety of methods for dividing childhood into stages. Some experts separate childhood into stages based on changes in the ways children think or acquire skills. Others identify stages based on periods of major physical or social development.

This section examines childhood in three stages: (1) the toddler stage, (2) the preschool years, and (3) the school-age years. Within this framework, the section will discuss the major physical, social, and behavioral changes that take place throughout childhood. It will also follow the child's movement through the four stages of mental development identified by the Swiss psychologist Jean Piaget. Piaget's stages are (1) the *sensorimotor period,* (2) the *preoperational period,* (3) the *period of concrete operations,* and (4) the *period of formal operations.*

The toddler stage, or *toddlerhood,* marks the end of infancy and beginning of childhood. It lasts from about 18 months to 3 years of age. By the start of the toddler stage, most children can feed themselves, walk and run a short distance, and say a few meaningful words.

As they begin toddlerhood, children are still in the sensorimotor period, the first of Piaget's stages of mental development. During the sensorimotor period, children gain a basic knowledge of objects through their senses. They spend much of their time playing and experimenting with various actions and movements. For instance, a toddler might drop a toy to see how such an action impacts his or her surroundings.

Around the age of 2, children enter what Piaget called the preoperational period. During this period, which lasts until about age 7, children develop such skills as drawing and language ability. By 3 years of age, most children can link several words together to form fairly complete sentences. Their vocabulary during this period grows by about nine words a day.

Another major development during toddlerhood involves the child's awareness of himself or herself as an individual and as a member of a family. Most toddlers take comfort in their family connections and seek the approval of their parents and other adults. Outside of the family, toddlers' social relationships develop gradually, with some children more outgoing and engaging than others.

The preschool years extend from about 3 to 5 years of age. By this stage, the child's brain has grown to about 80 percent of its adult size. Preschoolers have a remarkable capacity for learning and constantly explore the world around them. The toddler stage and the preschool years belong to the period known as *early childhood.*

During the preschool years, children continue to advance through the preoperational period of mental development. They gradually develop their understanding of time, space, symbols, and other concepts. The use of such concepts enables children to engage in more sophisticated thought processes. Preschoolers learn new words every day, and their vocabulary grows to between 8,000 and 15,000 words by the time they are 6 years old. They also have significant improvements in motor development and hand-eye coordination.

Children at this stage begin to identify themselves with particular roles within the family and the community. They learn that there are certain *standards of behavior*—that is, things they should and should not do. Specific standards vary from culture to culture, but many are common throughout the world. Children are generally expected to be obedient, truthful, and respectful toward those around them. During the preschool years, children are also expected to develop control of their bowels and bladder, through a process called *toilet training.* In most societies, children learn the basic standards of behavior by the age of 5.

As early childhood progresses, children start building more fully developed social relationships. Preschoolers begin to recognize how they are similar to, or different from, other individuals. The play activities of toddlers are often solitary in nature, but preschoolers increasingly play with other children. Early schoollike settings—such as nursery schools and day-care centers—provide a wide range of intellectual and social experiences.

The school-age years. In the United States, Canada, the United Kingdom, and most other developed countries, children start school at about 5 or 6 years of age. The years from about age 5 to 8 are often called the *early school years.* The years from about age 9 to 12 are called the *preteen-age years.* Many experts describe the school-age years from about age 7 to 11 as *middle childhood,* because they represent the period between early childhood and adolescence. Most children in developed countries remain in school well into adolescence.

The early school years mark a major turning point in childhood. This period brings important advances in mental, emotional, and social development. Children also continue to improve their physical skills during this stage.

Around age 7, children enter the period of concrete operations, the third of Piaget's stages of mental development. During this stage, which usually lasts until about age 11, children develop the ability to think logically. They learn to organize their knowledge, classify objects, and solve problems. For instance, a 5-year-old child might try to solve a problem by choosing the first solution that comes to mind. But a child in the period of concrete operations thinks about several possible solutions and considers why one is better than another.

Before the period of concrete operations, the child's manner of thinking is largely *egocentric*—that is, the child's thought processes are limited to his or her own point of view. Around the age of 7, however, the child becomes increasingly able to distinguish his or her point of view from the points of view of others. The decline in egocentrism helps children evaluate situations from multiple perspectives. It also helps them understand and communicate with others.

During the school-age years, children receive formal instruction and become active members of social

Learning to read is a major challenge for young children. Many parents read stories to preschoolers and early school-age children to help them build vocabulary and develop language skills.

groups outside the family. Children also increasingly compare themselves with other youngsters. Such comparisons contribute to a child's *self-image* (the view one has of oneself) and *self-esteem* (the way one feels about oneself).

The preteen-age years, sometimes called *preadolescence,* begin the transition into adolescence. During the preteen-age years, the rate of physical growth increases sharply. Most girls grow rapidly between the ages of 9 and 12. Girls are normally heavier and taller than boys during these years. At about age 12, however, most boys start to grow rapidly, and the girls' growth rate declines. By early adolescence, most boys are heavier and taller than most girls their age.

As preteens grow, they begin to develop the sexual characteristics of adults. The period during which a person matures sexually is called *puberty.* Some children reach sexual maturity before age 13. But others do not become sexually mature until adolescence.

The preteen-age years are an especially important period of social development. During this stage, a child's circle of friends and acquaintances, or *peer group,* plays an important role in the child's life. Preteens begin to look chiefly to their peer group, rather than to their parents, for acceptance and approval. A child's behavior may change noticeably under *peer pressure*—that is, social pressure and expectations from people of the child's own age.

During the preteen-age years, the child's manner of thinking continues to develop. Around the age of 11, children enter the period of formal operations, the fourth of Piaget's stages of mental development. During this period, children begin to think reasonably about the future and learn to deal with *abstractions.* Abstractions are ideas about qualities and characteristics viewed apart from the objects that have them. The growing complexity of the child's thought processes helps prepare the child for the challenges of adolescence and adulthood.

Individual differences among children

Children vary greatly in appearance, behavior, personality, and other characteristics. Two main forces—*heredity* and *environment*—account for individual differences among children. Heredity is the process by which children inherit physical and mental traits from their parents. Environment consists of all the factors in a child's surroundings that affect the child's development. Such factors include relations with family members, lessons and activities at school, nutrition and exercise, and interactions with people in the community.

This section examines the physical, psychological, and cultural characteristics that make every child unique.

Physical differences include differences in appearance, physical ability, and rate of growth. Many children experience physical growth and development months or years earlier or later than most others. In addition, individuals vary greatly in body type, coordination, and athletic ability.

In general, heredity limits what the environment can do in influencing a child's physical development. For example, every child inherits a tendency to grow to a certain height. But children need the right conditions—including proper nourishment and exercise—to grow as tall as their heredity allows. Not even the best environmental conditions will enable a child to grow much taller than this height. In some cases, sickness or disease can limit a child's development.

Psychological differences involve differences in the ways children think, learn, and behave. A child's *temperament* (emotional make-up and manner of behavior) is apparent during infancy and becomes increasingly established throughout childhood. Children possess varying degrees of such qualities as anxiety, sociability, moodiness, and aggression. Many of the traits or tendencies of a child's temperament are inherited from parents and influenced by environmental factors. Such factors include school experiences and interactions with parents, siblings, and friends.

Intelligence—often defined as the ability to adapt to the environment—is another quality that varies from one child to another. Children who are highly intelligent can learn quickly and understand what goes on around them. Many experts believe that general mental ability is mostly inherited. Others, however, believe that environment has a strong influence on a child's intelligence. Most of what is considered intelligent behavior involves a complex interaction of heredity and environment.

Traditionally, differences in intelligence among children have been measured by *IQ* (intelligence quotient) tests. These tests are designed to indicate a child's general mental ability in relation to other children of the same age. However, many experts argue that intelligence has many dimensions that cannot be accurately measured by a single test. For instance, the American psychologist Howard E. Gardner suggested in the 1990's that there are eight distinct "intelligences," including linguistic intelligence, musical intelligence, and *interpersonal intelligence* (the ability to get along with others). A child may have below-average intelligence in some of these areas but exceptional intelligence in other areas.

Cultural differences result from the beliefs, customs, arts, languages, technology, and conditions that surround the child as he or she develops. Every nation has a national culture. But, within each nation, there are various cultural groups with their own distinct sets of values and traditions. Cultural factors greatly influence children's social behavior, manner of dress, religious beliefs, and style of learning.

People are not born with cultural knowledge. Instead, they acquire the knowledge through the use of language and by watching and imitating behaviors in society. The process by which children learn about their culture is called *enculturation.*

All societies have specific ideas about what abilities, behaviors, and characteristics are considered "normal" for children. In many developed countries, for example, children are expected to attend schools and learn how to read and write. In less developed countries, however, children may instead learn skills needed for farmwork or household chores. Societies also differ in the values and personality traits that are emphasized in children. For instance, in many Western nations, such traits as competitiveness and independence are encouraged. In many other countries, however, these traits are considered abnormal. The roles of parents and educators vary depending on the skills and characteristics that children are expected to develop.

© Stephanie Maze, Corbis

Organized activities help children develop new skills while learning to work with others. Many schools and communities offer special programs for youngsters interested in music, sports, the arts, and other areas.

The role of the family

The family is the basic unit of social organization in all human societies. It is the primary institution responsible for raising children, providing them with food and shelter, and satisfying their needs for love and support. The responsibility of caring for children and helping them develop is commonly called *child-rearing.* Parents typically play the central role in child-rearing. However, in many households, aunts, uncles, grandparents, family friends, and other caregivers are actively involved.

Parents and caregivers can guide a child's development in a variety of ways, including (1) understanding the child's basic needs, (2) motivating the child's behavior, and (3) serving as models of appropriate behavior. In addition, siblings play a major role in the development of many boys and girls.

Understanding the child's basic needs. Every child has basic physical and psychological needs that must be met if he or she is to develop normally. Parents are expected to understand and satisfy these needs.

Basic physical needs. Children need nourishing meals, proper clothing, and a clean, comfortable home. They also require a reasonable amount of play and exercise. In addition, parents should teach their children good health habits and standard safety practices to reduce the risk of diseases and injuries.

Parents should also ensure that their children receive regular medical check-ups and proper health care. In the United States, most children get their first *immunizations*—vaccinations against such diseases as diphtheria, polio, tetanus, measles, and mumps—before 18 months of age. Most experts recommend that children be reimmunized at 4 to 6 years of age.

Basic psychological needs. Children need to feel loved, wanted, and respected by parents and other family members. They need close contact with adults whom they like and admire. Such contacts help promote normal emotional development. Parents assist and encourage young children as they develop language ability and other skills. When parents make a practice of reading to children during the toddler and preschool years, the children are more likely to achieve success in school.

Motivating the child's behavior. Parents motivate a child when they encourage the child to adopt a certain type of behavior. Parents might use rewards to reinforce good behavior and punishments to discourage bad behavior. Appropriate rewards and punishments vary depending on the child's age, the type of behavior, and other circumstances. Rewards for good behavior may include a word of praise, a hug, the gift of a toy, or a special privilege. Special privileges typically involve activities the child enjoys, such as watching television, playing video games, or visiting a favorite store or park. Punishments may include a strong "no," a scolding, or the removal of privileges.

Some parents and child-rearing experts believe that mild *corporal* (bodily) punishment—such as light slapping or spanking—can be effective in disciplining a child. However, others believe that such punishments should never be used. Many experts believe that corporal punishment will likely lead to increased resistance or aggressive behavior from the child.

By making sure that children understand the reasons for punishments, parents help children learn better standards of behavior. Children are likely to be upset if they feel they are being punished unfairly or too severely. Punishments that make children feel unloved or unwanted do not promote healthy development.

Serving as models of appropriate behavior. Because children closely identify with their parents, parents should seek to provide good examples of how to act. The things parents do and say—and the ways they do and say them—strongly influence a child's behavior and sense of right and wrong. Parents' actions also affect a child's self-image. Children who see mainly good qualities in their parents will likely learn to see themselves in a favorable way. Children who observe bad qualities in their parents may have difficulty seeing good qualities in themselves.

In addition to serving as examples themselves, parents monitor and supervise other factors that influence their child's attitudes and behavior. Such factors include interactions with friends, peers, and teachers, as well as books, music, video games, and television. Parents can shape and monitor a child's TV habits and encourage the child to discuss the programs that he or she views.

The influence of siblings. In many families, older siblings act as teachers, caregivers, and role models for their younger brothers and sisters. Siblings also serve as friends and peers. The nature of a sibling relationship depends largely on the individual characteristics of the siblings. Although siblings have much of the same genetic makeup, they can vary greatly in personality and temperament. A relationship in which siblings cooperate and help one another helps each child's development. However, quarrels, rivalries, and disagreements between siblings are common. Parents address conflicts between siblings, teach them to manage their emotions, and help them resolve their differences. Sibling relationships help children develop important social skills that they will use in later stages of life.

The influence of the child's environment

Although the family is the traditional center of the childhood experience, numerous other people, places, conditions, and events contribute to a child's development. Children do not grow up in isolation. Instead, they experience a wide range of meaningful and complex interactions with their environment.

The Russian-born American psychologist Urie Bronfenbrenner examined these interactions using his *bioecological model* of human development. The model, introduced in 1979, presents the child's environment as four interconnected layers: (1) the *microsystem,* (2) the *mesosystem,* (3) the *exosystem,* and (4) the *macrosystem.*

The microsystem, the innermost layer of Bronfenbrenner's model, consists of the people, places, and institutions in the child's immediate environment. The child's family is at the center of the microsystem. But the system may also include teachers, doctors, and peers, as well as such places as schools, playgrounds, and day-care centers. Elements of the microsystem regularly and directly affect the child's life.

The mesosystem is the complex system of interactions between various elements of the microsystem. These interactions can have a significant impact on a child's development. For example, meetings between a child's parents and teachers can strongly affect the child's happiness in school and at home.

The exosystem involves factors that exist beyond the child's immediate environment yet still affect the child. Elements of the exosystem include parents' workplaces, community organizations, social and health services, and school boards. The mass media—including television, motion pictures, the Internet, and advertising—are also an important aspect of the exosystem. Elements of the exosystem can have a powerful, though often indirect, influence on the child's life. For instance, a child may not be directly involved with a parent's workplace, but the child's life will be affected if a parent is promoted, laid off, or asked to work overtime.

The macrosystem is the broad cultural context in which the other systems operate. It involves such elements as government policies, economic conditions, and world events. For instance, government policies regarding education and health care affect the conditions of a child's development.

World events in the macrosystem can drastically alter a child's surroundings. A war, for instance, can threaten a child's safety, emotional well-being, and access to food and shelter. Similarly, a major economic slump can force children to live under conditions of poverty, where many of their needs cannot be met.

Special challenges and concerns

Many children face significant problems and obstacles in the course of development. A number of childhood problems may result from physical or psychological disorders. However, many are normal aspects of the childhood experience. Common childhood concerns include (1) emotional problems, (2) physical disabilities and challenges, (3) obstacles to learning, (4) social problems, (5) aggressive behavior, and (6) problems in the home. Most children can overcome their challenges with the help of parents, friends, and others, or through special therapy or assistance programs.

Emotional problems. One of the most common emotional problems in children is *depression.* Depression is a condition in which a child suffers long periods of sadness and other unpleasant feelings. Depressed children may feel fearful, guilty, or helpless. They often cry, and many lose interest in school and other activities. Treatments for depression include hospitalization, med-

Parents play a vital role in the development of children. They provide for the basic physical and psychological needs of children, motivate good behavior, and serve as models for appropriate behavior. Activities involving parents are important as children develop their self-image. Children who observe good qualities in their parents are more likely to see themselves in a favorable way.

ication, and *psychotherapy* (psychological treatment).

Some children suffer from unrealistic fears—that is, fears that occur regularly in the absence of real danger. In many cases, such fears can interfere with a child's everyday activities. Some fears are directly related to a frightening past experience. For example, a child who has been attacked by an animal may develop an unrealistic fear of all animals. Children who experience such fears may benefit from professional counseling.

Physical disabilities and challenges. A disability is a condition that affects a child's ability to perform the activities of everyday life. Common physical disabilities include blindness, deafness, deformity, loss of limbs, and muscular, nervous, and sensory disorders. A physical disability may make it difficult for a child to perform daily activities, such as dressing, eating, and maintaining personal hygiene. However, with *assistive* (aid-giving) devices and help from others, most children with disabilities can have a healthy and fulfilling childhood.

Many children develop health problems that can increase the risk of illness later in life. *Obesity* is the condition of having an excessive amount of body fat. Obesity is influenced by both hereditary and environmental factors. Two of the main environmental factors are unhealthy eating habits and physical inactivity. Children who spend large amounts of time watching television are more likely to develop weight problems than children who are more active. Parents, teachers, and others can help children improve their physical health by demonstrating and encouraging healthy eating habits and providing regular opportunities for exercise.

Obstacles to learning. One of the central tasks of childhood is to advance in school and become a successful learner. However, many children face barriers to learning. In some cases, the barrier is a psychological condition that interferes with the child's ability to pay attention in class, develop skills, or understand concepts. In other cases, the barrier is a feature of the child's environment. For instance, the child might attend a school that lacks the resources needed for effective instruction.

Learning disabilities are disorders that limit a child's ability to learn. They can interfere with the development of such skills as concentration, coordination, language, and memory. *Attention deficit disorder* is a condition in which children have unusual difficulty paying attention, sitting still, or controlling impulses. The formal term for attention deficit disorder is *attention-deficit/hyperactivity disorder* (ADHD). Difficulties in school may also result from emotional disturbances, mental retardation, or poor hearing or vision. Therapies, medication, assistive devices, and specialized teaching techniques can help children overcome most physical and psychological conditions that interfere with learning.

Social problems. A child may have difficulty making friends or establishing social relationships if he or she differs from his or her peers in certain ways. For instance, a child with a physical disability might become socially isolated from—or even ridiculed by—other children. A child might also become isolated if he or she performs poorly in school activities or differs greatly from classmates in terms of social class or cultural background. In some cases, a child might become socially isolated if he or she displays exceptional talent in a particular area.

Children who have difficulty building friendships may become victims of *bullying*. Bullying is the repeated use of aggression by one or more people against another person or group. Bullying may involve name-calling, pushing or hitting, or preventing an individual from participating in an activity. Bullied children may experience anxiety, low self-esteem, difficulty sleeping, or other problems. School policies, parental supervision, and open communication between children and trusted adults can help address problems with bullying. Bullies and victims need attention to resolve these problems.

Aggressive behavior. Some children develop patterns of aggressive behavior that are a problem to themselves and to the people around them. Such behavior can result from the frustration children feel when their feelings of worthiness and self-respect are threatened.

Most children learn to control aggression by channeling their energies into hobbies, sports, schoolwork, and other activities. Some children, however, do not learn to deal with aggression effectively. Instead, they relieve feelings of frustration through antisocial behavior, such as stealing, bullying, or destroying property. Such forms of behavior worsen if the peer group encourages them.

Problems in the home often involve strained or unhealthy relationships between family members. One of the most severe childhood problems is *child abuse*—that is, mistreatment of a child by a parent or another adult. Child abuse may take the form of physical violence or any other treatment harmful to the child. Many experts believe that abused children will more likely become abusive as adults, a development sometimes called the *cycle of abuse*. Family members, friends, and neighbors—as well as people in the medical, psychological, social, and legal professions—have a responsibility to report any suspected cases of abuse to a government authority.

Violence in the home can harm a child even if the child is not the target of the violence. *Domestic violence*—that is, abuse between marital partners or other adults in close relationships—is a major source of emotional and psychological distress in children.

When parents divorce, the children usually live with either the mother or the father. Divorce breaks apart the family unit and affects many children deeply. However, many experts believe that living with one parent is less harmful to a child than living with both parents in an unhappy environment. Donald Wertlieb

Related articles in *World Book* include:

Child development

Adolescent
Aggression
Attention deficit disorder
Baby
Behavior
Day care
Depression
Developmental psychology
Disability
Family
Growth
Health
Intelligence
Lisping
Mental retardation
Motivation
Nutrition
Obesity
Parent
Personality
Physical fitness
Safety
Sexuality
Socialization
Stuttering

Education

Character education
Early childhood education
Education
Gifted children
Kindergarten
Learning
Learning disabilities
Library (Services for children)
Literature for children
Nursery school
Parent education
Physical education
Reading
School
Sex education
Special education

Recreation

Doll	Play	Television
Game	Recreation	Toy
Hobby	Sports	Video game

Other related articles

Adoption	Divorce (Child custody arrangements)
Bullying	Foster care
Child abuse	Heredity
Child labor	Homosexuality
Child welfare	Human being
Childhood Education International, Association for	Juvenile delinquency
Children's Bureau	Minor
Children's home	Pediatrics
	UNICEF

Outline

I. The stages of childhood
- A. The toddler stage
- B. The preschool years
- C. The school-age years

II. Individual differences among children
- A. Physical differences
- B. Psychological differences
- C. Cultural differences

III. The role of the family
- A. Understanding the child's basic needs
- B. Motivating the child's behavior
- C. Serving as models of appropriate behavior
- D. The influence of siblings

IV. The influence of the child's environment
- A. The microsystem
- B. The mesosystem
- C. The exosystem
- D. The macrosystem

V. Special challenges and concerns
- A. Emotional problems
- B. Physical disabilities and challenges
- C. Obstacles to learning
- D. Social problems
- E. Aggressive behavior
- F. Problems in the home

Questions

What two main forces account for individual differences among children?
What are some responsibilities of parents?
What is often the cause of a child's poor performance in school?
At what ages does childhood begin and end?
What are some key developments during the toddler stage?
How do siblings influence a child's development?
What methods do parents use to motivate a child's behavior?
What changes take place during Piaget's period of concrete operations?
How can children learn to control aggression?
What is the *cycle of abuse*?

Additional resources

Allen, K. Eileen, and Marotz, L. R. *Developmental Profiles: Pre-Birth Through Twelve.* 4th ed. Thomson Delmar Learning, 2003.
Charlesworth, Rosalind. *Understanding Child Development.* 6th ed. Thomson Delmar Learning, 2004.
Children's Hospital Boston. *The Children's Hospital Guide to Your Child's Health and Development.* Perseus Pub., 2001.
Kagan, Jerome, and Gall, S. B., eds. *Gale Encyclopedia of Childhood and Adolescence.* Gale, 1997.
Kaul, Chandrika. *Statistical Handbook on the World's Children.* Oryx, 2002.
Mayes, Linda C., and Cohen, D. J. *The Yale Child Study Center Guide to Understanding Your Child.* Little, Brown, 2002.
Rogoff, Barbara. *The Cultural Nature of Human Development.* Oxford, 2003.
Shonkoff, Jack P., and Phillips, D. A., eds. *From Neurons to Neighborhoods: The Science of Early Childhood Development.* National Academy Pr., 2000.

Child, Lydia Maria (1802-1880), was an American abolitionist, author, and editor. She became known for her book *An Appeal in Favor of That Class of Americans Called Africans* (1833), which condemned slavery.

Lydia M. Francis was born on Feb. 11, 1802, in Medford, Massachusetts. In 1826, she founded *Juvenile Miscellany,* the nation's first magazine for children. In 1828, she married David Child, a Boston lawyer and abolitionist. She became involved in abolitionism in 1831, when she met the famous abolitionist William Lloyd Garrison.

From 1841 to 1843, Child served as editor of the *National Anti-Slavery Standard,* the weekly publication of the American Anti-Slavery Society. She wrote a series of letters supporting John Brown, the noted abolitionist, after he led his historic raid at Harpers Ferry, Virginia, in 1859. Child also edited *Incidents in the Life of a Slave Girl* (1861), the recollections of a former slave named Harriet Ann Jacobs. Child died on Oct. 20, 1880.

Child wrote several books on American Indians, one of her earliest interests. She also wrote the famous poem "Boy's Thanksgiving" (1845), which begins "Over the river and through the woods...." Nancy Woloch

Child abuse is a term that generally refers to mistreatment of a child by a parent or another adult. There is no standard definition of child abuse, however. A narrow definition is limited to life-threatening physical violence, including severe beatings, burns, and strangulation. A broader definition includes any treatment other than the most favorable care.

No one knows how many instances of child abuse occur each year because many cases of child abuse are never reported. However, the National Center for Child Abuse and Neglect estimates that nearly 1 million children in the United States suffer nonaccidental, life-threatening physical violence each year.

Views about the causes of child abuse have changed through the years. Many social scientists once believed that only people with severe emotional problems would abuse children. However, studies indicate that most individuals who abuse children do not suffer from traditional psychiatric illnesses. Another common view is that abused children grow up to be abusive adults, a development referred to as the *cycle of abuse.* But research has shown that abused children do not necessarily become abusers as adults.

Today, many experts believe child abuse is widespread because society regards physical punishment by parents as a reasonable way of changing children's behavior. Thus, adults who hurt children sometimes only intend to correct them and do not realize how easily children can be injured.

Another cause of child abuse is stress. Parents who are unemployed, very isolated, or under great stress for other reasons are more likely to abuse their children than parents who do not have such problems. Children who are difficult to care for, such as premature infants and children with disabilities, create more stress for parents. Thus, such children are more likely to be abused than are other children. Parent support groups, such as Parents Anonymous, and other professional services can help relieve many of the stresses that lead to abuse. In extreme cases, a juvenile court may place children in a foster home.

The problems of *pedophilia* and sexual abuse have received much attention in the media. Pedophilia is sexual attraction in an adult toward children. Adults who are sexually attracted to children are called *pedophiles*. Children are warned not to let people, even family members, touch them in ways that make them uncomfortable. Children also are told to tell a trusted adult if they are sexually abused. Children should be urged to discuss anything that bothers them with a trustworthy adult. But experts point out that frightening warnings about something small children cannot understand can terrify and confuse them.

Before the 1800's, little was done to prevent child abuse. In the late 1800's, citizens of some large cities set up agencies to deal with social problems, including poverty, overcrowding, and child abuse.

Child abuse gained major attention in the United States in the 1960's. This increased attention was linked to the identification of the *battered child syndrome* by C. Henry Kempe, a professor of pediatrics, and his associates. Kempe's studies pointed out the responsibilities of people in medical, psychological, social, and legal professions to help control child abuse. All 50 states soon required physicians to report suspected cases of abuse to a government authority.

In 1974, the United States Congress organized the National Center on Child Abuse and Neglect. The center helps support programs that deal with child abuse. Today, state welfare experts investigate abuse cases and counsel families of abused children. Edward Zigler

See also **Bullying; Domestic violence; Shaken baby syndrome.**

Additional resources

Clark, Robin E., and others. *The Encyclopedia of Child Abuse*. 2nd ed. Facts on File, 2001.
Grapes, Bryan J., ed. *Child Abuse*. Greenhaven, 2001.

Child-care center. See **Day care; Nursery school.**

Child labor is the employment of children as wage earners. It became a serious social problem during the Industrial Revolution in Britain (now the United Kingdom) during the 1700's, and the problem spread to other countries as they became industrialized. The problem arose when children, many below the age of 10, were employed by factories and mines. The youths were forced to work long hours under dangerous and unhealthy conditions, and their wages were very small.

Social reformers began to condemn child labor practices because of their ruinous effect on children's health and welfare. The most effective attack on the evils of child labor may have come from Charles Dickens's novel *Oliver Twist* (1837-1839). The book was widely read in both the United States and the United Kingdom.

Gradually, countries passed laws to correct the abuses of child labor. Children still work today. In Canada, the United Kingdom, the United States, and many other countries, most working children are teen-agers who hold part-time jobs. Their working conditions are carefully regulated by law. However, in Asia and other parts of the world, millions of boys and girls still hold full-time jobs. In some countries, children under 15 form a large part of the total working force, and there is little or no control over their working conditions.

Abuses of child labor. Since ancient times, children have worked to help support their families, especially on farms. But child labor created no major social problems until the factory system of labor began.

During the 1700's, many British businesses began to hire children. Children worked for lower wages than adults, and were not so likely as adults to cause labor troubles. Factory owners wanted to use their small, nimble fingers for tending machines. Children worked for low pay in dirty, poorly lighted factories, mills, and mines. They often performed jobs that really required adult strength. Many children worked to help support their unemployed parents. Orphans were pressed into labor. Similar conditions became common in the United States during the late 1700's.

Child workers were often deprived of the chance to attend school. Uneducated, the only work they were capable of doing was unskilled labor. Thus, they had little chance to better themselves.

Early child labor laws. In 1802, the British Parliament passed the first law regulating child labor. The law prohibited the employment of *pauper children* (children dependent on charity) under 9 years of age in cotton mills. Pauper children under 14 could not work at night, and their workday was limited to 12 hours. In 1819, the law was extended to include all children. No real provision for enforcing these laws was made until 1833. Germany was the second country to pass national child labor laws. It did so in 1839.

The development of the textile industry in America depended heavily on children. In 1832, about 40 percent of all factory workers in New England were between the ages of 7 and 16.

In 1836, Massachusetts passed the first state child labor law in the United States. The law prohibited the employment of children under 15 in any factory unless the children had attended school for at least three months during the preceding year. But by 1860, only a few states had outlawed factory employment of children under 10 or 12 years old. Enforcement of these laws proved difficult due to the large number of poor families and government reluctance to offend employers. By 1890, nearly 20 percent of U.S. children were employed full-time.

U.S. federal laws. The first federal child labor law was passed by the U.S. Congress in 1916. It set standards for the hiring of children by industries involved in interstate or foreign commerce. The standards included a 16-year minimum age for work in mines and quarries, a 14-year minimum age for other types of work, an 8-hour day, and a 48-hour week. The law prohibited night work for children under the age of 16. But in 1918, the Supreme Court of the United States declared the law unconstitutional.

In 1924, Congress passed a constitutional amendment to authorize federal laws for regulating the labor of persons under 18. But this amendment failed to receive the required approval of three-fourths of all the states.

The Fair Labor Standards Act of 1938 helped to promote child labor reform. The law included basic standards for the employment of minors. Later upheld by the Supreme Court, this law declared that boys and girls 16 and over may be employed in any occupations except those declared hazardous by the U.S. secretary of labor. The minimum age for hazardous occupations was set at 18. Children 14 and 15 years old were permitted to work in only a limited number of occupations outside of school hours. This law firmly established the constitutional legality of child labor laws.

The Fair Labor Standards Act also requires employers to pay child laborers the U.S. minimum wage. Since the early 1970's, the minimum wage has generally failed to keep pace with inflation. During the early 1980's, Congress considered proposals that would permit payment below the minimum wage to increase the number of jobs available to young minority workers.

U.S. state laws. All 50 states, the District of Columbia, and Puerto Rico now have child labor laws that regulate the employment of children. Most state laws set a minimum age for general employment, a higher minimum age for hazardous work, and limitations on the daily and weekly hours of work. Federal and state child labor laws vary widely. When both federal and state laws apply, the higher standard must be observed.

However, legislative reform has had little effect on the lives of child farmworkers. Because they travel and work with their parents, they get little schooling. They suffer from long hours, poor sanitation and housing, and possible exposure to dangerous pesticides.

Canadian laws. The provinces of Canada have child labor laws that regulate employment in mines, factories, and shops. The first of these laws came in 1873, when Nova Scotia set 10 as the minimum age for mineworkers. The law limited boys under 12 years old to 60 hours of work a week belowground. In time, the minimum age was raised and the hours of work lowered. In most of the provinces today, a higher minimum age is fixed for work in mines than in other places of work.

Most provinces have laws regulating child labor in factories. The standards vary, but all provinces set minimum ages for employment and limit the hours that boys and girls can work. The minimum age for employment in factories varies from 14 to 16. School attendance laws restrict the employment during school hours of children who are still required to attend school. David Brody

See also **Coal** (picture: A Pennsylvania mine of the late 1800's); **Industrial Revolution.**

Additional resources

Bartoletti, Susan C. *Kids on Strike!* Houghton, 1999.
Hindman, Hugh D. *Child Labor: An American History.* M. E. Sharpe, 2002.
Schlemmer, Bernard, ed. *The Exploited Child.* Zed Bks., 2000.

Child welfare is a system of financial, medical, psychological, and social services for children and parents. Such services—commonly provided by governments, international organizations, and private agencies—seek to ensure the safety and healthy development of children. They work to help children meet their basic needs, resolve their psychological and social problems, and attain their full potential.

Child welfare services vary from one community to another. Some child welfare programs fund health care for children, help prepare young children for school, or provide day care for children whose parents both have jobs. Others seek to prevent adolescent pregnancy, violence, drug use, or other problems. Many child welfare agencies provide services specifically for children who have been abused or neglected, or who have not received adequate care. Such agencies may administer *child protection* programs, which protect children from cruelty; *family preservation* services, which help families resolve their problems; or *out-of-home* programs, which find new homes for children through foster care, residential group care, and adoption.

Important child welfare organizations include the Child Welfare League of America, the Child Welfare League of Canada, and the British Association for the Study and Prevention of Child Abuse and Neglect. The United Nations Children's Fund, commonly called UNICEF, works with governments throughout the world to meet children's needs. Many countries also have government agencies devoted to child welfare. In the United States, for instance, the Children's Bureau oversees a variety of programs that assist children and families.

Many schools of social work offer child welfare as a specialized field of study. Students in child welfare programs learn how to provide counseling, support, and other services for children in need and their families.

Derrik R. Tollefson

See also **Child abuse; Day care; Foster care; Social work.**

Childbirth is the process by which a woman gives birth to a baby. A pregnant woman carries a baby within her body inside a hollow, muscular organ called the *uterus.* After about nine months, the baby passes out of the uterus and through the *vagina,* also called the *birth canal.* Childbirth can be painful, but the severity of the pain varies among women.

The birth process is called *labor.* The process begins when the muscles of the uterus start to tighten and relax in a rhythmic pattern. As labor progresses, these muscle contractions become stronger and more frequent, causing the *cervix* (lower part of the uterus) to open. After the cervix has opened about 4 inches (10 centimeters), the contractions gradually force the baby through the cervix and out of the woman's body through the vagina. Many women assist the process by "pushing" with their abdominal muscles in time with their contractions. The *amniotic sac,* a membrane containing fluids that surround the baby, breaks before or during labor. The fluids flow out through the vagina.

In most births, the baby's head is the first part that comes out of the mother's body. But in some deliveries, called *breech births,* the feet or buttocks come out first. After the baby has fully come out of the mother's body, the *umbilical cord* is cut, and the infant starts to breathe. The umbilical cord is a tubelike structure that connects the baby to the *placenta,* an organ attached to the wall of the uterus. Food and oxygen from the mother's blood go through the placenta to the baby during pregnancy.

After the baby is born, the muscles of the uterus continue to contract until the placenta separates from the uterus and is expelled through the vagina. The discharged placenta is also called the *afterbirth.*

The length of labor varies greatly among women. It averages 13 to 14 hours for women having their first babies and lasts 7 to 8 hours thereafter.

Some women need an operation called a *cesarean section* to deliver a baby. In this operation, a surgeon removes the baby and the placenta through an incision in the abdomen and uterus. Cesarean sections are performed for a number of reasons, but chiefly because the baby cannot pass through the birth canal. The woman's pelvis may be too small, or the baby may be too large.

Methods of childbirth. Most women in developed countries deliver their babies in hospitals, which have specially equipped birth facilities. During childbirth, a woman may receive medication to relieve her labor pains. In some cases, a physician will administer a drug to induce (bring on) labor. Before delivery, the physician may widen the woman's vaginal opening by making a small incision called an episiotomy.

In many cases, physicians use an electronic *fetal monitor* to record the baby's heartbeat during labor. Disturbances in the heartbeat may signal that the baby is in danger and that a cesarean section may be necessary.

During the 1960's and the 1970's, many hospitals developed educational programs to prepare women for childbirth and parenting. These programs instruct both mothers and fathers on pregnancy, childbirth, and infant care. In addition, such programs as *natural childbirth* and the *Lamaze method* teach relaxation exercises and breathing techniques to lessen the discomfort of labor, thus reducing the need for painkilling drugs. Many such drugs pass to the baby through the placenta, so some women choose to avoid them. Some women also avoid drugs so they can remain alert throughout labor.

A type of anesthesia called an *epidural* is another popular method for relieving labor pain. This form of pain relief does not affect the baby or reduce the mother's alertness, but it must be given by a specially trained doctor. Epidural anesthesia is injected through a small tube that is inserted into the back next to the spinal cord. When the anesthesia is absorbed by nerves that go from the spine to the uterus, it almost completely eliminates labor pains.

At many hospitals, *birthing rooms* offer an alternative to traditional labor and delivery rooms. Most birthing rooms resemble a home bedroom and are used for labor, delivery, and sometimes recovery. Birthing rooms provide a relaxed and intimate atmosphere where the hospital's facilities are still at hand if complications occur. Susan R. Johnson

Related articles in *World Book* include:

Apgar score	Preeclampsia
Midwife	Pregnancy
Neonatology	Premature birth
Postpartum depression	Reproduction, Human

Childhood Education International, Association for, is an international organization that promotes the education, rights, and welfare of children. The group's members are educators, parents, and others who work with children in the home, at school, and in the community.

The association, sometimes called ACEI, works to improve the quality of education and to help children reach their full potential. It sponsors an annual conference, issues statements on educational topics, and publishes resources for educators and parents.

The association was founded in 1892. Its headquarters are in Olney, Maryland. Critically reviewed by the Association for Childhood Education International

Children. See **Child.**

Children and Families, Administration for, is a part of the United States Department of Health and Human Services (HHS). It works to improve the economic and social conditions of low-income children and families, and conditions of American Indians, refugees, disabled people, and others with special needs.

The administration's programs include Child Support Enforcement, Head Start, and the Job Opportunities and Basic Skills Training Program (JOBS). Other programs work to prevent, identify, and treat child abuse and neglect; provide shelter and other services to runaway and homeless youth; find permanent homes for foster children; help low-income families pay for quality child care; and assist low-income households with home heating and cooling costs. Still other programs promote economic and social development for American Indians and help refugees find jobs.

The Administration for Children and Families was formed in 1991. It was established by the joining of two HHS divisions—the Office of Human Development Services and the Family Support Administration.

Critically reviewed by the Administration for Children and Families

See also **Head Start.**

Children's Bureau is a unit of the United States Department of Health and Human Services (HHS). The bureau works with local and state agencies to develop programs that assist children and families.

The bureau administers many programs to improve child welfare services. These include the Adoption Assistance, Child Welfare Services, Foster Care, and Independent Living programs. Through them, the bureau works with states to develop programs that strengthen troubled families; find permanent homes for children who cannot remain in their own homes; provide services to foster children 16 years old or older to help them live independently; and improve the skills and quality of the staff administering child welfare services.

The Children's Bureau was established in 1912. It is part of the Administration on Children, Youth and Families in HHS's Administration for Children and Families.

Critically reviewed by the Administration on Children, Youth and Families

See also **Lathrop, Julia C.; Wald, Lillian D.**

Children's Crusade. See **Crusades.**

Children's home is an institution that cares for homeless children. Such institutions are often called *orphanages,* especially in Eastern Europe, Asia, and less developed countries. Religious groups and government agencies provide funds for many children's homes.

Children cared for in a children's home may be left alone after both their parents die. Others may be abandoned by their parents because of poverty, or may be removed from their homes because of neglect or abuse. Some children may be homeless because their parents do not want the responsibility of rearing them.

Many child welfare specialists in Western countries try to place children with foster families instead of in children's homes. These authorities believe that children should live in a family environment. Also, supporting children in foster families costs less than caring for them in children's homes. The parents in a foster family volunteer to care for a child in their own home while a permanent adoptive family is sought for the child.

If a foster home or adoptive parent is unavailable, authorities may place a child in a *group home* or *residential school* rather than in a children's home. In a group home, a professional staff cares for a small number of children. Residential schools are institutions at which children both live and attend classes. Alice Page Eyman

See also **Foster care.**

Children's literature. See **Literature for children; Writing** (Literature for children).

© Ric Ergenbright

Southern Chile's rugged coast is battered by strong winds and cold waters. The country's spectacular landscape also includes vast deserts, majestic mountains, and fertile river basins.

Chile

Chile, *CHIHL ee* or *CHEE lay,* is a long, narrow country on South America's west coast. It is more than 10 times as long as it is wide and stretches about 2,650 miles (4,265 kilometers) from Peru in the north to the southern tip of the continent. Chile's name probably comes from *chilli,* an Indian word meaning *where the land ends.*

Chile is a land of great variety. The Atacama Desert in the north is one of the driest places in the world, but parts of the south are among the rainiest. The towering Andes Mountains form Chile's eastern boundary, and low mountains rise along the country's Pacific coast. A series of fertile river basins called the Central Valley lies between the mountain ranges in central Chile. The landscape of southern Chile is breathtaking. There are snow-capped volcanoes, thick forests, and huge glaciers. Many rocky, windswept islands dot the rugged shore.

Most Chileans are of mixed Spanish and Indian ancestry. Many others are of unmixed European descent. Indians—descendants of Chile's original inhabitants—form another group. Nearly all Chileans speak Spanish, the nation's official language, and about three-fourths of the people are Roman Catholics.

Michael Monteón, the contributor of this article, is Professor of History at the University of California, San Diego.

Santiago is Chile's capital and largest city. It lies in the Central Valley, where the great majority of Chile's people live. The Central Valley also has the country's other largest cities, major factories, and best farmland.

Since about 1900, poor, rural Chileans have poured into the cities in search of a better life. But there are not

Facts in brief

Capital: Santiago.
Official language: Spanish.
Official name: República de Chile (Republic of Chile).
Area: 292,135 mi² (756,626 km²). *Greatest distances*—north-south, 2,650 mi (4,265 km); east-west, 265 mi (427 km). *Coastline*—3,317 mi (5,338 km).
Elevation: *Highest*—Ojos del Salado, 22,572 ft (6,880 m) above sea level. *Lowest*—sea level.
Population: *Estimated 2006 population*—16,366,000; density, 56 per mi² (22 per km²); distribution, 87 percent urban, 13 percent rural. *2002 census*—15,116,435.
Chief products: *Agriculture*—apples, barley, beans, beef cattle, citrus fruits, corn, grapes, nuts, oats, peaches, potatoes, poultry, rice, sheep, sugar beets, wheat. *Fishing industry*—anchovettas, jack mackerel, salmon, sardines. *Manufacturing*—beverages, cement, chemicals, clothing, food products, iron and steel, metal products, paper products, textiles, transportation equipment, wood products. *Mining*—copper, gold, iron ore, lithium, manganese, molybdenum, natural gas, petroleum, silver, sodium nitrate.
National holiday: Independence Day, September 18.
Money: *Basic unit*—Chilean peso.

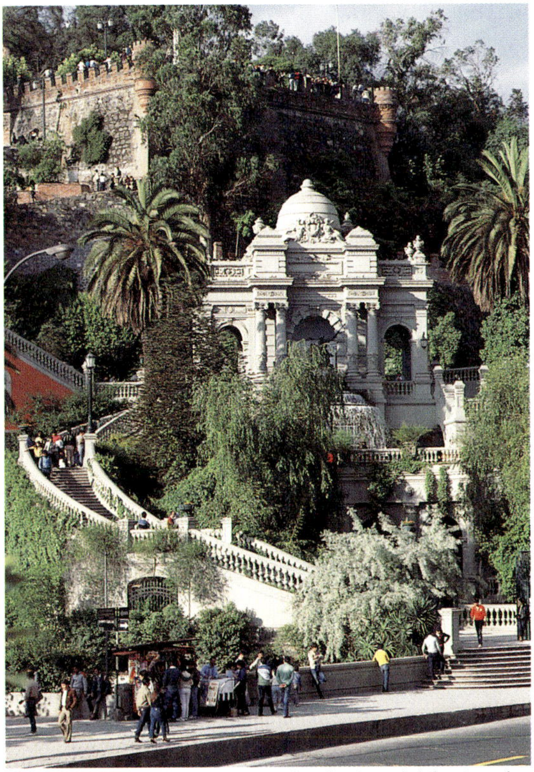

© Matthias Oppersdorf, Photo Researchers

Santiago, Chile's capital and largest city, has a landscape dominated by hills. One of these is Cerro Santa Lucía, a park with gardens, fountains, and winding stairs and pathways.

enough jobs in the cities. Also, many rural Chileans lack the skills needed for available city jobs. As a result, Chile's large urban areas have had such problems as poverty and unemployment.

Chile is the world's leading copper-producing nation. Its economy depends on copper exports. Farms in the Central Valley produce plentiful crops, but most fruit grown there is exported. Chile imports much of its food, manufactured goods, and petroleum.

For nearly 300 years, Chile was a Spanish colony. It gained independence from Spain in 1818. In 1833, a long period of constitutional rule began in Chile. Except for a few civil wars in the 1800's and a dictatorship from 1927 to 1931, the country became increasingly democratic. In 1973, military leaders overthrew the civilian government and set up a dictatorship. In 1990, however, a democratically elected civilian government was reestablished.

Government

National government. Chile is a republic. The president serves as head of state. The president is elected by the people to a four-year term and may not be elected to two consecutive terms. A Cabinet appointed by the president helps carry out government functions.

The Chilean legislature consists of two houses—the Chamber of Deputies and the Senate. Voters elect 120 deputies and 38 senators to terms of four and eight years, respectively.

Local government. Chile is divided into 12 regions, plus the Santiago metropolitan area, for purposes of local government. The regions are further divided into 51 provinces. The provinces are divided into more than 300 municipalities. The national government appoints the regional and provincial administrators. The people elect municipal officials to four-year terms.

Courts. The Supreme Court, Chile's highest court, consists of 21 judges appointed by the president. It reviews decisions made by lower courts. A separate body called the Constitutional Tribunal rules on the constitutionality of laws and reviews constitutional amendments. The court system also includes courts of appeal, criminal courts, and district courts.

Armed forces. Chile's army, navy, and air force have about 87,000 members. Men aged 18 or 19 are drafted to serve for one year in the army or air force or two years in the navy. Women may volunteer to fill noncombat military roles, such as nurses or paramedics. Both men and women attend military academies in Chile.

People

Population. Chile's population is unevenly distributed. Relatively few people live in the northern desert or in the rugged Andes. Southern Chile, with its many is-

Chile's flag. The white star stands for progress and honor. The red stands for the blood of heroes, the white for the snow of the Andes, and the blue for the sky.

The Chilean coat of arms bears the motto *By Right or by Might* in Spanish.

WORLD BOOK map

Chile lies along the west coast of South America. It borders Argentina, Bolivia, Peru, and the South Pacific Ocean.

lands and thick forests, is also thinly populated. More than three-fourths of all Chileans live in the Central Valley, which has a pleasant climate and rich soil.

Ancestry. Indians lived in what is now Chile long before Spaniards arrived in the 1500's. Over the years, many Spanish settlers and Indians intermarried. Their descendants are called *mestizos.* Today, mestizos make up about 65 percent of Chile's population. About 25 percent of the people are of unmixed European descent, chiefly Spanish. About 7 percent of all Chileans are of unmixed Indian ancestry.

About 1 million Mapuche Indians form the largest *indigenous* (native) group in Chile. The Spanish called the Mapuche *Araucanians.* They fought the Spaniards and their descendants for about 350 years. Today, most indigenous Chileans live in urban areas, but about one-fifth of the Mapuches still live in rural areas of southern Chile. The indigenous population also includes small groups of Atacameños, Quechua, and Aymara Indians, most of whom live in the north.

Social classes in Chile are based chiefly on wealth, not ancestry. But nearly all members of the small, rich upper class are of European descent. Mestizos make up most of the middle class. The lower class consists mainly of poor mestizos and most of Chile's Indians.

Language. Nearly all Chileans speak Spanish, the country's official language. Many Araucanians speak their own Indian language in addition to Spanish.

Way of life

City life. In Santiago and other major Chilean cities, modern steel and glass skyscrapers rise in busy commercial districts. The cities also have many Spanish-style buildings with red tile roofs and patios. Monuments and impressive public buildings border treelined streets. The cities are also known for their parks, gardens, and large *plazas* (public squares).

Wealthy city dwellers in Chile live in luxurious high-rise apartment buildings or spacious houses with fenced-in lawns and gardens. The well-to-do include business executives, industrialists, and owners of country estates who prefer to live in the city. Many middle-class city dwellers work in business or industry or have government or professional jobs. They live in apartments or comfortable single-family houses. Working-class city dwellers include salesclerks, factory workers, and other Chileans with low-paying jobs. Many of them live in run-down buildings in older neighborhoods. Some build their own homes out of discarded materials.

Since about 1900, poor rural Chileans have come to the cities—especially Santiago—to find work. By the 1930's, Chile had become a mostly urban society. But there have been too few jobs and inadequate housing for the poor migrants. During much of the 1900's, many of them resided in slums called *callampas* (mushrooms) because, like mushrooms, the slums seemed to spring up overnight. Since the 1970's, the poor have been pushed to the outskirts of Santiago and other cities. Government-subsidized programs in these areas have steadily replaced the substandard dwellings of the callampas with adequate housing and public services. But the new settlements are relatively isolated. Residents must travel far to work, increasing traffic and pollution.

Rural life. Most people who live in Chile's rural areas

© Ric Ergenbright

At a colorful river market in rural Chile, merchants bring boatloads of goods to be sold in nearby villages. At the same time, they pick up locally grown produce to sell in the cities.

Chile map index

Cities and towns*

City or town	Population	Key	
Ancud	39,946	G	1
Andacollo	10,288	D	2
Angol	48,996	H	5
Antofagasta	296,905	B	2
Arauco	34,873	G	4
Arica	186,488	A	2
Buin	63,419	D	6
Bulnes	20,595	G	5
Calama	138,402	B	3
Calbuco†	31,070	K	4
Cañete	31,270	H	4
Carahue	25,696	H	4
Casablanca†	21,874	D	5
Castro	39,366	K	4
Cauquenes	41,217	F	5
Chañaral	13,543	C	2
Chimbarongo	32,316	E	5
Chiguayante	81,302	G	4
Chillán	161,953	F	2
Coihaique	50,041	H	2
Colina	77,815	D	6
Concepción	216,061	F	2
Constitución	46,081	F	5
Copiapó	129,091	C	2
Coquimbo	163,036	D	2
Coronel	95,528	G	4
Curacautín	16,970	H	5
Curacaví†	24,298	D	5
Curanilahue	31,943	G	4
Curicó	119,585	E	6
El Monte†	26,459	D	6
Graneros	25,961	E	6
Illapel	30,355	D	2
Iquique	214,586	A	2
Isla de Maipo†	25,798	D	6
La Calera	49,503	D	6
La Laja	22,404	G	5
La Ligua	31,987	C	5
La Serena	160,148	D	2
La Unión	39,447	G	2
Lautaro	32,218	H	5
Lebu	25,035	H	4
Limache	39,219	D	5
Linares	83,249	F	2
Llaillay†	21,644	D	6
Llanquihue†	16,337	K	4
Loncoche	23,037	I	5
Lonquimay	10,237	H	5
Los Andes	60,198	D	6
Los Ángeles	166,556	F	2
Los Vilos	17,453	C	5
Lota	49,089	G	4
Mariá Elena	7,530	B	2
Maullin	15,580	K	4
Melipilla	94,540	D	6
Molina	38,521	F	5
Monte Patria†	30,276	D	2
Mulchén	29,003	H	5
Nacimiento	25,971	G	5
Nueva Imperial	40,059	H	4
Osorno	145,745	G	2
Ovalle	98,089	D	2
Panguipulli	33,273	I	5
Parral	37,822	F	5
Peñaflor	66,619	D	6
Penco	46,016	G	4
Pichilemu	12,392	E	5
Pitrufquén	21,988	I	5
Puente Alto†	492,915	D	6
Puerto Aisén	22,353	H	2
Puerto Montt	175,938	G	2
Puerto Natales	19,116	J	2
Puerto Varas	32,912	K	5
Punta Arenas	119,496	K	2
Quillota	75,916	D	5
Quilpué	128,578	D	5
Quintero†	21,174	D	5
Rancagua	214,344	E	2
Rengo	50,830	E	6
Río Bueno	32,627	J	5
Rio Negro	14,732	J	4
San Antonio	87,205	D	5
San Bernardo	246,762	D	6
San Carlos	50,088	G	5
San Felipe	64,126	D	6
San Fernando	63,732	E	6
San Javier	37,793	F	5
San Vicente†	40,253	E	5
Santa Cruz	32,387	E	5
Santiago	4,668,473	E	2
Talagante	59,805	D	6
Talca	201,797	F	2
Talcahuano	250,348	F	1
Taltal	11,100	C	2
Temuco	245,347	H	5
Tocopilla	23,986	B	2
Tomé	52,440	G	4
Traiguén	19,534	H	5
Valdivia	140,559	G	2
Vallenar	48,040	D	2
Valparaíso	275,982	E	2
Victoria	33,501	H	5
Vicuña†	24,010	D	2
Villa Alemana	95,623	D	5
Villarrica	45,531	I	5
Viña del Mar	286,931	D	5
Yumbel	20,498	G	5

*Population includes urban and rural areas.
†Does not appear on map; key shows general location.
Source: 2002 census.

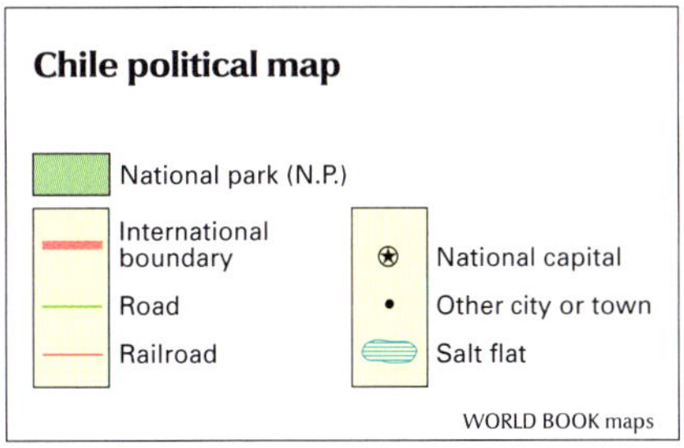

© Ric Ergenbright

© Carl Purcell

Housing in Chile includes sturdy wooden homes that perch on the steep, rocky south coast, *left,* and slum shacks on the outskirts of large cities, *right.* Many slumdwellers have moved from rural areas to the cities in an unsuccessful search for jobs and a better way of life.

are small farmers or farmworkers. Before the 1960's, large estates called *fundos* filled the countryside. Farmworkers called *inquilinos* lived on the fundos. In exchange for their labor, the inquilinos received a small wage, housing, and a plot of land on which to grow food. Women and children often worked as servants in the fundo household. In the 1960's, a government land reform program began to break up the fundos. In addition, many rural workers invaded the fundos and demanded land. Chile's governments often sided with the workers. But reforms were stopped when the military took over the government in 1973. The military returned some lands to fundo owners, kept some lands as a public reserve, and left the rest with small farmers. Many rural poor were left with nothing. Those who had farms often lacked the credit or facilities needed to succeed. As a result, rural people continued to migrate to the cities.

Clothing. Chileans dress much as people do in the United States and Canada. For rodeos and other special events, Chilean cowboys, called *huasos,* wear big flat-topped hats, ponchos, colorful sashes, fringed leather leggings, and boots with spurs. The clothing of the Mapuche women of south-central Chile includes brightly colored shawls and heavy silver jewelry.

Food and drink. Most Chileans have enough to eat, though many poor people lack a well-balanced diet. The Chilean diet is based on bread, beans, and potatoes. Most people also regularly eat at least a little meat in addition to many kinds of fish and shellfish. Meat and vegetables are often combined in stews or thick soups. Chileans enjoy a number of traditional dishes. *Cazuela de ave* is a hearty soup consisting of chicken, rice, and vegetables. *Pastel de choclo,* a baked corn casserole, is made of grated corn, minced meat, raisins, and onions. Other favorite dishes include a fish chowder called *paila marina* and *empanadas*—pastry turnovers stuffed with meat or seafood, eggs, vegetables, and fruit.

Coffee and tea, including an herb tea called *agüita,* are popular beverages. Many of the wealthier people enjoy fine Chilean wines with their meals.

Recreation. Movies are a popular form of recreation in Chilean cities. In Santiago and other major cities, concerts, plays, ballets, and operas also attract large audiences. Rural Chileans enjoy family outings and visits with friends and neighbors. Chileans also celebrate various religious holidays with parades and festivals.

Chile's long Pacific coastline is dotted with scenic beaches. Vacationers from many countries flock to the luxurious coastal resort of Viña del Mar during the warmer months of December through March. South-central Chile's Lake Country offers fishing, boating, and hiking. Portillo and other ski resorts in the Andes attract wealthy Chileans and foreigners.

Soccer is Chile's most popular spectator sport by far. Fans crowd the stadiums to watch professional games and cheer their favorite teams. Chileans also enjoy such sports as horse racing, basketball, and tennis.

Religion. Spanish colonists brought the Roman Catholic religion to Chile. Today, about 75 percent of all Chileans are Catholics. The Catholic Church operates many schools in Chile, and church leaders have actively promoted political and social reforms.

The number of Protestants in Chile is growing. Today, about 12 percent of the people are Protestants. Protestant groups include Baptists, Lutherans, Methodists, and an increasing number of Pentecostal churches.

Education. Most Chileans aged 15 and older can read and write. For the country's literacy rate, see **Litera-**

cy (table: Literacy rates for selected countries). Chile provides free public elementary education, and children must attend eight years of elementary school. Many elementary school graduates do not go to high school because they must work to help support their families. Most of the high school students come from upper middle-class or upper-class families. Chile has both public and private high schools. The private high schools charge tuition. Most of them are operated by the Catholic Church. Public high schools are free. The University of Chile, in Santiago, is the country's oldest and largest institution of higher learning.

The arts. Chile's greatest achievements in the arts have been in literature. *La Araucana,* written by Alonso de Ercilla y Zúñiga in the late 1500's, ranks as one of the great epic poems in Latin American literature. It tells of the Mapuche Indians' fight against the Spanish conquerors of Chile. In 1945, the Chilean poet Gabriela Mistral became the first Latin American writer to win the Nobel Prize in literature. Her works express great sympathy for the needy. One of her students, Pablo Neruda, won the 1971 Nobel Prize in literature. His poems express the joys, dreams, struggles, and frustrations of ordinary Latin Americans. Ariel Dorfman gained international recognition for his fiction and nonfiction works that explore the terrors of political dictatorship.

The land

Chile lies along South America's Pacific coast. It extends 2,650 miles (4,265 kilometers) from north to south but is only 265 miles (427 kilometers) wide at its widest

© Ric Ergenbright

At a village elementary school, Chilean youngsters learn to read and write. Chile provides free public elementary education, and children must attend eight years of elementary school.

Michael Minardi, Black Star

Early worshipers arrive for Mass at a small Roman Catholic church in the town of Castro. About 75 percent of the people of Chile are Roman Catholics.

Jack Fields, Photo Researchers

Skiing in the Andes Mountains is a popular form of recreation among well-to-do Chileans. Such ski resorts as Portillo, *shown here,* also attract many vacationers from other countries.

point. A low range of mountains rises along the coast. The lofty Andes Mountains form the country's eastern boundary with Bolivia and Argentina. Chile lies along a major earthquake belt and is frequently struck by earthquakes and huge destructive waves called *tsunamis.*

Chile can be divided into three land regions. They are, from north to south: (1) the Northern Desert, (2) the Central Valley, and (3) the Archipelago. In addition, Chile owns a number of small islands in the Pacific Ocean.

The Northern Desert stretches 1,050 miles (1,690 kilometers) south from the Peruvian border to the Aconcagua River, just north of Valparaíso. The Atacama Desert, which Chileans call the Norte Grande (Great North), covers the northern half of the region. The Atacama is one of the world's driest places. It gradually gives way to a slightly less arid area in the south called the Norte Chico (Little North).

Except for crops grown on a few oases, the Atacama has almost no plant life. However, the desert has huge deposits of copper. It also contains vast deposits of sodium nitrate, which is used for fertilizers and explosives.

The Loa is the only river in the Atacama. It flows from the Andes to the Pacific. Several rivers cross the Norte Chico. However, many of them are dry part of the year.

Some cities and towns in the Northern Desert are scattered along the coast, where fishing is an important occupation. Other towns are near mining areas in the interior. The large coastal cities, such as Antofagasta and Arica, also serve as seaports. Water and other supplies for many of the region's settlements must be brought in from other areas. A few oases in the Atacama support small farming communities. Farmers in the Norte Chico raise livestock and grow crops in irrigated river valleys.

The Central Valley extends about 600 miles (970 kilometers) from the Aconcagua River to the city of Puerto Montt. The Central Valley is the heartland of Chile. Industry, agriculture, and most of the nation's population

F. Gohier, Photo Researchers

Chile's Northern Desert region includes one of the world's driest places, the Atacama Desert, *shown here.* The Atacama has little plant life, but it contains huge deposits of valuable minerals.

WORLD BOOK map

Physical features

Aconcagua River	D	2
Andes Mountains	E	2
Atacama Desert	B	2
Bió-Bió River	E	2
Cape Horn	H	3
Chiloé Island	F	2
Domeyko Range	B	2
Gulf of Corcovado	F	2
Juan Fernández Islands	D	1
Lake Llanquihue	E	2
Loa River	B	2
Maipo River	D	2
Mapocho River	D	2
Maule River	D	2
Norte Chico	C	2
Ojos del Salado (mountain)	C	3
Point Lavapié	E	2
San Ambrosio Island	B	1
San Félix Island	B	1
South Atlantic Ocean	G	3
South Pacific Ocean	C	1
Strait of Magellan	H	3
Tierra del Fuego (island group)	H	2
Uspallata Pass	D	2

Hans Silvester, Photo Researchers

Chile's Central Valley is crossed by several rivers fed by runoff water from the Andes. The fertile soil of the river basins makes the Central Valley Chile's richest agricultural region. The region also has much of the country's industry and most of its population.

are concentrated in the region.

Runoff water from the Andes Mountains is channeled through several rivers that cross the Central Valley. The rivers include the Aconcagua, Mapocho, Maipo, Maule, and Bío-Bío. The river valleys contain Chile's richest soil. Orchards, vineyards, pastures, and croplands cover much of the Central Valley. The region also has large deposits of coal, copper, and manganese.

An area of spectacular beauty lies south of the Bío-Bío River. Snow-capped volcanoes—some of which are still active—rise on the Andes' western slopes. Sparkling lakes and deep valleys made by glaciers lie among heavily forested mountains. This area, called the Lake Country, is a popular vacation spot during the dry summers.

The Archipelago extends about 1,000 miles (1,600 kilometers) from Puerto Montt to the southernmost tip of South America, Cape Horn. It is a wild region of steep, rocky slopes, dense forests, glaciers, and lakes. The region's western edge is broken into thousands of islands pounded by the sea. In the far south, the Strait of Magellan separates mainland Chile from the group of islands known as Tierra del Fuego, which are divided between Chile and Argentina. Cape Horn, on Chile's Horn Island, is the southernmost point of Tierra del Fuego.

Relatively few people live in the Archipelago region. Punta Arenas, on the Strait of Magellan, is the only major settlement. Most of the land is unsuitable for growing crops. However, farmers graze large numbers of sheep on pastures at the southern end of the mainland and on Tierra del Fuego. The far south is also important for its oil fields. Most petroleum produced in Chile comes from the Strait of Magellan and Tierra del Fuego.

Outlying territories. Chile owns several small islands far out in the Pacific, including Easter Island and the Juan Fernández Islands. Easter Island, about 2,300 miles (3,700 kilometers) west of the mainland, is famous for its huge stone carvings. The Juan Fernández Islands lie about 400 miles (640 kilometers) west of Chile. See **Easter Island; Juan Fernández.**

Chile also claims a large pie-slice-shaped area of Antarctica. But other nations do not recognize this claim.

Climate

Chile lies south of the equator, and so its seasons are opposite those of the Northern Hemisphere. Summer lasts from late December to late March, and winter from late June to late September.

Parts of Chile's Northern Desert may not have rain for years. But the region is not especially hot. Winds that blow across the cold Peru Current bring cool, cloudy weather and frequent fogs to the coastal area. In Antofagasta, temperatures average 69 °F (20 °C) in January and 57 °F (14 °C) in July.

The Central Valley has a mild climate, with rainy winters and dry summers. Santiago gets about 14 inches (36 centimeters) of rain annually. Temperatures in the city average 69 °F (20 °C) in January and 48 °F (9 °C) in July.

Cold rains, piercing winds, and frequent storms characterize the Archipelago. In Puerto Montt, temperatures average 59 °F (15 °C) in January and 46 °F (8 °C) in July. The city's average annual precipitation is 86 inches (218 centimeters). Parts of the Archipelago receive up to 200 inches (500 centimeters) of rain a year.

Economy

Service industries and manufacturing account for most of Chile's *gross domestic product* (GDP)—the total value of goods and services produced within a country in a year. However, mining plays a more important role in the economy of Chile than in the economies of most other countries. Copper is the most valuable resource and export. Many other industries of Chile are dependent on the country's mineral production.

In 1971, Chile's government began to take control of many industries and to regulate prices, wages, and trade. These actions aroused opposition among some business and military leaders. After military leaders overthrew the Chilean government in 1973, they reduced the government's role in the economy. By 1990, when Chile returned to civilian rule, the government had sold most industries and utilities to private owners. The civilian leaders continued the privatization process.

Service industries account for more than half of Chile's GDP and employ more than half of the country's workers. Many service workers are employed by businesses that engage in trade, including stores and restaurants. Government agencies, banks, health care facilities, and social service organizations also employ many Chileans. Many other service workers in Chile are employed in transportation and communication and in such professions as teaching and law.

Manufacturing accounts for about one-sixth of Chile's GDP and employs about one-seventh of the nation's work force. Most Chilean factories produce consumer goods, such as beverages, clothing, processed foods, textiles, and wood products. Other manufactured goods include cement, chemicals, paper products, steel, and transportation equipment. Concepción, Santiago, and Valparaíso are Chile's main industrial centers.

Agriculture employs almost as many workers as manufacturing but produces only about half as much of the nation's GDP. Almost all farmland lies in the Central Valley. Wheat is the most valuable crop. Other crops include corn, barley, rice, and oats. Farmers grow beans, potatoes, sugar beets, and other vegetables, as well as apples, citrus fruits, grapes, peaches, and nuts. Cattle, poultry, sheep, and other livestock make up about a third of the value of Chile's agricultural production.

Chile does not produce enough food for all its people, partly because only about 3 percent of its land can be cultivated. Old-fashioned farming methods also limit Chile's agricultural output.

A few wealthy landowners held most of Chile's farmland until the 1960's. In the late 1960's and early 1970's, a rural reform movement led to the division of large estates. Today, most land is owned by small farmers or large corporations. Most of Chile's farms cover less than 25 acres (10 hectares). Small farmers are often too poor to purchase modern technology to work their land. But corporate farm production is increasing. Many corporate farms grow fruits and vegetables that are exported to Europe and North America during their winters.

Mining. Chile has about a fifth of the world's known copper reserves and ranks as the world's leading copper-producing nation. Chuquicamata in the Atacama Desert is the largest open-pit copper mine in the world. The world's largest underground copper mine, El Teniente, lies southeast of Santiago.

Chile ranks among the leading countries in molybdenum production. Chile is also a significant producer of natural sodium nitrate and iodine. The country's mineral products also include gold, iron ore, lithium, manganese, natural gas, petroleum, and silver.

Fishing industry. Chile has one of the world's largest fishing industries. This industry yields an annual catch of about 6 million tons (5.4 million metric tons) of fish and shellfish. Most fishing takes place off the north coast. The catch consists mainly of anchovettas, jack mackerel, and sardines. Most fish are processed into fish meal and fish oil for export. Chile also exports fresh fish, especially salmon and bass, to Europe, Japan, and North America.

Energy sources. Chile uses far more petroleum than it produces. As a result, the country must import more than 90 percent of the petroleum it uses.

Hydroelectric power plants generate about two-thirds of Chile's electric power. Plants that burn petroleum produce most of the rest.

International trade. Minerals—mainly copper, molybdenum, and iron ore—account for nearly half of the total value of Chile's exports. Other leading exports

Chile's gross domestic product

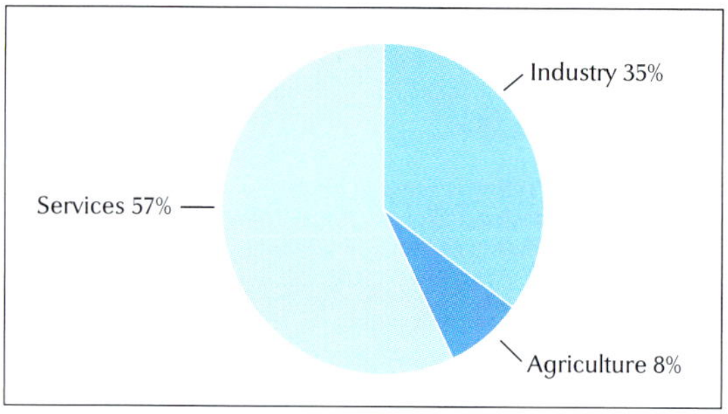

Chile's gross domestic product (GDP) was $75,515,000,000 in United States dollars in 2000. The GDP is the total value of goods and services produced within a country in a year. *Services* include community, government, and personal services; finance, insurance, real estate, and business services; transportation and communication; and wholesale and retail trade. *Industry* includes construction, manufacturing, mining, and utilities. *Agriculture* includes agriculture, forestry, and fishing.

Production and workers by economic activities

Economic activities	Percent of GDP produced	Employed workers: Number of people	Employed workers: Percent of total
Wholesale & retail trade	19	995,500	18
Finance, insurance, & real estate	19	425,800	8
Manufacturing	16	754,200	14
Mining	11	70,300	1
Transportation & communication	10	430,200	8
Community, government, & personal services	9	1,494,200	28
Agriculture, forestry, & fishing	8	770,000	14
Construction	5	406,100	8
Utilities	3	28,400	1
Total	100	5,374,700	100

Figures are for 2000.
Sources: Chile National Institute of Statistics; International Monetary Fund.

© Ric Ergenbright

Jack Fields, Photo Researchers

Ranching and fishing provide food for many Chileans. At the left, a cowboy, called a *huaso,* herds cattle in central Chile. Many ranches in southern Chile raise sheep. At the right, fishermen sell their catch from the boat. Chile has one of the world's largest fishing industries.

include beverages, chemical products, fish meal, fruits, metal products, and wood products. The chief imports include chemicals, electronic equipment, machinery, motor vehicles, petroleum, and wheat. The United States is Chile's major trading partner. Since the 1970's, Chile also has expanded its trade with other Latin American countries and with Asian and European countries.

Transportation and communication. The Atacama Desert, the Andes Mountains, and the many islands in the south have hampered the development of transportation in Chile. In addition, most of the country's rivers are too short and swift to serve as inland transportation routes. Until the 1900's, ships traveling from one coastal port to another provided the main links between Chile's regions. Today, railroads, highways, and airlines connect cities and towns in northern and central Chile. In the south, ships are still a chief means of transportation. Between the late 1970's and mid-1990's, a road was built from Puerto Montt to the far south.

Most Chileans rely on automobiles and buses for transportation. International railways connect Chile to Argentina, Bolivia, and Peru. Santiago has a fine underground railway system. Valparaíso is the country's leading port. Other major ports include Antofagasta, Arica, Puerto Montt, and Punta Arenas. Chile's busiest airport, Arturo Merino Benítez Airport, is near Santiago.

More than 90 percent of all Chilean households have at least one radio, and most also have a television set. More than 40 daily newspapers are published in Chile.

Hans Silvester, Photo Researchers

A huge copper smelter purifies copper from the world's largest open-pit copper mine, Chuquicamata, in northern Chile. Chile ranks as the world's leading copper-producing nation.

History

Early days. Indians lived in what is now Chile long before the first white people arrived in the 1500's. The Atacama, Diaguita, and other small groups lived along the north coast and at the southern edge of the Atacama Desert. These Indians hunted game, tended llamas and alpacas, and grew a variety of crops. In the late 1400's, they were conquered by the Inca Indians of Peru.

Chile's largest Indian group, the Mapuche, lived in the Central Valley. Their warriors defeated the Inca, who tried to push southward into the region. The Mapuche fished and grew such crops as corn, beans, and potatoes. In the cold, wet south, the Ona and Yahgan Indians lived by hunting and fishing.

In 1520, the Portuguese navigator Ferdinand Magellan

became the first European to reach what is now Chile. He sighted the area as he sailed through the strait that now bears his name near the tip of South America.

Spanish conquest. The Spaniards defeated the Inca of Peru by 1533 and seized their gold and silver. One of the Spanish conquerors, Diego de Almagro, set out in 1535 to explore the land south of Peru. Almagro and his men hoped to find more gold and silver. They traveled as far as the area around present-day Santiago but found only scattered Indian settlements with no riches.

In 1540, another Spaniard, Pedro de Valdivia, led a group of men from Peru to Chile's Central Valley. Valdivia founded Santiago on Feb. 12, 1541. Six months later, the Mapuche destroyed it. The Spaniards rebuilt Santiago and also founded La Serena, Valparaíso, Concepción, Valdivia, and Villarrica. The Mapuche refused to give in to the Spaniards, however. In 1553, they killed Valdivia and most of his men in battle. The determined resistance of the Mapuche made southern Chile a battleground for more than 300 years.

Colonial period. Spain ruled Chile from the 1500's to the early 1800's. Chile was part of a large Spanish colony called the Viceroyalty of Peru, which included other parts of Spanish South America. The king of Spain appointed a captain-general to govern Chile, but he was under the authority of the viceroy of Peru.

Chile attracted few settlers because the Spanish explorers had found little gold or silver there. But many colonists who did come grew rich raising cattle and wheat in the Central Valley. The king of Spain granted the settlers huge tracts of land. The Spaniards forced the Indians who lived on the land to work as slaves. But many Indians—especially Mapuche in the south—fought the Spaniards. A frontier army was formed in southern Chile to protect settlers from Indian attacks.

During the colonial period, the Roman Catholic Church sent missionaries to Chile to convert the Indians. In time, the church became a powerful institution in the colony. It owned vast estates and controlled education.

Independence. In 1808, the French emperor Napoleon Bonaparte seized control of Spain. He removed King Ferdinand VII from the throne and appointed his brother Joseph Bonaparte king of Spain. Meanwhile, a movement for independence had been growing in Chile and other Spanish colonies in South America. With the French army occupying Spain, the colonies took the opportunity to revolt.

On Sept. 18, 1810, a group made up chiefly of large landowners formed a *junta* (council) and declared that it would serve as an independent government. A Chilean aristocrat named José Miguel Carrera became head of the government in 1811. His rule was challenged by Bernardo O'Higgins Riquelme, son of an Irish immigrant who had been viceroy of Peru. While Carrera and O'Higgins feuded, Spanish forces loyal to Ferdinand entered Chile from Peru and regained control of the colony in 1814. Carrera and O'Higgins fled to Argentina.

O'Higgins returned to Chile in 1817 with the Argentine general José de San Martín. They led an army that defeated the Spanish at Chacabuco, near Santiago. On April 5, 1818, O'Higgins and San Martín won a final victory over the Spanish at the Maipo River. O'Higgins became the new nation's first leader.

Building the nation. O'Higgins supervised the drafting of two constitutions for Chile—one in 1818 and the other in 1822. He established a Chilean navy, set up a system of elementary schools separate from the Catholic Church, and founded the National Library of Chile. O'Higgins also made reforms that angered some of his supporters. For example, he abolished titles of nobility, tried to break up landowners' huge estates, and worked to reduce the power of the Catholic Church.

Soon after independence, two political parties arose in Chile. The Conservatives favored a strong central government that would carry on many of the policies of the colonial period. The Liberals supported constitutional government, land reform, and restrictions on the power of the Catholic Church. The Conservatives felt O'Higgins was too liberal, and many Liberals felt he wanted too much power. Because of this lack of support, O'Higgins was forced to resign in 1823. Weak, heavily indebted governments ruled from 1823 to 1830. The Conservatives gained control of the government in 1830 after a brief civil war and stayed in power for the next 30 years.

During the 1830's, a businessman named Diego Portales Palazuelos controlled Chile's government through his role as a presidential adviser. Portales supervised the writing of the Constitution of 1833, which remained in effect until 1925. The Constitution established a strong central government and gave the president widespread powers. It also made Catholicism the state religion. Under this Constitution, only men older than 25 who earned more than a certain amount of income or owned more than a minimum amount of property could vote.

In 1836, Chile declared war on Peru and Bolivia to prevent them from forming a confederation. Chile won the war in 1839. A dispute over control of the nitrate deposits in the Atacama Desert broke out between Chile and Bolivia in the 1870's. Peru sided with Bolivia, and the three nations fought the War of the Pacific from 1879 to 1883. Chile won the war and increased its land area by more than a third. The new territory held valuable deposits of copper as well as nitrates.

Important dates in Chile

Late 1400's	Indian groups in northern Chile were conquered by the Inca Indians of Peru.
1520	Ferdinand Magellan, a Portuguese navigator, became the first European to sight Chile.
1541	Pedro de Valdivia, a Spaniard, founded Santiago.
1818	Chile won independence from Spain.
1833	A new Chilean Constitution established a strong central government and made Roman Catholicism the state religion.
1925	Another new Constitution separated church and state and strengthened individual rights.
1939	The Chilean government created an economic development corporation.
1970	Salvador Allende Gossens was elected president of Chile. He became the first democratically elected Marxist to head a nation in the Western Hemisphere.
1973	Military leaders overthrew the Allende government.
1980	A new Constitution provided for a gradual return to democratic government in Chile in the 1990's.
1989	Elections for president and a legislature led to a return to a democratic civilian government.
2006	Chileans elected Michelle Bachelet president. She was the first woman to be elected president of Chile.

Museum of Modern Art of Latin America, Organization of American States, Washington, D.C.

Bernardo O'Higgins was a hero of Chile's war of independence. With the Argentine general José de San Martín, O'Higgins led an army to final victory over the Spanish in 1818.

Era of changes. Chile's new mineral wealth provided the resources for economic development in the late 1800's. But political conflicts continued. For years, many Liberal political leaders had resented the broad powers of the presidency. In 1890, the situation reached a crisis when the National Congress refused to approve President José Manuel Balmaceda's spending plans. Civil war broke out 1891, and over 10,000 Chileans died in the fighting. Balmaceda's forces were defeated, and he took his life. After the civil war, Congress voted to increase its powers and limit those of the president. Congress remained the strongest force in Chilean politics until 1925.

Beginning in the late 1800's, earnings from nitrate exports fueled industrial growth in Chile. This growth led to an enlarged middle class of clerks, professional workers, and shopkeepers. Many workers, however, did not share in Chile's prosperity. Rising prices led workers to strike, and sometimes to riot, to demand better working conditions and higher pay.

Chile remained neutral during World War I (1914-1918). The nation's economy boomed because of the wartime demand for nitrates, which were used to make explosives. After the war, Germany began to export synthetic nitrates, and Chile's export market collapsed. Unemployment surged. Strikes and riots disrupted the presidential election campaign of 1920. Many middle-class people joined forces with factory workers and miners to elect Arturo Alessandri Palma president. Alessandri pushed for political and social reforms, but Congress rejected most of his proposals. Eventually, some reforms were passed under pressure from the military. In 1924, the military seized control of the government, and Alessandri resigned. But his supporters in the military led a second coup in 1925, and he returned to the presidency. That year, a new constitution was passed that included many of Alessandri's reforms.

The Constitution of 1925 reduced the power of Congress and restored many presidential powers. It called for the president to be elected directly by the voters. The Constitution strengthened individual rights, including freedom of religion. Church and state became separate. The Constitution also lowered the voting age so that all men older than 21 who could read and write could vote. The income and property requirements for voters had been abolished in 1885.

In 1927, General Carlos Ibáñez del Campo became president in a rigged election. He governed as a dictator. He made several domestic reforms, expanded social welfare programs, and promoted industry. He also cracked down on labor unions and left-wing political activity. He increased government revenues but eventually began borrowing heavily to sustain high public spending. The worldwide Great Depression that began in 1929 led to economic collapse in Chile. Demonstrations forced Ibáñez to resign in 1931.

Years of progress. Alessandri was again elected president of Chile in 1932. The country made a slow economic recovery during his administration.

Chileans elected Pedro Aguirre Cerda president in 1938. The next year, the government created an economic development corporation called the Corporación de Fomento de la Producción (CORFO). With loans from the United States, CORFO built a steel mill near Concepción, developed hydroelectric facilities, and established a sugar beet industry.

Chile was neutral at the start of World War II (1939-1945), but it broke relations with Germany and Japan in 1943. Chile sold copper, nitrates, and other war supplies to the Allies. Economic development projects continued during the 1940's under Presidents Juan Antonio Ríos and Gabriel González Videla. Chilean women gained the right to vote in national elections in 1949.

Chile's economy began having problems in the 1940's and 1950's. The economy was too dependent on income from copper export taxes. High inflation in the late 1940's led to worker rebellions, which the government crushed. Deep political divisions developed between conservative, moderate, and left-wing groups. Former President Ibáñez became president again in 1952. He pledged to rise above party politics, curb inflation, and address the problems of Chile's poor. But government mismanagement and continuing economic problems led Chileans to be discouraged by his administration.

In 1958, Jorge Alessandri Rodríguez, a son of Arturo Alessandri, was elected president. He reduced taxes on businesses and attracted some foreign investment. Although his conservative policies initially helped stabilize the economy, inflation remained a problem. In 1960, a series of earthquakes and a tsunami struck Chile. These disasters killed thousands, caused several hundred million dollars in damage, and added to Chile's economic difficulties.

Chileans elected Eduardo Frei Montalva president in 1964. Frei set up programs for land reform, public housing construction, and investment in education. During

Frei's presidency, the United States provided financial aid to Chile through the Alliance for Progress, a cooperative economic development program (see **Alliance for Progress**). This aid allowed Frei to spend more on social reforms and to buy partial control of copper mines from their U.S. owners. Frei's programs did not satisfy Chile's conservative and left-wing parties, who became even more divided over the pace of change.

Marxism and military rule. Salvador Allende Gossens, who ran on a program to make Chile a socialist state, was elected president in 1970. He was the first Marxist to be elected democratically to head a nation in the Western Hemisphere. The Allende government took over ownership of the copper mines, many banks, and numerous other industries. It also implemented a broad land reform program. Many rural Chileans seized land illegally while the program was being carried out.

The Allende government approved sharp increases in the minimum wage at the same time that it tried to prevent price increases in consumer goods. Food shortages became widespread. Inflation soared from about 20 percent in 1971 to more than 350 percent in 1973. Strikes became common, and both supporters and opponents of Allende staged violent demonstrations. Opposition from Congress and the middle and upper classes further weakened Allende's government. The Soviet Union and Cuba supported Allende, but the United States and U.S. firms in Chile assisted Allende's opponents. The U.S. government cut off aid to the Chilean government. Also, U.S. intelligence agencies encouraged right-wing paramilitary groups and military leaders who were plotting to seize control of the government.

On Sept. 11, 1973, the military overthrew the government. As jets and troops attacked the presidential palace, Allende reportedly committed suicide rather than surrender and resign.

The military junta that then ruled Chile dissolved Congress, censored the press, cracked down on labor and land reform movements, and banned political parties. Many left-wing party, union, and peasant leaders were murdered. Thousands of people were tortured. Supporters of Allende were imprisoned or forced into exile. Most industries that the Allende government had taken over were returned to the previous owners. The military government, however, kept control of the copper mines.

General Augusto Pinochet Ugarte became the dominant figure of the junta and eventually president of Chile. He radically changed Chile's economy to promote capitalism. He cut government spending and social subsidies, lowered tariffs, and opened Chilean markets to massive imports. Wages fell, industries closed, and the working poor faced starvation.

Gradually, however, private industry recovered, prospering between 1976 and 1981. Chile began exporting more fruits, vegetables, fish, and forestry products to advanced economies. Except for brief periods, the U.S. government supported the Pinochet regime with financial aid.

Crisis and democracy. In 1980, a new constitution was approved in a *plebiscite* (vote of the people) controlled by Pinochet. Under the new set of laws, presidential powers were greatly expanded, and the military's role in government was formally established. The 1980 Constitution also provided for a vote in 1988 on whether Pinochet's rule should continue.

In 1982 and 1983, Chile's economy collapsed. Strikes and demonstrations threatened to end Pinochet's government. But a renewed crackdown on government opponents allowed Pinochet to hang on to power until the economy began to recover later in the 1980's. In 1987, he allowed some political parties to reenter public life. Many people in exile began returning to Chile.

In 1988, Chile held a plebiscite on Pinochet's rule. The vote resulted in his defeat. Another plebiscite in 1989 approved constitutional reforms that restored civil liberties. Later that year, elections were held for a civilian president and a two-house Congress. Patricio Aylwin Azócar, a member of the centrist Christian Democratic Party, won the presidency. Aylwin represented the Concertación, or Coalition of Parties for Democracy, which included Christian Democrats and Socialists.

Despite the 1989 reforms, the 1980 Constitution limited what the new government could do. Rules had been imposed to prohibit a return to socialist policies. Pinochet remained head of the army, and his supporters dominated the Senate. Aylwin created some social programs to ease the poverty that had existed throughout Pinochet's rule. However, Aylwin did not change the free-market basis of the economy.

Recent developments. During the 1990's, the economy boomed. Chile had low inflation and unemployment, an expanding middle class, and steady investment in education and basic social welfare measures. Concertación candidates won each of the next two presidential elections. Eduardo Frei Ruíz-Tagle, a Christian Democrat and son of the earlier President Frei, became president in 1994. Ricardo Lagos Escobar, a Socialist, became president in 2000. The 1980 Constitution remains the basic law of Chile, and the country continues to function under the free-market system that had been imposed by Pinochet.

Pinochet remained head of Chile's army until 1998, when he became a senator for life. That year, while seeking medical treatment in the United Kingdom, he was arrested on an international warrant for crimes against humanity. In 2000, British officials allowed Pinochet to return to Chile, saying he was unfit to stand trial. In 2002, Pinochet resigned from the office of senator for life.

During the early 2000's, Chilean courts stripped Pinochet of legal immunity and ruled that he could be prosecuted for human rights abuses committed while he was in power and for tax fraud. But higher courts later ruled that Pinochet was too ill to stand trial in most of the cases.

In 2006, Chileans elected Michelle Bachelet the country's first woman president. Bachelet belongs to the Socialist Party and leads the center-left Concertación coalition. Michael Monteón

Related articles in *World Book* include:

Biographies

Allende Gossens, Salvador
Bachelet, Michelle
Mistral, Gabriela
Neruda, Pablo
O'Higgins, Bernardo
Pinochet Ugarte, Augusto

Cities

Santiago
Valparaíso
Viña del Mar

Other related articles

Andes Mountains
Atacama Desert
Cape Horn
Easter Island
Juan Fernández
Latin America
Mapuche
Ojos del Salado
San Martín, José de
South America
Tierra del Fuego

Outline

I. Government
- A. National government
- B. Local government
- C. Courts
- D. Armed forces

II. People
- A. Population
- B. Ancestry
- C. Language

III. Way of life
- A. City life
- B. Rural life
- C. Clothing
- D. Food and drink
- E. Recreation
- F. Religion
- G. Education
- H. The arts

IV. The land
- A. The Northern Desert
- B. The Central Valley
- C. The Archipelago
- D. Outlying territories

V. Climate

VI. Economy
- A. Service industries
- B. Manufacturing
- C. Agriculture
- D. Mining
- E. Fishing industry
- F. Energy sources
- G. Trade
- H. Transportation and communication

VII. History

Questions

Why did Chile attract few settlers after the Spanish conquest?
What is *La Araucana*?
Where do most of Chile's people live?
What is Chile's most popular spectator sport?
When did Chile win independence from Spain?
Why did Chile's economy boom during World War I?
Who was Bernardo O'Higgins? Diego Portales?
Why have Chile's cities grown in population since about 1900?
What is Chile's most valuable resource?
Who was the first Marxist to be democratically elected to head a nation in the Western Hemisphere?

Additional resources

Chile: A Country Study Guide. International Business Pubns., published annually.
Collier, Simon, and Sater, W. F. *A History of Chile, 1808-1994.* Cambridge, 1996.
Graham, Melissa, and others. *Chile.* Rough Guides, 1999.
Hickman, John. *News from the End of Earth.* St. Martin's, 1998.
Lomnitz, Larissa A., and Melnick, Ana. *Chile's Political Culture and Parties.* Notre Dame, 2000.
McNair, Sylvia. *Chile.* Children's Pr., 2000. Younger readers.

Chimborazo, *CHIHM buh RAH zoh,* is a volcanic mountain in the Andes of Ecuador, about 120 miles (193 kilometers) from the Pacific coast (see **Ecuador** [map]). Snow-covered Mount Chimborazo rises 20,561 feet (6,267 meters) above sea level. It is the highest of about 35 peaks in northern Ecuador that form an "avenue of volcanoes." See also **Mountain** (diagram: Major mountains). Gregory Knapp

Chimera, *ky MIHR uh* or *kuh MIHR uh,* was a fire-breathing monster in Greek mythology. The name is also spelled *Chimaera.* The Chimera was the offspring of the monsters Typhon and Echidna. It had the head of a lion, the body of a goat, and the tail of a serpent.

The Chimera terrorized the kingdom of Lycia. Iobates, the Lycian king, ordered the hero Bellerophon to destroy the monster. Bellerophon tamed the winged horse Pegasus with the help of a golden bridle provided by the goddess Athena. Then Bellerophon flew over the Chimera and killed it with arrows. The words *chimera* and *chimerical* are often used to describe anything that is wildly fanciful or absurd. Justin M. Glenn

Chimes, also called *tubular bells,* are a percussion instrument that consists of 18 to 20 brass or steel tubes hung on a frame. The tubes have a range of 1 ½ octaves. The tubes are arranged with low notes on the left and high notes on the right. The player strikes the tubes with one or two mallets made of pressed leather. The chimes produce deep, ringing sounds. The musician can sustain the sounds by operating a *sustaining pedal* with the foot. Chimes made of stone were used in the Far East as early as 2300 B.C. In 1885, John Hampton of Coventry, England, developed the kind of chimes used today in bands, orchestras, and other musical groups. John H. Beck

See also **Bell** (Chimes and carillons); **Music** (picture: Percussion instruments).

Chimney sweep is a worker who cleans the soot out of chimneys. A brush on a long handle is also sometimes called a chimney sweep. In earlier times, many chimney sweeps worked in Europe and in North America. A few of them still work at the trade.

Chimney swift. See Swift.

Chimpanzee is an African ape that shares many characteristics with human beings. Chimpanzees are intelligent, playful, curious, and easy to train. Scientific evidence suggests that chimpanzees and their closest relatives, the *bonobos* or *pygmy chimpanzees,* are more closely related to human beings than any other animal. Chimpanzees are also related to gorillas, orangutans, and gibbons.

The chimpanzee lives in tropical Africa from Lake Victoria in the east to Gambia in the west. Members of this species differ enough that scientists divide them into three *subspecies* (kinds). They are the *central chim-*

Randall L. Susman

The body of a chimpanzee is covered with long, dark hair. Chimpanzee faces generally grow darker with age. The face of the young chimpanzee pictured here has partially darkened.

Richard Wrangham, Anthro-Photo

Chimpanzees live together in groups. The chimpanzees shown in the background are grooming each other. They pick through each other's hair to remove any dirt, burs, or insects. Adult chimpanzees spend about an hour a day grooming.

panzee, the *eastern* or *long-haired chimpanzee,* and the *western chimpanzee.*

The body of a chimpanzee. Chimpanzees range in height from 3 ¼ feet (100 centimeters) to 5 ½ feet (170 centimeters). An adult male weighs about 110 pounds (50 kilograms), while an adult female weighs about 90 pounds (41 kilograms).

The chimpanzee's body is covered with long, dark hair. Like other apes, the chimpanzee does not have a tail. It has large ears, and its arms are longer than its legs. The chimpanzee's long hands are well shaped for powerful grasping and for holding on to branches. In addition, the big toes of the chimpanzee face sideways and work like thumbs to help the animal climb trees.

The life of a chimpanzee. Chimpanzees live mainly in forests. Their territories range from humid rain forests to dry grasslands with few trees. Some chimpanzees even make their homes in desertlike places. But more chimpanzees live in wet areas than in dry areas. They move about in search of food and usually range over an area of about 10 to 20 square miles (26 to 52 square kilometers). The size of their range is larger in areas with less forest cover.

Scientists believe chimpanzees form loosely tied groups called *communities,* which share the same territory. Within these communities, the apes travel in smaller groups that vary in number and change members frequently. There are three types of groups: (1) all-male bands, (2) bands of mothers and their infants, and (3) mixed bands consisting of both sexes. The dominant male or males usually control a chimpanzee community's territory.

Chimpanzees live both in trees and on the ground. They spend from 50 to 75 percent of each day in the trees, depending on the forest covering and the season. They sleep in tree nests made of branches, leaves, and twigs. The animals make new nests each night. They build them at least 15 feet (4.6 meters) above the ground.

Like gorillas, chimpanzees travel in an unusual way called *knuckle walking.* The apes walk on all fours, supporting the upper part of their bodies with their knuckles. They occasionally stand upright to walk or run. Chimpanzees will walk on two legs when excited, carrying food, or looking over tall grass.

Chimpanzees' main foods are fruits, leaves, seeds, and stems. They also eat ants, bird's eggs, and termites. Sometimes the apes will kill and eat larger prey, including baboons, *bush pigs* (wild hogs), monkeys, and small antelope.

Chimpanzees in the wild mate throughout the year. Most females bear their first young at the age of 11 or 12 years. The pregnancy lasts about 230 days. Female chimpanzees generally give birth to a single baby once every three or four years.

The females raise their young by themselves. The infants ride under the mother's body, supported by her arm, until they are about 5 months old. Then they ride on the mother's back. Chimpanzees leave their mothers at about 6 years of age.

The skeleton of a chimpanzee

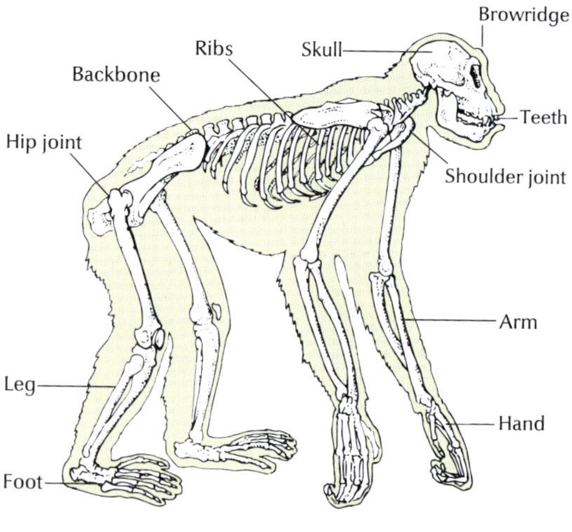

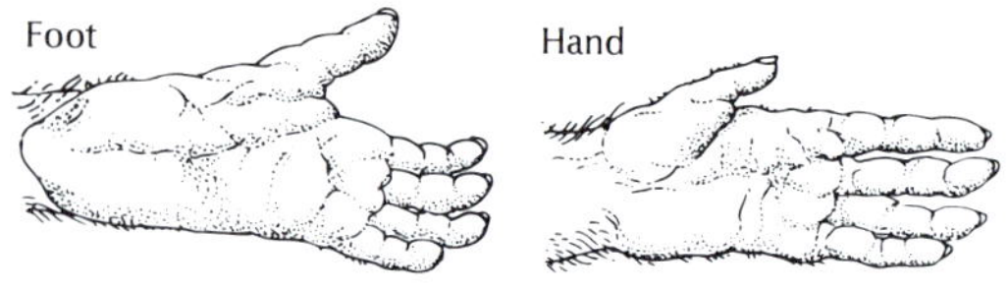

WORLD BOOK illustrations by Marion Pahl

A chimpanzee's hands and feet are well adapted for grasping branches and other objects. The hands have long, muscular fingers. The big toes of the feet face sideways like thumbs, which helps the chimpanzee grasp branches while climbing.

Adult chimpanzees spend about an hour each day in a friendly, social activity called *grooming.* During this time, two or more of them sit and pick through each other's hair. They remove such objects as dirt, insects, leaves, and burs from each other. Chimps occasionally fight among themselves, usually to establish their rank within the social group. They are also aggressive toward chimpanzees from other territories and will sometimes kill them.

Chimpanzees communicate by barks, grunts, and screams. When they find a large food supply, the apes jump through the trees, hoot loudly, and beat on tree trunks. The activity alerts all other chimpanzees within hearing distance. They also communicate with body postures, facial expressions, and hand gestures. Chimpanzees greet each other by embracing or by touching various parts of the other's body. Their facial expressions cover many emotions, including excitement, fear, and rage. Sometimes the males make an aggressive show of strength by such methods as walking upright, making their hair stand up, waving branches, and screaming.

Chimpanzees make and use simple tools more than any other creatures except human beings. For example, they strip the leaves from stems and use the stems as tools to catch termites. In addition, chimpanzees use leaves to make "sponges" for soaking up water to drink. Some chimps employ stones as "hammers" to crack open nuts.

Biologists believe chimpanzees live from 30 to 40 years in their normal surroundings. The natural enemies of chimpanzees include such predators as leopards and large eagles, which prey on young animals. Wild chimpanzees also die from accidents, such as falling from trees. Chimpanzees frequently succumb to various diseases.

Human beings, however, rank as the greatest threat to wild chimpanzees. In some areas, people hunt chimpanzees for food or capture the apes to sell them as household pets. People also have destroyed many of the forests where the animals once lived to obtain wood and create farmland.

Concern about shrinking chimpanzee populations led to a restriction on international trade in the animals during the late 1970's. Some African countries established game preserves to protect chimpanzees. Conservationists also proposed captive-breeding programs for chimpanzees to replace some of the decreasing population in the wild. Today, the chimpanzee is considered an endangered species.

Chimpanzees and people. Because of the similarities between chimpanzees and human beings, people have conducted many studies of these animals in the wild and in laboratories. Scientists have observed chimps in their natural habitats since the 1890's. By the 1960's, biologists had begun studying wild chimpanzees extensively.

British biologist Jane Goodall made some of the most important chimpanzee studies while working in northwestern Tanzania. Goodall discovered that the animals fashioned their own tools. She also became the first scientist to document hunting and warfare among chimpanzees.

Scientists use chimpanzees in medical and psychological research because the apes share many physical and social characteristics with human beings. For example, human and chimpanzee DNA are between about 95 percent and 99 percent identical. In addition, many scientists believe that *HIV-1,* one of the viruses that causes AIDS, developed from a virus found in chimpanzees called *simian immunodeficiency virus* (SIV).

Breese, Gamma/Liaison

Jane Goodall uncovered many similarities between human beings and chimpanzees through years of observation.

Psychologists use chimpanzees to study such behavior as communication, learning, and problem solving. In one experiment, chimpanzees were shown an object and then given two objects to touch. The chimpanzees learned to identify by touch the object that was identical to the one they had seen. Scientists once believed that only human beings had this ability.

During the 1970's and 1980's, many other chimpanzees were taught sign language. At the Yerkes Primate Research Center, located in Atlanta, Georgia, a chimpanzee named Lana learned to use symbols on a computer keyboard to ask for food, companionship, and music. Such studies suggest that chimpanzees may use symbols in the same way that people use words to represent objects, individuals, and emotions.

Randall L. Susman

Scientific classification. Chimpanzees belong to the anthropoid ape family, Pongidae, and the genus *Pan.* The scientific name of the chimpanzee is *P. troglodytes.* The central chimpanzee is *P. troglodytes troglodytes.* The eastern or long-haired chimpanzee is *P. troglodytes schweinfurthi,* and the western chimpanzee is *P. troglodytes verus.*

See also **Ape; Bonobo; Culture** (The culture of animals); **Goodall, Jane.**

Additional resources

Banks, Martin. *Chimpanzee: Habits, Life Cycles, Food Chains, Threats.* Raintree Steck-Vaughn, 2000. Younger readers.

Boesch, Christophe, and Boesch-Achermann, Hedwige. *The Chimpanzees of the Tai Forest.* Oxford, 2000.

Goodall, Jane. *Through a Window: My Thirty Years with the Chimpanzees of Gombe.* 1990. Reprint. Mariner Bks., 2000.

Greenberg, Daniel A. *Chimpanzees.* Benchmark Bks., 2001.

Hofer, Angelika, and others. *Mahale: A Photographic Encounter with Chimpanzees.* Sterling Pub., 2000.

Wrangham, Richard W., and others, eds. *Chimpanzee Cultures.* 1994. Reprint. Harvard Univ. Pr., 1996.

Ch'in dynasty. See Qin dynasty.

Crops grow in terraced fields cut into these hillsides in central China. Agriculture remains the country's leading economic activity, but China also has many modern industries. The busy city of Chengdu lies just across the river, *upper left.*

China

China is a large country in eastern Asia. It is the world's largest country in population with over 1 billion people—about 20 percent of all the people in the world. China is the third largest country in area. Only Russia and Canada have more territory. China is also one of the world's oldest countries, with a rich history that stretches over thousands of years.

The Chinese call their country *Zhongguo,* which means *Middle Country.* This name probably came from the ancient Chinese belief that their country was the geographical center of the world and the most cultured civilization. The English name *China* probably came from *Qin* (pronounced *chihn),* the name of an early Chinese *dynasty* (series of rulers from the same family).

Over 90 percent of China's people live in the eastern half of China, which has most of China's major cities and nearly all the land suitable for farming. Western China, by contrast, has far fewer people and resources. It is home to many of the country's minority groups.

Agriculture has always been the chief economic activity in China. Most of the people live in rural villages, and over half of all workers are farmers. However, China has some of the world's largest cities. They include Shanghai and Beijing (also spelled Peking), the nation's capital.

China is one of the world's oldest living civilizations. Its written history goes back about 3,500 years. The Chinese were the first to develop the compass, paper, porcelain, and silk cloth. They undertook huge construction projects, such as the Great Wall. Over the centuries, Japan, Korea, Vietnam, and other Asian lands borrowed from Chinese art, language, literature, religion, and technology.

In early times, the country that is now China was divided into small states, which were sometimes allied and sometimes at war. In 221 B.C., the Qin dynasty conquered the states and created a strong central government, forming the first united Chinese empire. Such empires continued to rule for more than 2,000 years. Chinese empires expanded the country's territory, built great cities, and sponsored magnificent works of literature and art. Nomadic groups from the north sometimes conquered all or part of the country. But the invaders generally adopted more from Chinese civilization than the Chinese adopted from them.

In the 1800's, China's last empire, the Qing, began to

The contributors of this article are Richard Louis Edmonds, Senior Lecturer in Geography at King's College, University of London, and Associate Member of the Center for East Asian Studies, University of Chicago; and Richard J. Smith, Professor of History and George and Nancy Rupp Professor of Humanities at Rice University.

François Perri, Getty Images

Shanghai ranks as China's largest city in population. Like most large Chinese cities, Shanghai suffers from overcrowding. Pedestrian bridges such as the one pictured here span the city's busy streets to help relieve traffic congestion. China has more people than any other country.

weaken. In 1911, revolutionaries overthrew the Qing, and the next year, China became a republic. But the *Kuomintang* (Nationalist Party), which ruled the republic, never established effective government over all of China. In 1949, the Chinese Communist Party defeated the Nationalists and set up China's present government. The Communists called the country *Zhonghua Renmin Gongheguo* (People's Republic of China). The Nationalists fled to the island of Taiwan, where they reestablished their government. The People's Republic claims that Taiwan should be part of its territory. This article discusses only the People's Republic of China. For information about Taiwan, which Nationalists call the Republic of China, see the *World Book* article on **Taiwan**.

The Communists made many major changes in China. They placed all important industries under state ownership and direction. The government also took control of most trade and finance. In the late 1900's, the Communists began to loosen their grip on the nation's economy and to allow more free enterprise. China has one of the world's largest economies, and many of its people prosper. But the majority of Chinese still live modestly.

Government

China's government is dominated by the Chinese Communist Party, the military, and a branch of government known as the State Council. The Communist Party is the most powerful group. All people who hold mid-

© Felix Stensson, Alamy

China's artistic heritage dates back thousands of years. This sculpture of a lion stands outside a Buddhist temple in Beijing that was built over 300 years ago.

China in brief

General information

Capital: Beijing.
Official language: Northern Chinese (Mandarin, or *putonghua*).
Official name: *Zhonghua Renmin Gongheguo* (People's Republic of China).
National anthem: "March of the Volunteers."
Largest cities:

Shanghai (14,348,535)	Chongqing (9,691,901)
Beijing (11,509,595)	Guangzhou (8,524,826)

Symbols of China. China's flag was adopted in 1949. The large star represents the leadership of the Communist Party. The four small stars stand for groups of workers. The state emblem, *right,* shows the Gate of Heavenly Peace in Beijing framed by grains of rice and wheat that stand for agriculture and a cogwheel that represents industry.

Land and climate

Land: China lies in eastern Asia and borders the Pacific Ocean. Forests and fertile lowlands cover much of northeastern China. The Qin Ling, a range of mountains, rise in east-central China. Hills and tropical lowlands extend over much of the southeast. Dry, rocky plateaus divided by mountain ranges extend over western China. The Himalaya rise along the southwest border. Other high western ranges include the Tian Shan, Altai Mountains, and Kunlun Mountains. Desert covers much of the northwest. Major rivers include the Huang He, Xi Jiang, and Yangtze.

Area: 3,692,671 mi² (9,563,974 km²). *Greatest distances*—east-west, 3,000 mi (4,828 km); north-south, 2,500 mi (4,023 km). *Coastline*—4,019 mi (6,468 km), including 458 mi (737 km) for Hainan Island.
Elevation: *Highest*—Mount Everest, 29,035 ft (8,850 m); *Lowest*—Turpan Depression, 505 ft (154 m) below sea level.
Climate: China has a wide range of climates. Northern and western China have long, bitterly cold winters. However, central and southern China have mild to warm winters. Summers are hot and humid in eastern China and southern Manchuria and extremely hot and dry in the northwestern deserts. January temperatures average below 0 °F (218 °C) in Manchuria and Tibet, and about 20 °F (27 °C) throughout much of eastern China. January is much milder on the country's southeastern coast, with temperatures averaging about 60 °F (16 °C). July temperatures average about 80 °F (27 °C) throughout much of China but may reach over 100 °F (38 °C) in the northwestern deserts. Rainfall varies from light in the northern deserts to heavy in the southeast.

Government

Form of government: Control by Communist Party.
Head of state: President (largely ceremonial).
Head of government: Premier.
Executive: Premier, assisted by State Council.
Legislature: National People's Congress of almost 3,000 members. Congress has little independent lawmaking power; it usually follows suggestions of party leaders.
Judiciary: Highest court is the Supreme People's Court.
Political subdivisions: 22 provinces, 5 autonomous regions, 4 special municipalities, 2 special administrative regions.

People

Population: *2006 estimate*—1,338,331,000. *2000 census*—1,242,612,000.
Population density: 362 per mi² (140 per km²).
Distribution: 59 percent rural, 41 percent urban.
Major ethnic/national groups. About 92 percent Han. Smaller groups include Kazakhs, Mongols, Tibetans, and Uygurs.
Major religions: The government discourages religious practice. But some people still practice religion. Traditional Chinese religions include Confucianism, Taoism, and Buddhism. Also, about 2 percent of the Chinese people are Muslims, and about 1 percent are Christians.

Population trend

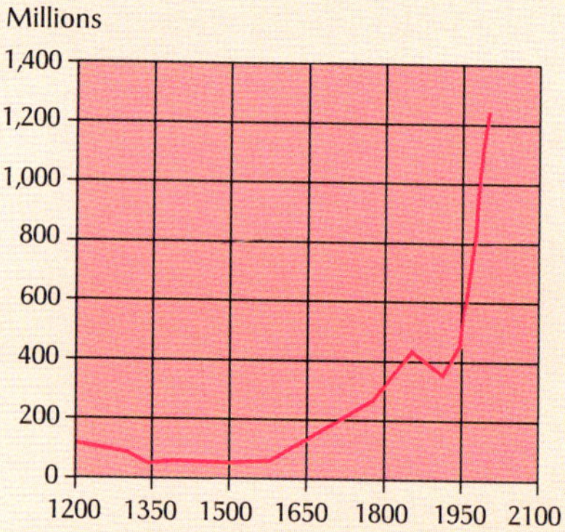

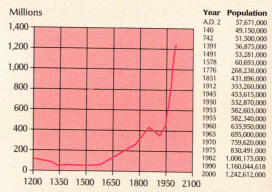

Year	Population
A.D. 2	57,671,000
140	49,150,000
742	51,500,000
1391	56,875,000
1491	53,281,000
1578	60,693,000
1776	268,238,000
1851	431,896,000
1912	353,260,000
1945	453,615,000
1950	532,870,000
1953	582,603,000
1955	582,340,000
1960	635,950,000
1965	695,000,000
1970	759,620,000
1975	830,491,000
1982	1,008,175,000
1990	1,160,044,618
2000	1,242,612,000

Sources: Official censuses and other population studies.

Economy

Chief products: *Agriculture*—corn, cotton, eggs, fruits, hogs, peanuts, potatoes, rice, soybeans, sweet potatoes, tea, tobacco, tomatoes, wheat. *Manufacturing*—cement, chemicals, clothing and textiles, iron and steel, machinery, processed foods. *Mining*—coal, copper, iron ore, petroleum, salt, tin, tungsten.
Money: *Basic unit*—yuan (also called renminbi). One hundred fen equal one yuan. See also **Yuan**.
International trade: *Major exports*—clothing, textiles, tea, food. *Major imports*—metals, machinery, grain, cotton, fertilizers. *Major trading partners*—Germany, Japan, United States.

dle- or lower-level positions in the party or the government are called *cadres* or *ganbu.*

The Communist Party. China remains a one-party state. A number of minor political parties exist, but they have no power. Millions of Chinese belong to the Communist Party, but members make up only about 5 percent of the total population. In 2002, the party began allowing business owners to join. Admitting business owners was a major change because Communists traditionally had considered the owners of businesses and other means of production to be enemies of the working class. Although the party still supports Communist ideals, it recognized that business owners play an important role in modern China.

The Communist Party has four main administrative bodies: the National Party Congress, the Central Committee, the *Politburo* (Political Bureau), and the Secretariat. The National Party Congress has more than 2,100 representatives, selected by party members throughout the nation. The Central Committee consists of about 200 leading party members, elected by the National Party Congress. The Politburo has about 25 members, who are top party leaders elected by the Central Committee. The Standing Committee is a smaller group within the Politburo and is made up of some of the most important members of the Communist Party. In addition, several powerful leaders belong to the Secretariat, which is chosen by the Central Committee.

The Communist Party's constitution states that the National Party Congress and the Central Committee are the most important bodies, but they have little real power. In general, they automatically approve party policies and guidelines set by the Politburo and its Standing Committee. The Secretariat is responsible for carrying out the day-to-day activities of the party.

The highest post in the Communist Party is that of general secretary, who serves as head of the Secretariat. But other high-ranking government officials sometimes hold more power. For example, Deng Xiaoping was China's most influential leader from the late 1970's until the early 1990's, though Hu Yaobang and others held the post of general secretary.

National government. China's Constitution establishes the National People's Congress as the highest government authority. Members of the National People's Congress are elected by local and regional people's congresses and by the armed forces. The members of the National People's Congress serve five-year terms. The chief function of the congress is legislative. Its powers include adopting laws, approving the national budget, and appointing government officials. A standing committee of about 150 members handles the work of the congress when it is not in session.

The State Council serves as the executive branch. It carries on the day-to-day affairs of the government. The council is led by the premier, China's head of government. The premier is chosen by the National People's Congress, upon nomination by the president. The president's duties are largely ceremonial. The premier is assisted by several vice premiers, state councilors, and a number of ministers and heads of special commissions. The ministers are in charge of government departments, such as the ministries of defense, education, and finance.

Political divisions. China has 33 major political divisions—22 provinces, 5 *autonomous* (self-governing) regions, 4 nationally governed municipalities, and 2 special administrative regions. The autonomous regions—Guangxi, Inner Mongolia, Ningxia, Tibet, and Xinjiang—have many people who belong to China's minority ethnic groups. Although the regions are called autonomous, they are actually governed much like the rest of the nation. The nationally governed municipalities—Beijing, Chongqing, Shanghai, and Tianjin—are large metropolitan areas that are administered by the national government. Each of these municipalities consists of an urban center and a rural area. The special administrative regions are Hong Kong and Macao, which were controlled for many years by the United Kingdom and Portugal, respectively. Hong Kong and Macao have their own executive, legislative, and judicial bodies. China handles their defense and foreign policy.

China has three levels of local government. The 33 major political units are divided into more than 300 prefectures and more than 650 major cities. Counties, other cities, and districts of major cities make up the next level. The counties are subdivided into thousands of townships and towns. Each political unit has a people's congress with a standing committee, and an executive body patterned after the State Council.

Courts in China do not function as a completely independent branch of government as they do in many

New China Pictures

China's capitol is the Great Hall of the People in Beijing. The National People's Congress and other governmental bodies meet in its chambers.

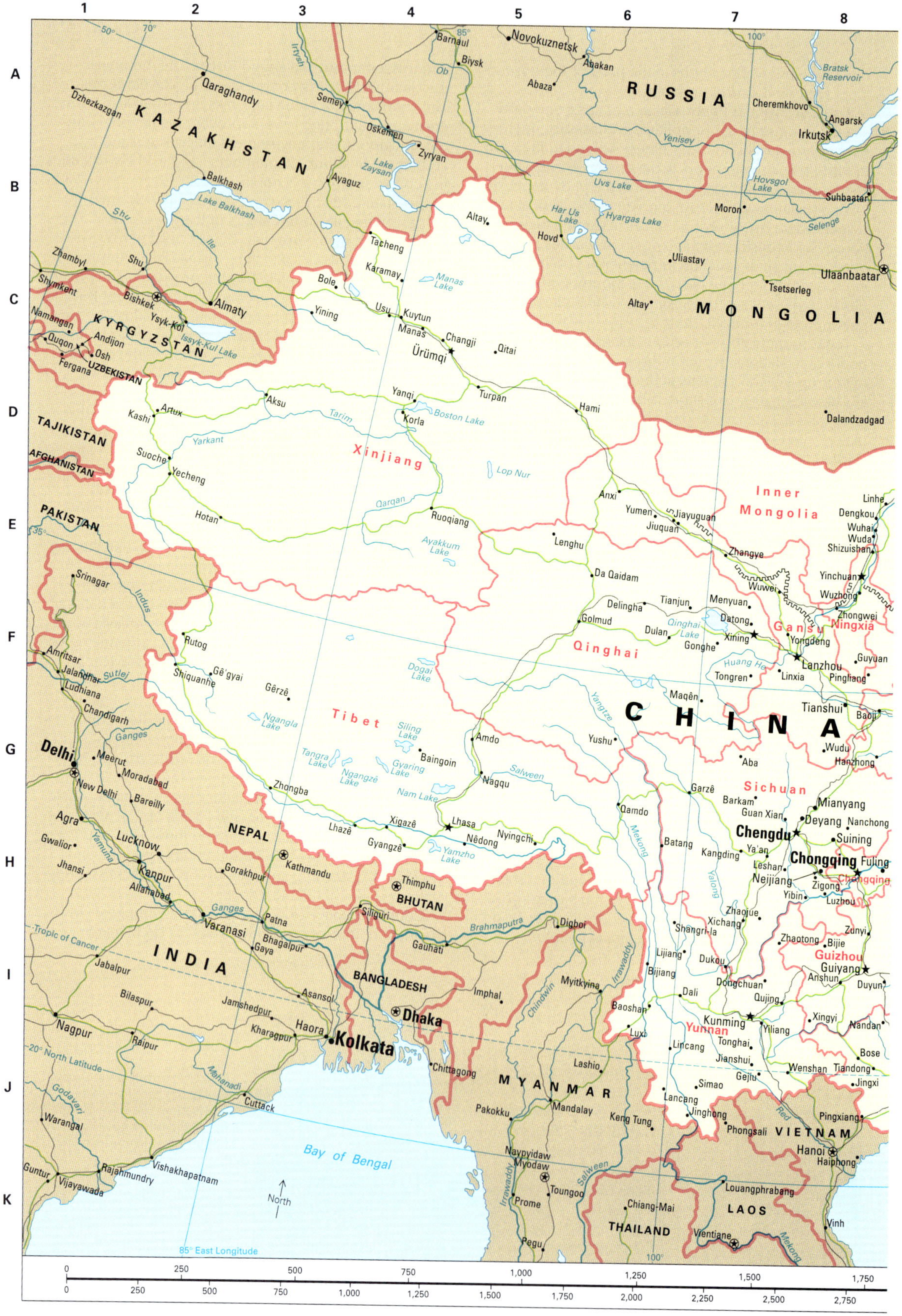

1
2
3
4
5
6
7
8
A
B
C
D
E
F
G
H
I
J
K
RUSSIA
KAZAKHSTAN
KYRGYZSTAN
UZBEKISTAN
TAJIKISTAN
AFGHANISTAN
PAKISTAN
INDIA
NEPAL
BHUTAN
BANGLADESH
MYANMAR
THAILAND
LAOS
VIETNAM
MONGOLIA
CHINA
Xinjiang
Tibet
Qinghai
Inner Mongolia
Gansu
Ningxia
Sichuan
Chongqing
Guizhou
Yunnan
Novokuznetsk
Barnaul
Biysk
Abakan
Abaza
Cheremkhovo
Angarsk
Irkutsk
Bratsk Reservoir
Yenisey
Ob
Irtysh
Semey
Oskemen
Zyryan
Lake Zaysan
Ayaguz
Qaraghandy
Dzhezkazgan
Balkhash
Lake Balkhash
Shu
Ile
Zhambyl
Shymkent
Bishkek
Almaty
Ysyk-Kol
Issyk-Kul Lake
Namangan
Andijon
Quqon
Osh
Fergana
Uvs Lake
Har Us Lake
Hyargas Lake
Hovsgol Lake
Moron
Hovd
Uliastay
Tsetserleg
Altay
Suhbaatar
Selenge
Ulaanbaatar
Dalandzadgad
Tacheng
Karamay
Manas Lake
Bole
Yining
Usu
Kuytun
Manas
Changji
Qitai
Ürümqi
Turpan
Hami
Yanqi
Boston Lake
Korla
Aksu
Artux
Kashi
Tarim
Yarkant
Suoche
Yecheng
Hotan
Qarqan
Ruoqiang
Lop Nur
Ayakkum Lake
Anxi
Yumen
Jiayuguan
Jiuquan
Zhangye
Lenghu
Da Qaidam
Delingha
Tianjun
Menyuan
Golmud
Qinghai Lake
Dulan
Gonghe
Datong
Xining
Wuwei
Linhe
Dengkou
Wuhai
Wuda
Shizuishan
Yinchuan
Wuzhong
Zhongwei
Yongdeng
Lanzhou
Guyuan
Pingliang
Linxia
Tongren
Huang He
Maqên
Tianshui
Baoji
Srinagar
Indus
Rutog
Shiquanhe
Gê'gyai
Gêrzê
Dogai Lake
Ngangla Lake
Siling Lake
Tangra Lake
Ngangzê Lake
Gyaring Lake
Baingoin
Amdo
Nagqu
Salween
Nam Lake
Zhongba
Lhazê
Xigazê
Lhasa
Nêdong
Nyingchi
Gyangzê
Yamzho Lake
Yangtze
Yushu
Qamdo
Mekong
Garzê
Aba
Barkam
Guan Xian
Mianyang
Deyang
Nanchong
Chengdu
Suining
Ya'an
Kangding
Batang
Yalong
Leshan
Neijiang
Chongqing
Fuling
Zigong
Yibin
Luzhou
Wudu
Hanzhong
Amritsar
Jalandhar
Sutlej
Ludhiana
Chandigarh
Ganges
Delhi
New Delhi
Meerut
Moradabad
Bareilly
Agra
Gwalior
Yamuna
Jhansi
Lucknow
Kanpur
Allahabad
Gorakhpur
Kathmandu
Thimphu
Varanasi
Patna
Bhagalpur
Gaya
Siliguri
Brahmaputra
Gauhati
Dibrugarh
Tropic of Cancer
Jabalpur
Bilaspur
Jamshedpur
Asansol
Haora
Kolkata
Kharagpur
Dhaka
Imphal
Chindwin
Myitkyina
Irrawaddy
Nagpur
Raipur
20° North Latitude
Godavari
Mahanadi
Cuttack
Warangal
Guntur
Vijayawada
Rajahmundry
Vishakhapatnam
Bay of Bengal
North
85° East Longitude
Chittagong
Lashio
Mandalay
Pakokku
Keng Tung
Naypyidaw
Myodaw
Toungoo
Prome
Pegu
Chiang Mai
Vientiane
Louangphrabang
Shangri-la
Xichang
Zhaojue
Lijiang
Jijiang
Dukou
Dali
Baoshan
Luxi
Lincang
Lancang
Jinghong
Simao
Tonghai
Jianshui
Gejiu
Kunming
Yiliang
Qujing
Dongchuan
Zhaotong
Bijie
Zunyi
Guiyang
Anshun
Duyun
Xingyi
Nandan
Bose
Wenshan
Tiandong
Jingxi
Phongsali
Pingxiang
Hanoi
Haiphong
Vinh
Red
50°
70°
85°
100°
35°
0
250
500
750
1,000
1,250
1,500
1,750
2,000
2,250
2,500
2,750

China political map

China map index

Provinces

Name	Population	Area		Capital	Map key
		In mi²	In km²		
Anhui	58,999,948	54,000	139,900	Hefei	G 11
Fujian	34,097,947	47,500	123,100	Fuzhou	I 11
Gansu	25,142,282	141,500	366,500	Lanzhou	E 7
Guangdong	85,225,007	76,100	197,100	Guangzhou	J 10
Guizhou	35,247,695	67,200	174,000	Guiyang	I 8
Hainan	7,559,035	13,200	34,300	Haikou	K 9
Hebei	66,684,419	78,300	202,700	Shijiazhuang	E 10
Heilongjiang	36,237,576	179,000	463,600	Harbin	B 12
Henan	91,236,854	64,500	167,000	Zhengzhou	G 10
Hubei	59,508,870	72,400	187,500	Wuhan	G 10
Hunan	63,274,173	81,300	210,500	Changsha	I 9
Jiangsu	73,043,577	39,600	102,600	Nanjing	G 11
Jiangxi	40,397,598	63,600	164,800	Nanchang	I 10
Jilin	26,802,191	72,200	187,000	Changchun	C 12
Liaoning	41,824,412	58,300	151,000	Shenyang	D 11
Qinghai	4,822,963	278,400	721,000	Xining	F 6
Shaanxi	35,365,072	75,600	195,800	Xi'an	F 9
Shandong	89,971,789	59,200	153,300	Jinan	F 11
Shanxi	32,471,242	60,700	157,100	Taiyuan	F 10
Sichuan	82,348,296	188,000	487,000	Chengdu	G 7
Yunnan	42,360.089	168,400	436,200	Kunming	I 7
Zhejiang	45,930,651	39,300	101,800	Hangzhou	H 12

Autonomous regions

Name	Population	Area		Capital	Map key
		In mi²	In km²		
Guangxi	43,854,538	85,100	220,400	Nanning	J 9
Inner Mongolia	23,323,347	454,600	1,177,500	Hohhot	C 11
Ningxia	5,486,393	25,600	66,400	Yinchuan	E 8
Tibet	2,616,329	471,700	1,221,600	Lhasa	G 4
Xinjiang	18,459,511	635,900	1,646,900	Ürümqi	D 4

Nationally governed municipalities

Name	Population	Area		Map key
		In mi²	In km²	
Beijing	13,569,194	6,490	16,800	E 10
Chongqing	30,512,763	31,700	82,000	H 8
Shanghai	16,407,734	2,400	6,200	G 12
Tianjin	9,848,731	4,360	11,300	E 11

Special administrative regions

Name	Population	Area		Map key
		In mi²	In km²	
Hong Kong	†6,708,389	1,126	2,916	J 10
Macao	†435,235	10	27	J 10

Cities and towns

Aksu	561,822	D 3
Altay	178,510	B 5
Anda	473,091	C 12
Ankang	843,426	G 9
Anlu*	611,990	G 10
Anqing	582,751	H 11
Anqiu*	1,096,782	F 11
Anshan	1,556,285	D 12
Anshun	767,307	I 8
Anyang	768,992	F 10
Baicheng	484,979	C 12
Baiyin*	460,982	F 8
Baoding	902,496	E 10
Baoji	600,377	G 8
Baotou	1,671,181	E 9
Bei'an	442,474	B 12
Beihai	558,635	J 9
Beijing	11,509,595	E 10
Beiliu*	1,049,035	J 9
Bengbu*	809,399	G 11
Benxi	980,069	D 12
Bijie	1,128,230	I 8
Bole	224,869	C 3
Boshan	846,865	F 11
Boutou*	550,880	E 11
Cangzhou	443,561	E 11
Changchun	3,225,557	C 12
Changde	1,346,739	H 10
Changji	387,169	C 4
Changsha	2,122,873	H 10
Changzhi	648,981	F 10
Changzhou	1,081,845	G 12
Chaohu*	778,864	G 11
Chaoyang	2,470,812	J 11
Chaozhou	363,582	J 11
Chengde	437,251	E 11
Chengdu	4,333,541	H 8
Chenzhou*	655,014	I 10
Chifeng	1,153,723	D 11
Chongqing	9,691,901	H 8
Chuxiong*	503,682	I 6
Chuzhou*	493,735	G 11
Da'an*	430,512	C 12
Dali	521,169	I 7
Dalian	3,245,191	E 12
Dandong	780,414	E 12
Dangyang*	495,946	H 10
Danjiangkou*	501,126	G 9
Daqing*	1,380,051	C 12
Datong	1,526,744	E 10
Dengzhou*	1,290,656	E 12
Deyang	628,876	H 8
Dezhou	552,445	F 11
Dingzhou*	1,107,903	E 10
Dongguan	6,445,777	J 10
Dongsheng	252,566	E 9
Dongying*	788,844	F 11
Dunhua*	480,834	C 13
Dunhuang*	187,578	E 6
Duyun	463,426	I 8
Enshi	755,725	H 9
Ezhou*	1,023,285	H 10
Fengcheng*	1,216,412	H 11
Foshan	768,656	J 10
Fu'an	554,057	I 12
Fujin*	420,579	B 13
Fushun	1,434,447	D 12
Fuxin	627,855	D 11
Fuyang	628,633	G 10
Fuzhou	2,124,435	I 12
Ganzhou	494,600	I 10
Gaocheng*	758,269	E 10
Gejiu	453,311	J 7
Guangshui*	885,936	G 10
Guangyuan*	905,057	G 8
Guangzhou	8,524,826	J 10
Guilin	804,571	I 9
Guiping*	1,359,035	J 9
Guiyang	2,985,105	I 8
Haikou	830,192	K 9
Hailar	262,184	B 11
Hailun	720,008	B 12
Haimen	942,952	H 11
Hami	388,714	D 6
Hancheng*	387,041	F 9
Handan	1,329,734	F 10
Hangzhou	2,451,319	H 12
Hanzhong	503,871	G 8
Harbin	3,481,504	C 12
Hebi	495,336	F 10
Hechi	318,348	I 9
Hefei	1,659,075	G 11
Hegang	694,640	B 13
Heihe*	192,764	B 12
Hengshui*	422,761	F 10
Hengyang	879,051	I 10
Hetian*	186,127	I 11
Heyuan	227,773	J 10
Heze*	1,280,031	F 10
Hohhot	1,406,955	E 9
Hong Kong	†1,335,469	J 10
Houma	225,123	E 9
Huaibei*	741,195	G 11
Huainan	1,357,228	G 11
Huaiyin	555,052	G 11
Huangshan*	406,200	H 11
Huangshi*	653,722	H 10
Huazhou	1,007,796	J 9
Huizhou	591,686	J 10
Hulin	311,509	C 14
Hunjiang	335,400	D 12
Jiamusi	859,944	B 13
Ji'an	473,113	I 10
Jiangmen*	536,317	J 10
Jian'ou	478,651	H 11
Jianyang	317,848	H 11
Jiaozuo	747,299	F 10
Jiaxing	881,923	G 12
Jiayuguan	159,541	E 7
Jieshou*	640,878	G 10
Jieyang	633,570	J 11
Jilin	1,953,134	C 12
Jinan	2.999,934	F 11
Jinchang*	204,902	E 7
Jincheng*	304,221	F 10
Jingdezhen	444,720	H 11
Jinghong	443,672	J 7
Jingmen	583,373	H 10
Jinhua	424,859	H 12
Jining	1,050,522	F 11
Jining	272,448	E 10
Jinzhou	861,991	D 11
Jishou	294,297	H 9
Jiujiang	551,329	H 11
Jiuquan	346,258	E 7
Jixi	910,782	C 13
Kaifeng	796,171	F 10
Kaili	433,236	I 9
Kashi	340,640	D 2
Kowloon*	†2,023,979	J 10
Kunming	3,035,406	I 4
Laiyang	897,681	F 11
Langfang*	715,388	E 11
Lanzhou	2,087,759	F 8
Leiyang	1,180,235	I 10
Lengshui-jiang*	339,701	I 9
Lianyuan	996,893	I 9
Lianyungang	687,242	F 11
Liaocheng*	950,319	F 10
Liaoyang	728,492	D 12
Liaoyuan	462,233	D 12
Lichuan*	786,984	H 9
Linfen	724,403	F 9
Linhai	948,618	H 11
Linhe	510,965	E 8
Linqing*	694,247	F 10
Linxia	202,498	F 8
Linyi	1,938,510	F 11
Lishui	348,241	H 12
Liupanshui*	995,055	I 8
Liuzhou	1,220,392	J 9
Longyan*	543,731	I 11
Loudi*	398,577	I 10
Lufeng	1,164,767	J 10
Luohe	304,105	G 10
Luoyang	1,491,680	F 10
Luxi	337,406	I 6
Luzhou	1,252,884	H 8
Ma'anshan	567,576	G 11
Macao	†435,235	G 11
Macheng*	1,129,047	H 10
Manzhouli	181,112	B 10
Maoming	644,301	J 9
Meizhou	354,302	I 11
Mianyang	1,162,962	G 8
Mishan*	438,277	C 13
Mudanjiang	1,014,206	C 13
Nanchang	1,844,253	H 10
Nanchong	1,771,920	H 8
Nangong*	467,356	F 10
Nanhai*	2,133,741	J 10
Nanjing	3,624,234	G 11
Nanning	1,766,701	J 9
Nanping	488,818	I 11
Nantong	771,386	G 12
Nanxiong	372,844	I 10
Nanyang	1,584,715	G 10
Neijiang	1,391,931	H 8
Ningbo	1,567,499	H 12
Ningde	400,293	I 12
Panzhihua*	690,739	I 7
Pingdingshan	900,903	G 10
Pingliang	454,996	F 8
Pingxiang	783,445	I 10
Putian	443,926	I 11
Puyang*	448,290	F 10
Qianjiang*	992,438	H 10
Qingdao	2,720,972	F 12
Qingtongxia*	248,640	F 8
Qingyuan	506,680	J 10
Qinhuangdao	817,487	E 10
Qinzhou	1,035,504	J 9
Qiqihar	1,540,089	C 12
Qitaihe*	486,704	C 13
Quanzhou	1,192,286	I 11
Qujing	648,956	I 7
Quzhou	286,271	H 11
Rizhao	1,148,190	F 11
Rui'an	1,207,788	H 11
Sanmenxia	288,746	F 9
Sanming	337,105	I 11
Sanya	482,296	K 9
Shahe*	474,260	E 10
Shanghai	14,348,535	G 12
Shangqiu	1,428,983	F 10
Shangrao	327,703	H 11
Shangzhi*	582,764	C 13
Shantou	1,270,112	J 11
Shanwei*	409,677	J 11
Shaoguan	535,979	I 10
Shaowu*	288,401	I 11
Shaoxing	633,118	H 12
Shaoyang	607,868	I 9
Shashi	243,242	H 10
Shenyang	5,303,053	D 12
Shenzhen	7,008,831	J 10
Shihezi*	590,115	C 4
Shijiazhuang	1,969,975	E 10
Shishou*	602,649	H 10
Shiyan	589,824	G 9
Shizuishan	314,296	E 8
Shuangcheng	749,182	C 12
Shuang-yashan	487,294	B 13
Shunde*	1,694,152	J 10
Simao	230,834	J 7
Siping	492,841	D 12
Suihua	800,207	C 12
Suining	1,355,388	H 8
Suizhou*	1,598,752	H 10
Suzhou	1,601,181	F 11
Suzhou	1,344,709	G 12
Tai'an	1,538,211	F 11
Taiyuan	2,558,382	E 10
Taizhou	607,660	G 11
Tangshan	1,711,311	E 11
Taonan	441,096	C 12
Tianjin	7,499,181	E 11
Tianmen	1,613,739	H 10
Tianshui	1,146,986	G 7
Tieli*	354,601	B 12
Tieling	433,799	D 12
Tongchuan	404,257	F 9
Tonghua	460,148	D 12
Tongliao	793,913	D 12
Tongling	362,477	H 11
Tongren	308,583	I 9
Tumen	132,368	D 13
Ürümqi	1,753,298	C 4
Wanxian	474,260	H 9
Weifang	1,380,300	F 11
Weihai	609,219	E 12
Weinan*	888,866	F 9
Wenzhou	1,915,548	H 12
Wuhai	427,553	E 8
Wuhan	8,312,700	H 10
Wuhu	697,197	G 11
Wuwei	946,506	E 8
Wuxi	1,425,766	G 11
Wuxue*	719,426	H 10
Wuzhong	355,442	E 8
Wuzhou	381,043	J 9
Xiamen	2,053,070	I 11
Xi'an	4,481,508	G 9
Xiangfan	871,388	G 10
Xiangtan	707,783	I 10
Xianning*	567,598	H 10
Xiantao	1,474,078	H 10
Xianyang	953,860	G 9
Xiaogan	883,123	H 10
Xichang	651,212	F 7
Xingyi	719,605	I 8
Xining	854,466	F 7
Xinji*	623,219	E 10
Xinxiang	775,941	F 10
Xinyang	1,255,750	G 10
Xinyi*	962,656	F 11
Xinyu*	778,391	H 10
Xuanzhou*	822,707	G 11
Xuchang	373,387	G 10
Xuzhou	1,679,626	G 11
Ya'an	334,475	H 7
Yan'an	403,868	F 9
Yangjiang*	538,069	J 10
Yangquan	655,317	F 10
Yangzhou	711,993	G 11
Yanji	432,339	D 13
Yantai	1,724,404	E 12
Yibin	809,099	H 8
Yichang	712,738	H 9
Yichun	814,016	B 13
Yichun*	920,357	I 10
Yinchuan	807,487	E 5
Yingcheng*	650,485	H 10
Yingkou	698,059	E 12
Yining	357,519	C 3
Yiyang	1,228,881	H 10
Yongzhou*	976,539	I 10
Yueyang	912,993	H 10
Yulin	451,337	E 9
Yumen	188,931	E 6
Yuncheng*	604,381	F 9
Yushu	1,155,670	G 6
Yuxi*	409,044	I 6
Yuyao	852,719	H 12
Zaozhuang	1,996,798	F 11
Zhangjiakou	903,348	E 10
Zhangye	486,688	E 7
Zhangzhou	567,884	I 11
Zhanjiang	1,350,665	J 9
Zhaoqing*	507,834	J 10
Zhaotong*	727,959	H 11
Zhengzhou	2,589,387	G 10
Zhenjiang	695,663	G 12
Zhongshan	2,363,322	J 10
Zhoukou*	323,738	G 10
Zhoushan*	715,685	H 12
Zhuhai	833,908	J 10
Zhumadian*	338,036	G 10
Zhuzhou	879,996	H 10
Zibo	2,817,479	F 11
Zigong	1,051,384	H 8
Zixing*	351,831	I 10
Zunyi	691,694	I 8

*Does not appear on map; key shows general location.
†2001 census data from Census and Statistics Department, Hong Kong.
Sources: 2000 census; United Nations and *World Book* estimates, except where indicated by †.

Western nations. Instead, the courts base their decisions largely on the policies of the Communist Party.

The highest court in China is the Supreme People's Court. It interprets the national laws and supervises the local people's courts. It also makes the final judgment on cases that have been appealed from lower courts. The Supreme People's Procuratorate hears cases that involve violations by government officials and sees that the national Constitution and the regulations of the National People's Congress are observed.

The armed forces of China are jointly commanded by the Central Military Commission of the Communist Party and the Central Military Commission of the government. China has an army, navy, and air force, which together make up the People's Liberation Army (PLA). The PLA has about 2 ¼ million male and female regular members. About 1 ½ million men and women serve in China's *militia* (citizens' army). There are also about 800,000 army reserves. Men and women between 18 and 22 years of age may be drafted for military service.

The armed forces hold enormous political power in the People's Republic of China. Military officers make up a large percentage of the members on the Communist Party's Central Committee. In addition to its military duties, the People's Liberation Army helps carry out party policies and programs.

People

Population. About a fifth of the world's people live in China. Shanghai is China's largest city and one of the world's largest as well. Beijing, the country's capital, is the second largest city. About 100 Chinese cities each have more than a million people. However, most of the country's people live in rural villages and small towns in eastern China. The western half of China has less than 10 percent of the population.

China's government sees the country's population as both a great resource and a great burden. China's huge work force could make its economy the most powerful in the world. But unless China limits its population growth, far more children would be born than China could adequately feed, house, educate, or employ under present conditions. By law, to limit population increases, men may not marry until they are 22 years old, and women until they are 20. People are encouraged to postpone marriage until they are in their late 20's and to have no more than two children.

Nationalities. About 92 percent of the people belong to the Han nationality. The rest of the population consists of over 50 minority groups, including Kazakhs, Mongols, Tibetans, Uygurs, and Zhuang. The different nationality groups are distinguished chiefly by language and culture.

Most of China's minority peoples live in the border regions and western China. A few groups, such as the Mongols in the north and the Kazakhs in the northwest, have a long tradition of herding sheep, goats, and other livestock. Some are still nomads, moving from place to place during the year to feed their herds on fresh pastures. The Uygurs raise livestock and grow crops on oases in the deserts of northwestern China. The Tibetan people practice simple forms of agriculture and herding in China's southwestern highlands. Many Koreans are farmers near the border with North Korea.

A number of minority groups inhabit the far southern parts of China. Some of these groups, such as the Zhuang, live much like their neighbors, the Han. Other minority groups are related to the peoples of Laos, Myanmar, Thailand, or Tibet. Many of these people, who live in less developed mountain areas, retain their traditional language and way of life.

Languages. Chinese, the native language of the Han, is actually a group of closely related languages. Early in the 1900's, China's government made northern Chinese, which was spoken in Beijing, the official language. This version of Chinese is often called Mandarin in English, but the Chinese call it *Putonghua* (common language). Most people in northern China speak Putonghua, and it

Photri

Colorful folk dances are part of the cultural heritage of China's minority peoples, such as the Mongols, *shown here.* Many Mongols still follow their old way of life as nomadic herders.

Population density and major ethnic groups

About 92 percent of the Chinese people belong to the Han ethnic group and live crowded together in eastern China. The rest of the population consists of about 55 minority groups. They live chiefly in the border areas and in western China.

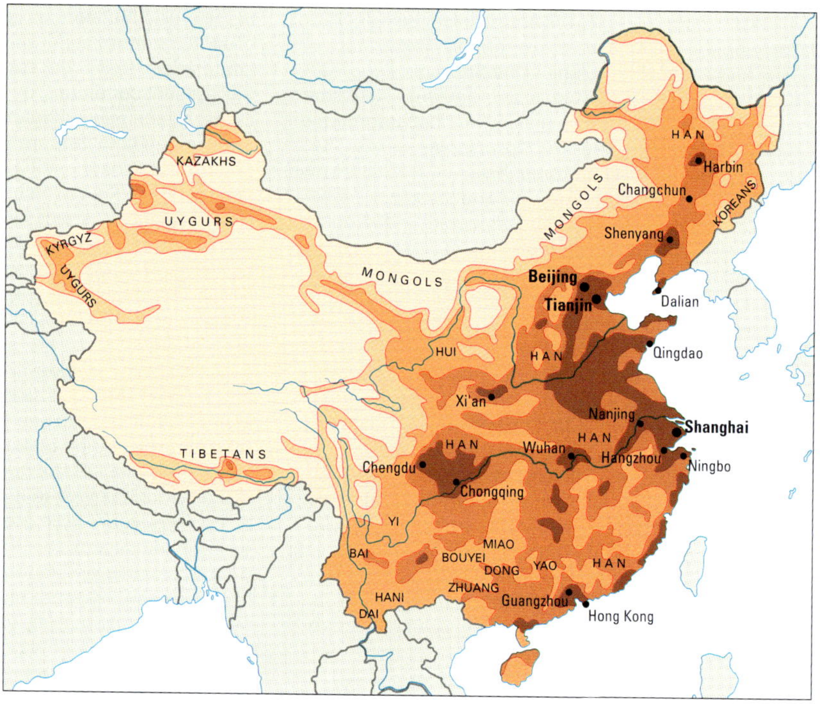

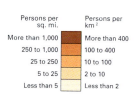

WORLD BOOK map

is the language of instruction in almost all schools. Other varieties of Chinese include Northern Min (spoken in Fujian province), Southern Min (spoken mainly in Guangdong and Hainan), Wu (spoken in Shanghai, Jiangsu, and Zhejiang), and Yue or Cantonese (spoken in Guangdong and Guangxi). Each language has several local dialects.

Although each version of Chinese has its own pronunciation, all Chinese is written in a similar way. The Chinese writing system uses *characters* instead of an alphabet. Each character is a symbol that represents a word or part of a word. For more information, see **Chinese language**.

The minority peoples of China speak many languages, including Korean, Mongolian, Uygur, and Zhuang. Many groups use their own language in their schools and publications. Many members of China's minority groups learn Chinese as a second language. A few minority groups speak Chinese as their primary language.

Way of life

Family life has always been extremely important in Chinese culture. For thousands of years, the Chinese people practiced loyalty to family, obedience to the father, and reverence for ancestors. Chinese philosophy and religion emphasized these values. In the mid-1900's, the Communists tried to replace loyalty to the family with loyalty to the work group. Other social and economic changes in the late 1900's further disrupted traditional family values.

Relationships within Chinese families have become less formal, and parents no longer expect their children to show unquestioning obedience. In the past, parents arranged marriages for their children and chose whom the children would marry. Many young people today choose their own marriage partners, although usually with the consent of their parents. Parents still help arrange some marriages in rural areas.

Chinese families traditionally valued sons far more than daughters. A husband could divorce his wife if she failed to give birth to sons. In some cases, daughters were killed at birth to save resources for the sons. Today, social policy in China stresses that families should value girls and boys equally. The Communist government strongly supports the idea that women should contribute to the family income and participate in social and political activities. Women do many kinds of work outside the home. Many young husbands share in the shopping, housecleaning, cooking, and caring for the children. However, equality between the sexes is more widely accepted in the cities than in the countryside.

Rural life. Traditionally, most Chinese lived in small villages. Many families owned their land, though it was often not large enough to support them. Many other families owned no land but worked as tenants or laborers for landowners and rich farmers.

After the Communists took control of China, they organized a collective ownership system, in which large groups of peasants owned land, tools, work animals, and workshops in common. The highest level of the collective system was the *commune,* which administered the economic activity for groups of about 5,000 families. Smaller units called *production brigades* were further divided into *production teams,* which were the equivalent of a small village. These units planned and performed most day-to-day farm work. In some cases, each family owned its house and a plot on which it could grow vegetables and raise chickens or hogs for its own use. If a family grew a surplus of crops, it could sell the surplus in a local market.

In 1979, the government began a new system to gradually abolish communes, brigades, and teams. Now, cooperative groups known as *collectives* make contracts with individual families. The contract tells how much land a family can work, what crops and livestock the family will raise, and how much it will sell to the government at a set price. After fulfilling its contract, the farm family may use the remainder of its production as it wishes. Most families use some for food and sell the rest on the open market.

Some rural families sign contracts as *specialized households.* These households may specialize in raising only one commodity, such as chickens or silk. Or they may provide farm machinery, repairs, or handicrafts on the free market instead of doing full-time farm work. After paying an agreed amount to the government, the specialized household keeps any profit. Some households operate businesses or small factories and hire employees. Some of them have become relatively wealthy.

The standard of living in rural China today is much higher than it was before the Communists came to power. The average income in rural areas is still low, but most families have enough food and clothing and also own a bicycle or motor scooter, a radio or television set, and a sewing machine. Some rural families own a refrigerator or a washing machine. Most rural families live in five- or six-room houses. Older houses are made of wood or mud bricks and have a tile or thatched roof. Newer houses are made of clay bricks or stone and have a tile roof. Some villages have apartment buildings. Except in remote areas, most houses and apartments have electric power.

Rural people work many hours a day, especially at planting and harvesting time. They also attend meetings and night classes, where they learn to read and write or how to use scientific farming methods. Even so, the people have time for recreation. Many villages have a small library and a recreation center with a television or a film projector, and sometimes a computer. Villages may also have sports facilities, music groups, or theater groups.

City life. China's cities are crowded, and housing is in great demand. Many city residents live in older neighborhoods where the houses resemble those in the countryside. Many other city dwellers live in large new apartment complexes. City governments construct some apartment buildings, and large businesses build others to house their workers. Most families pay rent for their apartments, but some have the opportunity to buy them.

Most city neighborhoods or apartment complexes have an elected residents' committee, also called a neighborhood committee. The committee supervises various neighborhood facilities and programs, such as day-care centers, evening classes, and after-school activities for children. When fights, petty crimes, or acts of juvenile delinquency occur in the neighborhoods, committee members talk with the people involved and try to help them solve the problem. These neighborhood organizations seek to keep crime from becoming a serious problem despite the overcrowding in China's cities.

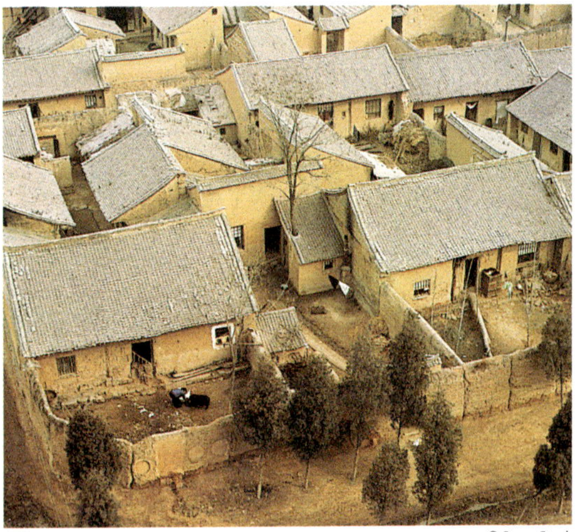

© SuperStock

Typical Chinese farmhouses are built of mud bricks, clay bricks, or stone, and have a tile or straw roof.

AP/Wide World

Family life has been an important part of Chinese culture throughout the country's history. In this picture, a factory worker and his family share lunch in their apartment in Shenzhen.

© Steve Vidler, eStock

WORLD BOOK photo by Robert Borja

The housing in China's cities is a mixture of new and old, as shown by these two photographs taken in the city of Guilin. Some city residents live in modern apartment complexes, *left*. Others live in older neighborhoods where the houses resemble those in rural areas, *right*.

In general, people in China's cities have a higher standard of living than people in the countryside. Their wages are low compared with those of workers in Western industrial countries. But most households have at least two wage earners, and rents and the cost of food are low. Most city people can afford a bicycle or motor scooter, a television set, and some household appliances. Some are able to buy a computer or a car. City people also have more cultural advantages than do rural people. They can attend a greater variety of classes and meetings, and cities typically have more theaters, museums, and other cultural activities.

Food. Grains are the main foods in China. Rice is the favorite grain among people in the south. In the north, people prefer wheat, which they make into dumplings and noodles. Corn, millet, and sorghum are also eaten. Vegetables, especially cabbages and *tofu* (soybean curd), rank second in the Chinese diet. Pork and poultry are favorite meats. People in China also like eggs, fish, fruits, and shellfish. Fast food, such as hamburgers and french fries, has become popular in China's cities.

Breakfast foods in China include rice porridge, stuffed pocket bread, or deep-fried pastries that taste like doughnuts. Favorite lunchtime foods include egg rolls and dumplings stuffed with meat or shrimp. A typical main meal includes vegetables with bits of meat or seafood, soup, and rice or noodles. Chopsticks and soup spoons serve as the utensils at Chinese meals.

Tea is the traditional favorite Chinese beverage. But soft drinks and beer have also become popular beverages. Ice cream is a favorite treat in China's cities.

Fancy Chinese cooking varies from region to region. *Beijing* (also spelled *Peking) duck* is a northern specialty. It consists of slices of crisp roast duck eaten with thin rolled pancakes and a sweet sauce made from soybean paste. Foods from the coastal areas include fish, crab, and shrimp. The spiciest foods come from Sichuan and Hunan. Chinese cooks vary the texture of dishes by adding crunchy bamboo shoots and *water chestnuts* (thickened stems of an aquatic plant). The Chinese occasionally eat things rarely used as food elsewhere, such as tiger lily buds, sea animals called *sea cucumbers,* and

© Jeff Greenberg, The Image Works

Dining at a restaurant is a popular activity in China. This group of friends shares a meal at an outdoor restaurant on Cheung Chau Island in Hong Kong.

snake meat. Shark's fin soup is an expensive delicacy.

Recreation. The Chinese enjoy many recreational activities that are popular throughout the world. Watching television, listening to radio, reading, going to the movies or opera, and shopping are common. *Karaoke* clubs, where guests sing along to recorded music, have become popular. Badminton, basketball, soccer, and table tennis are favorite sports. Chinese often invite guests over for meals, but going to restaurants is also popular. Many Chinese urban youth use computers at Internet cafes.

Traditional Chinese martial arts, such as *t'ai chi ch'uan* (also written *taijiquan*), are popular. Ballroom dancing parties take place both indoors and outdoors. In parks, the Chinese play *xiang qi* (a Chinese version of chess) and Chinese card games. Another favorite game is *mahjongg,* which is played with engraved tiles.

Clothing. Most Chinese wear clothing similar to that of Europeans and North Americans. In urban areas, fashionable designs are popular, especially among younger people. Members of certain religious and ethnic groups may wear special costumes and headgear. In rural areas, people often make their own clothes.

Health care in China combines traditional Chinese medicine and modern Western medicine. Traditional medicine is based on the use of herbs, attention to diet, and ancient treatments, such as *acupuncture.* In acupuncture, thin needles are inserted into the body at certain points to relieve pain or treat disease (see **Acupuncture**). From Western medicine, the Chinese have adopted many drugs and surgical methods.

Hospitals and clinics in China may be either publicly or privately owned. Hospitals in large cities provide access to advanced medical technologies. In rural areas, some villages have medical workers or rural doctors, although some of them do not have much medical training. Village health care providers can treat simple cases and prescribe drugs. For more advanced care, rural Chinese may have to travel a great distance to reach a township health center or a county hospital.

Beginning in the late 1970's, China's government greatly reduced health care funding. Now, patients are expected to pay more of their health care expenses. Most urban residents live near good facilities and can afford to pay for their care. But many rural Chinese no longer have access to affordable health care.

Religion is tolerated, but restricted, by the Communist government of China. However, it played an important part in traditional Chinese life. Confucianism, Taoism (also spelled Daoism), and Buddhism were major religions throughout most of China's history. The religious beliefs of many Chinese people included elements of all three.

Confucianism is based on the ideas of Confucius, a Chinese philosopher born about 550 B.C. More a moral code than a religion, it stresses the importance of ethical standards and of a well-ordered society. In the ideal Confucian society, parents have the right to rule their children, men to rule women, and the educated to rule the common people. Confucianism strongly emphasizes deep respect for one's ancestors and for the past. See **Confucianism**.

Taoism, also native to China, teaches that a person should live in harmony with nature. Taoism began during the 300's B.C. and is based largely on the book *Tao Te Ching (The Classic of the Way and the Virtue).* Taoism came to include many elements of Chinese folk religion and so became a religion with many protective gods. See **Taoism**.

Buddhism reached China from India before A.D. 100 and became well established throughout the country during the 300's. Under the influence of Taoism, Chinese varieties of Buddhism developed. They taught strict moral standards and the ideas of rebirth and life after

AP/Wide World

A basketball game takes place on a playground in Beijing. Basketball is one of the most popular sports in China. Other popular sports include badminton, soccer, and table tennis.

© Cheng Zhishan, New China Pictures

Ancient Chinese exercises called *t'ai chi ch'uan* (also spelled *taijiquan*) are performed by many Chinese every morning. T'ai chi emphasizes relaxation, balance, and breathing techniques.

death. The Chinese Buddhists worshiped many gods and appealed to them for help. See **Buddhism**.

China's Communist government regarded religion as part of China's past that would die out. It expected scientific and Marxist thought to replace religion and for many years persecuted religious believers. The Communists destroyed some Taoist and Buddhist temples and other religious buildings, and it turned others into museums, schools, and meeting halls. Beginning in the 1970's, the government adopted a more tolerant attitude toward religion. The government now allows the open practice of religion and the publication of religious works. It restored and reopened some religious buildings. But the government still tries to control religious organizations.

Christian missionaries worked in China for many years before the Communists came to power. The Communists expelled foreign missionaries and closed most Christian churches. In the late 1900's, the government permitted many Christian churches to reopen, but it suppressed Christian movements that organized outside of government control.

Muslims make up a small percentage of the Chinese population. They live mainly in northwestern China.

A spiritual movement called Falun Gong appeared in China in the early 1990's and grew rapidly. Falun Gong teaches techniques of meditation through exercises as a means of improving physical health and spiritual purity. The movement claims to have millions of followers in China. Members of Falun Gong staged a 10,000-person demonstration outside central government buildings in Beijing in 1999. This demonstration led the Chinese government to suppress Falun Gong and to issue an arrest warrant for its founder.

Education. The Chinese have always prized education and respected scholars. The Confucians believed that people could perfect themselves through study. They made no sharp distinction between academic education and moral education. For many years, candidates for government jobs had to pass an examination based on the Confucian works.

The Communists regard education as a key to reaching their goals. They have conducted literacy programs in rural areas in an effort to teach all Chinese to read and write. In the 1950's, they began a language reform program to help reduce illiteracy. The program included simplifying more than 2,000 of the most basic Chinese characters by reducing the number of strokes in each character. Such changes helped make Chinese easier to write. Today, most Chinese 15 years of age or older can read and write. For the country's literacy rate, see **Literacy** (table: Literacy rates).

Moral education is important in China. However, the Chinese teach morality as defined in a Communist sense. They say students should be both politically committed to Communist ideas and technically skilled. Courses in China combine the teaching of academic facts and political values.

In the mid-1980's, China's government began trying to get children to attend school for at least nine years. Students who show outstanding ability on nationwide examinations go to *key schools,* which have the best faculties and facilities. Key schools offer education at the elementary, secondary, and college levels. Some private schools exist, although their fees are high.

Elementary and secondary schools. Children in China enter elementary school at the age of 6 or 7. Nearly all of the country's children attend elementary school, which lasts for 5 or 6 years. Elementary school courses include art, Chinese, English, geography, history, mathematics, music, science, physical education, and political education.

After completing elementary school, students may enter secondary schools called *middle schools.* Junior middle school lasts three years, and senior middle school continues for another two or three years. Middle school courses include many subjects studied in elementary school plus biology, chemistry, physics, and foreign languages. Vocational and technical middle schools offer training in agriculture, industrial technology, and other work-related subjects. Almost all elementary school graduates enter middle school, but far fewer continue on to the senior level.

Higher education. Nationwide examinations deter-

Students read and study in a library at Tsinghua University in Beijing. China has about 2,000 institutions of higher learning but not enough to meet the demand for higher education. Nationwide tests determine who can attend state-sponsored universities.

mine who may advance to higher education and at what kind of school. Students study intensely for the tests. Those who do best on the tests enter a university. Some wealthier students who do not qualify may pay to attend private universities. The chief university subjects include economics, education, engineering, literature, medicine, and science.

Others who pass the examination with lower scores may enter a technical college or vocational university. These schools train students for jobs in business and industry. Many students complete two- or three-year programs in such fields as agriculture, industrial arts, and nursing.

China has about 2,000 institutions of higher learning, including both universities and schools for adult education. The number of students who desire a university education exceeds the number of openings available. But in addition to technical and vocational schools, adult students can continue their education at "workers' colleges" run by factories. These schools offer short-term courses for employees. Other adult education includes part-time study, radio, television, and correspondence courses, and distance learning programs conducted over the Internet.

The arts

The Chinese have one of the longest and greatest artistic traditions in the world. Chinese pottery and jade from the 4000's B.C. showed a great deal of technical skill and artistic refinement. During the Shang (1766-1045 B.C.) and Zhou (1045-256 B.C.) dynasties, Chinese metalworkers excelled in bronzework. Late in the Zhou dynasty, the Chinese produced remarkable textiles and lacquered items. Most early Chinese art reflected the power and mystery of nature. But around 200 B.C., Chinese art and literature began to focus on mythical and historical figures, and human situations and values.

By the Song dynasty (A.D. 960-1279), nature had again become a prominent theme in Chinese art and literature. Chinese artists emphasized the balance between two principal forces of nature, called *yin* and *yang*. Landscape painters, for example, aimed for harmony, rhythm, and balance in their compositions. Chinese writers, musicians, and architects also tried to capture these qualities in their work.

In the late 1800's and early 1900's, European and American culture began to influence Chinese life, including the arts. But after the Chinese Communists gained control of the country in 1949, they required art and literature to express Communist values and ideals. Since the late 1970's, the government has relaxed its demands, allowing the revival of Chinese traditions in the arts and permitting experimentation in non-Chinese styles.

Literature. The earliest Chinese literature was inscribed on pieces of bone or turtle shell called *oracle bones* from about 1500 to 1045 B.C., during the Shang dynasty. These inscriptions recorded the administrative duties, dreams, and future concerns of the royal families. A period of great philosophical activity in the latter part of the Zhou dynasty produced the Confucian, Taoist, and other classic writings. These classics, written in a highly refined script known as *wenyan* (patterned words), became models of Chinese literature.

For most of Chinese history, poetry was considered the highest form of literary achievement. It was esteemed not only on its own, but also as an important part of dramas, stories, and novels. Poetry was even inscribed on paintings. For more information on China's rich literary heritage, see **Chinese literature**.

Painting. Chinese potters painted sophisticated designs on their vessels as early as the 4000's B.C. Painting on silk began during the Shang dynasty. Painting on paper began after the Chinese invented paper in the 200's B.C. Early paintings showed people, animals, spirits, or abstract designs. But landscapes became the chief subject of Chinese painting by the A.D. 900's. During the Song dynasty (960-1279), many artists painted landscapes showing towering mountains and vast expanses of water. These artworks expressed a harmony between nature and the human spirit.

Chinese *calligraphy* (fine handwriting) has long been closely linked with the arts of poetry and painting. The use of a brush for writing became common during the Han dynasty (206 B.C.-A.D. 220). The Chinese traditionally considered calligraphy as the highest form of art.

In the A.D. 1000's, painters began to combine landscapes and other subjects with written inscriptions that added to the overall design. These inscriptions typically described the artist's feelings about the scene or the circumstances under which the painting was created. Owners of such paintings would often add inscriptions to the work, recording their own reactions.

In traditional Chinese painting, artists use the same kind of brush for painting as for calligraphy. It consists of a wooden or bamboo handle with bristles of animal hair arranged to form an extremely fine point. The artist can paint many kinds of lines by adjusting the angle of the brush and the pressure on it. Chinese artists paint chiefly with black ink made of pine soot and glue. They sometimes use plant or mineral pigments to add color to their paintings. Chinese painters have created many

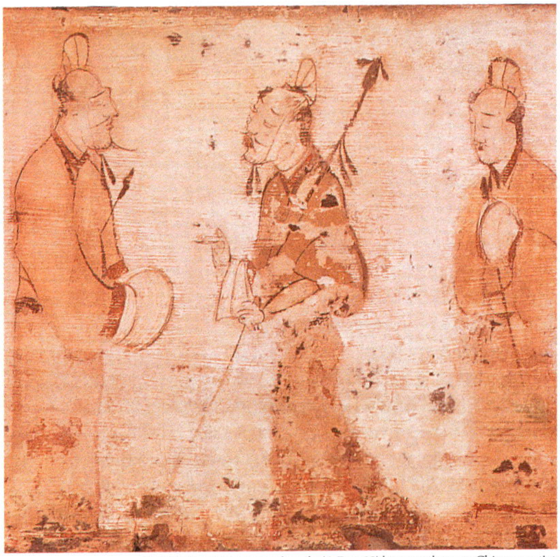

Detail of a painting on clay tile (A.D. 1-99) by an unknown Chinese artist; Museum of Fine Arts, Boston, Denman Waldo Ross Collection

Paintings on the tiles of tombs during the Han dynasty were done in a graceful, lively style. This tomb tile shows two officials of the Chinese emperor's court.

Buddhist Temple Amid Clearing Mountain Peaks (A.D. 967), an ink painting on silk attributed to Li Cheng; Nelson-Atkins Museum of Art, Kansas City, MO, Nelson Fund

Landscapes became the chief subject of Chinese painting by the A.D. 900's. This work is a fine example of the *shanshui* (mountain-water) style developed during the Song dynasty.

works on paper or silk scrolls, which can be rolled up for storage and safekeeping. Other paintings have been done on plaster walls or on flat pieces of silk or paper. See **Painting** (Chinese painting).

Bronze and jade. The earliest Chinese bronzes were highly decorated vessels created for use in rituals during the Shang and Zhou dynasties. Bronze workers cast the vessels in *piece molds,* clay molds made of separate pieces of baked clay, which had to be destroyed to free the vessels. Art collectors have prized early Chinese bronzes for centuries, valuing them both for their exquisite design and their antiquity.

The Chinese have always held jade in high regard. Their language has many words built on *yu,* the word for jade. These words often convey notions of beauty, virtue, long life, and purity. The Chinese used various

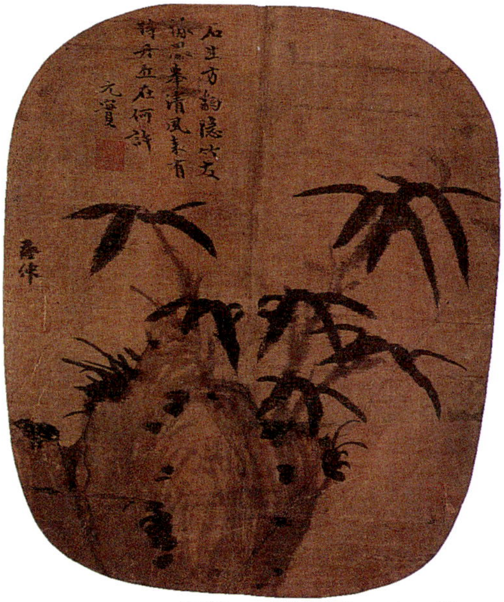

Ink painting on silk (1279-1368) by an unknown Chinese artist; National Museum, Taipei, Taiwan (Wan-go H. C. Weng)

Fine handwriting called calligraphy forms an essential part of many Chinese paintings. Artists of the Yuan period often combined calligraphy with paintings of bamboo, as on this fan.

forms of jade in ceremonies, buried it with the dead, displayed it in homes and palaces, and wore it for both decoration and protection. Jade *amulets* (charms) supposedly provided protection from evil spirits and preserved the owner's "life force." The Chinese esteemed jade chimes for their clear and uplifting sound.

Sculpture and pottery. Most Chinese sculptures are associated with ritual and religion. They often stand as tomb guardians above ground or as burial attendants in or near graves. Since 1974, thousands of earthenware figures of people, horses, and chariots have been discovered near Xi'an in burial pits near the tomb of Shi Huangdi, the first emperor of the Qin dynasty. These figures, the earliest known life-sized Chinese sculptures, date from the late 200's B.C. See **Archaeology** (picture: An army of life-sized statues).

Buddhism reached China from India toward the end of the Han period (206 B.C. to A.D. 220), and sculptors began to turn their skills to the service of this new religion. The Buddhists built temples in or near cities. In rural areas, they hollowed out cliffsides to form chapels. Sculptors decorated the chapels with figures of Buddha and his attendants. Some sculptures were carved from local stone. Others were molded of clay, fired, painted, and glazed. Still other sculptures were cast of bronze and coated with gold. See **Sculpture** (China).

The Chinese have made pottery since prehistoric times. They began to use the potter's wheel before 3000 B.C. and produced glazed pottery as early as the 1300's B.C. The Chinese developed the world's first porcelain in the A.D. 100's, during the Han dynasty. They admired porcelain, and wrote many essays and poems about it. Among the most esteemed types of porcelain were "official ware" *(guanyao),* produced for the emperor's household; bluish-white *qingbai* ware; and crackled *ge* ware.

Bronze vessel (1100's B.C.) by an unknown Chinese artist; Freer Gallery of Art, Smithsonian Institution, Washington, D.C.

Jade disk (400-200 B.C.) by an unknown Chinese artist; Nelson-Atkins Museum of Art, Kansas City, MO, Nelson Fund

Chinese ceremonial art included works created in bronze and jade. Bronze vessels like the one above were used in ceremonies for the dead during the Shang dynasty. The carved jade disk on the right, called a *bi,* was used as a symbol of heaven in religious ceremonies. It dates from the Zhou dynasty.

Gilded bronze statue by an unknown Chinese sculptor; Asian Art Museum of San Francisco, Avery Brundage Collection

© Steve Vidler, eStock

Chinese sculpture was greatly influenced by Buddhism. A seated Buddha, *left,* one of the oldest Chinese Buddhist sculptures, dates from A.D. 338. Sculptors also created huge figures of Buddha and his attendants for cliffside chapels, such as the Fengxian cave in Henan province, *right.*

White pottery made during the Shang dynasty had a polished surface with carved designs. This jar is a fine example of this pottery.

Unglazed clay jar (about 1200 B.C.); Freer Gallery of Art, Smithsonian Institution, Washington, D.C.

Fine white porcelain was produced during the Ming dynasty. Like much Ming porcelain, this bowl has a blue underglaze.

Bowl (late 1400's); Freer Gallery of Art, Smithsonian Institution, Washington, D.C.

Multicolor ceramics were developed in the Tang era. Potters combined color glazes to form patterns like the one on this vase.

Vase (A.D. 618-907) by an unknown Chinese artist; Nelson-Atkins Museum of Art, Kansas City, MO, Nelson Fund

Other kinds of porcelains were decorated with folk symbols and the bright colors of folk and religious art. Some featured beautifully painted flowers, landscapes, historical scenes, and calligraphic inscriptions. Porcelain dishware and vases produced during the Tang (618-907), Song (960-1279), and Ming dynasties (1368-1644) and the early part of the Qing dynasty (1644-1912) are among the greatest treasures of Chinese art.

Architecture. Traditionally, most of the public buildings in China were constructed of wood on a stone or earthen platform. The most outstanding feature of Chinese architecture was a large tile roof with extending edges that curved gracefully upward, a development dating from the Tang dynasty. Wooden columns were connected to the ceiling beams by wooden brackets that branched out to support these roofs. Walls did not carry weight but merely provided privacy. Most buildings had only one story, but the Chinese also built many-storied towers called *pagodas* (see **Pagoda**). Today, Chinese architects seldom construct buildings in the traditional styles, and new buildings in Chinese cities look much like those in any modern city.

China's traditional landscape gardens were designed primarily to serve as Taoist retreats. They combine artistic design, complex symbolism, and careful arrangement. Their structure reflects the interplay between the principles of yin and yang. For example, garden designers place angular buildings among rounded natural features and rock formations next to water. Light areas alternate with dark, and empty spaces with solids.

Music was extremely important in traditional Chinese society, both for ritual and recreational purposes. The *Record of Rites,* an ancient Confucian text, states that music is the best way to achieve harmony in the universe. The occasions for music in China ranged from grand public ceremonies and festivals to marriages, funerals, and simple social gatherings.

Traditional Chinese music sounds much different from the music of Europe and America because it uses a different scale. The scales most commonly used in Western music have eight tones, but most Chinese scales have five tones. Melody is the most important element in Chinese music. Instruments and voices follow the same melodic line instead of following different lines that harmonize.

Traditional Chinese instruments include the *qin,* a seven-stringed instrument, and the *sheng,* a mouth organ made of 17 bamboo pipes. The Chinese also have a lute-like instrument called the *pipa* and two kinds of flutes, the *xiao* and the *di.* Today, Chinese musicians also play non-Chinese instruments and perform the music of many American and European composers, jazz artists, and rock stars.

Theater. There are several types of Chinese drama: classic *zaju* (variety performance) of the Yuan dynasty (1279-1368); southern drama *(xiwen* and *chuanqi);* various regional styles, such as *Kunqu,* from the region of Suzhou; and a Qing dynasty hybrid form known as *jingxi* or Beijing opera. Although each of these traditional dramatic forms has its own special features, all combine spoken language, music, acting, and sometimes mime, dance, or acrobatics.

Chinese drama often uses poetry to convey dramatic mood. Characters that appear frequently in traditional Chinese drama include scholars, military men (both good and bad), heroic women, and silly comic characters. Since the late 1800's, forms of drama from Europe and the United States have influenced Chinese plays.

The land

China is the world's third largest country in area. Only Russia and Canada are larger. China's land is as varied as it is vast. It ranges from subarctic regions in the north to tropical lowlands in the south and from fertile plains in the east to deserts in the west.

Northeastern China was once called Manchuria, but today it is called the Northeast *(Dongbei* in Chinese). Xinjiang covers the far northwest, and Tibet (or *Xizang)* covers the far southwest. Inner Mongolia lies in the north. The eastern half of China, south of the Northeast and Inner Mongolia, is sometimes called *China proper.* It has always had most of China's people.

China can be divided into eight major land regions. They are (1) Tibetan Highlands, (2) Xinjiang-Mongolian Uplands, (3) Inner Mongolian Border Uplands, (4) Eastern Highlands, (5) Eastern Lowlands, (6) Central Uplands, (7) Sichuan Basin, and (8) Southern Uplands.

Much of China is so densely populated that little wildlife remains. But rugged mountain forests at the eastern edge of the Tibetan Highlands shelter pandas, golden monkeys, takins, and other rare animals. A few elephants and gibbons inhabit the tropical Southern

WORLD BOOK photo by Robert Borja

Chinese musicians play Western and Chinese instruments. In the group shown here, the girl on the left is playing a cello, and her friends are playing traditional Chinese instruments.

Beijing opera, the most popular form of drama in China, combines dialogue and songs with dance and symbolic gestures. The plays are based on Chinese history and folklore.

© Steve Vidler, eStock

Uplands region. A few Amur, or Siberian, tigers live in remote forests of the Northeast.

The Tibetan Highlands lie in southwestern China. The region consists of a vast plateau bordered by towering mountains—the Himalaya on the south, the Karakoram Range on the west, and the Kunlun on the north. The world's highest mountain, Mount Everest, rises 29,035 feet (8,850 meters) above sea level in the Himalaya in southern Tibet. Two of the world's longest rivers, the Huang He and the Yangtze, begin in the highlands and flow eastward across China to the sea. The Yangtze River is called the Chang Jiang in China.

Tibet suffers from both drought and extreme cold. Most of the region is a wasteland of rock, gravel, snow, and ice. A few areas provide limited grazing for hardy yaks—woolly oxen that furnish food, clothing, and transportation for the Tibetans. Crops grow only in a few lower-lying areas, largely in the east. See **Tibet**.

The Xinjiang-Mongolian Uplands occupy the vast dry stretches of northwestern China. The region has plentiful mineral resources. However, it is thinly populated because of its remoteness and harsh climate.

The eastern part of the region consists of two deserts, the Mu Us and part of the Gobi. The western part of the region is divided into two areas by the Tian Shan range, which has peaks over 20,000 feet (6,096 meters) above sea level. South of the mountains lies one of the world's driest deserts, the Taklimakan. The Turpan Depression, an oasis near the northern edge of the Taklimakan, is the lowest point in China. It lies 505 feet (154 meters) below sea level. To the north of the Tian Shan, the Junggar Basin stretches northward to the Altai Mountains along the Mongolian border.

The Inner Mongolian Border Uplands lie between the Gobi and the Eastern Lowlands. The Greater Hinggan Range forms the northern part of the region. The terrain there is rugged, and little agriculture is practiced. The southern part of the region is a plateau thickly covered with *loess,* a fertile, yellowish soil deposited by the wind. Loess consists of tiny mineral particles and is easily worn away. The Huang He and its tributaries have carved out hills and steep-sided valleys in the soft soil.

© Jean DeLord, eStock

The Xinjiang-Mongolian Uplands are a vast area of deserts and rugged mountains in northwestern China. This photograph shows the edge of the Gobi, a desert in the eastern part of the region.

The name *Huang He* means *Yellow River* and comes from the large amounts of silt carried by the river.

The Eastern Highlands consist of the Shandong Peninsula and the eastern part of the Northeast. The Shandong Peninsula is a hilly region with excellent harbors and rich deposits of coal. The hills of the eastern part of the Northeast have some of China's best forests. The highest hills are the Changbai Mountains (Long White Mountains) along the border with North Korea. To the north, the Amur River forms the border with Russia. Just south of the Amur is the Lesser Hinggan Range.

The Eastern Lowlands lie between the Inner Mongolian Border Uplands and the Eastern Highlands and extend south to the Southern Uplands. From north to south, the region consists of the Northeastern Plain, the North China Plain, and the valley of the Yangtze River. The Eastern Lowlands have China's best farmland and many of the largest cities.

The Northeastern Plain has fertile soils and large deposits of coal and iron ore. Most of the Northeast's people live on the southern part of the plain near the Liao River.

Farther south, the wide, flat North China Plain lies in the valley of the Huang He. Wheat is the main crop in this highly productive agricultural area. Major flooding formerly occurred in the valley, which earned the river

Physical features

Altai Mountains ....B 3
Altun Mountains ....C 2
Amur River ....A 6
Changbai
Mountains ....B 7
Daxue Mountains ....D 4
Dongting Lake ....E 5
Gobi (desert) ....C 4
Grand Canal ....D 6
Greater Hinggan
Range..................A 6
Hainan Island ....F 5
Himalaya
(mountains) ....D 1
Huai River ....D 6
Huang He
(Yellow River) ....D 5
Junggar Basin ....B 2
K2 (mountain) ....C 1
Kunlun
Mountains ....C 2
Lesser Hinggan
Range...................A 6
Liao River ....B 6
Loess Hills ....C 5
Northeastern Plain ......B 6
Mekong River ....D 3
Mount Everest ....E 2
Mu Us Desert ....C 5
Nan Ling
(mountains) ....E 5
North China Plain ....D 6
Pamirs
(mountains) ....C 1
Peak Pobedy ....B 2
Poyang Lake ....D 6
Qaidam Basin ....C 3
Qilian Mountains ....C 3
Qin Ling
(mountains) ....D 5
Qinghai Lake ....C 4
Shandong
Peninsula ....C 6
Sichuan Basin ....D 4
Taklimakan
Desert ....C 2
Tarim Basin ....C 2
Tibet, Plateau of ....D 2
Tian Shan
(mountains) ....B 1
Turpan
Depression ....B 3
Wuyi
Mountains ....E 6
Xi Jiang
(West River) ....E 5
Yangtze River
(Chang Jiang) ....D 5
Yellow Sea ....C 6
Yunnan Plateau ....E 4

© Zhou Lixin, Imaginechina

Three Gorges Dam, under construction on the Yangtze River in Hubei province, will be the world's largest dam. The dam will help control flooding and generate hydroelectric power.

the nickname *China's Sorrow.* Today, dams, dikes, and reservoirs, and the use of river water for irrigation, control most floods. The Grand Canal, which is the world's longest artificially created waterway, extends more than 1,000 miles (1,600 kilometers) across the North China Plain.

The lower Yangtze Valley has the best combination of level land, fertile soil, and rainfall anywhere in China. In the so-called Fertile Triangle between Nanjing, Shanghai, and Hangzhou, the population density is extremely high. The Yangtze River and its many tributaries have long formed the most important water route for trade within China.

The Central Uplands are an area of hills and mountains between the Eastern Lowlands and the Tibetan Highlands. The Qin Ling, a mountain range, are the chief physical feature of the region. Peaks in the range rise more than 12,000 feet (3,658 meters) above sea level. The Qin Ling cross the region from east to west. They form a natural barricade against seasonal winds that carry rain from the south and dust or cold air from the north. To the north of the mountains are dry wheat-growing areas. To the south lie warm, humid areas where rice is the major crop.

The Sichuan Basin, a large basin surrounded by high mountains, lies southwest of the Central Uplands. Its mild climate and long growing season make it one of China's main agricultural regions. Most crops are grown on *terraced fields*—level strips of land cut out of the hillsides. The name *Sichuan* means *Four Rivers* and refers to the four streams that flow into the Yangtze River in the region. The rivers have carved out deep gorges in the region's red sandstone, which makes land travel difficult. Small ships can travel on the Yangtze into central Hubei, but only boats and other small craft can navigate farther west into Sichuan and the river's swift-flowing tributaries.

The Southern Uplands cover southeastern China, including the island of Hainan. The Southern Uplands are a region of green hills and mountains. The deltas of the Xi Jiang (West River) and Min rivers are almost the only flat areas in the region. The Xi Jiang and its tributaries form the main transportation route for southern China.

© SuperStock

The Central Uplands include dry wheat-growing areas like this one near the city of Xi'an. To the south of this area, the Qin Ling Mountains cross the Central Uplands from west to east.

The Southern Uplands are a region of green hills and mountains. This picture shows part of the city of Guilin and the Li River, one of the many important waterways in the central part of the region.

© SuperStock

Deep, rich soils and a tropical climate help make the delta area an extremely productive agricultural region.

Much of the Southern Uplands is so hilly and mountainous that little land can be cultivated, even by terracing. The central part of the region, near the city of Guilin, is one of the most scenic areas in China. It has many isolated limestone hills that rise 100 to 600 feet (30 to 182 meters) almost straight up.

Climate

China has a wide range of climates because it is such a large country and has such a variety of natural features. The most severe climatic conditions occur in the Taklimakan and Gobi deserts. Daytime temperatures in these deserts may exceed 100 °F (38 °C) in summer, but nighttime lows may fall to −30 °F (−34 °C) in winter. Tibet and Heilongjiang province in northeastern China have long, bitterly cold winters. In contrast, coastal areas of southeastern China have a tropical climate.

Seasonal winds called *monsoons* greatly affect China's climate. In winter, monsoons carry cold, dry air from central Asia across China toward the sea. These high winds often create dust storms in the north. From late spring to early fall, the monsoons blow from the opposite direction and spread warm, moist air inland from the sea. Because of the monsoons, more rain falls in summer than in winter throughout China. Most parts of the country receive more than 80 percent of their rainfall between May and October.

Summers tend to be hot and humid in southeastern China and in the southern parts of the Northeast. In fact, summer temperatures average about 80 °F (27 °C) throughout much of China. However, northern China has longer and much colder winters than the south has. In January, daily low temperatures average about −13 °F (−25 °C) in Heilongjiang and about 20 °F (−7 °C) throughout much of the eastern third of the country. However, the coastal areas of the Southern uplands are much warmer. Mountains shield southern China and the Yangtze Valley west of Wuhan from the winter winds. The Sichuan Basin is especially well protected, and frost occurs only a few days each winter.

The amount of precipitation varies greatly from region to region in China. The deserts of Xinjiang and Inner Mongolia receive less than 4 inches (10 centimeters) of rain yearly. More than 40 inches (100 centimeters) of

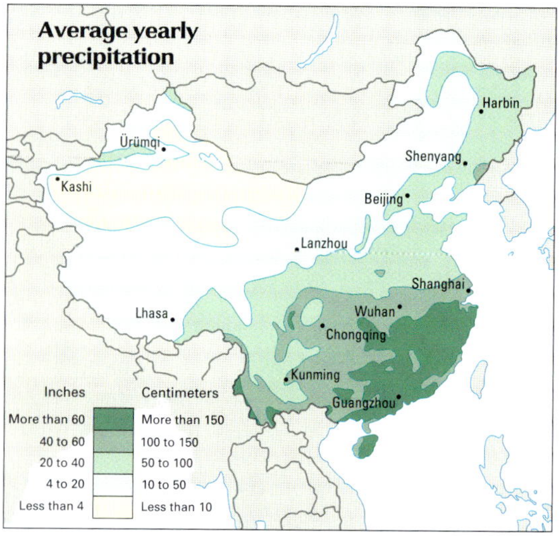

WORLD BOOK map

Rainfall in China is heaviest in the southeast, where it averages from 40 to 80 inches (100 to 200 centimeters) yearly. In the north, the amount of precipitation varies widely from year to year.

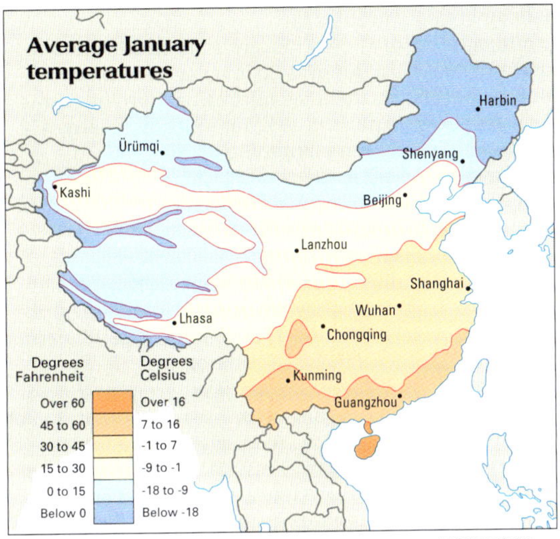

WORLD BOOK map

Northern and western China have far colder winters than the south. January temperatures average below 0 °F (−18 °C) in Manchuria and Tibet but over 60 °F (16 °C) on the south coast.

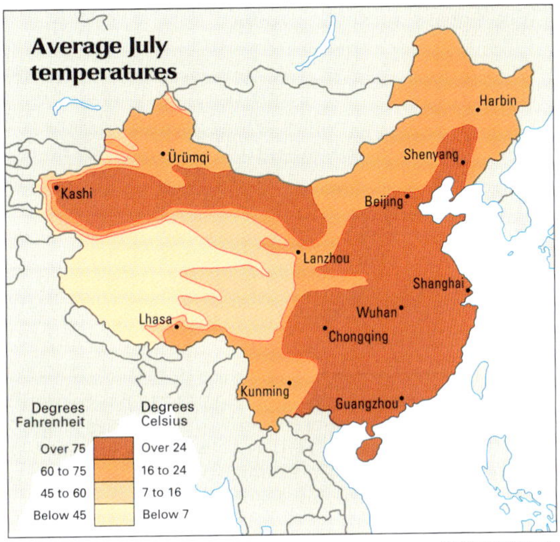

WORLD BOOK map

Temperatures in July average above 75 °F (24 °C) throughout southeastern China and in southern Manchuria. Daytime temperatures may exceed 100 °F (38 °C) in the northwestern deserts.

rain falls each year in many parts of southeastern China. Some areas near the southeastern coast receive up to 80 inches (200 centimeters) annually. In northern China, the amount of precipitation varies widely from year to year. However, most areas in northern China receive less than 40 inches (100 centimeters) yearly. For example, annual precipitation averages about 25 inches (63 centimeters) in Beijing and 28 inches (70 centimeters) in Shenyang. Snowfalls occur only in the north. But even there, they are infrequent and usually light.

Economy

China has one of the world's largest economies in terms of its *gross domestic product* (GDP), the value of all goods and services it produces in a year. But in terms of *per capita* (per person) GDP, China ranks low. More than half of the world's countries have a higher per capita GDP than China. Because of this, many economists still consider China a developing country.

The national government exercises much control over China's economy. It controls the most important industrial plants and operates most of the nation's banks, most long-distance transportation, and foreign trade. It also sets the prices of certain key goods and services.

China's government makes national economic plans that cover five-year periods. These plans determine how the government will work to improve different areas of the economy. Through the end of the 1900's, the Communist government achieved an impressive record of economic growth.

In the early 1980's, the Chinese government began a series of economic reforms that led to less government control over some business activities. Since then, the number of privately owned and operated businesses has increased dramatically. Many experts believe the increased ownership of business has contributed significantly to China's economic growth. However, it has also led to increased unemployment and labor migration.

In the 1990's, the government began spending huge amounts of money to improve China's *infrastructure* (roads, bridges, dams, and other public works). These projects include the Three Gorges Dam, canals to bring water from the south to the north, and subway systems in major cities.

Manufacturing and mining contribute more to China's GDP than any other category of economic activity. Shanghai is one of the world's leading manufacturing centers. Its industrial output far exceeds that of any other place in China. Beijing and Tianjin are also important industrial centers. Others include Shenyang and Harbin in the Northeast; Guangzhou, Hangzhou, Suzhou, and Wuhan in southeastern China; and Kunming, Chengdu, and Chongqing in southwestern China.

After the Communists came to power, they began to rebuild China's factories in an effort to make the nation an industrial power. They concentrated on the development of heavy industries, such as the production of metals and machinery. Today, China has one of the world's largest steel industries. The machine-building industry provides metalworking tools and other machines for new factories. Other major manufactured products include cement and other building materials, fertilizer and other chemicals, irrigation equipment, military equipment, ships, tractors, and trucks.

The largest consumer goods industries are the textile industry, the food-processing industry, and electronics. As the standard of living in China improves, demand is growing for such consumer goods as automobiles, refrigerators, and television sets. As a result, the Chinese are increasing their production of consumer items.

To help continue the country's industrial expansion, China's leaders made contracts with foreign companies to modernize factories and to build new ones. The government is also improving and expanding scientific and technical education in China and sending students abroad for training. However, waste and inefficiency in

China's gross domestic product

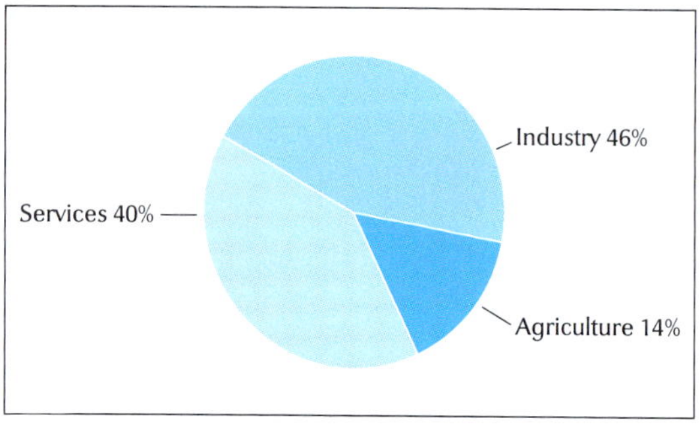

China's gross domestic product (GDP) was $1,355,321,000,000 in 2001. This figure includes Hong Kong, which the United Kingdom returned to China in 1997. The GDP is the total value of goods and services produced in a country in a year. *Services* include community, social, and personal services; finance, insurance, and real estate; government; wholesale and retail trade; transportation and communication. *Industry* includes construction, manufacturing, mining, and utilities. *Agriculture* includes agriculture, forestry, and fishing.

Production and workers by economic activities

Economic activities	Percent of GDP produced	Employed workers* Number of people	Employed workers* Percent of total
Manufacturing, mining, & utilities	39	89,662,300	14
Community, social, & personal services	20	100,698,900	16
Agriculture, forestry, & fishing	14	329,747,200	52
Trade	10	48,351,100	8
Construction	6	36,981,400	6
Transportation & communication	7	20,723,400	3
Finance, insurance, & real estate	3	3,838,100	1
Total†	100	630,002,400	100

*Figures are for 2001 and include Hong Kong.
†Figures may not add up to 100 percent due to rounding.
Source: International Labour Office.

industry remain problems.

China is one of the world's largest producers and users of coal. Coal deposits lie in many parts of China, but the best fields are in the north. Coal-burning plants provide about 75 percent of China's electric energy. Hydroelectric plants and oil-burning plants supply the rest. The largest oil field in China is at Daqing in Heilongjiang. Other major Chinese oil fields include those at Dagang, near Tianjin; at Liaohe, in Liaoning; and at Shengli on the Shandong Peninsula.

China is a leading producer of iron ore. Most of the ore comes from large, low-grade deposits in the northeastern provinces. Mines in the central and southwestern parts of the country also yield iron ore.

China outranks all other countries in the production of magnesium, tin, and tungsten. It is a leading producer of aluminum, copper, gold, lead, silver, and zinc.

Service industries provide services rather than produce goods. They include trade; banking and finance; communication; education; health care; insurance; recreation; and transportation. Together, they contribute about two-fifths of China's GDP.

Tourism has become an important part of this group. Each year, tens of millions of tourists visit China from other countries, and tens of millions of Chinese travel within their country. More information on transportation and communication appears later in this section.

Agriculture contributes only a small part of China's GDP, but it ranks as the country's largest employer. Almost half of China's workers are farmers. In southern China cotton, rice, sweet potatoes, and tea are the major crops. Wheat is the chief crop in the north, followed by millet and sorghum. China produces more apples, cabbages, carrots, cotton, pears, potatoes, rice, tobacco, tomatoes, and wheat than any other country. It grows 85 percent of the world's sweet potatoes. In addition, it is a leading producer of corn, melons, rubber, soybeans, sugar beets, sugar cane, and tea. Farmers in the far south grow tropical crops, such as bananas, oranges, and pineapples.

In rural areas, many families raise chickens and ducks. China has more domesticated ducks than any other country. Nearly every household has a hog. Hogs pro-

AP/Wide World

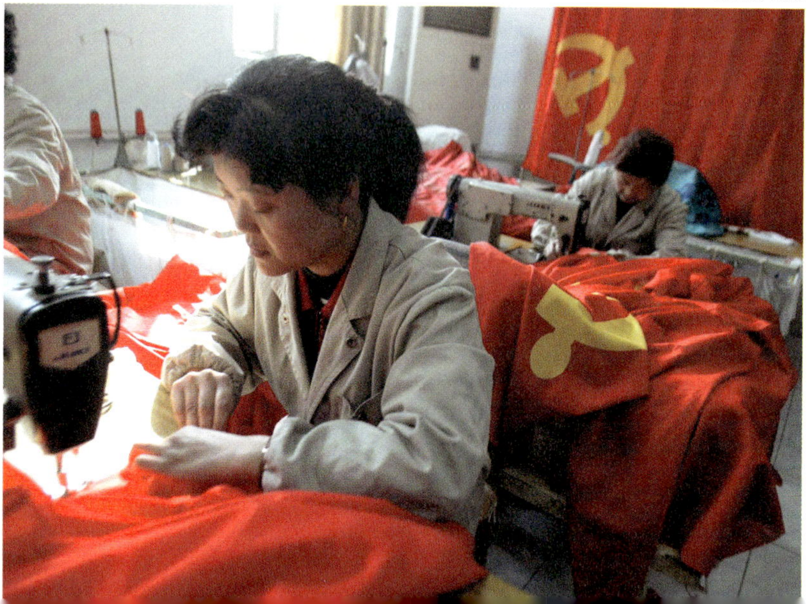

Workers sew Communist Party flags at a factory in Beijing. China's textile industry employs millions of people and contributes greatly to the country's economy. Clothing and textiles are among China's leading exports.

© Gao Feng, Imaginechina

China's steel industry ranks among the largest in the world. In this picture, workers walk past rolled sheets of steel on the floor of a plant in Shanghai.

vide both meat and fertilizer. China has about 450 million hogs, nearly half of all the hogs in the world. China also has many cattle, goats, horses, and sheep.

Only about 14 percent of China's land area can be cultivated. Thus, farmers have little cropland on which to grow food for themselves and the rest of the country's huge population. However, they manage to provide almost enough food for all the people. Southern China has a long growing season, so farmers there can grow two or more crops on the same land each year. However, droughts and floods often interrupt production. Chinese farmers do most of their work by hand with simple tools. They use irrigation and fertilizers and practice soil conservation.

During the 1950's, the Communists *collectivized* China's agriculture. They organized the peasants to farm the land cooperatively in units called *communes.* In the 1980's, emphasis on communes declined, and individual families farmed more of the land. The families must pay taxes on their land and must sell an agreed amount of farm products to the state at a fixed price. They may then sell their surplus crops at farm markets, sometimes to city dwellers.

Fishing industry. China has the world's largest fishing industry. The Chinese catch tens of millions of tons of fish, shellfish, and other seafood annually. Fish farming is an important industry in China. Fish farmers raise fish in ponds both for food and for use in fertilizer.

Forestry. China is a world leader in producing forest products. Its timber industry is concentrated in the far Northeast, in western Sichuan, and in eastern Tibet. But China does not produce enough timber to meet its own needs and must import many forest products.

International trade is vital to China's economic development. Foreign investments help China increase its imports and exports. In 1999, China signed a landmark trade agreement with the United States that lowered many barriers to trade. In 2001, China joined the World Trade Organization, a group that promotes international trade.

China imports machinery and other technology needed to modernize the economy. Other leading imports include chemicals, fertilizers, grain, metals, and plastics. China's main exports include clothing, furniture, electronic devices, textiles, and toys. China also exports tea and such foods as fruits, pork, and vegetables. Much of China's international trade passes through Hong Kong. China's chief trading partners include Germany, Japan, South Korea, and the United States.

Transportation. Many Chinese still rely on simple, traditional means for transportation over short distances. Rural people carry loads fastened to their back or hanging from poles carried across their shoulders.

© Geoffrey Morgan, Alamy

Chinese farmers, like this rice grower, do much of their work by hand with simple tools. About half of China's workers are farmers who live in rural villages similar to this one in Yunnan province.

© Jiang Ren, Imaginechina

Brokers at the Shanghai Stock Exchange conduct their business using computers. Financial services and other service industries contribute significantly to China's economy.

Carts and wagons are pulled either by people or by donkeys, horses, mules, or oxen. Bicycles, motor scooters, taxis, and buses are widely used for local travel.

Railroads make up the most important part of China's modern transportation system. Rail lines link the major cities and manufacturing centers. The railroads transport both freight and passenger traffic.

China has an extensive network of roads that reaches almost every town in the nation. However, most roads are unpaved. Highway traffic in China consists mostly of trucks and buses. On rural roads, tractors are common. Many cars are owned by government agencies or taxi companies, but growing numbers of Chinese are buying them for personal use.

Ships transport freight and boats carry passengers and light loads on several Chinese rivers, especially the Yangtze. The Grand Canal, completed about A.D. 610, extends more than 1,000 miles (1,600 kilometers) from Hangzhou in the south to Beijing in the north. However, silt deposits clog the canal, and only part of it still serves as a water route.

China's major ports include Dalian, Guangzhou, Hong Kong, Ningbo, Qingdao, Shanghai, Shenzhen, and Tianjin. The chief airports are at Beijing, Guangzhou, Hong Kong, and Shanghai, but many other cities have airports. Chinese and foreign airlines link China with cities around the world.

Communication in China comes under strict govern-

China land use

This map shows the major uses of land in China. Nearly all of China's cropland is in the eastern half of the country. Extremely dry conditions in western China make much of the land there unproductive.

- Intensively cultivated land
- Other cultivated land
- Grazing land
- Forest land
- Generally unproductive land
- Fishing
- Manufacturing center
- Mineral deposit

WORLD BOOK map

Bicycles are a popular means of transportation in China. These people cycle through downtown Chengdu during rush hour. One cyclist, *center,* uses her cellular telephone as she rides.

© Mark Henley, Panos Pictures

ment control. During the early years of Communism, newspapers, radio, and television were devoted mostly to political propaganda. But in the 1980's, the government began allowing the media to provide general information and entertainment. Educational programs, concerts, plays, and films often appear on television.

Hundreds of daily newspapers and many weeklies are published in China. The government and the Chinese Communist Party publish or support most of these. China's leading newspaper is *Sichuan Ribao (Sichuan Daily)* of Chengdu.

In 1978, many people began to express political opinions using posters with large writing called *big-character posters.* These posters were pasted on walls that came to be known as *democracy walls.* Many posters complained about China's political system. In 1979, the government forbade posters that criticized its policies. Now, posters typically give such information as tips on health and physical fitness.

Radios and televisions are widespread throughout China, although they are much more common in urban areas. Radio programs are still broadcast over loudspeakers in some rural areas. A village or other group of people sometimes buys a television set and places it in a common area for public use.

Since the 1990's, the telephone system that had been reserved for official purposes has been expanded to allow private use. Cellular telephones are popular, especially among city dwellers. People also use the state-run postal system for personal communication.

The Internet is popular in China, but the government tightly regulates its use. Yet some people in China use the Internet to express their political views, much as the big-character posters were used in the late 1970's.

History

The oldest written records of Chinese history date from about 1500 B.C., during the Shang dynasty. These records are in the form of *oracle bones*—notations scratched on thousands of turtle shells and animal bones. About 100 B.C., a Chinese historian named Sima Qian wrote the first major history of China. Through the centuries, the Chinese always kept detailed records of the events of their times.

Beginnings of Chinese civilization. People lived in what is now China long before the beginning of written history. Primitive human beings probably inhabited parts of eastern China about 2 million years ago. Prehistoric human beings known as the *Peking* (or *Beijing) people* lived between about 600,000 and 400,000 years ago in what is now northern China. By about 10,000 B.C., a number of cultures had developed in this area. From two of them—the Yangshao and the Longshan—a distinctly Chinese civilization gradually emerged.

The Yangshao culture reached the peak of its development about 3000 B.C. The culture, which extended from the central valley of the Huang He to the present-day province of Gansu, was based on millet farming. About the same time, the Longshan culture spread over much of what is now the eastern third of the country. The Longshan people lived in walled communities, cultivated rice, and raised cattle and sheep.

The first dynasties. The Xia culture, which some scholars consider China's first dynasty, arose during the 2100's B.C. For many years, experts doubted that the Xia really existed and thought it was only part of Chinese mythology. But archaeologists found evidence of its existence in what is now Henan province.

The Shang dynasty arose from the Longshan and Xia cultures about 1766 B.C. The Shang kingdom was centered in the eastern Huang He Valley. It became a highly developed society governed by a hereditary class of aristocrats. The dynasty's accomplishments included magnificent bronze vessels, horse-drawn war chariots, and a system of writing.

About 1045 B.C., the Zhou people overthrew the Shang from the west and established their own dynasty. The Zhou dynasty ruled China until 256 B.C. The dynasty directly controlled only the western part of their territory. To the east, the Zhou gave authority to certain follow-

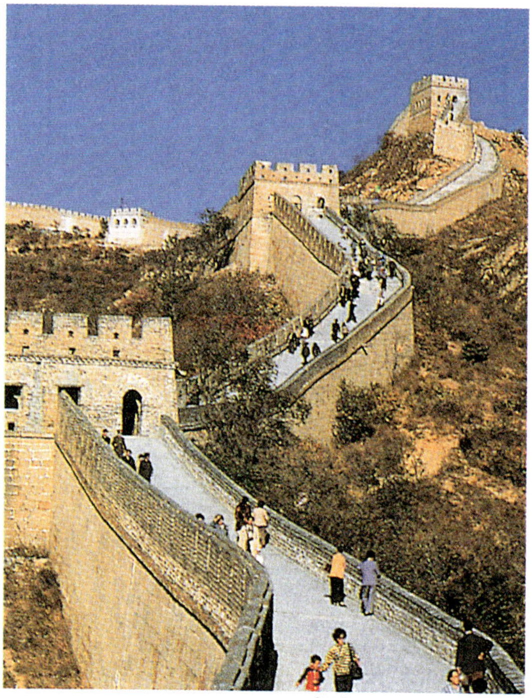

© Dallas & John Heaton, Stock, Boston

The Great Wall of China, built, added to, and rebuilt over many centuries, was intended to keep out central Asian invaders. It extends about 4,500 miles (7,240 kilometers) across northern China.

ers. These followers became lords of semi-independent states. As time passed, these lords grew increasingly independent of the royal court and so weakened its power. In 771 B.C., invaders forced the Zhou to abandon their capital, near what is now Xi'an, and move eastward to Luoyang. Battles between the Zhou rulers and with non-Chinese invaders further weakened the dynasty.

About 500 B.C., the great philosopher Confucius proposed new moral standards to replace the magical practices of his time. During the later Zhou period, there were seven eastern states. The rulers of these states fought one another for the control of all China. In 221 B.C., the Qin state defeated the last of its rival states and established China's first empire controlled by a strong central government. The Qin believed in a philosophy called *Legalism,* and their victory resulted partly from following Legalistic ideas. Legalism emphasized the importance of authority, efficient administration, and strict laws. A combination of Legalistic administrative practices and Confucian moral values helped the Chinese empires endure for more than 2,000 years.

The Qin dynasty lasted only until 206 B.C., but it brought great changes that influenced all later empires in China. The first Qin emperor, Shi Huangdi, abolished the local states and set up a strong central government. His government standardized weights and measures, the currency, and the Chinese writing system. To keep out invaders, he ordered the construction of the Great Wall of China. Laborers built the wall by joining shorter walls constructed during the Zhou dynasty. The Great Wall, which was added to, rebuilt, and moved by later dynasties, extends from the Bo Gulf of the Yellow Sea to the Lop Nur region in what is now Xinjiang in western China. Its many sections and branches cover about 4,500 miles (7,240 kilometers).

Shi Huangdi taxed the Chinese people heavily to support his military campaigns and his vast building projects. These taxes and the harsh enforcement of laws led to civil war soon after his death in 210 B.C. The Qin dynasty collapsed four years later.

The Han dynasty then gained control of China. It ruled from 206 B.C. to A.D. 220. During the Han period,

Important dates in China

c. 1766-c.1045 B.C. The Shang dynasty ruled China.

c. 1045 B.C. The Zhou people from the west overthrew the Shang and set up a new dynasty that ruled until 256 B.C.

c. 500 B.C. The philosopher Confucius developed a system of moral values and responsible behavior that influenced China for more than 2,000 years.

221-206 B.C. The Qin dynasty established China's first strong central government.

206 B.C.-A.D. 220 China became a powerful empire under the Han dynasty. Chinese culture flourished.

581-618 The Sui dynasty came to power and reunified China after almost 400 years of division.

618-907 The Tang dynasty ruled China during a period of prosperity and great cultural accomplishment.

960-1279 The Song dynasty ruled the empire and made Neo-Confucianism the official state philosophy.

1279-1368 The Mongols conquered and controlled all of China.

1368-1644 The Ming dynasty governed China.

1644-1912 The Manchus ruled China as the Qing dynasty.

1842 The Treaty of Nanjing gave Hong Kong to the United Kingdom and allowed British trade at five Chinese ports.

1850-1864 Millions of Chinese died in the Taiping Rebellion.

1900 Members of a secret society attacked and killed Westerners and Chinese Christians during the Boxer Rebellion.

1912 The Republic of China was established.

1928 The Nationalists, led by Chiang Kai-shek, united China under one government.

1931 The Japanese seized Manchuria (the Northeast).

1934-1935 Mao Zedong led the Chinese Communists on their Long March to Shaanxi.

1937-1945 War with Japan shattered China.

1949 The Chinese Communists defeated the Nationalists and established the People's Republic of China.

1958 The Communists launched the Great Leap Forward, which severely weakened China's economy.

1966-1969 The Cultural Revolution disrupted education, the government, and daily life in China.

1971 China was admitted to the United Nations (UN).

1972 U.S. President Richard M. Nixon visited China.

1976 Communist Party Chairman Mao Zedong and Premier Zhou Enlai died.

1979 China and the United States established normal diplomatic relations.

Early 1980's The Communist Party began reforms toward reducing government economic controls.

1989 Demonstrations across China called for more democracy and an end to corruption in government. The military crushed the movement, killing hundreds of protesters.

1997 China regained control of Hong Kong from the United Kingdom.

1999 China regained control of Macao from Portugal.

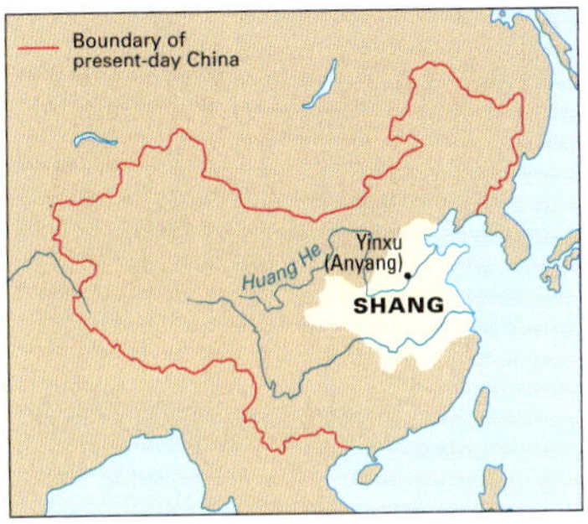

China's first dynasty, the Shang, arose in the Huang He Valley during the 1700's B.C. It ruled China until about 1045 B.C.

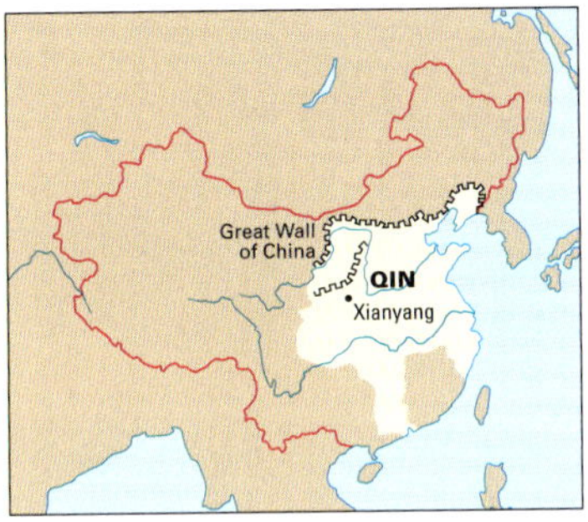

The Qin dynasty, in 221 B.C., established China's first empire controlled by a strong central government.

WORLD BOOK maps

The Han dynasty gained control of China in 206 B.C. Han rulers expanded the Chinese empire into Central Asia.

Confucianism became the philosophical basis of government. Aristocrats held most important state offices. However, a person's qualifications began to play a role in the selection and placement of officials. Chinese influence spread into neighboring countries, and overland trade routes linked China with Europe for the first time.

In A.D. 9, a Han official named Wang Mang seized the throne and set up the Xin dynasty. However, the Han dynasty regained control of China by A.D. 25. Art, education, and science thrived. Writers produced histories and dictionaries. They also collected classics of literature from earlier times. During the late Han period, Buddhism was introduced into China from India.

Political struggles at the royal court and administrative dishonesty plagued the last century of Han rule. In addition, powerful regional officials began to mistreat the peasants. As a result, large-scale rebellion finally broke out, and the Han dynasty fell in 220.

The period of division. China then split into three competing kingdoms. Soon afterward, nomadic groups invaded northern China. A series of Chinese and non-Chinese dynasties ruled all or part of the north from 304 to 581. Six dynasties followed one another in the south from 222 to 589. During this period of division, Buddhism spread across China and influenced all aspects of life.

The brief Sui dynasty (581-618) reunified China when it absorbed the last southern dynasty in 589. By 610, the Grand Canal linked the Yangtze Valley with northern China. The canal made the grain and other products of the south more easily available to support the political and military needs of the north.

The Tang dynasty replaced the Sui in 618 and ruled China for nearly 300 years. The Tang period was an age of prosperity and great cultural accomplishment. The Tang capital at Chang'an (now Xi'an) had more than a million people, making it the largest city in the world. It attracted diplomats, traders, poets, and scholars from throughout Asia. Some of China's greatest poets, including Li Bo and Du Fu, wrote during the Tang period. Buddhism, in forms adapted to Chinese ways, remained an enormous cultural influence. Distinctly Chinese schools of Buddhism spread, including *Chan* (Zen) and *Qingtu* (Pure Land).

In 755, a rebellion led by a northern general named An Lushan touched off a gradual decline in Tang power. A series of rebellions in the late 800's further weakened the Tang empire, which finally ended in 907. During the period that followed, a succession of "Five Dynasties and Ten Kingdoms" struggled for control of the empire. In 960, the Song dynasty reunified China.

The Song dynasty brought major changes that affected China throughout the remaining empires. The Song rulers firmly established a system of civil service examinations that had begun during the Han period. They thus completed the shift of social and political power from aristocratic families to officials selected on the basis of talent. Another significant change was the development of *Neo-Confucianism,* which combined the moral standards of traditional Confucianism with elements of Buddhism and Taoism. The philosopher Zhu Xi was largely responsible for this new Confucianism. The Song dynasty established Neo-Confucianism as the official state philosophy, and all later Chinese dynasties continued to support it.

During the Song period, the introduction of early ripening rice made it possible to grow two or three crops a year in the south. The increased rice production helped support the population, which for the first time exceeded 100 million. Chinese inventions during this period included the handgun and movable type for printing. Literature, philosophy, and history flourished. In the fine arts, the great Song achievements were hard-glazed porcelains and magnificent landscape paintings.

The Song dynasty suffered from frequent attacks by nomadic peoples from the north. By 1127, it had lost its hold in northern China to a rival dynasty from northeastern China. The Song then moved their capital from Kaifeng to Hangzhou on the wealthy lower Yangtze Delta. The dynasty that ruled from 960 to 1127 is often called the Northern Song, and the dynasty that ruled after 1127 is called the Southern Song.

Mongol rule. During the 1200's, Mongol warriors swept into China from the north. The Mongol leader Kublai Khan established the Yuan dynasty. It controlled all of China from 1279 to 1368, the first time that the entire country had come under foreign rule. During the Yuan period, Europeans became increasingly interested in China because of the reports of travelers and traders. The most enthusiastic reports came from Marco Polo, a trader from Venice. He claimed that he traveled widely in China from 1275 to 1292, and he gave glowing accounts of the highly civilized country known by Europeans as *Cathay.*

The Mongols ruled China harshly. During the mid-1300's, rebellions drove the Mongols out of China and led to the establishment of the Ming dynasty.

The Ming dynasty ruled from 1368 to 1644, a period of stability, prosperity, and revived Chinese influence in eastern Asia. Literature and art flourished again. When European traders and Roman Catholic missionaries visited China during the late 1500's and the 1600's, the Ming rulers distrusted them. The Chinese considered the Europeans to be a threat to the country's stability.

The early rule of the Manchus. In 1644, the Manchus from northeastern China invaded Beijing, the Ming capital, and established the Qing dynasty. The Manchus ruled China until 1912. Like the Mongols, the Manchus came from beyond the Great Wall. But unlike the Mongols, the Manchus had adopted many elements of Chinese culture before they gained control of the empire. The Manchus strongly supported Neo-Confucianism and modeled their political system after that of the Ming.

From 1669 to 1796, the Qing empire prospered. Chinese influence extended into Mongolia, Tibet, and other parts of central Asia. Commerce and the handicraft industry built up the economy. Agricultural output increased as China's population expanded rapidly, doubling from about 150 million in 1700 to about 300 million by 1800.

By the late 1700's, the standard of living in China began to decline as the population grew faster than agricultural production. In the 1770's, political dishonesty began to plague the Qing administration. In 1796, the worsening conditions touched off a rebellion, led by an anti-Manchu secret society. The rebellion lasted until 1804 and greatly weakened the Qing dynasty.

The dynastic cycle. Chinese historians noticed a pattern to the rise and fall of China's dynasties. They saw that dynasties usually began with a strong ruler who established an empire, often using ruthless means. Once established, the dynasty would expand and make great contributions to Chinese culture. Later rulers would become corrupt and neglect the empire, which eventually would weaken and fall after a rebellion. From the chaos that followed, a new strong leader would emerge, and the cycle would begin again.

Many Chinese believed the cyclic pattern could help them predict what would happen next to a dynasty. Peasants added the idea that natural events, such as earthquakes, were signs that things were about to change. These ideas continue to influence Chinese thought today.

Clash with the Western powers. Merchants from Europe and North America had little effect on China before the 1800's. The Chinese government permitted foreign trade only at the port of Guangzhou and severely limited contact between foreigners and Chinese. China exported large quantities of tea and silk to the West but purchased few goods in return. To balance their trade, European merchants began to bring opium to China during the late 1700's. The Chinese had outlawed the importation of opium, so the Europeans smuggled the drug.

Opium smuggling created much local disorder in China, and the large outflow of money to pay for the opium seriously disturbed the economy. In March 1839, Chinese officials tried to stop the illegal trade by seizing over 20,000 chests of opium from British merchants in Guangzhou. The Opium War then broke out between China and the United Kingdom. The United Kingdom easily won the war, which ended with the Treaty of Nanjing in 1842.

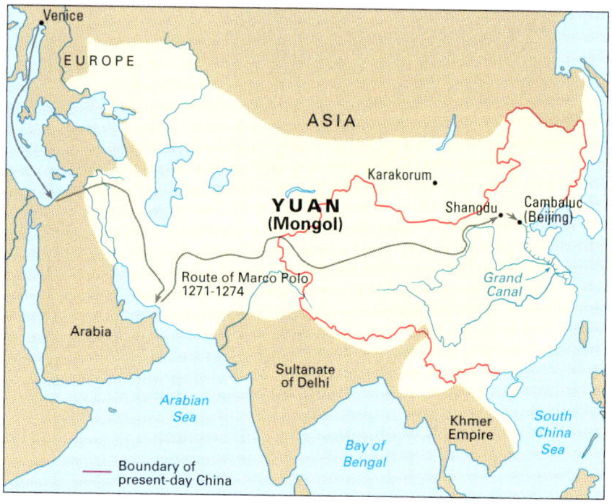

WORLD BOOK map

The Yuan (Mongol) dynasty ruled China from 1279 to 1368. During this period, China was part of the vast Mongol Empire. Marco Polo, a trader from Venice, visited China during the Yuan period and carried home reports of a highly civilized country.

The Treaty of Nanjing was the first of what the Chinese called the *unequal treaties.* It gave the Chinese island of Hong Kong to the United Kingdom and opened four more Chinese ports to British residence and trade. The Treaty of Nanjing also granted British officials the right to deal on equal terms with Chinese officials and to try criminal cases involving British citizens. China signed similar treaties with France and the United States in 1844. These treaties stated that any rights granted to one foreign power must also be given to the other nations. The Western nations thus acquired a common interest in maintaining their special privileges in China.

In 1858 and 1860—after China lost another war, against the United Kingdom and France—China signed more treaties with France, Russia, the United Kingdom, and the United States. These treaties opened additional ports to trade, permitted foreign shipping on the Yangtze, and allowed missionaries to live on and own property in the interior of China. The treaties also called for the Western nations to establish permanent diplomatic offices in Beijing. The United Kingdom added the Kowloon Peninsula to its Hong Kong colony, and Russia received all Chinese territory north of the Amur River and east of the Ussuri River.

The Taiping Rebellion. A series of uprisings in the mid-1800's posed a serious threat to the survival of the Qing dynasty. The most important uprising was the Taiping Rebellion. It lasted from 1850 to 1864 and cost millions of lives. The Taipings were a semireligious group that combined Christian beliefs with ancient Chinese ideas for perfecting society. They challenged both the Qing dynasty and Confucianism with a program to divide the land equally among the people. During the rebellion, local Chinese officials organized new armies, which defeated the Taipings. The Qing received some military aid from the foreign nations that had signed the treaties. These nations wanted the dynasty to survive so the unequal terms of the treaties could remain in effect.

The Open-Door Policy. A disastrous war with Japan in 1894 and 1895 forced China to give up its claim on Korea. China also had to give the Japanese the island of Taiwan, which the Qing had controlled since 1683. France, Germany, Italy, Japan, Russia, and the United Kingdom then forced the crumbling Qing empire to grant them more trading rights and territory. The division of China into a number of European colonies appeared likely. But the Chinese people had begun to develop strong feelings of national unity. This growth of nationalism helped prevent the division of the country, as did rivalry among the foreign powers. None of the foreign powers would allow any of the others to become dominant in China. Beginning in 1899, the United States gradually persuaded the other Western powers and Japan to accept the *Open-Door Policy,* which guaranteed the rights of all nations to trade with China on an equal basis.

The Boxer Rebellion. By the 1890's, some Chinese violently opposed the spread of Western and Christian influences in China. Chinese rebels formed secret societies to fight these influences. The best-known society was called the *Boxers* by Westerners because its members practiced Chinese ceremonial exercises that resembled shadowboxing. In the Boxer Rebellion of 1900, the Boxers attacked and killed Westerners and Chinese Christians. Although initially neutral, the Manchu court eventually supported the rebellion. A rescue force from the Western nations crushed the rebellion.

In the years following the Boxer Rebellion, the Manchus set out to reform the Chinese government and economy. They abolished the Confucian civil service examinations, established modern schools, and sent students abroad to study. They also organized and equipped a Western-style army. In addition, the Qing court reorganized the central government, promised to adopt a constitution, and permitted the provinces to elect their own legislatures.

The fall of the Manchus. The Manchu reforms came too late to save the dynasty. A movement to set up a republic had been growing since the Japanese defeated China in 1895. In 1905, several revolutionary organizations that wanted China to become a republic combined to form the Revolutionary Alliance. They chose as their leader Sun Yat-sen, a Western-educated physician.

From 1905 to 1911, the rebels staged a series of unsuccessful armed attacks against the Manchus. Finally, on Oct. 10, 1911, army troops loosely associated with the Revolutionary Alliance revolted at Wuchang. By the year's end, all the southern and central provinces had declared their independence from Manchu rule.

The early republic. On Jan. 1, 1912, the leaders of the revolution formally established the Republic of China in Nanjing. They named Sun Yat-sen temporary president of the republic. The Manchus then called upon Yuan Shikai, a retired military official, to try to defeat the supporters of the republic. But Yuan arranged a secret settlement with Sun and his followers. The last Manchu emperor, a 6-year-old boy named Pu Yi, gave up the throne on Feb. 12, 1912. The following month, Yuan became president in place of Sun, who stepped down. Yuan quickly moved to expand his personal power.

Photoworld

Troops from eight nations crushed the Boxer Rebellion of 1900—an anti-Western campaign waged by Chinese secret societies. Victorious foreign troops paraded in Beijing, *shown here.*

In 1912, the former revolutionaries established the *Kuomintang* (Nationalist Party, also spelled Guomintang). In 1913, they organized a revolt against Yuan. The revolt failed, and the Nationalist leaders fled to Japan. Yuan's presidency became a dictatorship, and he took steps to establish himself as emperor. But even Yuan's own followers opposed the revival of the empire. A rebellion by military leaders in the provinces forced him to abandon his plans.

The war lord period. Yuan Shikai died in 1916, and the power of the central government quickly crumbled. Presidents continued to hold office in Beijing, but the real power in northern China lay in the hands of *war lords* (local military leaders). In 1917, with the support of southern war lords, Sun Yat-sen set up a rival government in Guangzhou. By 1922, the republic had failed hopelessly and civil war was widespread.

Meanwhile, great changes occurred in Chinese culture and society. A journal called *New Youth* attacked Confucianism and presented a wide range of philosophies and social theories. On May 4, 1919, students in Beijing demonstrated against the Versailles Peace Conference. The conference permitted Japan to keep control of the German holdings it had seized in China during World War I (1914-1918). Other demonstrations that followed helped spread ideas presented by *New Youth* and other journals. This revolution in thought became known as the *May Fourth Movement.* It contributed greatly to the growth of Chinese nationalism and so

The Qing dynasty, an empire established by the Manchu people of Manchuria, ruled China from 1644 to 1912.

In 1934, the Nationalists forced the Communists to flee their bases in southern China and begin their Long March.

WORLD BOOK maps

Japanese expansion into China reached its greatest extent in 1944, when the Japanese controlled much of eastern China.

strengthened the drive for political revolution.

In 1919, Sun began to reorganize the Nationalist Party and to recruit supporters from among students. At almost the same time, the first Communist student groups appeared in Beijing and other major cities. The Soviet Union, which had been formed in 1922 under Russia's leadership, sent advisers to China in 1923 to help the Nationalists. The Soviets persuaded the Chinese Communists to join the Nationalist Party and to help it carry out the revolution. The party began to develop its own army and to organize workers and peasants to prepare for an attack on the northern war lords.

Sun Yat-sen died in 1925, and leadership of the Nationalist Party gradually passed to its military commander, Chiang Kai-shek. In 1926, the Nationalists began a campaign to defeat the northern war lords and soon won some major victories. In 1927, Chiang and his troops turned against the Communists and executed hundreds of members of Communist-backed labor unions in Shanghai. More attacks followed in other cities. Communist survivors fled to the hills in the province of Jiangxi in southern China. In 1928, the Nationalists captured Beijing and united China under one government for the first time since 1916.

Nationalist rule. The Nationalist government was a one-party dictatorship that never gained full control of China. Communist opposition and Japanese aggression severely limited its power and accomplishments.

By 1931, the Communists had established a number of rural bases and set up a rival government in southern and central China. In 1934, Chiang Kai-shek's armies forced the Communists to evacuate their bases and begin their famous journey called the *Long March.* By the fall of 1935, the Communists had marched more than 6,000 miles (9,700 kilometers) over a winding route to the province of Shaanxi in northern China. Of the approximately 100,000 Communists who began the march, only a few thousand survived to reach Shaanxi. During the march, Mao Zedong became the leader of the Chinese Communist Party.

While Chiang fought the Communists, the Japanese seized more Chinese territory. In 1931, the Japanese occupied Manchuria (which the Chinese now call *Dongbei* or the Northeast) and made it a puppet state that they called *Manchukuo.* The Japanese then extended their military influence into Inner Mongolia and other parts of northern China. Chiang agreed to a series of Japanese demands because he felt unprepared to fight the Japanese until he had defeated the Communists.

Many students and intellectuals opposed Chiang's giving in to Japan. They organized demonstrations and anti-Japanese associations. Dissatisfaction spread to troops from Manchuria who were blockading the Communist-held areas in the northwest. In 1936, the Manchurian forces kidnapped Chiang in Xi'an. He was released only after agreeing to end the civil war and to form a united front against the Japanese.

War with Japan. The Japanese army launched a major attack against China in 1937. The Chinese resisted courageously, but Japanese armies controlled most of eastern China by the end of 1938. The Nationalist forces withdrew to the province of Sichuan, where they made Chongqing the wartime capital.

China joined the Allies in World War II on Dec. 9, 1941, two days after Japan attacked the United States at Pearl Harbor, Hawaii. In that war, the United Kingdom, the United States, the Soviet Union, and the other Allies fought Germany, Japan, and the other Axis powers. The Allies gave aid to China, but constant warfare against Japan exhausted China's resources and strength. The cost of the war caused severe inflation, which led to government corruption and weakened the Chinese people's support for the Nationalists.

For the Communists, the war against Japan provided an opportunity for political and military expansion. In northern China, they gained control of large areas that the Japanese army had overrun but lacked the forces to defend. The Communists enlarged their army and organized and trained the people to become productive party members. They also began a social revolution in the countryside, which included redistributing land to the peasants in Communist-controlled areas. When the war against Japan ended in August 1945, the Communists held an area in northern China with a population of about 100 million. In addition, they claimed to have an army of nearly 1 million soldiers.

Civil war. In 1945, the United States sent General George C. Marshall to China to attempt to arrange a political settlement between the Nationalists and the Communists. However, neither the Nationalists nor the Communists believed that they could achieve their goals by coming to terms with the other side. In mid-1946, full-scale fighting began.

The superior military tactics of the Communists and

the social revolution they had started in the countryside gradually turned the tide against the Nationalists. After capturing Tianjin and Beijing in January 1949, Mao Zedong's armies crossed the Yangtze River and drove the Nationalists toward southern China. On Oct. 1, 1949, Mao proclaimed the establishment in Beijing of the People's Republic of China. In December, Chiang Kai-shek and his followers fled to the island of Taiwan.

The beginning of Communist rule took place under the direction of Mao Zedong, the chairman of the Communist Party. Premier Zhou Enlai directed all government departments and ministries. Military, technical, and economic help from the Soviet Union helped support the new government. From 1949 to 1952, the new government firmly established its control over China and worked to help the nation's economy recover.

The new Communist government seized farmland from landlords and redistributed it among the peasants. Angry mobs, resentful of the way landlords had mistreated them, killed many of the landlords. Estimates of the number of landlords killed range from 200,000 to several million.

In 1953, China began its First Five-Year Plan for economic development. From 1953 to 1957, Chinese industry grew at the rapid rate of about 15 percent a year. By 1957, the Communists had brought all important industries under the control of the government. In addition, peasants were forced or persuaded to combine their landholdings into agricultural cooperatives. But agricultural production increased much more slowly than industrial output.

The Great Leap Forward was the name given to China's Second Five-Year Plan. Launched in 1958, this plan was designed to accelerate China's economic development. It was based on Mao's belief that human willpower and effort could overcome all obstacles. Thus, the government tried to speed development by greatly increasing the number of workers and their hours while ignoring China's lack of capital and modern technology. It combined the agricultural cooperatives into huge communes to improve the efficiency of farmworkers. The plan also set up many small factories and increased the industrial work force. Laborers worked long hours, sometimes sleeping at their machines.

Eastfoto

Chinese Communists, led by Mao Zedong, defeated the Nationalist government in a war from 1946 to 1949. Mao is shown here on horseback, moving across Shaanxi in 1947.

The Great Leap Forward shattered China's economy. From 1959 to 1961, China suffered economic depression, food shortages, and a decline in industrial output. By 1962, the economy began to recover. However, the Chinese had not solved the problem of achieving economic growth while maintaining the Communist ideals.

Disagreement over this issue produced a major split within the Communist Party between *radicals* and *revisionists.* The radicals called for China to strive for a classless society in which everyone would work selflessly for the common good. The revisionists stressed that division of labor was necessary for economic development. They believed that the policies of the radicals were unrealistic and hampered the modernization of China.

Break with the Soviet Union. Friendly relations between China and the Soviet Union ended in the early 1960's. China had criticized the Soviets as early as 1956 for their policy of "peaceful coexistence" with the West. Unlike the Soviets, the Chinese believed that war with the West was inevitable. They also accused the Soviet Union of betraying the aims of Communism. In 1960, the Soviet Union stopped giving assistance to China. In 1962, the Soviets refused to support China in a border war with India. The Soviet Union signed a nuclear test ban treaty with the United States and the United Kingdom in 1963. The Chinese then broke off relations with the Soviets, whom they accused of joining an anti-Chinese plot.

The Cultural Revolution. In 1966, Mao Zedong gave his support to the radicals in the Communist Party. Mao thus began what he called the Great Proletarian Cultural Revolution, a drive to enforce strict Communist principles and to rid China of revisionists. The radicals accused many top party and government officials of failing to follow Communist ideals and removed them from their positions. Students and other young people formed semimilitary organizations called the Red Guards. They demonstrated in the major cities against revisionists, intellectuals, scientists, and others whom they called anti-Maoists. Most universities were closed from 1966 to 1970. Radicals seized control of many provincial and city governments. Violence frequently broke out as competing radical groups struggled for power.

Mao's attempt to put China back on a revolutionary path wrecked the government and economy so severely that he had to call out the army in 1967 to restore order. By 1970, the Communist Party, the government, and the educational system had begun to resume their normal activities. But the conflict between radicals and revisionists within the party continued.

Improved relations with the West. During the early 1970's, Canada, Japan, and several other nations established diplomatic relations with the People's Republic of China. The United States continued officially to recognize only the Nationalist government on Taiwan. But in 1971, the United Nations voted to admit the People's Republic in place of Taiwan.

In 1972, U.S. President Richard M. Nixon traveled to China and met with Premier Zhou Enlai and Communist Party chairman Mao Zedong. During Nixon's visit, the United States and China signed the Shanghai Communiqué, which looked forward to the establishment of normal relations. The following year, the two nations sent representatives to serve in each other's capital. Japan established diplomatic relations with China in 1972.

Deng Xiaoping. Both Zhou Enlai and Mao Zedong died in 1976. A power struggle followed between radicals led by Mao's widow, Jiang Qing, and moderates led by Deng Xiaoping. The moderates emerged from the revisionist movement and promoted a more relaxed form of Communism. As a compromise, Hua Guofeng succeeded Zhou as premier and Mao as chairman of the Communist Party. Hua's government imprisoned Jiang and three other radicals, who were labeled the Gang of Four.

In 1977, Deng Xiaoping became vice premier and vice chairman of the Communist Party. On Jan. 1, 1979, China and the United States established normal diplomatic relations.

By 1980, Hua had lost most of his power, and Deng had become China's most powerful leader. Hua resigned as premier in 1980 and as party chairman in 1981. Deng helped Zhao Ziyang become premier and helped Hu Yaobang become chairman of the party. Zhao and Hu were moderates. Deng resigned as vice premier in 1980. In 1982, the party's new constitution abolished Deng's post of vice chairman and Hu's post of chairman. It created the position of general secretary as the top party post, and Hu continued in that office. However, Deng remained China's most influential leader.

Deng and the other moderates sought to reduce the people's admiration of Mao. The moderates praised Mao's leadership but denounced the idea that all his policies should be followed. They greatly increased trade and cultural contact with foreign countries. They set out to modernize China's economy with technical help from abroad.

Protests. In the late 1980's, uprisings against Chinese rule broke out in Tibet. In March 1989, China sent troops there to restore order.

In December 1986, many Chinese university students began demanding increased freedom of speech and a greater voice in the selection of officials. Students held demonstrations in a number of cities to promote their demands. In January 1987, Hu Yaobang was removed from his post of Communist Party general secretary. Conservative leaders had criticized Hu for his liberal views on freedom of expression and political reform. Zhao Ziyang then became general secretary of the party. Li Peng became premier in 1988.

Hu Yaobang died in April 1989. University students held marches to honor Hu and mourn his death. They called for a reevaluation of Hu by the country's leaders. These events led to large demonstrations by students and other citizens in Beijing's Tiananmen Square and on the streets of other Chinese cities. The protesters called for more democracy in China and an end to corruption in government. The military crushed the demonstrations and killed hundreds of protesters. The government later arrested many people suspected of involvement in the pro-democracy movement. The government executed a number of those arrested. In addition, the Communist Party dismissed Zhao Zhiyang from his post for not doing more to suppress the pro-democracy movement.

© Eric Bouvet, Getty Images

Student protesters erected a statue called the Goddess of Democracy in a 1989 protest for greater democracy in China. Chinese soldiers later attacked the students and killed hundreds.

Jiang Zemin replaced Zhao as general secretary.

Also in 1989, officials of China and the Soviet Union met to improve relations. When the Soviet Union broke apart in 1991, China established diplomatic relations with the former Soviet republics.

Deng resigned from his remaining party and government posts in 1989 and 1990. But he continued to have influence through the early 1990's. In 1993, Jiang was named to another high office, the largely ceremonial post of president. Deng died in 1997.

Hong Kong and Macao. In 1984, China and the United Kingdom signed an agreement regarding the return of Hong Kong to China when the United Kingdom's lease expired in 1997. China agreed that Hong Kong would retain a high degree of *autonomy* (self-rule) and keep its free-enterprise economy for 50 years, or until 2047. In 1990, the Chinese government approved the Basic Law, the new framework for Hong Kong's administration. On July 1, 1997, Hong Kong became a special administrative region of China.

In 1987, China and Portugal signed a similar agreement for the return of Macao to Chinese administration. On Dec. 20, 1999, Macao became the second special administrative region of China.

Recent developments. In 1998, Zhu Rongji succeeded Li Peng as premier. Zhu had been a vice premier in charge of economic policy. Li Peng was named chairman of China's national legislature.

Construction of Three Gorges Dam on the Yangtze River began in 1994. When completed, it will be the world's largest dam. It is intended to generate electric power, to provide an inland waterway, and to control flooding. The dam's huge reservoir has forced the resettlement of more than 1 million people. The project has many critics, who charge that it will create environmental problems, drown some of China's best farmland, and cover thousands of historical sites.

In 2001, China became a member of the World Trade Organization, which promotes international trade. China's entry into the organization marked progress in freeing the Chinese economy from government control.

Jiang Zemin stepped down as general secretary of China's Communist Party in 2002. He stepped down as China's president in 2003 and as head of China's military in 2004. Hu Jintao replaced him in all three positions. Also in 2003, Wen Jiabao replaced Zhu Rongji as premier, and Wu Bangguo succeeded Li Peng as chairman of China's legislature.

Richard Louis Edmonds and Richard J. Smith

Related articles in *World Book* include:

Biographies

Chen Rong
Chiang Ching-kuo
Chiang Kai-shek
Chiang Soong Mei-ling
Confucius
Deng Xiaoping
Genghis Khan
Gu Kaizhi
Hu Jintao
Hu Yaobang
Huizong
Jiang Qing
Jiang Zemin
Kublai Khan
Laozi
Lee, Tsung Dao
Li Bo
Li Peng
Li Yuan
Lin Biao
Lin Yutang
Liu Bang
Ma Yuan
Mao Zedong
Mencius
Pu Yi
Shi Huangdi
Sun Yat-sen
Wang Wei
Wu, Chien- shiung
Wu Daozi
Xunzi
Yang, Chen Ning
Zhao Ziyang
Zheng He
Zhou Enlai
Zhuangzi

Cities

Beijing
Chengdu
Chongqing
Fuzhou
Guangzhou
Hangzhou
Harbin
Lanzhou
Lhasa
Lüshun
Nanjing
Ningbo
Shanghai
Shenyang
Suzhou
Tianjin
Wuhan
Xiamen
Xi'an

History

Boxer Rebellion
Burma Road
Cathay
Cold War
Communism
Cultural Revolution
Great Wall of China
Han dynasty
Indochina
Korean War
Ming dynasty
Mongol Empire
Nanking Massacre
Open-Door Policy
Polo, Marco
Qin dynasty
Shang dynasty
Silk Road
Sino-Japanese War of 1894-1895
Sino-Japanese War of 1937-1945
Song dynasty
Stilwell, Joseph W.
Sui dynasty
Tang dynasty
Trans-Siberian Railroad
Treaty Port
World War II
Zhou dynasty

Physical features

Amur River
China Sea
Gobi
Himalaya
Huang He
Mekong River
Mount Everest
Mount Makalu
Three Gorges Dam
Tian Shan
Xi Jiang
Yalu River
Yangtze River
Yellow Sea

Regions

Hong Kong
Manchuria
Macao
Tibet
Turkestan
Xinjiang

Religions

Buddhism
Confucianism
Taoism

Other related articles

Air force (The Chinese Air Force)
Architecture (Chinese architecture)
Army (The Chinese army)
Asia (Way of life in East Asia)
Book (History)
Bronze (pictures)
Calendar (The Chinese calendar)
Chinese language
Chinese literature
Chinese New Year
Clothing (picture: Traditional costumes)
Dance (Asian theatrical dance)
Drama (China)
Exploration (The Chinese)
Flag (picture: Historical flags)
Houseboat
I Ching
Invention (China)
Iron and steel (In China)
Jade
Jinrikisha
Kite
Lacquerware
Mah-jongg
Mandarin
Martial arts (Chinese martial arts)
Mathematics (Chinese mathematics)
Money (How money developed; pictures)
Monsoon
Music (Asian music)
Opium
Pagoda
Painting (Chinese painting)
Paper (History)
Peking fossils
Porcelain
Printing (History)
Sampan
Sculpture (China)
Silk
Soybean
T'ai chi ch'uan

Outline

I. Government
A. The Communist Party
B. National government
C. Political divisions
C. Languages
E. The armed forces

II. People
A. Population
B. Nationalities
C. Languages

III. Way of life
A. Family life
B. Rural life
C. City life
D. Food
E. Recreation
F. Clothing
G. Health care
H. Religion
I. Education

IV. The arts
A. Literature
B. Painting
C. Bronze and jade
D. Sculpture and pottery
E. Architecture
F. Music
G. Theater

V. The land
A. The Tibetan Highlands
B. The Xinjiang-Mongolian Uplands
C. The Inner Mongolian Border Uplands
D. The Eastern Highlands
E. The Eastern Lowlands
F. The Central Uplands
G. The Sichuan Basin
H. The Southern Uplands

VI. Climate

VII. Economy
A. Manufacturing and mining
B. Service industries
C. Agriculture
D. Fishing industry
E. Forestry
F. International trade
G. Transportation
H. Communication

VIII. History

Questions

What are some typical breakfast foods in China?
What is the highest post in the Communist Party?
When was the People's Republic of China established?
Why did the Chinese have a high regard for education in the past? Why do the Communists value it today?
Name and describe some traditional Chinese musical instruments.
Which dynasty established China's first empire controlled by a strong central government?
How does China rank in the world in population? In area?
Who led China's Communists from about 1934 to 1976?
The majority of Chinese people belong to what nationality?
Why do economists consider China a developing country?

Additional resources

Level I

Deedrick, Tami. *China.* Steck-Vaughn, 2001.
Field, Catherine. *China.* Raintree Steck-Vaughn, 2000.
Italia, Bob. *China.* Checkerboard Lib., 2001.

Level II

Hutchings, Graham. *Modern China: A Guide to a Century of Change.* Harvard Univ. Pr., 2001.
Mackerras, Colin. *The New Cambridge Handbook of Contemporary China.* Cambridge, 2001.
Rutherford, Scott, ed. *Insight Guide: China.* 9th ed. APA Pubns., 2002.

China, porcelain ware. See **Porcelain.**

China Sea is the name of two seas of the Pacific Ocean along the east coast of Asia. Both seas and some of their islands were scenes of important battles during World War II (1939-1945). These conflicts included the Battle of Okinawa in 1945. The East China Sea (area 482,300 square miles, or 1,249,200 square kilometers) extends north from Taiwan to Japan and the Koreas. Shanghai, China, and Nagasaki, Japan, are the sea's main ports.

The South China Sea (area 1,300,000 square miles, or 3,370,000 square kilometers) is connected to the East China Sea by the Taiwan Strait. The South China Sea includes the Gulf of Tonkin and Gulf of Thailand on the west and Manila Bay on the east.

Violent tropical storms called *typhoons* sweep over the sea. The Mekong and Xi Jiang rivers empty into the sea, and the seaports of Guangzhou (also called Canton) and Hong Kong, China; Singapore; and Manila, in the Philippines, lie along its coasts.

David A. Ross

Chinaware. See **Porcelain.**

Chinch bug is a small insect that feeds on plants. It sucks the juices of plants and is a pest of corn, sorghum, wheat, and other grains. Chinch bugs are found throughout the United States, Canada, Central America, and the West Indies. An adult chinch bug has a black body with whitish wings and measures about ⅙ inch (4 millimeters) long.

WORLD BOOK map

Location of the China Sea

Adult chinch bugs spend the winter in grass or rubbish. In early spring, they move to pastures or fields of newly planted grain and lay eggs on roots and stems. The eggs hatch in about a week, and the young bugs feed on the roots and stems.

In the middle of the summer, young chinch bugs crawl or fly into nearby fields of ripening grain. There, they lay eggs that become the next generation of chinch bugs. This second generation often causes extensive damage to crops, especially corn and sorghum. Chinch bugs develop most rapidly in warm, dry climates. In such climates, more than two generations of bugs may occur each year.

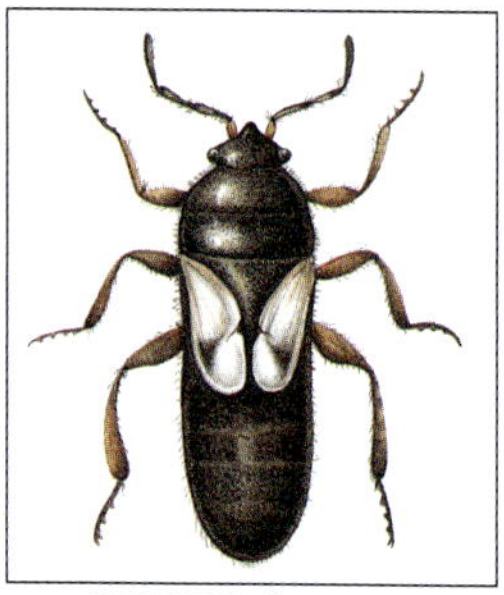
WORLD BOOK illustration by Shirley Hooper, Oxford Illustrators Limited

Chinch bug

The chinch bug was once considered the most serious pest of corn and many other grains. Today, the bug is controlled by a variety of methods, including careful weed control, early planting of crops, and the use of plant varieties that are resistant to chinch bugs. Many farmers prevent damage to corn and sorghum by planting these crops away from grain fields where the chinch bugs feed. Insecticides may be sprayed or dusted on fields to control a severe infestation of chinch bugs.

John R. Meyer

Scientific classification. The chinch bug belongs to the order Hemiptera and the lygaeid bug family, Lygaeidae. Its scientific name is *Blissus leucopterus.*

Chinchilla is the name of two small animals known for their soft, thick fur. Chinchillas are *rodents,* small mammals with teeth suited for gnawing. Their chunky bodies measure about 11 to 18 inches (28 to 46 centimeters) long, including the bushy tail. Females grow larger than males. The animals' thick, shiny, blue-gray fur is 1 inch (2.5 centimeters) or more in length. People have long used chinchilla pelts to make soft, luxurious coats.

The two types of chinchillas are the *long-tailed chinchilla* and *short-tailed chinchilla.* They are native to the snow-capped Andes Mountains, especially the high valleys from Peru and northern Bolivia to southern Chile. Their heavy fur helps keep them warm in these cold, rocky environments. Long, strong hind limbs enable them to run and jump easily on rocky surfaces. Wild chinchillas live in large groups, sleeping during the day in dens. The animals come out at night to search for such food as grasses, bulbs, and roots.

Chinchillas begin to breed at about 9 to 12 months of age. Females typically give birth twice a year to two or three young at a time. Some individuals may bear as many as seven babies at a time. The babies weigh about 1¼ ounces (35 grams) each and are born with their eyes open, fully furred, and with all their 20 teeth. Young chinchillas reach adult size at around 12 months of age. In the wild, chinchillas may live about 10 years.

People have long valued chinchillas. The Chincha and Inca Indians ate chinchillas and used their fur for clothing. Spanish explorers who came to South America in

© Ulrike Schanz, Nature Picture Library

A chinchilla has a soft, thick, blue-gray coat and a bushy tail. Its fur measures 1 inch (2.5 centimeters) or more deep. Chinchilla pet owners sometimes feed the animals fruit as a special treat.

the 1500's named the animals after the Chinchas. They introduced the fur into Europe.

By the 1940's, demand for chinchilla fur had become so great that the animals were almost wiped out in the wild. As a result, people in Europe and North and South America began captive breeding programs to supply Chinchilla fur to the clothing industry. Several South American countries also passed laws to protect the remaining wild chinchilla populations. Today, the animals remain extremely rare in their natural habitats.

People also keep chinchillas as pets. The animals make relatively clean, gentle, and quiet companions. Owners should feed pet chinchillas scientifically prepared pellets, as well as grains, vegetables, and timothy hay. Chinchillas may receive fruit as a special treat. Pet chinchillas may live as long as 20 years. Paul W. Sherman

Scientific classification. Chinchillas belong to the chinchilla family, Chinchilladae. The long-tailed chinchilla is *Chinchilla lanigera,* and the short-tailed chinchilla is *C. brevicaudata.*

See also **Animal** (picture: Animals of the mountains).

Chinese, language. See **Chinese language.**

Chinese cabbage is a cabbagelike vegetable that has been grown in China since the A.D. 400's. It has wide, thick leaves that form a long, cylindrical head. Some varieties, such as *pak-choi,* have a loose, open head. Others, such as *Michihli* and *wong bok,* have a more compact head.

WORLD BOOK illustration by Kate Lloyd-Jones, Linden Artists Ltd.

Chinese cabbage

Each leaf of a Chinese cabbage has a thick celerylike stalk. The leaves range in color from green on the outside of the head to white on the inside. Many people prefer the inside leaves. Chinese cabbage tastes somewhat like lettuce and often is eaten raw in salads. People also cook it in casseroles and Chinese-style dishes.

Chinese cabbage grows best in cool weather. It can withstand frost but requires rich, moist soil. It thrives as an autumn crop in many areas of eastern Asia and the northern United States. George R. Hughes

Scientific classification. Chinese cabbages belong to the mustard family, Brassicaceae or Cruciferae. Michihli and wong bok are varieties of the *Pekinensis* group. Pak-choi is a variety of the *Chinensis* group.

Chinese crested is a breed of small dog. It stands from 11 to 13 inches (28 to 33 centimeters) high at the shoulder and weighs from 5 to 10 pounds (2.3 to 4.5 kilograms). There are two varieties of Chinese cresteds, *hairless* and *powderpuff.* The hairless variety has soft, flowing hair only on the head, tail, legs, and feet. Hairless skin covers the rest of the body. The skin can be any color or combination of colors. The powderpuff variety has a soft, fluffy coat of hair over the entire body. Both varieties can be born in the same litter.

© Norvia Behling

The hairless variety of Chinese crested has hair only on the head, feet, legs, and tail.

Chinese cresteds are agile and alert and make good pets. The breed probably originated in Africa during the 1000's or 1100's. The dogs were kept as pets by *mandarins* (high-ranking officials) in China. Chinese merchants carried the dogs on sailing vessels and thus introduced them to other countries throughout the world.

Critically reviewed by the American Chinese Crested Club

Chinese-Japanese wars. See **Sino-Japanese War of 1894-1895; Sino-Japanese War of 1937-1945.**

Chinese language is one of the world's oldest languages. Almost all of the people of China and Taiwan speak Chinese, and about three-fourths of the people of Singapore speak it.

Chinese is written the same way throughout China. However, the language consists of seven major dialect groups with some variations within each group. These dialects differ so greatly that a person who lives in one area may not be able to converse with someone from another area. The pronunciation of many words depends on the dialect being spoken.

Chinese belongs to the Sino-Tibetan family of languages. This family includes Burmese, Thai, and Tibetan. See **Language** (Other language families).

Written Chinese has no alphabet. Instead, it consists

of about 50,000 *characters.* The Chinese writing system is *logographic,* meaning that each character stands for a word or part of a word. A person who knows about 4,000 of the most frequently used characters can read a Chinese newspaper or modern novel. Scholars who read ancient Chinese literature and documents must learn many more characters.

The earliest forms of Chinese script were *pictographs.* The characters, also called *graphs,* were drawings or pictures of the objects they represented. For example, the character for *water* was 水 and the one for *deer* was 鹿. As Chinese script developed, characters became more simplified and less pictographic.

Some characters are not pictures but represent abstract words. Examples include the characters for *up* (上) and *down* (下). Such characters, called *simple graphs,* are few in number. *Compound graphs,* however, are more numerous. Compound graphs are formed by two or more characters. For example, the character 吠 (to bark) is a compound graph formed by the characters 口 (mouth) and 狗 (dog).

The Chinese also developed a technique called *character borrowing.* It involves "borrowing" the character of one word to represent another word that has a similar pronunciation. For example, 然 means *burn,* but it also is used to represent *yes.* The character is pronounced *rahn* for both meanings.

The meaning of a character that stands for more than one word may be difficult to determine. To make the meaning of such a character clear, the Chinese developed *phonetic compounds.* A phonetic compound is a character that has an additional character or an additional marking to help the reader determine which word it represents.

Kinds of Chinese characters

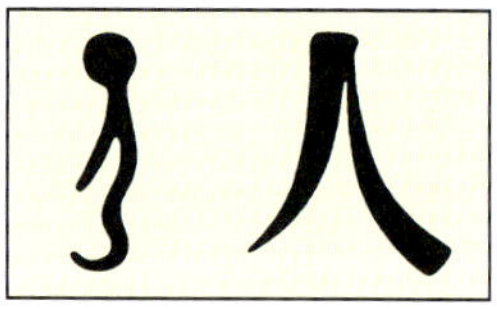

Pictographs are ancient characters that resembled the objects they represented. The pictograph on the far left stands for *man.* The second character is the modern symbol.

Ancient character from *Chinese Calligraphy,* 3rd ed., by Chiang Yee, 1973, Harvard Univ. Press.

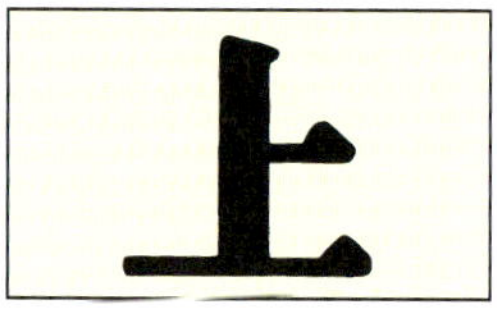

Simple graphs are single characters that represent abstract words. The character on the left is a simple graph that stands for the word *up.*

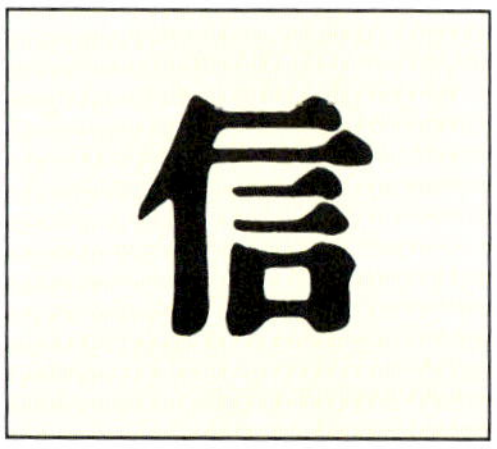

Compound graphs have two or more characters that represent a word. The word *trust,* shown on the left, is a compound graph. It consists of the character for *man* and the one for *word.*

Phonetic compounds consist of two elements. One gives the character's meaning and the other its pronunciation. The character on the left means *nephew.* The right-hand element indicates the meaning and the left-hand one the pronunciation, *sheng.*

Spoken Chinese. The common dialect of Chinese is *Northern Chinese* or *Mandarin.* The Chinese call the dialect *putonghua,* which means *common* or *standard language.* Northern Chinese is the official language of China and is taught in all the nation's schools. About 600 million people speak it. They live throughout northern China and in several southwestern provinces. Other major Chinese dialects include *Yue* or *Cantonese, Xiang, Gan, Hakka, Min,* and *Wu.* They are spoken in many areas of China and in the Chinese communities of various cities in other countries.

Chinese dialects differ in the use of *tones.* A tone is the pitch used in saying a particular word. Northern Chinese has four tones—*high-level* (high and unwavering), *rising, low-dipping* (falling and rising), and *falling.* Some other dialects have as many as nine tones. The use of tone is an important means of separating words of different meanings but similar pronunciation. For example, *ma* means *mother* in a high-level tone, *horse* in a low-dipping tone, *scold* in a falling tone, and *hemp* in a rising tone. Each of these words has a different character when written in Northern Chinese.

Chinese is spoken with no tenses. For example, the sentence *Ta shi xuezhe* could mean *He is a scholar* or *He was a scholar,* depending on how it is used.

Many language experts consider Chinese to be *monosyllabic*—that is, almost all the words have only one syllable. Even words of more than one syllable can be broken down into single-syllable words. For example, *xuezhe* (scholar) consists of two single-syllable words—*xue* (learn) and *zhe* (one who).

Development. The earliest known examples of Chinese are inscriptions carved in bones and shells during the Shang dynasty (about 1766 to about 1045 B.C.). This early language had a simple structure. It was the basis of a later language called *classical,* or *literary, Chinese.*

Present-day Chinese dialects developed from classical Chinese. Northern Chinese began to be used during the A.D. 1300's. Northern Chinese became China's official language because it was spoken in Beijing, the capital. But it was not widely used in writing until the Literary Revolution, a cultural movement that began in 1917.

Through the years, the government has promoted the use of Northern Chinese through the nation's educational program. In 1919, Chinese schools began to use a system of *phonetic signs* to teach standard pronunciation. This method involved books that taught the pronunciation in Northern Chinese of Chinese characters. In 1949, Chinese educators began to simplify characters to make them easier to learn and write.

In the mid-1950's, the government introduced *pinyin,* a system of writing Chinese using the Roman alphabet. This alphabet consists of the 26 letters used to write English and many other languages except the letter *v.* In 1978, the government directed that Chinese names and words used in English and other foreign language publications be written in pinyin. Pinyin replaced the *Wade-Giles system* and other writing systems that use the Roman alphabet. Two British diplomats, Thomas Wade and

Herbert Giles, developed this system during the late 1800's and early 1900's. David R. Knechtges

See also **China.**

Additional resources

Chen, Ping. *Modern Chinese.* Cambridge, 1999.
Wu, Sha-hsiung, and Hoss, Ulrich. *Travelwise Chinese.* Barron's, 1998.

Chinese literature is one of the oldest and greatest of the world's literatures. Chinese writers have produced important works for almost 3,000 years.

During most of China's history, the Chinese did not consider literature a separate art form. They expected all cultured people to write in a graceful, elegant style, regardless of the topic. Many masterpieces of Chinese literature deal with subjects that some Western writers regard as nonliterary. These topics include history, philosophy, politics, religion, and science.

Until the 1900's, government service was the occupation of greatest prestige in China. For more than 1,000 years, people gained a government position primarily by passing an examination that tested their ability to compose both poetry and prose. Almost all of China's greatest writers before the 1900's were government officials. Most of them received their appointments because of their skill with words.

Many works of Chinese literature teach a moral lesson or express a political philosophy. These themes appear especially in the writings of Confucians. Confucianism is a philosophy founded by Confucius, who lived from about 551 to 479 B.C. It was the dominant Chinese philosophy until the 1900's. Many other writers were Buddhists or Taoists, rather than Confucians. Buddhism was a major Chinese religion, and Taoism was both an important religion and a philosophy. The Buddhists and Taoists were less interested than the Confucians in morality and politics. But they used literature to express religious and philosophical ideas.

During the 1900's, Chinese literature made a sharp break with the past. This break resulted partly from the influence of Western culture on Chinese writers. But the rise of the Communist Party to power in China made an even greater impact. After the Communists took control of mainland China in 1949, the party required writers to conform to the ideals of socialist and revolutionary realism. Beginning in the 1980's, the party relaxed its control over writers, and some authors even started to criticize the government.

Early Chinese literature

Beginnings. One of the earliest works of Chinese literature was a collection of 300 poems called the *Book of Songs.* The earliest of these poems date back to the 1000's B.C. Some of them may have originated as songs about farming, love, and war. Others were used in weddings and religious sacrifices. An early prose work was a collection of historical writings called the *Book of Documents.* It consisted largely of speeches supposedly made by the earliest Chinese rulers. However, the speeches were probably fiction written during the Zhou dynasty (about 1045 to 256 B.C.).

The *Book of Songs* and the *Book of Documents,* along with three other books, formed the *Five Classics* and became the basis of Confucianism. The Confucians considered these books to be models of literary excellence. They also honored them as works of moral wisdom because the books emphasized Confucian ideals of duty, moderation, proper conduct, and public service.

Taoism probably began during the 300's B.C., partly as a reaction against Confucianism. Unlike the Confucians, the Taoists believed people should avoid social obligations and live simply and close to nature. Taoist ideas influenced poets who wrote about the beauties of nature. Taoism produced two literary masterpieces. *The Classic of the Way and the Virtue* was probably written by Laozi, founder of Taoism. Most of the other work, the *Zhuangzi,* is credited to Zhuangzi, a philosopher.

An important collection of poems called the *Songs of Chu* appeared during the 300's B.C. Most of them were probably written by a poet named Qu Yuan. Many of the poems describe flights to imaginary regions inhabited by mythical creatures, gods, and spirits. The ornate style of poems by Qu Yuan led to the development of the important literary style called *fu* or *rhapsody* during the Han dynasty (206 B.C.-A.D. 220). These long works, written in difficult language, celebrate the majesty and splendor of the Han empire.

Poetry. Perhaps the four greatest Chinese poets lived during the Tang dynasty (A.D. 618-907). They were, in the order of birth, Wang Wei, Li Bo, Du Fu, and Bo Juyi.

Wang Wei wrote four-line poems that describe scenes from nature. His works, which emphasize quiet and contemplation, show the influence of Buddhism.

Li Bo wrote imaginative poems about his dreams and fantasies and his love of wine. Unlike most poets of his time, he wrote in the style of old Chinese ballads.

Du Fu is considered China's greatest poet by many critics. He surpassed all other Tang poets in range of style and subject matter. In some of his early poems, Du Fu expressed disappointment at failing an examination for government service. A bloody rebellion from 755 to 757 inspired him to write poems condemning the absurdity he saw in war. In his late poems, Du Fu emphasized clever use of language, developing a style that influenced Chinese poets for centuries.

Bo Juyi wrote satiric poems in ballad style. He protested against various government policies of his day.

Drama and fiction developed as important forms of Chinese literature during the 1200's. Chinese plays resemble European opera, combining singing and dancing with dialogue. The two most famous Chinese plays are *The Western Chamber,* written by Wang Shifu, and *Injustice to Tou O,* written by Guan Hanqing. Both plays were written in the 1200's. Tang Xianzu ranks as the greatest Chinese playwright. His most notable play was *Peony Pavilion* (about 1600).

Unknown professional writers rewrote traditional historical tales into complicated stories that resemble novels written by Western authors. *Romance of the Three Kingdoms,* by an unknown author, is credited to Luo Guanzhong. It describes the struggle for power among three rival states during the late A.D. 100's and early 200's. *Water Margin,* also known as *All Men Are Brothers,* is probably wrongly credited to Luo Guanzhong and Shi Naien. It tells about an outlaw gang that may have existed in the A.D. 1100's.

A great comic novel, *The Journey to the West,* appeared in the 1500's. Often called *Monkey* in the West, it is attributed to Wu Cheng'en. It describes a pilgrimage of a Buddhist monk in the A.D. 600's. An unknown writer of the 1500's wrote *Golden Lotus,* a famous novel about moral corruption. *Dream of the Red Chamber,* also called *Story of the Stone,* was perhaps the greatest Chinese novel. It was written by Cao Xueqin in the 1700's. It traces the decline of an aristocratic family.

Modern Chinese literature

Until the 1800's, China was almost isolated from the West. Many European missionaries and traders traveled to China during the 1800's, and the Chinese were gradually exposed to Western culture. By the early 1900's, the works of most Chinese authors showed some influence of Western literature. The most important Chinese author of the early 1900's was Lu Xun, who wrote satiric short stories of social criticism.

The Chinese Communists, led by Mao Zedong, came to power in 1949 after a long civil war. They demanded that all literature serve the new state and ordered writers to create works that could be easily understood by the peasants, soldiers, and workers. In addition, the heroes of literary works had to represent the working class. Some older writers in China attacked the new literature, which they considered dull. The government prohibited these writers from publishing their works.

During the Cultural Revolution (1966-1969), the Communist Party persecuted all intellectuals in China. Unskilled workers and peasants wrote most of the works that were published. In 1976, the government began to allow writers more artistic freedom. Political and social themes dominated published works, and some writers dared to write works that criticized the government. Important writers included Liu Binyan, Zhang Jie, and Wang Meng. Starting in the 1990's, writers in China have been relatively free as long as they do not openly criticize party policy. Important fiction writers include Wang Shuo, Mo Yan, and Su Tong. The poet Bei Dao (Zhao Zhenkai) is widely read in China and in other countries.

Writers from Taiwan, Hong Kong, and Singapore have produced important works of Chinese literature. Major Taiwanese authors include the poets Yang Mu (C. H. Wang), Yü Kuang-chung, and Lo Ch'ing (who is also a famous painter); and the fiction writers Bai Xianyong, Wang Wenxing, and Chen Ruoxi. Jin Yong of Hong Kong, who writes martial arts fiction, is the most widely read Chinese author in the world. In 2000, Gao Xingjian, a Chinese writer living in Paris, became the first Chinese author to win the Nobel Prize in literature.

David R. Knechtges

Related articles in *World Book* include:

Chinese language	Drama (Asian drama)	Lin Yutang
Confucianism	Laozi	Taoism
Confucius	Li Bo	Zhuangzi

Additional resources

Mair, Victor H., ed. *The Columbia Anthology of Traditional Chinese Literature.* Columbia Univ. Pr., 1994. *The Columbia History of Chinese Literature.* 2001.

Nienhauser, William H., Jr., ed. *The Indiana Companion to Traditional Chinese Literature.* 2 vols. Ind. Univ. Pr., 1985, 1998.

Chinese New Year is the most important festival of the Chinese calendar. The date of the Chinese New Year is based on the cycles of the moon. It begins between January 21 and February 20. In ancient China, the monthlong festival marked the end of one farming season and the beginning of a new one. Today, the Chinese New Year festival usually lasts only a few days.

Chinese people prepare for the new year by thoroughly cleaning and decorating the house. Decorations include *spring couplets,* red paper scrolls with phrases praising the renewal of life and the return of spring.

Family reunions are an important part of the celebration. Family members join in a festive New Year's Eve dinner. Places are set at the table for absent family members to symbolize the unity of the family. Special foods that symbolize good fortune for the new year are served. For example, rice cakes, called *nian gao,* are a popular food for New Year's Eve dinners. The Chinese word *nian* means *year,* and *gao* means *high.* This food signifies achievement in the new year. Children bow to their parents and grandparents to wish them a long life. Gifts of money in red envelopes are given to children to wish them luck and wealth in the new year.

On New Year's Day, people visit relatives, neighbors, and friends. Dances featuring colorful dragon and lion costumes are often performed on this day. Parades are a popular New Year's custom among Chinese communities in the United States and Canada.

Tung-Ling Li Chen

See also **Calendar** (The Chinese Calendar); **New Year's Day** (picture).

Chinese shar-pei, *shahr pay,* is a breed of dog that originated in China about 200 B.C. It is also known simply as the *shar-pei.* This compact dog has short ears and a short, harsh coat of a solid color. Its skin is loose, and wrinkles cover the head, neck, and shoulders. The skin of puppies is especially loose and wrinkled. Most shar-peis stand 18 to 20 inches (46 to 51 centimeters) tall at the shoulder and weigh 40 to 55 pounds (18 to 25 kilograms). The tongue is blue-black. Shar-peis originally were used as guard dogs and later may have been bred to fight. They are alert, independent, intelligent, and loyal. Critically reviewed by the Chinese Shar-Pei Club of America, Inc.

© Yann Arthus-Bertrand, Corbis

A Chinese shar-pei has loose, wrinkled skin. Puppies, such as the one pictured here, lose some of their wrinkles as adults.

Chinook, *shih NOOK,* is a warm dry wind that blows down the eastern slopes of the Rocky Mountains, usually in winter and early spring. It was named by early settlers who thought it came from the country of the Chinook Indians along the Columbia River. Chinooks blow in the Northwestern United States and in southwestern Canada. They usually blow from the west.

A chinook gets warmer as it moves down the mountain slope. Its temperature increases by about 1 degree Fahrenheit for every 180 feet (1 degree Celsius for every 99 meters) of descent. For example, a chinook that descends 5,500 feet (1,680 meters) is about 30 °F (17 °C) warmer when it reaches the foot of the mountain. The dry wind takes up moisture by evaporation. It often rapidly melts and evaporates snow as it spreads out at the mountain base. For this reason, chinooks are sometimes called *snow eaters.* Similar winds that blow in other parts of the world are called *foehns* (see **Foehn**).

Residents along the Pacific Coast in Washington and Oregon use the name *wet chinook* for warm, moist winds that blow from the southwest. Richard A. Dirks

Chinook Indians are a people of the Pacific Northwest. Most live in Washington and Oregon. They once lived in fishing villages at the mouth of the Columbia River in what is now Washington. The Chinook belong to a larger group of Indians that anthropologists call *Chinookans.* The Chinookans include other peoples who lived along the Columbia and Willamette rivers and spoke languages similar to the Chinook language. The Chinookans have intermarried with members of other Indian groups or with non-Indians. They now make a living by fishing, ranching, and other activities.

In traditional Chinook society, people were divided into three groups. The chiefs and their families belonged to the wealthy, dominant class. The common people had fewer possessions of their own. Slaves, captured in raids or acquired by trading with other Indian groups, formed the lowest group and were considered as property. The Chinook made their living by trading, by fishing, and by gathering berries, nuts, and roots.

European explorers encountered Chinook in 1792 when the whites sailed into the mouth of the Columbia River. In the 1800's, both whites and other Indians in the region learned a simplified form of the Chinook language to make trading easier. The Chinook became known for their skill in dealing with explorers and settlers. But a series of epidemics in the 1800's destroyed most Chinookan societies. During the early 1900's, the remaining Chinookans moved to reservations and small towns in Oregon and Washington. Michael Silverstein

Chipmunk is any of a group of small mammals with stripes on their face, back, and sides. Nearly all *species* (kinds) of chipmunks live in North America. One species inhabits Asia and Europe.

Chipmunks are *rodents,* mammals with gnawing teeth. They grow about 7 to 10 inches (18 to 25 centimeters) in length, including the long tail. The animals have largely reddish-brown coloring with black stripes bordered by white, brown, or gray stripes. Their underside is light gray or white.

Chipmunks take shelter and spend the night in *burrows* (tunnels) that they dig. They spend much of the day outdoors searching for food, including nuts, seeds, fungi, and even birds' eggs and insects. The animals eat by holding a piece of food in their small, slender forepaws and nibbling at it with their sharp front teeth. In the autumn, chipmunks collect large quantities of food for the winter, which they carry to their burrows in cheek pouches. They sleep through much of the winter.

Female chipmunks often bear four to six *pups* (young) at a time. Chipmunks may live 4 or 5 years. Such animals as coyotes and hawks eat chipmunks. Paul W. Sherman

Scientific classification. Chipmunks belong to the squirrel family, Sciuridae. They make up the genus *Tamias.*

See also **Animal** (picture: Animals of the temperate forests); **Rodent; Squirrel.**

Chippendale, Thomas (1718-1779), was an English furniture maker and designer. His reputation today is based on his book of furniture designs called *The Gentleman and Cabinet-Maker's Director* (1754). The *Director* was the first book devoted entirely to designs for household furniture. It popularized a number of styles in London during the mid-1700's and spread the English Rococo style to furniture makers outside London. Much of the furniture produced in America between 1755 and 1790 was modeled on designs in the *Director* and became known as Chippendale. Chippendale's furniture company produced a wide range of furniture in the Rococo, Neoclassical, Gothic, and Chinese styles. He made many pieces for interiors designed by the Scottish archi-

WORLD BOOK illustration by George Suyeoka

The chipmunk begins its underground nest by digging a hole, *left.* It carves a tunnel and may make another opening, *right.* The chipmunk then builds a nesting area, pushes the dirt out, and may plug the first entrance to its nest.

tect Robert Adam. Chippendale was born in Otley, near Bradford. He died on Nov. 13, 1779. Nancy E. Richards

See also **Furniture** (English styles; picture: The Chippendale style).

Chippewa Indians, *CHIP uh wah,* form one of the largest tribal groups in North America. They once lived in the forest country around the shores of Lake Superior. The American poet Henry Wadsworth Longfellow based many of the customs in his poem *The Song of Hiawatha* on the Chippewa. The Chippewa are also called the Anishinabe, Ojibwa, Ojibway, Ojibwe, or Otchipwe.

The Chippewa were skilled in fishing. They also hunted in the forests and gathered wild plants, especially the wild rice of the lake country. They used much of the plentiful birchbark in the northern forests to cover their wigwams and make beautiful bark canoes, boxes, dishes, and baskets.

Many Chippewa belonged to a secret religious organization, the Midewiwin Society. Members tried to gain long life by using herbs and magic. The priests kept records by scratching symbols on birchbark.

The Chippewa lived in isolated areas, and so they had few battles with white people. But they often fought the Sioux and the Fox tribes, especially over possession of wild-rice fields. During the 1800's, the Chippewa ceded their tribal lands to the federal governments of Canada and the United States, and these governments established federal reservations for the tribe.

According to the 2000 census, there are about 106,000 Chippewa. About 67,000 live in Michigan, Minnesota, or North Dakota. The largest Chippewa communities are the Turtle Mountain Reservation in North Dakota and the Red Lake Reservation in Minnesota. But most Chippewa live outside reservations. Chippewa work in a wide range of occupations, including agriculture, the arts, and such professions as education, law, and medicine. Many make a living by hunting, trapping, lumbering, or working as guides. Chippewa harvest much of the wild rice eaten in the United States. Gerald Vizenor

Chirac, *shee RAK,* **Jacques René** (1932-), won election as president of France in 1995 and was reelected in 2002. He is a member of the conservative political party Union for a Popular Movement (UPM).

As president, Chirac has sought to advance France's role as a leading country of Europe and the world. He gave France a strong voice in European Union affairs. He also became a leading opponent of the Iraq War, the United States-led war on Iraq that began in 2003.

Chirac was born in Paris on Nov. 29, 1932. In 1959, he graduated from the National School of Administration and began a career in government service. During the 1960's and 1970's, he held various offices in the cabinets of several prime ministers of France. His offices included minister of agriculture and minister of the interior.

In 1976, Chirac founded the political party Rally for the Republic (RPR), which became one of France's leading conservative parties. In 2002, RPR merged with several other conservative parties to form the UPM.

Chirac served as prime minister of France from 1974 to 1976 and from 1986 to 1988. He served as mayor of Paris from 1977 to 1995. He ran unsuccessfully for the presidency in 1981 and 1988. Wayne Northcutt

Chirico, *KEY rih koh,* **Giorgio de** (1888-1978), was an Italian painter. He did his most significant work between 1910 and 1920. Most of his paintings during this period show a vast city square in bright afternoon light. The square is empty except for a statue, or one or two lonely human figures. Chirico created a puzzling or even menacing atmosphere by combining the emptiness of the square with irregular perspectives, brilliant light, and long shadows. His scenes resemble the paintings of the Surrealists, whom he influenced during the 1920's. But Chirico was not an active participant in that movement.

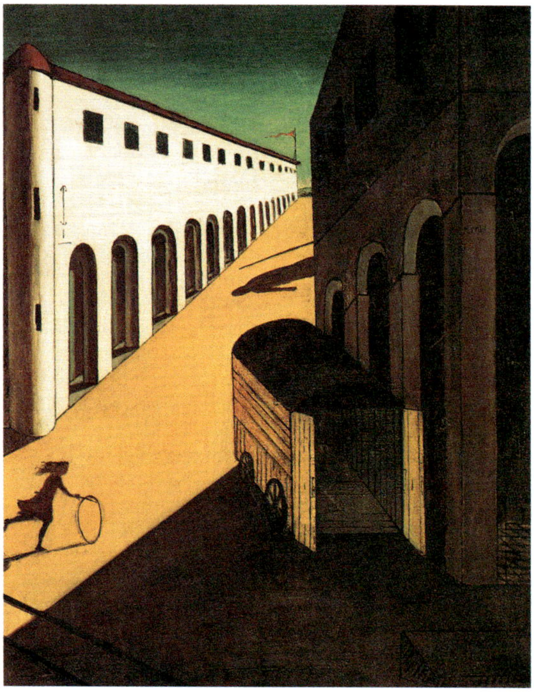

Mystery and Melancholy of a Street (1914), an oil painting on canvas; private collection, WORLD BOOK photo by Henry Beville

Chirico's major paintings express hidden danger by combining shadows, isolated figures, and exaggerated perspective.

Chirico was born on July 10, 1888, in Vólos, Greece. He studied art in Munich, Germany, for three years before moving to Italy in 1910. In the 1920's, he began painting in a more traditional style and disclaimed his earlier work. He died on Nov. 20, 1978. Nancy J. Troy

See also **Painting** (Surrealism).

Chiropractic, *KY ruh PRAK tihk,* is a system of health care that emphasizes the relationship between structure and function in the body. Doctors of chiropractic believe good health depends, in part, on the normal alignment of the body's parts, and that misalignments—known as *subluxations*—can be a major factor in illness. Chiropractors consider proper alignment of the spine to be of critical importance because of its central role in the function of the nervous system. Proper nerve function is essential in restoring and maintaining good health.

Chiropractic treatment often consists of manual manipulation of the spine or other body parts to restore proper alignment. Such manipulations are called *adjustments.* Studies have shown that chiropractic adjustments can relieve pain and structural disorders in the joints and muscles and ease lower back pain. Techniques of *physical therapy* are often used to promote the effects of treatment (see **Physical therapy**). Claims that chiropractic can cure diseases have never been proved scientifically.

In the United States and in several other countries, the practice of chiropractic is regulated. The laws of all U.S. states and Canadian provinces prohibit chiropractors from prescribing drugs or performing major surgery. Some states permit chiropractors to do minor surgery.

The American Medical Association (AMA) has a long history of opposition to chiropractic. In 1967, the AMA ruled that it was unethical for physicians to associate professionally with chiropractors. In 1987, however, a federal judge ordered the AMA not to interfere with relationships between physicians and chiropractors. In 1992, the AMA changed its code of ethics to allow referral of patients to chiropractors whenever the physician feels it may benefit the patient. Many hospitals now allow chiropractors to practice in their facilities. The granting of hospital privileges has led to the development of a new procedure called "manipulation under anesthesia." This procedure, performed while the patient is under anesthesia, allows the chiropractor to make more vigorous adjustments of the spine.

Daniel David Palmer, an Iowa merchant, founded the chiropractic method in 1895. Two years later, he opened the first college of chiropractic in Davenport, Iowa.

Today, the United States has 14 accredited chiropractic colleges. Each offers a four-year program that leads to the degree of Doctor of Chiropractic (D.C.). Additional information may be obtained from the American Chiropractic Association, which has headquarters in Arlington, Virginia. Thomas H. Maugh II

Chisholm, *CHIHZ uhm,* **Shirley** (1924-2005), became the first African American woman to serve in the United States Congress. Chisholm, a New York Democrat, was a member of the U.S. House of Representatives from 1969 to 1983. She served in the New York State Assembly from 1964 to 1968. Chisholm campaigned for, but did not win, the 1972 Democratic presidential nomination.

Chisholm worked for the reform of U.S. political parties and legislatures to meet the needs of more citizens. She was a severe critic of the seniority system in Congress and protested her 1969 assignment to the House Agriculture Committee. She won reassignment to a committee on which she felt she could be of greater service to her Brooklyn inner-city district.

Shirley Anita St. Hill Chisholm was born on Nov. 30, 1924, in the Brooklyn section of New York City. She graduated from Brooklyn College and earned a master's degree at Columbia University. She taught nursery school and directed day-care centers in New York City. From 1959 to 1964, Chisholm was a consultant for the city's Bureau of Child Welfare. She wrote an autobiography, *Unbought and Unbossed* (1970). Chisholm died on Jan. 1, 2005. Charles V. Hamilton

Mount Holyoke College

Shirley Chisholm

Chisholm Trail, *CHIHZ uhm,* was a famous route that Texas cowboys used in driving cattle herds north to the railroads in Kansas. In 1866, Jesse Chisholm, a mixed-blood Cherokee Indian trader, drove a wagon through Indian Territory (now Oklahoma) to his trading post near Wichita, Kansas. A year later, cattle drivers followed Chisholm's wagon tracks to Abilene, Kansas, and named the trail after him. The trail began about 1,000 miles (1,600 kilometers) south of Abilene, near San Antonio, where herds of longhorn cattle abandoned by Mexican ranchers roamed wild.

The Chisholm Trail and its users are celebrated in Western stories and songs. Cowboys began a series of long trail drives in 1867 and moved about 1 ½ million cattle over the trail in three years. They liked the route because it had no towns, hills, or wooded areas.

As the railroads moved west across the plains, settlers soon followed, and the route of the trail shifted westward. Ellsworth, 60 miles (97 kilometers) west of Abilene on the Kansas Pacific Railroad, and later Newton, farther south on the Atchison, Topeka and Santa Fe Railway, became terminal points for cattle drives between 1872 and 1875. For the location of these towns, see **Kansas** (political map). Saloons, houses of prostitution, and gambling halls lined the streets of these "cow towns." The cattle drives ended and the trail fell into disuse as the railroads pushed across the plains and farmers built fences on their homesteads. Dan L. Flores

See also **Western frontier life in America** (The cattle drive).

Chisinau, *KEE shee NUH oo* (pop. 676,000), is the capital and largest city of Moldova, formerly the Soviet republic of Moldavia. The city lies in central Moldova along the Byk River (see **Moldova** [map]). The older section of the city borders the river, and the newer section extends to the surrounding hills.

Chisinau is a major industrial center. Its products include prepared foods and construction equipment.

Chisinau was founded near a monastery about 1420. Control over Moldova switched several times between the Ottoman Empire, Romania, and Russia during the next 500 years. In 1940, the Soviets seized Moldova and made it part of the Soviet Union. The Soviets called Moldova the Moldavian Soviet Socialist Republic. Chisinau, which they called Kishinev, was the capital. Over half the buildings in the city were destroyed in World War II (1939-1945), but Chisinau was rebuilt after the war. In 1991, Moldova declared its independence from the Soviet Union. Vladimir Tismaneanu

Chiton, *KY tuhn,* is a marine animal protected by a tough, eight-pieced shell. The shell's hard pieces are known as *valves.* Leathery flesh called the *girdle* holds the valves together. There are about 800 kinds of chitons worldwide. They live mostly in shallow waters, where they use their *foot,* a broad, muscular organ, to cling to rocks. Most are sluggish animals that feed on plantlike organisms called *algae.* They eat with their *radula,* a ribbon of hard teeth. Chitons grow from about ⅓ to 12 inches (1 to 30 centimeters) long. Robert S. Prezant

Scientific classification. Chitons belong to the phylum Mollusca. They make up many families of the class Polyplacophora.

See also **Mollusk** (picture); **Shell** (Chitons).

Chivalry. See **Etiquette; Knights and knighthood.**

Chive is a green vegetable that is closely related to the onion. The chive plant is native to Siberia and Southeast Asia. It grows wild in Europe and Asia and is cultivated in most parts of the United States. The root is a small, egg-shaped bulb from which grow long, thin, tubelike leaves. The plant bears showy lavender flowers.

People chop the leaves and use them to flavor food. For example, chive leaves may be used in salads, soups, and cheeses. Chives contain a fairly large amount of vitamin C. The plants are often potted and grown indoors.

W. E. Splittstoesser

Scientific classification. The chive plant belongs to the onion family, Alliaceae. Its scientific name is *Allium schoenoprasum.*

WORLD BOOK illustration by Jill Coombs

Flowering chive plants

Chlamydia, *kluh MIHD ee uh,* is the common name for a group of bacteria that cause disease in animals and human beings. In the United States, genital chlamydia infection is the most common bacterial sexually transmitted disease (STD). It is caused by the bacterium *Chlamydia trachomatis,* which also causes another STD called *lymphogranuloma venereum.* Medical experts estimate that chlamydia strikes about 4 million Americans each year, mostly young people under 25 years of age.

In men, symptoms of chlamydia appear about 7 to 21 days after infection. Most infected men develop a white or colorless discharge from the penis, accompanied by painful urination. The symptoms may go unnoticed, and they usually disappear after several months. Left untreated, the patient may infect other people.

In women, chlamydia can cause a vaginal discharge or pelvic pain, but many have no symptoms. The consequences of untreated infection in women can be especially severe. Infection can spread through the uterus and into the fallopian tubes, causing *pelvic inflammatory disease* (PID), a condition that may result in sterility, and rarely, death (see **Pelvic inflammatory disease**). Pregnant women who have chlamydia can transmit it to their babies during delivery. The germ may infect the baby's lungs, causing pneumonia, and the eyes, causing *conjunctivitis* (see **Conjunctivitis**).

In some developing countries, certain varieties of *C. trachomatis* can infect the eyes, especially in children. These germs are spread by nonsexual contact and perhaps by flies. People infected in this way may develop *trachoma,* which can lead to blindness (see **Trachoma**).

Chlamydial infection can be diagnosed by laboratory tests done on a swab of genital fluids or a urine sample. Doctors often assume a patient has chlamydia if symptoms are present and gonorrhea infection cannot be confirmed. Doctors treat chlamydia with antibiotics. Treatment is most effective when given early in the disease. Strategies for avoiding the infection include using condoms during intimate sexual contact.

Other species of chlamydia cause disease in human beings. *Chlamydophila pneumoniae* is a common cause of respiratory infections. Scientists think it may also have a role in the development of heart disease. *Chlamydia psittaci* is usually transmitted from birds to people and can cause pneumonia or fever. Janet N. Arno

See also **Gonorrhea; Sexually transmitted disease.**

Chloramphenicol, *KLAWR am FEHN uh kohl,* is an antibiotic once used for the treatment of many kinds of infections. It has proved lifesaving in such serious infections as meningitis, typhoid fever, Rocky Mountain spotted fever, and typhus. Chloramphenicol can cause a fatal side effect, however. Because other equally effective and safer antibiotics have become available, chloramphenicol is now seldom used in the United States.

Chloramphenicol was discovered in 1947. It was one of the first widely used antibiotics. During the 1950's, it became evident that chloramphenicol can cause *aplastic anemia,* a potentially fatal condition in which the bone marrow fails to make blood cells. Richard W. Sloan

See also **Antibiotic.**

Chloride is a chemical compound that contains the chlorine ion (Cl^{-1}). Chlorine atoms readily attract electrons from other elements to form chlorides. Chlorides are widely distributed on Earth's surface.

Chlorides may be *organic* or *inorganic.* Organic chlorides contain the element carbon. They include the dry-cleaning agent perchloroethylene. Inorganic chlorides may contain a metallic or a nonmetallic element. Most metals combine with chlorine by losing an electron to form chlorides known as salts. Chloride salts have high melting and boiling points and conduct electric current well when dissolved in water or melted. Chloride salts include sodium chloride, or common table salt, and silver chloride, which is used in photography. Nonmetallic elements and some metals form chlorides by sharing a pair of electrons with chlorine atoms. These chlorides have low melting and boiling points and react with water to form hydrochloric acid. One of these compounds, aluminum chloride, is used in manufacturing detergents. Marianna A. Busch

See also **Carbon tetrachloride; Hydrochloric acid; Salt; Salt, Chemical.**

Chlorine, *KLAWR een,* is a poisonous, yellowish-green gas with a strong, unpleasant odor. Chlorine causes irritation to the nose, throat, and lungs. However, when combined with the metal sodium, chlorine forms sodium chloride, or table salt.

The Swedish chemist Carl Wilhelm Scheele first made chlorine in 1774 by treating *muriatic acid* (hydrochloric acid) with manganese dioxide. In 1810, the English chemist Sir Humphry Davy determined that chlorine was a chemical element. He named it from a Greek word meaning *greenish-yellow.*

Sources of chlorine. In nature, chlorine exists only in compounds. It is found mainly in chloride minerals, of which the best known is sodium chloride. Chlorides occur in seawater, salt lakes, and deposits of rock salt.

Uses of chlorine. Chlorine kills bacteria in water, and so it is widely used to purify drinking water and the water in swimming pools. In sunlight, chlorine can react explosively with hydrogen to form hydrogen chloride. This compound dissolves in water to become hydrochloric acid. People use hydrochloric acid in dyeing and in cleaning metal. When chlorine is dissolved in sodium hydroxide, it becomes a mixture of sodium chloride and sodium hypochlorite. This mixture has often been used as a bleach and disinfectant.

Manufacturers also use chlorine compounds to produce paper, plastics, insecticides, cleaning fluids, and antifreeze. In addition, chlorine is used in the manufacture of medicines, paints, and petroleum products.

Manufacturers produce chlorine gas chiefly by passing an electric current through solutions of sodium chloride in water (see **Electrolysis**). *Sodium hydroxide* (also called caustic soda, or lye) forms at the same time. This process is the basis of one of the largest chemical industries, the *chlor-alkali* or *chlorine-caustic* industry. Chlorine can be put under pressure and made a liquid.

Chemical properties. Chlorine is a member of the *halogen* (salt-forming) group of nonmetallic elements. Pure chlorine is extremely active chemically. Like the other halogens, it tends to combine with other elements by accepting electrons from them. Chlorine acts as a powerful *oxidizing agent* by causing substances to give up electrons. Chlorine has the chemical symbol Cl. It has an *atomic number* (number of protons in its nucleus) of 17. Its *relative atomic mass* is 35.453. An element's relative atomic mass equals its *mass* (amount of matter) divided by $\frac{1}{12}$ of the mass of carbon 12, the most abundant form of carbon. At 20 °C, chlorine gas has a density of 0.00295 gram per cubic centimeter at sea level. Chlorine may be condensed to a liquid that boils at −34.05 °C and freezes at −100.98 °C. Evan H. Appelman

Related articles in *World Book* include:

Bleach	Salt (Uses of salt)
Chlorofluorocarbon	Sewage
Halogen	Water (Purifying and treating water)
Hydrochloric acid	

Chlorofluorocarbon, *KLAWR uh FLOOR uh KAHR buhn,* is any of a group of synthetic organic compounds that contain chlorine, fluorine, and carbon. The two most common chlorofluorocarbons (CFC's) are *trichlorofluoromethane* (CCl_3F), also called CFC-11, and *dichlorodifluoromethane* (CCl_2F_2), or CFC-12. They are used as refrigerants in air conditioners and refrigerators and to make plastic foams for furniture and insulation.

CFC-11 and CFC-12 are nonpoisonous and nonflammable under normal conditions, and they are easily converted from liquid to gas or from gas to liquid. These properties make them useful as propellants in aerosol spray products. Scientific studies indicate, however, that CFC's harm the environment by breaking down ozone molecules in Earth's upper atmosphere. Ozone (O_3), a form of oxygen, protects plants and animals from the harmful ultraviolet rays of the sun. As CFC's reach the upper atmosphere, they break apart and release chlorine atoms. These chlorine atoms can react chemically with the ozone and convert it to ordinary oxygen (O_2).

In 1978, the United States government banned chlorofluorocarbon aerosols for most uses. In 1988, the DuPont Company, the world's largest producer of CFC's, announced plans to phase out production of these chemicals. DuPont sold CFC's under the registered trademark *Freon.* The United States and most other industrialized countries that produced CFC's agreed in 1990 to end production by 2000. There are two exceptions to the ban in the United States: (1) use as a propellant in inhalers for asthma patients, and (2) use in the manufacture of methyl chloroform to clean O-ring seals for the space shuttle. In late 1992, the industrialized countries agreed to move the deadline to the end of 1995. By 1996, most of these countries had complied with this deadline. Other countries planned to end production by 2010. Robert C. Gadwood

See also **Ozone hole.**

Chloroform is a dense, colorless liquid that is used as a solvent in the manufacture of pharmaceuticals, dyes, and pesticides. It is also used as a starting material for the manufacture of fluorocarbons. Physicians once used chloroform as an anesthetic.

Until 1976, chloroform was an ingredient in some cough medicines, liniments, and toothpastes. That year, the United States Food and Drug Administration (FDA) banned the use of chloroform in drugs and cosmetics. The FDA took this action after tests showed that high doses of chloroform could cause cancer in laboratory animals. Chloroform is an unwanted by-product formed in small amounts in drinking water when chlorine is added to kill disease-causing bacteria. In 1979, the Environmental Protection Agency (EPA) issued regulations to limit the amount of chloroform in drinking water.

Chloroform was discovered in 1831 by three chemists, each working independently of the others. They were Eugène Soubeiran of France, Justus von Liebig of Germany, and Samuel Guthrie of the United States. Sir James Simpson of Scotland publicly demonstrated chloroform as an anesthetic in 1847. Queen Victoria helped win acceptance for the medical use of chloroform to deaden pain and to produce general anesthesia. But since chloroform can damage the heart, liver, and kidneys, less toxic anesthetics have replaced chloroform in modern medical practice.

Chloroform has the chemical formula $CHCl_3$. It boils at 62 °C and freezes at −64 °C. Robert C. Gadwood

See also **Anesthesia.**

Chlorophyll, *KLAWR uh fihl,* is the green pigment in plants that absorbs light energy for use in photosynthesis. Chlorophyll also is found in simple organisms called *algae* and in some bacteria. Most plant cells do not produce chlorophyll unless the plant is exposed to light. This is why plants kept away from light are white or yellow rather than green.

Chlorophyll is in disk-shaped membranes called *thylakoids* within cells. In most plants, thylakoids are contained in tiny cell bodies called *chloroplasts.* The chloroplasts in the leaves of plants carry out all the essential processes of photosynthesis. Light energy absorbed by chlorophyll is channeled to *reaction centers* in the thylakoids. The reaction centers, along with *electron-carrier molecules,* convert the light energy to chemical energy. Oxygen is released in the process. Chemical energy is needed for taking carbon dioxide from the air, eventually leading to the production of sugars and such other food substances as starch, fat, protein, and vitamins.

There are several forms of chlorophyll. The most common forms in plants are *chlorophyll a* and *chlorophyll b.* They absorb most of the long wavelengths (red rays) and the short wavelengths (blue-violet rays) of visible light. They absorb the middle wavelengths (green rays) least effectively. Some bacteria, just as plants do, make their own food by photosynthesis. These bacteria have special chlorophylls that can absorb longer wavelengths called *infrared rays,* which lie beyond the visible light spectrum. When dried, chlorophyll looks like blue or green-black powder. Elisabeth Gantt

See also **Chloroplast; Leaf** (Photosynthesis); **Photosynthesis.**

Chloroplast, *KLAWR uh plast,* is a specialized structure within the cells of plants. Chloroplasts serve as the site of photosynthesis. They contain *chlorophyll,* the green pigment that absorbs energy from sunlight for use in photosynthesis. Chlorophyll also gives green plants their color. In the fall, the production of chlorophyll in woody plants ceases. The colors of yellow pigments in the chloroplasts then become visible.

The chloroplasts of most plants are shaped like disks or lenses. Under a microscope, they can be suspended in the part of a cell called the *cytoplasm.* Except for the cell nucleus, chloroplasts are the most visible structures in a plant cell.

Chloroplasts are one of several types of specialized plant-cell structures called *plastids.* Other plastids contain yellow, orange, or red pigments, and provide the colors of many flowers and fruits. Plastids also store oil, protein, and starch. Joseph E. Armstrong

See also **Chlorophyll; Photosynthesis.**

Chlorpromazine, *klawr PROH muh zeen,* is a drug used to reduce hallucinations and delusions in mentally ill persons. It also helps control nausea, vomiting, and continuous hiccuping. The drug may also produce drowsiness and lower the patient's blood pressure. Chlorpromazine was developed in France in the 1950's. It was the first medication to effectively treat *psychoses* (severe mental disorders). Its use enabled many thousands of patients to leave mental hospitals. Chlorpromazine's trade name is *Thorazine.* Mark S. Gold

Chocolate is a food made from the seeds of a tropical tree called the *cacao.* Botanists believe the cacao tree originated between southern Mexico and the Amazon River Basin in South America. The word *chocolate* comes from *chocolatl,* a word Spanish conquerors may have created by combining the Maya word *chocol,* which means *hot,* with the Aztec word *atl,* which means *water.*

The cacao tree produces the seeds, or cacao beans, from which all chocolate is made. The scientific name of the cacao tree is *Theobroma cacao.* The trees flourish in tropical climates within 20 degrees latitude north and south of the equator. Most of the world's cacao beans come from the west coast of Africa. Côte d'Ivoire is, by far, the world's leading cacao bean producer. Other major producers include Ghana, Indonesia, and Brazil.

The cultivated cacao tree grows about 25 feet (7.6 meters) high. It produces leaves, flowers, and fruit in all seasons of the year. The flowers are small. They grow singly and in clusters on the main stem of the branches and on the trunk. The ripe fruit, or pod, may be red, yellow, golden, pale green, or a combination of these colors. The melonlike pod contains 20 to 40 almond-shaped seeds. When these seeds are fermented and dried, they become the commercial cacao bean. Because of a mistake in spelling, probably made by English importers many years ago, these beans became known as *cocoa beans* in English-speaking countries.

Harvesting the cacao beans. Workers cut the pods from the trees with knives attached to long poles, or with machetes. They gather the pods into heaps, cut them open, and scoop out the beans. The beans are placed in piles, covered with banana leaves, and allowed to ferment for 2 to 9 days. Some large operations ferment the beans in boxes instead of piles. Next, the beans are dried in the sun or with warm air to prevent mold. Workers then place the beans in bags or bulk containers for shipment.

Hershey Foods Corporation

Milk chocolate is stirred for 72 hours to help develop its flavor and make it smooth for molding into bars.

Manufacturing chocolate. Chocolate manufacturers receive many types of beans. They blend them to yield the flavor and color desired in the final product. The first steps in processing the beans include cleaning, roasting, hulling, blending, and grinding. Cacao seeds with the shells removed are called *nibs.* The nibs are quite dry, even though they contain about 54 percent *cocoa butter,* the natural fat of the cacao bean. The grinding process releases the cocoa butter from within the nibs. The mixture of cocoa butter and finely ground nibs forms a free-flowing substance called *chocolate liquor.*

Chocolate products are all manufactured from chocolate liquor. They include baking chocolate, cocoa, milk chocolate, and sweet and semisweet chocolate.

Baking chocolate is the commercial form of chocolate liquor. Manufacturers cool and solidify the chocolate liquor into cakes. This bitter, unsweetened form of chocolate is used in many baked goods.

Cocoa. In making cocoa powder, workers use huge hydraulic presses to force some of the cocoa butter out of the heated chocolate liquor. The mass remaining in the presses forms large, hard cakes called *press cakes.* Manufacturers grind press cakes into fine, reddish-brown cocoa powder. People can prepare a hot beverage from the cocoa powder by adding sugar, hot milk, and sometimes vanilla. Confectioners, bakers, ice cream manufacturers, and other food producers use cocoa in many of their products.

Milk chocolate ranks as the most popular of all chocolate products. Chocolate liquor, additional cocoa butter, whole milk solids, and sugar are the basic ingredients in this form of chocolate. Manufacturers may also add small amounts of flavoring, such as vanilla and salt.

The ingredients are mixed well. The mixture then

passes through a series of large, steel roll refiners that crush the sugar and milk powder to produce a fine paste. Machines called *conches* then process the chocolate for up to 72 hours. The mixing action of the conch helps develop the smooth texture and desired flavor as it blends the chocolate. Milk chocolate is sold in the form of bars and as the coating on some candies.

Sweet chocolate and semisweet chocolate are processed in the same way as milk chocolate. But manufacturers do not add milk solids to the mixture. Manufacturers sell large amounts of both sweet and semisweet chocolate to confectioners for making chocolate-covered candies. These types of chocolate, often called *dark chocolate,* are commonly used in baking.

Food value of chocolate. Chocolate ranks high in calories but also high in food value. It contains carbohydrates, fats, protein, and several vitamins and minerals. Many people whose work requires physical endurance, including soldiers, explorers, and athletes, rely on chocolate as a source of quick energy.

History. The Olmec Indians, who flourished in southern Mexico between about 1200 and 400 B.C., may have been the first to cultivate cacao. The Maya Indians of Central America may have begun using cacao beans as early as 600 B.C. The Aztec Indians of Mexico cultivated cacao by A.D. 1500. The cacao bean played an important role in Aztec traditions and religion. Members of the Aztec elite and warrior classes drank a beverage made of ground cacao mixed with ground corn and other seeds. They may have added honey to sweeten the drink, or mixed in vanilla or chili powder to add flavor. The Aztec also used cacao beans as a currency and in religious rituals.

Spanish explorers and conquistadors in Mexico first tasted cacao during the early 1500's, but it is not known whether they brought the beans back to Spain. However, chocolate had arrived in Spain by the mid-1500's. The first commercial shipment of cacao beans to Europe arrived in Spain in 1585. Chocolate became a popular drink of European nobility soon afterward. In London, the first establishment to sell cocoa opened in 1657. Europeans added sugar, vanilla, cinnamon, and milk to the beverage to reduce the bitter taste.

The British chocolate company J. S. Fry and Sons is credited with developing solid eating chocolate. The company first made the confection in 1847. In 1876, the Swiss chocolate manufacturer Daniel Peter invented a method to produce milk chocolate. Today, chocolate is popular around the world. Countries in which large amounts of chocolate are eaten include Belgium, France, Germany, Norway, Switzerland, the United Kingdom, and the United States. Gregory R. Ziegler

See also **Carob; Hershey, Milton Snavely.**

Choctaw Indians, *CHAHK taw,* are a tribe that originally lived in what is now Alabama and Mississippi. They hunted and raised corn and other crops. One of their chief religious ceremonies was a harvest celebration called the Green Corn Dance. According to one legend, the Choctaw were created at a sacred mound called Nanih Waiya, near Noxapater, Mississippi.

In 1540, the Spanish explorer Hernando de Soto led the first European expedition through Choctaw territory. Fighting broke out after the Choctaw refused to supply the Spaniards with a guide and transportation. Several Spaniards and many Indians were killed.

In 1830, the United States government passed the Indian Removal Act. This act called for eastern Indians to be moved west to make room for more white settlers. The government then forced the Choctaw to sign the Treaty of Dancing Rabbit Creek. The treaty exchanged the tribe's eastern land for an area in the Indian Territory, in what is now Oklahoma. About 14,000 Choctaw moved there in several groups during the early 1830's. About a fourth of the Indians died on the journey. About 5,000 Choctaw remained in Mississippi.

The Choctaw who moved to the Indian Territory established their own government and school system. During the American Civil War (1861-1865), the Choctaw fought for the Confederacy. After the South lost the war, the Indians were forced to give up much of their land. The tribal government was dissolved by 1907, when Oklahoma became a state. In the 1970's, Congress again recognized the tribe's right to elect its own chief.

According to the 2000 census, there are about 87,000 Choctaw. About 44,000 live in Oklahoma. About 6,400 live in Mississippi as a separate tribe. Clara Sue Kidwell

See also **Five Civilized Tribes; Indian Territory.**

Cholera, *KAHL uhr uh,* is an infectious intestinal disorder. It is common in southern Asia, and outbreaks also occur occasionally in other parts of the world. Cholera is caused by a comma-shaped bacterium called *Vibrio cholerae.* The microorganism is transmitted by water or food that has been contaminated with the *feces* (solid body wastes) of people who have the disease.

Cholera occurs when *Vibrio cholerae* enters the intestines and releases cholera toxin. The toxin causes the intestine to secrete large amounts of water and salt. Because the intestine cannot absorb the water and salt at

Archives and Manuscripts Division, Oklahoma Historical Society

Choctaw Indians play a traditional game in a photo taken in Oklahoma in 1902. The United States government had forced most of the Choctaw to move from the Southeast to the Oklahoma region in the 1830's.

the rate they are secreted, the patient suffers severe diarrhea. This loss of fluid causes severe dehydration and changes in the body chemistry. If untreated, the illness can lead to shock and eventually death. With proper treatment, cholera lasts only a few days.

Doctors treat cholera with special solutions that help replace the patient's lost fluids. The solutions may be taken orally or *intravenously* (by injection). Intravenous treatments are more effective, but they often are not available in rural areas where the illness frequently occurs. An easily prepared household solution for treating cholera consists of 5 grams (1 teaspoon) of salt and 20 grams (4 teaspoons) of sugar per 1 liter (0.95 quart) of water. The amount of fluid given to the patient should match the amount lost in diarrhea.

Prevention of cholera requires adequate sanitation facilities. A vaccine against the illness has been developed, but it is not very effective. People who travel in areas where cholera is widespread should not drink the local water. In addition, they should cook all foods that may have been exposed to water. Andrew G. Plaut

Cholesterol, *kuh LEHS tuh rohl,* is a fatty substance found in animal tissues. The human body produces cholesterol, but this substance also enters the body in food. Meats, egg yolks, and milk products, such as butter and cheese, contain cholesterol. Such organs as the brain and liver contain much cholesterol.

Cholesterol is a type of *lipid,* one of the classes of chemical compounds essential to human health (see **Lipid**). Cholesterol makes up an important part of the membranes of each cell in the body. In addition, the liver uses cholesterol to make *bile acids,* which aid digestion. The body also uses cholesterol to produce vitamin D and certain hormones, including sex hormones.

Cholesterol and *triglycerides,* another lipid, are two of the major fatty substances in the blood (see **Triglyceride**). Triglycerides may be used by cells for energy, or they may be stored for later use. Doctors often measure the amount of cholesterol and triglycerides in blood to help determine a patient's overall health. High levels of cholesterol, particularly if accompanied by high levels of triglycerides, increase the risk of heart disease.

Both cholesterol and triglycerides are carried through the bloodstream in large molecules called *lipoproteins.* There are two chief types of cholesterol-carrying lipoproteins, *low-density lipoprotein* (LDL) and *high-density lipoprotein* (HDL). Cholesterol in blood can thus be identified as either LDL-cholesterol or HDL-cholesterol, depending on which lipoprotein carries it. High levels of LDL-cholesterol in blood are a primary cause of heart attacks. LDL can be found in the wall of heart arteries. Low levels of HDL-cholesterol also increase the risk of heart attack. Scientists believe that HDL's help remove cholesterol from tissues.

Factors that cause high cholesterol levels. The amount of cholesterol in the human body is controlled by cellular molecules that are called *LDL-receptors.* These molecules allow LDL-cholesterol to attach to and be used by the cell. LDL-cholesterol accumulates in blood in large amounts when the LDL-cholesterol in the body far exceeds the number of available LDL-receptors. This condition most commonly occurs in people whose diets are high in cholesterol or in *saturated fats.* Saturated fats are found primarily in animal fats and in certain vegetable fats, such as coconut oil and palm oil.

People also may have high cholesterol levels if they have an abnormal gene that prevents a full number of LDL-receptors from forming. This inherited disorder is called *familial hypercholesterolemia.* Other factors that can cause high blood cholesterol include a malfunctioning thyroid gland, kidney disease, diabetes, and the use of various medicines, including certain diuretics.

Cholesterol and heart disease. In adults, a cholesterol level of less than 200 milligrams per 1 deciliter (3 ounces) of blood is considered desirable. Above that level, the risk of heart disease increases dramatically. Adults also are at an above-average risk of heart disease if they have an LDL-cholesterol level of more than 160 milligrams per deciliter of blood or an HDL-cholesterol level of less than 40 milligrams per deciliter.

Besides cholesterol levels, other factors increase the risk of heart disease. These factors include cigarette smoking, high blood pressure, diabetes, a family history of premature heart disease, and being a male over 44 years of age or a female over 54. Individuals with two or more of these factors have high risk of heart attack, particularly if they also have *atherosclerosis* (narrowing of the arteries because of fatty deposits).

Treatment of high blood cholesterol consists of first reducing the amount of saturated fat and cholesterol in the diet. Poultry and fish are low in cholesterol. Cereals, fresh fruit, and vegetables contain no cholesterol. Regular aerobic exercise—such as bicycling, running, and swimming—can further lower the cholesterol level.

Medication should be considered only for people who are at high risk of heart disease and who have been unable to control their cholesterol with diet. Medications shown to reduce cholesterol levels and the risk of heart disease include cholestyramine, colestipol, gemfibrozil, lovastatin, and niacin.

Clinical research trials have indicated that lowering the amount of cholesterol in the blood can reduce the risk of heart attack in middle-aged men who had no history of heart disease. In men and women with atherosclerosis, reducing cholesterol in blood prevents further narrowing of the heart arteries. Neil J. Stone

See also **Heart** (Coronary artery disease).

Chomsky, *CHAHM skee,* **Noam,** *nohm* (1928-), is an American linguist, philosopher, and political activist. He revolutionized the study of language with his introduction of *generative grammar,* also called *transformational grammar.* Generative grammar is a set of largely unconscious rules that speakers use to produce and understand sentences in their language. Chomsky argued that certain universal properties underlie all languages, and that these properties are *innate* (inborn). His research has influenced theories of innate ideas in philosophy, psychology, mathematics, and education.

Chomsky is also known for his *dissident* political beliefs—that is, beliefs that disagree with those who hold power. His lectures and writings have sought to expose what he views as government misinformation and the hidden influence of big business. Chomsky's work has influenced socialist movements that favor limiting government activities.

Avram Noam Chomsky was born in Philadelphia. He graduated from the University of Pennsylvania in 1949, and he earned his Ph.D. there in 1955. He then joined the faculty of the Massachusetts Institute of Technology.

Chomsky has written over 80 books. Some of them include *Syntactic Structures* (1957); *Aspects of the Theory of Syntax* (1965); *Reflections on Language* (1975); *Lectures on Government and Binding* (1981); *Deterring Democracy* (1991); and *Hegemony or Survival: America's Quest for Global Dominance* (2003). Anne Lobeck

See also **Linguistics** (The generative theory of language); **Socialism** (The New Left).

Chongqing, *chuhng chihng* (pop. 9,691,901), also spelled *Chungking* or *Ch'ung-ch'ing,* is one of China's leading commercial, transportation, and industrial centers. The city served as the capital of the Republic of China from 1938 to 1946. Chongqing stands in a mountainous region in south-central China at the junction of the Yangtze and Jialing rivers (see **China** [political map]).

In 1997, Chongqing and its surrounding area became one of China's four municipalities that are governed directly by the national government. These metropolitan areas have a political status similar to that of a province. Beijing, Shanghai, and Tianjin are the other nationally governed municipalities. The Chongqing Municipality covers about 31,700 square miles (82,000 square kilometers) and has over 30 million people. It is China's largest nationally governed municipality in area and population.

Chongqing has been a major inland port since ancient times. Goods produced there include automobiles, iron and steel, leather, medicine, motorcycles, and silk. The city also has several copper and petroleum refineries.

Gray-walled, ancient Chongqing city has a history of more than 4,000 years. It became part of China in 220 B.C., when the Emperor Shi Huangdi brought the territory under his rule. Chongqing served as the wartime capital of China from 1938 to 1946. The Chinese Nationalist government moved to Chongqing after Japanese forces had overrun the capital at Nanjing and then the temporary capital of Wuhan. Chongqing was the most heavily bombed city in China during World War II (1939-1945). Bombs destroyed many of Chongqing's old, narrow streets, which go up hillsides in stairsteps. Nanjing again became the capital in 1946, after World War II ended.

In the late 1960s, China's government developed military industries near Chongqing as part of its "third line" strategy. Under this strategy, the government planned to retreat to central China in case of an attack on the east coast. Richard Louis Edmonds

See also **Yangtze River.**

Chopin, *SHOH pan* or *shaw PAN,* **Frédéric François,** *FREHD uh rihk frahn SWAH* (1810-1849), a Polish-born composer, was one of the masters of piano composition. He wrote *chamber music* (music for small groups of instruments), songs, and pieces for piano and orchestra. But his fame rests almost entirely on his more than 200 compositions for solo piano.

His life. Chopin was born in Zelazowa-Wola, near Warsaw, probably on March 1, 1810. A child prodigy, Chopin played the piano in public when he was only 8 years old. He began to compose soon afterward. Chopin studied at the Warsaw Conservatory from 1826 to 1829 before leaving Poland in 1830. He settled in Paris in 1831.

In 1837, Chopin began a famous love affair with George Sand, a French woman novelist. The affair ended with a quarrel in 1847. He was then seriously ill with tuberculosis. Chopin died on Oct. 17, 1849.

His works. Chopin was a master of small musical forms. His works for solo piano include three sonatas, four ballades, four scherzos, about 40 mazurkas in a Polish $\frac{3}{4}$ dance rhythm, 25 preludes, and about 15 polonaises in a stately Polish dance rhythm. His other solo pieces include more than 25 études, 18 waltzes (including the famous "Minute Waltz"), a barcarole, a berceuse, a bolero, a tarantella, and several rondos. His fantasia is perhaps his greatest single work. His études are valuable for their music and for teaching piano. Chopin also composed two pianos concertos and a funeral march.

Chopin is unique among composers because his music has always been as highly esteemed by musicians as by the public. Chopin was a creator of melody, and some of his pieces now seem as familiar as folk music.

Chopin did much to influence piano composition. He had a keen appreciation for the piano's ability to produce beautiful music. He designed his compositions to display the resources of the instrument to full effect. His best works were written in patterns that he worked out or perfected himself. Chopin also influenced the future of music by including Slavic folk harmonies and rhythms in his work. Chopin's music expresses Polish patriotism in the Polish harmonies and rhythms of his mazurkas and polonaises. However, the rest of his music is essentially international in style. Daniel T. Politoske

Additional resources

Azoury, Pierre H. *Chopin Through His Contemporaries.* Greenwood, 1999.
Samson, Jim. *Chopin.* 1996. Reprint. Oxford, 1998.

Chopin, *SHOH pan,* **Kate** (1851-1904), was an American novelist and short-story writer. She was the first American female novelist to write frankly about women's feelings toward their roles as wives and mothers. Chopin's best-known novel, *The Awakening* (1899), deals with a woman who is dissatisfied with her passionless husband. The woman gradually gives in to her strong desires for other men and commits adultery. The novel focuses on the restrictions that social and religious institutions of the late 1800's placed on women. Chopin's novel was severely criticized for her realistic treatment of the subject of adultery.

Kate O'Flaherty Chopin was born on Feb. 8, 1851, in St. Louis. For many years, she lived in or near New Orleans. Many of her stories appear in the collections *Bayou Folk* (1894) and *A Night in Acadie* (1897). They give a frank picture of life in the Cajun, Creole, and African American communities of central Louisiana. Chopin died on Aug. 22, 1904. Alan Gribben

Chopsticks are utensils used in many Asian countries to eat and to serve food. Most of the food in those countries is served in small pieces. These pieces can be easily handled with a pair of chopsticks. The Chinese name for chopsticks, *kuaizi,* is a pun on *kuai,* a word that means both *quick* and *piece.* The English word may come from pidgin English, a dialect used by early traders in China. *Chop* means *quick* in pidgin English.

Chopsticks are about 10 inches (25 centimeters) long. Most are wood or bamboo, but some are ivory or silver. A person using chopsticks holds the top stick by the thumb, index, and middle fingers, like a pencil. The top stick moves up and down. The bottom stick rests at the base of the thumb and is braced against the top of the fourth finger. The ends of the chopsticks thus hold the food securely. Many non-Asians use chopsticks when eating Asian food. Norma Diamond

Chorale, *kuh RAL,* is the music for a hymn, in particular the hymns of German Protestant churches. Chorales developed during the early 1500's as part of the Protestant movement. The earliest chorales were single-line melodies with texts in German. Congregations sang them in unison and without accompaniment. Over time, chorales became more elaborate. Composers added harmony and counterpoint as well as instrumental accompaniment to the simple melodies. Many composers also used chorales in larger works, such as cantatas, oratorios, passion music, and compositions for organ. Martin Luther, the founder of Protestantism in Germany and an accomplished musician, wrote many chorales. One was the famous "A Mighty Fortress Is Our God." See also **Hymn.** Katherine K. Preston

Chordate, *KAWR dayt,* is the name of a large *phylum* (group) of land, marine, and freshwater animals. Chordates include lancelets, amphibians, fish, reptiles, birds, and mammals. At some time during their life cycle, all chordates have a *notochord* (a rodlike, flexible cord that runs down the back of the body). In vertebrates, the notochord is surrounded or replaced by a bony structure called a *vertebral column.* Chordates also have a hollow nerve tube that runs above the notochord. Chordates are segmented in some way, and they have left and right sides that are alike. Chordates also have gill slits, but in many cases these appear only during the undeveloped stage. See also **Vertebrate.** William N. Eschmeyer

Chorea, *kaw REE uh,* is any of a number of disorders characterized by brief, rapid, uncoordinated movements. The word is often used to mean *acute chorea,* a condition associated with rheumatic fever (see **Rheumatic fever**). Acute chorea was formerly called *St. Vitus's dance.* Chorea occurs most commonly in children between the ages of 7 and 15 years. Doctors do not know exactly what causes chorea, and there are no specific laboratory tests to diagnose it. The infectious agent may be in the patient's body for weeks or months before symptoms of chorea develop.

Chorea develops gradually. The patient becomes inattentive, nervous and irritable, and cries easily. The patient has difficulty writing, often stumbles, and falls easily. Uncoordinated movements of the face, limbs, and body soon develop. These movements are completely without purpose. They become worse when the patient is excited, but disappear during sleep. The symptoms may last from two to four months or more, but the patient eventually recovers. Doctors treat chorea with sedatives. Patients must remain in bed, have a nutritious diet, and avoid fatigue. Doctors try to prevent chorea by treating infections promptly.

The word *chorea* comes from a Greek word meaning *dance.* The disease probably was named for the muscular twitchings of the limbs and body that resemble a grotesque dance. The name *St. Vitus's dance* comes from a form of hysteria that was widespread in Europe during the 1500's. People with this condition sought cures at shrines of St. Vitus. Thomas J. Gill III

Chou dynasty. See Zhou dynasty.

Chou En-lai. See Zhou Enlai.

Chouart, Médard. See Groseilliers, Sieur des.

Chouteau, *shoo TOH,* **Jean Pierre,** *jhahn pyair* (1758-1849), who went by his middle name, was an American fur trader and a United States Indian agent. Indian agents represented the government in its dealings with American Indians. Chouteau spent much of his life among Indians, many of whom liked and respected him.

Chouteau was born on Oct. 10, 1758, in New Orleans. From 1794 to 1802, he and his half-brother René Auguste shared a monopoly of trade with the Osage Indians in what are now Arkansas, Kansas, Missouri, and Oklahoma. Following the Louisiana Purchase in 1803, Jean Pierre became the first U.S. agent to the Indians west of the Mississippi River (see **Louisiana Purchase**). He was especially influential among the Osage and was their agent for many years. In 1809, Chouteau and other business people formed the St. Louis Missouri Fur Company to develop the fur trade on the American frontier. Chouteau's son Pierre, Jr., became a leading American fur trader and financier. William E. Foley

Chouteau, *shoo TOH,* **Pierre, Jr.** (1789-1865), often called *Cadet,* acquired great wealth from the fur business and was one of the most powerful financiers of his day. He headed the western department of the American Fur Company for the American businessman John Jacob Astor. In 1834, Chouteau bought the department from Astor and created a fur-trading monopoly in the Missouri River Valley. He pioneered the use of steamboats in the fur trade. It became the first fur-trading firm to take a steamboat up the Missouri River to Montana. When the fur trade declined, Chouteau moved to New York and invested in iron and steel works.

Chouteau was born on Jan. 19, 1789, in St. Louis, Missouri. He served as a member of the Missouri State Constitutional Convention in 1820. Pierre, South Dakota, and Chouteau, Montana, were both named for him. His father, Jean Pierre Chouteau, also was an American fur trader (see **Chouteau, Jean Pierre**). William E. Foley

Chouteau, *shoo TOH,* **René Auguste,** *ruh NAY aw GOOST* (1749-1829), was a French fur trader and merchant who helped found St. Louis, Missouri. Chouteau was born on Sept. 7, 1749, in New Orleans. In 1763, he traveled up the Mississippi River with his stepfather, Pierre Laclède Liguest, and visited the site of what is now St. Louis. The next year, at age 14, Chouteau helped set up a permanent settlement there. St. Louis became a center of the fur trade, and Chouteau the city's most influential trader. Chouteau helped American explorers Meriwether Lewis and William Clark prepare for their famous expedition to the Pacific Ocean. The journey began near St. Louis in 1804. Chouteau also helped the federal government negotiate treaties with Indian tribes. His younger half-brother, Jean Pierre Chouteau, also played an important role in settling the American frontier. William E. Foley

Chow chow, commonly called *chow,* is one of the oldest breeds of dogs. It originally was bred in China about 150 B.C. The chow may have long or short hair. Its coat is solid black, blue, red, cinnamon, or cream, with lighter shadings underneath, on its tail, and on its legs. The chow is medium-sized with a sturdy build. Its blue-black tongue is unique among dogs. Chows are strong, active, and intelligent. See also **Dog** (picture: Some breeds of dogs). Critically reviewed by the Chow Chow Club

Jean Chrétien

Prime minister of Canada
1993-2003

Campbell
1993

Chrétien
1993-2003

Martin
2003-

Office of the Leader of the Opposition

Chrétien, *kray TYEHN,* **Jean,** *zhahn* (1934-   ), served as prime minister of Canada from 1993 to 2003. He became prime minister in late 1993, when the Liberal Party beat the Progressive Conservatives, led by Kim Campbell, in a general election. Chrétien remained in office following general elections in 1997 and 2000.

Chrétien became active in Canada's Liberal Party at age 12. In 1963, at 29, he was elected to Canada's House of Commons. He remained a member of the Commons for the next 23 years. During this time, he held various posts in the cabinets of Prime Ministers Lester B. Pearson, Pierre Elliott Trudeau, and John N. Turner.

In 1984, Chrétien campaigned for leadership of the Liberal Party, but he lost to Turner. In 1986, Chrétien resigned from the House of Commons after a dispute with Turner. Following his resignation, Chrétien practiced law in Ottawa and Montreal. He reentered politics in 1990, when he was elected leader of the Liberal Party. Later that year, Chrétien returned to the House of Commons after winning a by-election, a special election to fill a vacant seat.

Chrétien's forceful speaking style, passionate patriotism, sense of humor, and ability to identify with the Canadian people made him one of the most popular political figures in English-speaking Canada. But his earthy populism and his opposition to Quebec nationalism made him unpopular in his home province of Quebec.

When Chrétien first became prime minister, Canada's economy was struggling to recover from a recession that had started in 1990. Chrétien made economic growth and the creation of jobs his top priorities. He also aimed to cut the federal deficit.

Early life

Boyhood. Joseph-Jacques Jean Chrétien was born on Jan. 11, 1934, in Shawinigan, Quebec. He was the 18th of 19 children of Wellie Chrétien and Marie Boisvert Chrétien. Ten of his siblings died in infancy, leaving him with five brothers and three sisters. His father was a machinist in a paper mill and an organizer for the Liberal Party.

A childhood disease partially paralyzed Chrétien's mouth and left him permanently deaf in his right ear. Jean's parents sent him and his brothers and sisters to boarding schools. They felt the children would get a better education there than in Shawinigan. By the age of 12, Jean was distributing Liberal Party pamphlets.

College years and early career. Chrétien earned a B.A. degree from the College of Three Rivers in Trois-Rivières in 1955. He then entered Laval University in Quebec City to study law. He became president of the university's Liberal Club and organized the Liberal Party's campaign in Quebec for the 1956 general elections. Chrétien earned his law degree from Laval in 1958. That same year, he helped found the law firm of Chrétien, Landry, Deschenes, Trudel and Normand in Shawinigan.

In 1957, Chrétien married Aline Chaîné. The couple had a daughter, France, and a son, Hubert. They adopted an American Indian boy, Michel, in the early 1970's.

Important dates in Chrétien's life

1934	(Jan. 11) Born in Shawinigan, Quebec.
1957	(Sept. 10) Married Aline Chaîné.
1958	Graduated from Laval University with a law degree.
1963	Elected to House of Commons.
1977	Became first French-Canadian minister of finance.
1986	Resigned from House of Commons.
1990	(June 23) Elected leader of Liberal Party.
1990	(Dec. 10) Elected to House of Commons again.
1993	(Nov. 4) Became prime minister of Canada.
1997	Led the Liberal Party to a second election victory.
2000	Led the Liberal Party to a third election victory.
2003	(Dec. 12) Resigned as prime minister.

Political career

Member of Parliament. In 1963, Chrétien won election to the House of Commons, representing the *riding* (district) of St.-Maurice-Laflèche, which included Shawinigan. At that time, Chrétien spoke French but knew little English. He immediately began studying English so he could function effectively in the national government. A majority of Canada's people speak English. Chrétien was reelected in 1965. In 1968, he won election to the new riding of St.-Maurice and was reelected in 1972, 1974, 1979, 1980, and 1984.

Early posts. In the Commons, Chrétien was quickly recognized as a promising politician. Prime Minister Lester B. Pearson appointed him as his parliamentary secretary in 1965 and as secretary to the minister of finance in 1966. In 1967, Chrétien served as minister of state in the ministry of finance, where he helped prepare the federal budget. He became minister of national revenue in 1968. Pearson retired that year, and Chrétien supported Minister of Justice Pierre Elliott Trudeau's successful bid for the Liberal leadership. As party leader, Trudeau succeeded Pearson as prime minister. The Liberals retained power after winning most of the seats in the House of Commons in a general election in June.

In Trudeau's Cabinet, Chrétien held several important posts. Trudeau appointed him minister of Indian affairs and northern development in 1968. Chrétien held this post for six years. During this time, he improved government relations with Canada's native peoples and reorganized the governments of the Yukon and Northwest territories. He also created 10 national parks.

In 1974, Trudeau appointed Chrétien president of the Treasury Board of Canada, where Chrétien made huge cuts in government spending. Chrétien's success in this post led to his appointment as minister of industry, trade, and commerce in 1976. In 1977, he became the first French-Canadian minister of finance. At that time, Canada's economy was suffering from a recession, growing unemployment, and soaring inflation. Chrétien tried to stimulate the economy by cutting taxes, but the recession continued. In 1979 elections, the Progressive Conservative Party, led by Joe Clark, gained control of the government, and Clark became prime minister.

In a 1980 general election, the Liberals regained control of the government. Trudeau returned as prime minister. He appointed Chrétien minister of justice, attorney general, and minister of state for social development. Trudeau also gave Chrétien the task of organizing federal opposition to a growing independence movement in Quebec. The government of Quebec called a provincial referendum for May 1980, asking voters for the authority to negotiate Quebec's political independence. Chrétien campaigned vigorously to preserve national unity, and the people of Quebec voted against independence.

During the next two years, Chrétien worked with representatives from the 10 provinces to develop a plan to give Canada complete control over the Canadian constitution. At that time, all amendments to the constitution required the approval of the British Parliament. In November 1981, after extended negotiations, Trudeau and Chrétien won acceptance of the proposed changes to the constitution from the premiers of all the provinces except Quebec. The proposals became part of the Constitution Act of 1982, passed by the British Parliament in March. The act took effect on April 17, when Queen Elizabeth II approved it. Later that year, Trudeau named Chrétien minister of energy, mines, and resources.

Canapress

Chrétien filled a number of important Cabinet posts under Prime Minister Pierre E. Trudeau. Trudeau and Chrétien, then minister of justice, stroll in Ottawa in 1981.

First bid for party leadership. In February 1984, Trudeau announced he would resign as leader of the Liberal Party. Chrétien announced his candidacy for leadership of the party in March. He ran against six others, including John N. Turner, a former finance minister.

Although Chrétien and Turner ran a close race, Turner won the leadership at a convention in June. Chrétien placed a strong second. Turner succeeded Trudeau as prime minister and appointed Chrétien deputy prime minister and secretary of state for external affairs. But in a general election in September, Brian Mulroney led the Progressive Conservatives to a landslide victory over the Liberals. After the election, Chrétien wrote a best-selling autobiography, *Straight from the Heart* (1985).

Resignation from Parliament. In February 1986, a dispute arose between Chrétien and Turner over the leadership of the Liberal Party in Quebec. Chrétien supported Francis Fox, a former minister of communications. Turner, however, favored another candidate and persuaded Fox to withdraw from the race. Chrétien felt Turner had betrayed him by failing to consult him in the matter. He angrily accused Turner of interfering in the election and working to keep experienced Liberals out of the party organization in Quebec. In late February, Chrétien resigned from the House of Commons. He then worked for the law firm of Lang, Michener, Lawrence, and Shaw in Ottawa and for Gordon Capital Corporation, an investment firm in Montreal.

Election as party leader. The Progressive Conservatives again won a majority of seats in the House of Commons in a general election in 1988. In 1990, Turner resigned as Liberal Party leader. Chrétien then ran against four other candidates to replace Turner as party leader.

Debate about the Meech Lake accord overshadowed Chrétien's campaign. The Meech Lake accord was an agreement between Mulroney and the 10 provincial premiers to amend the 1982 constitution. The proposed amendment would have recognized the province of Quebec as a distinct society in Canada. It also would have given provincial governments the power to veto future amendments. Chrétien had criticized the accord before he became a candidate, claiming it weakened the federal government. But during his campaign, he avoided speaking against the plan. The accord was not ratified. But disagreement about it divided Canada and the Liberal Party and made Chrétien less popular in Quebec.

In June, Chrétien was elected head of the Liberal Party by a wide margin. He vowed to help reunify both the country and the Liberal Party. In December 1990, he won a seat in a by-election to the House of Commons from the riding of Beauséjour in New Brunswick.

In 1992, Mulroney and the provincial premiers agreed on a second plan for amending the constitution, and Chrétien supported it. Like the Meech Lake accord, this plan—called the Charlottetown accord—recognized Quebec as a distinct society in Canada. In addition, it called for replacing Canada's appointed Senate with an elected Senate, granting self-government to the native peoples of Canada, and transferring some federal powers to the provinces. In a nationwide referendum held in October 1992, Canadian voters rejected the reforms.

The 1993 election. In 1993, Mulroney resigned as prime minister and Progressive Conservative Party leader. Kim Campbell succeeded him. She called a general election for Oct. 25, 1993. In the election campaign, Chrétien led the Liberals against the Progressive Conservatives; the Bloc Québécois, led by Lucien Bouchard; the Reform Party, led by Preston Manning; and the New Democratic Party, led by Audrey M. McLaughlin.

During the campaign, Chrétien criticized the way the Progressive Conservatives had run the government. He pointed out the growth of the budget deficit under the Progressive Conservatives. Chrétien promised to reduce the federal budget deficit. He also insisted that the North American Free Trade Agreement (NAFTA) be renegotiated to get terms more favorable to Canada. The pact called for the gradual elimination of tariffs and other trade barriers among Canada, the United States, and Mexico. It had been signed by leaders of the three countries but required ratification by the national legislatures.

In the general election in October, the Liberal Party won a majority of seats in the House of Commons, and Chrétien became the prime minister on November 4. The Bloc Québécois, which favors sovereignty for Quebec, came in second. The Progressive Conservative Party came in last, winning only two seats in the Commons.

Prime minister. As prime minister, Chrétien concentrated chiefly on economic matters and national unity. Chrétien's budgets focused mainly on reducing the federal budget deficit. They included cuts in unemployment benefits and defense spending, reductions in federal spending for welfare and some other social programs, and changes in the federal pension system.

Brian Willer

Chrétien and his wife, Aline, were surrounded by supporters at the Liberal Party convention in Calgary, where Chrétien won a landslide election as leader of the party in 1990.

In January 1994, NAFTA went into effect with Chrétien's support, though he did not get the changes he had sought. But he did win agreement from the United States to continue negotiations on certain issues.

Canadian unity. The issue of Canadian unity gained worldwide attention in October 1995, when Quebec held a referendum on whether it should become independent from the rest of Canada. Chrétien was a leading opponent of Quebec independence. The separatist proposal was defeated by an extremely narrow margin.

In December 1995, Chrétien proposed several parliamentary resolutions aimed at promoting national unity. In late 1995 and early 1996, Parliament passed two resolutions. One recognized Quebec's unique language, culture, and civil law. The second granted five regions what amounted to a veto over changes in the Canadian constitution. The regions are the Atlantic Provinces, British Columbia, Ontario, the Prairie Provinces, and Quebec.

The 1997 election. With public opinion polls favoring the Liberal Party, Chrétien decided to call an early election for June 1997. During the campaign, he stressed his success in reducing the federal budget deficit. The Liberals again won the election, but with a reduced majority of seats in the Commons. Chrétien remained prime minister. The Reform Party, which strongly opposed special constitutional status for Quebec, came in second and replaced the Bloc Québécois as the official opposition. In 2000, members of the Reform Party voted to join the newly created Canadian Alliance. The new party, officially called the Canadian Reform Conservative Alliance, then became the official opposition.

The 2000 election. In 2000, Chrétien again called an early election, which was held on November 27. The Liberal Party increased its majority in the Commons, and Chrétien remained prime minister.

Resignation. In 2002, Chrétien announced he would resign as prime minister and Liberal Party leader in February 2004. During 2003, Chrétien made a number of controversial decisions. He refused to support a United States-led invasion of Iraq and ended contributions to political parties by corporations and labor unions. He also introduced legislation in favor of gay marriage and decriminalization of possession of marijuana.

In November 2003, former finance minister Paul Martin was elected leader of the Liberal Party. Chrétien then decided to step down on December 12, and Martin succeeded him as prime minister. After retiring as prime minister, Chrétien began practicing law and working as a consultant. Graham Fraser

See also **Campbell, Kim; Canada, History of; Martin, Paul; Prime minister of Canada.**

Chrétien de Troyes, *kray TYEHN duh TRWAH,* was a French poet who wrote from about 1160 to about 1190. He introduced the tales of King Arthur and the Knights of the Round Table into French literature, using legends told by Welsh and Breton *bards* (poet-singers) of his day. Chrétien wrote long verse romances of love and adventure that show the spirit of medieval chivalry, the splendor of festivals and tournaments, and the importance of courtly love. Chrétien's *Perceval,* or *The Tale of the Grail,* is the earliest known literary version of the Holy Grail legend. Chrétien's other romances include *Lancelot,* or *The Knight of the Cart; Erec and Enide; Cligès;* and *Yvain,* or *The Knight of the Lion.* Little is known of Chrétien's life. He probably wrote at the courts of Champagne and Flanders in northern France. Edmund Reiss

Christ, Jesus. See **Jesus Christ.**

Christchurch (pop. 316,227) is one of the largest cities in New Zealand and a major technology center. It lies on the east coast of the South Island. For location, see **New Zealand** (political map). Tunnels through the nearby Port Hills link the city with Lyttelton, the South Island's chief port. The Avon River winds through Christchurch. The city has many parks and gardens, and a Gothic-style Anglican cathedral stands in the central square. Christchurch's chief products include electrical and electronic goods, fertilizers, leather, and processed meat and wool. Tourism is an important industry. Railroads and an international airport serve the area. The Canterbury Association, an Anglican church group from the United Kingdom, founded Christchurch in 1850. Tim Pankhurst

Christening. See **Baptism.**

Christian IV (1577-1648) was king of Denmark from 1588 until his death on Feb. 28, 1648. His 60-year reign was the longest of any Danish king. Christian inherited a strong, wealthy nation but involved it in wars that left it weak and bankrupt. However, he became known as Denmark's greatest builder, and he encouraged the arts.

Christian was born on April 12, 1577, in Frederiksborg. He succeeded his father, Frederik II, as king. Christian sponsored the construction of many elegant buildings in Copenhagen, Denmark's capital, including the Rosenborg Palace (1606) and the Stock Exchange (1624). He also promoted music and ballet. The king licensed trading companies that helped establish Danish colonies in Africa, India, and the West Indies.

From 1625 to 1629, Danish forces helped Protestants fight Roman Catholics in Germany (see **Thirty Years' War** [The Danish period]). From 1643 to 1645, Denmark fought Sweden. These wars brought defeat and losses and drained Denmark's treasury. H. Peter Krosby

Christian IX (1818-1906) was king of Denmark from 1863 to 1906. He was the country's first ruler from the House of Glücksborg. Denmark lost about a third of its territory during his reign.

Christian IX was born on April 8, 1818, at Gottorp, near Flensburg, in what is now northern Germany. He was a descendant of Danish kings and succeeded King Frederik VII, who had no children. In 1863, under political pressure, Christian signed an act that tied the duchy of Schleswig more closely to Denmark. This led to an invasion by Prussia and Austria in 1864. They won a quick victory and took Schleswig and the duchy of Holstein.

Christian's conservative politics made him unpopular. But when, in 1901, he agreed to appoint a liberal government, his popularity increased. He died on Jan. 29, 1906. His descendants have sat on the thrones of Denmark, Norway, the United Kingdom, Greece, and Russia. Kirsten Wolf

Christian X (1870-1947) was king of Denmark from 1912 to 1947. A member of the House of Glücksborg, he became an important symbol of Danish resistance to the German occupation during World War II (1939-1945).

Christian X was born on Sept. 26, 1870, at Charlottenlund, near Copenhagen. He succeeded his father, Frederik VIII, to the throne. During Christian's reign, the Danish government passed social security laws and many other reforms. In 1915, he signed a new constitution that ended special rights for the upper classes in Denmark.

The German army invaded Denmark in 1940. The Danish forces quickly surrendered, but Christian remained on the throne. He inspired the Danish people by riding his horse through Copenhagen daily. From 1943 to 1945, the Germans held him captive in Sorgenfri Palace near Copenhagen. He died on April 20, 1947. Kirsten Wolf

Christian, Charlie (1916?-1942), an American musician, established the guitar as a solo instrument in jazz. Before Christian, jazz guitarists usually limited themselves to rhythmic chord backgrounds or accompaniments in rhythm sections. Christian's playing freed them from these limitations and paved the way for later generations of solo guitarists.

Charles Christian was born in Dallas and grew up in Oklahoma City, Oklahoma. In 1939, a New York talent scout and jazz enthusiast named John Hammond arranged for Christian to audition for the Benny Goodman band. Goodman hired Christian and featured him on weekly broadcasts and recordings. Christian also played with such jazz experimenters as trumpeter Dizzy Gillespie and pianist Thelonious Monk. Christian died of tuberculosis on March 2, 1942. Eddie Cook

See also **Jazz** (picture: Benny Goodman).

Christian Coalition is a conservative political organization in the United States devoted to preserving what it considers traditional values in American life. It seeks to elect public officials who agree with its philosophy.

Most members of the Christian Coalition are Protestants, but the organization is open to all faiths. In politics, the coalition promotes conservative candidates, usually Republicans. Partly due to the Christian Coalition's help in the 1994 national elections, Republicans won control of both houses of Congress for the first time in 40 years.

In 1995, the Christian Coalition issued a social program called the Contract with the American Family and urged its adoption by Congress. The program's goals included laws to restrict abortion and pornography, and to allow voluntary prayer at such public places as courthouse lawns and public high school graduation ceremonies. The program also called for the use of government funds to help parents who choose to send their children to parochial or other private schools. It favored an end to the government's financial aid to the arts and public broadcasting.

The Christian Coalition was founded in 1989 by Pat Robertson, an evangelical Protestant religious broadcaster. Later that year, Robertson named Ralph Reed to head the organization as executive director. Reed did much to build up the organization. He resigned in 1997. Robertson headed the organization again from 1999 to 2001. The Christian Coalition has headquarters in Chesapeake, Virginia. Carl L. Davis

Christian Endeavor International is a ministry that assists local churches in reaching young people with the gospel of Jesus Christ. The goal of the organization is disciplining young people in the Christian faith and equipping them for Christian ministry and service in their churches and community and in the world. Christian Endeavor International also produces materials for program enrichment and conducts seminars, conferences, and conventions.

Francis E. Clark began the movement in 1881 in Portland, Maine. In 1991, it became Christian Endeavor International. Headquarters are in Mount Vernon, Ohio.

Critically reviewed by Christian Endeavor International

Christian Era is the period from the birth of Jesus Christ to the present. During the A.D. 500's, the monk Dionysius Exiguus introduced the present custom of reckoning time by counting the years from the birth of Christ. This method was in use in Christian countries by about 1400. James Jespersen

See also **B.C.; A.D.**

Christian Reformed Church was founded in 1857 in the United States by a group of Dutch Protestants. They broke away from the Dutch Reformed Church (now the Reformed Church in America) but continued to follow the teachings of John Calvin. The Christian Reformed Church adopted its name in 1894. Headquarters are in Grand Rapids, Michigan.

Critically reviewed by the Christian Reformed Church

Christian Scientists are members of a religious movement that stresses spiritual healing. Mary Baker Eddy, a New England woman, founded the Christian Science movement in the 1800's. The religion has deep roots in Protestant Christianity. It is "designed to commemorate the word and works of our Master, which should reinstate primitive Christianity and its lost element of healing." See **Eddy, Mary Baker**.

The central institution of Christian Science is The First Church of Christ, Scientist, in Boston. Eddy and a group of followers founded it in 1879. After a reorganization in 1892, it became known as the *Mother Church.* There are about 2,000 branch churches worldwide.

Beliefs. Eddy's principal book, *Science and Health with Key to the Scriptures* (1875), contains the full statement of Christian Science beliefs. Church members study this book and the Bible every day. *Lesson-sermons* compiled from these two books are the chief feature of Sunday worship at all churches.

Christian Science is based on the teaching that God is wholly good and all-powerful, the basis of all true being. In this teaching, *reality* refers to everything derived from God, eternal and spiritual. Whatever is unlike God—including evil, sickness, and injustice—reflects a distorted human sense of reality that has no true foundation. Through prayer and by learning more about God, people can begin to see and increasingly experience the divine reality, not just as a future hope but as a present spiritual power in their lives.

Christian Scientists view healing as an awakening to this reality. To understand truth means not to ignore evil and sickness, but to wipe them out through prayer and spiritual understanding. They teach that this message is essentially the message of Jesus. No church *dogma* (belief) or penalty enforces reliance on prayer for healing, but it is a natural part of their way of life.

Organization. The Church of Christ, Scientist, took its final form in 1892. The church has no clergy. Services are conducted by members elected to serve as *readers.* The church is administered by the Board of The Mother Church in Boston. Local churches govern themselves democratically. There are about 2,750 *practitioners,* who devote their full time professionally to healing.

The church maintains reading rooms in many cities and provides printed materials about the religion in many public places. A publishing society in Boston supervises the publications printing Christian Science teachings. The monthly *Christian Science Journal* provides a directory of local churches and practitioners. The *Journal*, the weekly *Christian Science Sentinel*, and the monthly *Herald of Christian Science* contain accounts of Christian Science healing. *The Christian Science Quarterly* contains citations from the Bible and the religion's textbook for Sunday services and daily study. In 1908, Eddy founded *The Christian Science Monitor.* This famous daily newspaper is published in Boston.

Critically reviewed by the Christian Scientists

Additional resources

Fraser, Caroline. *God's Perfect Child: Living and Dying in the Christian Science Church.* Metropolitan Bks., 1999. A critical look at Christian Science practices.
Knee, Stuart E. *Christian Science in the Age of Mary Baker Eddy.* Greenwood, 1994.
Williams, Jean K. *The Christian Scientists.* Watts, 1997.

Christian Socialism. See **Kingsley, Charles.**

Christiania. See **Oslo.**

Christianity is the religion based on the life and teachings of Jesus Christ. Most followers of Christianity, called Christians, are members of one of three major groups—Roman Catholic, Protestant, or Eastern Orthodox. These groups have different beliefs about Jesus and His teachings. But all consider Jesus central to their religion. Most Christians believe God sent Jesus into the world as the Savior. Christianity teaches that humanity can achieve salvation through Jesus.

Jesus lived in Judea (later called Palestine), a Middle Eastern land ruled by the Romans. The Romans crucified Jesus about A.D. 30. Jesus's followers were convinced that He rose from the dead, and they soon spread Christianity to major cities throughout the Roman Empire. Today, Christians make up the largest religious group in the world. Christianity has about 2 billion followers worldwide. It is the major religion in Europe, the Western Hemisphere, and Australia. Many Christians also live in Africa and Asia.

Christianity has had an enormous influence on Western civilization, especially on art, literature, and philosophy. The teachings of Christianity have had a lasting effect on the conduct of business, government, and social relations.

Beliefs

Christians believe that there is one God, and that He created the universe and continues to care for it. The belief in one God was first taught by the Jewish religion.

Christianity teaches that God sent His Son, Jesus, into the world as His chosen servant, called the *Messiah* (*Christos* in Greek), to help people fulfill their religious duties. Christianity also teaches that after Jesus's earthly life, God's presence remained on earth in the form of the *Holy Spirit,* or *Holy Ghost.* The belief that in one God there are three Persons—the Father, the Son, and the Holy Spirit—is known as the *doctrine of the Trinity.* Roman Catholic and Eastern Orthodox Churches and many Protestant churches accept this doctrine as the central teaching of Christianity.

Some Christians regard Jesus as a great but human teacher. However, most Christians view Jesus as *God incarnate*—that is, a divine being who took on the human appearance and characteristics of a man. They believe that Jesus is the Savior who died to save humanity from sin. According to this view, Jesus's death made salvation and eternal life possible for others.

Christians gather in churches because they believe that God intended them to form special groups for worship. They also meet in churches to encourage one another to lead upright lives according to God's moral law.

Two practices important to Christian worship usually take place in churches. These practices are (1) baptism and (2) the Eucharist, also called Holy Communion or the Lord's Supper. The ceremony of baptism celebrates an individual's entrance into Christianity. The Eucharist represents the Last Supper, the final meal that Jesus shared with His disciples. Worshipers share bread and wine in the Eucharist as a sign of their unity with each other and with Jesus.

Christians see Jesus as continuous with the God of Judaism. A collection of Christian writings was added to the Jewish scriptures known as the Old Testament, or Hebrew Bible. The Christian writings, called the New Testament, record the life and teachings of Jesus. They also describe the development of the early church and explain what faith in Jesus means. The Christian Bible includes both the Old and New Testaments. Some Christian groups also accept as part of the Bible a collection of writings called the Apocrypha.

The origin of Christianity

Jesus's ministry. Christianity originated in Jesus's ministry. During His lifetime, Jesus preached the gospel, meaning *good news,* that God was coming to Earth to

Mosaic (500's) in the Church of Saint Cosmas and Saint Damian, Rome (SCALA/Art Resource)

Jesus Christ is the central figure of Christianity. This mosaic shows Saint Peter, in white on the left, and Saint Paul, in white on the right, presenting Saints Cosmas and Damian to Jesus. Saints Felix IV and Theodore stand at the far left and far right, respectively.

be among His people in a special way. Jesus called this special way the Kingdom of God. He warned His listeners to repent their sinful ways to be ready for the approaching Kingdom of God. In urging repentance for sin, Jesus gave His own interpretation of Jewish law to show how people could obey God and achieve righteousness.

For a time, Jesus's teaching brought Him great popularity. Reports spread that He performed such miracles as healing the sick and bringing the dead back to life. Jesus's popularity caused opposition from Jewish and Roman officials. The Romans charged Jesus with treason, and they crucified Him as a criminal.

Resurrection and Pentecost. The followers of Jesus did not accept His death as His end. Jesus's followers were certain that Jesus came back from the dead. They believed that He later rose to heaven. Many stories circulated about Jesus's appearance among His disciples after His death.

Reports of the Resurrection convinced many people that Jesus was the Son of God. Some followers began to call Jesus the Messiah, the Savior of the Jewish people promised in the Old Testament. Followers of Jesus came to believe that they, too, could receive eternal life because of Jesus's Resurrection.

Jesus had chosen 12 men, known as the *apostles,* to preach the gospel after His death. About 50 days after the Crucifixion, the apostles and other followers of Jesus claimed that the Holy Spirit had entered them and given them the ability to speak foreign languages. This ability enabled them to spread Jesus's teachings to all lands. Christians date the beginning of the church to this event, which they celebrate as Pentecost.

The first Christians were Jews. Soon, many *gentiles* (non-Jews) converted to the new faith. Peter and the other apostles urged people to accept Jesus as the divine Christ who had conquered sin and death. Peter founded churches in Palestine and, according to Christian tradition, headed the church in Rome.

Paul, an early convert to Christianity, preached mainly to gentiles outside Palestine. Paul believed that human nature is basically sinful. For that reason, he felt that people are unable to repent and live according to God's law. Yet Paul believed that human nature can be changed through faith in Jesus as the Son of God and belief in His power to forgive sin. According to Paul, people can share in Jesus's life through baptism and the Eucharist. Paul's version of Christianity has survived in his *epistles* (letters) to the young Christian churches. The epistles form part of the New Testament.

At first, there were many kinds of Christian leaders, both men and women. No central authority regulated their activities. But by A.D. 100, churches began to distinguish between religious leaders, called *clergy,* and the general membership. The most important leader in every large church was a bishop who supervised other clergy. Christians relied on bishops to interpret Christian teachings and ensure correct belief.

The spread of Christianity

The early church. At first, the Roman government considered Christianity a legal Jewish sect. However, beginning in A.D. 64, and continuing for the next 250 years, various Roman emperors persecuted the followers of Christianity. Rather than weakening the young religion, persecution strengthened it. Persecution gave believers of Christianity an opportunity to prove their faith by dying for it.

The Roman Emperor Constantine the Great gave Christians freedom of worship in 313. He called the first *ecumenical* (general) church council in 325 to make doctrine uniform throughout the empire. The council adopted a statement known as the Nicene Creed, which said that Jesus Christ was of the same substance as God. The council condemned *Arianism,* a belief that Jesus was not completely divine.

By 392, Christianity had become the official religion of the Roman Empire. The church then grew more involved in worldly affairs. In protest, some believers adopted a way of life known as *monasticism.* They withdrew from everyday life to concentrate on prayer and meditation. During the 500's, Saint Benedict of Nursia established monasteries where monks and nuns lived in separate communities. He also set down rules for the monastic way of life. For 500 years, most monastics in Europe belonged to the Benedictine religious order. The Benedictines helped spread Christianity throughout western Europe.

The Roman Empire became the West and East Roman empires in 395. The last West Roman emperor fell from power in 476. German chieftains carved up the West Roman Empire. The East Roman Empire survived as the Byzantine Empire until 1453, when Ottoman Turks claimed its capital, Constantinople (now Istanbul). Christianity also had a Western and an Eastern church. The center of the Western church was in Rome. The center of the Eastern church was in Constantinople. The most powerful church leaders were the bishop of Rome, called the

Detail of a fresco by Giotto di Bondone in the Church of Saint Francis, Assisi, Italy (SCALA/Art Resource)

Saint Francis of Assisi established the influential Franciscan religious order during the Middle Ages. In this fresco, Francis and his followers kneel before Pope Innocent III.

pope, in the West and the patriarch of Constantinople in the East.

The Middle Ages began after the fall of the West Roman Empire and continued for about 1,000 years. During the Middle Ages, Christianity replaced the Roman Empire as the unifying force in western Europe.

After the fall of the West Roman Empire, the pope had more authority than any other person in Europe. The most influential early pope was Gregory the Great, whose reign began in 590. Gregory sent missionaries to convert the people of England. He also established rules of conduct for the clergy.

The pope exercised political as well as spiritual authority. In 800, Pope Leo III crowned the Frankish ruler Charlemagne emperor of the Romans. Charlemagne had united much of western Europe. He wanted to restore the stability of Roman rule in an empire built on the Christian faith. Charlemagne's empire declined after his death in 814. But Leo III had established the pope's right to make an emperor's authority lawful.

After Charlemagne, disputes arose over the distribution of power between the church and the state. Many kings and nobles insisted on the right to appoint church officials. The desire for an independent clergy led Pope Nicholas II to establish the Sacred College of Cardinals in 1059. The college assumed responsibility for electing a pope. In 1075, Pope Gregory VII announced that the pope would appoint clergy free from outside interference. He also outlawed *simony,* the practice of buying and selling church posts.

Medieval religious scholars called *scholastics* expanded Christian doctrine into a complete body of thought that included science and philosophy. The scholastics wished to reach a better understanding of Christian faith through reason. Saint Anselm, an early scholastic, attempted to prove God's existence through logic. In the 1200's, Saint Thomas Aquinas produced the most important scholastic work, the *Summa Theologica.* In it, he brought Christian doctrine into harmony with the teachings of the ancient Greek philosopher Aristotle.

Monasteries were centers of learning throughout the Middle Ages. In the 1200's, members of new religious orders, called *friars,* began to work among the people. Franciscan friars followed the selfless example of Saint Francis of Assisi, who founded their order in 1209. Franciscans were noted for their loving service to others. The Dominican order, which was founded in 1216 by Saint Dominic, became noted for its scholarship.

In the Middle Ages, Christian armies tried to recapture Palestine, which had been conquered by Muslim Turks. These military expeditions, known as *Crusades,* began just before 1100 and ended in the late 1200's. The crusaders failed to hold the Holy Land. But their contact with the East greatly influenced European culture.

The division of the church

The split between East and West. The two centers of Christianity—Rome and Constantinople—drifted further apart during the early Middle Ages. Eastern Christians enjoyed political stability, and they tolerated a wide range of religious discussion. Western believers supported many different kingdoms, but they insisted on complete agreement over doctrine. Disagreements over the pope's authority in the East produced a *schism* (split) in 1054 between the Eastern Orthodox Churches and the Roman Catholic Church. The schism still exists today. However, some Eastern churches eventually reunited with the Roman Catholic Church, forming what are now called the Eastern Catholic Churches. See **Eastern Catholic Churches.**

Decline of papal authority. In 1309, a French pope moved the *papacy* (office of the pope) from Rome to Avignon in what is now France. The papacy remained in Avignon until 1377. French kings and nobles exerted influence on the papacy and greatly reduced its prestige. This decline in the institution of the papacy made many members of the clergy impatient for reform.

In 1378, a disagreement among the cardinals resulted in the election of two rival popes. For a time, three men opposed one another as the rightful pope. Finally in 1417, the Council of Constance elected a pope who was accepted by all the rival groups.

The Reformation. The desire to reform Christianity grew stronger during the 1500's. In 1517, a movement called the Reformation began when Martin Luther, a German monk, criticized certain church practices. The Reformation divided Western Christianity into the Roman Catholic Church and Protestantism.

Luther disagreed with church teaching about the role of human effort in salvation. Appealing to the theology of Saint Paul, Luther emphasized solely God's role in salvation. Luther's position contrasted with Roman Catholic views that humanity must freely cooperate with God's grace. According to Luther, the Bible alone and not traditional church doctrine should guide Christians. The Lutheran movement based on his teachings spread rapidly through northern Germany and the Scandinavian countries during the 1520's.

The teachings of John Calvin, a French Protestant thinker, greatly influenced the Reformation in Switzerland, England, Scotland, France, and the Netherlands. Calvin agreed with Luther about salvation through faith. But Calvin was more interested in how Christianity could reform society. Calvin urged Christians to live in communities according to the divine law expressed in the Bible.

In England during the 1530's, King Henry VIII influenced Parliament to end the pope's authority in England and recognize the king as the supreme head of the Church in England. But Calvinists in England wanted further reform. Their disputes with the Church of England led to the formation of the Presbyterian and Congregationalist churches in the 1600's.

Some smaller, more radical religious groups claimed that the Lutherans and Calvinists had not gone far enough in reforming Christianity. Some of these groups, including the Baptists, Quakers, and Mennonites, developed their own forms of worship.

The Counter Reformation. Some Christians wanted to reform the Roman Catholic Church without leaving it. To renew Catholic worship, the pope and other Catholic bishops called the Council of Trent, which met at various times from 1545 to 1563. Many decrees issued by the council deliberately opposed Protestant viewpoints. For this reason, the movement for reform within the church has been called the Counter Reformation. It is also known as the Catholic Reformation. The council emphasized church tradition as having equal authority with the Bible. The bishops at the council also stressed the role of human effort in achieving salvation.

A leading force in the Counter Reformation was the Society of Jesus, or Jesuit order, founded by Saint Ignatius Loyola in 1534. The Jesuits quickly restored religious zeal among believers in southern Europe. Jesuit missionaries helped spread Roman Catholicism to many peoples throughout the world.

The 1700's and 1800's

The spread of Protestantism contributed to a series of religious wars between Catholics and Protestants that ended in 1648. Christianity faced many challenges in the periods that followed, even though conflicts among Christians lessened.

Rationalism and pietism were two viewpoints that reduced religious controversy during the 1700's. Rationalism was the belief in an orderly universe that could be explained by human reason, especially by scientific principles. Rationalist thinkers urged religious people of all beliefs to agree on certain basic ideas. These ideas included the existence of a purposeful God or maker of the world, the existence of the soul, and the certainty of rewards and punishment in a life after death. Rationalists thought that disputes over belief involved matters of opinion rather than reasoned truths. But they came into conflict with many Christians because they rejected the Bible and church tradition as sources of truth.

Pietism avoided controversy in another way. Rather than appealing to reason, it emphasized the strong emotional power of personal religious experience. The pietists believed such experience was more important than intellectual formulas. They considered a private relationship with God more important than doctrinal precision or correct forms of worship. The most important figure in the pietist movement was John Wesley, an English clergyman. Wesley's followers, called *Methodists,* separated from the Church of England in the late 1700's.

The rise of nationalism during the 1800's weakened the influence of Christianity, especially the Roman Catholic Church. After the French Revolution began in 1789, the forces of nationalism and democracy swept across Europe. New governments tended to separate the powers of church and state. Nationalist movements questioned the supreme authority of the pope.

In the mid-1800's, Pope Pius IX took steps to uphold the authority of the Roman Catholic Church. The *Syllabus of Errors* issued by Pius in 1864 condemned republican government, rationalism, and other ideas that threatened the power and authority of the church. In 1869, Pius assembled Vatican Council I. It produced the most controversial act of his reign—the declaration of *papal infallibility.* According to this declaration, the pope cannot be in error when he speaks as head of the church on matters of faith or morals.

Science also challenged Christian belief. The evolutionary theory of biological development proposed by the British naturalist Charles Darwin conflicted with the Biblical version of creation.

Christianity today

Science and technology have changed the modern world and have created some new problems while solving old ones. Many people question whether religion can meet human needs in today's world of technology. In response, many Christians try to deal with basic issues of human welfare, and Christian leaders speak out on such issues as world peace and human rights. Some Christians seek a more emotional form of religious worship and turn to *charismatic Christianity* and other movements that stress a personal response to Jesus.

A search for unity, known as the *ecumenical movement,* became a major concern of Christians during the 1900's. Protestants began meeting to explore closer cooperation in 1910. Protestant leaders formed the World Council of Churches in 1948. This organization works to reduce differences on doctrine and to promote Christian unity. Today, the World Council of Churches also represents Eastern Orthodox Churches. The Roman Catholic Church expressed its support for the ecumenical movement at Vatican Council II, which met from 1962 to 1965. Henry Warner Bowden

Related articles in *World Book.* See the separate articles **Jesus Christ; Bible; Roman Catholic Church; Protestantism;** and **Eastern Orthodox Churches** and their lists of *Related articles.* See also the following articles:

Church
Cross
Crusades
Education (Christian education in the Middle Ages)
Monasticism
Religion
Religious life

Additional resources

Chadwick, Henry, and Evans, G. R., eds. *Atlas of the Christian Church.* Facts on File, 1987.
Cooper, Jean C., ed. *Dictionary of Christianity.* Fitzroy Dearborn, 1996.
McManners, John, ed. *The Oxford Illustrated History of Christianity.* Oxford, 1990.
Mursell, Gordon, ed. *The Story of Christian Spirituality.* Fortress, 2001.
Olson, Roger E. *The Story of Christian Theology.* InterVarsity, 1999.
Penney, Sue. *Christianity.* Raintree Steck-Vaughn, 1997. Younger readers.

Christie, Agatha (1890-1976), was an English writer of detective stories noted for their clever plots. She introduced the Belgian private investigator Hercule Poirot in her first detective novel, *The Mysterious Affair at Styles* (1920). Poirot is also featured in her most famous detective novel, *The Murder of Roger Ackroyd* (1926), and in many later novels. Miss Marple, an elderly Englishwoman, is in many stories, including *The Murder at the Vicarage* (1930) and *Nemesis* (1971). Tommy and Tuppence Beresford are the amateur detectives in several of Christie's novels, including *N or M?* (1941) and *By the Pricking of My Thumbs* (1968).

Christie's mystery and detective fiction consists of 67 novels and almost 150 short stories. She also wrote 16 plays. Her best-known plays include the suspense dramas *The Mousetrap* (1952) and *Witness for the Prosecution* (1953). She wrote six novels under the name Mary Westmacott and *An Autobiography* (published in 1977, after her death).

Christie was born Agatha Mary Clarissa Miller on Sept. 15, 1890, in Torquay (now part of Torbay), Devon. Queen Elizabeth II made her a Dame Commander in the Order of the British Empire in 1971, and she became known as Dame Agatha Christie. David Geherin

WORLD BOOK photo by Dan Miller

A Nativity scene, also called a *crèche,* shows figures of Mary and Joseph praying over the Christ child. The wise men, shepherds, and various animals surround the Holy Family.

Christmas

Christmas is a Christian holiday that celebrates the birth of Jesus Christ. No one knows the exact date of Christ's birth, but most Christians observe Christmas on December 25. On this day, many go to church, where they take part in special religious services. During the Christmas season, they also exchange gifts and decorate their homes with holly, mistletoe, and Christmas trees. The word *Christmas* comes from *Cristes maesse,* an early English phrase that means *Mass of Christ.*

The story of Christmas comes chiefly from the Gospels of Saint Luke and Saint Matthew in the New Testament. According to Luke, an angel appeared to shepherds outside the town of Bethlehem and told them of Jesus' birth. Matthew tells how the wise men, called *Magi,* followed a bright star that led them to Jesus.

The first mention of December 25 as the birth date of Jesus occurred in A.D. 336 in an early Roman calendar. The celebration of this day as Jesus' birth date was probably influenced by *pagan* (unchristian) festivals held at that time. The ancient Romans held year-end celebrations to honor Saturn, their harvest god; and Mithras, the god of light. Various peoples in northern Europe held festivals in mid-December to celebrate the end of the harvest season. As part of all these celebrations, the people prepared special foods, decorated their homes with greenery, and joined in singing and gift giving. These customs gradually became part of the Christmas celebration.

Robert J. Myers, the contributor of this article, is coeditor of American Christmas *and the author of* Celebrations: The Complete Book of American Holidays.

In the late 300's, Christianity became the official religion of the Roman Empire. By 1100, Christmas had become the most important religious festival in Europe, and Saint Nicholas was a symbol of gift giving in many European countries. During the 1400's and 1500's, many artists painted scenes of the *Nativity,* the birth of Jesus. An example of these works appears in the **Jesus Christ** article.

The popularity of Christmas grew until the Reformation, a religious movement of the 1500's. This movement gave birth to Protestantism. During the Reformation, many Christians began to consider Christmas a pagan celebration because it included nonreligious customs. During the 1600's, because of these feelings, Christmas was outlawed in England and in parts of the English colonies in America. The old customs of feasting and decorating, however, soon reappeared and blended with the more Christian aspects of the celebration.

In the 1800's, two more Christmas customs became popular—decorating Christmas trees and sending Christmas cards to relatives and friends. Many well-known Christmas carols, including "Silent Night" and "Hark! The Herald Angels Sing," were composed during this period. In the United States and other countries, Santa Claus replaced Saint Nicholas as the symbol of gift giving.

The celebration of Christmas became increasingly important to many kinds of businesses during the 1900's.

Today, companies manufacture Christmas ornaments, lights, and other decorations throughout the year. Other firms grow Christmas trees, holly, and mistletoe. Many stores and other businesses hire extra workers during the Christmas season to handle the increase in sales.

The word *Xmas* is sometimes used instead of Christmas. This tradition began in the early Christian church. In Greek, *X* is the first letter of Christ's name. It was frequently used as a holy symbol.

Christmas around the world

Christmas is the happiest and busiest time of the year for millions of Christians throughout the world. People of different countries celebrate the holiday in various ways, depending on national and local customs.

In the United States and Canada, people decorate their homes with Christmas trees, wreaths, and ornaments. City streets sparkle with colored lights, and the sound of bells and Christmas carols fills the air.

During the weeks before Christmas, children write letters to Santa Claus and tell him what presents they would like to receive. Many department stores hire people to wear a Santa Claus costume and listen to children's requests. People share holiday greetings by sending Christmas cards to relatives and friends. Many companies give presents to their employees.

A Christmas tree is the main attraction in most homes. Relatives and friends may join in trimming the tree with lights, tinsel, and colorful ornaments. Presents are placed under the tree. Many young children believe the presents are brought by Santa Claus, who arrives on Christmas Eve in a sleigh pulled by reindeer. Some youngsters hang up stockings so Santa can fill them with candy, fruit, and other small gifts. Families open their presents on Christmas Eve or Christmas morning.

In many parts of the United States and Canada, groups of carolers walk from house to house and sing Christmas songs. Some people give the singers money or small gifts or invite them in for a warm drink.

Many people attend church services on Christmas Eve or Christmas morning. Churches are decorated with evergreen branches, red poinsettias, and scenes of the Nativity. Churchgoers listen to readings from the Bible and join in singing Christmas carols.

A traditional Christmas dinner includes stuffed turkey, mashed potatoes, cranberry sauce, and a variety of other dishes. Some families have ham or roast goose instead of turkey. Favorite desserts include mince pie or pumpkin pie, plum pudding, and fruitcake. Eggnog is a popular Christmas beverage in many homes.

In some parts of the United States and Canada, various ethnic groups observe Christmas customs of their ancestors. For example, Spanish traditions are popular in the Southwestern United States. Many families in the province of Quebec follow French customs. Some black Americans combine Christmas with *Kwanzaa,* an African American holiday. Kwanzaa lasts seven days, from December 26 through January 1. Each day, families light a candle symbolizing one of seven principles, including creativity, faith, and unity. See **Kwanzaa**.

"Merry Christmas" around the world

Country	Greeting
China	**Sheng Dan Kuai Le**
Denmark	**Glaedelig Jul**
Finland	**Hauskaa Joulua**
France	**Joyeux Noël**
Germany and Austria	**Fröhliche Weihnachten**
Greece	**Kala Christougenna**
Hungary	**Kellemes Karácsonyi Ünnepeket**
Italy	**Buon Natale**
Japan	**Meri Kurisumasu**
Netherlands	**Zalig Kerstfeest**
Norway	**Gledelig Jul**
Poland	**Wesolych Swiat**
Portugal and Brazil	**Boas Festas**
Russia	**'S Rozhdestvom Khristovym**
Spain, Mexico, and other Spanish-speaking countries	**Feliz Navidad**
Sweden	**God Jul**
United States, Canada, and other English-speaking countries	**Merry Christmas**

Owen Franken, Stock, Boston

The Christmas parade in many U.S. communities includes hundreds of colorful floats. The highlight of the parade is the float featuring Santa Claus in his sleigh pulled by reindeer.

Ted Spiegel, Black Star

Outdoor decorations brighten many public buildings during the Christmas season. This picture shows strings of lights on the British Columbia Parliament buildings in Victoria, Canada.

© Susan McCartney

Christmas carolers provide holiday entertainment in many public places. An English choir, dressed in clothing of the 1800's, sings carols near Tower Bridge in London, *shown here.*

In England, Ireland, Scotland, and Wales. Many Christmas customs that are popular in the United States and Canada originated in England, Ireland, Scotland, and Wales. These customs include sending Christmas cards and hanging a sprig of mistletoe in a room or hallway. According to tradition, a person may kiss anyone standing under the mistletoe. On Christmas Eve, children hang up stockings for *Father Christmas,* the British version of Santa Claus, to fill with presents. On the afternoon of Christmas Day, most British families watch their monarch give a special Christmas message on television. In England, dinner on Christmas Day features roast turkey and dessert of mince pie and plum pudding.

During the days before Christmas, children or groups of adults go from house to house singing Christmas carols. Children ask for money for themselves, but adults usually ask for money for charity. This tradition began many years ago, when visitors sang carols in return for a drink from the *wassail bowl.* The bowl contained hot punch made from ale, apples, eggs, sugar, and spices. The word *wassail* comes from *Was haile,* an old Saxon greeting that means *Be healthy.* Today, English people at large parties still drink punch, but it is usually made from wine and other alcoholic beverages, fruit, and spices.

In Ireland, people put a lighted candle in their window on Christmas Eve as a sign of welcome to Mary and Joseph. In Wales, people have caroling contests during the weeks before Christmas. Roast turkey is the main course for dinner. People in Scotland also have roast turkey and exchange small gifts. Some Scottish families decorate a Christmas tree and sing carols, but most hold their main celebrations on New Year's Day.

In France, children put their shoes in front of the fireplace so *Père Noël* (Father Christmas) can fill them with gifts. Many families attend midnight Mass and then have a festive supper called *Le réveillon.* Large numbers of French families also decorate their homes with small Nativity scenes. In these scenes, clay figures called *santons* (little saints) portray the story of Jesus' birth. Some people put additional santons in their Nativity scenes every year. They buy these figures at special holiday fairs that are held before Christmas.

In Germany, Saint Nicholas visits children's homes on St. Nicholas Eve, December 5, and delivers candy and other sweets to be opened on December 6, St. Nicholas Day. According to one tradition, the *Christkind* (Christ child) sends the gifts on Christmas Eve. This tradition is most popular in the mainly Roman Catholic region of southern Germany. In the northern, mainly Protestant areas, parents usually say the *Weihnachtsmann* (Christmas Man) brings the gifts.

Most German families have a Christmas tree that they decorate with lights, tinsel, and ornaments. Spicy cakes called *lebkuchen* are made in various shapes and used as decorations.

© Gaston Malherbe from Louis Mercier

Christmas fairs in France feature a variety of holiday gifts and decorations. The most popular are handmade clay figures called *santons* (little saints), such as those shown in this photograph. The French use santons in Nativity scenes.

Betty Crowell, Atoz Images

Mummers act out Christmas plays in parades and festivals. These Austrian mummers wear masks to frighten evil spirits.

Netherlands Information Service

Saint Nicholas, accompanied by his servant *Swarte Piet* (Black Pete) and other attendants, arrives in the Netherlands by boat from Spain, *shown here.* According to legend, Saint Nicholas brings gifts to children on the eve of December 6.

Fred Ward, Black Star

On St. Lucia Day, December 13, Swedish girls carry lighted candles and bring coffee and buns to their families.

In Spain, people dance and sing in the streets after midnight Mass on Christmas Eve. Most Spanish homes and churches display a miniature Nativity scene called a *Nacimiento.* During the evening of January 5, children put their shoes on a balcony or near a window. The next day is Epiphany, the last day of the Christmas season. It celebrates the visit of the Magi to the infant Jesus. According to legend, the Wise Men arrive during the night before Epiphany and fill the children's shoes with small gifts. See **Epiphany**.

In the Netherlands, Belgium, and Luxembourg, according to legend, Saint Nicholas gives presents to children on St. Nicholas Eve, December 5, which they open on December 6, St. Nicholas Day. Wearing a red robe, he arrives on a boat from Spain and rides down the streets on a white horse. His servant, *Swarte Piet* (Black Pete), accompanies him. Saint Nicholas goes down the chimney of each house and leaves gifts in shoes that the children have put by the fireplace.

In Italy, most homes and churches have a *presepio* (Nativity scene). On Christmas Eve, the family prays while the mother places a figure of the *Bambino* (Christ child) in the manger. Many Italians serve eels for dinner on Christmas Eve. They also bake a Christmas bread called *panettone,* which contains raisins and candied fruit. Italian children receive gifts from *La Befana,* a kindly old witch, on the eve of Epiphany.

In Poland, people attend *Pasterka* (Shepherd's Mass) at midnight on Christmas Eve. Many Polish families follow the Christmas tradition of breaking an *opłatek,* a thin wafer made of wheat flour and water. Nativity scenes are stamped on the opłatek. The head of the family holds the wafer, and each person breaks off a small piece and eats it. The Christmas Eve meal features fish, sauerkraut, potato pancakes, and beet soup.

In Denmark, Norway, and Sweden, Christmas dinner includes rice pudding, called *julgröt,* which has an almond in it. According to tradition, whoever gets the almond will have good luck throughout the new year.

Santa Claus is a familiar figure in the Scandinavian countries. But many children there believe that a lively elf brings them gifts from Santa on Christmas Eve. The Danes and Norwegians call this elf *Julenissen,* and the Swedes refer to him as *Jultomten.*

The Christmas season in Sweden begins on St. Lucia Day, December 13. In the morning of this day, the oldest daughter in the home dresses in white and wears a wreath with seven lighted candles on her head. She

Fritz Prenzel

Christmas comes in summer in Australia and New Zealand. Many people there go to the beach on Christmas Day. These children are chatting with Santa Claus in Sydney, Australia.

A Mexican tradition at Christmastime is breaking the piñata. A piñata is a paper or clay figure filled with candy and small gifts. It is hung from the ceiling, and the children take turns trying to break it with a stick while blindfolded. The piñata can be raised and lowered, which makes the task more difficult.

© Michael A. Vaccaro from Louis Mercier

serves the other members of the family coffee and buns in bed.

A popular Christmas custom in Norway is *ringe in Julen* (ringing in Christmas). Throughout the country, people ring church bells at 5 p.m. on Christmas Eve. In Denmark, people decorate their Christmas tree with small paper cones filled with candy. Children are not allowed to see the tree until Christmas Eve.

In Australia and New Zealand, December comes during the summer. Many people celebrate Christmas by going on a picnic or to the beach. Schoolchildren have a six-week summer vacation at Christmastime. Caroling takes place in many cities and towns. Popular Christmas foods include turkey and plum pudding. Both Father Christmas and Santa Claus are popular symbols of gift giving in Australia and New Zealand.

In Latin America. The nine days before Christmas have special importance in Mexico. These days are called *posadas,* which means *inns* or *lodgings.* On each day, Mexicans reenact Mary and Joseph's search for lodgings on the first Christmas Eve. Two children carrying figures of Mary and Joseph lead a procession of people to a particular house. The people knock on the door and ask for lodgings. They are refused at first but finally are admitted.

After each posada ceremony, Mexicans feast and celebrate. Children enjoy trying to break the *piñata,* a brightly decorated paper or clay figure containing candy and small gifts. The piñata may be shaped like an animal, an elf, a star, or some other object. It is hung from the ceiling, and the children take turns trying to hit it with a stick while blindfolded. When someone breaks the piñata, the gifts and candy fall to the floor, and the children scramble for them.

In Venezuela, people have a late supper after returning from midnight Mass on Christmas Eve. Most of these meals include *hallacas,* which are corn-meal pies stuffed with chicken, pork, beef, and spices. A favorite Christmas dish in Argentina is *niños envueltos* (wrapped children). It consists of rolled beef slices filled with seasoned mincemeat.

Children in some Latin-American countries, including Brazil, Colombia, and parts of Mexico, receive gifts on Christmas Day. In Argentina, Venezuela, Puerto Rico,

Leon V. Kofod

Japanese children sing carols while reenacting the Nativity during a Christmas play. Many Japanese also follow such Western customs as giving gifts and decorating Christmas trees.

Victor Englebert

Epiphany in Ethiopia celebrates the baptism of Jesus with a procession of priests the afternoon before the holiday. The next morning, the priests will baptize babies at a small natural pool.

WORLD BOOK photo

An Advent calendar and wreath help keep track of the four weeks before Christmas. A flap on the calendar is lifted each day, and a candle on the wreath is lit every Sunday.

and most areas of Mexico, the wise men leave the presents on the eve of Epiphany.

In Asia. Relatively small numbers of Christians live in the countries of Asia, and so Christmas is not widely celebrated there. In areas where Christmas is observed, people follow such Western customs as attending religious services, giving presents, singing carols, and decorating Christmas trees.

In Japan, Christians are a minority, yet the popular aspects of Christmas are increasingly seen. Gifts are exchanged, lights decorate business districts, and department stores often display Christmas trees. Even Santa Claus makes his appearance in the crowded stores.

In the Philippines, people attend *Misas de Gallo* (Masses of the Cock), which are celebrated early each morning the nine days before Christmas. On Christmas Eve, Filipinos parade through the streets carrying colorful star-shaped lanterns called *parols.* These lanterns are also displayed in the windows of most homes.

On Christmas Eve, Christians from throughout the world gather for midnight Mass in Bethlehem, the town near Jerusalem where Jesus was born. They kneel to kiss the silver star that is set in the ground at the spot where Jesus' birth is believed to have taken place.

In Africa, as in Asia, the celebration of Christmas is not widespread because most of the countries have a small Christian population. Missionaries brought Christmas customs to Africa and so people in the Christian communities generally follow Western traditions. However, Africans sing carols and hymns in their own languages. In Ethiopia, members of the Ethiopian Orthodox Church hold religious services on Christmas, January 7. The major celebration takes place nearly two weeks later at Epiphany.

The celebration of Christmas

Religious practices. For most Christians, the Christmas season begins on the Sunday nearest November 30. This date is the feast day of Saint Andrew, one of the 12 apostles of Christ. The nearest Sunday is the first day of *Advent,* a four-week period during which Christians prepare for Christmas. The word *advent* means *a coming* and refers to the coming of Jesus on Christmas Day.

Many Christians have an Advent wreath in their homes during the holiday season. Most of these wreaths are made of evergreen or holly branches and may lie on a table. Four candles, one for each Sunday of Advent, are placed among the branches. On the first Sunday, the family lights one candle and joins in prayer. They repeat this ceremony on each Sunday of Advent, lighting one additional candle each time. Three of the candles are purple, and the other one is pink. The pink candle is lit for the first time on the third Sunday, when people celebrate the beginning of the second half of Advent. On Christmas Day, all four candles may be replaced by four white ones, or a white candle may be added in the center. White symbolizes Jesus.

In many countries, people use special Advent calendars or Advent candles to keep track of the 24 days before Christmas. An Advent calendar has a colorful Christmas scene, and each date is printed on a flap. One flap is lifted daily to uncover a holiday picture or a Biblical verse. On an Advent candle, the dates appear in a row down the side. Each evening, the candle is lit and then burned down to the next date. By Christmas Day, the entire candle has melted.

During the Christmas season, many churches display a *crèche* (Nativity scene). It shows figures of Mary and Joseph praying over the infant Jesus in the stable. Figures of the Magi, angels, shepherds, and various animals surround the Holy Family.

WORLD BOOK photo by Dan Miller

Church services on Christmas morning are a highlight of the holiday season for millions of Christians. Many churches also hold midnight services on Christmas Eve.

For many Christians, the Christmas season reaches a climax at midnight Mass or other religious services on Christmas Eve. Churches are decorated with candles, lights, evergreen branches, and bright red poinsettias. People sing Christmas carols and listen to readings from the Gospels of Saint Luke and Saint Matthew. Priests and ministers speak to the congregations about the coming of Christ and the need for peace and understanding among all people. Most churches also hold services on Christmas Day.

The Christmas season ends on Epiphany, January 6. In Western Christian churches, Epiphany celebrates the coming of the Wise Men to the Christ child. Among Eastern Christians, this day celebrates Jesus' baptism. Epiphany falls on the 12th day after Christmas. The song "The Twelve Days of Christmas" refers to the 12 days between Christmas and Epiphany.

Gift giving. The custom of giving gifts to relatives and friends on a special day in winter probably began in ancient Rome and northern Europe. In these regions, people gave each other small presents as part of their year-end celebrations.

By 1100, Saint Nicholas had become a popular symbol of gift giving in many European countries. According to legend, he brought presents to children on the eve of his feast day, December 6. Nonreligious figures replaced Saint Nicholas in certain countries soon after the Reformation, and December 25 became the day for giving gifts.

Today, Santa Claus brings presents to children in many countries, including the United States, Canada, and Australia. A number of other countries have their own versions of Santa Claus, such as Father Christmas in the United Kingdom and Ireland, Père Noël in France, and Weihnachtsmann in Germany.

Saint Nicholas still brings presents in some countries, including the Netherlands, Austria, Belgium, and parts of Germany. Children fill shoes with straw and carrots for his horse and place them in front of the fireplace. By morning, the straw and carrots have been replaced by presents. Youngsters in many Spanish-speaking nations have a similar custom. However, they leave the food for the camels of the Wise Men and put the shoes outside a window on the eve of Epiphany. The Magi place small gifts in the shoes during the night. The custom of hanging stockings by the fireplace probably developed from those traditions.

WORLD BOOK photo by Dan Miller

A visit with Santa is a Christmas treat for children throughout the world. In many department stores, youngsters wait in line to tell Santa what presents they would like for Christmas.

In some areas of northern Germany, Saint Nicholas' assistant, *Knecht Ruprecht* (Servant Rupert), gives presents to good children. He gives whipping rods to the parents of bad ones. In Sweden, many children receive presents from the elf Jultomten, called Julenissen in Denmark and Norway.

In Italy, La Befana brings presents on the eve of Epiphany. According to legend, the Wise Men asked the kindly old witch to accompany them to see the infant Jesus. She refused, saying she was too busy and had to clean her house, and so she missed the wondrous sight. Each year, La Befana goes from house to house, leaving gifts and looking for the Christ child.

Christmas feasting. The year-end festivities of ancient European peoples included huge feasts, many of which lasted for several days. The preparation of special foods later became an important part of the Christmas celebration throughout the world.

At the first Christmas feasts, people roasted boars,

WORLD BOOK photo by Dan Miller

Opening Christmas gifts is one of the most exciting parts of the holiday celebration. Most people use colorful paper and shiny ribbons to wrap the presents they give.

pigs, and peacocks over large open fires. Today, roast turkey is the most popular main course in the United States, Canada, Australia, and New Zealand. In the United Kingdom and Ireland, people serve roast goose. Fish is the feature of Christmas Eve dinner in a number of countries. For example, Austrians eat baked carp and Norwegians dine on *lutefisk* (dried cod). Vegetables, relishes, hot breads, and a variety of other dishes accompany the main course of the Christmas feast everywhere.

Popular beverages served especially at Christmastime include eggnog in the United States and hot, spicy wassail in England. Many people in Sweden drink *glögg,* a hot punch made with spices, liquors, raisins, and nuts.

Favorite Christmas desserts in the United States include fruitcake, mince pie, and pumpkin pie. Plum pudding is traditional in Canada and the United Kingdom and Ireland. The French serve a Christmas cake called *bûche de Noël,* which looks like a miniature log. Italians finish their meal with *torrone,* a candy made of egg whites, honey, and nuts. Fruit-filled breads called *stollen* are favorites in Germany. In Mexico and other Latin American countries, thin, round pastries called *buñuelos* are usually eaten with cinnamon and sugar.

Christmas decorations. The traditional colors of Christmas are green and red. Green represents the continuance of life through the winter and the Christian belief in eternal life through Christ. Red symbolizes the blood that Jesus shed at His Crucifixion. Christmas decorations that feature these colors include the Christmas tree, the Christmas wreath, holly, and mistletoe.

The Christmas tree probably developed in part from the "Paradise Tree." This tree was an evergreen decorated with apples used in a popular play about Adam and Eve held on December 24 in medieval Germany. By 1605, some Germans decorated their homes with evergreens for Christmas. They trimmed the trees with fruits, nuts, lighted candles, and paper roses. Later decorations included painted eggshells, cookies, and candies.

The first Christmas trees in the United States were used in the early 1800's by German settlers in Pennsylvania. During the mid-1800's, the custom of trimming Christmas trees spread rapidly throughout the world. Today, some form of Christmas tree is part of every Christmas celebration. Decorations include tinsel, bright ornaments, and candy canes. A star is mounted on top of many Christmas trees and other Christmas displays. It represents the star that led the wise men to the stable in Bethlehem where Jesus was born.

WORLD BOOK photo by Dan Miller

A traditional Christmas dinner in the United States and Canada includes stuffed turkey, mashed potatoes, and various relishes. Fruitcake and mince pie are favorite desserts.

Robert H. Glaze, Artstreet

Strings of colored lights brighten millions of homes at Christmastime. Other outdoor decorations include candles, stars, wreaths, and figures of Santa Claus and carolers.

The Christmas wreath, like the evergreens used as Christmas trees, symbolizes the strength of life overcoming the forces of winter. In ancient Rome, people used decorative wreaths as a sign of victory and celebration. The custom of hanging a Christmas wreath on the front door of the home probably came from this practice.

Holly is an evergreen tree with sharply pointed, glossy leaves and red berries. It is used in making Christmas wreaths and other decorations. The needlelike points of the leaves were thought to resemble the crown of thorns that Jesus wore when He was crucified. The red berries symbolized the drops of blood He shed.

Mistletoe is an evergreen plant with dark leaves and shiny white berries. Ancient Celtic priests considered the plant sacred and gave people sprigs of it to use as charms. The custom of decorating homes with mistletoe probably came from its use as a ceremonial plant by early Europeans. In many countries, a person standing under a sprig of mistletoe may be kissed.

Christmas carols. The word *carol* came from a Greek dance called a *choraulein,* which was accompanied by flute music. The dance later spread throughout

Europe and became especially popular with the French, who replaced the flute music with singing. People originally performed carols on several occasions. By the 1600's, carols involved singing only, and Christmas had become the main holiday for these songs.

Most of the carols sung today were originally composed in the 1700's and 1800's. They include "O Little Town of Bethlehem" and "Hark! The Herald Angels Sing." The words of the famous carol "Silent Night" were written on Christmas Eve in 1818 by Joseph Mohr, an Austrian priest. Franz Gruber, the organist of Mohr's church, composed the music that same night, and the carol was sung at midnight Mass. "O Holy Night" was introduced at midnight Mass in 1847. Adolphe Adam, a French composer, wrote the music. Popular nonreligious carols include "Jingle Bells" and "White Christmas."

Christmas cards. The first Christmas card was created in 1843 by John Callcott Horsley, an English illustrator. It resembled a postcard and showed a large family enjoying a Christmas celebration. The message on the card read, "A Merry Christmas and a Happy New Year to You." About 1,000 of the cards were sold. By 1860, the custom of exchanging Christmas cards had spread throughout the United Kingdom. The first Christmas cards manufactured in the United States were made in 1875 by Louis Prang, a German-born Boston printer.

Other customs. In some countries, especially the United Kingdom, France, and the Scandinavian nations, many families burned a *Yule log* at Christmastime. The log was a large piece of a tree trunk, and people kept an unburned part of it to light the next year's log. Early Europeans believed the unburned wood had magic powers. It was thought that bad luck would follow if the Yule log fire went out. Today, these fires are confined to large public fireplaces, such as those in ski resorts.

Many people enjoy reading Christmas stories and poems during the holiday season. For example, *A Christmas Carol* (1843) by the English novelist Charles Dickens ranks as one of the most famous tales ever written. The poem "A Visit from St. Nicholas" (1823), popularly known by its first line, "'Twas the Night Before Christmas," is read aloud in many homes on Christmas Eve. Clement Moore, an American scholar, supposedly wrote this poem as a Christmas present for his children. Several musical productions are also Christmas traditions. They include *The Nutcracker,* a ballet by Peter Ilich Tchaikovsky of Russia, and *Amahl and the Night Visitors,* an opera by Gian Carlo Menotti of Italy. Robert J. Myers

Related articles in *World Book* include:

Advent
Boxing Day
Dickens, Charles (The first phase)
Holly
Jesus Christ
Mistletoe
Moore, Clement C.
Moses, Grandma (picture: Out for the Christmas Trees)
Nicholas, Saint
Santa Claus
Santa Claus (Ind.)
Twelfth Night
Yule

Outline

I. Christmas around the world
- A. In the United States and Canada
- B. In England, Ireland, Scotland, and Wales
- C. In France
- D. In Germany
- E. In Spain
- F. In the Netherlands, Belgium, and Luxembourg
- G. In Italy
- H. In Poland
- I. In Denmark, Norway, and Sweden
- J. In Australia and New Zealand
- K. In Latin America
- L. In Asia
- M. In Africa

II. The celebration of Christmas
- A. Religious practices
- B. Gift giving
- C. Christmas feasting
- D. Christmas decorations
- E. Christmas carols
- F. Christmas cards
- G. Other customs

Questions

What is the legend of *La Befana?*
Why are green and red associated with Christmas?
What does the Mexican tradition of *posadas* represent?
How did the Christmas tree probably develop?
What is a *Yule log?* An *Advent wreath?* An *Advent calendar?*
What are some special Scandinavian Christmas foods?
What does the word *Christmas* mean?
In what countries is *Boxing Day* observed?
What is *Epiphany?* When does it occur?
Why was the celebration of Christmas outlawed in the 1600's in England and in parts of the English colonies in America?

Hallmark Historical Collection

The first Christmas card, *shown here,* was created in 1843 by John Callcott Horsley, an English illustrator. It featured a drawing of a family enjoying Christmas together. Smaller drawings on the card showed people helping the needy. About 1,000 copies of Horsley's card were sold.

Additional resources

Level I

Edens, Cooper. *'Tis the Season: A Classic Illustrated Christmas Treasury.* Chronicle, 2003.
Ganeri, Anita. *The Christmas Story.* Evans Brothers, 2002.
Graham-Barber, Lynda. *Ho Ho Ho! The Complete Book of Christmas Words.* Bradbury, 1993.
Roop, Peter and Connie. *Let's Celebrate Christmas.* Millbrook, 1997.

Level II

Bowler, Gerald. *The World Encyclopedia of Christmas.* McClelland, 2000.
Christmas Around the World. World Book, 1974- . Multivolume work. One volume published per year, each featuring a different country or culture.
Crump, William D. *The Christmas Encyclopedia.* McFarland, 2001.
Walsh, Joseph J. *Were They Wise Men or Kings? The Book of Christmas Questions.* Westminster John Knox, 2001.

Christmas tree. See **Christmas** (Christmas decorations); **Fir.**

Christo (1935-), a Bulgarian-born American artist, creates huge, temporary art projects in collaboration with his wife, Jeanne-Claude. He aims to reach many people, including those not usually interested in art, and so he locates his works outdoors in or near urban centers. Christo's projects cost millions of dollars.

Some of Christo's projects involve wrapping buildings or other structures in canvas or plastic. Structures he has wrapped include the Museum of Contemporary Art in Chicago in 1968; the Pont Neuf, Paris's oldest bridge, in 1985; and the Reichstag building in Berlin in 1995. Other projects celebrate natural landscape. They often are called *wrapped art* or *environmental art.* For example, in *Surrounded Islands* (1983), he encircled 11 islands off the Florida coast with more than 6 million square feet (560,000 square meters) of floating flamingo-pink polypropylene. For a picture of *Surrounded Islands,* see **Sculpture** (Environmental sculpture).

Christo Javacheff was born on June 13, 1935, in Gabrovo, Bulgaria. He has lived in New York City since 1964.

Joseph F. Lamb

Christophe, *krees TAWF,* **Henri,** *ahn REE* (1767-1820), was a black king in northern Haiti in the early 1800's. He is one of Haiti's national heroes. Christophe was born a slave on Oct. 6, 1767, on either Grenada or St. Christopher (now St. Kitts), two Caribbean islands. In 1779, he fought for the Americans in the Revolutionary War in America. He later became a general in the French army in the French colony of Saint Domingue (now Haiti). He served under Generals Toussaint L'Ouverture and Jean-Jacques Dessalines.

Christophe fought in the Haitian Revolution, which led to the creation of the independent country of Haiti in 1804. He was named Haiti's president in 1806. But another general, Alexandre Pétion, challenged his authority. As a result, Christophe became president of northern Haiti, and Pétion became president of the south. In 1811, Christophe proclaimed himself king of northern Haiti.

Christophe was a strong and intelligent leader and became known as a great builder of forts and palaces. Under him, however, laws were passed that forced Haitian workers to continue to labor on plantations. The workers had hoped to work on their own private plots instead. They rebelled in 1820. Ill and unable to fight, Christophe shot himself to death. Patrick Bellegarde-Smith

Christopher, Saint, is the patron saint of ferry workers and travelers. It is not certain that he existed historically, but he may have been martyred about A.D. 250. Legend says he was a ferryman who carried people across a bridgeless river. One day, he carried over a child who seemed to grow heavier at each step. When they reached the shore, he remarked that one would think he had been carrying the burden of the world. To this the Christ child replied: "Thou hast borne upon thy back the world and Him who created it."

It is believed those who seek Saint Christopher's protection will not be harmed. For this reason, many people carry Saint Christopher medals.

Eastern Orthodox Churches celebrate Saint Christopher's day on May 9. Since the 1969 revision of the Roman Catholic ritual, Saint Christopher's feast no longer appears in the Roman Catholic liturgy. But he is still venerated as a saint. Stanley K. Stowers

Christopher, Warren Minor (1925-), served as United States secretary of state under President Bill Clinton from 1993 to 1997. His roles as secretary included negotiations to settle disputes between warring sides in Bosnia. Christopher had served as deputy secretary of state under President Jimmy Carter from 1977 to 1981. In that position, he acted as chief negotiator for the release of a group of Americans held hostage in Iran.

From 1967 to 1969, Christopher was deputy attorney general under President Lyndon B. Johnson. In that post, he managed federal efforts to restore order in Chicago and Detroit after riots broke out in predominantly black areas of those cities. In 1991, he headed a commission that investigated the use of force by the Los Angeles police against minorities. The investigation followed an incident in which white Los Angeles police officers beat Rodney G. King, a black motorist stopped after a pursuit. In 2000, Christopher represented Al Gore's presidential campaign as an observer to the vote recount in Florida.

Christopher was born on Oct. 27, 1925, in Scranton, North Dakota. He earned a bachelor's degree from the University of Southern California and a law degree from Stanford University. He practiced law in Los Angeles when not in government service. Andrew Bennett

Chromatography, *KROH muh TAHG ruh fee,* is a method of separating substances that make up a liquid or gaseous mixture. One use of it is to measure or identify low concentrations of substances, such as pollutants in air or water.

Chromatographic methods are based mainly on a process called adsorption. A mixture passes through a solid or liquid material that *adsorbs* (attracts to its surface) substances. This material is called an *adsorbent.* A liquid or gas added to the mixture helps move it through an adsorbent. Various substances are adsorbed at different rates of speed, so the substances in a mixture separate from one another as the mixture moves through the material. See **Absorption and adsorption.**

Common chromatographic methods are *liquid column, thin layer,* and *gas chromatography.*

Liquid column chromatography uses a *column* (tube), usually made of glass. Chemists fill the column with an adsorbent material. They then add the mixture to be separated and a liquid carrier at the top of the column. The substances move down through the column at different speeds.

Thin layer chromatography uses a *plate*—that is, a thin, flat sheet of glass or other material—coated with an adsorbent film. Chemists place a drop of the mixture on one end of the plate, then stand that end of the plate in a shallow pool of liquid. The liquid travels up the film, moving the mixture along with it. The substances separate from one another as they are adsorbed.

Gas chromatography uses a column of adsorbent material to separate gases and substances that are easily converted into gases by heating. Chemists use special equipment to inject the mixture and gaseous carrier into the column. The gas most often used to move a mixture through an adsorbent is argon. Computers play a key role in the analysis of chromatographic data, especially in gas chromatography. Computers can help tell how much of a substance is in a mixture and can help identify an unknown mixture by looking for various properties of the possible ingredients. Marvis E. Hartman

Chrome. See **Chromium**.

Chrome, *krohm,* is the name given to several combinations of chromium and lead that are used as paint pigments. These compounds produce bright green, orange, red, and yellow paints. Manufacturers limit their use of these substances because of the toxic lead content. One nontoxic pigment, not to be confused with leaded chromes, is *chrome oxide.* George J. Danker

Chromic acid, *KROH mihk,* is the common name for chromium trioxide, an important industrial compound. Its chemical formula is CrO_3. Most chromic acid is made by combining sulfuric acid with potassium dichromate. The two substances react to form dark red crystals. These crystals readily absorb water and react with other substances. Chromic acid is poisonous and *carcinogenic* (cancer-producing), and it can cause serious burns. Chromic acid is used in chrome plating, which produces a shiny protective finish for faucets and similar products. It is also used to make fungicides, fire-retardant chemicals, and industrial *catalysts* (substances that speed chemical reactions). Kenneth A. Bowman

Chromium, *KROH mee uhm,* a chemical element, is a glossy, fairly soft, gray metal. It is sometimes called *chrome.* Chromium resists corrosion, and becomes bright and shiny when polished. For these reasons, chromium is widely used to *plate* (coat) other metals, giving them a durable, shiny finish. Chromium is used to plate automobile bumpers, door handles, and trim.

Chromium hardens steel. Chromium-steel *alloys* (mixtures) are used to make armor plate for ships and tanks, safes, ball bearings, and the cutting edges of high-speed machine tools. Alloys that have over 10 percent of chromium are called *stainless steels.* Stainless steel is used to make eating utensils and kitchen equipment.

Chromium combines with other elements to form colored compounds. The word *chromium* comes from the Greek word *chroma,* meaning *color.* Traces of oxidized chromium give rubies and emeralds their characteristic red and green colors. Many chromium compounds are important in industry. Potassium dichromate ($K_2Cr_2O_7$) is used in tanning leather. Lead chromate ($PbCrO_4$) is a paint pigment called *chrome yellow.* Chromium compounds are used in the textile industry as *mordants* (substances that fix dyes permanently to fabrics).

Chromium is almost always found combined with iron and oxygen in a mineral called *chromite.* Major chromite-producing countries include Albania, South Africa, Turkey, and Zimbabwe.

Chromium has the chemical symbol Cr. Its *atomic number* (number of protons in its nucleus) is 24. Its *relative atomic mass* is 51.9961. An element's relative atomic mass equals its *mass* (amount of matter) divided by $\frac{1}{12}$ of the mass of carbon 12, the most abundant form of carbon. Chromium melts at 1900 °C and boils at 2690 °C. The density is 7.14 grams per cubic centimeter at 20 °C. Louis Nicolas Vauquelin, a French chemist, discovered a compound of chromium and oxygen in 1797. He prepared the free chromium metal in 1798. S. C. Cummings

See also **Stainless steel**.

Chromosome, *KROH muh sohm,* is a tiny, thin, threadlike structure found in cells of all organisms. Chromosomes are the carriers of *inheritance*—that is, the physical or behavioral characteristics offspring receive from parents. The passing of such characteristics is called *heredity.* The basic unit of inheritance is the *gene.* Genes are long sequences of DNA (deoxyribonucleic acid) molecules that make up most of the material in chromosomes. Proteins called *histones* bend and coil the long DNA molecules to form chromosomes.

Chromosomes come in various lengths and shapes, depending on the organism. Their characteristic shape allows scientists to identify individual chromosomes when viewed under a microscope. Every *species* (type) of organism has a certain number of chromosomes in each cell of its body. Human body cells, except for sperm or egg cells, typically have 46 chromosomes.

Chromosomes have an essential role in cell division. New cells are formed by division, so that there are two cells, often called *daughter cells,* where there once was only one cell. Before division begins, the chromosomes are duplicated. During division, each duplicated chromosome forms into a pair of rodlike structures. The new cells that are formed receive one of each pair of chromosomes. The new cells then each have a set of chromosomes exactly like those of the original cell.

For much of the time, a cell's chromosomes are partially uncoiled so that the genes can produce the various biological molecules necessary for cell function. When cells divide, the chromosomes condense into a compact state. As a result, different sections of DNA do not be-

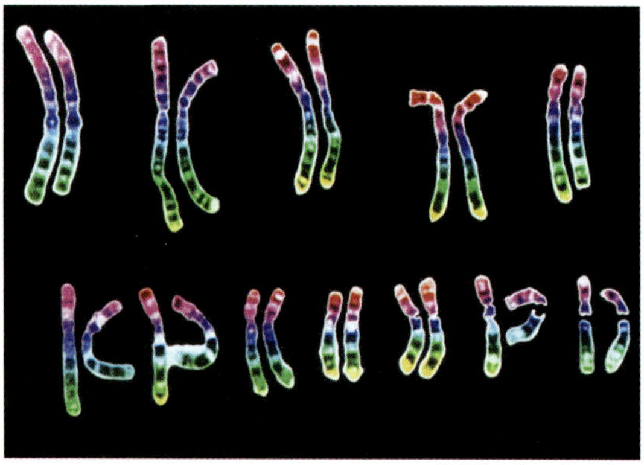

© L. Willatt, Photo Researchers

Chromosomes, made up of long strands of tightly coiled DNA, generally occur in pairs. This photograph shows 12 of the 23 pairs of chromosomes that occur in most human body cells.

come entangled as the chromosomes are split between the two daughter cells. On rare occasions, a fragment of a chromosome can break off and join to another chromosome. This process, called *rearrangement,* can cause problems in the development or proper functioning of cells. In human beings, rearranged chromosomes can cause certain diseases that can be passed on from a parent to a child. Many cancer cells also have changes in their chromosome number or structure.

Walter Flemming, a German scientist, first observed the role of chromosomes in cell division in 1882. He noticed that when salamander cells divided, the chromosomes were duplicated and divided equally into the two daughter cells. Perry B. Hackett, Jr.

See also **Cell** (Cell division); **DNA; Heredity** (Chromosomes and genes).

Chronic fatigue syndrome, also called CFS, is a disorder characterized by severe fatigue that significantly reduces a person's ability to do most normal daily activities. Rest or sleep does not relieve the fatigue. In fact, prolonged rest may actually make the condition worse. CFS affects men and women of all ages, but it occurs most often in women from 30 to 40 years of age.

Other symptoms of CFS include impaired memory or concentration, sore throat, muscle and joint pain, headache, difficulty sleeping, depression, and prolonged exhaustion following physical activity. A diagnosis of CFS requires the presence of at least four of the symptoms, in addition to severe fatigue lasting at least six months.

The cause of CFS is not known. In patients with CFS, all common laboratory tests are normal, and doctors find no other possible cause of fatigue. Symptoms often begin after a viral illness, such as flu, but researchers have not identified a disease-causing agent for CFS. Research shows that some patients have certain changes in the function of their immune system. But these changes also appear in patients with other disorders who do not have CFS. Some scientific studies suggest that people with CFS have a genetic makeup that affects the body's ability to adapt to change. There is no evidence that CFS can be transmitted from person to person.

CFS is often a long-lasting illness that may get better or worse over time. Physicians can give medicines to relieve pain, sleeping problems, and depression. Some patients have low blood pressure and get better when given drugs. Doctors recommend moderate exercise increased gradually to help patients regain former activity levels. Many patients also benefit from *cognitive behavioral therapy.* They learn to redirect their energy into physical activities within their limits and to replace depressing thoughts with cheerful ones. Nelson M. Gantz

Chronicles, Books of, are two books of the Bible that describe the history of the Jews from Adam to the 500's B.C. The books focus on the monarchies of Israel and Judah, especially the reigns of King David (I Chronicles 10-29) and King Solomon (II Chronicles 1-9). The events in the books parallel the accounts in the Biblical books from Genesis through Kings. The author of Chronicles probably drew on those books for material.

The books express the national and religious concerns of the period in which they were written. This period followed the Babylonian Exile of the 500's B.C. First Chronicles focuses on King David to reflect the hope that the community might be restored to the independence and glory it had in the days of David. Second Chronicles portrays King Solomon as the builder of the original Temple in Jerusalem to stress the importance of the Temple rebuilt there. The rebuilt Temple represented community life and the continued presence of God in His sanctuary in Jerusalem. Carol L. Meyers

See also **Bible** (Books of the Hebrew Bible); **David; Solomon.**

Chronometer, *kruh NAHM uh tuhr,* is an instrument that keeps time with extreme accuracy. Clockmakers developed it for use on ships because navigators needed an accurate clock to help determine their position at sea.

The *marine chronometer* is an accurate clock that has been specially mounted to remove the effect of a ship's motion. It is usually set to *Universal Time Coordinated* (UTC), an international time standard. To find a ship's position, a navigator notes the time and measures the positions of certain stars. The navigator compares these positions with tables that show the stars' positions at UTC, and then calculates the ship's position.

The first reliable chronometer was developed in 1735 by John Harrison, an English clockmaker. In 1776, Pierre LeRoy, a French watchmaker, built a chronometer that became the model for the modern chronometer. Today, many ships rely chiefly on radar and other electronic systems for navigation. Radio time signals and electric and atomic clocks have replaced mechanical chronometers in most other applications. James Jespersen

See also **Atomic clock; Clock** (picture: Marine chronometers); **Watch.**

Chrysalis, *KRIHS uh lihs,* is the third, or *pupal,* stage in the development of a butterfly. A *caterpillar* (butterfly larva) changes into a chrysalis after it is fully grown. It spins a small pad of silk and hangs from it by small hooks, called the *cremaster.* It then *molts,* or sheds its skin, to become the chrysalis form. Unlike many moth larvae, butterfly larvae do not form cocoons (see **Cocoon**). Adult butterfly features develop inside the chrysalis. Finally, the chrysalis skin splits open, and the butterfly emerges and spreads its moist wings to full size.

Edward S. Ross

Chrysalis

See also **Butterfly; Caterpillar; Metamorphosis; Pupa.** Charles V. Covell, Jr.

Chrysanthemum, *kruh SAN thuh muhm,* is a group of strong-scented shrubby herbs that grow in many temperate regions. Gardeners grow them for their beautiful and abundant blossoms, which usually appear in autumn. *Chrysanthemum* comes from two Greek words meaning *golden flower.* Many independent flowers make up each blossom. By careful *disbudding* (removing buds), flowers 8 inches (20 centimeters) across may be developed. Most blossoms are grown as clusters. Blossoms range from white or yellow to pink or red.

Chrysanthemums are easy to grow. They thrive in fertile, drained soil and full sunlight. Chrysanthemums grow from cuttings or root divisions. Most are perenni-

© Giuseppe Mazza

Many types of chrysanthemums have been developed. The flowers vary widely in color and they range in size from small multiple blossoms to large single blossoms.

al. In northern climates, a covering of *mulch* (straw, leaves, or loose materials) may be needed in winter.

Cultivated chrysanthemums are "short-day plants." They flower during the reduced daylight hours of autumn. Covering the plants in late afternoon will stimulate them to flower earlier in the season. Florists have learned to produce chrysanthemum flowers throughout the year by regulating the light in the greenhouse.

The chrysanthemum has been called the *flower of the East.* People in Asia have cultivated chrysanthemums for over 2,000 years. In China during the 400's, Tao Yuanming became a famous breeder of these plants. After his death, his native city was named Juxian *(City of Chrysanthemums).* Chrysanthemums also flourished in Japan. In 797, the *Mikado* (ruler of Japan) made this flower his personal emblem. He decreed that it could be used only by royalty. In October, Japan celebrates the Feast of the Chrysanthemums. W. Dennis Clark

Scientific classification. Chrysanthemums belong to the composite family, Compositae. They make up the genus *Chrysanthemum.*

See also **Flower** (picture: Garden perennials).

Chrysler, *KRYS luhr,* **Walter Percy** (1875-1940), an American automobile manufacturer, was a founder and the first president of the Chrysler Corporation (now part of DaimlerChrysler AG). Chrysler served as president of the company from 1925 to 1935, and as chairman of the board from 1935 to his death on Aug. 18, 1940.

Chrysler was born on April 2, 1875, in Wamego, Kansas. His great interest in automobiles began in 1908 when he bought his first car. He became works manager for the Buick Motor Company in 1912, and four years later became president of the company. Next, he became a vice president of General Motors Corporation, and retired as a millionaire in 1919. In 1920, Chrysler returned to business as manager of the Willys-Overland Corporation. In 1924, while president of the Maxwell Motor Corporation, he and his associates produced the six-cylinder Chrysler automobile. William L. Bailey

See also **DaimlerChrysler AG.**

Chrysostom, *KRIHS uh stuhm* or *krih SAHS tuhm,* **Saint John** (347?-407?), was one of the most beloved and celebrated of the fathers of the early Christian church. He was born at Antioch, Syria (now in Turkey). His talent in preaching earned him the title Chrysostom, which means *golden-mouthed.* In 398, John went to Constantinople as patriarch. His zeal for charity gained him the title John the Almoner, but his campaign for reform offended the Empress Eudoxia. As a result, the East Roman Emperor Arcadius banished him to Syria and then to the shores of the Black Sea for his preaching against worldliness. John's homilies on Scripture are among the best of early Christian writings. His feast day is celebrated on January 27. William J. Courtenay

Chuang Tzu. See **Zhuangzi.**

Chub is the common name of several small fishes. The *creek chub,* also called the *horned dace,* is found in streams, small rivers, and lakes from northern Florida to Canada and westward to eastern Texas, Colorado, and Montana. This chub grows up to 1 foot (30 centimeters) long, but it is usually smaller. It is blue on top and silver underneath. During the mating season, several female creek chubs lay eggs in a nest made by a male. The male then covers the eggs with small stones until they hatch. Chubs feed on small insects and sometimes on tiny fish. The *silver chub, flathead chub,* and *hornyhead chub* are also found in North America. See also **Fish** (picture: Fish of temperate fresh waters). Robert D. Hoyt

WORLD BOOK illustration by Colin Newman, Linden Artists Ltd.

The creek chub may grow to a length of 1 foot (30 centimeters). The fish is blue on top and silver underneath.

Scientific classification. Chubs are in the family Cyprinidae. The creek chub is *Semotilus atromaculatus.*

Chuck wagon was a mess wagon or rolling kitchen that provided food for cowhands trailing herds north from Texas or for roundup crews on Western ranches. The term comes from the slang expression *chuck,* meaning *food* or *grub.*

Two teams of horses usually pulled the chuck wagon, loaded with food, utensils, and bedding. It led the way from camp to camp. Some chuck wagons were farm wagons fitted with shelving and boxes. Others were specially built. A cook could quickly get a meal for 20 cowhands. William W. Savage, Jr.

Chuckwalla is the name of several kinds of large, harmless lizards found in rocky deserts of the United States and Mexico. The largest species grows to about 2 feet (60 centimeters) long and weighs about 2 pounds (0.9 kilogram). Chuckwallas live up to 25 years. They feed on leaves and flowers. Most other lizards eat insects. When chased by an enemy, a chuckwalla will run to a

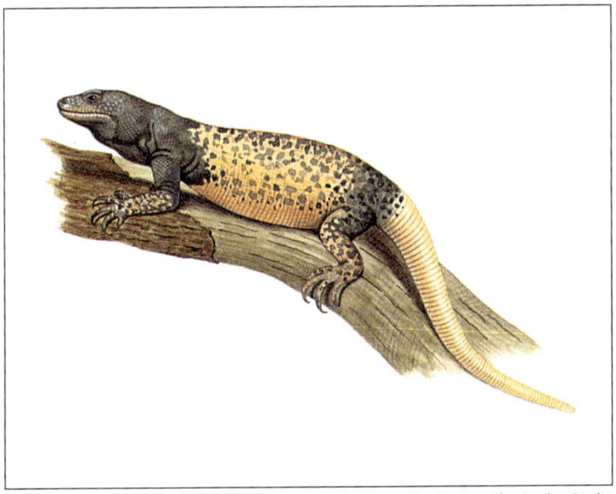

World Book illustration by Richard Lewington, The Garden Studio

The chuckwalla, one of the largest of American lizards, was at one time used for food by Indians in the Southwest.

crack in a rock or some other narrow opening and wedge itself in tightly by filling its lungs with air.

Raymond B. Huey

Scientific classification. Chuckwallas belong to the genus *Sauromalus* in the family Iguanidae.

Chumash Indians, *CHOO mash,* are a group of tribes in southern California. Traditionally, they lived along the Pacific coast between San Luis Obispo and Malibu (near Los Angeles) and inland to the western edge of the San Joaquin Valley. They also lived on the nearby Channel Islands. There were at least six Chumash groups, each with its own language. They built large oceangoing canoes called *tomols* and wove intricately decorated baskets. They also made cooking tools and bowls from stone and ceremonial paintings on rock.

The coastal Chumash lived in large grass-covered dwellings, each of which housed many related families. Most inland Chumash lived in smaller, single-family dwellings. Coastal Chumash caught fish, shellfish, marine birds, and sea mammals. Inland Chumash gathered plants and hunted deer and other animals. Acorns were also an important food for most Chumash.

The Spanish began building Roman Catholic missions on Chumash lands in the 1700's. By the early 1800's, most Chumash lived within the mission system. Diseases brought by Europeans reduced the Chumash population from as many as 22,000 in 1770 to about 300 in 1880. Some Chumash Indians live on the Santa Ynez Reservation near Santa Barbara, California. Most of the rest live in other places in their traditional homeland.

Victoria D. Patterson

Ch'ung-ch'ing. See **Chongqing.**

Chungking. See **Chongqing.**

Church, in Christianity, has two basic meanings. *Church* is the term for a community of Christians who share a specific set of beliefs. It also means the building that Christians use for worship and other religious activities. The word *church* comes from the Greek *kuriakon,* which means *of the Lord.*

In the early centuries of Christianity, *church* meant the community of all Christians. But in 1054, a split occurred between Christians in western Europe and those in eastern Europe and western Asia. The communities in eastern Europe and western Asia became known as the Eastern Orthodox Churches.

In the 1500's, a religious movement called the Reformation divided western Christianity into the Roman Catholic Church and Protestantism. The Protestants established a number of new churches—often called *denominations*—including the Anglican, Baptist, Lutheran, Methodist, and Presbyterian churches.

The early Christians had no church buildings. Because they feared persecution from the Roman rulers, they met secretly in private homes or in underground passages and rooms called *catacombs.* Christians began building churches in the 300's, when the Roman emperor Constantine the Great ended persecution of the Christians. Since then, most churches have reflected the architecture of their time and region.

During the 300's, the basilica became the most common form of church design. The basilica was originally a large hall built by the Romans for administrative and judicial purposes. Between 1000 and 1500, Christians built numerous majestic and richly decorated cathedrals. Many churches built today combine traditional and modern architectural styles. Jill Raitt

For more information about the church as a community, see **Eastern Orthodox Churches; Protestantism; Roman Catholic Church.** For information about church buildings, see **Architecture** (Medieval architecture; Renaissance architecture; Baroque architecture); **Basilica; Cathedral.**

Church, Frederick Edwin (1826-1900), was an American painter known for his huge, dramatic landscapes. Church traveled widely searching for subjects. He painted New York's Catskill Mountains, the Andes Mountains of South America, the wilderness of Ecuador, the lush vegetation of Jamaica, and icebergs near Labrador. Many of Church's paintings feature the vivid use of light, such as brilliant rainbows and fiery sunsets. Church carefully studied and sketched his subjects, using the sketches to paint large composite scenes in his studio. Church's most famous paintings include *Heart of the Andes* (1859) and *Icebergs* (1861).

Church was born in Hartford, Connecticut, on May 4, 1826. At age 18, he studied with the American landscape artist Thomas Cole. Early in his career, Church became a leading member of the first school of American landscape painting, the Hudson River School. His early works, like those of other members of the school, were

A Church painting of Niagara Falls is typical of the artist's panoramic, detailed treatment of scenes from nature early in his career. This style made him a leading member of the Hudson River School of American landscape painting.

Detail of *Niagara Falls* (1857), an oil painting on canvas; Corcoran Gallery of Art, Washington, D.C.

panoramic, detailed scenes of nature. Church's *Niagara Falls* (1857) is an example. Church died on April 7, 1900.

Sarah Burns

See also **Hudson River School**.

Church and state is a term that refers to the relations between churches and governments. The church-state relationship has been the subject of disagreements and conflicts throughout history. Today, the *separation of church and state* is a central principle of government in the United States and some other democracies. It seeks to protect religious freedom and to prevent discrimination or exclusion on the basis of religion.

In the United States, the separation of church and state has roots in the First Amendment to the Constitution. The amendment states that "Congress shall make no law respecting an establishment of religion, or prohibiting the free exercise thereof." Courts have ruled that this amendment forbids government from supporting an official or preferred religion, or interfering with the practice of faith. A number of other countries—including Australia, France, and Japan—also support separation of church and state. Some countries, such as the United Kingdom, maintain separation in some areas but recognize certain religions as *established* (national) churches.

The church-state debate. People have long disagreed over the extent of the separation of church and state. Many people believe that government should be entirely *secular* (nonreligious) and that churches should operate outside the government system. Other people believe that government should be able to fund or support some religious activities, as long as it does not favor one religion over another. Still others believe that religion improves the moral character of citizens and should therefore be actively promoted by government.

A number of church-state issues have generated intense debate, particularly in the United States. Such issues have included prayer in public schools, government funding for religious schools, government support for religious charities, and the display of religious symbols on government property.

History. In ancient Greece and Rome, closely related bodies handled both religious and governmental affairs. Church-state relations began to change after Christianity became the official religion of the Roman Empire about A.D. 380. In 494, Pope Gelasius I formulated a doctrine of coordination between church and state. He wrote that priests and kings ordinarily should not interfere with one another, but that religious officials should have the last word if a conflict arose. The Concordat of Worms in 1122 further defined the roles of religious and secular officials. Religious officials claimed the higher authority.

The Middle Ages, from about the 400's through the 1400's, saw a series of struggles between popes and European rulers. In 1302, during a dispute with King Philip IV of France, Pope Boniface VIII issued a famous *bull* (papal decree) called *Unam sanctam.* The bull affirmed papal authority over secular rulers. In response, Philip accused Boniface of a number of crimes and tried to force him to resign. Boniface died in 1303. In 1309, a French pope, Clement V, moved the papal court to Avignon, in what is now France. From that year to 1377, French kings often were able to influence the popes. By the end of the 1400's, the church and many of the governments of Europe had established an uneasy peace.

The Reformation, a religious movement of the 1500's, had a major impact on church-state relations. The emergence of numerous Christian denominations during this period led to conflicts over spiritual authority in many countries. Eventually, it became common for a country's ruler to determine the religion of the country's people. With minor exceptions, this arrangement prevailed until the American and French revolutions in the late 1700's.

After the United States declared its independence in 1776, it moved toward separation of church and state. This separation became a feature of democratic governments in the 1800's and 1900's.

Gregg Ivers

Related articles in *World Book* include:

Constitution of the United States (Article VI; Amendment 1)
Education (How should education be financed?)
Freedom of religion
Pope
Reformation
Roman Catholic Church
School prayer

Church of Christ. See **Churches of Christ**.

Church of Christ, Scientist. See **Christian Scientists**.

Church of England, also called the Established Church, is the official church in England. About half the people of England are baptized members. It is also the mother church of the worldwide Anglican Communion.

Doctrines. The Church of England recognizes the Old and New Testaments as its authority for doctrine. It also upholds traditional Christian teachings as expressed in the Apostles' Creed and Nicene Creed, and in its own Thirty-Nine Articles. The church does not insist on specific interpretations of these documents, but relies on its bishops to ensure consistent teaching. The bishops are regarded as successors to the apostles. The Book of Common Prayer, the church's official liturgy book, is also a major source of doctrinal unity. The Church of England has two sacraments—baptism and

Holy Communion—but other rituals are also important.

Organization. England is divided into two religious provinces, Canterbury and York. An archbishop governs each. Canterbury's archbishop bears the title *Primate of All England,* and is considered the Anglican spiritual leader. Provinces are divided into dioceses, each governed by a bishop. Dioceses are divided into parishes, each headed by a rector. Bishops, clergy, and laity all take part in setting religious policy. The church owns its property and is largely supported by endowments.

History. Christians in England recognized the spiritual authority of the pope until 1534, when King Henry VIII forced Parliament to pass the Act of Supremacy. The act declared the king to be head of the church in place of the pope, who resisted Henry's request to dissolve his marriage to Catherine of Aragon.

Under Henry's successors, King Edward VI and Queen Mary I, disputes took place over whether the church was to be primarily Protestant or Roman Catholic. Their successor, Queen Elizabeth I, established a compromise between the two positions. In 1559, she restored the independence of the Church of England with a new Act of Supremacy. During the 1600's, certain church members, called Puritans, sought more Protestant reforms. Another group, the Methodists, made their final break from the church by the late 1700's. The Oxford Movement, a reform movement that stressed Roman Catholic ideas, had great influence on the church in the 1800's. Today, a variety of theological opinions are represented in the church. In 1993, the church passed a measure to allow women to be ordained as priests. Peter W. Williams

Related articles in *World Book* include:

Anglicans	Hampton Court Conference	Puritans (History)
Augustine of Canterbury, Saint	Henry VIII	Reformation
Cranmer, Thomas	Methodists	Ridley, Nicholas
England (Religion)	Oxford Movement	Thirty-Nine Articles
Episcopal Church		

Additional resources

Doran, Susan, and Durston, Christopher. *Princes, Pastors, and People: The Church and Religion in England, 1500-1700.* 2nd ed. Routledge, 2002.

Hylson-Smith, Kenneth. *High Churchmanship in the Church of England.* T&T Clark, 1993.

Church of God in Christ, The, is one of the largest Pentecostal denominations in the world. The church has about 3,700,000 members in the United States and about 1,300,000 in more than 50 other countries. The base for the denomination's faith is the Bible, with emphasis on the experiences of the apostles on the Day of Pentecost (Acts 2:4). The church follows an episcopal form of government, with bishops at its head.

Bishop Charles Harrison Mason and others founded the church in 1895 in Lexington, Mississippi, as a Holiness church. Holiness churches are American Protestant churches that stress personal experience, morality, and usually a fundamentalist approach to the Bible. In 1907, influenced by the Pentecostal movement, Bishop Mason declared the church to be Pentecostal (see **Pentecostal churches**). The church's headquarters are in Memphis, Tennessee. Critically reviewed by The Church of God in Christ

Church of Jesus Christ of Latter-day Saints. See Mormons.

Church of the Brethren. See Brethren, Church of the.

Church of the Nazarene is a Protestant denomination that follows the teachings of early Methodism. The church was established in 1908 in Pilot Point, Texas, by a merger of three independent Holiness groups. The church has more than 12,000 congregations and a network of missions in all parts of the world.

The Church of the Nazarene supports graduate theological seminaries in the United States and the Philippines. It also maintains other schools, including several liberal arts colleges and universities in the United States and Canada. The Nazarene Publishing House produces books and periodicals. The official church newspaper, *Holiness Today,* is printed in English and Spanish. The church maintains worldwide radio ministry programs. International offices are in Kansas City, Missouri.

Critically reviewed by the Church of the Nazarene

Church school. See **Parochial school; Religious education.**

Churches of Christ are a group of religious congregations that accept the Bible as the inspired, authoritative word of God. The New Testament is the principal authority for church and Christian action, but the Old Testament contributes much to faith and understanding. The congregations recognize no creeds or manuals of doctrine. They regard Jesus Christ as the founder, head, and Savior of their church. Members believe that one is born again by faith, repentance, confession, and baptism. They also believe that one must lead a faithful Christian life to be saved.

The Churches of Christ are self-governing congregations. There are no central offices or officers. A group of elders leads each congregation.

During the early 1800's, many local movements in such areas as New England, North Carolina, South Carolina, West Virginia, and Georgia urged a return to the Bible. As a result of this effort to restore New Testament Christianity, congregations that make up the Churches of Christ are in all 50 states of the United States and in over 100 other countries. But most members live in the south-central part of the United States.

Member congregations operate hundreds of primary and secondary schools, as well as several junior colleges, colleges, and universities. They also sponsor several graduate schools of religion, many schools of preaching, and numerous children's homes and charitable agencies. F. Furman Kearley

Churches of Christ, National Council of. See **National Council of Churches.**

Churches of God consist of about 15 religious groups in the United States that use the same name—Church of God—but differ in faith and practice. Most trace their origins to the Pentecostal, Holiness, or Adventist movements. The largest, the Church of God with headquarters in Cleveland, Tennessee, was founded in 1886. It became one of the first Pentecostal churches. Another major group, the Church of God with headquarters in Anderson, Indiana, was established about 1880. This group developed into one of the largest Holiness churches. The Holiness Movement stresses sanctification and the literal interpretation of the Bible.

For more information on the historical background of the Churches of God, see **Adventists; Pentecostal churches;** and **Fundamentalism.** Charles H. Lippy

Churchill, John. See **Marlborough, Duke of.**

Oil painting on canvas (1945) by Lucile Rader; Winston Churchill Memorial and Library, Westminster College

Winston S. Churchill

Prime minister of the United Kingdom 1940-1945 ·1951-1955

Sir Winston Churchill

Churchill, Sir Winston Leonard Spencer (1874-1965), became one of the greatest statesmen in world history. Churchill reached the height of his fame as the heroic prime minister of the United Kingdom during World War II. He offered his people only "blood, toil, tears, and sweat" as they struggled to keep their freedom. Churchill also was a noted speaker, author, painter, soldier, and war reporter.

Early in World War II, the United Kingdom stood alone against Nazi Germany. The British people refused to give in despite the tremendous odds against them. Churchill's personal courage, the magic of his words, and his faith in victory inspired the British to "their finest hour." The mere sight of this stocky, determined man—a cigar in his mouth and two fingers raised high in a "V for victory" salute—cheered the people. Churchill seemed to be John Bull, the symbol of the English people, come to life.

Churchill not only made history, he also wrote it. As a historian, war reporter, and biographer, he showed a matchless command of the English language. In 1953, he won the Nobel Prize in literature. Yet as a schoolboy, he had been the worst student in his class. Churchill spoke as he wrote—clearly, vividly, majestically. Yet he had stuttered as a boy.

The vigor of Churchill's body equaled that of his

Quotations from Churchill

The following quotations come from some of Churchill's speeches.

I have nothing to offer but blood, toil, tears, and sweat.
Speech to the House of Commons, May 13, 1940, soon after Churchill became prime minister. The sentence refers to Great Britain's participation in World War II under Churchill's leadership.

... we shall not flag or fail. ... we shall fight in France, we shall fight in the seas and oceans, we shall fight with growing confidence and growing strength in the air, we shall defend our island, whatever the cost may be, we shall fight on the beaches, we shall fight on the landing-grounds, ... we shall fight in the hills; we shall never surrender. ...
Speech to the House of Commons, June 4, 1940

... the Battle of Britain is about to begin. ... The whole fury and might of the enemy must very soon be turned on us. ... Let us therefore brace ourselves to our duties, and so bear ourselves that, if the British Empire and its Commonwealth last for a thousand years, men will say, "This was their finest hour."
Speech to the House of Commons, June 18, 1940

A shadow has fallen upon the scenes so lately lighted by the Allied victory. ... From Stettin in the Baltic to Trieste in the Adriatic, an iron curtain has descended across the Continent.
Speech at Westminster College in Fulton, Mo., March 5, 1946

United Press Int.

Churchill's famous victory salute became an inspiring symbol during World War II.

Reproduced by kind permission of His Grace the Duke of Marlborough

Churchill was born at Blenheim Palace, *above,* near Woodstock, in Oxfordshire, England. He was the elder of two sons of Lord Randolph and Lady Churchill.

Important dates in Churchill's life

1874	(Nov. 30) Born in Oxfordshire, England.
1895	Graduated from Royal Military College.
1901	Entered House of Commons.
1908	(Sept. 12) Married Clementine Hozier.
1911	Appointed first lord of the Admiralty.
1915	Resigned from the Admiralty.
1939	Appointed first lord of the Admiralty.
1940	Became prime minister of Britain.
1945	Became leader of the opposition.
1951	Became prime minister of Britain.
1953	Knighted. Won Nobel Prize for literature.
1955	Retired as prime minister.
1963	Made honorary citizen of the United States.
1964	Retired from House of Commons.
1965	(Jan. 24) Died in London.

mind. His tremendous physical endurance allowed him to live a long, eventful life. In youth, his boundless energy found release on the battlefield. Churchill loved the rough and ready life of a soldier, but he also had great sensitivity. He expressed this side of his nature beautifully in his paintings.

Churchill entered the service of his country in 1895 as an army lieutenant under Queen Victoria. He ended his career in 1964 as a member of the House of Commons under Queen Elizabeth II, Queen Victoria's great-great-granddaughter. Few men ever served their country so long or so well.

Early life

Boyhood and education. Winston Churchill was born on Nov. 30, 1874, in Blenheim Palace in Oxfordshire, England. He was the elder of the two sons of Lord Randolph Churchill (1849-1895) and Lady Churchill (1854-1921), an American girl whose maiden name was Jennie Jerome. Lord Randolph was the third son of the seventh Duke of Marlborough. The first Duke of Marlborough had been one of England's greatest military commanders. Winston's mother was famous for her beauty. Her father, Leonard Jerome, made and lost several fortunes in business.

Young Winston, a chunky lad with a mop of red hair, had an unhappy boyhood. He talked with a stutter and lisp, and did poorly in his schoolwork. His stubbornness and high spirits annoyed everyone. In addition, his parents had little time for him.

Winston stood in fear and wonder of his father. Lord Randolph, a leader in the Conservative party, showed little affection for Winston. Winston's mother charmed everyone with her beauty and wit. As Lord Randolph's

Hulton Picture Library from Publix

Churchill's family included his brother, John, *left,* his mother, *center,* and young Winston, *right.*

Camera Press, Pix from Publix

As a war correspondent, Churchill, *far right,* was captured during the Anglo-Boer War of 1899-1902. He escaped and crossed 300 miles (480 kilometers) of enemy territory to safety.

wife, she had many duties. Little time was left for Winston. Churchill later wrote of his mother: "She shone for me like the Evening Star. I loved her dearly—but at a distance."

When Winston was 6 years old, his brother, John, was born. The difference in their ages prevented any real companionship. At the age of 12, Winston entered Harrow School, a leading English secondary school. Winston entered as the lowest boy in the lowest class, and in that unhappy position he stayed. At Harrow, however, his love of the English language began to grow. There, he said later, he "got into my bones the essential structure of the ordinary English sentence ..."

Lord Randolph noticed that Winston spent many hours playing with toy soldiers. He decided that soldiering was the only career for a boy of limited intelligence. In 1893, at the age of 18, Winston entered the Royal Military College at Sandhurst. He had failed the entrance examinations twice before passing them. But he soon led his class in tactics and fortifications, the most important subjects. He was graduated eighth in a class of 150. In 1895, Churchill was appointed a second lieutenant in the 4th Hussars, a proud cavalry regiment.

Soldier and reporter. Twenty-year-old Lieutenant Churchill ached for adventure. For a soldier, adventure meant fighting. But the only fighting at the moment was in Cuba, where the people had revolted against their Spanish rulers. Churchill was on leave from the army, and used his family's influence to go to Cuba as an observer with the Spanish. While there, he wrote five colorful articles on the revolt for a London newspaper. Churchill returned to London with a love for Havana cigars that lasted the rest of his life.

In 1896, Churchill's regiment was sent to Bangalore, in southern India. There he acquired a fondness for polo, and read many books he had neglected in school. The works of Edward Gibbon and Thomas B. Macaulay interested him the most.

In 1897, Churchill learned that fighting had broken out in northwestern India between British forces and Pashtun warriors. He obtained a leave from his regiment, and persuaded two newspapers to hire him as a reporter. Churchill joined the advance guard of the Malakand Field Force and took part in bloody hand-to-hand fighting. After returning to Bangalore, Churchill wrote about the campaign in his first book, *The Story of the Malakand Field Force* (1898).

Churchill's adventurous spirit made him restless again. A British force was being built up in Egypt to invade the Sudan. Churchill got himself transferred to the force, and again obtained a newspaper assignment. In 1898, he took part in the last great cavalry charge of the British army, in the Battle of Omdurman. Churchill returned to England and wrote a book about the Sudanese campaign, *The River War* (1899).

In 1899, while working on his book, Churchill resigned from the army and ran for Parliament as a Conservative from Oldham. But he did not impress Oldham's voters, most of whom were laborers belonging to the Liberal party. Churchill lost his first election.

The Anglo-Boer War of 1899-1902 began in South Africa. A London newspaper hired Churchill to report the war between the Boers—most of whom were Dutch settlers—and the British. Soon after Churchill arrived in South Africa, the Boers ambushed an armored train on which he was riding. He was captured and imprisoned, but made a daring escape. He scaled the prison wall one night, and slipped by the sentries. Then, traveling on freight trains, he crossed 300 miles (480 kilometers) of enemy territory to safety. He became a famous hero overnight.

Early political career

First public offices. In 1900, Churchill returned to England and to politics. Oldham gave him a hero's welcome, and the voters elected him to Parliament.

In January 1901, Churchill took his seat in the House of Commons for the first time. He soon began to criticize many Conservative policies openly and sharply. In 1904, Churchill broke with his party completely. He dramatically crossed the floor of Commons, amid the howls of Conservatives and the cheers of Liberals, to sit with the Liberals. In the next election, in 1906, Churchill ran as a Liberal and won.

With enormous energy, Churchill moved through

three government positions during the next few years. He served as undersecretary of state for the colonies (1906-1908), president of the board of trade (1908-1910), and home secretary (1910-1911). His appointment to the board of trade was his first cabinet position.

Churchill's family. In the spring of 1908, Churchill met Clementine Hozier (1885-1977), the daughter of a retired Army officer. Clementine and Churchill married on Sept. 12, 1908. Years later, Churchill wrote that he "lived happily ever afterwards." He also wrote: "My most brilliant achievement was my ability to persuade my wife to marry me." Churchill became a devoted parent to his four children: Diana (1909-1963), Randolph (1911-1968), Sarah (1914-1982), and Mary (1922-). Another daughter, Marigold, died in 1921 at the age of 3.

World War I. In 1911, Prime Minister Herbert H. Asquith appointed Churchill first lord of the admiralty. The build-up of German military and naval forces had convinced Asquith that the admiralty needed a strong leader. Churchill was one of the few people who realized that war with Germany would probably come. He reorganized the Navy, developed antisubmarine tactics, and modernized the fleet. He also created the Navy's first air service. When the United Kingdom entered World War I, on Aug. 4, 1914, the fleet was ready.

In 1915, Churchill urged an attack on the Dardanelles and the Gallipoli Peninsula, both controlled by Turkey. If successful, the attack would have opened a route to the Black Sea. Aid could then have been sent to Russia, the United Kingdom's ally. But the campaign failed disastrously, and Churchill was blamed. He resigned from the admiralty, although he kept his seat in Parliament. Churchill regarded himself as a political failure. "I am finished," he told a friend. In November 1915, Churchill joined the British Army in France. He served briefly as a major in the 2nd Grenadier Guards. Then he was promoted to lieutenant colonel and given command of a battalion of the 6th Royal Scots Fusiliers.

David Lloyd George became prime minister in December 1916. He appointed Churchill minister of munitions in July 1917. While in the admiralty, Churchill had promoted the development of the tank. Now he began large-scale tank production. Churchill visited the battlefields frequently. He watched every important engagement in France, often from the air.

Hulton Picture Library from Publix

Churchill and his bride, Clementine Hozier, married in 1908, soon after they met. Churchill wrote that his "most brilliant achievement" was persuading his wife to marry him.

Between wars

World War I ended in November 1918. The next January, Churchill became secretary of state for war and for air. As war secretary, he supervised the *demobilization* (release of men) of the British Army. In 1921, Lloyd George named him colonial secretary.

Three days before the 1922 election campaign began, Churchill had to have his appendix removed. He was able to campaign only briefly, and lost the election. He said he found himself "without office, without a seat, without a party, and without an appendix."

In 1924, Churchill was returned to Parliament from Epping after he rejoined the Conservative Party. He was later named chancellor of the exchequer under Prime Minister Stanley Baldwin. Churchill's father had held this office almost 40 years earlier. The Conservatives lost the 1929 election, and Churchill left office. He did not hold a Cabinet position again until 1939. He kept his seat in Parliament throughout this period.

During the years between World Wars I and II, Churchill spent much of his spare time painting and writing. He did not begin painting until in his 40's, and surprised critics with his talent. He liked to use bold, brilliant colors. Many of Churchill's paintings have hung in the Royal Academy of Arts.

Painting provided relaxation and pleasure, but Churchill considered writing his chief occupation after politics. In his four-volume *World Crisis* (1923-1929), he brilliantly recorded the history of World War I. In *Marlborough, His Life and Times* (1933-1938), he wrote a monumental six-volume study of his ancestor.

In speaking and in writing after 1932, Churchill tried to rouse his nation and the world to the danger of Nazi Germany. The build-up of the German armed forces alarmed him, and he pleaded for a powerful British air force. But he was called a warmonger.

Wartime prime minister

World War II begins. German troops marched into Poland on Sept. 1, 1939. The war that Churchill had so clearly foreseen had begun. On September 3, the United Kingdom and France declared war on Germany. Prime Minister Neville Chamberlain at once named Churchill first lord of the admiralty, the same post he had held in World War I. The British fleet was notified with a simple message: "Winston is back."

In April 1940, Germany attacked Denmark and Norway. The United Kingdom quickly sent troops to Norway, but they had to retreat because they lacked air support. In the parliamentary debate that followed, Chamberlain's government fell.

On May 10, King George VI asked Churchill to form a government. That same day, Germany invaded Belgium, Luxembourg, and the Netherlands. At age 65, Churchill became prime minister. He wrote later: "I felt as if I were walking with destiny, and that all my past life had been but a preparation for this hour and for this trial."

Rarely, if ever, had a national leader taken over in such a desperate hour. Said Churchill: "I have nothing to offer but blood, toil, tears, and sweat."

The months that followed brought a full measure of

AP/Wide World

During the Battle of Britain, German planes bombed the House of Commons. The next morning, on May 11, 1941, Churchill had tears in his eyes as he inspected the damage.

blood, toil, tears, and sweat. Belgium surrendered to Germany on May 28, and the defeat of France appeared likely at any moment. On June 4, Churchill told Commons that even though all of Europe might fall, "... we shall not flag or fail. We shall go on to the end ... we shall fight in the seas and oceans ... we shall fight on the beaches, we shall fight on the landing-grounds, we shall fight in the fields and in the streets, we shall fight in the hills; we shall never surrender. ..." On June 22, France surrendered to Germany.

The Battle of Britain. The United Kingdom now stood alone. A German invasion seemed certain. In a speech to the House of Commons on the day after France asked Germany for an armistice, Churchill declared: "Let us therefore brace ourselves to our duties, and so bear ourselves that, if the British Empire and its Commonwealth last for a thousand years, men will say, 'This was their finest hour.' "

The Germans had to defeat the Royal Air Force (RAF) before they could invade across the English Channel. In July, the German *Luftwaffe* (air force) began to bomb British shipping and ports. In September, the Luftwaffe began nightly raids on London. The RAF, though outnumbered, fought bravely and finally defeated the Luftwaffe. Churchill expressed the nation's gratitude to its airmen: "Never in the field of human conflict was so much owed by so many to so few."

While the battle raged, Churchill turned up everywhere. He defied air-raid alarms and went into the streets as the bombs fell. He toured RAF headquarters, inspected coastal defenses, and visited victims of the air raids. Everywhere he went, he held up two fingers in a "V for victory" salute. To the people of all the Allied nations, this simple gesture became an inspiring symbol of faith in eventual victory.

Churchill had a strong grasp of military reality. He had denied the pleas of the French for additional support from RAF planes, knowing that the United Kingdom needed the planes for its own defense. He decided that the French fleet at Oran in Algeria had to be destroyed. Otherwise, French warships might be surrendered and used to strengthen the German navy. He boldly sent the only fully equipped armored division in England to Egypt. Churchill reasoned that, if a German invasion of England could not be prevented, one armored division could not save the country. But that division could fight the Germans in Egypt.

Meetings with Roosevelt. In August 1941, Churchill and President Franklin D. Roosevelt met aboard ship off the coast of Newfoundland. They drew up the Atlantic Charter, which set forth the common postwar aims of the United States and the United Kingdom. Churchill and Roosevelt exchanged more than 1,700 messages and met nine times before Roosevelt's death in 1945.

The United States entered the war after Japan attacked Pearl Harbor on Dec. 7, 1941. Later that month, Churchill and Roosevelt met in Washington, D.C. On December 26, Churchill addressed the United States Congress. He stirred all Americans with his faith "... that in the days to come the British and American peoples will ... walk together side by side in majesty, in justice, and in peace."

Relations between Churchill and Roosevelt always remained friendly even though differences arose between them. Churchill gloried in the British Empire, but Roosevelt was suspicious of British colonial policies. Churchill distrusted the Soviet Union, but Roosevelt did not.

In August 1942, Churchill journeyed to Moscow to meet with Soviet Premier Joseph Stalin. The Soviet Union had entered the war in June 1941, after being invaded by Germany. Almost immediately, Stalin had demanded that the British open a second fighting front in western Europe to relieve the strain on the Soviet Union. Churchill explained to Stalin that it would be disastrous

UPI/Bettmann Newsphotos

The Big Three led the Allies during World War II. Churchill, United States President Franklin D. Roosevelt, *left,* and Soviet Premier Joseph Stalin met in Tehran, Iran, in 1943.

to open a second front in 1942 because the Allies were unprepared.

In January 1943, Churchill and Roosevelt met in Casablanca, Morocco. They announced that the Allies would accept only *unconditional* (complete) surrender from Germany, Italy, and Japan. After returning to England, Churchill fell ill with pneumonia. But he recovered with incredible vigor.

The Big Three. The first meeting of Churchill, Stalin, and Roosevelt took place in Tehran, Iran, in November 1943. The Big Three, as they were called, set the British-American invasion of France for the following spring. On his way home from Tehran, the 69-year-old Churchill was again struck down by pneumonia. Again he recovered rapidly.

In February 1945, the Big Three met in Yalta in the Soviet Union. The end of the war in Europe was in sight. The three leaders agreed on plans to occupy defeated Germany. Churchill distrusted Stalin. He feared the Soviet Union might keep the territories in eastern Europe that its troops occupied. Roosevelt, a close friend of Churchill's as well as an ally, died two months after the conference, and Harry S. Truman became president.

Germany surrendered on May 7, 1945, almost five years to the day after Churchill became prime minister. In July, Churchill met with Truman and Stalin in Potsdam, Germany, to discuss the administration of Germany. But Churchill's presence at the meeting was cut short. He had lost his post as prime minister.

An election had been held in the United Kingdom. The Conservatives suffered an overwhelming defeat by the Labour party. The Labour party's promise of sweeping socialistic reforms appealed to the voters. In addition, the people were voting against the Conservative party. Many blamed the Conservatives, who had been in office before the war, for failing to prepare the United Kingdom for World War II. The defeat hurt Churchill deeply. Clement R. Attlee succeeded him as prime minister.

Postwar leader

Leader of the opposition. Churchill took his place as leader of the opposition in the House of Commons. He urged Parliament to plan for national defense, and warned the western world against the dangers of Communism. On March 5, 1946, speaking at Fulton, Missouri, Churchill declared: "Beware . . . time may be short . . . . From Stettin in the Baltic to Trieste in the Adriatic, an iron curtain has descended across the Continent." Many people in the United States and the United Kingdom called the speech warmongering.

Politics, lecturing, painting, and writing kept Churchill busy. But these activities did not completely satisfy his great energy. He found much to do around Chartwell Manor, his country estate in Kent. He took pride in his cattle and his race horses. In 1948, the first volume of Churchill's *Second World War* was published. The sixth and last volume of these magnificent memoirs appeared in 1953.

Return to power. The Conservatives returned to power in 1951. Churchill, now almost 77 years old, again became prime minister. As usual, he concentrated most of his energy on foreign affairs. He worked especially hard to encourage British-American unity. He visited

Wide World

Churchill warned the world about the Soviet Union's Iron Curtain in a 1946 speech at Fulton, Mo. With him was United States President Harry S. Truman, *left.*

Washington in 1952, 1953, and 1954.

In April 1953, Churchill was knighted by Queen Elizabeth. The queen made him a knight of the Order of the Garter, the United Kingdom's highest order of knighthood. He had been offered this honor in 1945. He had refused it because of his party's defeat in the election. He had also refused an earldom and a dukedom. As an earl or a duke, he could not have served in Commons. In June 1953, Sir Winston suffered a severe stroke that paralyzed his left side. He made a remarkable recovery.

Late in 1953, Sir Winston won the Nobel Prize for literature. He was honored for ". . . his mastery of historical and biographical presentation and for his brilliant oratory. . . ."

On Nov. 30, 1954, Churchill celebrated his 80th birthday. Members of all political parties gathered to honor him. Gifts and congratulations poured in from all corners of the world. The show of affection and respect touched Churchill deeply. His eyes bright with tears, he denied having inspired the United Kingdom during World War II. "It was the nation and the race dwelling all round the globe that had the lion's heart," he said. "I had the luck to be called on to give the roar."

For some time it had been rumored that Churchill would retire due to his advanced age. But he showed no intention of doing so, and seemed to enjoy keeping people guessing. However, the years and two world wars had taken a toll. In April 1955, Churchill retired.

End of an era. Churchill went back to his painting and writing. He worked on his four-volume *History of the English-Speaking Peoples* (1956-1958). He had begun this study 20 years earlier. He still took his seat in Commons, his body now bent with age. Here, where his voice once rang eloquently, he now sat silently.

In 1963, Congress made Churchill an honorary U.S. citizen. The action reflected the American people's affection for the man who had done so much for the cause of freedom. Churchill's remarkable career ended in 1964. He did not run in the general election that year.

Topham Picture Library

After his retirement, Churchill returned to writing at his home in London, where he died in 1965.

Churchill had served in Parliament from 1901 to 1922, then from 1924 until his retirement 40 years later.

Churchill suffered a stroke on Jan. 15, 1965. He died nine days later, at the age of 90. He was buried in St. Martin's Churchyard in Oxfordshire, near his birthplace, Blenheim Palace. Carol L. Thompson

Related articles in *World Book* include:

Atlantic Charter
Caricature (picture)
Cold War
Potsdam Conference
Roosevelt, Franklin D.
Tehran Conference
United Kingdom (History)
World War I
World War II
Yalta Conference

Outline

I. **Early life**
 A. Boyhood and education B. Soldier and reporter
II. **Early political career**
 A. First public offices
 B. Churchill's family
 C. World War I
III. **Between wars**
IV. **Wartime prime minister**
 A. World War II begins
 B. The Battle of Britain
 C. Meetings with Roosevelt
 D. The Big Three
V. **Postwar leader**
 A. Leader of the opposition
 B. Return to power
 C. End of an era

Questions

What was the nationality of Churchill's mother?
How did Churchill join the Liberal Party in 1904?
How did the U.S. Congress honor Churchill in 1963?
Why did Churchill's father decide that Winston should become a soldier?
In what field did Churchill win a Nobel Prize?
How did Churchill become a hero in the Anglo-Boer War of 1899-1902?
How did Churchill feel about becoming prime minister of the United Kingdom in 1940?
Who were the Big Three?
What did Churchill mean when he held up two fingers in a "V"?
To whom did Churchill refer when he said: "This was their finest hour"?

Additional resources

Best, Geoffrey F. A. *Churchill.* 2001. Reprint. Oxford, 2003.
Blake, Robert, and Louis, W. R., eds. *Churchill.* Norton, 1993.
Gilbert, Martin. *Churchill: A Life.* Henry Holt, 1991. Condensed edition of the eight-volume biography by Martin Gilbert and Randolph S. Churchill.
Jenkins, Roy. *Churchill.* Farrar, 2001.
Keegan, John. *Winston Churchill.* Viking, 2002.
Kimball, Warren F. *Forged in War: Roosevelt, Churchill, and the Second World War.* 1997. Reprint. Ivan R. Dee, 2003.
Severance, John B. *Winston Churchill.* Clarion, 1996. Younger readers.

Churchill Downs. See **Kentucky** (Visitor's guide); **Kentucky Derby; Louisville** (History).

Churchill River is in Saskatchewan and Manitoba in western Canada (see **Canada** [terrain map]). Almost 1,000 miles (1,600 kilometers) long, the river flows east from Lac la Loche in northwestern Saskatchewan and empties into Hudson Bay. The river's mouth is almost entirely surrounded by land. This gives the town of Churchill, Manitoba, the best natural harbor on Hudson Bay. The river was discovered in 1619 by Danish explorer Jens Munk. It was later named for John Churchill, third governor of the Hudson's Bay Company and later Duke of Marlborough. John S. Brierley

Churchill River flows through the province of Newfoundland and Labrador in eastern Canada (see **Canada** [terrain map]). The chief river on the Labrador Peninsula, it flows east for about 600 miles (970 kilometers), and empties into Lake Melville—a part of Hamilton Inlet on the Atlantic Ocean. The river originates as the Ashuanipi River at Ashuanipi Lake on the Quebec border. Churchill Falls (formerly Grand Falls) is about 220 miles (354 kilometers) from the mouth of the river.

The river was called the Hamilton River until 1965, when it was renamed to honor Sir Winston Churchill, the former prime minister of the United Kingdom. A giant project to develop the river's hydroelectric potential was completed in 1974 at Churchill Falls. The power plant there has a capacity of more than 5 million kilowatts of electric power and is one of the largest power projects in the Western Hemisphere. Simon M. Evans

Churn is a container in which cream or milk is stirred or beaten. Rapid stirring in a churn causes the fat particles to separate from the liquid. They are then worked into a solid mass called butter (see **Butter**).

People use two main types of churns—continuous churns and conventional churns. Continuous churns keep a steady flow of butter moving through the various steps of the butter-making process. They can turn cream into butter in three minutes or less. Continuous churns produce most of the butter made in the United States.

Conventional churns have large stainless steel drums with paddles inside to stir the cream. These churns can make as much as 8,500 pounds (3,860 kilograms) of butter in 30 to 45 minutes. Michael F. Hutjens

Chyle. See **Lymphatic system** (Absorption of fats).